MW01010073

LUTHERAN BIBLE
COMPANION

Volume 2: Intertestamental Era, New Testament,and Bible Dictionary

LUTHERAN BIBLE COMPANION

Volume 2: Intertestamental Era, New Testament, and Bible Dictionary

A Practical Tool for Church Workers and Laypeople

Drawn from the consultant materials of 27 scholars for *The Lutheran Study Bible* project and from numerous faithful resources; supplemented in view of recent research, including articles by Horace D. Hummel, Paul L. Maier, Andrew E. Steinmann, and others.

GENERAL EDITOR
EDWARD A. ENGELBRECHT

FOREWORD BY GREGORY P. SELTZ

Whoever would know God and have eternal life should read [the Bible] with diligence and search for its testimony of Christ, God's Son.
—Martin Luther (*What Luther Says* § 245)

CONCORDIA PUBLISHING HOUSE · SAINT LOUIS

Copyright © 2014 Concordia Publishing House
3558 S. Jefferson Avenue, St. Louis, MO 63118-3968
1-800-325-3040 • www.cph.org

Manufactured in the United States of America

1 2 3 4 5 6 7 8 9 10   23 22 21 20 19 18 17 16 15 14

CONTENTS

VOLUME 1

Alphabetical Order of Biblical Books, Including Apocrypha xiii

Foreword xv

Editor's Preface xix

How to Use this Bible Companion xxv

How to Read and Study the Holy Bible . . . xxix
- An Introduction to Studying the Holy Bible xxx
- Law and Gospel: Identifying God's Ways with Mankind xxxix
- The Unity of the Scripture xliii
- The Purpose of the Bible xlvii

The Nature of Biblical Miracles liii

The Land of the Bible lxi

The Time of the Bible: A Chronology . . . lxxiii

General Tools for Studying the Bible ci

Reference Guide cvii
- Abbreviations cviii
- Maps and Diagrams cxi
- Transliteration Guidelines cxii

THE OLD TESTAMENT (39 books)
- Article: The Value of the Old Testament 1

The Books of Moses 5
- Article: The JEDP Theory 10

Genesis 13
- Outline 18
- Composition 21
- Doctrinal Content 24
- Lutheran Theologians on Genesis 40
- Questions People Ask about Genesis 43
- Further Study 56

Exodus 59
- Composition 61
- Article: The Date of the Exodus 62
- Outline 64
- Doctrinal Content 69
- Lutheran Theologians on Exodus 84
- Questions People Ask about Exodus 86
- Further Study 97

Leviticus 99
- Composition 101
- Doctrinal Content 103
- Outline 104
- Lutheran Theologians on Leviticus 114
- Questions People Ask about Leviticus 115
- Further Study 125

Numbers 127
- Composition 128
- Article: The Legislative Sections of Numbers 131
- Outline 134
- Doctrinal Content 136
- Lutheran Theologians on Numbers 148
- Questions People Ask about Numbers 150
- Further Study 155

Deuteronomy 157
- Composition 159
- Outline 163
- Doctrinal Content 166
- Lutheran Theologians on Deuteronomy 180
- Questions People Ask about Deuteronomy 183
- Further Study 187

The Books of History 189
Article: Prophets and Historians 194
Article: Hexateuch, Heptateuch, Octateuch, and Deuteronomic History 196

Joshua 199
Article: The Conquest and Archaeology 200
Composition 203
Article: Critical Views of Joshua 204
Outline 208
Doctrinal Content 209
Lutheran Theologians on Joshua 220
Questions People Ask about Joshua 222
Further Study 227

Judges 229
Article: Critical Views of Judges 232
Composition 233
Outline 236
Doctrinal Content 237
Lutheran Theologians on Judges 247
Questions People Ask about Judges 249
Further Study 251

Ruth 253
Composition 254
Outline 259
Doctrinal Content 260
Lutheran Theologians on Ruth 265
Questions People Ask about Ruth 267
Further Study 269

1 and 2 Samuel 271
Composition 274
Outline 284
Doctrinal Content 288
Lutheran Theologians on 1 and 2 Samuel 306
Questions People Ask about Samuel 309
Further Study 318

1 and 2 Kings 321
Composition 325
Article: The Books of Samuel and Kings Compared 327
Outline 335
Doctrinal Content 341
Lutheran Theologians on 1 and 2 Kings .. 364
Questions People Ask about Kings 366
Chart: Kings and Prophets of Judah and Israel 372
Further Study 378

1 and 2 Chronicles 381
Composition 382
Article: Chronicles and the Critics 384
Outline 392
Chart: Cycles in Chronicles 397
Chart: Differences with Samuel-Kings ... 398
Doctrinal Content 399
Lutheran Theologians on Chronicles 418
Questions People Ask about Chronicles 420
Further Study 421

Ezra and Nehemiah 423
Chart: Persian Rulers 426
Composition 426
Outline for Ezra 431
Outline for Nehemiah 435
Doctrinal Content 439
Lutheran Theologians on Ezra-Nehemiah 447
Questions People Ask about Ezra and Nehemiah 450
Further Study 457

Esther 459
Composition 460
Article: Major Historical Matters in the Book of Esther 464
Outline 468
Doctrinal Content 469
Lutheran Theologians on Esther 477
Further Study 479

The Books of Wisdom and Poetry 481
Chart: Categories of Wisdom 485
Article: The Writings 491

Job 495
Composition 499
Outline 508
Doctrinal Content 511
Lutheran Theologians on Job 524
Article: The Place of Wisdom in the Bible 528
Questions People Ask about Job 535
Further Study 538

Psalms .541
- Article: The Psalms in Israel's Worship .545
- Chart: Names in the Psalms .550
- Composition .551
- Outline .570
- Doctrinal Content .573
- Lutheran Theologians on Psalms .606
- Questions People Ask about Psalms .612
- Further Study .617

Proverbs .621
- Composition .622
- Doctrinal Content .631
- Outline .632
- Article: Extrabiblical "Wisdom" .645
- Lutheran Theologians on Proverbs .648
- Further Study .651

Ecclesiastes .653
- Composition .654
- Article: Misunderstanding Luther .655
- Outline .660
- Doctrinal Content .661
- Lutheran Theologians on Ecclesiastes .666
- Questions People Ask about Ecclesiastes .669
- Further Study .672

Song of Solomon .675
- Composition .676
- Article: Issues Raised by Critics .677
- Doctrinal Content .682
- Outline .683
- Article: History of Interpretation .685
- Lutheran Theologians on Song of Solomon .695
- Further Study .699

The Books of the Prophets .701
- Chart: Major and Minor Prophets .701
- Article: Definition of "Prophet" .703
- Article: Understanding Classic Critical Views .708

Isaiah .715
- Composition .716
- Outline .718
- Doctrinal Content .728
- Article: Did Jesus Bring Peace? .736
- Lutheran Theologians on Isaiah .743
- Further Study .748

Jeremiah .751
- Article: The House of Shaphan .754
- Composition .755
- Outline .760
- Doctrinal Content .761
- Chart: The Order of Jeremiah's Prophecies .763
- Article: Jeremiah and the Lachish Ostraca .767
- Lutheran Theologians on Jeremiah .774
- Further Study .779

Lamentations .781
- Composition .782
- Outline .785
- Doctrinal Content .786
- Lutheran Theologians on Lamentations .791
- Further Study .793

Ezekiel .795
- Composition .796
- Outline .801
- Doctrinal Content .804
- Lutheran Theologians on Ezekiel .813
- Further Study .816
- Article: Apocalyptic Literature .817

Daniel .823
- Composition .824
- Outline .828
- Doctrinal Content .833
- Lutheran Theologians on Daniel .840
- Further Study .843
- Article: Daniel and History .844

The Book of the Twelve .851

Hosea .853
- Composition .855
- Outline .858
- Doctrinal Content .860
- Lutheran Theologians on Hosea .863
- Further Study .865

Joel .866
- Composition .867
- Outline .870
- Doctrinal Content .871
- Lutheran Theologians on Joel .874
- Further Study .877

Amos 878
Composition 880
Outline 884
Doctrinal Content 886
Lutheran Theologians on Amos 889
Article: Is God the Author of Evil? 891
Further Study 893

Obadiah 895
Composition 896
Outline 898
Doctrinal Content 899
Lutheran Theologians on Obadiah 901
Further Study 903

Jonah 905
Composition 906
Outline 908
Doctrinal Content 910
Lutheran Theologians on Jonah 914
Article: The Prophet Jonah and the Great Fish 916
Further Study 919

Micah 921
Composition 922
Doctrinal Content 925
Outline 926
Lutheran Theologians on Micah 930
Further Study 933

Nahum 935
Composition 936
Outline 939
Doctrinal Content 940
Lutheran Theologians on Nahum 942
Further Study 945

Habakkuk 947
Composition 948
Outline 950
Doctrinal Content 953
Lutheran Theologians on Habakkuk 957
Further Study 959

Zephaniah 960
Composition 961
Doctrinal Content 963
Outline 964
Lutheran Theologians on Zephaniah 967
Further Study 969

Haggai 971
Composition 972
Outline 974
Doctrinal Content 976
Lutheran Theologians on Haggai 979
Further Study 981

Zechariah 983
Composition 983
Outline 986
Doctrinal Content 988
Lutheran Theologians on Zechariah 993
Further Study 995

Malachi 997
Composition 998
Doctrinal Content 1000
Outline 1001
Lutheran Theologians on Malachi 1006
Further Study 1010
Chart: Order of Books in Hebrew Bible 1011

Art Credits 1012

VOLUME 2

Alphabetical Order of Biblical Books, Including Apocrypha xiii
Abbreviations xiv
Maps and Diagrams. .xvii
Transliteration Guidelines. xviii
Editor's Preface. 1
THE APOCRYPHA (19 Books)
and the Time between the Testaments 3
Article: The Holy Scripture and Other Ancient Writings. 6
Article: Arrangement of the Apocrypha. . .11
Judith. 15
Composition. 16
Outline. 18
Doctrinal Content 20
Lutheran Theologians on Judith 23
Further Study 25
The Wisdom of Solomon 27
Composition. 28
Outline. 30
Doctrinal Content 32
Lutheran Theologians on the Wisdom of Solomon 35
Further Study 37
Tobit. 39
Composition. 40
Outline. 42
Doctrinal Content 45
Lutheran Theologians on Tobit 47
Further Study 49
Ecclesiasticus (Wisdom of Jesus son of Sirach) 51
Composition. 52
Outline. 54
Doctrinal Content 55
Lutheran Theologians on Ecclesiasticus . . .58
Further Study 59
Baruch. 61
Composition. 62
Outline. 64
Doctrinal Content 65
Lutheran Theologians on Baruch. 67
Further Study 69
The Letter of Jeremiah. 71
Composition. 72
Doctrinal Content 74
Outline. 75
Lutheran Theologians on The Letter of Jeremiah 76
Further Study 77
1 Maccabees. 79
Composition. 80
Outline. 82
Doctrinal Content 85
Lutheran Theologians on 1 Maccabees. . . .88
Further Study 90
2 Maccabees. 93
Composition. 94
Outline. 96
Doctrinal Content 97
Lutheran Theologians on 2 Maccabees. . .101
Further Study 103
Old Greek Esther 104
Composition. 105
Outline. 107
Doctrinal Content .111
Lutheran Theologians on Old Greek Esther 113
Further Study 115
Susanna. 117
Composition. 118
Outline. 120
Doctrinal Content .121
Lutheran Theologians on Susanna. 123
Further Study 125
Bel and the Dragon .127
Composition. 128
Outline. 129
Doctrinal Content .130
Lutheran Theologians on Bel and the Dragon 132
Further Study 133

The Prayer of Azariah and the Song of the Three Holy Children 135
- Composition 136
- Outline 137
- Doctrinal Content 138
- Lutheran Theologians on the Prayer and the Song 140
- Further Study 141

The Prayer of Manasseh 143
- Composition 143
- Outline 145
- Doctrinal Content 145
- Lutheran Theologians on the Prayer of Manasseh 147
- Further Study 148

The Apocrypha in Other Christian Traditions 149
- 1 Esdras 149
- 2 Esdras 150
- 3 Maccabees (Ptolemaika) 150
- 4 Maccabees 152
- Psalm 151 152

THE NEW TESTAMENT (27 books)
- New Testament Authority 155
- Article: The Canon of the New Testament 156
- Article: Demon Possession at the Time of Christ 165
- Article: The Resurrection of Jesus 169

The Gospels 175
- Article: The Synoptic Problem 178

Matthew 185
- Composition 187
- Outline 193
- Doctrinal Content 194
- Lutheran Theologians on Matthew 214
- Questions People Ask about Matthew 219
- Further Study 230

Mark 233
- Composition 234
- Outline 239
- Doctrinal Content 244
- Lutheran Theologians on Mark 255
- Questions People Ask about Mark 257
- Further Study 264

Luke 267
- Chart: The Temple in Luke 268
- Composition 269
- Outline 275
- Doctrinal Content 277
- Chart: Luke's Unique Contribution 285
- Lutheran Theologians on Luke 295
- Questions People Ask about Luke 297
- Further Study 315

John 319
- Composition 321
- Outline 331
- Doctrinal Content 333
- Lutheran Theologians on John 346
- Questions People Ask about John 350
- Further Study 356

The Acts of the Apostles 359
- Composition 362
- Article: Acts and the Critics 364
- Outline 369
- Doctrinal Content 374
- Lutheran Theologians on Acts 402
- Questions People Ask about Acts 405
- Further Study 408

The Epistles of Paul 411
- Chart: Paul's Letters and You 414

Romans 417
- Composition 419
- Outline 421
- Doctrinal Content 424
- Lutheran Theologians on Romans 433
- Questions People Ask about Romans 435
- Further Study 438

1 Corinthians 441
- Composition 442
- Article: Paul's Known Visits and Letters to Corinth 445
- Article: Speaking in Tongues 448
- Outline 456
- Doctrinal Content 459
- Lutheran Theologians on 1 Corinthians 468
- Questions People Ask about 1 Corinthians 471
- Further Study 477

2 Corinthians 479
Composition 482
Doctrinal Content 485
Outline 486
Lutheran Theologians on 2 Corinthians . . 494
Further Study 497

Galatians 499
Composition 502
Outline 504
Doctrinal Content 506
Lutheran Theologians on Galatians 512
Questions People Ask about Galatians . . . 514
Further Study 516

Ephesians 519
Article: Authenticity of Ephesians 523
Composition 524
Doctrinal Content 527
Outline 528
Lutheran Theologians on Ephesians 533
Article: Captivity Letters 534
Further Study 537

Philippians 539
Composition 540
Outline 543
Doctrinal Content 544
Lutheran Theologians on Philippians 548
Further Study 549

Colossians, ... 551
Composition 552
Outline 554
Doctrinal Content 555
Lutheran Theologians on Colossians 559
Further Study 561

1 Thessalonians 563
Composition 566
Outline 569
Doctrinal Content 570
Lutheran Theologians on 1 Thessalonians 574
Further Study 577

2 Thessalonians 579
Composition 580
Doctrinal Content 582
Outline 583
Lutheran Theologians on 2 Thessalonians 587
Questions People Ask about 2 Thessalonians 589
Further Study 591
Article: The Pastoral Letters 593

1 Timothy 597
Composition 599
Outline 606
Doctrinal Content 607
Lutheran Theologians on 1 Timothy 611
Further Study 613

2 Timothy 615
Composition 616
Doctrinal Content 617
Outline 619
Lutheran Theologians on 2 Timothy 621
Questions People Ask about 2 Timothy . . 622
Further Study 623

Titus 625
Composition 626
Doctrinal Content 627
Outline 629
Lutheran Theologians on Titus 631
Further Study 633

Philemon 635
Composition 636
Doctrinal Content 637
Outline 639
Lutheran Theologians on Philemon 641
Further Study 643

The General Epistles 645
Chart: Order of General Epistles 648

Hebrews 651
Composition 652
Outline 655
Doctrinal Content 659
Lutheran Theologians on Hebrews 666
Questions People Ask about Hebrews 670
Further Study 672

James 675
Composition 677
Outline 685
Doctrinal Content 687
Lutheran Theologians on James 694
Further Study 699

1 Peter .701
Composition .702
Outline .706
Doctrinal Content .709
Lutheran Theologians on 1 Peter .713
Further Study .716

2 Peter .719
Composition .720
Chart: Epistles Likely Prepared through a Scribe .721
Outline .725
Doctrinal Content .727
Lutheran Theologians on 2 Peter .730
Further Study .734

1, 2, and 3 John .737
Composition .738
Outline .742
Doctrinal Content .746
Lutheran Theologians on 1, 2, and 3 John .752
Further Study .754

Jude .757
Composition .758
Doctrinal Content .761
Outline .762
Lutheran Theologians on Jude .765
Further Study .769

Revelation .771
Outline .776
Composition .778
Doctrinal Content .783
Lutheran Theologians on Revelation .791
Further Study .794

Archaeology and the Bible .797
Chart: Common Archaeological Periods .814
Helpful Resources .815

Ancient Literature and the Holy Scriptures .817

The Church from Age to Age .823

How the Bible Came to Us .827

Bible Dictionary/Index .831

Art Credits .990

Alphabetical Order of Biblical Books, Including Apocrypha

Acts of the Apostles 2:359
Amos 1:878
Azariah, Prayer of 2:135

Baruch 2:61
Bel and the Dragon 2:127

Chronicles (1) 1:381
Chronicles (2) 1:381
Colossians, Letter to the 2:551
Corinthians, Letter to the (1) 2:441
Corinthians, Letter to the (2) 2:479

Daniel 1:823
Deuteronomy 1:157

Ecclesiastes 1:653
Ecclesiasticus (Wisdom of Jesus son of Sirach) 2:51
Ephesians, Letter to the 2:519
Esdras (1) 2:149
Esdras (2) 2:150
Esther 1:459
Esther, Old Greek 2:104
Exodus 1:59
Ezekiel 1:795
Ezra 1:423

Galatians, Letter to the 2:499
Genesis 1:13

Habakkuk 1:947
Haggai 1:971
Hebrews, Letter to the 2:651
Hosea 1:853

Isaiah 1:715

James, Letter of 2:675
Jeremiah 1:751
Jeremiah, Letter of 2:71
Job 1:495
Joel 1:866
John, Gospel of 2:319
John, Letter of (1) 2:737
John, Letter of (2) 2:737
John, Letter of (3) 2:737
Jonah 1:905
Joshua 1:199
Jude, Letter of 2:757
Judges 1:229
Judith 2:15

Kings (1) 1:321
Kings (2) 1:321

Lamentations 1:781
Leviticus 1:99
Luke, Gospel of 2:267

Maccabees (1) 2:79
Maccabees (2) 2:93
Maccabees (3; Ptolemaika) 2:150
Maccabees (4) 2:152
Malachi 1:997
Manasseh, Prayer of 2:143
Mark, Gospel of 2:233
Matthew, Gospel of 2:185
Micah 1:921

Nahum 1:935
Nehemiah 1:423
Numbers 1:127

Obadiah 1:895

Peter, Letter of (1) 2:701
Peter, Letter of (2) 2:719
Philemon, Letter to 2:635
Philippians, Letter to the 2:539
Proverbs 1:621
Psalm 151 ..... 2:152
Psalms 1:541

Revelation 2:771
Romans, Letter to the 2:417
Ruth 1:253

Samuel (1) 1:271
Samuel (2) 1:271
Song of Solomon 1:675
Song of the Three Holy Children 2:135
Susanna 2:117

Thessalonians, Letter to the (1) 2:563
Thessalonians, Letter to the (2) 2:579
Timothy, Letter to (1) 2:597
Timothy, Letter to (2) 2:615
Titus, Letter to 2:625
Tobit 2:39

Wisdom of Solomon 2:27

Zechariah 1:983
Zephaniah 1:960

ABBREVIATIONS

= . . . . means the wording is the same or virtually so
AD . . . . *anno Domini* (in the year of [our] Lord)
Aram . . . . Aramaic
BC . . . . before Christ
c . . . . circa
cf . . . . confer
ch . . . . chapter
chs . . . . chapters
esp . . . . especially
Grm . . . . German
Gk . . . . Greek
Hbr. . . . . Hebrew
lit . . . . literally
NT . . . . New Testament
OT . . . . Old Testament
p . . . . page
pp . . . . pages
v . . . . verse
vv . . . . verses

Canonical Scripture

Gn . . . . Genesis
Ex. . . . . Exodus
Lv . . . . Leviticus
Nu . . . . Numbers
Dt. . . . . Deuteronomy
Jsh . . . . Joshua
Jgs. . . . . Judges
Ru. . . . . Ruth
1Sm . . . . 1 Samuel
2Sm . . . . 2 Samuel
1Ki . . . . 1 Kings
2Ki . . . . 2 Kings
1Ch . . . . 1 Chronicles
2Ch . . . . 2 Chronicles
Ezr . . . . Ezra
Ne. . . . . Nehemiah
Est . . . . Esther
Jb . . . . Job
Ps . . . . Psalms
Pr . . . . Proverbs
Ec . . . . Ecclesiastes
Sg . . . . Song of Solomon
Is . . . . Isaiah
Jer. . . . . Jeremiah
Lm . . . . Lamentations
Ezk. . . . . Ezekiel
Dn . . . . Daniel
Hos. . . . . Hosea
Jl . . . . Joel
Am. . . . . Amos
Ob . . . . Obadiah
Jnh . . . . Jonah
Mi. . . . . Micah
Na. . . . . Nahum
Hab . . . . Habakkuk
Zep. . . . . Zephaniah
Hg . . . . Haggai
Zec. . . . . Zechariah
Mal. . . . . Malachi
Mt. . . . . Matthew
Mk . . . . Mark
Lk. . . . . Luke
Jn . . . . John
Ac. . . . . Acts
Rm . . . . Romans
1Co . . . . 1 Corinthians
2Co . . . . 2 Corinthians
Gal . . . . Galatians
Eph. . . . . Ephesians
Php. . . . . Philippians
Col . . . . Colossians
1Th. 1 Thessalonians
2Th. 2 Thessalonians
1Tm . . . . 1 Timothy
2Tm . . . . 2 Timothy
Ti . . . . Titus
Phm . . . . Philemon
Heb . . . . Hebrews
Jas. . . . . James
1Pt . . . . 1 Peter
2Pt . . . . 2 Peter

1Jn . . . . . 1 John
2Jn . . . . . 2 John
3Jn . . . . . 3 John
Jude . . . . . Jude
Rv . . . . . Revelation

The Apocrypha

Jth. . . . . . Judith
Wis. . . . . . The Wisdom of Solomon
Tob. . . . . . Tobit
Ecclus. . . . . . Ecclesiasticus (Sirach)
Bar . . . . . . Baruch
Lt Jer . . . . . . The Letter of Jeremiah
1Macc . . . . . . 1 Maccabees
2Macc . . . . . . 2 Maccabees
Old Grk Est. . . . . . Old Greek Esther
Sus . . . . . . Susanna
Bel . . . . . . Bel and the Dragon
Pr Az . . . . . . The Prayer of Azariah
Sg Three. . . . . . The Song of the Three Holy Children
Pr Man. . . . . . Prayer of Manasseh

Other Books

1Esd. . . . . . 1 Esdras
2Esd. . . . . . 2 Esdras
3Macc . . . . . . 3 Maccabees (Ptolemaika)
4Macc . . . . . . 4 Maccabees
Ps 151. . . . . . Psalm 151
1En. . . . . . *1 Enoch*
2En. . . . . . *2 Enoch*
Jub . . . . . . *Jubilees*

Commonly Cited Works and Authors

AB — The Anchor Bible Commentary series.

ACCS — Ancient Christian Commentary on Scripture. Thomas C. Oden, gen. ed. 29 vols. Downers Grove, IL: InterVarsity Press, 2000–2009.

AE — Luther, Martin. *Luther's Works*. American Edition. Vols. 1–30: Edited by Jaroslav Pelikan. St. Louis: Concordia, 1955–76. Vols. 31–55: Edited by Helmut Lehmann. Philadelphia/Minneapolis: Muhlenberg/Fortress, 1957–86. Vols. 56–75: Edited by Christopher Boyd Brown. St. Louis: Concordia, 2009–.

ANF — Roberts, Alexander, and James Donaldson, eds. *The Ante-Nicene Fathers: The Writings of the Fathers Down to AD 325*. 10 vols. Buffalo: The Christian Literature Publishing Company, 1885–96. Reprint, Grand Rapids, MI: Eerdmans, 2001.

Ant — Josephus, Flavius. *Antiquities of the Jews*. In *The Works of Josephus*. Translated by William Whiston. Peabody, MA: Hendrickson Publishers, 1987.

Ap — Apology of the Augsburg Confession. From *Concordia*.

ALEN — Engelbrecht, Edward A., gen. ed. *The Apocrypha: The Lutheran Edition with Notes*. St. Louis: Concordia, 2012.

CBCA — Cambridge Bible Commentaries on the Apocrypha.

CC — Concordia Commentary series. St. Louis: Concordia, 1996–.

CC 2Pt/Jude — Giese, Curtis P. *2 Peter and Jude*. CC. St. Louis: Concordia, 2012.

CC Col — Deterding, Paul E. *Colossians*. CC. St. Louis: Concordia, 2003.

CC Dn — Steinmann, Andrew E. *Daniel*. CC. St. Louis: Concordia, 2009.

CC Jnh — Lessing, R. Reed. *Jonah*. CC. St. Louis: Concordia, 2007.

CC Lk1 — Just, Arthur A. *Luke 1:1–9:50*. CC. St. Louis: Concordia, 1996.

CC Mt1 — Gibbs, Jeffrey A. *Matthew 1:1–11*. CC. St. Louis: Concordia, 2006.

CC Rv — Brighton, Louis A. *Revelation*. CC. St. Louis: Concordia, 2004.

Concordia — McCain, Paul Timothy, ed. *Concordia: The Lutheran Confessions*. 2nd ed. St. Louis: Concordia, 2006.

Ep — Epitome of the Formula of Concord. From *Concordia*.

FC — Formula of Concord. From *Concordia*.

GWFT — God's Word for Today. Bible study series. St. Louis: Concordia, 1994–.

ICC — International Critical Commentary.

K&D — Keil, C. F., and F. Delitzsch. *Biblical Commentary on the Old Testament.* Translated by J. Martin et al. 25 vols. Edinburgh, 1857–78.

KJV — King James Version of Scripture.

LBC — Engelbrecht, Edward A., gen. ed. *Lutheran Bible Companion.* St. Louis: Concordia, 2014.

LC — Large Catechism of Martin Luther. From *Concordia.*

LCHS — Lange, John Peter. Lange's Commentary on the Holy Scriptures. Edited by John Peter Lange and Philip Schaff. 25 vols. New York: Charles Scribner's Sons, 1893.

LL — LifeLight. Bible study series. St. Louis: Concordia, 1999–.

LSB — Commission on Worship of The Lutheran Church—Missouri Synod. *Lutheran Service Book.* St. Louis: Concordia, 2006.

LSB Altar Book — Commission on Worship of The Lutheran Church—Missouri Synod. *Lutheran Service Book: Altar Book.* St. Louis: Concordia, 2006.

LXX — Septuagint. Koine Greek Old Testament.

MT — Masoretic text.

NAC — New American Commentary. 38 vols. Nashville: Broadman & Holman, 1991–2010.

NCBC — New Century Bible Commentary.

NICNT — New International Commentary on the New Testament.

NICOT — New International Commentary on the Old Testament.

NIGTC — New International Greek Testament Commentary.

*NPNF*1 — Schaff, Philip, ed. *A Select Library of Nicene and Post-Nicene Fathers of the Christian Church,* Series 1. 14 vols. New York: The Christian Literature Series, 1886–89. Reprint, Grand Rapids, MI: Eerdmans, 1956.

*NPNF*2 — Schaff, Philip, and Henry Wace, ed. *A Select Library of Nicene and Post-Nicene Fathers of the Christian Church,* Series 2. 14 vols. New York: The Christian Literature Series, 1890–99. Reprint, Grand Rapids, MI: Eerdmans, 1952, 1961.

OTL — Old Testament Library.

PBC — People's Bible Commentary. 41 vols. St. Louis: Concordia, 1994, 2005.

RHBC — Reformation Heritage Bible Commentary. St. Louis: Concordia, 2013–.

SC — Luther, Martin. *Luther's Small Catechism with Explanation.* St. Louis: Concordia, 1986.

SD — Solid Declaration of the Formula of Concord. From *Concordia.*

Steinmann — Steinmann, Andrew E. *From Abraham to Paul: A Biblical Chronology.* St. Louis: Concordia, 2011.

StL — *Dr. Martin Luthers Sämmtliche Schriften.* Herausgegeben von Dr. Joh. Georg Walch. Neue revidirte Stereotypausgabe. St. Louis: Concordia, 1880–1910.

ThC E1 — Gerhard, Johann. *Theological Commonplaces.* Exegesis 1, *On the Nature of Theology and On Scripture.* Edited with annotations by Benjamin T. G. Mayes. Translated by Richard J. Dinda. St. Louis: Concordia, 2009.

TLSB — Engelbrecht, Edward A., gen. ed. *The Lutheran Study Bible.* St. Louis: Concordia, 2009.

TNTC — Tyndale New Testament Commentaries.

TOTC — Tyndale Old Testament Commentaries.

WA DB — *D. Martin Luthers Werke: Deutsche Bibel* [Luther's Works, Weimar Edition: German Bible]. 12 vols. in 15. Weimar: H. Böhlau, 1906–.

WA TR — *D. Martin Luthers Werke: Tischreden.* 6 vols. Weimar: H. Böhlau, 1912–21.

WBC — Word Biblical Commentary.

MAPS AND DIAGRAMS

Volume 1

The Land of the Bible
Ancient Trade Routes lxx

Genesis
Abraham's Travels. 25
Jacob's Travels 29

Exodus
The Tabernacle 72
The Ark of the Covenant. 75
The Exodus 81

Numbers
Wilderness Wanderings 140

Joshua
The Conquest of Canaan. 211
The Twelve Tribes. .212

Ruth
Journeys of Naomi and Ruth 260

1 and 2 Samuel
Kingdom and Battles of Saul 290
Saul Pursues David 292
Kingdom of David .293
Background of Jerusalem 305

1 and 2 Kings
Kingdom of David and Solomon. 331
Israel and Judah 345
Assyrian Exile of Israel 352
Solomon's Temple. .359
Art Forms of Solomon's Period 360

1 and 2 Chronicles
Solomon's Kingdom. 391
Babylonian Exile of Judah. 413

Ezra and Nehemiah
Zerubbabel's Temple 445

Job
Locations of Job 497

Hosea
Hosea's Setting 854

Amos
Amos's Ministry 880

Jonah
Travels of Jonah 907

Volume 2

The Apocrypha and the Time between the Testaments
The Empire of Alexander 12
The Hasmonean Conquest 13

Tobit
Israelite/Jewish Diaspora Settlements. 41

The New Testament
Herod's Temple. 159

Matthew
The Kingdom of Herod 195
Travels of the Holy Family 196
Key Locations in Jesus' Ministry 199

Acts
The Apostles' Ministry (Acts 1–12). 367
Plan of Ancient Antioch 377
Plan of Athens 379
The Temple of Herod. 382–83
Paul's Missionary Journeys (Acts 13–21) 388
The Roman Empire and Paul's Journey to Rome 391
Herod's Temple (Aerial View) 401

Romans
Plan of Ancient Rome 418

1 Corinthians
Corinth and Vicinity 443

1 Peter
Regions and Cities of Asia Minor 705

TRANSLITERATION GUIDELINES

References to the Hebrew, Aramaic, and Greek texts of the Bible appear at various places in *LBC*, especially in the Bible Dictionary. Transliterated terms were included to support in-depth study of the text. Readers who do not desire to study a foreign term or phrase may skip over it just as one may skip over etymological information in an English dictionary.

A transliterated word in *LBC* is usually a lexical form, but may also be (1) a form in a specific text, or (2) a form found in English usage (e.g., Baal).

Hebrew and Aramaic Transliteration

Hebrew Consonants	English Consonants
א : alef	ʼ
ב : bet	b
ג : gimel	g
ד : dalet	d
ה : he	h
ו : waw	w
ז : zayin	z
ח : chet	ch
ט : tet	t
י : yod	y
ך or כ : kaph	k
ל : lamed	l
ם or מ : mem	m
ן or נ : nun	n
ס : samek	s
ע : ayin	ʻ
ף or פ : pe	p; f; or ph
ץ or צ : tsade	ts
ק : qof	q
ר : resh	r
ש : sin/shin	s; sh
ת : taw	t; th

Hebrew Vowels	English Vowels
patach	a
furtive patach	a
qamets	a
final qamets he	ah
seghol	e
tsere	e
tsere yod	e
short hireq	i
long hireq	i
hireq yod	i
qamets chatuph	o
holem	o
full holem	o
short qibbuts	u
long qibbuts	u
shureq	u
chatef qamets	o
chatef patach	a

Greek Transliteration

Greek Letters	English Letters
α : alpha	a
β : beta	b
γ : gamma	g
γ : gamma nasal (before γ, κ, ξ, χ)	n
δ : delta	d
ε : epsilon	e
ζ : zeta	z
η : eta	e
θ : theta	th
ι : iota	i
κ : kappa	k
λ : lambda	l
μ : mu	m
ν : nu	n

Greek Letters	English Letters
ξ : xi	x
ο : omicron	o
π : pi	p
ρ : rho	r
ρ : initial rho (or in medial double rho)	rh
σ and **ς** : sigma	s
τ : tau	t
υ : upsilon (not in diphthong)	y
υ : upsilon (in diphthong)	u
φ : phi	ph
χ : chi	ch
ψ : psi	ps
ω : omega	o
ʽ : rough breathing mark	h

Adapted from *The SBL Handbook of Style* (Peabody, MA: Hendrickson Publishers), 1999, 28–29.

EDITOR'S PREFACE

Lutherans who study the Bible, preach, or teach in English have never had their own comprehensive handbook of the Bible. They have contented themselves with works of varying value by other Christians. From the respectable *Halley's Bible Handbook*, which first appeared as a pamphlet in 1922, to volumes that promote theology of glory, confusion of Law and Gospel, and criticism of the Bible—the Lutheran reader has had to settle for less than helpful resources or search a variety of works to get at the insights needed for basic Bible Study. For these reasons, a *Lutheran Bible Companion* was needed.

This volume is the last in a series of works that began in 2003 when we organized the Grow in His Word research project in the Adult Bible Study area at Concordia Publishing House. That research project focused on how people read the Bible and what questions came to mind for them as they read portions of the English Standard Version (ESV). The project led to our publication of *The Lutheran Study Bible* (*TLSB*; 2009) and *The Apocrypha: The Lutheran Edition with Notes* (*ALEN*; 2012).

Special thanks are due to our designer, Stacy Johnston, who contributed so greatly to the visual content, as well as our production editors, Laura L. Lane and Sarah J. Steiner, proofreader Kari Vo, and production coordinator Pam Burgdorf. Additional thanks to Rev. Roy Askins, who updated the Bible Dictionary and created the index. I praise God for their dedicated service.

We trust that you will enjoy getting to know the Bible better as you call on the Holy Spirit who inspired the Holy Scriptures and as you consult this volume to learn more about the history, culture, setting, and teaching of the Scriptures. May God grant you life by His Word (Psalm 119:25).

Rev. Edward A. Engelbrecht, STM
Concordia Publishing House
Senior Editor, Bible Resources
General Editor, *Lutheran Bible Companion*

An ancient olive tree in Gethsemane, though split by lightning, continues to flourish.

THE APOCRYPHA AND THE TIME BETWEEN THE TESTAMENTS

When the Prophets Ceased to Speak

The Time between the Testaments (c 430–2 BC)

Who are the Pharisees, and where did they come from? How did the Romans end up in Judea? Who wrote the Dead Sea Scrolls? The Old Testament books do not answer these questions or the many others that naturally come up when you read the New Testament.

This is because there is a gap or "silent period" from the last writing prophet, Malachi (c 430 BC), until the New Testament era. These four centuries abounded with historic, religious, and social developments—the most important being that the prophets ceased to speak (cf 1Macc 4:46; 9:27; 14:41). By learning about this intertestamental period, you will gain a much better understanding of the New Testament world and the culture in which Jesus conducted His earthly ministry. (A more thorough overview is provided by Raymond F. Surburg in *ALEN*; see pp xci–c.)

An ancient Greek amphora. During the Time between the Testaments, Alexander the Great brought increased Hellenistic (Greek) influence into the Holy Land.

Historical Events

The Time between the Testaments begins with the Persian emperor Cyrus the Great (d c 530 BC), who conquered Babylon and allowed the Judeans to return to Jerusalem. Cyrus and other Persian rulers demonstrated a tolerant attitude toward the Judeans and other religious and ethnic groups (see *TLSB* notes, Ezr 1:1–2). Cyrus supported the rebuilding of Jerusalem and its temple, which took several decades. The last Old Testament prophets (Ezra, Nehemiah, Haggai, Zechariah, and Malachi) supported this work. The Judeans made a new commitment to God's Word, and life for them was fairly peaceful.

About a century later (332 BC), the Macedonian general Alexander the Great took Judea away from the Persians. Alexander planned to unite his new empire by spreading the Greek language and Greek culture (a policy called "Hellenization," meaning "from the Greek"). But Alexander did not forcefully oppose the Judeans or their religious practices. After Alexander died in 323 BC, his vast empire was divided between four of his generals (cf Dn 8:22; 1Macc 1:5–9).

Ptolemy, one of Alexander's generals, ruled Israel and Egypt. Ptolemy's descendants allowed the Judeans to practice their religion and culture, while they also continued the policy of Hellenization. In 198 BC, descendants of Seleucus, another of Alexander's generals, conquered the region of Judea. The Seleucid rulers forcefully opposed the religion of the Judeans and outlawed its practice. For example, they made it illegal to possess a copy of the Hebrew Scriptures (1Macc 1:56–57). To circumcise someone was punishable by death (1Macc 1:60–61).

The worst Seleucid ruler, Antiochus IV Epiphanes (175–164 BC), caused a Judean revolt because he erected a statue of Zeus in the Jerusalem temple court, sacrificed a pig on its altar, and insisted that the Lord's priests participate in pagan sacrifices (1Macc 1:44–50; 2:15–18; 2Macc 6:1–2). A Judean named Mattathias rebelled against representatives of the Seleucid Empire (1Macc 2); faithful Judeans supported this rebellion (167 BC). Led by Mattathias's sons, the Judeans won independence. They regained Jerusalem and purified the temple (commemorated by the Jewish festival of Hanukkah).

Mattathias's descendants, the Hasmoneans, ruled the land until the Roman military helped settle a civil war between two Hasmonean brothers, each of whom claimed Israel's throne. The Roman Empire established control of the region in 63 BC. Rome and its Byzantine successors ruled Judea until AD 637. For more on religious and social developments, see *ALEN*, pp xiv–c.

Literature

Perhaps the most important work produced during this "silent period" was the Septuagint (LXX). Jewish scholars translated the Hebrew Scriptures into Koine, or "common," Greek, the language used in the Mediterranean world. As a result of Alexander's conquests and the process of Hellenization, this simplified Greek served as the business language for dozens of different people groups.

The LXX receives its name from the tradition that 72 Jewish scholars were responsible for the translation (attested by the *Letter of Aristeas*). New Testament writers frequently used the LXX when citing Scripture, and even Jesus may have used it (cf Gn 2:24; Mt 19:5).

The Dead Sea Scrolls were also produced during the Time between the Testaments. These were discovered in 1947 near Qumran, near the northwest shore of the Dead Sea, and have added greatly to our knowledge of the time. About one-third of the scrolls are copies of books from the Hebrew Scriptures and generally demonstrate the preciseness with which the Scriptures were passed down. Other scrolls include commentaries on books of Hebrew Scriptures and sectarian documents about the beliefs of the Qumran community.

A wide variety of other works were produced during the centuries leading up to Christ's birth. Most prominent are the Apocrypha, the books of which appear in the LXX. The Apocrypha helps readers understand the world in which the New Testament was born. For a thorough overview of the Apocrypha and the Time between the Testaments, see Surburg's introduction in *ALEN*, pp xiv–c. For more on other ancient literature that was not included in the Bible, read "The Holy Scripture and Other Ancient Writings" (pp 6–10).

The Holy Scripture and Other Ancient Writings

Curiosity about books that were not included in the Holy Bible has greatly increased in recent times. The discovery of the Dead Sea Scrolls (Jewish, first and second centuries BC), the Nag Hammadi Codices (Gnostic, AD second and third centuries), and other documents (see below) has also increased media attention on this issue. Just as some scholars and religious groups today question the authority or genuineness of some biblical books, ancient critics and later scholars of Renaissance humanism raised similar questions about books of Scripture.

The Lutheran reformers and theologians were fully familiar with such questions and the methods that the critics used. Although archaeologists have discovered new documents in recent decades, the methods for evaluating the historical and spiritual worth of such documents have changed little since the Renaissance and the Reformation. Like the early Christians, medieval Christians, and Luther during the Reformation, we face questions about distinguishing which writings are (1) Sacred Scripture; (2) useful writings, though not the same as Sacred Scripture; or (3) false and spiritually harmful writings.

The following essay summarizes how Lutherans have reflected on these issues. Luther's prefaces to the Apocrypha, which are cited in the introductions to specific books of the Apocrypha, illustrate these reflections in use.

What Is Holy Scripture?

> We believe, teach, and confess that the only rule and norm according to which all teachings, together with ‹all› teachers, should be evaluated and judged [2 Timothy 3:15–17] are the prophetic and apostolic Scriptures of the Old and New Testament alone. For it is written in Psalm 119:105, "Your word is a lamp to my feet and a light to my path." St. Paul has written, "even if we or an angel from heaven should preach to you a gospel contrary to the one we preached to you, let him be accursed" (Galatians 1:8). However, other writings by ancient or modern teachers—no matter whose name they bear—must not be regarded as equal to the Holy Scriptures. All of them are subject to the Scriptures. (FC Ep Sum 1–2)

The importance of Holy Scripture for Christian faith and life leads us to consider how it became "holy." What is it about Scripture that makes it sacred? Historically, Lutherans have recognized the following characteristics of the books of Sacred Scripture, summarized by Robert Preus:

> (a) the depth of the mysteries revealed in Scripture, (b) the majesty of God speaking to us in Scripture, (c) the truthfulness of Scripture, (d) the sufficiency of the teachings and precepts of Scripture, (e) the profound and yet simple manner in which Scripture speaks to us, (f) the power of Scripture to bend the hearts of sinful people and give them hope, (g) the fact that Scripture has maintained its authority in the face of time and opposition, (h) the remarkable harmony between the Old and the New Testament. (Robert D. Preus, The Theology of Post-Reformation Lutheranism [St. Louis: Concordia, 1970], 1:301)

Along with these features of Scripture, we should note that the Holy Scripture was written by prophets, evangelists, and apostles whom God chose and inspired to lead His people. The congregations of both the Old and New Testaments recognized this inspiration and authority so that the books of Scripture continued in use throughout Christian churches from the beginning.[1]

Luther, with his characteristic flair, draws all such thoughts together in his preface to the Old Testament and notes:

> Dismiss your own opinions and feelings, and think of the Scriptures as the loftiest and noblest of holy things, as the richest of mines which can never be sufficiently explored, in order that you may find that divine wisdom which God here lays before you in such simple guise as to quench all pride. Here you will find the swaddling cloths and the manger in which Christ lies, and to which the angel points the shepherds [Luke 2:12]. Simple and lowly are these swaddling cloths [of the Scriptures], but dear is the treasure, Christ, who lies in them. (AE 35:236)

Inspiration

> All Scripture is breathed out by God and profitable for teaching, for reproof, for correction, and for training in righteousness. (2Tm 3:16)

---

1 Though the Church recognized the Scripture as God's Word, it did not "create" the Scripture as God's Word on human authority. The Scripture is self-authenticating. For example, if a child sees an apple and declares, "There's an apple," no one would suggest that the child's declaration created the apple. He simply sees it for what it is.

The biblical teaching about inspiration of Scripture deserves special attention. When Paul wrote to Timothy about the inspiration of Scripture, he had in mind particularly the Hebrew Scripture, what we today call the Old Testament.[2] "Inspired" is simply a shorter way of saying "breathed out by God" and indicates the source of Sacred Scripture—God Himself.

God breathed His Spirit into His prophets (Old Testament) and apostles (New Testament), so that the words they wrote down would be God's words. Inspiration means that not just the thought or general idea came from God, but also the wording, the sentence structure, and the literary composition flowed from God as well as from the authors onto the written page. God worked with the personalities, skills, and abilities of these writers. As a result, the Scriptures reflect the writers' diversity of styles and perception. We get to know the authors as well as the message when we read God's Holy Word. Yet the Holy Scripture also displays a remarkable unity because God inspired it. (See "The Unity of Scripture," in *TLSB*, pp xlv–xlvii.)

Authority

Because the words of Holy Scripture come from God, they carry divine authority. The Law and Gospel of Scripture teach us about salvation and life. God's Word always accomplishes His purposes—it is reliable (Is 55:10–11). In the original languages of Hebrew, Aramaic, and Greek, as well as in accurate translations—whether the Word is written, spoken, or signed—Scripture effectively works faith and salvation in people.

God's Word presents itself with clarity and simplicity (Rm 10:9–11). Ironically, a person can spend a lifetime studying Scripture and never master it, yet a child can read or hear it and come to faith in Jesus right away (cf Mt 11:25–26).

The early Christians used the term *canon* (Gk *kanon*, "measuring rod" or "rule") to describe the collection of Holy Scripture that the Church uses for public reading, for teaching, and for judging doctrine and practice.

The Canon of the Hebrew Scripture

For many years, a list of the books that were considered Holy Scripture was not necessary. God had directed Moses to put a copy of the Ten Commandments into the ark of the covenant (Ex 25:16, 21). He had also told Moses to record the Law and told the priests to teach the Law (Ex 17:14; 34:27; Lv 10:11). The

---

2 Paul also considered New Testament Scripture inspired, as he sets Dt 25:4 and Lk 10:7 on equal footing in 1Tm 5:18.

Old Testament often refers to these texts but also mentions some books that were eventually lost (see *TLSB*, pp 3–5). Over time, the writings of the prophets and also the Psalms were preserved for use by God's people. Scrolls were likely kept in the temple archives (cf 2Ki 22:8; 1Macc 14:49; 2Macc 2:13; see *TLSB* note, 1Ch 26:20–28).

By the first century BC, the books of Holy Scripture were well established as the books we have in our Old Testament. According to the Mishnah, in c AD 100 (after the destruction of the Jerusalem temple), Jewish religious leaders in Jamnia also discussed qualities of the Old Testament books. (See rabbinic opinions in Mishna Yadayim 3:2–5; Bava Batra 14b; Shabbat 14a, 30b.)

Old Testament Apocrypha and Pseudepigrapha

During the Time between the Testaments, a variety of books related to themes and figures in the Hebrew Scripture were produced. Some of these documents claimed to be written by people in the Bible from long ago (*pseudepigrapha*, credited to people such as Enoch, Adam and Eve, and Moses). Other books contained history (1 and 2 Maccabees), supplements to recognized biblical books (Baruch, additions to Daniel and Esther), or contemporary religious thought (wisdom books). A number of the books were translated for the LXX.

Jerome included some of these books in his Latin translation of the Bible (Vulgate) in the fourth century AD. Roman Catholics, Eastern Orthodox, and some Protestants regard these books as a "second canon" (*deuterocanonical* books) or as part of the Old Testament. Luther thought these books were good to read but did not regard them as Holy Scripture.

Lutherans have labeled these books as the *Apocrypha* (Gk, "hidden away") and separated them from books universally recognized as Holy Scripture. Apocryphal books are not typically read in worship services, nor do they typically serve as sermon texts.

New Testament Pseudepigrapha

Just as many nonbiblical books appeared during the Time between the Testaments, so there were a variety of works that non-Christian sects produced during the Early Church period. Many of these books (e.g., the Nag Hammadi library) came from Gnostic groups that rejected all or part of biblical teaching.

Gnostics varied widely in their teachings and beliefs, but most emphasized the importance of a secret "knowledge" passed on to followers by a founding religious figure. Some Gnostic groups had little or nothing to do with Christianity (e.g., Sethian Gnostics were more Jewish in character), but many borrowed heavily from the New Testament and Christian traditions.

"Christian" Gnostics and other false teachers invented a "Jesus" who is very different from the real Jesus Christ. They preached a "gospel" that eliminated the cross as the atoning sacrifice for the sins of the world. They also produced numerous documents to support their philosophy. But the Gnostics eventually died out and were almost entirely forgotten. Because some of their literature was discovered in the nineteenth and twentieth centuries, people have shown a renewed interest in these odd religious sects. If you hear news reports about a recent or newly discovered "gospel," it is likely one of these Gnostic texts.

In the second century, the heretic Marcion of Sinope rejected the entire Old Testament Scripture and taught that the God who created the physical world was a lower-level spiritual being whose creation ineptly caused the creation of evil. Marcion taught that people should worship the supreme, loving God instead. Marcion created his own version of the Gospel according to Luke and rejected all the New Testament books except for some of Paul's Letters. Marcion denied the Christ of Scripture and taught that Jesus was a middle-level spirit-being who came to teach His disciples a body of secret knowledge. Marcion's teachings caused the Church to define and defend the books that are in the Bible.

Conclusion

The books of the Bible have authenticated themselves over many centuries. People have recognized the divine nature of Holy Scripture and spent time and money to make copies of God's Word, even when this was tedious and expensive. Recognizing Scripture's authority, churches and synagogues have read it in public worship services, preached its message, and taught its contents for generations. People have willingly died rather than surrender these books of Scripture to those who would destroy them (cf 1 Macc 1:56–57).

The Christian Church does not stand over the Scripture and decide what is or is not God's Word. The Christian Church merely recognizes the voice of its Good Shepherd in the biblical books and follows Him through His teaching (cf Jn 10:27–28; 14:23–24).

Arrangement of the Apocrypha

One should note that across the centuries the order of the books varies from tradition to tradition, and likewise varies in early manuscripts as described on p 3 of *ALEN*, which follows the order in the German Luther Bible. Some scholars express frustration in trying to understanding the order of the apocryphal books Luther used. The table of contents for the 1534 Luther Bible lists them in seven unnumbered entries as follows: Judith, the Book of Wisdom, Tobit, Jesus Sirach [Ecclesiasticus], Baruch, Maccabees, and Additions in Esther and Daniel. The title page for the Apocrypha in the Luther Bible follows the same order, though distinguishing the Additions to Esther and Daniel for a total of eight numbered entries. In his prefaces to the books of the Apocrypha, Luther gave some indication of the categories he assumed as he worked. These categories help us understand Luther's order.

Compositions. Judith, Wisdom of Solomon, Tobit, and Ecclesiasticus are placed together as compositions that teach the faith. For example, Luther called Judith "a beautiful religious fiction" (AE 35:338; "ein geistlich schön Geticht" in WA DB 12:5). Baruch and the Letter of Jeremiah are prophetic letters of warning against idolatry, which Luther also regarded as non-historical compositions and treated as one book (see p 67).

Histories. 1 Maccabees and 2 Maccabees are works of history (Grm *Geschichte*).

Additions. Luther regarded the additions (Grm *Stücke*) to Esther and Daniel as "cornflowers" (AE 35:353; "Kornblumen" in WA DB 12:493). These are compositions that grew up in the middle of existing works, though the Luther Bible does refer to Susanna as a *Historia* according to ancient custom.

Prayers/Songs. Luther grouped together the additions that were prayers or songs, rather than stories, and placed them at the end of the collection.

After the Prayer of Manasseh, one finds "End of the Books of the Old Testament." This shows that the editors of the 1534 Luther Bible included and described the books of the Apocrypha as a part of the Old Testament collection. In other words, they were compositions from the time of the old covenant that were "useful and good to read" (see 1534 heading), though not canonical.

The Empire of Alexander
Territory controlled by Alexander.
Approximate route of Alexander from the Battle at the Granicus River in 334 BC to his death in Babylon in 323 BC.
Danube R.
THRACE
MACEDONIA
Byzantium
BLACK SEA
Pella
Granicus R.
Gordium
333
Sardis
Ephesus
334
HELLAS
Miletus
Issus
Melitene
ARMENIA
Knossos
CRETE
CYPRUS
MEDITERRANEAN SEA
Tyre
Damascus
SYRIA
331
ASSYRIA
Nineveh
Asshur
Euphrates R.
Babylon
324/323
MEDIA
Ecbatana
Rhagae
Susa
330
ELAM
331
Pasargadae
Persepolis
324
CASPIAN SEA
ARAL SEA
CHORASMIA
PARTHIA
329
Bokhara
Bactra
BACTRIA
327
ARACHOSIA
DRANGIANA
PERSIA
GEDROSIA
325
Indus R.
SCYTHIA
INDIA
GULF OF OMAN
ARABIAN SEA
INDIAN OCEAN
Alexandria
Gaza
Jerusalem
Memphis
EGYPT
LIBYA
Nile R.
Thebes
RED SEA
ARABIA
ETHIOPIA [CUSH]
MACEDONIA
Pella
Thessalonica
THESSALY
AEGEAN SEA
AETOLIA
Delphi
Thebes
Marathon
Athens
Corinth
ACHAIA
IONIAN SEA
Sparta
GULF O
0 50 100 KM.
0 50 100 MI.

THE HASMONEAN CONQUEST. The Seleucid ruler Antiochus IV Epiphanes annexed Judea in c 175 BC and persecuted the Jews (1Macc 1:10–63). The Hasmonean priest Mattathias and then his son Judas Maccabeus organized an insurgency (1Macc 2:1–3:1). Judas reclaimed Jerusalem in 164 BC (1Macc 3–4), from whence the feast of Hanukkah dates.

After Judas died in battle (1Macc 9), his brother Jonathan was named ethnarch and high priest (1Macc 10–12). After Jonathan was killed, his brother Simon succeeded him, gaining complete independence for Judea in 142 BC (1Macc 13–14). Simon's remaining son, John Hyrcanus, expanded Hasmonean control after Simon's death. John's son Aristobulus established the Hasmonean kingdom. Aristobulus's brother Alexander Jannaeus reigned after him, expanding the kingdom to its greatest boundaries.

Alexander's son Hyrcanus II lost the kingship to his brother Aristobulus II, who in turn lost control of Judea to the Roman general Pompey in 63 BC.

JUDITH

Wait for His deliverance

The Book of Judith is supposed to describe the Babylonians' early sixth century advance into Judea. However, as the Church Fathers noted, the story is likely fictional. The story includes obvious historical inaccuracies that may have been intentional. For example, Nebuchadnezzar was a Babylonian king, not an Assyrian king reigning from Nineveh (1:1). The distance covered by Holofernes's troops from Nineveh to Cilicia is over 300 miles (2:21), a feat that is humanly impossible to accomplish in three days (2:28). Such depictions may be provided for literary effect to characterize the invincible aura of Judah's enemies, whom God will overthrow by the hand of one woman.

Cultural and Historical Setting

Features of the story point to its composition during the reign of Hellenistic kings over Israel or after the rise of the Maccabees. For example, the inaccuracies regarding Babylonian and Persian history speak against composition during those eras. The Judeans have already returned from exile and rebuilt the temple (4:3) so it had to be written after 519 BC. Other features of the book are characteristic of still a later period. The high priest and a Jerusalem council are ruling authorities (4:6–8; 11:14; 15:8), bringing the date into the Hellenistic or Maccabean period.

A Jewess decked out with a diadem of pearls, rows of pearls around her neck, and curly hair flowing to her shoulders. Carved in ivory during the Late Iron Age, found in the district of Hebron.

OVERVIEW

Author
An unnamed Judean

Date
Composed late second century BC

Place
"Bethulia," situated near Dothan

People
Achior; Holofernes; Judith; Joakim the high priest

Purpose
To describe how the Lord delivered Israel through the self-sacrifice and devotion of a beautiful widow, Judith

Themes
Contrast between the true God and false gods; trust in God's providential care; the importance of following the Lord's ways (Torah); deception

Memory Verses
Achior's report (5:17–19); wait for God's deliverance (8:16–17); God's Word and Spirit (16:14)

TIMELINE

722 BC	Assyrian Shalmaneser V takes Israel captive
681–669 BC	Reign of Esarhaddon
323 BC	Death of Alexander the Great
165–134 BC	Maccabean Revolt
2 BC	Birth of Jesus

Composition

Author

We do not know who wrote the Book of Judith. The author was most familiar with political and cultural aspects of life in Israel, the book's primary setting. Hebraic expressions point toward composition of the book in Hebrew. An Israelite author of the second century BC is most likely.

Date of Composition

Details such as reconsecration of the temple (4:3), the high priest as a military commander (4:6), and a "senate" in Jerusalem (4:8) point to a second century BC composition rather than the seventh century setting with which the author introduced the book. Other composition features, such as the generic name Judith, which means "Judean woman," point to an inspirational story that seeks to embody the bravery and devotion of Judeans in an era of persecution. As a consequence, scholars conclude that the author was a Judean writing in the second century BC.

Judith with the head of Holofernes, by Lucas Cranach the Elder.

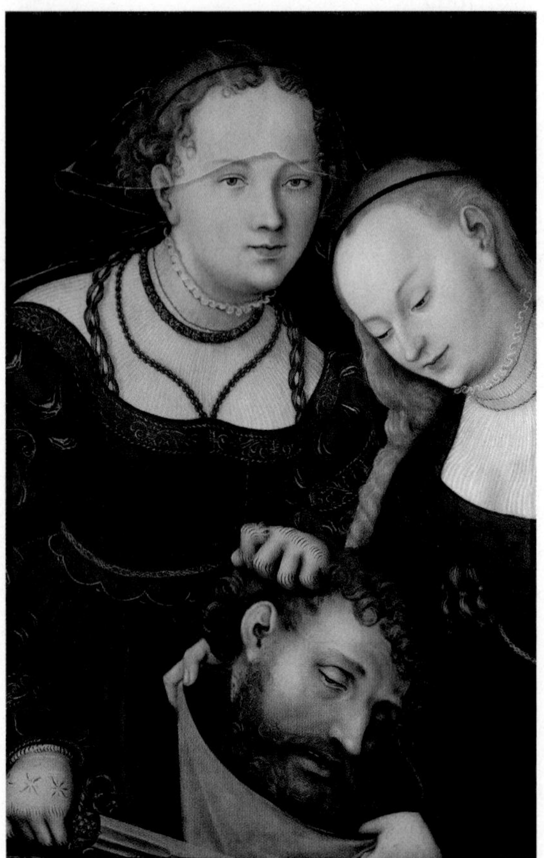

Purpose/Recipients

The book encourages hope in God and courage to act in one's defense, despite overwhelming opposition. It raises important questions about morality and goodness when faced with difficulty or even annihilation. For these reasons it makes compelling reading for God's people, who may also benefit from the expressions of prayer, faith, and worship that characterize the work.

Literary Features

Genre

The Book of Judith is presented as history. It is well composed, though the author does not introduce his heroine until nearly halfway through the story. As you read, watch for the storyteller's use of irony and contrast, which enriches the plot. The book is perhaps best compared with what we call today historical fiction.

Characters

The book has as its main character **Judith**, described as a beautiful young widow whom God suddenly calls to greatness. Although she is mournfully severed from her dear husband, God raises her up as a deliverer, such as the Old Testament heroines of Deborah, Jael, and Esther. The other chief character of the book is the Assyrian general **Holofernes**. In the beginning he is presented as an unstoppable leader who conquers his way toward Judah. When he meets Judith, however, he is captivated by her beauty, which leads to his downfall. Other significant figures are **Achior**, the leader of the Ammonites, who describes Israel and her God; and the **elders of Bethulia**, who despair and are pleased to follow Judith's plans and leadership.

A Seleucid era wine vessel.

Narrative Development or Plot

The Book of Judith is a story of deliverance—a rescue based ironically on ritual purity, on the one hand, and deceitfully outsmarting one's enemy, on the other. The first seven chapters describe the invincible threat as Holofernes's armies move closer and closer to Judah and the city of Bethulia. Achior's report foreshadows a possible escape for the people, if they will obey their God (5:17). When the collapse of Bethulia appears inevitable (ch 7), a ritually pure heroine arises to chide and comfort the community and to enact deliverance through prayer and deed. The heroine, Judith, allows the Assyrians to capture her. However, she carefully maintains her ritual purity so as to please God and serve as His instrument of deliverance. When Holofernes trusts her fully, he gets drunk in her presence. Judith quietly and privately executes him and departs with his head, which she uses to inspire the Judean resistance. The Assyrians panic after discovering the body of their headless leader. They flee before the Judeans. The book ends with Judith praising God for delivering the people.

Resources

As noted above, the stories of Deborah and Jael in Jgs 4–5 were likely contributors to the writing of the Book of Judith. The book also has charac-

Continued on p 20.

Outline

I. Introduction to Assyrian Conquests (ch 1)
- A. Nebuchadnezzar's War with the Medes (1:1–6)
- B. Nebuchadnezzar's Request for Allies (1:7–12)
- C. Nebuchadnezzar Defeats the Medes (1:13–16)

II. Holofernes's Campaign of Revenge (chs 2–7)
- A. Holofernes Appointed to Punish the Western Nations (2:1–3:8)
  1. Nebuchadnezzar's plan of revenge (2:1–3)
  2. Nebuchadnezzar's orders for Holofernes (2:4–13)
  3. Holofernes prepares for the campaign (2:14–20)
  4. Holofernes's campaign from Nineveh to Damascus (2:21–27)
  5. Holofernes accepts the surrender of coastal cities (2:28–3:8)
- B. Holofernes Resisted by Israel (3:9–4:15)
  1. Holofernes encamps near Dothan (3:9–10)
  2. Israelites fortify the hilltops and villages (4:1–5)
  3. Joakim's strategy and prayers (4:6–15)
- C. Holofernes Learns about Israel and Their God (chs 5–6)
  1. Holofernes consults local leaders (5:1–4)
  2. Achior describes Israel and their God (5:5–21)
  3. Achior's description rejected (5:22–24)
  4. Holofernes describes Nebuchadnezzar as God (6:1–4)
  5. Holofernes turns Achior over to the Israelites (6:5–13)
  6. Israel learns of the Assyrians' arrogance (6:14–21)
- D. Holofernes Besieges Bethulia (ch 7)
  1. Holofernes advances to Bethulia (7:1–5)
  2. Holofernes's allies and commanders counsel for siege (7:6–18)
  3. Bethulia's suffering during the siege (7:19–28)
  4. Uzziah contemplates surrender (7:29–32)

III. The Lord Delivers Israel through Judith (8:1–15:7)
   A. Judith's Counsel (ch 8)
      1. Judith introduced (8:1–8)
      2. Judith argues that the Lord will deliver Israel (8:9–31)
      3. Judith plans to visit the enemy (8:32–36)
   B. Judith's Prayers (ch 9)
   C. Judith Visits the Enemy (ch 10)
      1. Judith beautifies herself (10:1–5)
      2. Judith leaves Bethulia (10:6–10)
      3. Judith taken to Holofernes (10:11–23)
   D. The Lord's Will and Nebuchadnezzar's Will Contrasted (ch 11)
   E. Judith Conquers Holofernes (12:1–13:11)
      1. Holofernes's banquet (ch 12)
      2. Judith beheads Holofernes (13:1–10a)
      3. Judith returns to Bethulia (13:10b–11)
   F. Judith Guides Israel to Victory (13:12–15:7)
      1. Judith encourages the people of Bethulia (13:12–14:5)
      2. Achior believes in the Lord (14:6–10)
      3. Israel drives the Assyrians away (14:11–15:7)

IV. Celebration of Victory (15:8–16:25)
   A. Israel Celebrates (15:8–13)
   B. Judith Offers Thanksgiving (16:1–20)
   C. Judith's Renown (16:21–25)

teristics found in biblical Esther, such as her beauty, her role as a deliverer for Israel, and the story's use of irony. The author quoted from the books of Genesis, Exodus, and Numbers, while drawing on biblical teaching more generally.

Text and Translations

The LXX is the earliest available text. The character of the Greek makes it likely that the story was first composed in Hebrew, or perhaps Aramaic. Jerome stated that he prepared the Vulgate translation from an Aramaic manuscript, which he used to revise the Old Latin translation.

A medieval Hebrew summary of the story has Seleucus reigning as king rather than Nebuchadnezzar. Jerusalem is the scene of the action rather than Bethulia.

Doctrinal Content

Summary Commentary

Chs 1–7 Nebuchadnezzar commanded Holofernes to punish the rebel vassals of the king of Assyria. With a large army Holofernes conquered Cilicia, Mesopotamia, and the region of Damascus. On his way to northern Israel he devastated everything in his path. With the help of the Lord the Jews determined to resist the coming attack of Holofernes on Judean territory. The successes of the general terrified them. They prepared themselves spiritually by prayer and fasting and physically by the mobilization of their forces. The story then concentrates on the siege of Bethulia. At the end of 34 days the inhabitants are considering surrendering (7:1–7) because their water supply had recently been drained. The leaders are blamed by the people for the plight in which they find themselves. One of the elders, Uzziah, begs them to hold out five days longer, promising that help will come (7:30).

Chs 8–9 At this point in the story (8:1) Judith is introduced, a widow for more than three years and known for her piety and great beauty. When she is told of the plan of the elders to surrender the city, she becomes indignant, exclaiming: "God is not like man, to be threatened" (8:16). She announces that she has a plan that will bring about the defeat of the enemy. Chapter 9 contains the prayer she utters before her journey to the camp of Holofernes. After beautifying herself with all manner of cosmetics, she goes with her maid to the enemy camp. She informs the guards of Holofernes that she is a

Hebrew woman fleeing from the city about to fall, and that she has come to reveal a way in which the city can be taken.

Chs 10–13 Judith confirms an earlier report of Achior that the Jewish city would not fall while the Jews remained faithful to the Lord. But now they were planning to eat forbidden animals, which would bring God's punishment upon the city (10:14–11:23). Judith is offered refreshments from the general's table, but she requests to be allowed to eat only the food her maid had brought along. She is also granted permission to go outside the camp with her maid to bathe and pray. This Judith does for three nights. Finally, Holofernes arranges a banquet for Judith at which he hopes to enjoy her to the utmost. Again she abstains from eating unclean foods and eats only that which her maid had prepared. Left alone with Holofernes, who is intoxicated, she asks God's help and then takes Holofernes's sword and decapitates him. In the bag she has brought, she deposits his head and, as in previous nights, walks past the sentry beyond the camp.

Chs 14–16 After Judith and her maid arrive at the city of Bethulia, she displays Holofernes's head. She calls upon the people to praise and thank God for the deliverance He effected (13:14). The next day the besieged Jews put the enemy to flight. In the epilogue, the author relates the triumph of Judith and gives her hymn of praise (15:9–16:25).

Specific Themes

The story of Judith highlights the contrast of the true God over against the false gods of the nations. Although the nations fall one after another before the Assyrian onslaught, little Bethulia, where the true God is honored, becomes a stopping point. What is more, the true God accomplishes His victory over the gods by the hand of a woman rather than a mighty warrior, which illustrates His power all the more. Judith is the proper instrument for God's work because of (1) her faithfulness to the covenant, manifested by her purity, and (2) her trust in God's providential care. God hears her prayers, and the community welcomes her hymn of praise when all is accomplished.

An important element of the book is also Judith's planned deception whereby she gains victory over Holofernes.

Specific Doctrines

The Book of Judith rightly points out that we cannot set the time for God's deliverance; we learn to wait upon His timing (8:11–13). Confidence for life and work is drawn from trust in God and obedience to His teachings.

Judith places special emphasis on keeping the ceremonial law to maintain ritual purity or covenant righteousness before God. She described Israel as God's consecrated people (9:13). Those who fail to trust and serve God will face eternal torment (16:17). Some commentators describe the teachings of the book as Pharisaic, though there are no direct references to the Pharisees.

The book also presents a number of doctrinal problems, which prevent it from serving as a fully reliable guide to Christian teaching. For example, Judith celebrates the dishonesty and treachery of her forefather, Simeon, in dealing with foreigners who threatened the identity and future of Israel (9:2–4). She engages in seduction and deception to fulfill her plans. The story promotes a morality that is not in keeping with biblical teaching about God's Law. It teaches trust in God while also suggesting that one may seek success by every means.

Achior, an Ammonite leader and significant character in Judith, was depicted as fully versed in Israelite history and doctrine. This Iron Age bust depicts an Ammonite king.

Canonicity

Although Jews read and used the text down to the medieval era, mentioning it in the liturgy for Hanukkah, they never regarded it as the same as books of Scripture. Early Christians valued the book, and over time it was welcome among the books of the eastern and western churches. However, Jerome and others spoke against receiving the Book of Judith as Holy Scripture, the conclusion later reached by Luther and adopted by Protestant churches. In 1546, the Council of Trent described the book as canonical for Roman Catholics. The 1672 Synod of Jerusalem affirmed Judith as Sacred Scripture for Eastern Orthodox churches.

Lutheran Theologians on Judith

Luther

"If one could prove from established and reliable histories that the events in Judith really happened, it would be a noble and fine book, and should properly be in the Bible. Yet it hardly squares with the historical accounts of the Holy Scriptures, especially Jeremiah and Ezra. . . . Thus as to both time and name, error and doubt are still present, so that I cannot reconcile [the accounts] at all. Some people think this is not an account of historical events [*Geschichte*] but rather a beautiful religious fiction [*Gedicht*] by a holy and ingenious man who wanted to sketch and depict therein the fortunes of the whole Jewish people and the victory God always miraculously granted them over all their enemies. . . . Such an interpretation strikes my fancy, and I think that the poet deliberately and painstakingly inserted the errors of time and name in order to remind the reader that the book should be taken and understood as that kind of a sacred, religious, composition. Now the names fit into this sort of an interpretation extraordinarily well. [E.g.,] Judith means Judea, (that is) the Jewish people. . . . It may even be that in those days they dramatized literature like this, just as among us the Passion and other sacred stories are performed. . . . Therefore this is a fine, good, holy, useful book, well worth reading by us Christians. For the words spoken by the persons in it should be understood as though they were uttered in the Holy Spirit by a spiritual, holy poet or prophet who, in presenting such persons in his play, preaches to us through them." (AE 35:337–39)

Gerhard

"We demonstrate that *the Book of Judith* is outside the canon with the following arguments. [I] *It is not found in the Hebrew sources. . . .* [II] It does not agree with historical truth. . . . [III] The Book of Judith by no means agrees with the analogy of faith. In Judith 9:2 approval is given to the deed of Simeon and Levi, who killed the Shechemites with the sword, contrary to the treaty and promise they had made. . . . [IV] The Israelite church and the early Christian church exclude the Book of Judith from the canon. Josephus does not even touch on the entire history of Judith in his commentaries *De antiquitate.* In his preface to Judith, Jerome explicitly excludes it from the canon." (ThC E1 §§ 191–92, 194–95)

Further Study

Lay/Bible Class Resources

Burgland, Lane. *Study Guide to the Apocrypha.* St. Louis: Concordia, 2012. § Lutheran author. Eight-session Bible study, including leader's notes and discussion questions. Companion piece to *ALEN.*

Dancy, J. C. *The Shorter Books of the Apocrypha.* CBCA. Cambridge: Cambridge University Press, 1972. § Prepared by British scholars for the general reader. Includes the New English Bible translation along with commentary.

Engelbrecht, Edward A., gen. ed. *The Apocrypha: The Lutheran Edition with Notes.* St. Louis: Concordia, 2012. § Based on the ESV. Reflects the Luther Bible tradition of the Apocrypha. Prepared by Lutherans, with commendations from top scholars of intertestamental studies.

Church Worker Resources

deSilva, David A. *Introducing the Apocrypha: Message, Context, and Significance.* Grand Rapids: Baker Academic, 2002. § A thorough and informative introduction to the books of the Apocrypha from an evangelical scholar who served on the ESV Translation Committee of the Apocryphal Books.

Academic Resources

Bissell, Edwin Cone. *The Apocrypha of the Old Testament.* LCHS. New York: Charles Scribner's Sons, 1896. § Philip Schaff appears to have added this volume to the English edition of the Lange commentary. Still one of the most substantive one-volume commentaries on the Apocrypha available in English.

Charles, R. H. *The Apocrypha and Pseudepigrapha of the Old Testament.* Vol. 1. Oxford: Clarendon Press, 1913. § A standard scholarly reference work. Provides thorough introductions to the Apocrypha and substantive footnotes, commenting from the Greek, Hebrew, etc.

Moore, Carey A. *Judith.* Vol. 40 of AB. New York: Doubleday, 1985. § A thorough commentary and new translation of Judith prepared for a major academic series. Focuses on historical and literary interpretation.

Pietersma, Albert, and Benjamin G. Wright, eds. *A New English Translation of the Septuagint.* Oxford: Oxford University Press, 2007. § A literal revision of the NRSV translation prepared by an international team of Septuagint scholars. Includes thorough introductions focused on the text of the LXX.

Decree of the priests of Memphis
honours on Ptolemy V. Epiphanes, King of Egypt,
The inscription is in three forms: 1. in the "classical"
language, in hieroglyphics: 2. in the contemporary idiom of
in the cursive writing called demotic: 3. in the Greek language and
An account of the finding and history of the stone and of the
of the hieroglyphic writing associated with the name of Champollion
found in the pamphlet placed behind the stone.

THE WISDOM OF SOLOMON

To know You is complete righteousness

After the Jewish people settled in cosmopolitan Egypt, the artistry and learning of their new neighbors both fascinated and repulsed them. The author of the Wisdom of Solomon borrowed the literary artistry of Hellenism in order to illustrate the foolishness of their Hellenistic doctrines and outlook on life. He used their language and style to refute them and argue for the superiority of the biblical wisdom tradition. These tensions preoccupied the teachers of Israel in the time between the testaments.

Historical and Cultural Setting

The Wisdom of Solomon opens by addressing "rulers of the earth" (1:1) without specifying which rulers are in view, whose history would provide us with the specific historical and cultural setting. The character of the book makes it impossible for Solomon to have written it. The fact that it was written in Greek and that it often focuses on Egypt and the exodus suggests that Egypt was the homeland for the document.

Many Jews lived outside of Israel, especially after the exile, in the communities known as the Diaspora. One of the largest Jewish settlements was to be found in Egyptian Alexandria, the intellectual and scientific center of the Hellenistic world, with one of the great libraries of

The granite Rosetta Stone clearly displays Egyptian hieroglyphs, Egyptian demotic script, and Greek. It was created in the second century BC, about the same era as the Wisdom of Solomon was written.

OVERVIEW

Author
An Alexandrian Jew

Date
c second century BC–c AD 100

Place
Egypt (implied)

People
Rulers (kings, judges, monarchs); the author; the ungodly; the righteous; a holy people; oppressors; the fathers

Purpose
To teach rulers the contrast between wisdom and folly

Themes
Creation of all things through God's Word; the exodus as the redemption of Israel; the wisdom of God's people in contrast with the foolishness of the nations

Memory Verses
Creation, fall, and God's protection (2:23–3:1); death of the righteous (4:7, 14); surprise of the lawless (5:4–5); God's strength and will (12:18); knowing God (15:3); the Lord's Word heals (16:12)

TIMELINE

970–931 BC	Reign of Solomon
587 BC	Judeans flee to Egypt
332 BC	Alexander the Great proclaimed Pharaoh
198 BC	Egyptian Ptolemies lose control of Judea
2 BC	Holy family in Egypt

the ancient world. In Alexandria, Jewish religion and thought came to grips with heathen religion and philosophy. Often the Jews became defenders of their faith because of attacks made upon it and of persecution against them. It is believed that the Wisdom of Solomon was written to encourage the Jews to be faithful to their ancestral religion.

Composition

Author

The obvious Greek style and philosophical influences make it clear that the Hebrew king Solomon did not write the book. The author, likely a Jew living in Alexandria, chose the example and persona of Solomon, the wisest man of his tradition. The author's emphasis on the foolishness of the Egyptians makes Egypt a likely location of the writing. St. Augustine believed that Jesus son of Sirach, the author of Ecclesiasticus, was also responsible for penning Wisdom. However, the differences between the two apocryphal books make this unlikely. Jerome claims that "many old writers" of his time regarded Philo of Alexandria (c 20 BC–c AD 50) as the author, a view that Luther, Gerhard, and many Reformation scholars accepted. This is an interesting suggestion that remains unproven.

Some have tried to associate the book with Apollos, because he is considered by some to be the author of the Epistle to the Hebrews. But this conjecture cannot be verified. Specifically Christian ideas do not appear in Wisdom, which would constitute a serious objection to this theory.

The author is greatly indebted to the Books of Moses and the Hebrew wisdom literature. However, he is likewise greatly influenced by Greek philosophical ideals such as Stoicism and Platonism. He wished to present the strength of the biblical tradition in the manner of the respected Hellenistic tradition. At times this leads to compromises in biblical doctrine. (Cf 8:19–20.)

Date of Composition

Authorities are not agreed as to the date. Opinion ranges from the second century BC to AD 100. The persecution mentioned in 2:10–20 and the oppression referred to in 15:14 may be allusions to the measures taken by Ptolemy VIII Euergetes II against the Jews who opposed his government. The reference in 15:6 to the worship of idols and elsewhere to persecutions is interpreted as a reference to Emperor Caligula, who in c AD 40 wished to have himself recognized as a god. Other scholars argue that the influence of the Wisdom of Solomon on New Testament books requires a date earlier than AD 40, and they place the book back to 100 BC or earlier. As in the Books of the Maccabees, so in the Wisdom of Solomon the matter of defection from the Jewish faith was a problem in the second century BC when the orthodox Jews were frequently persecuted.

Cleopatra VII was the last Ptolemaic ruler of Egypt, regarded also as the last pharaoh.

Purpose/Recipients

The Wisdom of Solomon is partly polemical and partly apologetic. The opening chapters warn against "the ungodly," by whom most likely are meant the Sadducees. They did not believe in future life, and therefore were not deterred by the fear of punishment.

Hedonism was a great temptation for the Jews of the Greek-speaking world. One of the purposes of the author of Wisdom was to instruct and keep the Hellenistic Jews faithful to their ancestral religion. The author also addresses himself to the pagans with the idea of attracting them to Judaism. The veiled and mysterious ways in which he alludes to past Jewish history are designed to arouse their curiosity and hold their attention (chs 10–12; 16–19). This technique was also employed in the Sibylline Books.

Literary Features

Genre

This book is classified as belonging to the wisdom genre to which Ecclesiasticus is assigned.

Characters

Solomon is never explicitly mentioned, though the first person ("I") passages are best associated with him as the purported writer, as the ancient title for the book demonstrates. The writer addressed the work to rulers such as kings and judges who should gain divine wisdom for the sake of their rule. Like wisdom literature generally, the book contrasts the wise and

Continued on p 32.

Outline

The parts of the Wisdom of Solomon are not always easily distinguished. The flow of the author's style and thought create a unified whole rather than a clear step-by-step composition. This feature also makes it likely that the book is the unified composition of a single author. For more on structure, see the outline.

I. The Righteous and the Ungodly Contrasted (1:1–6:11)
- A. Love Righteousness (1:1–5)
- B. The Sinner Cannot Escape Punishment (1:6–11)
- C. God Does Not Willingly Afflict People (1:12–16)
- D. The Ungodly Prefer the Ways of Death (2:1–5)
- E. The Pact of the Ungodly (2:6–20)
- F. A Future Life Is in Store for the Righteous (2:21–3:9)
- G. The Ungodly Shall Be Punished (3:10–4:6)
- H. The Death of the Righteous and the Ungodly Contrasted (4:7–19)
- I. The Remorse of the Ungodly at the Judgment (4:20–5:14)
- J. The Bliss of the Righteous and the Miserable Fate of the Ungodly (5:15–23)
- K. Admonition to Rulers (6:1–11)

II. The Source and Benefits of Wisdom (6:12–11:1)
- A. Wisdom Desires to Be Found (6:12–16)
- B. Wisdom Leads to a Kingdom (6:17–20)
- C. Solomon Promises to Declare the Nature of Wisdom (6:21–25)
- D. Solomon Received Wisdom through Prayer (7:1–7)
- E. The Value of Wisdom (7:8–14)
- F. Solomon's Greatness Came from Wisdom (7:15–22a)
- G. The Attributes of Wisdom (7:22b–8:1)
- H. Only God Gives Wisdom (8:2–21)
- I. Prayer for Wisdom (ch 9)
- J. Wisdom from Adam to Moses (10:1–11:1)

III. Egypt and Israel Contrasted (11:2–19:22)
- A. Punishment to the Egyptians but Benefit to Israel (11:2–14)
- B. Punishment Was Appropriate (11:15–20)
- C. God, Though Almighty, Is Full of Mercy (11:21–12:2)
- D. God's Patience with the Canaanites (12:3–18)
- E. God's Mercy an Example to Mankind (12:19–22)
- F. Heavier Punishment for Persistent Folly (12:23–27)
- G. Mankind Cannot Know the True God (13:1–9)
- H. Idolaters Are without Excuse (13:10–19)
- I. Folly of the Navigator Who Prays to a Useless Piece of Wood (14:1–7)
- J. Idolaters Shall Be Punished (14:8–11)
- K. The Origin of Idolatry (14:12–21)
- L. Evil Results of Idolatry (14:22–31)
- M. Benefits of Worshiping the True God (15:1–6)
- N. Another Example of the Manufacture of Idols (15:7–17)
- O. Egyptians Were Punished by Means of Animals; Israelites Benefited (15:18–16:4)
- P. Israelites Admonished by Serpents (16:5–14)
- Q. Egyptians Were Punished by Fire but the Israelites Benefited (16:15–29)
- R. The Plague of Darkness (17:1–18:4)
- S. The Egyptians Counsel Death but Were Slain Themselves (18:5–19)
- T. Aaron's Intercession Stayed the Punishment of Death (18:20–25)
- U. Nothing Stayed Death in the Case of the Egyptians (19:1–5)
- V. Creation Fought for the Chosen People (19:6–12)
- W. Creation Fought against the Egyptians (19:13–17)
- X. The Transmutation of the Elements (19:18–22)

the foolish, the righteous and the ungodly. A chief example of the ungodly is the Egyptians who foolishly worship idols. Chapter 18 especially praises God for His work with the fathers of Israel.

Narrative Development or Plot

As wisdom literature, the book does not have a storyline or plot. However, in chs 11–19, the writer works with biblical stories of the exodus and wilderness wanderings in order to contrast Egypt and Israel. As a result, many elements of that history enter into the wise sayings, demonstrating how God worked all things for the benefit of Israel.

Resources

The author is greatly indebted to the Books of Moses and the Hebrew wisdom literature. Chapters 11–19 present a remarkable commentary and meditation on the events of Exodus and Numbers, which is fascinating to read. However, the writer is likewise greatly influenced by Greek philosophical ideas such as Stoicism and Platonism. He wished to present the strength of the biblical tradition in the manner of the respected Hellenistic tradition. At times this leads to compromises in biblical doctrine.

Text and Translations

The text is well preserved in the Greek manuscripts of the LXX as well as various early translations. The Old Latin version helpfully preserves readings from earlier Greek manuscripts.

Doctrinal Content

Summary Commentary

Chs 1–2 The first chapters are an exhortation to righteousness, whose pursuit is depicted as a prerequisite for the acquisition of wisdom, "because wisdom will not enter a deceitful soul or dwell in a body enslaved to sin" (1:4). Righteousness is not only concerned with this life but is portrayed as meriting life beyond the grave; therefore whatever a righteous person may suffer at the hands of his enemies in this world, eventual victory nevertheless rests with him.

Chs 3–5 The Jews learn that God made man for immortality. After death, the soul of the just lives, not in the pale, shadowy reaches of Sheol, but in a life of eternal happiness in the presence of God. Some critical scholars believe that this was the first time in the pre-Christian literature that the doctrine of immortality had been clearly and unequivocably taught.

Chs 6–9 The writer appeals to kings and judges to follow wisdom; he presents an account of Solomon's zeal for this quest. Wisdom is personified and comes close to being called a divine spirit. This is emphasized in 7:24–26.

Chs 10–19 The final chapters give illustrations of the power and value of wisdom, taken from the history of the Israelites. The miserable failure of the heathen, who lack righteousness, is contrasted with the triumph of God's elect. In chs 11–12 there is a prayer directed to God that rises to noble heights in expression. However, with this exception, it is believed that not much would have been lost if the writer would have condensed the latter part of Wisdom. Illustrations taken from the lives of the patriarchs and the early history of the nation show that wisdom has always been at the root of success, and the lack of wisdom resulted in failure.

Specific Themes

As in other wisdom literature, the doctrine of creation is important to the writer, who emphasizes that God created all things through His Word. The exodus is repeatedly discussed in the latter half of the book as it illustrates how God redeemed Israel as His people, whose wisdom distinguishes them from the foolishness of the nations—most especially the foolishness of idolatry.

Specific Doctrines

The writer of Wisdom emphasizes the importance of God's work in creating and sustaining the world. This is his most important contribution to theology. In interpreting and applying Gn 1:1–3, the author's theology of the Word of God anticipates New Testament doctrine and the blessings of Christ, our mediator and deliverer (Wis 9:1; 16:12, 26; 18:15, 22). The writer also describes the role of God's Spirit in creation and the Holy Spirit's presence everywhere (1:7). On the doctrine of sin, he teaches

Anubis, Egyptian god of the dead. The author of the Wisdom of Solomon regarded such idolatry as obvious foolishness.

that the devil—not God—is the cause of sin and death (2:24). Also, lying runs contrary to God's commands and leads to destruction (1:11). God will provide forms of punishment that appropriately match people's sins (11:17).

As noted above, the author is clearly indebted to elements of Greek philosophy. For example, in 8:19–20 he appears to teach the Platonic notion of pre-existing souls, which contradicts biblical teaching.

Canonicity

Early Christians valued the Wisdom of Solomon, and over time it was welcomed among the books of the eastern and western churches. For example, Augustine quoted from it extensively. However, Jerome and others spoke against receiving the book as Holy Scripture, the conclusion later reached by Luther and adopted by Protestant churches. In 1546, the Council of Trent described the book as canonical for Roman Catholics. The 1672 Synod of Jerusalem affirmed the Wisdom of Solomon as Sacred Scripture for Eastern Orthodox churches.

Plato's philosophy influenced some of the intertestamental writings, causing them to conflict with biblical teaching.

Lutheran Theologians on the Wisdom of Solomon

Luther

"For a long time this book has stood in the cross fire of controversy as to whether or not it should be included among the sacred Scriptures of the Old Testament, especially in view of the fact that the author suggests in chapter 9[:7] that throughout the book it is King Solomon speaking—he whose wisdom is also extolled in the Book of Kings [I Kings 4, 10].

"The ancient church fathers, however, excluded it outright from the sacred Scriptures. . . . They contend, however, that Philo is the author of this book. Undoubtedly he was one of the most learned and wisest men the Jewish people have had since the prophets, as he demonstrated in other books and deeds of his. . . . When the emperor was so embittered against the Jews that he turned them away and would not even hear them, then Philo—a man of courage and confidence—spoke up and said to his fellow Jews, 'Well, then, dear brethren, do not be afraid but take heart; just because human help fails us, God's help will surely be with us!'

"In my estimation, this book must have come out of such a situation or cause. . . . It came to be regarded by many as a genuine book of sacred Scripture. . . . There are many good things in this book, and it is well worth reading. . . . This book is timely for our day, because tyrants are now cocksurely abusing their authority against him from whom they have it. . . . It pleases me beyond measure that the author here [6:22] extols the Word of God so highly, and ascribes to the Word all the wonders God has performed, both on enemies and in his saints. . . .

"Finally, this book is a proper exposition and illustration of the first commandment. For here you see that the author throughout is teaching you to fear and trust God; he terrifies with examples of divine wrath those who are not afraid and who despise God, and he comforts with examples of divine grace those who believe and trust him." (AE 35:340–44)

Gerhard

"We admit that the Book of Wisdom is filled with many fine thoughts and precepts, and we say that, along with Ecclesiasticus, it excels the rest of the Apocrypha. Yet we can by no means reckon it among the properly and specifically canonical books, [I] because it is not written in the prophetic language but in Greek and [II] because it was not written by a prophet but by Philo. In his preface to Wisdom, Jerome says, 'this book has the scent of Greek eloquence,' in which Jerome says Philo was the most skilled (*Catalog.*). Jerome also says in his preface to the Books of Solomon: 'There is still another Book of Solomon, which was written by the son of Sirach, and still another falsely named book that is entitled "The Wisdom of Solomon." ' . . . Philo wrote the Book of Wisdom in which he treats in detail the duties of princes, the penalty for idolatry, the blessed death of the devout, the punishment of the wicked, etc., for the comfort of the Jews and the terror of tyrants. . . .

"The Book of Wisdom was not written before Christ's birth. Therefore the Book of Wisdom is not in the canon of the Old Testament. . . . [III] The Book of Wisdom contains some matters not in harmony with the analogy of faith. . . . [IV] The Book of Wisdom lacks the unanimous approval of the early Church." (ThC E1 §§ 209–12)

FURTHER STUDY

Lay/Bible Class Resources

Burgland, Lane. *Study Guide to the Apocrypha*. St. Louis: Concordia, 2012. ♦ Lutheran author. Eight-session Bible study, including leader's notes and discussion questions. Companion piece to *ALEN*.

Clarke, Ernest G. *The Wisdom of Solomon*. CBCA. Cambridge: Cambridge University Press, 1974. ♦ Prepared by British scholars for the general reader. Includes the New English Bible translation along with commentary.

Engelbrecht, Edward A., gen. ed. *The Apocrypha: The Lutheran Edition with Notes*. St. Louis: Concordia, 2012. ♦ Based on the ESV. Reflects the Luther Bible tradition of the Apocrypha. Prepared by Lutherans, with commendations from top scholars of intertestamental studies.

Church Worker Resources

deSilva, David A. *Introducing the Apocrypha: Message, Context, and Significance*. Grand Rapids: Baker Academic, 2002. ♦ A thorough and informative introduction to the books of the Apocrypha from an evangelical scholar who served on the ESV Translation Committee of the Apocryphal Books.

Academic Resources

Bissell, Edwin Cone. *The Apocrypha of the Old Testament*. LCHS. New York: Charles Scribner's Sons, 1896. ♦ Philip Schaff appears to have added this volume to the English edition of the Lange commentary. Still one of the most substantive one-volume commentaries on the Apocrypha available in English.

Charles, R. H. *The Apocrypha and Pseudepigrapha of the Old Testament*. Vol. 1. Oxford; Clarendon Press, 1913. ♦ A standard scholarly reference work. Provides thorough introductions to the Apocrypha and substantive footnotes, commenting from the Greek, Hebrew, etc.

Pietersma, Albert, and Benjamin G. Wright, eds. *A New English Translation of the Septuagint*. Oxford: Oxford University Press, 2007. ♦ A literal revision of the NRSV translation prepared by an international team of Septuagint scholars. Includes thorough introductions focused on the text of the LXX.

Winston, David. *The Wisdom of Solomon*. Vol. 43 of AB. New York: Doubleday, 1979. ♦ A thorough commentary and new translation prepared for a major academic series. Winston regards the Wisdom of Solomon as an expression of Hellenistic or Philonic philosophy rather than of traditional Judaism.

TOBIT

Perform deeds of charity

From the tree-lined banks of the Tigris River stretch fertile fields along the winding Khoser River that runs through the midst of Nineveh, the high-walled city. After the Assyrian conquest of Israel (722 BC), Nineveh became home to Israelite exiles. The Book of Tobit tells the story of one such family transplanted from Galilee into the heart of a foreign empire.

Tobit depicts the frustrations of Israelites in exile who sought to practice their faith and piety among unsympathetic Gentiles. This gives us a clear picture of how the people lived with fear and failure. The story also describes some key elements of marriage and its celebration, which provides important background for understanding the New Testament. The author had a strong sense that God was guiding the Israelites in the midst of affliction, leading them to genuine comfort and hope.

Historical and Cultural Setting

The writer knew about the succession of Assyrian rulers in the seventh and eighth centuries BC. He mentions cities from Jerusalem to Rages in Media. However, it is not likely that Tobit was either living during the secession of the northern tribes from Judah or that he was also among those deported under Tiglath-pileser. These events are separated by nearly 200 years. The writer's most specific geographical description is for Galilee, which may have been his homeland.

Helmeted Seleucus I (311–280 BC) succeeded Alexander the Great as ruler of Syria, where much of the story of Tobit unfolds.

OVERVIEW

Author
An Israelite or Judean in the Eastern Diaspora

Date
Written within the fourth to second centuries BC

Places
Thisbe; Kedesh Naphtali in Galilee; Nineveh; Israel; Jerusalem; Ecbatana in Media; Rages in Media; Ararat; Elymais; Tigris River

People
Tobit; Tobiel; Tobias; King Enemessarus; Gabael; Sennacherib; Sacherdonus; Ahikar; Anna; Sarah; Raguel; Edna; Nasbas; demonic and angelic characters such as Asmodeus, Azarias/Raphael

Purpose
To describe the affliction and mercy of God while encouraging Israelites/Judeans to practice righteousness and almsgiving (12:8–9) as they await the restoration of Israel and the conversion of the nations

Themes
Suffering of the righteous; giving alms to the poor; honorable burial; marriage; ministry of angels; duty to family; affliction and mercy of God

Memory Verses
Raphael's counsel (12:6–10)

TIMELINE

722 BC	Assyrian Shalmaneser V takes Israel captive
704–681 BC	Reign of Sennacherib
681–669 BC	Reign of Esarhaddon
538 BC	Cyrus decrees that exiles may return to Judah
323 BC	Death of Alexander the Great

Composition

Author

The writer was most likely an Israelite or Judean who had travelled to or settled in the Eastern Diaspora (Mesopotamia).

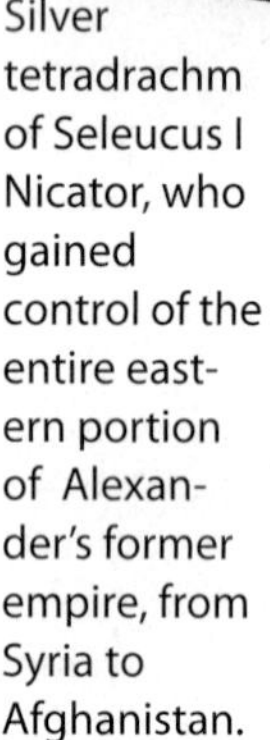

Silver tetradrachm of Seleucus I Nicator, who gained control of the entire eastern portion of Alexander's former empire, from Syria to Afghanistan.

Date of Composition

Although originally written in Hebrew or Aramaic, the earliest complete manuscripts for Tobit are in Greek. It may be one of the earliest writings of the Apocrypha. Scholars differ as to the time of composition, though it was probably written about 250–175 BC. The theory has also been advanced that Tobit was composed by a pious Jew in Egypt at the close of the third century BC. However, the setting for the story runs from Israel to the east, which makes Egyptian origin unlikely.

Purpose/Recipients

The story of Tobit is filled with a deep sense of obligation, that something must be attempted no matter what the consequences. The book also describes the author's deep conviction that God is watching us and that He is ready to reward the good deeds of the pious.

Modern Roman Catholic scholars contend that the purpose of Tobit is to give not history but "an edifying story." The historical blunders and chronological distortions, it is believed, indicate that the author was writing a moralizing story, one interrupted with suitable exhortations (4:3–21; 12:6–15; 14:8–11, and others).

Israelite/Jewish Diaspora Settlements

The map at right illustrates the spread of Israelites and Judeans from the Assryrian conquest and resettlements (722 BC) to the second Jewish revolt (AD 132–135). All cities shown contained some kind of Jewish presence. Trade routes provided the framework for expanding Jewish settlement. Close-knit communities allowed Jewish people to trade on stable credit throughout the known world and to stay in contact with one another.

The Diaspora also enabled the early spread of the Gospel as Paul and other Christian leaders visited Jewish settlements and preached that Jesus fulfilled the Old Testament promises of the Messiah.

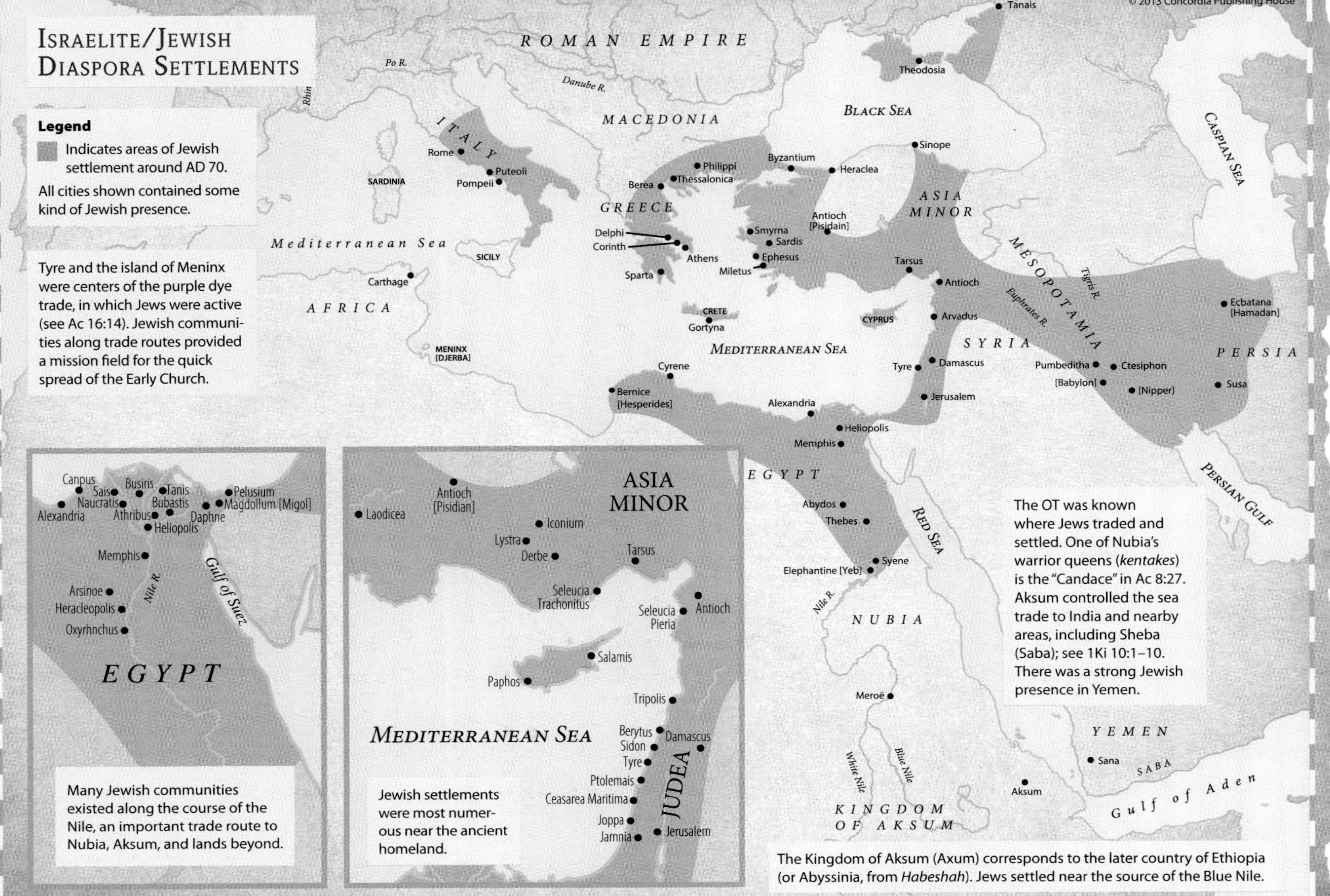

Israelite/Jewish Diaspora Settlements
Legend
Indicates areas of Jewish settlement around AD 70.
All cities shown contained some kind of Jewish presence.
Tyre and the island of Meninx were centers of the purple dye trade, in which Jews were active (see Ac 16:14). Jewish communities along trade routes provided a mission field for the quick spread of the Early Church.
The OT was known where Jews traded and settled. One of Nubia's warrior queens (kentakes) is the "Candace" in Ac 8:27. Aksum controlled the sea trade to India and nearby areas, including Sheba (Saba); see 1Ki 10:1–10. There was a strong Jewish presence in Yemen.
The Kingdom of Aksum (Axum) corresponds to the later country of Ethiopia (or Abyssinia, from Habeshah). Jews settled near the source of the Blue Nile.
Many Jewish communities existed along the course of the Nile, an important trade route to Nubia, Aksum, and lands beyond.
Jewish settlements were most numerous near the ancient homeland.
© 2013 Concordia Publishing House
ROMAN EMPIRE
MACEDONIA
GREECE
ITALY
AFRICA
Mediterranean Sea
MEDITERRANEAN SEA
BLACK SEA
CASPIAN SEA
PERSIAN GULF
RED SEA
ASIA MINOR
MESOPOTAMIA
SYRIA
PERSIA
EGYPT
NUBIA
YEMEN
SABA
Gulf of Aden
KINGDOM OF AKSUM
Rhin
Po R.
Danube R.
Tigris R.
Euphrates R.
Nile R.
White Nile
Blue Nile
SARDINIA
SICILY
CRETE
CYPRUS
MENINX [DJERBA]
Tanais
Theodosia
Sinope
Byzantium
Heraclea
Philippi
Thessalonica
Berea
Rome
Puteoli
Pompeii
Delphi
Corinth
Athens
Sparta
Smyrna
Sardis
Ephesus
Miletus
Antioch [Pisidain]
Tarsus
Antioch
Arvadus
Damascus
Tyre
Jerusalem
Carthage
Gortyna
Cyrene
Bernice [Hesperides]
Alexandria
Heliopolis
Memphis
Abydos
Thebes
Syene
Elephantine [Yeb]
Meroë
Aksum
Sana
Ecbatana [Hamadan]
Susa
Pumbeditha
Ctesiphon
[Babylon]
[Nipper]
EGYPT
Canpus
Sais
Busiris
Tanis
Pelusium
Naucratis
Bubastis
Magdollum [Migol]
Alexandria
Athribus
Daphne
Heliopolis
Memphis
Arsinoe
Heracleopolis
Oxyrhnchus
Gulf of Suez
Nile R.
ASIA MINOR
Laodicea
Antioch [Pisidian]
Iconium
Lystra
Derbe
Tarsus
Seleucia Trachonitus
Seleucia Pieria
Antioch
Salamis
Paphos
Tripolis
Berytus
Sidon
Damascus
Tyre
Ptolemais
Ceasarea Maritima
Joppa
Jamnia
Jerusalem
JUDEA
MEDITERRANEAN SEA

Outline

I. Preface (1:1–2)

II. Introduction (1:3–3:17)

A. Tobit's Earlier Life (1:3–3:6)

1. Tobit's previous fortunes (1:3–22)
2. Tobit's present story (ch 2)
3. Tobit's prefatory prayer (3:1–6)

B. Sarah's Previous History (3:7–15)

C. Union of Sarah's and Tobit's Destinies (3:16–17)

III. The Journey of Tobias (chs 4–13)

A. The Journey's Cause and the Preparations (4:1–5:17a)

1. The cause (4:1–2)
2. The teaching of Tobit (4:3–21)
3. The preparation (5:1–17a)

B. The Departure (5:17b–6:1)

C. The Events of the Journey (6:2–9:6)

1. Tobias's adventure with the fish (6:2–9)
2. Tobias at Raguel's home and his marriage with Sarah (6:10–9:6)

D. The Homecoming (chs 10–11)

1. Tobias's sorrowing parents (10:1–7a)
2. Tobias sets out for home (10:7b–13)
3. Tobias's reunion with his parents and the return of Tobit's sight (ch 11)

E. The Self-Revelation and Ascension of Raphael (chs 12–13)

1. The offer of wages (12:1–5)
2. Raphael's wisdom and self-revelation (12:6–15)
3. Raphael's commission and ascension (12:16–22)
4. Tobit's prayer of joy (ch 13)

IV. Conclusion (ch 14)

Literary Features

A wall painting in the synagogue at Dura Europos, Syria, depicts the angel of the Lord addressing Moses.

Genre

Tobit is introduced as "the book of the acts [literally, "words"] of Tobit," which presents it as a historical narrative. It is a fictional story about how God cares for and rewards the righteous. The work is written in biblical language and has many allusions to the Old Testament.

Characters

The story is told as the acts or words of **Tobit**, a member of the Israelite Diaspora resettled from Galilee into Nineveh by the Assyrians. Tobit pursues a virtuous life while living in a Gentile city. Despite his noble actions, he tragically suffers blindness. His wife, **Anna**, is forced to work in order to support the family.

Tobit sends his son **Tobias** on a trip to Ecbatana in order to repay a debt. Tobias's travelling companion is an angel, **Raphael**. He deceives Tobias and Tobit by introducing himself as Azarias, a member of Tobias's tribe (5:13–14). Later in the story, the angel reveals his true identity.

In Ecbatana, Tobias meets his cousins Raguel, Edna, and their daughter, **Sarah**. Sarah has suffered a series of disappointments because each time she marries, the demon Asmodeus kills her husband on their wedding night. The angel Raphael provides Tobias with a magical spell that drives away the demon, allowing Tobias to marry Sarah and fulfill the Levirite law of marriage. The couple travels with Raphael back to Tobit and Anna in Nineveh where the angel tells Tobias how to heal his father's eyes.

Narrative Development or Plot

Using a travel narrative, the story links the dilemmas faced by two families: (1) the family of Tobit and (2) the family of Raguel, Tobit's cousin. Through the guidance of an angel, the Lord brings the families together in the marriage of Tobias and Sarah. The Lord rewards them for faithfully observing the Law of Moses so that both families escape disaster.

Resources

Scholarly opinion differs as to the extent foreign sources were incorporated by Tobit's author. The reference to angels and demons is allegedly a new development of Judaism, coming from Zoroastrianism. For example, Asmodeus is supposed to be Aeshma Daeva of Persian demonology. The dog who follows Tobias on his journeys is reminiscent of the dog who in Zoroastrianism attends to Sraosha (another demon). In Judaism the dog was a despised animal, considered unclean. The writer must have been a Jew influenced by the Greeks, living under the Ptolemies in Egypt, who incorporated various strands in his fictional story.

Some scholars have argued that Tobit was written to counteract an Egyptian work, the *Tractate of Khons*, in which a demon is cast out by a woman with the aid of a Theban deity. *The Story of Ahikar* is also supposed to have influenced the contents of Tobit. Another source allegedly employed was the folklore of the grateful dead, who help those who show them respect. All the opinions listed above are speculative and unsatisfying.

In contrast, some Roman Catholic scholars believe that the main source for Tobit was Genesis and its stories of the patriarchs. In Genesis 24 is the story of Abraham's servant and Isaac's marriage. The scholars argue that Rebekah served as a model for the account of Tobias's journey and his wedding to Sarah. Raphael is the angel, who according to Gn 24:7, 40 was sent by the Lord to guide Abraham's servant in finding a wife for Isaac.

Text and Translations

Tobit was widely circulated in ancient times, as is attested by various translations among Jews and Christians. Cave 4 at Qumran included copies of one Hebrew and four Aramaic manuscripts of the book. Scholars disagree as to whether Hebrew or Aramaic was the original language of composition. There are extant three recensions in Greek, two in Latin, two in Syriac, four in later Hebrew, and one in Ethiopic. There are significant differences in the text of the Greek versions. The Codex Sinaiticus (S) has the longest text as contrasted with Codex Vaticanus (B), of which Alexandrinus is a revision. Jerome made his translation in the Vulgate from an Aramaic text.

Doctrinal Content

Summary Commentary

Chs 1–3 Tobit begins with a summary account of the early life of the devout Tobit. This is followed by an account of the hard trial which on the same day befell Tobit at Nineveh (2:1–3:6) and Sarah, the daughter of Raguel, at Ecbatana (3:7–15), prompting both to ask for help from God. God answers their prayers by sending the angel Raphael to aid both of them (3:16). At this point the main part of the story begins.

Chs 4–9 Tobias, the son of Tobit, is asked by his father to go to Rages in Media and collect a large sum of money deposited with a relative, Gabael. Raphael offers his services to Tobias, who needs a guide (5:1–22). In the Tigris River they catch a large fish whose heart, liver, and gall are removed by Tobias at the suggestion of Azariah (the angel Raphael). In Ecbatana they call on Raguel, father of Sarah. Tobias meets Sarah and asks for her hand in marriage, but he is told how a demon has killed all her previous suitors and husbands. Since Tobias has been instructed by Azariah how to defeat the demons, Tobias insists on marrying Sarah. On the wedding night Tobias follows instructions and burns the heart and liver of the fish with incense in the bridal chamber and drives the evil spirit to the uttermost parts of Egypt. After this Tobias sends Azariah to Rages to collect the money from his kinsman and then prepares for the wedding feast given by his father-in-law.

Chs 10–14 Upon the return of Tobias and Sarah to Nineveh, the eyesight of Tobit is restored by means of the gall taken from the same fish that has furnished the heart and liver for driving away the demon Asmodeus. Before Sarah reaches Tobit's home, he has regained his sight so that he is able to meet the bride at the gate of the city. Another wedding banquet of seven day's duration is held. Finally, when Tobit and Tobias endeavor to reward Azarias, who was mainly responsible for their happiness, they discover that their benefactor has been the angel Raphael, one of the seven angels who presents the prayers of men before God. The book concludes with a canticle of thanksgiving and the father's last instruction for a happy life for Tobias, who obeys his father's dying wish and lives to hear of Nineveh's destruction.

Specific Themes

A major theme in Tobit is the suffering of the righteous, described in terms of exile, illness, and demonic oppression. However, the book correspondingly teaches that God vindicates the righteous. He mercifully hears the prayers of His children and rewards their good deeds. Tobit includes special focus on the kindness of burying the dead and giving alms for the poor, the latter being equated with righteousness. The families in Tobit are especially concerned with marriage and their duties to one another as relatives. The description of marriage practices is one of the most thorough examples in biblical literature. An angel and a demon play key roles in the book. They live among people and substantially influence their lives.

Specific Doctrines

Tobit's objective is to show religious people the sufferings and trials a good person must endure. However, if one continues to be faithful, ultimately God will bless him with temporal goods (3:17; 4:21; 11:17). With this thesis there are combined instructions on the value of legal observances (1:4–9, 12; 4:6); the importance of prayer (3:1–6, 11–15); on chastity (3:16–18); marrying within one's tribe (4:13; 6:16–18); on doing works of mercy (2:1–2); the excellence of giving alms (4:7–11; 12:8b–9; 14:10), and also on manifesting respect for the dead.

This Hellenistic era ring shows a hunting dog pouncing on a hare. A dog accompanied Tobias on his journey, which is surprising given that the Old Testament associated dogs with impurity.

The book describes the spiritual conflict between good and evil angels (8:1–3) and how good angels carry our prayers to God (12:12). A unique feature of Old Testament teaching is its aversion to magical practices (cf Dt 18:10–11). In contrast, Tob 6:17–18 encourages a magical practice. The angel Raphael describes a smoke that could drive away a spiritual being. This use of magic is likely the influence of Near Eastern or Greek culture.

Canonicity

The discovery of one Hebrew manuscript and of Aramaic manuscripts in Cave 4 of Qumran seems to show that at the beginning of the Christian era Tobit was read and valued by Jews. The Christian Councils of Hippo (AD 393) and Carthage (AD 419) listed Tobit among the canonical books. However, Jerome and other Fathers spoke against receiving the book as Holy Scripture, the conclusion later reached by Luther and by Protestant churches. The Syriac Peshitta did not include Tobit. In 1546, the Roman Catholic Council of Trent reaffirmed the action taken by earlier church councils. The 1672 Synod of Jerusalem affirmed Tobit as Sacred Scripture for Eastern Orthodox churches.

Lutheran Theologians on Tobit

Luther

"What was said about the book of Judith may also be said about this book of Tobit. If the events really happened, then it is a fine and holy history. But if they are all made up, then it is indeed a very beautiful, wholesome, and useful fiction or drama by a gifted poet. . . . For Judith presents a good, serious, heroic tragedy, and Tobit presents a fine, delightful, devout comedy. . . . Tobit shows how things may go badly with a pious peasant or townsman, and there may be much suffering in married life, yet God always graciously helps and finally crowns the outcome with joy, in order that married folk should learn to have patience and, in a genuine fear of God and firm faith, put up gladly with all sorts of hardships because they have hope. . . . Therefore this book is useful and good for us Christians to read." (AE 35:345–47)

Gerhard

"We demonstrate that it is outside the canon with the following arguments: [I] Because it is not contained in the Hebrew sources. . . . It is extant only in the Greek and Latin languages. Jerome says that he saw a Chaldaic copy, but he attributes nothing to it. . . . [II] The Greek version does not agree with the Latin. . . . [III] The Greek edition conflicts not only with the Latin version but also with historical truth. . . . [IV] In some places this book contains material not in harmony with canonical truth and the analogy of faith. . . . [V] The fathers eliminate this book from the canon. Jerome, preface to Tobit: 'The Hebrews have cut this book from the catalog of divine Scripture and have given it up to those that they call "hagiographa." ' (Here we must read 'apocrypha' instead of 'hagiographa,' as we have shown earlier.)" (ThC E1 §§ 180–82, 187)

Further Study

Lay/Bible Class Resources

Burgland, Lane. *Study Guide to the Apocrypha*. St. Louis: Concordia, 2012. ♦ Lutheran author. Eight-session Bible study, including leader's notes and discussion questions. Companion piece to *ALEN*.

Dancy, J. C. *The Shorter Books of the Apocrypha*. CBCA. Cambridge: Cambridge University Press, 1972. ♦ Prepared by British scholars for the general reader. Includes the New English Bible translation along with commentary.

Engelbrecht, Edward A., gen. ed. *The Apocrypha: The Lutheran Edition with Notes*. St. Louis: Concordia, 2012. ♦ Based on the ESV. Reflects the Luther Bible tradition of the Apocrypha. Prepared by Lutherans, with commendations from top scholars of intertestamental studies.

Church Worker Resources

deSilva, David A. *Introducing the Apocrypha: Message, Context, and Significance*. Grand Rapids: Baker Academic, 2002. ♦ A thorough and informative introduction to the books of the Apocrypha from an evangelical scholar who served on the ESV Translation Committee of the Apocryphal Books.

Academic Resources

Bissell, Edwin Cone. *The Apocrypha of the Old Testament*. LCHS. New York: Charles Scribner's Sons, 1896. ♦ Philip Schaff appears to have added this volume to the English edition of the Lange commentary. Still one of the most substantive one-volume commentaries on the Apocrypha available in English.

Charles, R. H. *The Apocrypha and Pseudepigrapha of the Old Testament*. Vol. 1. Oxford: Clarendon Press, 1913. ♦ A standard scholarly reference work. Provides thorough introductions to the Apocrypha and substantive footnotes, commenting from the Greek, Hebrew, etc.

Fitzmyer, Joseph A. *Tobit*. Commentaries on Early Jewish Literature. Boston: Walter de Gruyter, 2003. ♦ Prepared for a new academic series by a well-known philologist.

Littman, Robert J. *Tobit*. Septuagint Commentary Series. Leiden: Brill, 2008. ♦ Includes the Greek text with a new English translation and commentary in light of the most recent scholarship.

Moore, Carey A. *Tobit*. Vol. 40A of AB. New York: Doubleday, 1996. ♦ A thorough commentary and new translation of Tobit prepared for a major academic series.

Pietersma, Albert, and Benjamin G. Wright, eds. *A New English Translation of the Septuagint*. Oxford: Oxford University Press, 2007. ♦ A literal revision of the NRSV translation prepared by an international team of Septuagint scholars. Includes thorough introductions focused on the text of the LXX.

Apamea was the military headquarters of the Seleucid kings and a vital city of Roman Syria. Grand ruins illustrate the powerful influence of pagan culture and governance over the lives of Diaspora Israelites, like those depicted in Tobit. For a sense of scale, note the persons walking near the right margin of the picture.

ECCLESIASTICUS (WISDOM OF JESUS SON OF SIRACH)

All wisdom comes from the Lord

As early as the third century, some Church Fathers called Jesus son of Sirach's book *Ecclesiasticus*, which means "churchly." They admired his wisdom and perhaps advocated for it to become required reading in the churches. This longest book of the Apocrypha—twice as long as the canonical Book of Proverbs—has much to commend it. Yet it also raises numerous questions.

Historical and Cultural Setting

When the Seleucid ruler Antiochus the Great took the region of Israel away from the Ptolemies at the beginning of the second century BC, Jesus son of Sirach likely lived and worked in Jeruslaem as a scribe and teacher. In ch 50 of his book, he wrote about the high priest Simon son of Onias (219–196 BC) called "the Just," as though he was an eyewitness of his priestly activities on the Day of Atonement. Simon renovated the temple, strengthened its walls, and dug a siege reservoir (Ecclus 50:1–4). Jesus son of Sirach wrote about Simon in the past tense, which would mean that he lived to witness the ministry of Simon's brother Eleazar. Jesus son of Sirach's grandson translated the collection of his sayings from Hebrew into Greek so that readers outside of Judea could benefit from his insights.

Like the author of Ecclesiasticus, the Jews who built the synagogue at Dura Europos (third century AD) celebrated the heroes of the Old Testament stories and built a shrine for the Torah as the focus of their devotion.

Ossuary with the name Jesus in Aramaic.

Composition

Author

This is the only apocryphal book of which the author is known. The writer tells his readers that his name is "Jesus son of Sirach," the son of Eleazar of Jerusalem (50:27). His grandson translated the book into Greek 50 years later. Jesus son of Sirach is described as a resident of Jerusalem; he likely taught there. He gives evidence of intimate knowledge of the Old Testament. The entire book is replete with ideas taken from the Old Testament and reflects the attitude and training of a person who enjoyed an excellent preparation for the position of scribe. From certain allusions in the book it has been inferred that he was a man of leisure, fond of travel, a man with a philosophical mind, and an adherent of a party that later came to be known as the Sadducees. Little else is known about the author or his grandson.

Date of Composition

The book was written before the outbreak of the Maccabean struggle. The translation of Ecclesiasticus was undertaken and completed around 132 BC. In the prologue the grandson states that he had come to Alexandria in Egypt in the thirty-eighth year of King Euergetes, or 132 BC. In the prologue he also states what prompted him to undertake the translation (para 3).

Purpose/Recipients

Jesus son of Sirach wrote to teach people the wise ways of God so that they may progress in living according to the Law of Moses, which embodies wisdom. At the end of the book, he writes, "Draw near to me, you who are untaught, and lodge in the house of instruction" (51:23). It is possible that this refers to an actual school where the author taught his addresses to students (see outline below).

Literary Features

Genre

Ecclesiasticus provides a helpful picture of how the wisdom tradition was continued after the biblical books of Proverbs and Ecclesiastes. Comments from the author reveal how formal education took place in the second century BC and illustrate the authoritative use of most books of the Old

Testament. Many sayings from Jesus son of Sirach relate genuine wisdom in keeping with the biblical tradition as well as a sincere piety. He especially shows the central place that God's written Word had taken in the lives of His people as the embodiment of true wisdom.

Characters

Aside from personal information about the author, Jesus son of Sirach (see "Author" above), chs 44–50 provide extensive comment on a list of "famous men" (44:1) from Israel's history. (The ESV headings provide a convenient listing.) These descriptions are based mostly on information from canonical Scripture. However, one of the most prominent figures is **Simon II**, son of Onias. Simon served as high priest in the late third century BC. The many teachings of Jesus son of Sirach include the common contrast between wise men and fools as well as other characters common to wisdom literature. For comment on Jesus son of Sirach's descriptions of women, see "Specific Doctrines" below.

Narrative Development or Plot

As a collection of wise addresses, the book does not have a storyline or plot. However, the hymn of the fathers (chs 44–50) celebrates the history of Israel in chronological order, culminating with the high priestly ministry of Simon the Just whose service the author likely witnessed. Jesus son of Sirach remembered the fathers as persons appointed by God, who preserved His people through the wisdom He gave them.

Resources

As noted above, the entire book is replete with ideas taken from the Old Testament and reflects the attitude and training of a person who enjoyed an excellent preparation for the position of scribe.

Text and Translations

Jesus son of Sirach originally wrote his book in Hebrew, which was later translated by his grandson into Greek

OVERVIEW

Author
Jesus son of Sirach (Yeshua Ben Sira)

Date
Early second century BC; translated in 132 BC

Places
Egypt; Zion; Jerusalem; the temple; a house of instruction; sites from Old Testament accounts

People
Jesus son of Sirach, son of Eleazar; the author's grandson (translator); Euergetes; teacher and student ("father" and "son"); people serving in various callings (e.g., physicians, scribes); a catalog of famous men from the Old Testament; high priest Simon son of Onias

Purpose
To instruct people in wisdom so that they may make even greater progress in living according to the Law of Moses

Themes
Fear of the Lord; the Law as wisdom; folly; friendship; wealth; creation; good and wicked women; famous forefathers; prayer; and God's care

Memory Verses
Fear of the Lord (1:16); testing (2:1); humility (3:11, 18, 22–23); mercy of the Lord (17:29); the Lord's care (34:19); benediction (50:22–24); labor and rest (51:27)

TIMELINE

198 BC	Seleucid rule of Judea begins
165–134 BC	Maccabean Revolt
132 BC	Ecclesiasticus translated into Greek
63 BC	Romans enter Judean politics
2 BC	Birth of Jesus of Nazareth

Outline

Ecclesiasticus is written as a series of wise addresses from a teacher to his student(s), which are presented as counsel from a "father" to "son(s)." The structure and presentation is similar to Proverbs 1–9, which likewise includes addresses and poems about wisdom. The addresses in Ecclesiasticus usually begin with praise for wisdom or recount the blessings of wisdom (1:1–30; 6:18–37; 14:20–15:20; 24:1–34; 39:12–35). An exception is the fifth address (33:20–39:11), which the author sets off from the preceding address by a personal statement (33:16–19).

The conclusion of Ecclesiasticus (42:15–51:30) differs from the earlier sections. It begins with a celebration of God's works in creation and in Israel (42:15–50:26). It ends with personal statements from the author.

The addresses in Ecclesiasticus cover a wide variety of themes, to which the author returns again and again. A detailed outline runs many pages. The outline below presents an overview. The ESV headings distinguish smaller units and themes of the work.

I. Prologue from Translator (three paragraphs)

II. Prologue in Praise of Wisdom (ch 1)

III. Wise Addresses to Students (2:1–42:14)

- A. First Set of Wise Addresses to Students (2:1–6:17)
- B. Second Set of Wise Addresses to Students (6:18–14:19)
- C. Third Set of Wise Addresses to Students (14:20–23:27)
- D. Fourth Set of Wise Addresses to Students (24:1–33:19)
- E. Fifth Set of Wise Addresses to Students (33:20–39:11)
- F. Sixth Set of Wise Addresses to Students (39:12–42:14)

IV. God's Work in Creation and in Israel (42:15–50:26)

V. Additions to the Book (50:27–51:30)

(Prologue, para 2–3). For many centuries the Greek text was widely used, and it was the foundational version available to Christians until the discovery of Hebrew texts at the Cairo Geniza (explored in the 1800s) and later found at Qumran and Masada (1940s to 1960s). More than two-thirds of Ecclesiasticus is now available in Hebrew.

Scholars regard the shorter edition, which appears in Hebrew and Greek manuscripts, as the original or earlier edition of Ecclesiasticus. A longer edition, with hundreds of more lines, is also found in Hebrew and in Greek manuscripts. The book was either expanded by the original author or by subsequent contributors. The Old Latin and Vulgate editions, which western Christians used for centuries, are based on the longer edition. The reader should be aware of great divergences between the King James Version, the Revised Version, and other more recent translations. The ESV translation is based on the shorter edition, with references to the longer edition in the translation notes.

The book seems to have been utilized in the Early Church as an instructional manual. It was so popular that it was translated into a number of Oriental languages, including Coptic (Sahidic, Bohairic, and Akhmimic dialects), Armenian, Ethiopic, Georgian, Old Slavonic, and Arabic.

Doctrinal Content

Summary Commentary

Ecclesiasticus is divided into several parts, unequal in length.

Prologue Written by Jesus son of Sirach's grandson as a preface to the Greek translation completed in 132 BC, the prologue introduces the author, his learning, and his reason for writing the book. It also explains some features of the translation.

Ch 1 The first chapter serves as an introduction. It introduces a favorite topic: God's wisdom manifested in creation. It then commends "the fear of the Lord" as the root of wisdom, which includes keeping God's commandments (Torah). Bear in mind that the biblical expression "fear the Lord" usually refers to trust in God and not to terror of Him.

2:1–42:14 The longest section of the work contains the "proverbs of Ben Sirach." It is a collection of proverbs loosely strung together, presenting the author's meditation and lectures on religious and ethical matters. There is a great similarity between the canonical Proverbs and this part of Ecclesiasticus, which may be divided into a collection of addresses to students of wisdom.

42:15–43:33 The poem of praise lauds the wonderful works of physical nature created by God.

44:1–49:16 This section begins with these famous words: "Let us now praise famous men and our fathers in their generations" and contains a recapitulation of the history of the Hebrew people and the accomplishments of their great leaders. This section may have furnished the author of Hebrews with a model for the great roll call of the heroes of faith given in Heb 11.

Chs 50–51 The last section has the nature of an appendix; it contains the best description of the temple services that has survived from ancient times (50:1–26) as well as personal information about the author.

Specific Themes

The themes of Ecclesiasticus are great in number and variety. The following is a list of prominent themes, which is far from comprehensive. As noted above, the introduction on the fear of the Lord sets forth a key teaching of the author and of Israelite wisdom literature generally. The book also includes the customary contrasts between wisdom and folly, righteousness and wickedness. The author repeatedly looks to creation as a source of examples for illustrating God's wisdom. In some sections he writes in praise of a good wife but with some bitterness toward women. Chapters 44–49 celebrate the fathers of Israel. The author commonly refers to prayer and faith in God's providential care.

Specific Doctrines

Due to the length and character of Ecclesiasticus, Church Fathers cited it more often than any other book of the Apocrypha, especially to lend support and context to interpretation of passages in Sacred Scripture. For example, Ecclus 15:11–20 was used to interpret Is 63:17, "O Lord, why do You make us wander from Your ways?" by pointing out that people are responsible for their own sin. The first sin was freely chosen by mankind, therefore, God is not the cause of sin and of evil. The Fathers also noted that the book consistently taught the Law of Holy Scripture and its doctrine of God as creator of all things. It was also valued for its practical counsel of matters of friendship, public etiquette, and other virtues.

Along with the many praiseworthy elements of Ecclesiasticus appear some that raise doctrinal concerns because they contrast with biblical teaching. These concerning passages are among the reasons why the book could not be received as Sacred Scripture by all Christians. For example, in some passages the author presents ideas about atonement that stray from biblical teaching (3:3, 30; 20:28; 35:3). These passages show a confidence in personal righteousness rather than in the forgiveness of sins that God promises through blood atonement, as described in the Law of Moses. In teaching about human responsibility, the author strongly emphasizes the freedom of the human will and overstates human ability to do what is right (15:15–17) without mentioning the debilitating consequences of the fall into sin.

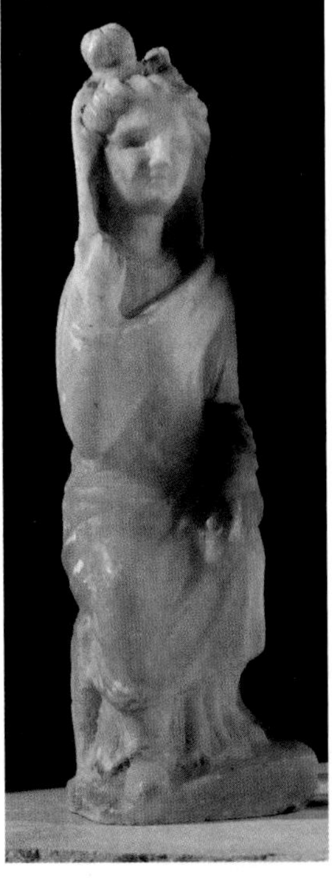
An alabaster figure of a traditional mother found at Babylon, heavily influenced by Greek style during the Seleucid era.

The author has sharp warnings concerning women, which may stem from negative personal experiences. He describes women causing anxiety for husbands and fathers because they are beguiling (9:1–9), given to sin (25:16–26; 26:5–12), morally inferior (42:9–14), and less valuable than men (22:3; 42:14). He also praises good wives (26:1–4, 13–18) but not with the same intensity or frequency with which he criticizes women. Readers should not conclude that Jesus son of Sirach's views were characteristic of early Jewish culture.

Jesus son of Sirach emphasized the permanence of death (17:27–28; 38:16–23) and did not clearly comment on punishment or reward in the afterlife. This has led some interpreters to conclude that he completely denied an afterlife. Other interpreters point to 44:16; 46:12; 48:11; and 49:10 as evidence that he did believe in an afterlife.

Canonicity

The book has exercised great influence on later Jewish literature. Although the great Rabbi Akiba prohibited its reading, Talmudic scholars assiduously studied Ecclesiasticus. The leading Tannaitic and Amoraic scholars quote liberally from it. More than 20 proverbs are cited in the Babylonian and Palestinian Talmuds. Some of the quotations in the Talmuds are introduced as if from the Bible: "It is written." In two places Ecclesiasticus is spoken of as belonging to the kethubim, or hagiographa, of the Hebrew Old Testament.

Early Christians valued Ecclesiasticus, and over time it was welcome among the books of the eastern and western churches. However, Jerome and others spoke against receiving the book as Holy Scripture, the conclusion later reached by Luther and adopted by Protestant churches. In 1546, the Council of Trent described the book as canonical for Roman Catholics. The 1672 Synod of Jerusalem affirmed Ecclesiasticus as Sacred Scripture for Eastern Orthodox churches.

Lutheran Theologians on Ecclesiaticus

Luther

"This book has heretofore carried the Latin title, *Ecclesiasticus*, which has been understood in German to mean 'spiritual discipline.' . . . Its real name is otherwise Jesus Sirach, after its author, as its own prologue and the Greek [50:27] indicate. This is how the books of Moses, Joshua, Isaiah, and all the prophets are named, after their authors. Yet the ancient fathers did not include this one among the books of sacred Scripture, but simply regarded it as the fine work of a wise man. And we shall let it go at that. . . .

"That the book must be a compilation is suggested also by the fact that in it one part is not fitted neatly to the next, as in the work of a single author. Instead it draws on many books and authors and mixes them together, much as a bee sucks juices out of all sorts of flowers and mixes them. . . .

"This is a useful book for the ordinary man. The author concentrates all his effort on helping a citizen or housefather to be God-fearing, devout, and wise; and on showing what the relationship of such a man should be to God, the Word of God, priests, parents, wife, children, his own body, his servants, possessions, neighbors, friends, enemies, government, and anyone else. So one might well call this a book on home discipline or on the virtues of a pious householder. This indeed is the proper 'spiritual discipline,' and should be recognized as such." (AE 35:347–48)

Gerhard

"[Ecclesiasticus] was not written by a prophet, . . . There are some things in this book that are not in harmony with the analogy of faith. [Gerhard lists the doctrine of wisdom (1:3; 24:9), almsgiving and atonement (3:30), misinterpretation of Scripture (46:20; 49:4), and return of Elijah (48:10).] Sirach lacks the unanimous approval of the early Church, as is clear from our general discussion of the apocryphal books. . . . Some of the Papists themselves entertain doubts about the canonical authority of this book." (ThC E1 § 216)

Further Study

Lay/Bible Class Resources

Burgland, Lane. *Study Guide to the Apocrypha*. St. Louis: Concordia, 2012. ✠ Lutheran author. Eight-session Bible study, including leader's notes and discussion questions. Companion piece to *ALEN*.

Engelbrecht, Edward A., gen. ed. *The Apocrypha: The Lutheran Edition with Notes*. St. Louis: Concordia, 2012. ✠ Based on the ESV. Reflects the Luther Bible tradition of the Apocrypha. Prepared by Lutherans, with commendations from top scholars of intertestamental studies.

Snaith, John G. *Ecclesiasticus, or the Wisdom of Jesus Son of Sirach*. CBCA. Cambridge: Cambridge University Press, 1974. ✠ Prepared by British scholars for the general reader. Includes the New English Bible translation along with commentary.

Church Worker Resources

deSilva, David A. *Introducing the Apocrypha: Message, Context, and Significance*. Grand Rapids: Baker Academic, 2002. ✠ A thorough and informative introduction to the books of the Apocrypha from an evangelical scholar who served on the ESV Translation Committee of the Apocryphal Books.

Academic Resources

Beentjes, P. C. *The Book of Ben Sira in Hebrew*. Leiden: Brill, 1997. ✠ A scholarly presentation of all the Hebrew texts discovered in the twentieth century.

Bissell, Edwin Cone. *The Apocrypha of the Old Testament*. LCHS. New York: Charles Scribner's Sons, 1896. ✠ Philip Schaff appears to have added this volume to the English edition of the Lange commentary. Still one of the most substantive one-volume commentaries on the Apocrypha available in English.

Charles, R. H. *The Apocrypha and Pseudepigrapha of the Old Testament*. Vol. 1. Oxford: Clarendon Press, 1913. ✠ A standard scholarly reference work. Provides thorough introductions to the Apocrypha and substantive footnotes, commenting from the Greek, Hebrew, etc.

Pietersma, Albert, and Benjamin G. Wright, eds. *A New English Translation of the Septuagint*. Oxford: Oxford University Press, 2007. ✠ A literal revision of the NRSV translation prepared by an international team of Septuagint scholars. Includes thorough introductions focused on the text of the LXX.

Skehan, Patrick W., and Alexander A. DiLella. *The Wisdom of Ben Sira*. Vol. 39 of AB. New York: Doubleday, 1985. ✠ A thorough work prepared for a major academic series. Translation and commentary based on the LXX and Hebrew manuscripts discovered in the twentieth century.

BARUCH

Righteousness belongs to the Lord

For the Israelites during the Persian and Hellenistic periods, there were no greater lessons to retain than those of the Babylonian exile. The downfall of the kingdom of Judah was a constant reminder that God's people may lose faith and fail. The history continually urged repentance and faithfulness to the covenant.

Although the Book of Baruch purports to be written in c 582 BC at Babylon (1:2), the historical circumstances do not match up with the content. The work certainly comes after the Babylonians destroyed Jerusalem (587 BC) yet the general content of the work, which is likely a composite of several compositions, makes it difficult to determine when it was composed or compiled.

Historical and Cultural Setting

The Book of Baruch assumes a resettled Jerusalem with active services at the temple site, a Jewish Diaspora interested in supporting the temple, and freedom to travel to and from Jerusalem. The people are instructed to serve in peace those who rule over them. These general circumstances often prevailed after the restoration of the temple in 516 BC during Persian rule. As a result, it is difficult to identify a more specific historical setting.

Judean families were torn apart in the days of exile. In the Book of Baruch, the writer wishes to capture sorrows over sin by recalling those most bitter experiences. Yet alongside the desolation, he adds prayers of repentance

Gates of Persepolis, Persia. Judean exiles passed through the regal gates of their conquerers and rulers, which reminded them of their failure to keep the covenant.

OVERVIEW

Author
A Judean in exile

Date
After 587 BC

Places
Babylon; Jerusalem; River Sud; Egypt; Canaan; Teman; Merran; Zion; Judah; Israel

People
Baruch; Chaldeans; King Jeconiah; Belshazzar; high priest Jehoiakim; King Zedekiah; Nebuchadnezzar; mighty men; princes; elders; prisoners; judges; prophets; sons of Hagar; merchants of Merran

Purpose
To call God's people to repentance and urge them to pray for their rulers

Themes
Exile among the nations; confession of sins; prayer; God's gift of wisdom; Zion; encouragement that salvation is coming; the everlasting God

Memory Verses
Prayers for mercy (2:6, 20)

TIMELINE

598–597 BC	Reign of Jehoiachin (Jeconiah)
587 BC	Babylonians take Jerusalem
538 BC	Cyrus decrees that exiles may return to Judah
332 BC	Alexander the Great takes Judea from Persians
165–134 BC	Maccabean rule

and hope that God would restore His people. Baruch described both the depth of pain and the depth of faith that his readers needed for reflection in their circumstances. They are urged to forget the past and not to plan vengeance but to serve the empire faithfully and seek blessings from the emperor.

Composition

Author(s)

It is unlikely that Baruch the son of Neriah, who served as the prophet Jeremiah's scribe (Jer 32:12), wrote this book (Bar 1:1). The author does draw deeply from the style of the biblical prophets such as Jeremiah, which may have suggested Baruch as a possible contributor. See Gerhard's comments below.

Sometimes this book is referred to as 1 Baruch to distinguish it from two apocalyptic books (*2 Baruch*, *3 Baruch*) as well as "Things Left Out of Jeremiah" (*4 Baruch*). The latter books are among the Old Testament Pseudepigrapha.

Date of Composition

Scholars are generally agreed that the book has nothing to do with the time of the Babylonian captivity. What then was the situation that prompted the writing? The answer scholars give is divided: one school of thought places its origin during the persecution of Antiochus Epiphanes, while another school assigns it to a time after the destruction of Jerusalem in AD 70. Still others date the origin of the latter portion of the book as late as AD 150. Although the second part may come from the second century AD, the first part is believed to be quite old. Although no Hebrew copy of Baruch exists, portions of the Greek text show signs of having been translated from Hebrew.

Purpose/Recipients

The stated purpose of Baruch is for reading at the Jerusalem temple at appointed feasts (1:14). It was to accompany a monetary gift for supporting the temple offerings, a message that could inspire Diaspora Jews to support the temple with gifts of their own. The confession of sins, prayers, and wise teachings of the book are addressed to Judah and to Israel, who require the Lord's admonition due to their rebellious past.

Baruch was written to persuade readers to be subservient and obedient to their Babylonian masters (cf 1:11–12), to urge repentance for their sins that had been responsible for the destruction of Jerusalem, and to create faith in God's ultimate purpose of eventually restoring the Jews from captivity.

Literary Features

Genre

Baruch is a composite work, uneven in quality and not harmonious, in the style of Israelite prophetic literature. It consists of two or even three distinct documents. The clearest and sharpest division of the book comes between 3:8 and 3:9. At this point the style changes from prose to poetry.

Characters

The Book of Baruch portrays itself as written by Jeremiah's friend and secretary, the son of Neraiah (1:1). According to the testimony of the book, it was written in the fifth year after the destruction of Jerusalem, 582 BC. **Baruch**, the faithful follower of Jeremiah, is among the deported exiles who is sent to his countrymen left behind in Jerusalem. He is entrusted with a sum of money to aid Jewish worship in Jerusalem and with a request that the Jews pray for Nebuchadnezzar and his son Belshazzar. Just how this was to be effected with the temple destroyed and its priesthood scattered is not made clear by the author.

Baruch, the son of Neraiah, came to occupy an important place in Jewish legends. Since he is reported to have rewritten the canonical Book of Jeremiah and also was an eyewitness of the destruction of Jerusalem, it was assumed natural that he should write about events connected with the downfall of the Southern Kingdom.

Narrative Development or Plot

The book opens with Baruch reading to the Judean exiles in Babylon in the year 582 BC, five years after the destruction of Jerusalem. The people respond to Baruch's message by fasting, prayer, and gathering money to support the offerings in Jerusalem. They send Baruch back to Judah with the money, the temple vessels that the Babylonians confiscated, and the book that Baruch would read at the temple services on feast days.

Outline

The structure of Baruch follows the familiar cycle of sin, punishment, repentance, and restoration noted in Dt 28–32 and illustrated throughout Judges. In this way, Baruch reconnected Judean exiles with a timeless message: follow the ways of the Lord and hope in His promised salvation.

I. Introduction (1:1–14)

II. Prayers of Confession (1:15–3:8)

III. Poems for Instructing Israel (3:9–5:9)
- A. The Law Gives Wisdom (3:9–4:4)
- B. Admonition about the Exile (4:5–5:9)

The story and the book may serve as a model for actions the Diaspora Jews should take in order to maintain their faith and their relationship to the Jerusalem temple as the focal point for expressing their faith.

Resources

The wording of Baruch is heavily dependent on expressions found in biblical prophetic books, passages of the biblical wisdom tradition (such as Jb 28; Pr 8; Ecclus 24), and Dt 30. As Luther and Gerhard note below, these points of consistency with the Bible have helped to commend the book, yet have also made it seem like unnecessary repetition.

Text and Translations

The earliest extent text of Baruch is in Greek. All other versions depend on the Greek edition, which circulated with the writings associated with Jeremiah (Book of Jeremiah, Lamentations, Letter of Jeremiah). It is possible that the latter half of Baruch (3:9–5:9) was composed in Greek or at least translated by the same LXX translator who worked on Jeremiah 29–52. However, good arguments have been made for Baruch 1:1–3:8 having been written originally in Hebrew. These observations contribute to the scholarly consensus that Baruch is a composite book.

Doctrinal Content

Summary Commentary

This golden head of a Persian deity is part of the Oxus treasure, the most important collection from the Achaemenid period, which shows the Persians' devotion to their idolatrous religion.

1:1–3:8 The first section contains the letter of Baruch (1:1–14) and a liturgical confession and prayer as well as a story of how the book came into use.

3:9–4:4 A second section consists of a short chapter on wisdom and is the reason why Baruch is often grouped with Ecclesiasticus and the Wisdom of Solomon in the category of the wisdom literature. In it the sufferings of the Jews are attributed to the fact that Israel forsook the fountains of wisdom.

4:5–5:9 The third and final section endeavors to encourage the people and promises them the final restoration of Zion. For example, in 4:5–35 the refrain "be of good cheer" or its equivalent (vv 5, 21, 27, 30) constantly recurs, and in 4:30–5:9 there is the regular repetition of "O Jerusalem." The final lines of the last part of the book end on an optimistic note:

> Arise, O Jerusalem, stand upon the height and look toward the east and see your children gathered from west and east, at the word of the Holy One, rejoicing that God has remembered them. (5:5)

This concluding passage fits with the opening message about the bond between the Jews in Jerusalem and the Diaspora Jews who send them their gifts in support of the temple.

Specific Themes

Baruch refers to the status of Judeans as exiles, which provides the historical basis for confessions of sin and prayers for God's help. Beginning at 3:9, Baruch celebrates the wisdom of God as a special blessing for Israel, God's chosen people. Jerusalem and Zion are important themes, especially in the latter portion of the book, where the Lord is described as the everlasting Savior (4:22).

Specific Doctrines

God is spoken of in different ways. In 1:1–3:8 the author uses the following names for God: Lord (22 times); Lord Almighty, the God of Israel (two times); Lord, our God (15 times). Not one of these names for the deity is employed in the second part (3:9–5:9).

Canonicity

Early Christians valued Baruch, and over time it was welcomed among the books of the eastern and western churches. However, Jerome and other Fathers spoke against receiving the book as Holy Scripture, the conclusion later reached by Luther and adopted by Protestant churches. In 1546, the Council of Trent described the book as canonical for Roman Catholics. The 1672 Synod of Jerusalem did not expressly mention the Book of Baruch. However, it appeared in editions of the LXX as an appendix to Jeremiah.

Ruins of Palmyra (Tadmor), an ancient caravan city.

Lutheran Theologians on Baruch

Luther

Luther's opening comment on Baruch was likely prompted by the order of the books of the Apocrypha as they appear in his translation of the Bible. The five chapters of Baruch appear just after the 51 chapters of Ecclesiasticus.

"Whoever the good Baruch may be, this book is very skimpy. It is hardly credible that the servant of St. Jeremiah, whose name is also Baruch (and to whom this letter is attributed), should not be richer and loftier in spirit than this Baruch. Furthermore, the book's chronology does not agree with the [accepted] histories. Thus I very nearly let it go with the third and fourth books of Esdras. . . . Baruch, however, we shall let run with the pack because he writes so vigorously against idolatry and sets forth the law of Moses." (AE 35:349–50)

Gerhard

"We admit that Baruch is to be preferred to the rest of the apocryphal books because in it are many quite majestic subjects that are rather close to sacred character. Yet we are scarcely able to list it among the properly canonical books for these reasons. . . . Baruch 6:2 says, 'You will be there for seven generations.' Yet this is alien to Hebrew style, for nowhere in Hebrew literature is the word 'generation' taken to include a period of ten years. The epistle that is attributed to Jeremiah in c. 6 has little flavor of his style. Jerome says (preface to Jeremiah): 'The Hebrews neither have nor read this book.' . . . Baruch conflicts with the canonical books. This Baruch says that 'he composed his writing in Babylon after Jerusalem had been destroyed' (1:1). Canonical history, however, testifies that Baruch, the son of Neriah, the servant of Jeremiah, along with his master 'had been deported into Egypt' (Jer. 43:6) by the stubborn Jews after the destruction of the city. This Baruch says that 'after the city was abandoned, money was sent to the priests at Jerusalem that with it they might buy burnt offerings, incense, and myrrh and offer sacrifices at Jerusalem to the Lord for the sake of the captive Jews' (1:7). But sacred history nowhere says that after the temple had been burned that there was any external worship there. Rather, it contradicts this fabrication when it mentions that the feasts were discontinued and the temple completely destroyed. Lam. 2:6: 'He has broken down his booth like that of a garden. He has demolished His tabernacle. The Lord has consigned feast and Sabbath to forgetfulness in Zion,' etc. Verse 7: 'The Lord has driven away His altar and has removed His sanctuary far from Himself.' Ezra 3:[2] relates that after seventy years of captivity the Jews returned home and 'built the altar of the God of Israel to offer burnt offerings upon it.' " (ThC E1 § 222)

Further Study

Lay/Bible Class Resources

Burgland, Lane. *Study Guide to the Apocrypha*. St. Louis: Concordia, 2012. ❧ Lutheran author. Eight-session Bible study, including leader's notes and discussion questions. Companion piece to *ALEN*.

Dancy, J. C. *The Shorter Books of the Apocrypha*. CBCA. Cambridge: Cambridge University Press, 1972. ❧ Prepared by British scholars for the general reader. Includes the New English Bible translation along with commentary.

Engelbrecht, Edward A., gen. ed. *The Apocrypha: The Lutheran Edition with Notes*. St. Louis: Concordia, 2012. ❧ Based on the ESV. Reflects the Luther Bible tradition of the Apocrypha. Prepared by Lutherans, with commendations from top scholars of intertestamental studies.

Church Worker Resources

deSilva, David A. *Introducing the Apocrypha: Message, Context, and Significance*. Grand Rapids: Baker Academic, 2002. ❧ A thorough and informative introduction to the books of the Apocrypha from an evangelical scholar who served on the ESV Translation Committee of the Apocryphal Books.

Academic Resources

Bissell, Edwin Cone. *The Apocrypha of the Old Testament*. LCHS. New York: Charles Scribner's Sons, 1896. ❧ Philip Schaff appears to have added this volume to the English edition of the Lange commentary. Still one of the most substantive one-volume commentaries on the Apocrypha available in English.

Charles, R. H. *The Apocrypha and Pseudepigrapha of the Old Testament*. Vol. 1. Oxford: Clarendon Press, 1913. ❧ A standard scholarly reference work. Provides thorough introductions to the Apocrypha and substantive footnotes, commenting from the Greek, Hebrew, etc.

Moore, Carey A. *Daniel, Esther, and Jeremiah: The Additions*. Vol. 44 of AB. New York: Doubleday, 1977. ❧ A thorough commentary and new translation prepared for a major academic series. Focuses on historical and literary interpretation.

Pietersma, Albert, and Benjamin G. Wright, eds. *A New English Translation of the Septuagint*. Oxford: Oxford University Press, 2007. ❧ A literal revision of the NRSV translation prepared by an international team of Septuagint scholars. Includes thorough introductions focused on the text of the LXX.

THE LETTER OF JEREMIAH

They are not gods

The new surroundings must have awed the Judeans in exile. But those who remembered Zion mocked the stolid faces of the idols. The Letter of Jeremiah is a rant against idolatry, with humorous turns and taunts.

The source of inspiration for the writing of the alleged Letter of Jeremiah was the canonical Book of Jeremiah 10:11, the only verse in the entire book that is in Aramaic. "Thus shall you say to them: 'The gods who did not make the heavens and the earth shall perish from the earth and from under the heavens.' " The second person plural, "You shall say unto them," refers to the men of Israel giving this truth to the Gentiles.

Historical and Cultural Setting

The experience of the Judeans during the exile, when they transitioned from rule by a familiar power to rule by a foreign power, was repeated numerous times from the sixth century BC to the first century BC when the Romans acquired Judea for their empire. The Letter of Jeremiah perhaps reflects on one of these experiences and the tensions caused by the religion of the new rulers.

Grimacing idols greeted the Judeans exiled to Babylon and other foreign lands. This dog symbolized Gula, a goddess of healing.

OVERVIEW

Author
Judean or Babylonian Jew

Date
After 587 BC

Place
Babylon

People
Jeremiah; captives from Judea; foreigners/heathen; Babylonian priests; harlots; Chaldeans; various artisans

Purpose
To warn Judeans that they will be in exile for many years, tempted by idolatry

Themes
Exile in Babylon; idols are not real gods

Memory Verses
Refrain (vv 64–65)

TIMELINE

628 BC	Jeremiah called to be a prophet
587 BC	Judeans flee to Egypt
538 BC	Cyrus decrees that exiles may return to Judah
332 BC	Alexander the Great takes Judea from Persians
305 BC	Seleucid Dynasty rules over Judea

Composition

Author

Ancient and modern scholars agree that Jeremiah did not compose this letter.

Date of Composition

The advocates of Hebrew as the original language for this letter put the time of composition at the end of the fourth century BC. According to this view the Babylon referred to is the actual Babylon, and the letter itself was sent to the Jews of Babylon to warn them against assimilation. The proponents of Greek as the original language claim the letter was written in Alexandria as an attack on paganism. They place the writing around 70 BC. They believe that the idolatry referred to was the kind practiced at the temple of Serapis. Still others believe that Vespasian is the Nebuchadnezzar of the letter, and Rome is Babylon.

The Letter of Jeremiah is part of a literature specifically directed against the idolatrous practices of paganism, together with the stories of Bel and the Dragon, the second part of the Wisdom of Solomon, and the implications of the Prayer of Manasseh.

Purpose/Recipients

The book shows the folly of idol worship. In verse 43 there seems to be a reference to the licentious fertility rites connected with the worship of the Babylonian god Tammuz, to whom writers such as Herodotus, Strabo, and Lucian allude.

A cylinder seal depicting a shepherd feeding his flock. Mesopotamians associated shepherds with the fertility god Dumuzi/Tammuz, whose name became the name of a month (June/July) in the Israelite calendar due to influences of the Babylonian exile.

Literary Features

Genre

As the name of the book implies, the writing is presented as a letter from Jeremiah to the exiles who would go to Babylon. However, the text is written in a sermonic style, presenting Jewish apologetic teaching against idolatry.

Characters

The biblical prophet Jeremiah is introduced as the writer. The letter is addressed to Judeans who are conquered and imprisoned. Their captors, the Babylonian idolaters, will lead them away into a prolonged exile.

Narrative Development or Plot

Since the Letter of Jeremiah is written as a series of apologetic arguments, it does not have a storyline or plot. However, the opening of the book assumes the story of Israel's fall into sin and punishment from God by the Babylonian conquest. The writer warns those going into exile that they will be there for up to seven generations. During this time they must recognize the uselessness of the idols and resist temptations to participate in worship of them. The Lord promises to provide them with the ministering presence of His angel, who will also judge them.

Resources

Most of the author's thoughts are biblical in character, if not borrowed directly word for word from the Bible.

Text and Translation

Scholarly opinion is divided about the nature of the original language of the Letter of Jeremiah. Some have advanced the view that it was written in Hebrew. Others, however, contend that the advocates of Hebrew have not proven their case and argue for Aramaic, from which the present Greek text would have been translated. Still others argue for a Greek original.

The Letter of Jeremiah was originally a separate writing but subsequently became attached to the Book of Baruch, likely because the historical Baruch and Jeremiah were friends and co-workers. Scholars are certain that the prophet Jeremiah had nothing to do with the authorship of the letter. The Letter of Jeremiah may appear as the sixth chapter of the Book of Baruch and is found inserted in different places of various manuscripts of the Apocrypha. In the Vulgate it is attached to the apocryphal Book of Baruch.

Doctrinal Content

Summary Commentary

Jeremiah 29 portrays the prophet writing a letter to the Jewish exiles in Babylon. With this background it is not difficult to imagine a later Jew writing a letter incorporating the idea of Jer 10:11. The author elaborates on this verse, showing by a variety of arguments the foolishness of the sin of idolatry. Ridicule of the heathen gods is found in Hebrew literature in Is 44:9–20 and Pss 115 and 135. Examples of sarcasm are seen in the comparison between Yahweh and the wooden deity being used as a roost for bats, birds, and cats. The writer says that the food offered the idol by their devotees is sold by the priests, whose wives even salt a portion of it (Lt Jer 28). The heathen deities are useless even as "a scarecrow in a cucumber bed" (v 70). If a fire breaks out in the temple, the god burns as does the timber.

The Letter of Jeremiah gives glimpses into daily religious practices in the Near East, which Judean exiles encountered. It also shows the creativity of the exiles, who sought to defend their faith at a time when they were disadvantaged in every way alongside the religions of their neighbors. The writer carefully examines the practices and appearance of false religion and churns through a list of absurdities that make the dominant religion seem weak. The author portrays the idols as senseless, worthless, powerless, meaningless, useless objects of human creativity and imagination, not to be feared or worshiped, but ridiculed. Only the just and loving Lord is worthy of faithful worship.

Specific Themes

Like other apologetic literature during or following the exile in Babylon, the writer counsels the people about how to cope under their difficult circumstances, making ridicule of idols his chief theme.

Specific Doctrines

In apologetic style, the book expounds thoughts related to the First Commandment and the general doctrine of God and His attributes.

Canonicity

Early Christians valued the Letter of Jeremiah, and over time it was welcomed in the eastern and western churches, where it was placed with Lamentations

Outline

The Letter of Jeremiah divides into clear sections, though the sections often have overlapping themes or statements. The author consistently concludes sections with the following or similar lines: "They are not gods; so do not fear them," or "Why then must anyone think that they are gods or call them gods?"

- I. Introduction (vv 1–7)
  - A. Author and Addressees (v 1)
  - B. Reason for the Exile and Admonition (vv 2–7)
- II. Sermon against Idolatry (vv 8–73)
  - A. Idols Appear like Mere Humans (vv 8–16)
  - B. Senseless Idols Patiently Endure Insult (vv 17–40)
    - 1. First set of examples (vv 17–23)
    - 2. Second set of examples (vv 24–29)
    - 3. Third set of examples (vv 30–40a)
  - C. Chaldeans Insult Their Idols (vv 40b–44)
  - D. Idols Are Merely Works of Art (vv 45–52)
  - E. Things Idols Cannot Do (vv 53–69)
  - F. Concluding Comparisons (vv 70–73

and Baruch among the writings associated with Jeremiah. However, Jerome and other Fathers spoke against receiving the book as Holy Scripture, the conclusion later reached by Luther and adopted by Protestant churches. In 1546, the Council of Trent described the book as canonical for Roman Catholics. The 1672 Synod of Jerusalem did not expressly mention the book. However, it appeared in editions of the LXX as an appendix to Jeremiah.

Lutheran Theologians on the Letter of Jeremiah

Luther

Following the Vulgate tradition, Luther placed the Letter of Jeremiah as chapter 6 of Baruch. The LXX and earlier manuscript traditions treated the letter as an independent document as it appears in *ALEN*. For Luther's comments on Baruch, see p 67.

Gerhard

See Gerhard's comments on ch 6 of Baruch, pp 67–68.

Further Study

Lay/Bible Class Resources

Burgland, Lane. *Study Guide to the Apocrypha.* St. Louis: Concordia, 2012. ⸎ Lutheran author. Eight-session Bible study, including leader's notes and discussion questions. Companion piece to *ALEN.*

Dancy, J. C. *The Shorter Books of the Apocrypha.* CBCA. Cambridge: Cambridge University Press, 1972. ⸎ Prepared by British scholars for the general reader. Includes the New English Bible translation along with commentary.

Engelbrecht, Edward A., gen. ed. *The Apocrypha: The Lutheran Edition with Notes.* St. Louis: Concordia, 2012. ⸎ Based on the ESV. Reflects the Luther Bible tradition of the Apocrypha. Prepared by Lutherans, with commendations from top scholars of intertestamental studies.

Church Worker Resources

deSilva, David A. *Introducing the Apocrypha: Message, Context, and Significance.* Grand Rapids: Baker Academic, 2002. ⸎ A thorough and informative introduction to the books of the Apocrypha from an evangelical scholar who served on the ESV Translation Committee of the Apocryphal Books.

Academic Resources

Bissell, Edwin Cone. *The Apocrypha of the Old Testament.* LCHS. New York: Charles Scribner's Sons, 1896. ⸎ Philip Schaff appears to have added this volume to the English edition of the Lange commentary. Still one of the most substantive one-volume commentaries on the Apocrypha available in English.

Charles, R. H. *The Apocrypha and Pseudepigrapha of the Old Testament.* Vol. 1. Oxford: Clarendon Press, 1913. ⸎ A standard scholarly reference work. Provides thorough introductions to the Apocrypha and substantive footnotes, commenting from the Greek, Hebrew, etc.

Moore, Carey A. *Daniel, Esther, and Jeremiah: The Additions.* Vol. 44 of AB. New York: Doubleday, 1977. ⸎ A thorough commentary and new translation prepared for a major academic series. Focuses on historical and literary interpretation.

Pietersma, Albert, and Benjamin G. Wright, eds. *A New English Translation of the Septuagint.* Oxford: Oxford University Press, 2007. ⸎ A literal revision of the NRSV translation prepared by an international team of Septuagint scholars. Includes thorough introductions focused on the text of the LXX.

1 MACCABEES

Strength comes from heaven

The gentle slopes of the Shephelah hills surrounding Modein are the home ground of one of the greatest conflicts in Israel's history: the Maccabean revolt. When the priest Mattathias slew an unfaithful Judean and tore down the pagan altar erected at Modein, he propelled his sons and his countrymen into a one-hundred-year struggle for Israel's purification from Gentile rule.

First Maccabees provides a most helpful historical account about the lives and struggles of God's people in the second century BC. It illustrates the ongoing struggle for faithfulness in an ever changing world. To learn more about how the accounts of 1 Maccabees relate to 2 Maccabees, see *ALEN*, pp 195–96. See also Gerhard's ThC E1 § 233, which describes five "discordant matters." Both Luther and Gerhard favored 1 Maccabees over 2 Maccabees.

Historical and Cultural Setting

Seleucus I Nicator (311–280 BC) and his descendants ruled the region of Syria following the breakup of Alexander the Great's empire in the late fourth century BC. In 198 BC, Antiochus III the Great, a fourth generation Seleucid, secured Judea for his kingdom at the Battle of Paneas (Panium) by defeating the Egyptian Ptolemies. Antiochus treated his Jewish subjects tolerantly, allowing them to maintain their ancestral religion and laws. After the Second Punic War, Antiochus welcomed Hannibal of Carthage as a military advisor and became entangled in Greco-Roman affairs. But the Romans decisively defeated Antiochus at the Battle of Smyrna (190 BC) and imposed a heavy financial penalty upon the Seleucids, which led

The rock-cut tombs of the Maccabees in Modi'im, Israel.

OVERVIEW

Author
A Judean supporter of the Maccabees

Date
Late second century BC, after 134 BC

Places
Regions from Spain to India, centering in the traditional territory of Israel

People
Antiochus IV Epiphanes; Ptolemy VI; Mattathias and his sons: John, Simon, Judas, Eleazar, Jonathan; Hasideans; "friends of the king"; Lysias; Antiochus; Nicanor; Romans; Spartans; Alexander Epiphanes (Balas); Demetrius II; Trypho; Onias the High Priest

Purpose
To record the trials and victories of the Judeans led by Mattathias, Judas, Jonathan, and Simon against their oppressors

Themes
Lawlessness; idolatry; persecution; zeal for God's Law; God's deliverance through the Maccabees; the Jerusalem temple; politics; war

Memory Verses
Strength from heaven (1Macc 3:19, 60)

TIMELINE

332 BC	Alexander the Great takes Judea from Persians
167 BC	Antiochus IV Epiphanes desecrates Jerusalem temple
164 BC	Maccabees cleanse the temple
63 BC	Romans establish Idumean dynasty in Judea
2 BC	Birth of Jesus

Antiochus to confiscate temple treasuries throughout his empire. The continued debt to Rome ensured conflict between the Seleucid rulers and their subjects. When Antiochus's son, Antiochus IV Epiphanes (175–164 BC), forced Greek customs and religion on the Judeans in order to create greater unity in his realm, this provoked the Maccabean revolt led by Judas Maccabeus, for whom the Books of Maccabees are named.

Composition

Author

The author of 1 Maccabees was a good historian and perhaps an eyewitness of some of the events he recorded. He undoubtedly had many opportunities to secure firsthand information about the events and personalities he reported. He grasped the deep significance of the deadly battle his countrymen were waging against great odds. As a participant in various campaigns, he obtained an excellent knowledge of the topography and geography of Israel.

Some scholars believe it strange that 1 Maccabees does not refer to the immortality of the soul or to the resurrection of the dead in such places where reference to these matters would have been in place. This has caused scholars to infer that 1 Maccabees was written by a Sadducee because they were known to reject these doctrines. Other scholars, however, caution against acceptance of this conclusion, for omission of these doctrines may have been for other reasons—the author of 1 Maccabees may not have been interested in stating doctrines but merely in giving events.

Date of Composition

The First Book of Maccabees was certainly written after 134 BC. Some suggest a more specific range of possible dates, between 100 and 90 BC, probably after the death of John Hyrcanus in 104 BC.

Purpose/Recipients

The book does full justice to its traditional name, for it obviously aims at the glorification of the Maccabean family, who are depicted as liberators of Judaism. Furthermore, 1 Maccabees is anti-Greek, portraying not only the Seleucids as the enemies of God's people, but including with the latter the apostate Jews who were trying to adjust to Hellenism.

Literary Features

Genre

First Maccabees is a historical account of the Jewish struggle against the persecution of Antiochus Epiphanes, king of Syria, which resulted in the liberation of the Jewish nation in the days of the Hasmoneans. The period covered by the body of the book is c 323–134 BC, from the outbreak of the Maccabean revolt until the death of Simon, the last of the five sons of Mattathias.

Characters

Although 1 Maccabees presents villainous characters such as **Antiochus IV Epiphanes**, its focus is on the leaders of the Hasmonean dynasty. Beginning with the heroic acts of the priest **Mattathias**, it describes the victories and struggles of his sons **Judas**, **Jonathan**, and **Simon**. The brothers are presented as faithful Israelites who oppose and overcome Seleucid and Ptolemaic generals and kings while forming major political alliances with powers such as Sparta and Rome. The book ends with the death of Simon and two of his sons due to a treacherous plot against them, threatening the succession of the dynasty to the second generation. However, Simon's son **John Hyrcanus** learns of the plot and destroys the perpetrators. He ensures that he will succeed his father and maintain the dynasty.

Antiochus IV Epiphanes.

Narrative Development or Plot

As noted under "Characters" above, the author's plan is that each portion of the book treat one particular member of the house of Maccabees. Chapter 1 is introductory to the Maccabean conflict; ch 2 relates the revolt of Mattathias; 3:1–9:22 records the exploits of Judas; 9:23–12:53 depicts the activities of Jonathan; and the last part of the book, 12:53–16:23, gives the account of Simon's career.

Resources

Preserved in 1 Maccabees are about a dozen state papers, decrees, proclamations, and some letters to Rome and Sparta. If they are genuine, they belong to a later date than is ascribed to them in the book. The decrees of

Continued on p 84.

Outline

- I. Introduction (1:1–9)
  - A. Alexander the Great's Victory over the Persians (1:1–4)
  - B. The Sickness and Death of Alexander; the Division of His Empire (1:5–9)
- II. The Cause of the Maccabean Revolt (1:10–64)
  - A. Antiochus Epiphanes and the Hellenistic Party in Judea (1:10–15)
  - B. Antiochus Subdues Egypt (1:16–19)
  - C. The Desecration of the Temple; Slaughter of the Jews (1:20–28)
  - D. Jerusalem Occupied by Apollonius and Desecrated (1:29–40)
  - E. Edict of Antiochus Forbidding Jewish Worship (1:41–53)
  - F. Idolatry forced upon the people of Judah (1:54–64)
- III. Mattathias (ch 2)
  - A. The Genealogy of the Maccabees (2:1–5)
  - B. A Dirge over the Desecration of the Holy City (2:6–14)
  - C. The Commencement of the Maccabean Revolt (2:15–28)
  - D. Strict Sabbath Observance Results in Massacre of a Thousand Jewish People (2:29–38)
  - E. Mattathias, Supported by the Chasidim, Continues War with Success (2:39–48)
  - F. The Last Words of Mattathias; His Death (2:49–70)
- IV. Judas Maccabeus (3:1–9:22)
  - A. A Song of Praise in Honor of Judas Maccabeus (3:1–9)
  - B. Victories of Judas Maccabeus over Apollonius and Seron (3:10–26)
  - C. Lysias Continues the War against the Jews while Antiochus Is in Persia (3:27–37)
  - D. Judas Maccabeus Prepares for the Coming Struggle with Lysias's Army (3:38–60)
  - E. Victory of Judas over Gorgias (4:1–25)
  - F. Victory of Judas over Lysias (4:26–35)
  - G. The Rededication of the Temple and New Fortifications (4:36–61)

- H. Victories of Judas over the Edomites, the Sons of Baean, and Ammonites (5:1–8)
- I. Victories of Simon in Galilee, and of Judas in Gilead (5:9–68)
- J. Death of Antiochus Epiphanes, and Accession of His Son, Antiochus Eupator (6:1–17)
- K. The Struggle for the Possession of Jerusalem and Beth-zur (6:18–54)
- L. An Abortive Treaty of Peace (6:55–63)
- M. Demetrius Becomes King of Syria; Bacchides and Alchimus Sent against the Jews (7:1–20)
- N. Judas Takes Vengeance on the Deserters; His Victories over Nicanor (7:21–50)
- O. Judas Concludes a Treaty with the Romans (ch 8)
- P. Death of Judas Maccabeus (9:1–22)

V. Jonathan Maccabeus (9:23–12:53)

- A. Jonathan Succeeds Judas (9:23–31)
- B. Jonathan's Struggle with Bacchides (9:32–73)
- C. Jonathan Supports Alexander Epiphanes (Balas) in His Struggle with Demetrius I (10:1–66)
- D. Victory of Jonathan over Apollonius, the General of Demetrius II (10:67–89)
- E. Alliance between Ptolemy VI and Demetrius II (11:1–19)
- F. Jonathan Secures the Favor of Demetrius II (11:20–37)
- G. Jonathan Assists Demetrius in Opposing Trypho (11:38–53)
- H. Friendship between Jonathan and Antiochus VI (11:54–74)
- I. Jonathan Renews His Alliance with Rome and Enters into a League with the Spartans (12:1–38)
- J. The Capture of Jonathan through Treachery (12:39–53)

VI. Simon Maccabeus (chs 13–16)

- A. Simon Elected Leader (13:1–11)
- B. Simon Defeats Trypho (13:12–24)
- C. Jonathan's Sepulchre at Modein (13:25–30)

D. Murder of Antiochus; Treaty between Simon and Demetrius II (13:31–42)
E. Simon Captures Gazara and the Citadel of Jerusalem (13:43–53)
F. Demetrius II Imprisoned by Arsaces, King of Persia (14:1–3)
G. Simon's Beneficent Rule; an Ode in His Honor (14:4–15)
H. Renewal of the Alliance with Rome (14:16–24)
I. The Hereditary High Priesthood Conferred upon Simon (14:25–49)
J. Antiochus VII Sidetes Seeks the Throne and Solicits the Help of Simon (15:1–9)
K. Antiochus VII Besieges Trypho in Dor (15:10–14)
L. The Return of the Jewish Envoys from Rome (15:15–24)
M. Antiochus VII Breaks His Covenant with Simon (15:25–41)
N. Judas and John, the Sons of Simon, Defeat Cendebeus (16:1–10)
O. Ptolemy Murders Simon, Mattathias, and Judas; John Hyrcanus Escapes (16:11–24)

the Syrian kings, considered by most scholars as interpolations, may have been inserted in the history of the Hasmoneans by some other writer who obtained them from the history of Jason of Cyrene, mentioned in 2Macc 2:23. Some scholars believe that chapters 14–16 were not originally a part of 1 Maccabees. This deduction is based on the fact that Josephus, who in *Antiquities of the Jews* follows 1 Maccabees very closely, does not go beyond chapter 13; after that he employs some other source of reference. However, H. W. Ettelson's *The Integrity of 1 Maccabees* has argued that chapters 14–16 are a part of 1 Maccabees.

Text and Translations

The earliest manuscripts of 1 Maccabees are in Greek. Nevertheless, scholars agree that the character of the Greek indicates that it was translated from a Hebrew or Aramaic original. Unfortunately, none of the great manuscript discoveries in the twentieth century brought a Hebrew or Aramaic manuscript to light. Jerome in his *Prologus Galeatus* makes the assertion that he had seen a copy of 1 Maccabees in Hebrew. In the Septuagint, 1 Maccabees has survived in a text represented by Codex Sinaiticus, Codex Venetus, and some other manuscripts. The translation in the Vulgate is regarded as a revision of the Old Latin text.

Doctrinal Content

Summary Commentary

Chs 1–2 The narrative follows a chronological order: 1 Maccabees opens with a brief account of Alexander the Great's conquests, death, and the division of the empire. The events of 1 Maccabees begin with Antiochus IV Epiphanes as king of Syria in 175 BC and go to the death of Simon Maccabeus in 134 BC. Included is the formation of a Hellenizing party in Jerusalem that is willing to adopt the heathen practices in violation of Judaism. Antiochus Epiphanes, called by the Jews Epimanes ("the madman"), embarks upon a plan of forcing Greek culture, civilization, and religion on the Jews of Israel. This results in violent clashes between the soldiers of Epiphanes and the Jewish patriots. After the temple in Jerusalem is desecrated, Mattathias and his sons at Modein kill the king's officers and flee to the mountains.

3:1–9:22 Judas Maccabeus is the hero. These chapters describe him fighting Syrian generals and defeating Apollonius, Seron, Gorgias, Lysias, and Nicanor. Within three years after the desecration of the temple, Judas and his brothers rededicate its altar and have the traditional worship resumed. Judas sends ambassadors to Rome to conclude a treaty with the Romans. The political aspirations of Judas lead the Chasidim, who later became the Pharisees, to break with him. In 160 BC Judas is defeated and killed in battle with the Syrian commander Bacchides.

9:23–12:53 Jonathan, Judas's youngest brother, succeeds him as leader of the Jews (160–142 BC). This section describes his reign. Although Jonathan is powerless for a long time, he finally prevails over the Syrian general Bacchides. As a result, Judah enjoys peace. Jonathan exploits the rivalry between Demetrius II and Alexander Balas, receiving from the latter the title of high priest. Jonathan also shows great cleverness in exploiting the rivalries between Demetrius II and Antiochus VI, playing one against the other. Like his brother Judas, Jonathan is captured at Ptolemais and ultimately killed (*Ant* 13). John Hyrcanus, Simon's son, succeeds Jonathan in the position of high priest and combines in one office the civil, military, and religious leadership of the Jewish nation.

Chs 13–16 An older Maccabean brother, Simon (leader from 142–134 BC), leads the resistance of the Jews to Syria. He drives the Syrian garrison out of Jerusalem and makes alliance with Demetrius II and other foreign powers. The Sadducean dream of the political independence of Judah is recognized by Syria, and Simon is made general, ethnarch, and high priest. During his seven-year rule the country enjoys peace and prosperity. Simon, together with his two sons, is assassinated by his son-in-law, Ptolemy. John Hyrcanus, the third son of Simon, becomes his successor.

Specific Themes

First Maccabees opens with concern about the rise of "lawless men" (1:11) in Israel who would lead the people to adopt the ways of the Gentiles who do not know or follow God's Torah. This concern about the lawless men persists throughout the book, along with stories about devout zeal for the Law (e.g., Mattathias). The author illustrates how divided Israel was as a people. Like many books of the Apocrypha, 1 Maccabees opposes idolatry and records the cleansing of the temple from idols as a major event (chs 1, 4). The temple is a focal point of the history and the subject of political intrigue as different leaders struggle over the high priesthood of the temple. War and making peace alternate constantly. Victory and peace are the blessings of heaven (3:19), with the author mentioning the realm of God rather than God Himself (see "Specific Doctrines" below).

A Hellenistic terra-cotta figure of a war elephant trampling a warrior from Galatia (second century BC).

Specific Doctrines

Reading 1 Maccabees can help God's people today reflect on the value and limitations of the use of force when combating evil and changes in culture. One may consider the strategies of the Maccabean leaders so as to compare and contrast them with examples of leaders in the Old and New Testaments. Note especially their prayers, which reveal their hearts and teach readers to call upon the Lord in every trouble.

First Maccabees, like the Book of Esther, focuses on relating history as God's people experience it rather than history from a heavenly or theological perspective. As a result, there are only a few explicit references to God (see e.g., 1Macc 4:30; 7:37, 41). More often the text refers to "heaven" as a substitute for God's name (cf 3:18–19, 50; 4:10, 24, 40, 55; 5:31; 9:46; 12:15; 16:3). Chapters 1 and 6 illustrate the consequences of violating God's house and profaning the Sabbath. The reader senses the belief that God is guiding the destinies of the Jewish nation. As history, 1 Maccabees is very valuable and interesting to read, but it has less substantial devotional content. The religious interests of the writer are also shown in his concern for the temple and priesthood, and for the Law rather than for the refinements connected with it. The author continues his history after religious liberation has been effected and relates how political freedom was also achieved.

Canonicity

Early Christians valued 1 Maccabees, and over time it was welcomed among the books of eastern and western churches. Clement of Alexandria, Hippolytus of Rome, Origen, and Eusebius all refer to it as being a part of Scripture. In Egypt it is found together with 2 Maccabees in the Clermont list of the books of Scripture. From the LXX, 1 Maccabees passed into the Vulgate, Peshitta, and Coptic biblical manuscripts. It was widely considered a part of the Old Testament canon throughout the Middle Ages. However, Jerome and other early Fathers spoke against receiving the book as Holy Scripture, the conclusion later reached by Luther and adopted by Protestant churches. In 1546, the Council of Trent described the book as canonical for Roman Catholics. The 1672 Synod of Jerusalem affirmed 1 Maccabees as Sacred Scripture for Eastern Orthodox churches.

Lutheran Theologians on 1 Maccabees

Luther

"This is another book not to be found in the Hebrew Bible. Yet its words and speech adhere to the same style as the other books of sacred Scripture. This book would not have been unworthy of a place among them, because it is very necessary and helpful for an understanding of chapter 11 of the prophet Daniel. For the fulfillment of Daniel's prophecy in that chapter, about the abomination and misfortune which was going to befall the people of Israel, is here described—namely, Antiochus Epiphanes—and in much the same way that Daniel [11:29–35] speaks of it: a little help and great persecution by the Gentiles and by false Jews, which is what took place at the time of the Maccabees. This is why the book is good for us Christians to read and to know. . . .

"We should take heart that God helped those people not only against Antiochus and the Gentiles but also against the traitorous and disloyal Jews who had gone over to the Gentiles and were helping to persecute, kill, and torment their own people and brethren. . . . However those same enemies and traitors are amply punished by God at the end; their tyranny and treachery does not go undetected." (AE 35:350–52)

Gerhard

"We admit that the first book is to be preferred to the second. The first is written with gravity; the second was cut by an uncertain author from the five books of Jason of Cyrene with an affected style. . . . However, that they are not canonical we demonstrate from the following arguments. They are not written in Hebrew but in Greek and thus do not have a prophet as their author. They were written after the time of Malachi, who was the last prophet of the Old Testament. Therefore they were not written by a prophet. Jerome (*Catal. vir. illustr.*; *Contra Pelag.*, bk. 2) and others claim that 'Josephus is the author of these books.' Josephus, however, lived after Christ and was not renowned for prophetic authority. How, then, could he have written a prophetic book of the Old Testament? . . . The Books of the Maccabees have the testimony of neither Christ nor the apostles of the New Testament. . . . Although the second book again goes over the same accounts that were described in the first, it adds many things, such as the astonishing apparitions in the battles, for example, which neither 1 Maccabees nor Josephus had mentioned. Although the first book speaks modestly about the numbers of those slain, the second exaggerates everything immensely. Furthermore, regarding the number of years, as well as other matters, we detect the obvious contradiction of the second book against the first. . . . They were not accepted into the canon by the Israelite church, to which 'the oracles of God' were entrusted (Rom. 3:2)." (ThC E1 §§ 230, 231, 233, 236)

Further Study

Lay/Bible Class Resources

Bartlett, J. R. *The First and Second Books of the Maccabees*. CBCA. Cambridge: Cambridge University Press, 1973. ⸎ Prepared by British scholars for the general reader. Includes the New English Bible translation along with commentary.

Burgland, Lane. *Study Guide to the Apocrypha*. St. Louis: Concordia, 2012. ⸎ Lutheran author. Eight-session Bible study, including leader's notes and discussion questions. Companion piece to *ALEN*.

Engelbrecht, Edward A., gen. ed. *The Apocrypha: The Lutheran Edition with Notes*. St. Louis: Concordia, 2012. ⸎ Based on the ESV. Reflects the Luther Bible tradition of the Apocrypha. Prepared by Lutherans, with commendations from top scholars of intertestamental studies.

Church Worker Resources

deSilva, David A. *Introducing the Apocrypha: Message, Context, and Significance*. Grand Rapids: Baker Academic, 2002. ⸎ A thorough and informative introduction to the books of the Apocrypha from an evangelical scholar who served on the ESV Translation Committee of the Apocryphal Books.

Academic Resources

Bissell, Edwin Cone. *The Apocrypha of the Old Testament*. LCHS. New York: Charles Scribner's Sons, 1896. ⸎ Philip Schaff appears to have added this volume to the English edition of the Lange commentary. Still one of the most substantive one-volume commentaries on the Apocrypha available in English.

Charles, R. H. *The Apocrypha and Pseudepigrapha of the Old Testament*. Vol. 1. Oxford: Clarendon Press, 1913. ⸎ A standard scholarly reference work. Provides thorough introductions to the Apocrypha and substantive footnotes, commenting from the Greek, Hebrew, etc.

Goldstein, Jonathan A. *1 Maccabees*. Vol. 41 of AB. New York: Doubleday, 1998. ⸎ A thorough commentary and new translation prepared for a major academic series.

Pietersma, Albert, and Benjamin G. Wright, eds. *A New English Translation of the Septuagint*. Oxford: Oxford University Press, 2007. ⸎ A literal revision of the NRSV translation prepared by an international team of Septuagint scholars. Includes thorough introductions focused on the text of the LXX.

The city of Maresha includes a Hellenistic period (fourth to third century BC) Colombarium. It contained more than 2,000 stone-carved chambers in which pigeons were raised for food and ritual purposes.

2 MACCABEES

Reverence of the divine laws

The Greek letters that open 2 Maccabees bear witness to a stream of correspondence between the Judeans who settled in ancient Egypt and the Judeans who rebuilt the temple at Jerusalem (516 BC). Just as there was correspondence from Jerusalem to Judeans exiled in Babylon and the east (cf e.g., Jer 29), there was likely ongoing correspondence from Jerusalem to Egyptian Jews in the west (specific examples are found in the Elephantine Papyri; see Appendix 1 in *ALEN*, p 334; such practices are assumed by the apocryphal Letter of Jeremiah, p 72). Second Maccabees illustrates the enduring support that God's people of that era showed toward one another while also describing the latest threat to their faith and future: the Hellenization program of the Seleucid ruler Antiochus IV Epiphanes.

Historical and Cultural Setting

For an overview of the historical context, see the setting described for 1 Maccabees, pp 79–80. The uncompromising devotion of the Jews greatly offended and enraged the Hellenistic rulers. They suppressed the day-to-day habits of Jewish life using the harshest, most violent measures. Second Maccabees tells the story of not only the unspeakable suffering for those who followed God's covenant but also their trust that God was chastening His disobedient people and that He would deliver them. God's faithful servants withstood evil and overcame pain and error by God's grace alone. God is the true hero of those who published 2 Maccabees, who were probably Jews of Alexandria, Egypt. They left us this lively testimony of deliverance from evil.

This structure, wrongly titled "David's Tower," dates from the Maccabean period (after 167 BC). Its high walls defended the northwest corner of the city, which had no natural defenses. Note the squarish blocks used in that era. The round-topped minaret is from the Muslim era.

OVERVIEW

Authors
The epitomizers of Jason of Cyrene (2:23–26)

Date
Compiled after 160 BC; summarized c 124

Places
Locations from Rome to Ecbatana, centering on the traditional territory of Israel. See map, p 13.

People
Jews; Aristobulus; Antiochus IV Epiphanes; Judas Maccabeus; Antiochus V Eupator; Jason of Cyrene; Onias the high priest; Seleucus; Simon, brother of Judas; Heliodorus; Menelaus; Ptolemy VI Philometor; Lysias; Nicanor

Purpose
To summarize and simplify Jason of Cyrene's account of the rise of the Maccabees, illustrating the importance of continuing in the covenant and the use of the Jerusalem temple

Themes
Stipulations of the covenant; apostasy; chastening from God; nobility of martyrdom and suffering; trust in God's deliverance; God's intervention through angels; bodily resurrection

Memory Verse
Reverence (4:17)

TIMELINE

332 BC	Alexander the Great takes Judea from Persians
167 BC	Antiochus IV Epiphanes desecrates Jerusalem temple
164 BC	Maccabees cleanse the temple
63 BC	Romans enter Judean politics
2 BC	Birth of Jesus

Composition

Authors

Scholars commonly refer to the author of 2 Maccabees as the "compiler" or "epitomizer," based on 2Macc 2:23. He describes his work as a condensation of five volumes by Jason of Cyrene, a Jewish writer from a Greek colony west of Egypt in Libya. No other confirmed information about Jason exists apart from this mention in 2 Maccabees.

Date of Composition

Second Maccabees was probably written in Alexandria about 125 BC. The work was known to Philo, who died c AD 50. Although the precise date of composition is unknown, it must be earlier than the capture of Jerusalem by Pompey in 63 BC. Some scholars wish to find traces of influence in the New Testament Book of Hebrews where Heb 11:35 seems to refer to 2Macc 6–7.

Purpose/Recipients

With great warmth and energy the author endeavors to admonish his readers, the Alexandrian Jews, to be conscious of their Jewish race and religion, which they have in common with their brethren in Israel. The author continues his admonitions by vividly portraying the courage of the martyrs and of those who defend their nation and faith. He also explains the reasons for celebrating the Feast of Lights (Hanukkah) and the Day of Nicanor. Regarding the purpose of the volume, the author himself asserts:

> Now I urge those who read this book not to be depressed by such calamities, but to recognize that these punishments were designed not to destroy but to discipline our people. In fact, to punish the ungodly quickly rather than leave them alone for very long is a sign of great kindness. For in the case of the other nations the Lord waits patiently to punish them until they have reached the full measure of their sins; but He does not deal in this way with us, in order that He may not take vengeance on us afterward when our sins have reached their height. Therefore He never withdraws His mercy from us. Though He disciplines us with calamities, he does not forsake His own people. (6:12–17)

Second Maccabees argues for the importance of the temple and the covenant, which must be kept holy. The author celebrates the lives and the sacrifices of Jewish leaders and martyrs who illustrate these values. He often recounts miraculous and providential examples of how God intervenes to rescue and support His people.

The menorah lampstand became an enduring symbol of Judaism and the Feast of Hanukkah.

Literary Features

Genre

Second Maccabees begins with two letters (ch 1), interrupts the flow of the story with a compiler's preface (2:19–32), and describes itself as a condensation of a larger work by Jason of Cyrene, an obscure Jewish historian of the second century BC. Summarizing written works was a student exercise in Hellenistic education. However, this book is not simply the result of a student exercise. The compiler's preface expressly states the desire to present a more readable account of Judas Maccabeus and his brothers. The style and emphasis of 2 Maccabees are considerably different from that of 1 Maccabees. The question is still disputed among scholars whether or not the author of 2 Maccabees was acquainted with the contents of 1 Maccabees. Although 1 Maccabees rests upon the personal experiences of the writer, 2 Maccabees does not represent the efforts of historical research but is merely an abridgment of a longer history of Jason of Cyrene (2:23).

As Luther noted (see below), the book differs in details from 1 Maccabees but also supplies information that 1 Maccabees does not.

Characters

The scope of 2 Maccabees is limited in comparison with 1 Maccabees. Portrayal of the Hasmonean heroes is confined to **Judas**; the careers of Jonathan and Simon are ignored. In order to have his book end on a happy note, the author concludes his account with the victory of Judas over **Nicanor**. A most influential portion of the book describes the faith, devotion, torture, and martyrdom of **a mother and her seven sons** (ch 7). This story set the pattern for future accounts of martyrdom in Jewish and Christian literature.

Narrative Development or Plot

Second Maccabees describes how Judeans and their temple are threatened by oppressive foreign rulers and how God delivers them from corrupting

Outline

- I. Preface Documents (1:1–2:18)
  - A. Letter from Jerusalem to Jews in Egypt (1:1–9)
  - B. Letter from Jerusalem to Aristobulus and Jews in Egypt (1:10–2:18)
- II. Preface of the Epitomist (2:19–32)
- III. Jason of Cyrene's History Summarized (3:1–15:36)
  - A. Attack of Seleucus and Heliodorus against the Jerusalem Temple Repelled (ch 3)
  - B. Intrigues of Simon and Jason over the High Priesthood (4:1–22)
  - C. Intrigues of Menelaus (4:23–50)
  - D. Profanation of the Temple and Oppression of Jews by Antiochus IV Epiphanes (ch 5)
  - E. Enforced Hellenization of the Jews (ch 6)
  - F. Martyrdom of Seven Brothers and Their Mother (ch 7)
  - G. Revolt and Early Successes of Judas Maccabeus (ch 8)
  - H. The Miserable Death of Antiochus IV Epiphanes (ch 9)
  - I. The Temple Purified and the Feast of Dedication Instituted (10:1–9)
  - J. Further Campaigns of Judas (10:10–38)
  - K. Defeat of Lysias; Terms of Peace Arranged (ch 11)
  - L. Fresh Campaigns of Judas (ch 12)
  - M. Lysias and Eupator Forced to Make Terms with Jews (ch 13)
  - N. Intrigues and Threats of Nicanor (ch 14)
  - O. Attack, Defeat, and Death of Nicanor (15:1–36)
- IV. Epilogue of the Epitomist (15:37–39)

threats and intrigues. The opening letters (ch 1) and description of Old Testament figures (ch 2) draw the reader's attention to the temple and its sanctity. The book then proceeds to give a history of threats against the temple and its priesthood with the Lord intervening to preserve or restore their sanctity, chiefly through the leadership of Judas Maccabeus.

Resources

On the letters cited and the epitome of the history by Jason of Cyrene, see "Genre" above.

Text and Translations

Most modern scholars dealing with the intertestamental literature are convinced on the basis of style that 2 Maccabees was written in Greek. The two letters introduced in the work were also composed in Greek, though the letters are said to bear the stamp of Hebrew genius.

Doctrinal Content

Summary Commentary

Chs 1–2 At the beginning of 2 Maccabees there are inserted two letters sent from Jerusalem to the Egyptian Jews, calling upon them to commemorate the feast of dedication of Hanukkah (1:1–2:16). The second of the two letters tells a legend about the altar in Jerusalem and a strange story about the prophet Jeremiah. In the author's preface that follows, he announces that his narrative of the Maccabean wars is only an abridgment (2:20–23). The narrative is divided into two sections.

3:1–10:9 The first part covers events of the reign of Antiochus Epiphanes (3:1–10:9), including the struggles for the office of high priest, the attempt of Antiochus Epiphanes to Hellenize the Jews, the desecration of the temple, the defeat of the Syrians, the death of Antiochus Epiphanes, and the purification of the temple. The celebration of a feast commemorating the cleansing of the temple was to be an annual observance.

10:10–15:36 The second part deals with events that happened during the reigns of Antiochus V Eupator and Demetrius I: the struggle against neighboring peoples, the Syrians, and particularly against Nicanor. When the latter was defeated by the Jews, it led to the institution of a feast called the Day of Nicanor.

15:37–39 The conclusion of the book is reminiscent of the preamble (2:20–23).

An artist's depiction of a mounted angel trampling Heliodorus, representative of King Seleucus IV.

Specific Themes

Second Maccabees contrasts faithfulness to the covenant with apostasy by fellow Israelites who choose to support Gentile rulers and culture. The suffering that the Israelites experience is meant for the cleansing of the nation, received as a sign of God's mercy on them. Therefore, the author boldly celebrates martyrdom and defiant faith that will not compromise, no matter how terrible the consequences. The writer looks for God's intervention on behalf of His people and looks forward to the final resurrection of the body on Judgment Day, when all the righteous will be vindicated.

Specific Doctrines

If 1 Maccabees may be said to represent a Sadducean standpoint, 2 Maccabees is certainly written from a Pharisaic point of view. There is no reserve or reticence on the part of the author of 2 Maccabees. He never misses an opportunity to point out the moral of the story. The most interesting feature of the theology of this book is its teaching regarding the resurrection of the dead. In fact, the doctrines of the immortality of the soul and the resurrection of the dead are nowhere so clearly taught in the intertestamental literature as they are here, save in Wisdom of Solomon, where there are passages from which these doctrines may be inferred (4:20–5:14). In 2 Maccabees, doctrines covering rewards and punishment after death (6:26; 7:36; 12:45), prayer for the dead (12:43–45), and the intercession of the saints are taught.

Second Maccabees includes noteworthy teaching about creation. Augustine and later Church Fathers regarded 2Macc 7:22 as helpful counsel against forming dogmatic views on the origin of the soul. Second Maccabees 7:28 described creation out of nothing, as affirmed elsewhere in Scripture (Gn 1:1; Rm 4:17–20). The traditional prayer that God would send His protecting angel, as also found in Luther's Small Catechism, is derived from 2Macc 11:6; 15:23–24. In keeping with applications of the Seventh Commandment, 2Macc condemns examples of bribery and love of money over one's brethren (e.g., 10:20–22).

Some passages of 2 Maccabees stray beyond the teachings of Holy Scripture and have been used to teach harmful doctrines. For example, 2Macc 14:41–42 describes the violent suicide of Razis the Elder as a noble, manly death. Such a description contradicts what Scripture teaches (Ex 20:13) and the way Scripture describes other suicides (e.g., Saul in 1Sm 31 and Judas in Mt 27:3–10; Ac 1:18–20).

Second Maccabees 12:41–45 explains that Judas Maccabeus commanded his troops to pray for the Jews who were killed at Adullam because it was discovered that these Jews were wearing forbidden, idolatrous "sacred tokens." The prayers were intended to atone for the sins of the dead in anticipation of the resurrection and final judgment. Judas also took up a collection to pay for a sin offering, which was likewise intended to atone for the sins of the dead. On the one hand, the passage illustrates Judas's noble piety and personal concern. On the other hand, his actions introduced doctrines and practices that conflicted with the teachings about atonement and repentance described in the Books of Moses (see Lv 4 and its emphasis on realizing one's guilt). Ironically, Judas's instructions violated the laws of the covenant he sought to uphold. They introduced gross misunderstanding of repentance and forgiveness, which ultimately led to the doctrine of purgatory, the sale of indulgences, and other abuses that subsequently divided Christendom. Cf Ap XXI.

Despite the doctrinal and historical weaknesses of 2 Maccabees, the book is valuable for understanding events not mentioned in 1 Maccabees. It illustrates the origin of the Jewish festival of Hanukkah as well as Christian attitudes about bearing witness to God's Word and suffering martyrdom rather than denying the Lord.

Canonicity

Early Christians valued 2 Maccabees, and over time it was welcomed among the books of the eastern and western churches. For example, it appears in the LXX manuscripts Codex Sinaiticus and Alexandrinus as well as the Vulgate, Peshitta, and Coptic manuscripts. However, Jerome and other Early Church Fathers spoke against receiving the book as Holy Scripture, the conclusion later reached by Luther and adopted by Protestant churches. In 1546, the Council of Trent described the book as canonical for Roman Catholics. The 1672 Synod of Jerusalem affirmed 2 Maccabees as Sacred Scripture for Eastern Orthodox churches.

Lutheran Theologians on 2 Maccabees

Luther

"This book is called, and is supposed to be, the second book of Maccabees, as the title indicates. Yet this cannot be true, because it reports several incidents that happened before those reported in the first book, and it does not proceed any further than Judas Maccabaeus, that is, chapter 7 of the first book. . . . But we include it anyway, for the sake of the good story of the seven Maccabean martyrs and their mother, and other things as well.

"It appears, however, that the book has no single author, but was pieced together out of many books. It also presents a knotty problem in chapter 14[:41–46] where Razis commits suicide, something which also troubles St. Augustine and the ancient fathers. Such an example is good for nothing and should not be praised, even though it may be tolerated and perhaps explained. So also in chapter 1 this book describes the death of Antiochus quite differently than does First Maccabees [6:1–16]. . . . However the whole thing is left and referred to the pious reader to judge and to decide." (AE 35:352–53)

Gerhard

See his comments on p 89.

A la louenge de dieu tout
puissant nre createur
et redempteur qui par
sa saincte misericorde
voult en ce mortel monde
naistre homme de mere vierge et souffrir
mort et passion par les mains des
Juifz pour nous tous rachecter denfer
auquel par le peche du premier home
nous feusmes soubzmis et obligiez
Et pour avoir entendement par
langaige francois de listoire de la
destruction des Juifz et de la cite de
ihrlm ensemble de toute la tre diceulx
Juifz ce que plusieurs appellent la
vengence de la mort et passion de nre

Further Study

Lay/Bible Class Resources

Bartlett, J. R. *The First and Second Books of the Maccabees*. CBCA. Cambridge: Cambridge University Press, 1973. § Prepared by British scholars for the general reader. Includes the New English Bible translation along with commentary.

Burgland, Lane. *Study Guide to the Apocrypha*. St. Louis: Concordia, 2012. § Lutheran author. Eight-session Bible study, including leader's notes and discussion questions. Companion piece to *ALEN*.

Engelbrecht, Edward A., gen. ed. *The Apocrypha: The Lutheran Edition with Notes*. St. Louis: Concordia, 2012. § Based on the ESV. Reflects the Luther Bible tradition of the Apocrypha. Prepared by Lutherans, with commendations from top scholars of intertestamental studies.

Church Worker Resources

deSilva, David A. *Introducing the Apocrypha: Message, Context, and Significance*. Grand Rapids: Baker Academic, 2002. § A thorough and informative introduction to the books of the Apocrypha from an evangelical scholar who served on the ESV Translation Committee of the Apocryphal Books.

Academic Resources

Bissell, Edwin Cone. *The Apocrypha of the Old Testament*. LCHS. New York: Charles Scribner's Sons, 1896. § Philip Schaff appears to have added this volume to the English edition of the Lange commentary. Still one of the most substantive one-volume commentaries on the Apocrypha available in English.

Charles, R. H. *The Apocrypha and Pseudepigrapha of the Old Testament*. Vol. 1. Oxford: Clarendon Press, 1913. § A standard scholarly reference work. Provides thorough introductions to the Apocrypha and substantive footnotes, commenting from the Greek, Hebrew, etc.

Goldstein, Jonathan A. *II Maccabees*. Vol. 41A of AB. New York: Doubleday, 1983. § A thorough commentary and new translation prepared for a major academic series.

Pietersma, Albert, and Benjamin G. Wright, eds. *A New English Translation of the Septuagint*. Oxford: Oxford University Press, 2007. § A literal revision of the NRSV translation prepared by an international team of Septuagint scholars. Includes thorough introductions focused on the text of the LXX.

Schwartz, Daniel R. *2 Maccabees*. Commentaries on Early Jewish Literature. Berlin: Walter de Gruyter, 2008. § Updated from the Hebrew version published in 2004. New translation and commentary, based on current scholarship. Schwartz argues for an earlier date and departs from other long held scholarly opinions.

A medieval illuminated French edition of Flavius Josephus's *The Wars of the Jews*, which begins by describing persecution of the Jews by Antiochus IV Epiphanes. The left panel depicts Antiochus. The right panel depicts the arrest of the seven brothers (2Macc 7). Second Maccabees influenced Christian ideas of martyrdom and is the source of the word *macabre*, which comes from a French spelling of "Maccabees."

OLD GREEK ESTHER

The Lord knows all things

The Old Testament Book of Esther is a strong nationalistic book, recording that the Jews, at the instigation of Haman, were to be killed. However, the canonical Book of Esther does not mention the name of God, while the

The synagogue frescoes at Dura Europos depict Queen Esther and her cousin Mordecai, enthroned as leaders in the Medo-Persian Empire.

name of the Persian king is referred to 175 times. Nor is a word said about prayer; in fact, the book mentions very little of religion.

The apocryphal Esther aims to supplement the canonical book. Esther faced personal and national dilemmas that Old Greek Esther intensifies: When does one speak out against evil? How much should an individual risk to rescue others? The writer(s) or compiler(s) of Old Greek Esther present a challenging message to all who are conscious of their responsibilities before God, fellow believers, and the world. Through the heroism of Esther, the Jews were able to defend themselves against their enemies in the Persian Empire and kill 75,000 of them.

Historical and Cultural Setting

For information about the likely cultural setting that contributed to the writing of Old Greek Esther, see the setting of 1 Maccabees, pp 79–80.

Composition

Author(s)

It is feasible that the various additions were written by different men. For example, the superscription in chapter 11 asserts that these letters were explained by Lysimachus son of Ptolemy of Jerusalem and were brought to Egypt by a Levite priest named Dositheus in the fourth year of Ptolemy and Cleopatra.

Date of Composition

The Greek version of Esther includes reference to the Macedonians (16:14), associating them with a time when the Macedonian kingdom was little engaged with the Persian Empire. This reference to the Macedonians likely

OVERVIEW

Author
Judean; Lysimachus, translator for at least a portion

Date
Second century BC

Places
Susa; Babylon; Jerusalem; Judea; India; Ethiopia; Israel; Egypt

People
Artaxerxes the Great; Mordecai; Nebuchadnezzar; Jeconiah; Gabatha and Tharra; Haman; Israel; Judea; Esther; Persians; Ptolemy and Cleopatra; Dositheus the Priest; Ptolemy; Lysimachus

Purpose
To fill in theological and historical setting not found in Hebrew version of Esther

Themes
God's intervention; Israel as the Lord's inheritance; providential care; facing persecution; prayer; divine justice

Memory Verses
Mordecai's heart (13:12–14); Esther's prayer (14:19)

TIMELINE

516 BC	Second temple completed at Jerusalem
478 BC	Ahasuerus (Xerxes) marries Esther
474 BC	Mordecai issues edict about Judeans
332 BC	Alexander the Great takes Judea from Persians
167 BC	Antiochus IV Epiphanes desecrates Jerusalem temple

shows the late composition of the additions, at a time when the Macedonians were a significant factor in Persian politics.

It is difficult to determine the exact date and place of the origin of apocryphal Esther. Some authorities believe the additions to Esther were written somewhere in Egypt between 180–145 BC. The references to Ptolemy and Cleopatra are inconclusive. Since there were four different kings named Ptolemy who had wives named Cleopatra, it is difficult to ascertain the exact date.

Golden Greek myrtle wreath.

Esther's Hebrew name, Hadassah, means myrtle.

The Greek edition of Esther was well-known to Josephus around AD 90, for he had paraphrased its contents in the *Antiquities of the Jews* 11:184–296. Clement of Rome, author of one book of the Apostolic Fathers, spoke of Esther as entreating the all-seeing Lord with her fasting and humiliation (55:6, cf Old Gk Est 15:2 [Vulgate]), which likely refers to Old Greek Esther rather than to the canonical Book of Esther.

Purpose/Recipients

The new additions to Esther are calculated to add a strong religious element to the biblical version; thus Mordecai and Esther speak long prayers, and Mordecai explains the word *Purim*, "lots," by the two lots that God had made, one for the people of God, one for the heathen. The additions also endeavor to clarify what is obscure in the biblical account.

Literary Features

Genre

The additional content in Old Greek Esther does not change the literary genre of the Hebrew book, which provides a history of how Esther and Mordecai delivered the Judeans in Babylon and includes reasons for celebrating the Feast of Purim. However, Greek Esther adds some unique compositions to the overall history, including the following: Mordecai's dream and its interpretation, letters sent out by the king of Persia, and prayers of Mordecai and Esther.

Outline

The Greek version of Esther varies considerably from the Hebrew version because later writers inserted 107 verses of new material to create a unique composition, as represented on the second line of the chart below, which illustrates how the materials appear in the ESV translation (see *ALEN*). In the ESV translation, the chapter and verse numbering of Greek Esther is based on both the traditional Hebrew chapters and the chapter divisions used for Greek Esther in the King James Bible.

The following outline is based on the Old Greek form of Esther, which appears in LXX manuscripts and editions. To simplify matters somewhat, the divisions are based on the chapter headings of the ESV Apocrypha and include reference to the A–F designation of additions used by scholars. Readers should understand that they are experiencing Old Greek Esther in its usual verse-by-verse order.

Also, readers should recognize that the ESV Apocrypha text includes chapter divisions from the KJV tradition (labeled chs 11, 12, 13a, 13b, 14, 15, 16, 10:4–11:1 because the additions to Esther were treated as appendices in the KJV). To these the ESV editors have added the traditional nine chapter divisions of the Hebrew form of Esther. This makes it easier to compare the Hebrew and LXX forms of Esther. The result is a presentation of c 17 chapter divisions, depending on how one counts. However, because the two numeration systems are merged, the presentation of chapters does not flow in strict numerical order. This may confuse first-time readers. It is due to the complex history of the text and not to the indifference of the editors. Use the chart to gain a basic idea of the sequence of material.

Hbr Est			1	2	3:1–13		3:14–15	4				5	6	7	8:1–12		8:13–17	9	10	
Gk Additions	11:2–12	12				13:1–7			13:8–18	14	15					16				11:1

I. God Warns Mordecai about an Assassination Plot (11:2–12:6)

A. Mordecai's Dream (11:2–12; Addition A:1–11)

B. Mordecai Discovers the Plot of the Two Eunuchs (12:1–6; Addition A:12–17)

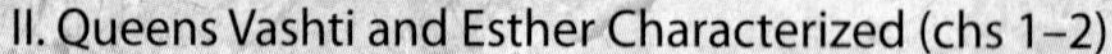

- II. Queens Vashti and Esther Characterized (chs 1–2)
  - A. King Artaxerxes Deposes Queen Vashti (ch 1)
  - B. Esther Becomes Queen (2:1–18)
  - C. Mordecai Discovers a Plot (2:19–23)
- III. God Overturns Haman's Plot (3:1–9:19)
  - A. Haman Undertakes to Destroy the Jews (3:1–13)
  - B. The King's Letter (13:1–7; Addition B:1–7)
  - C. Posting of the Letter (3:14–15)
  - D. Esther Agrees to Help the Judeans (ch 4)
  - E. Mordecai's Prayer (13:8–18; Addition C:1–11)
  - F. Esther's Prayer (ch 14; Addition C:12–30)
  - G. The King Receives Esther (ch 15; Addition D:1–16)
  - H. Esther's Invitations (5:3–8)
  - I. Haman Plans to Have Mordecai Hanged (5:9–14)
  - J. The King Honors Mordecai (6:1–13)
  - K. Haman's Downfall (6:14–7:10)
  - L. Esther Saves the Judeans (8:1–12)
  - M. Decree of Artaxerxes (ch 16; Addition E:1–24)
  - N. Decree of Artaxerxes Posted (8:13–17)
  - O. Destruction of Enemies of the Judeans (9:1–19)
- IV. Conclusion (9:20–11:1)
  - A. Feast of Purim Inaugurated (9:20–31)
  - B. Mordecai Succeeds Artaxerxes (10:1–3)
  - C. Mordecai's Dream Fulfilled (10:4–13; Addition F:1–10)
  - D. Postscript (11:1; Addition F:11)

Characters

As in the canonical account, the key figures are the heroine **Esther**, for whom the book is named; her uncle **Mordecai**, who upholds biblical standards and counsels Esther to faithful action on behalf of her people; the villain **Haman**, who hates the Judeans and plots to destroy them; and **King Artaxerxes**, who is an authority figure playing a largely passive role until provoked. The most important character in Old Greek Esther is **the Lord**. In contrast to Hebrew Esther, where God is not even named, Old Greek Esther explicitly turns on His responses to prayer and His intervention.

Narrative Development or Plot

For the plot of biblical Esther, see *LBC* vol. 1, p. 467. Old Greek Esther opens with Mordecai's dream wherein God reveals to him what will happen. This prepares Mordecai to guide Esther. The book then provides further information about how Mordecai discovered and reported the plot against the king. The prayers of Mordecai and Esther provide the theological basis for God's intervention. The decree of Artaxerxes depicts how the Judeans might live peaceably with Gentile neighbors who promote good governance. The end of Old Greek Esther affirms God's intervention and His will in all these matters.

Resources

Two long letters of Artaxerxes are introduced in the decree mentioned in canonical Est 3:13–15; the other is referred to in 8:13, which abrogates the previous decree. The additional materials, such as letters, may have derived from other documents or adaptations of them.

Text and Translations

The Hebrew edition of Esther has nine chapters, which stand together as a well-composed history of how Esther delivered her people from destruction by Haman. However, later writers sought ways to improve upon the story by adding more material. They did this for a variety of reasons, such as making the story more clearly religious and answering questions about the activities and motives of persons in the story.

Greek versions of Esther, which appear among the traditional apocrypha, have two basic forms. Scholars are not sure which of the two forms is older or how they might have influenced each other as they were copied over the centuries. Even the scholarly names for the forms have changed over time so that one may read about A-Text, B-Text; Old Greek, Lucianic Greek, or Alpha Text, etc.

The ESV Apocrypha presents the common LXX text called "Old Greek." Because of the complex history of the additions, *The Apocrypha: The Lutheran Edition with Notes* includes references for readers who wish to consult other versions.

The Vulgate

The Greek Version of Esther, which Jerome used when making the Vulgate translation, has 107 verses not represented in the Hebrew text. Jerome removed these passages from the body of Esther and arranged them in an appendix in the order found in the English version.

The different versions of Esther do not always present all the additions or put them in the same places. For example, the Old Latin translation included some of the additional material but not all of it. Scholars variously describe the passages as six or seven additions (cf Gerhard's reference to "seven chapters" below). Modern scholars label them A through F, and some divide C into two chapters. Although some of the additions may have been composed originally in Hebrew, additions B and E were likely composed in Greek, which suggests that different authors worked at different times on creating and ordering the material.

The Luther Bible

The Luther Bible tradition does not include Old Gk Est 12:1–6. This passage details the circumstances of the assassination plot that Mordecai reported (cf Hbr Est 2:19–23). Although the LXX and Vulgate texts commonly include the six verses of Old Grk Est 12, the verses are missing from Old Latin manuscripts. Researchers believe that the Old Latin manuscripts represent an early version of Greek Esther. (See *The Old Testament in Greek*, vol. 3, pt. 1 [Cambridge: Cambridge University Press, 1940], 2; see also *Vetus Latina*, vol. 7, pt. 3, "Hester" [Freiburg: Herder, 2003], 112.)

It is possible that the edition of the Septuagint that Luther used did not include the verses of Old Gk Est 12, which would explain why the verses did not appear in his translation. Other passages, such Ecclus 22:19, are also different in Luther's edition of the Apocrypha. These circumstances have led to confusion about what Luther actually did in his translation work. (See, e.g., Helmut Lamparter's conclusion that Luther had mixed editions in *Die Apocryphen I: Das Buch Jesus Sirach* [Stuttgart: Calwer Verlag, 1972], 13 n. 4.) Scholars of Luther's Bible publishing believe that Luther used the "Aldine

Septuagint" begun by Aldus Manutius (1449–1515; see Hans Volz's mention of the edition in WA DB 12:XX, n. 6; see also M. Reu, *Luther's German Bible* [Columbus, OH: The Lutheran Book Concern, 1934], 185; Willem Jan Kooiman, *Luther and the Bible*, trans. John Schmidt [Philadelphia: Muhlenberg Press, 1961], 131). The Aldine edition became the first complete printing of the Greek Bible, published at Venice in 1518. (The Greek text of the Complutensian Polyglot was compiled earlier, but was not released until 1521 or 1522.) The Aldine Septuagint was the base text for German editions of the Septuagint. (See notes by Henry Barclay Swete in *An Introduction to the Old Testament in Greek* [Cambridge: Cambridge University Press, 1914], 174.)

Doctrinal Content

Summary Commentary

The following list briefly characterizes the additions to the Greek text of Esther. For more commentary, consult *ALEN*, pp 227–40.

1. Mordecai's dream, and the episode where the conspiracy against the king is brought to naught. This portion of 17 verses is placed before chapter 1 of the canonical book.
2. The letters sent out by the king of Persia to the effect that all Jews in the Persian Empire are to be killed. It follows chapter 3:13 of the Hebrew text. In the Vulgate it is 13:1–7.
3. The prayers of Mordecai and Esther follow chapter 4 of the Hebrew text. In the Vulgatem Mordecai's prayer is 13:8–17 and Esther's is 14:1–19.
4. Esther's audience with the king in the LXX covers 16 verses, whereas the Masoretic text has two. In the Latin Bible this is found in 15:1–16.
5. A copy of the letter of the king of Persia, which gives the Jews permission to defend themselves against their enemies, follows 8:12. In the Vulgate it is 16:1–24.
6. This part contains different subjects. The first consists of an interpretation of Mordecai's dream. It is climaxed by a discussion of the purpose of the Feast of Purim. This follows the Hebrew text and closes the Greek version of Esther. In the Vulgate it is 10:4–13. The second part of this section, a historical note added to the Greek version, is 11:1 in the Vulgate.

Specific Themes

Old Greek Esther describes how the Lord works in and through the challenges faced by His people in order to bring about His good purposes for them. In contrast with much of biblical and apocryphal literature, Israel in Esther is largely innocent and suffering unjust mistreatment by the Gentiles. The tragedy of the Babylonian exile stands in the background of the story with settled, hardworking, and pious Judeans in the foreground. They are the Lord's inheritance, which He will jealously protect with providential care. In contrast to Hebrew Esther, Greek Esther emphasizes the role that prayer plays in the lives of God's people. Yet, like Hebrew Esther, the implied message of the story overall describes God's justice in delivering the righteous from persecution while repaying the wicked persecutors.

Specific Doctrines

In contrast with Hebrew Esther, which never directly mentions God, the writers and editors of Old Greek Esther make God a clear character in the story. The LXX refers directly to God more than fifty times. This concern to make the story expressly theological was likely an important factor in the creation of the Greek versions of Esther.

Canonicity

According to Jerome, the Greek additions to Esther were not accepted by the Jews, but in his *Letter to Africanus* he stated that they were able to edify those who read them. Greek Esther introduced significant contradictions with the Hebrew edition, a matter carefully described by Gerhard (see below). Although some of Gerhard's criticisms might be softened, he presented a helpful illustration of how Old Greek Esther simply does not piece together well with the nine chapters of the Hebrew text. Following the counsel of Jerome and Luther, Protestant churches did not receive the additions as canonical. Editions of the Greek, Latin, Syriac, and Coptic Bible include the additions among the canonical Scriptures.

Lutheran Theologians on Old Greek Esther

Luther

"Here follow several pieces which we did not wish to translate [and include] in the prophet Daniel and in the book of Esther. We have uprooted such cornflowers (because they do not appear in the Hebrew versions of Daniel and Esther). And yet, to keep them from perishing, we have put them here in a kind of special little spice garden or flower bed since much that is good . . . is to be found in them." (AE 35:353)

Gerhard

"We say that a distinction must be made between the genuine and *canonical Book of Esther*, which contains nine chapters written in the Hebrew language, and the *appendix*, which contains the seven final chapters that we do not have in Hebrew. We are speaking about these last seven chapters when we deny that that section connected to the Book of Esther as an appendix is canonical. . . .

"It contains some things that conflict with the canonical Book of Esther. Therefore it cannot be canonical because the Holy Spirit never contradicts Himself. (1) In the canonical Book of Esther (2:16), the plot of the eunuchs was detected by Mordecai 'in the seventh year' of Ahasuerus. The supplement (11:2) refers this 'to the second year.' . . . (2) The canonical Book of Esther says that 'Mordecai received no rewards for detecting the plot' (Esther 6:3). The supplement (12:5) says that 'they were given to him.' . . . (3) The supplement to Esther (12:6) says that 'Haman wanted to kill Mordecai because of the eunuchs who were put to death.' Canonical Esther 3:5 refers the cause for this to Mordecai's denial of Haman's speech. . . . (4) In the canonical Book of Esther, it says that the king looked favorably on the queen (Esther 5:2). In the supplement, he is said to have looked at her with anger ([15]:10). . . . (5) In canonical Esther, the day appointed for the destruction of the Jews is said to have been the thirteenth day of Adar (Esther 3:13; 8:12; 9:1). The supplement says it was the fourteenth day of Adar (13:6). (6) In canonical Esther 8:3, Haman is called an Agagite, that is an Amalekite, but the supplement calls him a Macedonian (16:[10]). (7) In the supplement (13:14), Mordecai says that he was unwilling to bow down to Haman because he 'was afraid, lest he transfer the honor of his god to a man and worship someone besides his God.' Yet canonical Esther nowhere says that the rest worshiped Haman as a God or that Haman wanted to be worshiped as God. Rather, it was this civil honor that Mordecai denied to wicked Haman because of the singular and heroic impulse of the Holy Spirit." (ThC E1 §§ 198, 201)

The Apadana (audience hall) columns of Persepolis, which were nearly 80 feet tall and topped with animal sculptures. The army of Alexander the Great destroyed this grand Persian structure when the Greeks took the city in 331 BC.

Further Study

Lay/Bible Class Resources

Burgland, Lane. *Study Guide to the Apocrypha*. St. Louis: Concordia, 2012 ❧ Lutheran author. Eight-session Bible study, including leader's notes and discussion questions. Companion piece to *ALEN*.

Dancy, J. C. *The Shorter Books of the Apocrypha*. CBCA. Cambridge: Cambridge University Press, 1972. ❧ Prepared by British scholars for the general reader. Includes the New English Bible translation along with commentary.

Engelbrecht, Edward A., gen. ed. *The Apocrypha: The Lutheran Edition with Notes*. St. Louis: Concordia, 2012. ❧ Based on the ESV. Reflects the Luther Bible tradition of the Apocrypha. Prepared by Lutherans, with commendations from top scholars of intertestamental studies.

Church Worker Resources

deSilva, David A. *Introducing the Apocrypha: Message, Context, and Significance*. Grand Rapids: Baker Academic, 2002. ❧ A thorough and informative introduction to the books of the Apocrypha from an evangelical scholar who served on the ESV Translation Committee of the Apocryphal Books.

Academic Resources

Bissell, Edwin Cone. *The Apocrypha of the Old Testament*. LCHS. New York: Charles Scribner's Sons, 1896. ❧ Philip Schaff appears to have added this volume to the English edition of the Lange commentary. Still one of the most substantive one-volume commentaries on the Apocrypha available in English.

Charles, R. H. *The Apocrypha and Pseudepigrapha of the Old Testament*. Vol. 1. Oxford: Clarendon Press, 1913. ❧ A standard scholarly reference work. Provides thorough introductions to the Apocrypha and substantive footnotes, commenting from the Greek, Hebrew, etc.

Moore, Carey A. *Daniel, Esther, and Jeremiah: The Additions*. Vol. 44 of AB. New York: Doubleday, 1977. ❧ A thorough commentary and new translation prepared for a major academic series. Focuses on historical and literary interpretation.

Paton, L. *A Critical and Exegetical Commentary on the Book of Esther*. ICC. Edinburgh: T&T Clark, 1908. ❧ Written from a highly critical perspective. Includes a detailed discussion of textual issues.

Pietersma, Albert, and Benjamin G. Wright, eds. *A New English Translation of the Septuagint*. Oxford: Oxford University Press, 2007. ❧ A literal revision of the NRSV translation prepared by an international team of Septuagint scholars. Includes thorough introductions focused on the text of the LXX.

SUSANNA

God discerns what is secret

The story of Susanna characterizes the trials faced by young women and communities when power and privilege are abused. The villains are older, respected men of the community, and the heroes should be subject to their judgment—except that the Lord reveals the truth and vindicates the righteous.

Historical and Cultural Setting

The specific historical and cultural setting for the story of Susanna is unknown, though it likely is from the Persian or Hellenistic periods of Israel's history. The LXX editors placed the story of Susanna after Dn 12, where it does not fit well with biblical Daniel. This is because biblical Daniel is a wise, older statesman by the end of the book, and the Daniel of the Susanna story is an impetuous young man. In the Theodotion edition, the Susanna story appears at the beginning of the Book of Daniel as an introduction to the young man. This fits better with the order of biblical Daniel but introduces another problem: the context of the story assumes a settled Judean community in Mesopotamia rather than the newly arrived Judean exiles described in the biblical book of Daniel. These factors, along with the manuscript evidence, indicate that the story was independent of the biblical Book of Daniel and was added to it at a later time.

OVERVIEW

Author
Jewish author in Judea or Mesopotamia

Date
Persian or Hellenistic periods

Places
Babylon; Joakim's garden; Israel; Judah; Canaan

People
Joakim; Susanna; Susanna's father, Hilkiah, and mother; two elders/judges; maids and servants; the assembly; Daniel

Purpose
To illustrate the dangers and the virtues of public justice among God's people

Themes
Justice; truth; marital faithfulness; defending the defenseless; prayers answered

Memory Verses
Susanna's prayer answered (42–46)

TIMELINE

605 BC	First Judeans, including Daniel, exiled to Babylon
536 BC	Daniel's final vision
332 BC	Alexander the Great takes Judea from Persians
165–134 BC	Maccabean Rule
67 BC	Romans enter Judea

Wild lilies grow on the Israeli coast of the Mediterranean.
The Hebrew name Susanna means "lily."

Composition

Author

We do not know who wrote Susanna, though it was likely a Jewish writer in Israel or Mesopotamia. Stories like Susanna, as well as other Daniel traditions at Qumran, show how popular Daniel was as a genuine prophet. To date, there are no Hebrew or Aramaic manuscripts for the popular Daniel stories that are found in the Apocrypha. Writers as early as Julius Africanus (c 160–c 240) have suggested that the additions to Daniel were never written in Hebrew or Aramaic but were composed in Greek, since they include plays on Greek words (see Gerhard's comment below), though translators might also have introduced such wordplay. The earliest manuscripts have confirmed the reliability of the traditional Hebrew/Aramaic text of Daniel 1–12, and these manuscripts do not include the Apocrypha Daniel stories. For more on these issues, see CC Dn 17–18, 62–73.

Date of Composition

Some scholars believe the story to be a parable written during the reign of Alexander Jannaeus (103–76 BC), illustrating the kinds of controversies that existed between the Pharisees and Sadducees. However, the themes of the book are simply too broad for such precise dating and could reflect circumstances in either the Persian or Hellenistic periods of Israelite history.

Purpose/Recipients

The story of Susanna was likely inspired by circumstances such as those described in Jer 29:21–23 where leading men among the Judeans in Babylon were condemned for lying and for marital unfaithfulness. Such sins are a perpetual temptation to leaders, which makes the story lively and compelling for readers of any era.

Various opinions have been expressed as to the purpose for this piece of fiction written in the best tradition of storytelling. The author of Susanna seems to urge a more rigid examination of witnesses, especially where there is suspicion of collusion. He further recommends that it become a rule to inflict the same punishment on those guilty of perjury as the prescribed punishment for the victims of false testimony. Ultimately, the goals of the story seem to be praise for the prophet Daniel and ideals for marital faithfulness.

Literary Features

Genre

The Church Fathers appreciated the story of Susanna, some of whom gave it an allegorical interpretation. Hippolytus, Bishop of Rome, wrote in the third century as follows: "Susanna is a type prefiguring the Church; Joakim, her husband, prefigures the Christ. The garden is the election of the saints, who like trees that bear fruit are planted in the Church, Babylon is the world; the two elders are typical of the two nations that plot against the Church—the one being of the circumcision, and the other from the Gentiles."[1] This type of interpretation seems to have been responsible for the manner in which Susanna is represented in art. Many painters have portrayed the story on canvas. The famous statement in *The Merchant of Venice*, where Shylock addressed Portia as "a Daniel come to judgment," rests on the role of Daniel in the Susanna legend.

Characters

Although the story is commonly named for Susanna, it appeared within manuscripts of the Book of **Daniel**, who dominates the outcome of the story. The virtuous **Susanna** plays a fairly passive role in the story, though she calls out against the elders and calls on the Lord to discern the truth of the matter. She is pursued by the **corrupt elders** who ogle her and testify against her. Daniel arrives with the court assembly to oppose the testimony of the elders and the initial verdict of the community.

The judgment of Daniel.

Narrative Development or Plot

Susanna presents a story of scandal and justice in which corrupt leaders abuse their privileges to obtain sexual favors. The story's high point is

1 Greek text in Pitca, *Analecta sacra*; quoted in R. H. Charles, *The Apocrypha and Pseudepigrapha of the Old Testament* (New York: Oxford University Press, 1913), 1:645.

Outline

The two ancient versions of Greek Daniel arrange the additional stories in different ways, one placing Susanna at the beginning and the other near the end of the book. The order in the Vulgate matches Old Greek Daniel.

Theodotion	Susanna	Dn 1:1–3:23	Pr Az & Sg Three	Dn 3:24–12:13	Bel & Dragon	
Old Greek		Dn 1:1–3:23	Pr Az & Sg Three	Dn 3:24–12:13	Susanna	Bel & Dragon

Modern versions of the Apocrypha likewise arrange the material in different ways. The sequence of stories in our edition matches that of the Luther Bible tradition.

Luther Bible		Susanna	Bel & Dragon	Pr Az & Sg Three
King James Bible	Pr Az & Sg Three	Susanna	Bel & Dragon	

I. Preface (vv 1–4)

II. The Elders and Susanna (vv 5–14)

III. The Attempted Seduction (vv 15–27)

IV. The Elders Judge Susanna (vv 28–46)

V. Daniel Questions the Elders (vv 47–59)

VI. The Elders Condemned (vv 60–62)

VII. Susanna Delivered (vv 63–64)

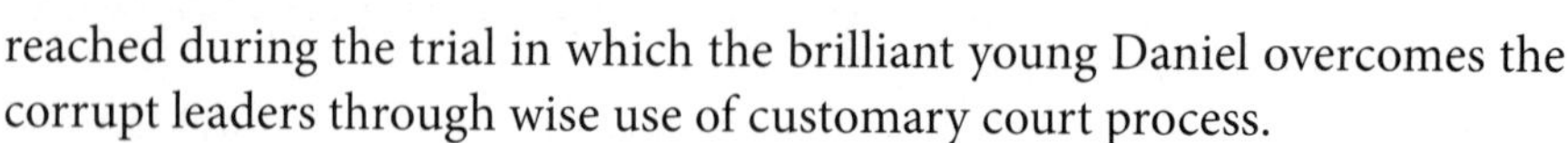

reached during the trial in which the brilliant young Daniel overcomes the corrupt leaders through wise use of customary court process.

Resources

See "Purpose/Recipients" above.

Text and Translations

There are two forms of the Susanna story. The LXX form was largely unused, though it is likely older. The favored form was from the Greek edition of the Old Testament by Theodotion (second century). This version was adopted for the Greek Bible around the fourth century and provides a fuller story. The ESV text is based on the LXX.

Doctrinal Content

Summary Commentary

Vv 1–43 The setting of the story is in Babylon and takes place during the exile. Susanna is the beautiful wife of a rich Jew who resides in Babylon. Two Jewish elders are inflamed to passion by her beauty, greatly coveting her. One day the two men meet each other as they are spying on Susanna. They confess to each other their secret lust for Susanna and decide upon a plot designed to make her accept their improper advances. They hide themselves in the garden where she is bathing, and when her attendants leave her alone, they surprise her, threatening to accuse her of adultery if she fails to comply with their demands. Susanna refuses, and the next day she is brought to trial before the court of Israel. Because she is unable to defend herself against the false accusations of the two elders, she is condemned to death.

Vv 44–64 As Susanna is led away to be killed, suddenly the proceedings are halted by the shout of Daniel, a young man who asks for the privilege of questioning the witnesses. The young man examines each of the two elders separately and succeeds in showing that their testimony is not in agreement; they have perjured themselves. Susanna is acquitted, the two elders are executed in her place, and Daniel's fame spreads among the people.

Specific Themes

Essential features of the story include the importance of marital faithfulness, pursuit of truth and justice in opposition to worldly authority, and the defense of defenseless persons. Theological themes include God's attention to our prayers and the goodness of keeping God's commandments against adultery and bearing false witness.

Specific Doctrines

Susanna sets forth a wonderful depiction of marital faithfulness, willingness to suffer injustice rather than sin against God and one's spouse, and God hearing the prayers of His people. The story of Susanna also illustrates the misuse and proper use of the Mosaic Law for justice and for leadership in community life. Like Bel and the Dragon, this story shows a positive use of wisdom and reason in the service of justice and truth.

Canonicity

Early Christians valued Susanna, and over time it was welcomed among the books of the eastern and western churches. However, Jerome and others spoke against receiving it as Holy Scripture, the conclusion later reached by Luther and adopted by Protestant churches. In 1546, the Council of Trent described the fuller form of Daniel as canonical for Roman Catholics. The 1672 Synod of Jerusalem affirmed Susanna as Sacred Scripture for Eastern Orthodox churches.

An early Christian fresco in which Susanna stands between her accusers.

Lutheran Theologians on Susanna

Luther

"Here follow several pieces which we did not wish to translate [and include] in the prophet Daniel and in the book of Esther. We have uprooted such cornflowers (because they do not appear in the Hebrew versions of Daniel and Esther). And yet, to keep them from perishing, we have put them here in a kind of special little spice garden or flower bed since much that is good, . . . is to be found in them.

"But the texts of Susanna, and of Bel, Habakkuk, and the Dragon, seem like beautiful religious fictions, such as Judith and Tobit, for their names indicate as much. For example, Susanna means a rose, that is, a nice pious land and folk, or a group of poor people among the thorns. . . . Be the story as it may, it can all be easily interpreted in terms of the state, the home, or the devout company of the faithful." (AE 35:353–54)

Gerhard

"Those plays on words [about the trees] argue clearly that the story of Susanna was written in Greek. This argument against the canonical authority of that story is used by Jerome in his preface to Daniel. . . . [Jerome also] calls the narrative about Susanna 'a story.' In so doing he does not remove all trustworthiness from it, as far as the truth of the occurrence is concerned." (ThC E1 § 224)

FURTHER STUDY

Lay/Bible Class Resources

Burgland, Lane. *Study Guide to the Apocrypha*. St. Louis: Concordia, 2012. ❧ Lutheran author. Eight-session Bible study, including leader's notes and discussion questions. Companion piece to *ALEN*.

Dancy, J. C. *The Shorter Books of the Apocrypha*. CBCA. Cambridge: Cambridge University Press, 1972. ❧ Prepared by British scholars for the general reader. Includes the New English Bible translation along with commentary.

Engelbrecht, Edward A., gen. ed. *The Apocrypha: The Lutheran Edition with Notes*. St. Louis: Concordia, 2012. ❧ Based on the ESV. Reflects the Luther Bible tradition of the Apocrypha. Prepared by Lutherans, with commendations from top scholars of intertestamental studies.

Church Worker Resources

deSilva, David A. *Introducing the Apocrypha: Message, Context, and Significance*. Grand Rapids: Baker Academic, 2002. ❧ A thorough and informative introduction to the books of the Apocrypha from an evangelical scholar who served on the ESV Translation Committee of the Apocryphal Books.

Academic Resources

Bissell, Edwin Cone. *The Apocrypha of the Old Testament*. LCHS. New York: Charles Scribner's Sons, 1896. ❧ Philip Schaff appears to have added this volume to the English edition of the Lange commentary. Still one of the most substantive one-volume commentaries on the Apocrypha available in English.

Charles, R. H. *The Apocrypha and Pseudepigrapha of the Old Testament*. Vol. 1. Oxford: Clarendon Press, 1913. ❧ A standard scholarly reference work. Provides thorough introductions to the Apocrypha and substantive footnotes, commenting from the Greek, Hebrew, etc.

Collins, John J. *Daniel*. Hermeneia: A Critical and Historical Commentary on the Bible. Philadelphia: Fortress, 1993. ❧ A thorough, critical commentary on biblical Daniel as well as the apocryphal stories, with special emphasis on the structure of the narratives. Includes a helpful overview of apocalyptic literature.

Moore, Carey A. *Daniel, Esther, and Jeremiah: The Additions*. Vol. 44 of AB. New York: Doubleday, 1977. ❧ A thorough commentary and new translation prepared for a major academic series. Focuses on historical and literary interpretation.

Pietersma, Albert, and Benjamin G. Wright, eds. *A New English Translation of the Septuagint*. Oxford: Oxford University Press, 2007. ❧ A literal revision of the NRSV translation prepared by an international team of Septuagint scholars. Includes thorough introductions focused on the text of the LXX.

Mastic trees cling to the edge of a hill. This species of tree features importantly in the story of Susanna.

BEL AND THE DRAGON

You are great, O Lord God of Daniel

In centers such as Alexandria and Babylon, where a heavy concentration of Gentiles lived, great pressures were brought upon the Jews to adjust themselves to their environment by adopting the practices of the land, including the heathen religion. Bel and the Dragon resorts to ridicule to demonstrate the folly of trusting in man-made idols. The episodes of Bel and the Dragon stand at the end of Daniel in the Septuagint.

Historical and Cultural Setting

In the two stories incorporated in Bel and the Dragon we have interesting examples of Jewish apologetic that belittled the worship of idols and discredited heathen priestcraft. The Jews were attracted to the gods and goddesses of surrounding nations, especially those of the conquerors. Many felt that the victory of the heathen over Israel was achieved because of the superiority of the heathen gods. Furthermore, a majority of the Jews lived in the Diaspora, where since the time of the conquest of Alexander the Great there was a universal tendency to adopt Greek customs and civilization.

Achaemenid figure from the Oxus treasure (fifth to fourth century BC). Horned dragons or other fantastic creatures were associated with the supreme Babylonian god Marduk, whose title Bel (cf Hbr *ba'al*) gives this story its name.

OVERVIEW

Author
Jewish author in Israel or Babylon

Date
Perhaps second century BC

Places
Babylon; Judea

People
King Astyages; Cyrus the Persian; Daniel; friends of the King; priests of Bel; Judeans; Habakkuk

Purpose
To show the God of Daniel is great and there is no other god besides Him

Themes
The living God; idolatry; use of wisdom and of reason; suffering for the sake of truth; the Lord remembers

Memory Verse
The king's confession (v 41)

TIMELINE

605 BC	First Judeans, including Daniel, exiled to Babylon
536 BC	Daniel's final vision
332 BC	Alexander the Great takes Judea from Persians
165–134 BC	Maccabean Rule
67 BC	Romans enter Judea

Composition

Author(s)

The author(s) of Bel and the Dragon remain(s) unknown; neither can it be stated definitively whether the stories were written in Hebrew or Aramaic. Some scholars believe the original language was Greek.

Date of Composition

Since the stories of Bel and the Dragon seem to draw on similar events in the canonical Book of Daniel, it is likely that the stories were written after the biblical book. However, there are great differences of thought on the dating of canonical Daniel, since conservatives attribute the book to the prophet himself while liberal scholars assume a long process of composition well beyond the time of the prophet. Scholars settle on the second century BC as a likely date for the additional stories, perhaps due to the specific challenges with idolatry at that time and the responses of other Jewish writers to such challenges. (Cf e.g., the composition of 4QPsDan from that era, which was found at Qumran.)

Purpose/Recipients

The stories ridicule idolatry while raising up the virtues of the Hebrew prophets who worship the only true God. In this way, they reinforce one of the most basic of biblical teachings: you shall have no other gods.

Literary Features

Genre

Like Susanna, the stories of Bel and the Dragon read like little detective novels, showing the early development of this literary genre and Christian interest in its development.

Characters

The chief characters in each story are **a Gentile king**, who trusts in and worships idols, and **Daniel**, who devises a clever means for showing the king that his trust in idols is misplaced. Daniel uses divine wisdom rather than prophetic revelation in order to teach about idolatry. However, revelation enters the second story when an angel takes the prophet **Habakkuk** to Daniel in order to relieve his hunger.

Outline

I. The Story of Bel (vv 1–22)
  A. Introduction (vv 1–2)
  B. The King and Daniel (vv 3–5)
  C. The Contest (vv 6–20)
  D. Conclusion (vv 21–22)
II. The Story of the Dragon (vv 23–42)
  A. The Living God and the Dragon (vv 23–27)
  B. The Conspiracy (vv 28–32)
  C. God Calls Habakkuk (vv 33–39)
  D. The King Worships Daniel's God (vv 40–42)

Narrative Development or Plot

Both stories describe contests between the Lord's servant, Daniel, and idolaters. In the first story, Daniel uses wisdom to win. In the second story, he depends upon both wisdom and divine intervention.

Resources

Bel and the Dragon consists of two distinct stories that are variations of episodes narrated in the Book of Daniel. The first has as its basis Dn 3, the episode about the golden image; the second rests on Dn 6, the story of Daniel in the lions' den. Scholars have noted some passages in the prophets that present themes similar to Bel and the dragon (e.g., Is 45:1–46:7; Jer 51:34–58). However, these passages do not lead naturally to the stories. Knowledge of the biblical prophet Habakkuk is clearly reflected in the story of the dragon, though it does not include details about the prophet from the Book of Habakkuk.

Text and Translations

Bel and the Dragon exists in two accounts: the Theodotion and the LXX versions.

Doctrinal Content

Summary Commentary

Vv 1–15 In the story of Bel, King Cyrus is depicted as coming to the Persian throne. One day he asks his friend Daniel why he does not worship the god Bel, who is the chief Babylonian god and daily consumes large quantities of flour and oil and many sheep. Daniel persuades Cyrus to place the usual amount of goods in the temple and then to close and seal it. To prove that the image of Bel does not eat the food, Daniel has wood ashes scattered on the floor to record the footprints of the priests, who with their families and by means of a trap door beneath the idol make nocturnal visits and consume the food and offerings.

Vv 16–22 When Daniel and the king return to the temple in the morning, the food is gone. The king announces triumphantly that Bel is a living god, but Daniel points to the many footprints on the floor made by men, women, and children, clearly showing that people have entered by a secret door and consumed the large quantity of food placed there for the idol. For this deception, so the story runs, the priests are killed, and Daniel is given permission to destroy the idols.

Vv 23–40 The story of the dragon is similar to that of Bel. Here the king is described as worshiping a living serpent—reminiscent of the practice of the Greeks who worshiped serpents at Oriental shrines, such as that of Aesculapius at Epidaurus. Daniel, who is summoned to pay homage to the dragon, denies its divinity. He feeds it with a concoction of pitch, fat, and hair, which causes the serpent to burst open. The people become angry at the treatment accorded their god and compel the king to have Daniel cast into a den of lions, who have been deprived of their food to make them more ferocious. For six days Daniel eats nothing, and the lions do not eat Daniel. On the seventh day the prophet Habakkuk is carrying food and drink to some reapers in Judea. Suddenly an angel takes him by the hair and carries him to the lions' den to give Daniel the food. Then, in the twinkling of an eye, the angel returns Habakkuk to Judea. On the seventh day the king has Daniel removed from the lions' den. He orders Daniel's enemies to be thrown in, and they are devoured immediately.

Specific Themes

The stories of Bel and the dragon oppose the servants of the living God to idolaters. The servants of God use wisdom and divine revelation to overcome false teaching and superstition. The chief character, Daniel, endures threats and suffering to reveal the truth.

Walking dragon, symbolizing the god Marduk, from the Ishtar Gate in Babylon.

Specific Doctrines

The Judeans in exile felt pressured by the pagan culture that surrounded them. Whereas most cultures of the Near East accepted and accommodated the gods that others worshiped, faithful Judeans worshiped only one God—the living God—who is unlike all others. This truth made them a people unlike all others, alone in a crowd.

The Daniel character uses careful reasoning and appeals to evidence in defense of his confession of faith. The writer illustrates the compatible use of wisdom and reason in the service of faith.

Canonicity

Early Christians valued these stories, and over time they were welcomed among the books of the eastern and western churches. However, Jerome and others spoke against receiving them as Holy Scripture, the conclusion later reached by Luther and adopted by Protestant churches. In 1546, the Council of Trent described the fuller version of Daniel as canonical for Roman Catholics. The 1672 Synod of Jerusalem affirmed the fuller version of Daniel as Sacred Scripture for Eastern Orthodox churches.

Lutheran Theologians on Bel and the Dragon

Luther

"Here follow several pieces which we did not wish to translate [and include] in the prophet Daniel and in the book of Esther. We have uprooted such cornflowers (because they do not appear in the Hebrew versions of Daniel and Esther). And yet, to keep them from perishing, we have put them here in a kind of special little spice garden or flower bed since much that is good, . . . is to be found in them.

"But the texts of Susanna, and of Bel, Habakkuk, and the Dragon, seem like beautiful religious fictions, such as Judith and Tobit, for their names indicate as much. . . . Daniel means a judge, and so on. Be the story as it may, it can all be easily interpreted in terms of the state, the home, or the devout company of the faithful." (AE 35:353–54)

Gerhard

"These additions do not have a prophetic author. To be sure, they are called 'the additions of Daniel,' but a comparison shows that the name 'Daniel' cannot be taken to mean the famous prophet whose canonical prophecy is extant. The true Daniel was thrown into the lions' den because he invoked the true God of Israel from the open windows of his room (Dan. 6:11). This fictitious Daniel, however, was thrown down into the lions' den for overturning Bel and killing the dragon (14:30). The true Daniel spent only one night in the lions' den (Dan. 6:19). This fictitious Daniel, however, is said to have spent six days in the lions' den (14:30). The true Daniel was sent into the lions' den under King Darius (Dan. 6:1); the fictitious one, under King Cyrus (13:65). . . . These additions conflict with historical truth. The account of Habakkuk bringing a meal to Daniel in the lions' den does not fit chronology, because the prophet Habakkuk lived before the Babylonian captivity." (ThC E1 §§ 225–26)

Further Study

Lay/Bible Class Resources

Burgland, Lane. *Study Guide to the Apocrypha*. St. Louis: Concordia, 2012. § Lutheran author. Eight-session Bible study, including leader's notes and discussion questions. Companion piece to *ALEN*.

Dancy, J. C. *The Shorter Books of the Apocrypha*. CBCA. Cambridge: Cambridge University Press, 1972. § Prepared by British scholars for the general reader. Includes the New English Bible translation along with commentary.

Engelbrecht, Edward A., gen. ed. *The Apocrypha: The Lutheran Edition with Notes*. St. Louis: Concordia, 2012. § Based on the ESV. Reflects the Luther Bible tradition of the Apocrypha. Prepared by Lutherans, with commendations from top scholars of intertestamental studies.

Church Worker Resources

deSilva, David A. *Introducing the Apocrypha: Message, Context, and Significance*. Grand Rapids: Baker Academic, 2002. § A thorough and informative introduction to the books of the Apocrypha from an evangelical scholar who served on the ESV Translation Committee of the Apocryphal Books.

Academic Resources

Bissell, Edwin Cone. *The Apocrypha of the Old Testament*. LCHS. New York: Charles Scribner's Sons, 1896. § Philip Schaff appears to have added this volume to the English edition of the Lange commentary. Still one of the most substantive one-volume commentaries on the Apocrypha available in English.

Charles, R. H. *The Apocrypha and Pseudepigrapha of the Old Testament*. Vol. 1. Oxford: Clarendon Press, 1913. § A standard scholarly reference work. Provides thorough introductions to the Apocrypha and substantive footnotes, commenting from the Greek, Hebrew, etc.

Moore, Carey A. *Daniel, Esther, and Jeremiah: The Additions*. Vol. 44 of AB. New York: Doubleday, 1977. § A thorough commentary and new translation prepared for a major academic series. Focuses on historical and literary interpretation.

Pietersma, Albert, and Benjamin G. Wright, eds. *A New English Translation of the Septuagint*. Oxford: Oxford University Press, 2007. § A literal revision of the NRSV translation prepared by an international team of Septuagint scholars. Includes thorough introductions focused on the text of the LXX.

In this early Christian fresco (sixth century AD), Hananiah, Mishael, and Azariah extend their hands in prayer, as the Lord protects them from the heat of the fiery furnace.

THE PRAYER OF AZARIAH AND THE SONG OF THE THREE HOLY CHILDREN

No shame for those who trust in God

The songs added to the Book of Daniel present a defiant, confident people who will hold to their God despite the worst kinds of suffering. The songs describe the Lord as ruler of heaven and all the earth in opposition to the people's experience under foreign rulers.

Historical and Cultural Setting

These two prayers or songs did not belong originally to the Book of Daniel since they do not appear in the Hebrew manuscript tradition. They are found after Dn 3:23 in the LXX. Some prose verses (vv 1–2, 23–28) link the prayers/songs with the story in Daniel and with one another. The author or authors may have composed the prayers/songs in Hebrew or Aramaic. They could be older than the other additions to Daniel. (See "Author," p 118.) However, scholars note that some features of the Prayer of Azariah seem to fit the character of Jewish concerns and teaching in the second century BC. For example, the opening of the prayers is similar to other prayers of the postexilic period (e.g., Tob 8:5). An unjust, wicked king is mentioned in v 9, who could be Antiochus IV Epiphanes. Also, the prayer describes a time when there is "no prince or prophet or leader" or offerings (v 15). This conflicts with the account of Daniel, which is attributed to a time when there were prophets in Judah. In fact, the Jerusalem temple continued to function for some years after Daniel entered into exile. Therefore, the circumstances of v 15 may refer to the time when the temple was in the hands of the Gentiles in the second century BC.

OVERVIEW

Author
A resident of Judea, or a Judean exiled in Babylon

Date
Perhaps composed second century BC

Places
Babylon; Jerusalem

People
Hananiah, Azariah, and Mishael; Nebuchadnezzar; the king's servants

Purpose
To commend the practice of praying in the midst of suffering and even during torture

Themes
Prayer; God's truth and justice; confession of sins; deliverance; praising God with all creation

Memory Verses
The Lord's mercy (vv 15–17)

TIMELINE

605 BC	First Judeans, including Daniel, exiled to Babylon
536 BC	Daniel's final vision
332 BC	Alexander the Great takes Judea from Persians
165–134 BC	Maccabean Rule
67 BC	Romans enter Judea

Composition

Author(s)

Some scholars believe that the two prayers were not written by the same author and were not originally together. Azariah, one of the four friends of Daniel, is considered by some scholars to be another Azariah, a hero of the Maccabean struggle.

Date of Composition

These two additions to Dn 3 are believed to have been composed during the Maccabean age, probably in the reign of the Seleucid king Antiochus IV Epiphanes (about 175–164 BC). During these years the Jewish people suffered great affliction. In verse 9 the writer laments: "You have given us into the hands of lawless enemies, most hateful rebels, and to an unjust king, the most wicked in all the world." This seems to be a reference to the renegade Jews in 1Macc 1:1–15 and the cruelties of King Antiochus. (See 1Macc 1:20–24; 41–64.)

Purpose/Recipients

The two poems were likely composed for general liturgical use during the services of God's people. In the story, they illustrate the humility of the Lord's servants who suffered exile along with their countrymen. In the first poem, they enter their suffering in a sacrificial manner, pleading for the deliverance of their people (vv 15–17). In the second song, they praise the Lord as creator over all, setting His character in contrast with the limited deities and regional deities of the idol worshipers who torment them.

Outline

- I. The Prayer of Azariah (vv 1–22)
  - A. Introduction (vv 1–2)
  - B. The Prayer (vv 3–22)
    1. Praise to God (vv 3–10)
    2. First request for deliverance (vv 11–19)
    3. Second request for deliverance (vv 20–22)
- II. The Song of the Three Holy Children (vv 23–68)
  - A. The Furnace (vv 23–27)
  - B. The Song with First Refrain (vv 28–34)
  - C. The Song with Second Refrain (vv 35–68)

Literary Features

Genre

Liturgical hymns or prayers of confession.

Characters

The chief character in both compositions is **the Lord**, who is presented as judge and redeemer in the first hymn and creator in the second.

Narrative Development or Plot

The first hymn presents the typical example of restoration through repentance and faith in the Lord's redemption. It culminates with defeat of the wicked. The second hymn is primarily a litany, describing God but also ending with the hope of redemption.

Resources

The hymns are similar to others in the Bible and the Apocrypha (e.g., Dn 9:4–19; Pss 136, 148; Bar 1:15–2:15).

Text and Translations

The Prayer of Azariah and the Song of the Three Holy Children are found in all Greek manuscripts of Daniel between vv 23 and 24 of ch 3. There are two versions of these additions to the Book of Daniel: that of the LXX proper and that of Theodotion, which is translated in the English versions. This block of material does not appear in the Aramaic text. Some modern translations introduce the passages with headings to distinguish them from the canonical text (e.g., editions of KJV; Revised Version of 1885).

Doctrinal Content

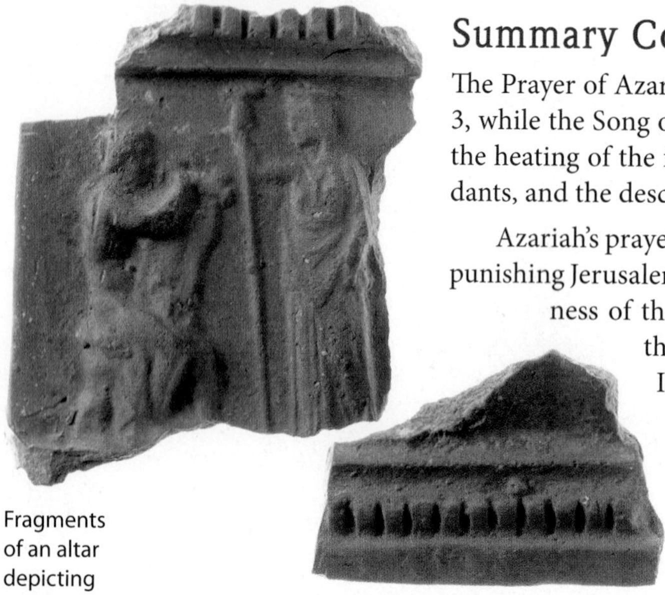

Summary Commentary

The Prayer of Azariah is linked to the context of Dn 3, while the Song of the Three Holy Children relates the heating of the furnace, the burning of the attendants, and the descent of the Angel of the Lord.

Azariah's prayer acknowledges that God is just in punishing Jerusalem, bewails the cruelty and wickedness of the enemy, brings to remembrance the promises made to Abraham, Isaac, and Jacob, and describes the forlorn condition of the Jews, who are portrayed as having "no prince or prophet or leader, no whole burnt offering or sacrifice or oblation or incense, no place to make an offering before You or to find mercy" (v 15). The author hopes that the penitence of the people will bring about restoration and judgment on the enemy.

Fragments of an altar depicting Apollo playing a lyre. Found at Tel Maresha, Israel, it illustrates the ancient love of music as well as competing religions in Hellenized Israel.

Verses 29–68 contain a blessing of God by the three friends of Daniel. Verse 35 begins, "Bless the Lord, all works of the Lord." This canticle is used as an alternative to the Te Deum in the Morning Prayer in Episcopalian churches and is hymn 931 in *Lutheran Service Book*.

The Song of the Three Holy Children is considered a splendid example of Jewish devotional literature. The refrain "[The Lord is] to be praised and highly exalted forever," occurs 32 times throughout the song.

Specific Themes

See "Literary Features" above.

Specific Doctrines

Consider thoughtfully the example of faith in the face of persecution, which the songs in Daniel describe. Their songs endured and passed from one generation to the next, reaching your eyes this day. They are a testimony that neither fire nor the sands of time can destroy the faith the Maker of heaven and earth creates in our hearts by His enduring Word. Give thanks and bless His name!

The influence of these additions to the canonical Book of Daniel has been considerable throughout the Christian Church. Not only were they a part of the Latin and Greek versions, but these additions were also translated into languages such as Syriac, Coptic, Ethiopic, Armenian, Georgian, and Arabic. The Song of the Three Holy Children has also influenced the liturgical history of the Medieval Church. Roman Catholics, Episcopalians, and Lutherans use it as a canticle. The Benedictus (vv 35–65) has been employed since Christian antiquity as a hymn of praise. In 1549, it was prescribed in the First Prayer Book as a substitute for the Te Deum during Lent. In the revision of the *American Prayer Book* in 1928 the opening part of the prayer was included in the Morning Prayer under the name of Benedictus.

Canonicity

Early Christians valued these poems, and over time they were welcomed among the books of the eastern and western churches. However, Jerome and others spoke against receiving them as Holy Scripture, the conclusion later reached by Luther and adopted by Protestant churches. In 1546, the Council of Trent described them as canonical for Roman Catholics. The 1672 Synod of Jerusalem affirmed the fuller version of Daniel as Sacred Scripture for Eastern Orthodox churches.

Lutheran Theologians on the Prayer and the Song

Luther

"Here follow several pieces which we did not wish to translate [and include] in the prophet Daniel and in the book of Esther. We have uprooted such cornflowers (because they do not appear in the Hebrew versions of Daniel and Esther). And yet, to keep them from perishing, we have put them here in a kind of special little spice garden or flower bed since much that is good, especially the hymn of praise, *Benedicite*, is to be found in them." (AE 35:353)

Gerhard

Gerhard's comments on the additions to Daniel focus almost entirely on the stories of Bel and the Dragon and of Susanna. He does note briefly that "the Song of the Three Children [does] not belong to the canon" (ThC E1 § 224).

Further Study

Lay/Bible Class Resources

Burgland, Lane. *Study Guide to the Apocrypha*. St. Louis: Concordia, 2012. ✠ Lutheran author. Eight-session Bible study, including leader's notes and discussion questions. Companion piece to *ALEN*.

Dancy, J. C. *The Shorter Books of the Apocrypha*. CBCA. Cambridge: Cambridge University Press, 1972. ✠ Prepared by British scholars for the general reader. Includes the New English Bible translation along with commentary.

Engelbrecht, Edward A., gen. ed. *The Apocrypha: The Lutheran Edition with Notes*. St. Louis: Concordia, 2012. ✠ Based on the ESV. Reflects the Luther Bible tradition of the Apocrypha. Prepared by Lutherans, with commendations from top scholars of intertestamental studies.

Church Worker Resources

deSilva, David A. *Introducing the Apocrypha: Message, Context, and Significance*. Grand Rapids: Baker Academic, 2002. ✠ A thorough and informative introduction to the books of the Apocrypha from an evangelical scholar who served on the ESV Translation Committee of the Apocryphal Books.

Academic Resources

Bissell, Edwin Cone. *The Apocrypha of the Old Testament*. LCHS. New York: Charles Scribner's Sons, 1896. ✠ Philip Schaff appears to have added this volume to the English edition of the Lange commentary. Still one of the most substantive one-volume commentaries on the Apocrypha available in English.

Charles, R. H. *The Apocrypha and Pseudepigrapha of the Old Testament*. Vol. 1. Oxford: Clarendon Press, 1913. ✠ A standard scholarly reference work. Provides thorough introductions to the Apocrypha and substantive footnotes, commenting from the Greek, Hebrew, etc.

Collins, John J. *Daniel*. Hermeneia: A Critical and Historical Commentary on the Bible. Philadelphia: Fortress, 1993. ✠ A thorough, critical commentary on biblical Daniel as well as the apocryphal stories, with special emphasis on the structure of the narratives. Includes a helpful overview of apocalyptic literature.

Moore, Carey A. *Daniel, Esther, and Jeremiah: The Additions*. Vol. 44 of AB. New York: Doubleday, 1977. ✠ A thorough commentary and new translation prepared for a major academic series. Focuses on historical and literary interpretation.

Pietersma, Albert, and Benjamin G. Wright, eds. *A New English Translation of the Septuagint*. Oxford: Oxford University Press, 2007. ✠ A literal revision of the NRSV translation prepared by an international team of Septuagint scholars. Includes thorough introductions focused on the text of the LXX.

THE PRAYER OF MANASSEH

I bend the knee of my heart

The practice of repentance was ongoing among the pious in ancient Israel. It was prescribed by the Law of Moses, governed with the Old Testament sacrifices, and described by many of the psalms throughout the history of their composition (cf e.g., the Penitential Psalms: 6, 32, 38, 51, 102, 130, and 143). The Prayer of Manasseh is a good example of this practice of worship and confession from a later time in Israel's history.

Historical and Cultural Setting

Although the prayer presents itself as the words of a seventh-century king of Judah, scholars agree that it was most likely composed later, by an author in a different setting. For more on this issue of setting, see "Date of Composition" below.

OVERVIEW

Author
An unknown Israelite

Date
Perhaps composed in the second century BC

Places
Babylon; Judah

People
Manasseh, king of Judah

Purpose
To illustrate the mercy of God toward even the most hardened sinners in Judah

Themes
Order of God's creation; God's great mercy; God's wrath; confession of sins and repentance

Memory Verses
Bending the knee of my heart (vv 11–15)

TIMELINE

696–642 BC	Reign of Manasseh
605 BC	First Judeans, including Daniel, exiled to Babylon
332 BC	Alexander the Great takes Judea from Persians
165–134 BC	Maccabean Rule
67 BC	Romans enter Judea

Composition

Author

The prayer is attributed to Manasseh, who ruled Judah in the seventh century BC. Second Chronicles 33:12–13, 18–19 states three times that he repented and that his

The Mediterranean shore defined the western border of Israel and Judah. Its sandy beaches reminded the writer of the Prayer of Manasseh that his sins were "more in number than the sand of the sea" (v 9).

prayer was recorded either in "the Chronicles of the Kings of Israel" (v 18) or in "the Chronicles of the Seers" (v 19). These texts are not available today. The content of the Prayer of Manasseh could be from such an early time, though scholars question whether the prayer was originally written in Greek rather than Hebrew or Aramaic. If the prayer was written in Greek, it naturally dates from a later period and cannot be attributed to Manasseh. Most scholars think that a later writer composed the prayer as a guide to sincere repentance.

Date of Composition

Scholars differ regarding the time of origin of this short apocryphal book. Some believe that an unknown Jew composed this prayer between 150 and 50 BC. Others place it much later, arguing for the second or third century of the Christian era. This is based upon the belief that part or all of the prayer was written in Greek. Nothing in the prayer indicates its provenance.

Purpose/Recipients

The Prayer of Manasseh is meant to fill in the material missing from Chronicles by giving the words of the king's prayer.

Literary Features

Genre

Prayer of repentance.

Characters

Manasseh, who "led Judah and the inhabitants of Jerusalem astray, to do more evil than the nations whom the LORD destroyed before the people of Israel" (2Ch 33:9).

Narrative Development or Plot

The prayer begins by praising God for the kindness He has shown to the patriarchs before proceeding to confess sins in personal ("I") terms but in a general way. It concludes with a request for forgiveness and the promise to praise God for "all the days of my life."

Resources

See "Author" above.

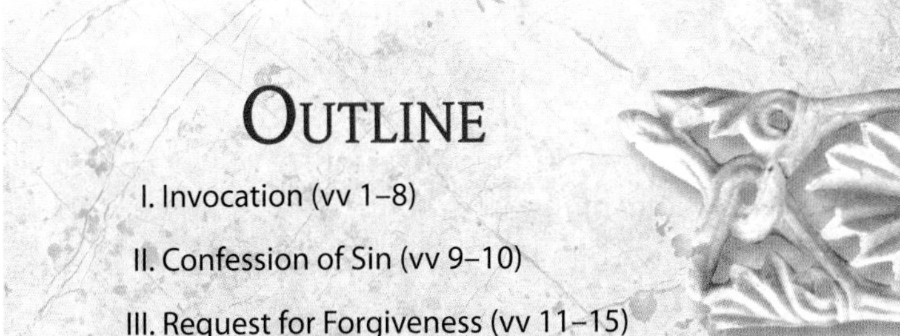

Outline

I. Invocation (vv 1–8)

II. Confession of Sin (vv 9–10)

III. Request for Forgiveness (vv 11–15)

Text and Translations

The Prayer of Manasseh is found in most manuscripts of the Septuagint and Vulgate. It has been incorporated in the Ethiopic version of Scripture. It was also rendered into Syriac, being found in the Didascalia, a third-century work translated from the Greek. The Greek text is found for the first time in the *Apostolic Constitutions* II, 22, a work from the fourth century AD.

Doctrinal Content

A prophet confronts a king, urging him to repent. The woodcut appeared in editions of Luther's 1519 tract on *How Confession Should Be Made*, which also included the Prayer of Manasseh.

Summary Commentary

The Prayer of Manasseh consists of only 15 verses, and includes standard elements of invocation, confession, and pleas for forgiveness. Evaluated from a literary point of view, it is a fine prayer of penitence that may reflect Pharisaic coloring.

Specific Themes

The prayer describes the order with which God created the universe, whose glory reminds the author of how powerful God is to judge and condemn him. In contrast, the Lord is known for His great mercy that appoints repentance for the sake of sinners. This twofold introduction leads naturally to the confession of sins and prayer for forgiveness that follow.

Specific Doctrines

The Prayer of Manasseh expresses genuine, heartfelt grief, acknowledging the bondage and burden of sin, which afflicts us. As Luther suggested, this prayer provides a helpful model of sincere confession. Note the outline that the writer used and adapt it for your personal use.

The Prayer of Manasseh awkwardly states that the patriarchs Abraham, Isaac, and Jacob did not sin against the Lord, though Genesis clearly records examples of both Abraham and Jacob deceiving other people (Gn 12:17–20; 27:18–24). The prayer also states that God "did not appoint repentance for the righteous" (Pr Man 8), which when taken literally conflicts with biblical teaching. The author may intend these statements to show how great his sins are in contrast with other Israelites. (See Gerhard's comment below.) Cf also Jesus' comment in Mt 9:13; Mk 2:17; and Lk 5:32.

Canonicity

Early Christians valued the prayer, and over time it was welcomed among the books of the Greek and Roman churches. However, the prayer is not commonly listed in Latin medieval manuscript surveys. Jerome and others spoke against receiving the book as Holy Scripture, the conclusion later reached by Luther and adopted by Protestant churches. The prayer is included in an appendix of the Vulgate for Roman Catholics. It was not listed among the books approved at the 1672 Synod of Jerusalem for Eastern Orthodox churches.

Lutheran Theologians on the Prayer of Manasseh

Luther

As a 1520 tract during the early years of the Reformation, Luther wrote *A Discussion on How Confession Should Be Made*, which included a copy of the Prayer of Manasseh for the reader's use (AE 39:46–47). Luther likewise referred to the prayer as a valuable example of repentant prayer in other writings. However, Luther did not include any comments on the prayer in the introduction to his translation of the Apocrypha or in his marginal note about Manasseh in the 1545 German Bible.

Gerhard

"That this book is outside the canon is obvious. (1) It is contained neither in the Hebrew text nor in the Greek Bible. (2) It lacks the testimony of the Church. (3) The Papists themselves reject it. . . . However, it is added to the Books of Chronicles as a part of them, and the fathers occasionally quote something from it. . . . (4) Some add that it conflicts with the analogy of faith because it denies that 'repentance has been set for the righteous.' But this agrees with the statement of Christ in Luke 15:7 and should be explained in the same way, namely, that it should be taken not *absolutely* but *comparatively*, unless someone prefers to take 'righteous' in Christ's statement to mean those who consider themselves righteous." (ThC E1 § 176)

Further Study

Lay/Bible Class Resources

Burgland, Lane. *Study Guide to the Apocrypha*. St. Louis: Concordia, 2012. § Lutheran author. Eight-session Bible study, including leader's notes and discussion questions. Companion piece to *ALEN*.

Dancy, J. C. *The Shorter Books of the Apocrypha*. CBCA. Cambridge: Cambridge University Press, 1972. § Prepared by British scholars for the general reader. Includes the New English Bible translation along with commentary.

Engelbrecht, Edward A., gen. ed. *The Apocrypha: The Lutheran Edition with Notes*. St. Louis: Concordia, 2012. § Based on the ESV. Reflects the Luther Bible tradition of the Apocrypha. Prepared by Lutherans, with commendations from top scholars of intertestamental studies.

Church Worker Resources

deSilva, David A. *Introducing the Apocrypha: Message, Context, and Significance*. Grand Rapids: Baker Academic, 2002. § A thorough and informative introduction to the books of the Apocrypha from an evangelical scholar who served on the ESV Translation Committee of the Apocryphal Books.

Academic Resources

Bissell, Edwin Cone. *The Apocrypha of the Old Testament*. LCHS. New York: Charles Scribner's Sons, 1896. § Philip Schaff appears to have added this volume to the English edition of the Lange commentary. Still one of the most substantive one-volume commentaries on the Apocrypha available in English.

Charles, R. H. *The Apocrypha and Pseudepigrapha of the Old Testament*. Vol. 1. Oxford: Clarendon Press, 1913. § A standard scholarly reference work. Provides thorough introductions to the Apocrypha and substantive footnotes, commenting from the Greek, Hebrew, etc.

THE APOCRYPHA IN OTHER CHRISTIAN TRADITIONS

Luther did not include all books called apocryphal in his translation of the Bible because he did not regard all of them as worthwhile reading. The following are books that appear in the biblical manuscripts or Bible publications of other Christian traditions, along with brief information about such books. For more information, see *The Apocrypha: The Lutheran Edition with Notes* (pp 261–332) and David A. deSilva's *Introducing the Apocrypha: Message Context, and Significance* (Grand Rapids: Baker Academic, 2002).

1 ESDRAS

OVERVIEW

Author

A Jewish author rewriting portions of 2Ch, Ezr, and Ne

Date

Perhaps second century BC

Places

Locations in the Assyrian, Babylonian, and Persian empires, from Egypt to India but centered in Judah and Jerusalem

People

Kings Josiah and Zedekiah of Judah; pharaohs; Esarhaddon of Assyria; Nebuchadnezzar of Babylon; Cyrus, Artaxerxes, and Darius of Persia; Zerubbabel; the prophets Jeremiah, Haggai, and Zechariah; Ezra the scribe and other priests and Levites

Purpose

To describe the decline, fall, and restoration of Judah and the temple, which God restored through rulers and leaders, especially Zerubbabel and Ezra

Themes

Decline and fall of Judah; destruction of the temple; exile; return from exile; rebuilding of Jerusalem and the temple; purifying of the Judeans

2 ESDRAS

OVERVIEW

Author

Likely Jewish and Christian contributors

Date

After AD 70

Places

Babylon; field of Ardat; Euphrates River; Media; Persia; Egypt; Assyria; Jerusalem; Zion; Israel; Mount Horeb; Arzareth; Lebanon; Arabia; Asia

People

Ezra (Salathiel); King Artaxerxes; Israelites in Babylon; Phaltiel, chief of the people; the elect; the scribes Sarea, Dabria, Selemia, Elkana, and Asiel; Carmonians; Assyrians

Purpose

To prepare God's people for the end

Themes

Visions; Israel's unfaithfulness; God's wrath against the wicked; God's mercy; prayer; signs of the end; coming Messiah

3 MACCABEES (PTOLEMAIKA)

OVERVIEW

Author

An Egyptian Jew

Date

After 217 BC

Places

Egyptian cities of Raphia, Alexandria, Schedia, Ptolemais; Jerusalem; Asia [Minor]; Coelesyria; Phoenicia

People

Ptolemy IV Philopator; Antiochus III; Arsinoë; Theodotus; Dositheus; Drimylus; high priest Simon; Hermon; Priest Eleazar

Purpose

To describe God's miraculous deliverance of His temple and His people from the violations of Ptolemy IV Philopator

Themes

The rise of Ptolemy IV Philopator; Ptolemy's attempt to enter the Jerusalem temple; political and religious oppression of the Jews; the stampeding of elephants; efficacious prayer; God's miraculous intervention to overturn the plans of evil rulers; Ptolemy's change in policy toward the Jews

Colorful fishing boats line the Alexandria harbor, founded by Alexander the Great in the fourth century BC. The Ptolemaic rulers who succeeded Alexander made the city a center of Hellenistic learning and trade which attracted many Jewish settlers.

4 MACCABEES

OVERVIEW

Author
A Jewish philosopher, likely in Israel

Date
Perhaps first century AD

Places
Israel; Jerusalem; Syria; Phoenicia; Cilicia

People
Eleazar, the seven brothers, and their mother; Seleucus Nicanor; Simon; High Priest Onias III (Jason); Antiochus IV Epiphanes; Ptolemy VI Philometor; references to numerous Old Testament figures

Purpose
To demonstrate from argument, but especially from examples in Israelite history, that reason rules over intemperate emotions

Themes
Reason is sovereign over emotion; Law of Moses; persecution, torture, and martyrdom; reverence for God is greater than life

PSALM 151

OVERVIEW

Author
Attributed to David

Date
Prior to AD 68; likely intertestamental

Places
Israel

People
David, his brothers, and their father; children of Israel; God's messenger (Samuel); the Philistine, Goliath

Purpose
To celebrate God's choice of and victory through David

Themes
David's humble origins; God's election of David

In the brief Psalm 151, the writer celebrates young David's defeat of the giant Goliath in the Valley of Elah, on the border between Philistia and Judah.

Nicholas of Verdun completed the 51 copper and enamel pieces of an altar triptych in 1181. The middle and right hand panels include stories from the New Testament, illustrating the Church's focus on the life and teaching of Christ and the apostles. This scene shows the Baptism of Jesus.

THE NEW TESTAMENT

New Testament Authority

Scripture declares that the New Testament is of divine origin. As the titles of the various books indicate, they came from the pens of apostles and their assistants. These men were endowed with the Holy Spirit and were made the infallible teachers of the Church. When they spoke and wrote the Scriptures, it was really the Spirit of God who was speaking—and writing. For proof of this important, far-reaching statement we look to Jn 14:26: "But the Helper, the Holy Spirit, whom the Father will send in My name, He will teach you all things and bring to your remembrance all that I have said to you." Matthew 10:20 affirms: "For it is not you who speak, but the Spirit of your Father speaking through you." In 1Co 2:13 Paul declares: "And we impart this in words not taught by human wisdom but taught by the Spirit, interpreting spiritual truths to those who are spiritual."

Let the reader furthermore remember that the Christian Church, according to the words of Paul, is built not only on the prophets but also on the apostles; in fact, the latter are mentioned first (Eph 2:20). They rank with the inspired prophets of old, their writings being as much God-breathed as those of Moses and Isaiah. Compare 2Pt 3:2: "That you should remember the predictions of the holy prophets and the commandment of the Lord and Savior through your apostles." In addition we must cite: "As [Paul] does in all his letters when he speaks in them of these matters. There are some things in them that are hard to understand, which the ignorant and unstable twist to their own destruction, as they do the other Scriptures" (2Pt 3:16). Let the reader here note the words "the other Scriptures." Peter assigns Paul's epistles the rank of Scripture; for in speaking of the rest of the Bible, he uses the term "the other Scriptures." It is clear, then, that if we regard the writings of the apostles in the light of New Testament teaching, they must be viewed as being of divine origin, having been produced by the Holy Spirit.

THE CANON OF THE NEW TESTAMENT

By the end of the first century, all the New Testament writings were in existence; the Word of the Lord grew in written form in various places and at various times in the first, decisive half-century of the existence of the apostolic Church. But the 27 New Testament writings did not then exist as a completed collection that was the authority for the faith and life of the Church. That is, the New Testament writings did not yet exist as the New Testament *canon*. The Greek word *kanon* developed a wide range of meanings from its original sense of "reed." It came to mean "measuring rod," "rule," "plumb line"; and from this physical sense there arose the sense of "measure," "standard," "norm," or "model." A law, for instance, could be called a *kanon*. From the practice of compiling lists of standard, normative literary works, *kanon* acquired the sense of "list." In the New Testament itself we find the word used in the sense of "rule" (Gal 6:16). In the Christian literature of the first three centuries it is used in various combinations to express the idea of "revealed truth as normative for the Church." About AD 350 we find established the practice of referring to biblical books as "canonical" or as "belonging to, or in, the canon." Two senses of canon seem to have merged here: a book is called canonical both because it is included in a list and because it has the character of a norm or standard. When we today speak of the New Testament canon, therefore, we speak of the New Testament writings as an aggregate, as a list or collection of books that is normative for the Church.

Agreed Upon and Spoken Against

When we speak of the canonicity of a New Testament book, we refer to its position in this normative list. Those books that were always and everywhere recognized as canonical are termed "agreed upon" (*homologoumena*);

those books whose position in the canon was for a time disputed or doubtful are "spoken against" (*antilegomena*). The teachers Origen (third century) and Eusebius (fourth century) gave the Early Church this terminology; they used the terms to sum up the history of the 27 books up to their time. The terms are therefore a description of the history of the books in the life of the Church, not primarily or even necessarily a judgment on their value. The *homologoumena* are the four Gospels and Acts, the 13 letters of Paul, the First Letter of Peter and the First Letter of John. The *antilegomena* are the Letter to the Hebrews, the Letter of James, the Second Letter of Peter, the Second and Third Letters of John, the Letter of Jude, and Revelation.

In a very real sense the New Testament Church always had a canon, namely in the Old Testament Scriptures, which Jesus and His apostles had interpreted as fulfilled in Jesus Christ and had given to the Church as its "Holy Scriptures." Christianity did not develop from a religion of Spirit into a religion of the Book, as some have claimed. It was from the beginning a "book religion," and the new book, our New Testament, took its place beside the old, not suddenly and magically, but by a gradual historical process over the years as the Church worshiped, did its work, and fought its battles. The story of that process is a complicated one and sometimes difficult to trace, for the process was not uniform throughout the churches, and our information is often tantalizingly incomplete. It will be traced here only in broadest outline.

Growth of the Canon: First Stage, AD 100–170

In this period there is at first no discussion of the canon as such; that is, no one explicitly asks or answers the question, "Which books are to be included in the list of those that are normative for the Church?" What we do find in the writings of the Apostolic Fathers (Clement of Rome, the Epistle of Barnabas, Ignatius, Polycarp, Hermas, the Teaching of the Twelve Apostles) is, first, a witness to the fact that the books destined to become the New Testament canon are *there*, at work in the Church from the first. The books are quoted and alluded to, more often without mention of author or title than by way of formal quotation. Second, we find a witness to the fact that the thought and life of the Church were being shaped by the content of the New Testament writings from the first, and moreover by the content of all types of New Testament writings. The influence of all types of New Testament writings (Synoptic Gospels, Johannine works, Pauline Letters, the Catholic Letters) is clearly discernible. To judge by the evidence of this period, the four Gospels and the letters of Paul were everywhere the basic units in the emerging canon of the New Testament.

And, third, there is some specific witness in these writings to the fact that the New Testament writings assumed a position of authority in the churches that they share with no other writings. "The Lord" and "the apostles" appear as authoritative voices besides the Old Testament Scriptures, at first usually without any mention of the fact that these voices are preserved in writings. But these voices of authority are also found directly associated with the writings that contain them, and once or twice a saying of Jesus is introduced by the formula regularly used to introduce Old Testament citations: "It is written." This is high testimony, for the authority of the Old Testament was unquestioned in the Early Church.

Further evidence for the authority exercised by the New Testament writings is found in the fact, recorded by Justin Martyr, that the New Testament writings (or at least the Gospels) were read in the worship services of the churches, interchangeably with the Old Testament. This is perhaps the most significant bit of evidence for this period—for one thing, Justin records it as a well-established regular practice, so that we may fairly assume that the practice had been long established in the churches. For another, the fact of public reading in the churches became for later generations one of the prime criteria of canonicity. This phenomenon is typical of the quiet, unplanned, and unofficial way in which the New Testament writings established themselves in the Church. One might almost say that the Church had a canon before she began to think about the canon.

Another piece of evidence for the authority exercised by the New Testament writings is the fact that heretics, such as the gnostics Basilides and Valentinus, appealed to them and sought by reinterpretation to base their teachings upon them. They used other sources of their own also, but the fact that they could not simply turn their backs on writings that were, after all, less directly useful to them than their own "tradition" speaks eloquently of the authority that the New Testament writings possessed for the Church.

Indeed, it was a heretic who brought the question of the New Testament canon into clear focus and made it a theological concern for the Church. Marcion dealt more radically with the New Testament books than did other heretics. He was not content merely to reinterpret and to supplement the existing books. He constructed a canon of his own, a canon consisting of the Gospel of Luke, radically revised by himself, and ten letters of Paul (his canon did not contain the Pastoral Letters). With this revised canon he con-

In Old Testament times, the temple treasury likely served as a repository for biblical manuscripts. The Early Church did not have such a central repository. Yet the Lord preserved the New Testament writings and all the Scriptures for us to read today.

Herod's Temple

20 BC–AD 70

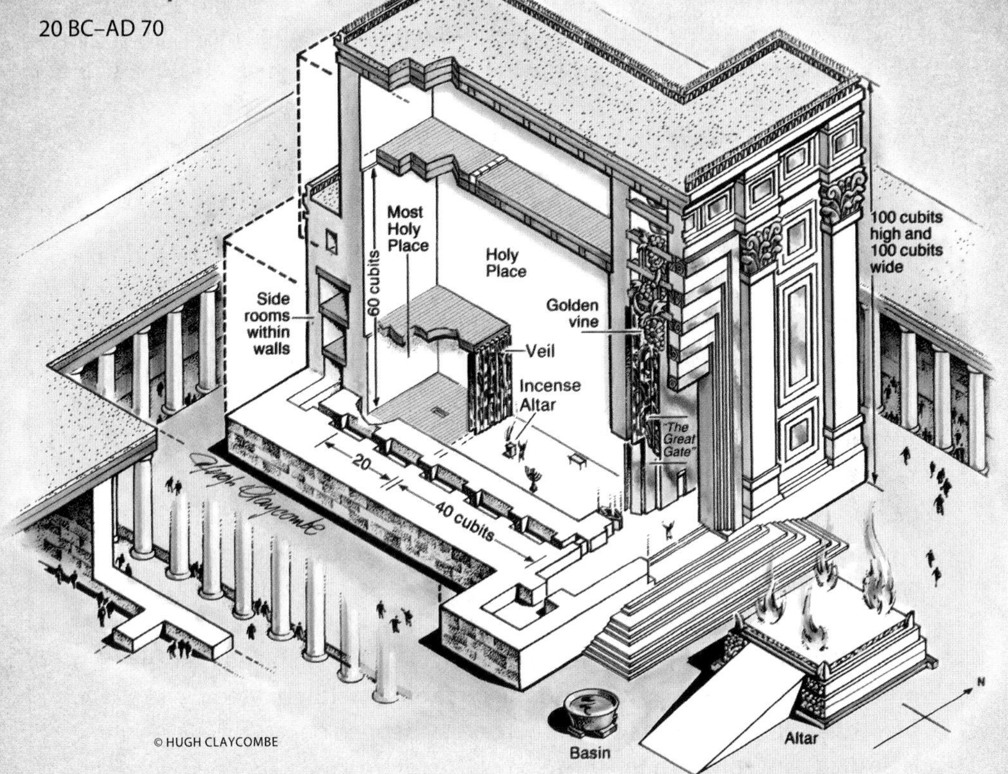

Most Holy Place
Holy Place
60 cubits
Side rooms within walls
Golden vine
Veil
Incense Altar
"The Great Gate"
100 cubits high and 100 cubits wide
20
40 cubits
Basin
Altar
N

© HUGH CLAYCOMBE

Begun in 20 BC, Herod's new structure towered 15 stories high, following the floor dimensions of the former temples in the Holy Place and the Most Holy Place. The high sanctuary shown here in a cutaway view was built on the site of the former temples of Solomon and Zerubbabel and was completed in just 18 months.

The outer courts surrounding the temple mount were not completed until AD 64. The entire structure was demolished by the Romans in AD 70.

Dimension of rooms, steps, doorways, cornices, and exterior measurements are mentioned in history (Josephus and the Mishnah) but are subject to interpretation, and all drawings vary.

Was the ark still present during the Roman period? Josephus describes the Most Holy Place as having "nothing at all," which was accurate on the day he wrote it. The Mishnah hints that the ark was hidden (Shekalim 6:12). On the ark of the covenant, cf Ex 25.

Slanted tunnel within walls ascends to upper levels
Most Holy Place
Holy Place

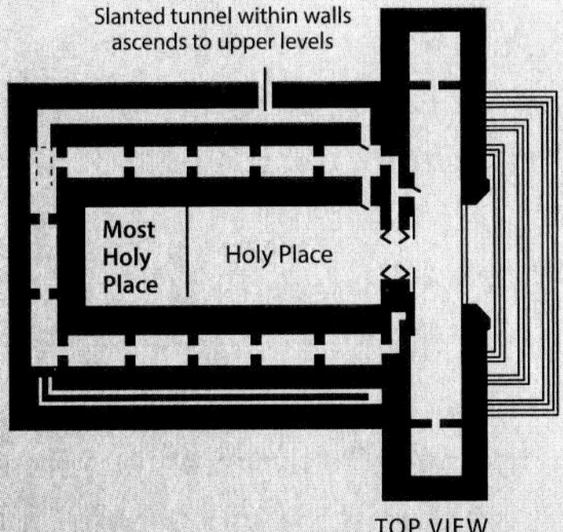

TOP VIEW

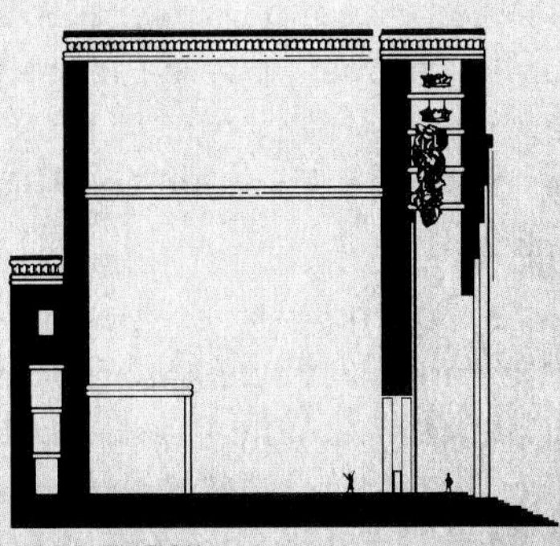

SIDE ELEVATION

fronted the Church; these books, he claimed, and only these, contained the unadulterated Gospel. The Church, which rejected the heresy of Marcion, was thus forced to deal explicitly with the question of the canon. From this time onward the canon is not merely the self-evident but undefined possession of the Church; the Church now becomes conscious of its embattled possession, and the canon emerges into the clear light of history.

Growth of the Canon: Second Stage, AD 170–220

In this period elements already present earlier seem to crystallize and take more definite shape. There is no longer any question as to the existence of the canon as a more or less definite quantity and as a decisive standard; only the extent of the canon is still open to question. Even that question is limited in scope, for about four-fifths of the eventual canon of the Church is already so firmly established as to be beyond debate.

Two documents from near the beginning of this period are an illustration of the remarkable agreement in various churches concerning the basic limits of the canon. The one is a description of a recent persecution that the churches of Vienne and Lyons in Gaul sent to Asia Minor (*NPNF*2 1:211–18). The other is the work of a bishop, Theophilus of Antioch in Syria (*ANF* 2:89–121). The Syrian bishop and the Gallic churches have, so far as we can see, a practically identical basic New Testament, though neither of them cite all the present 27 books—the absence of some may happen because neither source is dealing explicitly with the question of the canon. And in neither of them is there any apocryphal New Testament material.

Three fathers of this period have in their writings left us a fairly complete picture of the situation in various churches: Irenaeus of Lyons in Gaul (who was acquainted with the life of the churches also in Asia and Rome), Clement of Alexandria, and Tertullian of Carthage. Their writings indicate that all but one of the 27 books were somewhere known and accepted in the Christian Church; the exception is the Second Letter of Peter. They show also that there was practical unanimity in the churches on all except seven of the New Testament books—the Letter to the Hebrews, the Letter of James, the Second Letter of Peter, the Second and Third Letters of John, the Letter of Jude, and Revelation.

The growing self-consciousness of the Church regarding its canon is most strikingly reflected in a document called the Muratorian Fragment or the Muratorian Canon. The document gets its name from the librarian of the Ambrosian Library in Milan, Muratori, who discovered the document in 1740. The beginning of the document has been lost, and its curiously corrupt and enigmatic Latin text (probably a rough translation of a Greek original) presents many problems. But the document does give us a clear and fairly complete picture of the canon of the church of Rome about AD 170. That canon includes 22 books. The five books omitted are: the Letter to the Hebrews, the First and Second Letters of Peter, the Letter of James, and one of the shorter letters of John.

The most startling omission is that of the First Letter of Peter; it is startling because this letter is otherwise so widely attested and so generally accepted in the Early Church. This omission may be due to the mutilated state of the text. The canon includes also a Revelation of Peter, although the document notes that "some of us do not want it read in the church"—another indication of the importance of public reading in the question of canonicity. The Wisdom of Solomon is also included, without comment. The Shepherd of Hermas is rejected because of its recent origin; there is no objection to its content, but it is not to be used in the worship of the church alongside the prophets and apostles. The works of heretics are decisively rejected, as are letters written in support of Marcion's heresy and falsely attributed to Paul: "Gall is not to be mingled with honey." It is clear: the canon is not yet a finished thing. The content is to a large extent fixed, but some books still have not found their place in the canon, and there are some either in the canon or on the fringe of the canon that will not maintain their place.

Growth of the Canon: Third Stage, AD 220–400

The first part of this period, the third century, marks no decisive stage in the growth of the canon. The three chief witnesses for the state of the canon in this century are Origen, Dionysius of Alexandria, and Cyprian of Carthage. Origen is of special importance because of the immense range of his learning and because of his wide knowledge of the various branches of the Early Church; he knew what writings were normative for the Church, not only in his home Alexandria, but also in Rome, Antioch, Athens, and Caesarea. Origen knew and used all 27 books of our New Testament canon. He is the first ancient authority to take notice of the Second Letter of Peter; there is none of the *antilegomena* that he rejects, though he knows that they have not all won equal acceptance in the churches. His tendency is to be inclusive rather than exclusive; consequently, it is difficult to determine the outer limits of his canon.

Dionysius of Alexandria, the pupil and successor of Origen, likewise was in communication with many branches of the Early Church. His canon includes, besides the *homologoumena*, the Letter of James, the Letter to the Hebrews (which he, unlike Origen, considers Pauline) and the Second and Third Letters of John. He argues, on the basis of vocabulary, style, and content, that Revelation is not by the apostle John, but he is not inclined to question its authority; the author is in his view another John, "a holy and inspired man," who "beheld the revelation and had knowledge and the gift of prophecy." Dionysius does not notice the Second Letter of Peter or the Letter of Jude.

Cyprian of Carthage is our witness for the West in this century. In his writings he cites all books of the New Testament except Paul's Letter to Philemon, the Letter of James, the Second Letter of Peter, the Second and Third Letters of John, the Letter of Jude, and the Letter to the Hebrews. This does not necessarily mean that these books were all unknown at Carthage or unacknowledged. There is evidence that the Second Letter of John, for instance, was accepted at Carthage during Cyprian's time. Of the *antilegomena*, Cyprian frequently used and held in high esteem the Revelation to John.

Two things are noteworthy in the third century. One is the fact that the *antilegomena* are slowly gaining ground in the churches. The other is the absence of any official action on the canon: no church council defines the canon or imposes a canon on the Early Church. The canon is not being *made*; it is growing and being recognized. This remains the case in the fourth century also, when the canon assumed the form that it was destined to retain ever after in the Western Church. When the historian Eusebius of Caesarea early in the fourth century (AD 325) came to consider the canon of the Early Church, he had nothing "official" to which he could appeal, no conciliar decrees, no definitive pronouncements that had behind them the authority of the whole Church. His discussion of the canon is in essence a historical survey of what had happened to the various books in the churches (*NPNF*2 2:133–25, 155–57; 6:272–73). What had happened was this: 27 books had assumed a place of authority in the life of the Early Church. But the evidence indicated that the process had not been uniform, and Eusebius seeks to deal fairly with the evidence by dividing the books into three classes, the *homologoumena*, the *antilegomena*, and the "spurious." (This third classification is really a subdivision under *antilegomena* and includes the Acts of Paul, the Shepherd of Hermas, the Revelation of Peter, and the Epistle of Barnabas.) He lists 21 books as *homologoumena:* the four Gospels, 14 letters of Paul (Eusebius includes the Letter to the Hebrews among the Pauline Letters), the First Letter of Peter, and the First Letter of John; he includes the Revelation to John also, but with the reservation, "if it seems good," and indicates that he will give his own opinion on this point later. He lists five books as "*antilegomena*, but known to (or acknowledged by) the majority," namely, the Letter of James, the Second Letter of Peter, the Second and Third Letters of John, the Letter of Jude. He lists Revelation twice, once among the *homologoumena* and again under the "spurious" books, noting that some reject the work while others list it among the *homologoumena*. This hesitation is curious—Eusebius attempts to be scrupulously fair in assessing the evidence both for and against the book without being unduly swayed by his own opinion of the book, which was not favorable to it.

Some 25 years later (AD 350) Cyril of Jerusalem in his catechetical lectures recommends to his catechumens a 26-book canon of the New Testament. His canon differs formally from that of Eusebius in the omission of Revelation. More remarkable is the fact that the distinction between *homologoumena* and *antilegomena* plays no role whatever in the canon of Cyril. The 26 books *are* the *homologoumena*, "the books agreed upon by all," in contrast to apocryphal works against which he warns his hearers: "Do not read for yourself what is not read in the churches." Again it is noteworthy that Cyril appeals to no official action of the Early Church but only to the general consensus of the churches.

In AD 367 Athanasius, bishop of Alexandria, in his Thirty-Ninth Paschal Letter (so-called because it announced the official date of Easter to the churches) warns the churches against heretical writings and lists the 27 books of Eusebius's canon as the "well-springs of salvation, from which he who thirsts may take his fill of sacred words." Like Cyril, he draws a sharp line between canonical and heretical works with their fictitious claim to antiquity and authenticity. Also like Cyril, he makes no distinction between *homologoumena* and *antilegomena*. Like Eusebius, he finds the authority for the canon in the history of the canon, not in any decree of the Early Church. It is noteworthy, too, that Athanasius expressly states that he is not introducing any novelty in thus defining the canon: "Permit me," he says, "to remind you of what you know." With the Paschal Letter of Athanasius the canon of the Church is practically determined. The 27-book canon remained the canon of the Greek Church. Before the end of the fourth century, the Western Church, strongly influenced herein by Jerome and Augustine, likewise had a definitive 27-book canon. Local divergences persisted here and there for a time, as the content of some of our New Testament manuscripts indicates, but only the Syrian Church persisted in using an essentially different canon, one in which the Catholic Letters and Revelation had no firm position.

St. Athanasius, great teacher of the Church.

The sketchy and incomplete account here given indicates that the New Testament as a collection has a curiously informal and almost casual sort of history. The book that was destined to remain the sacred book for millions of Christians for century upon century came into the Church without fanfare, in a quiet, shuffling sort of way. Its history is not at all what *we* should expect the history of a sacred book to be. The story of the Book of Mormon is a good example of how some people think a sacred book should come about—miraculously, guaranteed by its miraculousness. The canon is a miracle indeed, but a miracle of another sort, a miracle like the incarnation of our Lord, a miracle in servant's form. Only a God who is really Lord of all history could risk bringing His written word into history in the way in which the New Testament was actually brought in. Only the God who by His Spirit rules sovereignly over His people could lead His weak, embattled, and persecuted churches to ask the right questions concerning the books that made their claim upon God's people and to find the right answers: to fix with Spirit-led instinct on that which was genuinely apostolic (whether written directly by an apostle or not) and therefore genuinely authoritative. Only God Himself could make people see that public reading in the churches was a sure clue to canonicity; only the Spirit of God could make people see that a word which commands the obedience of God's people thereby established itself as God's Word and must inevitably remove all other claimants from the scene.

This the 27-book canon did. It established itself in the early centuries of the Church and maintained itself in the continued life of the Church. It survived the questionings of both humanists and reformers in the sixteenth century; it is a remarkable fact that a Scripture reading in Lutheran churches on the Feast of the Reformation is taken from one of the books that Martin Luther himself seriously questioned, the Book of Revelation. And it will maintain itself henceforth. The question of the limits of the canon may be theoretically open, but the history of the Church indicates that it is for practical purposes closed. In the Lutheran Church, the Luther Bible more or less established which books would be read and regarded as Holy Scripture, even if the Lutheran Confessions never provided an official list (the Apocrypha were not typically included in public readings since Lutherans do not regard them as canonical). The 27 New Testament books are *there* in the Church, at work in the Church. They are what Athanasius called them—"the wellsprings of salvation" for all Christendom. And in the last analysis, the Church of God can become convinced and remain assured that they are indeed the wellsprings of salvation only by drinking from them.

Jesus driving out the unclean spirit.

Demon Possession at the Time of Christ

Many New Testament passages speak of persons who were possessed by demons. Frequently Jesus heals such unfortunate people by expelling the demons. Several questions arise in this connection. We inquire, "What is meant by demon possession? Why were instances of this affliction so frequent in those days? How was it possible for some of the Jews who were not followers of Jesus to practice exorcism, that is, expulsion of demons?"

We must distinguish between being controlled morally and being controlled physically by the devil. It is said of Judas Iscariot in Jn 13:2: "The devil had already put it into the heart of Judas Iscariot, Simon's son, to betray Him"; and again in v 27: "Then after he had taken the morsel, Satan entered into him." Luke says likewise: "Then Satan entered into Judas called Iscariot, who was of the number of the twelve" (22:3). What we see here is the inexpressibly sad condition of a person who is under the moral or spiritual control of Satan, yielding to the evil impulses that Satan arouses in him. However, when we speak of persons as being possessed by the devil, we do not refer to the service that is rendered Satan by every wicked person, but the term is meant to denote a state in which the person afflicted is physically controlled by the prince of darkness. Frequently such possession may have been due to a life of sin; at times, however, as in the case of the boy spoken of in Mk 9:14–21, there may have been no moral depravity on the part of the victims to which the extraordinary power of Satan over them could be attributed.

The persons who were possessed by demons at times, in some cases probably continuously, were not masters of their own bodies, their limbs, and their organs of speech. There were hours when someone else directed their actions and spoke out of their mouths. The demoniac in the country of the Gadarenes, when asked by Jesus what his name was, replied, "My name is Legion, for we are many," referring to the number of demons who were living there (Mk 5:9). It was the mouth of the demoniac that was speaking, but the statement that was made came from the demons that were residing in him. We may describe the state of such persons, then, as being that of a dual personality, the victims' own personality now and then becoming entirely submerged and the devil assuming control of all their organs and faculties. A remarkable phenomenon found with persons so possessed was that they, through the devil inhabiting them, recognized Jesus as the Son of God and hailed Him as such when He came near them. Thus when Jesus entered the synagogue at Capernaum, as related in Mk 1:23–24, a man with an unclean spirit, that is, a demon, cried out: "What have You to do with us, Jesus of Nazareth? Have You come to destroy us? I know who You are—the Holy One of God." It is plain that here more than human insight was manifesting itself. In such cases Jesus always forbade the spirits to speak, and though the Scriptures do not inform us as to the reason why He took such a course, we can easily find an explanation. He did not wish to build His kingdom with the help of Satan, and hence He refused to profit by what the devil could divulge about His person.

In addition to supernatural insight, possessed persons sometimes exhibited superhuman strength. The demoniac in the country of the Gadarenes had pulled chains apart and had broken shackles in pieces (Mk 5:4). This action confirms the view that here we are dealing with a phenomenon that must be classified as supernatural. We are aware that this matter deserves great caution, for who will fix the limits of a person's strength when under the influence of extreme mental stress? But it seems that we are not going too far in describing the strength of this man as superhuman.

Demon Possession Different From Insanity

From the above it is obvious that we reject the view that the so-called demoniacs were merely insane and that possession of the devil was a figment of the imagination of the people living in the first century AD. Such a view cannot be held by those who look upon the Bible as the inerrant Word of God and upon Jesus, who bade the demons depart, as the omniscient Lord. Sometimes it is asserted that Jesus knew quite well that there was no such thing as demon possession and that He, in expelling the demons, merely accommodated Himself to the ideas and the language of His contemporaries. But this theory of accommodation ill suits Him who insisted on honesty and sincerity and who used very strong language in dealing with the hypocrisy of the scribes and Pharisees. How can we assume that He deliberately deceived the people who surrounded Him and were guided by His message? Whether now and then insane persons were mistakenly regarded as being possessed by demons is a different question. Quite likely the dividing line between these two states was not always carefully observed. But that there was in those days an affliction which was properly described as possession by evil spirits, biblical Christians must consider true.

When we ask why cases of this sad state apparently were very frequent at the time when Jesus visibly moved among people, we are driven to conjecture, because the Scriptures do not furnish us information on this matter. A very plausible explanation is that the devil realized that the Redeemer had come for the salvation of the world and the destruction of his kingdom, and that hence he made very determined efforts to counteract the work of Jesus and the apostles, using all means at his command, physical and spiritual, in opposing the coming of the kingdom of God. The situation is very aptly described in the words of Jesus: "When a strong man, fully armed, guards his own palace, his goods are safe; but when one stronger than he attacks him and overcomes him, he takes away his armor in which he trusted and divides his spoil" (Lk 11:21–22). Warfare was on between Jesus and Satan when the former began His earthly ministry. Satan was aware of the intention with which the Son of God had appeared on earth, to storm the citadel that Satan was occupying. There had to come a gigantic conflict between the Prince of life and light and the prince of death and darkness, and demon possession was one of the weapons that the latter employed in this struggle. Taking this view, we shall not think it strange that cases of this affliction were so frequent in the days of the earthly life of our Savior. There is, of course, no reason why we should hold that demon possession cannot occur today; but to enter upon that subject would take us beyond the scope of this book.

Jewish Exorcists

There remains the question of how we shall account for the fact that demons were expelled not only by our Lord and His disciples, but likewise by persons who did not belong to His circle. Such was the case in Lk 11:19 and parallel passages. What is indeed remarkable is that Jesus Himself here acknowledges that demons were being exorcised by people other than Himself and His disciples. The statement of our Lord is so definite that we cannot describe these persons simply as imposters who were probably enriching themselves at the expense of credulous people. That a good deal of fraud was practiced under the mantle of exorcism we may readily grant, knowing from our own observations that the occult furnishes quacks of all kinds with a fruitful field for fleecing the public. But there must have been some genuine cases of expulsion of demons by these exorcists. How could they perform such things? Evidently through the power of Yahweh, the true God. We have to think of their endeavors the same way in which we regard the exorcism of demons by the apostles. The latter performed this miracle not through their own power, but through the power of God; the genuine exorcists mentioned by Christ did their work in no other way. God was merciful to the distressed and permitted healings to be performed by these people.

Christ drives out an evil spirit. Italian; fifteenth century.

The Resurrection of Jesus

Perhaps nothing in the Bible is pointed to with greater frequency in the attempt to prove that our Sacred Book contains contradictions than the four accounts of the resurrection of our Savior: Mt 28:1–10, Mk 16:1–11, Lk 24:1–12, and Jn 20:1–18. We are told that in a number of points these accounts are at variance with one another. First, every person must admit without hesitation that not one of the four accounts of the resurrection is complete, reporting all the facts. None of them makes the claim of being exhaustive. Each one reports actual occurrences, but none states that it includes all the pertinent occurrences. Hence the reports may be fragmentary, incomplete, and yet true. If this simple principle is borne in mind, most of the difficulties contained in the resurrection story will vanish.

For example, Matthew relates that Mary Magdalene and the other Mary came to the tomb on that great morning. Mark mentions Mary Magdalene, Mary the mother of James, and Salome. Luke has the names of Mary Magdalene, Joanna, and Mary the mother of James. John records in this connection the name of but one woman, that of Mary Magdalene. Is there a contradiction here? All four accounts have the name of Mary Magdalene. Mark and Luke name Mary the mother of James as belonging to that company. It is she to whom Matthew refers in the term "the other Mary" (cf Mt 27:56). Thus this Mary appears in the narrative of three of the Gospels. Therefore there is a remarkable agreement between the accounts as far as the women who visited the grave are concerned. It is true that Mark is the only one to state that Salome belonged to this group on Easter morning, while Luke is the only one who mentions Joanna in his account. But that does not mean that Mark and Luke contradict each other. Their reports are supplementary, that is all. Salome was among those women, so was Joanna. It is interesting to note that although John mentions the name of but one woman in his account, Mary Magdalene, he indicates that she had companions as she went to the grave; for he writes that she reported to Peter and John when she had found the tomb empty: "They have taken the Lord out of the tomb, and we do not know where they have laid Him" (Jn 20:2). The plural "we" sufficiently indicates that she did not go alone. Besides, this plural is a striking witness to the correctness of the view that John presupposes that his readers are acquainted with the first three Gospels, the Synoptic Gospels. For that reason we need not be surprised that he does not relate incidents and details reported by the other evangelists.

Stone-hewn tomb with rolling stone door.

In respect to the time when the women came to the grave, it might seem that John and Mark contradict each other. Mark says that the women came to the grave when the sun had risen. John relates that Mary Magdalene came to the grave when it was still dark. The difficulty is easily solved when the actual situation is looked into. To go to the grave, the women had to walk some distance. This was the case whether we assume that they lodged in Jerusalem or that they stayed at Bethany. When they left their quarters, it was still dark, and when they arrived at the tomb, which was outside the city walls, the sun was just coming into view. John is thinking of the time of departure for the grave, Mark of the time of arrival there.

The item that probably has caused more discussion than any other in these accounts is the reference to the angels who appeared to the women and announced the resurrection of Jesus. Matthew and Mark say that an angel spoke to the women, while Luke and John report that two angels were seen and broke the good news to the visitors at the grave. The critics usually present their charge as follows: "The first two Gospels say that only one angel was present at the grave on Easter morning. The last two inform us that two were there. This is an evident discrepancy." The careful reader will notice that this is a misstatement of the case. Do Matthew and Mark say that only one angel was at the tomb? That little, but important word "only" is missing in their accounts. While their reports do not mention the presence of several angels, but of merely "an angel" or of "a young man clothed in a long white robe," they do not deny that more may have been there and were seen by the women. That Matthew describes only one angel seems to be due to his having related that "an angel of the Lord descended from heaven and came and rolled back the stone and sat on it" (Mt 28:2). It was this angel who spoke to the women. His role was so important that Matthew contents himself with the reference to this one messenger of God and does not dwell on the presence of any other. In similar manner the silence of Mark with respect to another angel at the tomb may be due to the fact that he is thinking only of the angel who conveyed the news of the resurrection of Christ to the women and is disregarding the presence of the other angel who was in the tomb when the women entered. The vital feature for him evidently is that the women received the news of the resurrection not from a human being, not from a disciple, but from an angel; whether one or more angels appeared was a matter of secondary importance.

Let us assume a hypothetical example of today. Walking the streets of Washington, you might meet the president of the United States and his secretary of education. Let us assume that the president speaks to you and gives you some interesting information on a pending question. Upon meeting a friend, you would be likely to say, "I saw the president, and this is what he said." A few minutes later you might meet another friend and tell him, "I saw the president and the secretary of education, and this is what the president said." To a third person you might say: "I met the president and his secretary of education, and this is the information that I received from them." Note that in the third statement the plural of the pronoun is used. Will anyone maintain that in speaking to these three friends you have presented three contradictory accounts of your meeting with the president? Let us accord the Bible the same fair treatment that we demand for ourselves.

The previous paragraph dismisses the objection that the one set of narratives says that an angel spoke to the women, while the other set relates that they (the angels) spoke to them. It may be that only one angel did the actual speaking, while the other nodded assent. Or it may be that the second one verbally confirmed the message of the first. Whatever the case may have been, the evangelists were justified in using either the singular or the plural in their reports. One would have to entirely disregard the laws of language and of logic to insist on a discrepancy here.

Fifth-century ivory carving of empty sepulchre; likely made in Rome.

Another alleged contradiction in the resurrection story involves Jesus' appearance(s) on Easter morning. John records that Jesus appeared to Mary Magdalene at the tomb after she returned from informing Peter and John about Jesus' resurrection. Matthew relates that Jesus appeared to the women after they had been at the tomb, as they were on their way to tell the disciples the Easter message. The matter need not detain us long. When Mary Magdalene had hurried away from the tomb to inform the apostles of the removal of the Lord's body, the other women went into the tomb and saw the angels, from whom they heard the glorious Easter tidings. As they were hastening back to bring the message to the disciples, Mary Magdalene returned to the grave, and then and there the risen Lord appeared to her. Immediately after this event He appeared to the other women while they were still on the way home, as Matthew reports. It is true that Mary Magdalene was not with them when this occurred, but is it fair to insist that Matthew's account, to be correct, ought to have read, "And as they went to tell His disciples, behold, Jesus met them, excepting Mary Magdalene" (28:9)?

One more item may be mentioned. Matthew records that the women "ran to tell His disciples" (28:8), while Mark relates: "And they said nothing to anyone, for they were afraid" (16:8). The first passage seems to imply that the women brought the news reported to them by the angels to the disciples. The second says they did not say anything to anyone. The solution of the difficulty is immediately apparent. The statement from Mark refers to the attitude of the women while they were returning home. They were so overawed (which is a better translation than "afraid") that they did not stop at the houses of friends and acquaintances to report what they had seen and heard, but they hastened back to their abode as quickly as they could. Mark certainly does not wish to create the impression that they did not inform the disciples of the message of the angels. According to his narrative, the angels had told the women, "But go, tell His disciples and Peter that He is going before you to Galilee" (16:7). If they had not told the disciples, that would have meant disobedience to the command given them by the messenger of God, and these God-fearing women would not have become guilty of such disobedience.

THE GOSPELS

Jesus Christ brought the Gospel (from older English, "Good-spel," "good news") to the world. He announced that in His person the kingdom of God was coming to mankind and that through faith in Him people might find new and eternal life. He was Himself the Good News, or Gospel.

The word *gospel* was an ancient word when Christians first put it to use with their special meaning. Originally it had meant the reward given to the person who brought good news, and then came to mean the good news itself. On an inscription prepared for the birthday of Octavian Augustus (9 BC) one can still read: "The birthday of the god [that is, the Caesar] was for the world the beginning of glad tidings, which have gone forth for his sake."

When the Christians adopted the term, they related its meaning to Jesus Christ, and they also understood the word to mean that this good news was to be spoken and proclaimed. In the New Testament, *Gospel* usually means to speak the Good News in the power of the Spirit. In the second century the word gradually came to mean a book containing the story of Jesus' life.

The Christian Gospels were a new kind of book. Nothing exactly like them had been written previously. Many biographies of great heroes were in existence. One might think first of biographical sections of the Old Testament, such as the story of Joseph, the calling of Moses, the leadership and adventures of Joshua, the Judges, and David, or the miracle stories of Elijah and Elisha. Several books of the Apocrypha provide similar heroic accounts.

Golden dawn melts the Galilean hills, lights the sea, and illumines the shore where Jesus called fishermen to follow Him.

Alexander the Great was a favorite subject of biographies in the Greek-speaking world. But these stories differed from the New Testament Gospels in several ways. Such Greek biographies paid considerable attention to the facts of the hero's birth, life, and death. They contained character sketches, careful chronological reports, and considerable background material. The Gospels are not this kind of biography.

It would be impossible to construct a week-by-week account of Jesus' life on the basis of the four Gospels. It is, for example, not easy to construct a completely satisfactory record of the order of Jesus' post-resurrection appearances (see pp 169–73). The Gospel writers did not have purely historical purposes in mind. The Christian Gospels are also different from the Greek "miracle biographies," which were very popular in the world of the New Testament. The miracle biographies resembled the Gospels in that they were not attempts to write full historical accounts of the miracle worker's life, but they differ from the Gospels in the often fantastic miracles they report, in the exaggerated difficulties that confront the healer, and in other respects. The Christian Gospel writers are sober and restrained in comparison. In other words, the good news that God was in Christ, reconciling the world unto Himself, could not be told in writing by using any existing book form.

Apostolic Preaching

The Gospels include all that the apostolic preaching (Gk *kerygma*) included: the sending of the Messiah by God in fulfillment of His promises; the Messiah's ministry to mankind, culminating in His death for the sins of all; His resurrection; His exaltation; and the promise of His return. They have the same basic historical outline as apostolic preaching, as a comparison between Peter's sermon in the house of Cornelius (Ac 10:34–43) and the Gospel according to Mark shows at a glance. Their content is more than a biography of Jesus. It is the Way of the Messiah from the time that John the Baptist prepared the way before Him to the time when God raised Him from the dead. They lay bare the redemptive meaning of the Way of the Messiah.

From the start, apostolic teaching was the natural and necessary extension of the missionary Gospel, an organic growth of the growing Word of the Lord. As our Gospels show, this teaching took the form of an ever fuller recital of the words and deeds of Jesus, the concrete details of what Jesus taught and did. This teaching thus satisfied the natural desire of the believing and hoping Church to have a distinct and rounded-out picture of Him who was the object of her faith and hope; but the satisfaction of the historical interest was not the primary concern of this teaching. If it had been, one would expect the accounts to be much fuller, more nearly complete. As it is, the accounts are anything but complete; John in his old age was able to supplement the first three Gospels from his own recollections, and even he makes plain that there is much that remains unwritten (Jn 20:30; 21:25). Likewise, if the historical interest were primary, we should expect the accounts to be more detailed; as it is, they are sparse and terse even in Mark, the most dramatic narrator of them all, while Matthew cuts away everything that is not religiously essential. And in all the evangelists, much that is invaluable from a historical point of view is disregarded (e.g., they do not always set out to establish an exact sequence of events). The basic interest of the teaching is religious—its aim is to confront people with the Christ (Mt 1:1; Mk 1:1), to preserve and strengthen their faith in Him (Jn 20:31), and to bring people into a disciple's total obedience to Him (Mt 28:20).

Fourth-century portrait of Jesus with longer hair, beard, and large eyes. One of the earliest standard portraits, from the catacomb of Commodilla, Rome.

The Gospels are genuinely historical; they record facts, and their account of Jesus' words and deeds follows a historical sequence that is common to the first three Gospels (ministry in Galilee; a period of wanderings; last days; death and resurrection at Jerusalem). But their interest and intent are not merely historical; they do not aim merely at reconstructing a piece of the past. For them, history is the clothing in which the Messiah of God comes in order that He may be revealed and may enter people's lives as the present and potent Christ. The Gospels reflect both halves of Jesus' last words to His disciples, both the command that looks backward, "Teaching them to observe all that I have commanded you," and the promise that marks Him as perpetually present, "Behold, I am with you always" (Mt 28:20).

The Synoptic Problem

The first three Gospels (Matthew, Mark, and Luke) are called the Synoptic Gospels. The word *synoptic* means "presenting or taking the same or a common view," and these Gospels are called "synoptic" because they offer a view of the life, death, and resurrection of Jesus that is basically common to all three of them. One can set down the materials of these three evangelists in parallel columns and study them together, whereas the Gospel according to John would not lend itself to such a form of study.

The Synoptic Problem is posed by the fact that the Synoptic Gospels, for all their basic similarity, present a complex set of agreements and differences in detail. The questions naturally arise: What is the historical relationship between these three writings? How is their striking similarity and dissimilarity to be explained? The modern obsession with this problem has been under discussion for two centuries, and a vast literature has grown up around the subject, but it can hardly be said that a really satisfactory solution has as yet been found. It is neither possible nor necessary to go into detail on this complex problem here; a brief indication of the types of solution that command the widest acceptance, together with a critique that indicates the strength and the inadequacies of each, will suffice by way of introduction.

The Two-Source Hypothesis (or, Two-Document Theory)

The chief proposals of the Two-Source Hypothesis are: (a) Mark is the earliest of the Gospels, and the authors of the first and the third Gospels both used his work as a source in constructing their Gospels. This is based on the observation that Matthew and Luke largely incorporate Mark's subject matter, wording, and sequence of events. Both follow Mark's basic outline and hardly depart from it together; where one departs from it, the other preserves it. (b) Matthew and Luke are assumed to have drawn on another source for the material that they have in common; this source was a document containing chiefly sayings of Jesus and is for convenience labeled Q (from the German word *Quelle*, meaning "source"). (c) The author of this document Q may have been the apostle Matthew. Papias, writing about AD 130, reports that "Matthew compiled the *oracles* in the Hebrew language and individuals translated them as they were able." A Greek translation of this document served as source for the first Gospel, and since that Gospel incorporated Matthew's "Oracles" more fully than any other Gospel, it came to be known as Matthew's Gospel. Its actual author or compiler is unknown.

The Four-Source Hypothesis

The Four-Source Hypothesis is an elaboration of the Two-Source Hypothesis and a recognition of the fact that the Two-Source Hypothesis is too simple to account for all the facts. According to this hypothesis the author of the first Gospel utilized another source in addition to Mark and Q, which is labeled M (material peculiar to Matthew). He also made use of material preserved by oral tradition, probably at Antioch. The third Gospel also utilized another document in addition to Mark and Q, which is labeled L (material peculiar to Luke), and an oral tradition that furnished the materials for the first two chapters of the Gospel.

Critique of the Hypotheses

It should in fairness be said that these theories are much more persuasive when presented in detail, with all the acumen and ingenuity that characterize many of the experts in this field, than in the skeleton form given above. But both theories, no matter how fully and ingeniously argued, suffer from basic weaknesses that must be noted here.

Both theories work with the assumption that the Gospel according to Mark was the first to be written. The arguments for the priority of Mark are certainly strong, but they are based wholly on internal evidence, that is, on the nature of the documents themselves. There is no external evidence to support it, that is, no ancient source says that Mark was written first or that the other evangelists made use of Mark. Internal evidence, like circumstantial evidence in law, is a slippery business, and conclusions based on it alone are bound to be somewhat uncertain. One sees something of this uncertainty in the fact that some scholars believe that Matthew and Luke used an earlier form of Mark, not the Mark that we have today, or an early document having the basic outline of Mark, but not identical with our Mark.

Still others see in Matthew the earliest Gospel and can support their case with a mass of data that cannot simply be dismissed out of hand, especially since the ancient tradition tends to make Matthew the first Gospel in point of time. Unless new evidence is discovered, there will probably always remain a reasonable doubt concerning the priority of Mark. Q is, of course, purely hypothetical, a sort of "X" used to identify an unknown quantity. One may rightly question whether such a document, consisting exclusively or predominantly of sayings of Jesus, ever existed. The apostles and the early apostolic Church never thought of Jesus or proclaimed Jesus merely as a teacher; consequently His words were never thought of as a body of teaching that could be divorced from His acts or from His person as the crucified, risen, and exalted Christ. Jesus was remembered and proclaimed as the Christ, mighty in word and deed, whose works and words were organically bound up together. In all the sermons in Acts, Jesus is quoted just once (Ac 20:35), and it is at first glance a surprising fact that in the whole New Testament outside the Gospels Jesus is so seldom quoted directly, though His word and person dominate and permeate the whole. One can collect the sayings of a rabbi and have in them the distillate of his life's work; the words of the Christ are part of the seamless robe of His Christhood and have their true meaning only as part of the texture of that robe. The way in which Matthew has built the discourses into the structure of His Gospel testifies to this, as does the intimate connection between work and word in the Gospel of John (e.g., Jn 6, the feeding of the five thousand and the discourse on the bread of life).

Fifth-century mosaic inside the Church of the Multiplication, Tabgha, Israel.

One may also legitimately question the way in which the problem of the authorship of the first Gospel is treated in these theories. The ancient church unanimously attributed the first Gospel to Matthew, the tax collector and apostle. It is hard to find a reason for this attribution in anything except the fact that Matthew did write the Gospel. The theory that the Gospel was called Matthew's because it incorporated so much material from his supposed collection of the "oracles of the Lord" can hardly stand up; for the ancient church understood from Papias that Mark's Gospel incorporated the preaching of Peter and emphasized that fact, but the ancient church did not for that reason call it the Gospel according to Peter. Even if the priority of Mark were established beyond all doubt, and the literary relationship between Matthew and Mark could be explained only by assuming that Matthew used Mark as one of his sources, that would not yet disprove the Matthean authorship of the first Gospel. The apostles were practical, praying, hard-working men, not literary men concerned about their reputation as authors. What would have prevented Matthew from utilizing a document by a nonapostle, a document that, moreover, incorporated the preaching of Peter the apostle?

The more elaborate the theories become, the larger the hypothetical element in them becomes. The Two-Source Hypothesis operates with one unknown quantity, Q; the Four-Source Hypothesis (which is really a six-source hypothesis) operates with five unknowns. Where is the evidence by which these conjectures are to be controlled?

Form Criticism

It was perhaps the sterility of synoptic studies of the type treated above that turned some scholars from the investigation of literary relationships in terms of documents to an investigation of the oral Gospel that preceded written documents and in the last analysis underlies all of them. This type of investigation is known as form criticism (Grm *Formgeschichte*). Its aim is to penetrate beyond the written Gospels and the documents underlying the written Gospels to the Gospel as it was proclaimed by missionaries, preached by evangelists, and taught by catechists in the Church.

Basic to this type of investigation is the perception of the fact that our present Gospels are made up of a series of relatively short, self-contained units of narrative and discourse. These units, it is thought, follow rather definite patterns similar to those in which the traditions of other primitive communities are cast. The task of the form critic is, first, to classify these units according to their characteristic forms. Once he has classified them (e.g., as pronouncement stories, miracle stories, myths, legends, wisdom sayings, parables, etc.), he seeks to recover the original form of the story by stripping the present written account of what he considers to be additions and modifications introduced in the course of oral transmission or by the compilers of the written Gospels. When he has recovered the original form of the unit, he seeks to establish its life situation (Grm *Sitz im Leben*); in other words, he attempts to answer the question: For what purpose or to meet what need did the first church preserve, shape, modify, or even invent the story or saying? The critic's ultimate aim is to reconstruct the history of the unit from the time of its oral telling, through the time when modifications were imposed upon it in the process of constant retelling, to the time when it was fixed in writing in our present Gospels.

The merits of this approach are readily seen: it has again called attention to something which, for all its obviousness, has often been lost sight of when the Gospels were studied merely as literary documents, namely to the *preaching* character of the Gospels, their historical connection with the living voice of the proclaiming church. And it has called attention to another pretty obvious feature of the Gospel materials, namely to their practical, church-centered character. Our Gospels are again seen to be books that gather up and perpetuate the "teaching" by which the churches lived and died.

But when one has recognized these legitimate concerns of the method and has appreciated these legitimate emphases, one has said about all that can positively be said for the method. In practice the emphasis of form criticism is all on the Christian community as the creator and bearer of the Gospel tradition; the fact of the apostolate, the fact that Jesus Himself prepared men to be witnesses to Him with divinely given authority and equipped them for their task by His gift of the illumining and empowering Spirit—this fact is largely, if not entirely, ignored. The teaching tradition of the Church is treated as if it were completely parallel to the folklore and the myth-making of all primitive communities, and classifications derived from non-Israelite folklore are applied to the Gospel materials without regard for the uncertainty of these classifications and without questioning their applicability to the Gospel materials. Form critics attribute to the "community" a creative power that is really incredible; while the Gospels themselves and the Book of Acts with one voice proclaim that Jesus the Christ created the Church, the form critics seem to conclude that the Church somehow created the Christ. The net result of their study is the conclusion that the Gospels, which incorporate the tradition of the Christian community, tell us a great deal about the faith of the early Christian community, but very little about Jesus of Nazareth! Not all practitioners of the method are equally radical and negative, of course, but the main current of form criticism does set in that direction.

Conclusions

One wonders whether the Church of God is well served by any of these attempts to penetrate into the substrata of the Gospels which it has pleased God to give to His Church. All of the theories must, in view of the paucity of the evidence, remain highly speculative. None of them in the last analysis contributes much to the understanding of the Gospels as we have them.

Jeffrey Gibbs, in his multi-volume commentary on the Gospel according to Matthew, provides helpful observations on these issues. He notes that the flexibility of the critical theories about the Synoptic Problem makes it difficult to either confirm them or deny them. After undertaking his own careful word-for-word comparison of Matthew and Mark, Gibbs concludes:

> Everyone who has studied parallel passages among the Synoptic Gospels has noticed the slight differences of detail and emphasis that so often characterize units common to two or three of the Gospels. The kind of "controlled" oral transmission that was surely at work in first-century Judea and Galilee offers a ready explanation for such minor differences. Moreover, when one prefers (as I do) fairly early dates in the 50s or early 60s for all three Synoptics, it is likely that the apostles and other eyewitnesses of the Lord Jesus' ministry played a significant role in handing down authentic dominical material to the evangelists and to the church.
>
> All this is merely to say that the "solution" to the Synoptic Problem is likely a complex one. We need to reckon with a number of factors and forces, all operating under the guiding hand of the Holy Spirit, whose inspiration is ultimately responsible for the Synoptic Gospels, and indeed for all of Scripture. (CC Mt1 1:29–30)

The three Synoptic Gospels loom in large and mysterious grandeur, like three great mountains, before the eyes of the Church. The Lord of the Church has given us in our generation abundant materials for the study of their geography; He has given us practically none for the study of their geology. Perhaps our main business is geography, not geology; perhaps it is our business to understand the three Gospels, each on its own terms, in their individual and yet consentient witness to Jesus Christ the Son of God, without exercising ourselves overmuch about the unanswerable question of their origins and their historical interrelationships. There will be unanswered questions and unrelieved tensions enough even so; but the big questions, the question of life-and-death import, the question of the Christ, will be answered; and people can learn to live well and die peacefully without having answers to the others.

MATTHEW

Jesus opened His mouth and taught them

The first book of the New Testament begins in a manner similar to the first book of the Old Testament: focused on genealogy (cf Mt 1:1–17; Gn 5). Matthew sketches for us a human landscape from Abraham, the patriarch of Israel, to Jesus, the Savior of Israel and of the nations. He bridges us from the great eras and figures of sacred history to the climax of all history, "the birth of Jesus Christ" (1:18; cf Gal 4:4).

Matthew is keen to tell both the glorious elements of the story as well as the tragic ones. Jesus is a descendant of the great king David but also a descendant of a defeated people, deported to Babylon. Jesus will grow up in "Galilee of the Gentiles," where a subject people struggled to make a living and to keep the Lord's Word. Throughout the book, Matthew emphasizes how Jesus taught and fulfilled the Word of the Lord for the sake of the people.

Historical and Cultural Setting

If the tradition that the Gospel of Matthew was originally written in Hebrew or Aramaic is correct, Israel is, of course, an obvious and natural place of writing. However, a Greek Gospel would not be an impossibility. When Alexander the Great passed through Israel on his way to conquer Egypt, he brought with him Greek language and learning, which would be preferred by rulers of the region for centuries. The books of Maccabees tell the story of the Greek lan-

The Tree of Jesse bordered by scenes from the life of King David and John the Baptist, who were members of Jesus' broader kinship.

OVERVIEW

Author
Matthew Levi the apostle

Date
Written c AD 50

Places
Galilee; Judea; Nazareth; Capernaum; Tyre and Sidon; Jerusalem; Jericho; Bethany; Jordan River; Mount of Olives; Gethsemane

People
Jesus; John the Baptist; the 12 apostles; Jesus' family; scribes; Pharisees; Sadducees; Herod the Great; Herod Antipas; Mary Magdalene; Mary the mother of James and Joseph; the mother of James and John

Purpose
To proclaim that God's end-times rule has come in the person and ministry of Jesus Christ

Law Themes
God's rule in judgment; repentance; political and religious opposition; authoritative teaching; confronting a brother who sins

Gospel Themes
God's rule in mercy; Gospel; Baptism; compassion; authoritative teaching; ransom; Lord's Supper; forgiving a brother who sins

Memory Verses
Jesus' birth (1:18–25); the Beatitudes (5:1–12); prayer and the Golden Rule (7:7–14); rest from Jesus (11:28–30); parable of the net interpreted (13:47–50); forgiveness and the Church (18:15–20); make disciples (28:18–20)

TIMELINE

2 BC	Birth of Jesus
AD 29	Baptism of Jesus
AD 33	Resurrection, Ascension, Pentecost
c AD 50	Matthew written
AD 68	Martyrdom of Peter and Paul

guage in Israel, which many people eagerly adopted. Even when the Romans conquered Israel, Greek continued as a language of business and learning; it had to be inscribed by the Romans upon Jesus' cross in order to communicate fully with residents of Jerusalem (Jn 19:20).

Although the rulers of Israel favored Greek language and culture, the discovery of the Dead Sea Scrolls and other documents illustrates the tenacity of Jewish culture and language. The local people may have used Greek for business, but their home language, their heart language, was rooted in the languages of their Scriptures.

Jesus was born into an empire ruled by distant Caesar Augustus, who enforced his wishes through local kings: Herod the Great and his descendants. These Idumean (Edomite) rulers maintained control by pleasing Rome and the priestly families in Israel, while resorting to violence as needed. Matthew, who as a tax collector would have cooperated with and served the Herods, does not fail to tell us about their fears and rivalries, which eventually conspired in Jesus' crucifixion. Yet he is equally clear that this was the will of heaven's ruler (Mt 26:36–46) and the fulfillment of Old Testament prophecy.

Caesar Augustus.

Theodotus inscription, which describes the founding and first century AD restoration of a Jerusalem synagogue.

Synagogue and Church

Matthew is the only Gospel that attributes the word *church* to the teachings of Jesus (16:18; 18:17), a point that receives much attention from critical scholars. Some conclude that this is evidence the Gospel was written later in the first century to meet the needs of the later Christian community (e.g., Syrian Antioch) that was emerging from the synagogue.

Composition

Author

The book itself does not name its author. The Early Church, which read and used the first Gospel more often than any other, is unanimous in attributing it to Matthew. No other claim to authorship is ever put forward by anyone. Little is known of Matthew. The Gospels tell us that he was a tax collector at Capernaum and therefore a member of the outcast class publicly branded by the Jewish community as "sinners." Mark and Luke call him Levi (Mk 2:14; Lk 5:27), the son of Alphaeus; only the first Gospel calls him Matthew. It may be that he was originally called Levi and that Jesus gave him the name Matthew (Hbr or Aramaic for "Gift of God"), just as He named the sons of Zebedee "Boanerges" and gave Simon his significant name "Peter." Or Matthew may have had two names to begin with. At any rate, we may assume that "Matthew" was the name by which he was best known in the Jewish Christian community and thus became the name attached to the Gospel attributed to him.

Matthew is not prominent in the New Testament record of the twelve apostles. All three of the early evangelists tell the story of his call and of the feast that he gave to celebrate this turning point in his life, and all three record that he was among the Twelve; but they tell the story of his calling (the only one recorded after the calling of the first four disciples) not as a part of the record of a prominent apostle, but as a testimony to the supreme grace of the Christ, who called into His fellowship and made His messenger one whom Judaism expelled and degraded (Mt 9:9–13; Mk 2:13–17; Lk 5:27–32). As a tax collector, either under the Roman government or under Herod Antipas at Capernaum, he would be a man of some education, skilled in numbers, speaking both Aramaic and Greek, and a man of substance. Early tradition has it that he first preached the Gospel to his countrymen in Israel, originally wrote his Gospel in their tongue, and later went abroad as a missionary to other nations. The tradition concerning his later career is relatively late, tends to be fantastic and legendary in character, and often confuses Matthew with Matthias, so that it offers little or no basis for constructing a reliable history of Matthew the evangelist.

The evangelist Matthew visited by an angel.

Date of Composition

The Early Church generally deemed the Gospel according to Matthew the earliest of the Gospels; somewhere between AD 50 and 60 is a probable date. The book itself offers no certain data for determining the time of writing.

Purpose/Recipients

The Gospel according to Matthew was apparently written for religious instruction, perhaps for Jewish Christians. Matthew helps his readers understand the Old Testament Scriptures correctly in view of Jesus' fulfillment of Old Testament prophecies (c 35 times). Within a generally chronological framework that is common to the first three Gospels, the arrangement of the deeds and words of the Christ is more topical than chronological. The facts are massed and marshaled in impressive and easily remembered units of three, five, and seven. Thus we have in Matthew three major divisions in the genealogy of Jesus with which the Gospel opens (Mt 1:1–17), three illustrations of hypocrisy and pure piety (6:1–18), and three parables of planting and growth (13:1–32). Jesus' words are presented in five great discourses (chs 5–7, 10, 13, 18, 23–25), and within the Sermon on the Mount Matthew records five examples that illustrate the full intention of God's Law (5:21–48; note the repetition of "you have heard"). Jesus in this Gospel pronounces seven woes upon the scribes and Pharisees (23:13–36), and the great parable chapter (ch 13) contains just seven parables. This topical arrangement is not absolutely peculiar to Matthew; Mark, for instance, twice gives a grouping of five disputes between Jesus and His Judaic adversaries, once in Galilee (Mk 2:1–3:6) and again in Jerusalem (Mk 11:27–12:44). But it is found in Matthew in a fuller and more highly developed form than in any of the other evangelists.

Matthew used what one may call an "extreme case" method; that is, Matthew illustrates the bent of Jesus' will by means of words and deeds that indicate the extreme limit to which Jesus went (as we illustrate a man's generosity, for instance, by saying, "He'd give you the shirt off his back"). The first public address (discourse) of Jesus in Matthew begins with the blessings upon the "poor"—Jesus promises the Kingdom and all its blessings to the beggar, to the "poor in spirit" (Mt 5:3); this removes every limitation from the grace of God and makes it as wide and as deep as the need of mankind. In Matthew's account of Jesus' miracles the first three are extreme-case miracles, which illustrate the lengths to which the compassion of Jesus will go (8:1–15). Jesus heals the leper whom the Law cannot help, but must exclude from the people of God; He helps the Gentile who is outside the pale of God's people; and He restores to health the woman whom some in Judaism degraded to the rank of a second-rate creature of God. Now people can take the measure of the potent grace of God present and at work in the Christ. And they can measure the greatness of the divine forgiveness that Jesus brings by another extreme case, by the fact that Jesus calls a tax collector (whom the synagogue branded as sinner and excluded) to be His disciple and His apostle and His table companion (9:9–13).

How rigorous and all-inclusive Jesus' call to repentance is can again be seen by an extreme case: Jesus calls just the righteous to repentance; more, He imposes the call to repentance upon the men who have become His disciples too (18:1–4). When Jesus bids His disciples love their *enemies*, He has removed every limitation from their loving (5:44). When He threatens Peter (the disciple who was ready to forgive seven times) with the wrath of the divine King if he will not forgive without limit, the fullness of the fraternal charity that Jesus both inspires in and demands of His disciples is spelled out in unmistakable clarity. How completely Jesus binds the disciple to Himself can be seen in the fact that Jesus makes His own cross (the climax of His life of ministry) the impulse and the standard of the disciple's ministry (10:38;

16:24; 20:25–28). In all these ways, the Gospel amplifies the uniqueness of Jesus' teaching and mercy, which create a distinct body of disciples.

Literary Features

Genre

Matthew's work is a Gospel—theology presented in a biographical format (see pp 175–77). A unique feature of Matthew's account is His arrangement of Jesus' sayings and teachings into five long speeches, commonly called "discourses." These collections of Jesus' sayings likely indicate that Matthew was less concerned about preserving specific chronological order and more concerned about illustrating consistency of themes in Jesus' teaching at different times during His ministry.

Characters

A prominent feature in Matthew's teaching about **Jesus** is the use of contrasts, similar to that process in the pictorial arts that creates its impression not by the clearly drawn line, but by the skillful blocking out of figures and features by means of contrasting areas of light and shade (chiaroscuro). For example, in the genealogy of Jesus, Matthew marks Jesus as son of Abraham and son of David, the crowning issue of Israel's history (Mt 1:1–17). The immediately following section is in sharp contrast to this: here it is made plain that God gives to Israel what her history cannot; the Messiah is not the product of Israel's history, but God's creative intervention in that history of guilt and doom; Jesus is conceived by the Holy Spirit (1:18–23). Jesus in the Beatitudes promises to His disciples all the blessings of the kingdom of the heavens, all the glory of the world to come (5:3–9)—and puts them under the yoke of persecution "for righteousness' sake" (5:10–12). The Christ miraculously multiplies the loaves and fishes and sets a table for thousands in the wilderness (15:32–39)—and yet refuses to show a sign from heaven when the leaders of Judaism demand one (16:1–4). The woman who spent her money lavishly in order to anoint the dying Christ is put in close and sharp contrast with the disciple who betrayed Him for money (26:6–13; 26:14–16). The Messiah who in sovereign grace gives Himself, His body and His blood, to His disciples and goes freely into death to inaugurate the New Covenant is set side by side with the Messiah whose "soul is very sorrowful, even to death" in Gethsemane (26:26–29; 26:36–46). The Son of Man who claims a seat upon the very throne of God and proclaims that He will return upon "the clouds of heaven" (26:64) upon the cross cries out, "My God, My God, why have You forsaken Me?" (27:46).

Thus the Christ portrays the absoluteness of His grace for mankind and the absoluteness of His claim upon them by recording both His claim to an absolute communion with God, which strikes His contemporaries as blasphemous, and His full and suffering humanity, which makes Him a stumbling block to His contemporaries. It is the historical Jesus of Nazareth who is being portrayed, but He is in His every word and work portrayed and proclaimed as Christ the Son of God: He is *the* Son who alone of men gives God the glory that is due Him, who alone does battle with Satan and overcomes him, who alone gives His life a ransom for many. He is not a sage, so that His significance for mankind can be told in His words alone; He is not a hero, whose deeds alone can signify what He means in history. He is the Christ, and His whole person, His words and works as a unity, must be recounted if we are to know Him, believe in Him, and have eternal life in His name.

Matthew records that Jesus was bound and scourged before going to the cross, as depicted by Caravaggio in this chiaroscuro painting of Jesus (c 1605-1607).

The deep interest in the **disciples** of Jesus displayed by all the Gospels is further testimony to their "teaching" character. In all the Gospels Jesus' first messianic act (after His Baptism and temptation) is the calling of disciples; in all of them the story of Jesus' ministry is told in terms of the widening cleavage between Jesus and Israel on the one hand and the deepening communion between Jesus and His disciples on the other. And in all the Gospels the supreme revelation of the Messiah, the appearance of the risen Lord, is granted to the disciples alone. But Matthew gives us the fullest account of the creation of the disciples, how Jesus called them, how He trained them, how they failed in the face of the cross, and how the risen Lord forgave and restored them. The five discourses of Jesus, which determine the structure of Matthew's Gospel, are all addressed to disciples; and the last word of Jesus in Matthew's record of Him is "Make disciples" (28:19). The thought that is in all the Gospels, that Jesus sought nothing and found nothing in the world except the men whom the Father gave Him, His disciples, comes out with special force and clarity in Matthew. As God is known by His works, so the Christ becomes known to others by His disciples, by the men whom He called and molded in His own image.

Narrative Development or Plot

Jeffrey A. Gibbs, whose commentaries take a narrative approach to reading Matthew, summarizes the development of Matthew's Gospel in the following way:

> Matthew's narrative consists of three major blocks, which extend from 1:1 to 4:17, from 4:17 to 16:20, and from 16:21 to 28:20. The first block introduces, in seminal form, the person and significance of Jesus. The second section narrates both his eschatological ministry of word and deed in Israel as well as the contrast between those who confess his true identity (albeit imperfectly) and those who increasingly oppose and seek to destroy him. The third major block is dominated explicitly by the goal of the Gospel, namely, the death and resurrection of Jesus. (CC Mt1 1:40)

For more details of Matthew's narrative, see CC Mt1 1:40–47.

Resources

The resources that Matthew clearly drew upon were the Scriptures of the Old Testament, to which he referred repeatedly. For critical theories about how the Gospel was written, see pp 178–83.

Text and Translations

As noted above, early tradition held that Matthew originally wrote the Gospel in Aramaic or Hebrew (see p 185). If true, our Greek text of Matthew would necessarily be a translation from the original. Although some scholars have suggested examples of wording in the Greek that points to a Hebrew or Aramaic original, the matter is inconclusive, so that the state of the Greek text interests us most. The text of the Gospel appears in numerous early Greek manuscripts, some dateable as early as the second century. Only the Gospel of John is better represented in Greek papyri. Matthew includes no longer additions to its account, like the long ending of Mark (Mk 16:9–20 and variations) or the story of the woman caught in adultery (Jn 7:53–8:11, or after Lk 21:38). Matthew had a favored status in antiquity likely due to its usefulness for teaching, which contributed to its priority in the order of the canon.

Outline

Matthew divides at 4:17 and again at 16:21 with these words: "From that time Jesus began to . . ." Another important dividing phrase appears at the end of each discourse: "And when Jesus had finished . . ." (7:28; 11:1; 13:53; 19:1; 26:1). The outline below reflects these natural divisions within the text.

- I. The Person of Jesus Christ (1:1–4:16)
    - A. The Genealogy, Birth, and Childhood of Jesus Christ (chs 1–2)
    - B. The Ministry of John the Baptist and of Jesus (3:1–4:16)
- II. The Proclamation and Ministry of Jesus Christ to Israel (4:17–16:20)
    - A. Jesus Begins Ministry to Israel (4:17–25)
    - B. First Discourse: The Sermon on the Mount (chs 5–7)
    - C. The Deeds of Jesus Christ (chs 8–9)
    - D. Second Discourse: The Missionary Discourse (10:1–11:1)
    - E. Jesus' Ministry Meets with Opposition and Prompts Division (11:2–12:50)
    - F. Third Discourse: The Parable Discourse (13:1–52)
    - G. Continuing Opposition and Jesus' Identity (13:53–16:20)
- III. The Suffering, Death, and Resurrection of Jesus Christ for Israel and All People (16:21–28:20)
    - A. Jesus Approaches Jerusalem, Where He Will Suffer, Die, and Be Raised (16:21–17:27)
    - B. The Fourth Discourse: The Church Is Founded on the Forgiveness of Sins (ch 18)
    - C. Jesus Continues toward Jerusalem in the Face of Opposition (chs 19–20)

D. Jesus' Ministry in Jerusalem, Where He Meets Confrontation and Rejection (chs 21–23)
E. Fifth Discourse: The Eschatological Discourse (chs 24–25)
F. Jesus' Passion (chs 26–27)
  1. The plot against Jesus (26:1–16)
  2. Passover becomes the Lord's Supper (26:17–29)
  3. Jesus foretells Peter's denial (26:30–35)
  4. Jesus' arrest and trial (26:36–27:26)
  5. Jesus is mocked, crucified, and buried (27:27–66)
G. Jesus Rises from the Dead and Sends the Eleven (ch 28)

Doctrinal Content

Summary Commentary

Chs 1–2 In the genealogy of Jesus Christ, Matthew makes no effort to hide sinners and scandals. Instead, he highlights them. Jesus' ancestors include prostitutes, adulterers, violent men, and other sinners of all descriptions. The story of Jesus' origins continues with Joseph, who serves as a model for believers. Before Joseph knew the reason for Mary's pregnancy, he wanted to treat her justly but mercifully. However, when God's angel reveals the unique miracle of a virginal conception, Joseph believes, and he fulfills his responsibilities by marrying his betrothed and raising Jesus.

The Adoration of the Magi (fresco), third century AD.

THE KINGDOM OF HEROD. Appointed as King of Judea by the Romans, Herod the Great was staunchly loyal to Rome during his reign (37–1 BC). By c 20 BC, Herod controlled the purple area on this map. He rebuilt some 22 cities and fortresses, including Caesarea Maritima, Sebaste, Herodium, and Masada. His greatest monument was the Jerusalem temple.

After Herod's death, the bulk of his kingdom was divided among three of his sons. Archelaus succeeded him in Judea, Idumea, and Samaria. Antipas became tetrarch of Galilee and Perea. Philip received Ituraea, Gaulanitis, Batanea, Trachonitis, and Auranitis. Archelaus was deposed in AD 6, and his lands became a Roman imperial province governed from Caesarea Maritima and Jerusalem.

Agrippa I (Herod's grandson) would rule almost all of Herod's former lands through the favor of Gaius Caesar (Caligula) and, later, Claudius Caesar. Agrippa II ruled some of this territory, but not Judea. Paul appeared before Agrippa II on his way to Rome (Ac 25:13–26:32).

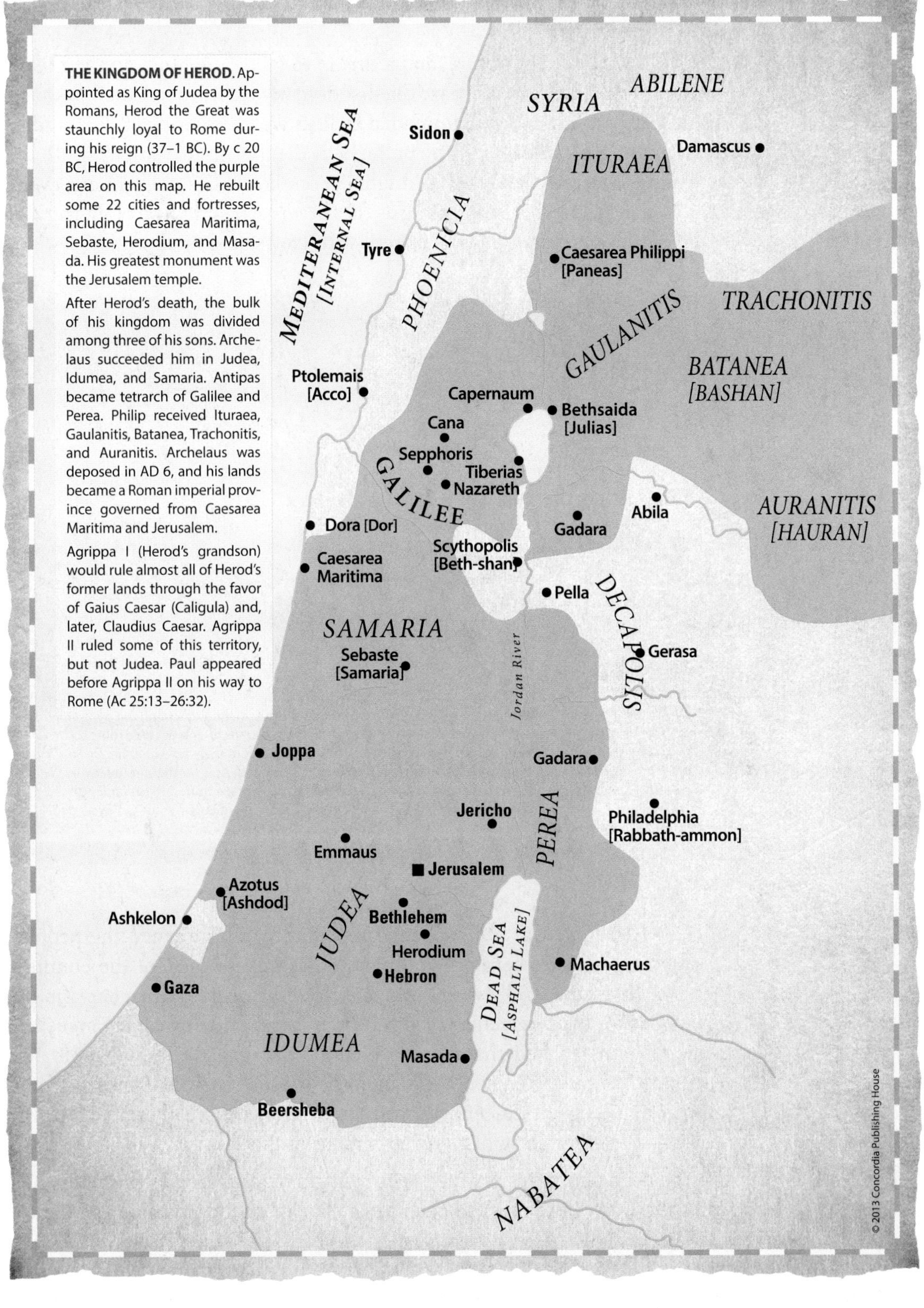

God uses a star, Scripture, and a dream to guide the Magi on their way to and from Bethlehem. They are the first of many Gentiles to worship Jesus. After God's warning, Joseph immediately flees with his family in the middle of the night. The young boys of Bethlehem die, but Jesus escapes death at the hands of Herod, that later He might die on the cross for all sinners, even ones as cruel as Herod or as young as these two-year-olds. The Holy Family finally settles permanently in Nazareth with God's guidance.

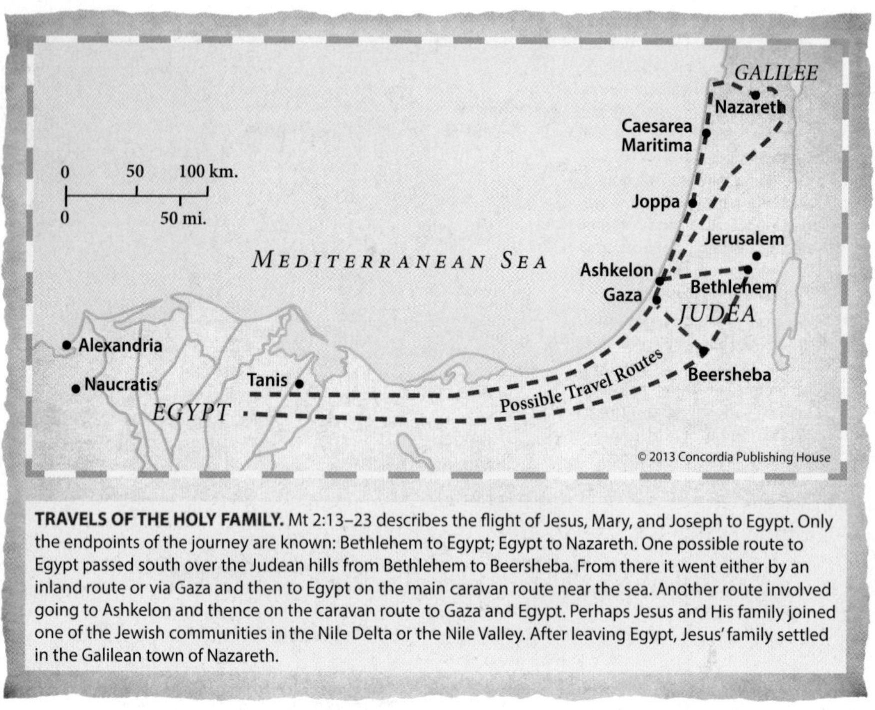

TRAVELS OF THE HOLY FAMILY. Mt 2:13–23 describes the flight of Jesus, Mary, and Joseph to Egypt. Only the endpoints of the journey are known: Bethlehem to Egypt; Egypt to Nazareth. One possible route to Egypt passed south over the Judean hills from Bethlehem to Beersheba. From there it went either by an inland route or via Gaza and then to Egypt on the main caravan route near the sea. Another route involved going to Ashkelon and thence on the caravan route to Gaza and Egypt. Perhaps Jesus and His family joined one of the Jewish communities in the Nile Delta or the Nile Valley. After leaving Egypt, Jesus' family settled in the Galilean town of Nazareth.

3:1–4:16 John was a preacher of repentance, who warned the people of Israel about God's coming wrath as well as His promise of the coming Messiah. To escape God's wrath, John baptized the people with a baptism of repentance for the forgiveness of sins. When Jesus suddenly came to receive baptism, John realized that he was unworthy to baptize Jesus, whom he recognized as the promised Messiah. When Jesus received Baptism from John, the Holy Spirit descended on Jesus, and God the Father spoke from heaven—a manifestation of all three persons of the Trinity.

The devil tempts Jesus to seek His own glory. Jesus refuses this path and walks the way of the cross to become the Savior of those walking in darkness and the shadow of death, who are unable to find their way and lacking the ability to help themselves. He is the light of the world, whose great light shines first in humble Galilee.

4:17–25 Ch 4 ends with a transitional passage in which Jesus takes up the message of repentance and the kingdom of heaven that John had preached. He also calls disciples and heals the sick, attracting great crowds and fulfilling Old Testament prophecies.

Ch 5 Jesus' first discourse (chs 5–7), the Sermon on the Mount. He introduces it with nine beatitudes that detail the future blessedness of His disciples. Only after Jesus has assured His disciples of God's goodness to them does He call on them, in the rest of His sermon, to be good and do good. Luther noted: "At this point you will discover how hard it is to do the good works God commands. . . . You will find out that you will be occupied with the practice of this work for the rest of your life" (AE 44:109). Some people, when confronted with the strict demands of the Law, will whittle off a point here, another there. They suggest that we do the best we can, and God will be satisfied. But God demands perfection, which sinners cannot achieve (cf Rm 7:21–25; 1Tm 1:15).

Ch 6 Jesus calls us to hide our good works when we are tempted to show them. Our works must glorify the Father. After Jesus warns His disciples not to pray in an ostentatious or merely repetitious manner, He provides them with an ideal prayer. Jesus does not command His disciples to discontinue acts of piety such as fasting, but to make sure that they are done to God's glory (cf 1Co 10:31). As with Jesus' parables, we need to look for His central teaching about treasures and worry: seek God's salvation first, and then entrust your daily life to His loving care.

Ch 7 One of the most difficult tasks for a Christian is to speak to a fellow believer about some personal fault (cf Mt 18:15). This is especially difficult within a family or a congregation. Jesus sets forth a basic rule that needs to be observed: first, practice self-examination. Jesus also emphasizes the blessings and importance of prayer. Most important is our heavenly Father's eagerness to give His children "good things." Jesus' teachings in the Sermon on the Mount show us our sins and describe the path on which we, as repentant children of God, seek to walk. Just as there are two ways, the good and the bad, so there are two kinds of prophets. Jesus begins this sermon by declaring that God blesses the poor in spirit, the mourning, the meek, and those who are hungry for God's saving righteousness (5:3–12). He concludes by picturing the secure future guaranteed to the wise disciple who hears His words and does them.

Ch 8 Cleansing the leper is the first of 10 miracles that Jesus performs in chs 8–9. Jesus' words possess power and authority. The centurion believes this, and his faith is not in vain. However, other would-be disciples of Jesus fail to count the cost. One disciple is too quick in promising to follow, while the other is too slow to follow. By calming a storm, Jesus shows His faithful disciples that He has divine authority (cf Ps 65:7; 89:9). The great calm that the disciples experienced is a foretaste of the truly blessed conditions that all believers will enjoy in the new creation. Demons are especially active in opposing Jesus' ministry. But they cannot stymie God's Son, who repeatedly shows His authority over them.

Ch 9 A paralytic brought to Jesus hopes for physical healing. He receives an even greater blessing: absolution—the sacred act of loosing a person from sin, freeing him or her from guilt. Matthew records the shock people felt when Jesus ate with tax collectors and sinners, even calling Matthew to be His disciple! Jesus also overturns the religious teachings and practices of the day by not fasting and by showing special care for a woman and a girl. He answers the blind men's cries for mercy by restoring their sight. When the mute man speaks, the crowds recognize that Jesus is someone special. As He travels around Galilee, the need for partners to preach the Gospel becomes more and more obvious.

10:1–11:1 Jesus' missionary (second) discourse. He selects representatives to extend His gracious kingdom. They are named individually and given divine authority, demonstrating Jesus' personal care for each disciple. He warns them that not everyone will receive them hospitably or listen to their message. However, enemies of the Gospel can persecute believers only within limits set by our heavenly Father. The radical nature of following Jesus may even result in conflict and divisions within families and sacrificing earthly benefits. He concludes His sermon by promising a reward to those who support the Gospel message and fellow disciples.

11:2–30 Jesus encourages John's disciples by noting the progress of the Kingdom that both He and John proclaimed, demonstrating that He is indeed the Messiah promised through John. However, Jesus is deeply grieved that some who have had the greatest opportunity to hear the Gospel stubbornly refuse to repent and believe. God's gracious plan of salvation, hidden from the wise and understanding, relieves those burdened by the Law.

Ch 12 God's purpose in giving the Sabbath law was to provide physical rest for His people. The accusations of the Pharisees provide another example of how Jesus took on Himself the sins of the world. As the Servant of the Lord, Jesus proclaims justice to all nations, a justice that rightfully

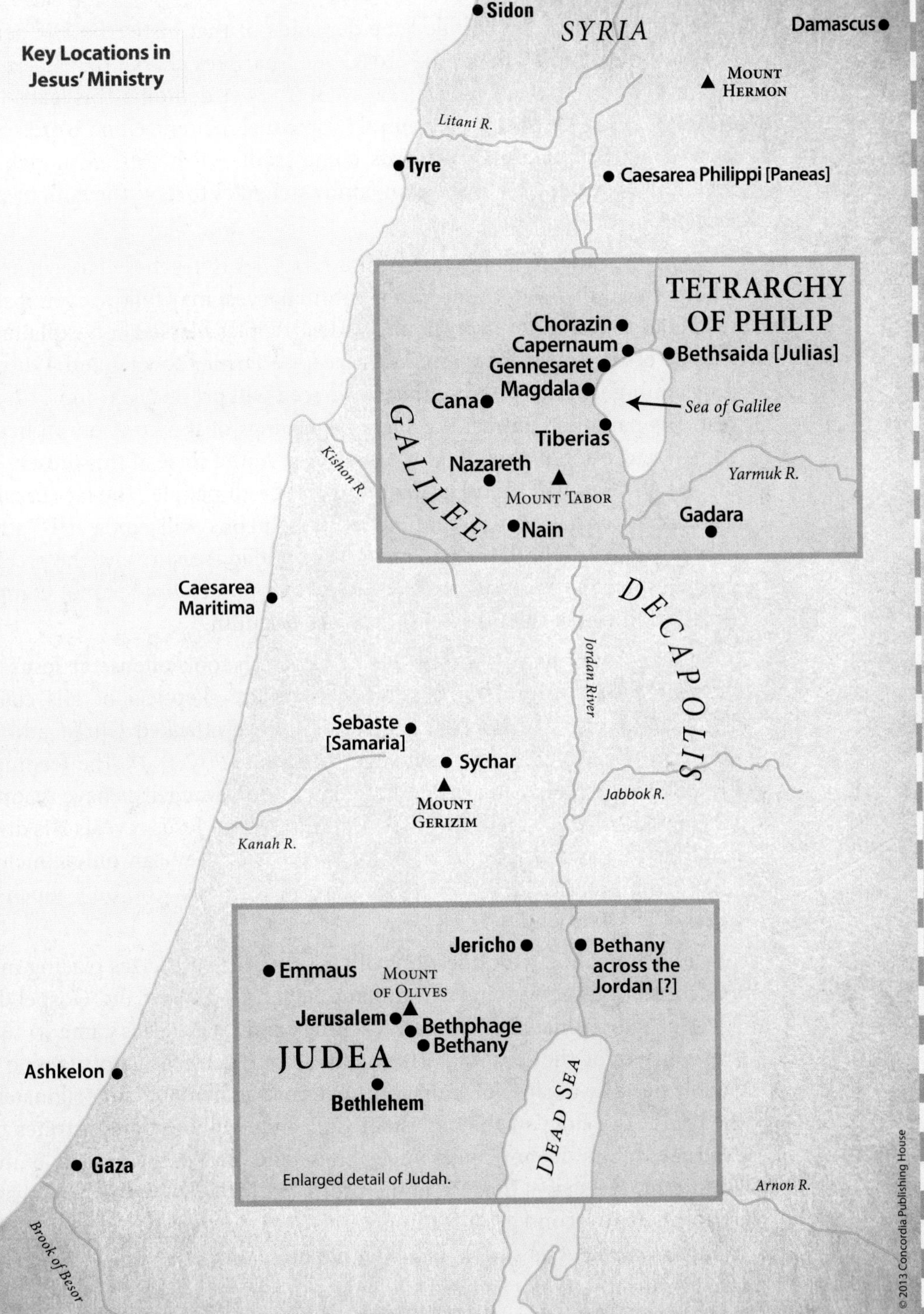

Key Locations in Jesus' Ministry
Sidon
SYRIA
Damascus
Mount Hermon
Litani R.
Tyre
Caesarea Philippi [Paneas]
TETRARCHY OF PHILIP
Chorazin
Capernaum
Bethsaida [Julias]
Gennesaret
Magdala
Cana
Sea of Galilee
GALILEE
Tiberias
Kishon R.
Nazareth
Yarmuk R.
Mount Tabor
Gadara
Nain
Caesarea Maritima
DECAPOLIS
Jordan River
Sebaste [Samaria]
Sychar
Mount Gerizim
Jabbok R.
Kanah R.
Jericho
Bethany across the Jordan [?]
Emmaus
Mount of Olives
Jerusalem
Bethphage
Bethany
JUDEA
Ashkelon
Bethlehem
Dead Sea
Gaza
Enlarged detail of Judah.
Arnon R.
Brook of Besor
© 2013 Concordia Publishing House

condemns sinners. He fulfilled the demands of that justice by His perfect life and innocent death on the cross. The Pharisees charge that Beelzebul, the prince of demons, enables Jesus to overpower demons. This leads Jesus to declare that one cannot be neutral in spiritual matters. Good words come from good hearts, and evil words come from evil hearts. Although His greatness is evident, even His own family struggles to have the faith basic to discipleship.

13:1–52 The parable (third) discourse. Jesus teaches that when His laborer faithfully sows the seed, a plentiful harvest may follow, even if some seed goes to waste. Jesus pronounces His disciples blessed and explains the parable of the sower for them. What keeps a farmer sowing and a disciple proclaiming is Jesus' promise that some seed will produce a wonderful harvest. His parables contrast the small beginnings of the kingdom of heaven with its exceptional, though hidden, growth. At the close of this present age, the Son of Man will send His angels to gather all people. The law-breakers will suffer eternal punishment, and the righteous will enjoy the Father's heavenly glory. In both the parables of the hidden treasure and the precious pearl, Jesus reinforces this basic truth: earthly possessions cannot compare with the immense value and cost of God's kingdom.

13:53–16:20 Just as the people of Nazareth took offense at Jesus and refused to believe in Him, so today many are skeptical of His claims. Throughout history, wicked earthly rulers have attacked Christ and His kingdom (cf 2:16–18). But their rage is in vain (Ps 2:1–2). The feeding of the 5,000 is obviously important because all four evangelists have recorded this miracle that bolstered the disciples' faith. When Jesus reveals His divine presence to His disciples by walking on the sea, they can only conclude: "Truly You are the Son of God." He even heals many who only touch the tassel of His garment!

Jesus is dealing with questions of Law when He criticizes placing man-made traditions above God's Commandments. God's Law and Gospel dare never be subordinated to human teachings and rules. Jesus came to fulfill every aspect of the Law that He might be our perfect Savior. People are unholy because of sin, not from some external defilement. Sin originates in the heart. The story of the persistent Canaanite woman demonstrates that external factors do not cause uncleanness and that faith in Jesus is most important. He shows that He is the promised Messiah by the healings He performs. The second great feeding miracle of Jesus reminds us of how God miraculously fed His people Israel with manna and quail in the wilderness (Ex 16; Nu 11).

When miracles fail to lead the Pharisees and Sadducees to faith, Jesus points them to the sign of Jonah, Jesus' death and resurrection. He warns the disciples against the teaching of the Pharisees and Sadducees. Peter confesses faith in Jesus as the Messiah and Son of God, a climax in the Gospel.

16:21–17:27 Peter genuinely thinks he is helping Jesus when he tries to talk Him out of suffering and death. Talk of suffering and death, taking up one's cross, and losing one's life sounds strange and foreboding to Jesus' disciples. The transfiguration of Jesus confirms for the disciples that He truly is the Messiah, the Son of the living God, as Peter confessed (16:16). The transfiguration is a foretaste of coming glory: Christ's resurrection and His earthly appearances afterward, His ascension, and finally heaven. When Jesus heals a demon-possessed boy, whom His disciples were unable to help, He shows them how their faith is still faltering. He tells His disciples repeatedly that He is going to suffer, die, and rise. Despite His greatness and glory, He humbly submits to paying the temple tax so as not to cause offense, continuing to fulfill the requirements of the Law and noble expectations.

A Hebrew/Aramaic ostracon letter requesting payment of a very large debt, similar to the circumstances of Jesus' parable in Mt 18.

Ch 18 The forgiveness (fourth) discourse. Jesus demonstrates that humility is the hallmark of greatness in the kingdom of heaven. One need look no further than Jesus' words about temptation to see how much the holy God hates sin. Yet Jesus compares the Father's love for His little ones to that of a shepherd who left his 99 sheep to search for the one who went astray. He commands the Church to do all it can to regain an unrepentant sinner. To humbly and lovingly speak to such a brother or sister is to follow the example of the shepherd who searched for one lost sheep. Christ has promised to stand behind the actions of the Church in either forgiving or refusing to forgive sins. God has forgiven us far more than we will ever be called on to forgive.

Ch 19 Sin has deeply affected our human relationships to the point that its effects seem normal, but they are not. When questioned about marriage and divorce, Jesus emphasizes that a lifelong, monogamous union is God's intent for a man and a woman. He instituted marriage to be a gift and a blessing. (Jesus also affirms the value of a single lifestyle.) Jesus welcomes children and makes it clear that they, too, have a place in the Kingdom. We cannot earn eternal life through our good works; we can only receive it by God's grace. But Jesus still rewards our sacrifices and service for Him.

Ch 20 Serving the Lord's kingdom is a privilege and labor of love, not something undertaken to gain a reward. For a third and final time, Jesus predicts His Passion. (Ironically, Jesus' three predictions will match the number of Peter's denials.) Jesus continues to convince His disciples that in His kingdom, humility and service, not acclaim and power, are most highly valued. Though the nearness of the crowd and His own impending death weigh heavily on Him, Jesus is not too preoccupied to help two blind men.

Ch 21 Palm Sunday is another high point, as a crowd at the Jewish capital openly acclaims Jesus as Messiah. It is also a turning point, however, since it galvanizes His opponents. Immediately after being acclaimed Messiah, Jesus further provokes the Jewish leaders by driving merchants and money-changers out of the temple. By cursing a fruitless fig tree, Jesus reveals symbolically God's judgment against the faithless and fruitless portion of His covenant people. When His opponents challenge the source of His authority, Jesus exhibits divine wisdom. He warns His opponents that rejecting Him will ultimately lead to their exclusion from the Kingdom.

Ch 22 Jesus contends again with the leaders in Jerusalem by teaching that although God earnestly invites all to His Son's feast, some refuse to accept His invitation and so fail to enjoy its richness. Jesus' followers owe loyalty and obedience not only to Him but also to the human rulers that God Himself has established. Though Christians may be tempted to avoid taxes and shirk civic responsibilities, they must "render to Caesar." Jesus next vindicates Israel's resurrection hope by masterfully interpreting the Scriptures given them through Moses. He avoids every trap set by His opponents, correctly identifying love for God and for neighbor as the two main concerns of the divine Commandments. Jesus' authoritative interpretation of the Old Testament proves that the Messiah is not merely human but also divine.

Ch 23 Jesus sharply criticizes the scribes and the Pharisees for hypocrisy and obstinacy. Just days before His sacrificial death for all people, He laments the fact that so many of His people reject Him and the gift of eternal life. In the end, those who reject Jesus and refuse His offer of eternal life will be judged.

Ch 24 Jesus' (fifth) discourse about the end times fills chs 24–25. In response to His disciples' admiring comments about the temple, Jesus predicts its destruction. He further prophesies about things leading up to the end of the world. Jesus warns His disciples against being deceived by false messiahs. He describes the manner (though not the exact time) of His second coming. He will come in glory on the clouds of heaven as the Savior. For those who reject Jesus and the Gospel, the reminder that He is standing at the gate is a threat of judgment and condemnation. The suddenness of Christ's second coming, along with His promise that faithfulness will be richly rewarded, moves us to watch eagerly for Jesus.

Ch 25 Jesus warns that many invited to share in the eternal joy of His kingdom will miss out by failing to have a living faith at the end. Though some will be condemned for heinous crimes and gross sins, many more will fail to enter heaven because they neglected their faith. Our relationship to God and the world is one of stewardship. We are to use everything entrusted to us in such a way that it benefits God's kingdom. On the Last Day, Jesus will separate true believers from hypocrites and those who reject Him. The faithful will be vindicated and welcomed into heaven, while unbelievers will be condemned.

Last Supper, sixth-century Ravenna mosaic. The figures closest to Jesus look to Him while the other disciples look at the figure on the right, who may be Judas.

Ch 26 Both Jesus and His enemies long for His impending death. They plot to kill Him, but He determines to offer up His life for them and for the whole world. A woman anoints Jesus, which greatly offends His disciples. Jesus, however, commends the woman, because her action points to His death. Judas then agrees to betray Jesus for 30 pieces of silver. As Jesus transforms the Passover into the Lord's Supper for the forgiveness of sins, He warns Judas against betraying Him. The disciples, especially Peter, do not perceive the danger of that night. They think they are strong enough to face anything without denying Christ. While Jesus prays three times in Gethsemane, His disciples give themselves over to sleep rather than to prayer. Judas betrays Jesus, but Jesus refuses to allow His disciples to use vio-

Third century fresco of a child being baptized. Catacombs of San Callisto, Rome.

lence to defend Him. Jesus stands trial before the Council. He notes that He will come again to judge them and all who have sinned. He makes this confession so He can go to the cross and die for all who have perverted justice. Peter denies Jesus three times.

Ch 27 Morning brings another climax in the story and in all of history as the leaders in Jerusalem hand Christ over to Pilate for judgment. Jesus silently listens to His accusers. The crowd chooses Barabbas instead of Jesus, and Pilate condemns Jesus to death while he seeks to absolve himself of responsibility for it. The Roman soldiers mock Jesus as a false king. He is crucified and reviled on every hand. After Jesus cries in agony at His abandonment, He dies. His death is followed by supernatural signs. After Jesus is buried, the chief priests and their allies secure Jesus' tomb to prevent a faked resurrection. Their act, done out of unbelief, will ironically give compelling evidence for the resurrection.

Ch 28 The story concludes with the testimony of various witnesses. The women see the empty tomb and the angel, who proclaims that Christ has risen. The guards report His resurrection to the authorities, but the authorities prefer to create and spread a lie. Christ commissions His disciples as witnesses, to go and make disciples of all nations through Baptism and teaching. He promises to be with all who believe and bear witness to Him.

Specific Law Themes

Matthew focuses his readers on Jesus' message of God's rule or kingdom. With God's rule comes His Word of the Law, authority, and judgment. Even the King's presence alone may provoke trembling as He drives out demons and rebukes the self-righteous. The message of the Kingdom is one of repentance. Jesus and the disciples consistently face political and religious opposition, which ultimately brings suffering and the cross. Chapter 18 describes the challenges of dealing with sin and sinners in the community of faith.

Specific Gospel Themes

The message of God's rule is also a message of mercy. The King constantly displays compassion to the outcasts and the ill. He proclaims Good News and sanctifies Baptism for hallowing His disciples. A key element of Jesus' authoritative teaching is the forgiveness of sins, which may accompany His miracles of healing. The King comes to ransom His people from bondage to sin and institutes a new Passover for forgiveness and nurture of faith: the Lord's Supper. Every sinner will be welcomed back into the fellowship of the community of faith through the call to repentance and the forgiveness of sins.

Specific Doctrines

Jesus called Matthew as a tax collector. Like Paul, Matthew vividly experienced the call of Jesus as the absolute divine grace that it was. Matthew no doubt deserved the title that the synagogue gave him—he was a "sinner." He had, in becoming a tax collector, turned his back upon the promise and the blessing given to Israel and had expressed his indifference toward the Law; he had turned to a life whose basic note was a self-seeking materialism. Jesus' call therefore meant for him a radical break with a sinful past. Repentance was for him a complete 180-degree turn from sin and self to the grace of God that grasped him in Jesus. Matthew's own experience had given him an unusually keen awareness of how completely and hopelessly man's sin can separate him from God and had impressed upon him with unforgettable sharpness the fact that only the grace of the Christ can recall someone from that separation into fellowship with God. This gave Matthew a keen perception of two significant features in the words and works of Jesus, features that are consequently prominent in his Gospel.

First, Matthew clearly saw and recorded with emphasis the fact that Jesus' call to repentance is an absolute call, demanding the whole man wholly. His Gospel is marked by a stern and unsparing opposition to any compromise with evil, whether that compromise be a Jewish one or a Christian one. He makes it clear that the call to communion with the Christ is a call to a never-ending struggle against the evil in mankind that is perpetually threatening that communion. It is no accident that the words of Jesus, which impose on the disciple the duty of correcting and winning the sinning brother, are peculiar to Matthew and that the necessity of perpetual forgiveness toward the errant brother is reinforced by one of Jesus' most powerful parables, again peculiar to Matthew (18:15–35) in a chapter that explores the boundaries and burdens of forgiveness. Matthew 18 might even be titled the "forgiveness chapter" of the Bible. No other point in Scripture teaches more or more practically on the topic.

Second, Matthew saw that the way to obedience can only be the way of faith, faith that is seen in the attitude and action of the beggar who receives the grace of God. Jesus' call had taught him: "There is only one who is good" (19:17). But God is surely and wholly good; no one may therefore doubt His goodness and come to God with a divided heart or serve Him with half a devotion. That was the sin of scribe and Pharisee, and Matthew's Gospel is therefore the severest indictment of scribe and Pharisee in the New Testament. Matthew indicts the scribe and Pharisee not out of personal animus but on religious grounds. He knew the hollowness and falsity of a religion that could and did degrade the sinner and thus hold him fast in his sin but could not help him by forgiving him. Scribe and Pharisee had shut up the Kingdom before him; Jesus had called him into the Kingdom. Matthew 15:9 is a key passage for this distinction between following God's teaching or self-willed forms of worship.

If the call of Jesus set Matthew free from all the authorities that were leading Israel to her doom (ch 23), it did not separate him from the Old Testament or from the God of Abraham, Isaac, and Jacob. Jesus made a true Israelite of Matthew: his Gospel is marked by a rich and constant use of the Old Testament, the fullest of any of the Gospels. He sees in the Christ the consummation of Israel's history and the fulfilling of Old Testament prophecy. Of the 29 Old Testament prophecies recorded in the first Gospel, ten are peculiar to Matthew. And the influence of the Old Testament is not confined to the direct citation of the Old Testament. The Old Testament constitutes the ever-present background and the all-pervasive atmosphere of the Gospel. For example, the grouping of the words of Christ in five great discourses is no doubt intended to recall the five books of the Law and the five divisions of the Psalter. The Gospel according to Matthew is fittingly placed at the beginning of our New Testament, for it constitutes the New Testament's most powerful link with the Old. Jesus comes to fulfill the Law—the old covenant—as He emphasizes near the beginning of His first discourse (5:17–20) where He also describes those blessed with the new life God grants through His reign (5:2–12).

The Gospel according to Matthew is the most austere of the Gospels, stern in its denial toward evil, uncompromising in spelling out the inexorable claim of God's grace upon the disciples, almost fearfully conscious of how precarious our hold upon that grace is, summoning us to a sober and responsible adoration of the Christ. The austerity of the message is reflected in the style, which is sober and restrained. A monumental quiet seems to brood over the work. He allows the Church to see how this Jesus of Nazareth once confiscated people by His gracious call (11:27–28). Finally, Matthew recorded the Words of Institution for the Sacraments (26:26–28), through which the Lord founds His Church and gives it the means and authority to carry out His mission (16:18–19; 28:18–20). For all these reasons, Christians of every generation have turned to this Gospel.

Application

Chs 1–2 Only sinners to make up Jesus' genealogy. His ancestors needed a Savior just as much as we do. If God, in His grace, can use such flawed and sinful people, how much more can He bless and use sinners who witness the Messiah's sinless sacrifice and believe in Him today! Some people struggle to believe the virgin birth, but it takes no more faith for us to believe than it did for Joseph. In fact, we have the evidence of Joseph's testimony to help us. Through His Word, the Father guides people of all nations to Christ. When threatening challenges surround us, we trust that God is in control and that He will protect us. Jesus sacrificed His innocent life to redeem all people from sin, death, and the power of the devil. Trusting in Jesus, we have perfect innocence before our Father in heaven.

Chs 3–4 We believers must not only sincerely confess our sins but also be certain of forgiveness. Because Jesus is our substitute, we need not fear God's wrath and punishment for our sins. We are washed clean by the blood of the Lamb (Rv 7:14), who prepared the waters of Baptism for us. He did all this for the sake of Israel, who had failed God's test. He did all this for our sake because we, too, have failed God's test. His great light continues to shine in our darkness. The Good News of God's reign continues to be sounded in Word and Sacrament.

Ch 5 When we recognize our own spiritual poverty, when the Lord leads us to hunger and thirst for God's righteousness, when He makes us pure in heart so that we seek to worship only the true God, then we are blessed, now and forever. The words we speak in praise of our heavenly Father need the support of our deeds. Jesus' stern preaching of the Law causes us to take stock of our own behavior and to confess that we often, through sinful anger, fall. When reconciled to God, we may be reconciled with one another. Jesus also teaches that there may be times when Christians will be asked to take an oath in their earthly affairs or contacts with governing authorities. Out of loving consideration for this request, Christians may comply. Thanks be to God that He vowed to save us (cf Ti 1:2) and fulfilled that vow by His Son's life, death, and resurrection for our salvation. Our perfection is in Christ alone.

Ch 6 The only blessing that counts is the one received from the Father's generous hand. His grace perfects even the least of our good works. We may at times utter the Lord's Prayer thoughtlessly. Yet, our Father is fully attentive at all times to our needs and desires. He hears us as we fast and pray. Jesus gave generously, prayed, and fasted for our salvation. As children of light, God now calls us to be generous with our possessions and to serve God as our master rather than live as slaves to possessions. For our sake, Christ became the servant of all—to save all—by bearing all of our sins and granting us rich, surpassing, eternal forgiveness.

Ch 7 If you do not realize your own sins and faults, you cannot offer admonition to a fellow Christian. Because of the blindness caused by sin, we do not always recognize that God answers every prayer for our good (Rm 8:28). God regards those works as good that give evidence of saving faith in Jesus, our Lord. Saving faith is living and active, eager to do what He says.

Ch 8 Jesus' miracles are signs that anticipate the day when every disease and even death itself will be no more (Rv 21:4). The examples of would-be disciples invite us to ask, "What kind of disciple am I?" When we evaluate our lives as Jesus' disciples, we must confess that we often fail in our words and actions. Though we fall short, our Savior did not. He stilled the storms of life and He went all the way to the cross for us. We are citizens of God's kingdom only because of what Jesus has done for us. Baptism into Christ ensures that His victory is our victory.

This sixth-century mosaic of Christ healing the paralytic at Capernaum is similar to a third-century fresco found at Dura Europas, which includes one of the earliest known pictures of Jesus.

Ch 9 When we confess our sins, whether publicly or privately, and hear God's word of forgiveness spoken to us, then, like the paralytic, we are absolved. The Lord calls to faith people who are conscious of their unrighteousness. Jesus sits with them, not because they are worthy, but because He is merciful. He wants sinners included in His kingdom. The Bride of Christ is the Church—all those who by repentance and faith are united with the Bridegroom. Jesus' miracles confirm His care for all manner of people and His will to extend the Kingdom. All Christians are called to be witnesses of the surpassing compassion Jesus shows them by the forgiveness, life, and salvation He offers.

10:1–11:1 The compassionate authority of forgiveness is given to each of Christ's followers. We are sent with the message of God's love to a world of sinners. When we experience abuse because of our loyalty to Jesus, we have His assurance that the Holy Spirit will help us to speak the right words. Because He is in charge of our lives, we need not be afraid of those who oppose us because we confess Christ. No reward can match the blessings of grace given to those who repent of their sins and believe in Jesus as their Savior (Eph 2:8–10). He gives peace with God, patience in time of tribulation, confidence to pray, and finally eternal life.

11:2–30 To guard against false expectations, focus on Jesus and on what He has said and done. He is the fulfillment of all our hopes. "All the promises of God find their Yes in Him" (2Co 1:20). Day by day, Jesus patiently invites us to repent of our sins and hear His word of forgiveness. He invites us to receive the yoke of the Gospel, which guarantees true rest.

Ch 12 Though we have many faults, for which we deserve condemnation, He has declared us guiltless by His innocent suffering and death. As Christ's present-day ambassadors, we do well to follow His example as we proclaim His message. We will not save anyone by being argumentative and quarrelsome. The Gospel of Christ alone is the power of God for salvation (Rm 1:16). Only faith in Jesus, the Word of God, produces good hearts, from which flow words of praise and confession. One sign is sufficient for faith, the sign of Jonah. In this sign we find peace, joy, and hope. Our Savior's arms, once extended on the cross, now embrace us as His beloved family.

13:1–52 Let us not grow weary in doing good, knowing that at the right time we will reap, because God provides the harvest (Gal 6:9). The Holy Spirit has given us eyes that see and ears that hear. We dare never take our spiritual blessings for granted, for then we put ourselves in danger of losing them. The blessings of God's kingdom come through the seed of God's Word. A mark of God's rule is His patience (2Pt 3:8–15). For us sinners, this is a great comfort and also an encouragement for us to endure evil patiently (2Tm 2:24). God uses even our small efforts to accomplish His purposes. We inherit the Kingdom by grace through faith in Christ, who purchased and redeemed us with His precious blood.

13:53–14:36 People may agree that Jesus was a good religious teacher whose example we should follow. Only the Spirit, working through the Word, can change an unbeliever's heart. Whenever you have doubts about God's power, recall His miracles. Jesus is able to provide for us in the greatest hardships. Although we know the Son of God is with us and provides for all our needs, we still worry and fear. Jesus states, "Take heart; it is I. Do not be afraid" (14:27). His powerful arm reaches out to steady us and guide us into His safe harbor. Thank and praise Him for the multitude of His undeserved favors that we daily receive.

15:1–16:20 Although traditions may be a blessing and complement to biblical teaching, they must not supercede God's commands. At our birth, we were already sinful and condemned by the Law. But through Holy Baptism and the Word, the Spirit has renewed our hearts and washed away all our sins (Ti 3:4–7). In time of need, we often either fail to pray with determination or only ask hesitantly. Jesus brings eternal salvation, but He also helps and heals us when we are physically afflicted. God also works through His creation to provide our daily bread. We dare not take His blessings for granted. The sign of Jesus' cross and resurrection sustains us in our faith and is the sign to which we must point in our witness (Ac 2:23, 31–32). To confess Jesus as Savior and Lord is also essential in every believer's life.

16:21–17:27 At times, like Peter, we also fail to understand God's ways, thinking we know better. Jesus knows that He has to take up the cross for our salvation. Peter will learn that truth later—a truth that continues to give us comfort and peace. We continue to behold the spread of the message of Christ's cross into all the world. Though we are still troubled by the cares and ills of earthly life, every believer shares in the vision of what is to come (1Jn 3:2). Comfort one another with these words. Our prayer must ever be: "Lord, increase our faith." May we never grow weary of hearing this story of God's love and our salvation, for His righteousness sets us free.

Ch 18 Humility means confessing our inability to do anything at all to become worthy before God and earn salvation. Who of us can say that our hand or foot or eye has not caused us to sin? Thank God that Jesus' hands and feet were pierced for our iniquities and that His eyes beheld our sin in order to turn the Father's face from it. Do we show similar concern when fellow Christians stray from faith in Christ? We need personally to cherish

His gifts and to present His Law and Gospel to anyone caught in the grip of sin. Our willingness to forgive a brother or sister is grounded in God's abundant mercy toward us. Pray for such simplicity of heart; trust likewise in the simple, enduring love of your gracious heavenly Father, who daily forgives all your debts.

Ch 19 Few problems afflict the Church and society more than those of marital infidelity and divorce. With His forgiveness, grace, and guidance, our relationships can be a blessing. For a variety of reasons—some unavoidable and others the result of selfishness—many children today are not nurtured as they ought to be. Because of His special love for children, Jesus not only allows children into His kingdom, but He also gives them pride of place! Through faith in Christ, God freely gives His children the gift of eternal life. And if that were not enough, He rewards the sacrifices made for His kingdom a hundredfold!

Ch 20 Through forgiveness and the renewing work of God's Spirit, we can indeed be used by God for vital service in His kingdom. Jesus willingly laid down His life in order to save us. No one took Jesus' life from Him, as His Passion predictions make clear. Though many things make Jesus great—among them His role in creating and preserving all things—it is His sacrificial death that is most wonderful for us. He painstakingly extended His ministry to all in need, showing care and concern for them.

Ch 21 Like the crowds in Jerusalem, we are prone to fickleness—today all for the Lord, tomorrow turning from Him. Sometimes financial concerns eclipse the Church's real priority: faithfully teaching the Word and administering the Sacraments. Jesus responds to our misuse of holy things not by yanking them away from us but rather by correcting us and calling us to receive them worthily, unto faith and salvation. Though faithlessness rightly deserves God's wrath, God Himself works faithfulness in us and grants a rich reward of blessings. In God's kingdom, no repentant sinner is ever turned away. Repentant tax collectors and prostitutes were welcomed; so are we! In His great wisdom and mercy, God used the murder of His Son to work salvation, and He used the rejection of Israel's leaders to hasten the extension of the Kingdom to Gentiles.

Ch 22 Coming from a long line of believers does not guarantee anyone a place in God's kingdom. Ingratitude and presumption ever threaten to lead us away, as the teachings in this chapter warn. Among our many sins, none is more grievous than our failure to love God above all else. Thankfully, God does not respond to our selfishness by reciprocating. Instead, He gives us the greatest gift: His only-begotten Son. Jesus Christ, God's eternal Son, descended from heaven, assumed our flesh, suffered, died, and rose again, that we might share in His glory.

Ch 23 Even Jesus' most acrimonious denunciations are motivated by His sincere desire that people turn from sin and death and receive the gift of eternal life. Even when hated and rejected by many, Jesus never stopped loving and sincerely reaching out to them. He does the same with us.

Ch 24 The things of this world do not endure. All earthly splendor will be forgotten on the Last Day. All this should remind us of the nearness of the end of this age. In that we may rejoice! Though the world is indeed increasingly evil, hostile to God, and plagued with false prophets, Christians are ever nearer the great day of Christ's return. In an instant, He will raise the dead, transform believers into His likeness, and so effect our final deliverance. Sadly, many Christians today seem to have lost their expectation of Christ's imminent return. Countless sins and vices follow. Christians who are found faithful when called home will be unbelievably privileged: they will share in Christ's everlasting reign!

Ch 25 No matter how depleted our faith is, Jesus' grace can fill us to overflowing with a single word. An unfailing promise attaches to faithful stewardship: if we use the things entrusted to us for God and His purposes, we will be blessed here and in heaven. Having received forgiveness through faith in Christ, God's flock eagerly await the day on which they shall be publicly vindicated and receive eternal life.

Ch 26 Pray for those who oppose the Gospel. Despite such opposition, the Lord is at work for the good of His people. How often we, too, have betrayed Christ and sent Him to the cross for a lot less than 30 pieces of silver. God warns us daily not to yield to sin and thus betray Him. He also invites us to partake of fellowship with Him, as Christ did with His disciples at the Passover, freely offering His forgiveness. He continues to offer His body and His blood for us Christians to eat and to drink for the forgiveness of sins whenever we come to His Table. Jesus knows our weaknesses and is ready to restore us, even as He restored Peter. Pour out your heart to the Lord in sincere prayer again and again. Christ's prayer and obedience to the Father open the portals of heaven to your prayers. As Jesus restored Peter, even so He forgives us when we fall into sin.

Ch 27 When others betray you or falsely speak evil against you, take counsel with Jesus. He knows your sorrows and has borne your sins. When foes accuse you, curb your tongue. Loose your tongue in prayer to the One who takes away your sin. The silent Lamb of God would lead us away from the ways of the world to walk in His ways. He was condemned to death, that we might go freely into His kingdom. How different are the Lord's ways by which He rescues us! The pain of the cross and the reviling of the whole world shows us the full depth of God's mercy in that Jesus willingly submitted Himself to this torture for our sakes. His cry shows the abandonment that we should have experienced. But by His death, He destroyed the power of death and removed the barrier that separated us from God. By sharing our human grave, He sanctifies our tombs and makes them places where our bodies can rest, confident in the resurrection.

Ch 28 Christ's resurrection terrifies His enemies, such as the guards at the tomb, but it brings great joy to His followers. Rejoice today in His resurrection and pray for His reappearing. The Good News of Christ's resurrection has triumphed over the skepticism of Christianity's critics. Today, remember your Baptism and confirmation in the faith, which are precious blessings for the Lord's disciples. His love and care are new for you every morning.

Canonicity

Like the Gospel of John, the number of early manuscript copies of Matthew indicates it was used more often than Mark and Luke. At least one manuscript, Papyrus 104, dates from as early as the second century AD. As Gerhard indicates below, the canonical character of Matthew's Gospel was never challenged. See comments above on *homologoumena*, p 156–57.

Christian sarcophagus decorated with scenes of the Passion of Christ, including the arrest and Christ before Pontius Pilate; from the the catacombs of St. Domitilla.

Lutheran Theologians on Matthew

Luther

In his prefaces to the New Testament (1522, 1546, etc.) Luther wrote that there is only one Gospel, which is proclaimed throughout the Scriptures. He introduced the four Gospels as follows:

"The notion must be given up that there are four gospels and only four evangelists. . . . 'Gospel' [Euangelium] is a Greek word and means in Greek a good message, good tidings, good news, a good report, which one sings and tells with gladness. For example, when David overcame the great Goliath, there came among the Jewish people the good report and encouraging news that their terrible enemy had been struck down and that they had been rescued and given joy and peace; and they sang and danced and were glad for it [I Sam. 18:6].

"Thus this gospel of God or New Testament is a good story and report, sounded forth into all the world by the apostles, telling of a true David who strove with sin, death, and the devil, and overcame them, and thereby rescued all those who were captive in sin, afflicted with death, and overpowered by the devil. Without any merit of their own he made them righteous, gave them life, and saved them, so that they were given peace and brought back to God. For this they sing, and thank and praise God, and are glad forever, if only they believe firmly and remain steadfast in faith.

"This report and encouraging tidings, or evangelical and divine news, is also called a New Testament. For it is a testament when a dying man bequeaths his property, after his death, to his legally defined heirs. And Christ, before his death, commanded and ordained that his gospel be preached after his death in all the world [Luke 24:44–47]. Thereby he gave to all who believe, as their possession, everything that he had. This included: his life, in which he swallowed up death; his righteousness, by which he blotted out sin; and his salvation, with which he overcame everlasting damnation. A poor man, dead in sin and consigned to hell, can hear nothing more comforting than this precious and tender message about Christ; from the bottom of his heart he must laugh and be glad over it, if he believes it true.

"Now to strengthen this faith, God has promised this gospel and testament in many ways, by the prophets in the Old Testament, as St. Paul says in Romans 1[:1], 'I am set apart to preach the gospel of God which he promised beforehand through his prophets in the holy scriptures, concerning his Son, who was descended from David,' etc. . . . [Editor's note: Luther cites Gn 3:15; 22:18; Gal 3:8, 16; Jn 11:26; 2Sm 7:12–14; Mi 5:2; and Hos 13:14 to make this point.]

"The gospel, then, is nothing but the preaching about Christ, Son of God and of David, true God and man, who by his death and resurrection has overcome for us the sin, death, and hell of all men who believe in him. Thus the gospel can be either a brief or a lengthy message; one person can write of it briefly, another at length. He writes of it at length, who writes about many words and works of Christ, as do the four evangelists. He writes of it briefly, however, who does not tell of Christ's works, but indicates briefly how by his death and resurrection he has overcome sin, death, and hell for those who believe in him, as do St. Peter and St. Paul.

"See to it, therefore, that you do not make a Moses out of Christ, or a book of laws and doctrines out of the gospel, as has been done heretofore and as certain prefaces put it, even those of St. Jerome. For the gospel does not expressly demand works of our own by which we become righteous and are saved; indeed it condemns such works. Rather the gospel demands faith in Christ: that he has overcome for us sin, death, and hell, and thus gives us righteousness, life, and salvation not through our works, but through his own works, death, and suffering, in order that we may avail ourselves of his death and victory as though we had done it ourselves.

"To be sure, Christ in the gospel, and St. Peter and St. Paul besides, do give many commandments and doctrines, and expound the law. But these are to be counted like all Christ's other works and good deeds. To know his works and the things that happened to him is not yet to know the true gospel, for you do not yet thereby know that he has overcome sin, death, and the devil. So, too, it is not yet knowledge of the gospel when you know these doctrines and commandments, but only when the voice comes that says, 'Christ is your own, with his life, teaching, works, death, resurrection, and all that he is, has, does, and can do.'

"Thus we see also that he does not compel us but invites us kindly and says, 'Blessed are the poor,' etc. [Matt. 5:3]. And the apostles use the words, 'I exhort,' 'I entreat,' 'I beg,' so that one sees on every hand that the gospel is not a book of law, but really a preaching of the benefits of Christ, shown to us and given to us for our own possession, if we believe. But Moses, in his books, drives, compels, threatens, strikes, and rebukes terribly, for he is a lawgiver and driver.

"Hence it comes that to a believer no law is given by which he becomes righteous before God, as St. Paul says in I Timothy 1[:9], because he is alive and righteous and saved by faith, and he needs nothing further except to prove his faith by works. Truly, if faith is there, he cannot hold back; he proves himself, breaks out into good works, confesses and teaches this gospel before the people, and stakes his life on it. Everything that he lives and does is directed to his neighbor's profit, in order to help him—not only to the attainment of this grace, but also in body, property, and honor. Seeing that Christ has done this for him, he thus follows Christ's example.

"That is what Christ meant when at the last he gave no other commandment than love, by which men were to know who were his disciples [John 13:34–35] and true believers. For where works and love do not break forth, there faith is not right, the gospel does not yet take hold, and Christ is not rightly known. See, then, that you so approach the books of the New Testament as to learn to read them in this way." (AE 35:357–61)

For more of Luther's insights on Matthew, see collections of his sermons, especially his commentary on Mt 5–7, *The Sermon on the Mount* (AE 21:1–294).

Gerhard

"To the canonical books of the New Testament of the first rank belongs: *the Gospel of Matthew*. There has never been any doubt about it in the Church. Tertullian calls Matthew 'the most faithful interpreter of the Gospel' (*De carne Christi*, p. 37). In his preface to the *Opus imperf.*, Chrysostom asserts that '[Matthew] preached the Gospel to sinners not [only] with speech but also by the improvement of his own life.' Eusebius (*Hist. eccles.*, bk. 3, c. 24) and, from him, Nicephorus (bk. 2, c. 45) explain the occasion at which he wrote his evangelical history: 'When Matthew had first preached to the Hebrews and now was about to go to others, he put his Gospel into writing. What those he was leaving might long for, his presence being removed, he filled in with his writing.' He wrote his Gospel in the eighth year after Christ's ascent, as Eusebius would have it; or in the fifteenth year after Christ's ascent, according to the reckoning of Nicephorus (bk. 2, c. 45); or in the twenty-first year, according to Irenaeus (bk. 3, c. 1).

"Some testify that he wrote in Hebrew: Irenaeus (loc. cit.), Athanasius (*Synopsis*, p. 141), Eusebius (bk. 3, c. 24), Nazianzen (*Carmina*), Jerome (preface to the four evangelists, *ad Damas.*; in c. 11, Hosea), Augustine (*De consens. evang.*, bk. 1, c. 2), and Nicephorus (bk. 4, c. 32)—all of whom Baronius (*Annal.*, ann. 34, n. 165) and Bellarmine (*De verbo Dei*, bk. 2, c. 7) follow. Some attribute the translation of it to the evangelist John, some to the apostle James, some to Luke and Paul, some to Mark. However: (1) The ancient writers only say this; they do not prove it. Chrysostom, on Matthew, does not dare make a firm declaration. He says, 'It is said,' and adds: 'I would rather it exist than prove it.' Also, no one bears witness of having seen any trace of that Hebrew volume. In fact, that which they call the Book of the Nazarenes had not been written in Hebrew but in Chaldaic, only using Hebrew forms, according to Jerome. Also, it is listed among the apocryphal writings, for only the Nazarenes and Ebionites claimed it for themselves, according to Epiphanius and Jerome; the Catholics embraced the Greek. What Munsterus published does not belong to Matthew himself, for its author, whoever he may have been, was not even learned in Hebrew. (2) The same authors who say that Matthew wrote in Hebrew admit that that Gospel was published in Greek at the time of the apostles and was commended to the Church as authentic; Irenaeus (bk. 3, c. 39), Jerome (*Catal. illustr.*), and Eusebius (bk. 3, c. 34, 39; bk. 5, c. 10) attribute the translation of it to Mark. In *Synopsis*, Athanasius declares that the apostle James translated it from Hebrew to Greek. Theophylact attributes it to John. Anastasius (*Genes.*, sermon 8) claims Luke and Paul as authors of that translation. (3) The rest of the apostles first wrote in the Greek language not only indiscriminately for all Jews and Gentiles but also specifically for the Jews. Why, then, would we want to make a different claim for Matthew? His calling to the apostolate required him to write in a familiar language. (4) Jerome believes that Matthew wrote with 'a pure Hebrew language' (*Catal.*, on Matthew). However, Widmanstadius, Guido Fabricius, and Bellarmine (*De verbo Dei*, bk. 2, c. 4) think he wrote it in Syriac. (5) The pen of Matthew clearly is in harmony with that of Mark and is not far removed from the style of John. (6) Matthew interprets the Hebrew name Immanuel in Greek (1:23); therefore he did not write his Gospel in Hebrew. After all, if he were writing in Hebrew, why would he interpret it for people who understood Hebrew? (7) Whatever it may be, the Greek edition of Matthew is authentic. In fact, he produced it while the apostles were still living, and the apostles themselves approved of it. The ancients also confirm this. Therefore one cannot approve what Baronius writes in the passage we recently cited: 'I say that we cannot declare of what trustworthiness the Greek text is without a comparison with the Hebrew original.' Casaubonus explains carefully (*Exerc.* 15, c. 12, p. 338) what must be thought about this pronouncement.

"The evangelical history of Matthew has twenty-eight chapters in which Christ's person and His prophetic, priestly, and royal office are described.

"In other instances, the older Latins divide it according to the division of Hilary into thirty-three canons and according to the division of Christian Druthmar into sixty-seven canons. The more recent Latins, however, divide it into eight chapters. Among the Greeks, they divide it into sixty-eight chapters, according to Euthymius or Oecumenius; according to Suidas, into sixty-eight titles and 355 chapters. Ammonius and Eusebius also divide it into 355 chapters." (ThC E1 § 243)

Questions People Ask about Matthew

Genealogies of Christ

In the beginning of the New Testament we meet a much-discussed difficulty when comparing the genealogy of Christ given in Mt 1:1–17 with that found in Lk 3:23–38. A first reading creates the impression that in both, the lineage of Jesus is traced by enumerating the ancestors of Joseph, His earthly father, and that hence in both instances we have before us the genealogy of Joseph. But according to Mt 1:16, the father of Joseph was a man by the name of Jacob, while Lk 3:23 seems to say that Heli was the father of Joseph. A discrepancy, say the critics of the Bible!

Let the case be calmly considered. Joseph was the son of Jacob, says Matthew. "Joseph was the son of Heli" is apparently what Luke states. We say apparently, for his words allow a different construction. If we translate Lk 3:23–24 literally from the Greek, the passage reads thus: "Jesus Himself, when He began, was about 30 years old, being the son of Joseph, as it was thought, of Heli, of Matthat." This statement could indicate that Joseph was the son of Heli, but it does not necessarily do so. The meaning of the holy writer may be that Jesus was indeed considered to be the son of Joseph, but in reality He was the son of Heli, of Matthat, etc. According to this view the words "Jesus being the son of" may be implied before at least the next name, Heli, and the term "son" would have the wider significance of "descendant." Note that "son" is used in a wide sense in Lk 3:38: "Adam, the son of God." Accepting this interpretation, we assume that Heli was the father of Mary, the mother of Jesus, and hence the actual ancestor of our Lord according to the flesh. If we adopt this view, the difficulty that confronted us vanishes. Luke desires to give the actual genealogy of Jesus and enumerates the persons from whom Christ is descended according to His human nature. He mentions Joseph, but he immediately eliminates him with the statement that it was only through error that he was considered as belonging to the ancestors of Jesus. We may conclude, then, that Luke does not present the genealogy of Joseph at all, but that of Mary, and that he must not be understood to say that Joseph was the son of Heli.

The question may be asked, "Why does Luke not mention Mary in the genealogy of Jesus?" Luke had mentioned a number of times in the first two chapters of his Gospel that Mary was the mother of Jesus. No more words were needed on that point. Furthermore, a genealogy ordinarily includes the names of the father, grandfather, great-grandfather, etc., of the person concerned. Luke follows this rule and mentions not the name of Mary but the name of the "father," adding that it was only in the opinion of the people that Joseph was the father of Jesus, not in reality. The longer one ponders the genealogy given by Luke, the more strikingly apt and well considered it will appear to be. The contention, then, that there is a discrepancy between Mt 1:1–17 and Lk 3:23–38 may safely be dismissed as having no foundation in fact.

A minor difficulty is Matthew's omission of the names of four kings—Ahaziah, Joaz, Amaziah (not included in 1:8–9), and Jehoiakim (not included in 1:11). This fact would hardly require comment if Matthew did not say that there were three sets of 14 generations from Abraham to Christ (1:17). The second set of names in the list, it seems, ought to embrace 18 instead of 14 links. First, it must be said that Matthew cannot have been ignorant of the names of the kings whom he does not mention, because every page of his Gospel shows a thorough acquaintance with the Old Testament. Furthermore, it would be absurd to suppose that Matthew tried to deceive his readers. His book was intended for people who knew the Old Testament, and a juggling of the facts would immediately have been detected. The names of the kings in question were well-known, and Matthew could not have made this omission in the hope that it would remain unnoticed. But what could have induced him to draw up a list of this kind? A simple explanation is that he used current genealogical tables, in which certain names had been dropped, probably to retain symmetry. He wished to present proof that Jesus was the Messiah, who was to be a descendant both of Abraham and of David. Therefore, he appeals to the genealogical tables of the Jews themselves and shows that their own official documents prove that Joseph, the legal father of Jesus, was a son of Abraham and a son of David. If viewed thus, we shall no longer find the omission of these names inexplicable. Let it be said in conclusion that the Bible, in the two genealogies of Jesus, shows Him to have been in the most full and perfect sense a descendant of David, namely, by law in the royal line of kings through His reputed father, and in fact by direct personal descent through His mother.

Are Good Works to Be Done Openly or in Secret?

Matthew 5:16 reads: "Let your light shine before others, so that they may see your good works and give glory to your Father who is in heaven."

Matthew 6:1 asserts: "Beware of practicing your righteousness before other people in order to be seen by them, for then you will have no reward from your Father who is in heaven."

In one and the same sermon Jesus says that we must let our light shine so that people can see our good works; and again, that we must do our good works in secret, so that people cannot see them. How are we to harmonize these two statements? In Mt 5:16 and the preceding verses Jesus urges His disciples to engage in good works. He tells them that they are equipped for serving their God and other people; they are the salt of the earth and the light of the world; and the good qualities with which they are endowed are not to lie dormant, but they are to be put to use. As salt they can heal and purify, and as a light they can lead. And being thus equipped, they must not be idle. In Mt 6:1, however, Jesus is discussing the motives from which our good works are to flow, and in very forcible language He tells us that if our good works are to be pleasing to God, they must not be done in the spirit of vanity or of glorification of self, but in humility, our aim being to advance the glory of God and the best interests of our neighbors. In Mt 5:16 Jesus tells us to do good works; they will be seen and will help to exalt the name of your great God. In Mt 6:1 He tells us not to do good works in order to be seen doing them. In that case they lose all ethical value. Putting it briefly, we might say that in the one passage Jesus prescribes good works, in the other He warns against the wrong motive for doing good works.

Jordanian reenactors dressed as soldiers of the sixth legion, which was stationed in the Near East during the New Testament era. The man at center is dressed as a centurion.

How Did the Centurion Bring His Request Before Jesus?

Matthew 8:5–13 and Lk 7:1–10 form a pair of passages that have been puzzling to Bible readers. The centurion, seeking the help of the Lord for his sick servant, is spoken of in both texts. Matthew says that the centurion came to Jesus. Luke declares that he entreated the Savior through delegations of elders and other friends. However, there is no disagreement here.

This presents the case clearly: the centurion came to Jesus, says the one evangelist, and the centurion sent for Jesus, says the other. One explanation is that the term "came" may not necessarily mean that he came in person; it may have a wider significance, namely, that of putting oneself in touch with someone else. Therefore, the language of Matthew may not compel us to understand him to say that the centurion appeared before Jesus in person. This point is satisfactorily explained by the legal maxim: what our agent does, we do ourselves (*Qui facit per alium, facit per se*). Matthew narrates briefly; Luke gives the circumstances more fully. Similarly in Jn 4:1 Jesus is said to have baptized when He did it by His disciples (v 2). In Jn 19:1 and elsewhere Pilate is said to have scourged Jesus—certainly not with his own hands. In Mk 10:35 James and John come to Jesus with a certain request; in Mt 20:20 it is their mother who presents the request. We say, similarly, that the president went to the senate with this difficulty. We do not necessarily wish to imply that he appeared before the senate in person, but merely that he in some way or another, probably by means of a written communication, apprised the senate of a pending difficulty and asked its advice.

Another equally valid solution to the apparent difficulty is that Luke adds a detail which Matthew does not contain; yet both accounts are accurate. Perhaps the centurion, being a Roman, hesitated to approach Jesus. He may have had doubts about the reception a Gentile would receive. Therefore he sent a delegation of Jewish elders who knew him personally to intercede with Jesus on his behalf. Only after the elders had explained that the Roman officer was worthy of Jesus' consideration (Lk 7:4–5) did the centurion speak directly to Jesus, who had come partway to the house in which the sick servant was lying. Probably this construing of the events is preferable to that of the previous paragraph on the basis of Mt 8:13, which implies that the centurion was present in person: "And to the centurion Jesus said, 'Go; let it be done for you as you have believed.' "

The Unpardonable Sin

Matthew 12:31–32 states: "Therefore I tell you, every sin and blasphemy will be forgiven people, but the blasphemy against the Spirit will not be forgiven. And whoever speaks a word against the Son of Man will be forgiven, but whoever speaks against the Holy Spirit will not be forgiven, either in this age or in the age to come."

Acts 13:39 asserts: "And by Him everyone who believes is freed from everything from which you could not be freed by the law of Moses."

The difficulty here is caused by the statement that there is an unpardonable sin, which seems to contradict the many passages of which Ac 13:39 is typical, saying that all who believe in Jesus will receive forgiveness of their sins. It seems that the Gospel promises, which offer pardon for the sins we commit when we turn to Jesus in true faith, are so comprehensive that no sin can be excluded. This view is correct. Not a single sin is excluded from the category of those that will be forgiven when the sinner seeks refuge in Jesus. Believe, and you are pardoned. But the unpardonable sin of which Jesus speaks has this characteristic: that the one committing it does not, and will not, believe in Jesus Christ. The Lord is describing the sin as blasphemy directed against the Holy Spirit. The Holy Spirit is that person of the Trinity who converts us. If a person blasphemes against Him and does not let the Holy Spirit do and sustain His work, this person cannot be a believer and hence cannot receive forgiveness of sins. The words of Jesus may be paraphrased thus: "Beware of opposing the Holy Spirit who seeks to bring about, or has brought about, your regeneration. If the Holy Spirit does not regenerate you, you cannot receive forgiveness." Therefore the texts quoted are not contradictory. It will be observed that Mt 12:31–32 does not oppose the statement that every sinner who believes in Jesus will be forgiven. The sin it describes is simply such that it excludes repentance and faith in Christ. Perhaps the most important point to remember is that no one who repents of his or her sins and seeks refuge in the wounds of Christ has committed the sin against the Holy Spirit.

How Long Was Jesus in the Grave?

Some people hold that there is a discrepancy between the prediction of Jesus that He would be in the sepulchre three days and three nights (Mt 12:40) and the account of His death and resurrection, according to which He was put to death on a Friday afternoon and raised from the dead on the following Sunday morning. If we compute the time in which the body of our Lord lay in the grave, we have a few hours remaining of Friday, which ended at sunset on the day of crucifixion, then the night and the day which constituted Saturday or the Sabbath, and finally that part of Sunday which lay between sunset on Saturday and the resurrection on Sunday morning. In other words, Jesus was in the grave a part of a day, a whole 24-hour day, and another part of a day. It must be remembered that the Jews began their day at sunset. Does the resurrection account contradict the prophecy of Jesus that states that He would be in the grave three days and three nights?

The question evidently turns upon the expression "three days and three nights." If that expression cannot have any other meaning than three 24-hour days, then we are confronted with a real difficulty. But is this the case? We may confidently say that it is not. With the Jews "one day and one night" was simply an idiom for designating a day, and they would use this expression even when they referred to only a part of a day. This practice is evident from 1Sm 30:12, where we are told of an Amalekite who had not eaten or drunk anything for three days and three nights. The following verse indicates that the day that he was found was the third day of his being sick and left behind by his master, which is equivalent to "the day before yesterday." It is for this reason that Jesus says to His disciples that He must suffer many things and "after three days rise again" (Mk 8:31), and that He will "on the third day be raised" (Mt 16:21). The terms "after three days" and "the third day" were used synonymously, part of a day being reckoned as a whole day. One would have to entirely ignore this idiomatic usage to maintain that a discrepancy exists between these passages.

Another fact to be considered is that many people in New Testament times counted inclusively. That is, in the Roman calendar the second day before the first day of the following month was listed as "the third day before the Calends," a term for the first day of a month. For example, January 30 was called the third day before the Calends of February—thus counting January 30, 31, and February 1—when in reality it is the second day before February 1. This inclusive terminology is present in the German expression *"heute in acht Tagen"* ("today in eight days") which comes from the Roman inclusive numbering of days and means "a week from today." Likewise Pentecost, also called the Feast of Weeks, was celebrated on the forty-ninth day after the Feast of Unleavened Bread, but it was known as Pentecost, the Greek word for fiftieth.

Did Jesus Oppose Marriage?

That is an interpretation that has been put on the words of our Lord in Mt 19:12. Let us remember that the words were spoken when He had given information on the question of divorce. Against the loose practice prevailing at the time among the Jews with respect to divorce, Jesus insisted that the marriage bond should be considered indissoluble by husband and wife. Instead of belittling or destroying the sanctity of marriage, He exalted and defended it. No one can truthfully say that the statements of Jesus in Mt 19:1–12 reflect a low view of the married state.

When the disciples say that it is not good or profitable to marry if the marriage vow is binding until death and a husband cannot at will rid himself of an unworthy, troublesome wife, Jesus has a word to say about the unmarried state. Edgar Goodspeed's translation of Mt 19:10–12 brings out the meaning quite well, and therefore we quote it here:

> The disciples said to Him, "If that is a man's relation to his wife, it is better not to marry!" He said to them, "It is not everyone who can accept that, but only those who have a special gift; for some are incapable of marriage from their birth, and some have been made so by men, and some have made themselves so for the sake of the kingdom of heaven. Let him accept it who can." (*The Bible: An American Translation* [Chicago: The University of Chicago Press, 1935])

Jesus elaborates on the statement of the disciples that, if He had correctly given the meaning of marriage, it is not good or profitable to marry. He does not say that they are wrong, but He asserts that the principle they have just uttered cannot be accepted and acted upon except by those who have received a special gift from God, referring to the gift of celibacy. There are three classes of people who refrain from marriage—those who are unfit for it through physical defect, those who have been rendered unfit by cruel mutilation, and those who have made themselves unfit for it for the sake of the kingdom of heaven, that is, who voluntarily, in order to assist more effectively in extending the kingdom of heaven, forego marriage, having been equipped for such a course by a special divine endowment enabling them to remain chaste without the married relation.

In all this there certainly is no condemnation of matrimony. Furthermore, Jesus here does not even advise people to remain unmarried, nor does He say that those who do not marry manifest greater godliness and piety than those who marry. Whoever imputes such sentiments to Jesus is reading things into His words which are not there. His words rather contain the warning: "If you think that for yourself an unmarried life is preferable, be sure that you have the gift of celibacy." The charge that our Lord is recommending horrid self-mutilation rests on a misapprehension of His words. It entirely ignores the consideration that the statement of Jesus may well be taken in a figurative sense, making oneself a eunuch simply meaning the determination to remain unmarried. In fact, there are strong reasons showing us that in this instance the literal sense must be discarded and a figurative sense adopted. In Mt 19:12 Jesus uses the term "eunuch" in three senses: (1) people born with impaired sexuality; (2) castrated males; (3) people who refuse marriage for the sake of God's kingdom. Luther very acutely remarks that if, in speaking of people of the third class, Jesus likewise referred to self-mutilation, He would be repeating what He says about people of the second class. Besides, mutilation of one's own body is clearly forbidden in the divine commandment "You shall not murder." It is certain that Jesus would not have commended such a course.

Jesus enters Jerusalem on Palm Sunday; from the Winchester Psalter.

The Entry of Jesus into Jerusalem

Matthew 21:1–9 records that Jesus' entry into Jerusalem on Palm Sunday involved two animals—a donkey and her colt. The parallel accounts (Mk 11:1–10; Lk 19:28–38; Jn 12:12–16) mention only the colt. All four evangelists agree that Jesus rode on the colt, as we shall show. But first we shall discuss the number of animals.

The King James Bible has at Mt 21:5: " . . . meek, and sitting upon an ass, and a colt the foal of an ass." The New King James Version reads (in poetic form):

> Lowly, and sitting on a donkey,
>
> A colt, the foal of a donkey.

The New International Version, again as poetry, renders it thus:

> Gentle and riding on a donkey,
>
> and on a colt, the foal of a donkey.

This difference in translation between "an ass, and a colt" and "a donkey, a colt" reflects the fact that the Greek text has between "donkey" and "colt" a word (*kai*), which may be interpreted to mean either "and" or "even" in the sense of "namely." Thus the Greek may signify only one animal in Mt 21:5, which is a quotation from Zec 9:9. The same situation exists in the Hebrew text of Zechariah—a connective particle between "donkey" and "colt" may mean either "and" or "or." This similar difference in translation is present between the King James Version on the one hand and the New King James Version and the New International Version on the other, parallel to their respective renderings of Mt 21:5.

The basic question then in Zechariah is whether the mentioning of both donkey and colt is to be taken as Hebrew poetic parallelism or as an indication of two animals. Likewise does the Greek text in Mt 21:5 reflect Hebrew poetic parallelism or does it refer to two donkeys? The answer is clearly the latter on the basis of the entire passage in Matthew. Jesus requests two animals (21:2–3), and two disciples brought two animals (21:7).

Our Savior, however, rode on only one animal, the young colt, as Mark, Luke, and John state and as Matthew agrees when he is correctly construed on the basis of the Greek text in 21:7. The English rendition unfortunately is misleading: "They brought the donkey and the colt and put on them their cloaks, and He sat on them." The pronoun "them," which occurs twice, may refer either to the two animals or to the clothes according to the context. The Greek sentence may mean: "They brought the donkey and the colt, laid their clothes on them [on both animals], and He sat on them [on the clothes placed on the colt]."

A probable reconstruction of the event and of Matthew's purpose in involving the mother donkey should be helpful. Since the colt had never been ridden before (Mk 11:2; Lk 19:30), its emotional dependency on the mother donkey is an important factor, although the colt may have been weaned. It would be logical to lead the mother donkey toward the gate of Jerusalem. The colt would follow her even though he had not been trained to pursue a path and previously had not carried a rider. Matthew, an eyewitness (rather than Mark or Luke), implies the additional detail that the mother donkey preceded Jesus, who was on the colt, in the procession to Jerusalem.

The Cursing of the Fig Tree

The cursing of the fig tree (Mt 21:18–19) is a miracle on which critics have pounced, declaring it unworthy of our Lord. One of them even remarks that Jesus, "out of humor after the controversy with His enemies, finds a target for His wrath in an innocent tree which bare naught but leaves and flowers at this season." For the most part, the miracles of Jesus were acts of healing, helping people in their distress, and bringing joy to oppressed hearts. When He worked wonders in the sphere of external nature, for instance, when He stilled the storm on the sea, it was for the purpose of rendering aid to those who needed it.

The one seeming exception is the cursing of the fig tree. A little reflection will help clear up the difficulty. In the first place, this miracle did not cause any pain or suffering. Furthermore, it showed the apostles the omnipotence of their Master and furnished Him an opportunity to instruct them on the power of faith. Some Bible students have conjectured quite plausibly that Jesus here wished to furnish His disciples in a symbolical way a description of the Jewish nation, devoid of God-pleasing fruit as it was.

Jeremiah or Zechariah?

In 27:9–10, Matthew seems to be contradicting the Old Testament. The words read: "Then was fulfilled what had been spoken by the prophet Jeremiah, saying, 'And they took the thirty pieces of silver, the price of Him on whom a price had been set by some of the sons of Israel, and they gave them for the potter's field, as the Lord directed me.' "

Matthew ascribes a prophecy to Jeremiah which apparently was uttered by Zechariah (Zec 11:13). A number of solutions have been suggested. It will suffice to mention two of them. Reading Jeremiah, we find that while he does not have the exact words quoted here, he has words that are somewhat similar (Jer 32:6–15). It will be noted that he is speaking of the purchase of a field, although he is not alluding to 30 pieces of silver. The purchase of a field is certainly an important item in the prophecy quoted by Matthew. We are justified, then, in saying that a prominent feature of the prophecy as placed before us by Matthew is found in Jeremiah. Turning to Zechariah, we find that he does not speak of the buying of a field, but makes mention of 30 pieces of silver. We see, then, that Matthew has drawn together two prophecies, the one taken from Jeremiah, the other from Zechariah. We could not find any fault with Matthew if he had written: "Then was fulfilled what was written by Jeremiah and Zechariah," because, inasmuch as buying a field is alluded to in the prophecy quoted, the Book of Jeremiah may justly be said to contain a part of it. If this must be granted, then we cannot accuse Matthew of contradicting the Old Testament in his statement as to the source of his quotation. No one will take it amiss if a work that has two authors is, in a brief allusion to it, ascribed to merely one of them, especially if this writer happens to be the more prominent of the two. (Thus *A Greek-English Lexicon of the New Testament* might be referred to as "Bauer," who originally published the book [1949–52] or as "Danker," the latest editor to revise and contribute to it [2001].) Jeremiah is a far more prominent prophet than Zechariah, and thus it is not surprising that a prophecy that can be traced back to both of them is called a prophecy of Jeremiah, even though the greater part of it is taken from Zechariah.

The other explanation is that there is good evidence that the Jews, in their arrangement of the books of the prophets, placed Jeremiah first. In all ages people often have designated a collection of writings by the name of the first one, which in such cases usually is one of importance. An old edition, for example, of Luther's commentary on the Epistle of Paul to the Galatians bears the title *Luther's Commentary on Galatians*, but it contains a number of other writings in addition. Therefore any passage in the writings of the prophets might quite properly be said to be taken from the Book of Jeremiah. From this point of view, too, every vestige of a contradiction between Mt 27:9–10 and the Old Testament must disappear.

Did the Risen Lord Appear to His Disciples in Jerusalem?

Matthew 28:10, 16–17 relates, "Then Jesus said to them, 'Do not be afraid; go and tell My brothers to go to Galilee, and there they will see Me.' . . . Now the eleven disciples went to Galilee, to the mountain to which Jesus had directed them. And when they saw Him they worshiped Him, but some doubted."

John 20:19 records: "On the evening of that day [resurrection day], the first day of the week, the doors being locked where the disciples were for fear of the Jews, Jesus came and stood among them and said to them, 'Peace be with you.' "

These texts deal with the appearances of Jesus after His resurrection. The only peg on which one might hang a charge of discrepancy is that Matthew does not mention the appearance of Jesus to His disciples in the city of Jerusalem. But does Matthew deny that the risen Jesus was seen by the apostles in the capital? Not at all. We do not know the reason he is silent on the appearance of Jesus in Jerusalem. And we need not speculate on it. But there is no collision between his account and that of John. Matthew is more fragmentary, that is all.

Further Study

Lay/Bible Class Resources

Albrecht, G. J., and M. J. Albrecht. *Matthew*. PBC. St. Louis: Concordia, 2004. ♦ Lutheran author. Excellent for Bible classes. Based on the NIV translation.

Carson, D. A. *The Sermon on the Mount: An Evangelical Exposition of Matthew 5–7*. Grand Rapids: Baker, 1982. ♦ A masterful study of Matthew 5–7 in simple language, letting the text speak for itself.

Carter, Stephen, Donna Streufert, Dale Meyer, Roland Ehlke, and Jesse Yow. *Matthew, Parts 1 and 2*. Leaders Guide and Enrichment Magazine/Study Guide. LL. St. Louis: Concordia, 1999. ♦ In-depth, nine-session Bible studies with individual, small group, and lecture portions.

Erdman, Leonard. *Matthew: His Kingdom Forever*. GWFT. St. Louis: Concordia, 1994. ♦ Lutheran author. Ten-session Bible study, including leader's notes and discussion questions.

France, R. T. *The Gospel According to Matthew: An Introduction and Commentary*. TNTC. Grand Rapids: Eerdmans, 1985. ♦ Compact commentary interacting with the Greek text in a popular format. Generally helpful evangelical treatment of the text by a British scholar who supports authorship by the apostle Matthew.

Life by His Word. St. Louis: Concordia, 2009. ♦ More than 1,500 reproducible one-page Bible studies covering each chapter of the canonical Scriptures. Page references to *The Lutheran Study Bible*. CD-Rom and downloadable.

Church Worker Resources

Garland, David E. *Reading Matthew: A Literary and Theological Commentary*. Macon, GA: Smyth & Helwys Publishing, 2001. ♦ Garland's work is not a technical commentary. It is filled with insightful and useful observations about the text.

Hendriksen, William. *New Testament Commentary: Exposition of the Gospel According to Matthew*. Grand Rapids: Baker, 1973. ♦ This helpful resource keeps in mind the meaning of the text then as well as its meaning for today. Technical materials often appear in the footnotes.

Luther, Martin. *The Sermon on the Mount and The Magnificat*. Vol. 21 of AE. St. Louis: Concordia, 1956. ♦ Presents the great reformer's verse-by-verse sermon series on Mt 5–7, originally published in 1532.

Academic Resources

Davies, W. D., and D. C. Allison. *Matthew 1–7, 8–18, 19–28*. 3 vols. ICC. London: T&T Clark, 1988, 1991, 1997. ♦ A very solid and competent treatment of basic exegetical issues. Their presentation is encyclopedic in its breadth and depth. It is invaluable in providing the various necessary backgrounds and contexts for verses. At times, their exegetical judgments tend toward more speculative positions.

Davies, W. D. *The Sermon on the Mount*. New York: Cambridge University Press, 1966. ♦ A somewhat critical study. Davies' inclusion of helpful materials from Judaica, Qumran, and Pauline studies sheds light on the total context of this discourse.

Farmer, William R. *The Synoptic Problem: A Critical Review of the Problem of the Literary Relationships between Matthew, Mark, and Luke*. Rev. ed. Dillsboro, NC: Western North Carolina Press, 1976. ♦ A careful study of the theoretical priority of Mark, which shows that historically Matthew was the first Gospel written.

France, R. T. *The Gospel of Matthew*. NICNT. Grand Rapids: Eerdmans, 2007. ❧ Written from an evangelical, though critical, perspective by a Matthew scholar at the University of Wales. France focuses on the first century context and text as received by the Church.

Gibbs, Jeffrey A. *Matthew 1:1–11:1. Matthew 11:2–20:34*. CC. St. Louis: Concordia, 2006, 2010. ❧ A detailed commentary on the Greek text and theology of Matthew, written by a Lutheran scholar, who questions the idea that the Gospel has direct, literary dependence on the Gospel of Mark. The author is currently working on the final volume.

Guelich, Robert A. *The Sermon on the Mount: A Foundation for Understanding*. Waco, TX: Word, 1982. ❧ A verse-by-verse study, drawing in part on the two-source hypothesis.

Hagner, Donald A. *Matthew*. 2 vols. WBC. Nashville: Thomas Nelson, 1993, 1995. ❧ Hagner provides a helpful survey of exegetical options and consistently makes solid choices. The commentary displays sufficient depth without getting lost in the details.

Hill, David. *The Gospel of Matthew*. NCBC. Grand Rapids: Eerdmans, 1981. ❧ Moderately critical; brings in pertinent material from Judaica. Reflects Jeremiah's work on the parables.

Kingsbury, Jack Dean. *Matthew as Story*. 2nd ed. Minneapolis: Augsburg Fortress, 1988. ❧ An influential study of the narrative structure of Matthew.

Lange, John Peter. *Matthew*. LCHS. New York: Charles Scribner's Sons, 1865. ❧ A helpful older example of German biblical scholarship, based on the Greek text, which provides references to significant commentaries from the Reformation era forward.

Lenski, R. C. H. *The Interpretation of St. Matthew's Gospel*. 2 vols. Minneapolis: Augsburg Fortress, 2008. ❧ A standard resource by a noteworthy Lutheran interpreter, concerned with being faithful to the text and with its implications for today.

Luz, Ulrich. *Matthew 1–7. Matthew 8–20. Matthew 21–28*. 3 vols. Hermeneia: A Critical and Historical Commentary on the Bible. Minneapolis: Augsburg Fortress, 2001, 2005, 2007. ❧ Luz provides a very solid and competent treatment of basic exegetical issues. In particular, his treatment of the history of interpretation for each pericope supplies very helpful background.

Nolland, John. *The Gospel of Matthew*. NIGTC. Grand Rapids: Eerdmans, 2005. ❧ Careful study of the Greek text of the Gospel, assuming Markan priority and that the apostle Matthew was not the author.

Overman, J. Andrew. *Matthew's Gospel and Formative Judaism: The Social World of the Matthean Community*. Minneapolis: Augsburg Fortress, 1990. ❧ A compact introduction to sociological reading of Matthew.

Plummer, Alfred. *An Exegetical Commentary on the Gospel According to St. Matthew*. Grand Rapids: Baker, 1982 reprint. ❧ Although somewhat old, still a helpful resource by a well-known scholar of an earlier generation. Follows to a degree the two-source hypothesis.

Powell, Mark Allan, ed. *Methods for Matthew*. Methods in Biblical Interpretation. Cambridge: Cambridge University Press, 2009. ❧ Collection of essays from scholars of Matthean studies, who describe critical, literary, feminist, historical, social, and postcolonial approaches to interpretation.

Saldarini, Anthony J. *Matthew's Christian-Jewish Community*. Chicago: University of Chicago Press, 1994. ❧ Argues that the author of the Gospel is a Jewish teacher writing from within the Jewish tradition.

Scaer, David P. *Discourses in Matthew: Jesus Teaches the Church*. St. Louis: Concordia, 2004. ❧ Argues that Matthew was written as catechesis with the five discourses summarizing the message the disciples are to carry to all nations (Mt 28:19–20).

Scaer, David P. *The Sermon on the Mount: The Church's First Statement of the Gospel*. St. Louis: Concordia, 2000. ❧ A careful study of Matthew 5–7, exploring each unit of the sermon to present its Law and Gospel content. Argues that the sermon was used to train catechumens in the Early Church.

MARK

The Son of Man came to give His life as a ransom for many

The Jordan River rushes 65 miles from the Sea of Galilee to the Dead Sea. It tumbles from an elevation of 695 feet below sea level to 1,300 feet below sea level. Along its banks walked Joshua, leading Israel to the conquest; the prophets Elijah and Elisha, who ministered during the decline of Israel's Northern Kingdom; and Jonathan the Maccabee, who fought for his life against the Seleucids. Yet the Jordan River is best known as the font for John the Baptist and the followers of Jesus who sought the Word of life and cleansing from sin.

Mark's Gospel, which begins on Jordan's bank, likewise rushes. Forty-one times Mark describes the events flowing around Jesus' life with the word *immediately* (Gk *euthus*), propelling the reader toward the cross where Jesus would die, giving His life as a ransom for many. Mark uniquely focuses on the action in the story of Jesus' life, making His account both short and compelling to read.

Historical and Cultural Setting

For the political circumstances surrounding the life of Jesus, see pp 185–86.

According to early Fathers, Mark wrote his Gospel at the heart of the empire: Rome. The accounts hold that Mark drew the content from Peter's sermons. The character of the book is suited for a Gentile readership, and its active content would please a Roman audience. For more on this point, see "Purpose/Recipients" below.

The Jordan River flowing down the fault line of the Great Rift Valley into the north end of the Sea of Galilee.

OVERVIEW

Author
John Mark

Date
Written c AD 50–60

Places
Galilee; Judea; Nazareth; Capernaum; Tyre; Sidon; Jerusalem; Jericho; Bethany; Jordan River; Mount of Olives; Gethsemane; see map, p 199

People
Jesus; John the Baptist; the 12 apostles; Jesus' family; scribes; Pharisees; Herodians; Herod Antipas; Mary the mother of Joses; Mary Magdalene; Mary the mother of James; Salome

Purpose
To proclaim Jesus the Son of God, who calls disciples to repent, to believe the Gospel, and to bear the cross

Law Themes
Repentance; political and religious opposition; uncleanness; authoritative teaching; hard-heartedness

Gospel Themes
Gospel; Baptism; compassion; mercy; cleansing; authoritative teaching; ransom; Lord's Supper

Memory Verses
Jesus' message (1:14–15); prayer for faith (9:23–24); Jesus' mission (10:42–45); a centurion's confession (15:39)

TIMELINE

2 BC	Birth of Jesus
1 BC	Death of Herod the Great
AD 29	Baptism of Jesus
AD 33	Resurrection, Ascension, Pentecost
AD 36	Conversion of Paul
AD 68	Martyrdom of Peter and Paul

Composition

Author

Mark, referred to in the New Testament also as John and as John Mark (Ac 13:5, 13; 12:12), was the son of a certain Mary, who owned a house in Jerusalem. At the time of Peter's imprisonment (AD 41), Jerusalem Christians assembled at Mary's house for prayer, and it was there that Peter turned when he was miraculously released from prison. Peter evidently knew the family, and since he calls Mark his "son" in 1Pt 5:13, it is possible Peter was instrumental in Mark's conversion. In c AD 47 Mark accompanied Paul and Barnabas on the first missionary journey as far as Perga in Pamphylia, whence he returned to Jerusalem (Ac 13:13). Barnabas wished to take his cousin Mark along on the second missionary journey also, but Paul objected so strongly that the two missionaries parted ways (Ac 15:37–39). Barnabas took Mark with him to Cyprus. Mark was with Paul again during the first Roman imprisonment, according to Phm 24 (AD 59–61) and Paul bespeaks a warm welcome for him on the part of the Christians of Colossae (Col 4:10). In 1Pt 5:13 Peter includes greetings from his "son" Mark to the Christians of Asia Minor; apparently he had worked there and was known there. According to Papias, Mark was with Peter in Rome at the time of writing, in the early sixties. A few years later, at the time of Paul's last imprisonment, he was again in Asia Minor. Paul urges Timothy to bring Mark with him when he comes to Rome (2Tm 4:11). This is the last New Testament notice of Mark. According to the church historian Eusebius, Mark was the founder of the church at Alexandria in Egypt and its first bishop. He is said to have died a martyr's death there.

The evangelist Mark accompanied by a lion, since his Gospel begins in the wilderness.

Early tradition is unanimous in ascribing the second Gospel to Mark, the interpreter of Peter. There is one bit of evidence in the Gospel itself that may also point, though only indirectly, to Mark. Only this Gospel records the incident of the young man who ran away naked at the arrest of Jesus (Mk 14:51–52). Since no other convincing reason can be found for the inclusion of this detail, many scholars assume that the young man was Mark himself; the evangelist is thus appending his signature, as it were, to the Gospel. It may even be that the house of Mark's mother, Mary, was the house in whose Upper Room our Lord celebrated the Passover with His disciples on the night in which He was betrayed.

Date of Composition

The style and character of the Gospel of Mark, which make it probable that the book was written for Gentile readers, affirm the tradition that Mark wrote his Gospel in Rome. The Gospel is therefore to be dated in the sixties of the first century, since Peter did not reach Rome until his later years. Some of the early witnesses declare that Mark wrote after the death of Peter. This would necessitate a date after AD 68. But since the tradition is not unanimous on this point, there can be no absolute certainty on it.

Papias, bishop of Hierapolis, writing about AD 130 and citing as his authority the "Elder John" (perhaps John the apostle, certainly a man close to the apostolic age), writes concerning the second Gospel: "Mark, having become Peter's interpreter, wrote down accurately, though not in order, as many as he remembered of the things said or done by the Lord. For he neither had heard the Lord nor followed Him, but at a later time, as I said, [he followed] Peter, who delivered his instructions according to the needs [of the occasion]." Other early notices locate this preaching of Peter's and Mark's recording of it in Italy, more specifically in Rome. An early prologue to the Gospel (one of the so-called Anti-Marcionite prologues) says that Mark wrote his record of Peter's preaching "in the regions of Italy."

Purpose/Recipients

Clement of Alexandria reports an early tradition that Mark wrote his Gospel in Rome at the request of those who had heard Peter preach there. Since Christianity had been established in Italy and Rome before Peter ever worked there, both these notices are taken most naturally as referring to a teaching activity of Peter in Rome rather than to a strictly missionary activity.

The ancient tradition that Mark wrote his Gospel for Gentiles, specifically at the request of Roman Christians, is confirmed by the Gospel itself. Hebrew and Aramaic expressions are elucidated (3:17; 5:41; 7:11; 15:22), and Jewish customs are explained (7:2–4; 15:42). The evangelist himself quotes the Old Testament explicitly but once (1:2), though his narrative shows by allusion and echo that the narrator is conscious of the Old Testament background of the Gospel story (e.g., 9:2–8, cf Ex 24:12; 12:1–12, cf Is 5:1). Mark reduces Greek money to terms of Roman currency (12:42) and explains an unfamiliar Greek term by means of a Latin one (15:16, *praetorium*). Latinisms, that is, the direct taking over of Latin terms into the

Nero Caesar Augustus persecuted Christians at Rome in AD 64.

Greek, are more frequent in Mark's language than in that of the other evangelists.

Christians lived in Rome at the time of Nero, an emperor who had ordered persecution of the Christians shortly after Rome had been largely consumed by fire. Indeed the threatening sword of Nero may have been hanging over the head of Mark and his readers when he wrote the Gospel. Perhaps his friends were faced with the real danger of losing all their possessions and even their lives. They needed to have the story of Jesus before their eyes in concrete form, and the Holy Spirit, who always knows the needs of His people, gave this picture to them in the Gospel according to Mark.

The second Gospel begins with the words, "The beginning of the gospel of Jesus Christ, the Son of God." This is too comprehensive and solemn a phrase to be the title of the opening section only, as some have thought—the part which deals with John the Baptist, and Jesus' baptism by John, and His temptation, the preparation for Jesus' messianic ministry. It is designed to be the title to the whole work, and it is a significant one. Mark's book aims to set before the readers the record of the beginning and origin of that Good News which they knew and believed, that powerful and saving Word of God which the Son of God first proclaimed in word and deed (1:14–15), a word which was still the voice of Christ when proclaimed to people by human apostles and evangelists. Mark is answering the question of converts who, once they had heard the basic message, naturally and rightly asked, "How did this great Good News that has revolutionized our lives begin? What is its history? Tell us more of the strong Son of God who loved us and gave Himself for us. Recount for us His words and works, which will make clear His will for us, who have become His own."

Literary Features

Genre

Mark is doing what Luke did when he wrote "an orderly account" for Theophilus, in order that he might know the truth concerning the things of which he had been informed (Lk 1:3–4). Mark's book is "teaching" in the sense defined above. This is confirmed by many details in the book itself; for instance, the noun "Gospel" occurs eight times in Mark, while it occurs only four times in Matthew's much longer work and not at all in Luke and John. And it is in Mark's Gospel that Jesus identifies "Gospel" so closely with

His own person that the two are practically one entity, as when He says, "Whoever loses his life for My sake and the Gospel's will save it" (Mk 8:35; cf 10:29).

Characters

As compared with Matthew, Mark emphasizes the deeds of **Jesus**. The deeds of Jesus are by no means isolated from His words; the word is Jesus' instrument in His deeds too—He speaks, and it is done. And Mark, besides giving two longer discourses of Jesus (4:1–34; 13:1–37), repeatedly emphasizes the centrality of the word in the ministry of Jesus and the effect of its authority upon people (1:14, 22, 38; 2:2, 13; 4:1; 6:1–7; 9:7; 10:1; 11:18; cf also 8:38). But it is chiefly by His works that Jesus is marked as the proclaimer and the bringer of the almighty grace of the kingdom of God, as the Anointed King in whom we can trust, the Son of God in whom we can believe.

Jesus is also presented as the Son of Man who united Himself with mankind to deliver them from all their troubles. He is the Son of Man who had to suffer many things and be put to death (8:31; 9:12; 10:33, 45). He is the Son of Man who called His disciples to follow Him and to walk where He walked (2:14). He is the Son of Man who did not want to be remembered chiefly for His miracles.

It is important to note how often in this Gospel Jesus tells people to keep silent about His miracles. In this same connection, note that He makes no claim to be the Messiah until after 8:27, but even after that point He still asks the disciples to keep this secret. This characteristic has been called the "messianic secrecy motif" or the "hidden Son of Man motif." This secrecy is more noticeable in Mark than in the other Synoptic Gospels. Many explanations have been offered. It may be that the perilous situation of his Roman readers led Mark to develop this explanation of the person and work of Jesus Christ. Perhaps he wants to remind his readers that God's ways with men are often hidden rather than overwhelming, just as Jesus worked in a low-key way and refused to overpower His followers with many proofs of His deity. Perhaps this secrecy motif reminded the Roman Christians that their faith had not given them special power that protected them from suffering, but that they, too, might be called to follow in the footsteps of their Master, who relied on His Father instead of trusting in worldly power and success. They, too, would understand the way of Christian faith in the light of the resurrection (9:9–10).

The Gospel according to Mark is also the Gospel of **Peter**. Papias's statement that Mark "became Peter's interpreter" can be variously interpreted, but his assertion that Mark's Gospel incorporates the preaching of Peter is certainly confirmed by the character of the Gospel itself: it begins with Peter's call (1:16); it reaches its critical point when Peter in the name of the Twelve confesses the Christ (8:29); it closes with a message from the risen Lord to "His disciples *and Peter*" (16:7). Peter's house is the center of operations at Capernaum (1:29), the followers of Jesus are called "Simon and those who were with him" (1:36), and Mark's use of an indefinite "they" for the disciples is most naturally understood as reproducing Peter's use of "we" (e.g., 1:21; 6:53). The resemblance of the structure of the Gospel to that of Peter's sermon in the house of Cornelius (Ac 10:34–43) points in the same direction.

First century AD sandals found at Masada.

The many vivid and dramatic touches in the Gospel that distinguish the account as that of an eyewitness also reflect the preaching of Peter and are quite in keeping with what we know of his warm, vivacious, and volatile nature. The expressions, bearing, gestures, and feelings of Jesus are often noted, as is the effect of His words and deeds on the disciples and the multitudes. The narrative frequently drops into the vivid historical present, and Jesus' words are usually given in direct speech. The occasional reproduction of Jesus' words in Jesus' own tongue is probably also an echo of Peter's concrete and vivid narrative (e.g., 5:41; 7:34).

Narrative Development or Plot

Mark's Gospel begins with a significant introduction concerning the ministry of John the Baptist and the Baptism and temptation of Jesus (1:1–13). The evangelist relates the first part of Jesus' ministry in Galilee, which is marked by miracles, conflicts with the Pharisees, and several parables (1:14–5:43). This is followed by the second part of the Galilean ministry, during which John the Baptist is killed, Jesus feeds the 5,000, walks on the water, brings the Gospel to several people outside the flock of Israel, is confessed by Peter to be the Christ, is transfigured before three disciples, and begins His journey to Jerusalem (6:1–9:50). Jesus prepares His disciples for His passion by predicting His sufferings as they journey toward Jerusalem. He teaches on such topics as marriage, riches, and discipleship (10:1–52). Mark then relates the events of Holy Week and Jesus' discourse about the last times (11:1–13:37). The climax contains the narrative of His betrayal, arrest, crucifixion, and resurrection (14:1–16:20). The events of Holy Week receive much greater attention compared with other elements in Mark's account.

Outline

The simplest outline of Mark has two parts: Jesus' public ministry and Jesus' Passion. The outline below provides greater detail.

I. Prologue: "The Beginning of the Gospel of Jesus Christ, the Son of God" (1:1–13)

- A. The Ministry of John the Baptist (1:1–8)
- B. The Baptism and Temptation of Jesus (1:9–13)

II. Jesus' Public Ministry of Preaching and Miracle Working (1:14–8:30)

- A. Jesus Begins His Ministry in Galilee with Authority, but Meets Opposition (1:14–3:12)
  - 1. Jesus proclaims the rule of God and calls disciples (1:14–20)
  - 2. Jesus begins His ministry on a Sabbath Day in Capernaum (1:21–39)
  - 3. Jesus continues His ministry amid growing opposition (1:40–3:6)
  - 4. Large crowds follow Jesus (3:7–12)
- B. Jesus Is Received with Both Unbelief and Faith (3:13–6:6)
  - 1. Jesus appoints the 12 apostles (3:13–19)
  - 2. Jesus confronts the unbelief facing His ministry (3:20–4:34)
    - a. Jesus confronts unbelief both from the scribes and His family (3:20–35)
    - b. Jesus teaches the crowds and His disciples in light of the unbelief of the religious authorities ("The Parabolic Discourse"; 4:1–34)
  - 3. Jesus performs miracles on and around the Sea of Galilee (4:35–5:43)
    - a. Jesus calms a storm (4:35–41)
    - b. Jesus heals a Gerasene demoniac (5:1–20)
    - c. Jesus heals a sick woman and raises a dead girl (5:21–43)

4. Jesus is rejected at Nazareth (6:1–6)

C. Jesus Withdraws from His Public Ministry in Galilee (6:7–8:30)

1. Jesus sends the 12 apostles; John the Baptist dies (6:7–30)
2. A first cycle of parallel events (6:31–7:37)
   a. Jesus feeds 5,000 in the wilderness and walks on water (6:31–56)
   b. Jesus confronts the Pharisees and scribes and teaches on the distinction between clean and unclean, but His disciples misunderstand (7:1–23)
   c. Jesus heals a Syrophoenician woman's daughter near Tyre (7:24–30)
   d. Jesus heals a deaf man in the region of the Decapolis (7:31–37)
3. A second cycle of parallel events (8:1–26)
   a. Jesus feeds 4,000 in the wilderness (8:1–10)
   b. Jesus confronts the Pharisees and warns against the yeast of the Pharisees and Herod, but His disciples misunderstand (8:11–21)
   c. Jesus heals a blind man in Bethsaida (8:22–26)
4. Peter confesses that Jesus is the Christ in Caesarea Philippi (8:27–30)

III. Jesus Prepares His Disciples for His Passion, Death, and Resurrection (8:31–16:8)

A. Jesus Reveals His Passion, Death, and Resurrection and Teaches on Discipleship (8:31–10:52)

1. The first Passion prediction and subsequent teaching and events (8:31–9:29)
   a. Jesus predicts His suffering, death, and resurrection, and rebukes Peter (8:31–33)
   b. Jesus teaches His disciples and the crowd on discipleship (8:34–9:1)
   c. Jesus is transfigured before three of His disciples (9:2–13)
   d. Jesus casts out an unclean spirit from a boy after His disciples' failure (9:14–29)
2. The second Passion prediction and subsequent teaching (9:30–10:31)

a. Jesus predicts His suffering, death, and resurrection (9:30–32)

b. Jesus teaches His disciples on greatness in the kingdom of God (9:33–50)

c. Jesus teaches in the region of Judea and across the Jordan (10:1–31)

3. The third Passion prediction and subsequent teaching and events (10:32–52)

a. Jesus predicts His suffering, death, and resurrection (10:32–34)

b. Jesus responds to the request of James and John and teaches on greatness in the kingdom of God (10:35–45)

c. Jesus heals blind Bartimaeus (10:46–52)

B. Jesus Enters Jerusalem and Confronts the Religious Authorities (chs 11–13)

1. Jesus enters Jerusalem to the praise of the crowds (11:1–11)

2. Jesus curses the fig tree, cleanses the temple, and teaches the disciples on faith (11:12–26)

3. Jesus confronts the religious authorities (11:27–12:40)

a. Jesus responds to the question of His authority (11:27–33)

b. Jesus teaches the parable of the tenants (12:1–12)

c. Jesus responds to the question about paying taxes to Caesar (12:13–17)

d. Jesus responds to the Sadducees on the resurrection (12:18–27)

e. Jesus responds to the question on the greatest commandment (12:28–34)

f. Jesus questions them about the relationship of David and the Christ (12:35–37)

g. Jesus warns against the scribes (12:38–40)

4. Jesus teaches His disciples through the widow's offering (12:41–44)

5. Jesus teaches His disciples in light of His rejection by the religious authorities ("The Eschatological Discourse"; ch 13)

   a. Jesus predicts the temple's destruction (13:1–2)
   b. The signs and warnings (13:3–37)

C. Jesus' Passion, Death, and Resurrection (14:1–16:8)

1. Jesus is anointed at Bethany amid a plot to have Him arrested and killed (14:1–11)
2. Jesus celebrates the Passover with His disciples, predicts His betrayal, and institutes the Lord's Supper (14:12–25)
3. Jesus predicts Peter's denial (14:26–31)
4. Jesus prays in Gethsemane and is arrested (14:32–52)
5. Jesus is tried before the high priest and is denied by Peter (14:53–72)
6. Jesus is tried before Pilate (15:1–15)
7. Jesus is mocked by the soldiers, crucified, and dies (15:16–41)
8. Jesus is buried (15:42–47)
9. The women find the empty tomb and hear that Jesus is risen (16:1–8)

IV. The Long Ending (16:9–20)

Resources

On the tradition that Mark built his account from Peter's preaching, see pp 237–38.

Text and Translations

A question of integrity concerns the last 12 verses of the Gospel, as the mode of printing or notes in modern versions indicates. Most scholars doubt that these verses were a part of the original text of Mark's Gospel, for two reasons: (1) the attestation of these verses in the early manuscripts and Church Fathers; (2) the content and style of the verses in question.

As for the attestation, we may confine ourselves to the most important facts. The verses were apparently known to the second-century fathers Irenaeus and Justin and seem to have been included in the first attempt at Gospel harmony, the *Diatessaron* of Tatian. They are included in some of the early Latin and Syriac translations and in a number of important manuscripts from the fourth century on. But, on the other hand, the verses are omitted from reliable and important manuscripts as well as from some of the early translations. Eusebius, writing in the fourth century, tells us that the "exact" Greek manuscripts known to him closed with 16:8. The fact that another, shorter ending exists in some manuscripts is, of course, also evidence against the originality of 16:9–20; the shorter ending would hardly have found acceptance anywhere if the longer ending had been known to be original.

The content and style of the last 12 verses also make it doubtful whether they were part of the Gospel originally. The narrative of 16:1–8 is not really continued in them. Mary Magdalene is introduced anew (16:9), though she has already been mentioned (16:1); the promised reunion in Galilee (16:7) is not referred to again. Instead there is a listing of appearances of the risen Lord that looks very much like a summary of the appearances recorded in Matthew, Luke, and John. The compressed and colorless style of these verses is in marked contrast to Mark's usually rather broad and vivid narrative, and a number of expressions occur that are not found elsewhere in Mark.

It may be that the Gospel originally ended at 16:8, as some scholars maintain. It is difficult to explain how an original ending, if one existed, could have disappeared so completely as it apparently did. If it was lost or destroyed early, Mark himself could have supplied the loss; if later, how did it happen that it was lost from *all* copies of the Gospel? Still, it is hard to believe that a Gospel with the title "The beginning of the gospel," did not include a record of the meeting of the risen Lord with His disciples and of His missionary command to them. The ending that someone in the Early Church supplied to make good the loss of the original ending was probably never intended to pass as the original ending. It was a substitute for the ending, made up from the other Gospels. And it does, with its record of the commissioning of the apostles by the risen Christ, carry out the intentions of the Gospel according to St. Mark.

Doctrinal Content

Summary Commentary

1:1–13 Mark begins by telling of (1) John's call to repentance, (2) Baptism, and (3) eager expectation of the Messiah's coming. The Father declares Jesus is His Son as the Spirit descends on Jesus—note all three persons of the Trinity in the account. However, Jesus' status as God's Son makes Him a target of Satan's assaults (1:12–13). Jesus' successful struggle against temptation in the wilderness prefigures His final victory at the cross over our ancient foe.

1:14–3:12 At first, Jesus' message sounds much like the message of John and the prophets. On the other hand, the arrival of the Messiah fulfills prophecy and ushers in a new era. The first thing Jesus does in His public ministry is call two pairs of brothers. They respond by dropping everything, following Him, and becoming "fishers of men." Jesus' authoritative teaching and power over the unclean spirits create an immediate stir among those beholding Him in the early days of His ministry in Galilee.

First-century fishing boat found in the mud of the Sea of Galilee.

Jesus' first day of public ministry—the Sabbath—is a busy one. Though Jesus has much more to do among the people of Capernaum, He makes time for private devotion and then insists on moving on to visit other towns and villages. When a leper seeks Jesus' help, the Lord not only heals him but also makes sure that the man is restored to his rightful place in society.

In the presence of many who doubt Jesus' ability, He forgives and heals a paralyzed man simply by speaking the word. Jesus outrages His critics by calling Levi the tax collector to follow Him, then eats with a houseful of equally "defiled" people. Jesus stresses that the time of fulfillment has arrived, and thus totally new ways of thinking and acting are in order. When the Pharisees accuse Jesus and His disciples of violating the Sabbath, Jesus uses the opportunity to claim divine authority and assert His messianic status. In contrast to the Pharisees' and Herodians' hostility, the crowds enthusiastically press around Jesus to listen and be healed.

Clay brick found in Jerusalem, stamped with LEG X F (Legion 10 Fretensis) and the symbol of a wild pig. This legion served in Samaria, Edom, and Judah and took part in the seige of Jerusalem in AD 70.

3:13–6:6 Even as Jesus seeks to expand His ministry by appointing and sending 12 apostles, His family comes and tries to make Him stop what He is doing. Those who refuse to recognize Jesus as God's Son and acknowledge His works as manifestations of the Holy Spirit remain under the dominion of Satan. Loyalty to God takes precedence over loyalty to blood relations.

The parable of the sower helps explain why not everyone who hears the Gospel believes it and bears the fruit of faith. Jesus interprets the parable and builds on the theme of producing for the Kingdom by comparing His people to lamps set on a stand and by promising that faithfulness will be rewarded. God's kingdom grows mysteriously of itself, at its own pace, through the power of the Word. Jesus' parables reassure believers that over time the kingdom of God will grow incredibly large, far beyond its unassuming beginnings.

When Jesus rebukes the wind and waves, the lifeless storm shows a greater recognition of His divine power than do the disciples. Despite Jesus' magnificent work of deliverance, the reaction to Him is mixed. The demon-possessed man eagerly wishes to follow Jesus and then enthusiastically furthers His cause, while the townspeople ask Jesus to go away. Jesus heals Jairus's daughter and a woman with a chronic ailment. Two very different astonishments stand side by side: Jesus' teachings amaze His hometown neighbors; yet their close-minded hard-heartedness leaves Jesus amazed.

6:7–8:30 The disciples multiply Jesus' healing and revealing ministry, building on the foundation laid by John the Baptist and anticipating their own ministries, which will bear full fruit after Jesus' ascension. Even as Jesus sends the Twelve, He anticipates that not everyone will welcome the Gospel. Coming just after the story about Jesus' rejection in Nazareth, the tragic story of John gives an unmistakable foreshadowing of what awaits Jesus: rejection and even violent hostility.

When a multitude of Jesus' followers have far too little food for all to eat, Jesus multiplies five loaves and two fishes so that all are satisfied. Demonstrating mastery over the winds and waves for a second time, Jesus calms another storm. Even more amazing, however, is the fact that Jesus' disciples still do not recognize His divine nature. In contrast, the people of Gennesaret show great faith by receiving Jesus and clamoring for His healing power.

A traditional mikveh, a ritual bath, discovered in Jericho near Herod's palace. Their use is described in the Mishnah tractate Mikwaoth. Jesus describes the Jewish interest in washing in Mk 7.

Jesus criticizes the Pharisees for being overly concerned with man-made observances while failing to fulfill God's Commandments. Jesus teaches that people are not defiled by food or other things entering the body from the outside, but rather by their own evil inclinations and sinful behaviors. In the regions of Tyre and Sidon, Jesus reveals that He has come to save the ritually unclean Gentiles along with the Jews. Jesus heals another person in a Gentile region, further emphasizing His love for every race and kind of people.

Jesus' compassion moves Him to feed another hungry crowd by means of a second miraculous multiplication of bread. When Jesus confronts the disciples with feeding the crowds for a second time, they again fail to see that His power provides the way forward. Even though the Pharisees have already rejected Jesus, they still try to demand that He prove His identity. The disciples remember their lack of bread but forget about the One who is with them, the very Lord and Creator of all. Jesus heals a blind man as His disciples continue to struggle with the issue of who Jesus is and what He has come to do. For the first time in Mark, one of the Twelve recognizes Jesus as the Christ, God's Anointed One.

8:31–10:52 At the heart of the Gospel, Jesus warns that He has come to suffer, die, and rise and that everyone who follows Him must carry the cross. Jesus is transfigured to display His divine glory and to prepare His disciples for His death and resurrection. When Jesus descends from the transfiguration, He meets a defiant demon, an anxious father, an astonished crowd, and despairing disciples. Jesus repeats the prophecy of His Passion and resurrection while the disciples listen in frightened silence. Confused by Jesus' prediction of His death, the disciples return to a subject they know well—their own greatness. Jesus shows them that true status is found in serving those whom God values. Jesus opens the disciples' eyes to see those who do God's work in dramatic or simple ways. Nothing is more important than retaining the faith unto eternal life.

Jesus teaches that God wants a man and a woman in marriage to be exclusively committed to each other for life. The next story shows us that salvation is a gift of grace through faith in Jesus Christ. We trust the Lord as a child trusts a parent. Jesus teaches His disciples that not even people with the greatest worldly means (e.g., a rich man) can enter the kingdom of God on their own merit. Jesus then predicts His trial, execution, and resurrection for the third time in Mark (cf 8:31–32; 9:30–32) while walking boldly to His death. Jesus puts our welfare and needs ahead of His own as He conducts His ministry, showing us what real leadership is. Though Jesus is intent on going to the cross, He pauses to have mercy on Bartimaeus, who cries out to the Lord in a childlike manner, "Have mercy!"

Chs 11–13 Jesus enters Jerusalem triumphantly as King, openly accepting messianic titles and fulfilling several Old Testament prophecies. The disciples and the crowds expect Jesus to establish an earthly kingdom. They celebrate His arrival at Jerusalem without a clear view of His express purpose: to die for the sins of the world. The curse and destruction of the fig tree warns Jesus' disciples of impending judgment against the temple and the unfruitful people. As prophesied in Mal 3:1–5, Jesus purifies the temple of those who use religion to line their pockets. He does so in the temple court, where genuine worship has been disrupted. Jesus teaches that saving faith rescues us from God's judgment and that, through faith, we have the power to do the work God gives us. Opponents of Jesus confront Him and question His authority. Jesus refuses to engage them since He confidently knows the true character of His authority.

Jesus tells a parable about God's patience. But eventually God's patience runs out, and every person must face judgment. Jesus challenges the hypocritical Pharisees to examine their own hearts and repent. When the Sadducees try to trap Jesus with a hypothetical question, Jesus turns their question upside down and shows them that they deny God's power and reject His Word. Jesus also challenges an expert in the Scriptures to consider the entire Law and to turn to the Lord in faith. Only Jesus has kept the entire Law perfectly. Jesus invites His audience to think about the Messiah and realize that He is more than a man; He is God as well. Self-serving religion does not elevate us above others, as the example of the widow's offering shows.

Jesus begins to talk about the fall of Jerusalem and the end of the world with a prediction of the temple's destruction. Jesus warns His disciples about the coming troubles they will face as they bring the Gospel into the world. He encourages them to trust God and rely on the Holy Spirit, especially when they face opposition and persecution. Jesus warns His followers of the imminent destruction of Jerusalem, which was fulfilled during the Jewish revolt against the Romans (AD 66–70). These events foreshadowed the end of the world. Jesus tells us these things so that we may be prepared to resist evil and proclaim the Gospel more fervently while we have time to do so. When Jesus returns on the Last Day, He will judge all people. Prior to that glorious and victorious day, evil will erupt and bring destruction. Jesus answers the original question of "when?" about the destruction of the temple (13:4). In contrast to the fall of Jerusalem (13:5–23), which will happen within a generation, no one knows the day when Jesus will return to judge the world (13:24–27).

14:1–42 The Jewish leaders desperately try to find a way to execute Jesus quickly and quietly before He gains full support for His mission. A woman anoints Jesus for His burial, sacrificing expensive ointment out of love for Him. Judas, one of the Twelve whom Jesus appointed, decides to betray Him to the authorities. Jesus arranged for the Passover to be eaten at a secret location in Jerusalem. He establishes the Lord's Supper, giving communicants His true body and blood for the forgiveness of sins under the bread and wine. Jesus fulfills the Scripture that promises the forgiveness of sins through the sacrifice of the Shepherd, even though all His sheep desert Him. On the eve of His Passion, Jesus prays in agony, yet He concludes by praying that the Father's will be done. The disciples fall asleep while praying, unfaithful in the critical hour.

14:43–15:15 Representatives of the Jewish ruling Council arrest Jesus, apprehending Him at night outside the city to avoid causing a riot among His supporters. Jesus is abandoned by His disciples, including a young man (possibly Mark) who has witnessed the arrest. The Jewish ruling Council convicts Jesus of blasphemy for claiming to be the messianic King. While Jesus stands firm before Caiaphas, on trial for His life, Peter three times denies knowing Jesus. The Jewish leaders bring Jesus to Pilate, hoping to get a death penalty conviction from him. The world does not understand the kingdom of God, where God rules by grace through faith in Jesus Christ, nor does the world understand its King. Jesus endures His trial silently, without making a legal defense. Despite knowing that Jesus is innocent, Pilate condemns Him to death by crucifixion under pressure from the Jewish leadership and the crowds. Even though Pilate wants to release Jesus, he sentences Him to death to keep himself out of trouble.

15:16–16:8 Roman soldiers mock Jesus as the King of the Jews, inflicting terrible physical and emotional pain. Jesus is crucified, bearing the punishment for the sins of the world. He opens the way to God through faith in Him. Friends bury the body of Jesus quickly because the approaching Sabbath Day is holy to the Lord, and no work can be done on it (Ex 20:8–11). On the third day, the women undertake the job of properly preparing Jesus' body for burial, which the press of time prevented earlier. When they arrive at the tomb, they find it empty and hear the wonderful (and temporarily paralyzing) message that Jesus has risen from the dead and the tomb is empty. Despite Jesus' clear predictions on at least three occasions (8:31–32; 9:31; 10:33–34), His disciples do not understand or believe.

A Jerusalem ossuary contained the above heelbone of a crucified man pierced by a nail. The model at left show how the nail was driven through the outside of the foot into the side of the verticle crosspost.

16:9–20 This is the "long ending" of Mark, which may not be part of the original composition. Mary Magdalene sees the resurrected Jesus and tells the disciples about Him, but they do not believe it. The pattern of unbelief continues despite additional eyewitness accounts. Jesus commissions His followers to proclaim the message of salvation throughout the world.

Specific Law Themes

Mark begins with the message of repentance, preached by both John the Baptist and Jesus. The political and religious opposition that the two preachers face illustrates the sins and errors of the people. Ritual and spiritual uncleanness abounds. Jesus addresses these problems through His authoritative teaching, yet many remain hard-hearted. They fail to repent or recognize Him as the Messiah.

Specific Gospel Themes

The Gospel of Mark proclaims the coming of the Lord with His salvation. It begins with Baptism, offered for the forgiveness of sins. Throughout the Gospel, Jesus demonstrates God's compassion by healing people or providing for them in other ways. God's desire is to have mercy on sinners, to ransom them. To that end, Jesus teaches about God's mercy with authority and promise. He likewise institutes the Lord's Supper.

Specific Doctrines

The Gospel of Mark is the least doctrinal of the canonical accounts, focusing primarily on Jesus' deeds. Nonetheless, the Church has turned to several key texts in Mark's account. The first is Mark's summary of Jesus' teaching, calling for repentance and faith (1:15), which agrees with the broader preaching themes of Law and Gospel found in the Old Testament prophets. Mark 9:24 wonderfully summarizes the struggles faced by many of Jesus' disciples who believe and yet stumble in their faith. Along with faith, the Lord promises rewards, even for this life. However, He also notes that the blessings of the Gospel will be attended by persecutions and trials, despite which we long for everlasting life (Mk 10:30).

Mark 10:45 is a key verse to the Gospel itself, also noting that Christians from the earliest times regarded the cross and death of Jesus as redemptive and not merely as an example of suffering. Lay people and scholars alike have pondered 13:22, what it tells us about the person of Jesus and also how we are to anticipate His return. Ironically, one of the most referenced passages of the Gospel for doctrinal purposes (16:16 on the importance of Baptism) likely was not part of Mark's original composition.

On Mark's emphasis on the "messianic secret," see p 259.

Application

1:1–13 John warns us not to adopt worldly values and expectations. Satan does all that he can to tempt the baptized. Yet, our own Baptism joins us to Christ and clothes us with His righteousness. Jesus, after uniting Himself with fallen humans through Baptism, won a preliminary victory over the evil foe's temptations. At the cross, Jesus gained an even more wonderful victory for us. His resurrection proves that Satan cannot prevail.

1:14–3:12 The Church's message today focuses on the age-old problem of sin and human failure. However, the Gospel delivers the forgiveness of sins and with it the hope of an eternal future with God. As Jesus invited disciples to follow Him, He confronts people today: either drop everything and, in faith, follow Jesus and make sacrifices, or run the risk of missing out on the Kingdom. We often see the same thing. People continue to be interested in and even amazed by Jesus' teaching, and yet many fail to depend on Him for life and salvation. He commands us to lay all our needs before Him and stands ever willing and able to help us. But Jesus' healing will remedy our alienation. His grace makes peace with God, restores our broken relationships, and thus puts us right with one another.

Some doubt the power of Jesus' Word—there will always be such naysayers. But, as Peter reminds us, though our flesh will perish, the Word of the Lord stands forever (1Pt 1:24–25). His story invites the modern hearer to reflect: am I more like the manifest sinners in the Gospel or like those who criticize Jesus' openness to be with the unworthy? Either way, you stand in need of forgiveness. Thankfully, the Lord offers such surpassingly great promises that the old way of life is made obsolete. That is what Paul meant when he said, "If anyone is in Christ, he is a new creation" (2Co 5:17). He knows all our burdens and desires to grant us rest. Call on Him in earnest prayer. When the Lord is for us, no one can oppose us! Jesus attends to people's physical and spiritual needs. He continues to bless those who seek Him today.

3:13–35 How ironic that those who think they know Jesus best are trying to stop Him from fulfilling His mission! Unfortunately, similar examples are still seen, as when lifelong Christians undermine sound mission strategies. Those baptized into Christ have received not only Him but also His promised Holy Spirit. The Lord now calls us to have sound relationships with family and friends as well as with the heavenly Father. Jesus stands first in our lives because He placed Himself last, to humbly bear our sins and make us children of God.

4:1–34 The Word of the Lord accomplishes His good purpose. It works miracles in lives where the Spirit has His way. The failures of the various soils to produce for the Lord are still common: people even now refuse to hear, fall away when hardship comes, and allow worldly concerns to overwhelm their faith. Yet, by God's grace, many receive the Word in good faith and produce richly. The Lord calls us to focus on His mission. Though we are generous, He is more generous still and blesses more and more. It is a great blessing that things ultimately depend on Him and not us, for only He is able to bring home a great harvest for life eternal. Precisely because the Kingdom grows so slowly and its Lord is so patient, believers tend to become discouraged and its enemies are emboldened. But in the end, the Kingdom alone will stand, and everything else will be overthrown. Thank God, He shelters His people of every nation in its eternal shade.

4:35–6:6 The brute forces of nature invariably obey the Lord's commands better than people—including God's own children—obey them. But the Lord nonetheless continues to love and care for us, despite our dullness and doubts. He not only calms all of the storms in our lives but actually does so in ways that mature our faith and lead us to trust Him more deeply. But what remarkable kindness Jesus shows! He rescues people from the devil's power and even the grave itself, and then allows them to be witnesses to the wonders of His

First-century ossuary with the inscription "Jacob (James) son of Joseph brother of Jesus." Although the genuineness of the inscription was challenged, a 2012 trial revealed that critics misrepresented their knowledge of the discovery. Top paleographers have defended the inscription, though debate about its authenticity is likely to continue. The photo's inscription is enhanced.

grace. The Eternal One, who overcame death by rising from the dead, never runs out of time. His gracious promise is that we shall share eternal life with Him.

6:7–56 God unfailingly opens hearts and doors to the disciples' ministry, and He promises to do the same until the end of time. Rejection and violence cannot overcome the risen Lord. When problems threaten us and needs overwhelm our resources, how do we react? We should turn first to the Lord, as His Word makes clear, for He still treats His flock with compassion and more than provides for every need of body and soul. Jesus remains devoted to us even when our commitment wavers or fails. His resolve to suffer and die for all is ample proof of that.

7:1–37 Hypocrisy abounds today, as most people worry more about human opinions than what God thinks. Jesus' teaching exposes the uselessness of our own excuse-making. However, Jesus does not merely condemn; He sets and He reaches out to all people. No one lies beyond the scope of His love and grace. The Gospel accounts of Jesus' healing people underscores that He desires to love, cleanse, and heal all people.

8:1–30 How slowly we sometimes respond in faith! Yet how graciously Jesus continues to provide. Scoffers may demand signs. Believers, however, know that God's goodness in Christ is real, and they see the depth of His love in Christ's suffering and the glory of His promises in the resurrection. His gracious touch opens our eyes so that, despite our weaknesses, we recognize Him as the Christ and believe in Him unto life everlasting.

8:31–9:50 A safe life tempts us to deny Christ and His cross. We cannot imagine the glory of God, especially in Christ, as we consider His humanity. Jesus loses none of His divine majesty in the incarnation, but His glory shines through His human nature. His glory reminds us that He freely chose death and resurrection for our sakes. Despair threatens to overwhelm our faith by pointing out how we fail to change or improve, suggesting that God neither cares for us nor has power to help. Yet, Jesus bears our fears as well as our sins on the cross in order to deliver us. Our Master hangs on the cross. He represents us before the Father in order to redeem us, and He leads us by the cross into a new life. He shows His power and kindness through great life-changing miracles and simple cups of water.

Ch 10 Attempts to alter or get around God's good intentions bring condemnation, not greater liberty.

We do not earn God's love and favor by keeping the Law, especially when we look for loopholes to excuse our sinful behavior (cf 10:1–12). We cannot justify ourselves; we receive salvation ("inherit eternal life") solely by grace through faith in Jesus, just like a little child (10:13–16). Faith looks to Christ crucified and risen and says "for me." He leads by laying down His life as the sacrifice for our sins and calls us to similar sacrifice. Like Bartimaeus, learn to call on the Lord and trust in His power to deliver you. Jesus will hear and respond compassionately.

Ch 11 Jesus enters Jerusalem in humility to fulfill the plan of salvation by laying down His life for sinners. True faith, and the life that flows from it, cannot be separated. They are the good and gracious gifts of our heavenly Father. Today, Jesus challenges us to eliminate all barriers to God's Word in our lives and in our congregations. Without faith in Jesus, it is impossible to please God or pray to Him. We know God hears our prayers even if we do not receive an answer immediately. Confident prayer, based on faith in Christ crucified and risen, trusts God to answer in His own time and way (cf Rm 8:32).

Ch 12 God planned the death of His Son for the sins of all people. Though sin shattered the image of our Maker in us, the Lord still wants us for His very own people (Rm 8:29; Eph 4:24; Col 3:10). Like the Sadducees, people today want to limit God to doing what makes sense to them, as if human limitations or reason could bind Him! Unbelief binds people so they do not see Christ in the Old Testament (cf 2Co 3:12–18). God became man, born of Mary, born under the Law, to redeem sinners such as we (cf Gal 4:4–5). Jesus' love and sacrifice motivate us to offer our whole lives to Him as our daily offering of gratitude. He gave up everything, including His life, on the cross for us.

Ch 13 What makes a house of worship worthy is not its outward appearance but the Word of God in it. As Christians proclaim Law and Gospel, they need to be ready to endure the loss of everything, including their church and their lives. Yet, God holds on to His people throughout trying events, anchoring believers in Jesus Christ by His Holy Spirit. We can be sure of our salvation no matter how fearsome the Last Day may be. Focus on the calling we have as Christ's Church: Gospel proclamation and outreach (cf Mt 28:18–20). God has created this time before the second appearing of Jesus so that we may come to faith and call others to faith and salvation. Jesus promises to be with us always, and He has poured out on us His Holy Spirit for the work of evangelizing the nations.

14:1–42 Devote yourself to Jesus by prayer and service. He now stands at the Father's throne, praying for you, serving as your Savior. God is at work, using even the opposition of His enemies for His gracious purposes. Even Judas's betrayal of Jesus plays an important role in the plan of salvation, culminating in the cross and empty tomb. Opposition to the Gospel comes from Satan, the world, and even from within the ranks of Jesus' followers. The sacrifice of the Passover lamb would foreshadow the sacrifice of our beloved Redeemer for us. Jesus creates a new relationship between God and sinners through His suffering and death on the cross. By His blood, He seals His testament of peace and forgiveness, which we receive in this Sacrament. Only through God's strength can any Christian face trial. Even though Jesus' sheep will run away, He will lay down His life for them. Our Savior is ever vigilant and interceding on our behalf, that the Lord might answer our prayers in mercy.

14:43–16:8 God's plan of salvation moves forward, using the "success" of His enemies. We cannot count on our own courage or strength in the face of Satan and his forces. God uses the plans and plots of His enemies to accomplish our salvation. Only God can give us the courage to face difficult situations, especially persecution.

We can pray that the Lord would grant us courage to trust His will and share His will. He has promised to give us His Holy Spirit to strengthen us for every challenge. Paying for the sin of the world was costly. Jesus' tremendous love for us kept Him on course to the cross. Even in the tomb, death does not conquer Jesus—His body does not decay (cf Ac 2:31). Jesus completes His mission with this last step in His state of humiliation. He has fully paid for the sins of the entire world! Jesus rises from the dead, proclaiming His victory to all creation and providing for all believers a resurrection to eternal life on the Last Day.

16:9–20 Faith, like life, comes as a pure gift from God. He keeps us in the true faith unto life everlasting. Jesus rose for us and commissioned us to proclaim the Gospel everywhere. Only through faith in Jesus Christ can anyone be saved. The Gospel invitation is open to all. God wants all people to be saved through Jesus (1Tm 2:3–4).

Canonicity

Although Mark was not used as much as Matthew and John, it was unquestioningly received as a canonical Gospel (*homologoumenon*). On the history of the long ending (16:9–20), see p 243.

Lutheran Theologians on Mark

Luther

See pp 214–16.

Gerhard

"Irenaeus calls Mark 'the interpreter and follower of Peter' (bk. 3, c. 1, p. 183). Nicephorus writes this about him: 'Peter dictated the Gospel to him and sanctioned that it then be read in the churches' (bk. 2, c. 45). Epiphanius states: 'Peter ordered Mark to publish the Gospel in Rome' (*Haeres*. 51, p. 192). In *Hist.*, bk. 6, c. 11, Eusebius also cites these things from Clement of Alexandria. Jerome, *Catal. illustr.*: 'Mark was the disciple and interpreter of Peter. When the brethren at Rome asked him, he wrote in brief form the Gospel according to what he had heard Peter tell. When Peter heard it, he approved of it and stated under his authority that it should be read in the Church.' (Cf. Eusebius, *Hist.*, bk. 1, c. 15, and Nicephorus, bk. 2, c. 15.)

"Others relate concerning him that he was Peter's nephew from his sister; that he was one of the seventy disciples of Christ; and that he preached the Gospel in the Egyptian city of Alexandria. Baronius claims: 'Mark wrote his Gospel in Latin, not in Greek. The first copy of it is preserved in Venice among the treasures of San Marco' (vol. 1, *Annal.*, ann. 45). In his preface to *Gramm. Arab.*, p. 36, Kirstenius agrees with Baronius in part. However: (1) He does not prove this by any suitable and old witness. Damasus, whom he is quoting, has many fables. (2) The same reasons that prove that Matthew did not write his Gospel in Hebrew demonstrate that Mark did not write in Latin. (3) The copy preserved at Venice is not of sufficiently proved trustworthiness. (4) In *De verbo Dei*, bk. 2, c. 7 and 15, Bellarmine frankly admits that 'the entire Greek edition of the New Testament has the apostles and the evangelists as their authors.' Therefore let us hold on to what is certain; let us abandon what is uncertain, that is, let us accept the Greek texts of Matthew and Mark as authentic.

"We gather that the last chapter of Mark was not accepted by all as canonical at the time of Jerome from his Epistle *ad Hebidiam* 150, q. 3, where he says, 'Almost all the books in Greek do not have this brief chapter at the end.' There appears to be a twofold reason for doubt: (1) It seems to conflict with the description of the Lord's resurrection among the rest of the evangelists. We have shown the contrary, however, in our *Harmonia evangelica*, 'On the Resurrection.' (2) According to the statement of Jerome in *Dial. 2 adv. Pelag.*, heretics inserted in it some apocryphal sentences that have the smell of Manichaeanism: 'And they were apologizing, saying, "This is the age of iniquity and the substance of unbelief. It did not permit the true power of God to be grasped through the unclean spirits. Therefore reveal your righteousness now." ' Let the apocryphal and foreign parts be removed, however, and let the remaining canonical portions be kept. Irenaeus (bk. 3, c. 11), Athanasius (*Synopsis*), Augustine (*De cons. evang.*, bk. 3, c. 24), Bede (commentary [on Mark]), and others of the ancients acknowledge that this chapter is genuine.

"The Gospel account of Mark has sixteen chapters in which is also explained the threefold *office of Christ: prophetic, priestly, and royal*." (ThC E1 § 244)

Christ victorious, raising the dead.

Questions People Ask about Mark

The Beginning of the Public Ministry of Jesus

Mark 1:14 reads: "Now after John was arrested, Jesus came into Galilee, proclaiming the Gospel of God."

John 3:22–24 relates: "After this Jesus and His disciples went into the Judean countryside, and He remained there with them and was baptizing. John also was baptizing at Aenon near Salim, because water was plentiful there, and people were coming and being baptized (for John had not yet been put in prison)."

There might seem to be a contradiction between Mark and John, as the former places the beginning of the ministry of Jesus apparently after the imprisonment of John the Baptist, the latter before it. The solution is that while Mark does not relate the activity of Jesus before John was cast into prison, his account does not exclude the possibility that Jesus preached and taught quite extensively before persecution fell upon the Baptist. When Mark says, "Now after John was arrested, Jesus came into Galilee," he does not deny that Jesus had been in Galilee before and had been teaching there. But it is true that the main activity of Jesus as a prophet did not commence until John's enforced retirement from the scene, and on that account probably the first three evangelists do not mention the work He had done previously. We must repeat here that the Gospel according to John was written a considerable time later than the other Gospels, and that one of its purposes plainly is to supplement the narratives of Matthew, Mark, and Luke, adding such details as they had passed over in silence; hence what is given us by John is additional and not contradictory information. We would have a contradiction here if Mark or Matthew or Luke had said that Jesus did not do any preaching until after the imprisonment of John, but none of them makes that statement, and hence it is idle to speak of a discrepancy here.

The Voice from Heaven at the Baptism of Jesus

Matthew 3:17 states: "And behold, a voice from heaven said, 'This is My beloved Son, with whom I am well pleased.'"

Mark 1:11 says: "And a voice came from heaven, 'You are My beloved Son; with You I am well pleased.'"

It has been charged that there is a discrepancy here because the one evangelist reports the voice as saying, "This is My beloved Son," and the other, "You are My beloved Son." Everyone will have to admit that in the substance of the words spoken in this connection there is no difference. The meaning conveyed is the same in both cases. There is a difference in the form, that is true. According to Mark, the words are spoken to Jesus; according to Matthew, they are spoken of Him. The difference is explained very readily if we conclude that Mark records the words of God the Father with literal exactness, while Matthew merely gives the meaning. Shall we say that two people contradict each other in their reports of a political meeting when the one states that the audience shouted, speaking to the candidate, "You are our man!" and the other informs us that the shout went up, "This is our man!"? Both reports are correct. The one is merely a trifle more literally accurate than the other.

Few Miracles in Nazareth

A passage requiring some comment is Mk 6:5–6, which refers to Jesus' visit to Nazareth. We are told: "And He could do no mighty work there, except that He laid His hands on a few sick people and healed them. And He marveled because of their unbelief." Does this passage deny that Jesus is omnipotent and the true God? Nothing of the sort! It simply points out that if the gifts of God are to be received, there must be a receptive attitude on the part of people, that our Lord will not force His beneficient ministrations on anybody, that those who persistently refuse to accept what He offers will not receive it. It is very true that this receptive attitude itself is a gift of God. But what we are concerned with here is the truth that God's wonderful works are not performed for those who spurn them.

Equipment of the Disciples on Their Missionary Journey

Matthew 10:9–10 reads: "Acquire no gold or silver or copper for your belts, no bag for your journey, or two tunics or sandals or a staff, for the laborer deserves his food."

Mark 6:8–9 states: "He charged them to take nothing for their journey except a staff—no bread, no bag, no money in their belts—but to wear sandals and not put on two tunics."

A careful comparison of these texts reveals that according to Matthew Jesus forbids His disciples to "acquire" staffs or sandals (the Greek term may imply "shoes"), while in Mark the disciples may take along staffs and sandals (here the Greek may not mean "shoes"). The difference between the verbs that the evangelists use is important. In Matthew, Jesus forbids the purchase or acquisition of equipment; in Mark, He speaks not of what they should not provide for themselves but of what they might take along or not take along on their journey.

What the Lord says to the disciples in Mark is practically: "Go as you are." If they had staffs, they could take them with them, but they were not to provide themselves with additional ones. They should consider their sandals sufficient and not procure more footwear. Hence a careful reading of the two texts reveals that we are dealing with two statements that supplement each other and were both spoken when Jesus gave His disciples instruction for their first missionary tour.

Was Jesus Omniscient?

Mark 13:32 reads: "But concerning that day or that hour, no one knows, not even the angels in heaven, nor the Son, but only the Father."

John 21:17 records: "He said to him the third time, 'Simon, son of John, do you love Me?' Peter was grieved because He said to him the third time, 'Do you love me?' and he said to Him, 'Lord, You know everything; You know that I love You.' Jesus said to him, 'Feed my sheep.' "

The one passage ascribes omniscience to Jesus; the other denies that He, the Son, knew the day and the hour when the last judgment will take place. One must remember that Scripture teaches that Jesus is both God and man in one person and that He might speak according to the strength of His divine nature or according to the weakness of His human nature. Let the reader also carefully note when each one of these statements was made. When Peter said to Jesus, "Lord, You know everything" the days of suffering for our Lord were past and the resurrection had taken place; but the words of Jesus Himself, saying that the Son did not know the time of the last judgment, were spoken before His Passion and His victorious return to life. Here we have the key to the whole situation. The Bible distinguishes between Jesus before and after His resurrection. A consideration of all pertinent Scripture passages will show that, while Jesus before His suffering and death was invested with all the divine attributes, He did not during this period of humiliation use His divine majesty fully and uninterruptedly. Before His resurrection He had made Himself of no reputation, took upon Himself the form of a servant, and humbled Himself (Php 2:7–8). He possessed omniscience, but according to His human nature He was content to forego its use except on certain occasions. When He says that the Son does not know the date of the judgment, a glimpse is afforded into the depth of His humiliation entered upon for us, which made Him refrain from exercising the divine powers He possessed and which reached its climax when He, apparently powerless and defenseless, hung on the cross. After His resurrection, however, His status is changed; "God has highly exalted Him and bestowed on Him the name that is above every name" (Php 2:9).

The Denial of Peter

Second century child's pull toy with reconstructed wheels.

Among the passages that cause some Bible readers great difficulty are those that contain the prediction and the account of Peter's denial. In Mt 26:34 we read: "Jesus said to [Peter], 'Truly, I tell you, this very night, before the rooster crows, you will deny Me three times.' " In vv 74 and 75 of the same chapter Matthew relates: "And immediately the rooster crowed. And Peter remembered the saying of Jesus, 'Before the rooster crows, you will deny Me three times.' And he went out and wept bitterly."

Mark 14:30 states: "And Jesus said to him, 'Truly, I tell you, this very night, before the rooster crows twice, you will deny me three times.' " Verse 68 says: "And he went out into the gateway and the rooster crowed," while v 72 records: "And immediately the rooster crowed a second time. And Peter remembered how Jesus had said to him, 'Before the rooster crows twice, you will deny Me three times.' And he broke down and wept." Here it has been imagined that a discrepancy has slipped into the New Testament. Matthew has "before the rooster crows," and Mark has "before the rooster crows twice."

It is very easy to harmonize the two accounts. Jesus made both statements: that Peter would deny Him before the crowing of the rooster and that he would do it before the rooster had crowed twice. Matthew records the one statement, Mark the other. Luke (22:34, 60–62) and John (13:38; 18:25–27), it ought to be added, report the words of Jesus practically in the same form as Matthew. Before we could be justified in accusing the evangelists of contradicting one another, positive proof would have to be brought that the prediction of Jesus was made only once. We may well imagine that the situation was as follows: Jesus informs Peter that the latter will deny Him, saying, "Before the rooster crows, you will deny Me three times." Impetuous Peter becomes very excited. He deny his Lord? That is impossible! So he declares, "Never! I shall rather die than deny You." Thereupon Jesus, with warning voice, repeats His statement, adding another detail: "Peter, before the rooster crows twice, you will deny Me three times." It seems so natural to reason that with respect to this serious subject a number of remarks should have been exchanged between the Lord and Peter; there is no difficulty in holding that Jesus spoke both the words reported by Matthew, Luke, and John and those recorded by Mark.

Here, too, we may add an alternative view, which has found favor with many Bible students. Matthew, Luke, and John are reporting the prediction of Jesus in general terms, while Mark, as is his custom, is more specific. Just as in other narratives he frequently adds little touches that the other evangelists do not mention, so here Mark reports a detail that is not found in the other Gospels. Furthermore, we must bear in mind that Mark's Gospel is reported to have been written under the guiding influence of Peter and is spoken of as having a Petrine character. Therefore, we need not be surprised to find that the important words spoken to Peter on that solemn occasion are in this book given with greater completeness than in the other Gospels.

One more word may be required. It might seem that there is a discrepancy between the prediction of Jesus, "before the rooster crows, you will deny Me three times," and the account of the fulfillment as given by Mark, which says that when Peter had denied once, the rooster crowed (14:68). When Jesus says that Peter would deny Him three times before the rooster crows, He is speaking in the conventional way of the rooster's crow as the signal announcing that the morning is about to arrive. The "time of the rooster's crow" is simply another term for daybreak. However, when Jesus speaks of the rooster's crowing twice, He is predicting that in that night of terrors the phenomenon of the rooster's crow in the deep of the night would occur preceding the rooster's crow at the dawn of morning by some time. There is nothing here that makes harmonization difficult.

Drink Given to Jesus before the Crucifixion

In the King James Version Mt 27:34 reads: "They gave him vinegar to drink mingled with gall: and when he had tasted thereof, he would not drink." The English Standard Version, however, has: "They offered Him wine to drink, mixed with gall, but when He tasted it, He would not drink it."

Mark 15:23 records: "And they offered Him wine mixed with myrrh, but he did not take it."

In this instance modern scholarship has shown that no discrepancy exists concerning the liquid offered to Jesus, for textual research has made it clear that also in Mt 27:34 the word should be wine (Gk *oinos*) as it is in Mk 15:23. Another Greek word (Gk *oxos*), used later when Jesus does accept a liquid presented to Him, means wine vinegar or sour wine (Mt 27:48; Mk 15:36; Lk 23:36; Jn 19:29).

A careful reader of Mt 27:34 and Mk 15:23 might question the difference between "wine mixed with gall" and "wine mixed with myrrh." Both phrases say essentially the same thing. Gall (Gk *thole*) is not a substance but refers to something bitter. Mark informs us that the substance was myrrh (Gk *myron*)—which has a bitter or slightly pungent taste. Thus there is no discrepancy concerning the liquids offered to Jesus on the cross—either the one He rejected or the other that He accepted.

The Hour of Christ's Crucifixion

It has often been charged that Mark and John are in disagreement as to the time when Jesus was crucified. In Mk 15:25 we read: "And it was the third hour when they crucified Him." John 19:14 reports that when Jesus was standing before Pilate, as the latter had sat down in his judgment seat in the place called Gabbatha, after ineffectual attempts to procure the Jews' consent for the dismissal of Jesus, "it was the day of Preparation of the Passover. It was about the sixth hour. He said to the Jews, 'Behold your King!' "

A. T. Robertson writes:

> The most satisfactory solution of the difficulty is to be found in the idea that John here uses the Roman computation of time, from midnight to noon and noon to midnight, just as we do now. Hence the sixth hour would be our six o'clock in the morning. If this hour was the beginning of the last trial of Jesus, we then have enough, but not too much, time for the completion of the trial, the carrying away of Jesus outside the city walls, together with the procuring of the crosses, etc. All the events, moreover, narrated by the evangelists could have occurred between dawn (John 18:27) and six or seven. For a long time it was doubted whether the Romans ever used this method of computing time for civil days. Farrar vehemently opposes this idea. But Plutarch, Pliny, Aulus Gellius, and Macrobius expressly say that the Roman civil day was reckoned from midnight to midnight. So the question of fact may be considered as settled. The only remaining question is whether John used this mode of reckoning. Of course, the Romans had also the natural day and the natural night just as we do now. In favor of the idea that John uses the Roman way of counting the hours in the civil day several things may be said. (*A Harmony of the Gospels for Students of the Life of Christ* [New York: Harper, 1922], pp 285–86)

If we adopt the interpretation of John 19:14 that this scholar puts before us so convincingly, the two passages are in complete harmony. It is logical, moreover, for John to adopt the Roman reckoning of time since he wrote at or around Ephesus, the capital of the Roman province of Asia, at a time and place in which the Christian Church was predominantly Gentile, not Jewish.

Sunrise over the Dead Sea.

Further Study

Lay/Bible Class Resources

Cole, R. Alan. *The Gospel According to Mark.* 2nd ed. TNTC. Grand Rapids: Eerdmans, 1989. ❧ Compact commentary interacting with the Greek text in a popular format. Generally helpful evangelical treatment of the text by an Australian scholar.

Dargatz, Robert A., and Steven Roberge. *Mark.* Leaders Guide and Enrichment Magazine/Study Guide. LL. St. Louis: Concordia, 2009. ❧ In-depth, nine-session Bible study with individual, small group, and lecture portions.

Dumit, Julene. *Mark: The Serving Christ.* GWFT. St. Louis: Concordia, 1995. ❧ Lutheran author. Ten-session Bible study, including leader's notes and discussion questions.

Life by His Word. St. Louis: Concordia, 2009. ❧ More than 1,500 reproducible one-page Bible studies covering each chapter of the canonical Scriptures. Page references to *The Lutheran Study Bible.* CD-Rom and downloadable.

Wicke, Harold E. *Mark.* PBC. St. Louis: Concordia, 2004. ❧ Lutheran author. Excellent for Bible classes. Based on the NIV translation.

Church Worker Resources

Dowd, Sharyn. *Reading Mark: A Literary and Theological Commentary on the Second Gospel.* Macon, GA: Smyth & Helwys Publishing, Inc., 2000. ❧ Not a full commentary but an easy-to-read literary and theological overview of the book. Presents Mark as a Greco-Roman biography written with apocalyptic perspective.

Lane, William L. *The Gospel according to Mark.* NICNT. Grand Rapids: Eerdmans, 1974. ❧ Perhaps the finest commentary on Mark. Pays close attention to the total context, also Judaica. Clearly and simply written.

Martin, Ralph. *Mark: Evangelist and Theologian.* Contemporary Evangelical Perspectives. Grand Rapids: Zondervan, 1986. ❧ A valuable overview by an evangelical scholar.

Academic Resources

Anderson, Hugh. *The Gospel of Mark.* NCBC. Rev. ed. Grand Rapids: Eerdmans, 1981. ❧ Written by a critical scholar with clear exposition from that perspective.

Bryan, Christopher. *A Preface to Mark: Notes on the Gospel in Its Literary and Cultural Settings.* New York: Oxford University Press, 1993. ❧ Bryan provides a very helpful introduction into questions of Mark's genre and original literary purpose, how Mark would have been received in the first century AD as a work of literature. Basically Bryan argues that Mark would have been recognized as an example of a "Greek Life" and it was written to be read aloud.

Cranfield, C. E. B. *The Gospel According to St Mark: An Introduction and Commentary.* Cambridge Greek Testament Commentary. Edited by C. F. D. Moule. New York: Cambridge University Press, 1959. ❧ This is an old standard commentary. Cranfield has a critical bent, but this commentary still provides an excellent interaction with the Greek text and the various ways it can be interpreted.

France, R. T. *The Gospel of Mark: A Commentary on the Greek Text.* NIGTC. Grand Rapids: Eerdmans, 2002. ❧ France interacts with the Greek text and makes his own text critical decisions at certain points that disagree with "the received text" of the Nestle-Aland edition. France provides a narrative reading and his general approach is conservative. Most of the time he identifies the various ways a text has been or could be interpreted before making his own decision. France's understanding of the theme of the cross in Mark's Gospel runs counter to traditional Lutheran reading since he sees the cross in Mark's Gospel as theology of glory.

Hendriksen, William. *New Testament Commentary: The Gospel of Mark.* Grand Rapids: Baker, 1975. § A reasonably detailed commentary from an evangelical scholar.

Kingsbury, Jack Dean. *Conflict in Mark: Jesus, Authorities, Disciples.* Minneapolis: Augsburg Fortress, 1989. § Provides a narrative critical reading of Mark's Gospel and identifies the major characters and their function in Mark.

Lange, John Peter. *Mark.* LCHS. New York: Charles Scribner's Sons, 1868. § A helpful older example of German biblical scholarship, based on the Greek text, which provides references to significant commentaries from the Reformation era forward.

Lenski, R. C. H. *The Interpretation of St. Mark's Gospel.* Minneapolis: Augsburg Fortress, 2008. § A standard resource by a noteworthy Lutheran interpreter, concerned with being faithful to the text and with its implications for today.

Mann, C. S. *Mark: A New Translation with Introduction and Commentary.* AB. Garden City, NY: Doubleday, 1986. § The general articles summarize critical scholarship. Mann sees Mark as the third Gospel account written that, together with Matthew and Luke, dates to the pre-AD 70 period. Stresses the great difficulty of the attempts to separate Jesus' actual words and deeds from what Jesus' followers later shared. Valuable extensive bibliographies.

Marcus, Joel. *Mark.* Vols. 27 and 27A of AB. New York: Doubleday, 1999; New Haven, CT: Yale University Press, 2009. § A massive critical commentary that proposes the Gospel was written after AD 70 as a liturgical drama for a Syrian congregation.

Moloney, Francis J. *The Gospel of Mark: A Commentary.* Peabody: Hendrickson Publishers, 2002. § Moloney provides a narrative approach to interpreting Mark. He assumes the four source hypothesis for the origin of the Synoptics. Moloney's introduction, especially his treatment of Mark's audience, plot, and literary shape are very helpful.

Stein, Robert H. *Mark.* Baker Exegetical Commentary on the New Testament. Grand Rapids: Baker, 2008. § An evangelical commentator who defends traditional Markan authorship but uses redaction criticism methods.

Taylor, Vincent. *The Gospel According to St. Mark: The Greek Text with Introduction, Notes, and Indexes.* London: Macmillan, 1952. § A classic commentary, provides much detailed information on textual variants; somewhat neo-orthodox in approach.

Witherington III, Ben. *The Gospel of Mark: A Socio-Rhetorical Commentary.* Grand Rapids: Eerdmans, 2001. § Explores the literary character of Mark's Gospel in view of its Jewish and Greco-Roman contexts.

LUKE

An orderly account from eyewitnesses and ministers of the Word

The Jerusalem temple was overlaid with so much gold that persons who saw it described its blinding effects as it glistened in the sun. Herod the Great was its builder. He surrounded it with a massive court, turning the Temple Mount into a sacred complex far larger than other temples of the ancient world. The project was ongoing when Mary and Joseph brought the infant Jesus to the temple for purification (Lk 2:22–38). It was still going some 30 years later when Jesus cleansed the temple from the money-changers at the beginning of Holy Week. During those days, Jesus would prophesy the temple's destruction and His own resurrection.

Historical and Cultural Setting

Unlike the other Gospel writers, Luke pays special attention to the temple of Herod, which was celebrated by Israel as the hallowed dwelling place of God and by Gentiles for its impressive size and majesty. Jesus and His followers gathered there for the rites, feasts, and teachings that marked Jesus' progress toward Good Friday when He would be crucified outside the city walls. After the resurrection, Jesus' disciples would again gather at the temple for prayer.

Luke's unique focus on the temple as the context for Jesus' life and ministry is exhibited in the chart on pp 268–69.

For the political circumstances surrounding the life of Jesus, see pp 185–86.

Although Herod the Great's redesign of the Jerusalem temple was completely destroyed by the Romans in AD 70, stunning examples of his building program survived. The Herodium, an artificial hill, contains his fortress palace. The ruins at left included a Roman-style bath and possibly Herod's tomb.

OVERVIEW

Author
Luke

Date
Written c AD 55–60

Places
Galilee; Judea; Samaria; Nazareth; Capernaum; Bethlehem; Jerusalem; Jericho; Bethany; Emmaus; Jordan River; Mount of Olives; see map, p 199

People
Jesus; the 12 apostles; Joseph; Mary; Zechariah; Elizabeth; John the Baptist; Simeon; Anna; Mary Magdalene; Zacchaeus; Herod the Great; Herod Antipas; Pilate

Purpose
To affirm Theophilus in the Gospel of Jesus, which he learned through catechesis

Law Themes
The lost; the mighty brought low; destruction of the temple; repentance; call to pray

Gospel Themes
The found; the humble exalted; God's presence at the temple; work of the Spirit; promises fulfilled; fellowship meals; call of the Gentiles

Memory Verses
The annunciation (1:30–33); the Magnificat (1:46–55); the Gloria in Excelsis (2:10–14); the Nunc Dimittis (2:29–32); parable of the lost sheep (15:1–7); Jesus fulfills the Scriptures (24:44–49)

TIMELINE

3 BC	Annunciation to Mary
2 BC	Birth of Jesus
AD 29	Baptism of Jesus
AD 3	Resurrection, Ascension, Pentecost
AD 36	Conversion of Paul
c AD 55–60	Luke written

The Temple in Luke

Luke's Gospel begins and ends with events at the Jerusalem temple.

Outline	Passages	Events	Comment
Birth and Boyhood of Jesus	1:5–25	Angel of the Lord appears to Zechariah	A major theme in the birth narratives is the shift in location of God's presence from the temple to the body of Jesus as God's temple (cf Jn 2:19–22; see CC Lk2, p 681).
	2:21–35	Jesus presented at the temple	
	2:25–35	Simeon blesses Jesus	
	2:36–38	Anna blesses Jesus	
	2:41–52	Visit to the temple at age 12	
Preparation for Ministry	4:9–11	Satan tempts Jesus to cast Himself down from the temple	We know from other Gospels that Jesus continued to visit the temple for various feasts. However, Luke contrasts Jesus' commitment to teaching outside Jerusalem and the temple with the role of the temple at the beginning and end of Jesus' life.
Ministry	13:1–3	Jesus reminds His followers about deaths at the temple	In these accounts, Jesus refers to tensions and struggles that have taken place at the temple. He would soon confront the political and self-righteous powers that gathered at the temple.
	18:9–14	Parable of the Pharisee and the tax collector at the temple	
Passion	19:45–48	Cleansing of the temple	Jesus cleansed the temple and made it once again the site of His teaching.
	20–21	Jesus' teaching at the temple and prophesying of its destruction	
	22:3–4, 52–53	Jesus arrested by leaders from the temple	

Outline	Passages	Events	Comment
Exaltation	23:45	Curtain of the temple torn	When Jesus died, the temple's curtain tore open, showing that the separation between God and mankind ended through the death of Christ.
	24:53	Disciples continue to pray at the temple	After the resurrection, the disciples continued to gather at the temple for worship.

Conclusion

God's mighty deed promised to Abraham and his descendants is fulfilled in the coming of Jesus Christ, salvation in visible form. Jesus' work of reversing the worldly order begins at His birth and culminates with His death on the cross. By His incarnation and death, Jesus puts fallen creation back into the realm of the magnificent. His life is God's great reversal. In God's grace and mercy, He came to reverse the low estate of His servants, namely the poor, the sick, the captive, the hungry, and the sinful. He came to send away the rich and proud with empty hands. How He does this in His ministry and continues that work in the Church is detailed in the rest of Luke and in Luke's second writing, the Acts of the Apostles.

Composition

Author

The Early Church, from the second half of the second century onward, uniformly ascribes the third Gospel and the Acts of the Apostles to Luke, "the beloved physician," Paul's companion on his journeys and his faithful friend in his imprisonment. He was probably a Gentile, for Paul distinguishes him from his Jewish co-workers (Col 4:10–11, 14). Luke joined Paul at Troas during the second missionary journey, as the use of the first person plural in Ac 16:11 indicates, accompanied Paul as far as Philippi on that journey, and apparently remained there for the next seven years. He rejoined Paul in AD 55 when Paul passed through Philippi on his last journey to Jerusalem and

The evangelist Luke portrayed with an ox, one of the animals offered in sacrifice at the temple, which is a focus of Luke's account.

was with him continually thereafter. According to 2Tm 4:11 he was with Paul in his last imprisonment also.

The evidence of the two books themselves confirms the ancient tradition. The Gospel and Acts have one author, both are addressed to Theophilus, and they are markedly alike in language and style; they also show structural similarities. As noted above, the author of Acts in a number of places speaks in the first person plural (the so-called "we" passages, e.g., Ac 16:11–17; 20:5–21:18; 27:1–28:16), thus indicating that he was an eyewitness of the events recorded. Since these "we" passages are in the same style as the rest of the work and fit naturally into the whole narrative, they can hardly be assigned to another author. This marks the author as a companion of Paul. Of all the known companions of Paul, only Titus and Luke come seriously into consideration; the rest are excluded by the content of the narrative itself or made unlikely by their obscurity. If the Early Church were guessing at the author, it might well have picked Titus, who is more prominent than Luke in the letters of Paul. The tradition that assigns the third Gospel and Acts to Luke is therefore in all probability a genuine tradition and is to be trusted.

Scholars have naturally examined the language of Luke to see whether it betrays the influence of a physician. The first findings of research in this area greatly exaggerated the medical character of Luke's language. Later investigation has shown that much which had been labeled "medical" was not peculiarly medical at all but part of the common language of cultured men of the day. But if the language of Luke is not sufficiently medical in character to prove that he was a physician, it does confirm the ancient tradition in so far as there is nothing in it that makes it unlikely or impossible that the writer was a physician.

Date of Composition

Neither the time nor the place of writing can be fixed accurately. The ancient sources are either silent or vague about the place of writing. As to the time of writing, Irenaeus and the Anti-Marcionite Prologue imply that Luke wrote after the death of Paul, which would mean a date in the late sixties.

Many scholars date the books considerably later, AD 75–80, but the reasons for this later dating are hardly compelling. This later dating is supposed to allow time for the writing of the "many" Gospel narratives to which Luke refers in his preface to the Gospel (Lk 1:1–4). But is there really any reason to assume that these many accounts could not have been written in the 30-odd years after the resurrection? It is said that Jesus' words in Lk 19:43–44 (His lament over Jerusalem) and in Lk 21:20, 24 concerning the fall of Jerusalem are so precise, compared with the statements in Matthew and Mark, that Luke must have given them a form dictated by the fulfillment of the prediction in AD 70. One may doubt whether Luke felt free to deal so freely with the words of Jesus as this argument presupposes. More important, the words of Jesus in both passages are strongly colored by Old Testament language, a characteristic feature of Jesus' predictions in the other evangelists also; they are therefore not conspicuously more specific than is His language in the parallel accounts.

An even later dating period proposed by some scholars (AD 95–100) is based on arguments even less tenable: It is alleged that Luke in some passages in Acts (e.g., Ac 5:34–39) is dependent on, or shows acquaintance with, the *Antiquities* of Josephus, published about AD 94. The argument is singularly weak, for if Luke did use Josephus, he either read him very carelessly or consciously differed from him.

Ultimately, composition before the death of Paul seems most likely. The Gospel was clearly written before the Book of Acts, as the opening to that book makes clear (Ac 1:1). Moreover, Acts ends with Paul at Rome in c AD 58–60 before his martyrdom. Since the Gospel was written first, it was most likely composed in the 50s AD.

Purpose/Recipients

The third Gospel is the most outspokenly "teaching" Gospel of them all. This is already obvious from the dedicatory preface (Lk 1:1–4), in which the author promises Theophilus a full and orderly account of things that Theophilus to some extent already knows, in order that he may have reliable information concerning the things that he has been taught. Luke is not proclaiming the Gospel for the first time to Theophilus and his Gentile readers generally; rather, he intends to expand and fill in the already familiar basic outline of the Gospel message with a full account of what Jesus did and taught (cf Ac 1:1). This is borne out by the fullness and completeness of his narrative; it is likewise confirmed by the fact that Luke extends his narrative in the Acts of the Apostles to include not only what Jesus "began to do and teach," but also the continued activity of the exalted Lord through His messengers by the power of the Spirit. The words of the preface, "accomplished *among us*," indicate that Luke had this extension of the account in mind from the very beginning; he is, like Mark, going to tell the beginning of the Gospel of Jesus Christ, but he is going to carry on the account of it to include that triumphant progress of the Gospel from Jerusalem to Rome, the center of the western world. He is recording the mighty growth of the Word of the Lord that he and his readers have come to know as the power of God in their own experience. The Spirit of God led the mind of Luke to see that a man has not come to know the Christ fully until he has come to know also the Church that the exalted Christ by His Word and through His messengers creates.

Literary Features

Genre

The Gospel according to Luke, with its companion volume, the Acts of the Apostles, is teaching designed for Gentiles. The name Theophilus is best taken as a real name, not merely as a symbolical designation of the Christian reader; the adjective "most excellent" (1:3) would mark him as a man of some standing in society—Paul and Tertullus use the same term in addressing the Roman procurators Felix and Festus (Ac 24:2; 26:25). Luke was following a literary custom of antiquity in dedicating his work to Theophilus. The man to whom the book was dedicated often bore the cost of the publication and the distribution of the book, which may well have been the case with Theophilus. Since the work follows the contemporary conventions of Greek literature, it would follow that it was designed for Greek readers. And the content of the work confirms this inference.

Characters

Arthur Just summarizes Luke's presentation of **Jesus** in the following ways:

> Jesus journeys to Jerusalem as the Prophet whose destiny is to fulfill the prophetic pattern of the OT (Lk 13:31–35). As he makes his way to Jerusalem, a *prophet Christology* develops that stretches back to the OT prophets, comes to fulfillment with Jesus, and continues with the NT apostles. Jesus reveals himself as the antitype for whom the prophets prepared: as teacher and miracle worker he is rejected and killed. All the OT prophets, corporately, prefigure him, with various individuals representing various features: Moses as leader and teacher; Elijah and Elisha as miracle workers; Isaiah and Jeremiah as persecuted, suffering servants; the priest Ezekiel and Hag-

gai, Zechariah, and Malachi as prophets concerned with the temple and sacrificial atonement. The pattern of Luke's Christology follows the prophetic categories that Jesus embraced and fulfilled: first teaching and miracles, then rejection.

First, Jesus' teaching and miracles demonstrated that the new era of salvation was present in his messianic ministry. His teaching proclaimed that in him the new aeon, the kingdom of God, had arrived; his miracles showed that this was true. Christ's preaching and teaching "declared that God was doing among them today: This day is this scripture fulfilled" (Lk 4:21). At the same time, however, Jesus is rejected by many because of his teaching and miracles, i.e., for proclaiming that in him the kingdom of God had come. This rejection led to suffering and the shameful death that became the ultimate expression of the essence of the kingdom in all its poverty and humility. This horrible rejection was overcome by the resurrection, which proclaimed to the world that God in Christ was making all things new. (CC Lk1, pp 25–26)

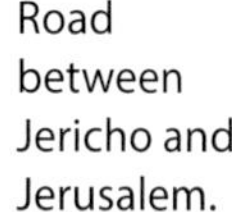
Road between Jericho and Jerusalem.

On the identity of Theophilus, see "Genre" above.

Narrative Development or Plot

Like Matthew, Luke begins his Gospel with the narrative of Jesus' birth and the remarkable incidents that precede and accompany it. He includes three great songs of the Church in the first two chapters. In chapters 3 and 4 Luke relates the beginning of Jesus' ministry in considerable detail. The description of Jesus' Galilean ministry begins with 4:14 and continues through 9:50. This account is quite similar to Matthew and Mark. Luke follows this with a full description of Jesus' journey toward Jerusalem. Most of this material is found only in the Gospel of Luke. It contains special training given to the disciples, instructions about prayer, and conflicts with the members of that "evil generation." The section concludes with Jesus' solemn words about the prophet who must die in Jerusalem.

The Jerusalem journey continues to emphasize the growing conflict. Several parables are found in this section, also several miracles and Jesus' teaching on a variety of topics. At regular intervals the readers are reminded that Jesus is going to Jerusalem (17:11; 19:28). In the final section Luke relates the events in Jerusalem, and here his account again is like that provided by Matthew and Mark.

Resources

In 1:1–4, Luke tells us that he was familiar with the work that "many" had written regarding Jesus. He researched his topic, perhaps drawing on the testimony of "eyewitnesses and ministers of the word." Luke may have done his research while Paul was a prisoner at Caesarea in Israel for two years (cf Ac 21:33 with 27:1; note "we"—Luke is with Paul). Here Luke may have heard the beautiful stories and songs about the birth of Jesus that he alone reports. The grammar and vocabulary of chs 1 and 2 are noticeably different from the rest of the book, and this may be because Luke had these stories before him in a Hebrew or Aramaic copy that he then translated into Greek.

Text and Translations

Luke wrote with a range of Greek from a classical style introduction (1:1–4), to a more Semitic style, to Koine (common) style, which he used most generally. Texts of the Gospel appear in manuscripts dated as early as the third century.

Although copies of the Gospel are not as numerous as those for Matthew and John, the Gospel of Luke was valued for its "orderly account" and continuity with Luke's second book: Acts. Alongside the usual textual variants, ch 22 includes more substantial variations at vv 17–20 (words leading up to the Lord's Supper) and vv 43–44 (mentioning an angel ministering to Jesus on the Mount of Olives).

Outline

Luke's Gospel can be divided into a prologue and seven sections:

I. Prologue (1:1–4)

II. Infancy of John and Jesus (1:5–2:52)

III. Preparation for the Public Ministry of Jesus (3:1–4:13)

IV. Ministry of Jesus in Galilee (4:14–9:50)

V. Journey to Jerusalem (9:51–19:27)

VI. Ministry of Jesus in Jerusalem (19:28–21:38)

VII. Passion of Jesus (22:1–23:56a)

VIII. Resurrection of Jesus (23:56b–24:53)

The following is a more detailed outline:

I. Prologue (1:1–4)

II. Infancy of John and Jesus (1:5–2:52)
- A. Announcement of John's Birth (1:5–25)
- B. Announcement of Jesus' Birth (1:26–38)
- C. Visitation (1:39–45)
- D. Magnificat (1:46–56)
- E. Birth and Circumcision of John (1:57–66)
- F. Benedictus (1:67–80)
- G. Birth of Jesus (2:1–21)
- H. Infant Lord Comes to His Temple (2:22–40)
- I. Young Jesus Returns to His Temple (2:41–52)

III. Preparation for the Public Ministry of Jesus (3:1–4:13)
- A. Ministry of John the Baptist (3:1–20)
- B. Baptism of Jesus (3:21–22)
- C. Genealogy of Jesus (3:23–38)
- D. Temptation of Jesus in the Wilderness (4:1–13)

IV. Ministry of Jesus in Galilee (4:14–9:50)

A. Jesus the Cornerstone (4:14–44)

B. Peter as First among the Twelve; Matthew (Levi) as First among the Gospel Writers (5:1–6:11)

C. Apostolic Foundation and Ways of Life and Death (6:12–49)

D. Jesus Heals and Teaches at Table (ch 7)

E. Parable of the Sower and Mysteries of the Kingdom (ch 8)

F. Climax of Jesus' Galilean Ministry (9:1–50)

V. Journey to Jerusalem (9:51–19:27)

A. Part 1 (9:51–13:21)

1. Turning point of Jesus' ministry (9:51)
2. Rejection in Samaria and the sending of the Seventy-two (9:52–10:24)
3. Jesus' teachings about mercy, worship, and prayer; Pharisaic opposition (10:25–11:54)
4. Discourse on persecution, possessions, and hypocrisy (12:1–13:21)

B. Part 2 (13:22–17:10)

1. Teachings about the end times (13:22–14:24)
2. Teachings in parables (14:25–17:10)

C. Part 3 (17:11–19:27)

1. Teaching from the final travel notice to the final Passion prediction (17:11–18:34)
2. Teachings near Jericho and Jesus' approach to Jerusalem (18:35–19:27)

VI. Ministry of Jesus in Jerusalem (19:28–21:38)

A. Triumphant Entrance into Jerusalem (19:28–48)

B. Conflict with Religious Establishment in the Temple (20:1–21:4)

C. Signs and Warnings about the End Times (21:5–38)

VII. Passion of Jesus (22:1–23:56a)

A. Last Supper (22:1–38)

B. Temptation and Testing of Disciples (22:39–62)

C. Trials of Jesus (22:63–23:25)

D. Final Hours (23:26–56a)

VIII. Resurrection of Jesus (23:56b–24:53)

A. Sabbath Rest in the Tomb and Sunday Announcement to the Women (23:56b–24:12)

B. Emmaus Journey and Recognition of Jesus (24:13–35)

C. Risen Lord Eats with and Teaches His Disciples; Ascends (24:36–53)

Doctrinal Content

Summary Commentary

1:1–4 Luke introduces the Gospel as a well-written, researched, and historical record of Jesus' life and teachings.

1:5–2:52 The theme of ch 1 is fulfillment. Zechariah receives word that the Lord will bless him and Elizabeth with a son who has a special calling. The angel Gabriel announces Jesus' birth to Mary, who responds in faith. As Mary greets Elizabeth, baby John leaps for joy in Elizabeth's womb. Mary rejoices that the Lord delivers His people amid suffering and disappointment. Elizabeth gives birth to John; Zechariah confirms his son's name. God faithfully keeps His promises by sending one like Elijah to prepare His people, and then by announcing the advent of the Son of God and Savior of all humankind.

Joseph and Mary travel from Nazareth to Bethlehem, where Jesus is born in humble circumstances. Angels reveal to shepherds the Good News of the Savior's birth. The shepherds in turn announce the Good News to others. As confirmed by prophecy, Simeon, and Anna, Jesus is appointed as the Savior. Jesus matures as a normal child and also has the blessings of God's wisdom and favor. Luke's account of Jesus' birth and childhood repeatedly sets the ordinary beside the miraculous (e.g., a youth from the hinterland stuns the Jerusalem rabbis with His wisdom).

3:1–4:13 Luke's account of John the Baptist's ministry and Jesus' ancestry hints at the universal nature of the Messiah's kingdom. The Holy Spirit leads Jesus and abides with Him through His temptation, affirming that Jesus truly is the Son of God.

4:14–44 Jesus begins to teach publicly for the first time. Jesus' ministry begins with victories over Satan and his minions, but also with an episode

Octagonal chapel built over the ruins of St. Peter's house. It allows a view over the site.

Fourth-century synagogue.

Fourth century AD synagogue at Capernaum built on top of the remains of the earlier synagogue where Jesus taught and healed.

in Nazareth that foreshadows His rejection at the hands of His own people. With authoritative words, Jesus silences and sends away unclean spirits. Jesus heals many people by a word and a touch. People chase after Jesus as though they could possess Him and keep Him for themselves.

5:1–6:11 A miraculous catch of fish and other events show the disciples that Jesus is more than a great teacher—God is working mightily through Him. Jesus cleanses a leper by touching him and sends him to fulfill the Law of Moses. Jesus then asserts His authority to forgive sins by healing a paralyzed man. Though Jesus could easily say, "Your sins are forgiven you," the price of that forgiveness cost Him His life. Jesus teaches the people that He came to save sinners by leading them to repentance.

Jesus fulfills God's promise to make all things new: He makes fishermen and a tax collector into disciples, He makes a leper and a paralytic whole, and He forgives sins. Unfortunately, some resist such changes. Jesus reapplies the Third Commandment to reveal the blessings of the Sabbath.

Despite facing severe criticism, He has mercy on the man with a withered hand.

6:12–49 Jesus chooses 12 men as His apostles, an office specifically appointed by Jesus for the early years of the Church. Jesus blesses the crowds and describes their estates in this life and the life to come. He condemns those who live for today, neglecting the ways of God and the care of His people. Jesus overthrows the common ethics of human culture to emphasize the Father's ways of love and mercy. He teaches the disciples to judge mercifully and lead faithfully. A person's words and deeds—not appearances—are the true marks of one's character. Jesus authoritatively teaches about the ways of God's kingdom. Unfortunately, His teachings are so radically demanding and countercultural that even the most dedicated believers fail to live up to them. It is good news indeed, then, that Jesus does not merely command long-suffering, forgiveness, and love of enemies. He Himself puts them into practice, lovingly bearing with us and forgiving us.

Ch 7 Jesus reveals His authority over every threatening foe, even death, by healing a centurion's servant. Out of compassion for a widow who lost her only son, Jesus raises the young man back to life. In response to doubt and criticism, Jesus affirms that He is indeed the Messiah announced by John, and that John, who heralded His advent, is Israel's greatest prophet. Yet, many will accept neither John's thunderous warnings nor Jesus' proclamation of the Good News of the Kingdom. Jesus teaches that even notorious sinners can be forgiven and restored; indeed, they sometimes become all the more devoted to God for having received greater deliverance.

A Sepphoris mosaic shows the Hellenistic culture in Galilee.

Ch 8 Jesus breaks with rabbinic tradition and allows women to become disciples. Jesus warns that not everyone hearing God's Word will have an enduring faith. Tragically, some hear the life-giving Gospel of Jesus but fail to produce the fruit of a Christian life, eventually dying in unbelief. Jesus uses an agricultural metaphor to explain how the

Gospel ministry works and why it is sometimes thwarted. He calls His followers to be just as transparent in their attitudes and irreproachable in their behavior as He is. By faith, we inherit the kingdom of God.

After calming a storm, Jesus challenges His disciples to consider the answer to their question, "Who then is this?" Luke's lengthiest report of an exorcism is also his most dramatic: in the Gerasene region, Jesus frees a deranged and menacing demoniac. The magnitude of this man's suffering leads some—especially the pious—to dread evil spirits and wonder what prevents any of us from being the object of their attacks. After displaying His mastery over nature and demons, Jesus shows His authority over incurable illness and even death.

9:1–50 Jesus sends out the 12 apostles to preach the Gospel, heal diseases, and cast out evil spirits. After the Twelve are sent, there is such an outburst of activity that even Herod takes notice. In a miracle reminiscent of the manna in the wilderness, Jesus feeds the multitude that have come out to the wilderness to hear Him. For the first time in the Gospel, Peter makes a clear confession of Jesus as the Messiah. Jesus then challenges His disciples' understanding of that role by revealing His impending suffering and death. Because Jesus is the only way to eternal life, following Him demands that we reorder our priorities, putting Him in first place and setting aside whatever does not accord with His way. Through the transfiguration, Jesus allows His disciples to catch a glimpse of the glory that will again be His after His resurrection. On the way down from the transfiguration, Jesus rescues a demon-possessed boy. He once more predicts His suffering and death, and once more the disciples fail to understand Him. He clarifies that true greatness comes from faith and service.

9:51–10:24 When Jesus' overture to the Samaritans is rejected, His apostles imagine that harsh retribution is in order. In three brief exchanges with would-be disciples, Jesus shows that the cost of discipleship is high. Having previously sent out the Twelve (9:1–6), Jesus expands the breadth of His Gospel outreach by sending out 72 more workers. He warns that whoever rejects Him will be in danger of eternal condemnation. Empowered by Jesus, the Seventy-two advance into Satan's territory as people believe the Gospel. Although rejoicing that His disciples have received the gift of life-saving faith, Jesus stresses that He is the chief content and unique mediator of the Gospel revelation.

10:25–11:54 Jesus tells the famous parable of the Good Samaritan to clarify that He expects His followers to do good to all people. However, His concluding exhortation, "Go, and do likewise," reminds us just how far we are from the loving, self-sacrificing behaviors the Lord expects. In contrast with Jesus' demand for great works (vv 25–37), the story of Mary and Martha shows the importance of simple faith and rest in Jesus and His Word.

Jesus teaches that Christian prayers are unfailingly heard because God has promised to hear us. He then responds to accusations that He performs exorcisms by Satan's power. A person healed of demon possession could fall into such trouble again. Thus, it is a grave mistake to imagine that we can receive the Gospel, come to Jesus, and yet continue in destructive ways and return to our sins. Jesus teaches that hearing His Word and faithfully putting it into practice heaps praise on Him. He contrasts the stubborn unbelief of His own people with Gentiles who believed God's Word and turned to Him in repentance. Some people remain in darkness because they reject the Gospel and will not allow the message of salvation to penetrate and dispel the darkness of their souls. The Lord moves us to appreciate that it is God Himself, through His Spirit, who illumines souls and preserves faith in hearts. Jesus' harshest criticisms are directed at those religious leaders and experts in Scripture who place their traditions above God's Word and refuse God's call to repentance.

12:1–13:21 Jesus warns His disciples about the pitfalls of religious hypocrisy, and identifies fear as its root cause. He assures us that His Father's children have nothing to fear from others. Jesus teaches about the blessedness of confessing Him and the great dangers in denying Him and resisting His grace. He underlines the great danger of being rich in earthly things but poor toward God. He warns against the self-destructive nature of covetousness and encourages His disciples to trust in God, their heavenly Father, since He will provide for all their needs. Jesus then urges those in positions of leadership to faithfully discharge their duties. He expresses a deep desire to fulfill God's plan of salvation once for all, even though it means going to the cross. He condemns the unbelief of those beholding His miraculous signs who yet reject the obvious implications.

Jesus encourages His followers to repent and make peace quickly, lest a budding conflict escalate and spin out of control. He points out tragedies as occasions for self-examination and reflection on our sinful frailty. Jesus warns that His audience needs to begin producing works consistent with the Gospel. Though His critics saw His miracle as a clear violation of the Sabbath, Jesus' work, in fact, fulfilled the Sabbath Day's purpose: to provide blessing for God's people. Although the kingdom of God has humble beginnings, it grows to embrace all creation.

13:22–14:24 People can enter God's kingdom only through Jesus Christ. The Father beseeches one and all to come into the great wedding banquet of His Son. Jesus then repeats His determination to press toward Jerusalem and God's will for Him there. Unfortunately, the impenitence mentioned in this passage continues today, keeping people out of God's kingdom. Jesus exposes His enemies' inconsistencies and cruelty. He illustrates how pride leads to humiliation. God's invitations overcome people's rejections.

14:25–17:10 Jesus illustrates the unconditional nature of discipleship. Christ's people are "the salt of the earth" (Mt 5:13), purifying and seasoning it, because Christ is within them. In the first of three similar parables, Jesus uses the devotion of a shepherd to illustrate God's willingness to find the wayward sinner. The unrepentant sinner is like a coin lost in the darkness. God found us when we were far from Him.

Guard against becoming enslaved to the pursuit of wealth. Instead, use money for godly and eternal purposes. It is tempting to lay aside the inconvenient portions of God's Law. Yet, every Word of God is precious and for our edification. Marital fidelity is to be preserved, for marriage is the blessing of a lifelong partnership. Jesus challenges the belief that earthly blessings are a sign of God's eternal favor. He teaches us to heed the Word of God now while faithful mercy can be shown, for this is God's good and gracious will. Disciples need to guard the faith of others with for-

Pharisee and tax collector, sixth-century Ravenna mosaic.

giveness and a helping hand. The tiniest faith accomplishes remarkable things. We owe God our full service and truly can do Him no favors.

17:11–18:34 Jesus commends the faith of a Samaritan leper who alone gives thanks for his healing. Daily God's mercy extends to the unworthy; His kingdom will come unexpectedly, but surely, to all. If even an unworthy judge responds to persistence, God certainly hears His people's faithful prayers. The Pharisee excludes himself from God's gift of righteousness, while the penitent tax collector embraces it. Jesus includes children in His kingdom and teaches that we must be like them to enter the kingdom of heaven. Wealth, works, and personal sacrifice cannot save. However, any sacrifice made for God's kingdom is amply compensated in this life and in the life to come. As in Lk 9, Jesus explains the culmination of His ministry in suffering, death, and resurrection.

18:35–19:27 A blind beggar overcomes the crowd and cries for sight. Jesus then saves Zacchaeus by visiting him with mercy. Followers of Jesus dare never begrudge the mercy others have received. Our returning King will abolish all opposition to His kingdom and will honor those who faithfully served Him.

19:28–21:4 Entering Jerusalem, Jesus fulfills Old Testament prophecy and is acclaimed the messianic King. He weeps over Jerusalem's present blindness and future fate. He goes directly to the temple to cleanse it for proper services: the hearing of God's Word. Jesus would not allow detractors to take away His right to teach in the temple. By parable and psalm, Jesus warns against rejecting the Messiah.

Jesus outwits His opponents and teaches the proper relationship between earthly authority and God. He demonstrates that the Lord is the God of the living. The patriarchs, though dead from an earthly perspective, are still alive with God. Only the incarnation can answer Jesus' question. He is both man (David's son) and God (David's Lord). Jesus warns His disciples not to be impressed by the scribes' display; do not practice the faith simply to impress others. He then highlights a widow's offering in order to teach what God values.

21:5–38 Jesus prepares His disciples for the temple's destruction and the final judgment. The disciples will endure various persecutions along with Jerusalem's fall. He also points ahead to the judgment of all the world and to signs preceding His return. The sure coming of God's kingdom is like the budding of a fig tree. Jesus promises that His teachings will abide forever and warns His disciples to be ready for His return.

22:1–62 The Jewish leaders seek Jesus' death. Prompted by Satan, Judas negotiates the price for Jesus. Nevertheless, Jesus directs His disciples in preparing the Passover meal and transforms the meal into the Sacrament of His body and blood, by which He brings forgiveness to His people. Jesus points His arguing apostles to true greatness in serving others, promising they will share His honor. He warns a self-confident Peter that he will deny his Lord, but also assures him of His intercession. Jesus then warns all His disciples about the hostile times they will face, similar to His own rejection. While the disciples sleep, Jesus, in prayerful agony, shrinks from His coming ordeal and yet submits to His Father's will. Judas then betrays Jesus with a kiss, and Jesus, in mercy, heals a servant's severed ear. During Jesus' interrogation, Peter denies Jesus three times. But Jesus' word and look bring Peter to tears and finally to repentance.

22:63–23:25 Jesus is mocked as a prophet by those holding Him. Previously accused of blasphemy, Jesus, the Son of God, is now blasphemed. Jesus, before the Council, points to His exaltation. He acknowledges that He is the Son of God and is condemned. The Jewish leaders then bring Jesus before Pilate, seeking a death penalty. Pilate and Herod declare Jesus innocent but do not believe in Him. Pilate, frightened of the crowd and blind to Jesus' identity, releases Barabbas and hands Jesus over to be crucified.

23:26–56 Jesus was crucified so that we may be spared the coming judgment, hear His word of absolution, and enter into paradise with Him. He not only interceded for others, but He is also the messianic King who

Luke's Unique Contribution

Luke records many passages that are similar to passages in Matthew and Mark. However, Luke also records unique sayings and events from Jesus' life. This chart will help you investigate Luke's unique contribution.

	Passages	Sayings, Parables, and Events	Insights
Birth Narratives	1:1–4	Luke's Prologue	Luke carefully details the events surrounding the births of John and Jesus. He writes from Mary's perspective and perhaps bases his presentation on interviews with Mary (Lk 1:2).
	1:5–25	Event: An Angel of the Lord Visits Zechariah	
	1:26–38	Event: Gabriel Visits Mary	
	1:39–56	Event: Mary Visits Elizabeth	
	1:57–80	Event: The Birth of John the Baptist	
	2:1–7	Event: The Birth of Jesus	
	2:8–21	Event: An Angel of the Lord Visits the Shepherds	
	2:22–40	Event: Jesus Presented at the Temple	
	2:41–52	Event: The Boy Jesus at the Temple	
Preparation for Ministry	3:10–14	Saying: John the Baptist Answers the Crowds	Luke records this unique example of John the Baptist's teaching.
Galilean Ministry	4:16–30	Event: The Synagogue at Nazareth	These sayings and events broaden the picture of Jesus' early ministry.
	6:24–26	Saying: Four Woes	
	7:11–17	Event: Raising of the Widow's Son	
Journey to Jerusalem	9:52–56	Event: Rejection by the Samaritans	In this portion of the Gospel, Luke presents events and sayings of Jesus in a unique way, focusing on the journey toward the Passion in Jerusalem. He records several parables not found in the other Gospels, as well as numerous sayings.
	10:29–37	Parable: The Good Samaritan	
	10:38–42	Event: Visit with Mary and Martha	
	11:5–8	Parable: The Inconsiderate Friend	
	11:27–28	Saying: True Blessedness	
	12:13–15	Saying: Warning about Greed	
	12:16–21	Parable: The Rich Fool	
	13:1–5	Saying: Murder of the Galileans	
	13:6–9	Parable: The Fruitless Fig Tree	
	13:10–17	Event: Healing of a Disabled Woman	
	13:22–30	Event: Teaching on Road to Jerusalem	
	14:28–33	Saying: Teaching about Commitment	
	15:8–10	Parable: The Lost Coin	
	15:11–32	Parable: The Prodigal Son	
	16:1–12	Parable: The Dishonest Manager	
	16:14–15	Saying: Rebuke of the Pharisees	
	16:19–31	Saying: The Rich Man and Lazarus	
	17:7–10	Saying: Unworthy Servants	
	17:11–19	Event: The Cleansing of 10 Lepers	
	18:1–8	Parable: The Unrighteous Judge	
	18:9–14	Parable: The Pharisee and the Tax Collector	
	19:1–10	Event: The Salvation of Zacchaeus	

	Passages	Sayings, Parables, and Events	Insights
Jerusalem Ministry	21:37–38	Event: Ministry in Jerusalem	Luke reminds his readers of Jesus' popularity and that he has not recorded everything Jesus taught during that week.
Passion	22:35–38	Saying: Two Swords	Luke records these details from the hours before Jesus' death.
	23:13–16	Event: Pilate Declares Jesus Innocent	
Resurrection and Ascension	24:13–35	Event: Journey to Emmaus	Luke not only records unique information about the events following the resurrection, but he also prepares his readers for the next part of the story, which he covers in Acts.
	24:44–49	Saying: Final Instructions	
	24:50–53	Event: The Ascension	

Luke's introduction shows that the original audience for his Gospel had already received teaching about Christ from within the Church by her ministers and writings. Luke was writing to the Church for the benefit of those already in the Church. Arthur Just writes in his commentary on Luke:

> The gospel was used in catechesis, which we may define broadly as the instruction of those who have come to faith and who look forward to Baptism or who have been baptized already. Catechesis is centered in Jesus Christ of Nazareth, who was promised in the OT and became incarnate to accomplish the Father's plan of salvation. . . .
>
> Luke's gospel is a book of the church, written for the church, to be used by the church in its proclamation of the Gospel to the unbaptized and the baptized. (CC Lk1, p 5)

saves us. In the darkness, when the temple curtain is torn, Jesus commits His spirit into His Father's hands. The centurion praises God, the crowds become remorseful, and Jesus' followers observe from a distance. Joseph of Arimathea secures the body of Jesus and places it in a newly hewn tomb. The women make preparations for a final burial after the Sabbath.

Ch 24 On the third day, the women find the stone has been rolled away from the tomb. They discover not the body of Jesus but two angels who say that Jesus is alive. Jesus later joins two disciples discussing what happened in Jerusalem. He interprets His death and resurrection through the Old Testament before revealing Himself in the breaking of the bread. Jesus then dispels all doubt when He offers absolute proof of His resurrection. Again, He points to Himself as Scripture's center, but now includes the mission to all nations through the Holy Spirit's power. Jesus leads His disciples to Bethany, where He blesses them and is taken up into heaven. They worship Him and return to Jerusalem where they regularly worship God in the temple.

Specific Law Themes

The Gospel of Luke uniquely highlights the plight of those lost to God and the Church. It warns that the mighty will be brought low and that even the temple, the focal point of Israel's faith, will be destroyed. In view of these truths, the Gospel calls people to repentance and faithfulness in prayer.

Specific Gospel Themes

Luke emphasizes that the Lord seeks and finds the lost; He raises up the lowly. God is present in His temple to bless His people. However, and more important, God is present in His holy child, Jesus. Through Jesus, the Spirit works and the Father fulfills His promises. Luke also describes a number of fellowship meals, illustrating how Jesus welcomes people into God's kingdom. Finally, the Lord calls not only Israel to be saved through Jesus but also the nations.

Specific Doctrines

Luke's emphasis on the temple has already been noted (see pp 268–69). Other passages and themes include Luke's teaching about the work of the Holy Spirit (1:35; 11:13), whose role in the incarnation and the Christian life is highlighted in the early Christian creeds due to Luke's influence. The canticles that Luke includes in chs 1–2 began to be used consistently for worship as early as the fourth century. Expressions such as "tender mercy" (1:78) characterize God's compassion in view of the New Testament.

Jesus' practical teaching about judgment, fairness, and rewards (6:37–38) deserve special notice. Luke 7:50 describes the importance of faith in more than conversion, since one lives by faith in ongoing relationship with God. Luke 8:1–3 highlights a way that Luke's Gospel differs from the others. He gives special attention to women and their service to Jesus. Luke 10:16 teaches the authority of the apostolic Church as God's voice in a fallen world—God chooses to work through His servants.

Luke includes several influential and popular parables of Jesus that are not found in the other Gospels. Alongside Luke's account of Jesus' birth, these parables are his most important contribution to the story of Jesus' life. The parable of the Good Samaritan continues Luke's theme of compassion (10:25–37) as do the parables of the lost, which are foundational to Christian attitudes about mission work (ch 15). The parable of the Pharisee and the tax collector illustrates the contrast between false repentance and true repentance, which is essential to justification by grace through faith alone.

In Luke's Gospel, Jesus also characterizes the attitude of believers, who see their lives humbly as unworthy service (17:10). The book closes with Jesus' teaching about how He fulfills the Scripture for our sakes. He is the key to understanding the Word, which is ultimately about repentance and salvation, Law and Gospel. The chart on pp 285–86 summarizes Luke's unique contributions to the Gospel story.

Application

1:1–4 God's people need clear, accurate teaching in order to grow in faith and in service. As you study Luke's account, pray that the Lord would make you a faithful "friend of God" through Jesus, who has accomplished your salvation by His birth, life, death, and resurrection.

1:5–80 Children are a blessing from God to be treasured and raised according to His good purposes. The work of God's Spirit is not limited by age, gender, or socio-economic status. He is poured out for all people according to the good and gracious will of God, who blesses motherhood and children and, through them, all humanity, even as He promised Eve (Gn 3:15). Rejoice in His surpassing mercy through the Holy Child, who delivers the generations from sin and sorrow. Do not doubt, but dare to proclaim what the Lord has accomplished for your salvation. His blessings never cease to amaze! Nothing is impossible with God!

Ch 2 The birth of a child always comes with great hardship (Gn 3:16). The birth of this Child comes with great blessings for sinners. As you reflect on the wonder of Jesus' birth, pray also for a humble and pure heart. The mighty Lord will have mercy on you and exalt you by grace alone (Lk 1:49–52). As you celebrate the glory of Christmas, be sure to announce Jesus' saving work to others also. Pray that the Lord would grant you the enduring faith of Simeon and Anna. Pray also for the children in your family or neighborhood, that they would grow in the knowledge of their Savior and receive His favor. He who has blessed and kept you in faith will likewise hear and bless them too.

3:1–4:13 The Gospel is for everyone! Jesus' death and resurrection bring life and salvation to all who repent and call on His name. The blessed Trinity likewise abides with us, that we may withstand Satan's temptation of our flesh, our pride, and our will. Through Holy Baptism in God's name, we are truly His beloved children.

4:14–44 Pray that the Holy Spirit would bless your speech and lead others to the Lord through you. Focus on the end of the Gospel story, for there we see God's greatest victory over sin and the devil, and the revelation of His grace and mercy for us. Revel in Jesus' teaching and its great blessings for you. Pray that Jesus would deliver you from evil and protect you from the effects of sin. Christ can forgive and restore you by His grace.

5:1–32 As with the disciples, the mundane struggle for daily bread, and the sin and doubt it fosters, may make you feel distant from God. He still touches lives today and has mercy according to His good and gracious will. Bring your requests to Jesus and trust in His good purposes for you. He bore the cross and your sins willingly, and He will also bear with you in all infirmities. No matter what your past, whether you are a notorious sinner or smugly self-righteous, Jesus calls you to a life of daily repentance. As the great physician, He can forgive all manner of sins.

5:33–6:11 Jesus calls us to wholly embrace the Gospel and the new life it brings. When we consider laws and their application, God would have us see not simply how laws restrict but also who and what they protect. All God's Word is written for our benefit, that we may enjoy the inherited blessings of His mercy.

6:12–49 Jesus continues to call people for various roles of service in the Church, depending on God's order, our gifts, and the Church's needs. He continues to touch our lives today through the ongoing ministry of His life-giving Word of blessing. When pride and self-interest allure you, turn to the Lord in repentance. God calls you to have self-sacrificing love. Pray for wisdom and patience with yourself as you put God's ways into practice. We can never outgrow our good teacher, who by grace judged and declared us not guilty while we were yet dead in our sins. His grace in our lives—measured, pressed, and shaken—always runs over. He is our refuge.

Ch 7 How often we try everything else before turning to the Lord when we find ourselves in desperate straits! Tragedy knows no bounds, striking people of every nation, age, and station in life. Thank God for His great compassion, that Jesus is the Savior for all people. Both life and conversion are God's works through His Word. God's Spirit continues to enlighten, sanctify, and keep us in the true faith. His teaching also challenges us to consider: Do we trust that God can truly change people's lives? By God's Spirit, we grow daily in our appreciation of the fact that "where sin increased, grace abounded all the more" (Rm 5:20).

8:1–21 The Lord has appropriate forms of service for every member of His kingdom, regardless of gender, ethnicity, or social standing. Genuine faith so transforms our lives that we joyfully serve the Lord in this world and enjoy eternal life. By God's grace our faith not only withstands trial and temptation but even grows stronger. We often fare poorly under such a glaring light, where our failures seem magnified. Nevertheless, when we confess our sins, He is faithful and just to forgive our sins and call us members of His household.

8:22–56 When we are overwhelmed, the risen Christ comes to our aid. His resurrection has disarmed the forces of sin, death, and even Satan. Jesus can deal with any problem.

Catacomb portrait of a woman praying in cross-shaped manner.

9:1–50 Wherever the Gospel is delivered and received, the greatest healing follows. By God's Spirit and grace, our hearing of the Gospel will result in faithful commitment and the eager expectation of Jesus' life-giving blessings. Just as He miraculously fed the 5,000, He is also willing and able to provide for us in time of need. All of our words and actions should confess the One who is the only life and hope of the world. Following Him proves impossible for us but not for our Lord, who embraces and bears our crosses. Jesus has not called us out of the world, but rather to overcome it. Accordingly, He lifts us up and strengthens us when we are challenged, reminding us that He has already overcome the world for us. By the power of God's Spirit, our humble service produces things great in His eyes. Jesus left the comfort of heaven to stand with us, bear our burdens, and deliver us from evil.

9:51–10:24 Age-old conflicts die hard. We may easily resort to bad judgment. Were it up to us to achieve our place in the kingdom of God, we would never make it. How heartening to know that Jesus continues to reach out with compassion through the Gospel ministry He has established. In Christ, we cannot lose, even though put to death, for in the end Christ grants us eternal life. Oh, that we would have the grace to rejoice with Him and to appreciate fully the great privilege that is ours in the Gospel!

10:25–42 Jesus became the Good Samaritan for us. He laid down His life and befriended us while we were yet His enemies. What we can never earn for ourselves, no matter how much we scramble, God freely provides through faith in Jesus Christ.

Ch 11 We can depend on God to keep His promise to hear us and answer us because He never breaks His word. Jesus has overcome the devil and opened God's kingdom to all who hear His Word and follow Him. We enjoy the privilege of being called God's people today. Happily, the One who called us is faithful. Give thanks to God for faithful traditions that agree with His Gospel, which alone grants us salvation in Christ.

12:1–21 Though justified by faith, Christians still have a sinful nature and so struggle daily with the challenge of living the faith sincerely. If we are honest about the things that trouble us most, we will have to admit that fear and worry are near the top of the list. In a culture increasingly hostile to traditional Christian belief, Jesus provides timely warnings, as the temptation to compromise our confession becomes more intense every day. He is the very source of life and goodness, who fills us with joyful satisfaction through the Gospel.

12:22–59 God's faithfulness far exceeds our needs. The depth of God's commitment naturally forces His followers to decide what is most important for them. As you wrestle with so great a challenge, take comfort in the One who calls you. He is faithful. Only by God's grace can we see clearly, as the Spirit opens our eyes through faith in Jesus Christ. Jesus promises mercy and blessings for those who repent and receive His peace.

13:1–21 In His wisdom, God allows and uses even tragic events to warn of judgment, that He might bring us to repentance. He enables us to repent and to produce the fruit that flows from His salvation. He calls us to keep the Sabbath by gladly receiving God's Word, which delivers to us the blessings of Jesus' victory over sin and death. He extends His realm in His way with His timing.

13:22–14:24 The time for every human being—and indeed the world—is quickly slipping away. Yet the Lord still reaches out to His wayward children, earnestly seeking to gather them under His protective wing. He reaches out to us in mercy, despite the indifference or rejection of others. No matter what others say or do, your greatest promotion is when the heavenly Father calls you His beloved child, through Christ. And God is persistent; He reaches out again and again wherever His servants carry the Good News, so that all may receive His gracious invitation.

14:25–15:32 Consider well the radical demands of following Jesus, and be ready to meet them. God does not abandon us to our foolishness but seeks us out, calling us to repentance and to faith in the Gospel. The good news of Christ gives "light to those who sit in darkness and in the shadow of death" (1:79). We are in no position to begrudge His grace similarly given to others, no matter how unworthy they appear to us. God calls us to a joyful celebration, not only of our own salvation, but also for the salvation of our brothers and sisters.

16:1–17:10 God offers us lasting treasure in Christ, and so a true perspective on money and goods. The good news of His kingdom releases us from sin and gives new life. His Word and faithfulness avails for our forgiveness and salvation. How ready God is to forgive, as He demonstrates in the love of Christ. Pray for the Lord's strength. His gift of faith is anything but weak, and He will grant you strength to accomplish the impossible. When He returns, we will eat and drink in His kingdom as He has served us.

17:11–18:34 Give praise to Him who bears no grudge toward you but came to save you. Live in daily repentance rather than put off repentance or take confidence that you can discern the day of Christ's return. Pray without ceasing (1Th 5:17). God will answer speedily as He has promised in Christ. Beware of the complacency of measuring your goodness against others. Measure yourself against God's standards—then repent. No one has a greater claim to the Kingdom than a newly baptized infant. Heaven is our inheritance by our loving Father's grace alone. God has fulfilled His glorious promises of prophecy in His Son.

18:35–19:27 Persist in prayer and in faith. The Gospel can save one sinner who repents just as well as another. The saving love of Jesus seeks and reaches out to all people. Christ calls you to share in His Word, and He is ever generous and merciful toward you.

19:28–20:18 Take joy in the reign of your Savior. Pray for your family, friends, and neighbors that they would receive Jesus, who came in compassion to seek and save the lost. Beware of worldly distractions from the Lord's Word. Hang on to it, for Jesus cleanses our hearts by faith in His Holy Word. Subject all things to His reign and the wisdom of His Word. He claims you as His holy temple that He may rule your heart in forgiveness, peace, and love. God's mission in Christ will succeed. Despite all opposition, God will build His Church on the crucified and resurrected Jesus.

20:19–21:4 Not even the legitimate claims of government usurp our loyalty to God. Also, our human reason dare not come between us and God's sure promises. Jesus—David's son—has become our Lord through His death and resurrection, and the Father has exalted Jesus to His right hand. Receive Him in humility and give of yourself freely for the good of His kingdom.

21:5–38 Do not be so impressed with the world's splendor that you lose sight of the eternal. Jesus promises guidance in the persecutions His dis-

Stone with the inscription "To the place of trumpeting" found in the Temple Mount excavation.

ciples face. We can face the judgment unafraid, because Jesus has already borne God's vengeance for our sakes and takes away the cause of judgment: our sins. Pray earnestly for Jesus' return. More firm than this creation is His promise of return and new creation for you.

22:1–62 Those who conspire against God's plans ultimately fail, as Pharaoh learned at the first Passover. To neglect the Lord's Supper is to ignore the forgiveness Christ earned for us. We have the Lord's promise that He always sees and will reward our service. Jesus, who interceded for Peter, is even now at the right hand of God interceding for us (Rm 8:34; Heb 7:25). He comes to us, again and again, to strengthen us against temptation. God used the night of betrayal to overcome darkness and usher in His everlasting light. Jesus now and ever looks at us in love to call us to repentance, forgiving our sins.

22:63–23:25 We mock Jesus whenever we withhold the honor that is rightfully His as God's Son. It is for us to receive Him for who He is, as described in Scripture. For us and for our lives, Jesus makes great claims. He would be our Savior and King. We thank God that others have brought Jesus into our lives and that, through His Spirit, He enables us to cling to Him always.

23:26–56 We all justly deserve God's judgment because of our sinful deeds. Jesus died bearing the darkness of God's judgment on the world's sins. Out of the darkness of judgment, Jesus ushers in the bright day of grace. The work of redeeming the world is done.

Ch 24 "He is not here, but has risen" means that someday the graves of all His followers will be opened, and they, too, will rise to live with Him. God, who has given us the Scriptures to make us "wise for salvation" (2Tm 3:15), opens our eyes to believe Jesus. The resurrected Christ truly equips us for our witness to Him with the Holy Spirit, whom He provides. We are led to repentance and renewed faith each day, and Jesus continues to bless us with salvation and puts joy into our lives as we serve Him.

Canonicity

Although Luke was not used as much as Matthew and John, it was unquestioningly received as a canonical Gospel (*homologoumenon*). On its essential role in Christian teaching, see "Specific Doctrines" (pp 287–88).

Lutheran Theologians on Luke

Luther

See Luther's general comments on the Gospels, pp 214–16.

For Luther's insights on Lk 1, see *The Magnificat* (AE 21:295–358); on Lk 6, see *The Sermon on the Mount* (AE 21:1–294).

Gerhard

"Irenaeus, bk. 3, c. 14, p. 198: 'Luke was inseparable from Paul and was his co-worker in the Gospel.' Chapter 11, p. 181: 'Luke was a follower and disciple of the apostles.' Tertullian (*Adv. Marcion.*, bk. 4, p. 224) likewise calls him 'a follower of Paul,' from which it is by no means incorrect to believe that he wrote his Gospel account at the command of the apostle Paul. As a result, some think that Paul calls this 'his Gospel' (Rom. 2:16; 2 Tim. 2:8). Eusebius testifies (*Hist. eccles.*, bk. 3, c. 21): 'The Gospel of Luke, no less than those of Matthew and Mark, was approved by John.' This Luke is mentioned in Col. 4:14; 2 Tim. 4:11; Philem. 24; and especially, according to the opinion of some, in 2 Cor. 8:18: 'With him we have sent the brother whose praise is in the Gospel among all the churches.' From this, one gathers that the Gospel of Luke was known and approved in the Church already at the time when, under Claudius, Paul was going from Macedonia to Jerusalem. Irenaeus (bk. 3, c. 14, p. 198) mentions everything that Luke recorded as compared with the rest of the evangelists.

"He was a native of Antioch, a physician by profession, according to Eusebius (*Hist.*, bk. 3, c. 4) and Jerome (*Catalog. script.*), which agrees with Col. 4:14. If we have confidence in Nicephorus (*Hist.*, bk. 6, c. 6), he added the ability to paint to his medical skill. Jerome (on Isaiah 6) gives him this praise: 'He was highly skilled in the Greek language,' something that the character of the language in which he wrote his Gospel account clearly witnesses. Casaubonus (*Exerc.* 2, c. 1, p. 161) says, 'It is well-known to the learned that he observed pure Hellenism more carefully than the rest of the evangelists.' Epiphanius numbers him among the seventy-two disciples. This can be doubted with good cause because in his Gospel account (1:2) he says he is writing that which was told him by others—among whom he was not. He lived for eighty-four years, according to Jerome (*Catalog.*), and according to the same author (on Acts) he died in Bithynia. Some say that he was hanged from an olive tree in Greece and died as a martyr.

"He himself makes clear in his preface the reason that drove him to write his Gospel history. Eusebius points out (*Hist.*, bk. 3, c. 21): 'Luke describes those things that Christ began to do and teach up to the captivity of John the Baptist and describes the things that happened in the third year of Christ's ministry only somewhat. Hence John was later compelled to supply those things in his Gospel.' Ambrose (on Luke 2) writes this about him: 'Luke believed that he would be rich enough if he claimed for himself only the manger and cradle of the Lord.'

"From Luke 22, the account of Christ's bloody sweat and the comfort of the angel was at one time called into doubt, according to Hilary (*De Trinit.*, bk. 10) and Jerome (*Contra Pelag.*, bk. 2)—doubtlessly because those things seem to conflict with the divinity of the Son, just as some Catholics with wrongheaded zeal strike out the words 'He wept' from Luke 19 of their Bibles, as Epiphanius relates (*Ancorat*). This, however, is not sufficient cause for doubt. You see, we must make a distinction between the divine and human nature of Christ, a distinction between the state of exaltation and humiliation, a distinction between the infirmities that Christ voluntarily underwent for our sake and sin with its vicious effects, from which He was completely free. Augustine (*De cons. evang.*, bk. 3, c. 4) proves that this passage is evangelical. In *Ad Theoph.*, bk. 6, Athanasius pronounces an anathema on those who deny that Christ sweat blood.

"The Gospel of Luke contains twenty-four chapters in which he accurately describes the birth, circumcision, upbringing, and office both of the forerunner John the Baptist and of Christ." (ThC E1 § 245)

Questions People Ask about Luke

The Reference to Quirinius

We now come to the charge that Luke is guilty of an error in ascribing the governorship of Syria at the time of the birth of Jesus to Quirinius, since Josephus reports that Quirinius took a census in AD 6. That we are here facing a difficulty is undeniable. But it is by no means an insuperable one. A glance at the Greek New Testament will convince all who are somewhat acquainted with its language that Luke does not say that Quirinius was governor of Syria at the time. A literal translation of Lk 2:2 implies that the census took place with "Quirinius controlling (being at the head of) Syria."

A very plausible solution of our difficulty here suggests itself. While Quirinius may not have been the titular governor of Syria at the time of Jesus' birth, it is well possible that he actually administered affairs. The reference to Quirinius does not convict Luke of historical error. After all, we need not prove that our interpretation is the only right one; our task here is to demonstrate that the words of Luke do not compel us to assume that he was in error.[1]

The Census of Luke 2:1–5

In the New Testament perhaps no matter involving a date has been more discussed than the census mentioned in Lk 2:1–5. The King James Version speaks of a taxing being decreed by the emperor, but it is now recognized that "census" and "registering" (with a view to taxation) are better translations of the Greek words.[2] Luke is said to have blundered seriously in this account. The critics charge him with being in error on the following points: (1) that Augustus ordered a general census of the empire and that a census of Israel was taken at the time of the birth of Christ; (2) that Quirinius was governor of Syria when the birth of Jesus occurred; and (3) that a Roman emperor ordered the Jews to go to their native city for the enrollment, since it was the Roman custom to regis-

Roman calvaryman carved into carnelian gemstone.

1 Another explanation of v 2 is possible based on the following two points of Greek grammar: (1) the absence of an article with "this"; and (2) taking the superlative "first" as the comparative degree "prior," as is done in Jn 20:4, 8. Luke 2:2 could then be translated: "This took place as a census prior to Quirinius being governor of Syria."

2 This is the translation adopted in the New King James Version.

ter people at the place of their actual residence. These points sound formidable enough, it must be admitted. The question is whether they can be proved to be valid.

We begin our investigation with the decree of Augustus referred to by Luke. Critics argue that the history of Augustus is enveloped in much obscurity and that our knowledge concerning his reign is not nearly so complete as that of other periods of ancient Roman history. It is true that the secular sources that are available to us do not speak at all of a general census ordered by Augustus. But neither do they deny that a decree for such a census was issued. It is a subject on which they are silent. Now, since information admittedly is very scanty, leaving us in the dark on many a question, it is not surprising that no mention is made of a general census undertaken by Augustus to establish the extent of his power and resources. Here, then, we are not facing a great difficulty. The fact that certain documents do not refer to a certain event does not prove that it did not occur. The argument from silence, as it is called, has but little weight.

But more serious seems the accusation that Luke has entirely misdated the census, that the census of Augustus, carried out by Quirinius, occurred years after the birth of Christ and that there was no such undertaking at the time when Jesus was born. From the works of Josephus we learn that when Archelaus, the son of Herod (Mt 2:22), had been deposed by the Romans, his lands were annexed to the province of Syria, and Quirinius came "to take an account of their substance," and that the Jews, "although at the beginning they took the report of a taxation heinously," finally submitted and gave an account of their estates (*Ant* 18:1–3). It is the same census that Luke speaks of in Ac 5:37, and its date is AD 6. Other writers of antiquity, it seems, do not dwell on it. To this census, whose historicity is not doubted, Luke is said to have erroneously referred in his famous statement about the time of the birth of Jesus. But even the casual reader will at once have several objections. Luke, knowing, as his reference in Ac 5:37 shows, the circumstances of the Judean census of AD 6, would not be likely to misdate it. Also, Luke (in Lk 2:2) apparently is at pains to differentiate the census mentioned there from the later one, occurring AD 6, saying that the census of the time when Jesus was born was the first one. From this it seems very plain that no person is justified in accusing Luke of simply misdating the census.

But at the time Jesus was born, so someone may object, Herod was the king of the Jews, as is evident not only from Luke's account (1:5) but especially from Mt 2:1–12. How, then, could Augustus at this period order a census that would affect Israel? The answer is easy. Although Herod nominally was the ruler of Israel, in reality he was merely a subject of Rome and occupied the throne by the permission of the Roman emperor. The relations between the latter and Herod are perhaps best reflected in a letter which Augustus in indignation sent to Herod when he learned that the Jewish king had led an army into Arabia. Josephus says of this letter: "The sum of this epistle was this, that whereas of old he had used him as his friend, he should now use him as his subject" (*Ant* 16:290). The tone of this letter should silence the objection that Augustus would not in a census of his dominions include the territory over which Herod reigned.

"Each to His Own Town"

Critics charge that Luke is guilty of a misstatement when he says that all went to be enrolled, "each to his own town," because the Roman system required people to be registered in the town or city where they lived, not in their ancestral home. The statement of Lk 2:3, however, does not have to be understood as referring to the whole world, but can well be taken as bearing on Israel alone. The question, then, is whether the Romans, contrary to their custom, would conduct an enrollment in Israel in the manner indicated by Luke. Papyri finds from the first century AD give an affirmative answer. Documents have come to light that show that in Egypt the census was taken by the Romans just as described by Luke. If they did it in Egypt, it is only fair to assume that they could adopt this method also for Israel. We must remember that the Romans were very shrewd in ruling their colonies and provinces, adapting themselves, as much as safety permitted, to the customs and traditions of the subject peoples. In Israel the census method handed down from previous generations required that people be entered in the lists in that city which was looked upon as the home of their family. The Romans evidently did not see any reason that would compel them to carry out the enrollment in a manner not in keeping with the old customs of the Jews. Here, then, we have an instance where archaeology vindicates the reliability of the biblical record.

It is pertinent to add that, according to census records dating back to the early period of the Roman Empire, a census was taken by the Roman emperors every 14 years, the earliest one of these records coming from AD 20. If we count back 14 years from this date, we arrive at AD 6, when the census recorded by Josephus and in Ac 5:37 was held. Going back another 14 years, we would arrive at 8 BC, a date that does not match the census spoken of in Lk 2:1–5. Its execution in Israel may have been delayed. The lack of modern communication methods and the newness of the undertaking would probably be important factors in such delay.

Does Luke Deny the Flight into Egypt?

Matthew 2:1–23 is often said to be at variance with Lk 2:39–40. Matthew narrates the visit of the Magi; the flight of Joseph, Mary, and Jesus to Egypt; the slaughter of the babes in Bethlehem by the mercenaries of Herod; the death of Herod; the return of Joseph and his family; and their making their home in Nazareth. Luke does not relate the incidents mentioned. He simply says: "And when they had performed everything according to the Law of the Lord, they returned into Galilee, to their own town of Nazareth" (2:39). It is maintained that there is evidently a discrepancy here. But let the matter be pondered a minute, and it will appear how untenable the charge is.

In Matthew we are told, to put it briefly, that after the visit of the Magi, Joseph and his family went to Egypt and from there to Nazareth. Luke records that after they performed the rites prescribed in the law, Joseph and his family returned to Nazareth. Where is the contradiction? Luke does not deny that the family of Joseph sought refuge in Egypt. He merely does not mention this episode in the life of the Christ Child. There is no contradiction between two accounts if the one mentions more details than the other.

Furthermore, it must be remembered that the two statements are not necessarily parallel in respect to the time when the events spoken of occurred. No year or month is specified by either evangelist. Matthew dates the flight into Egypt after the visit of the Magi; Luke relates that Joseph and his family return to Nazareth after fulfilling all the requirements of the law. It is possible that the events of Mt 2 occurred after the return to Nazareth, which Luke mentions in 2:39. In that case Joseph and his family, after they had come back to Nazareth, moved to Bethlehem to live in the ancestral city and received there the visit of the Magi, but they could not make Bethlehem their permanent home on account of the enmity of Herod against the Christ Child. Another possibility is that the designation of time in Luke, which is indefinite and broad, covers all the events related in Mt 2.

Let it also be observed that what Luke wishes to emphasize is that all the commandments of the Law were adhered to by Joseph and Mary; the parents of Jesus returned home not before but only after they had performed everything the Law prescribed in the case of a firstborn son. If Luke's statement is viewed thus, one will find it very natural that other events that happened in the meantime are passed over in silence.

Matthew, on the other hand, presents Jesus to Jewish readers as a new Moses and the leader of the new Israel, the Christian Church. So Matthew includes the flight of Jesus into Egypt and compares Jesus to Moses in several respects: both went to Egypt under a Joseph, stayed in Egypt, and escaped from Egypt. Both in the account concerning Moses and in the event involving Jesus, male children were killed. Other parallelisms are: Jesus and Moses fast 40 days (Mt 4:2; Ex 34:28); both undergo temptations (Mt 4:1–11; Ex 16–17), spend time in the wilderness (Mt 4:1; Ex 15:22), and experience an episode on a mountain (Mt 5:1; 8:1; Ex 24:15–17). It is essentially Matthew's theme that compels him to include Jesus' flight into Egypt, while Luke's focus on the temple allows him to omit the incident—otherwise his volume, if he were not selective, would be too large for one scroll.

Annas and Caiaphas, High Priests

Perhaps some Bible reader has wondered at the statement in Lk 3:2 that Annas and Caiaphas were high priests when John began His ministry. The high priestly office was not simultaneously held by two persons. How strange, then, that Luke mentions two men as high priests for that period! The surprise will disappear when one studies the history of the times. Annas had been high priest from AD 7 to 14, the Romans having deposed him in the latter year. In spite of having incurred the displeasure of the Roman government, he remained very powerful. A son of Annas was among the high priests who preceded Caiaphas, and four sons of his were among those that followed Caiaphas, the latter himself being the son-in-law of Annas. While these facts alone would suffice to make Annas a force to reckon with as long as he lived, there is the additional consideration that many of the Jews would not approve of his being removed from his sacred office by the foreign masters and would continue to address him as high priest. When occasion arose, he would probably be invited by his son-in-law temporarily to fill the high priestly office.

The Caiaphas Ossuary, which likely contained the remains of the high priest mentioned in the Gospel. First century, Jerusalem.

We may point to the custom of addressing someone who has served as governor with this title long after he or she has ceased to hold this office. While Caiaphas was actually the high priest during the years of the earthly ministry of our Savior, Annas continued to be regarded as the one who was the high priest according to the Law of God. Thus it was natural for Luke to speak of two priests for this period. The Jew who had been asked at this time about the incumbent of the high priestly office would have replied, "Caiaphas is the man who wears the high priestly garments, but really Annas is our high priest, whom the Romans deposed, ignoring our sacred ancestral rules, according to which the high priest serves for life." The more one probes into Luke's narrative, the more trustworthy and reliable it is seen to be.

The Lists of the Apostles

Some accuse the Bible of containing contradictions by asserting that the names of the 12 apostles are given differently in Mt 10:2–4 and Lk 6:13–16. The names are the same in both lists, except in one instance. Matthew's list mentions Thaddaeus while Luke has Judas, the son of James. Thaddaeus must be the same person as Judas the son of James. This person evidently had two names, which was a custom of some prevalence in that age, as we see from the case of Peter, whose real name was Simon, to which was added the name of Cephas or Peter by our Lord Himself (Jn 1:42; Mt 16:16–18). Likewise the disciple who was a tax collector had two names: Matthew and Levi (Mt 9:9; Mk 2:14; Lk 5:27), while the apostle to the Gentiles was called Saul and Paul (Ac 13:9).

Can Jesus Be Accused of Occasional Undue Harshness?

We are all familiar with the strong language that Jesus used against the scribes and Pharisees as reported in Mt 23, where He denounced them as hypocrites and charged them with various other sins. No Christian holds that Jesus was too vehement in these utterances; for not only do we know that the Savior was sinless, being the Son of God, but that He was dealing with a set of men for most of whom religion had become a matter of outward observance and who, while they were interested in hundreds of little rules of conduct, neglected the chief things in the Law (Mt 23:23; Lk 11:42).

There is another occasion in the life of Christ where some people think He displayed extraordinary severity. Luke 9:59–60 states: "To another He said, 'Follow Me.' But he said, 'Lord, let me first go and bury my father.' And Jesus said to him, 'Leave the dead to bury their own dead. But as for you, go and proclaim the kingdom of God.' " A superficial reading gives the impression that Jesus forbade this person to attend the funeral of his father, who was about to be buried, and that He demanded from him the apparently altogether unnecessary sacrifice of foregoing the highly prized privilege of joining friends and relatives in according his father the last honors. A little reflection and study, however, will show that such a view does not grasp the real meaning of the passage.

First, Jesus' command "Follow Me" had the significance, as the present tense of the Greek verb shows, of "Be My follower; be My constant companion." What Jesus requests is not that the young man at once forsake all tasks and duties with which he at the moment was confronted, but that he become His disciple and travel about with Him and the Twelve, listening to the instruction of the Master, who had come from God. It was not imperative that this be done the next minute or the next hour. Jesus would be satisfied if it were done as soon as possible.

Furthermore, we must not assume that the father of this young man had died and that the corpse was awaiting burial. If that had been the situation, it is more than doubtful that there would have been any contact between the young man and Jesus. In Israel the burial as a rule took place on the same day the person died. A few hours after the news had spread that a certain member of the community had passed away, the funeral procession would be seen going to the tomb. Therefore, the father of this man was probably still living, but perhaps was old and near the end of his earthly life, and the son quite naturally expresses the wish to be permitted to stay with his father as long as the latter was among the living and to attend to the funeral rites, which were regarded as a matter of great importance. Filial respect and love were, and still are, a prominent trait in Near Eastern countries. The son in this case expresses the desire to do what custom and sentiment demanded of him, but Jesus tells him that he must put first things first. God has a higher claim on us than our parents and other relatives. This young man was now called by Christ to take a part in the spreading of the heavenly Kingdom, and this call had to be given first consideration. When we remember that Jesus is here not refusing to let this man attend the funeral of his father, but is merely telling him that he must not delay entering His service and becoming a minister of the Gospel until the death of his father, the charge of unnatural harshness against Jesus collapses.

In this connection the saying of the Lord, "Leave the dead to bury their own dead," may be given a little attention. What does the Savior mean when making this strange statement? The explanation commonly given seems to be the right one, the words of Jesus having this significance: "Let those who are spiritually dead bury their people who are bodily dead." That is work which they can do and which is in keeping with their character. They cannot be used for the proclamation of the kingdom of God, so let them attend to the funeral of their relatives.

Another similar saying of Jesus causes difficulty for some people. We read: "Yet another said, 'I will follow You, Lord, but let me first say farewell to those at my home.' Jesus said to him, 'No one who puts his hand to the plow and looks back is fit for the kingdom of God' " (Lk 9:61–62). A superficial reading may conclude that Jesus here is denying a person the privilege of bidding farewell to his parents and other relatives before he starts out on a tour intended to further the spreading of the kingdom of God. Does not the attitude that the Lord here takes seem unnatural and even inhuman? The man offers himself to Jesus as a disciple and servant, but before joining the Master he requests to be given the privilege of saying farewell to the members of his family. It should be noted that Jesus does not tell him that the permission that he asks for cannot be granted. Not one word of that. To interpret this text as saying that Jesus told this man, "You must not bid those at your house farewell," is reading something into the passage that is not contained in it. But Jesus issues a warning to this man. When the latter speaks of willingness to follow Jesus, but in the same breath refers to earthly ties that have a claim upon him, it was very proper that the admonition should be given him that whoever wishes to serve Jesus must do it wholeheartedly, placing such ministry higher than everything else here on earth. The words of Jesus, then, tell us that whoever enters the Gospel ministry must know that the service that Jesus wants is not a divided service, one half going to the Lord and the other half to persons and objects here on earth. His messengers must enter the work with a sincere and complete devotion to their heavenly Lord. The saying of Jesus indeed sounds a very earnest note, but not one of undue harshness, as though it insisted on the smothering of all natural affections.

Does the Bible Inculcate Hatred Toward One's Relatives?

Critics of the Bible point to Lk 14:26, where Jesus, in discussing the cost of true discipleship, said: "If anyone comes to Me and does not hate his own father and mother and wife and children and brothers and sisters, yes, and even his own life, he cannot be My disciple." There our great Master, we are told, demands of His followers that they hate those who are near and dear to them. What a religion! Who would want to be among its advocates?

The close-up of an early third-century sarcophagus includes three Christian symbols: the fish, the Good Shepherd, and the anchor cross.

Such talk should not impress the Christian. We know that our Lord taught love, urging His disciples to love even their most bitter enemies. In Mt 15:4–6 Jesus emphasizes that the commandment "Honor your father and your mother" must not be set aside. Whatever may be the sense of the passage referred to, it cannot be intended to make us entertain hatred toward our relatives. For many centuries, disciples of Jesus have been reading this saying of their Lord, and they have never been led by it to become neglectful of loving-kindness toward the members of their family circle. Nor do we know of a single instance where any one of them was shaken in faith by what critics of the Gospel call a cruel or inhuman saying. But it is true that some followers of Jesus have found it difficult to explain adequately the strong language Jesus uses.

To account for the terminology of our Lord, we must remember that the word *hate* is used in the Scriptures in the sense of "to love less." We find it thus employed in Gn 29:31, where the sacred writer says that the Lord saw Leah was "hated" (ESV) or "unloved" (NKJV). The preceding verse, however, states that Jacob loved Rachel more than Leah, from which we conclude that "loving less" and "hating" were terms that at times were used synonymously.

The meaning of the words of Jesus in Lk 14:26, then, simply is that we must love Him more than anybody else, be He ever so dear to us and His claim upon our affection ever so strong. It signifies that, if we have to choose between loyalty to Christ and loyalty to friends and relatives, Christ always must be given the preference. Knowing our proneness to give first place to earthly ties and values, He employs heroic language, as it were, to make us realize the significance of true discipleship, involving, as it does, willingness to suffer for His sake the loss of everything one here cherishes.

It was not very difficult for His disciples to see what He meant and to harmonize this saying of His with others from His lips in which faithful observance of filial and conjugal duties had been stressed.

In Lk 14:12–14 we find another statement of Jesus that belongs to the class of hard or strong sayings. We read: "He said also to the man who had invited Him, 'When you give a dinner or a banquet, do not invite your friends or your brothers or your relatives or rich neighbors, lest they also invite you in return and you be repaid. But when you give a feast, invite the poor, the crippled, the lame, the blind, and you will be blessed, because they cannot repay you. For you will be repaid at the resurrection of the just.' " Looking at these words of Jesus, one is inclined to ask, "Does the Lord forbid us to invite our friends and relatives to be our guests and enjoy a meal at our table? Is the only kind of hospitality He sanctions that which we classify as charity?" To begin with, let us note that our Lord certainly would not approve of gluttonous eating and drinking where the desire to satisfy one's appetite for delicious food and drink is the ruling passion and, to use the phrase of Paul, people make their bellies the god that they worship.

But the question confronting us here is whether Jesus opposes innocent gatherings of friends and relatives where food and fellowship is enjoyed. At once the Christian reader will say that Jesus cannot have meant to interdict all entertaining of one's friends, rich neighbors, and relatives, for He Himself at times was the guest at such meals. The wedding at Cana can be mentioned here, likewise the occasion when He was anointed by Mary (Jn 12:1–3). Furthermore, when we examine the Greek of the passage, an important consideration presents itself. "Do not invite your friends," says the Savior. The verb in this case is in the present tense, so that the significance is, "Do not always or regularly or habitually invite your friends." Again, let it be observed that the tenor of the saying is directed not against hospitality toward one's kin but against that selfish hospitality that is practiced with the motive of serving one's own earthly interests. The finest exhibitions of friendship are spoiled when they are motivated by selfishness.

Persistence in Prayer

Matthew 6:7–8 states: "And when you pray, do not heap up empty phrases as the Gentiles do, for they think that they will be heard for their many words. Do not be like them, for your Father knows what you need before you ask Him."

Luke 18:5, 7 asserts: "Yet because this widow keeps bothering me, I will give her justice, so that she will not beat me down by her continual coming. . . . And will not God give justice to His elect, who cry to Him day and night? Will He delay long over them?"

The one text seems to urge: "Pray perseveringly, incessantly"; the other: "Pray briefly." Are we confronted with a contradiction? Matthew speaks of outward prayer, consisting in mere words. The Gentiles thought that in prayer quantity counted for much, and hence they repeated certain forms and words over and over again in a mechanical fashion, their hearts not joining in the utterances of their mouths. That is a practice that Jesus condemns in the plainest and severest of terms. But there is an incessant prayer that is right and acceptable in the sight of God, namely, when the heart cries to Him in all sincerity and is not daunted by the seeming unwillingness of the Lord to answer. If our requests are not granted immediately, we are in danger of doubting that God hears us at all and of ceasing to pray. To continue sending up our petitions even when heaven seems closed to us is what Jesus enjoins in Lk 18:5, 7. To sum up, Jesus condemns the meaningless, repetitious "prayers" of unbelievers and all prayers that are like them. But Jesus commends the insistent prayer of the true believer. Bearing this in mind, we see that the two texts quoted can well stand side by side.

It will be remembered in this connection that Paul in 1Th 5:17 urges constant prayer. "Pray without ceasing," he says, that is, let your whole life be a life of prayer; be in constant communion with your God. At first sight this might seem to conflict with the statement of Jesus on the futility of much speaking (Mt 6:7). Does not God know all our wants? Why keep repeating them? The explanation is that in Mt 6:7 Jesus forbids us to think that many words can better inform God as to our needs than few words can. As for that matter, no words are needed at all, because the Lord knows our wants before we ourselves are aware of them. But in 1Th 5:17 Paul refers to the attitude of our heart. It should be a prayerful attitude at all times, like that of a child toward his or her beloved parents, an attitude implying an earnest longing to discuss all plans and problems with Him and to be ever guided by His Word and Spirit. Hence the texts with which we are here concerned do not contain conflicting statements, but they merely emphasize two important truths. First, prayer is not something mechanical or magical, depending for its efficacy on the utterance of certain sounds. Second, prayer is something that we Christians should engage in at all times, letting our heart hold communion with God incessantly.

The Blind Man at Jericho

The texts in question are Mt 20:29–34, Mk 10:46–52, and Lk 18:35–43. It is well-known that the three accounts of the healing of blind men at Jericho by Jesus, when He was making His last journey to Jerusalem, are not alike in some details. According to Matthew, Jesus healed two blind men as He was leaving the town. Mark mentions one blind man, whose name was Bartimaeus, and he says that this man was healed by Jesus when He was departing from the town. Luke relates that the miracle took place as Jesus was drawing near to Jericho. In his account one blind man is spoken of. That Matthew mentions two blind men while Mark's and Luke's narratives refer to only one need cause no difficulty. The two statements are no more contradictory than the following two sentences: "It rained today" and "It rained and hailed today." The one is simply more complete than the other. It is clear, then, that Jesus healed two blind men at Jericho. Mark mentions the name of the one blind man probably because Bartimaeus

Jesus healing two blind men outside Jericho; protrayed in the Codex of Predis, 1476.

lived for several decades after he received his sight and was a familiar personage to the early Christians.

But what shall we say with respect to the fact that one evangelist says that the miracle occurred when Jesus was approaching the town, while the other two report that He performed it as He was leaving it? It is possible that Jesus healed one man as He was coming near the town and two others when He departed. In that case Luke would be reporting a different miracle than Matthew and Mark, and Jesus would have given sight to three blind men at Jericho.

Some suggest another solution. Luke 18:35 reads: "As He drew near to Jericho, a blind man was sitting by the roadside begging." Let it be noted that Luke does not absolutely say where the miracle itself occurred. It is possible that the beggar sat at the roadside when Jesus approached Jericho, but he was not healed until our Lord left the town. This interpretation presupposes either that Jesus left Jericho by the same gate through which He entered or that the beggar changed his station and was at the other side of Jericho when Jesus was leaving. But why should that be considered improbable? With the multitude, Bartimaeus had passed into town, and as Jesus and His companions were proceeding on their way, he and a blind companion uttered their cry for help. Instances of anticipation like the one assumed here are very frequent in books of history and biography. Luke uses a conspicuous example of it in 3:19–20.

There is still another explanation that many will hold more appealing. At the time of Christ there were two Jerichos, one on the site where a city had grown up during the period of the kings and another somewhat closer to Jerusalem at the very edge of the wilderness of Judea, which was built by Herod the Great and was a very attractive place. The traveler, going eastward from Jerusalem, arrives first at the city of Herodean Jericho and then, continuing on the road for another mile or two, approaches the older town. The blind man may have been at a place between the two Jerichos. When he was healed, a person reporting the miracle could say either that the healing had taken place when Jesus left Jericho, that is, the older town, or that it was performed when Jesus was approaching Jericho, that is, the Herodean creation. This explanation fully removes the difficulty.

Bengel and many other prominent theologians set forth still another solution. According to the view of these scholars, Matthew is giving a condensed account of what happened at Jericho. For the sake of brevity, instead of stating that Jesus healed a blind man when he entered and that He healed a blind man when He left, he merely mentions that Jesus healed two blind men who were sitting by the wayside and does not deem it necessary to give further particulars as to the place and time of the miracle performed upon them. This assumption likewise removes the discrepancy.

Twelfth-century column capital showing Judas hanging from a tree.

When Did Satan Enter Judas?

Luke 22:3–4, 7 states: "Then Satan entered into Judas called Iscariot, who was of the number of the twelve. He went away and conferred with the chief priests and officers how he might betray Him to them. . . . Then came the day of Unleavened Bread, on which the Passover lamb had to be sacrificed."

John 13:27 says: "Then after he had taken the morsel, Satan entered into him. Jesus said to him, 'What you are going to do, do quickly.' "

Why should it be thought that there is a discrepancy here? Quite true, in the one instance Satan is said to have entered Judas at the Last Supper; in the other, the entering takes place at an earlier time, namely, before Judas promised the enemies of Jesus to betray his Master. But is it not possible or even probable that Satan entered Judas more than once, or again and again? From Jn 13:2 it is evident that Satan had conquered the heart of Judas before the bread was given to him. Instead of writing, "The devil had already put it into the heart of Judas Iscariot, Simon's son, to betray him," John might have written, "the devil had entered Judas." The narrative of John, therefore, also indicates that Satan entered Judas repeatedly. (Cf references to God's Spirit coming upon Samson repeatedly; Jgs 14:6, 19; 15:14.)

Every time this unfortunate disciple determined anew to become the traitor of Jesus, Satan may be said to have seized him.

The Date of Christ's Death

Luke 22:7 says: "Then came the day of Unleavened Bread, on which the Passover lamb had to be sacrificed."

John 18:28 states: "Then they led Jesus from the house of Caiaphas to the governor's headquarters. It was early morning. They themselves did not enter the governor's headquarters, so that they would not be defiled, but could eat the Passover."

These two passages draw attention to a famous problem in the harmonization of the Gospels. The question involved is whether the death of Jesus occurred on the 15th or on the 14th of Nisan. The Synoptic Gospels (Matthew, Mark, and Luke) give the impression that it was on the 15th when our Lord died; but John seems to imply that the great sacrifice was offered up on the 14th. The synoptic evangelists relate that Jesus instituted the Lord's Supper the night in which He was betrayed. This institution took place in connection with the observance of the Passover when Jesus and His disciples were gathered to eat the meal prescribed for this festival. The paschal lamb was killed in the afternoon of the 14th of Nisan (cf Ex 12:6, where "at twilight" means the time between three and five o'clock in the afternoon). The meal was eaten "that night" (Ex 12:8). It must be remembered that the Jewish day began with sunset. Hence while the lamb was slaughtered on the 14th, the meal was held on the 15th of Nisan (called Abib in the early days of Israelite history).

When one peruses what Luke and the other synoptic writers say of the evening before Christ's death, the picture that presents itself fits the brief remarks made above on the Jewish Passover. Jesus sends two disciples to prepare the paschal meal. It is done on the day when the paschal lamb had to be killed, and in the evening that followed, Jesus and His disciples eat the ceremonial meal. This latter act must be dated as occurring on the 15th of Nisan. The following afternoon, hence still on the 15th, Jesus died on the cross.

When we read John's Gospel, the situation appears to be different. The high priests bring their prisoner to Pontius Pilate early in the morning, and from what is related in Jn 18:28, it seems that the Passover had not yet been observed and that hence it was on the 14th of Nisan when Pilate tried Jesus, condemned Him, and put Him to death on the cross. The high priests apparently had not yet eaten the paschal meal, but they were intending to do so in the evening of that day. A number of solutions of the apparent discrepancy have been proposed.

First, it has been held that the crucifixion of Jesus took place on the 14th of Nisan and that His death occurred about the same time as the slaying of the paschal lamb, which prefigured Him. The notices in the synoptic writers are explained in a way to harmonize with this view. It seems that the difficulties besetting this explanation are very formidable because the synoptic writers are quite explicit and definite in stating that the day before Christ's death was the day appointed for the killing of the paschal lamb, that is, the 14th of Nisan.

Second, other theologians have taken the view that the day of Christ's death was the 15th of Nisan and that what John says must be interpreted in such a way as to harmonize with this position. Very forcefully this opinion is championed by A. T. Robertson in his *Harmony of the Gospels* (New York: Harper, 1922), p. 283. He believes that Jn 18:28, the chief text appealed to by those who date Christ's death on the 14th of the month, does not say what these people find in it. "Eating the Passover," he points out, may well be considered an expression designating participation in the festive meal held on the 15th of Nisan; for this day was a holiday and was observed with a special celebration. Besides, he states that the pollution that the high priests feared according to Jn 18:28 would not have kept them from eating the paschal meal the coming evening because pollutions made a person unclean for the day when they occurred, but ended with sundown, and the paschal meal was eaten after sundown, hence the following day. Robertson concludes that therefore Jn 18:28 must not be interpreted as saying that the paschal meal had not yet been held. Since it can be proved that "Passover" may be a term pointing to a festive meal on the 15th of Nisan (cf our Christmas dinner), Robertson's explanation seems perfectly tenable.

A third view has gained prominence. On the basis of sound evidence there seem to have been two calendars that determined the date of the Passover by different methods. In a calendar used by the Essenes in the Qumran community, the Passover always occurred on the same day of the week (Wednesday), as the Book of Jubilees indicates. Another calendar, employed by the Pharisees, adjusted the time for the Passover according to lunar calculations. Thus in the year of our Savior's Passion, the Essene community and Galilee were celebrating the Passover, as related by the Synoptic Gospels, before the observance by the Pharisees in Jerusalem, as reflected in John's account. Thus it is logical for Jesus and His disciples, who were from Galilee, to have kept the Passover before the official feast in Jerusalem. In any case, scholarship shows that no real discrepancy exists between the accounts of the synoptic writers and John on the date of Jesus' crucifixion.

Nonresistance and Private Revenge

Matthew 5:39 records: "But I say to you, Do not resist the one who is evil. But if anyone slaps you on the right cheek, turn to him the other also."

Luke 22:36 reports: "He said to them, 'But now let the one who has a moneybag take it, and likewise a knapsack. And let the one who has no sword sell his cloak and buy one.' "

These two texts do not contradict each other. Matthew says in effect: "If any wrong is committed against you, bear it patiently rather than avenge it." That is the obvious meaning of the passage. These words in the Sermon on the Mount immediately precede the injunction of Jesus that His disciples must love their enemies. When Jesus says "not to resist evil," He simply points to one of the ways in which love must manifest itself toward the enemy. If we are wronged, the proper reaction is not revenge, but love. Instead of hurting those who are injuring us, we should lovingly minister to their needs.

A number of difficult questions arise in this connection, it is true. When our house is burglarized, should we forego calling the police and weakly submit to being dispossessed of our belongings? The course that we are to pursue must be dictated in each individual case not by feelings of revenge, but by pity and love. When our enemy has set our house on fire, love of our family certainly requires that we try to extinguish that fire. Even love toward the enemy demands such a course; for if we fail to check the fire, the injury the person inflicted will be all the greater. Evidently the words of Jesus are meant to inculcate this general principle: "Overcome evil with good" (Rm 12:21). The particular manner in which love is to manifest itself in dealing with the enemy is to be determined by the circumstances, which are hardly ever the same in any two cases.

The other text listed above by no means contradicts the teaching we have been considering. It is a warning to the disciples that troublesome times, days of suffering and persecution, are coming for them and that they will have to arm themselves to withstand the onslaughts that are impending. The connection makes it clear that our Lord is not speaking of swords of iron or steel in this admonition. The disciples thought that He was referring to such physical weapons, and they said, "Look, Lord, here are two swords" (Lk 22:38). Jesus, seeing that they were still very dull in their understanding of the spiritual teaching He had been giving them, said: "It is enough." He did not pursue the instruction any further, leaving it to the Holy Spirit to open up the full meaning of this matter to them later on. To put it briefly, the words of Jesus in Lk 22:36 are a figurative way of saying: "Perilous times are coming; prepare for them." The swords He had in mind are the spiritual weapons of strong faith, fervent love of the Savior, fortitude, patience, and hope. This text, then, treats an altogether different subject than the one touched on in Mt 5:39.

Crucifixion carving on the door of the Basilica of Santa Sabina;
Rome, fifth century.

Did Both Criminals Revile Jesus?

Matthew 27:44 reads: "And the robbers who were crucified with Him also reviled Him in the same way."

Mark 15:32 states: "Those who were crucified with Him also reviled Him."

Luke 23:39–40 records: "One of the criminals who were hanged railed at Him, saying, 'Are You not the Christ? Save Yourself and us!' But the other rebuked him, saying, 'Do you not fear God, since you are under the same sentence of condemnation?' "

The difficulty that confronts us here is readily solved. There are two possibilities of harmonizing the statements. Matthew and Mark say that the thieves who were crucified with Jesus blasphemed Him. They do not say that the criminals continued in this attitude toward the Lord to the very end. We may well assume that the thief on the right, after seeing the patience with which Jesus bore His suffering and hearing the words of love, imploring God to forgive those who were causing His torments, repented of his initial blasphemous utterances and spoke the words of rebuke reported by Luke. We, then, would have another case where one account supplements the other two: Matthew and Mark relate that at first both criminals crucified with Jesus joined in the maledictions and blasphemies hurled at Him by the populace, while Luke reports that one of the thieves after a while experienced a change of heart and became a worshiper of Jesus. If we adopt this view of the situation, every vestige of a discrepancy disappears.

The other way of harmonizing the statements assumes that only one of the robbers was guilty of contemptuous statements, but that Matthew and Mark use the plural because they intend to enumerate the classes of people who were reviling our Lord when He was in the depths of woe—passers-by, priests, scribes, and condemned criminals. In that case, Matthew and Mark would not be wishing to specify whether one or whether more robbers were reviling Jesus, but they merely indicate that from this class, too, came the taunts that helped to fill the cup of bitterness that He was emptying. Whether a person prefers the first or the second explanation, either one removes the difficulty.

Trees at the base of the Mount of Olives.

The Place of the Ascension

Luke 24:50–51 records: "Then He led them out as far as Bethany, and lifting up His hands He blessed them. While He blessed them, He parted from them and was carried up into heaven."

Acts 1:9, 12 reports: "And when He had said these things, as they were looking on, He was lifted up, and a cloud took Him out of their sight. . . . Then they returned to Jerusalem from the mount called Olivet, which is near Jerusalem, a Sabbath day's journey away."

These accounts are easily harmonized if one is somewhat familiar with the topography of the vicinity of Jerusalem. Bethany was located on the eastern slope of Mount Olivet. One may say, therefore, either that Jesus ascended to heaven from the Mount of Olives or that He ascended from Bethany.

Further Study

Lay/Bible Class Resources

Knolhoff, Wayne, Curtis Moermond, Mark Etter, Arthur Just, David Brazeal, and Gary Dunker. *Luke, Parts 1 and 2.* Leaders Guide and Enrichment Magazine/Study Guide. LL. St. Louis: Concordia, 2007, 2008. ✎ Two in-depth, nine-session Bible studies with individual, small group, and lecture portions.

Life by His Word. St. Louis: Concordia, 2009. ✎ More than 1,500 reproducible one-page Bible studies covering each chapter of the canonical Scriptures. Page references to *The Lutheran Study Bible.* CD-Rom and downloadable.

Miller, Donald G. *Luke.* Layman's Bible Commentary. Atlanta: John Knox, 1966. ✎ Somewhat brief; stresses prophecies of the Messiah and fulfillment, also in the light of Jewish messianic expectations.

Morris, Leon. *The Gospel according to St. Luke.* TNTC. Downers Grove, IL: Eerdmans, 1988. ✎ A valuable resource by a famous evangelical scholar. Based on the Greek text but written in a non-technical style.

Prange, Victor H. *Luke.* PBC. St. Louis: Concordia, 2004. ✎ Lutheran author. Excellent for Bible classes. Based on the NIV translation.

Scaer, Peter, and Derek Roberts. *God's Abiding Word: Luke.* St. Louis: Concordia, 2003. ✎ Developed by a Lutheran New Testament scholar. Eleven-session downloadable Bible study provides a thorough and thought-provoking look at the Gospel; includes leader's notes, discussion questions, time lines, map, charts, illustrated outline, and glossary.

Weidenschilling, J. M. *Luke: To All Nations.* GWFT. St. Louis: Concordia, 2006. ✎ Lutheran author. Twelve-session Bible study, including leader's notes and discussion questions.

Church Worker Resources

Bailey, Kenneth E. *Finding the Lost: Cultural Keys to Luke 15.* St. Louis: Concordia, 1992. ✎ As a sojourner in Palestine for many years, this interpretation of parables brings a cultural reading that provides insights into how the first century hearer would have understood Jesus' parables. By attempting to recover the culture of the parables, he provides insights that are excellent for preaching.

Esler, Philip Francis. *Community and Gospel in Luke-Acts: The Social and Political Motivations of Lucan Theology.* Cambridge: Cambridge University Press, 1987. ✎ A sociological exegete who explores the cultural insights that have often been overlooked. He takes on many of the critical assessments of the previous decades, deconstructing them from his sociological reading. Excellent for preaching.

Kingsbury, Jack Dean. *Conflict in Luke: Jesus, Authorities, Disciples.* Minneapolis: Augsburg Fortress, 1991. ✎ A retelling of the story of Luke intended to bring out the significance of the chief characters.

Stein, Robert H. *Luke.* NAC. Nashville: Broadman, 1992. ✎ A very conservative commentary that is safe and sane. Stein surprises with his occasional stunning insight.

Academic Resources

Bock, Darrell L. *Luke.* Baker Exegetical Commentary on the New Testament. 2 vols. Grand Rapids: Baker, 1994, 1996. ✎ Bock is a significant voice in Lukan scholarship who has published extensively on the Gospel.

———. *Proclamation from Prophecy and Pattern: Lucan Old Testament Christology.* Sheffield: Sheffield Acadmic Press, 1987. ✎ Shows how the language of typology is expressed in a prophetic pattern. Not only what the prophet says points to Jesus, but also the prophet's life points to our Lord as the prophet suffers for speaking God's word of Law and Gospel to his generation.

Further Study

Bovon, F. *Luke 1: A Commentary on the Gospel of Luke 1:1–9:50*. Hermenia. Minneapolis: Augsburg Fortress, 2002. § Commentary from a celebrated critical scholar whose *Luke the Theologian* (updated 2006) is a standard survey of Lukan literature. Strong powers of analysis and description.

Brown, Raymond E. *The Birth of the Messiah: A Commentary on the Infancy Narratives in the Gospels of Matthew and Luke*. New York: Doubleday, 1977. § Brown's treatment is the most comprehensive commentary on the infancy narratives, but not necessarily the most helpful. Fitzmyer's commentary distills much of Brown's book.

Cadbury, Henry J. *The Making of Luke-Acts*. London: SPCK, 1958. § This groundbreaking study opened up the field of Lukan scholarship to consider Luke as a significant Gospel.

Conzelmann, Hans. *The Theology of St. Luke*. New York: Harper, 1967. § A flawed but insightful study of Luke that scholars responded to for decades.

Creed, John Martin. *The Gospel according to St. Luke: The Greek Text with Introduction, Notes, and Indices*. London: Macmillan, 1930. § A significant older work that provided a standard for all Lukan commentaries that followed. In reading Creed's exegesis, one is struck on how fresh it seems after so many years.

Danker, Fredrick W. *Jesus and the New Age according to St. Luke: A Commentary on the Third Gospel*. St. Louis: Clayton, 1972. § Danker sees inaugurated eschatology at the center of Jesus' incarnation, death, resurrection, and ascension (thus the title). Focused on critical issues, the grammatical work is unsurpassed; theologically insightful.

Ellis, E. Earle. *The Gospel of Luke*. Eugene, OR: Wipf & Stock, 2003. § Helpful resource by a well-known evangelical scholar. Notes the two-source hypothesis in his introduction.

Fitzmyer, Joseph A. *The Gospel according to Luke*. Vols. 28 and 28A of AB. New York: Doubleday, Vol. 1, 1981; Vol. 2, 1985. § Noted Semitic scholar; critical, with a careful understanding of the importance of Judaica. The best introduction there is on Luke's Gospel. Thorough, critical analysis of the text is evident throughout the commentary, especially in notes. His theological analysis is always insightful; however, he does not relate his theological interpretation to the Church. Use with discernment.

Green, Joel B. *The Gospel of Luke*. NICNT. Grand Rapids: Eerdmans, 1997. § Green is a formidable exegete writing for an excellent series.

———. *The Theology of the Gospel of Luke*. Cambridge: Cambridge University Press, 1995. § Presents the Gospel as narrative theology and describes its major themes.

Hendriksen, William. *New Testament Commentary: Exposition of the Gospel According to Luke*. Grand Rapids: Baker, 1983. § A helpful resource, mindful of the meaning also for today.

Johnson, Luke Timothy. *The Gospel of Luke*. Sacra Pagina 3. Collegeville, MN: Liturgical Press, 1991. § Johnson's approach is literary-critical, reflecting the more conservative exegesis of Yale scholars. His comments read more like a narrative than a commentary. In some ways, they are like mini-sermons with refreshing perspective.

Just, Arthur A. *Luke*. 2 Vols. CC. St. Louis: Concordia, 1996–97. § A narrative and theological commentary by a Lutheran theologian who applies the text for today. Thorough examination of the Greek text. An excellent resource for preachers.

Karris, Robert J. *Luke: Artist and Theologian*. New York: Paulist, 1985. § Karris attempts to restore Luke's status as a significant Gospel alongside Matthew and Mark. He also stresses Luke as theologian. One of the first to highlight Luke's literary artistry. He shows how Luke exploits themes to record the historical events in a literary framework.

Keck, Leander E., and J. Louis Martyn, eds. *Studies in Luke-Acts*. Philadelphia: Augsburg Fortress, 1966. ✠ These essays were a direct response to Conzelmann's *The Theology of St. Luke*. Some of the essays are supportive of Conzelmann; others begin the extensive critique of Conzelmann's provocative book. This book of essays placed Luke back in the forefront of synoptic studies.

Lenski, R. C. H. *The Interpretation of St. Luke's Gospel*. Minneapolis: Augsburg Fortress, 2008. ✠ A standard resource by a noteworthy Lutheran interpreter, concerned with being faithful to the text and with its implications for today.

Marshall, I. Howard. *The Gospel of Luke: A Commentary on the Greek Text*. NIGTC. Grand Rapids: Eerdmans, 1978. ✠ Presupposes the two-source hypothesis, arguing at times as to how much Luke borrowed from Mark; provides much helpful information on varying views of individual pericopes. Marshall's exegesis is careful, precise, and reasonable.

———. *Luke: Historian & Theologian*. New Testament Profiles. Grand Rapids: InterVarsity Press, 1970. ✠ A very valuable overview and evaluation of earlier studies and views. Marshall shows that Luke's historical theology demonstrates that history is where salvation emerges, placing history and eschatology on the same plain. Luke does this by careful calibration of time and a faithful rendering of the tradition.

Navone, John. *Themes of St. Luke*. Rome: Gregorian University Press, 1970. ✠ A simple, straightforward presentation of the themes of Luke's Gospel. Since Luke exploits the use of motifs, this book highlights Luke's literary genius in weaving a tapestry of various themes throughout his Gospel.

Neyrey, Jerome H. *The Passion according to Luke*. New York: Paulist, 1985. ✠ A classic redactional study of Luke's passion narrative. Neyrey, along with Luther and Léon-Dufour, shows that Luke's version of the Last Supper is part of the testamentary tradition where Jesus as the testator gives His last will and testament to His disciples as the testatees.

———, ed. *The Social World of Luke-Acts: Models for Interpretation*. Peabody, MA: Hendrickson, 1991. ✠ A groundbreaking work that highlights the cultural world of the first century. Demonstrates that to understand Luke one must enter the biblical worldview.

Nolland, John. *Luke*. 3 vols. WBC. Dallas: Word Books, 1989, 1993. ✠ An exhaustive treatment of Luke's Gospel; ponderous and predictable.

Plummer, Alfred. *St. Luke*. ICC. Edinburgh: T&T Clark, 1985 reprint. ✠ Reprint of an old masterpiece (1922) with careful grammatical analysis.

Talbert, Charles H. *Literary Patterns, Theological Themes, and the Genre of Luke-Acts*. Missoula: Scholars, 1974. ✠ Emphasizes literary structural analysis over/against redaction, describing architecture analysis as a variety of the species style or rhetorical criticism within the genus of literary criticism. Of particular interest to Talbert is Luke's utilization of the principle of balance, a common literary practice in the Mediterranean.

Tannehill, R. *The Narrative Unity of Luke—Acts: A Literary Interpretation. Volume One: The Gospel according to Luke*. Philadelphia: Augsburg Fortress, 1986. ✠ An example of literary criticism that reads like a novel, eschewing the normal pattern of verse by verse analysis. Tannehill uncovers Luke's literary genius. The introduction makes some outrageous critical claims.

van Oosterzee, J. J. *A Commentary on the Holy Scriptures: Luke*. LCHS. New York: Charles Scribner's Sons, 1868. ✠ A helpful older example of German biblical scholarship, based on the Greek text, which provides references to significant commentaries from the Reformation era forward.

JOHN

The Word became flesh and dwelt among us

The plain bows into the Sea of Galilee where families of fishers settled and built their homes. The villagers prospered and, with the help of a centurion, built a synagogue. The settlement became known as Capernaum, "Village of Comfort" or perhaps "Village of Nahum," though there is no clear association with the Old Testament prophet by that name. Since the settlers built no wall to defend themselves, their lives must have been peaceful until the teacher from Nazareth arrived.

Crowds followed Jesus into Capernaum, which became the hub of His travels throughout Galilee. He stayed at the home of Simon Peter and gathered about Him other fishermen as His disciples. Among them was John the son of Zebedee, who most likely wrote the fourth Gospel in his old age, while ministering at distant Ephesus.

Historical and Cultural Setting

For the political circumstances surrounding the life of Jesus, see pp 185–86.

Five times the Gospel of John referred to "the disciple whom [Jesus] loved." This title invites a closer look at Jesus as teacher and John as a disciple, including John's background as a writer. Growing up on the shores of the Sea of Galilee where much of Jesus' ministry took place, John would have known well both the sea and his father's fishing trade. Zebedee's family prospered

Black basalt stones line the shore of the Sea of Galilee at Capernaum. The Capernaum synagogue where Jesus taught was built with basalt.

OVERVIEW

Author
John the apostle

Date
Written c AD 90

Places
Bethsaida; Nazareth; Cana; Capernaum; Aenon near Salim; Galilee; Samaria; Tiberias; Mount of Olives; Jerusalem; Bethany; see map, p 199

People
Jesus and His family; the Twelve (especially "the disciple whom Jesus loved," Andrew, Simon Peter, Philip, Nathanael, Thomas the Twin, Judas Iscariot); Caiaphas, Annas, and chief priests; "the Jews"; Nicodemus; Samaritan woman; blind man; Lazarus, Mary, and Martha; Pilate

Purpose
To lead people to believe that Jesus is the Christ, the Son of God

Law Themes
Darkness; slavery to sin; condemnation; demand for signs; death; fleshly desire; unbelief; Judas's example; spiritual blindness; unclean; command to love; the world's hatred

Gospel Themes
Light; grace; truth; Baptism; Lamb of God; born of the Spirit; life; resurrection; Jesus' flesh and blood; the Shepherd's care; clean; forgiveness; God's love; sanctification

Memory Verses
Jesus, the Word (1:1–5); born of God (1:12–14); water and the Spirit (3:5–8); God so loved the world (3:16–17); Jesus' flesh and blood (6:53–58); Peter's confession (6:67–69); Father and Son are one (10:27–30); resurrection and life (11:25–26); the way to the Father (14:1–6); gift of the Spirit (20:22–23)

TIMELINE

AD 33	Resurrection, Ascension, Pentecost
AD 41	Martyrdom of James, brother of John
AD 68	Martyrdom of Peter and Paul
c AD 90	Gospel of John written
AD 132	Bar Kokhba revolt begins

and was able to afford servant labor (Mk 1:20). Fishermen would have worked alongside their father and his servants in every aspect of the father's business. For example, Matthew describes how John and his brother James helped Zebedee prepare the nets by washing, mending, and hanging them out to dry at the end of the day (cf Mt 4:21).

Details about John's mother show the devoted upbringing of the children. She followed Jesus and ministered to Him when He taught in Galilee (she may be Salome; cf Mt 27:56; Mk 15:40–41). She saw Jesus die on the cross and brought spices to His tomb on Easter Sunday morning. (Based on Jn 19:25, some think she was the sister of Mary the mother of Jesus.) She was probably a protective and forceful personality in John's life. She asked Jesus to enthrone James and John alongside Him in His kingdom (Mt 20:20–24; cf Mk 10:35–41)! Not surprisingly, John never mentions this incident or the ill feelings it created among the disciples.

Fish mosaic from remains of a third-century church near Megiddo, one of the oldest churches in the region.

The extent of prosperity John's family experienced in their fishing business may be illustrated by the fact that John was known by the high priest and gained access to his household during Jesus' trial (Jn 18:15; note that Peter, another fisherman, did not have easy access). Also, from the cross, Jesus entrusted Mary to John's care. The closeness and wealth of the family probably made John the best choice to assume Jesus' family responsibility for His mother. (According to church historian Eusebius, John took care of Mary for 15 years.)

As noted above, John had a special relationship with Jesus. At crucial moments in His ministry, Jesus invited John to accompany Him (transfiguration: Mt 17:1; Mk 9:2; Lk 9:28; raising of Jairus's daughter: Mk 5:37; Lk 8:51; prayers at Gethsemane: Mt 26:37; Mk 14:33). At the Last Supper, John sat closest to Jesus, reclining on the floor or couch next to a short table according to Near Eastern custom (Jn 13:23). When Peter, another disciple close to Jesus, needed information, he tried to work through John to get to Jesus (vv 24–25). John appears to have been the only disciple to overcome his fear of arrest and stand by Jesus at the crucifixion (19:25–27). On Easter Sunday, John is the first of the disciples to reach the empty tomb and ponder its message (20:1–9). He clearly demonstrates a special closeness to the Lord. This is an important feature that distinguishes the Gospel of John from the other accounts.

Composition

Author

Because the Fourth Gospel differs so strikingly from the Synoptic Gospels in both form and matter, and because it gives so high and exalted a picture of the Christ, critical scholarship has questioned or denied the possibility that it is the work of the son of Zebedee; there has been a strong tendency to discount or discredit the evidence for the apostolic authorship of the Gospel. But both the tradition of the Early Church and the witness of the Gospel itself are very strong, and both point unambiguously to John the son of Zebedee as the author of the Gospel.

Acts and Early Traditions

John the apostle long outlived the other apostles. In all his writings, John is at pains to underscore the fact that he is freely giving what he has received freely, that in all his life and ministry it is the Christ who has taken and retains the initiative, and that this initiative is pure grace: "From His fullness we have all received, grace upon grace," he writes in his Gospel (1:16); the incarnate Word has given him the new birth which makes him a child of God (1:12, 13); it was the Son of God who made known to him the Father (1:18); it was the risen Christ who breathed on John and gave him the gift of the Holy Spirit, the Spirit who made his word a divinely valid word, effectual for forgiveness and for judgment (20:22–23).

The evangelist John accompanied by an eagle, a creature that soars into the heavens, symbolizing the lofty content of John's account.

"I chose you and appointed you that you should go and bear fruit and that your fruit should abide" (15:16). The elective grace of the Christ gave John a long and fruitful apostolic ministry, both in Israel and in Asia Minor. The Book of Acts gives us glimpses of his ministry in Israel: we find him associated with Peter in the healing of the lame man at Jerusalem (Ac 3:1–26), in his subsequent trial and defense before the Sanhedrin (4:1–22), and in his ministry to the young church in Samaria (8:14–25). Paul can speak of John as one of the three men "who seemed to be pillars" of the church in Jerusalem (Gal 2:9). He was associated with Peter in Israel; like Peter, he left Israel when the skies grew dark with judgment and it became increasingly clear that his apostolic mission to Israel had been fulfilled and the debt of love to Israel had been paid. Early Christian tradition, a tradition which there is no real reason to doubt (a tradition that archeological discoveries in Ephesus have, moreover, served to confirm) says that John went to Asia Minor and settled at Ephesus. John's rich literary activity falls in this period.

By the end of the second century we find the Gospel of John established as an authority in the Early Church alongside the first three Gospels. It is included in the first Gospel harmony of Christendom, the *Diatessaron* of Tatian (c AD 170), which opens with the first sentence of John and closes with the last. About AD 170, Theophilus of Antioch quotes from the Fourth Gospel and names John as its author. About AD 180, Irenaeus testifies expressly to the Johannine authorship of the Gospel; as was noted above, his testimony is particularly valuable, for he had in his youth known Polycarp of Smyrna, who in turn had known John the apostle in his youth. About the same time the Muratorian Canon, a listing of the New Testament books accepted as authoritative by the Church of Rome, attributes the Fourth Gospel to John the apostle. A little later Clement of Alexandria records a tradition of the "elders" (that is, the generation before him) on the sequence of the four Gospels and adds that John wrote his Gospel last of all at the urging of his friends.

We have, then, at the close of the second century, evidence from various quarters of the church (Gaul, Rome, Asia Minor, Egypt) in favor of the apostolic authorship of the Gospel. And there is really no historical evidence to the contrary. The Gospel was rejected by members of an obscure sect whom Epiphanius calls the Alogi and by a certain presbyter Gaius of Rome; but their reasons for so doing were doctrinal and not historical. There is no indication that they had any historical evidence that called into question the Johannine authorship of the Gospel.

Some scholars maintain, on the basis of an ambiguous fragment of Papias, that there were two Johns of note in Ephesus in the early days, the apostle John and an Elder (or Presbyter) John, and that Irenaeus mistakenly attributed the Gospel to the apostle, while it was in reality written by the Elder. If this be so, not only was Irenaeus mistaken, but he also succeeded in making the whole ancient church share in his mistake. Yet it is not even certain that the Papias fragment speaks of two Johns at Ephesus; Eusebius so interprets it and assigns Revelation to the Elder. However, even if Eusebius is right in distinguishing two Johns, it should be noted that he does not assign the Gospel to the Elder, and neither does anyone else in the ancient church. In fact, on any interpretation, the Elder remains a very shadowy figure; and the theory that he is the author of the Fourth Gospel leaves us with the unanswered question: How could a relatively unknown person, not an apostle, have added a Gospel (and so different a Gospel) to the existing three so late and yet win universal acceptance for it so easily?

Internal Evidence

The evidence of the Gospel itself is strongly in favor of apostolic authorship. It indicates that the author was a Jew; his style and thought are fundamentally Semitic, and he gives evidence of familiarity with the Hebrew Old Testament (Jn 13:18; 19:37). Scholars of Judaism have regarded this Gospel as an important example for rabbinical ideas current in Israel before the destruction of the temple in AD 70. And even scholars who reject the apostolic authorship insist on the fundamentally Jewish character of the work.

Last Supper, from a fifteenth-century illuminated manuscript at Mount Athos, Greece.

The Gospel likewise indicates that the author was an Israelite. He is familiar with the culture and geography of Israel; he identifies unimportant places with exact detail (e.g., 3:23). His notices concerning the pool of Bethesda (5:2) have been confirmed by excavations (1932). And he shows himself to be familiar with the arrangements of the Jerusalem temple (8:20; 10:23). The literature of Qumran has confirmed the findings of scholars who saw in the Fourth Gospel a product of Israel as over against those who disputed the apostolic authorship on the grounds that its language and thought betray alien influences.

The Gospel further indicates that its author was an eyewitness to the events that he records; many graphic details attest this (e.g., 9:2–7), and in a number of passages this fact of eyewitnessing is directly claimed by or for the author (19:35; cf 1:14; 21:24). The Gospel indirectly declares that this eyewitness is John the son of Zebedee. In the Fourth Gospel, and in it alone, there figures prominently a disciple who is left unnamed but is referred to as "the disciple whom Jesus loved" (13:23; 19:26; 20:2; 21:7, 20–23). In two passages an unnamed disciple likewise figures, and he is probably to be identified with the disciple whom Jesus loved (1:40; 18:15). Since this disciple is present at the Last Supper (13:23), he is one of the Twelve. Since he is on terms of peculiar intimacy with the Lord and appears together with Peter on a number of occasions (13:23; 20:2; 21:20), we may conclude that he is one of the favored three (Peter, James, and John) referred to in the Synoptic Gospels. Since Peter is excluded by the narrative itself and James is excluded by his early death (Ac 12:2), there remains only John the son of Zebedee as "the disciple whom Jesus loved"; thus Jn 21:24 points to John the son of Zebedee as the author of the Gospel (cf 21:20): "This is the disciple who is bearing witness about these things, and who has written these things." This identification is supported by the fact that the author of the Gospel never mentions John the son of Zebedee by name and calls John the Baptist simply "John."

In the face of such evidence it seems idle to raise the question whether a Galilean fisherman, an associate of Jesus in the days when He walked the ways of Israel, could have written so exalted a record and so profound an interpretation of the Christ. The life of Jesus is without parallel in the annals of mankind; the sending of the Spirit is without analogy in the experience of mankind—it is the unprecedented, end times act of God. Who is to say what a man who has beheld that life and has been led by that Spirit into all truth could or could not have written?

Date of Composition

Ancient tradition assigns the works of John to the time of his ministry at Ephesus in Asia Minor at the end of the first century AD. If it can be shown, therefore, that John the apostle never reached Ephesus and never worked there, the ancient testimony concerning the authorship of the works attributed to John is, of course, greatly weakened. Some scholars maintain that John the apostle never did reach Ephesus, but died a martyr's death in Judea, either at the same time as his brother James (c AD 41) or in the 60s at the latest. The following are the chief arguments used to support this contention: (a) The prophecy of Jesus (Mk 10:39) that the sons of Zebedee would drink His cup and share His Baptism is held to imply that both James and John must have died a martyr's death. But it should be noted that even if John did die a martyr's death (a question which need not be discussed here), there is nothing in the prophecy to indicate that he died early, in Judea. (b) A ninth-century chronicler, George Hamartolos, following a fifth-century source, the Chronicle of Philip of Side, quotes Papias (second century) to the effect that John was killed "by Jews." This, it is contended, points to an early martyrdom of John and marks the tradition of his Ephesian ministry as legendary. However there is not a syllable, either in the quotation from

Papias or in George's own words, to indicate that John was martyred early, in Judea. Hamartolos, in fact, states that John lived on into the reign of the emperor Nerva (AD 96–98). (c) Calendars of the ancient church seem to indicate that John was martyred at the same time as his brother James (c AD 41). A Syrian martyrology (a listing of martyrs' festivals) remarks on December 27: "John and James, the apostles [died as martyrs], in Jerusalem." However, scholars have long ago noted that the ancient martyrologies are not trustworthy guides to history: a Carthaginian martyrology, for instance, contradicts the Syrian one by linking John the *Baptist* with James in the commemoration of December 27. Besides, if the Syrian martyrology is taken at face value, it proves too much; for John, according to the evidence given by Paul (Gal 2:9), outlived his brother James and was in Jerusalem at the time of Paul's second post-conversion visit to Jerusalem, which falls later than the death of James, the son of Zebedee.

This will perhaps suffice to indicate the nature and the strength of the arguments used to discredit the tradition of the Ephesian ministry of John. The tradition of John's ministry at Ephesus is found first in Irenaeus (c AD 180), who is linked by a direct line of tradition to John himself: Irenaeus drew on the eye-and-ear witness of Polycarp, who had been a disciple of John in his youth. Irenaeus also knew other "elders," men of the previous generation who had associated with John in Ephesus. This tradition is never questioned or contradicted in the ancient church. Until more valid arguments are brought forward to overthrow it, we may accept it with confidence.

Purpose/Recipients

The central and controlling purpose of the Gospel is stated by the evangelist himself: "Now Jesus did many other signs in the presence of the disciples, which are not written in this book; but these are written so that you may believe that Jesus is the Christ, the Son of God, and that by believing you may have life in His name" (Jn 20:30–31). Yet the book is not a missionary appeal; it addresses people who are already Christians, and it seeks to deepen and strengthen their faith in Jesus as the Christ. It does so by interpretatively recounting the words and deeds of Jesus, His "signs," or significant actions. It is, therefore, like the first three Gospels, teaching in the sense of Ac 2:42. Like the other Gospels, it no doubt had behind it a long history of oral teaching; it is, as ancient tradition also indicates, the final precipitate of John's many years of oral apostolic witness to Christ in the churches of Asia Minor.

The Gospel of the Crucified was a stumbling block to the Jew and folly to the Greek in John's day as it had been in Paul's (1Co 1:23). The fierce hatred of the Jews of Asia had pursued Paul (Ac 20:19; 21:27); we find the same embittered Jewish offense at the cross active against Christians a generation later than John in Smyrna at the time of the martyrdom of Polycarp (*Mart. Pol.* 13:1). And in the letters to the churches at Smyrna and Philadelphia in Revelation (possibly written within a few years of the time of the Gospel of John), we find references to Jews opposed to the Church, "those who say that they are Jews and are not, but are a synagogue of Satan" (Rv 2:9; 3:9; cf Jn 8:44). Conflict with the Jews had not ended with the death of Jesus nor with the death of Paul. Rather, according to the witness of the Fourth Gospel, it persisted in intensified form; the Gospel of John presents the conflict between Jesus and the Jews in even stronger colors than does the Gospel of Matthew.

The Gospel was a stumbling block to the Jew; it was foolishness to the Greek. And the Gospel of John is also directed against a Greek perversion of the Gospel which was in effect a denial of the Gospel. According to the second-century father Irenaeus, the Gospel of John was written to combat the heresy of Cerinthus. This is hardly the whole purpose of the Gospel, but John's emphatic declaration that the eternal Son, the Word, "became *flesh*" (Jn 1:14) does seem to be aimed at one of the tenets peculiar to the sect of Cerinthus. For Cerinthus denied that the "heavenly Christ" had been identified with man, the creature of flesh, in any real and lasting way; he maintained that not the Christ but only the man Jesus (in whom the Christ had dwelt guest-fashion from the time of His Baptism onward up to the eve of His Passion) had suffered and died. This could also be the historical background to the fact that in the Fourth Gospel, and in it alone, Jesus is hailed at the very beginning of His ministry as the dying Christ, as "the Lamb of God" (Jn 1:29), and is at the end of His ministry worshiped by Thomas as the crucified: Thomas says, "My Lord and my God" to the Christ who bears on His body the marks of the crucifixion (Jn 20:27–28). Perhaps John's insistence, in the opening verses of his Gospel, that "all things were made through Him [the Word], and without Him was not any thing made that was made" (Jn 1:3) is also pointed at Cerinthus, who maintained that the world was created not by the highest God who sent the heavenly Christ into the world, but by a Power that had separated itself from God. The fact that the First Letter of John is patently directed against a heresy like that of Cerinthus lends great plausibility to the suggestion that the Gospel, too, has a polemical point that is aimed at Cerinthus.

Literary Features

Genre

John's work is a Gospel—theology presented in biographical form (see pp 175–77). Like the other Gospels, his book is teaching that supports and sustains the disciples' faith in Jesus. See "Purpose/Recipients," p 325.

The differences between the Fourth Gospel and the Synoptic Gospels strike every reader. In the Synoptic Gospels, for example, most of Jesus' public ministry takes place outside Judea; and Matthew, Mark, and Luke mention no visits to the Holy City between His temptations and His triumphal entry. John devotes considerable space to Jesus' activity in Judea and reports four visits to Jerusalem and one to Bethany in Judea. With one exception, the appearances of the resurrected Lord in John's Gospel take place in the vicinity of Jersualem, while Matthew and Mark emphasize His appearance in Galilee.

Different emphases are found in the Fourth Gospel in comparision with the Synoptic Gospels. The Fourth Gospel contains very few of Jesus' words or advice for daily living. His speeches in John are long and profound compared with the simple, direct speeches and parables contained in the other Gospels. The Fourth Gospel relates only a few events that show Jesus' meek and loving nature. In John, the Lord does not reserve His anger for the scribes and Pharisees, as had been the case in the Synoptics, but in several passages He directs His criticism to the Judeans as a whole.

The most striking difference between John and the Synoptic Gospels is each one's language about Jesus. The Synoptics talk in ordinary historical language about what Jesus did. Although John's Gospel has some plain language in it, it is filled with talk about light and darkness, falsehood and truth, above and below, of pictures of Jesus as the Water of Life, the Bread of Life, the Light of the World, of Jesus as the One who has been sent by the Father and is returning to the Father.

Jesus transforming water into wine at the wedding in Cana, part of a fifth-century ivory altar.

Enigmatic Sayings

Whereas Matthew and Luke tend to record Jesus' parables, John records many difficult sayings of Jesus that appear throughout the Gospel and unify its composition (e.g., 2:4, 19; 3:3, 8; 4:10, 32; 5:17; 6:35, 51, 53, 70; 7:6, 34, 37–38; 8:21, 58; 9:39; 13:33; 14:4; 15:17; 18:36–37; 21:18, 22). John often notes the trouble the disciples and the crowds have deciphering Jesus' intent by recording their questions. In some cases the disciples only understood Jesus' words much later (cf 2:22; 21:19). Jesus refers to His sayings as "figures of speech" (Gk *paroimia*, 16:25), an expression that commonly describes proverbs. But Jesus' sayings are more than traditional proverbs. They are often prophetic or have the character of riddles, demanding deep reflection. Jesus' many "I am" statements should be included among these enigmatic sayings.

Characters

John knows the distinctive coloring of the various Jewish parties, but the distinction between Pharisees and Sadducees is no longer of import to him or his readers. John speaks of **Judeans** simply as the people who rejected Jesus as their Messiah, and "Jew" is practically equivalent to "unbelieving Jew" (2:18, 20; 5:10, 16, 18; 6:41, 52; 7:13; 9:22, etc.). Unlike the Galileans, who are somewhat open to Jesus (4:45), the Judeans are the opponents of Jesus—blind and stubborn in their refusal to recognize Him—persecuting Him with an ever-mounting hatred. They deny that He is the Son of God (5:18; 8:40–59); they seek His life (5:18; 8:40, 59; 10:31, 39; 11:8, 50), and in all things show themselves not as true children of Abraham, but as children of the devil (8:39–44). Jesus predicts that this hatred will persist; they will deem it a service rendered to God if they kill Jesus' disciples (16:2). The Spirit whom Jesus will send will enable His disciples to continue the struggle that He had in His lifetime carried on against them (16:2–4, 7–11).

This feature of John's Gospel may be due in part to the fact that he devotes so much space to Jesus' ministry in Jerusalem, where opposition to Jesus was concentrated most strongly. But only in part—it is due chiefly to the fact that the lines have been drawn by Israel's rejection of her Messiah, that judgment has been executed on Jerusalem and a gulf has been fixed between the ancient people of God and the new Israel, the Church. But this does not mean that the Fourth Gospel has an anti-Semitic bias. John is at one with the other evangelists and with Paul (Rm 9:1–5) in his positive appreciation of what the Jew had by the grace of God received and in his hope that the Jew may still receive of that grace. John's harsh indictment of the Jew is therefore to be construed as a call to repentance. It is in the Fourth Gospel that Jesus declares to the Samaritan woman that "salvation is *from the Jews*" (Jn 4:22); the Scripture given to the Jews is for the Jesus of John the supreme authority as it is for the Jesus of Matthew (e.g., 10:35). The flock for which the Good Shepherd dies is a flock gathered out of Israel (10:16); the hour of the Gentiles, the hour for the Greeks who would see Jesus, is yet to come (10:16; 12:20, 32). Israel's own high priest must declare that Jesus is the One who dies for the whole people (11:50, 51). The title of the crucified is "King of the Jews" (19:19). Jesus is "King of Israel" (1:49), and the Gospel still pleads with the Jew to become an "Israelite indeed," an Israelite "in whom there is no deceit," by acknowledging Israel's King as Nathanael acknowledged Him (1:47). Indeed, this motif is so strong that one modern scholar has advanced and defended the theory that the Fourth Gospel is primarily a missionary appeal addressed to the Jew—an overstatement, of course, but an indication of the tendency of the Gospel.

Another less direct form of Judaic opposition to Jesus and His Church is combated by the Fourth Gospel also. There were those in Israel who became disciples of John the Baptist but did not accept his witness to Jesus as the Christ. These continued to exist as a separate group or sect, and apparently their reverent esteem for the Baptist was such that they assigned to him the titles and functions of the Messiah. The incident recorded in Ac 19:1–7 (Paul's encounter with "disciples" who knew only the baptism of John) would seem to indicate that this movement had spread as far as Ephesus, where the Fourth Gospel was written. This would account for the fact that the Fourth Gospel enunciates with special emphasis the fact that the Baptist has his significance and his honor in his subordination to Jesus as the Christ: "He was not the light, but came to bear witness about the Light" (Jn 1:8); in John's account of him, the Baptist will accept no title of honor at all, but calls himself merely the voice in the wilderness—his whole significance lies in his function as the herald of the Christ (1:19–23). He must decrease, as the Messiah must increase; and he finds his perfect joy in the Christ's increasing (3:28–30). He points his disciples to the Lamb of God who takes away the sin of the world (1:29–36). But the evangelist is not minded to belittle the true stature of the Baptist; he sees in him "a man sent from God" (1:6), a valid and mighty witness to the only Son from the Father (1:14–15). John alone records the witness of the people to John ("Everything that John said about this man was true," 10:41), and he alone records the words with which Jesus Himself places His seal upon the Baptist's mission: "You sent to John, and he has borne witness to the truth. . . . He was a burning and shining lamp" (5:33, 35).

Narrative Development or Plot

The Gospel opens with a rich introduction that presents Jesus as the Logos, the Word of God that came into the world. This is followed by the description of the ministry of John the Baptist and the calling of the first disciples (1:1–51).

The word *sign* is used 17 times in chs 2–12, and this fact has led many to call this part of the Gospel "The Book of Signs." The signs are Jesus' miracles, which the author describes as proof that Jesus is the Son of God deserving of the reader's trust and faith. These signs include the miracle of the wedding at Cana, the healing of the centurion's son, the healing of the lame man at the pool of Bethesda, the feeding of the 5,000, the walking on water, the healing of the man born blind, and the raising of Lazarus. These miracles provide the framework for powerful discourses by the Lord. Included is His conversation with Nicodemus about the new life, with the woman of Samaria about true religion, with a large crowd about how He would give His flesh for the world so that all who eat of it will live forever, about Himself as the true Shepherd, and with Martha about how He is the resurrection and the life (2:1–12:50).

Third-century sarcophagus with scene of Christ raising Lazarus.

The raising of Lazarus prompted the Jews to proceed against Jesus, and so the next portion of the Gospel relates the story of His suffering and death and the discourses He delivered during His last days. No miracles are found in this section, except for the miracles of His own resurrection. Here we find His discourse on humility, illustrated by washing His disciples' feet; an explanation of the meaning of His departure and return; a description of the Comforter who will come to the disciples; a discussion about the relationship between the individual believer and the Lord Jesus; and His High Priestly Prayer (13:1–17:26).

This is followed by the events of Holy Week told in much the same order as the three Synoptic Gospels relate this material. John adds a number of important postresurrection appearances of our Savior, notably the one to Thomas (18:1–20:31).

The last chapter is usually called a postscript to the Gospel. It relates Jesus' appearance to the disciples at the Sea of Galilee and concludes with a testimonial from the author to the effect that he had told only a small portion of Jesus' life, but that his record was absolutely trustworthy (21:1–25).

Outline

I. John's Prologue: The Word Became Flesh (1:1–18)

II. Jesus' Ministry (1:19–10:42)
- A. John the Baptist and the First Disciples (1:19–1:51)
  1. The testimony of John the Baptist (1:19–34)
  2. Jesus calls the first disciples (1:35–51)
- B. Early Ministry (chs 2–4)
  1. The wedding at Cana (2:1–12)
  2. Jesus cleanses the temple (2:13–25)
  3. Jesus teaches Nicodemus (3:1–21)
  4. John the Baptist exalts Christ (3:22–36)
  5. Jesus teaches a Samaritan woman and a Galilean official (ch 4)
- C. Rising Opposition to Jesus' Ministry (chs 5–10)
  1. The healing at the pool on the Sabbath (ch 5)
  2. Jesus feeds and teaches the 5,000 (ch 6)
  3. Jesus at the Feast of Booths (7:1–52)
  4. The woman caught in adultery (7:53–8:11)
  5. Jesus testifies about the Father before the Pharisees (8:12–59)
  6. Jesus heals a man born blind (ch 9)
  7. Jesus is the Good Shepherd (10:1–21)
  8. Jesus and the Father are one (10:22–42)

III. A Death and Resurrection; Persistent Unbelief (chs 11–12)
- A. Raising Lazarus (ch 11)
- B. The Triumphal Entry and People's Doubts (ch 12)
  1. Mary anoints Jesus for His death (12:1–11)
  2. Jesus' public teaching before the Passover (12:12–50)

IV. Passover and Holy Week (chs 13–19)
   A. Jesus Bids His Disciples Farewell (chs 13–16)
      1. Jesus washes the disciples' feet (13:1–20)
      2. Jesus predicts Judas's betrayal (13:21–30)
      3. Jesus gives a new commandment (13:31–35)
      4. Jesus foretells Peter's denial (13:36–38)
      5. Jesus is the way and the truth and the life (14:1–14)
      6. Jesus promises the Holy Spirit (14:15–31)
      7. Jesus is the true vine, hated by the world (15:1–16:4a)
      8. The work of the Holy Spirit (16:4b–15)
      9. Sorrow will turn into joy, and Jesus has overcome the world (16:16–33)
   B. Jesus' Prayer for the Disciples (ch 17)
   C. Jesus' Trial and Passion (chs 18–19)
      1. Betrayal and arrest of Jesus (18:1–11)
      2. Jesus faces Annas, Caiaphas, and Pilate (18:12–40)
      3. The crucifixion (19:1–27)
      4. The death and burial of Jesus (19:28–42)
V. Jesus' Resurrection (ch 20)
VI. Epilogue (ch 21)

Resources

The distinct content of John's Gospel has sparked discussion of potential sources used for its composition. Its opening regarding the Word may be related to the Israelite wisdom tradition (cf e.g., Pr 8; Ecclus 24) but does not require that his Word theology existed in a separate source.

In Rudolph Bultmann's 1941 commentary on the Gospel, he championed the view that John is compiled from a signs source, a revelation source, and a Passion Narrative of Jesus' death and resurrection. Although it is true that John uniquely presents Jesus' miracles as a series of signs (chs 2–12) and that he includes long unique discourses, these facts do not require that the signs or revelations existed in independent sources as Bultmann proposed. The signs may be viewed as organizational elements for the writer, who complemented Jesus' acts with personal accounts of His teaching. John may have consulted one or all of the other canonical Gospels for his account of Jesus' Passion, though scholars debate which one(s) he may have used.

Text and Translations

There is general agreement among scholars that Jn 7:53–8:11, the story of the woman taken in adultery, is a later insertion into the text of the Gospel. Many of the ancient manuscripts omit this section, and it is unknown to the commentators of the Greek church down to the eleventh century. Further doubt is thrown upon this section as constituting a part of the Fourth Gospel by the fact that other manuscripts insert the story at Lk 21:38, and still others at Jn 7:36 or Jn 21:24. Besides, the section differs from the Gospel in language and style. The story is probably true, a genuine part of the story of Jesus preserved by the early Christians, but it is not a part of the Gospel that John wrote.

Many scholars are of the opinion that ch 21, too, is not an original part of the Gospel but the work of a second hand. But here the situation is quite different from that of the story of the woman taken in adultery: every ancient manuscript and translation contains the contents of ch 21; it is linguistically and stylistically in harmony with the first 20 chapters. Although ch 2 is a sort of appendix to the Gospel proper, which obviously closes at 20:31, it is an appendix written by the author himself.

Doctrinal Content

Summary Commentary

1:1–18 By taking on human flesh, God the Son comes into the world He created. He graciously brings deliverance from spiritual darkness and authorizes believers to become God's children.

1:19–51 John the Baptist testifies to Jewish leaders that he is not the Christ but was sent to prepare the way for Him. John then testifies that Jesus is the Lamb of God, who takes away the sin of the world—the very Son of God, on whom the Holy Spirit rested at His Baptism. When Jesus calls the first disciples, He reveals Himself to be the Messiah—the Son of God and Son of Man—the way to heaven.

Chs 2–4 Jesus, through whom all things were made (1:3), performs His first miracle ("sign") at a wedding at Cana in Galilee, manifesting His glory by turning water into wine. With holy zeal, Jesus cleanses the temple, which

Judeans had turned into a marketplace, and He predicts His resurrection to those questioning His authority. In Jerusalem, many come to believe in Jesus with a superficial faith based mainly on the miracles they see.

Nicodemus, though "the teacher of Israel," shows that he cannot comprehend the Spirit's miraculous work of new birth through Baptism. Jesus teaches that the Father gives His only Son as a sacrificial gift to deliver the world from condemnation and to give eternal life to those who believe in Him. John the Baptist steps aside when Christ comes because Jesus is the Son of God from heaven and possesses the Holy Spirit without measure. God reveals His wrath against those who do not believe in His Son and deprives them of everlasting life. But He gives everlasting life to all who trust in Jesus.

A ring-shaped carrying cushion made of goat hair. It was used to stabilize and support a heavy load, such as a jar of water carried on a head, a common practice in the Near East.

Jesus then graciously reaches out to a Samaritan woman, leads her to recognize Him as the Messiah, and through her brings other Samaritans to receive His life-giving blessings. An official, whose dying son Jesus heals in Galilee, comes to a genuine faith in Him before the sign, the wonder, is done.

Ch 5 After Jesus heals an invalid, Jewish leaders accuse Him of breaking Sabbath law and begin to persecute Him. The Jews plot to kill Jesus for what they understand to be a blasphemous claim: equality with God. Failure to acknowledge Christ's deity despite Scripture's clear testimony places one in opposition to the Lord. Equal to the Father in deity and honor, God's Son makes people spiritually alive through His Word and raises believers from the grave at the hour of His coming to judge. Those who refuse to believe in God's Son will come under judgment, and their evil deeds will become known. The Father gives binding witness to His Son's true identity, which is revealed in the works He performs and in the Scriptures that everywhere speak of Him.

Ch 6 Jesus' feeding of 5,000, the next sign recorded in John, reveals Jesus as the Christ, the Son of the living God (20:30–31). By walking on the storm-tossed sea, Jesus also shows His disciples that He is the eternal King, ruler of all creation. Unlike the perishable manna God gave to Israel through Moses, Jesus comes down from heaven as the true bread to give life to all who believe in Him. Faced with Jesus' true identity and the necessity of faith in Him, many stop following Him, and even one of the Twelve aligns himself with Satan against Jesus.

7:1–52 Despite growing opposition from Jewish leaders and unbelief within His own family, Jesus enters Jerusalem during the Feast of Booths as the time of His death draws near. Because Jesus does not fit their preconceived notions of the Messiah's identity, residents of Jerusalem reject Him and join in the effort to kill Him for blasphemy. Jesus teaches that when He dies, He will return to His Father and become inaccessible to His enemies. Yet, He remains gracious toward all. On the final day of the Feast of Booths, Jesus promises that believers will receive the Holy Spirit (at Pentecost) after His death. Jewish leaders and the populace hold sharply different opinions regarding Jesus.

7:53–8:11 This is the famous story of the woman taken in adultery, which was likely added to John's Gospel. The scribes and Pharisees fail to trap Jesus by requesting a hasty judgment against a woman caught in the act of adultery. Jesus reveals the hypocrisy of His detractors and calls them to self-examination, even as He calls the sinful woman to consider her error.

8:12–59 Jesus claims to be the light of the world, through whom people may have life, which prompts the Pharisees to question His authority. Jews with a weak faith in Jesus balk when He says that true freedom comes through Him and His teaching. Jesus then traces the people's refusal to believe in Him and His Word to their spiritual "father," the devil himself. The confrontation between Jesus and the Pharisees reaches a climax when the Pharisees attempt to stone Him for claiming to be the preexistent Son of God.

The third-century Good Shepherd fresco in the catacombs of Saint Priscilla, Rome.

Ch 9 Jesus gives physical and spiritual sight—faith—to a man born blind, though the Pharisees accuse Jesus of violating the Sabbath and remain spiritually blind to who Jesus is.

Ch 10 Jesus calls Himself the Good Shepherd to describe His intimate relationship with His followers and the love that moves Him to lay down His life for them. In the colonnade of Solomon during the Jewish Feast of Dedication, Jesus declares His oneness with the Father, which the unbelieving crowd understands to be blasphemous and worthy of death.

Ch 11 Jesus, the Son of God, will raise Lazarus from the dead so that He might be glorified. When Jesus comes to Mary and Martha's house and sees great mourning, He is moved to tears over the situation and because of love for His friends. Yet Jesus assures Martha that all who believe in Him, though they die physically, will live forever. By raising Lazarus, Jesus reveals God's glory and that He is truly the resurrection and the life. After Jesus raises Lazarus, Jewish leaders become hardened in their opposition to Him and plot to kill Him before the Passover.

Ch 12 In humble devotion, yet with extravagant expense, Mary anoints Jesus, while Judas the betrayer and thief covers his greed with seemingly pious intentions. Jesus' popularity grows again as crowds hear about the raising of Lazarus, but the chief priests plot against Jesus and Lazarus. Riding on a donkey, Jesus enters Jerusalem on the Sunday of Passion Week. Leaders of the Jewish nation react with frustration and fear. When some Greeks want to see Jesus, He uses the occasion to proclaim His death and the fruit it will bear. Jesus faces the moment of His glory, confirmed by His Father's voice from heaven: the hour when He would be lifted up on the cross so that He could draw all people to Himself. Some Jews reject Jesus and, under God's judgment, are hardened in unbelief; others believe in Him but refuse to confess Him openly for fear of being removed from the synagogue community. As Jesus concludes His public ministry, He reminds His hearers that He has come to save the world.

Chs 13–16 Jesus teaches His disciples privately on the night He will be betrayed. He washes His disciples' feet, thereby showing His willingness to serve them. Jesus then predicts that one of His disciples will betray Him. He gives Judas a morsel of food, a gesture of friendship, but Judas leaves to carry out his plot. The disciples cannot follow Jesus to the cross, but He asks them to imitate His love for them as they love one another. Peter thinks he is fully ready to follow Jesus, but Jesus says Peter will only deny Him. Peter's boldness was not due to faith but to egotistical bravado. In the end, Peter did offer his life for Jesus, but only because Jesus first offered His life for Peter.

Through Jesus' death and resurrection, He goes to prepare a place for us in heaven, where we will dwell with God forever. Jesus promises that He and His Father will come to dwell in those who hear and believe His Word, and that He will send to them the Holy Spirit as the Helper. Jesus is the true vine, and His disciples are the branches, vitally connected to Him and spontaneously bearing fruit under His purifying care. Jesus predicts that His disciples will face hostility from the unbelieving world.

Jesus then comforts the disciples by promising to send them the Helper (the Holy Spirit), who will guide them into a deeper understanding of His Word. He promises to return after His resurrection and turn the disciples' sorrow into joy. The disciples confidently claim they understand Jesus' parting words, but Jesus utters the sober prediction that they will soon abandon Him.

Ch 17 Knowing that He is going to the cross, Jesus prays for His disciples and asks that they be united by faith in Him. He likewise prays for future believers, including us today.

Ch 18 Jesus powerfully confronts those who come to arrest Him in the garden, even while He voluntarily accepts the suffering that lies before Him. Jewish officials arrest Jesus with the assistance of soldiers and lead Him to the high priest Annas for questioning. Despite Peter's brave promise to lay down his life for Jesus (13:37), Peter denies that he is Jesus' disciple because of his concern for self-protection. After Jesus' arrest, Annas conducts the preliminary interrogation of Jesus. In sharp contrast to Jesus' forthright self-disclosure ("I am," 18:5, 8), Peter denies Jesus a third time ("I am not"), leaving Jesus alone on the way to suffering and death. To avoid religious contamination, the Jewish leaders refuse to enter Pilate's residence, but they unjustly seek to use Pilate's authority to put Jesus to death. Pilate tries to dismiss the case before him by accommodating a Jewish custom calling for the release of a prisoner at Passover—in this instance, an insurrectionist called Barabbas.

Ch 19 Pilate succumbs to political pressure exerted by Jewish leaders and delivers Jesus over to death by crucfixion. As Jesus is crucified on the Place of a Skull near Jerusalem, He entrusts His mother Mary to John's care. Jesus the Christ dies, finishing the work of salvation that His Father sent Him to accomplish. His death fulfills John the Baptist's earlier description of Jesus, the "Lamb of God, who takes away the sin of the world" (1:29). Joseph of Arimathea and Nicodemus, secretly Jesus' disciples for fear of the Jews, honor Jesus by attending to His burial.

First-century dice made of stone or bone. Cf Jn 19:23–24.

Ch 20 The first witnesses of Jesus' resurrection see an empty tomb bearing all the signs of the fulfillment of the Old Testament promises and Jesus' own declaration that He "must rise from the dead" (20:9). The disciples were slow to believe. But after His resurrection, Jesus first appears to Mary Magdalene, who is led to recognize Him and goes to tell the disciples she has seen the Lord. The once-crucified Jesus appears to His disciples, commissioning them for their work and equipping them with the Holy Spirit. Jesus then appears before a skeptical Thomas, who upon seeing Jesus is moved to confess Him as Lord and God.

Ch 21 During Jesus' third appearance after the resurrection, He performs another miracle and serves as host at a meal for the disciples. In Jesus' threefold exchange with Peter—who in pride and weakness failed to confess His Lord on three occasions—Jesus restores His disciple for service to Him and His flock. In the closing exchange between Jesus and Peter, Jesus kindly reminds Peter that God is in control of matters related to his future.

Specific Law Themes

The Gospel of John opens with a theme of pervading darkness, which describes sin and its affects upon humanity. People are by nature slaves to sin and therefore stand under the condemnation of God. Unbelievers demonstrate the darkness that grips them by demanding signs from Jesus rather than heeding His teaching. Fleshly desire controls them and so death is their end. An example of these themes is embodied in Judas, who knows Jesus' teaching and signs intimately, but departs from them. The Pharisees are described as spiritually blind. Jesus must command His disciples to love as He explains the life to which God calls them and the hatred they will experience from the world.

Specific Gospel Themes

The Gospel themes speak in sharp contrast to the gloomy picture of sin and its affects. In the ministry of Jesus, the light of God penetrates the darkness, which cannot overcome the light. John emphasizes the grace and truth of God in Jesus, who is baptized and is declared to be "the Lamb of God, who takes away the sin of the world!" (Jn 1:29). Those born of the Spirit trust in Jesus. He grants them life and resurrection to eternal life. In ch 6, Jesus used words that anticipated the Lord's Supper and its benefits. He compared His work to that of a shepherd. The Gospel closes with forgiveness and the promised Spirit as well as His personal care for all the disciples.

Specific Doctrines

In John's writings, basic notes of the New Testament proclamation are sounded with thunderous fullness and insistence by the apostle whom Jesus surnamed a "Son of Thunder" (Mk 3:17). He proclaims Jesus as Lord; his whole Gospel is a rich and manifold explication of what His Lordship signifies, a full and varied witness to the glory of Him who is God's incarnate Word, very God; the life and light of men; the only Son; the Lamb of God; the Anointed of God; the bread of life from heaven; the eternal Son who can say, "Before Abraham was, I am"; the resurrection and the life; the light of the world; the way, the truth, and the life. The cry which the appearance of the risen Christ wrung from Thomas the doubter is the free, witnessing cry of John: "My Lord and my God!" And the Gospel spells out with unequaled insistence that He alone is Lord, that there is no other name under heaven whereby man may be saved but His alone, that there can be no way to the Father but by Him; he confronts people with the ultimate and inescapable alternative of life or death: "Whoever believes in Him is not condemned, but whoever does not believe is condemned already, because he has not believed in the name of the only Son of God" (Jn 3:18).

John is at one with the whole New Testament also in proclaiming the reality and the power of the Holy Spirit. His Gospel gives us Jesus' promise of the Spirit in an unrivaled fullness and clarity. And his book is itself a monument to the fulfillment of the promise of his Lord, who said: "When the Spirit of truth comes, He will guide you into all the truth. . . . He will glorify Me" (Jn 16:13–14). His Gospel is the witness of one in whom the Spirit has through all his years done His gracious revelatory work; it is the witness of one before whose eyes the Christ loomed in ever greater grace and majesty.

The Word of the Lord as spoken and written by John is also, finally, focused on living in the world's last days. The words of Jesus in John's Gospel mark out with peculiar clarity the fact that the end of all things presses hard upon the present and gives the present its decisive eschatological character: "An hour *is coming, and is now here*, when the dead will hear the voice of the Son of God, and those who hear will live" (5:25). Eternal life, as Jesus proclaims and promises it, is not merely a far-off possibility; it has, in Jesus, moved into the present: "Truly, truly, I say to you, whoever hears My word and believes Him who sent Me has eternal life. He does not come into judgment, but has passed from death to life" (5:24). The resurrection of the dead is no longer a remote event; it is, in Jesus, a present reality: "I am the resurrection and the life" (11:25). And this reality moves surely toward its final consummation; Jesus' promise to the believer is: "I will raise him up on the last day" (6:40).

John's writings constitute a résumé of the New Testament proclamation, but they are anything but a mere résumé. They are a new and fresh revelation of the "unsearchable riches of Christ" (Eph 3:8). This growth of the apostolic word is, to many hearts and minds, the richest growth and the finest flowering of them all.

Key Texts

John 1:1–18 is arguably the deepest theological passage in all of Holy Scripture. Its confessions of God's nature, Christ's incarnation, and the relationship between the Old and New Testaments are unparalleled in simplicity yet profundity of language. Jesus' teaching on Baptism in ch 3 is foundational to the Sacrament and to the doctrine of the Holy Spirit. Luther described 3:16 as "the Gospel in a nutshell," and modern evangelicalism has made it one of the most widely recognized texts of the Bible. Similar themes appear in other portions of the Gospel. The promise of 6:40 echoes that of 3:16. John further describes the work of the Holy Spirit in conversion and the Christian life, while also contributing to the doctrine of the Holy Trinity (16:4b–15; see also 15:26). As noted for Matthew, John's Gospel presents the Sacraments to the Church in chs 3, 6, and 20:22–23, though Jesus speaks more enigmatically about them, as is typical of His discourses in John.

In 3:6 and 8:34–47, Jesus ominously describes the nature of sin and its origins in terms of inheritance and bondage. In contrast, ch 10 warmly presents the Good Shepherd imagery of God's love; Jesus revisits the theme of

Large household water vessel like those used in Roman era Israel.

love in chs 14–15, while noting the hatred of the world. Augustine developed the passages about love for his teaching about the Trinity, which has contributed greatly to Christian theology. Chapter 17 is known as Jesus' High Priestly Prayer, which pleads for the sanctity and unity of the Church. As Jesus goes to the cross, He notes that His kingdom is not like the political kingdoms of this world (18:36). While on the cross, He declares the fulfillment of our salvation (19:30; cf 1:29). The world that hates is also the world He came to save, which the Father draws to Himself through the cross (12:32; cf 6:44).

Application

1:1–18 Those who do not receive Christ by faith remain in darkness. Christ, the true light, has overcome the darkness, and He promises His forgiving grace to you and all people.

1:19–51 As a faithful servant, John the Baptist sets an example of humility and reverence for us. Ironically, the One whose sandal John was unworthy to untie became the Suffering Servant, who bore all our sins. In Baptism, Jesus Christ has taken away our sin, and the Spirit daily assures us of His merciful goodness toward us. Jesus overcomes unbelief through the Gospel testimony and graciously opens the way to heaven through His Word.

Ch 2 Take your concerns to Jesus in prayer and do not disrespect God's Word and sacred things. Christ's suffering, death, and resurrection reveal God's heart, which is zealous for those He loves. The all-knowing Christ calls us to abandon all outward pretense, to repent truly, and to trust Him fully. The Lord Jesus offers Himself in mercy and forgiveness to those who trust in Him.

Ch 3 Human reason, darkened by sin, cannot accept that God can grant spiritual rebirth through ordinary water used with His Word. But such a great promise has come from none other than the Son of Man, lifted up on the cross for our salvation! When we continue in an immoral lifestyle, we naturally resist divine disclosure of our sin and thus our need for a Savior. Do not flee the light, but repent. God has revealed His strong love in His Son, Jesus Christ, to forgive your sins and give you life.

Ch 4 Christians sometimes allow social and cultural barriers to hinder their witness to Christ and His love for all people. Just as Christ forgave the woman her past and present sins, He now freely offers His forgiving love to us and calls us to spread this Good News. The Lord Jesus hastens to call all people to faith; He would forgive them and bear their burdens and needs.

Ch 5 Legalistic rigidity can also keep us from showing mercy to those in need. The Lord calls us to repentance, sincere faith, and compassionate service. Jesus cares deeply for us, helping us in our physical and spiritual needs. He is indeed God and has given us the right to become God's children (1:12); nothing will ever take us from His hand (10:28). Christ has the authority to give you life now and on the day of your resurrection to everlasting life.

Ch 6 Like those who had "eaten their fill," we also are tempted to seek the Lord only for the earthly things He can give us. Today, when life's problems overwhelm us, fear may cause us to lose faith in God's protection and care. But Jesus is true God and true man in one person; Jesus has saved us from sin and evil, assuring us of His divine protection in every situation. Those united by faith to Christ will be raised up on the Last Day to enjoy eternal communion with the Father. Jesus' words bring life; they are the means the Father uses to draw people to Himself.

7:1–52 People today still fail to see that Jesus is not just another lawgiver but a merciful Savior. The fact that Jesus is true God and true man still remains a stumbling block for those who judge Him by earthly standards. Yet, the "window of opportunity" for the Gospel will soon close, both for the individual and for the world. God now graciously extends the time for the Gospel's proclamation that many others may hear and be saved (2Pt 3:9). Jesus' teaching exceeds all human expectations, imparting grace to those who hear.

7:53–8:11 The Lord's greatest desire is to deliver us from sin through repentance and faith, rather than condemn us for our sins. Jesus Christ came into the world to save sinners, even the worst of us, by His sacrifice on the cross.

8:12–59 Humans are self-centered from birth—in bondage to sin and spiritual darkness—unable to please God (Rm 8:8). Through Jesus' sacrificial death and resurrection, He provides liberation from sin, death, and the devil to all who believe and are baptized into His name. God's love revealed in the Gospel explains why His children by faith love their Savior and His Word. Pray for those confused or offended by the truth about Jesus, for "God shows His love for us in that while we were still sinners, Christ died for us" (Rm 5:8).

Ch 9 We are all born spiritually blind, unable to see our sin and unwilling to do things God's way. But through Baptism and the Word, God has delivered us from the domain of darkness through His beloved Son and has enlightened our hearts to know and follow Him.

Ch 10 Sheep who ignore the Good Shepherd's voice (His Word) have only themselves to blame and will fall prey to Satan. Unlike human love motivated by self-interest, Christ's love for His own moved Him to voluntarily endure even death on a cross for our sake (Php 2:8). Believers can rest secure that they belong to Jesus Christ and will never perish; all of Jesus' works affirm this truth.

Ch 11 Christians will have difficulty at times accepting God's promise to strengthen faith through adversity. Death is the consequence of sin (Gn 2:17; Rm 5:12; 6:23) and eventually takes everyone. No human being can overcome it. Apart from faith in Christ, the fear of death brings hopelessness and despair. Believers, however, can eagerly look forward to the day when Jesus will call them from their graves to live with Him forever (cf Jn 5:28–29). Rejoice that nothing stopped Jesus from graciously giving His life for all people at God's appointed time and gathering His children to Himself.

Ch 12 Sinners may appear to have pure motives, but inwardly they have greedy hearts. Those who hate Christ also hate His friends. Christ came in a humble and gentle manner, eager to listen to our prayers for salvation. Too often we are tempted to think that we are really "living" when we are indulging in life's sinful pleasures. But now is the day of salvation (2Co 6:2); people ignore it at their great peril. Thanks be to God, Christ remains committed to His mission to save the world in spite of its unbelief. Yet, take heart. God has revealed His saving presence (His glory) in the person of His Son, that we may glorify Him before all people. Believers see in Jesus a loving Savior who has our salvation ever on His heart.

Ch 13 Often we think that greatness means having others serve us. But Christ shows His true greatness and His love toward us in that He came to wash away our sins, even though it cost Him His life. Christians bring dishonor to Christ and His love when they deal with one another in a loveless manner. Christ redeemed us through His self-sacrificial love that we may in turn imitate His love (Eph 5:1–2).

Ch 14 The true God cannot be known apart from Jesus Christ. Because of Christ's work, we can know the Father and enter His eternal presence. Those who neglect Christ's Word isolate themselves from God. Jesus Christ reveals God's grace in His Word, dispelling our fear and unbelief.

15:1–16:4a Christians must love one another as friends, not regard one another as enemies. By grace, God has dwelt among us in His Son (1:14) and has joined us together in a fellowship of self-giving love. Those who think it is easy to be a Christian fail to understand the real consequences of following Jesus Christ. In the face of persecution and the world's hatred, Christ promises to strengthen and keep us from falling away.

16:4b–33 Mistakenly, we sometimes think that Jesus' physical absence places us at a disadvantage. In fact, Jesus is present with us through the witness of the Spirit, who works among us through God's Word and Sacraments. Human sorrow can become an expression of self-pity, hindering genuine prayer for God's help and deliverance. Yet, God knows how to turn our sorrow into joy, and He promises to hear our prayers for Jesus' sake. When we face temptation and trouble in this world, we can take heart that Christ has overcome the world for our sake.

Ch 17 Whenever Christians ignore God's Word, they foster divisions within the Church and diminish their witness. But God's Word is the truth that will unite His Church, glorify Him, and enable His people to fulfill their calling in a troubled world.

Ch 18 Jesus suffered and died not as a martyr for a noble cause but as the Savior whose sacrifice atoned for our sin. The arrest of God's Son reveals the depths to which sinful humans will go to remove Him from their lives. As in the case of Jesus' accusers, sinful human beings are prone to dealing unfairly with others. Jesus calls us to honest dealings. Christ's love is greater than our sin, and with His forgiveness He will restore a broken heart. God willed that the guilt of sin be laid on His innocent Son so we might receive God's forgiveness.

Ch 19 All human beings, by virtue of their participation in Adam's sin (Rm 5:12), bear responsibility for Christ's death. Death is not merely a natural process but is God's just punishment for sin (Rm 6:23). However, Jesus died not because He sinned but because He came to bear sin's punishment for us. That the Son of God should become a corpse and be entombed appears offensive and even scandalous to human reason. But Jesus' burial proclaims the depth of Christ's utter humiliation for the sake of our salvation. Like Mary and John, we also become members of Jesus' family by faith. From the cross, Jesus reigned with love for the world; now He reigns in the hearts of those who love Him.

Ch 20 Christ overcame the grave and death, confirming His own words, "I am the resurrection and the life" (11:25). When death confronts us, sorrow and a sense of loss may overcome us. But because Christ is risen, Christians can confidently assure one another that God will wipe away our tears (Rv 21:4). Pray that the Lord would grant you boldness. God raised Jesus, the great Shepherd of the sheep, and will equip us with every good thing to

Madaba mosaic showing the Jordan emptying into the north end of the Dead Sea. Although the sea was useless to fisherman, it was valuable for shipping goods.

do His will (Heb 13:20–21). Those who believe receive God's divine favor, for whoever believes has everlasting life (Jn 3:36).

Ch 21 Jesus shows once again His servant heart, teaching us to follow in His way. We bless and serve one another because our gracious Savior continues to bless and serve us, especially in His Holy Supper. Our own past sins and failures make us feel unworthy to serve God. But Jesus continues to comfort shepherds and the souls they serve with the forgiveness of sins and with compassion.

Canonicity

Like the Gospel of Matthew, the number of early manuscript copies of the Gospel of John indicates that it was used more often than Mark and Luke. In fact, the earliest dated New Testament papyrus manuscript (P^{52}) contains a fragment of Jn 18. The Gospel was unquestioningly received as canonical (*homologoumenon*). For more about the story of the woman taken in adultery (7:53–8:11), see p 333.

Lutheran Theologians on John

Luther

"From the very beginning the evangelist teaches and documents most convincingly the sublime article of our holy Christian faith according to which we believe and confess the one true, almighty, and eternal God. But he states expressly that three distinct Persons dwell in that same single divine essence, namely, God the Father, God the Son, and God the Holy Spirit. The Father begets the Son from eternity, the Holy Spirit proceeds from the Father and the Son, etc. Therefore there are three distinct Persons, equal in glory and majesty; yet there is only one divine essence. . . . The first man to attack the doctrine of the divinity of Christ was the heretic Cerinthus, a contemporary of the apostles. He presumed to fathom and comprehend this article with his reason. Therefore he declared that the Word was not God. And in order to support this view he cited the verse from Deuteronomy (6:4): 'The Lord our God is one God'; and also (Deut. 5:7): 'You shall have no other gods before Me.' With this sham he worked great harm. He gained a powerful following. Many Jews attached themselves to him, even some of those who had believed in Christ. It must be viewed as a manifestation of divine grace that Cerinthus assailed this article during the lifetime of the apostles; for this is what prompted John, the foremost of the apostles still living at the time, to write his Gospel. In it he proves this article conclusively: that Christ, our Lord and Savior, is true, natural, and eternal God with the Father and the Holy Spirit. John had a very good reason for basing his proof on Moses, since it was he of whom Cerinthus and his followers had boasted. Wresting Moses from their hands, mouth, and heart, John now quotes Moses in an attack against their blasphemous heresies and refutes them completely. This was a veritable masterstroke." (AE 22:5, 7)

"Therefore the evangelist John is a master above all the other evangelists, for he treats of this doctrine of Christ's divinity and His humanity persistently and diligently. He joins these two natures together. When Christ becomes man, He speaks to us, performs miracles, and dies according to His humanity. And then His divinity is also established with plain words." (AE 23:77)

For more of Luther's insights on this book, see *Sermons on the Gospel of St. John* (AE 22–24, 69).

Gerhard

"The writers of the Church say that John had two reasons in particular for putting together his Gospel account: (1) To refute the blasphemies of Ebion and Cerinthus, who were attacking the divinity of Christ. For this reason, he lifts himself up as an eagle and begins with a declaration and description of the divinity of Christ. Irenaeus, bk. 3, c. 11, p. 184: 'John, the disciple of the Lord, wanted by the declaration of his Gospel to remove the error that Cerinthus and, much earlier, those who were called "Nicolaitans," had planted among people, etc. In order to confound and persuade them that there is one God, who made all things through His Word, etc., and to establish the rule of truth in the Church, [John] began his Gospel in that way.' Jerome, introduction to his commentary on Matthew:

> When John was in Asia—where even then the seeds of heretics were sprouting, of Cerinthus, Ebion, and others who deny that Christ came in the flesh, whom he even calls "antichrists" in his Epistle and against whom the apostle Paul frequently lashes out—he was compelled by almost all the bishops of Asia at that time and by the representatives of many churches to write something quite lofty about the divinity of the Savior and to break forth to the very Word of God, so to speak, with not so much bold as blessed rashness. As a result, ecclesiastical history narrates that when the brethren compelled him to write in this way, he responded that he would do this if they would declare a fast and if all in common would pray to God. When this had been done, he was filled with revelation and uttered that introduction that came from heaven: "In the beginning was the Word."

This agrees with the brief statement he adds to his Gospel account (John 20:31).

"(2) After reading the volumes of the other three evangelists, he indeed approved what they had written. He affirmed, however, that they had mentioned the activities of only the one year after the imprisonment of John, the year when Christ also suffered. Eusebius, *Hist.*, bks. 6, 13, from Clement of Alexandria: 'Because John, the last, knew that in the rest of the evangelists the bodily activities of Christ were declared, he was invited by his friends and led by the Spirit to provide his spiritual Gospel.' Nazianzen sings of him in this way:

In the sacred book of John, you will find few miracles
But many discourses of Christ the King.

"The Gospel of John contains twenty-one chapters, in which he describes the person of Christ, consisting of divine and human nature, and the activities according to the four journeys to Jerusalem that He made.

"The *Valentinians* used to accept no Gospel except John's, according to Irenaeus (bk. 3, c. 11). Bellarmine (*De verbo Dei*, bk. 1, c. 6, heresy 14), Feuardentius (notes to bk. 3, c. 2 of Irenaeus), and Sandaeus (*Thema secular. de deserenda synagog. protest.*, thesis 22) try to draw our blessed Luther into the company of this latter error because he says in his preface to the New Testament: 'We must get rid of that false idea that there are only four Gospels.' Also: 'The Gospel of John is the one, beautiful, true, and principal Gospel. It is to be preferred far and wide to the other three.'

"We respond. (1) In that preface Luther with clear words did not establish only one historical account of the teaching and deeds of Christ, but he wanted to indicate this alone: that all four of the historical accounts of the evangelists are one and the same Gospel with regard to their theme and purpose. You see, as Chrysostom writes (on Galatians 1): 'Even if a thousand men were to write Gospels, yet if they write the same thing, the many are one.' These two ideas are completely different: that there is one evangelist and that there is only one Gospel.

"(2) He does not prefer the Gospel of John as if the accounts of the other evangelists were not divinely inspired. Rather, as he makes a comparison of the articles treated therein, he gives the trophy to John's Gospel because of his brilliant argument of the eternal deity of Christ and the mystery of the incarnation. Therefore, with regard to canonical authority, the writings of all four evangelists are equal, but with regard to the main points of Christian doctrine treated therein, one stands ahead of another. In this way the Epistle to the Romans surpasses the Epistle to Philemon; the Psalter surpasses the Book of Ruth.

"(3) The fathers cited in § 246 attribute a certain prominence to John and his Gospel, yet up to this time no one, I say, has charged them with this accusation.

"Although the orthodox have had no doubt about the entire Gospel account that John wrote, some people nevertheless have held the pericope about the adulteress in John 8 to be of doubtful credibility. Eusebius, *Hist.*, bk. 3, c. 39: '(Papias) adds some account about the adulterous woman whom the Jews accused before the Lord. But we find that parable written in the Gospel that is called "according to the Hebrews." ' Chrysostom (on John, homily 51) omits it. Theophylact does the same. It does not appear in the Syriac paraphrase; Nonnus, likewise, does not paraphrase it. Jerome cites it but admits (*Dial. 2 adv. Pelag.*): 'This account is not contained in all the codices.' However, the oldest and most serious writers among the ancients, Greek as well as Latin, acknowledge it as a genuine part of canonical Scripture. Among these are Ammonius (*Monotessar.*), Athanasius (*Synopsis*), Ambrose (bk. 7, Epistle 58), and Augustine (on John, treatise 33). This last, in *De adulter. conjug. ad Pollent.*, bk. 2, thinks: 'This account belongs to John, but cruel husbands saw to it that it was taken out so that adulterous wives might be killed.' Robertus Stephanus finds this account in two Greek copies—quite old ones. Bellarmine writes (*De verbo Dei*, bk. 1, c. 16, § *Initium*, etc.): 'Chrysostom, homily 60 on John, acknowledges this account.' But no such thing appears there in Chrysostom. (Cf. our *Disput. 1 ex dicto 1 Johan. 5.*)

"Chapter 21 of John. Some people think that John did not write it, but that someone else added it to the Gospel account because John added the general conclusion of his account at the end of the preceding chapter. But we have shown in our *Harm.*, 'On the Resurrection,' that it is contrary to reason for that final chapter to be torn away from the rest of the corpus of the account, since v. 24 of that chapter is clearly added: 'This is that disciple who is bearing witness to these things and who has written these things.' In the same place we showed that the conclusion in c. 20 is not a general one that applies to the entire Gospel account but a specific one that applies primarily and properly to the account of [Jesus'] appearance to the disciples, which happened after His resurrection." (ThC E1 §§ 247–49)

Questions People Ask about John

Does John Deny the Temptation of Jesus?

Mark 1:12–13 states: "The Spirit immediately drove Him out into the wilderness. And He was in the wilderness forty days, being tempted by Satan. And He was with the wild animals, and the angels were ministering to Him."

John 2:1–2 says: "On the third day there was a wedding at Cana in Galilee, and the mother of Jesus was there. Jesus also was invited to the wedding with His disciples."

These two texts are cited by critics who claim that the Scriptures contradict themselves. The passage from Mark shows, so they say, that Jesus was in the wilderness 40 days after His Baptism. And the text from John informs us, so they continue, that He returned to Galilee immediately after His Baptism. If these assumptions were right, we would be confronted here with an instance of a contradiction. But is the case stated correctly by critics? Does John say that Jesus returned to Galilee immediately after His Baptism? The careful reader will search in vain for a statement of that kind. John mentions the third day. The third day after what? Not after the Baptism of Jesus, but after His return to Galilee (cf Jn 1:43). To say that the third day after the Baptism of Jesus is meant is altogether arbitrary and does not rest on the narrative of John. It is true that the fourth evangelist does not make mention of the temptation of Jesus. But this is altogether in keeping with the purpose of his Gospel, which is of a supplementary character, narrating such events and discourses of Jesus as had been passed over in silence by the other evangelists. The Baptism and the temptation of Jesus apparently had taken place before the events referred to in 1:29–34. There is, then, no trace of a discrepancy here, if one is fair-minded and does not make the Scriptures say something that they do not say.

Jesus Both Equal and Subordinate to God

John 14:28 asserts: "The Father is greater than I."

Philippians 2:6 reports: "Who, though he was in the form of God, did not count equality with God a thing to be grasped."

The Bible says that Christ is equal to the Father and that He is subordinate to the Father. "A contradiction!" say some of its critics. Jesus has two natures, we are informed, the divine and the human (cf Jn 1:14; 1Tm 2:5). According to the former He is equal to the Father; according to the latter He is subordinate to Him.

Thus every vestige of a discrepancy disappears as soon as we let the full light of the Scriptures fall on these texts.

Panel of an ivory casket, one of the earliest known depictions of the crucifixion in story form; fifth century, Rome.

The Superscription on the Cross

A set of passages which critics often point to are the four versions given of the superscription on the cross of Jesus. It is maintained that they do not agree. We find the respective passages in Mt 27:37 ("This is Jesus, the King of the Jews"), Mk 15:26 ("The King of the Jews"), Lk 23:38 ("This is the King of the Jews"), and Jn 19:19 ("Jesus of Nazareth, the King of the Jews"). One glance suffices to show that among the four versions there is no difference in meaning. John's account is simply more complete than those of the others. Matthew ranks next to John in this respect. The opponents say, however, that verbal inspiration implies absolute accuracy: if the Bible had been given by verbal inspiration, then John could not have written that the superscription on the cross was, "Jesus of Nazareth, the King of the Jews," while Mark simply says the superscription was "The King of the Jews." This criticism arbitrarily lays down the principle that when one quotes a statement, one must, in order to be faithful to the original, give every word of it. Nothing is more common, however, than to abridge a speech or a remark that one is quoting. Besides, we must remember that the superscription was written in three languages, and that it may have been more complete in two of the languages than in the third. The evangelists probably did not all follow the same version in their account. Mark, moreover, does not assert that he is giving the superscription in full; he merely says, "The inscription of His accusation was written above: 'The King of the Jews.'" He reports the charge as it was proclaimed on the superscription; that is all.

Although the principle that abridgement of a quotation is acceptable practice would be a sufficient reply to critics, it may prove interesting to consider what could have developed when the superscription was written in three languages. John 19:19–20 records: "Pilate also wrote an inscription and put it on the cross. It read, 'Jesus of Nazareth, the King of the Jews.' Many of the Jews read this inscription, for the place where Jesus was crucified was near the city, and it was written in Aramaic, in Latin, and in Greek." That the Greek term *hebraisti* ("Hebrew") indicates Aramaic, the daily language of the Jews of that time, is clear from other passages of John (5:2; 19:13, 17; 20:16) where the respective words are in the Aramaic form, transliterated into Greek.

Note that John writes: "Pilate also wrote an inscription." Pilate (or an official under his authority) would be well versed in Latin, his native language, and in Greek, the language he would have had to use in dealing with non-Italians in Israel. He would likely not have been able to write Aramaic. We would expect, therefore, that the inscription was composed first in Latin in a brief form: "Rex Iudaeorum Hic." The last word could be rendered either "This (is)" or "Here," depending on whether one pronounced it with a short or long "i" respectively. The Latin would mean either "This is the King of the Jews" or "Here is the King of the Jews." Then as Pilate (or his official secretary) wrote in Greek, he could have added the name of Jesus and His city, for the Greek version would be legible to and understood by all people who passed by regardless of race or nationality. The Greek could have been: "Jesus of Nazareth, the King of the Jews." The Aramaic version may have followed the Greek with the omission of "Nazareth" and would have been: "Jesus the King of the Jews" or "This is Jesus the King of the Jews."

It is reasonable for Matthew to cite the Aramaic title since he wrote his Gospel originally in Aramaic according to Papias, a church leader within a generation after John's death. Hence Matthew has "This is Jesus, the King of the Jews." Mark, who wrote his Gospel in Rome under the tutelage of Peter, would be expected to follow the Latin version, the official and daily language in Rome. Since the last word (*hic*) allowed two interpretations, he could have omitted it and cited it as

"The King of the Jews." Likewise Luke followed the Latin title, interpreting the last word (*hic*) as "this": "This is the King of the Jews." We might expect Luke to have used the Latin version, for he had in mind "most excellent Theophilus" (Lk 1:3; cf Ac 1:1) and "most excellent" is a title that Luke reserves for Roman officials of high standing in the Roman government, such as Felix (Ac 23:26; 24:2) and Festus (26:25). Furthermore there are good reasons to conclude that Luke put the finishing touches on, if not composed much of, Luke/Acts in Rome while Paul was experiencing his two-year house arrest in the capital of the Roman empire (Ac 28:30–31). John, however, wrote later, probably in the last decade of the first century, at or near Ephesus, a center of Greek civilization. He naturally would quote the Greek title: "Jesus of Nazareth, the King of the Jews." We conclude by repeating that the previous three paragraphs represent speculation based on the various languages and writers, not fact, and that the common practice of abridging a quotation is a sufficient reply to critics.

The Touching of the Risen Lord

John 20:17 reports: "Jesus said to [Mary], 'Do not cling to Me' ['Touch Me not' in KJV], for I have not yet ascended to the Father.' "

John 20:27 records: "Then He said to Thomas, 'Put your finger here, and see My hands; and put out your hand, and place it in My side.' "

Why is Mary forbidden to "touch" (KJV) Jesus, but a week later Jesus invites Thomas to touch His wounds? Numerous—even silly—solutions have been offered concerning this supposed contradiction: (1) Mary cannot touch Jesus because His wounds have not yet healed. (2) Mary would be ceremonially defiled by touching a "dead" body. (3) Mary is told not to touch Jesus because He left His grave clothes behind and is naked. (4) The Greek text is wrong; it should read "fear not." (5) Mary is not to make physical contact because Jesus has not yet ascended to His Father—which apparently He did temporarily during the week, before His meeting with Thomas.

These vain attempts at harmonizing the two passages are unnecessary, and quite misleading, when the grammar of the Greek is considered. The key lies in the tenses of the verbs. The present imperative, connoting continuous action, cautions Mary not to continue to touch, or to stop clinging to Jesus—for there was work to be done. The aorist imperative to Thomas, denoting "snapshot" action, instructs him to make physical contact with the risen Christ—a new action that Thomas as yet had not dared to do. Thus later translations, such as ESV, are more correct than the former King James Version and solve the supposed discrepancy.

When Was the Holy Spirit Given to the Apostles?

John 20:22 reads: "And when He had said this, He breathed on them and said to them, 'Receive the Holy Spirit.'"

Acts 2:1, 4 asserts: "When the day of Pentecost arrived, they were all together in one place. . . . And they were all filled with the Holy Spirit and began to speak in other tongues as the Spirit gave them utterance."

Does the pouring out of the Holy Spirit on the apostles on Pentecost mean that this gracious gift was never given to them before? Every Christian has the Holy Spirit and yet asks God each day to be made the dwelling place of the Spirit of God. These apostles had the Holy Spirit before the death and resurrection of their Lord, as is very evident from their possessing the gift to expel demons and to heal diseases. Jesus Himself says that He was driving out demons through the Spirit of God (Mt 12:28). His apostles must have done it through the same agency. Jesus renewed this gift after His resurrection when He breathed on the apostles and assured them again that they, as true disciples, having the Holy Spirit, had authority to forgive and to retain sins. On the day of Pentecost they were filled with the Holy Spirit, being granted a special measure of His gifts and graces. In all of these passages there is nothing contradictory. In Eph 5:18, Paul exhorts his readers: "Be filled with the Spirit," and yet he had assured the same readers that they have the Holy Spirit, that they have been sealed with that Holy Spirit of promise (1:13). The difficulty supposed to be inherent in the above texts is removed if we remember that God sends His Holy Spirit again and again, now and then in a greater measure than at other times.

Resurrected Christ with Disciples.

Further Study

Lay/Bible Class Resources

Baumler, Gary P. *John*. PBC. St. Louis: Concordia, 2005. ◈ Lutheran author. Excellent for Bible classes. Based on the NIV translation.

Kruse, Colin G. *John*. TNTC. Downers Grove, IL: InterVarsity Press, 2008. ◈ Compact commentary interacting with the Greek text in a popular format. An evangelical treatment of the text by an Australian scholar.

Life by His Word. St. Louis: Concordia, 2009. ◈ More than 1,500 reproducible one-page Bible studies covering each chapter of the canonical Scriptures. Page references to *The Lutheran Study Bible*. CD-Rom and downloadable.

Reinisch, Richard. *John: The Word Became Flesh*. GWFT. St. Louis: Concordia, 1996. ◈ Lutheran author. Thirteen-session Bible study, including leader's notes and discussion questions.

Rudnick, Milton, Roger Sonnenberg, Richard Kapfer, Erwin Kolb, Gary Dunker, and Lane Burgland. *John, Parts 1 and 2*. Leaders Guide and Enrichment Magazine/Study Guide. LL. St. Louis: Concordia, 2001–2002. ◈ Two in-depth, nine-session Bible studies with individual, small group, and lecture portions.

Westcott, B. F. *The Gospel according to St. John*. Grand Rapids: Eerdmans, 1950 reprint. ◈ An old standard; a helpful resource by a scholar of New Testament Greek.

Church Worker Resources

Carson, D. A. *The Farewell Discourse and Final Prayer of Jesus: An Exposition of John 14–17*. Grand Rapids: Baker, 1980. ◈ A topical, devotional exposition with emphasis on the theology of the cross.

Culpepper, R. Alan. *The Gospel and Letters of John*. Interpreting Biblical Texts Series. Nashville: Abingdon Press, 1998. ◈ Although his introduction is higher critical, his treatment of the Gospel as an ancient biography in dramatic form is a fine example of a narrative critical approach to John. Written on a popular level.

Academic Resources

Ashton, John. *Understanding the Fourth Gospel*. 2nd ed. New York: Oxford University Press, 2009. ◈ An introduction by a critical scholar.

Barrett, C. K. *The Gospel according to St. John: An Introduction with Commentary and Notes on the Greek Text*. 2nd ed. Philadelphia: Westminster, 1978. ◈ Much information on higher critical views on authorship and theology of John; holds to a version of the so-called "Johannine School" hypothesis. Valuable information shed on the text by Judaica. Use with discernment.

Bauckham, Richard. *The Testimony of the Beloved Disciple: Narrative, History, and Theology in the Gospel of John*. Grand Rapids: Baker Academic, 2007. ◈ A collection of scholarly essays by a British evangelical.

Beasley-Murray, George. *John*. 2nd ed. WBC. Nashville: Thomas Nelson, 1999. ◈ Written for pastors by a British evangelical. Includes the author's interests on some academic debates about the Gospel.

Brown, Raymond E. *An Introduction to the Gospel of John*. New Haven: Yale University Press, 2003. ◈ An extremely thorough and current introduction. Higher critical in orientation.

———. *The Gospel according to John*. Vols. 29, 29A, and 30 of AB. New Haven: Yale University Press, 1995, 1970. ◈ Noted Roman Catholic scholar who holds to his own version of the "Johannine School" hypothesis. Helpful if used discerningly.

Bruce, F. F. *The Gospel of John*. Grand Rapids: Eerdmans, 1983. ◈ A helpful resource by a famous scholar. Fails to note that John uses Roman time references. This affects his interpretation of several passages, including the Passion Narratives.

Carson, D. A. *The Gospel according To John*. Pillar New Testament Commentary. Grand Rapids: Eerdmans, 1990. ◈ An evangelical commentary, which includes some reflections on secondary literature.

Elowsky, Joel C., ed. *John*. 2 vols. ACCS. Downers Grove, IL: InterVarsity Press, 2007. ❦ Includes insights from the homilies of John Chrysostom, many other ancient fathers, and liturgical texts.

Gruenler, Royce G. *The Trinity in the Gospel of John: A Thematic Commentary on the Fourth Gospel*. Eugene, OR: Wipf & Stock, 2004. ❦ A thematic, chapter-by-chapter commentary.

Hendriksen, William. *New Testament Commentary: Exposition of the Gospel according to John*. Grand Rapids: Baker, 1953. ❦ A helpful resource in simple English.

Keener, Craig S. *The Gospel of John: A Commentary*. 2 vols. Grand Rapids: Baker Academic, 2010 reprint. ❦ A thorough treatment from a socio-historical and literary perspective.

Koester, Craig R. *Symbolism in the Fourth Gospel: Meaning, Mystery, Community*. Minneapolis: Augsburg Fortress, 2003. ❦ A significant thematic study.

Köstenberger, Andreas J. *Encountering John: The Gospel in Historical, Literary, and Theological Perspective*. Encountering Biblical Studies. Grand Rapids: Baker Academic, 2002. ❦ An introduction for academic readers.

———. *John*. Baker Exegetical Commentary on the New Testament. Grand Rapids: Baker Academic, 2004. ❦ Includes the author's translation of the Greek text and verse by verse comments, also interacting with ancient texts and other interpreters.

Lange, John Peter. *John*. LCHS. New York: Charles Scribner's Sons, 1868. ❦ A helpful older example of German biblical scholarship, based on the Greek text, which provides references to significant commentaries from the Reformation era forward.

Lenski, R. C. H. *The Interpretation of St. John's Gospel*. Minneapolis: Augsburg Fortress, 1961. ❦ A standard resource by a noteworthy Lutheran interpreter, concerned with being faithful to the text and with its implications for today.

Morris, Leon. *The Gospel according to John*. NICNT. Rev. ed. Grand Rapids: Eerdmans, 1995. ❦ Perhaps the best commentary on John; demonstrates a wide and careful knowledge of the total context. Written in a simple style with many valuable excurses.

———. *Studies in the Fourth Gospel*. Grand Rapids: Eerdmans, 1969. ❦ A careful, scholarly study of the authorship, history, and theology of John and its relationship to the Synoptics, in the light of New Testament studies.

Plummer, Alfred. *The Gospel according to St. John*. Thornapple Commentary Series. Grand Rapids: Baker, 1981 reprint. ❦ A helpful resource first published in 1891. Includes brief, to-the-point comments.

Ridderbos, Herman. *The Gospel of John: A Theological Commentary*. Grand Rapids: Eerdmans, 1997. ❦ An evangelical commentary written by a Dutch scholar and translated into English.

Schnackenburg, Rudolf. *The Gospel according to St. John*. New York: Crossroad, Vol. 1, 1980; Vol. 2, 1981; Vol. 3, 1982. ❦ Schnackenburg holds to a unique view of the "Johannine School" hypothesis. Volume 1 is a helpful resource when used discerningly. Volume 2 is increasingly critical. Volume 3 suffers heavily from the author's use of form and redaction criticism.

The Madaba Map is the oldest floor mosaic map including the Holy City of Jerusalem. On the left (north) appears the Damascus gate and plaza. Running down the center from left to right is the western cardo street, flanked by colonnades. At its center appears the Church of the Holy Sepulchre (upside down, red roof, three openings on its facade). The street ends on the right (south) at the Nea Church (also with red roof and two openings). On the top (east) runs the eastern cardo street with a short connecting street to the Lion's Gate. At the bottom right (west side) appears the Jaffa Gate, with its street running up and angling right, toward the Nea Church. The temple Mount stood in the empty, upper right corner of the image (southeast).

THE ACTS OF THE APOSTLES

You will be My witnesses

"The word of God increased," Three times in the Book of Acts Luke uses this sentence to sum up a period of the history of the Early Church (6:7; 12:24; 19:20). These words are a telling expression of the biblical conception of the divine Word. Our Lord Himself compared the Word with a seed that is sown and sprouts and grows: "The seed is the word of God" (Lk 8:11; cf Col 1:6; 1Pt 1:23). The Word of the Lord is powerful and active; it "prevails mightily," as Luke puts it in Ac 19:20.

If, then, we are to hear the divine Word of the New Testament on its own terms (and that is the whole task and function of interpretation), we must study it historically. We must learn to see it as the growing and working divine Word, as God Himself active in history (Ac 2:11).

The Book of Acts is unique in the history of religions. Nowhere else do we find this sober and religious sense of history, this absolute conviction that God is the God of history, who clothes Himself in a garment of mighty deeds in order to reveal Himself to us. Here only do we find the conviction of faith that His Word is a force, is in fact *the* force in history. The Book of Acts is therefore uniquely valuable for our study of the whole New Testament. It is valuable because it provides us with the historical information

OVERVIEW

Author
Luke

Date
Written c AD 60–62

Places
Jerusalem; Samaria; Syrian Antioch; cities in Asia Minor and Greece; Rome; see map, p 388

People
Jesus; Peter, John, and the other apostles; James the brother of Jesus; Saul/Paul; Barnabas

Purpose
To link the Gospel of Jesus and the service of the 12 apostles with the missionary work of the apostle Paul

Law Themes
Kingdom of God; way of God; call to bear witness; repentance; devotion to the Law; turn to God; call to preach; condemnation of lying, magic, simony, and superstition; resisting the Spirit; persecution; generosity urged

Gospel Themes
Kingdom of God; way of God; God's promises fulfilled; resurrection; filled with the Spirit; salvation; Jesus' name; forgiveness; fear of God; grace; Gospel proclamation

Memory Verses
The mission (1:7–9); the name of Jesus (4:11–12); Stephen's prayer (7:59–60); saved by grace (15:10–11); counsel for church elders (20:28–32); Paul's mission (26:15–18)

TIMELINE

AD 33	Resurrection, Ascension, Pentecost
AD 36	Conversion of Paul
AD 49	Jerusalem Council
AD 57–58	Paul journeys to Rome
AD 70	Romans destroy Jerusalem

that is indispensable for reconstructing the historical background of many New Testament books, especially the letters of Paul; but not only for that reason. We appreciate and value the Book of Acts as students of history, of course, but we are never merely historians when we seek to interpret the New Testament. We are always first and foremost believers, for whom the historical is a means to a higher end, namely, that we hear the New Testament speak to us as the living voice of God *now*. And it is to the theologians and believers that the Book of Acts is really uniquely valuable. Since it is the history of the Early Church, conceived of and told not as the history of another religious society but as the history of the growth, the progress, and the triumph of the divine Word, the Book of Acts can determine not only the method of our study but also the basically religious attitude of our study.

Thus the first 12 chapters of the Book of Acts will provide us with the materials that enable us to reconstruct the historical setting and the original function of the Epistle of James, and will give us an insight into the genesis and the background of the mission to the Gentiles that gave rise to the letters of Paul. However, we shall do well to use these 12 chapters first as a means of getting a basic, theological insight into the character of the New Testament Word of God. This does not mean that we ignore the historical; it does mean that we see in history the revelation of God—our God. "When my love walks, she treads upon the ground," a poet once said. We might say the same of our God: "When our God walks, He treads upon the ground." He does not remain a remote and shadowy sort of philosopher's God; He condescends to enter history and does His gracious work there, for us men and for our salvation. If we study historically the life of the Early Church and the nature of the apostolic proclamation that called that First Church into being, we shall be enabled to hear God speaking to us now.

Christ grants preaching and teaching authority to Paul (on the left) and Peter (on the right) with other disciples. Titled "Sarcophagus of the Handing of the Keys." Fourth century.

Historical and Cultural Setting

What sort of life was this life of the Early Church, that life which was the historical framework of our New Testament, the seedbed in which it sprouted and grew? Its first and most obvious characteristic is that it is a life wholly dominated by the Lord Jesus Christ. Luke makes it very plain that the Book of Acts (which is the second book of a two-volume work, of which his Gospel is the first) is the direct continuation of the Gospel of Jesus Christ: "In the first book, . . . I have dealt with all that Jesus *began* to do and teach" (Ac 1:1). The human figure of Peter may loom large on the stage of history in the first part (chs 1–12) and that of Paul in the second (chs 13–28); but they are both dwarfed by, and completely subordinated to, Him who is the real and sole Actor in this Book of Acts—this Jesus who continues to do and to teach. It is His Word that grows and speeds and triumphs here, not Peter's or Paul's, a fact that Peter and Paul are the first to assert.

Second, the Book of Acts has aptly been called the Gospel of the Holy Spirit. The book opens with the promise of the Spirit (1:5, 8), and the New Testament Church is born when the Spirit is given in the fullness and universality that neither the Old Testament people of God nor the disciples of Jesus had as yet experienced (2:1–42). The third major aspect of the history which is the seedbed of our New Testament is the fact that the Church is conscious of being the end times people of God, that is, the people of God in the world's last days. The Spirit is the gift of God given "in the last days" (2:17). And the gift is given in order that we may bear witness to the fact which decisively ushers in the last days, the resurrection of Jesus from the dead (2:32–36). That fact means that Jesus is enthroned as Christ and Lord (2:36), soon to return (3:20). The "day of the Lord" of which Joel had spoken is full in view (2:20), and it is for the new people of God "the day of our Lord Jesus Christ." The kingdom of God is "at hand" more imminently and more urgently than when John the Baptist cried out in the wilderness (Mt 3:2) or even when Jesus proclaimed it in Galilee (Mt 4:17). The risen Lord is proclaiming it; the word of His messengers is establishing it (Ac 1:3, 6, 8). When the "good news about the kingdom of God and the name of Jesus Christ" is being proclaimed (8:12), the Kingdom is there, the Christ is taking up His power and is beginning to reign; it is the beginning of the end. The last days have dawned.

The Book of Acts pictures the new people of God as living by the apostles' word. The Church thus lives in faith and love under the Lordship of Jesus, animated by the Spirit, which He has poured out upon all believers, in joyous, active, and responsible expectancy of the return of the Lord in glory. The impress of this first history of God's people is on the whole new New Testament, and the first apostolic preaching (often referred to by its Greek name *kerygma*, "herald's news, proclaimed Gospel") has given all the New Testament writings their characteristic color and contour.

The whole New Testament is the rich and various unfolding of "The word of God increased." The Gospels expand it; the Epistles restate, point up, and apply it; the Book of Revelation unfolds its utmost eschatological reach. And nowhere, in any aspect of it, does this Word lose its character as history. It has a history, being the crown and fulfillment of God's previous actions and promises; it is history—the recital of the mighty works of God that culminate in that epochal history when God dealt decisively with the sin of mankind in His Servant Jesus of Nazareth; and it makes history—it is the Word of the Lord, and the Spirit of the Lord moves creatively in it. It calls upon people to turn, and turns them, and thus catches them up into God's last great movement in history toward God's last goal.

Composition

Author

According to early tradition, borne out in the headings of early manuscripts, Luke the evangelist wrote the Book of Acts. Since the questions surrounding Lukan authorship are closely tied to questions regarding the Gospel of Luke, see pp 269–70 for further information.

Date of Composition

The content of Acts requires that it was composed after Paul reached Rome. Since Paul and Peter were later executed at Rome in AD 68 and Acts does not record these monumental events, the book was most likely written before their executions. For more on the date of composition, see pp 270–71.

Purpose/Recipients

It may be, as some scholars have supposed, that Acts has an apologetic purpose: to make plain to the Roman world that Christianity is no treasonable, subversive movement but is innocent of any politically dangerous intent. Its preachers may be turning "the world upside down" (Ac 17:6), but not in any sense that threatens the stability of the empire. It has often been pointed out that Luke repeatedly notes the fact that Roman officials find Christianity politically neutral (e.g., 18:14, 15; 23:29; 25:18, 19; 26:32). But the apologetic purpose is at most a secondary one for the book. The prime intent of the work is religious. It portrays the impact of the risen and exalted Christ upon the entire world. Christ confronts all people in the inspired word of the messengers whom He Himself has chosen. He confronts all sorts and conditions—Jews, Samaritans, Greeks, Romans, the high and the lowly, suave metropolitan philosophers and superstitious, excitable louts of the hinterland. Christ confronts them all with the gracious claim of His saving Lordship. Whether the response be the joyous and absolute submission of faith or the embittered resistance of unbelief or the polite mockery of skepticism, He looms divinely large as the Lord before whom the ways of men divide, since they must welcome or reject Him. He is the Christ who is gathering the new people of God from among all the nations of the earth.

Literary Features

Genre

The Book of Acts is to be thought of as the direct continuation of Luke's Gospel, with the exalted Christ as its solely dominant figure (Ac 1:1). The book does not pretend to be a history of the Early Church or even a history of early missions; it would be woefully incomplete as either of the two. It is the continuation of the story of the Christ, and can therefore be as selective in recording the facts of history as the Gospel itself. Of all the ways that the Gospel went, Luke selects just one, the high road to Rome. And even that segment of the total history of missions is not fully portrayed but is leanly

Continued on p 368.

Acts and the Critics

The historical accuracy of Acts has been seriously questioned by critical scholarship in modern times for the following reasons: (1) The ancient tradition concerning Lukan authorship is heavily discounted by critics. Only the "we" sections, at most, are attributed to an eyewitness and companion of Paul, probably, but not necessarily, Luke. This material, it is asserted, has been utilized by a writer of much later date. (2) The aim of the work, it is said, is obviously not primarily to convey historical information. Since its purpose is edification (or apologetics), one cannot expect historical accuracy. For example, it is argued that the parallelism between the accounts of Peter (Ac 1–12) and Paul (Ac 13–28) is too complete and too pat to be convincing as history. (3) The account of Acts concerning Paul cannot, it is alleged, be squared with what the letters of Paul tell us of his life. (4) Most important, it is argued that no one who had really known Paul could have portrayed him as he is portrayed in Acts; for example, it is thought to be inconceivable that the man who wrote the Letter to the Galatians would make it a point to preach first to the Jews wherever he went or would so completely and unabashedly associate himself with Judaism as he does in 21:23–26 or would call himself a Pharisee (23:6). The author of Acts has, so the argument runs, distorted the picture in order to give the impression that the development within the Early Church was more peaceful and harmonious than it in reality was. It is likewise maintained that Paul in 17:22–31 makes concessions to pagan thought that cannot be paralleled in his letters.

To these arguments the answer is: (1) It is a good principle in historical study that a tradition stands until valid reasons have been given for rejecting it. Can any really valid reason be advanced for skepticism regarding the tradition of the Lukan authorship of Acts in the Early Church?

(2) Acts is obviously written for the edification of the Church; its preface already indicates that. But the argument that a book designed for edification is for that very reason not trustworthy as a record of facts rests on a false conception of what constitutes "edification." The New Testament itself is emphatic on the point that the apostles built and edified the Church, not with myths and dreams and fancies but with the facts of God's wonderful works; the Gospels by their very title (Good News) assert that they want to be taken seriously as history. Paul stakes the whole case for his apostolate, the apostolic message, and the Church on the factuality of the Resurrection (1Co 15:1–19). As for Luke, it should be remembered that Lk 1:1–4, with its claim to historical accuracy based on careful research and recourse to primary sources, is the preface to the whole two-volume work, which the secondary preface of Ac 1:1 is designed to recall. A feature such as the parallelism between the lives of Peter and Paul does not, therefore, call into question the accuracy of the report concerning them. The parallelism was no doubt designed by the author and designed for edifying purposes. But the parallels do not prove that he falsified the facts in order to produce the report. (For example, without falsifying history, a man may point out that Handel and Bach, both musicians, were born in the same year, were both treated by the same eye doctor, and both went blind.) Moreover, the accuracy of Luke's account in many details has been strikingly confirmed by historical and archaeological investigation. Luke, for instance, gets the titles of Roman officials right—and they varied not only from place to place, but also from time to time in the same place. And what is even more difficult for a noncontemporary, he accurately reproduces the atmosphere of the various places that are the scenes of events recorded by him—the fanatical Jewish nationalistic fervor at the time

A Roman trireme, typically used for war, but here used to transport cargo. Paul likely traveled on a much larger Alexandrian grain ship (Ac 27–28).

of a great festival in Jerusalem, the civic self-consciousness of the Philippian "colonists," the intellectual curiosity and rationality of Athens. The details of the narrative of Paul's voyage to Rome and his shipwreck on Malta in ch 27 have been checked by experts and not found wanting.

(3) The most remarkable feature about the relationship between Acts and the Letters of Paul is the amount and kind of correspondence between the two. The notices of Paul and Luke frequently dovetail, and in such a manner as to exclude a calculated agreement on the part of Luke. It is only natural and, indeed, inevitable that there should remain unresolved tensions and unanswered questions in this area. The two men write from different points of view, and neither Paul nor Luke is writing a complete biography of Paul, so that we are often left ignorant of facts that might supply the connecting and unifying links between the Lukan and the Pauline notices.

(4) If Acts has drawn a false picture of Paul, one that cannot be harmonized with the self-portrait of the letters, that would constitute a most serious indictment of its historical trustworthiness. But one may fairly ask whether those who have found Acts wanting in this respect have made the *whole* self-portrait of Paul's Letters the standard for comparison. Have they not forgotten the Paul who spoke of the Gospel as the power of God for salvation "to the Jew first" (Rm 1:16) when they question Luke's veracity in portraying the Paul who preached first in the synagogue? If Paul avoided the synagogue, how are we to account for the fact that he in his apostolic ministry received the 39 lashes at the hands of the Jews no less than five times (2Co 11:24)? Paul writes, "To the Jews I became as a Jew" (1Co 9:20); was that a mere theory, or did he put it into practice? And if Paul once calls himself a Pharisee, the situation in which he does so must be borne in mind. He was not thereby saying, and his Pharisaic judges did not understand him to say, that he was returning to Judaism; he was saying with typically Pauline incisiveness that he shared with the Pharisees what he did not share with the Sadducees, the messianic hope and the hope of the resurrection (Ac 23:6). And as for Paul's alleged concessions to paganism, does his speech on the Areopagus in Ac 17, rightly understood, really go beyond what he says in the first chapter of his Letter to the Romans (Rm 1:19)? And is there not a remarkable agreement between his speech on the Areopagus and the description that he himself gives of his missionary preaching in 1Th 1:9–10?

The historical accuracy of Acts cannot be checked and verified at all points; where it can be checked, the results have been generally favorable to Luke. In many points, no verification is possible; the miracles attributed to Peter and to Paul, for instance, lie quite outside the realm of historical verification. And what historical investigation can determine that which is for Luke the controlling fact of history, the fact of the presence and power of the Spirit? These realities can neither be proved nor disproved, and assent to the message that the facts spell out does not depend on the possibility of historical verification. Luke's appeals to faith; deep calls to deep and speaks a speech for which shallow rationality has no ear.

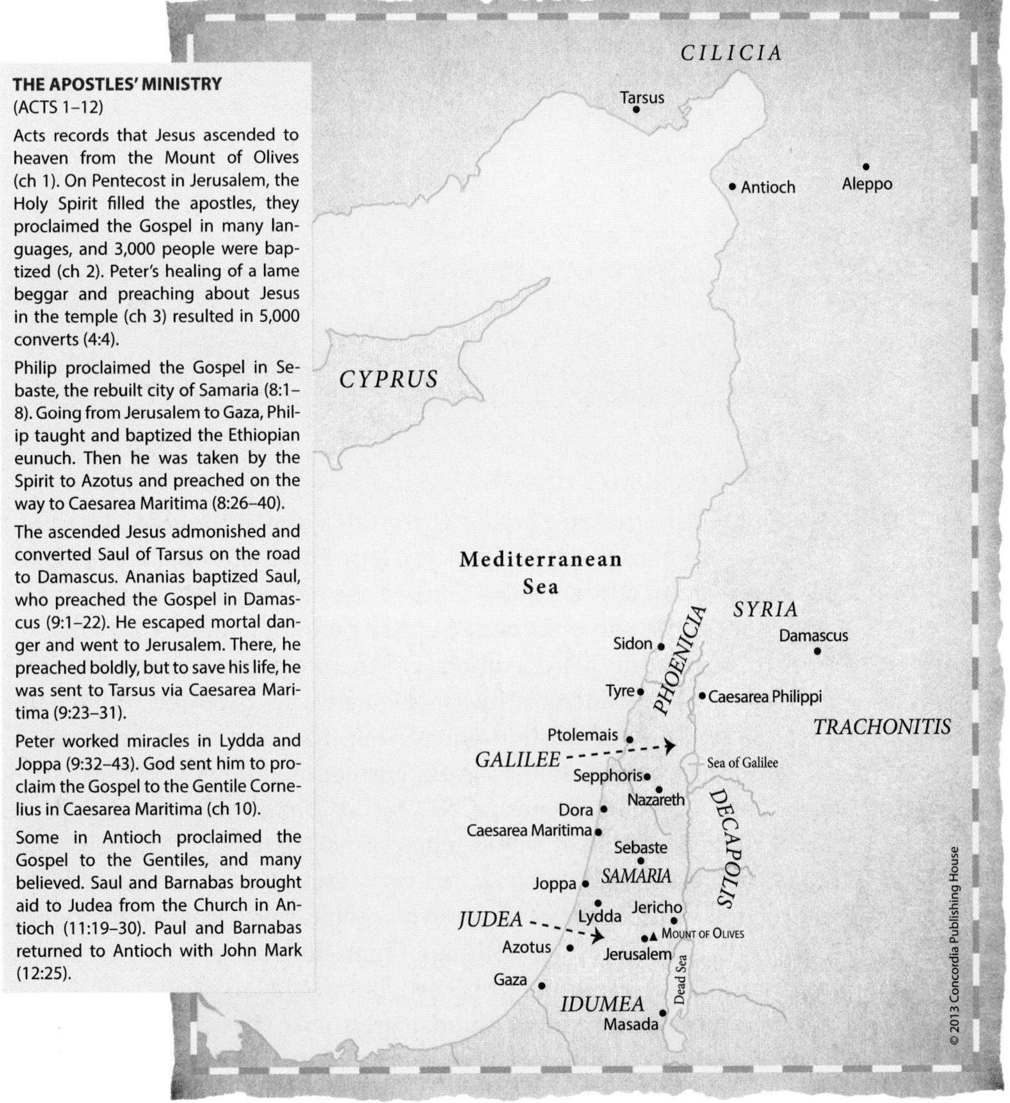

THE APOSTLES' MINISTRY
(ACTS 1–12)

Acts records that Jesus ascended to heaven from the Mount of Olives (ch 1). On Pentecost in Jerusalem, the Holy Spirit filled the apostles, they proclaimed the Gospel in many languages, and 3,000 people were baptized (ch 2). Peter's healing of a lame beggar and preaching about Jesus in the temple (ch 3) resulted in 5,000 converts (4:4).

Philip proclaimed the Gospel in Sebaste, the rebuilt city of Samaria (8:1–8). Going from Jerusalem to Gaza, Philip taught and baptized the Ethiopian eunuch. Then he was taken by the Spirit to Azotus and preached on the way to Caesarea Maritima (8:26–40).

The ascended Jesus admonished and converted Saul of Tarsus on the road to Damascus. Ananias baptized Saul, who preached the Gospel in Damascus (9:1–22). He escaped mortal danger and went to Jerusalem. There, he preached boldly, but to save his life, he was sent to Tarsus via Caesarea Maritima (9:23–31).

Peter worked miracles in Lydda and Joppa (9:32–43). God sent him to proclaim the Gospel to the Gentile Cornelius in Caesarea Maritima (ch 10).

Some in Antioch proclaimed the Gospel to the Gentiles, and many believed. Saul and Barnabas brought aid to Judea from the Church in Antioch (11:19–30). Paul and Barnabas returned to Antioch with John Mark (12:25).

and monumentally sketched. There are, for instance, large gaps in the record of the career of Paul; both his two years' ministry at Corinth and his three years' ministry at Ephesus are merely illustrated by means of typical incidents rather than chronicled. Indeed, the whole work illustrates rather than chronicles the course of the Word that proclaims and presents Christ. Luke selects incidents and actions that illumine and bring out in clear outline the impact of that Word upon people, the tensions and conflicts that ensue when the Word of the Lord is heard, and the triumphant progress of that Word despite tensions and conflicts.

Fourth-century engraving of Peter and Paul, key figures in Acts.

Characters

"Acts of the Apostles" can hardly be the title given to the second part of his work by Luke himself. Of the apostles, only **Peter** and **Paul** are really leading figures. **John** appears a few times in the early chapters and then disappears; **James the son of Zebedee** appears only as a martyr, with one short sentence devoted to his execution. On the other hand, men who are not apostles play a considerable role in the narrative: **Stephen**, **Philip**, **Barnabas**, **Silas**, **Agabus**. Furthermore, if the title were to be understood in the sense suggested by similar works current in antiquity, such as *The Acts of Alexander* by Callisthenes or *The Acts of Hannibal* by Sosylus, it could actually be misleading. It would suggest a narrative of human heroism and human achievement. Of course, the very term *apostle*, as defined by Jesus and as used by the apostles themselves, should have excluded that idea, for the apostle is by definition nothing of himself and everything by virtue of the commission given him by his Lord. But would Luke have selected a title that even suggested the idea of human greatness? His book tells the story of men, only because, and insofar as, men are instrumental in the growth and triumph of the Word of the Lord.

Outline

The Book of Acts may be divided most easily between the work of Peter (chs 1–12) and the work of Paul (chs 13–28). Also, 1:8 provides a helpful outline for the progress of the 25 years of history presented in Acts (c AD 33–58):

From Jerusalem (1:1–6:7)

To Judea and Samaria (6:8–9:31)

To the ends of the earth (9:32–28:31)

The following detailed outline takes into account the main characters as well as the progress from Jerusalem out to the broader Roman Empire and its capital.

I. Prologue (1:1–2) (Links Acts to Luke and Shows That Christ's Work Continues as the Spirit Works In and Through the Church)

II. Peter and the Church's Foundation: The Gospel Spreads from Judea to Galilee and Samaria (1:3–14:28)

- A. The Church Is Born (1:3–2:47)
  1. Jesus teaches about the kingdom of God, promises the Holy Spirit, and ascends into heaven (1:3–11)
  2. Matthias chosen to replace Judas: the foundation of the 12 apostles is restored (1:12–26)
  3. Pentecost: the descending Spirit gives birth to the Church (ch 2)
- B. Peter and John Carry on the Work of Christ in Jerusalem (chs 3–5)
  1. Peter and John's first trial and its effects (3:1–5:11)
  2. Peter and John's second trial and its effects (5:12–42)
- C. The Martyrdom of Stephen and Initial Spread of the Gospel (chs 6–8)
  1. Stephen and his martyrdom (6:1–8:1a)

2. The persecution of the Church leads to the Gospel's spread (8:1b–40)

D. The Conversion of Paul and the Vision of Peter Pave the Way for Outreach to the Gentiles (chs 9–14)

1. Saul's conversion on the road to Damascus (9:1–31)
2. Peter's vision and the extension of the Gospel (9:32–11:18)
3. The Church in Antioch (11:19–30)
4. Peter's escape; Herod's death (ch 12)
5. Paul's first missionary journey (chs 13–14)

III. The Jerusalem Council: Paul's Work Endorsed by Peter and James (15:1–35)

A. Paul's Missionary Work Sparks Controversy (15:1–5)
B. Paul's Missionary Work Evaluated (15:6–21)
C. The Council Sends a Letter to the Churches (15:22–35)

IV. Paul Carries the Gospel to the Ends of the Earth (15:36–28:31)

A. Paul's Second Missionary Journey (15:36–18:22)
B. Paul's Third Missionary Journey (18:23–21:16)
C. Paul Goes to Rome (21:17–28:31)

1. Paul's imprisonment in Jerusalem (21:17–23:35)
   a. Paul's arrest (21:17–22:29)
   b. Trial before the Council (22:30–23:11)
   c. Transfer to Caesarea (23:12–35)
2. Paul's imprisonment in Caesarea (chs 24–26)
   a. Trial before Felix (ch 24)
   b. Trial before Festus (25:1–12)
   c. Hearing before Festus and Agrippa (25:13–26:32)
3. Voyage to Rome (27:1–28:15)
4. House arrest in Rome: the Gospel is preached (28:16–31)

Paul is pictured as a loyal friend of the Jews, devoting some time on his second and third journeys to raise money for Christian Jews in Jerusalem. Perhaps Luke hoped that these emphases in his book would serve to heal the growing breach between Jewish and Gentile Christians. Peter was as important as Paul, Luke seems to be saying. God used Peter in the same way

He used Paul. Both Peter and Paul performed acts of healing; both raised people from the dead; both overcame sorcerers; both were offered divine worship by superstitious admirers; both were agents of divine judgment on impenitent sinners.

Narrative Development or Plot

Acts opens with (1) the believers in Jerusalem waiting for the gift of the Spirit and (2) Luke presenting the history of their work in that city. The history presents the journey of faith and of mission that led the early Christians from Jerusalem to the heart of the Roman Empire. In the early chapters, Peter emerges as a key character. Persecution and the death of the deacon, Stephen, moves the story from Jerusalem to Judea and Samaria, where a second key character is introduced: Saul/Paul, whom God calls to preach Christ.

For a few chapters, the story turns back to Peter, through whom God performs miracles, and begins ministry to the Gentiles (chs 9–12). The story then describes the mission to the Gentiles through Paul, with ch 15 recording how the Christians in Jerusalem settled doctrinal and practical disputes that arose due to the Gentile mission. The rest of the book records two missionary journeys of Paul and his companions until Paul reaches Rome, fulfilling an important aspect of Jesus' stated goal in Ac 1:8.

Many have found the ending of Acts puzzling and inadequate: why is the outcome of Paul's trial not told? Either his release or his martyrdom would seem to constitute a more fitting conclusion to the work than the one Luke has seen fit to give it. Some scholars have suggested that Luke perhaps intended to add a third volume to his work, one that would round out and conclude the story by recounting Paul's release, his voyage to Spain, and his martyr's death. But there is no real indication that Luke intended such a continuation of his book; neither is the suggestion very plausible that Luke did not record the outcome of Paul's trial because that outcome was martyrdom and he did not wish to conclude his account of the victorious Gospel on a sad and negative note. To judge from Luke's account of the martyrdom of Stephen (Ac 7:54–60) and from Paul's own attitude toward martyrdom as recorded by Luke (Ac 20:24; 21:13), neither Luke nor Paul looked on martyrdom as something negative and depressing.

The fact is that the present ending makes sense, both as the conclusion of Acts and as the conclusion of the two-part work. The goal noted in Ac 1:8 has been reached: the Gospel is being proclaimed in Rome, the capital of the western world; it has stepped through the door that opens into all the world.

That is *the* fact, the fact that counts; before it anyone's fate, even Paul's fate, pales into insignificance. And the present ending is a meaningful conclusion to the whole work also. When Jesus "began to do and to teach" in His own city, Nazareth, He offered His people God's free forgiveness on the basis of a word from Isaiah (Lk 4:18–21). He had met with objection and resistance from His own people even then (4:22, 23, 28–30). And He had hinted even then that the word they were rejecting would go to the Gentiles (4:24–27). Jesus' prediction is now being fulfilled; the Jews of Rome are following the course set by the Jews of Galilee and Jerusalem and the cities of Asia and Macedonia and Achaia. They are rejecting the proffered Good News of God. The prophet Isaiah is heard once more, this time uttering words of fearful judgment upon a people who will not hear (Ac 28:25–27). But God's purposes are being worked out nevertheless: "This salvation of God has been sent to the Gentiles; they will listen" (28:28).

Resources

What sources has the author of Acts used for his history? This question has been assiduously investigated by scholars, especially by those who are convinced that Luke is not the author. But since conjecture plays so large a role in this kind of investigation, it is not surprising that no satisfactory or generally accepted answer has as yet been given to the question. If Luke is the author, as the ancient tradition asserts, he of course himself witnessed a large portion of the events recorded in the latter half of the work. And as a companion of Paul he had access to firsthand information from Paul and his co-workers (e.g., Silas and Timothy). And since he was with Paul in Jerusalem and during Paul's two-year imprisonment in Caesarea, Luke had abundant opportunity for obtaining information on the early events in the Church in Israel from the apostles and men such as Philip, Agabus, the "early disciple" Mnason, James the brother of our Lord, and the Jerusalem elders. He may, of course, have also utilized written sources (cf Lk 1:1–4), both Aramaic and Greek, but as to their nature and extent we can only guess. It is generally agreed that he did not utilize the Letters of Paul—a fact that makes the remarkable agreement between Acts and the historical notices in the Pauline Letters all the more remarkable.

Sea of Galilee.

An ossuary (bone box) inscribed with both Greek and Hebrew, illustrating the bilingual setting of early Roman era Israel.

Text and Translations

The so-called "Western" text of Acts is about 12 percent longer than the early manuscripts associated with Alexandria and includes numerous interesting readings that reach back to at least the second century AD. It was named "Western" because some of its major witnesses were likely scribed in the western Mediterranean (e.g., Codex Bezae, uncial D, likely comes from Italy or France), though the so-called Western readings may likewise occur in manuscripts of Syria. Antioch, the Roman capital of Syria and one of the largest cities of western Asia, may have been the connecting point between these western and eastern manuscripts.

A minority of scholars have argued that the Western text is more original than the more polished Alexandrian texts; much of this discussion centers around the passages in Acts. In some passages, the Western text is shorter, leading to speculation about whether the Alexandrian texts included additions at those points. The majority of scholars conclude that the Western text is a looser and inclusive tradition of copying New Testament manuscripts rather than an earlier, more original form of the manuscripts. On the style of Luke's Greek, see p 274.

Doctrinal Content

Summary Commentary

Ch 1 The resurrected Christ advances the kingdom here and now. He will return in full sight of all in the Father's good time. In view of this, the disciples and others seek the Lord's will concerning the candidate of His choice to replace Judas as a leader of the Church, the new Israel.

Ch 2 The Holy Spirit descends as a gift, sounding forth one message in many languages, showing that Israel will soon burst its ethnic bounds. In faith, Peter shows from the Scriptures that Jesus is Israel's Lord as well as

Savior of the nations. The early Christians lived only for their Lord and for the other members of His Body, the Church.

3:1–4:31 In this highest form of almsgiving, Peter and John dispense God's own gift: mercy. Present through the Spirit in His holy name, the exalted Jesus makes the crippled man stand, that he may leap for joy. Peter then shows the crowd at the temple that all the prophets have pointed to Jesus as the Christ. The religious authorities close their eyes and cover their ears to silence the Word. But the crippled man still stands, the name of Jesus displays its power, and salvation resides in Him alone. Mounting pressure drives the apostles to prayer. They recite God's sure Word and ask Him for boldness and a demonstration of His presence.

4:32–5:42 As the early Christians loved their Lord, they loved His Bride, the Church, giving of themselves freely. Ananias and Sapphira paid a high price for their hypocrisy, taking grace for granted and forgetting that Christ will return in judgment. God heals many people through the apostles. This massive outpouring of God's love and power comes with His serious appeals for repentance. God's patience with Israel (Rm 2:4) is running out. Yet the leaders are dangerously close to judgment. Under fire, the Church holds firm, confesses the truth, and accepts the suffering that follows.

Chs 6–8 The apostles deal with complaints about the relief of the Church's poor, instituting the office of deacon. Yet one of the deacons, Stephen, is the new target of persecution. Synagogue leaders twist his words, accusing him of treason against Judaism. Stephen's reply recounts how God's chosen people, by rejecting Moses, rejected God. Israel's refusal to follow God ended in their dismissal of God's Son. Stephen displays the heart of one touched and changed by Jesus' love. His death and Saul's persecution of Christ's followers illustrate the fulfillment of the prophecy that the world would hate the Gospel and kill those who believed it (Mt 24:9–10). Yet the omnipotent God makes the world's fanatical hatred serve His purpose in proclaiming the Gospel throughout the entire world. The power of the Gospel, which reaches even the most unlikely people, is illustrated in the lives of the Samaritans. Then God leads Philip to bear witness to and baptize an important official from Ethiopia, ensuring that Jews in Africa and also Ethiopians would likewise receive the Gospel.

9:1–31 Jesus confronts Saul and converts him through the Gospel and Baptism. Though Saul was convinced of his righteous mission of persecution, he learned that true righteousness comes only through Christ. The Holy Spirit opened Saul's eyes and heart to forgiveness through Christ so he boldly confessed His name to his fellow Jews. Due to Saul's past, Christians

Remnants of the Roman era road to Damascus that Paul would have traveled (Ac 9).

are suspicious of him. Due to his new faith, enemies of the Christian faith plot to kill him. Nevertheless, the Holy Spirit brings Saul to other believers who help him escape. Through the power of the Gospel, the Church continues to grow.

9:32–11:18 Through the power of the Gospel, Peter heals Aeneas, paralyzed for eight years. Seeing this miracle, the residents of Lydda and Sharon repent and believe in the Lord. An untimely death comes to Tabitha, a beloved servant. However, those who mourn Tabitha's death witness the power of Christ when Peter prays for her restoration to life. The Lord also prepares Cornelius to learn more about Jesus. Through a vision, the Lord teaches Peter that holiness is not determined by people, but by what God Himself has ordained as holy and clean. Peter then affirms for devout Cornelius that Jesus is truly the Christ; the Spirit affirms for Peter that the Gospel applies to all people without partiality. Finally, the Holy Spirit demonstrates to the Jewish believers that God indeed desires to pour out His Spirit on "all flesh" (2:17), even Gentiles. So Peter urges that the Gentiles be baptized right away, without concern for circumcision or ritual purity according to the old covenant.

11:19–30 Though persecution scatters the believers, the Lord uses the persecution to proclaim the Gospel even more broadly. As believers grow in faith, they commit themselves to acts of service. Men of God, such as Barnabas, not only confirm the work of the Holy Spirit among believers but also ensure that new believers are nurtured in the faith.

Ch 12 As Christ had prophesied, His disciples share in His suffering, being arrested, beaten, and even killed. The death of James at the hand of Herod and the imprisonment of Peter demonstrate the world's hatred of the Gospel. Herod's violence and intrigue illustrate how evil breeds evil.

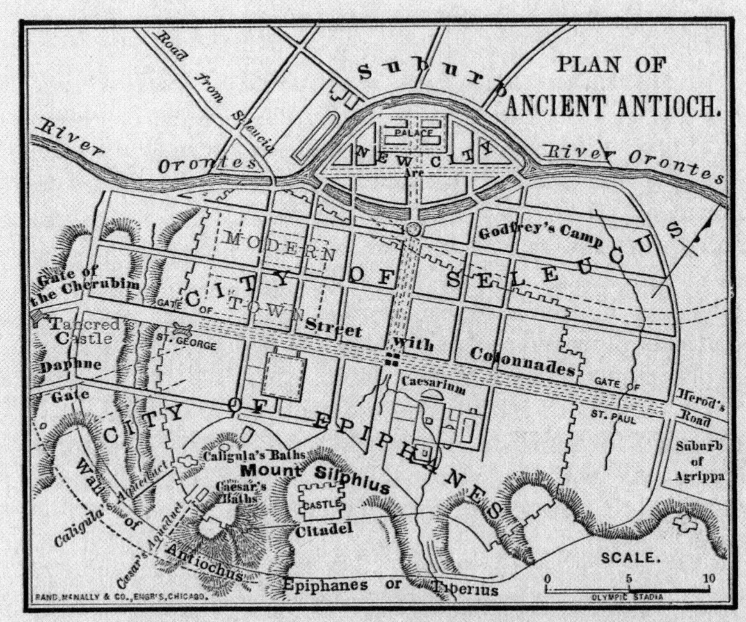

Following the first persecution (Ac 7–8), Syrian Antioch became the center for outreach to Gentiles (Ac 11:19–30; 13:1–3). From here, Paul and Barnabus traveled westward on their first missionary journey as far as Pisidian Antioch in Asia Minor.

Chs 13–14 The momentous missionary journeys of Saul (later Paul) begin with the calling and equipping by the Spirit. At the first mission stop, there is both opposition to and belief in the Gospel. Paul's visit to the synagogue at Pisidian Antioch is typical of his missionary technique and preaching. His visit to Iconium follows the same pattern, and the message of grace again encounters violent opposition. Lystra has no synagogue, so when God miraculously heals someone through Paul, he testifies to the people that God graciously blesses all creation. When he must interrupt their pagan sacrifices, they stone him! The conclusion of Paul's work in Lystra illustrates both suffering for the Gospel and the power of the Gospel as he rises up again. Paul and Barnabas end their journey by reporting to those who sent them everything God has done.

15:1–35 The Jerusalem Council resolved the critical issue of who God's chosen people are and affirmed that Jews and Gentiles are saved by grace alone (v 11). Then the decision reached in Jerusalem is delivered by delegation and by letter to the believers in Syrian Antioch, affirming the teaching of the council.

15:36–18:23 After disagreement over John Mark, two missionary teams are sent out from Antioch. Paul begins his second journey with Silas and Timothy. Through them, God continues to reach out with His message, using people as His messengers. God guided Paul and his companions in

Taurus Pass, which Paul likely used on the second missionary journey (Ac 15:41). Seeing the rugged terrain helps one realize the apostles' determination to spread the Gospel.

unexpected directions, leading them to Europe. Paul begins his work in Philippi through Lydia. He next heals a demon-possessed girl, and as a result, he and Silas are beaten and jailed. When the Lord frees Paul and Silas from prison, He also brings a Philippian jailer and his family to faith. At Thessalonica, Paul and Silas continue the pattern of preaching at the synagogue. Persecution follows the Gospel, even when the Bereans eagerly receive it. At Athens, Paul engages the dominant religious and philosophical teachings of the day. Paul reaches out to Athenians who do not know the Scriptures. He uses teachings from their philosophy and literature to point them to the God of creation, who sent His Son, Jesus. His stay in Corinth demonstrates two lessons: (1) The Gospel is the power of God for salvation, even in the face of rejection. (2) Opposition to the Gospel—not the Gospel itself—disrupts proper authority. These travels conclude Paul's second missionary journey.

18:24–21:16 Apollos is a gifted teacher with sincere faith, yet he needs to grow in his knowledge of the faith. Paul arrives at Ephesus and begins a very productive period of his ministry. God continues to work through mighty miracles and His Word. Yet a riot shows that opponents of the Gospel continually cause the troubles associated with the Christian faith. Paul and his companions begin the trip back to Jerusalem, encouraging fellow Christians along the way. The end of Paul's time in Troas is noteworthy for the resurrection of Eutychus. His farewell address to the Church leaders of Ephesus emphasizes the significance of the work of the ministry. Paul continues to journey toward Jerusalem despite warnings about the dangers he will encounter there.

21:17–23:35 The Church at Jerusalem rejoices at what God has done through Paul. The leaders ask him to dispel rumors among Jewish Christians about his ministry by taking part in an Old Testament purification ceremony. Paul's enemies unjustly accuse him of defiling the temple, and the Roman authorities intervene. Paul addresses an angry mob of Jews, vividly describing his life-changing encounter with the risen Jesus on the road to Damascus as well as another time when Christ appeared to him. Paul's address does not avert the crowd's hatred. However, as a Roman citizen, he receives help from a Roman tribune. When brought before the Council, Paul boldly speaks of Christ's resurrection. In so doing, he cleverly divides the Council since the Pharisees support his views while the Sadducees oppose them. Forty Jews, in conjunction with their leaders, create a plot to kill Paul, but Paul's nephew intervenes. Claudius Lysias turns Paul's case over to Felix the governor. All circumstances point to the apostle's innocence of any crimes against the state.

Ch 24 Paul defends himself before the Roman governor, Felix. He claims to follow what is written in the Scriptures, focusing especially on the resurrection of the dead. Paul uses this opportunity to bear witness concerning Jesus, who has given him new life. Although Felix listens as Paul proclaims God's Word, Felix is most interested in a bribe. So he ignores Paul's message and leaves him in custody.

Chs 25–26 The lack of justice in Paul's trial continues under Festus, who moves Paul to appeal to Caesar's court in Rome. Festus brings Paul's case

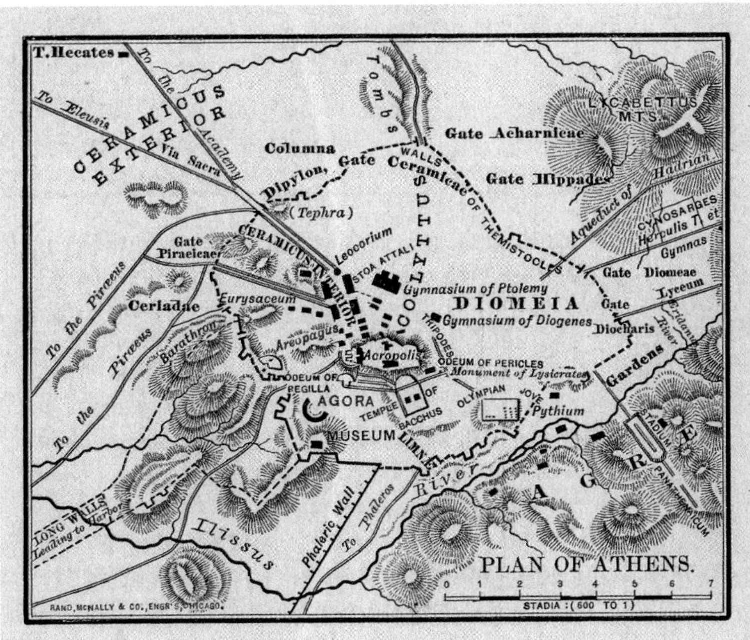

Acts 17:16–34 describes Paul addressing Athenians at the marketplace (Agora) and Areopagus.

before King Agrippa and Bernice so they may formulate charges to send with Paul to Rome. Festus fails to set Paul free, even though he knows Paul is innocent. When Paul makes his defense before King Agrippa, he describes his zealous opposition to Jesus and the Gospel message. Then he recounts how the Lord converted him from an ardent persecutor of the faith to an avid apostle.

Chs 27–28 Grave difficulties beset Paul's journey to Rome, yet the Lord assures Paul that he will reach his journey's goal. After a harrowing storm, the ship carrying Paul wrecks on the island of Malta. However, all the passengers are saved. Paul amazes the native people by surviving a snakebite, and they believe he is a god. As he heals many sick people, they will learn that his power comes from the one true God, not from Paul himself. Paul eventually reaches Rome safely and peacefully. Although not all of Paul's fellow Jews believe the Gospel, Paul proclaims it without hindrance to the Gentiles, thus fulfilling Christ's promise that the Gospel would be proclaimed to all nations.

Specific Law Themes

Describing the Christian life, Acts refers to Christianity as "the way" of God, which included rejection of idols, devotion to the Law and the Prophets, and the call to repentance. Acts emphasizes repeatedly, through commission and examples, that Christians must bear witness to the crucified and resurrected Christ as well as offer hospitality to those who travel for that purpose. As the apostles urge people to turn to God, they likewise condemn the sins of the nations. Those who resist the Spirit and persecute God's people are subject to His special judgment.

Specific Gospel Themes

"Kingdom of God" and "way of God" are also used in Acts to describe the way of salvation and the gracious reign of heaven, which breaks forth in a unique way as God fulfills His promises in Jesus and the gift of the Holy Spirit. The Spirit fills the disciples, who boldly proclaim salvation in Jesus' name through baptizing and teaching the Gospel. The story continually shows God's direct involvement in the life of His Church.

Specific Doctrines

The Book of Acts has special interest for every Christian. It tells how Christ's Church developed and matured in the crucial years between AD 30 and AD 60 as it preached the Gospel in the world, and it tells the story of the apostle

Paul, the missionary theologian whom God used to shape and mold the Church during this period. Acts serves to remind Christians that the Holy Spirit is active and powerful in the Church and that He gives them power to be witnesses to Jesus to "the end of the earth," including both Jews and Gentiles. The following pages will explore how Acts teaches these great themes.

The New People of God under the Lordship of Jesus Christ

His Word grows; His will is done. For He is the exalted Lord of invincible majesty, the Lord who has been "taken up" into heaven, to the world of God (Ac 1:2, 9, 11), "exalted at the right hand of God" (2:33) as "Leader and Savior" (5:31), the "Lord of all" (10:36). The dying Stephen prayed to this Lord, just as Jesus Himself had on the cross prayed to His Father (7:59, 60; cf Lk 23:34, 46).

He is the exalted Lord by virtue of His resurrection from the dead: "This Jesus God raised up. . . . Being therefore exalted at the right hand of God, . . . God has made Him both Lord and Christ" (2:32, 33, 36). It is the God who has raised Him from the dead who has exalted Jesus as Leader and Savior at His right hand (5:30, 31). "God raised Him on the third day and made Him to appear" (10:40). The exalted Lord is the Lord risen from the dead; that ties Him firmly and forever to the Lord who was made man for us men and for our salvation, to the Lord Jesus who went in and out among His disciples, whom John the Baptist heralded and proclaimed (1:21, 22), the *man* Jesus of Nazareth whom God attested to Israel with mighty works done in the midst of the men of Israel (2:22), the Jesus of Nazareth whom God anointed with the Holy Spirit and with power, who went about doing good and healing all who were oppressed by the devil (10:38).

He is Lord because He went that way of gracious ministry to the utmost. He is the chief stone of the new temple of God because He was the stone rejected by the builders (4:10, 11), because He was betrayed by His own disciple, arrested by His own people (1:16), and killed and crucified (2:23; 3:13–15; 4:10; 7:52).

The new people of God know and proclaim their Lord as the Servant of God. The term *Servant* is used more frequently of Him in these early chapters of Acts than anywhere else in the New Testament (3:13, 26; 4:27, 30; cf 8:32, 33). No other single term could, perhaps, so fully denote His peculiar and all-encompassing Lordship as this one. For with this term, Jesus was proclaimed as the fulfillment of those prophecies of Isaiah that fixed the hope of God's people on the Servant of the Lord, that servant whom the

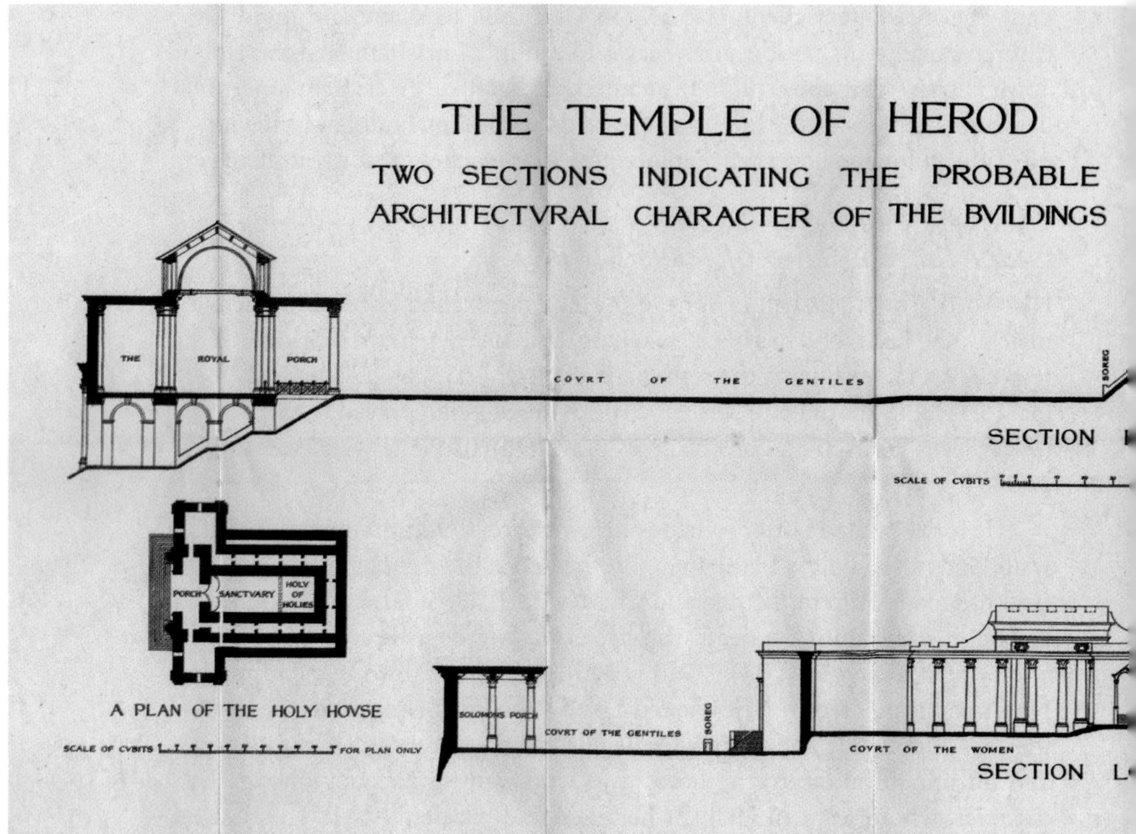

Two profiles of the temple and its courts. References to the temple in Acts may describe the entire complex or refer to the inner portion beyond the Soreg wall that separated the court of the Gentiles from the inner courts. Christians gathered for worship at Solomon's Porch (cf Ac 3:11; 5:12).

Lord endowed with His Spirit for a mission of merciful ministry to all nations in order that He might be "a covenant for the people" (Is 42:6) Israel (that is, that He might bring about fully and forever the intent of God's covenant-mercy and covenant-fidelity for God's chosen people), and in order that He might be "a light for the nations" (42:6)—that in Him the dawn of God's great day of salvation might break on all people everywhere (42:1–9). The Servant is described by the prophet Isaiah as going down into the depths of humiliation and rejection in His ministry (49:4, 7; 50:6), a ministry whose goal is the restoration of Israel and the salvation of all nations, that the Lord's "salvation may reach to the end of the earth" (49:6). The Servant is pictured by the prophet as going through ministry and humiliation to a triumphant exaltation (52:13, 15).

But the triumph is not His until He has gone the downward way of ministry to the full, not only "despised and rejected by men" (Is 53:3), but bruised and put to grief by the Lord

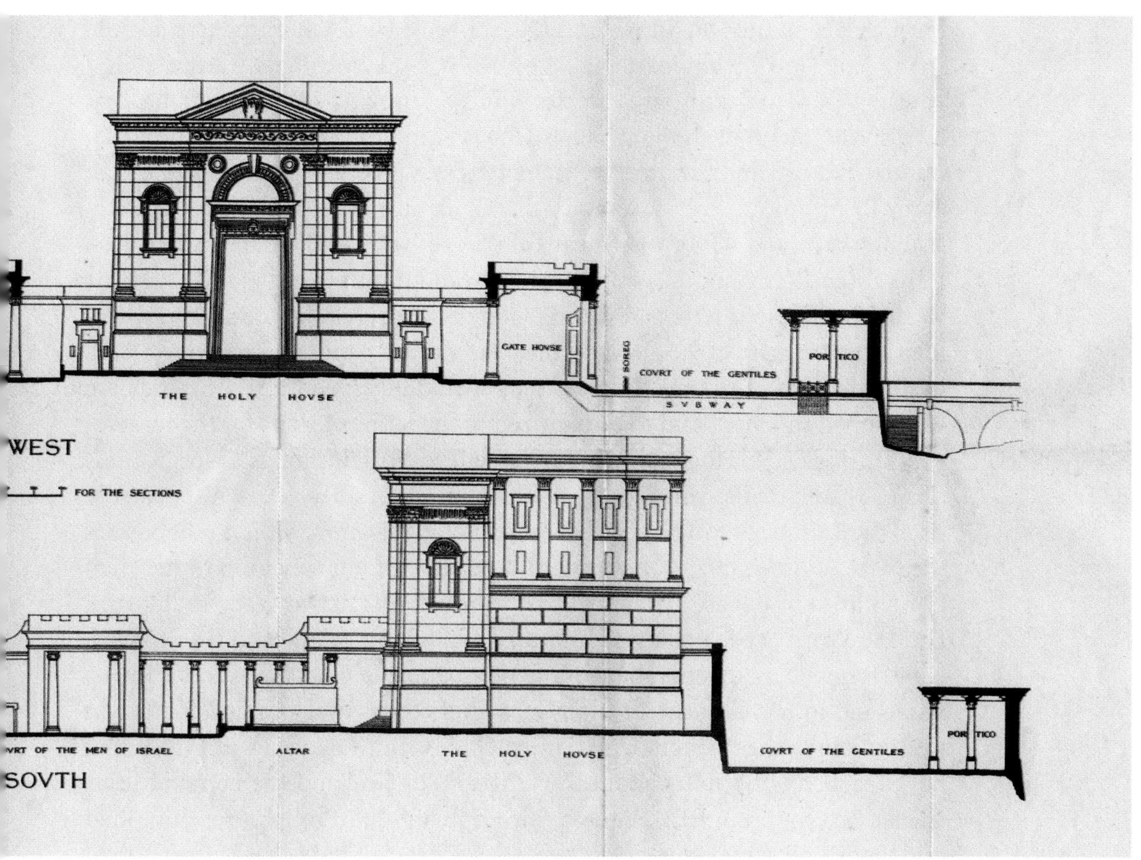

Himself (53:10), who numbers Him with the transgressors (53:12) and lays upon Him and punishes in Him the iniquity of all (53:5, 6). Only when the Servant has gone down into a vicarious, penal, atoning death for a sinful people, only when He has borne the sins of many, led like a lamb to the slaughter for their guilt, only then does He rise to new life and triumph (53:10–12). With the term *Servant* the apostles and the new people of God after them could sum up the whole glory of their Lord. The glory of the ministering Messiah, the crucified Messiah, the risen Messiah, the exalted Messiah was all comprehended in that term; and the dark mystery of His cross was illumined by it.

The Servant-Messiah of the new people of God is anything but a mere memory for them; He is for them no departed hero, no commemorated martyr. He is their present, living, and actively working Lord. Peter told the people, "God, having raised up His servant, sent Him to you first, *to bless you*" (Ac 3:26). We can see this actively blessing character of the Church's

Lord clearly in the way in which Luke spoke of His "name" in Acts; for the "name" of God in biblical language means God turning toward us, God entering into communion with us, God making and shaping our history. So also the name of the Lord Jesus Christ signifies the Lord in action. If a miracle is done "in the name" of the Lord Jesus, if Peter said to the lame man at the Beautiful Gate of the temple, "In the name of Jesus Christ of Nazareth, rise up and walk" (3:6), that means the Lord, who in the days of His flesh went about doing good, is still graciously and omnipotently at work in the world; the Author of life is restoring God's ruined creation to full and whole life (3:15, 16; 4:10; cf 9:34). Men must call on the name of Him whom God has made both Lord and Christ if they would be saved (2:21, 36); they are summoned to repent and to be baptized in the name of Jesus for the forgiveness of sins (2:38); for "everyone who believes in Him receives forgiveness of sins through His name" (10:43). The Church has been drawn repeatedly over the centuries to the conclusion of Peter's sermon, which emphasizes the place of Baptism and the work of the Spirit for our salvation rather than our abilities or deeds. In Jesus Christ, through His active grace in Baptism and the Word, we are saved from judgment (2:40), brought to God, reconciled, forgiven, made members of the new people of God. Salvation is in His name and in His alone (4:12), for He is God's own royal and lavish grace in person. He is the present kingdom of God; when Luke said of Philip that he "preached good news about the kingdom of God and the name of Jesus Christ" in Samaria (8:12), he was not implying that Philip's preaching had two themes (Philip had but one theme—he "proclaimed to them the Christ," 8:5) but was describing the one theme of his preaching in two ways. "The name of Jesus Christ" is another way of saying "the kingdom of God." Where the Lord Jesus is at work, there God Himself is at work establishing His royal reign of grace among us.

The exalted Lord works in history, through men. Men are His "instruments" (9:15) whom He chooses in sovereign grace—the persecutor Saul must bow before that royal grace and carry this Lord's name "before the Gentiles and kings and the children of Israel" and must suffer for the sake of that name (9:15, 16). He makes men His apostles, messengers who are determined wholly by the will of the sender and are completely dependent upon Him, wholly obedient to Him. As such they speak His word and represent Him and confront people with Him. The apostles' deeds of power are therefore the Lord's deeds; "many wonders and signs were done *through the apostles*" (2:43; cf 5:12). Concerning the lame man whom he had healed, Peter told the rulers, elders, and scribes, "By the name of Jesus Christ of Nazareth, whom you crucified, whom God raised from the dead—*by Him* this man is standing before you well" (4:10). Perhaps the most striking expression of the fact that the apostle is the "chosen instrument" of the Lord Jesus Christ (no less than that, but also only that) is in the words that Peter spoke at the bedside of the paralytic man at Lydda: "Aeneas, *Jesus Christ heals you*" (9:34). As instruments of the Lord, the apostles are completely selfless: "Why do you stare at us, as though by our own power or piety we have made him walk?" Peter asked the astounded people in Solomon's portico (3:12). And when Cornelius fell down at Peter's feet, Peter responded with, "Stand up; I too am a man" (10:25, 26). It is because the apostles are the self-effacing, chosen instruments of the Lord, because they are no more and no less than the human vehicles of the Lord's presence, that their word shaped and directed the whole life of the new community: "They devoted themselves to the apostles' teaching" (2:42).

The apostles were not religious geniuses, whose insights enriched and enlarged the accumulated religious stores of mankind. They were recipients of revelation, witnesses to a Person and an act in history—and this Person and this act completely overshadowed and dominated them. They were important, not for themselves, but for what they bore witness to. They received divine power for one purpose only, for witnessing (1:8). In fact, the Lord had to completely invert their own human thinking before He could use them as chosen instruments. They were curious as to times and seasons, and they thought of a reign in Israel: "Lord, will You at this time restore the kingdom to Israel?" (1:6). He turned their thoughts from curiosity about times and seasons to a sober submission to the sovereign will of the Father, from the idea of reign to the duty of ministry, from the narrow horizon of Israel to the wide world. They were to be His witnesses not only in the land and among the people they knew and loved but also to the Samaritans whom they hated, and to the ends of the earth, the wide world of the Gentiles, about whom they were by nature indifferent (1:8). The Lord set them to witnessing to Jew and to Gentile, for He is Lord of all (10:36) and determines all history. Acts 1:8 not only indicates the plan of the Book of Acts; it marks out the course of all history for the Church, until the time when the Son of Man returns to end and judge and crown all history.

Thus the life of the new people of God was a life under the Lordship of Jesus Christ; the men upon whom God's new day has dawned behold "the light of the knowledge of the glory of God *in the face of Christ*," as Paul put it (2Co 4:6). But they beheld the glory of God; the Lordship of Jesus does not obscure God but reveals Him. The name of Jesus is the revelation of the kingdom of God (Ac 8:12; cf 28:31); to be under the Lordship of Jesus is to live a life in communion with God.

The same history that reveals Jesus as Lord and Christ reveals God the King as the gracious and omnipotent Lord of history. God foretold the coming of His Christ, His anointed King, "by the mouth of all the prophets" (Ac 3:18; cf 4:25, 26). God attested the man Jesus of Nazareth with mighty works and wonders and signs (2:22); God anointed Jesus with the Holy Spirit and with power; God "was with Him" (10:38). When Jesus went down in death at the hands of His enemies, God was still in control; they crucified and killed Him "according to the definite plan and foreknowledge of God" (2:23). When they wrought their rebellious will upon God's Servant, they were still doing what God's hand and God's plan had predestined (4:27, 28). God, we hear it again and again, raised Jesus from the dead (2:24; 3:15; 10:40). God exalted Him on high and glorified His Servant (2:33; 3:13; 5:31). God has ordained Him to be Judge of the living and the dead (10:42). The exalted Christ has received from the Father the promised Holy Spirit that He pours out upon His own—and that Spirit moves men to tell of "the mighty works of *God*" (2:11). The persecuted and praying Church bowed before God as the absolute and sovereign Lord of history, whose enemies cannot but do His will (4:24–28). They chose to obey God, even before the legitimate authorities He established for government (5:29).

The Church that submitted itself wholly to God as the Lord of history (4:28–29) also adored Him as Creator; the Church's prayer began, "Sovereign Lord, who made the heaven and the earth and the sea and everything in them" (4:24). When God sent His Son into the created world, into history, into humanity, He was speaking an unmistakable yes to His very good creation; and not only the prayer of the Church, but the whole life of the Church is witness to the joyous conviction that "everything created by God is good" (1Tm 4:4). The witness of the Church did not pass over or seek to minimize the full humanity of Jesus, His very human history, His sufferings, His death. Moreover, the new community did not withdraw to a wilderness asylum, but stayed and worked and witnessed where the Creator of the world and the Lord of history had placed them. And there was nothing sequestered or monastic about their fellowship. Their fellowship was a table fellowship; "they received their food with glad and generous hearts, praising God" (2:46, 47). It was a fellowship of families—they broke bread from house to house (2:46). It was a fellowship from which women were not excluded (1:14; 6:1; 8:3), but in which women played a rich and honorable part, as the example of Tabitha shows (9:36–41). A common care for the physical needs of the community was an important part of the church's life from the beginning (2:44, 45; 4:32–35). The apostles did not permit it to encroach upon or overshadow their prime task of prayer and the ministry of the word, but they did recognize its importance and made provision for it as a work that only the Holy Spirit could enable a man rightly to do (6:1–6).

These men knew God the Creator as the Father of the Lord Jesus Christ and therefore as their Father too; they knew Him as men living under the heaven of the forgiveness of sins. This transformed their lives and gave them a remarkable freedom from care and anxiety. It gave them "glad and generous hearts" (2:46). It enabled them to welcome suffering in their lives as another good gift from the Creator's hand (5:41). It filled their lives with the music of prayer, which accompanied all that they did and all that befell them (2:42; 4:24–30; 6:4; 12:5, 12). It set them free for love toward one another, so that "the full number of those who believed were of one heart and soul, and no one said that any of the things that belonged to him was his own" (4:32). It was no wonder that people felt a certain awe for them (2:43; 4:21; 5:13, 26); they lived lives that were an enacted doxology to God the Father of our Lord Jesus Christ.

The Church has rightly called our New Testament, the book that incorporates the word that grew on this soil, "The New Testament of our Lord and Savior Jesus Christ"; for it is the book that on every page calls Jesus Lord and gives to us the light of the knowledge of the glory of God in the face of Christ. But it is for that very reason the book of the Holy Trinity, for in it Jesus is called Lord to the glory of God the Father. And the New Testament is a book of the Holy Spirit, too, an inspired book. This brings us to the second major aspect of the life of the Early Church.

First-century Roman jug with bird head pattern.

The New People of God under the Power of the Spirit

The disciples knew the Holy Spirit from the Old Testament as the creative personal presence of God, which makes and shapes and interprets history, the power that moved over the face of the waters at creation (Gn 1:2); the power that came upon the Judges of Israel (Jgs 6:34; 14:6) and upon Israel's kings (1Sm 16:13, 14) and enabled them to do great things for the Lord and the Lord's people. They knew the Spirit as the power that enabled the prophets to say, "Thus says the LORD"—to interpret history as the arm of the Lord laid bare and to foretell what the Lord would yet do for the salvation of His people and all nations (Ac 1:16; 4:25). They knew that when the children of Israel resisted the leaders and prophets sent to

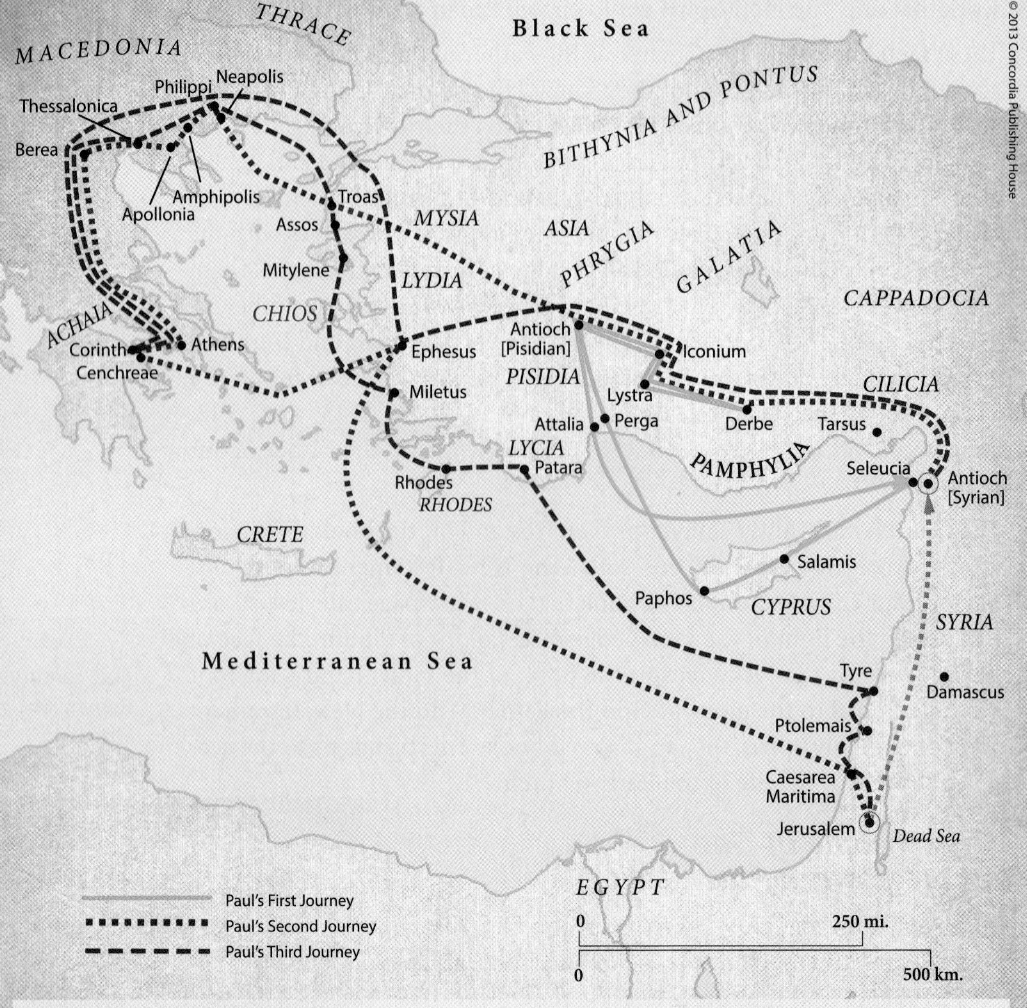

PAUL'S MISSIONARY JOURNEYS (ACTS 13–21)

First journey (AD 47–48): The Holy Spirit sent Saul, Barnabas, and John Mark from Antioch in Syria via Seleucia to Salamis, then overland to Paphos (Ac 13:1–12). The three continued to Perga, where John Mark left them for Jerusalem (13:13). Saul, also called Paul (13:9), and Barnabas continued to Antioch in Pisidia (13:14–50), Iconium (13:51–14:6a), Lystra, and Derbe (14:6b–20), from whence they retraced their steps back to Pisidian Antioch, then went to Attalia and Syrian Antioch (14:21–28).

Second journey (AD 49–51): Paul and Barnabas separated (15:36–39) while in Syrian Antioch. Paul and Silas went through Syria and Cilicia (15:40–41). They came to Derbe and Lystra, where Timothy joined them (16:1–5). The Spirit led them throughout Galatia and Phrygia to Troas, where they continued, via the island of Samothrace (not shown), to Macedonia; then they traveled to Neapolis and Philippi (16:6–40). They continued via Amphipolis and Apollonia to Thessalonica, Berea, Athens, and Corinth (17:1–18:17). Paul stayed 18 months there (18:11). He journeyed via Cenchreae and Ephesus to Caesarea Maritima, Jerusalem, and Syrian Antioch (18:18–22).

Third journey (AD 52–55): Paul took the inland route from Syrian Antioch and eventually arrived in Ephesus, where he stayed for two years and three months (18:23–19:41). He visited Macedonia and Achaia, and then sailed from Philippi to Troas (19:21; 20:1–12) on his way to Jerusalem. From Troas, he sailed via Assos, Mitylene, Miletus (where he met the Ephesian elders), Rhodes, and Patara to Tyre (20:13–21:6). He sailed to Ptolemais and Caesarea Maritima, and went on foot from there to Jerusalem (21:7–17).

them by God, they were resisting the Holy Spirit (7:51). They knew that the Spirit of the Lord was to rest upon the Messiah-Prince of the line of David and enable Him to establish God's rule of right over His people and to restore God's ruined creation to the peace of paradise (Is 11:1–10), that the Spirit of the Lord would come upon the Servant-Messiah and make Him the Covenant of the people and the Light to lighten the Gentiles (Lk 2:32). They knew that Jesus of Nazareth had been anointed by God with the Holy Spirit and had thus performed the mighty works that attested Him as Messiah and Savior (Ac 10:38). They knew that it was "through the Holy Spirit" that their risen Lord had given commandment to His chosen apostles (1:2). They had received the promise of the Spirit for themselves from Him, both in the days of His flesh (Lk 12:12) and in the 40 days after the resurrection (Ac 1:5, 8). But it was not until Pentecost had come that they experienced what their Lord had promised, what the prophet Joel had foretold for the last days (Ac 2:16, 17), the "pouring out" in unprecedented fullness of the Spirit of God upon "all flesh."

The 12 apostles received the Spirit (Ac 2:4; 4:8; 5:32; 10:19; 11:12). Paul, the apostle "untimely born" (1Co 15:8), received the Spirit, too, in peculiar fullness and strength. But what they received was not given to them to have and to hold as their private possession and prerogative; they were not only recipients of the Spirit but they also became vehicles of the Spirit (e.g., Ac 2:38; 8:18). The Spirit was poured out not only on apostles but also on prophets such as Agabus (11:28), on the seven chosen to serve (6:3, 5, 10) and on evangelists (7:55; 8:29, 39); on great and kindly leaders like Barnabas (11:24), on all believers (2:38; 4:31), on Jews, on Samaritans (8:15–18), and even (to the amazement of some Jewish Christians) on Gentiles (10:44, 45, 47; 11:15).

The Spirit filled the whole Church. The Spirit animated and governed the whole life of the new people of God. It is not only in utterance and in enraptured vision that the Spirit's working was manifested (though these are found in the life of the Early Church too); the men who spoke in other language at Pentecost were so far carried beyond the way of normal and ordinary speech that mockers could call them drunken (2:13). When the Spirit "fell" on the men of Samaria, the results were so striking that Simon the sorcerer wanted to purchase the power of the Spirit from the apostles—it seemed to him a very potent kind of magic (8:17–19); when the Spirit fell on Cornelius and his friends at Caesarea, they spoke "in tongues," in doxology (10:44–46; 11:15). Stephen, "full of the Holy Spirit," saw "the heavens opened, and the Son of Man standing at the right hand of God" (7:55–56).

But Luke's record attributes to the working of the Holy Spirit utterances and actions that our secularized thinking would consider ordinary and normal. Not only was the enraptured Peter of Pentecost filled with the Holy Spirit, but the Peter who would speak in sober defense before the Sanhedrin was no less Spirit-filled (4:8). As his Lord had promised, the Spirit taught him in that hour what he ought to say (Lk 12:12). The Spirit gave to the apostles functional power, a power that equipped them for their task of witnessing to the act of God in Christ, to the fact in history that spells the salvation of mankind (Ac 1:8; 5:32; 9:17, 20). The Spirit worked guidance for the apostle (10:19) and for the evangelist (8:29, 39). When the Spirit inspired the prophet Agabus, he produced no startling and exciting apocalyptic novelties to satisfy religious curiosity; he foretold a famine, in order that the Church might carefully plan and duly carry out her work of charity (11:28–30). The Spirit enabled men to "serve tables" in the Church, to provide for the widow and the fatherless in wise and sober charity; the seven chosen for this task must be, Peter told the Church, "men . . . full of the Spirit and of wisdom" (6:1–6). The martyr's vision of the opened heavens is not the only fruit of the Spirit in the life of Stephen, one of these seven men; the Spirit enabled him to do his work as servant of the Church for the poor and to acquit himself well in his disputes with the men of the synagogue (6:10).

The Church prayed in her hour of need (4:23) for courage to endure persecution, not for escape from persecution. God manifested His presence among them: "the place in which they were gathered together was shaken, and they were all filled with the Holy Spirit" (4:31). What was the fruit of the Spirit? What was the result of this inspiration? The result was characteristic of the whole piety of the First Church under the power of the Spirit; the aim and goal of its religious life was not self-enrichment or self-fulfillment; there was no trace of egotistical piety here. The result was the will to unity and the will to witness: "They . . . continued to speak the word of God with *boldness*" (4:31). The word we are forced to translate with "boldness" is the outstanding characteristic of the Spirit-filled Church in action. It signifies that free, glad, courageous confidence, that robust health of faith that comes from the assurance of free access to God the Father given in Christ by the Spirit. It is the energetic religious health that made Peter and John say, "We cannot but speak of what we have seen and heard" (4:20); it is that high confidence of faith that made Saul, when he had received the Holy Spirit (9:17), proclaim Jesus as Son of God in the synagogue "immediately" (9:20), "preaching boldly" both in Damascus and in Jerusalem (9:27–29).

This boldness is boldness under the Lordship of Jesus. It is the Church that walks "in the fear of the Lord," which enjoys the "comfort of the Holy

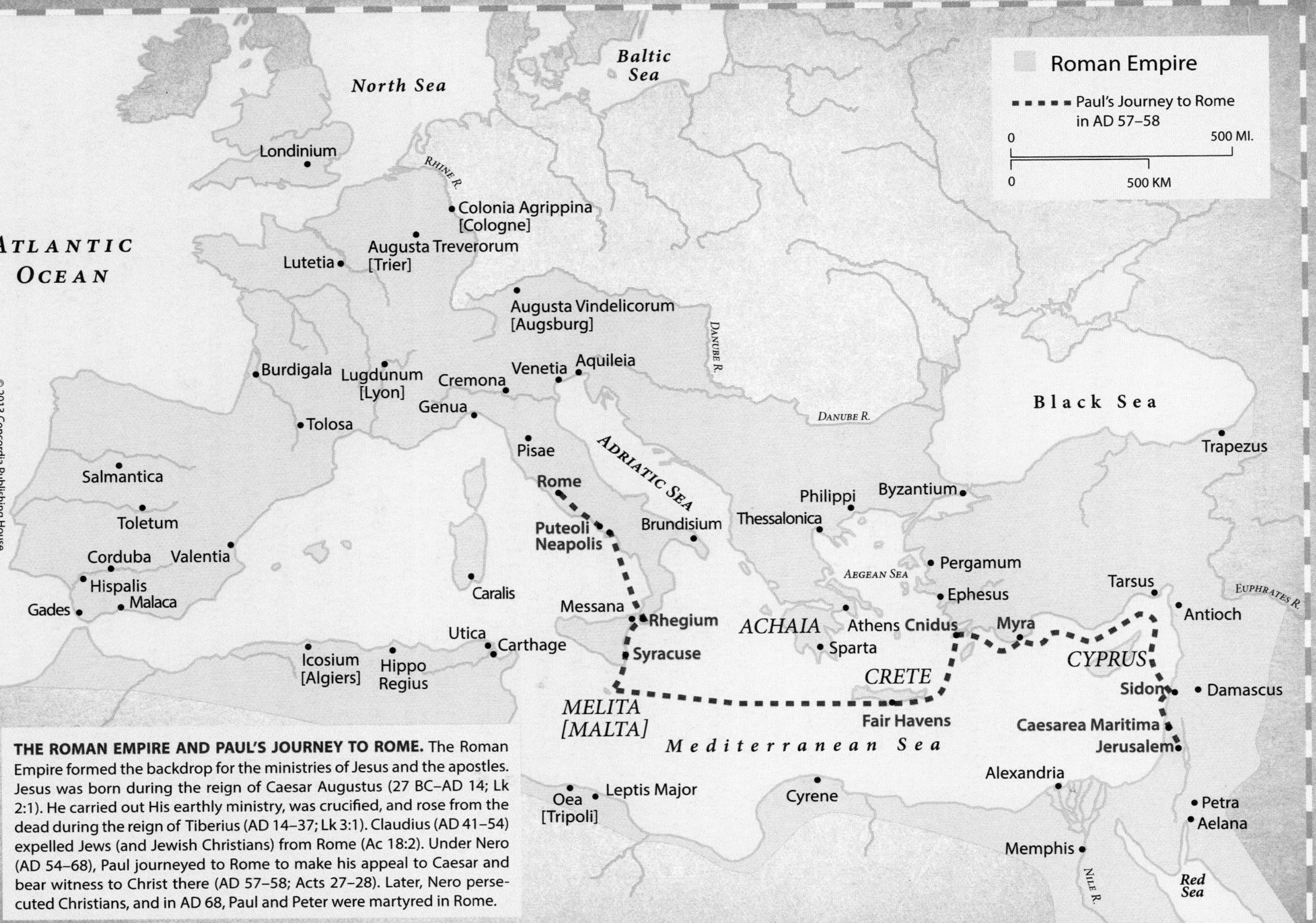

THE ROMAN EMPIRE AND PAUL'S JOURNEY TO ROME. The Roman Empire formed the backdrop for the ministries of Jesus and the apostles. Jesus was born during the reign of Caesar Augustus (27 BC–AD 14; Lk 2:1). He carried out His earthly ministry, was crucified, and rose from the dead during the reign of Tiberius (AD 14–37; Lk 3:1). Claudius (AD 41–54) expelled Jews (and Jewish Christians) from Rome (Ac 18:2). Under Nero (AD 54–68), Paul journeyed to Rome to make his appeal to Caesar and bear witness to Christ there (AD 57–58; Acts 27–28). Later, Nero persecuted Christians, and in AD 68, Paul and Peter were martyred in Rome.

Spirit" (9:31). It is a boldness under the reign of God, who gives His Spirit "to those who *obey* Him" (5:32). This disciplined and obedient character of the Church's boldness is especially apparent in the Church's use of the Old Testament. As Jesus in the days of His flesh was led by the Spirit not beyond Scripture but into it, so that He repelled Satan with "It is written" (Lk 4:1–13), so the apostles were led into Scripture by the guidance of the Spirit. They used the Old Testament gladly and freely, in the confidence that in it God was by His Spirit speaking to them there and then in their own day; they appropriated it fully as *their* book, the book of the New Testament people of God. Peter's sermon at Pentecost is typical. "The man is crammed with Scripture" is Luther's comment on it. And when Philip, prompted by the Spirit, joined the eunuch who was reading from the prophet Isaiah, he opened his mouth, and "*beginning with this Scripture* he told him the good news about Jesus" (Ac 8:35). The Spirit-filled Church under the living word of the apostles was far from feeling any aversion to the written Word of God's elder revelation; she perceived in the written Old Testament the voice and the operation of the Holy Spirit and gratefully used the inspired book.

The robust religious health of mind and will that the Spirit gave the Early Church is apparent also in the language of the Church. In a sense, the Holy Spirit did create a new language in the last days; as every student of the New Testament learns, a language richly individual, with forces and connotations all its own. But there is nothing strained, far-fetched, or esoteric about it; there is no mumbo-jumbo. It is a perfectly natural and open language, rooted in the life and history of the Jew and Greek to whom the Church bore witness.

That is the second major aspect of the history that produced our New Testament. It is a history in which the Spirit of God moves creatively upon the waters. To speak of the word that grew on this soil and sped and triumphed in this history as an *inspired* word, wholly inspired, is not to impose an alien theory upon the word; it is simply a recognition of its character as a part of the history of the New Testament people of God. It is inspired because God the Lord of history made it so; it is verbally inspired because God deals with men on person-to-person terms, in terms of converse with men; it is the product of the Spirit of the living God and vehicle of that Spirit still, inspired and inspiring.

The New People of God in the World's Last Days

All previous revelation of God has led up to and prepared for this: "All the prophets who have spoken . . . also proclaimed these days" (Ac 3:24). The prophets, whom a rebellious Israel persecuted, "announced beforehand the coming of the Righteous One" (7:52). All subsequent history is determined by this single, unparalleled, eschatological fact, the fact of the resurrection of Jesus. For this is not merely the fact that Jesus of Nazareth is alive, that "He presented Himself alive to them after His suffering" (1:3). His resurrection is the great turning point, from death to life, for all people and all creation. He is the Author of life (3:15). The apostles proclaimed *the resurrection from the dead* "in Jesus" (4:2)—they proclaimed that the man Jesus had crossed the frontier of death into everlasting life for all. All history is moving with divine inevitability, with the "must" of the will of God (3:21), toward the goal of all God's ways, toward the return of the Christ, the time of "refreshing . . . from the presence of the Lord," and the restoration of all creation, the establishing of all things that God spoke by the mouth of His holy prophets from of old (3:19–21).

With the resurrection of Jesus, the new life—the real and eternal life of the world to come—has become a present reality, breaking miraculously into the present world of people living under the sign of death. To proclaim and to impart this new life was the mission of the apostles. To the apostles, the witnesses of the resurrection of Jesus (1:3; 1:22; 10:41), the angel of the Lord said, "Go and stand in the temple and speak to the people all the words of this life" (5:20). The signs and wonders done through them were the enacted proclamation of "this life." They were "the powers of the age to come" (Heb 6:5), active even now, tokens and predictions of the new world of God, in which disease and death shall be no more. The "name of Jesus" is strong to save and can restore the lame man to perfect health because God has raised Him from the dead and made Him to be the Author of life (Ac 3:15, 16).

This consciousness of being the people of God in the world's last days, of being witnesses to the accomplished fact of the Resurrection, the fact that is the dawn of the last day and the assurance of its perfect coming, filled the Church with a joy that nothing could quench, not even death. The dying Stephen was the characteristic representative of the New Testament Church. The Church sees the heavens opened, the world of God welcoming mankind, and sees the Son of Man standing at the right hand of God, about to return, that Son of Man who came to seek and to save (Lk 19:10); and the Church knows that He will save to the uttermost, that His coming will be the end of the world's agony and the time of eternal refreshing for His people (Ac 3:19, 20). The Church is "born again to a living hope through the resurrection of Jesus Christ from the dead" (1Pt 1:3).

The Church knows, too, that "the Son of Man is going to come" in judgment and "will repay every person according to what he has done" (Mt 16:27); and the Church lives and works and hopes with a sober sense of responsibility. The Church knows that the present is pregnant with the future and has in it the issues of salvation and judgment. The Lord God has in Jesus raised up the Prophet whom Moses had foretold; people must give heed to His Word or be destroyed (Ac 3:22, 23). The apostles' cry was: Repent! Be saved from the judgment now, be saved in Him whose name alone can save (2:21, 38, 40; 4:12), before He comes to judge the living and the dead (10:42).

The New Testament that grew up amid this history, history interpreted by the Spirit of God and understood by faith as events in time moving surely toward God's goal of ultimate salvation and final judgment, is a book of buoyant end times hope and a book of sober and realistic end times responsibility. It is a book of the last days through and through, and speaks with the urgency and finality of the last days.

The Apostolic Proclamation in the First Church

The first 12 chapters of Acts give us the best and fullest examples of that apostolic *kerygma* in their record of the preaching of Peter (2:14–40; 3:12–26; 4:8–12; 10:34–43) and Stephen (7:2–53). We may round out the record with the sermon of Paul in the synagogue at Pisidian Antioch recorded in 13:16–41. The message of these sermons is essentially a reproduction of the basic proclamation of Jesus Himself, now told in the light of His resurrec-

An example of a Roman basilica preferred for early Christian architecture, beginning in the fourth century. The earliest church buildings were houses.

tion and exaltation. Jesus had opened His messianic ministry in Galilee with the words, "The time is fulfilled, and the kingdom of God is at hand; repent and believe in the gospel" (Mk 1:15).

Jesus marked His appearance as the fulfillment of the prophet's prediction and of Israel's hope. And the most obvious fact about the apostolic *kerygma* is the assertion that what happened to Jesus of Nazareth happened "according to the Scriptures," the assertion that He is in the whole compass of His history the fulfillment of Old Testament prophecy. Whether it be Peter preaching it to Jews (Ac 2:16, 25; 3:18, 22, 24; 4:11) or to Gentiles (10:43), or whether it be Paul (13:23, 27, 32), or whether it be the Spirit-filled Stephen (7:52), the apostolic *kerygma* was unanimous in proclaiming: all the voices of the Old Testament, all the hopes of Israel are fulfilled in Him whom we proclaim as Lord and Christ. As Paul put it: "All the promises of God find their Yes in Him" (2Co 1:20).

"The kingdom of God is at hand" (Mk 1:15). When Jesus spoke these words, He meant nothing less than this: "The kingdom of God is present in My person." The whole record of Him in the Gospels says just this, that God is establishing His reign in these last days by making Jesus Lord in the power of the Holy Spirit. Jesus can say to those who blasphemously reject Him: "But if it is by the *Spirit* of God that *I* cast out demons, then the kingdom of *God* has come upon you" (Mt 12:28). If, then, the apostolic proclamation asserts that Jesus is Lord and Christ, it is proclaiming the kingdom of God, just as Jesus' word had proclaimed it. If Peter says, "God has made Him both Lord and Christ, this Jesus whom you crucified" (Ac 2:36), or if Philip preaches "good news about the kingdom of God and the name of Jesus Christ" (8:12), that is consentient witness to one great fact, one great act of God. For Jesus is Lord to the glory of God the Father, the Father who did great works through Jesus, who gave Him up into death as the Servant who makes "many to be accounted righteous" (Is 53:11), exalted Him at His right hand, and gave Him the Spirit to pour out upon His own. To proclaim the kingdom of God and the Lordship of Jesus is therefore necessarily to proclaim the Holy Spirit too, for the Spirit is indissolubly connected with both. The presence of the Spirit in the earthly life of Jesus is the evidence of His Lordship even then (Ac 10:38); the gift of the Spirit is the witness to His exaltation (2:33–36) and the means whereby the exalted Lord exercises His gracious Lordship for the salvation of all (2:28; 5:32).

The kingdom of God, the Lordship of Jesus the Christ, the outpouring of the Holy Spirit, all mark the days in which this news is uttered as the last great days, the age of fulfillment, the beginning of the end, the time when the new life of the world to come has broken into the old world of death in the person of Him who is the Author of life. And this life becomes man's possession by the Spirit, the Lord and Giver of life. All history now moves from this event with a new and unheard-of urgency toward the end of the end, toward the judgment on all who refuse this new life, toward the consummation of all things, the new heaven and the new earth in which the righteousness of God is forever and fully at home.

"Repent, and believe in the Gospel." Jesus by His words and deeds demanded a decision: "Whoever is not with Me is against Me" (Mt 12:30). The apostolic proclamation of Jesus' words and deeds is news, is history. It is real, vital news; the story of the life, death, and exaltation of Jesus of Nazareth is not a tale that can be told or left untold at will. It does not diminish in immediacy and importance as the passage of days removes it from the present. It is an ever-present reality in the inspired Word that conveys it; it confronts, stirs, shakes, and moves us now. It calls for repentance, and it moves us to repentance and faith. In Jesus, the Lord God has laid bare His arm for the last time in history, and mankind is confronted with the choice, now, of having that almighty arm for him or against him. There is no neutral corner where we may stand, no place where we may stay and await developments, as Gamaliel hoped to do (Ac 5:38–39). In Acts, the apostles proclaim justification in Jesus Christ, respecting the role of human traditions and the role of Israel in first receiving God's Law, but insisting that salvation is through faith (10:43; 15:9–11).

Application

Ch 1 Boldly pray to Jesus, and acknowledge Him as your Lord. Your good standing today and your eternal tomorrow flow from Jesus' victory over the grave, His ascension, and His enthronement at the Father's right hand. He will prepare your way before you. Since our Lord is present with us till the end of the age, He will knit together in love His faithful people with Himself and with one another.

Ch 2 Humility before the Holy Spirit is in order, along with sheer wonder that God gives Himself to people of all nations. Rejoice that God pours out His Spirit in Baptism and multiplies His blessings to us in daily repentance and forgiveness. He makes a new Israel, a new house of David—the Church! How sad is our indifference and our compromises with the world. Yet the Holy Spirit still dwells and works among us; we still have the apostles' teaching embodied in the New Testament Scriptures. How blessed are we in such heavenly fellowship!

3:1–4:31 Shudder when you hear people use Jesus' holy name as a curse rather than as a cure. Call on Him in all your needs, and use His name reverently and gladly to bestow the Father's gifts on others. The risen Lord brings to light our hidden guilt and lifts the burden that crushes every sinner. Though His Word points out your shame, His grace will wipe away your sin. He pledges His life and blessing to you in the midst of all difficulties. Remember to pray for boldness when faced with persecution. Rejoice that the Lord refashions you in His image by His Word and Spirit.

4:32–5:42 Lavish love on your brothers and sisters in Christ, just as Jesus lavished His love on us all and gave Himself unto death for the worst of sinners. Woe to those who disturb and deceive the Lord's Church! God's power to change lives is still at work today. His greatest work always remains the forgiveness of sins. Pray for bold witness and the blessing of peaceful service. When trouble threatens, have confidence that the crucified and risen Savior will keep us steadfast in His grace.

Chs 6–8 Church conflict can often be resolved for the benefit of the ministries, preaching, teaching, and physical care of God's people. If your congregation is experiencing conflict, take counsel and comfort from this passage. Also, rest your heart and confidence in the Lord, who sends His Spirit and heals His Church. When persecution confronts you, be faithful to Jesus, whatever the consequences may be. Remember that He is always faithful to you and can deliver you. Trust that your Lord is at work in the midst of such circumstances. As the cross shows, He can work blessings for you and for others, despite all curses and condemnations. View people of every race and kind as precious to Jesus. His blood washes away all sin, and His Spirit makes us one. God and His grace cannot be bought. He will transform you and bless your service according to His gifts and good pleasure. Rejoice in the Word and Baptism you have received, through which the Holy Spirit continues to work in your life.

9:1–31 All we are and all we do depends on His blessing and calling. Trust that the Lord is able to change people's lives—even people you regard as utterly lost and despicable. How great is our Lord and His grace! For the sake of the Gospel, support and defend the witness of your brothers and sisters in Christ. The Lord your Savior is your defender. The Lord will likewise watch over the future of your congregation. Proclaim Christ! The Savior will bless and keep you.

9:32–11:18 As God grants you opportunity, share the love of Jesus by caring for the sick. His abiding care will sustain you in every need. He prepares and guides our lives in accordance with His good purposes. Therefore, commend your life and ways to your Lord, who at all times has you on His heart. We are powerless to hallow anything. Pray that God's gifts and blessings may be hallowed among us. Through the Gospel, the Lord cleanses and hallows us. The Holy Spirit unites one and all in the Body of Christ. Therefore, live a life of daily repentance, and glorify God for His lavish blessings and gifts to you and all people.

11:19–30 As believers grow in faith, they commit themselves to acts of service. Men of God, such as Barnabas, not only confirm the work of the Holy Spirit among believers but also ensure that new believers are nurtured in the faith through instruction (Mt 28:19–20). Barnabas becomes for us a beloved example of one who encourages others in the faith.

Ch 12 By His crucifixion and resurrection, Christ has passed through death and draws us safely through to life. He alone holds the keys of death and will leave none of His own behind. Nothing can separate believers from the love of Christ. He fulfills His purpose for us in life and in death; therefore, we have joy. Yet God can also decisively topple evil. In mercy to us, He sent His Son to the cross to condemn evil and rescue us. Living in forgiveness, we eagerly await the day when our Lord and Savior Jesus Christ takes us to live with Him forever in heaven.

Chs 13–14 The Holy Spirit calls us by the Gospel and enlightens us with His gifts, especially those of teaching and spreading God's Word, which we use in God's service and to the benefit of others (cf 1Co 12). The unbelieving world often responds in opposition to the message of salvation. Yet, the Gospel of Christ's death and resurrection, which fulfilled the Old Testament promises of salvation, "is the power of God for salvation to everyone who believes" (Rm 1:16). The word of grace from God is sufficient for us (2Co 12:9), but the Lord may accompany His message with miraculous signs that testify to its power. Neither our faith nor our missionary achievements are ultimately our doing. It is God who opens the door of faith—for us and for those to whom we witness.

15:1–35 Obedience to the Law is a burden or yoke no one can bear, neither Jew nor Gentile (v 10; cf 13:39). However, our salvation through faith alone also empowers us to live with care and respect for others. Seek peace based on God's Word and mutual care of fellow believers. The Lord, who cares deeply for you, will bless and provide for you in Christ, our peace.

15:36–18:23 God promises to work all things for good, even our faults and failings (cf Rm 8:28; Gn 50:20), as He forgives our sins in Christ. Encouragement is still a great blessing to our faith. Share your hope and joy! Jesus is our strength amid all troubles and challenges. God directs us as His

An early depiction of martyrdom in which St. Lawrence, a Roman deacon, approaches a gridiron upon which he was cast. The Greek word for "witness" (martyr) came to mean one who died while bearing witness to Christ.

messengers to the people and places He would have us go. His grace is not bounded by our weakness but serves His good purposes in Christ. Although the Gospel message is foolishness to people of this world, God desires to engage all people with His Word and, by the Spirit's power, to open their hearts and minds to the good news of Jesus and His resurrection.

18:24–21:16 While our knowledge in this life will always be incomplete, teachers should strive to learn everything God has revealed and teach it fully and properly to His people. God's Word, including His Word in the Baptism instituted by Jesus Christ, is the power by which we believe. Jesus Christ is the fulfillment of God's promises of eternal salvation for all. By the power of Jesus' name, you have been forgiven of all sin (Ac 2:38) and rescued from the fiercest evil, the devil himself! Believers in Christ may still suffer unjustly or, at times, justly because of their sins. In either case, the Lord brings us through suffering to His eternal kingdom, even while giving us opportunities to serve. Jesus has given—and still gives—temporal and eternal blessings, so we likewise are to give of ourselves to others. Yet, we can never outgive our generous Savior. Contrary to all human logic, God's plan of salvation was carried out through Christ for the forgiveness of all our failures. This shows us that God can make all things—however fearful or illogical they may seem to us—work out for our good. We are always on His heart.

21:17–23:35 We are often tempted to judge fellow Christians on the basis of things not specifically directed in God's Word. As God's forgiven people, we are motivated and inspired to seek the truth in all matters, especially as we interact with our neighbor. Pursuing our own agenda often leads to a dead

Inscription forbidding entry to the temple.

end. But because Christ washes away our sin, like Paul we can pray, "What shall I do, Lord?" And we can be sure that our Lord will hear and guide us. God established the governing authorities to bring a degree of peace and civil righteousness to our troubled world. However, our ultimate hope is in the Lord. Christ's Gospel brings eternal peace and righteousness before the highest court: heaven. Paul's family is an example to us of how family members may support one another in trying times and call upon legitimate authority in support of God's people. Good government and family are blessings of God's providence that enable the Gospel to spread among us.

Ch 24 God's Law can hurt our pride; we would rather avoid hearing about our sins and eternal judgment. Though God's Law and judgment are sharp, His Gospel grants full release. Through Jesus' sacrificial death and His resurrection from the dead, God forgives us and builds us up. He empowers us to proclaim His mercy. Rather than eternal death, Jesus grants us the riches of eternal life.

Chs 25–26 Governments exist to punish evil and promote good in this life. Support the proper functions of government. Because we are born in sin (Ps 51:5), we all have an ungodly past, even if we have never persecuted Christians the way Paul did. Be assured that Christ forgives and delivers us, just as He did Paul. The Lord turns us from darkness to light when we hear and believe the beautiful message of Jesus' life, death, and resurrection.

Chs 27–28 Have you ever blamed God for the problems in your life? Have you forgotten that even through hardships, God is working for your benefit (Rm 8:28)? Rejoice today that His love and care for you and other believers are infinite (Rm 8:38–39)! When the trials of life weigh us down, it is easy for us to lose hope and stop trusting God. Yet God promises He will never leave us nor forsake us (Dt 31:6, 8; Heb 13:5). By God's miraculous power in Christ, He rescues His people from sin, death, and ignorance. Pray that the Lord would break up the hardness of your heart. Rejoice in the message of forgiveness and life through Jesus Christ that is for all people, including you.

Canonicity

For more on the history of Acts as a canonical book, see Gerhard's comments below.

Herod's Temple Aerial view showing outer courts

20 BC–AD 70

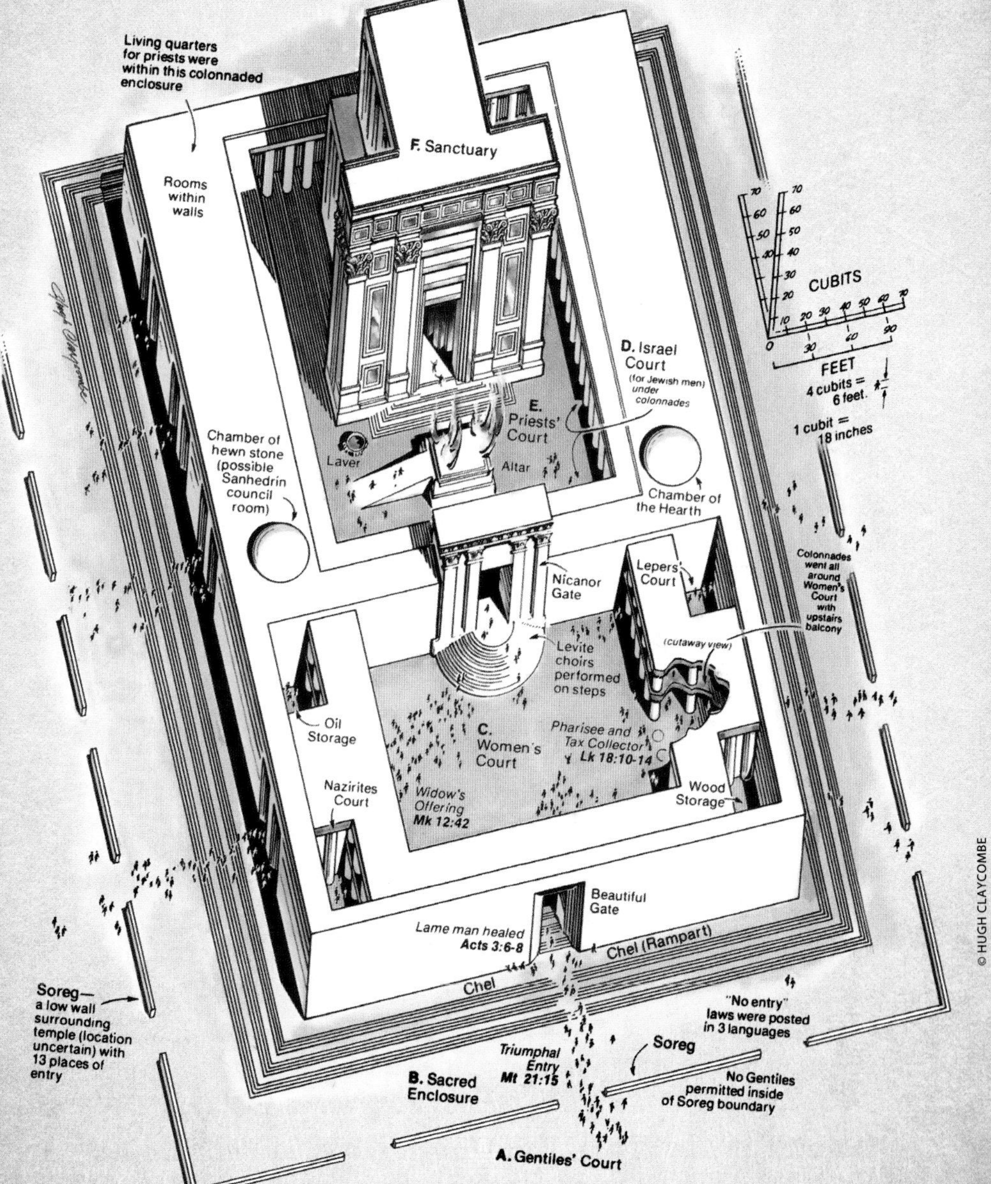

Living quarters for priests were within this colonnaded enclosure

Rooms within walls

F. Sanctuary

D. Israel Court (for Jewish men) under colonnades

E. Priests' Court

Laver

Altar

Chamber of hewn stone (possible Sanhedrin council room)

Chamber of the Hearth

Nicanor Gate

Lepers' Court

Levite choirs performed on steps

(cutaway view)

Colonnades went all around Women's Court with upstairs balcony

Oil Storage

C. Women's Court

Pharisee and Tax Collector Lk 18:10-14

Nazirites Court

Widow's Offering **Mk 12:42**

Wood Storage

Beautiful Gate

Lame man healed **Acts 3:6-8**

Chel (Rampart)

Chel

Soreg—a low wall surrounding temple (location uncertain) with 13 places of entry

"No entry" laws were posted in 3 languages

Soreg

Triumphal Entry **Mt 21:15**

No Gentiles permitted inside of Soreg boundary

B. Sacred Enclosure

A. Gentiles' Court

CUBITS

0 10 20 30 40 50 60 70

FEET

0 30 60 90

4 cubits = 6 feet.

1 cubit = 18 inches

Lutheran Theologians on Acts

Luther

"Contrary to what has sometimes been the practice, this book should not be read or regarded as though St. Luke had written about the personal work or history of the apostles simply as an example of good works or good life. Even St. Augustine and many others have looked upon the fact that the apostles had all things in common with Christians [Acts 2:44–45; 4:32–37] as the best example which the book contains. Yet this practice did not last long and in time had to stop. Rather it should be noted that by this book St. Luke teaches the whole of Christendom, even to the end of the world, that the true and chief article of Christian doctrine is this: We must all be justified alone by faith in Jesus Christ, without any contribution from the law or help from our works.

"This doctrine is the chief intention of the book and the author's principal reason for writing it. Therefore he emphasizes so powerfully not only the preaching of the apostles about faith in Christ, how both Gentiles and Jews must thereby be justified without any merits or works, but also the examples and the instances of this teaching, how the Gentiles as well as Jews were justified through the gospel alone, without the law.

"As St. Peter testifies in chapters 10[:34–47] and 15[:7–11], in this matter God made no distinction between Jews and Gentiles; just as he gave the Holy Spirit through the gospel to the Gentiles who were living without the law, so he gave him to the Jews through the gospel, and not through the law or because of their own works and merits. Thus in this book St. Luke puts side by side both the doctrine about faith and the examples of faith.

"Therefore this book might well be called a commentary on the epistles of St. Paul. For what Paul teaches and insists upon with words and passages of Scripture, St. Luke here points out and proves with examples and instances to show that it has happened and must happen in the way St. Paul teaches, namely, that no law, no work justifies men, but only faith in Christ. Here, then, in this book you find a beautiful mirror in which you can see that this is true: *Sola fides justificat*, 'faith alone justifies.' For all the examples and incidents contained in this book are sure and comforting testimonies to this doctrine; they neither deceive nor lie to you.

"For consider how St. Paul himself was converted [Acts 9:1–19], and how the Gentile, Cornelius, was converted through St. Peter's word—the angel telling him beforehand that Peter would preach to him and that thereby he would be saved [Acts 10:1–8, 30–33]. Look at the proconsul Sergius [Acts 13:7] and at all the cities where Paul and Barnabas preached. Look at the first council of the apostles at Jerusalem, in chapter 15; look at all the preaching of SS. Peter, Paul, Stephen, and Philip. You will find that it all adds up to one thing: we must come into grace and be justified only through faith in Christ, without law and works.

"By means of this book, used in this way, we can silence in a masterly and effective way the loquacity of opponents who [keep on] pointing us to the law and to our own works, and reveal their foolish unwisdom before all the world. Therefore St. Luke says too that these illustrations of faith amazed the pious Jews who had become believers, and that the unbelieving Jews became maddened and foolish over it. And this was no surprise, for they had been raised in the law and had been accustomed to it ever since Abraham. So it was bound to vex them that the Gentiles, who were without law and God, should be equal to themselves in God's grace." (AE 35:363–64)

Gerhard

"In his commentary, Chrysostom notes that already at his time there was doubt as to 'who is the author of that account.' Erasmus, however, rightly admonishes that 'only the unlettered and inept' doubted or could have doubted it. For in fact, with careful planning, immediately in the introduction to Acts, Luke mentions the Gospel that he wrote to declare that he was the author of both writings and, by the memory of the Gospel that many already accepted with praise and veneration, to obtain the same confidence and grace for the book of the 'Acts of the Apostles.' From this, in his preface to this book, Jerome writes: 'There is no doubt that Luke, the physician from Antioch, wrote this book.' Jerome again, *De vir. illustr.*: 'Luke, the disciple of the apostle (Paul) and his companion on every journey, wrote a Gospel. . . . He also published another fine book that is known by the title the "Acts of the Apostles," ' etc. Sophronius, on Luke: 'He wrote his Gospel in accord with what he had heard; however, the Acts of the Apostles he arranged in accord with what he himself observed.' Bede, on Acts: 'Luke wrote the things that the apostles did, which he believed were enough to edify the faith of those who read and heard. He did this in such a way that this is the only book worthy of confidence in the Church that tells about the activities of the apostles, whereas all those are reproved who have dared to write what the apostles said and did without that faithfulness which was necessary.' This monostich is prefixed to the scholia of Oecumenius: 'The Book of Acts that Luke wrote.' Bishop Dorotheus of Tyre relates that Luke wrote this book 'at Paul's command,' and Nicephorus also confirms this (*Hist.*, bk. 2, c. 43). The primary, predisposing [*proegoumene*] cause, however, is the Holy Spirit Himself, who wanted to have down in writing what is contained in this book for the advantage of the Church until the end of the world. Therefore He impelled His instrument to do this holy work.

"In *De vir. illustr.*, Jerome mentions that Luke wrote this book in Rome. The time of writing they set as AD 60, in the fourth year of Nero's rule and the twenty-seventh year after Paul's conversion. They also note that it contains as many chapters as records of years contained therein. Although Luke was Syrian by nationality, he nevertheless wrote this account in Greek, as he did also his Gospel. Epiphanius reports (*Haeres.* 30, *contra Ebionaeos*): 'This book was formerly preserved in Hebrew in the treasuries of the Jews in Tiberias.' Let the trustworthiness of this matter be in the hands of the reader. Even if there were such a thing, it has to be certain that it was a translation rather than the original writing. Jerome points out (on Isaiah 6): 'The Greek language that Luke uses is quite elegant, in which Hebraisms are scattered occasionally.' Anyone who reads it will grasp that Luke used a style not unlike that which is used in the Greek version of the Old Testament. From this, one concludes that Luke was studiously explaining [the Greek Old Testament]." (ThC E1 § 253)

Questions People Ask about Acts

Theudas

In Acts 5:36 we find a statement of Luke's that certain critics see as an error on his part. It is the reference to a revolutionary by the name of Theudas, who before the days of the census of AD 6 fomented trouble and perished with his followers. Those who here accuse Luke of making a misstatement quote Josephus (*Ant* 20:97–98), according to whose account a certain Theudas arose in revolt during the procuratorship of Fadus (AD 44–46). Luke, it is alleged, in reporting the speech of Gamaliel, fell into an anachronism, dating the career of Theudas too early by about 40 years. One at once inquires why Josephus should be thought to be more reliable than Luke, when the latter has now, especially by the research of Sir William Ramsay, been shown to be a historian of the first order. On the other hand, the famous German scholar Theodore Zahn has shown that the work of Josephus at times lacks accuracy.

There are a number of other considerations, however, that entirely remove the suspicion that Luke here has committed a blunder. To begin with, the mere fact that Josephus does not mention this particular Theudas is no proof that Luke in Ac 5:36 is not speaking of a historical person. Again, the years before AD 6 and this year itself saw many disturbances in Israel, as the narrative of Josephus bears out. Theudas may have been one of the unnamed insurrectionists alluded to by this historian. The name Theudas was a fairly common one; there is no reason why there should not have been another man thus named around AD 6, as well as in AD 45. Or it may be that Theudas was the second name of a disturber whose misdeeds Josephus has mentioned under a different name. Our attention is especially attracted by a slave called Simon, who at the time of the death of Herod the Great (4 BC) attempted to seize control of Israel (*Ant* 17:273–77; *War* 2:57–59), but instead of attaining his objective, came to a miserable end. It is quite possible that he originally bore the name Theudas and changed it to the popular name Simon when he came forward with his claims. Those who are particularly interested in this question can consult the passages in Josephus that relate to this period, and various possibilities accounting for Gamaliel's reference to Theudas as given in Ac 5:36 will easily suggest themselves.

Purchase of Potter's Field

Matthew 27:3, 7–8 reports: "Then when Judas, His betrayer, saw that Jesus was condemned, he changed his mind and brought back the thirty pieces of silver to the chief priests and the elders. . . . So they took counsel and bought with them the potter's field as a burial place for strangers. Therefore that field has been called the Field of Blood to this day."

Acts 1:18 records: "Now this man acquired a field with the reward of his wickedness, and falling headlong he burst open in the middle and all his bowels gushed out."

Is there a disagreement between the account of Matthew and the words in Acts? The former says that Judas returned the 30 pieces of silver paid him for the betrayal of Jesus and that the Jewish leaders purchased a field with this sum of money. The latter implies that Judas himself bought a field with the reward of iniquity. If we turn to the Greek text of Ac 1:18, we find that a more accurate rendering of the original would be: "Now this man obtained (or acquired) a piece of land with the wages of iniquity." What the money of Judas did is here ascribed to Judas himself. We have here a figure of speech with which we are all familiar and that we ourselves frequently employ. For example, let us say that Mrs. Hatfield bequeaths a large sum of money to the city, leaving it to the officials to decide how the money is to be invested. The city council decides to use it for the purchase of a park. What would be more natural than to say, "Mrs. Hatfield procured that park"? Of course it was not for herself but for the city. Hence the language employed in Acts is not contradicting the account of Matthew, but it relates merely the result of the incident, ascribing to Judas what his money accomplished. The Greek verb for "obtain" or "acquire" is the same as in Mt 10:9 concerning the equipment of the disciples on their missionary journey (see previous discussion under that topic). It is quite probable that the Jewish officials considered the money legally to be Judas's property and therefore bought the field with it in his name.

The Death of Judas

Matthew 27:5 states: "And throwing down the pieces of silver into the temple, he departed, and he went and hanged himself."

Acts 1:18 says: "Now this man acquired a field with the reward of his wickedness, and falling headlong he burst open in the middle and all his bowels gushed out."

People have been perturbed at finding that apparently Matthew describes the manner in which Judas Iscariot died differently from the Book of Acts. Matthew says that Judas hanged himself; Acts states that Judas fell headlong and was crushed by the impact. The two statements made about the death of Judas are different. But is there a discrepancy here? Does Matthew say that Judas did not fall? Does Acts say that Judas did not hang himself? The reader may immediately see that this is simply another instance where both versions are true, one supplementing the other.

Judas, who zealously followed Jesus, ultimately betrayed him. This early mosaic depicts Judas using his pallium garment to hold a crown, perhaps representing his apostleship or the eternal life he did not inherit.

It should be noted, however, before we harmonize the two passages, that the phrase in Acts for "falling headlong" occurs only in the Scriptures in Ac 1:18 (known as a *hapax legomenon*). In this case it occurs nowhere else in Greek literature either. The literal meaning of the Greek word that the ESV translates as "falling" is "becoming." The word translated as "headlong" has two possible meanings: (1) prone, face downward, headfirst, or headlong; or (2) swollen.

In either case the harmonization of Matthew and Acts poses no serious problem. Either Judas hanged himself from a tree on the brink of a precipice overlooking a valley, and the limb or rope gave way, causing him to fall and to be mangled as Acts describes; or Judas's body hung unnoticed for some time, until swelling resulted in his body bursting in the middle.

FURTHER STUDY

Lay/Bible Class Resources

Balge, Richard. *Acts*. PBC. St. Louis: Concordia, 2004. ❧ Lutheran author. Excellent for Bible classes. Based on the NIV translation.

Barry, A. L. *To the Ends of the Earth: A Journey through Acts*. St. Louis: Concordia, 1997. ❧ Written as a travel guide. Companion to Acts and the Christian life of witness and service by a former president of The Lutheran Church—Missouri Synod.

Engfehr, Lois M., ed. *Acts: The Gospel throughout the World*. GWFT. St. Louis: Concordia, 1996. ❧ Lutheran author. Ten-session Bible study, including leader's notes and discussion questions.

Life by His Word. St. Louis: Concordia, 2009. ❧ More than 1,500 reproducible one-page Bible studies covering each chapter of the canonical Scriptures. Page references to *The Lutheran Study Bible*. CD-Rom and downloadable.

Maas, Korey, Edward Westcott, Donna Streufert, Jerald C. Joersz, Paul Maier, Erwin Kolb, and Edward A. Engelbrecht. *Acts: Parts 1 and 2*. Leaders Guide and Enrichment Magazine/Study Guide. LL. St. Louis: Concordia, 2001, 2004. ❧ Two in-depth, nine-session Bible studies with individual, small group, and lecture portions.

Marshall, I. Howard. *Acts*. TNTC. Downers Grove, IL: InterVarsity Press, 2008. ❧ Compact commentary interacting with a variety of English translations. A popular but generally helpful evangelical treatment of the text containing some mildly critical overtones.

Church Worker Resources

Harrison, Everett F. *Acts: The Expanding Church*. Chicago: Moody, 1976. ❧ A very helpful exposition written in a simple style.

Lenski, R. C. H. *The Interpretation of the Acts of the Apostles*. Columbus, OH: Wartburg Press, 1944. ❧ An old standard by a Lutheran scholar concerned to reflect carefully the text and its meaning and significance for faith and life.

Longenecker, Richard N. *Acts*. The Expositor's Bible Commentary. Grand Rapids: Zondervan, 1995. ❧ From an Evangelical scholar, based on the NIV.

Academic Resources

Bruce, F. F. *The Acts of the Apostles: Greek Text with Introduction and Commentary.* 3rd revised and enlarged ed. Grand Rapids: Eerdmans, 1990. ❧ A verse-by-verse exposition on the basis of the Greek text; helpful introductory articles. This work has gone through many editions, and is a solid, conservative, Evangelical commentary.

———. *The Book of the Acts.* NICNT. Revised ed. Grand Rapids: Eerdmans, 1988. ❧ Carefully explores each event recorded in the Book of Acts. A valuable resource.

Cadbury, Henry J. *The Book of Acts in History.* London: A. & C. Black, 1955. ❧ A survey of historical issues in Acts.

Conzelmann, Hans. *Acts of the Apostles.* Philadelphia: Fortress Press, 1987. ❧ Though the reader should be wary of Conzelmann's liberal theology, nevertheless, he has good insights into the Book of Acts, especially as it relates to the theology of Luke.

Fitzmyer, Joseph A. *The Acts of the Apostles.* Vol. 31 of AB. New York: Doubleday, 1998. ❧ One of the classic commentaries on Luke from a scholar of Aramiac and Christian origins, who writes from a historical-critical perspective. This commentary should not be overlooked.

Foakes-Jackson, F. J., and Kirsopp Lake, eds. *The Beginnings of Christianity: Part I. The Acts of the Apostles.* 5 vols. Grand Rapids: Baker, 1979 reprint. ❧ Volumes 1 and 2 offer essays on Jewish, Gentile, and Christian backgrounds of the New Testament, and on the composition and authorship of Acts. Volume 3 is a dated study of the texts of Acts. Volume 4 is an exegetical exposition. Volume 5 contains very valuable articles on a wide variety of topics; it is the most valuable of the five volumes.

Gallagher, Robert L., and Paul Hertig, eds. *Mission in Acts: Ancient Narratives in Contemporary Context.* Maryknoll, NY: Orbis Books, 2004. ❧ A unique resource on the book's mission themes.

Hemer, Colin J. *The Book of Acts in the Setting of Hellenistic History.* Tübingen: Mohr, 1989. ❧ Helps readers recognize the Greco-Roman background of Acts.

Hengel, Martin. *Acts and the History of Earliest Christianity.* Philadelphia: Fortress, 1979. ❧ Hengel supports the historical integrity of Acts. In doing so, he interacts with the varying stances of critical scholars.

Johnson, Luke Timothy. *The Acts of the Apostles.* Collegeville, MN: Liturgical Press, 1992. ❧ This is a fairly conservative, solid Roman Catholic commentary. Johnson is good at showing how the Holy Spirit works within the life of the Church.

Lechler, Gotthard Victor, and Karl Gerok. *The Acts of the Apostles: An Exegetical and Doctrinal Commentary.* LCHS. New York: Charles Scribner's Sons, 1868. ❧ A helpful older example of German biblical scholarship, based on the Hebrew text, which provides references to significant commentaries from the Reformation era forward.

O'Toole, Robert F. *The Unity of Luke's Theology: An Analysis of Luke-Acts.* Wilmington, DE: Michael Glazier, 1984. ❧ Alerts the reader to more general Lukan theological themes.

Talbert, Charles H. *Reading Acts: A Literary and Theological Commentary on the Acts of the Apostles.* Macon, GA: Smyth and Helwys, 2001. ❧ Considers how the original audience would have understood the book in its precanonical and canonical contexts.

Witherington III, Ben. *The Acts of the Apostles: A Socio-Rhetorical Commentary.* Grand Rapids: Eerdmans, 1998. ❧ Written by an Evangelical scholar; good when defending the historicity of a certain passage. However, the commentary is not very original and often misses the churchly and sacramental import of a passage.

THE EPISTLES OF PAUL

"When you received the word of God, which you heard from us, you accepted it not as the word of men but as what it really is, the word of God, which is at work in you believers. . . . You received from us how you ought to walk and to please God. . . . For you know what instructions we gave you through the Lord Jesus" (1Th 2:13; 4:1, 2).

The earliest collection of New Testament documents was the 13 Epistles, or Letters, of the apostle Paul. The early Christians immediately regarded these letters as God's Word, like the writings of the prophets (2Pt 3:15–16).

The Apostle Paul

The apostle Paul grew up as Saul of Tarsus in Cilicia (Ac 9:11; see map, p 367). His father was a Diaspora Jew and a freedman in Roman society (16:37–38; 22:25–29). Paul was apprenticed as a tentmaker (18:3) but also studied the Scriptures as a Pharisee at Jerusalem under Rabbi Gamaliel the Elder (22:3). Gamaliel was the grandson of Rabbi Hillel, who was known for his progressive attitudes toward proselytes and for founding a key school of Jewish thought, Beth Hillel.

Paul zealously defended his Jewish faith by arresting Christians and supporting their execution, since he regarded them as false teachers (7:58; 8:1–3; 26:9–11). In AD 36, Jesus confronted Paul while he traveled to Damascus to arrest Christians there (9:1–9). Jesus turned Paul's heart. Paul was baptized and immediately began to proclaim Jesus as the Messiah (9:10–22). Retreating from persecution, Paul spent some years east of Damascus in the Arabian Desert before returning to Damascus and to Antioch as a teacher (11:25–26; Gal 1:17–18). In AD 47, the Holy Spirit directed the congregation at Antioch

Portrait of a young Roman holding a papyrus scroll. Fresco painted c AD 55–79.

Coin of Emperor Nero (AD 54–68).

to send Paul out as a missionary (Ac 13:1–3; see map, p 388), a calling he fulfilled until AD 68, when the Roman emperor Nero ordered Paul's execution. Paul's letters were written during his missionary journeys and while he was in prison for proclaiming Christ (see *TLSB*, p 2042). He typically had the help of a scribe (see *TLSB* notes, Rm 16:22; Gal 6:11); friends hand-delivered the letters (see *TLSB* note, Ti 3:13).

The Format of the Epistles

Early Christian scribes began to gather, copy, and circulate the apostle Paul's letters almost immediately. In this respect, Paul's 13 epistles shaped the New Testament, earliest Christian teaching (e.g., the Apostles' Creed), and earliest practice. After Jesus Himself, no other leader had greater influence on Christianity's direction. Using the Old Testament, Paul helped the other apostles recognize the full implications of Jesus' teaching, sacrifice, resurrection, and commission to spread the Gospel (Ac 15:1–29). Though the claim of some critics that Paul "created" Christianity is bizarre, one can hardly exaggerate Paul's importance. Luther wrote, "No one stresses the grace we have through Christ so valiantly as St. Paul does" (AE 30:4).

Paul established the format and style for Christian letters until the fourth century. Paul's letters still greatly influence how Christians relate to one another today. These should be among the first books of Scripture people study. To support the spread of the Gospel and the faith of new believers, the apostle Paul made letter writing an important activity for the earliest Christians.

Ancient Letters

Paul's letters are not the first to appear in the Bible. In Old Testament times, letters in Hebrew or Aramaic were common means for administration (cf 2Sm 11:15; 1Ki 21:8–10; 2Ki 5:5–6; 10:1–3, 6; 19:10–14; 2Ch 2:11–16; 21:12–15; Ezr 1:1–4; Ne 6:5–7; Jer 29:1–23, 25–28). Archaeologists have also discovered numerous ostraca (potsherd) letters for brief, official communications in Israel.

Prayer written in Greek on a potsherd (ostraca): "Have mercy on me in flesh and bone." Found at Capernaum, which became a place of pilgrimage for early Christians.

The Apocrypha shows how the tradition of letter writing continued after the tribe of Judah returned from exile in Babylon. For example, the priestly leadership in Judah sent letters to Jewish communities in Egypt and elsewhere to organize the Jewish feasts (cf 2Macc 1:1–9). Jewish "encyclicals" were delivered by envoys who ensured that the letters' contents were applied among those who received them (cf Ac 9:1–2; 15:22–32; 28:21). Elements of these Jewish letters influenced the way Paul wrote and worked as a spiritual leader.

However, the format and rhetoric of Greek letters also greatly influenced Paul. Archaeologists have discovered "handbooks" for writing Greek letters that illustrate various styles and occasions for writing, much as one may adapt and use form letters today. Paul likely studied such Greek letters.

The Style of Paul's Letters

Paul commonly wrote his letters in an exhortative or sermonic style, admonishing and encouraging his readers on the basis of biblical doctrines and stories. By applying God's Law and Gospel, Paul called his readers to account when they strayed and announced God's forgiveness for them when they repented.

Paul's letters are clearly more intimate than administrative letters of the time. They are more like family letters, since he viewed the churches as households. Paul's letters are also much longer than most Greek letters. Christian letters were carefully written to convey apostolic instruction, which flowed from Christ, the Head of the Church. Not all apostolic letters were preserved, since not every letter would always apply for future congregations. However, the New Testament apostolic letters were received as God's Word.

Paul's Letters and You

Below are listed typical elements of Paul's letters. As you study the letters, be sure to compare the outline of each with the elements below to discover the character of Paul's work. Many of these features also appear in the General Epistles, written by other apostles and Christian leaders.

TYPICAL ELEMENTS	NOTES
I. Opening	
Correspondent and his office	Writer declared authority or relationship.
Recipients	Paul usually addressed individual congregations.
Greeting with Christian blessing	Paul invoked Christ, making the greeting explicitly Christian.
Thanksgiving for the readers	Typical in Jewish letters.
Prayer for the readers	Celebrated the readers' blessings and qualities.
II. Body	
Instruction in doctrine	Christ called the apostles to teach the Law and the Gospel from Holy Scripture and divine revelation. Cf Lk 24:44–48.
Instruction in practice	Paul's counsel flowed from doctrinal instruction.
Responses to reports or letters	Problems were addressed point by point (e.g., 1Co).
Call to repentance	Used when the readers had strayed from God's teaching.
Travel plans	Travelers relied on the hospitality of the congregations in order to extend mission work.
III. Conclusion	
Blessing	A request for God's grace or presence.
Wish for peace	"Shalom" was a common Semitic greeting that Paul included in his Greek letters.
Request for prayer	Expressed with travel plans or descriptions of suffering.

Greetings extended to others	From the writer or his companions. Such greetings broadened and deepened the relationships between congregations and between leaders.
Holy kiss greeting	This may describe a liturgical action (see *TLSB* note, Rm 16:16).
Autographed greeting	Paul usually dictated his letters to a scribe, as was typical in ancient times. Sometimes he also signed his own greeting (e.g., Gal 6:11).

First-century Roman writing tools.

ROMANS

The righteousness of God through faith in Jesus Christ

Stepping from the shadows of the Ausoni Mountains, walking northward along the famous Appian Way, the apostle Paul reached the coastal plains of Italy that stretched all the way to Rome. Some five years earlier, Paul had expected to see the empire's capital and preach the Gospel there (Ac 19:21). Now drawing near the city and under guard, news of his arrival preceded him. Members of the church at Rome came more than 40 miles to greet him and escort him into the imperial city (28:11–16). They knew the apostle not merely by reputation but also by his most famous letter, penned on their behalf: the Book of Romans.

Only a year before Paul arrived at Rome, Emperor Nero succeeded to the throne. When Paul arrived, the new emperor was peacefully following the counsel of his advisors. The opportunities to preach and teach that Paul enjoyed and Luke described (28:17–31) did not hint at the time, 13 years later, when Nero would order citizen Paul silenced by the sword. The Letter to the Romans presents Paul as the most gifted early Christian theologian and, ironically, as a respectful supporter of the young Emperor Nero's governance (Rm 13).

The Appian Way by which Paul first reached Rome in c AD 57–58 (Ac 28). Paul wrote the Letter to the Romans as preparation for visiting them and seeking their support to proclaim Christ in Spain (Rm 15:22–29).

OVERVIEW

Author
Paul the apostle

Date
AD 55

Places
Rome; Cenchreae; Jerusalem; Spain

People
Paul; Jews; Gentiles; true "Israel"; Paul's co-workers (Rm 16)

Purpose
To defend an essential teaching of Christianity and its mission: justification through God's righteousness in Christ

Law Themes
Wrath against sinners; death's reign through sin; believers struggle with sin; hardened hearts; submission to authorities; owe one another love

Gospel Themes
God declares us righteous through faith in Christ; alive through Baptism; the Spirit is life; election; God's gifts; united in Christ

Memory Verses
The Gospel's power (1:16–17); none righteous (3:10b–18); justified through Jesus (3:21–26); peace through Christ (5:1–2); buried by Baptism (6:3–4); struggle with sin (7:21–25); the Spirit is life (8:1–2, 9–11); more than conquerors (8:31–39); living sacrifices (12:1–2); pursue peace (14:17–19)

TIMELINE

AD 36	Conversion of Paul
AD 52–55	Paul's third missionary journey
AD 55	Paul writes Romans
AD 57–58	Paul journeys to Rome
AD 58–60	Paul imprisoned at Rome

Historical and Cultural Setting

The historical situation of the Letter to the Romans is clear in outline and presents relatively few problems. Paul had been looking toward Rome and westward for some years before he wrote his letter to the church (or churches) at Rome (Rm 15:23). He had met Aquila and Priscilla as early as the year 49, when the edict of Claudius banishing all Jews from Rome brought that couple, destined to be so dear and so valuable to him, to Corinth (Ac 18:1–3). They could tell him of the church in that capital and key city of the empire, its problems and possibilities, especially its possibilities as a missionary center for the western half of the Roman Empire.

When Paul was in the act of concluding his work at Ephesus in the late summer of AD 55 and was about to return to Jerusalem by way of Macedonia and Achaia, he gave expression to a long-cherished hope, saying: "After

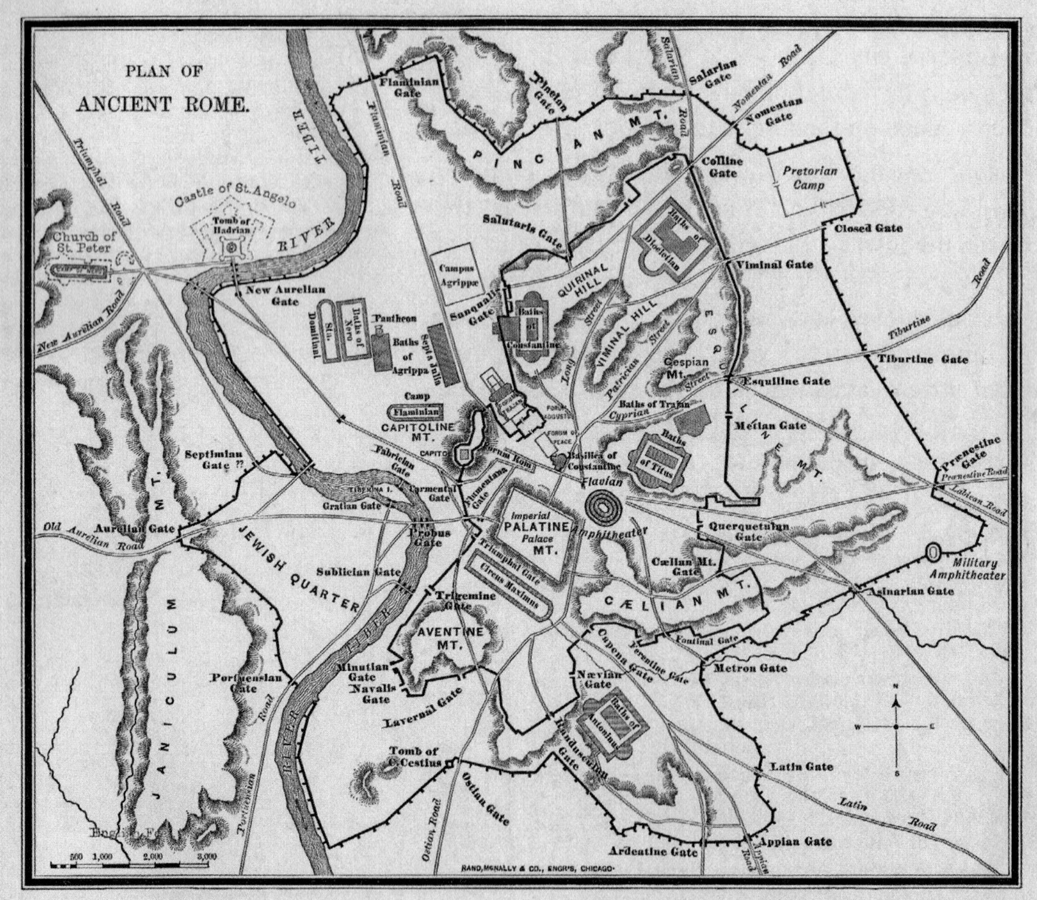

I have been there, I must also see Rome" (Ac 19:21). The same hope finds expression in the letter that he wrote to the Corinthians from Macedonia soon afterward: "Our hope is that as your faith increases, our area of influence among you may be greatly enlarged, so that we may preach the Gospel in lands beyond you" (2Co 10:15, 16). "Lands beyond you," coming from men who had lived and worked in the eastern Mediterranean area, points westward.

Paul did not reach Rome in the way he had hoped and intended, but the Lord who comforted him when he was taken prisoner in Jerusalem told him, "Take courage, for as you have testified to the facts about Me in Jerusalem, so you must testify also in Rome" (Ac 23:11). The Lord made good His promise. So Paul reached Rome, years later than he had hoped, and not as a free missionary, but as a prisoner. But the Letter to the Romans had not been written in vain. As Paul approached Rome, the brethren there, having heard of his coming, came out 30 and 40 miles to meet him at Three Taverns and the Forum of Appius. "On seeing them, Paul thanked God and took courage," Luke writes (Ac 28:15). Whatever Rome might hold for Paul, whatever the future might bring—death or work in Rome and beyond—Paul knew that the church of Rome was one with him in the Gospel; and for that he thanked God.

First–century Roman gladius sword, which became an icon for the apostle Paul in Christian art.

Composition

Author(s)

The apostle Paul, a Jew from Tarsus who studied under Rabbi Gamaliel at Jerusalem, is regarded as the author of the letter. Romans 16:22 makes clear that Paul dictated the letter to Tertius, who acted as his scribe and may have contributed in some fashion to the composition. However, some scholars have questioned the integrity of the last chapter, speculating that it may not have been part of the original work. On this opinion, see pp 435–37.

Date of Composition

The close of the third missionary journey would seem to be the fitting time for the writing of the Letter to the Romans, and the notices in the letter itself confirm this. According to the letter, Paul was about to conclude his work in the East; he had fully preached the Gospel of Christ "from Jerusalem and all the way around to Illyricum" (Rm 15:19). He was about to go to Jerusalem with a collection gathered in Macedonia and Achaia (Rm 15:25–27; cf 2Co 8 and 9). All this points to the end of the third missionary journey in the winter of AD 55.

Paul probably wrote the letter in Corinth, during his three months' stay in southern Greece (Ac 20:2–3). He sent greetings to the Romans from "Erastus, the city treasurer" (Rm 16:23); this Erastus is associated with Corinth in 2Tm 4:20, and an inscription has been found in Corinth that mentions an Erastus as a city official there. Furthermore, Paul commended to the Roman church a woman named Phoebe, a deaconess of the church at Cenchreae, the eastern harbor town of Corinth (Rm 16:1). Paul was at the time of writing the guest of a man named Gaius (Rm 16:23), and we know of a Gaius who was a member, and apparently a prominent one, of the church at Corinth (1Co 1:14). Gaius was, of course, a very common Roman name, and one should not make too much of the coincidence; but it does serve as cumulative evidence. Paul, then, most likely wrote to Rome from Corinth during the winter of AD 55–56.

Purpose/Recipients

Paul's aim in writing is delicately but clearly stated in the letter itself. His letter was to prepare for his visit to Rome, but Rome was not the ultimate goal of his travels. It could not be, for Paul had made it his ambition as apostle to the Gentiles "to preach the gospel, not where Christ has already been named," lest he build on another man's foundation (Rm 15:20). The apostle's task was to lay foundations, not to build on foundations already laid by others (1Co 3:10). And the foundation had long since been laid in Rome; Paul's words in his Letter to the Romans indicate that the church there had been in existence for a considerable time ("Your faith is proclaimed in all the world," Rm 1:8. "Your obedience is known to all," Rm 16:19. "I have longed *for many years* to come to you," Rm 15:23). Acts 2:10 notes that Jews from Rome were among those who heard Peter's Pentecost sermon in AD 33—about 22 years earlier. Non-Christian sources indicate that there was a church in Rome at least as early as AD 49 and probably considerably earlier. Since neither Paul nor any other early source points to any single outstanding personality as the founder of the Roman church, we may assume that the Word of the Lord grew and produced a church in Rome through the agency of a number of nameless men, such as the "visitors from Rome" who were present in Jerusalem at Pentecost and later returned to Rome, probably at the time when Saul persecuted the churches of Judea.

Paul planned to spend some time in Rome and to proclaim the Gospel there, to enrich and to be enriched by his association with the Roman Christians (Rm 1:11–13). But he was looking beyond Rome to Spain (15:24, 28); Paul hoped to be sped on his way there by the Romans (15:24). The passage

Outline

I. Introduction (1:1–15)

II. Theme of the Epistle: The Righteous Shall Live by Faith (1:16–17)

III. Who Is Righteous? The Wrath of God Revealed against All (1:18–3:20)

- A. Wrath against Unrighteousness without the Law (1:18–32)
- B. Wrath against the So-Called Righteousness by the Law (2:1–3:20)

IV. God Is Righteous! The Righteousness of God Revealed for All (3:21–4:25)

- A. Righteousness Revealed in Christ and by Faith (3:21–31)
- B. Example: Abraham Is Declared Righteous by Faith before Circumcision and the Law (ch 4)

V. The Righteous by Faith Truly Live (chs 5–8)

- A. Live at Peace with God: Reconciliation through Christ (ch 5)
- B. Live Dead to Sin and Alive to God: Baptism and Sanctification (ch 6)
- C. Live at War with the Sinful Flesh (ch 7)
- D. Live Victoriously in the Spirit for Eternity (ch 8)

VI. Righteousness by Faith That Leads to Life Is for "All Israel" (chs 9–11)

- A. The Promise Is Only to Believers (9:1–29)
- B. Jewish Rejection Is Not God's Fault (9:30–10:21)
- C. Jewish Rejection Is Not Final (ch 11)

VII. The Life Lived by the Righteous by Faith (12:1–15:13)

- A. Live as Living Sacrifices (12:1–2)
- B. Live as the Body of Christ (12:3–8)
- C. Love One Another (12:9–21)

D. Live Subject to Authorities (13:1–7)
E. Love Your Neighbor (13:8–10)
F. Cast Off Evil and Put On the Lord Jesus Christ (13:11–14)
G. Live Sensitive to the Weak in Faith (14:1–15:13)

VIII. Conclusion (15:14–16:27)

A. Paul's Travel Plans (15:14–33)
B. Greetings and Salutation (ch 16)

may cover anything from a simple "God speed!" to something more concrete and material in the way of support for a journey, both moral and material, given to missionaries by established churches or individual Christians (Ac 20:38; 21:5; 1Co 16:6, 11; 2Co 1:16; Ti 3:13; 3Jn 6). Paul evidently hoped that Rome would become his missionary base in the West, what Syrian Antioch had been for him in the East. The Letter to the Romans, the most elaborate and most systematic exposition of the Gospel as Paul proclaimed it, is written in the interests of Paul's missionary work, testifying to the harmony between theology and practice in the great apostle's mind.

Literary Features

Genre

Much of the Letter to the Romans reads like a doctrinal treatise. Some scholars have seen a problem in the fact that the treatment of the Gospel in the letter is of such unparalleled breadth and depth. Why should just this letter, written merely to *prepare* for a visit to Rome and work in the West, deal so searchingly and so comprehensively with the Gospel? The answer is not far to seek. Everything that we know of Paul's missionary preaching and his missionary methods (e.g., his practice of revisiting already established churches and his continued contact with them by letter and by means of personal emissaries) makes it clear that he did not aim at creating a vague, emotional, and enthusiastic movement but rather the firmly rooted, grounded, and established Church of God, in which the Word of Christ dwelt richly. What he sought therefore in a church that was to be his base in the West was a full and complete common understanding of the Gospel and a common obedience to the Gospel. At his former base in the East, this common understanding was something he could presuppose and rely on. Antioch had been deeply influenced by Barnabas, and Paul himself had preached and taught at Antioch for a full year before the Holy Spirit sent him forth from Antioch (Ac 11:26). What a year's ministry had accomplished in the East, a single letter had to accomplish in the West. That letter had of necessity to be a full and rich one.

Another unique feature of Romans is the nature of its sentences. Fully one-fourth of the sentences in the Greek text are questions. In other words, Paul composed Romans as a doctrinal and practical catechism for which the balance of the letter provides his answers and texts drawn from the Old Testament. See "Resources," p. 424.

Characters

Abraham features prominently in Romans 4 as the Old Testament's chief example of justification by grace through faith, making him a most important character in the doctrinal section of Paul's letter. The last chapter of the book includes the most extensive **list of persons** in the New Testament, some of whom we recognize from Acts and Paul's other letters (e.g., Prisca and Aquila; Timothy) but most of whom are little known to us. Paul greets dozens of people as he prepares to travel to Rome and meet the congregation. **Phoebe**, the deaconess mentioned at the opening of ch 16, has served as an important figure in discussions of women's service from the Early Church to today. In modern times, **Junia** has become the subject of debate as advocates of women's ordination have argued that this person served as an apostle, though the basis for such an argument is ambiguous at best (16:7; see *TLSB*, p 1942).

Abraham offering a calf to his heaven-sent guests, through whom God promised the birth of Isaac. Abraham received God's promise in faith. Sixth-century mosaic in Ravenna, Italy.

Narrative Development or Plot

Since the Book of Romans is written as a letter, with the character of a doctrinal treatise, it does not have a storyline or plot. However, the book does move through the order of one's salvation, from rebellion and wrath, to righteousness and peace through faith, to ongoing struggles against the flesh, overcome by the work of the Holy Spirit. The letter also divides into

Paul's typical approach of presenting doctrine first (chs 1–11) and practice second (chs 12–16).

Resources

Paul cited the Old Testament about 60 times while writing Romans. There are considerably more citations than in any of his other letters, including 1 Corinthians, which is of similar length but only cites the Old Testament about 16 times. About half of Paul's citations in Romans are from Isaiah and the Psalms. Romans 3:10–18 is an example of a "catena" or chain of situations, which he or someone else collected while reading the Scriptures. Paul regarded the Old Testament as the source and revelation of the Gospel, about which he preached and wrote.

Text and Translations

The text of Romans is well established through a wealth of early manuscripts dating as early as c AD 200 (Papyrus 46) and from Early Church Fathers who cite the letter. As with Paul's other letters, scholars discuss the possible influence of the early heretic Marcion on causing some of the textual variants. One reading that receives significant attention from scholars is 9:5: "who is God over all, blessed forever." The inconsistency of punctuation in early Greek manuscripts raises the question of whether Christ or the heavenly Father is intended.

Key doctrines in Romans teach that all are sinners (Rm 3:9–20) and that the wages of sin is death (6:23). Roman mosaic from Pompeii.

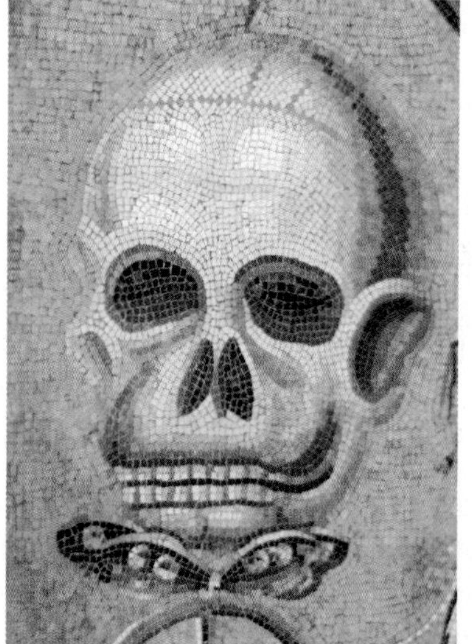

Doctrinal Content

Summary Commentary

1:1–17 Paul affirms three callings from God: he is called to be an apostle, the Romans are called to belong to Christ, and they are called to be saints. Paul was sent to the Greeks and barbarians, to the wise and foolish. The righteousness of God removes our shame and is the basis for life and salvation.

1:18–3:20 We might not have committed some of the acts Paul condemns in Romans, but we all have sinned. We have exchanged God's truth for human foolishness. When we pass judgment on another, we condemn ourselves (2:1). Paul's teachings are clear: without God's patience and forbearance, we would all be condemned. He warns against being praised by people but not by God (2:29). Pride desires recognition and praise from the world, but this may come in ways that are inconsistent with God's will. Human sinfulness shows the radical difference between God's holiness and humanity's unrighteousness.

3:21–4:25 Having condemned human sinfulness, Paul unfolds the basis for our righteousness or justification, using the story of Abraham. Abraham's circumcision did not save him; it was a response to his salvation. Abraham trusted that God was able to do what He promised, especially in sending him an heir through whom all nations would be blessed (Gn 12:3).

Ch 5 Jesus is the source of our peace with God. He is the second Adam through whom all mankind is reconciled. God will use afflictions for our good and to bless others. He will keep His promises, and we will overcome our sufferings by faith. Adam's sin brought guilt, the desire to sin, and mortality to all humans. He sent a Second Adam to begin a new humanity. Christ fulfilled the Law.

Chs 6–7 Although many people consider freedom to be the ultimate human right, no one is truly free spiritually. We were slaves to sin and bound to death. As the Law confronts fallen human nature, it still accuses and condemns believers, revealing sinfulness and the unreachable standard of God's holiness. Faithless people may be driven to sin and despair by the Law (7:5). Thanks be to God, in Christ we have died to the Law (7:4). Our struggle with sin is not a past event; it is a present reality. We know God's will and desire to serve Him, but we cannot overcome sin by our own means.

Ch 8 Because Christ justifies sinners, God's life-giving Spirit dwells in believers. He frees us from the bondage of sin and death. The Holy Spirit leads us to trust confidently that we are heirs, privileged to call God "our Father" and to receive eternal glory at the end of present suffering. The Holy Spirit ministers to God's dear children by giving us hope in our suffering, help in our weakness, and assurance that all things work out to fulfill God's eternal purposes in our lives. Christ's death, resurrection, and exaltation at God's right hand guarantees our victory over anything and everything that would separate us from His love.

Chs 9–11 The unbelief of his fellow Jews, to whom God had given so much, caused Paul great sorrow. Countering likely objections, Paul insists that God's Word has not failed and He is not unjust in His choices. Paul looks backward to God's election of Israel in history (9:1–29) and forward to the necessity of faith and the guilt of unbelief (10:5–21). Like a loving father waiting for his children to come home, God yearns to show mercy on all (cf Lk 15:11–32). Those who refuse to accept God's gracious invitation to share in the riches of His grace are accountable to Him for their unbelief. Paul, chosen by God's grace revealed in Jesus Christ, is a living example that God has preserved for Himself a remnant in Israel. Paul warns the Gentile believers against pride and reminds them of their role in God's mission to Jewish unbelievers. In ways beyond our understanding, God has acted in mercy to bring salvation to Jews and Gentiles. Human beings cannot exchange roles with God, presuming to sit in judgment of Him.

12:1–15:13 Paul urges us to present ourselves as living sacrifices because it is the proper response to "the mercies of God" (12:1). He repeatedly emphasizes the gracious gifts of God that are received in faith. Here is what a life of genuine love (12:9) looks like in specific detail. It is a life that follows Christ's example (Php 2:1–11) and models His words from the Sermon on the Mount (Mt 5–7).

While all governments fall short, Paul implies that the first-century Roman government was adequately carrying out its two essential functions: approving those who do good and punishing evildoers. Paul acknowledges that all authority comes from God, to whom ultimate obedience is due. Paul also continues to deal specifically with first-century controversial issues among Jewish and Gentile Christians (foods and holy days). Paul knows all foods are clean, but flaunting his freedoms will give offense in the presence of Jewish Christians who still observe Old Testament food laws. The Old Testament looked ahead to a day when Jews and Gentiles would worship God together.

15:14–16:27 Paul lays out the practice and scope of his mission work as well as his current travel plans. He greets 26 people by name and warns against those who cause divisions, whom God will overcome. Those who advocate a false Gospel are to be avoided entirely. Paul's closing words encompass the entire Good News of God, from the prophetic Old Testament writings to the proclamation of Jesus Christ being made known to all nations. God's eternal being, His wisdom, knowledge, and power, are all far beyond ours. He calls those of faith to respond in obedience to His will.

Specific Law Themes

The opening chapters of Romans emphasize God's wrath against sin and sinners. Death reigns over mankind through sin and will not release its grip. Even after coming to faith in Christ, believers continue to struggle against sin and suffer the sorrows of death. God breaks up our hardened hearts through the accusations of the Law. He teaches us that we owe love toward one another and even obedience to the worldly authorities He has established.

Specific Gospel Themes

In Romans, Paul proves from Scripture that God declares us righteous through faith in Christ alone, who is the fulfillment of God's Old Testament promises of redemption and the evidence of God's love for all. He has made us alive through Holy Baptism and given us His Holy Spirit. In fact, God has chosen us in Christ, through whom He gives us victory and gifts for service in His kingdom. We are united with Christ.

Specific Doctrines

Pointing up the theological value of this letter is like commenting on the depth of the Grand Canyon. Anything written here is at best a mere glimpse at the topic.

A Missionary Letter

A word or two on the letter as a missionary document (an aspect of the letter not always sufficiently appreciated) may be in place. The breadth and depth of this exposition of the Gospel of Christ is a perpetual warning against the temptation, which the Church has not always resisted, to make of its missionary endeavors a vague and sentimental humanitarian activity, in which penicillin becomes a substitute for the power of God, the Gospel. It is the most obvious and natural thing in the world that the Gospel should march through the world with steps of mercy, that faith should document itself in a love that comprehends all people's need and agony; but the temptation to "give up preaching the word of God to serve tables" (Ac 6:2) is particularly strong in missionary work, and the Letter to the Romans is the Church's salutary monitor concerning the primacy of the Word. The letter is therefore also a reminder that the content of missionary preaching is of critical importance, that a perversion or dilution of the divine Word is no more permissible here than anywhere else in the life of the Church. Cooperation in mission work cannot proceed based on an ill-defined or undefined minimum of agreement on the substance of the missionary proclamation. The confessional question is an acute question in missionary work.

Paul expounds the Gospel in the Letter to the Romans by setting it in antithesis to Judaism (the works of the Law, circumcision, descent from Abraham, etc.). Why should Paul choose to expound his Gospel in just this form to the Roman church? Why should just this letter deal at length (chs 9–11) with the tragic fate of Israel, the people of God who have rejected the righteousness of God that the Gospel reveals? We do not know the situation at Rome so well that we can be positive in our answers here. But two reasons may be suggested as probable. One reason would be Paul's personal experience. Paul had become a Christian by way of a radical and total break with Judaism. It would be natural for him to make clear to others the absolutely free grace of God's acquittal of the guilty in the Gospel by showing how that grace had come home to him, as the absolute antithesis to a religion of human performance and merit. He was, of course, not giving the Gospel a new or alien form by so portraying it. For the Gospel is always God's great *Nevertheless* after we fail to keep His Law.

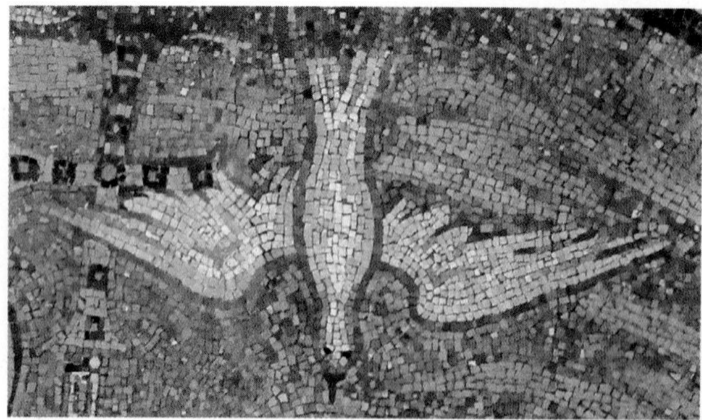

Holy Spirit descending as a dove. Sixth-century mosaic in Ravenna, Italy

The other reason is to be found in Paul's experience as missionary. Paul had seen, with sorrow and indignation, how the Judaizers had sought to make Christianity a compromise between legalistic Judaism and the Gospel of free grace in Christ; this was for him the classic form of rebellion against the free grace of God freely given, without condition and without price. If Judaism is exposed for what it is, the Judaizers are refuted; if the Judaizers are refuted, that is the refutation of every attempt, in whatever form, to make man as man somehow count in the relationship between God and man—and the air is cleared for the proclamation of the true Gospel of grace.

Possibly the situation in Rome also made this emphasis necessary; the church at Rome had come out of the synagogue and seems to have been, to begin with, predominantly Judaic—although at the time when Paul wrote, it had become a predominantly Gentile church, as Paul's letter makes clear (1:13–15; cf 1:5, 6; 11:13, 28–31). As members of an originally Judaic church, the Roman Christians had probably heard slanderous misinterpretations of Paul's preaching and needed to be disabused of false notions concerning it.

Key Doctrines Drawn from Romans

Since Romans is the most systematic and doctrinal of Paul's letters, the Church has naturally drawn from it to support key aspects of its teaching. For example, Augustine and Luther found here the doctrinal order of salvation, describing how God converts sinners, and setting a precedent for all Christian theology. The first chapters of Romans define the Gospel as "the power of God for salvation to everyone who believes" (1:16) making justification through faith in Christ the chief doctrine. Paul expounds the Old

Testament teaching about the "righteousness of God" throughout the opening chapters of the letter, reaching a climax in 3:21–28. Running parallel to this chief doctrine is the doctrine of original sin, since God wrote the Law into human hearts at the beginning of creation (2:15), revealing the depth of human sinfulness and our need for His gracious salvation (3:10–20). Paul traces the problem of human sin back to Adam (5:12) while also affirming the guilt of our sin. Justification through faith in Christ is thus shown to be the only means of peace with God, who grants us salvation by grace (5:1–2).

In chs 7–8 the apostle describes the Christian life, noting first the endless struggle against sin and the accusations of the Law (ch 7), which leads one to cry out to God through Jesus (cf 7:25). The Lord sends His Spirit, who leads us to walk in life and peace (ch 8), setting aside the torments of our sinful nature so that we may see God as our Father and the blessings of eternity He has prepared in Christ for those who love Him. It is noteworthy that ch 8 refers to the Holy Spirit and His work more than any other chapter in the Bible, distinguishing the doctrines of justification and sanctification while making them likewise inseparable from one another in the Christian life. For chs 9–11, Paul expounds the mystery of election by grace, which for many has served as a stumbling block since they have tried to approach the matter by reason rather than by faith. One should note the important place that Paul gives the Word of God and faith at the heart of these chapters: he notes that "faith comes from hearing, and hearing through the word of Christ" (10:17; cf 10:10).

Application

1:1–17 We sinners are prone to think that we control every aspect of our lives, and we tend to live only for ourselves. Knowing the futility of this, Christ Jesus sacrificed Himself on the cross that we might be redeemed. He calls us out of sin and death and into life. Once we are redeemed, we may be tempted to keep the Gospel to ourselves or limit it to people who are like us. However, Jesus did not limit His work. He redeemed the whole world—even barbarians and fools like us. He commissions us to reach out to all people. Receiving His gifts by faith, and empowered by the Spirit, we are no longer ashamed of the Gospel. We know it is God's power "for salvation to everyone who believes" (v 16).

1:18–3:20 Seeing sin, we ought not respond defensively but in confession. We know God's response to sin: He sent His Son to die for sinners. Our priorities are misplaced when we seek the world's acclaim. We are blessed when we place God first, knowing He loves and forgives us. He approves of us because of Jesus. That's all the praise we will ever need. God made covenants with His people, but we have broken our promises. How blessed we are that our unfaithfulness cannot nullify His faithfulness. He redeems us because He is gracious. Only when we see this are we prepared for the Good News of what Christ has done for us.

3:21–4:25 We are alike in our corruption and fallenness. But all humanity has also been redeemed by Christ. Sinners may draw distinctions between people, but God does not. He would save us all through Christ. We are constantly tempted to give our works a role in salvation, but this detracts from God's work. Christ saves us apart from our works, so anything we do responds to what He has already done for us. Trials and challenges may tempt us to doubt God's promises. As He did with Abraham, God will strengthen our faith, assure us of His promises, help us to trust, and fulfill all He said He would do.

Ch 5 We naturally seek to avoid pain and suffering. Yet, there are times when suffering is unavoidable. Focused on Christ's suffering, death, and resurrection, we know that suffering is not the whole story. We continue to sin and deserve condemnation. Praise God, He did not stop with Adam. Christ was obedient to the Father, and He paid the penalty for our sin. One man—Christ—has redeemed us and changed humanity forever.

Chs 6–7 Jesus came to serve us by giving His life on the cross and rising for us. Freed from sin, we can now serve God. Only when we are "slaves" to God will we have freedom to be the people He created us to be. Now we need not live in bondage and fear, but in a new life in the Spirit. Even if we try, we fail. We cry out, "Who will deliver me from this body of death?" (7:24). There is only one answer: "Thanks be to God through Jesus Christ our Lord!" (7:25). Jesus rescues us. Though we sin daily, He continues to forgive and restore us.

Ch 8 Those who are preoccupied with satisfying their selfish desires often become angry with God and rebel against Him. God promises release from this deadly cycle and brings life and peace. The path to glory, however, is not an easy street, for it entails daily rejection of personal sins. When God's judgment frightens us, the Spirit assures us that God loves us in Christ. When our hope in God dims, we easily succumb to impatience in distress. The Spirit helps us in our frailty, assuring us of God's steadfast love. When following Christ brings distress, we sometimes distance ourselves from Him. But Christ never draws back from us.

Chs 9–11 Unbelievers sit under God's judgment, placing themselves in spiritual peril. Yet God is patient, desiring to show mercy on us all. Every effort to get right with God by works of the Law, however sincere, is doomed to failure. God is the giver of righteousness to everyone who believes. However, Christ Jesus is always near to us in His Word. He stands ready to forgive and renew us. Those who become hardened and spiritually callous are in danger of God's frightening judgment. Yet, through the suffering for sin that Christ endured, even the sin of unbelief is forgiven in those who trust in His grace. To look down on any nonbeliever is sinful rejection of God's gracious purposes. In goodness and kindness, God can restore to faith those who have fallen. But we in whom His Spirit dwells praise Him for His inexhaustible kindness toward us in Christ Jesus.

Ch 12 Keep Paul's earlier words in mind as you study the last chapters of the book. On this side of heaven, we are not fully renewed (7:14–25). As a result, the exhortations of these show us that we still sin and fall short (3:23). But that is not the only purpose for this section; it is a guide for Christian living (see FC Ep and SD VI). God has shown us His undeserved mercies in Christ. God has transformed our lives in Baptism and continues to renew us daily by His Spirit. Our abilities can cause us to think of ourselves too highly. We all fail to live up to this standard. However, as living sacrifices, we have been transformed to live according to God's loving will (12:1–2). This serves as a powerful witness to others (cf Mt 5:16; Jn 13:34–35). God in Christ has first loved us in this way and, by His mercies (Rm 12:1), our salvation is secure and not dependent on how we love.

13:1–15:13 Believers are to honor those in authority, obey the government, and pay their taxes (cf 1Pt 2:13–17). To fail to do so is to suffer the consequences from those in authority and possibly from God as well. God is the ultimate authority; He used His power to save us (Rm 1:16). The Gospel

This inscription, likely from the time of Constantine (AD 280–334), marks the traditional tomb of the apostle Paul who died as a martyr at Rome.

calls us to rely on God's mercy in Christ, which then motivates us to love as we have been loved. Christians may judge the conduct of others only on the basis of God's Word (see FC Ep and SD X). We should not go beyond it and pronounce judgment in matters of Christian freedom. Those who do so wound other believers and will have to account for such behavior before God Himself. Freedom in Christ is not simply freedom from the Law, but freedom given for a purpose, to serve others in love (Gal 5:13). God's kingdom (14:17) has been given to us through Jesus Christ and by the Holy Spirit. There are strong and weak among us in the Church. We should follow Christ's example of accepting and striving to please others. Despite your sin and weaknesses, Christ bore the reproaches your sins deserved and welcomed you into God's family (15:7).

15:14–16:27 Apart from God's intervention through servants such as Paul, we would not have seen, heard, or understood God's grace. Christ's servants are to respond to His calling and use their gifts in dedicated service as Paul did. Anything we do is simply "what Christ has accomplished through" us (15:18). It is all by grace and is sanctified and empowered by the Holy Spirit. Christ empowered Paul's mission work and gave it the fullness of His blessing (15:29). He will give us joy, refreshment, and peace as well.

Many believers (ch 16) have labored long and hard for Christ with Paul. They serve as examples and role models for us. Christ unites Jew and Gentile, male and female. He breaks through all other human bonds in His Church. He also establishes a committed and dear relationship among believers. The Gospel of Jesus Christ was entrusted to Paul and faithfully proclaimed among the nations in accordance with God's will.

Canonicity

Like Paul's other biblical letters, which were collected and copied as authoritative already in the middle of the first century AD (2Pt 3:15–16), Romans quickly gained canonical status. Even critical scholars regard the book as a genuine letter of Paul.

Lutheran Theologians on Romans

Luther

The unique place that Romans has in theology generally and in the Lutheran Church is illustrated by Luther's preface to the letter for his German Bible. Whereas Luther typically introduced a book of Scripture with a page or two of summary and insights, his preface to Romans occupies 16 pages in the American Edition of his works (AE 35:365–80). This mini-commentary from the great reformer, which presents his mature interpretation of the letter, should not be overlooked. The following is just a few selections from his preface.

"This epistle is really the chief part of the New Testament, and is truly the purest gospel. It is worthy not only that every Christian should know it word for word, by heart, but also that he should occupy himself with it every day, as the daily bread of the soul. We can never read it or ponder over it too much; for the more we deal with it, the more precious it becomes and the better it tastes. . . .

"In this epistle we thus find most abundantly the things that a Christian ought to know, namely, what is law, gospel, sin, punishment, grace, faith, righteousness, Christ, God, good works, love, hope, and the cross; and also how we are to conduct ourselves toward everyone, be he righteous or sinner, strong or weak, friend or foe—and even toward our own selves. Moreover this is all ably supported with Scripture and proved by St. Paul's own example and that of the prophets, so that one could not wish for anything more. Therefore it appears that he wanted in this one epistle to sum up briefly the whole Christian and evangelical doctrine, and to prepare an introduction to the entire Old Testament. For, without doubt, whoever has this epistle well in his heart, has with him the light and power of the Old Testament. Therefore let every Christian be familiar with it and exercise himself in it continually. To this end may God give his grace. Amen." (AE 35:365, 380)

For more of Luther's insights on this book, see *Lectures on Romans: Glosses* and *Scholia* (AE 25); on Rm 9–11, see *The Bondage of the Will* (AE 33).

Gerhard

"Of the thirteen Pauline Epistles, the first is Romans, not in terms of the time of its writing but in dignity, for it is correctly called 'the key to theology' because of the majesty of the things with which it deals. The occasion for its writing was this: There were at Rome both Jews and Gentiles who had been converted to Christ. The Jews were taking for themselves a sort of prerogative because of the divine covenant and their circumcision, urging the ceremonies of the Law and seeking to be justified partly by faith in Christ, partly by their works. The Gentiles, on the other hand, with high arrogance held the Jews in contempt as if God had rejected them. Also, many of them were using their freedom under the Gospel as license for the flesh. The apostle, therefore, wished to advise both with this Epistle.

"Origen, preface to his commentary, concludes that Paul wrote this letter at Corinth on the basis of the following reasons: (1) Because he commends to the Romans Phoebe, whom he calls 'a servant of the church at Cenchreae' (Rom. 16:1). But Cenchreae is the port of Corinth. (2) He greets them in the name of a certain Gaius, his 'host,' about whom he writes to the Corinthians that he baptized him there (1 Cor. 1:14). (3) He greets them in the name of 'Erastus, the city treasurer,' who, he writes, had remained at Corinth (2 Tim. 4:20). (4) The postscript added to this Epistle bears witness to the same thing.

"Romans consists of sixteen chapters in which he joins to his introduction a treatment consisting both of a legal accusation of Gentiles and Jews—that both are guilty of sin—and of evangelical teaching concerning gratuitous justification and the consequent renewal of the life of justification. An epilogue follows this treatment." (ThC E1 § 257)

Questions People Ask about Romans

Integrity of the Letter

The one really debatable question concerning the integrity of the letter is the question of whether ch 16 was originally a part of the Letter to the Romans or not. The arguments used in questioning the integrity of the letter in this respect are chiefly the following:

a. The letter seems to come to a close at 15:33, with a benediction such as is common at the conclusion of Pauline Letters.

b. The closing doxology (16:25–27) is placed at various points in the ancient manuscripts. Some put it after 14:23; some after 15:33; some after 16:23; and some do not have the doxology at all. This would seem to indicate that ch 16 was not a fixed part of the letter in the manuscript tradition.

c. It seems unlikely that Paul would have so many acquaintances in Rome (26 names!) as the greetings of this chapter would indicate.

d. It seems unlikely that Aquila and Prisca (16:3) would change their place of residence as often as this chapter would require: they have moved from Rome to Corinth, from Corinth to Ephesus, are at the time of writing at Rome, and a few years later we find them once more at Ephesus (2Tm 4:19).

e. The content of 16:17–20, a warning against men who create dissensions and divisions, is not prepared for by anything in the first 15 chapters; and the tone of these verses, it is argued, is too brusque and authoritative for Paul to have used in addressing a church that he had not founded and does not know personally.

As for arguments (a) and (b), it should be noted that, while 15:33 does seem to be the closing benediction, a lengthy postscript is not improbable or impossible. The variant position of the doxology in the manuscripts would point to variations in the liturgical usage of the churches—the last chapters were probably not everywhere used in public reading in the services of the churches. It really says nothing about the length of the letter as preserved in various quarters of the church, for even the manuscripts that place the doxology early contain all the chapters of the letter as we have them today.

Regarding (c) (the number of Paul's friends and acquaintances in Rome), we have no way of determining whether Paul could have had some two dozen acquaintances in the Roman church or not. The edict of Claudius (AD 49) banning Jews from Rome affected Jewish Christians too; it brought Aquila and Prisca to Corinth, and it may have brought others into contact with Paul as he worked in Greece and Asia Minor or visited Antioch and Jerusalem.

The movements of Aquila and Prisca (d) are likewise no decisive argument against the integrity of the Letter to the Romans. They had moved from Corinth to Ephesus to be of assistance to Paul in his new field of labor; and a couple whose devotion to the missionary cause Paul could praise with such high words as those of Rm 16:4 might surely have preceded Paul to Rome as they had preceded him to Ephesus. What took them back to Ephesus later we do not know; perhaps they could have been of service to Timothy there (2Tm 4:19).

As for the content and tone of the warning against the disturbers of the church (e), we do not know the historical situation well enough to judge whether such a warning would be out of place or improbable in a letter to Rome or not. And is the tone of the warning, after all, any more brusque and authoritative than the many imperatives of chs 12 through 15? It should be noted, moreover, that in both sections (12–15 and 16:17–20) Paul qualifies the brusqueness of his imperatives, in the first case by recognizing his readers' Christian maturity and their capacity for mutual correction and admonition (15:14), in the second case by gratefully acknowledging their exemplary obedience to the Gospel (16:19).

The chief argument for the integrity of the letter in the form in which it has come down to us will always be the difficulty of explaining how a letter (or fragment of a letter) commending Phoebe to a church (Ephesus is usually taken to be the church addressed) should have become so firmly attached to the first 15 chapters that there is no single outright witness for its omission in all the manuscripts and versions that have been preserved.

Whether the closing doxology (16:25–27) was originally a part of the letter is a separate question. It is obviously more probable that a doxology should have been added to, or inserted in, the letter for liturgical use than that a fragment of a whole letter should have somehow become attached to it. But there is really nothing un-Pauline about the doxology: it fits the whole content of the letter, and there is only very slight evidence that the letter ever existed anywhere without it.

Paul and James

Paul affirms in Romans 3:28: "For we hold that one is justified by faith apart from works of the law."

James 2:24 asserts: "You see then that a person is justified by works and not by faith alone."

Many people think that Paul and James contradict each other with reference to the doctrine of justification, or forgiveness of sins, Paul teaching that a person is justified by faith apart from works, and James defending the thesis that a person is not justified by faith alone, but by faith plus good works. One simply has to read all that Paul has written on justification, and one will readily see that he and James are not in disagreement. Both apostles preach the same truth, but their perspective is not identical in the two passages mentioned above.

Paul uses the term *justification* for that act of God whereby a person's sins are forgiven the moment he or she believes in Jesus as his or her personal Savior. James, as his whole discussion shows, speaks of the state of justification into which the believer has been placed by the grace of God. Justification conceived of as a momentary act, as the reception into God's favor, is entirely by faith. No good works have as yet been performed that could possibly be pointed to as causing it. Justification conceived of as a state, however, embraces faith in the Redeemer and a godly life; for without such a life, as James correctly declares, faith is dead. Thus there is not the least contradiction between these two statements on the subject of justification. They proclaim one and the same truth; but the one emphasizes one aspect of it, the other another aspect. Paul says: "Do not rely on your good works." James says: "Do not neglect to perform good works."

It should also be noted that Paul is speaking of genuine faith, but the context implies that James has in mind faith in the sense of mere head knowledge, for he writes: "Even the demons believe—and shudder!" (2:19). Such believing by demons is far different from the faith that Christians possess. Such "faith" may exist without producing good deeds. But genuine faith in Jesus as our personal Redeemer cannot be present without a godly life. True faith and good works always are found together. Frequently we cite Ephesians 2:8–9: "For by grace you have been saved through faith. And this is not your own doing; it is the gift of God, not a result of works, so that no one may boast." Let us not omit what Paul adds immediately in the next verse: "For we are His workmanship, created in Christ Jesus for good works, which God prepared beforehand, that we should walk in them" (v 10).

Further Study

Lay/Bible Class Resources

Bruce, F. F. *The Epistle of Paul to the Romans: An Introduction and Commentary*. TNTC. Grand Rapids: Eerdmans, 1985. ✥ A helpful, succinct resource.

Franzmann, Martin H. *Romans: A Commentary*. St. Louis: Concordia, 1986. ✥ A brief verse-by-verse exposition of the text in its theological significance from a celebrated Lutheran writer.

Gieschen, Charles A. *God's Abiding Word: Romans*. St. Louis: Concordia, 2002. ✥ Lutheran New Testament scholar. Seventeen-session downloadable Bible study provides a thorough and thought-provoking look at St. Paul's greatest epistle; includes leader's notes, discussion questions, time lines, map, charts, illustrated outline, and glossary.

Life by His Word. St. Louis: Concordia, 2009. ✥ More than 1,500 reproducible one-page Bible studies covering each chapter of the canonical Scriptures. Page references to *The Lutheran Study Bible*. CD-Rom and downloadable.

Lumpp, David. *Romans: Alive in Christ*. GWFT. St. Louis: Concordia, 1996. ✥ Lutheran author. Thirteen-session Bible study, including leader's notes and discussion questions.

Panning, Armin. *Romans*. PBC. St. Louis: Concordia, 2004. ✥ Lutheran author. Excellent for Bible classes. Based on the NIV translation.

Popp, Kevin, David Marth, Jayne Fryar, David Lumpp, Dean Nadasdy, and Jesse Yow. *Romans, Parts 1 & 2*. Leaders Guide and Enrichment Magazine/Study Guide. LL. St. Louis: Concordia, 2001. ✥ Two in-depth, nine-session Bible studies covering the Book of Romans with individual, small group, and lecture portions.

Scharlemann, John. *Journeys through God's Word: Romans*. St. Louis: Concordia, 1999. ✥ An introductory course by a Lutheran pastor. Twelve-session Bible study, including leader's notes and discussion questions.

Church Worker Resources

Barrett, C. K. *A Commentary on the Epistle to the Romans*. New York: Harper & Row, 1958. ✥ A reasonably compact interpretation of Romans, with stress on the theological and historical issues of this Pauline letter.

Cranfield, C. E. B. *Romans: A Shorter Commentary*. Grand Rapids: Eerdmans, 1985. ✥ A condensation of the two-volume set. See below.

Nygren, Anders. *Commentary on Romans*. Philadelphia: Fortress, 1975. ✥ A readable and uplifting commentary written by a Swedish Lutheran bishop and theologian.

Academic Resources

Cranfield, C. E. B. *A Critical and Exegetical Commentary on the Epistle to the Romans*. 2 Vols. ICC. Edinburgh: T&T Clark, 1975; 1979. § A valuable set of resources from a critical scholar, perhaps more detailed than any other commentary on the Greek text. Use with discernment.

Donfried, Karl P., ed. *The Romans Debate*. Revised and expanded. Peabody, MA: Hendrickson, 2005. § A collection of articles by experts and introduced with an overview of the issues. Includes bibliography.

Dunn, James D. G. *Romans*. WBC. 2 Vols. Dallas: Word, 1988. § A more recent, detailed commentary on the Greek text that seeks to read Romans in its first century historical and cultural context.

Käsemann, Ernst. *Commentary on Romans*. Translated by Geoffrey W. Bromiley. Grand Rapids: Eerdmans, 1980. § Verse-by-verse commentary that stresses the theological meaning with emphasis on God's righteousness.

Lange, J. P., F. R. Fay, Philip Schaff, and M. B. Riddle. *The Epistle of Paul to the Romans*. LCHS. New York: Charles Scribner's Sons, 1869. § A helpful older example of German biblical scholarship, based on the Greek text, which provides references to significant commentaries from the Reformation era forward.

Lenski, R. C. H. *The Interpretation of St. Paul's Epistle to the Romans*. Minneapolis: Augsburg, 1936. § An old standard by a Lutheran scholar concerned to reflect carefully the text and its meaning and significance for faith and life.

Luther, Martin. *Lectures on Romans*. Vol. 25 of AE. St. Louis: Concordia, 1972. § Luther's glosses and scholia from his 1515–16 lecture series, during which he saw the full meaning of Romans 1:16–17. Readers should note that this represents Luther early in the Reformation, before his views and theological expression had fully matured. Nonetheless, for those familiar with medieval theology, this is a powerfully influential work of great historical significance.

Melanchthon, Philip. *Commentary on Romans*. Translated by Fred Kramer. 2nd ed. St. Louis: Concordia, 2010. § Melanchthon's 1540 commentary specializes in the study of Paul's rhetoric and its significance for interpreting the letter. Luther's early lectures influenced Melanchthon's approach, but this edition reflects the more mature theology of the Wittenberg Reformation, making a more practical volume for interpreters.

Middendorf, Michael P. *Romans 1–8*. CC. St. Louis: Concordia, 2013. § Thorough theological commentary by a Lutheran scholar of Pauline literature. Based on the Greek text with reference to many other technical resources.

Schreiner, Thomas R. *Romans*. Baker Exegetical Commentary on the New Testament. Grand Rapids: Baker, 1998. § A thorough recent commentary on the Greek text, written by an Evangelical scholar of Pauline theology.

Westerholm, Stephen. *Understanding Paul: The Early Christian Worldview of the Letter to the Romans*. 2nd ed. Grand Rapids: Baker, 2004. § An engaging overview of Paul's thought, based on the Book of Romans.

1 CORINTHIANS

Christ, our wisdom

Waves of the Aegean Sea lap the north shore of the Saronic Gulf in southeastern Greece. From Athens on the east end of the gulf to Cenchreae on the west, the apostle Paul had a 65-mile journey by sea or coastal road, which brought him to the Isthmus of Corinth, that low-lying neck of land that joins Attica (northeast) to the Peloponnese (southwest). High hills and cliffs line the route. But from Cenchreae to Corinth the ground is low enough that ancient merchants could draw their ships overland to the Gulf of Corinth, making that city rich from traders moving east and west. Corinth was a cosmopolitan city that attracted Asians, North Africans, and Westerners to its crowded markets. Along with their trade goods, they supplied a wealth of ideas to the wisdom-hungry Greeks.

In 1 Corinthians Paul writes to a congregation he established during his second missionary journey while visiting and teaching at the local synagogue (Ac 18:1–11). Paul devoted a year and a half to planting the congregation at this key city before returning to the congregation at Antioch that sent him out on mission trips. It was several years later—after Paul's third missionary journey—that he learned about serious divisions in the Corinthian congregation, which prompted his letters to them.

Historical and Cultural Setting

The Corinthian Church had never been tried, refined, and unified by persecution as had happened with other congregations to which Paul wrote. The policy of noninterference that the Roman proconsul Gallio had enunciated to the Jews (Ac 18:14–16) apparently remained in force with his successors. While the church no doubt had to endure the social pressures and animosities that any consistent opposition to the prevailing culture and religiosity evoked, it was safe from Jewish vindictiveness and from governmental coercion. The Christians of Corinth waited for the "revealing of our Lord Jesus Christ" (1Co 1:7), but they were tempted more than other churches to make themselves comfortable and at home in the world while they waited. They

Temple of Apollo at Lechaeum, the Aegean seaport for Corinth. The Lechaeum Way linked the port and the city in the first century AD.

OVERVIEW

Author
Paul the apostle

Date
AD 55, before Pentecost

Places
Corinth in Achaia; Macedonia; Galatia and Ephesus in Asia [Minor]; Jerusalem

People
Paul; Sosthenes; Chloe; Apollos; Cephas; Crispus; Gaius; Stephanas; Timothy; Barnabas; Fortunatus; Achaicus; Aquila; Prisca

Purpose
To explain that Jesus Christ crucified—who embodies the Gospel—creates the Church's unity, service, and hope

Law Themes
Rebukes against divisions; foolish human wisdom; struggles with sexual immorality, idolatry, and spiritual pride; the Lord's Supper abused; doubting the resurrection

Gospel Themes
Saved by Christ crucified; God's wisdom in Christ; the Spirit's work; Gospel ministry through the apostles; sanctified through Baptism; God's unity; the Lord's Supper; resurrection hope

Memory Verses
God's wisdom (1:26–2:2); the Lord's Supper (11:23–32); love's greatness (13:1–13); the resurrection (15:50–58)

TIMELINE

AD 36	Paul's conversion
AD 49–51	Paul plants congregation at Corinth (second missionary journey)
AD 52–55	Paul's third missionary journey
AD 55	Paul writes 1 Corinthians
AD 68	Martyrdom of Peter and Paul

enjoyed security, and they had leisure to speculate about the implications of the Gospel, since they were not called upon to affirm the Gospel in action in the face of persecution.

The city of Corinth developed as early as the tenth century BC and became an exporter of painted pottery. Kings and oligarchs ruled the city. Like other Greek cities, it resisted the Persian invasions and later sided with Sparta in the Great Peloponnesian War (431–404 BC). During the Corinthian War (395–386 BC), the Corinthians sided with Athens against Sparta. Philip of Macedon conquered the city for his empire, which his famous son, Alexander, assumed. The Romans destroyed Corinth in 146 BC but rebuilt it as a Roman colony in 44 BC when free Romans settled there. It was Roman Corinth that Paul visited in c AD 50 where he shared the Gospel at the synagogue established at an earlier, unknown date.

The Corinthian Church existed in a city that was notorious for its wickedness. To "corinthianize" meant to be immoral. Because the city was located on a major isthmus and travel route, sailors on leave thronged its streets. Sacred and secular prostitutes abounded. The Corinthians would have found the teachings of Paul quite different from those which prevailed in their city.

Composition

Author

The apostle Paul wrote 1 Corinthians. The letter, and the corresponding context from Acts and 2 Corinthians, tells us much about Paul personally. He was no bloodless saint on a gold background. He held life dear because he had committed it wholly to the Christ, and he hoped to live to see his Lord when He returned in glory (1Co 15:51; 2Co 5:1–5). Although Paul was ready to sacrifice his life (Ac 20:24), he was not ready to waste it. And so he suffered in a genu-

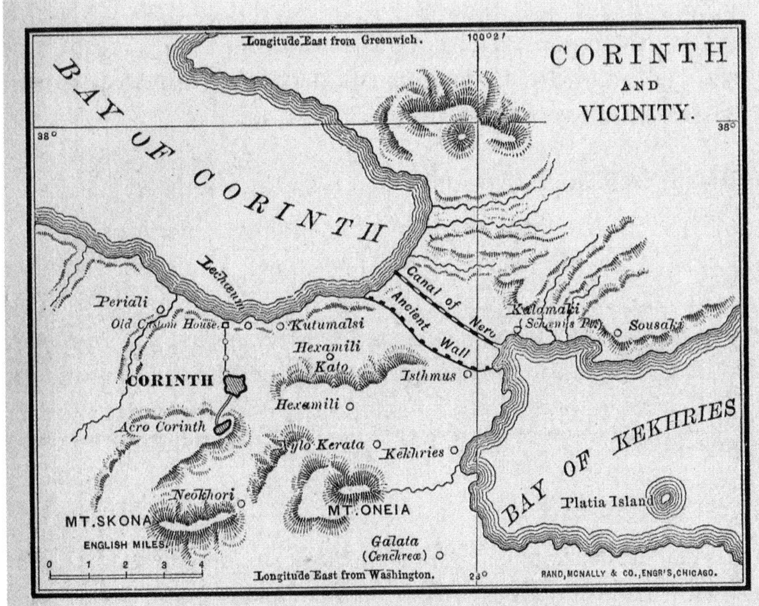

Map of Corinth showing its strategic location between the Ionian Sea (Bay of Corinth) and the Aegean Sea (Bay of Kekhries). Nero attempted unsuccessfully to build a canal connecting the bays. The Lechaeum road linked the city with the coast.

inely human way. He feared in the face of perils and was racked by his fears. But in his human frailty, which he never denied, but rather asserted (1Co 2:3, 4), he held in faith to the fact that all things that are and that happen are from God the Father and are mediated by the Lord Jesus Christ. Therefore, he saw in everything that befell him God's fatherly dealings with him and the Lordship of Christ exercised over him and through him (8:6). He experienced again and again the truth of what his Lord had told him: "My grace is sufficient for you, for My power is made perfect in weakness" (2Co 12:9). Thus a period singularly marked by perils was for Paul also an exhilarating one. We see him in the letters of this period exuberantly welcoming suffering as essential to the Christian life and a salutary part of it (Rm 5:3–5; 8:35–39) and triumphantly boasting of his perils and afflictions as being the glory of his life as an apostle. He employed high irony when he contrasted the assured complacency of the Corinthians with his own sorry and embattled existence (1Co 4:8–13), and the only boast he really permitted himself over against the boasting of his detractors in Corinth was a glorying in his sufferings (2Co 11:23–33). He saw in the paradox of "dying, and behold we live" (6:9) the culmination of his apostolate. The three mighty letters from this period are the golden products of faith and suffering.

Paul's dealings with his beloved, brilliant, and wayward child—the Corinthian Church—give us the most vivid picture of what Paul meant when he spoke of the daily pressure of "anxiety for all the churches" (2Co 11:28). If the growth of the Word of the Lord in this period meant conflict, if it meant "fighting without," it also meant for Paul an intense personal and pastoral anxiety; it meant "fear within" (7:5).

Date of Composition

Paul wrote his letters to Corinth during that strenuous, perilous, and exhilarating period of his life that is commonly known as his third missionary journey (AD 52–55). The heart of that journey was the nearly three years' ministry in the great metropolis of Asia Minor, Ephesus. This ministry was preceded by a revisitation of the churches founded on the first missionary journey and was followed by a revisitation of the European churches of Macedonia and Achaia founded on the second journey.

Purpose/Recipients

Paul had in an earlier letter prepared the Corinthian Church for Timothy's coming visit. That visit was designed by Paul to reinforce and to carry further the work that his letter was designed to do, namely, to bring the Corinthians back from their flight out of Christian reality and into an intoxicated and enthusiastic individualism, back to the cross, back to where Paul stood: "I urge you . . . be imitators of me. That is why I sent you Timothy . . . to remind you of my ways in Christ, as I teach them . . . in every church" (1Co 4:16, 17). The immediately preceding context makes plain what those "ways in Christ" were, Paul ironically contrasted the blissful state of the Corinthians—who had become kings, who were rich, wise, strong, and held in honor—with the apostles' wretched and unfinished state under the cross, sentenced to death, a spectacle for angels and others to gaze on, fools, weak, in disrepute, hungry, thirsty, ill-clad, homeless, the meekly enduring, toilworn refuse of the world (4:8–13). Paul anticipated that Timothy's task would not be a pleasant one and that his reception would be less than amiable (16:10, 11). Timothy's stay was brief, and since Corinthians doesn't mention it, we know nothing of its results except what we can infer from the events that followed.

The Corinthian Church was a brilliantly endowed church, "enriched . . . in all speech and all knowledge . . . not lacking in any gift" (1:5, 7). However, the church was full of tensions and ferment. And the church's outward situation did nothing to improve its inward state. This was because the church members lived in Corinth, where all the brilliance of the Greek mind and all the vagaries of the Greek will mingled with an influx of Eastern religiosity to produce a moral climate that even the Greeks found singularly vicious.

Paul's Known Visits and Letters to Corinth

Paul is known to have stayed in contact with the Corinthian congregation from c AD 50 through early AD 56. Paul's associates continued to visit the congregation, likely with Paul's directions for them (2Tm 4:20).

Church established (Ac 18:1–17) during Paul's second missionary journey (AD 49–51), when he stayed in Corinth a year and a half.

Reports of divisions (1Co 1:11) reached Paul during his third missionary journey (AD 52–55). Timothy also likely visited Corinth and reported to Paul about the congregation before Paul wrote to them, though when is not clear (cf 1Co 4:17; 16:10).

"Painful visit" (2Co 2:1) when Paul forcefully addressed problems in the congregation.

"Previous letter" (1Co 5:9); the date of this letter from Paul is unknown.

1 Corinthians written (AD 55, before Pentecost) in answer to questions the Corinthians sent to Paul.

Anguished letter (2Co 2:4), which some interpreters think was 1 Corinthians, but most think was a letter that Paul sent to follow up on matters addressed in 1 Corinthians. Titus visited the Corinthians and witnessed their anguish and repentance (2Co 7:6–8).

2 Corinthians written (AD 55, before winter).

Winter visit (Ac 20:1–2; 1Co 16:5; 2Co 1:16; 13:1; AD 55–56) when Paul likely wrote the Letter to the Romans, while staying at Corinth about three months.

That the Corinthian congregation survived their maladies is demonstrated by Clement of Rome's Letter to the Corinthians, which he wrote forty years later (c AD 96; *ANF* 1:5–21). However, one may sadly note that Clement wrote to the Corinthians because of divisions.

Literary Features

Genre

First Corinthians is in many respects like other letters Paul wrote to congregations. For more about typical elements of Pauline correspondence, see pp 411–15. First Corinthians clearly reveals that the congregation wrote Paul a letter (1Co 7:1) and laid before him a series of questions on points where it was becoming evident that the teaching of new leaders was not only different from Paul's, but was contradicting it. The fact that Paul interacted with the Corinthians' earlier letter and replied to its questions point by point makes this a unique instructional letter among Paul's writings. The following are a few examples of how Paul interacted with and replied to the congregation.

A plate depicting a couple with the inscription, "Devout in life" (fourth century AD).

Their first question concerned marriage (ch 7). The form that Paul's answer to their question takes makes it tolerably clear what direction the new teachers were taking here. Pursuing their ideal of religious self-fulfillment, they saw in marriage merely an impediment to the religious life and were intent on making the church an association of celibates, without regard for the moral dangers involved in this mass imposition of celibacy, without regard for the authority of the Lord Jesus, who had blessed little children and had declared the bond that united man and woman to be inviolable (Mt 19:3–9, 13–15) and made celibacy a gift reserved for those "to whom it is given" (19:11). They were running counter to the thinking and practice of the apostles also, for the apostles saw in the family and all natural orders primarily vehicles that the grace of God might employ—"You will be saved, *you and your household*," Paul told the jailer at Philippi (Ac 16:31). But the new teachers not only sought to keep men and women from marriage (the passage on the "unmarried" and the "betrothed" takes cognizance of this, 1Co 7:25–38); they also apparently permitted men and women to free themselves of their spouses, especially pagan spouses, in order to be "free" for the Lord, again in contradiction to the express command of Jesus (7:10, 11). Perhaps the license that they conceded with regard to association with harlots (6:12–20) is connected with this attitude toward marriage: if a man could not be continent and yet wished to be free of the impediment of marriage, the association with the harlot would be a solution, since "all things are lawful for me" (6:12).

To the question, "May a Christian eat food that has been offered as a sacrifice to idols?" (chs 8–10) the new teachers had a ready and simple answer: "All of us possess knowledge" (8:1). This meant, since knowledge gives liberty, that "all things are lawful," including the sacrificial meats consecrated to idols. In their self-centered piety, puffed up as they were by knowledge, they did not consider what harm their freedom might do to the brother whose knowledge was not yet deep and firm enough to make him capable of exercising such freedom. In their complacent self-assurance, they did not pause to consider that demonic powers are at work behind all false worship of false gods, though the gods themselves are nothing. They disregarded the warning example of Israel recorded for them in the Old Testament. They flouted the example of the apostles, whose knowledge was as great as theirs, whose wisdom was more profound and certainly more sober and realistic than theirs. Paul had to remind the Corinthians: "Be imitators of me, as I am of Christ" (11:1).

Characters

Corinth had the benefit of a much longer ministry by Paul than any of the other Greek cities. **Paul** was the "father" of the Corinthian Christians; their life in Christ had his unmistakable imprint upon it. We can gauge from Acts and from Paul's letters what it meant to have Paul for a father, how rich a heritage this father gave his children (cf 2Co 12:14). It appears that some of the Corinthians took special pride in their association with the apostle (1Co 1:12).

Among the Corinthians a second group defined itself, saying, **"I follow Apollos"** (1:12), that eloquent and fervent Alexandrian, powerful in the Scriptures (Ac 18:24). His coming to Corinth with letters of recommendation from Ephesus (18:27–28) apparently led to a renewed contact with the synagogue in Corinth, which had previously broken with Paul (18:6–8): "He powerfully refuted the Jews *in public*, showing by the Scriptures that the Christ was Jesus" (18:28). Perhaps it was Apollos who won for Christ the ruler of the synagogue, **Sosthenes**, whom the crowd had beaten before the tribunal of Gallio (18:17). Paul included Sosthenes with himself in the sending of his First Letter to the Corinthians (1Co 1:1). If this Sosthenes was a Corinthian, moreover, a Corinthian converted by Apollos, the fact that Paul thus singled him out is significant. Paul is telling the clique-ridden Corin-

Continued on p 450.

Speaking in Tongues

The issue of what "speaking in tongues" was at Corinth is long-standing. Many interpreters are content to offer no clear resolution. Nevertheless, there are three basic approaches to interpreting what Paul's letter says about "speaking in tongues." They are described below, beginning with the most recent views and concluding with views typically offered by the Church Fathers and the reformers.

Charismatic View

This approach is often associated with the rise of Pentecostalism in 1901 but has roots in the teachings of the French Prophets (Camisards; c 1702), Shakers (c 1747), Mormons, and Irvingites (c 1831). In this view, the Holy Spirit fills people and causes them to speak in human or angelic languages for the purposes of prayer or prophecy. Many charismatics view speaking in tongues as a necessary sign of being Spirit-filled, of perfect sanctification, or even of salvation. They regard such speaking in tongues as a normal activity for Christians that was lost in the early years of the Church. Some groups view Christians who do not speak in tongues as spiritually weak, cold, or dead.

Religious Psychology View

This approach stems from the comparative study of religions and from modern psychiatry (the latter arising c 1792). It began with C. G. Bardili (1761–1808), who compared speaking in tongues with records of ecstatic utterances by ancient Greek prophetesses at the oracle of Delphi. The critical scholar J. G. Eichhorn (1752–1827) popularized Bardili's opinion around the time that the experiences of Shakers, Mormons, and Irvingites began to be documented. In this view, speaking in tongues is an ecstatic, psychological state that is common to all radical religions and is evoked by religious fervor. The religious psychology view was important for the rise of the charismatic view because it legitimized religious ecstasy as common and blunted theological evaluation of the activity.

Cultural-Historical View

This approach was taught by the Church Fathers and the reformers, who viewed the gift of tongues as a special miracle for demonstrating God's acceptance of new believers (cf Ac 10:44–48; 11:17) and as a special ability to learn and use languages for the good of the Church. It holds that tongues are genuine human languages, as described in Ac 2:5–11. It points to the use and translation of various languages in the early Christian communities, which were culturally diverse.

The expression "to speak in a tongue" is common in Hebrew and Aramaic, where it means to speak or read another language (cf Dt 28:49; Ne 13:24; Es 1:22; Is 28:11; 33:19; Jer 5:15; Mishnah; Targums). Rabbis regarded Hebrew as the proper language for prayer (Sotah 7:1–2; Megillah 2:1) and the holy or heavenly language (spoken by angels, Babylonian Talmud, Sotah 33a). They wrestled with the issue of which language(s) to use during worship (see *Concordia Journal* 22:295–302). In the first century, Hebrew was still the language of temple liturgy in Jerusalem, but Aramaic or Greek was spoken by most people in Galilee and Judea (Mk 5:41; Jn 19:20; Ac 6:1; 21:37–22:2; 26:14). As Jewish Christians traveled, they naturally took their languages and synagogue practices with them.

The Corinthian congregation began from Paul's preaching at a Jewish synagogue (Ac 18:4–8). Members of the Corinthian congregation knew various languages. Paul's letters to them are written in Greek but include Hebrew or Aramaic liturgical terms and titles (1Co 1:12; 3:22; 9:5; 14:15; 15:5; 16:22; 2Co 1:20). Roman Jews were also present (Ac 18:2), and inscriptional evidence shows the importance of Latin at Corinth, since the Romans rebuilt Corinth as a colony. It is easy to see how language in worship could become an issue, especially when proud "Hebrews" came to teach at the church (2Co 11:13, 22).

Luther on Tongues

The cultural-historical view was what Luther had in mind as he interpreted 1Co 12–14, and was also the setting assumed in the Lutheran Confessions (AC XXIV 3–4; Ap XXIV 2–5; see also the notes in *TLSB*).

See also *The Charismatic Movement and Lutheran Theology* (CTCR Report, January 1972); *The Lutheran Church and the Charismatic Movement* (CTCR Report, April 1977); and *Spiritual Gifts* (CTCR Report, September 1994).

In Corinthians, Paul emphasized the need to preach the sacrifice of Christ for our sins. His letters interpret and apply the events recorded in the Gospel story.

thian Church: Here is one who received the Gospel from Apollos and is one with me in all that I am telling you, just as Apollos himself is (3:5–9; 16:12).

At the time when Paul wrote his letter, there was in the Corinthian Church a third group who said, **"I follow Cephas"** (1Co 1:12). They professed a special allegiance to Simon Peter, and they used the original Aramaic form of his official name (Cephas). This would indicate that they were Jews who had come to Corinth from one of the eastern Judaic churches that Peter had evangelized. The presence of these Christians from the fields where Peter had worked no doubt meant an enrichment for the Corinthian Church; but it also created tensions. The various components of the young church—the original converts of Paul, the converts of Apollos, and the new arrivals from the east—could not as yet, or would not, unite in that free and richly various oneness that Paul described as essential to the life of the church (ch 12). Apollos himself had worked in complete harmony with Paul; no shadow of blame attached to him, as every mention of him in the first letter shows. But there were those, converts or admirers of Apollos, who compared this personable, energetic, and brilliant preacher with Paul and found him more to their liking than Paul, the bondservant of God who had come to Corinth "in weakness and in fear and much trembling" (2:3), who candidly described himself as "unskilled in speaking" (2Co 11:6), and preached the *crucified* Christ with an almost monomaniac insistence (1Co 2:2). The new arrivals from the east, the Cephas people, quite naturally felt themselves to be the representatives of a mature, more original kind of Christianity than that of the churches founded by Paul. They had received the word from Peter, the "first" of the apostles, who had seen the Lord Jesus and had lived with Him. Paul was, in their eyes, an apostle of not quite equal rank with the Twelve, the child "untimely born" (15:8), not really a full member of the apostolic brotherhood. They felt as charter members of an old, honorable club might feel toward newer members, who besides being new would not be members at all if *they* had not generously relaxed the rules a bit.

It is noteworthy that along with the discussion of speaking in other languages (chs 12–14) one also finds specific Semitic names or liturgical expressions mentioned in the Letters to the Corinthians ("Cephas," 1Co 1:12; 3:22; 9:5; 15:5; "Amen," 1Co 14:16; 2Co 1:20; "Our Lord, come!" [*Maranatha*], 1Co 16:22) and that some of Paul's opponents were proud "Hebrews" (2Co 11:22).

All that was potentially harmful and disruptive in Corinth was crystallized and intensified by the emergence of a fourth group in the congregation. Since Paul never fully described this group, it is difficult to get a clear picture of these people, and sometimes it is impossible to see where the line between them and the Cephas people, for instance, is being drawn. But the following would seem to be a fair characterization of them. They came from outside the Corinthian Church. Paul distinguished them from those who professed allegiance to himself or to Apollos, the men who had worked at Corinth (1Co 1:12). His words in 2Co 11:4 explicitly marked this group as **new arrivals in Corinth**: "If someone *comes* and proclaims another Jesus than the one we proclaimed." Paul's contemptuous reference in 2Co 3:1 to "some" who need letters of recommendation makes it probable that they came with such letters from one of the eastern churches (which need not imply that any of the eastern churches was necessarily responsible for the teaching that they developed at Corinth). Like the Cephas people, they were Judaic and proud of it, Hebrews, Israelites, descendants of Abraham (2Co 11:22). But they were not Judaizers of the sort that had disturbed the churches of Galatia. We hear nothing of circumcision and the reimposition of the Mosaic Law in connection with these men. One can imagine that they claimed to be the inheritors of the true Judaic-Christian tradi-

The Syriac Rabbula Gospels (sixth century) include one of the earliest depictions of Pentecost.

tion and for that reason felt themselves uniquely qualified to lead the church beyond the first stages of that tradition into the full riches of knowledge and freedom in Christ.

What they brought into Corinth was a brilliant and persuasive kind of liberalism, which operated (as liberalism characteristically does) with genuinely Christian slogans and catchwords. If, according to Paul, they preached "another Jesus," *they* no doubt claimed that they were preaching the genuine Jesus. If they proclaimed a "different Gospel" and had and imparted a "different spirit," it was Paul who said so, not they. They claimed that their Gospel was the true Gospel and their spirit the true Spirit of God (2Co 11:4). The slogan they brought with them (or developed in the course of their activities at Corinth) was as Christian as a slogan can be: "I belong to Christ" (1Co 1:12; 2Co 10:7). Paul himself used the phrase to designate the Christian (1Co 3:23; cf Rm 8:9).

This fourth group exalted the Christ and awaited His return. They treasured His gift of the Spirit and set great store by the gifts given by the Spirit (cf 1Co 7:40). But they exalted the Christ as the Giver of knowledge and treasured the gifts of the Spirit primarily as a means to knowledge of God, as the way to wisdom (3:18–20; 8:1–3, 10, 11; 13:9). And this knowledge, they claimed, made them free; the knowledge and wisdom that they possessed carried them beyond any previous revelation of God, beyond the Old Testament Scriptures, beyond anything contained in the apostolic word. Before this ultimate knowledge of God, which they claimed to possess, all previous standards became meaningless, all former ties were dissolved, all the old taboos were gone: "All things are lawful for me"—that was their boast (6:12; 10:23). It was an intellectually appealing and an intoxicating message that they brought. It is not surprising that they attracted followers and deeply influenced the whole church.

Their influence on the life of the church went deep, and it was harmful in the extreme. We can trace its beginnings in Paul's reference to a letter (now lost) that he had written to the Corinthians before our present first letter (5:9). In that earlier letter Paul had demanded of the Corinthians that they refuse to have fellowship with "immoral people." This demand of Paul's was questioned by the church, perhaps even rejected as being unclear and impracticable (5:9–11).

Perhaps it was "Chloe's people" (to whom Paul refers in 1:11) who delivered Paul's earlier letter to Corinth; they would then have seen and could report to Paul how it was received, how the church broke up into factions over the issues involved (chs 1–4). It was probably Chloe's people who reported to Paul the conditions that resulted from this new proclamation of absolute liberty at Corinth; they could tell Paul why his letter was questioned and contradicted: the new teachers were saying that the new knowledge set people free. At least one Corinthian Christian had drastically used that liberty (5:1): Why should not a man be free to live with his father's wife (probably his stepmother) after his father's death? What the Old Testament said no longer bound him (Dt 22:30; 27:20), and the authority of Jesus and His apostles had been superseded by the new revelation of the Spirit. The Corinthian Church as a whole not only tolerated this immorality, but was even "arrogant" about it (1Co 5:2); these men felt that they were demonstrating their spiritual maturity in tolerating it. The people of Chloe could tell Paul, too, of the breakdown of discipline in the church, how differences between Christian brethren were no longer being settled within the church, but were being taken into pagan courts. The preachers of the new freedom had no interest in, and no taste for, the serious and painful business of keeping the church pure by calling erring brethren to repentance (6:1–11). Paul had to hammer home the most elementary moral facts in his attempt to pierce the complacency of the people intoxicated by the new freedom (6:9–11).

The new liberty preached in Corinth conceded to the Christian man the freedom to associate with prostitutes. The Law that demanded sexual purity of them was being put on the same level with the law concerning clean and unclean foods (6:12–20)—or, at least, the satisfaction of sexual desire was being put on the same level with the satisfaction of hunger (1Co 6:13). The fact that the Apostolic Council had expressly laid the abstaining from immorality on the consciences of the Gentile Christians (Ac 15:29) made no impression in Corinth.

Not everyone at Corinth was so completely swept away by the eloquent rationalism of the new teachers or so deeply intoxicated by the liberty that they offered that he asked no questions or raised no objections. Men such as **Stephanas** and **Fortunatus** and **Achaicus** (1Co 16:17) saw that it was high time that Paul be consulted explic-

A third-century sarcophagus relief of the Last Supper, when Jesus transformed the Passover meal into the Sacrament of Holy Communion.

itly and at length on the questions that were raised by the new theology of knowledge and freedom, and they saw to it that he was consulted.

But it was not only in the family and in private life that the intoxication of the new liberty was working mischief. It infected the worship life of the church too (chs 11–14). Women were asserting their newfound liberty by appearing at worship without the veil, which was the badge of their womanliness and their recognition of the role to which God the Creator and Redeemer (11:3, 8) had called them (11:2–16). They were also adding to the confusion of an already chaotic public worship by assuming a teaching authority to which neither Jesus nor the apostles had called them (14:33–36). But the voice of Jesus, the voice of His apostles, the practice of the churches of God (11:16) did not deter the proponents and adherents of the new liberty; they were "inclined to be contentious" nevertheless.

This spirit of rampant individualism made the common fellowship meals of the church a scene of feasting and carousing, in which the rich disregarded the poor and made of the Lord's Supper, celebrated in connection with the common meal, anything but the *Lord's* supper. The supper that commemorated and made effectively present the utter self-giving and self-sacrifice of the Lord Jesus Christ and was designed to unite the Lord's people in the eating of the one loaf and the partaking of the one cup became the scene and the means of the Corinthians' self-assertion and of division (11:17–34). When knowledge is the capstone of the religious structure and love no longer rules (ch 13), decency and order are sacrificed, edification is no longer possible, the salutary commands of the apostle are disregarded (14:37–38), and the example of the churches of God everywhere means nothing (14:36).

All that characterizes the "Christ-men" appeared in a concentrated and peculiarly clear form in their denial of the bodily resurrection of the dead (ch 15)—their false spirituality, which disregarded and degraded the body and all things natural; their false conception of knowledge, which made them manipulators of ideas who could disregard the central fact of all history, the bodily resurrection of Jesus Christ from the dead; their false conception of freedom, which moved them to oppose themselves and their ideas, not only to Paul but to all the apostles and to the Old Testament witness to Christ as well. In their intoxication of liberty (Paul had to tell them to come to their right mind, to sober up, 15:34), they felt free to sacrifice the central fact of the apostolic proclamation to Greek prejudice—to the Greek, the idea of a bodily resurrection was particularly offensive, as the reaction of the Stoics and Epicureans at Athens to Paul's preaching of the resurrection shows (Ac 17:32).

It became abundantly clear that when these men said, "We belong to Christ," they were saying it in an exclusive sense, as a fighting slogan. The liberty that their "knowledge" gave them, their "freedom" in the Spirit, necessarily involved a break with the authority of Paul, who had planted the word in Corinth. There is some evidence to indicate that they considered Paul superseded and unnecessary to the Corinthian Church and claimed that he would not come to Corinth again. Paul's words in 1Co 4:18–19 hinted as much: "Some are arrogant, as though I were not coming to you. But I will come to you soon, if the Lord wills, and I will find out not the talk of these arrogant people but their power." A break with Paul necessarily meant a break with Apollos, who had watered where Paul had planted; and it meant a break with all apostolic authority. Paul's words concerning their arrogance (1Co 4:18–19) and their contentiousness (11:16; 14:38) seem to indicate that they were highly autocratic and contemptuous of any power but their own, a fact that is confirmed by the bitter irony of Paul's reproach to the Corinthians in 2Co 11:20: "You bear it if someone makes slaves of you, or devours you, or takes advantage of you, or puts on airs, or strikes you in the face." They and those who were most completely taken in by them thus constituted a clique in the church; and as a clique produces more cliques by way of reaction, there ensued that sorry and divided state of the church that Paul dealt with so powerfully in the first four chapters of 1 Corinthians. At Corinth the line between the church (where Christ alone is Lord) and the world (where men head movements and command loyalties) was being perilously blurred.

Narrative Development or Plot

As a letter, 1 Corinthians is not written with a storyline or plot. Like Paul's other letters, it follows a pattern of addressing doctrinal topics followed by practical topics, though these two great themes from Paul are somewhat mixed in portions of the letter since the apostle was writing in answer to the Corinthians' questions.

Paul emphasized that the factions in the congregation would eventually destroy the Church of God because Christ's body is only where there is unity. In strong terms he affirmed that God had called them by the foolishness of preaching and not by the wisdom of human words. Paul also reminded them that he had resisted every temptation to use the high-flown language of his opponents and had determined to preach nothing except Jesus Christ and Him crucified (ch 3). True believers would be satisfied with this simple preaching because they would have no desire to know anything

Continued on p 458.

Outline

I. Greeting (1:1–3)

II. Thanksgiving (1:4–9)

III. Conflict over Divisions (1:10–4:21)
- A. Report of the Problem in Corinth (1:10–17)
- B. The Cross as the Power of God (1:18–2:5)
  1. The limits of human wisdom in light of the cross (1:18–25)
  2. The power of the cross shown among the Corinthians (1:26–2:5)
- C. The Transforming Work of the Spirit of God (2:6–3:4)
  1. True wisdom (2:6–9)
  2. The Spirit as revealer (2:10–16)
  3. Spiritual maturity in the Spirit (3:1–4)
- D. The Spirit at Work in the Church and Its Ministers (3:5–4:21)
  1. The work of the Spirit through the ministers of the Church (3:5–17)
     - a. Shared work in God's field (3:5–9)
     - b. Shared work in the building (3:10–15)
     - c. The temple and the indwelling Spirit (3:16–17)
  2. The work of God's ministers cannot be evaluated on the basis of human "wisdom" (3:18–4:5)
  3. The power of the Gospel made known in the weakness of the messenger (4:6–21)

IV. Compromise and Conflict in Corinth (chs 5–6)
- A. An Incestuous Relationship, with Further Implications (ch 5)
- B. Conflict and the Courts (6:1–11)
- C. Compromise in Sexual Relationships (6:12–20)

- V. Response to Questions Raised by the Corinthians (7:1–11:1)
  - A. Marriage, Status, Celibacy, and Widows (ch 7)
    - 1. Marriage and marital intimacy (7:1–7)
    - 2. Should a person remain unmarried? (7:8–9)
    - 3. Remaining together in marriage (7:10–16)
    - 4. The call of God and social status (7:17–24)
    - 5. About the unmarried (7:25–38)
    - 6. About widows (7:39–40)
  - B. Idols and Eating (8:1–11:1)
    - 1. Theological foundations (8:1–6)
      - a. The principle: love over knowledge (8:1–3)
      - b. The theology: all belongs to God (8:4–6)
    - 2. Situation 1: eating in temple dining rooms (8:7–13)
    - 3. Two examples: Paul and Israel (9:1–10:13)
      - a. Love of others shown by Paul (ch 9)
      - b. Idolatry by Israel and its consequences (10:1–13)
    - 4. Situation 2: sharing the Lord's Supper and avoiding temple worship (10:14–22)
    - 5. Situation 3: idol food from the marketplace (10:23–26)
    - 6. Situation 4: eating in the home of an unbeliever (10:27–30)
    - 7. Conclusion: giving glory to God and living for the salvation of others (10:31–11:1)
- VI. Freedom and Love in Worship and the Use of Gifts (11:2–14:40)
  - A. Gender and Public Worship (11:2–16)
  - B. The Unity Created by the Lord's Supper and Rebuke of the Status Distinctions in Corinth (11:17–34)
  - C. The Gifts of the Spirit for Service in Love (12:1–11)
    - 1. The Christocentric unity created by the Spirit (12:1–3)
    - 2. Diversity in unity: different gifts from one Spirit (12:4–7)
    - 3. The gifts of the Spirit (12:8–11)
  - D. The Unity of the Body of Christ (12:12–31)
  - E. The "Greatest" Way: Love (ch 13)
    - 1. Love as central to the gifts (13:1–3)
    - 2. Nature and practice of love (13:4–7)
    - 3. The permanence of love (13:8–13)

- F. Love for Others and the Use of Gifts (ch 14)
  - 1. Speaking must build up the community (14:1–25)
    - a. Speaking is not for one's own benefit (14:1–5)
    - b. The uselessness of speaking that cannot be understood (14:6–12)
    - c. Praying and speaking with the mind (14:13–19)
    - d. Speaking in the presence of outsiders (14:20–25)
  - 2. Speaking and order in worship (14:26–40)
    - a. Principles and examples (14:26–36)
    - b. Warning and encouragement (14:37–40)

VII. The Resurrection of the Dead (ch 15)

- A. The Resurrection of Christ (15:1–11)
- B. The Consequences of Denying the Resurrection (15:12–34)
  - 1. The consequences of denying any resurrection (15:12–19)
  - 2. Christ's resurrection is the foundation of present and future life (15:20–34)
- C. The Bodily Resurrection (15:35–58)

VIII. Final Matters (ch 16)

- A. The Collection for the Church in Jerusalem (16:1–4)
- B. Paul's Travel Plans (16:5–11)
- C. Concluding Exhortations and Greetings (16:12–24)

more than what God had revealed to them in the person and work of Jesus. After addressing a variety of doctrinal and practical issues, Paul concluded his letter with directions on the great collection for the poor believers in Jerusalem and with a brief report of his own future plans (ch 16).

Resources

As noted above, Paul composed this letter while interacting with an earlier letter from the Corinthians, which allowed him to reply to their questions or statements. The ESV translation has placed quotation marks around these Corinthian comments (e.g., 1:12; 3:4; 6:12–13; 7:1; 8:1; 10:23; cf 15:12). Paul also wrote in reaction to a report (cf 1:11).

As one of Paul's longest letters, 1 Corinthians includes a fair number of quotations from the Old Testament (c 16) though not nearly as many as appear in his other longer Letter to the Romans (c 60 quotations).

Text and Translations

The text of 1 Corinthians is well established through a wealth of early manuscripts dating as early as c AD 200 (Papyrus 46) and from Early Church Fathers who cite the letter. As with Paul's other letters, scholars discuss the possible influence of the early heretic Marcion on causing some of the textual variants. The largest variant is that some western manuscripts place 1Co 14:34–35 after v 40. For more on this text, see the notes in *TLSB*.

Doctrinal Content

Summary Commentary

1:1–2:5 Paul highlights the strengths of the congregation, strengths God extends to all believers by His grace. In contrast, divisions in the Church are a denial of the one Baptism into Christ, who was crucified for all. We should avoid pride and boasting about what we do for God or for others. The Good News is conveyed not through eloquence, but through humble messengers testifying about the cross.

2:6–4:21 The message of the cross is simple, but the spiritual wisdom that comes with it touches every area of life and faith. There is no ground for pride in human achievement in Christ's Church. Such an attitude undermines the very nature of His gifts of salvation and service. People may despise God's messenger because the Spirit's power is concealed in lowly, suffering leaders like Paul. The crowd always yearns for flashy leadership and despises those who teach the basics and lead by example.

The spotless Passover Lamb became one of the earliest Christian symbols of redemption (1Co 5:7; cf Jn 1:29; Rv 5:6).

Chs 5–6 Sins such as sexual immorality are out of place among the people of God. Christ, our Passover Lamb, has taken our sins upon Himself. Just as the old sinful nature rises to cause grievances between Christians, it also tempts us to seek satisfaction through secular processes. God calls churches to settle grievances through Law and Gospel before matters get out of hand. Because Christ has united us with Him and with one another, immorality has no place among us. Freedom to live in Christ excludes living in opposition to Him.

Ch 7 Marriage brings obligations, but being in Christ forms a new being. The Lord transforms believers from our previous existence and makes us members of His household. In view of this, Paul outlines two blessed estates, that of marriage and that of celibacy.

Chs 8–9 The rights and the freedom of the Gospel are wrongly promoted in the Corinthian Church, leading the believers to adopt too easily the behaviors and practices of the surrounding culture. No believer has the right or freedom to destroy the faith of others, especially those whom Paul describes as weak in the faith. Faith is not a private matter. As founder of the Corinthian Church, and as an apostle, Paul is perceived to have more "rights" than anyone else. Yet he consistently sets an example for the Corinthians, encouraging them to put off their own rights in order to serve one another.

10:1–11:1 "Flee from idolatry" (10:14) summarizes this section. Even Israel, who had seen God's mighty works throughout the exodus, acted as if God were not real, as if they could rely on gods of their own creation or even themselves to keep them safe. In Western culture, Christians rarely have to deal with food sacrificed to other gods, though Christians in Asia and Africa must deal with these issues directly. In either case, Paul's instructions show that our actions communicate something about who we are to those around us.

An ancient mosaic showing a Roman woman who has drawn her *palla* (outer garment) up over her head, a sign of modesty.

11:2–16 Corinthian women thought they could go along with cultural trends. However, removal of their hair covering would be similar to a woman in our culture removing her wedding ring: it symbolizes that she no longer intends to live in a faithful marriage relationship. Paul is concerned with outward conduct as well as with the roles God has given to each gender. The removal of the covering would eliminate the gender distinctions God established.

11:17–34 The Corinthians have turned the Sacrament into a supper of their own making. As a result, the community of believers formed by the Gospel and the Sacrament is being harmed, and individuals are falling under God's judgment. Recalling Christ's own institution of the Supper, Paul reminds the Corinthians to recognize what God has offered in the Sacrament: the body and blood of Christ, the forgiveness of sins, and through it the union of the Body of Christ, the Church, gathered around the altar.

Chs 12–14 God, who is one, unified and blessed the Corinthian congregation through His Spirit and gifts. Paul seeks to settle and unite the Corinthian congregation by emphasizing the order God established in creation and the priority of the Gospel. By so completely describing and advocating love's divine qualities, Paul reveals the Corinthians' immaturity. He sharply rebukes all noisy, clanging boasts of superiority. Yet, he alludes to the fact that the Father—who knows His children all too well—still loves them. Some Corinthians showed a lack of love by pursuing their own edification to the neglect of those around them. For example, issues of worship practice divided the Corinthians. Though Paul tolerates the Corinthians' personal interests, he insists that such interests have no place in congregational gatherings, which should clearly teach God's Word for all.

Ch 15 Because of zeal for more knowledge, the Corinthians have neglected what has first importance: the simple truths and application of the Gospel. They take pride in their wisdom, but Paul tears apart their arguments with basic logic and rhetoric defending the doctrine of the bodily resurrection. Logic, rhetoric, and even sarcasm have their uses in preaching and teaching the Gospel. Yet all our powers and wisdom must remain subject to the Lord, who is "all in all" (v 28). The body—corrupted by sin—declines, decays, and dies. Humanly speaking, we can extend our lives only by having children, whom we likewise corrupt with our inherited sin. The justification Jesus provided is our resurrection-hope against sin, death, and the Law's condemnation. Jesus delivers us from death's jaws.

Ch 16 Compassion leads the early Christian congregations to treasure up and distribute support for fellow Christians and ministries in need. As Paul closes the letter, he also clears the way for future work and for the work of his colleague Timothy. Paul urges the leaders at Corinth to recognize the service, calling, and authority of one another and to see themselves as part of a larger team. Paul's bittersweet conclusion illustrates his passion for the Gospel and for the congregation.

Specific Law Themes

Paul's opening chapters include rebukes against the divisions the Corinthians have introduced into the congregation, in part due to false teachings. Paul points out the foolishness of human wisdom, which offers solutions that inevitably lead to destruction. Paul also notes how the Corinthians struggle against issues of sexual immorality, idolatry, and spiritual pride: things typical of the environment in which they dwell but that should not be part of their lives as believers. Even the Lord's Supper is abused among them as they do not recognize the sacredness of the Sacrament—the body and blood of Christ—or the body of believers for which the Sacrament was intended. The false teachings they have entered into also undermine yet another central truth of the Christian faith: the resurrection of the body, which God has promised through raising His Son.

Specific Gospel Themes

In this letter Paul emphasizes the cross of Christ as the basis of our salvation—He would not have us know of Christianity in any other way. Christ crucified becomes the focal point of all his teaching and preaching such that the cross and Christ reveal the wisdom of God in starkest contrast to the wisdom of the world. The Almighty saves us through the weakness, suffering, and death of the cross. The Spirit whom we receive in Holy Baptism sanctifies us and enlightens us with His gifts for mutual edification. He works through the apostles whom God has called to preach the Word, even though by worldly standards they appear foolish and of no account, yet they are representatives of the true God. Paul emphasizes the unique character of the Lord's Supper, which is unlike any other meal or, indeed, any other experience. For in the Sacrament we partake of the very body and blood of Christ for the forgiveness of sins and for unity with the Lord and with one another. We are likewise united with the Lord in a bodily resurrection like His in which we will participate when He returns.

Specific Doctrines

Here is God's plenty; here in this severely functional, working theology of 1 Corinthians, a genuine letter, conditioned by history and directed to real-life situations from beginning to end, are inexhaustible riches for the Church to live by. We begin with the most obvious and most important fact about the letter: the entire New Testament is a chorus of grateful praise for the cross, but this letter drives home the centrality of the cross in a vital way. It proclaims the cross not as a tenet to be held or as an article to be believed, but as a power that makes possible, and demands, a life lived to God in all its parts and all its functions, a human life judged by the righteousness of God and a new life created and endowed by His grace.

The letter consequently draws the line between the Church and the world, between human wisdom and the Gospel, between the wisdom of this age and the "foolish," paradoxical wisdom of God, in a way that should have shattered once for all the attempts to make Christianity a rich and interesting blend of the two. The legacy of 1 Corinthians is a perpetual reminder to the Church that she must dare to be "other" if she is to be the apostolic Church of God, that she must dare to oppose the axioms and standards of this world if she is to do her divine work in the world. In a way, the first four chapters of the letter are a practical commentary on those words of our Lord in which He inverts the standards of this world, and does so by pointing to His cross:

> You know that the rulers of the Gentiles lord it over them, and their great ones exercise authority over them. It shall not be so among you. But whoever would be great among you must be your servant, and whoever would be first among you must be your slave, even as the Son of Man came not to be served but to serve, and to give His life as a ransom for many. (Mt 20:25–28)

First Corinthians is a rich explication of that word of Jesus. Jesus spoke these words to His disciples, to men who had received His promise that they should share royally in the enthronement of the Son of Man (Mt 19:28). Paul tells the congregation at Corinth, "All things are yours, . . . the world or life or death or the present or the future—all are yours" (1Co 3:21, 22); but he

Bodily resurrection is the chief topic of 1Co 15.

tells them in the same breath, "and you are Christ's" (3:23). He tells them that they belong to the Crucified, who gave Himself for all people. And so all their liberty in Christ and all the riches given them by the Spirit are theirs for ministry. They are enriched in all things in order that they may enrich their brethren.

First Corinthians has also impressed upon the Church the religious significance and the sanctity of the human body, the body as God's creation, as the abode of the Spirit, destined for glory, the expressive instrument of man's will in the service of God. Chapter 15, sometimes called the resurrection chapter, is the climax of these themes since it forcefully teaches the resurrection of the body. Paul's words on the bodily worship of the Christian in this letter are his practical application of the broad imperative in his Letter to the Romans: "Present your bodies as a living sacrifice, holy and acceptable to God, which is your spiritual worship" (Rm 12:1). These are the words of a man who worked with his hands to the glory of his Lord. Closely related to this religious appreciation of the body is Paul's sense of history as the vehicle of divine revelation: the "mighty acts of God," the cross, the resurrection, the hard, nonmalleable fact, the act of God that mankind cannot manipulate—these are for him the very essence of theology. The Gospel is not ideas and principles about which we may theorize and speculate; the Gospel is news of that culminating act of God that has transformed the relationship between God and man and will transfigure all creation.

This emphasis on the body and on history gives Paul that sober sense of reality that makes him the enemy of all enthusiasm and enables him to see both sides of a question, like the question of celibacy and marriage, and to deal fairly with both. It enables him to give a full and evangelical answer to a question such as meat offered to idols instead of a misapplied, standard reply. It enables him to do both, to give sober, down-to-earth directions for the worship of the church, and to carry his readers aloft in a hymn on the divinely given love that gives all gifts of the Spirit their value, spends itself in a reckless splendor of self-giving, and is a piece of the new world of God transplanted to this dying world even now.

As in Romans, Paul also teaches here about the bondage of the human will to sin (1Co 2:14) and Christ as our life and salvation (1:30), who has justified us through Baptism in His name (6:11). No other book in the New Testament teaches us more about the Lord's Supper, the topic of Paul's concern in chs 10–11, which he contrasts to the idolatrous offerings of pagan sacrifice. As the Church has turned to ch 7 for instruction on marriage and celibacy, it has likewise turned to ch 13 in celebration of divine love that excels all human love. Paul's words that "all things should be done decently and in order" (14:40) perpetually guide the Church's adaptation of traditions and practices for the sake of the Gospel rather than in spite of it.

Application

1:1–2:5 We rejoice in our relationship to God: He has called us and sanctified us, and He will sustain us. His faithful servants preach the Gospel and are not to become objects of unhealthy devotion. The triune God alone is the object of our faith and hope. We bring nothing but sin into our relationship with God but receive all good things from Him. We look to the cross of Jesus for God's power and rest in His wisdom.

2:6–4:21 In view of the cross, we see unbelievers with new compassion, as people with no true spiritual comprehension. The Holy Spirit grants such understanding only through the Gospel. God accomplishes everything for our good, living in us by His Spirit. He sends us spiritual fathers to nurture us, entrusting to them both the Law and the Gospel for our spiritual good.

Chs 5–6 Through repentance and absolution, the Lord renews us as His undefiled creation, even against sins such as sexual immorality. The Lord has judged us "not guilty" in view of Jesus' sacrifice, and He has washed us pure in Holy Baptism. When we fall into sin, we can repent of the disunity we have brought. Jesus Christ will restore and renew us as His very own.

Ch 7 In marriage, Christians can encourage one another, non-Christians may be drawn to belief, and children can be brought up in the faith. Whatever our station in life, we now live out the new life in the station to which God has appointed us. Marriage remains unique among God's blessings. It survived humanity's fall into sin. There are also responsibilities with marriage, and it is particularly important for the Christian to consider these when sitting down to "count the cost" of discipleship (Lk 14:28).

Chs 8–9 Faithful Christians will be zealous to pray for and carry out God's will that all be saved and come to the knowledge of the truth (1Tm 2:3–4). How marvelously our Savior bears with our weaknesses! Most important, He took away our sin and builds us up in love. The teaching and examples of Jesus Himself (Mk 10:45) urges us to set aside our own rights for the sake of others. His death and resurrection transform our lives so that we do not seek our own good but the good of others (Php 2:1–11).

Ch 10 In our age, there are many gods. Some are worshiped as such (e.g., Islam, Hinduism); others subtly become gods (e.g., money, pride). But the one true God does not tolerate shared allegiance. If we participate in the worship of false gods or support churches that do not faithfully confess the Gospel in all its purity, this would indicate that we assent to what those worshiping communities believe. For this reason, we avoid such false worship. At the Lord's Table, He offers His body and blood for the forgiveness of sins and through them creates a faithful community, one committed to Him and to one another. As we faithfully worship God, we are also called to build up both our fellow Christians and, ultimately, to lead all whom we meet to Christ. Our actions tell others about who we are in Christ, giving us an opportunity to witness to His love in all aspects of our lives. Christians are not forbidden from interacting with those who do not know Christ—far from it. By our actions and words among them we can testify to the one God and what His Son, Jesus Christ, has done for us.

11:1–16 The Lord has provided order in the family through faithful husbands and fathers and dedicated wives and mothers. When we seek to live in ways other than how He has called us to live, we move away from Him. Yet we are not abandoned to drift about in this world. God's Son loved us with a perfect love, sacrificing Himself on the cross for us. The forgiveness won for us there cleanses us from all our failures, even where we have failed those closest to us.

11:17–34 Paul reminds the Corinthians to recognize what God has offered in the Sacrament: the body and blood of Christ, the forgiveness of sins, and through them the union of the Body of Christ, the Church, gathered around the altar. The Lord's Supper is never just a private matter, something only between God and oneself, but it is a celebration of the whole Body of Christ.

Chs 12–14 Like the congregation at Corinth, we also suffer from divisions and party spirit, which undermine God's work among us. Yet the Lord still leads us to true confession through Jesus, our Savior, and the Spirit works among us. The sin of arrogance plaguing the Corinthians still disrupts congregations today when roles of service are not clearly defined or valued. Yet also today, Christ unites us in Baptism and makes us His very Body. Though wounded and afflicted, His Body can never be destroyed but carries out God's loving purposes. In love, God calls us together for mutual edification in His Word, which always richly applies to the mature as well as the immature. Through the Word, God is really among us, giving His Spirit, faith in Christ, and all blessings of salvation. The "God of peace" (Rm 15:33) has established our salvation and life in the cross of His dear Son, our only Savior, who makes us one and strengthens us in the one true faith.

Ch 15 How great is the temptation for us to overlook the Gospel today! A multitude of contemporary issues can crowd out the Gospel of life and forgiveness in Jesus until it grows unclear in our minds. Praise God for the wonderful creeds that our forebears have handed down across the centuries, which take up Paul's very words, summarize the Holy Gospel, and etch it into our memories. All our powers and wisdom must remain subject to the Lord, who is "all in all." The Lord refuted sin, death, Satan, and all our foes—not with reason but with acts: His death and resurrection for our redemption. He chose to establish a new order for us through Jesus' life, death, and resurrection. Jesus resisted all corruption and grants us His heavenly life. He now equips us to serve in His Church and to live eternally in His kingdom.

Ch 16 When we learn of brothers and sisters in need, God's Word leads us to demonstrate the bond of fellowship created by the Gospel. Christ treasured us by freely giving His life for us, and He grants us generous hearts. Effective ministry today also depends on clear planning and authority so that congregations may support the work of the Lord. That work is vital because faith, life, and salvation come only through the Lord's Word. No matter how or where you serve the Lord, you, too, are part of a larger team. Respect your fellow workers by listening to them and coordinating efforts with them. Our Savior's strong, firm love and leadership preserves the unity of His dear Church, for which He gave His life. He calls us to passionate service and love. Jesus, too, forcefully denounced those who abused God's Word (Mt 23:1–36); yet He poured out His love for all sinners, so that all might know His grace.

Canonicity

Like Paul's other biblical letters, which were collected and copied as authoritative already in the middle of the first century AD (cf 2Pt 3:15–16), 1 Corinthians quickly gained canonical status. Even critical scholars regard the book as a genuine letter of Paul.

Lutheran Theologians on 1 Corinthians

Luther

"In this epistle St. Paul exhorts the Corinthians to be one in faith and love, and to see to it that they learn well the chief thing, namely, that Christ is our salvation, the thing over which all reason and wisdom stumbles. . . .

"[St. Paul] had taught his Corinthians Christian faith and freedom from the law. But then the mad saints came along, and the immature know-it-alls. They broke up the unity of the doctrine and caused division among the believers. One claimed to belong to Paul, the other to Apollos; one to Peter, the other to Christ. One wanted circumcision, the other not; one wanted marriage, the other not; one wanted to eat food offered to idols, the other not. Some wanted to be outwardly free [*leiblich frey*]; some of the women wanted to go with uncovered hair, and so on. They went so far that one man abused his liberty and married his father's wife, some did not believe in the resurrection of the dead, and some thought lightly of the sacrament.

"In short, things got so wild and disorderly that everyone wanted to be the expert and do the teaching and make what he pleased of the gospel, the sacrament, and faith. Meanwhile they let the main thing drop—namely, that Christ is our salvation, righteousness, and redemption—as if they had long since outgrown it. This truth can never remain intact when people begin to imagine they are wise and know it all. . . .

"Therefore St. Paul most severely rebukes and condemns this shameful wisdom, and makes these connoisseur saints out to be fools. He says outright that they know nothing of Christ, or of the Spirit and gifts of God given to us in Christ, and that they had better begin to learn. It takes spiritual folk to understand this. The desire to be wise and the pretense of cleverness in the gospel are the very things that really give offense and hinder the knowledge of Christ and God, and create disturbances and contentions. This clever wisdom and reason can well serve to make for nothing but mad saints and wild Christians. Yet such people can never know our Lord Christ, unless they first become fools again and humbly let themselves be taught and led by the simple word of God. This is what St. Paul deals with in the first four chapters.

"In chapter 5 he rebukes the gross unchastity of the man who had married his father's wife. He would put this man under the ban and give him over to the devil. Thus he points out the right way of using the ban, that it should be laid with the consent of the believing congregation upon obvious transgressions, as Christ also teaches in Matthew 18[:17].

"In chapter 6 he rebukes contention and disputing in the courts, especially before heathen and unbelievers. He teaches them that they should settle their cases among themselves, or suffer wrong.

"In chapter 7 he gives instruction concerning chastity and married life. He praises chastity and virginity, saying that these are helpful in allowing closer attentiveness to the gospel, as Christ also teaches in Matthew 19[:12] concerning celibates who are chaste for the sake of the gospel or the kingdom of heaven. But Paul wills that it be practiced without force or compulsion, or the risk of greater sin; otherwise, marriage is better than a chastity which is continually aflame with passion.

"In chapters 8 to 12 he discusses many different ways in which weak consciences are to be guided and regarded in external matters such as eating, drinking, apparel, and receiving the sacrament. Everywhere he forbids the strong to despise the weak, since he himself, even though he is an apostle, has refrained from many things to which he really had a right. Moreover the strong may well be afraid, because in ancient Israel so many were destroyed, all of whom had been led out of Egypt by miracles. Besides this, he makes several digressions into worthwhile teachings.

"In chapters 12 and 13 he discusses the many different gifts of God, among which love is the best. He teaches the people not to exalt themselves but to serve one another in unity of spirit, since there is one God, one Lord, one Spirit, and everything is one, however great the diversity.

"In chapter 14 he teaches the preachers, prophets, and singers to use their gifts in an orderly manner; they are to display their preaching, skill, and understanding for edification only, and not in order to gain honor for themselves.

"In chapter 15 he takes those to task who had taught and believed wrongly concerning the resurrection of the body.

"In the last chapter he exhorts the people to give brotherly assistance to the needy in the form of material aid." (AE 35:380–83)

For more of Luther's insights on this book, see *Commentary on 1 Corinthians 7* (AE 28:1–56) and *Commentary on 1 Corinthians 15* (AE 28:57–213).

Gerhard

"To the extent that the Epistle to the Romans has authority in treating controversies of faith, so 1 Corinthians has authority in establishing church discipline. As a result, antiquity counts it in the second place among the Pauline Epistles. The occasion for its writing was this: The apostle had taught in Corinth for a year and a half (Acts 18:9–10). After the apostle's departure, various scandals of doctrine and behavior arose, as generally happens in densely populated, rich, and powerful cities such as Corinth, which Cicero calls 'the light and glory of all Greece' (*Pro leg. Manil.*). In the area of doctrine there were seducers who were eager to tear down Paul's authority and who were bringing up various questions—about which the Corinthians consulted Paul by special letter. In the area of behavior, ambition, discord, luxury, greed, and many sins of this sort were holding sway. In this letter the apostle wanted to meet both evils and to reestablish church discipline.

"Regarding the place where the Epistle was written, a certain discrepancy seems to occur in the final sentence of the Greek codex and in the account of the Acts of the Apostles. You see, the Greek text has that it was written at Philippi, where 2 Corinthians also was written. It is more likely, however, that it was written at Ephesus, for the apostle says, 'I shall remain at Ephesus until Pentecost' (1 Cor. 16:8), and he greets the Corinthians in the name of the churches of Asia, but Philippi is a city of Macedonia. Furthermore, this Epistle was written before he passed through Macedonia (1 Cor. 16:5), and at that time the apostle was at Ephesus (Acts 19:[22]). Finally, he greets the Corinthians in the name of Priscilla and Aquila, but he left them at Ephesus when he went down to Macedonia (Acts 18:19). Some people reconcile this apparent contradiction in this way: that it was written at Ephesus but sent from Philippi. There is a more simple answer: that those postscripts did not come from the apostle Paul but were added by later writers.

"It also has sixteen chapters in which, besides the introduction and epilogue, there is added in the middle a treatise partly censuring the schisms and sins that held sway in their behavior, partly teaching concerning adiaphora, matrimonial cases, the doctrine of the resurrection, etc." (ThC E1 § 258)

Questions People Ask about 1 Corinthians

Miracles in the Early Church

In the Early Church, many of the believers were endowed with miraculous powers, as is evident, for instance, from 1Co 12 and 14. (See especially 1Co 12:8–10.) It will be noticed that some of the spiritual gifts that Paul mentions must be classified as supernatural, while others would not be classified as such. But the apostle calls them all gifts of the Spirit. Some of the Corinthian Christians were given the word of wisdom. Their gift, it seems, consisted in the ability to give wise counsel resting on the words of God. Others had been given the word of knowledge, that is, the faculty to discern the deep things in the Scriptures and to give fitting utterance to their thoughts on these lofty themes. Some had received "faith," which perhaps means a special or extraordinary measure or degree of faith, strong to withstand vehement attacks. Others had been endowed with the gift of healing, with the ability to perform miraculous cures.

Then there was a group that had been given the ability to work miracles in general, that is, to do mighty, supernatural things. Some had the gift of prophecy. To them the Holy Spirit granted special revelations, which they proclaimed and applied with penetrating, gripping power; at times they also foretold future events. Others were able to discern spirits, that is, to tell whether teachers with whom they came in contact were sent by God or whether they came of their own or of Satan's accord. Perhaps the most extraordinary gift, from our perspective, was the gift that designated "various kinds of tongues" (12:28), which has caused so much discussion—and divisions—in modern churches. For more on this issue, see pp 448–49. The above list shows that it was a marvelously endowed congregation that Paul had founded at Corinth, and we need not assume that he presents an exhaustive list of the gifts with which its members were adorned. In other congregations there may have been similar manifestations of supernatural endowments. Bearing this in mind, we can more easily understand why the Early Church grew by leaps and bounds despite violent opposition from Jews and Gentiles.

Some Christians today insist that all manner of miraculous gifts and events must take place in churches, otherwise the churches are spiritually dead. Others hold that such miracles have ceased; therefore, the appearance of such events today is viewed with suspicion. It is helpful to note that the New Testament does not promise that miracles will always occur. Nor does it teach that miracles must disappear from our churches. In 2Co 12:12, Paul seems to indicate that miracles were especially part of the ministry of the apostles (cf Ac 2:43), which leads one to think of the apostolic era as a unique time for the Church without concluding that miracles must somehow cease today or that God's people may not pray for God's miraculous help. It is also important to note that when a historian like Luke recorded miracles in Acts, he tended to record extraordinary events rather than the day-in, day-out lives of God's people. The Book of Acts spans about 30 years of church history. Miracles feature prominently at points but so do struggle and suffering (Ac 14:22). Taking these points about the miraculous into consideration provides a well-balanced view of God's teaching.

Is Marriage Both Commended and Frowned On?

Genesis 2:18 records: "And the LORD God said, 'It is not good that the man should be alone; I will make him a helper fit for him.' "

1 Corinthians 7:27 reads: "Are you bound to a wife? Do not seek to be free. Are you free from a wife? Do not seek a wife."

People have wondered how Paul, in view of Gn 2:18, could give his readers the advice not to marry. Does he not thereby contradict the plain Word of God? The following discussion should remove all difficulties. In 1 Corinthians, Paul is not discussing whether marriage is right or wrong. The apostle's attitude on this matter is revealed in the following verse: "But if you do marry, you have not sinned, and if a betrothed woman marries, she has not sinned" (1Co 7:28). Paul clearly does not look upon marriage as something wrong or objectionable. It is essential that one bear this statement in mind if one wishes to understand the attitude of the apostle.

The fact stands that Paul advises against marriage. Why does he do it? Many people conclude that his position was that while marriage is not wrong, the single state is better, more holy, more God-pleasing. But not one syllable in this entire chapter justifies such an interpretation of Paul's words. The idea that an unmarried life is more acceptable to God than the married state is altogether foreign to Paul's letters, just as it is to the rest of the Bible. It was due to unsound, unscriptural asceticism that a later age invested the single life with special holiness. It is even possible that the Corinthians raise these questions (7:1, 25) because false teachers had been misleading them about the value of celibacy and marriage (cf 1Tm 4:3).

Paul's advice finds its explanation partly in v 26, partly in v 32. The earlier passage says: "I think that in view of the present distress it is good for a person to remain as he is." It was, in part, on account of the distress visiting the Christians of that age that Paul was writing as he did. The times were full of trouble for the Christians. If persecutions had not actually begun, Paul saw that they were coming. The "sect" following Jesus was being spoken against everywhere (Ac 28:22). If a Christian had a wife and children, naturally his suffering and anguish under persecution were greater than if he had been a single man, since he felt not merely the blows dealt out to him personally, but likewise those falling on his family. Because of this character of the times the unmarried Christian was likely to have greater peace than the married one (1Co 7:40). He wishes to spare his readers some trouble (cf v 28). The other passage (v 32) states: "I want you to be free from anxieties. The unmarried man is anxious about the things of the Lord, how to please the Lord." The apostle points out in this passage that the unmarried Christian will be able to do more for the spreading of the kingdom of God than the married one. That this is the meaning of his words is very clear from v 33. In making this statement, he presupposes that those who will remain unmarried in order to serve the Lord more efficiently have the gift of celibacy, which he refers to in the opening verses of this chapter. Those who do not possess this gift are urged by the apostle to marry, by all means. To conclude, Paul does not contradict the Word of the Lord: "It is not good that the man should be alone" (Gn 2:18). He simply says to the Corinthians that under the special circumstances in which you are placed, you will act wisely if you do not marry. In that case, too, you will be able to do more for the extension of the kingdom of God. But this advice always presupposes that you have the gift of continence.

Is 1 Corinthians Inspired?

First Corinthians 7:12 reports: "To the rest I say (I, not the Lord) that if any brother has a wife who is an unbeliever, and she consents to live with him, he should not divorce her."

Second Peter 1:21 records: "For no prophecy was ever produced by the will of man, but men spoke from God as they were carried along by the Holy Spirit."

Bible readers have now and then been perplexed to find that while Peter says that holy men of God spoke as they were moved by the Holy Spirit, Paul seems to disclaim divine inspiration for some of the statements he is making. There can be no doubt about the meaning of 2Pt 1:21. It says that holy men of God, the Old Testament writers, spoke or wrote as the Spirit gave them utterance, and therefore their prophecies are divine products. A comparison with

2Pt 3:16 will show that Paul's writings are given the same rank as the books of the Old Testament prophets; they are, by implication, termed Scripture, and therefore we must claim inspiration as the source of Paul's writings also. But how shall we harmonize with this view of his letters the statement that he himself makes in 1Co 7:12, that in the particular instance under discussion not the Lord, but he himself, was speaking?

Paul, let it be noted, is not saying that he is not inspired as he is writing these words. The question whether he is inspired or not while sending this message to the Corinthians does not enter into the discussion at all at this point. Paul is making a distinction between those precepts that Jesus had given during His earthly life and were being circulated among the first Christians and other precepts that had not been proclaimed by Jesus Himself, but that were now being enunciated by the apostle. Jesus, as 1Co 7:10–11 indicates, had forbidden divorce. Paul, the inspired apostle, in the passage which follows (vv 12–15) enjoins that if a Christian is married to an unbeliever, he or she should not seek a divorce, adding, however, that if the unbeliever should willfully desert the spouse, the marriage bond would be dissolved and the Christian would be free to marry again. Not with one syllable does the apostle hint that his words as given in vv 12–15 are less binding upon the Christians than those found in vv 10 and 11. What he does say is merely that one part of these pronouncements on divorce was proclaimed by Jesus personally, while another part was not given in this manner.

That Paul is not denying that he was inspired is evident from the second chapter of this letter, where in v 13 he writes: "And we impart this in words not taught by human wisdom but taught by the Spirit." It is likewise evident from ch 7 itself, where Paul concludes his discussion of the question pertaining to marriage by saying: "And I think that I too have the Spirit of God" (7:40). This claim indicates that everything that he placed before the Corinthians in the preceding instruction had been given to him by the Holy Spirit.

First Corinthians 7:25 may be discussed in this connection: "Now concerning the betrothed, I have no command from the Lord, but I give judgment as one who by the Lord's mercy is trustworthy." It has been thought that this verse amounts to a denial on the part of Paul that he was inspired when he wrote this section of 1Co 7. But again we must point out that Paul is not dwelling on the question of whether or not he is inspired. He is merely saying that in what he is writing now he is not transmitting a command of the Lord, but simply giving his opinion. Does that militate against the assumption that he wrote these words by inspiration of the Holy Spirit? Not at all. Inspiration means that the respective holy writer writes and hands down to posterity what the Holy Spirit wants him to write and to hand down. Paul's letters touch upon a great variety of subjects.

They place before us the great doctrinal truths of the Gospel; they relate many historical incidents; they depict the apostle's feelings and emotions; they contain many little personal items; they give advice as to the preservation of health (1Tm 5:23); they ask for personal favors (2Tm 4:13), etc. No one should maintain that all that Paul writes in his letters is of equal importance for our spiritual welfare. Nevertheless, all of it is inspired. It was the will of God that Paul should write just as he did write.

Returning to 1Co 7:25, we must say that it is true that the apostle is here voicing his personal opinion. But it is equally true that the Holy Spirit inspired him to write in this very fashion, since it was the will of God that in the matter that he is treating no command should be given to the church, but that the well-considered advice of the apostle should be submitted. This passage, then, does not conflict with the statement that holy men of God spoke as they were moved by the Holy Spirit. Paul was moved by the Holy Spirit when he wrote 1Co 7, and it was the Holy Spirit's design that the chapter should be written just as we have it.

The Sinfulness of the Children of Christian Parents

First Corinthians 7:14 says: "For the unbelieving husband is made holy because of his wife, and the unbelieving wife is made holy because of her husband. Otherwise your children would be unclean, but as it is, they are holy."

Ephesians 2:3 states: "Among whom we all once lived in the passions of our flesh, carrying out the desires of the body and the mind, and were by nature children of wrath, like the rest of mankind."

The teaching in Eph 2:3, that all people are born sinners, is found universally in the Scriptures. (Cf Gn 8:21; Ps 51:5; Jn 3:6.) How, then, can Paul say in 1Co 7:14 that the children of a Christian father or of a Christian mother are holy? The answer is that Paul in this passage does not dwell on the personal status or condition of the children of Christians, but he is speaking about the relationship between them and the Christian parents. The apostle says in this verse: "The unbelieving husband is made holy because of his wife." Obviously, the meaning is not that an unbeliever, through having a Christian wife, becomes a holy person; but Paul affirms that the wife is not contaminated through association with an unbelieving husband. An unbeliever is sinful before God; but that need not keep a Christian from maintaining relationships with unbelievers that previous family ties have brought about. Everything that a Christian uses and handles in the spirit of a child of God is sanctified. This great truth is expressed, for instance, in 1Tm 4:4–5: "For everything created by God is good, and nothing is to be rejected if it is received with thanksgiving, for it is made holy by the word of God and prayer." Evidently, then, the meaning of Paul with respect to the children of Christians is that to the Christian father or mother they are holy, that is, they are not defiling.

We must remember that the apostle in this section is considering a problem that was of tremendous importance in his age. When the Gospel was preached, it often happened that a person was converted whose spouse refused to embrace Christianity. The question immediately arose whether the converted party could continue to live in wedlock with an obstinate unbeliever. Would that not mean defilement? The apostle reassures his converts on that score and gives utterance to the great truth that Christianity does not require a severance of all connections with unbelievers; that it does not consist in the renunciation of all associations that have been caused by birth or marriage; that it does not mean that outward contact with unbelievers is rendering us obnoxious in the sight of the Lord; that, rather, all the earthly relations that we maintain in the fear of God and in obedience to His holy will are sanctified to us.

The apostle, of course, must not be understood to be advocating marriages between Christians and unbelievers. He is speaking of marriages that had been contracted before the conversion of his readers and is urging them not to consider this bond as something that would render them vile before God. It is in this connection that he says that their children are holy—holy to them in the sense that contact with their children was not something to be shunned. If anyone should still doubt the validity of the explanation just offered, consider the antithesis found in this verse between unclean and holy. The apostle evidently is not contrasting sinful and sinless beings, but those that cause pollution and those that do not. In this case, then, the context shows that Paul in 1Co 7:14 is not contradicting the scriptural doctrine that all are born sinful.

Further Study

Lay/Bible Class Resources

Engfehr, Lois. *1 Corinthians: One in Christ*. GWFT. St. Louis: Concordia, 1996. ֍ Lutheran author. Fourteen-session Bible study, including leader's notes and discussion questions.

Life by His Word. St. Louis: Concordia, 2009. ֍ More than 1,500 reproducible one-page Bible studies covering each chapter of the canonical Scriptures. Page references to *The Lutheran Study Bible*. CD-Rom and downloadable.

Morris, Leon. *1 Corinthians*. TNTC. Downers Grove, IL: InterVarsity Press, 2008. ֍ Carefully expounds the message of 1 Corinthians in a simple manner.

Rudnick, Milton, Erwin Kolb, Gregory Lockwood, and Gary Dunker. *1 Corinthians*. Leaders Guide and Enrichment Magazine/Study Guide. LL. St. Louis: Concordia, 2007. ֍ An in-depth, nine-session Bible study with individual, small group, and lecture portions.

Toppe, Carleton A. *1 Corinthians*. PBC. St. Louis: Concordia, 2004. ֍ Lutheran author. Excellent for Bible classes. Based on the NIV translation.

Church Worker Resources

Bruce, F. F. *Corinthians I and II*. NCBC. Rev. ed. Grand Rapids: Eerdmans, 1981. ֍ A compact, clear exposition, paying careful attention to the context of the readers in a masterful manner.

Lockwood, Gregory J. *1 Corinthians*. CC. St. Louis: Concordia, 2000. ֍ A faithful, theological approach from a Lutheran scholar, who probes contemporary controversies with an eye toward applying the text for pastoral care.

Witherington III, Ben. *Conflict and Community in Corinth: A Socio-Rhetorical Commentary on 1 and 2 Corinthians*. Grand Rapids: Eerdmans, 1995. ֍ Falls somewhere between a commentary and an overview; good, succinct discussions of the book, but without moving toward application.

Academic Resources

Barrett, C. K. *The First Epistle to the Corinthians*. Harper's New Testament Commentaries. New York: Harper & Row, 1968. ֍ Clear, comprehensive expositions; conscious also of the setting of the readers.

Fee, Gordon D. *The First Epistle to the Corinthians*. NICNT. Grand Rapids: Eerdmans, 1987. ֍ Fee's commentary has been the main academic resource for the book in recent years. However, his discussion of spiritual gifts, women in the church, and the Lord's Supper are far removed from Lutheran teaching.

Kling, Christian Friedrich. *The First Epistle of Paul to the Corinthians*. LCHS. New York: Charles Scribner's Sons, 1868. ֍ A helpful older example of German biblical scholarship, based on the Greek text, which provides references to significant commentaries from the Reformation era forward.

Lenski, R. C. H. *The Interpretation of St. Paul's First and Second Epistles to the Corinthians*. Minneapolis: Augsburg, 1963. ֍ A valuable resource from a Lutheran scholar, much concerned to be faithful to the text and its setting as he expounds on the problems Paul faced in Corinth.

Murphy-O'Conner, Jerome. *St. Paul's Corinth: Texts and Archaeology*. Good News Studies 6. Wilmington, DE: Michael Glazier, 1983. ֍ Excellent material on the total setting of Corinth, except for his comments on Gallio.

Robertson, A. T., and Alfred Plummer. *A Critical and Exegetical Commentary on the First Epistle of St. Paul to the Corinthians*. ICC. 2nd ed. Edinburgh: T&T Clark, 1978. ֍ A valuable standard resource, paying attention also to classical parallels.

Thiselton, Anthony C. *The First Epistle to the Corinthians*. NIGTC. Grand Rapids: Eerdmans, 2000. ֍ First Corinthians was virtually ignored by biblical scholarship for years. However, this large-scale commentary has become a most valuable new resource. While massive, and at times difficult to follow through an entire section, it addresses the many difficult issues in the book. It is weak, however, in the area of application.

2 CORINTHIANS

The ministry of reconciliation in Christ

The surpassing value of 2 Corinthians is the opportunity it gives us to view the great care—through both Law and Gospel—that Paul and his colleagues provided to a wayward congregation. We read about the sharpness of his rebuke by which he prodded the congregation toward repentance and the soothing comfort he poured out to them as they welcomed the Lord's Word. The introduction to 1 Corinthians (pp 441–44) prepares the reader for understanding 2 Corinthians. The "Historical and Cultural Setting" below provides further detail.

The Second Letter to the Corinthians is certainly one of the most difficult of Paul's letters—which is not to say that it was difficult or obscure for its first readers; they lived in the situation that we must laboriously reconstruct. Since the hints given by the letter itself are not always full enough to permit a complete and accurate reconstruction of the situation, the letter is for us difficult, an angel to be wrestled with if we would receive a blessing. But the blessing is a rich one and worth the wrestling.

Historical and Cultural Setting

One may begin to describe the events immediately preceding Paul's writing of 2 Corinthians with a report from Paul's colleague Timothy. Timothy reported to Paul how one of his letters had been received and how things stood at Corinth. What Paul heard moved him to interrupt his work at Ephesus and to proceed to Corinth at once. This is the second visit that is implied by 2Co 13:1–2; 12:21, the "painful visit" to which Paul alludes in 2:1 (see outline of events, p 445). Timothy's report had made clear to Paul that the influence of the new teachers had spread farther and gone deeper than he had realized. There were not only "some" who were arrogant (1Co 4:18), "some" who denied the central content of the apostolic proclamation (15:12); the whole church was infected and endangered—the very existence of "God's temple" (3:17) was being threatened. Immediate action was necessary, drastic action that had to be taken personally. The visit there-

The *Bema*, a public speaking platform at Corinth from which Paul would have addressed the people of the city (Ac 18:12–17). In the background (south) rises the Acrocorinth, site of the citadel and the temple of Aphrodite.

fore proved to be a painful one for the Corinthians, who were rudely shaken out of their dreaming self-assurance by the home truths that their apostle had to tell them (2Co 2:2; 13:2). It was a painful visit for Paul, too, for the opposition to him, under the leadership of the men who claimed to be Christ's, proved strong. They must have been bold, intellectually vigorous, and capable men—they were able to face Paul and to keep a sizable part of the congregation with them. Just what form Paul's dealings with the church took cannot be clearly made out, but this much is plain: Paul was convinced that fellowship with the new leaders was no longer possible, that a break had to be made (13:2). He left Corinth, however, without immediately forcing the issue. He still trusted that the church would come to see the necessity for the break as clearly as he himself saw it and left with the promise that he would return to Corinth when his work in Ephesus was done and would pay the church a double visit, both before and after the proposed revisitation of the Macedonian churches (2Co 1:15–16). This was, of course, a change from the travel plans that Paul had announced in 1Co 16:5–6.

The Severe Letter

What follows now is the obscurest part of an obscure history. Paul's trust that the church would see the light and would walk in that light was, apparently, disappointed. There occurred an incident that strained still further the already strained relations between Paul and the church. Paul spoke of one who did an injury that caused him pain (2Co 2:5), an injury not directly to Paul himself but affecting him. Since Paul did not indicate the nature of the wrong done him, we can only conjecture what it may have been. Perhaps one of the men loyal to Paul suffered violence at the hands of an opponent in the heat of party strife. At any rate, the offense was so flagrant and involved the authority of Paul so immediately that the church could not ignore it and still be in any sense "his" church, still

OVERVIEW

Author
Paul the apostle

Date
AD 55, before winter

Places
Corinth in Achaia; Macedonia; Troas in Asia [Minor]; Damascus; Judea

People
Paul; Timothy; Silvanus; Titus; King Aretas; super-apostles

Purpose
Paul guides the Corinthian congregation to evaluate his ministry truly as Christ's work among them

Law Themes
Divisions in congregations; false apostles; human frailty; poverty in sin; generosity; suffering; self-examination

Gospel Themes
Comfort in Christ; restoration through forgiveness; reconciliation; wealth in Christ; God's sufficient grace

Memory Verses
Amen in Christ (1:18–22); the Spirit gives life (3:4–6); eternal glory (4:16–18); the ministry of reconciliation (5:17–21); rich in Christ (8:9); a cheerful giver (9:6–8); God's sufficient grace (12:7–10)

TIMELINE

AD 36	Paul's conversion
AD 49–51	Paul plants congregation at Corinth (second missionary journey)
AD 52–55	Paul's third missionary journey
AD 55	Paul writes 2 Corinthians
AD 68	Martyrdom of Peter and Paul

A leather pouch for carrying letters, discovered at Nahal Hever, Israel,

esteem him as apostle and father in Christ. Paul therefore changed his plans once more; instead of going directly to Corinth from Ephesus, he first proceeded northward toward Macedonia by way of Troas. Before leaving Asia, he wrote a letter (now lost) to which he refers as a severe letter, a letter written "with many tears" (2:4). This letter summoned the church to repentance in no uncertain terms: the wrongdoer must be dealt with and disciplined, and the church must return in obedience to its apostle. Paul dispatched the letter by the hand of Titus and instructed Titus to rejoin him at Troas and report on its effect.

The Report of Titus

Titus had not yet returned to Troas when Paul arrived there (2Co 2:12); and so Paul, in an agony of doubt concerning the outcome of Titus's mission, left Troas and proceeded to Macedonia (2:13). And God, who comforts the downcast, comforted him by the coming of Titus (7:5–6). For Titus brought good news: the Church at Corinth had heeded Paul's summons to repentance, had bowed to his authority, and had disciplined the offender, who had also repented and asked for forgiveness. The church was ready to forgive him and only awaited Paul's assent to such a course before granting forgiveness. The church thus cleansed and restored by repentance longed to see Paul again, in order that the ties so long strained and endangered might be confirmed and strengthened once more (2:6; 7:7–16).

That was the positive side of Titus's report, and Paul welcomed it with that exuberant gratitude with which he received every good gift of God; he did not let the fact that there was another side to the report, a negative one, dampen his joy. Titus's news was not all good. The offender at Corinth had been punished by the "majority" of the congregation only, not by all (2:6). There were still those at Corinth who held to the new teachers. Neither Paul's visit nor his severe letter had silenced the men who maliciously misinterpreted his every word and action, for example, his change in his travel plans (1:17) or his letters (1:13), and sought always to undermine his apostolic authority. It was probably their influence that had brought to a standstill a project that Paul had promoted with such energy and with such good initial success: the collection for the poor saints at Jerusalem.

Paul spent the three winter months of AD 55–56 in Greece, shortly after 2 Corinthians was dispatched to Corinth (Ac 20:2–3). While in Greece, he wrote the Letter to the Romans, most likely at Corinth itself. These letters show Paul at a point of transition in his ministry. Second Corinthians and his winter visit had done the work they were intended to do, and the reconciliation with Corinth was complete. In the Letter to the Romans, Paul looked back over his work in the eastern Mediterranean area as finished and looked westward with serenity and confidence (Rm 15:14–33).

Composition

Author

Paul wrote 2 Corinthians, which resembles the Letter to the Galatians in being richly autobiographical; here we see Paul the man in all the human frailty and the human agony, which he never attempted to conceal. But Paul the man cannot be separated from Paul the apostle of Jesus Christ by the will of God. And the letter reveals the apostle with a fullness that even Galatians cannot rival. As in Galatians, we see the apostle engaged in battle, here a battle for his very existence as apostle to the Corinthians; and a man shows what he truly is in battle. The battle that Paul wages in this letter reveals him down to the very roots and bases of his apostolic existence. See pp 442–44.

Date of Composition

Paul wrote 2 Corinthians before the winter of AD 55. See the sequence of events on p 445.

During the reign of Claudius (AD 41–54), Israel suffered a famine. The Gentile churches collected money for the relief of their Jewish brethren (Ac 11:27–30; 2Co 9:1–5).

Purpose/Recipients

The unfinished task of the collection for the saints of Jerusalem was the occasion of Paul's fourth letter to the Church at Corinth, our present 2 Corinthians. But only the occasion; dear as the success of that undertaking was to Paul's heart and much as he valued the collection as an expression of the unity between the Gentile and the Judaic church, it is not the central concern of his letter. That is rather the re-establishment of a full and pure understanding of his authority as "apostle of Jesus Christ by the will of God" (2Co 1:1). His desire to make clear forever to the Corinthians wherein the glory and power of his ministry lay is the dominant impulse in his writing. This concern dominates the first section (chs 1–7), which looks to the past, wherein Paul welcomed the penitent advances of the majority of the church. He forgave the disciplined wrongdoer and bespoke the love of the church for him, then appealed for a renewal of the full communion of love that had been characteristic of his association with the Corinthian Church. These matters dominate the last section of the letter also, where Paul looked forward to his coming visit to Corinth and dealt rigorously and definitively with his detractors and their hangers-on (chs 10–13). And that concern has left its marks also on the chapters (8–9) that deal with the collection; here we see in action that peculiarly divine apostolic authority that seeks nothing for itself, but all for Christ, which will not autocratically lord it over men's faith, but works with men for their joy in Christ (1:24). This authority is essentially the vehicle of the potent claim of the grace of the Lord Jesus Christ; therefore, it will not command, but need only advise (8:8, 10). It is an expression of the Lordship of Christ, which can expect and claim obedience only because it is centered wholly in God the Father of the Lord Jesus Christ, in His power (8:5), His gifts and goodness (8:16; 9:7–8, 11–12, 15), and has His glory for its goal (9:13).

Literary Features

Genre

Second Corinthians is largely a letter of reconciliation through which Paul wished to strengthen ties with the congregation and divide them from the false teachers who caused them so many problems.

Characters

After **Paul**, the most important figures for understanding the letter are the **"super-apostles"** (11:5; 12:11). They claimed to belong to Christ but they stood in the way of full reconciliation between Paul and the congregation. Paul had reached the point in dealing with them where he realizes he must oppose them, even as he opposes the partisanship they create. Paul never identified them by name but noted that they boasted of their Israelite ancestry and their service to Christ (11:22–23).

Narrative Development or Plot

Since 2 Corinthians is a letter, it does not have a storyline or plot. However, the book clearly refers to a variety of historical events.

Some critical scholars have questioned the integrity of 2 Corinthians. They wonder whether the letter has come down to us in its original form, whether parts may have been lost, or whether sections may have been added, either by a later hand or from another work by the same author. The transition from 6:13 to 6:14 is so abrupt, and the change of mood at the beginning of ch 10 is so violent, that some scholars have conjectured that this book is a conglomeration of three letters, all of them admittedly by Paul. Section 6:14–7:1 is thought to be a fragment of the previous letter referred to in 1Co 5:9, and the last four chapters of the second letter are thought to be a part of the intermediate letter (or the severe letter) referred to in 2Co 2:3f.; 7:8.

These conjectures have a certain surface plausibility, but in the last analysis such critical constructions are neither convincing nor necessary:

a. All the ancient manuscripts and versions give us the second letter as we have it today.

b. The abruptness of transition and the change of mood are more readily understandable on the assumption that Paul wrote the letter as it stands. An editor patching up a number of letters into a unity would presumably avoid such harshnesses in the interest of obtaining a smoothly unified whole, whereas the apostle writing in the heat and passion of the situation would not be too much concerned about smooth transitions. And there remains always the unanswerable question: why were just these fragments of the letters preserved and not the complete letters?

c. Chapters 10–13 do not in fact fit into the situation presupposed for the so-called intermediate letter. There is no reference either to the person who committed the injury that so deeply affected Paul or to the sending of Titus.

d. Most important of all, the letter, as it stands, does have a natural sequence and an understandable order. As the outline given below indicates, Paul passed from the past (with its tensions and conflicts) to the present (with its concern for the work of charity that unites apostle and church), and then on to the future (with its unavoidable decision). The situation in Corinth as Paul pictures it in the first section of the letter calls for a section such as we have in the last four chapters. The success of Titus's mission had, after all, been only partial; Paul must still deal with the opposition and disobedience that remain to muddy the relationship between him and his church. That there should be a change of mood and tone corresponding to the change in topic is completely understandable.

Resources

See "Narrative Development or Plot" above.

Text and Translations

The text of 2 Corinthians is well established through a wealth of early manuscripts dating as early as c AD 200 (Papyrus 46) and from Early Church Fathers who cite the letter. As with Paul's other letters, scholars discuss the possible influence of the early heretic Marcion on causing some of the textual variants.

Doctrinal Content

Summary Commentary

1:1–2 Paul's ministry to the Corinthians has been "painful" (2:1). As Christ's representative, Paul calls them to repentance (cf 1Co 5–6; 10–11) for their willful disobedience of the Gospel of Jesus. Yet even for this church, there is grace and peace from "God our Father and the Lord Jesus Christ" (2Co 1:2), which establishes and sustains them anew as God's saints.

1:3–3:18 Paul puts suffering in the context of God's grace. Sharing the Gospel in the midst of a sinful world means that opposition is bound to come (Jn 15:20) and may even overwhelm God's people as they share the Good News with others. Paul defends his ministry to the Corinthians, not according to the standards of the world, but according to the gracious character of God's message delivered through self-sacrificing servants. Since the goal of church discipline is the restoration of the person, Paul calls the Corinthians, who have been diligent in punishment, to be even more diligent in forgiveness. Paul's spirit is restless and overwhelmed in the circumstances of his ministry. Nonetheless, he is confident that Christ will accomplish His work for the Corinthians. He describes the sufficiency, competency, and hope of the new covenant, which is the fulfillment of the old covenant.

4:1–5:10 The essence of Paul's ministry was "mercy" through the Lord Jesus alone. Such mercy compelled him to be straightforward, authentic, and transparent as a servant to God's people. Living and sharing the life of Christ with others often has a cost. Paul instructs us to look beyond the momentary affliction to the eternal glory of salvation in Jesus. He tells us to look to the treasure, not to the earthen vessel, for our confidence with God. God's promises of life and salvation are the most real things in our lives. Yet Paul also simply instructs the believer to please God. We, even as Christians, often live to please others and to please ourselves, neglecting the one thing that makes life worth living—pleasing Christ. Paul calls us to get our priorities straight.

Continued on p 488.

Outline

I. Salutation (1:1–2)

II. Blessed Be the God of Comfort (1:3–7)

III. Pastoral Reflection on Interaction with the Corinthians (1:8–5:10)

- A. Explanation of the Change in Travel Plans (1:8–2:2)
- B. Explanation of the Painful Letter (2:3–13)
- C. Theological Reflection on Paul's Apostolic Ministry (2:14–5:10)
  1. God leads His ministers to spread the knowledge of Christ (2:14–16a)
  2. Confidence and competence come from God, who establishes the ministry of the new covenant (2:16b–3:18)
  3. Consequent courage, integrity, and effectiveness of the ministry despite unbelief, personal weakness, and opposition (ch 4)
  4. Faith leads to a heavenly home (5:1–10)

IV. Apostolic Appeal to Be Reconciled to God and to His Ministers (5:11–7:16)

- A. We Live for God in the Service of Christ by Serving Others (5:11–15)
- B. The New Creation Gives a New Perspective of Others (5:16–17)
- C. God's Ministers of Reconciliation Urge Others to Be Reconciled to Him (5:18–21)
- D. The Apostle Appeals for Acceptance of God's Grace (6:1–13)
- E. Accepting God's Grace Means Separation from Unbelievers (6:14–7:1)
- F. Paul's Good Will toward Corinthians (7:2–16)

V. Logistics and Encouragement to Participate in the Jerusalem Collection (chs 8–9)

- A. Encouragement to Whole-Hearted Participation in the Collection (8:1–15)
- B. Titus and Two Other Brothers Represent the Church (8:16–24)
- C. Instructions for Other Congregations in Achaia (ch 9)

VI. Paul Appeals for Corinthians to Acknowledge His Apostolic Authority (ch 10)

VII. Paul Responds to the Accusations of the "Super-Apostles" (11:1–13:10)

- A. Corinthians Have Too Easily Turned from Pure Devotion to Christ (11:1–6)
- B. Paul's Motive in Not Accepting Support from the Corinthians (11:7–15)
- C. Though Boasting Is Foolish, the Request for Credentials Requires It (11:16–21a)
- D. Paul's Credentials Are His Sufferings in Ministry and for the Churches (11:21b–33)
- E. Paul Boasts Not in Revelations but in His Weaknesses (12:1–10)
- F. Boasting Is Foolish; Faithful Ministry Should Be Enough (12:11–13)
- G. Paul Did Not Take Advantage of the Church (12:14–18)
- H. Paul Warns That He Will Arrive with Christ's Power to Discipline (12:19–13:10)

VIII. Closing (13:11–14)

5:11–7:16 Christ's love compels Paul to persevere through all hardships in order to make God's offer of forgiveness and reconciliation plain to the people at Corinth. Our relationship with Jesus is intimate because we, as believers, are "the temple of the living God" (6:16). Paul also shares the ups and downs of ministry and his great joy in hearing that the Corinthians' faith in Christ was solid again.

Chs 8–9 The Macedonians forgot themselves as they gave to others as though there would be no tomorrow. God also calls us to give generously, because He endows us with earthly things for our neighbors' benefit. As Paul leads this great money-gathering effort, he takes care that clergy and laity work together to ensure that the Church's financial dealings are untainted by scandal. Because good intentions sometimes do not get acted on, Paul sends three representatives to Corinth to offer gentle encouragement to deliver what was promised. Paul urges the Corinthians to follow the example of God's self-giving in Christ by giving themselves to others, so that the downward and outward movement of grace comes full circle in an ascending symphony of thanksgiving.

Ch 10 Paul's opponents cut him to ribbons and paint themselves in glowing colors, but he presses forward in spiritual warfare, winning souls for Christ against all odds, rejoicing that the Lord prospers his work and opens doors for his ministry, giving all glory to Christ.

Chs 11–13 Paul went over the top in real ministry to bring the true Christ and the true Church to the Corinthians. He now grieves that they are falling for fake ministers who push a fake Christ. Paul gives sensitive personal information to prove that a genuine servant of Christ carries his Master's cross and drinks His cup. Like scarcely any other person before or since, Paul tasted the powers and bliss of heaven, but at the same time suffered bitterly under the curse of sin. The Corinthians should not have sat on their hands while the intruders tore Paul apart. The apostle wants to return for another visit, his heart and arms open wide with love, but he is also prepared to be firm if necessary. He will bind sins and excommunicate the unrepentant on his next visit. Yet he hopes examination of consciences will show the Corinthians that they hold the Lord's doctrine and that they forsake the way of death to cling to the Lord of life. If Christ dwells in them, then Paul will come in gentleness, for the Gos-

Fifth–century mosaic of St. Paul, showing the character thinness, high forehead, and partial baldness.

pel will hold sway. Confident that God's Word will do its work, Paul utters no more stern demand or harsh rebuke. He moves through gentle appeal to end on a triumphant note.

Specific Law Themes

Second Corinthians continues Paul's counsel and rebuke to a congregation badly divided by false teachers and partisanship. The temptations that exploit human frailty and sins that impoverish them spiritually are dealt with candidly by Paul. He urges his readers toward generosity, suffering for the sake of the truth, and toward self-examination to confirm whether they are in the true faith.

Specific Gospel Themes

This letter expresses repeatedly the sweet comfort of the Gospel for those who repent and are reconciled to God in Christ Jesus, who laid aside the riches of heaven and impoverished Himself so that we might receive the wealth of God's goodness and mercy (something Luther referred to as "the great exchange"). The Lord revealed to Paul that no matter what circumstances beset us, His grace is sufficient to save and sustain us.

Specific Doctrines

We learn from 2 Corinthians that there must be battle even within the Church that belongs to God and to the Prince of Peace, that lines must be drawn and where they must be drawn; we learn that Satan is at work even in that which passes for an advanced and superior form of Christianity, that his weapon is always the plausible lie that imitates the truth—one must never forget how very "nice" and very "Christian" the men of the Christ-party must have appeared to be. We learn that battle is necessary in the life of the Church and can be salutary for the life of the Church (10:4).

We learn also that the necessity of battle need not harden the battler; the church that fights for truth need not lose the love it had at first, as the Church at Ephesus did (Rv 2:4); the first seven chapters of this letter are a witness to the fact that the love which "does not rejoice at wrongdoing but rejoices with the truth" (1Co 13:6) is the only genuine love. Luther had these chapters especially in mind when he wrote of 2 Corinthians: "In his first epistle, St. Paul rebuked the Corinthians severely for many things, pouring sharp wine into their wounds [Luke 10:34] and frightening them. . . . Therefore in this epistle he praises them once more and pours oil into their wounds [Luke 10:34]. He shows himself wonderfully kind to them" (AE 35:383).

As an apostle, Paul is a "man in Christ" (2Co 12:2), a man whose whole existence and activity is shaped and formed by the single fact of Him in whom God reconciled the world to Himself. There is hardly a more vivid documentation of this lived Christianity than 2 Corinthians. No aspect of Paul's life is exempt from Christ; if he says, "Yes, I will come," or "No, I shall not come," he can say it only in the light of the great yes that God has spoken to all His promises in Christ (1:20). He can speak of Christian giving only in terms of the grace of our Lord Jesus Christ (8:9). His suffering is the mark of the Christ imprinted upon his life, the signature of Him whose strength is made perfect in weakness. Indeed, Christ is "the image of God" (4:4) who reveals the Father to us in the countenance of His Son (4:5).

As apostle, Paul is a man in whom Christ speaks (3:5–6); he is the earthen vessel that conveys the treasure of the Christ. Paul is here fighting for his apostolate; that means he is fighting for the Christ, for the apostolate is nothing less than the power and the presence of Christ among men. Men will find the treasure in this earthen vessel or they will not find it at all; they will behold the light of the knowledge of the glory of God in the face of Christ in the apostolate or they will not behold it at all. There is nothing like this letter to bind the Church to the apostolic word of the New Testament. The Reformation's embattled emphasis on *sola scriptura* finds powerful justification in this embattled epistle. Paul also distinguishes the letter and the Spirit, the deadly power of the Law from the life-giving Spirit (3:6), a key text for the ancient distinction between Law and Gospel.

Through conflict to triumph—2 Corinthians was born of conflict; and the triumph that Christ worked through it is not limited to the restoration of the Corinthian Church of the first century. By it the Church can triumph still.

Application

Chs 1–3 Like the Corinthians, we must also admit and repent of our misuse and neglect of the ministry of the Word. Too often, we trust in our own wisdom and strength to the detriment of our walk with God. Christ Jesus promises that in the midst of carrying crosses, burdens, and even the abuses and persecutions of others, His burden will be light (Mt 11:28–30). Sharing the Gospel message often exposes us as unworthy servants. In the midst of the hardships that Gospel ministry brings in a sinful world, the confidence of Christ, His encouraging, sustaining, forgiving presence, is a constant blessing for those who trust Him (1:20–21). When disciplining another, we often are tempted to do so legalistically, as if the person has to earn our forgiveness. Such an attitude actually destroys grace, both in the repentant believer and in us. To the one who is truly sorry for sin, we are to forgive as Christ forgives us and to remember the sin no more. As Christians, we often feel the very real weight of representing Christ to others. Our worries, sins, and frailties can overwhelm us. Our confidence and competency come from Christ, whose ministry truly gives life by the power of the Spirit. Therefore, we can be even bolder than Moses, the great prophet of the old covenant, as we proclaim Jesus, the one whom Moses yearned to see.

4:1–5:10 Merciful ministry exposes and binds us to the people we serve. We must never give in to the temptation to think that merciful ministry can be done from afar, as a master and not as a servant. Believers can look at afflictions and struggles purposefully as opportunities that make God's power more evident to those around them. Afflictions are temporary nuisances that will surely give way to the glory of life eternal with our Savior. His grace, His forgiveness, His gift of faith by the power of the Holy Spirit assures us that nothing in this world can separate us from God, and that Judgment Day will be a day of celebration for those who put their trust in Him.

5:11–7:16 Too often we mute the Gospel's power because of our pride, our carelessness, or our lack of concern for others. No greater honor can be given us than to be His ambassadors, His spokespeople. He not only saves us but also works through us. Our faith calls us to break from those things that would compromise our life with Jesus. The good news is that God's promises are sure even when we are unfaithful. God calls us to claim the promises of His gracious presence again and again through repentance and forgiveness. God has loved us with an everlasting love through Jesus Christ. To open up our hearts to others, to let them know of Christ's love, is to experience again the joy of that great love of God for all.

Chs 8–9 God's Son, the wealthiest of princes, became the most abject of slaves and gave His all to enrich poor sinners as His royal Bride. In our churches, we should honor those who undertake such servant-tasks. Thanks be to God for His gift of willing servants, who distribute the life-giving Gospel in all their service in Christ. The Lord has representatives to encourage us today as well. For example, we should listen to those who gently remind us to keep our baptismal vows. We open our hands to receive from God and extend them to give to our neighbor. We marvel that in Jesus it is always more and never less and rejoice that God's gifts multiply as we receive and share them.

Ch 10 Dear Christian, do not judge your ministers by the standards of secular business and entertainment, but go by whether they speak with the Shepherd's voice and give His care. As Christ endured the darts of the evil one to rescue the undeserving from his clutches, so Paul and faithful ministers submit to affliction in order to reach the lost and build up the flock.

Chs 11–13 Believers must wake up to the fact that pure doctrine, right worship, and genuine pastors cannot be taken for granted. Although Christ knew many would cast aside His mercy, He still bore the cross and He still sends out true shepherds with the genuine Gospel. We, too, must suffer with Christ now in order to reign with Him later. The Lord and His angels protect and accompany His servants even when they seem to have forsaken us. Remember your vows to God concerning one another, and keep them well. The Lord still comes into our troubled lives with His heart set to do His proper work of mercy. The blessed Trinity is not dry theory but the God of love in whom we have life now and forever.

Canonicity

Like Paul's other biblical letters, which were collected and copied as authoritative already in the middle of the first century AD (cf 2Pt 3:15–16), 2 Corinthians quickly gained canonical status. Even critical scholars regard the book as a genuine letter of Paul, though they question whether the work is a compilation of a number of Paul's letters (see "Genre," p 483).

Christ enthroned with cherubim, seraphim, and the angelic four living creatures. Paul refers to heavenly visions he received in 2Co 12:1–4.

Lutheran Theologians on 2 Corinthians

Luther

"In the first epistle, St. Paul rebuked the Corinthians severely for many things, pouring sharp wine into their wounds [Luke 10:34] and frightening them. But an apostle should be a preacher of comfort, to raise up terrified and fearful consciences, rather than to frighten them. Therefore in this epistle he praises them once more and pours oil into their wounds [Luke 10:34]. He shows himself wonderfully kind to them and bids them to receive the sinner back with love.

"In chapters 1 and 2 he shows his love toward them, how all that he said, did, and suffered was for their profit and benefit, and how they ought to trust him for the best.

"After that he praises the office of the gospel, which is the highest and most comforting of all works and is for the profit and benefit of men's consciences. He shows how it is nobler than the office of the law, also how it is persecuted, and yet increases among believers and produces through the cross a hope of eternal glory. But with all this he touches the false apostles, who were inculcating the law over against the gospel, teaching mere outward holiness—that is, hypocrisy—and allowing the inner shame of unbelief to continue. This he does in chapters 3, 4, and 5.

"In chapters 6 and 7 he exhorts them to implement this kind of preaching in the things they do and suffer. He concludes by praising them, so that he may encourage them to carry on.

"In chapters 8 and 9 he exhorts them to contribute also material aid and help in time of scarcity to the saints in Jerusalem, who from the outset had given over all their possessions, Acts 4[:34–35].

"In chapters 10, 11, and 12 he deals with the false apostles.

"In chapter 13 he threatens those who had sinned and not reformed." (AE 35:383–84)

Gerhard

"This Epistle was written in the eighteenth or nineteenth year after Paul's conversion and is almost entirely a defense. At that time he opposed false apostles and false teachers, as well as detractors who were interpreting his words and deeds in a sinister direction. Against both these groups he showed that he wrote nothing out of levity, ambition, or a desire to dominate—as the false teachers and detractors were portraying him—but out of a sincere concern for promoting their salvation. Yet mingled with his apologetic treatise are exhortation as well as rebukes of various kinds.

"It consists of thirteen chapters. In these, after his introduction, he excuses the delay of his coming and the intensity of his rebukes (c. 1–2); gives an account of his ministry (c. 2–3); exhorts them to patience in adversities (c. 3–4), to piety (c. 5), to purity and chastity (c. 6–7), to give alms (c. 8–9); and, finally, he asserts his own authority with an enumeration of the labors, visions, and perils he had endured for the sake of the Gospel of Christ (c. 11–13). At the end he adds an epilogue." (ThC E1 § 259)

Further Study

Lay/Bible Class Resources

Dunker, Gary. *2 Corinthians: God's Sufficient Grace.* GWFT. St. Louis: Concordia, 2007. ✠ Lutheran author. Eleven-session Bible study, including leader's notes and discussion questions.

Kapfer, Richard, William Schmelder, Timothy Rake, and Gary Dunker. *2 Corinthians.* Leaders Guide and Enrichment Magazine/Study Guide. LL. St. Louis: Concordia, 2007. ✠ An in-depth, nine-session Bible study with individual, small group, and lecture portions.

Kruse, Colin G. *2 Corinthians.* TNTC. Downers Grove, IL: InterVarsity Press, 1987. ✠ Compact commentary interacting with a variety of English translations. A popular but generally helpful evangelical treatment of the text.

Life by His Word. St. Louis: Concordia, 2009. ✠ More than 1,500 reproducible one-page Bible studies covering each chapter of the canonical Scriptures. Page references to *The Lutheran Study Bible.* CD-Rom and downloadable.

Valleskey, David. *2 Corinthians.* PBC. St. Louis: Concordia, 2005. ✠ Lutheran author. Excellent for Bible classes. Based on the NIV translation.

Church Worker Resources

Best, Ernest. *Second Corinthians.* Interpretation: A Bible Commentary for Teaching and Preaching. Atlanta: John Knox Press, 1987. ✠ This volume is valuable because it directs the academic discussions toward a more popular audience.

Academic Resources

Barrett, C. K. *The Second Epistle to the Corinthians.* Harper's New Testament Commentaries. New York: Harper & Row, 1974. ✠ Clear, comprehensive expositions, conscious also of the setting of the readers.

Furnish, Victor Paul. *II Corinthians.* Vol. 32A of AB. New York: Doubleday, 1986. ✠ Helpful for its treatment of the Greco-Roman setting for the letter.

Harris, Murray J., and W. Harold Mare. *1 & 2 Corinthians.* The Expositor's Bible Commentary. Grand Rapids: Zondervan, 1976. ✠ Includes a study of the sequence of events leading to the writing of 2 Corinthians.

Kling, Christian Friedrich. *The Second Epistle of Paul to the Corinthians.* LCHS. New York: Charles Scribner's Sons, 1868. ✠ A helpful older example of German biblical scholarship, based on the Greek text, which provides references to significant commentaries from the Reformation era forward.

Martin, Ralph P. *2 Corinthians.* WBC. Waco: Word, 1986. ✠ Describes both historical and theological aspects of the letter; includes the history of interpretation. Treats chs 1–9 as a unit, with chs 10–13 added later.

Plummer, Alfred. *A Critical and Exegetical Commentary on the Second Epistle of St. Paul to the Corinthians.* ICC. Edinburgh: T&T Clark, 1915. ✠ A rich standard resource.

Watson, Nigel. *The Second Epistle to the Corinthians.* Epworth Commentaries. London: Epworth Press, 1993. ✠ Brief; based on the Revised English Bible. Watson questions the original integrity of the letter.

Along the rugged Greek coast, the apostle Paul found fertile soil for the Gospel.

GALATIANS

Justified through faith in Jesus Christ

The Taurus Mountains of south central Asia Minor form the southern rim of a great basin in which one finds the central Anatolian steppe. Grass, shrubs, and salty lakes fill this dry, lower ground over which enterprising Greeks passed in search of Persian riches to the east. Greek (Hellenistic) settlements grew up at Pisidian Antioch, Iconium, Lystra, and Derbe alongside the Taurus Mountains.

But after the conquests of Alexander the Great, Celts came raiding out of central Europe (c 287 BC) and settled in the region. These Celts or Galatians ("people of Gaul") sided with the Romans against the Hellenists so that the great basin became the Roman province of Galatia in 25 BC. When the apostle Paul and Barnabus entered the great basin in c AD 47, they found Jewish synagogues in Greek speaking cities in a region named for Celts but ruled by the Romans. Is it any wonder that the inhabitants of the region found aspects of Paul's message confusing as the Book of Acts and the Letter to the Galatians describe?

Historical and Cultural Setting

The historical introduction given above has assumed that "Galatia" in Gal 1:2 means the Roman province of Galatia, which included not only the territory actually occupied by the old Galatian people but also other lands, including the territory in which lay the cities evangelized by Paul and Barnabas on the first missionary journey. This is known as the South

Lake Egridir, Antioch, in Pisidia, Turkey. Paul passed this way on his first missionary journey.

OVERVIEW

Author
Paul the apostle

Date
c AD 51–53

Places
Galatia; Jerusalem; Arabia; Damascus; Syria; Cilicia; Antioch

People
Galatians; Paul; Cephas (Peter); James, the Lord's brother; John; Barnabas; Titus; Gentiles; Jews; false brothers

Purpose
To demonstrate that faith in Christ accomplishes both justification and sanctification

Law Themes
The threat of subtle false teaching; hypocrisy; works cannot justify; the Law's curse; works of the flesh; the Law of Christ

Gospel Themes
One saving Gospel; God's gracious call; justified through faith in Christ; the gift of the Spirit; adoption as God's sons; freedom in Christ

Memory Verses
Only one Gospel (1:6–9); justification through faith, not works (2:16); life in Christ (2:19–20); the Law and the Gospel promise (3:23–29); freedom (5:1, 13–14); fruit of the Spirit (5:16–24); three crosses (6:14)

TIMELINE

AD 47–48	Paul's first missionary journey
AD 49	Paul confronts Peter in Antioch
AD 49–51	Paul's second missionary journey
c AD 51–53	Paul writes Galatians
AD 52–55	Paul's third missionary journey

Galatian Hypothesis. Other commentators take "Galatia" to mean the specific land occupied by the Galatian people in Asia Minor, whose chief cities were Tavium, Pessinus, and Ancyra. This view, known as the North Galatian Hypothesis, would necessitate a later dating of the letter, since Paul could not have touched this Galatian territory until the time of his second and third missionary journeys (AD 49–51 and 52–55). The South Galatian Hypothesis has seemed preferable, which will be treated following further introduction to the circumstances and content of Paul's letter. (See pp 502–3.)

The Judaizers

The immediate circumstances of Paul's letter stemmed from one of the first doctrinal controversies to affect the Early Church. Some early Jewish Christians believed that Jesus was the promised Messiah while they also clung to specific Jewish doctrines and practices that they believed were necessary for salvation. Paul referred to these teachers as "Judaizers," who visited other churches and spread their views, even in the churches that Paul and Barnabas had established in Southern Galatia on their first missionary journey to Pisidian Antioch, Iconium, Lystra, and Derbe (Ac 13–14). The Judaizers did so with considerable success, for what they proclaimed was a very plausible sort of substitute for the Gospel that Paul's converts had heard from him. To judge from Paul's polemics against them, the Judaizers did not in so many words deny any positive teaching that Paul had brought to the Galatians; they acknowledged and proclaimed Jesus as the Messiah, the Son of God, the risen and exalted Lord, the giver of the Spirit, in whose name is salvation; they did not deny that He would soon return in glory to consummate God's work in grace and judgment. The evidence does not even indicate that they completely ignored or obliterated the cross in its redemptive significance; Paul's repeated and passionate emphasis on the central and all-embracing significance of the cross in his letter does indicate that for them the Messiah of the cross was overshadowed by the Messiah in glory, that the cross of Christ tended to become an episode that His exaltation counterbalanced and reduced to relative insignificance.

The Judaizers did not, on their own profession, come to destroy Paul's work, but to complete it by requiring circumcision (cf Gal 3:3; 5:2–6). The coming of the Messiah, in their proclamation, crowned Israel's history and consummated Israel; it did not therefore by any means signify the end of the Law and such sacred ordinances as circumcision and the Sabbath, which God Himself had ordained as the mark and condition of the covenant between Himself and His people forever. The coming of the Christ did not free people from the Law; the Christ confirmed the teaching of the Law and deepened the obedience that it demanded. Salvation by the mediation of the Christ therefore most assuredly included the performance of the works of the Law. A Christian estate based on faith alone, without circumcision and without the Law, was a very rudimentary and unfinished estate; perfection lay in circumcision and in keeping the works that the Law required. Thus a man became a true son of Abraham and the inheritor of the blessing promised to Abraham, a member of God's true and ancient people. To dispense with the Law would mean moral chaos, or at best a very dubious and dangerous sort of liberty.

Paul, these men insinuated, had not told them all that was necessary for their full salvation. He was, after all, not an apostle of the first rank, not on a par with the original Jerusalem apostles, through whom he had received his apostolate. His failure to insist on the keeping of the Law was a piece of regrettable weakness on his part, due, no doubt, to his missionary zeal but regrettable nevertheless; he had sought to gain converts by softening the rigor of the genuine Gospel of God—he had, in other words, sought to "please men." They, the Judaizers, were now to complete what Paul had left unfinished, to lead them to that Christian perfection which Paul's Gospel could never give them.

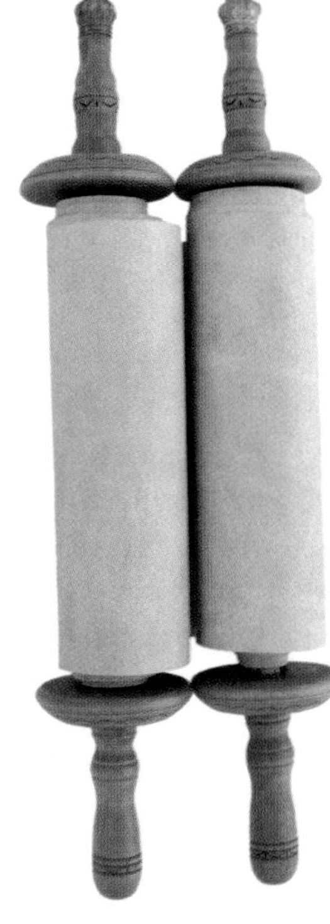

A Torah scroll, like those used in first-century synagogues.

Their attack was thus a three-pronged one. It was (1) an attack upon the apostolate of Paul, (2) an attack upon the Gospel of Paul as omitting essential demands of God, and (3) an attack that pointed up the moral dangers which would result from a proclamation of salvation by mere faith in an absolutely free and forgiving grace of God.

The attack was subtle; it was also, apparently, an organized attack, under a single leadership: Paul refers to one personality as particularly responsible for the harm that had been done in the Galatian churches (Gal 5:10). And the attack was ominously successful, understandably enough. For the converted Jew, this new form of the Gospel promised a more relaxed relationship with his unconverted fellow Jews; the Gentile converts would be impressed by the authority of the Jerusalem apostles which the new preachers invoked for their cause. And the zeal of these uncompromising extremists no doubt impressed both Gentile and Jew.

Composition

Author

The apostle Paul, a Jew from Tarsus who studied under the Rabbi Gamaliel at Jerusalem, is regarded as the author of the letter. See pp 411–13.

Date of Composition

Paul wrote the Letter to the Galatians after his first missionary journey (AD 47–48) but before the completion of his third missionary journey (AD 52–55). A reasonable date range is c AD 51–53.

The following questions and points reveal some of the problems with the North Galatian Hypothesis referred to under "Historical and Cultural Setting" above (pp 499–500).

1. Why would the Judaizers in their campaign against Paul bypass the South Galatian cities, readily accessible from Antioch, and go on into the wild, less civilized, and more remote regions of North Galatia?
2. Those who hold the North Galatian Hypothesis usually see in Gal 2:1–10 a reference to the Apostolic Council. But it is difficult to see how a meeting that Paul there describes as a *private* meeting (2:2) can be identified with the very public meeting described by Luke in Acts 15. And the question discussed in the meeting described by Paul in his letter, while no doubt related to the question up for discussion in the meeting of Acts 15, is hardly to be identified with it. Galatians 2:1–10 more likely refers to Paul's second visit to Jerusalem after his conversion. This took place during the time of famine (Ac 11:28–30).
3. If the proponents of the North Galatian Hypothesis raise the objection that the Roman province of Galatia had no fixed, official title (i.e., "Galatia") at the time of Paul's writing, that Paul therefore could not with propriety call the churches at Antioch or Derbe churches of Galatia and address men of Pisidia and Lycaonia as "Galatians" just because they lived in a province popularly known as Galatia, one must answer that there was no other single term that Paul could have used to cover all the churches addressed in the letter.

Many other subtle and ingenious arguments have been advanced on both sides, but they are rarely conclusive arguments. Thus, for example, the fact that Paul can assume that the Galatians whom he addresses know Barnabas (Gal 2:1) is used as evidence for the South Galatian Hypothesis, since Barnabas accompanied Paul only on the first missionary journey. But Paul assumes that the Corinthians, too, know Barnabas (1Co 9:6), though there is no evidence that Barnabas was ever in Corinth. Apparently Barnabas was prominent enough in the Early Church to be known in North Galatia as well as in Antioch, Iconium, Lystra, and Derbe.

Purpose/Recipients

Paul probably heard of the activity of the Judaizers and of their incipient success while he was still at Antioch on the Orontes. Since he could not go to Galatia in person, as he might have wished (Gal 4:20), to meet the attack and to combat the danger, he met it by writing the Letter to the Galatians, which may be dated AD 51–53.

Literary Features

Genre

The letter is a threefold fighting defense of Paul, his apostolate, and his proclamtion of the Gospel, corresponding to the threefold attack upon him by the Judaizers.

Characters

The most significant characters in the letter, after the apostle himself, are "**James**, the Lord's brother" and "**Cephas**," the Aramaic name of Simon Peter. Paul refers to these Galilean men, who were leading in Jerusalem, as "pillars" for the church there. According to Paul, James sent Judaizers to Antioch and they travelled there with Peter. Paul's letter highlights a conflict with these leaders who had approved of Paul's teaching. Acts 15 describes agreement between Paul and the Jerusalem leadership, which perhaps resolved their earlier tensions.

Paul also mentions his traveling companion and co-worker, **Barnabas**, as well as other figures.

Narrative Development or Plot

Although Galatians is a letter, it includes some stories and story elements through which the apostle teaches his readers. First, in 1:13–2:14, Paul relates the story of his conversion, his visits with the apostles at Jerusalem, and his confrontation with Peter at Antioch. This historical and biographical account demonstrates that Paul received his calling directly from Christ rather than from those at Jerusalem who, in fact, needed to be corrected by him on the topic of circumcision. Second, Paul relates the story of Abraham and Sarah from Genesis in order to show the priority that the Gospel-

Outline

Paul uses his rhetorical training in a most sophisticated way, as seen in this letter's structure and the argumentation. In 1:6–12, Paul confronts the chief problem: false teachers have come to Galatia and preached a different gospel, one that requires the reintroduction of Judaic practices (most prominently, circumcision) in order for the Gentile Christians in Galatia to truly be part of the "Israel of God" (6:16). Paul's solution is presented briefly in 2:15–21: faith in Christ accomplishes both justification (2:15–16) and sanctification ("endeavor to be justified"; 2:17–20). The rest of the book gives Paul's supporting argumentation for his solution (e.g., 2:15–16 is explained by 3:1–5:1; 2:17–20 is explained by 5:2–6:10).

I. Greetings (1:1–5)

II. The Problem (1:6–12)

- A. Is There Another Gospel? (1:6–10)
- B. The Gospel Preached by Paul Is the Only Gospel (1:11–12)

III. Background to the Problem, Moving toward a Solution (1:13–2:14)

IV. The Solution (2:15–21)

- A. How One Gets Justified (2:15–16)
- B. How One Lives as a Justified Person (2:17–20)
- C. The Gospel Preached by Paul Is the Only Gospel (2:21)

V. The Supporting Arguments for the Solution of 2:15–21 (3:1–6:10)

- A. First Argument about Receiving Justification (3:1–18): Foolish Galatians and Faithful Abraham
  1. Rebuke (3:1–5)
  2. Appeal to Scripture (3:6–14)
  3. Illustration of a human covenant (3:15–18)

- B. Second Argument about Receiving Justification (3:19–4:7): How One Becomes an Heir
  1. Why the Law? (3:19–22)
  2. The end of the Law's function as guardian, the coming of the inheritance by faith (3:23–29)
  3. Illustration of a human heir (4:1–7)
- C. Third Argument about Receiving Justification (4:8–20): Appeal to a Shared Past
  1. What the Galatians were before faith (4:8–11)
  2. Paul's anguish over a wayward child (4:12–20)
- D. Fourth Argument about Receiving Justification (4:21–5:1): Allegory of Sarah and Hagar—Be Free!
- E. First Argument about Living as a Justified Person (5:2–15): The Uselessness of Circumcision
  1. Paul's direct command (5:2–6)
  2. The Law divides the community (5:7–15)
- F. Second Argument about Living as a Justified Person (5:16–26): The Fruits of the Flesh and the One Fruit of the Spirit
  1. The community living by the flesh is divided (5:16–21)
  2. The community living by the Spirit is united (5:22–26)
- G. Third Argument about Living as a Justified Person (6:1–10): A Specific Application for the Community United by the Spirit
  1. Bearing and restoring one another (6:1–5)
  2. Serving one another (6:6–10)

VI. Summarizing Conclusion (6:11–18)

promise had in their lives over circumcision and the Law of Moses, which came later in Israel's history for the specific purposes of disciplining and training Israel (chs 3–4). Third, Paul briefly relates the example of his illness while visiting the Galatians to remind them of their close bond of mutual care (4:12–20).

Resources

The Old Testament books of Genesis and Exodus were key documents for Paul's letter. He also cites Isaiah 54.

This sixth-century floor mosaic from a Beth-Alpha synagogue depicts Abraham preparing to sacrifice his son, Isaac, when the angel of the Lord intervened. The life of Abraham was central to Paul's theology.

Text and Translations

The text of Galatians is well established through a wealth of early manuscripts dating as early as c AD 200 (Papyrus 46) and from Early Church Fathers who cite the letter. As with Paul's other letters, scholars discuss the possible influence of the early heretic Marcion on causing some of the textual variants.

Doctrinal Content

Summary Commentary

1:1–10 Paul's greeting anticipates the letter's central argument. According to His Father's will, Christ has graciously given Himself for our sins and delivered us from this present evil age; therefore, works of the Law are not necessary for salvation. Galatians begins not with an expression of thanksgiving but with a stern warning against defection from the one true Gospel.

1:11–2:21 Selecting key facts from his personal history, Paul proves that his apostleship comes from God, independent of human sources. For by divine revelation, Paul went to Jerusalem with Barnabas and Titus to visit Church leaders who, despite some opposition in their midst, approved of his message and mission to the Gentiles. Also, for the sake of the truth of the Gospel, Paul publicly rebuked Peter for his hypocritical conduct, which communicated that the Gentiles must keep Jewish laws. With this incident

In Galatians, Paul describes himself opposing Peter face-to-face before the congregation (2:11–14).

with Peter as the backdrop, Paul presented Galatians' core theological argument: justification is by faith in Christ and not by works of the Law.

Chs 3–4 The Galatians' experience (3:1–5) and Scripture's witness concerning Abraham (vv 6–9) teach that all believers are heirs of Abraham, to whom faith "was counted . . . as righteousness" (v 6). Paul warned against being mesmerized by the foolish notion that salvation is completed by works of the Law. Christ redeems us from the Law's curse by becoming a curse for us. Through Christ, God fulfills the promise He gave to Abraham. All united to Christ by Baptism become heirs of the promise and therefore are righteous before God. In this way, the Holy Spirit assures us that we are God's children, redeemed by Jesus Christ and made full heirs of the promise to Abraham. The Spirit never derides God's Son or spiritual matters (1Co 12:3).

Paul appeals to the Galatians as a pastor with affection and tenderness, genuinely desiring to restore their friendship and especially the freedom in Christ they once so gladly embraced. He reverses the Judaizers' definition of Abraham's true children. The uncircumcised Gentile Christians are Sarah's children (and thus free), not Hagar's (slaves).

5:1–6:10 Paul specifically argues that the acceptance of circumcision in principle violates Christian freedom and endangers a person's relationship to Christ. Christian freedom means walking (conducting oneself) by the Holy Spirit's power and leading. Members of God's family restore the erring, bear one another's burdens, support their teachers, and do good to all—especially to fellow Christians.

6:11–18 In a handwritten postscript, Paul leaves us with an interpretive lens through which to evaluate all Christian teaching and life: the message of the cross.

Specific Law Themes

Paul sharply warned against the threat of subtle false teachings and the way that even God's chosen servants can mask the problem through hypocrisy. He demonstrated from the Old Testament that our works cannot justify; we remain under the curse of the Law and the works of the flesh when we ought to fulfill the Law of Christ by bearing one another's burdens.

Specific Gospel Themes

Paul's Letter to the Galatians introduces one of the most thorough historical and doctrinal explanations of how the saving Gospel works. He relates how God graciously called him to proclaim the good news that we are justified through faith in Christ. Furthermore, God has given us His Holy Spirit and adopted us as His sons. Therefore, we enjoy freedom in Christ that only God can give.

Specific Doctrines

The Letter to the Galatians is one of the most personal and autobiographical of the letters of Paul, invaluable for the historical appreciation of his Gospel and his work. The chosen instruments of the Lord are anything but robots—they do their work and do the will of the Lord with the passionate intensity of personal involvement. The men who witness to the Christ are laid hold of by the Christ, and their mission becomes flesh of their flesh and bone of their bone.

Scarcely another epistle so emphasizes the "alone" of "by grace *alone*, through faith *alone*" as does this fighting exposition of the Gospel according to Paul, with its embattled stress on the fact that Law and Gospel confront people with an inescapable, not-to-be-compromised either/or. Paul's Letter to the Romans expounds the same theme more calmly and more fully and has a value of its own, but there is no presentation of the Gospel that can equal this letter in the force with which it presents the inexorable claim of the pure grace of God. Luther, who had to fight Paul's battle over again, said of the Letter to the Galatians: "The Epistle to the Galatians is my epistle, to which I am betrothed. It is my Katie von Bora" (AE 26:ix).

It should be remembered that the letter addresses itself to a very earnest and very pious heresy, then crushes it with an unqualified anathema. Our easy age, which discusses heresy with ecumenical calm over teacups, can learn in this letter of the terrible seriousness with which the all-inclusive Gospel of grace excludes all movements and all those who seek to qualify its grace.

Martin and Katharine Luther painted by Lucas Cranach the Elder. Galatians was a favorite book for Luther.

Key Texts

Paul's brief letter to the Galatians was an important contribution to defining the differences between the Law (3:19–24) and the Gospel (2:4–5) in opposition to false gospels (1:8–9). The letter emphasizes that we are justified through faith in Christ rather than the Law (2:16; 3:10–14; 5:4). As a result of the Gospel, Christ dwells in believers (2:20–21). They live as sons of God (4:6–7) freely exercising their faith through love (5:1, 6). Rather than continuing in the works of the flesh, they bear the fruit of the Spirit (5:17–22). When one of them falls, those led by the Spirit restore him in a spirit of gentleness (6:1).

Churchmen have also turned to Gal 2:11 as an example of what must be done when the truth of the Gospel is compromised. (However, cf Paul's action in 2:11 with his counsel in 6:1 in order to gauge the manner of one's response to sin and error.)

Application

1:1–10 Teachings that compromise the core truth of salvation rob God of His due glory and rob us of true peace, for God brings true peace to our hearts through the forgiveness of sins. Whoever falsifies the Gospel of Christ comes under God's curse. The Gospel, through which God calls us to be His own, proclaims God's grace in Christ.

1:11–2:21 Today, enemies of God's Church continue to question the divine origin of the Christian message, causing doubts and confusion among many believers in Christ. Christians continually face threats to the freedom they have in Christ, even from their own sinful flesh. The Word of God condemns hypocrisy (Mt 23:28; Lk 12:1; 1Pt 2:1; cf Lk 20:20). Yet this history shows that God is true to His promise of mercy toward sinners (1Co 1:9; 1Jn 1:9). The Gospel comes from God and thus cannot be deprived of its power to set us free. Those who appeal to the Law in addition to Christ as a means of salvation make His death meaningless—worse still, null and void. God's Son loves us and gave Himself for us to free us from the Law's condemnation.

Chs 3–4 God calls us by faith to be sons of Abraham rather than slaves of our flesh or of the Law. One sin, no matter how trivial it may seem to us, makes us a transgressor of the whole Law and accountable to God (Jas 2:10). The Law, as between Moses and Christ, still serves the good purpose of revealing sin and our need for a Savior. Through fulfilling the Law and through the cross, Christ earned for us the right to call God "our Father," a prayer taught only by the Spirit. When we hear the proclamation of the Gospel, Christ Himself is inviting all to return to Him for forgiveness and renewal of faith. Christianity sets people free, giving birth to heirs of eternal life in Christ.

5:1–6:10 Congregational strife often arises when issues in the area of Christian freedom are elevated to the level of biblical doctrine. Christ Jesus loved us to the end so that He might lift the burden of guilt that troubles our consciences. Our sinful flesh, consumed by self-importance, instinctively looks down on others and inevitably causes interpersonal tensions. At Baptism, we were united with Christ, who died to set us free from sin and the way of the Law. Nonetheless, the Son of God "loved me and gave Himself for me" (2:20), that I may be free to serve Him and my neighbor in need.

6:11–18 Against all self-righteous pride in spiritual accomplishments, the cross speaks a word of judgment. Yet to those who believe, the cross is God's power to make all things new.

Canonicity

Like Paul's other biblical letters, which were collected and copied as authoritative already in the middle of the first century AD (cf 2Pt 3:15–16), Galatians quickly gained canonical status (*homologoumenon*).

God calls us by faith to be sons of Abraham rather than
slaves of our flesh or of the Law.

Lutheran Theologians on Galatians

Luther

"The Galatians had been brought by St. Paul to the true Christian faith, from the law to the gospel. After his departure, however, false apostles came along. They were disciples of the true apostles, but they so turned the Galatians around that they believed they had to be saved by works of the law and were committing sin if they did not keep the law—as even several dignitaries in Jerusalem maintained, Acts 15.

"To refute them, St. Paul magnifies his office; he will not take a back seat to any other apostle. He boasts that his doctrine and office are from God alone, in order that he might silence the boast of the false apostles who helped themselves to the works and reputation of the true apostles. He says it is not true, even if an angel were to preach differently, or he himself, to say nothing of disciples of apostles, or of apostles themselves. This he does in chapters 1 and 2, and concludes that everyone must be justified without merit, without works, without law, through Christ alone.

"In chapters 3 and 4 he proves all this with passages of Scripture, examples, and analogies. He shows that the law brings sin and a curse rather than righteousness. Righteousness is promised by God, fulfilled by Christ without the law, given to us—out of grace alone.

"In chapters 5 and 6 he teaches the works of love that ought to follow faith." (AE 35:384)

For more of Luther's insights on this book, see *Galatians, Chapters 1–4; 5–6* (AE 26, 27).

Gerhard

"Galatians was written in the twenty-sixth year after his conversion, in AD 59. This was the occasion for its writing: The apostle had learned that the Galatians had allowed themselves to be misled by false apostles who were corrupting the pure teaching of the Gospel that the Galatians had received from Paul regarding justification by faith (or gratuitous justification through faith alone in Christ) by mixing in the righteousness of works. The false apostles were teaching that man is not justified by faith alone in Christ but that to attain righteousness before God and hence eternal life there is an additional need for the observance of the Law and, in fact, not only of the moral but also of the ceremonial law. With great strength, the apostolic spirit in this Epistle sets itself against their corrupting influences.

"It consists of six chapters, and it is completed in three parts. In the *first part* the apostle asserts the authority of his apostleship against the detractions of the false apostles who were attacking the person, office, and calling of Paul in order to make suspect the apostle's teaching about gratuitous justification by faith. In the *second part* he deals with the principal question by confirming the righteousness of faith and, on the other hand, by refuting the righteousness of works. In the *third*, he encourages them to pursue holiness because true faith reveals itself through good works." (ThC E1 § 260)

The apostle Paul holding the "sword of the spirit," which represents the Scriptures.

Questions People Ask about Galatians

Validity of the Ceremonial Law

Matthew 5:17–19 states: "Do not think that I have come to abolish the Law or the Prophets; I have not come to abolish them but to fulfill them. For truly, I say to you, until heaven and earth pass away, not an iota, not a dot, will pass from the Law until all is accomplished. Therefore whoever relaxes one of the least of these commandments and teaches others to do the same will be called least in the kingdom of heaven, but whoever does them and teaches them will be called great in the kingdom of heaven."

Galatians 4:10–11 says: "You observe days and months and seasons and years! I am afraid I may have labored over you in vain."

Paul says that the Jewish laws concerning days and months and seasons and years are no longer binding. Jesus says that not a single letter of the Law dare be ignored. Does not that constitute a conflict between Paul and our Lord? The Bible itself furnishes us all the data necessary to remove the difficulty. It points out that there is a holy law of God that will stand forever. We call this the moral law. Jesus has this in mind when He says that not one iota or dot of the Law shall pass away. Paul himself, in the very epistle from which the passage under discussion is taken, furnishes proof that the moral law of God is not abrogated. Paul in Gal 5:19–21 argues convincingly that the distinction between right and wrong has not been abolished (cf Rm 3:31). This Law condemns us because we have not kept it. Our comfort is not that it is a dead letter now in the time of the New Testament, but that it has been fulfilled by our Substitute, our Lord Jesus.

At the same time we must remember that many of the laws contained in the Old Testament were meant for the people of Israel only, to be valid until the Messiah came. The Old Testament itself contains instruction and promises to this effect (cf Jer 31:31–34). The New Testament writers, in a number of passages, set forth the glorious truth that proclaims freedom from an irksome bondage (cf Ac 15:7–11; Eph 2:15; Col 2:16–17). To this group of texts belong the words of Paul that chide the Galatians for holding the belief that the old ordinances, inculcating the observance of days, months, seasons, and years, are still binding. These ordinances, so runs the argument of Paul, had to be obeyed as long as the old covenant was in force; but when the fullness of time had come and God sent forth His Son (Gal 4:4), then the whole body of ceremonial ordinances that had been given by God through Moses was set aside (Col 2:16–17). It is the Bible itself, then, that clearly and emphatically declares that the ceremonial laws were to be effective only until the coming of Christ. To summarize briefly, both texts are true, but Paul speaks of the ceremonial laws and Jesus of the moral law.

Hospitality to Those Who Err

Galatians 6:10 urges: "So then, as we have opportunity, let us do good to everyone, and especially to those who are of the household of faith."

Second John 10–11 advises: "If anyone comes to you and does not bring this teaching, do not receive him into your house or give him any greeting, for whoever greets him takes part in his wicked works."

Can it be justly charged that Paul and John contradict each other here? Paul enjoins the Christians to do good to all. John forbids them to take into their houses a person who does not teach the true doctrine of Christ. Paul appears to be tolerant and abounding in love; John seems quite intolerant and hard-hearted. The simple fact is that the two apostles are speaking of two altogether different situations. Paul is discussing our duty toward those who are in need of our help; John speaks of our attitude toward false teachers. To understand the much-maligned injunction of John, we must remember that many false teachers were troubling the Christian Church in those days, attempting to impose their heretical notions about the person of Jesus on the Christians. When they came into a town to carry on their propaganda, was it right for one who believed in the deity of Jesus to offer them hospitality? A proper conception of truthfulness, sincerity, and devotion to a great cause will not approve of giving aid to false and dangerous doctrines. Can we assist advocates of a false religion as though they and we were allies? That would be denying the truth. John, the apostle of love, would have been the last one to urge that a false prophet, if he were in distress, should not receive our aid. But he is positive in demanding that his readers should not identify themselves with the wickedness of which these false prophets became guilty. In short, the principle is this: love everyone, love your enemies; but do not approve of and further false doctrine.

Further Study

Lay/Bible Class Resources

Cole, R. Alan. *Galatians.* TNTC. Downers Grove, IL: InterVarsity Press, 1990. ◈ Compact commentary interacting with key terms in the Greek text and a variety of English translations. A popular but generally helpful evangelical treatment of the text.

Doyle, Thomas. *Galatians: The Cost of Freedom.* GWFT. St. Louis: Concordia, 1994. ◈ Lutheran author. Eleven-session Bible study, including leader's notes and discussion questions.

Grebing, Diane, Mark Etter, and Erik Rottmann. *Galatians, Philippians, Colossians.* Leaders Guide and Enrichment Magazine/Study Guide. LL. St. Louis: Concordia, 2010. ◈ An in-depth, nine-session Bible study with individual, small group, and lecture portions.

Joersz, Jerald C. *Galatians, Ephesians, Philippians.* RHBC. St. Louis: Concordia, 2013. ◈ Verse-by-verse commentary on the ESV and KJV translations, presented in parallel columns. Written by a Lutheran theologian for lay readers and busy church workers. Includes quotations from prominent Reformers and articles about Reformation views. Excellent for Bible classes.

Life by His Word. St. Louis: Concordia, 2009. ◈ More than 1,500 reproducible one-page Bible studies covering each chapter of the canonical Scriptures. Page references to *The Lutheran Study Bible.* CD-Rom and downloadable.

Luther, Martin, and Philip Melanchthon. *Christian Freedom: Faith Working through Love, a Reader's Edition.* Trans. by Christopher J. Neuendorf and J. A. O. Preus II. Edward A. Engelbrecht and Charles P. Schaum, eds. St. Louis: Concordia, 2011. ◈ Luther's 1520 treatise presents an outstanding discussion of the Christian life. Although Luther's treatise does not claim to be a commentary on Galatians, it is so imbued with the spirit and aims of this letter that it may be the finest reflection on this key Pauline epistle ever written. This edition also includes further context from Luther's writings and from Melanchthon's *Chief Theological Topics.*

Panning, Armin. *Galatians, Ephesians.* PBC. St. Louis: Concordia, 2005. ◈ Lutheran author. Excellent for Bible classes. Based on the NIV translation.

Church Worker Resources

Luther, Martin. *Lectures on Galatians.* Vols. 26–27 of AE. St. Louis: Concordia, 1968. ◈ Luther's comments on Galatians underline the crucial importance of justification by faith alone. These lectures are a classic resource, though Luther's applications are very much focused on the battles being fought in his day.

Witherington III, Ben. *Grace in Galatia: A Commentary on Paul's Letter to the Galatians.* Grand Rapids: Eerdmans, 1998. ◈ Does not proceed verse-by-verse, but does offer helpful summaries of the sections and is especially helpful in beginning to make application of the individual sections and arguments.

Academic Resources

Bruce, F. F. *The Epistle to the Galatians.* NIGTC. Grand Rapids: Eerdmans, 1982. ◈ Very valuable, up-to-date resource for showing the erroneous basis for the North Galatian Hypothesis. The commentary portion is not as helpful.

Burton, Ernest DeWitt. *A Critical and Exegetical Commentary on the Epistle to the Galatians.* ICC. Edinburgh: T&T Clark, 1921. ◈ A valuable resource, especially his extended comments on key words and issues. A solid walk through the Greek text. It gives little application, however, and predates issues raised by the "New Look on Paul."

de Boer, Martinus C. *Galatians: A Commentary.* New Testament Library. Louisville, KY: Westminster John Knox, 2011. ◈ A recently published advocate of the North Galatian Hypothesis by a Dutch critical scholar, which aims at describing how Paul's first readers would have understood his letter.

Lenski, R. C. H. *The Interpretation of St. Paul's Epistle to the Galatians.* Minneapolis: Augsburg, 1946, 2008. ◈ A standard resource by a noteworthy Lutheran interpreter, concerned with being faithful to the text and with its implications for today. Most helpful on Galatians, always keeping in mind the central issue of works versus grace. Not clear on the relationship between Galatians 2 and Acts 15.

Lightfoot, J. B. *St. Paul's Epistle to the Galatians.* Charleston, SC: Forgotten Books, 2012 reprint. ⸙ First published in 1869. Despite its age, still a helpful resource. Holds that Galatians was written during Paul's third missionary journey rather than, correctly, after his first journey.

Longenecker, Richard N. *Galatians.* WBC. Nashville: Thomas Nelson, 1990. ⸙ Focuses especially on rhetorical analysis and the style of Paul's letter.

Martyn, J. Louis. *Galatians.* Vol. 33A of AB. New Haven, CT: Yale University Press, 2004. ⸙ Theological commentary from a critical Roman Catholic scholar. Occasionally offers flashes of brilliant insight, but is a bit dense and idiosyncratic. Some very helpful sub-discussions are presented, however, as "Comments" (e.g., nos. 37 and 40). These should be consulted for difficult problems, even if his solutions are not always the best. Martyn does, however, embrace the "New Look on Paul" and has an incorrect resolution of the "Faith of Christ/Faith in Christ" issue.

Matera, Frank J. *Galatians.* Sacra Pagina. Collegeville, MN: Liturgical Press, 2007. ⸙ Advocacy for the "New Look at Paul," written by a Roman Catholic scholar.

Nanos, Mark D., ed. *The Galatians Debate: Contemporary Issues in Rhetorical and Historical Interpretation.* Grand Rapids: Baker Academic, 2002. ⸙ Summarizes second literature on contemporary issues crucial to interpreting the epistle.

Sanders, E. P. *Paul and Palestinian Judaism: A Comparison of Patterns of Religion.* Philadelphia: Fortress Press, 1977. ⸙ Sanders is the primary exponent of the "New Look on Paul," which criticizes traditional interpretations of Paul's letters as incorrectly influenced by Martin Luther and the Reformation. Offers some valuable insights, but there are significant problems with Sanders' re-interpretation of Paul. Necessary reading for Pauline studies.

———. *Paul, the Law, and the Jewish People.* Philadelphia: Fortress Press, 1983. ⸙ Builds on his earlier study. See above.

Schmoller, Otto. *Galatians.* LCHS. New York: Charles Scribner's Sons, 1870. ⸙ A helpful older example of German biblical scholarship, based on the Greek text, which provides references to significant commentaries from the Reformation era forward.

Schreiner, Thomas R. *Galatians.* Zondervan Exegetical Commentary on the New Testament. Grand Rapids: Zondervan, 2010. ⸙ Thorough commentary by an evangelical scholar of Pauline studies.

———. *The Law and Its Fulfillment: A Pauline Theology of Law.* Grand Rapids: Baker Academic, 1998. ⸙ Schreiner's study helps to sift wheat from the chaff in current Pauline studies. An important response to Sanders' research.

Silva, Moisés. *Interpreting Galatians: Explorations in Exegetical Method.* 2nd ed. Grand Rapids: Baker Books, 2001. ⸙ Explores literary, historical, and theological factors for interpreting Paul's letter.

Westerholm, Stephen. *Perspectives Old and New on Paul: The "Lutheran" Paul and His Critics.* Grand Rapids: Eerdmans, 2003. ⸙ Reviews how Augustine, Luther, Calvin, and Wesley interpreted Paul before critiquing the twentieth century interpreters and the "New Look on Paul." An important response to Sanders' research.

EPHESIANS

Chosen in Christ before the foundation of the world

The mountain chains of western Asia Minor reach for the Aegean Sea. Where the Ayden range points finger-like toward the island of Samos and the Cayster River flows into the Sea, Ionian Greek colonists founded the prosperous port city of Ephesus (near modern Selcuk). In Roman times, the city continued to flourish and was regarded as the greatest commercial harbor along the coast facing Greece. No one can be sure when Jewish merchants first reached the city, but they established a prosperous community and a synagogue.

Paul prepared the way for his ministry in Ephesus by his visit there when returning from Corinth to Israel at the close of the second missionary journey (Ac 18:19–21). The men of the Ephesian synagogue were so much moved by his words that they asked him to stay on. He promised to return to Ephesus and left Aquila and Priscilla there. As this couple's contact with Apollos shows (18:24–26), they did not remain silent concerning the faith that was in them. The learned and eloquent Apollos became a full-fledged witness to the Christ through them (18:26–28) and thus further prepared the way for Paul. Perhaps Apollos won the twelve "disciples," who knew only the baptism of John and had not heard of the outpouring of the Holy Spirit in the last days (19:1–7). Paul baptized these twelve and laid hands on them, that they might receive the Holy Spirit. Thus his work at Ephesus began. The beginning was slight, only twelve men, but the foundation was, as always, essentially his own (Rm 15:20), and he built upon it with a will.

Historical and Cultural Setting

Luke's account of Paul's Ephesian ministry in the Book of Acts is anything but complete. He gives no chronicle of it, but presents it schematically, as a series of three conflicts, each of which results in a triumph for the cause of the apostle of Christ. The first conflict was with the synagogue (Ac 19:8–10). Paul was here permitted to witness in the synagogue for an unusually long

Overview of the street of Curetes in Ephesus, Turkey. Looking toward the plains where the port of Ephesus once stood by the Cayster River.

OVERVIEW

Author
Paul the apostle

Date
c AD 60

Places
Ephesus; Rome (from which Paul wrote)

People
Paul; Tychicus; "saints" and "brothers" at Ephesus

Purpose
Paul demonstrates that Baptism unites all Christians

Law Themes
Rivalry between believers; grieving the Spirit through unfaithfulness; marital unfaithfulness; spiritual warfare

Gospel Themes
Baptism; election by God's grace; justification by grace alone; the mystery of Christ revealed; unity in Christ's Body

Memory Verses
Election in Christ (1:3–10); saved by grace (2:8–10); unity through service (4:11–16); Bridegroom and Bride (5:22–33)

TIMELINE

AD 36	Conversion of Paul
AD 52–55	Paul's third missionary journey
c AD 60	Paul writes Ephesians
AD 65	Paul assigns Timothy to Ephesus
AD 68	Martyrdom of Peter and Paul

period (three months) and with considerable success. The Jews of the province of Asia were therefore particularly bitter against him, and it was they who later instigated the riot in Jerusalem that led to Paul's arrest and imprisonment (21:27–34). The break with the synagogue came, as it inevitably did: "Some became stubborn and continued in unbelief, speaking evil of the Way before the congregation" (19:9), and Paul withdrew from the synagogue to continue his teaching in the school of Tyrannus. He continued there for two years, and the conflict with Judaism proved to be a triumph for the Word of the Lord: "All the residents of Asia heard the word of the Lord, both Jews and Greeks" (19:10).

The second conflict generated by the Christ-centered will of Paul was the conflict with magic, for which Ephesus was notorious (19:11–20). The fact that "God was doing extraordinary miracles by the hands of Paul" (19:11) made the superstitious look upon Christianity as a new and more potent kind of magic; but the experience of the Jewish exorcists who sought to use the names of Jesus and Paul in their trade made it plain that Jesus is Lord in personal and august power, a Lord who can defend His name against misuse by those who deem Him a power that they can manipulate and employ. "The name of the Lord Jesus was extolled," and the conscience of believers was quickened—the line between magic and religion was sharply and critically drawn for them by this incident. They confessed their wrong and burned their infamous Ephesian books of charms and incantations, and "the word of the Lord continued to increase and prevail mightily" (19:20). The magical word by which men sought power grew impotent before the divine word.

The third and most dangerous conflict was the conflict with the commercialized state religion of Ephesus (19:23–41). The zeal of the silversmith Demetrius and his guild was something less than a

The great Roman theater in Ephesus where Paul's colleagues faced a riotous crowd (Ac 19:21–41).

purely religious fervor, but the fury of the guild members and of the huge, shouting city mob that they aroused is nevertheless an illustration of the demonic power that Paul describes as at work in the worship of gods that are no gods (1Co 10:19–20). The fury of that demonic power fell upon Paul and the Christians of Ephesus, but the conflict led to a vindication of Paul and his followers, so that Paul could leave Ephesus with an unsullied reputation and with the respect of men such as the Asiarchs and the town clerk (the most important city official of Ephesus). This was something which Paul valued; it was soon after he left Ephesus that he wrote the words: "We aim at what is honorable not only in the Lord's sight but also in the sight of man" (2Co 8:21; cf Col 4:5–6).

Luke hints that the Ephesian years were filled with difficulties and dangers beyond those noted by him in his account. He records the words of Paul to the elders of Ephesus which speak of the trials that befell him through the plottings of the Jews (Ac 20:19), tells of the Jewish plot against Paul's life at Corinth a little later (20:3), and notes that the Jews of Asia were especially rancorous in their hatred of Paul (21:27). Paul's letters of this period further fill in the picture of this time as a period of perils. Paul speaks of the fact that his great opportunity at Ephesus is shadowed by the presence of many adversaries (1Co 16:9), and that he has "fought with beasts at Ephesus" (15:32)—whether the expression is to be taken literally or, as is more probable, figuratively, it is a vivid expression of extreme peril. Paul gives thanks for an unlooked-for divine deliverance from desperate danger in the province of Asia (2Co 1:8–10). And when he speaks of the fact that Aquila and Priscilla have risked their necks for him, he is probably referring to the Ephesian period also (Rm 16:3–4).

Writing to the Ephesians

The best explanation of the historical background for the writing of the letter would seem to be the one suggested as early as the sixteenth century by Beza, Grotius, and Ussher: When Paul sent Tychicus to Colossae, he at the same time sent a general letter designed especially for a group of churches in Asia Minor that had been evangelized under his supervision during his Ephesian ministry, but had for the most part never been personally visited by him—places such as Colossae, Hierapolis, and Laodicea. Tychicus would leave a copy with each church in the towns through which he passed on his way to Colossae, and possibly he transmitted copies to towns that did not lie on his route. In the latter case, Paul's promise that Tychicus would inform the churches of his estate (Eph 6:21) would be fulfilled when Tychicus visited these churches after having completed his mission to Colossae. Each copy would bear the name of the church addressed. When Paul's letters were later collected and published, probably at Ephesus, the letter naturally came to bear the title "To the Ephesians," since Ephesus was no doubt included in the number of the churches addressed and was the most prominent among them. Some later copyist then probably inserted the words "in Ephesus" in the salutation, in order to bring the text of the letter into harmony with its title. Some scholars are inclined to see in the letter "from Laodicea," referred to in Col 4:16, the letter that we know as the Letter to the Ephesians. It may be; copying was an onerous task in antiquity, and it would be natural and sensible to make one copy do for the two churches, since Colossae and Laodicea lay only 13 miles apart.

Statue of the goddess Artemis found at Ephesus.

Authenticity of Ephesians

The authenticity of the Letter to the Ephesians is seriously questioned by many scholars. The case against authenticity is often supported by ingenious and elaborately worked out arguments. Many of these appear at first glance to be conclusive against authenticity, but a careful examination of all the data (including the ancient tradition that unanimously attributes the letter to Paul) will result in the realization that the arguments against authenticity are, after all, far from decisive.

Among the more important of the arguments advanced against the authenticity of the letter are: the peculiarities of its vocabulary and style, alleged differences in teaching between the letter and undoubtedly authentic letters of Paul, the peculiarly close relationship between the letter and the Letter to the Colossians (some 70 percent of the Colossian letter has parallels in the Letter to the Ephesians), and the generally derivative character of the Letter to the Ephesians (that is, the fact that it gives the impression of being a rehash or summary of teaching given by Paul in other letters). These and other arguments of less weight are said to make Pauline authorship impossible and to make it probable that the letter is the work of a disciple of Paul's, some man who was thoroughly familiar with his master's writings and was restating their teaching in terms of the needs and questions of his own day, probably in the last years of the first century. One American scholar even names the author Onesimus, and conjectures that he wrote the letter as a sort of preface to his edition of the collected letters of Paul, by way of expressing his own great indebtedness to Paul and in order to introduce later generations to the thought of the great apostle.

In general it may be said that the arguments have often been overstated in the eagerness of debate; that the differences in vocabulary and style are in themselves far from being conclusive proof that the letter is not authentic, as is being increasingly recognized by most scholars; that the alleged differences in teaching tend to disappear upon closer examination and that the novelties supposedly introduced by the imitator are seen to be fresh and original restatements of genuinely Pauline themes; that the connection between the Letter to the Colossians and the Letter to the Ephesians is so intricate and deep-rooted that the most natural explanation is that both letters were written by one man, Paul, at approximately the same time; that a later imitator should have so thoroughly assimilated the material of the Colossian letter and have distributed it so completely and haphazardly throughout the Ephesian letter remains historically very improbable. The argument concerning this imitation is, often enough, both confused and confusing: where the Ephesian letter is too much like the other letters of Paul, that is proof of its derivative character and therefore proof that an imitator wrote it; when it is unlike the other letters of Paul, that also is proof that an imitator wrote it. To sum up, all the arguments that have any validity at all point to the fact that the Letter to the Ephesians occupies a unique place among the Pauline Letters; they cannot be said to prove that the Letter to the Ephesians does not belong among the Pauline Letters.

Composition

Author

The apostle Paul, a Jew from Tarsus who studied under the Rabbi Gamaliel at Jerusalem, is regarded as the author of the letter. However, critical scholars have challenged this. See "Authenticity of Ephesians," above.

Date of Composition

Ephesians is linked by the evidence in the letter itself to the Letter to the Colossians and the Letter to Philemon. Tychicus is the bearer of the letter (Eph 6:21) and will give the readers fuller information concerning the imprisoned apostle (6:22). Since Tychicus is also the bearer of the Letter to the Colossians, and since Onesimus is returning to Colossae with Tychicus (Col 4:7–9), the three letters (to the Ephesians, to the Colossians, and to Philemon) have a common historical background; they proceed from Paul's Roman captivity and are to be dated somewhere within the time of that captivity, perhaps in the earlier part of it (see "Captivity Letters," pp 534–36).

Purpose/Recipients

The sending of Tychicus to Colossae thus provided the external occasion for the writing of the circular letter now called the Letter to the Ephesians. What Paul's motives in sending such a letter were, we can infer from the apostolic church's missionary practice and from a statement made by Paul toward the end of the letter itself. The apostolic church always sought contact with newly founded churches. John and Peter were sent to Samaria after the evangelist Philip had founded a church there (Ac 8:14). Barnabas was sent to the young Church at Antioch (11:22). Paul took representatives of the Jerusalem Church with him on his first two missionary journeys (Barnabas, Mark, Silas); he maintained contact with Jerusalem and Judaic Christianity and sought to express and to maintain the unity of the Spirit in the bond of peace by means of the Gentile collection for the Jerusalem saints; he regularly revisited the churches that he had founded. As Paul surveyed his work in the East from the vantage point of his position in Rome, and saw from the reports of his co-workers the temptations and the dangers to which the young churches were exposed, he might well be moved to do by letter what he could not do in person, to go through his territory once more, "strengthening the churches" (15:41). That would be one motive for writing to the churches in the East.

The other motive was provided by Paul's peculiar situation. Paul in Rome knew himself to be an ambassador for the Gospel, albeit "an ambassador in chains" (Eph 6:20). Again the strength of the Lord was being made perfect in weakness. The Gentile churches saw the human weakness of the imprisoned apostle more clearly than they saw the divine strength that worked through him; they had grown dispirited at the news of his imprisonment (3:13). Moreover, Paul was facing a crisis in his ambassadorship, one which would ask of him all the boldness he could muster (6:18–20). Paul therefore did two things in his letter: (1) He asked for the intercessions of the churches, thus removing them from the role of lamenting spectators and making them active participants in his great ambassadorial task. (2) He held up before them the greatness of that task, the greatness of the church that the mighty divine Word proclaimed by him had created and was sustaining. He had just written to the Colossians how God's act in the cross of Christ has made a peace that embraces the universe in all its parts and in all its powers (Col 1:20); he had just written to Philemon and had seen, in applying the power of the Gospel to heal the breach between master and runaway slave, how that peace heals all of a person's life and removes its ugly rancor. He spoke of Christ "our peace" (Eph 2:14) to all the scattered and troubled churches and held before them the greatness of the new people of God, which God had created by uniting Jew and Gentile, once enemies, in one church; he held up before them the glory of that one, Holy Church, thus keeping the churches conscious of their high privilege of unity in Christ and of the obligation that the high privilege of membership in the one church involves. If the Letter to the Colossians is the Letter of Christ the Head of the Church, the Letter to the Ephesians is the Letter of the Church, the Body of Christ. Its purpose and outreach are as universal as its destination is general.

Literary Features

Genre

Ephesians, which bears many similarities to Paul's Letter to the Colossians, may be an example of an encyclical letter. An encyclical was a communication meant for more than one location (see 2Macc 1:1–9 for an example of a Jewish encyclical). Paul or his scribe may have adopted an encyclical letter's contents especially for the Ephesian congregation. The letter includes the doctrinal and practical elements common to Paul's correspondence.

Characters

The only other person mentioned in the Letter to the Ephesians is the letter bearer, **Tychicus** (6:21).

Narrative Development or Plot

Since Ephesians is written primarily as a doctrinal letter, it does not have a storyline or plot.

Resources

As noted above, Ephesians bears some striking similarities with the Letter to the Colossians, which may mean that Paul was composing a general encyclical letter, which he then adapted to the specific needs of these congregations. Paul Deterding has described the relationship between the letters as follows:

> Ephesians employs many of the same concepts and terminology in a more general letter intended for wider circulation (as seen by the lack of "in Ephesus" in some manuscripts of Eph 1:1). This points to the following relationship between the two letters:
>
> 1. Paul writes Colossians in response to the heresy troubling that congregation. The distinctive vocabulary and more fully developed ideas of this letter are shaped in response to the vocabulary and ideas of the heresy.
>
> 2. With these newly formulated concepts and terms still fresh in his mind, the apostle writes the more general letter that we know as Ephesians. The new thoughts and language are there applied to the more general circumstances of the church at large.

> While there is extensive agreement between these letters, neither should be thought of as an expansion or epitome of the other, for each has its own emphasis. The letter to the Colossians is concerned with Christ as the head of his body, the church. Ephesians, on the other hand, emphasizes the church as the body of which Christ is the head. (CC Col, 12–13)

Text and Translations

The text of Ephesians is well established through a wealth of early manuscripts dating as early as c AD 200 (Papyrus 46) and from Early Church Fathers who cite the letter. As with Paul's other letters, scholars discuss the possible influence of the early heretic Marcion on causing some of the textual variants.

The earliest manuscripts do not have the words "in Ephesus" in the salutation (1:1), and their witness is confirmed by that of the Early Church Fathers; some English translations omit the words from their revision of the text. Moreover, the letter itself nowhere indicates that Paul and the readers whom he is addressing are personally acquainted with one another; there are passages that indicate the very opposite (1:15; 3:2). When we consider how long Paul ministered in Ephesus and what close ties that ministry established (Ac 20:36–38), the absence of any personal touches in the letter is very striking. Similarly the letter gives no hint that Paul is personally acquainted with the life of the church—there are no concrete details, no reminiscences of former personal contact. Paul's letters to the Corinthians, written to a church in which he had worked and with which he was intimately acquainted, present a striking contrast to the Letter to the Ephesians in this respect. One can hardly avoid the conclusion that the letter known as the Letter to the Ephesians was not originally addressed to Ephesus, at least not to Ephesus alone.

Doctrinal Content

Summary Commentary

Ch 1 Paul directs the Ephesians away from themselves, teaching them to trust in God's promises in Christ. He gives thanks for God's power at work in the Ephesians, whom God had chosen from the foundation of the world.

Chs 2–3 Judaizers threatened most early Christian communities, teaching that Gentiles had to obey the Old Testament Law in addition to having

Outline

I. Salutation (1:1–2)

II. Prologue on Unity (1:3–23)
  - A. Prayer (1:3–14)
  - B. Thanksgiving (1:15–23)

III. Proofs for Unity (chs 2–3)
  - A. New Creation by Grace Alone (2:1–10)
  - B. Gentiles and Israel (2:11–22)
  - C. Paul's Apostolic Mandate to the Gentiles (3:1–13)
  - D. Prayer and Doxology (3:14–21)

IV. Baptism Unites (4:1–5:20)
  - A. Baptism into One Body (4:1–16)
  - B. Baptism Clothes the Believer (4:17–32)
  - C. Baptism Directs the Believers' Walk (5:1–14)
  - D. The Liturgy of the Spirit (5:15–20)

V. Baptism Reorders Relationships (5:21–6:9)
  - A. Husband and Wife (5:22–33)
  - B. Parents and Children (6:1–4)
  - C. Masters and Servants (6:5–9)

VI. Baptism Equips with Armor (6:10–17)

VII. Conclusion (6:18–24)
  - A. Exhortation (6:18–20)
  - B. Commendation to Letter-Bearer (6:21–22)
  - C. Final Greeting and Blessing (6:23–24)

faith in Christ. But Paul insists that God saves both Jews and Gentiles by grace through faith, apart from any works. Christ has made us to be His one Body. Paul then defends his call as an apostle by emphasizing its basis in the Gospel. As He considers God's wisdom, grace, and love, he breaks out in prayer and praise.

4:1–5:21 Paul highlights the gifts of Christ that make us His Body; as one Body, we are protected from the dangers of our times. He describes the new life that results from the Gospel. Yet, the Law also continues to apply because of our sinful nature. We are confronted every day by a world rebelling against God's way.

5:22–6:24 Paul teaches that the husband is the "head" in a marriage and the wife is the "body." Both are necessary for life. He briefly describes the Christian life and gives common examples of vocations, or callings, in life. He exposes the demonic forces that battle against us, and he encourages us with the divine weapons that protect us. Paul concludes the letter by emphasizing prayer and by greeting the brethren briefly.

Paul warns that evil spirits are a real and constant threat to the good of believers, who can oppose them through the armor of God (Eph 6:10–20).

Specific Law Themes

Ephesians addresses the problem of divisions among Christians, especially divisions based on something other than true versus false doctrine. Paul explains that when we are unfaithful, we grieve God's Spirit. He treats also especially marriage and family, which God would not have us divide. Paul warns that the evil one is a constant threat.

A third-century image of a child being baptized.

Specific Gospel Themes

We are baptized into Christ, through whom the Lord chose us from the foundation of the world. Our justification before God comes by His grace, through faith alone. He has revealed the divine mysteries through the revelation of Jesus and made us one body—the Church.

Specific Doctrines

Paul is here singing hymns in prison, as he once did at Philippi. It is a hymn rich in content, a hymn that sings of the "manifold wisdom of God" and "the unsearchable riches of Christ." One very perceptive modern interpreter has compared the letter with the Letter to the Romans; in both letters, he points out, Paul elaborates the theme stated in 1Co 1:24, "Christ the power of God and the wisdom of God." Whereas the Letter to the Romans stresses the element of power (Rm 1:16), the Letter to the Ephesians emphasizes the wisdom of God. The Church, which is always prone to forget that it is God's creation and likes to think of itself as a structure of strength which *man* in his wisdom has reared and can in his wisdom control, will do well to immerse itself again and again in this hymn from prison and to learn from the ambassador in chains an awed humility in the presence of that awful, divine wisdom.

Key Texts

Ephesians opens with some of the boldest, straightforward statements about eternal election in the New Testament, affirming and commending this doctrine (1:4) rooted in Christ and God's love, which results in our holiness. The corruption and alienation caused by sin (2:1–3; 4:18–19) make God's grace the only basis of our salvation as well as our works (2:5–10). Delivered from God's coming wrath (5:5–6), the new man is stored in God's likeness (4:24), sealed by His Spirit (4:30), and therefore confident through faith (3:12).

For Paul in this letter, of central important is the Church, which is built upon Christ and His witnesses (2:20) and purely sanctified in Baptism (5:26–27). Christ bestows gifts of ministry to His Church for her edification and upbuilding (4:8–12). So equipped, the Church may carry on spiritual warfare against the forces of evil (6:12). Ephesians 5:22–33 teaches the doctrine of the Church while also commenting on the relationship between husband and wife, a passage increasingly discussed as social expectations for marriage changed during the twentieth century.

Application

Ch 1 Pride tempts us to trust in our commitment to God; doubt makes us worry that we are not committed enough. God's power is not automatically good news. It terrifies sinners, but it comforts us who know His love for us in Christ. Jesus blesses us spiritually by leading us to repent of sinful pride by the Law and calming our worried hearts through the Gospel.

Chs 2–3 Today's self-help culture tempts us to try to do it all ourselves. Though our personal credentials are important, our service in the church is based on God's gifts and calling, which stem from the Gospel. Study of God's Word naturally combines with prayer and praise in the Divine Service, where Christ's gifts are given out, and we receive them with thanksgiving.

4:1–5:21 Modern individualism and consumerism make it easy to treat the Church as "all about me." Thanks be to God, the Church is all about Jesus, who provides for our salvation and edification. As Luther explains the Ten Commandments in the Catechism, the Law both forbids sinful behavior ("shall not") and urges good works ("shall"). As we inevitably fail to live up to such demands, forgiveness preserves and restores the harmony of the Church. In our struggle against its temptations, we can rely on Christ's Word and Spirit to lead us.

5:22–6:24 We are inclined today to view our marriages selfishly: what can I get out of it? Instead, we should consider what we can offer to our spouse and see behind each action a picture of the Gospel itself. Today, God calls us to serve Him and other people selflessly, lovingly, and conscious of our relationship to Christ. We should examine our lives and our callings. The Lord will forgive our shortcomings and strengthen us to be Christlike. In the modern world, the spiritual dimension of life is often overlooked. We view our problems—and try to solve them—in purely human terms. But the Lord works in us by His Word and Spirit.

Canonicity

Like Paul's other biblical letters, which were collected and copied as authoritative already in the middle of the first century AD (cf 2Pt 3:15–16), Ephesians quickly gained canonical status (*homologoumenon*). However, most critical scholars do not regard the book as a genuine letter of Paul. For more on this issue, see pp 523–24.

In Ephesians Paul describes the Scriptures as the "sword of the Spirit" (Eph 6:17).

Lutheran Theologians on Ephesians

Luther

"In this epistle St. Paul teaches, first, what the gospel is, how it was predestined by God alone in eternity, and earned and sent forth through Christ, so that all who believe on it become righteous, godly, living, saved men, and free from the law, sin, and death. This he does in the first three chapters.

"Then he teaches that false teachings and the commandments of men are to be avoided, so that we may remain true to one Head, and become sure and genuine and complete in Christ alone. For in him we have everything, so that we need nothing beside him. This he does in chapter 4.

"Then he goes on to teach that we are to practice and prove our faith with good works, avoid sin, and fight with spiritual weapons against the devil, so that through the cross we may be steadfast in hope." (AE 35:385)

Gerhard

"For a two-year period Paul had preached the Gospel in Ephesus, the chief city of Ionia in Asia Minor (Acts 19:1), and had gathered quite a large church for Christ (1 Cor. 16:9), which after his departure he had entrusted to his disciple Timothy (1 Tim. 1:3) and of which the evangelist John is said to have been in charge later. [Paul] directed his letter to the inhabitants of that city. No schisms had been stirred up there; no false doctrine had been sown there, as among the Galatians. Rather, the impelling cause for writing was the far-seeing concern of the apostle lest they become weak and weary of the Gospel because of the chains that were binding him at Rome.

"It consists of six chapters and falls into two parts. The first is the teaching part, for it explains the foundation of our salvation, which consists in the gratuitous election of our God, in the redemption performed by Christ, in our calling by the Gospel, in justification and the gift of an eternal inheritance. The latter part is exhortation: (1) a generic one about the responsibility of the devout in general, that they should pursue piety, harmony, love, and the other Christian virtues; and (2) a specific one about the duty of husbands to wives, parents to their children, masters to their slaves, etc." (ThC E1 § 261)

Captivity Letters

Ephesians, Philippians, Colossians, and Philemon

The Captivity Letters issued from the Roman captivity of Paul (AD 58–60). A considerable number of scholars, however, favor other points of origin for all of them or for some of them. Some scholars are inclined to place at least the Letter to the Philippians into the Caesarean captivity of Paul (AD 55–57; cf Ac 23:33; 24:27). But this hypothesis really has very little to commend it. It is not likely that the runaway slave Onesimus would take refuge in a town like Caesarea, where he could hardly hope to escape detection. So far as we know, Paul never had any prospect of being released while at Caesarea, and he certainly never was in danger of being condemned and executed while there, something that Paul views as a distinct possibility in his Letter to the Philippians. Neither is it likely that Paul planned to visit his churches in Asia and Macedonia at this date; he was still turned Romeward and westward.

Scholars have also argued for Ephesus as the place where the letters were written. This theory has considerably more force. The following is a condensed survey of the most important arguments used to support the so-called Ephesian hypothesis. Counterarguments will be given after each argument.

The Ephesian Imprisonment of Paul

The Book of Acts records no imprisonment of Paul during his ministry at Ephesus. But, it is argued, Luke's account makes no pretense to completeness, and the following considerations make an imprisonment during this period at least possible if not probable: the whole period of Paul's activity at Ephesus was troubled by the machinations of his inveterate opponents, the Jews (Ac 19:9, 33; 20:19; 21:27; 1Co 16:9); it was obviously a time of desperate dangers for Paul (Rm 16:4, 7; 1Co 15:30; 2Co 1:8–10;). That is all the New Testament evidence. Later sources tell us that Paul once fought with a lion at Ephesus. A building in Ephesus was later pointed out as "Paul's prison." A set of introductory notes found in some ancient Latin manuscripts and dating from the third or fourth century (the so-called Monarchian Prologues) say of the Letter to the Colossians: "The apostle wrote it from Ephesus while already in prison."

However, the direct evidence for an imprisonment is admittedly slight; no New Testament document mentions an imprisonment at Ephesus. The references in later sources to Paul's fight with a lion at Ephesus seem to be simply inferences from Paul's figurative language in 1Co 15:32. The evidence of the Monarchian Prologue is made doubtful by the fact that this same source assigns the Letter to Philemon to Rome, and the Letter to Philemon cannot be separated from the Letter to the Colossians. Paul may possibly have been imprisoned at Ephesus, but it seems precarious to build a hypothesis on so shaky a foundation. It should be noted also that the events presupposed by the Letter to the Philippians demand an extended imprisonment; and the longer the imprisonment, the less likely it is that it should be wrapped in silence.

The Flight of Onesimus

Onesimus is more likely to have fled to Ephesus—only 125 miles from his home in Colossae and large enough to enable him to remain undetected—than to have undertaken the long, difficult, and (especially for runaway slaves) dangerous voyage to Rome.

However, we have no way of deciding whether Onesimus would have fled to Ephesus because it was near to Rome or because it was far. If he had lined his pockets with his master Philemon's money, the voyage to Rome would not have been so difficult as is often supposed. And Rome was notoriously the cesspool into which all the refuse of the Roman Empire flowed.

Paul's Request for Lodging at Colossae (Philemon 22)

Paul is more likely to have planned a visit to Colossae from Ephesus than from Rome.

However, one may reasonably doubt whether Paul's words, "Prepare a guest room for me," are to be taken quite so immediately as many interpreters seem inclined to do. In a letter as easy and informal in tone as the Letter to Philemon the words may be no more than a strong expression of the good hope of release from prison that animates Paul as he writes. As for the revisitation of the eastern provinces and churches, it is much more probable on the Roman hypothesis. By the time of Paul's imprisonment in Rome almost five years had elapsed since Paul had left his work in the East and turned to the West. He may have found it advisable, in the light of developments such as had arisen in Colossae and Laodicea, to revisit Asia and Macedonia once more—or it may have simply been the will of the Lord. The Pastoral Letters indicate that he did revisit the East.

The Companions of Paul during His Imprisonment

The large number of co-workers mentioned by Paul as being with him during his imprisonment seems unlikely for Rome but would be natural for the extended and intensive ministry at Ephesus.

However, the place where Paul was would naturally be headquarters for his co-workers. All calculations as to how many companions might or might not have been with Paul at Rome or at Ephesus, or which companions might more naturally be with him at either place, are bound to be highly speculative.

The Frequency of Communication Between Paul and Philippi

Since Ephesus is closer to Philippi, it is argued that frequent communication between Philippi and Paul is much more probable between Ephesus and Philippi than between Rome and Philippi. This is no doubt the strongest argument for the Ephesian hypothesis.

However, this, too, is not an overwhelming argument. It has been conservatively estimated that the communications that had taken place between Paul and Philippi by the time of the writing of the Letter to the Philippians need not have consumed more than six or seven months. They can be easily fitted into the two years of the Roman imprisonment. The journey between Philippi and Ephesus would require six or seven days, so that an imprisonment of considerable length would be necessary for the Ephesian hypothesis also.

Conclusions

The arguments (only typical examples have been given here) for the Ephesian imprisonment of Paul and for the dating of the Captivity Letters from that imprisonment range from the plausible and ingenious to the merely clever, but all are inconclusive. And until it can be shown that the Ephesian hypothesis better explains all the known facts concerning the Captivity Letters more than the Roman hypothesis, we are on safer ground in assigning the letters to the known and verifiable Roman imprisonment of AD 58–60. Two arguments for the Roman provenance of the letters deserve mention in closing: (a) according to the evidence of the letters themselves, Luke was with Paul during his imprisonment (Col 4:14; Phm 24); according to Acts, he was with Paul in Rome, but not in Ephesus; (b) in the Letter to the Philippians, Paul faces the possibility of an adverse verdict and death as a consequence (Php 1:20). This could happen only in Rome; in any provincial court, Paul could always appeal to the decision of the emperor, as he did at Caesarea under Festus (Ac 25:11–12).

Further Study

Lay/Bible Class Resources

Foulkes, Francis. *Ephesians*. TNTC. Downers Grove, IL: InterVarsity Press, 1989. § Compact commentary based on the RSV but interacting with a variety of English translations. A popular but generally helpful evangelical treatment of the text.

Joersz, Jerald C. *Galatians, Ephesians, Philippians*. RHBC. St. Louis: Concordia, 2013. § Verse-by-verse commentary on the ESV and KJV translations, presented in parallel columns. Written by a Lutheran theologian for lay readers and busy church workers. Includes quotations from prominent Reformers and articles about Reformation views. Excellent for Bible classes.

Life by His Word. St. Louis: Concordia, 2009. § More than 1,500 reproducible one-page Bible studies covering each chapter of the canonical Scriptures. Page references to *The Lutheran Study Bible*. CD-Rom and downloadable.

Nadasdy, Dean, and Roger Sonnenberg. *Ephesians, 1 & 2 Thessalonians*. Leaders Guide and Enrichment Magazine/Study Guide. LL. St. Louis: Concordia, 2011. § An in-depth, nine-session Bible study with individual, small group, and lecture portions.

Panning, Armin. *Galatians, Ephesians*. PBC. St. Louis: Concordia, 2005. § Lutheran author. Excellent for Bible classes. Based on the NIV translation.

Rosin, Walter. *Ephesians. The Church: God's Servant*. GWFT. St. Louis: Concordia, 1995. § Lutheran author. Thirteen-session Bible study, including leader's notes and discussion questions.

Church Worker Resources

Bruce, F. F. *The Epistles to the Colossians, to Philemon, and to the Ephesians*. NICNT. Grand Rapids: Eerdmans, 1984. § An excellent resource, carefully done.

Academic Resources

Abbott, T. K. *A Critical and Exegetical Commentary on the Epistles to the Ephesians and to the Colossians*. ICC. Edinburgh: T&T Clark, 1897. § Heavy stress on philology, and valuable from that viewpoint.

Arnold, Clinton E. *Ephesians*. Zondervan Exegetical Commentary on the New Testament. Grand Rapids: Zondervan, 2010. § A thorough evangelical commentary based on the Greek text, from an expert on the prison epistles.

Barth, Markus. *Ephesians*. Vols. 34 and 34A of AB. Garden City, NY: Doubleday, 1974. § Very detailed study; use with careful theological discernment.

Best, E. *A Critical and Exegetical Commentary on Ephesians*. ICC. Edinburgh: T&T Clark, 1998 reprint. § An older, detailed, valuable resource.

Braune, Karl. *Ephesians*. LCHS. New York: Charles Scribner's Sons, 1870. § A helpful older example of German biblical scholarship, based on the Greek text, which provides references to significant commentaries from the Reformation era forward.

Lenski, R. C. H. *The Interpretation of St. Paul's Epistles to the Ephesians and Philippians*. Minneapolis: Augsburg, 2008. § A standard resource by a noteworthy Lutheran interpreter, concerned with being faithful to the text and with its implications for today.

Lincoln, Andrew T. *Ephesians*. WBC. Dallas: Word Books, 1990. § Denies Pauline authorship, yet is a most useful commentary.

Stoeckhardt, George. *Commentary on Ephesians*. Concordia Classic Commentary series. St. Louis: Concordia, 1952. § Sound theologically, from a learned and experienced Lutheran exegete at Concordia Seminary.

Thielman, Frank. *Ephesians*. Baker Exegetical Commentary on the New Testament. Grand Rapids: Baker, 2010. § A thorough commentary on the Greek, written from an evangelical author who argues for Pauline authorship as crucial to interpreting the letter.

Westcott, Brooke Foss. *Saint Paul's Epistle to the Ephesians: The Greek Text*. Grand Rapids: Baker, 1979 reprint. § Still a helpful resource by a great New Testament scholar of the past. Introductory articles include in parallel columns the relationship of Ephesians to Colossians, other Pauline, and also other apostolic writings. Helpful excursuses appended.

PHILIPPIANS

Progress and joy in the faith

On the edge of the Datos plain, about six miles from the Aegean Sea, Greek colonists founded the city of Philippi in 356 BC. Philip II of Macedon soon took the city and named it after himself. The Roman Empire recognized the city's worth, making it one of the last points along the Egnatian Way, which linked Rome with the east and was strategically located in the system of Roman roads for the security of the empire.

In the first century AD, the Captivity Letters tell of a visitor who traveled from Paul's churches in the East to see Paul in Rome. His name was Epaphroditus, who came from Philippi in Macedonia, the first church Paul founded in Europe (Ac 16:6–40). Paul, Silas, Timothy, and Luke had arrived in Philippi early in the second missionary journey (AD 49–51). Philippi was a Roman "colony," that is, a settlement of Roman soldiers, enjoying Roman citizenship.

Historical and Cultural Setting

There were, apparently, not many Jews at Philippi; there was no regular synagogue, only a "place of prayer" (Ac 16:13), probably in the open air, at a river's side. It was there that Paul had begun his work. The Lord opened the ear of a proselyte named Lydia to his words, and we may suppose that the house of this wealthy and generous woman became the meeting place of the church (16:14–15). Paul knew "conflict" (Php 1:30) and suffering in Philippi; he had been beaten and imprisoned without the due process of law to which his Roman citizenship entitled him. He had known not only conflict, but also that joy in the midst of conflict and suffering which is the characteristic token of the apostolic and Christian existence (Ac 16:25). He had experienced triumph in conflict and suffering, the triumph of the Lord whose strength is made perfect in weakness and defeat; he was released from prison and vindicated, and he gained the jailer and his household for the Lord (16:25–40).

Early second century Greco-Roman style portait of a woman dressed in purple. The congregation at Philippi began with a proselyte, Lydia, "a seller of purple goods" (Ac 16:14). This portrait was found in Faiyum, Egypt.

OVERVIEW

Author
Paul the apostle

Date
c AD 60

Places
Philippi (Macedonia); Thessalonica

People
Paul; Timothy; Epaphroditus; Euodia; Syntyche; the imperial guard; "those of Caesar's household"

Purpose
Paul describes a life worthy of the Gospel (1:27)

Law Themes
Suffering, uncertainty, and personal sacrifice; rivalry over the Gospel; growth in humility and right-mindedness

Gospel Themes
Joy in Christ; Jesus' exaltation after the cross; righteousness through faith in Christ; heavenly citizenship

Memory Verses
To live is Christ (1:21–26); Christ's humility and exaltation (2:4–11); righteous through faith (3:7–11); press on (3:12–14); citizenship in heaven (3:20–21)

TIMELINE

AD 36	Paul's conversion
AD 49–51	Paul's second missionary journey
AD 52–55	Paul's third missionary journey
c AD 60	Paul writes Philippians
AD 68	Martyrdom of Peter and Paul

The church that grew, as the Word of the Lord grew, in Philippi was predominantly Gentile. And it was a church that remained peculiarly near and dear to Paul. It was Paul's firstborn in Europe; the faithful and consecrated Luke remained there when Paul continued on his journey and provided spiritual leadership of a high order; the impetuous generosity of Lydia in the first days evidently set the tone of the church's life for the years that followed. We recall how she viewed her Baptism as an initiation into a life of giving; she told Paul and his companions, "If you have judged me to be faithful . . . come to my house and stay," and "prevailed" on them to comply with her wish (16:15). The generosity of the Philippians was so genuinely rooted in Christ and His Gospel that Paul felt free to accept gifts from them; he can call them his "partners" in the proclamation of the Gospel (Php 1:5; 4:15). They supplied his wants in Thessalonica (4:16) and again in Corinth (2Co 11:9), and at some sacrifice to themselves; Paul told the Corinthians, "I robbed other churches by accepting support from them in order to serve you" (2Co 11:8). This same actively generous partnership in the Gospel had moved the Philippians (and the other churches of Macedonia), to contribute to the collection for the Jerusalem saints "beyond their means," even in the midst of a "severe test of affliction" and in the depths of poverty (8:1–5).

Composition

Author

The apostle Paul, a Jew from Tarsus who studied under the Rabbi Gamaliel at Jerusalem, is regarded as the author of the letter.

Date of Composition

The following events help fix the date of Paul's Letter to the Philippians more exactly within the limits of his two years' imprisonment at Rome (AD 58–60). There has been time for a series of communications between Rome and Philippi: news of Paul's imprisonment has reached distant Philippi; the Philippians' gift has been gathered, sent, and received; news of Epaphroditus's illness has reached Philippi and has caused great concern there; and news of this concern has again come to Paul and Epaphroditus at Rome. It has been calculated that this series of communications would require a total of five or six months at a minimum, and they may have taken considerably longer. Moreover, the letter itself indicates that Paul's long-deferred trial is at last in progress, that it has proceeded so far that Paul can with some confidence hope for an early release from imprisonment (Php 1:25–26; 2:24), though there is still real danger of an adverse verdict and death. All this points to a date toward the close of the two years' imprisonment, probably to the early months of AD 60.

Paul is about to return Epaphroditus to Philippi (2:25–30). He sends with him a letter in which he gives his partners in the Gospel news of himself, his trial, and his prospects of release; thanks them for their gift; and excuses and commends their messenger Epaphroditus, who through no fault of his own has been unable to carry out fully the ministry entrusted to him. He notices with pastoral concern and with kindly evangelical tact their internal troubles, a tendency to self-assertion on the part of some, with its consequent tendency to disunity. He encourages them in the persecution

A traditional location for Paul's prison in Philippi.

that presses on them from without, and he warns them, with passionate sternness, of the dangers that threaten them, alerting them to the threat posed by Judaistic and libertine perverters of the Gospel.

Purpose/Recipients

The coming of Epaphroditus was a link in the golden chain of Philippi's gracious generosity. Still suffering persecution (Php 1:29; 4:19), the men and women of Philippi had nevertheless gathered a gift for Paul, probably under the direction of their "overseers and deacons," whom Paul singles out in the salutation of his Letter to the Philippians (and only in this letter, 1:1). They had sent the gift to Paul by the hand of one of their number, Epaphroditus, and had instructed him to remain in Rome with Paul as a minister to his need (2:25). Epaphroditus had delivered the gift and had performed his task of ministry with such self-forgetting devotion that "he nearly died for the work of Christ, risking his life" to complete the service of the Philippian Christians to their apostle (2:30). In this letter, Paul writes to thank the Philippians as well as advise them on some matters.

Literary Features

Genre

Philippians is best characterized as a missionary thank you letter.

Characters

Timothy and Epaphroditus receive special mention as Paul's colleagues (2:19–30).

Narrative Development or Plot

Since Philippians is written as a letter, it does not have a storyline or plot. However, the book does illustrate the story of Paul's missionary activity, especially his imprisonment.

Resources

The sudden change of mood at 3:2 has led some scholars to conjecture that this portion of the letter (3:2–4:1) is a fragment of another Pauline letter. This conjecture receives some support from the fact that Polycarp in writing to the Philippians in the second century refers to "letter*s*" that they have received from Paul. We do not know the situation well enough to decide whether an abrupt change here (as in the Second Letter to the Corinthians, beginning at the tenth chapter) is so improbable as to demand a conjectural

Outline

I. Salutation (1:1–2)

II. Thanksgiving and Prayer (1:3–11)

III. News about Paul's Preaching (1:12–26)
- A. Paul's Imprisonment (1:12–18)
- B. Life in Christ (1:19–26)

IV. Exhortations (1:27–2:18)
- A. Behave as Citizens Worthy of the Gospel (1:27–30)
- B. Christ's Example of Humility (2:1–11)
- C. Lights in the Word (2:12–18)

V. Travel Plans for Timothy and Epaphroditus (2:19–30)

VI. Further Exhortations (3:1–4:9)
- A. Warning against Mutilators (3:1–11)
- B. Straining toward the Goal by Imitating Paul (3:12–4:1)
- C. Exhortation, Encouragement, and Prayer (4:2–9)

VII. Thanks for God's Provision and the Gifts Received (4:10–20)

VIII. Final Greetings (4:21–23)

partition of the letter. Even if Polycarp is referring to a number of letters written by Paul to the Church at Philippi (which is not certain), this does not yet prove that our present Letter to the Philippians is made up of two of them. All the ancient manuscripts and versions give the letter as we have it today.

The Christ hymn of 2:4–11 may have been an independent poem, perhaps even one familiar to the congregation.

Text and Translations

The text of Philippians is well established through a wealth of early manuscripts dating as early as c AD 200 (Papyrus 46) and from Early Church Fathers who cite the letter. As with Paul's other letters, scholars discuss the possible influence of the early heretic Marcion on causing some of the textual variants.

The Golden Cross of Essen; tenth century, Germany. In the Christ hymn (Php 2:4–11), Paul celebrates Christ's humble bearing of the cross.

Doctrinal Content

Summary Commentary

1:1–11 Paul introduces his Letter to the Christians in Philippi with descriptions of who they are and what that will mean in their lives. As a servant of Christ Jesus, Paul takes great pains to be faithful to the ministry entrusted to him. He continues the introduction by expressing his prayer, appreciation, and yearning for these fellow believers.

1:12–30 Paul demonstrates that his imprisonment does not defeat the Gospel, as some had feared. He turns his attention from the question of whether he will live or die to a more important issue: what it means to live in this world.

2:1–18 Paul couples the imperatives of a Christian life with a description of Christ, who makes that life possible. His exhortation flows from the previous section, revealing the significance of Jesus' life and sacrifice.

2:19–30 Paul takes a moment to inform the Philippians about the significance and well-being of two close associates, Timothy and Epaphroditus. These men provide remarkable examples of devotion to the Lord's mission and to His missionary Paul.

3:1–4:9 Paul reflects on his heritage and contrasts its value with the blessing of knowing Jesus, who sets us free to invest our lives in the lives of others. He holds out before us our upward calling, his example, and the promise of our transformation in the resurrection. As Paul concludes this letter, he uses imperative language to urge the reader to adopt practices of living that are in harmony with the Creator's will.

4:10–23 Paul cannot end this letter without a vibrant expression of gratitude toward God and the service of the Philippians. His last words in the letter are greetings and blessings.

Specific Law Themes

The Philippians faced suffering and uncertainty (Ac 16) as well as personal sacrifice as they sought to help their spiritual brothers and sisters in Jerusalem. Unfortunately, some of the Philippians also introduced rivalry over the Gospel. In view of these issues, Paul urges them to grow in humility and right mindedness.

Specific Gospel Themes

Paul's letter exudes joy and thankfulness in Christ for all that the Lord had done and would continue doing. Paul points the readers to Jesus' atoning sacrifice and His exaltation after the cross. He reminds the Philippians that they are declared righteous through Jesus their Savior. Through Him, they are already citizens of God's kingdom.

Specific Doctrines

Among the Captivity Letters, the Letters to the Colossians and to the Ephesians show us Paul the fighter for the truth, the thinker and theologian, the great strategist of church unity; the Letter to Philemon shows us Paul the man whose whole life is irradiated by the grace and glory of the Gospel. The content of the Letter to the Philippians, with its many and various facets, is harder to classify. One modern scholar has brilliantly used this letter as an introduction to the whole thought-world of Paul; he sees in it the characteristic union of Paul the believer, Paul the missionary, and Paul the theologian. Perhaps one might best use the bold joy of faith as the common denominator of its multiplicity, faith as Luther once described it: "Faith is a living, daring confidence in God's grace, so sure and certain that that believer would stake his life on it a thousand times. This knowledge of and confidence in God's grace makes men glad and bold and happy in dealing with God and with all creatures" (AE 35:370–71). An imprisoned apostle writes to a persecuted church, and the keynote of his letter is: "I rejoice. Do you rejoice?" Where under the sun is anything like this possible except where faith is, where the Holy Spirit breathes His wholesome and creative breath? The whole letter is a good illustration of a word Paul uses in Php 4:5, a word that we are obliged to translate with some such term as "reasonableness." But "reasonableness" expresses only a part of Paul's meaning; the Greek word that he uses points to a princely quality in man, to that largeness of heart, that spacious generosity, that freedom from the cruelly competitive scrabble of this world which only he possesses whose "commonwealth is in heaven," who is heir to all that is Christ's, heir to the new world of God, in which he shall reign with Christ.

Key Texts

Philippians has contributed to our understanding of the relationship between faith and works because Paul sprinkles comments about this relationship throughout the letter. He makes plain that we have no righteousness of our own but receive God's righteousness through faith in Christ (3:9). God is thus at work in we who believe (2:13) and Christ will bring to completion His work in us (1:6). For He owns us, and though we are not perfect in this life, God's work in us leads us to press for a Christlike life (2:12–13; 3:10–12).

One of the most studied passages in Philippians is the great Christ hymn (2:4–11), which teaches humility in the letter with rhetorical force but also teaches Christology and redemption succinctly. Elements of the poem led to debate in both ancient and modern theological discussions (esp 2:7).

Application

1:1–11 Paul encourages every reader by describing us as saints and by announcing that the words of the letter to follow, which are inspired by the Holy Spirit, will bring grace and peace to us. We who claim the Christian faith may see how far our thoughts, passions, and labors may miss the focus of the Christian life. Yet, God still welcomes our prayer. Confidence that God will complete the good work He has begun in us is still justified. Christ's righteousness is abundantly available to us in His Word.

1:12–30 God's wisdom and love so far surpass our abilities that He can and does still bring the truth of the Gospel to light despite all opposition, just as Jesus fulfilled all righteousness and conquered death by His resurrection. If God grants you a day in this world, it is because He would have you serve others by living and speaking in a way that is consistent with (worthy of) the Gospel. Our ability to live this way is a product of the salvation God lavishes on us in the very words we read here and in the Spirit that accompanies those words.

2:1–18 We are certainly not lords, nor have we any excuse for refusing to honor Jesus Christ as Lord. Yet the fulfillment of the imperative to live like Christ is supported by all that Christ gives freely: the encouragement, comfort, love, and mind of Christ, along with the participation of the Spirit. Like Paul, our labor would be meaningless and of no use to others if we lived crookedly and perversely as the world around us lives. But God is at work in us, moving us to hold fast to His Word of life, by which He extends His image and kingdom to others.

2:19–30 God's grace makes a person genuinely concerned for the welfare of others and sustains us in such service.

3:1–4:9 We often focus on earthly comforts, worldly examples of success, and maintaining a youthful appearance for this life. While doing this, we starve our souls. Only the life, suffering, death, and resurrection of Jesus Christ has the power to truly set us free to experience life to the fullest. Our citizenship is in heaven! Our life is in Christ, who reigns over all things in heaven and earth. The strength and clarity of Paul's exhortation reminds us that we often are to set our minds on God's will and the promises of God's blessing on our behalf.

4:10–23 Paul's outpouring of appreciation contrasts sharply with feelings of neglect, resentfulness, and even anger that can arise when we lack the privileges and comforts we expect. He invites us to see the blessings and fullness of God that are present in every situation. Christ multiplies those blessings by His grace. The grace of the Lord Jesus is so abundant that it flows over from Paul to us through this very Word and has the power to overflow from our lives into the lives of others, so that we genuinely greet others and then extend God's grace to them.

Canonicity

Like Paul's other biblical letters, which were collected and copied as authoritative already in the middle of the first century AD (cf 2Pt 3:15–16), Philippians quickly gained canonical status (*homologoumenon*).

Lutheran Theologians on Philippians

Luther

"In this epistle St. Paul praises and admonishes the Philippians that they abide and carry on in the true faith and increase in love. But since injury is always done to faith by false apostles and teachers of works, he warns them against these men and points out to them many different preachers—some good, some bad—including even himself and his disciples, Timothy and Epaphroditus. This he does in chapters 1 and 2.

"In chapter 3 he rejects that human righteousness not based on faith, which is taught and held by the false apostles. He offers himself as an example: he had lived gloriously in this kind of righteousness, and yet now holds it to be nothing, for the sake of the righteousness of Christ. For human righteousness makes the belly its god, and makes men enemies of the cross of Christ.

"In chapter 4 he exhorts them to peace and good outward conduct toward each other, and thanks them for the gift they sent him." (AE 35:385)

Gerhard

"The apostle had begun a church at Philippi, the chief city of Macedonia (Acts 16:12). This church had sent Epaphroditus, through whom it had offered help to Paul. In this letter, therefore, the apostle responds to them and makes known their devout eagerness.

"It consists of four chapters and falls into two parts. The first is exhorting, encouraging them to a steadfast faith and holy life; the second is of thanksgiving, in which he gives thanks for the benefits of the Philippians." (ThC E1 § 262)

Further Study

Lay/Bible Class Resources

Dumit, Julene. *Philippians: Joy in Christ*. GWFT. St. Louis: Concordia, 1996. ❧ Lutheran author. Six-session Bible study, including leader's notes and discussion questions.

Grebing, Diane, Mark Etter, and Erik Rottmann. *Galatians, Philippians, Colossians*. Leaders Guide and Enrichment Magazine/Study Guide. LL. St. Louis: Concordia, 2010. ❧ An in-depth, nine-session Bible study with individual, small group, and lecture portions.

Joersz, Jerald C. *Galatians, Ephesians, Philippians*. RHBC. St. Louis: Concordia, 2013. ❧ Verse-by-verse commentary on the ESV and KJV translations, presented in parallel columns. Written by a Lutheran theologian. Includes quotations from prominent Reformers and articles about Reformation views. Excellent for Bible classes.

Kuschel, Harlyn J. *Philippians, Colossians, Philemon*. PBC. St. Louis: Concordia, 2004. ❧ Lutheran author. Excellent for Bible classes. Based on the NIV.

Life by His Word. St. Louis: Concordia, 2009. ❧ More than 1,500 reproducible one-page Bible studies covering each chapter of the canonical Scriptures. Page references to *The Lutheran Study Bible*. CD-Rom and downloadable.

Martin, Ralph P. *Philippians*. TNTC. Downers Grove, IL: IVP Academic, 2008. ❧ Provides insight into the text and its meaning; some attention to critical views. Martin has a lengthy introduction. Comments on 2:7 are not entirely reliable.

Church Worker Resources

Bruce, F. F. *Philippians*. New York: Harper & Row, 1953. ❧ Holds to Pauline authorship. Brief, concise exposition. Needs to be supplemented by a more detailed commentary.

Academic Resources

Braune, Karl. *Philippians*. LCHS. New York: Charles Scribner's Sons, 1874. ❧ A helpful older example of German biblical scholarship, based on the Greek text, which provides references to significant commentaries from the Reformation era forward.

Lenski, R. C. H. *The Interpretation of St. Paul's Epistles to the Ephesians and Philippians*. Minneapolis: Augsburg, 2008. ❧ A standard resource by a noteworthy Lutheran interpreter, concerned with being faithful to the text and the theology of the New Testament.

Lightfoot, J. B. *St. Paul's Epistle to the Philippians*. Grand Rapids: Zondervan, 1953 reprint. ❧ Careful exposition on the basis of the Greek text.

Martin, Ralph P., and Gerald F. Hawthorne. *Philippians*. WBC. Waco, TX: Word, 1983. ❧ A careful, in-depth study; the most exhaustive commentary on Philippians. He uses the Greek, either in parentheses or followed by a translation into English. Opts for Caesarea as the place where Paul wrote the letter.

Martin, Ralph P. *Carmen Christi: Philippians 2:5–11 in Recent Interpretation and in the Setting of Early Christian Worship*. Rev. ed. Grand Rapids: Eerdmans, 1983. ❧ Surveys the history and exegesis of these verses and their varied interpretations in Christological debates.

———. *Philippians*. NCBC. Rev. ed. Grand Rapids: Eerdmans, 1980. ❧ An exposition conversant with a variety of critical theories. Use with careful discernment.

Reumann, John. *Philippians*. Vol. 33B of AB. New Haven: Yale University Press, 2008. ❧ A massive critical commentary from a recognized expert. A significant work for reference purposes.

Silva, Moisés. *Philippians*. Baker Exegetical Commentary on the New Testament. Grand Rapids: Baker, 1992. ❧ Commentary based on the Greek text (without being too technical). Silva has expertise in linguistics, particularly semantics, which was a twentieth-century development in the field of exegesis.

Vincent, Marvin R. *Philippians and Philemon*. ICC. Edinburgh: T&T Clark, 1897. ❧ Helpful for the Greek and for discovering classical references.

Witherington III, Ben. *Friendship and Finances in Philippi: The Letter of Paul to the Philippians*. NT in Context Commentaries. Trinity Press International, 1994. ❧ Written by a prolific (Methodist) New Testament scholar utilizing Duane Watson's rhetorical outline, with adaptations.

COLOSSIANS

All the fullness of God dwells in Christ

Travelers from the west coast of Asia Minor would walk up the Maeander River Valley on their journeys east. If they continued passed Laodicea, along the Lycos River, they would reach the Phrygian city of Colossae in a mountain valley about 125 miles from the coast along a major trade route to Persia.

In the first century AD, Colossae was the chief city of the Lycos Valley, famous for its purple-dyed wool. Paul passed near this region on his missionary trips, but we are never told whether he visited the Lycos Valley or Colossae in particular. Nevertheless, the Early Church has left us his Letter to the Colossians, which shares many characteristics with his Letter to the Ephesians.

Historical and Cultural Setting

Epaphras, among those who visited Paul during his Roman imprisonment, came from Colossae. He brought Paul news of the Gentile church that had been founded there, probably by Epaphras himself (Col 1:5–8), working under the direction of Paul or at least with Paul's full approval (1:7). Epaphras had good news to bring. He could speak warmly of the Colossians' faith and of their love; the Gospel had grown and borne fruit in Colossae as everywhere (1:6). But what had brought Epaphras to Rome was his anxiety for the Church at Colossae, not his pride in it. The Christians of Colossae and of neighboring

Rising nearly 100 feet and including 2,500 figures, Trajan's Column celebrates his military triumphs. Paul refers to a Roman triumphant celebration in Col 2:15 when describing Christ's victory on the cross.

OVERVIEW

Author
Paul the apostle

Date
c AD 60

Places
Colossae; Laodicea; Hierapolis

People
Paul; Timothy; Colossians; Laodiceans; Tychicus; Onesimus; Aristarchus; Mark; Barnabas; Jesus called Justus; Epaphras; Luke; Demas; Nympha; Archippus

Purpose
To guide the Colossian congregation away from heresy and into the truth about Jesus and His saving work

Law Themes
Threat of false teaching and self-made religion; Satan's domain; struggle to fulfill God's calling; God's coming wrath; the old self; admonish one another; God's order for families and labor

Gospel Themes
Gospel growth; the Son's kingdom and reign; mystery: Christ dwells in you; Baptism, the new circumcision; the new self; the Lord's inheritance

Memory Verses
Transferred to God's kingdom (1:11–14); hymn of Christ (1:15–20); the new circumcision (2:11–14); shadow and substance (2:16–17); glory above (3:1–4)

TIMELINE

AD 49	Paul confronts Peter in Antioch
AD 49–51	Paul's second missionary journey
AD 52–55	Paul's third missionary journey
c AD 60	Paul writes Colossians
AD 68	Martyrdom of Peter and Paul

Laodicea were still holding to the Gospel that they had received, but that pure loyalty was being threatened and undermined.

Composition

Author

The apostle Paul, a Jew from Tarsus who studied under the Rabbi Gamaliel at Jerusalem, is regarded as the author of the letter.

Date of Composition

Paul likely wrote to the Colossians during his imprisonment at Rome, in c 60 AD. See pp 534–36.

Purpose/Recipients

The Church at Colossae was threatened by a new teaching that was in many ways strikingly similar to the Gospel that Epaphras had preached there. Both the new teaching and the Gospel originally preached in Colossae proclaimed a non-national, universal religion. Both recognized the great gulf that exists between God and natural man. And both proffered a redemption that would bridge that gulf. But the new teaching was in the last analysis an utter distortion of the Gospel that Epaphras had proclaimed. Epaphras sensed the difference, but could not, perhaps, analyze and define it well enough to be able to oppose it vigorously and effectively. He therefore appealed to Paul, wise in the ways of Greek and Jew alike, keen in insight, and ready to do battle for the truth. Would Paul help him?

It is difficult to get a clear and consistent picture of the heresy that threatened Colossae, for Paul in his Letter to the Colossians does not so much oppose it argumentatively as overwhelm it by confronting it with the whole riches of the true Gospel of Christ. It seems to have been a religion of self-redemption of the "Gnostic" type. Built upon a Jewish or Jewish-Christian basis, it was a fusion of Greek and Asian ideas and combined at least three elements. One of these elements was theosophic, that is, the new teaching claimed to have and to impart a secret, profound knowledge derived from God; Paul speaks contemptuously of a "tradition" and a "philosophy" (Col 2:8). Another element was ritualistic: stress was laid on circumcision (2:11); questions of food and drink, festivals, new moons, and Sabbaths were deemed important (2:16). A third element was ascetic: Paul speaks of prescriptions of abstinence ("Do not handle, Do not taste, Do not

In the letter to Colossae, Paul mentions Hierapolis (pictured here) and Laodicea. These three cities were the chief settlments in the Lycos Valley, where Paul's colleague Epaphras served.

touch," 2:21) and of a "self-made religion," of "asceticism," and of "severity to the body" (2:23). We are left to conjecture how these elements were combined into a system.

Paul's references to the "worship of angels" (2:18) and to "elemental spirits of the world" (2:8, 20) indicate what was the heart of the danger present in this teaching. Other powers besides the Christ were being proclaimed and invoked as mediators between God and man; the ritual and ascetic aspects of this religion probably represent means of placating or of obtaining contact and communion with these powers. What Epaphras, with a sound Christian instinct, surely sensed and what Paul clearly saw was this: the new teaching called into question and obscured the unique greatness of the Christ and the complete sufficiency of His atonement. What made this heresy all the more dangerous was the fact that it claimed not to supplant, but to supplement, the Gospel that the Colossians had received. The new teaching would, so the new teachers claimed, carry the Colossian Christians beyond their rudimentary Christianity to fullness and perfection; hence Paul's repeated emphasis on the fact that the Colossians are complete and full in the Gospel that they have received, that in the Christ whom they know they can find all the treasures of divine wisdom (2:2–3, 9–10; cf 1:28).

Outline

- I. Preaching (chs 1–2)
  - A. Salutation (1:1–2)
  - B. Overture (1:3–20)
    - 1. Thanksgiving report (1:3–8)
    - 2. The source of knowledge: reason for intercession (1:9–14)
    - 3. The Christ hymn: creation and reconciliation (1:15–20)
  - C. Main Exposition and Resolution (1:21–2:23)
    - 1. Ministry of reconciliation (1:21–29)
    - 2. True knowledge (2:1–5)
    - 3. The fullness of Christ (2:6–15)
    - 4. True freedom (2:16–23)
- II. Paul's Instructions (chs 3–4)
  - A. The Christian Life (3:1–4:6)
    - 1. Death and life (3:1–4)
    - 2. Put off and put on (3:5–17)
    - 3. Table of duties (3:18–4:1)
    - 4. Watch and pray (4:2–6)
  - B. Concluding Matters (4:7–18)

Literary Features

Genre

The letter may have been adapted from an encyclical. See "Genre," p 526.

Characters

Paul writes with high praise for **Epaphras**, who was a teacher from Colossae and perhaps also served in Hierapolis and Laodicea, the other cities of the Lycos Valley (4:13). Epaphras, however, is only mentioned in Colossians and the Letter to Philemon, so we know little more about this fellow servant of the great apostle.

Narrative Development or Plot

Since Colossians is written as a letter, it does not have a storyline or plot.

Resources

See pp 526–27.

Text and Translations

The text of Colossians is well established through a wealth of early manuscripts dating as early as c AD 200 (Papyrus 46) and from Early Church Fathers who cite the letter. As with Paul's other letters, scholars discuss the possible influence of the early heretic Marcion on causing some of the textual variants.

Doctrinal Content

Summary Commentary

1:1–23 Faithful Epaphras established a tiny foothold for the kingdom of God at Colossae and nearby cities. Now this young church is threatened by false belief, which directs people away from Christ and His work to themselves. But God does not give up. He uses Paul, Timothy, and other faithful servants to establish the truth and love of Christ in their hearts.

Paul cares very much for these new Christians, and he knows that God cares for them even more. Unfortunately, false teachings that lead people to look to themselves instead of looking to God compete for the Colossians' attention. Paul says we have assurance that Christ's work reconciles us to

God because of who Christ is: the image of the invisible God, the Creator, the one who is preeminent over all things.

1:24–2:23 All people suffer because of the fallen nature of the world. But Christians are called to a special form of suffering for the sake of Christ: rejection, ridicule, and persecution. False teaching has infiltrated the Colossian Church, and it is not the teaching of Jesus Christ. Seeking guidance and security from creation rather than from the Creator will end in disaster. The Christian faith can not be replaced by man-made religion.

Chs 3–4 What is the good life? Prosperity, popularity, pleasure? No, it is the life we receive from Jesus, including gifts that we cannot make or purchase: forgiveness, love, peace, and thankfulness. People have to work together, but the heart of the old nature is to seek personal advantage, which causes frustration, resentment, and violence. Paul urges us to resist this temptation. He presents to the Colossians and to us a beautiful explanation of Christ's person and work.

Mosaic cross from Basilica of Saint Apollinare; sixth century. The inscription titles Jesus, "The Salvation of the World."

Specific Law Themes

All humanity must face God's wrath. False teaching and self-made religion would draw us away from Christ and into Satan's domain. In a sinful world, believers struggle to fulfill their calling, especially as the old sinful nature constantly manifests itself in them. God commands us to admonish one another, and to adopt His order for family and labor.

Specific Gospel Themes

The Gospel of Jesus provides us with growth. His kingdom and reign are rooted in a mystery: Christ dwells in believers. He has made our Baptism into the new circumcision. It creates a new self and promises us the inheritance of everlasting life.

Specific Doctrines

The new movement at Colossae meant evil, for it was an attack (all the more vicious because it was not a frontal attack) upon the fact that dominates the whole New Testament, the sole Lordship of the Lord Jesus Christ. God gave us in Paul's Letter to the Colossians a proclamation of the Lord Jesus Christ in unparalleled fullness and depth. The Church that in its creed intones, "God of God, Light of Light, very God of very God, begotten not made, being of one substance with the Father," is indebted not least to this letter.

The Letter to the Colossians is also a striking fulfillment of the promise of Jesus to His disciples: "Every scribe who has been trained for the kingdom of heaven is like a master of a house, who brings out of his treasure what is new and what is old" (Mt 13:52). The apostles of Jesus are not merely disciples of a scribe, whose sacred duty it is to pass on their master's words unchanged. They are witnesses to Him who has all authority in heaven and on earth, and they have the Spirit as His gift, the Spirit who leads them into all truth and thus glorifies the Christ. At the time of the Church's need the Spirit opened up to Paul dimensions of the glory of the Christ that the new people of God had not apprehended so fully before.

Key Texts

Like Paul's other letters, Colossians warns of God's coming wrath (3:5–6), the emptiness of self-made religion (2:23), and of mere ceremony (2:16–17). He describes the human condition as dead in sin, and salvation as a resurrection with Christ (2:13–14) who redeems us from the rule of darkness and transfers us into His kingdom. Christ is described as the Lord through whom all things were created; in Christ all the fullness of God dwells bodily (1:16–17; 2:9). Since Christ is our wisdom and assurance (2:3), Paul teaches us to mortify the flesh (3:5), obey parents (3:20), and attain maturity in Christ (1:28).

Application

1:1–23 What else would you look to for assurance? To an angel? To yourself? No, look to God Himself in Christ. Since we have all been tempted to look to other things instead of Jesus for our salvation, God is the only one who can overcome this evil. God does not give up on us when we or those we love are tempted by false teachings.

1:24–2:23 No one likes suffering. Nevertheless, the tears of Christian suffering reflect the glory of the cross of Christ. We can be drawn away from Christ by all sorts of attractive thoughts and words. Eventually, Christless or Christ-lite teachings will separate us from God and from one another. But the treasures of Christ's wisdom and knowledge overcome all temptation and defeat all deception. In Baptism, we have been raised up as a new creation. The waves of man-made religion always end up breaking apart upon God's truth in Jesus, who "is the same yesterday and today and forever" (Heb 13:8).

Chs 3–4 Jesus' life fills us with virtues rather than vices and enables us to be a blessing rather than a bane to others no matter what our calling in life may be. We live by faith "in the Son of God, who loved [us] and gave Himself for [us]" (Gal 2:20). In Christ, we know that we will not miss out on anything. We do not need to turn to ourselves, to angels, or to anything else. Jesus is our true God and Savior. Paul's "grocery list" of concluding instructions shows that the Gospel is not an abstract idea. It is the essential truth that transforms individual lives, such as those mentioned here, and continues to transform one person after another.

Canonicity

Like Paul's other biblical letters, which were collected and copied as authoritative already in the middle of the first century AD (cf 2Pt 3:15–16), Colossians quickly gained canonical status (*homologoumenon*). However, many critical scholars do not regard the book as a genuine letter of Paul. For more on this issue, see pp 523–24.

Lutheran Theologians on Colossians

Luther

"Just as the Epistle to the Galatians resembles and is modeled on the Epistle to the Romans, comprising in outline the same material that is more fully and richly developed in Romans; so this epistle resembles that to the Ephesians and comprises also in outline the same contents.

"First [Paul] praises and wishes for the Colossians, that they continue and increase in faith. He delineates what the gospel and faith are, namely, a wisdom which recognizes Christ as Lord and God, crucified for us, which has been hidden for ages but now brought into the open through his ministry. This is the first chapter.

"In chapter 2 he warns them against the doctrines of men, which are always contrary to faith. He depicts these doctrines more clearly than they are depicted anywhere else in Scripture, and criticizes them in a masterly way.

"In chapter 3 he exhorts them to be fruitful in the pure faith, doing all sorts of good works for one another, and he describes for some various stations in life the works which are appropriate to them.

"In chapter 4 he commends himself to their prayers and gives them greetings and encouragement." (AE 35:386)

Gerhard

"Colosse was the principal city of Phrygia in Asia Minor, near Laodicea. There Epaphras, a fellow worker of the apostles, had gathered a congregation by preaching the Gospel. The apostle directed this Epistle to the inhabitants of that city. Although the people of Rhodes are found to have been called 'Colossians' [*Colossenses*] because of their famous Colossus, the apostle nevertheless addresses not them but residents of Phrygia. The occasion for its writing was this: The Colossians had been attacked by false teachers.

Some of these, who had come from Judaism, were confusing Moses with Christ and were arguing that the ceremonies of the Law were necessary for salvation. Some, who had been converted to the Christian faith from heathenism, were urging human rules from the teachings of the philosophers. At Epaphras's request, therefore, Paul wrote this Epistle to them from his captivity in Rome to strengthen them in the true faith and safeguard them against the false teachers.

"It consists of four chapters in which, according to his usual method, (1) he fortifies the truth of the faith; (2) he hands down rules for life and behavior—both *general* rules, common to all Christians, as well as *specific* rules proper to certain groups, namely, to wives and husbands, to children and parents, to slaves and masters." (ThC E1 § 263)

The Resurrection.

Further Study

Lay/Bible Class Resources

Deterding, Paul E., and Edward A. Engelbrecht. *Colossians, Thessalonians*. RHBC. St. Louis: Concordia, 2012. ❧ Verse-by-verse commentary on the ESV and KJV translations, presented in parallel columns. Written by Lutheran theologians for lay readers and busy church workers. Includes quotations from prominent reformers and articles about Reformation views. Excellent for Bible classes.

Doyle, Thomas. *Colossians, Philemon: Take a New Look at Christ*. GWFT. St. Louis: Concordia, 1994. ❧ Lutheran author. Thirteen-session Bible study, including leader's notes and discussion questions.

Grebing, Diane, Mark Etter, and Erik Rottmann. *Galatians, Philippians, Colossians*. Leaders Guide and Enrichment Magazine/Study Guide. LL. St. Louis: Concordia, 2010. ❧ An in-depth, nine-session Bible study with individual, small group, and lecture portions.

Kuschel, Harlyn J. *Philippians, Colossians, Philemon*. PBC. St. Louis: Concordia, 2004. ❧ Lutheran author. Excellent for Bible classes. Based on the NIV translation.

Life by His Word. St. Louis: Concordia, 2009. ❧ More than 1,500 reproducible one-page Bible studies covering each chapter of the canonical Scriptures. Page references to *The Lutheran Study Bible*. CD-Rom and downloadable.

Wright, N. T. *Colossians and Philemon*. TNTC. Downers Grove, IL: InterVarsity Press, 1987. ❧ Compact commentary interacting with a variety of English translations. A popular but generally helpful evangelical treatment of the text.

Church Worker Resources

Bruce, F. F. *The Epistles to the Colossians, to Philemon, and to the Ephesians*. NICNT. Grand Rapids: Eerdmans, 1983. ❧ An invaluable resource.

Academic Resources

Abbott, T. K. *Ephesians and Colossians*. ICC. Edinburgh: T&T Clark, 1897. ❧ Helpful from the viewpoint of philology and the setting of the letters.

Braune, Karl. *Colossians*. LCHS. New York: Charles Scribner's Sons, 1874. ❧ A helpful older example of German biblical scholarship, based on the Greek text, which provides references to significant commentaries from the Reformation era forward.

Deterding, Paul E. *Colossians*. CC. St. Louis: Concordia, 2003. ❧ Faithful commentary on the Greek text by a Lutheran theologian who interacts with the best of other resources.

Lenski, R. C. H. *The Interpretation of St. Paul's Epistles to the Colossians and Thessalonians*. Minneapolis: Augsburg, 1946, 2008. ❧ A standard resource by a noteworthy Lutheran interpreter, concerned with being faithful to the text and with its implications for today.

Lightfoot, J. B. *St. Paul's Epistles to the Colossians and to Philemon*. Grand Rapids: Zondervan, 1957 reprint. ❧ Still a helpful resource; includes the views of some of the Early Church Fathers.

Martin, Ralph P. *Colossians and Philemon*. NCBC. Rev. ed. Grand Rapids: Eerdmans, 1981. ❧ An important resource; includes an analysis of the nature of the Colossian heresy, and a careful study of the provenance of these two letters.

Moule, C. F. D., ed. *The Epistles of Paul the Apostle to the Colossians and to Philemon*. CGTC. Cambridge: Cambridge University Press, 1957. ❧ Known for its careful study of the Greek text by a master exegete.

O'Brien, Peter T. *Colossians, Philemon*. WBC. Waco, TX: Word, 1982. ❧ Includes a full discussion of the pros and cons of debated matters, such as that of authorship, the setting of the letter, and the like.

Sumney, Jerry L. *Colossians: A Commentary*. New Testament Library. Louisville: Westminster John Knox Press, 2008. ❧ A thorough, recent commentary from a critical perspective, which rejects Pauline authorship.

1 THESSALONIANS

Blameless at the coming of our Lord Jesus Christ

Founded in 316 BC by Cassander, who ruled Macedonia on behalf of Alexander the Great, Thessalonica became an important harbor and leading city in the region. When the Romans built the Egnatian Way to connect Rome to its eastern interests, Thessalonica was a major stop and the first point of the road that reached the Aegean Sea. It was a natural stopping point also for the apostle Paul as he began mission work in Europe.

Historical and Cultural Setting

The Letters to the Thessalonians are part of that history of the growth of the Word of the Lord which we commonly designate as Paul's second missionary journey (AD 49–51). That journey took Paul, with his new companions Silas and Timothy, to Europe. The heart of the second missionary journey was the apostle's 18-month ministry in the great commercial center of Corinth. That ministry was preceded by a revisitation of the churches of Syria and Cilicia and of the Galatian churches founded on the first missionary journey; by missionary work in the European cities of Philippi, Thessalonica, and Berea, work again and again cut short by the malice of superstitious avarice or by the plottings of members of the synagogues who could not accept Paul's teaching; and by missionary activity at Athens, the great cultural center of Greece. It was followed by a brief exploratory visit to Ephesus that prepared for Paul's long ministry there on his third missionary journey.

The Word of the Lord sped on and was honored (2Th 3:1) in Europe, but in its peculiarly divine way. It sped on surely but not without opposition; it was honored with the inevitable honor of a work of God, but its history is not the history of an easy and effortless triumph—it is a history marked, rather, by the persecution, suffering, and internal difficulties of the human bearers and the human recipients of the Word. The history of the second missionary journey has left its mark on the Letters to the Thessalonians. Paul's companions on the journey, Silas (Paul calls him by his Roman name Silvanus) and Timothy, join in the sending of both letters. Paul's opening words in the first

Beach at Thessalonica, Greece, illustrating the rugged coastline.

OVERVIEW

Author
Paul the apostle

Date
c AD 51

Places
Thessalonica; Macedonia; Achaia; Philippi; Athens

People
Paul; Silvanus; Timothy; Thessalonian Church; persecutors

Purpose
To restore relations with the Thessalonian Christians after persecution separated Paul and his colleagues from the congregation

Law Themes
Imitation; affliction; parental care; God's Word at work; God's wrath; sanctification; idleness

Gospel Themes
The Gospel message; deliverance; God's Word at work; established blameless; resurrection of the dead; salvation; complete sanctification; God's faithfulness

Memory Verses
The resurrection of the dead (4:16–18); blameless in Christ (5:23–24)

TIMELINE

AD 36	Paul's conversion
AD 33	Resurrection of Jesus
AD 47–48	Paul's first missionary journey
AD 49–51	Paul's second missionary journey
c AD 51	Paul writes 1 Thessalonians
AD 52–55	Paul's third missionary journey

letter are a commentary on the history that brought him to Thessalonica: "We know, brothers beloved by God, *that He has chosen you*, because our Gospel came to you not only in word, but also in power and in the Holy Spirit and with full conviction" (1Th 1:4–5; emphasis added). Paul knew from his own experience that the existence of the Church at Thessalonica was due not to human planning and devising, but to the elective love of God which had become history in Paul's mission to Europe. Paul would recall, as he wrote these words, how he and his companions had been led, uncomprehending but obedient, by God's own hand and by the Spirit of Jesus (Ac 16:7), past the province of Asia, which would have seemed the logical next step on their missionary way, past Mysia, away from Bithynia, to Troas, to receive there the vision that summoned them to Europe (16:9); he would recall, too, how persecution had pushed him on with illogical haste from Philippi to Thessalonica. When Paul spoke of the elective love of God to the Thessalonians, he was not uttering a theoretical tenet of his faith; he was uttering that which God had woven into the living texture of his faith by a history in which he, Paul, had himself acted and suffered.

Paul bore the badge of suffering which was the mark of his apostolate when he came to Thessalonica from Philippi. The Paul and Silvanus who took to "praying and singing hymns to God" in the jail at Philippi after being beaten by the magistrates (Ac 16:25) had learned to see in their sufferings not the defeat, but the triumph of the Word of the Lord; and they spoke the word in Thessalonica with the robust and confident courage of men who know that they are bearers of the Word of God (1Th 2:13). They did not conceal from their Thessalonian hearers that their word would put the imprint of suffering upon the Church of God in Thessalonica too (1Th 1:6; 2:14; 3:3–4; 2Th 1:4–7). No small part of that suffering was due to the rancor of unbelieving Jews; and this, too, finds expression in the letter (1Th 2:14–16).

Paul experienced anew on this journey the power and activity of Satan, who plants weeds where the Lord plants good seed. Forced to leave Thessalonica before his work there was really finished, he tried again and again to return to the young church—"but Satan hindered us," he writes (1Th 2:18; cf 3:5). He experienced also the power for order and discipline which God had set into the world in the form of the Roman government (cf Rm 13:1–7); his Roman citizenship had procured him an honorable release from prison at Philippi (Ac 16:37–39), and the power of Rome was to stand between him and Judaic malice again at Corinth (18:12–17), when the proconsul Gallio refused to entertain the ambiguous and invidious Jewish charges against him. When Paul spoke to the Thessalonians of the power that restrains the anti-Christian attack upon God and God's people (2Th 2:6–7), he was writing a prophetic revelation that God had given him, to be sure; but God had written that revelation into the history and the experience of Paul the apostle too.

The Founding of the Church at Thessalonica

Thessalonica was the kind of place that Paul usually chose for an intensive and prolonged ministry. It was the capital of the Roman province of Macedonia and the residence of the Roman proconsul, commercially important as a harbor town, and an important communications center, lying on the *Via Egnatia*, the road that connected Rome (by way of Dyrrachium) with Byzantium and the East. It was thus naturally fitted to become a missionary center, a point from which the Word of the Lord, once established in people's hearts, might readily "sound forth" (1Th 1:8).

Paul, with his companions Silas and Timothy (one representing the old Jerusalem Church; the other, half Jew and half Greek, representing the young Church at Galatia), arrived at Thessalonica in AD 50 and began his work, as usual, in the synagogue. According to Luke, Paul's work in the synagogue lasted "three Sabbaths" (Ac 17:2), and Luke records no further activity in Thessalonica. But Paul's own account of his work as missionary and as pastor of the new Church at Thessalonica (1Th 2:1–12) suggests a more prolonged ministry among the Gentiles after the break with the synagogue had taken place (Ac 17:5). This is confirmed by a notice in Paul's Letter to the Philippians, where Paul recalls that the Philippians *twice* sent money for his needs when he was at Thessalonica (Php 4:16). Luke's account in Acts is therefore a highly compressed one; he gives an impression of Paul's ministry at Thessalonica by indicating only the initial and the final stages of his work there.

The break with the synagogue came early; the ministry among the Gentiles was perhaps prolonged for several months. The congregation at Thessalonica was therefore, as the Letters to the Thessalonians also indicate, predominantly Gentile who turned away from idolatry (1Th 1:9; 2:14; cf Ac 17:4). The life of that congregation was from the first a vigorous one, marked by the characteristically Christian joy that even severe trials cannot quench, an active faith that documented itself in a far-reaching missionary witness (1:3, 7), a brotherly love that Paul can speak of as taught them by God Himself (4:9–10), and an intense hope that longed for the return of "Jesus who delivers us from the wrath to come" (1:10; cf 4:13). Paul says of them (and Paul's generous recognition of what God has wrought in them never degenerates into empty flattery) that they "became an example to all the believers in Macedonia and in Achaia," all Greece (1:7). Only, they were still little children in Christ, good and gifted children, but not mature and stable men, when Paul was forced to leave them (Ac 17:5–10; 1Th 2:17).

Composition

Author

The apostle Paul, a Jew from Tarsus who studied under the Rabbi Gamaliel at Jerusalem, is regarded as the author of the letter.

Date of Composition

Paul wrote to the Thessalonian Church in c AD 51, about a year after he first ministered there. This makes 1 Thessalonians one of the earliest documents of the New Testament Scriptures.

Purpose/Recipients

While Paul was working at Corinth, the Church at Thessalonica remained in his thoughts and his prayers, and he was filled with a deep and restless anxiety for the brothers from whom he was "torn away . . . in person not in heart" (1Th 2:17). Would they stand fast under the persecution which had come upon them? Would they misunderstand his departure and his continued absence from them? In this connection it is well to remember that Paul and his companions were not the only propagandists and pleaders for a cause that traveled the Roman roads in those days; they were part of a numerous and motley troop of philosophers, rhetoricians, propagandists for various foreign and domestic cults, missionaries, charlatans, and quacks who went from town to town, all intent on getting a hearing, all eager for money or fame or both. These usually came and went, never to be heard from again. Paul would in the popular mind be classified with them. And Paul in Thessalonica, c AD 49, was not yet the apostle Paul as the Church has learned to see him since; he was simply a hitherto unknown Jewish teacher who had come and gone, like hundreds of brilliant and persuasive men before him. The Church of Thessalonica would of itself not be minded to classify Paul thus; but his enemies would, and they would thus undermine his apostolic authority and, with it, the faith in the Gospel with which he was identified as apostle.

Paul's anxieties and fears were well founded. He could not return to Thessalonica, though he attempted to do so more than once, to relieve his anxieties and to do the work that would obviate the dangers which gave rise to them. Satan hindered him (1Th 2:18); we can only guess as to what form this hindering took. Finally, when he could no longer endure the suspense, he sacrificed the aid and companionship of Timothy (a real sacrifice, for Paul's was a nature that needed the presence of friends and brethren) and sent him to Thessalonica, both to strengthen the faith of the church and to learn firsthand how they fared (3:1–5).

Neither the account in Acts nor Paul's account in his first letter makes it clear whether Timothy first joined Paul at Athens and was sent back to Thessalonica from there or whether Paul, alone at Athens, directed Timothy by letter to revisit Thessalonica before rejoining him at Corinth. At any rate, when Timothy returned from Thessalonica to Paul at Corinth with the good news of the Thessalonians' faith and love and fidelity to Paul (3:6), it meant for Paul the release from a long and agonizing tension. He threw himself with new vigor into his work at Corinth (Ac 18:5), and he wrote the letter which we call First Thessalonians. This letter is Paul's response to Timothy's report, a long thanksgiving for the good news that

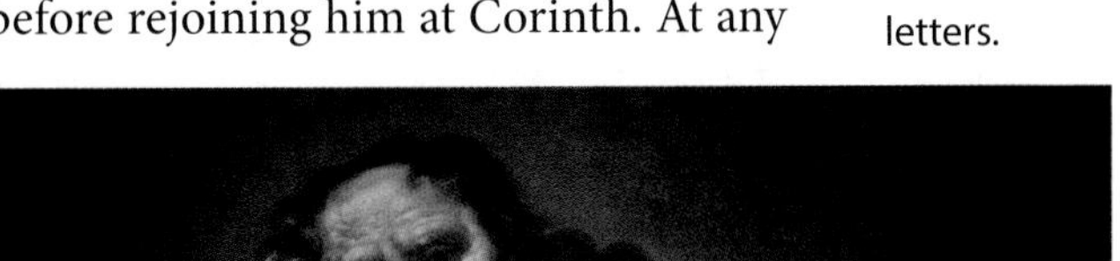

Paul with his letters.

Timothy had brought, a thanksgiving that looks back over the whole history of the Thessalonian Church since its founding and is at the same time a vindication of the purity and sanctity of his motives as their apostle and pastor (1Th 1–3). The thanksgiving is followed by a series of admonitions suggested by Timothy's report. Paul is doing by letter what he could not do face-to-face; he is supplying what is lacking in their faith (cf 3:10).

Timothy would have reported that these Christians in a Gentile environment, and in a Greek harbor town at that, where the idea of sexual purity was a complete novelty, were having difficulty in maintaining that chastity which a life of faith demands; that their past made it difficult for them to shed at once and altogether the unscrupulous craftiness which they had hitherto regarded as normal and prudent; that their fervent hope easily degenerated into an excited and irresponsible enthusiasm which led them to neglect the tasks and duties of daily life; that their imperfect grasp of the hope which the promised return of the Christ gave them made them despondent regarding their kin and brethren who had died before that return; that their hope was not content to be pure hope and leave the times and seasons of fulfillment in God's hands but sought to calculate and predict; that their life as a community bound together by faith and love and hope was not without its frictions and difficulties. To these difficulties Paul's warm and pastoral heart responded with a wisdom and a love that only the Spirit of God can bestow.

Literary Features

Genre

Paul's letter expresses both thanksgiving to God for sustaining the Thessalonians in the Christian faith and exhortations on how they are to conduct themselves in view of Christ's second coming.

Characters

Apart from the apostle's reference to his own pastoral passion for the Thessalonians, he thrice mentions his co-worker **Timothy**. Paul sent Timothy to enquire about the well-being of the congregation since the angry Jews at Thessalonica would not recognize him. Timothy could slip in, work with the Thessalonians, and return to Paul without stirring up further resistance.

Narrative Development or Plot

Since 1 Thessalonians is written as a letter, it does not have a storyline or plot. However, the book does describe the perils and the growth of the congregation as well as Paul's deep concern for them as the church's founder.

Outline

- I. The Greeting (1:1)
- II. Thanksgiving for the Congregation at Thessalonica (1:2–3:13)
  - A. The Conversion of the Thessalonians (1:2–10)
  - B. Paul's Ministry in Thessalonica (2:1–12)
  - C. The Word under Persecution (2:13–16)
  - D. Separations and Reestablishing Contact (2:17–3:10)
  - E. Prayer (3:11–13)
- III. Exhortations (4:1–5:22)
  - A. Introduction (4:1–2)
  - B. On Marriage (4:3–8)
  - C. On Brotherly Love and Self-Sufficiency (4:9–12)
  - D. On Clarifying Concerns about the End Times (4:13–5:11)
    - 1. Those who have fallen asleep (4:13–18)
    - 2. The coming of the day of the Lord (5:1–11)
  - E. On Life in the Congregation (5:12–22)
    - 1. Pastoral care among the congregation (5:12–15)
    - 2. The evaluation of prophecy (5:16–22)
- IV. Conclusion (5:23–28)

Resources

Paul's letter is built upon Timothy's report about the congregation (3:6), references back to his earlier teaching (4:2) and probably questions that the Thessalonians raised (4:13; 5:1).

Text and Translations

The text of 1 Thessalonians is well established through a wealth of early manuscripts dating as early as c AD 200 (Papyrus 46) and from Early Church Fathers who cite the letter. As with Paul's other letters, scholars discuss the possible influence of the early heretic Marcion on causing some of the textual variants.

Doctrinal Content

Summary Commentary

Ch 1 As a good shepherd, Paul wants to keep in touch with the flock of God. The Thessalonians become model Christians in words and deeds due to the impact of the Gospel in their lives and the fruit of the Spirit demonstrated in their faith, love, and hope.

Chs 2–3 Paul's experience, inner being, motives, and love toward the Christians is laid bare. He speaks about how he conducted himself (2:9–12). He commends the Thessalonians for receiving the Gospel preached by him as the Word of God and for enduring persecution for its sake (2:13–16). Paul is interested in the well-being of the Thessalonians, whether they stand firm in the Gospel or yield due to pressure from the opponents. When he can no more bear the lack of news, he decides to send Timothy, his co-worker and helper. Then Paul gives thanks and prays for the Thessalonians when he hears the good report from Timothy that they are standing in their faith and have the same kind of love for him as he has for them.

Ch 4 Paul gives advice on some practical matters dealing with sanctification so that their witness for the Lord may go forward blamelessly. He comforts the Thessalonians, saying that the dead in Christ will be the first to taste the resurrection and come with the risen Christ. At the second coming, we will all be together once more.

Ch 5 After describing the future glory of those who have died in Christ, Paul now proceeds to tell the Thessalonians about the coming Day of Judgment in which the Lord will give His final verdict. He gives both his final instruction about leadership and a benediction.

Empty tomb; Hierapolis, Turkey. Paul assured the Thessalonians that their loved ones who died would rise from the dead to meet Christ when He returned.

Specific Law Themes

Paul urged the Thessalonians to imitate his example as He followed the ways of the Lord. This would include the challenge of enduring hardship for the sake of the truth. He also warned them of God's coming wrath, admonishing with parental care. Among Paul's teachings is an emphasis on sanctification and a warning against idleness.

Specific Gospel Themes

Paul rejoices in the results of the Gospel message, which led to the deliverance of the Thessalonians. God continually worked among them through His life-giving Word, which establishes them blameless. He describes for them the coming resurrection of God's saints, who are saved and will be completely sanctified in eternity. He concludes by celebrating God's faithfulness to these new believers.

Specific Doctrines

The first three chapters give us a particularly vivid picture of Paul the missionary and pastor at work in a young Gentile church—how the Word of the Lord grows on pagan soil, which can guide our mission theology and efforts today. Paul's exhortations in the letter have furnished no less than three epistles in the ancient church's pericopal system, the epistle for the second Sunday in Lent (1Th 4:1–7), and for the twenty-fifth and twenty-seventh Sundays after Trinity (1Th 4:13–18; 5:1–11). This demonstrates the sage character of his teaching in so short a composition.

Key Texts

First Thessalonians teaches us the elementary practice of addressing both the Father and Jesus with our prayer requests (3:11), while describing the joyful habit of Christian prayer (5:16–18). It also describes the holiness that should adorn God's people and distinguish us from the world (4:3–8).

Few letters offer more sustenance for the hope of God's people than this one; besides the two great sections on the lot of the dead in Christ (4:13–18) and on the times and seasons of the Lord's return (5:1–11), the fact that practically every major section in the letter ends on the note of the return of the Lord (1:10; 2:12; 2:16; 2:19; 3:13; 5:23).

Application

Ch 1 Labor in God's kingdom is not a one-man job. We must not forget to visit and follow up with those who are in Christ Jesus. We must work in God's kingdom by joining hands with other brothers and sisters. Compared to the Thessalonians, we are much poorer in our faith, labor of love, and steadfastness of hope. Even without hardship or persecution, we are slow to confess our faith and live it out in love. The Lord knows each one of us and our specific situation. His Spirit has created faith in us and gives us power and full conviction. Despite our weaknesses and failings, His unfailing love and forgiveness will sustain us to be His witnesses.

Chs 2–3 The Lord wants us to share His Gospel boldly, even if there is suffering or conflict in our path. We should please God and be faithful to His message rather than speak what is pleasing for people to hear. Let us not make lack of financial resources an excuse. Pastors and leaders in God's Church need to follow up on their members. They should take practical steps to know how they are. The Lord seeks and wants to save and strengthen us through His servants, even in the midst of our problems. We are the apple of His eye. The Lord, who has promised to be with us until the end of time, will keep us in His faith and kindle His love in our hearts so that we may love Him and one another.

Ch 4 We Christians must lead a sexually pure life so that we may not grieve the Holy Spirit. Our love to one another should not be superficial but honest and from the heart. We should live by our labor without improperly depending on others for support. What is more, Christians grieve over the death of loved ones but not as those who have no hope. The resurrection of our Lord, and the victory we have over death through Him, gives us a living hope, despite the fact that death separates us from loved ones and causes great pain.

Ch 5 Let us walk in holiness and righteousness so that we may not be ashamed when our Lord appears to judge our work. The Lord who has chosen us for salvation and died for us will be on our side on the final Day of Judgment. Christians should support and encourage one another. We should, therefore, respect the elders and leaders of our congregations because of their work for the Lord and the whole people of God. The Lord Jesus, by humbling Himself to the point of washing His disciples' feet, showed to us the love He has for all believers.

Canonicity

Like Paul's other biblical letters, which were collected and copied as authoritative already in the middle of the first century AD (cf 2Pt 3:15–16), 1 Thessalonians quickly gained canonical status (*homologoumenon*).

Lutheran Theologians on 1 Thessalonians

Luther

"St. Paul writes out of especial love and apostolic solicitude. For in the first two chapters he praises them because they received the gospel from him with such earnestness that they remained steadfast in it despite suffering and persecution, and became a beautiful example of faith to all congregations everywhere, and suffered persecution from their own kinsfolk like Christ and his apostles did from the Jews—as St. Paul by way of example had himself also suffered and led a holy life when he was with them. For this he thanks God, that his gospel had borne such fruit among them.

"In chapter 3 he shows his care and solicitude that this labor of his and their praiseworthy beginning not be brought to nothing by the devil and his apostles through the doctrines of men. For this reason he sent Timothy to them beforehand to make sure about this. And he thanks God that things were still right among them and hopes that they continue to increase.

"In chapter 4 he exhorts them to guard against sin and to do good to one another. He also answers a question which they had presented to him through Timothy concerning the resurrection of the dead, whether all would rise at once, or whether some after others.

"In chapter 5 he writes of the Last Day, how it shall come suddenly and quickly. He gives them some good directions for governing other people and tells them what attitude they are to take toward the lives and teachings of others." (AE 35:386–87)

Gerhard

"Thessalonica was a town at the mouth of the Macedonian Bay, located at the middle of a bend in the coast. There the apostle, through his preaching of the Gospel, had converted some Jews and Gentiles to Christ (Acts 17:2). However, because of persecution that the still-unbelieving Jews had stirred up against him, he was not able to remain there long. When he realized that the church he had recently planted was falling into great danger because it was afraid of persecutions, he sent Timothy to it to strengthen the Thessalonians in their faith. Timothy noticed that they were not at all terrified by persecutions, that they were still constant in their faith and patient in their adversities, and he related everything to the apostle faithfully. So, in this Epistle, Paul praises them and bears witness of his faithfulness, care, and concern on their behalf. Later, he encourages them to a holy pattern of life, to love, and to a moderation of their grief over the dead, which occasion he uses to discuss the resurrection of the dead and the final judgment.

"It consists of five chapters and falls into two parts, the former of which is of praising; the latter, of exhorting." (ThC E1 §264)

Macedonian bay.

Paul wrote that a trumpet would sound on the Last Day to rouse those who fell asleep in Christ (1Th 4:16). Thirteenth-century Psalter shows the raising of the dead and the final judgment.

Further Study

Lay/Bible Class Resources

Deterding, Paul E., and Edward A. Engelbrecht. *Colossians, Thessalonians*. RHBC. St. Louis: Concordia, 2012. ✠ Verse-by-verse commentary on the ESV and KJV translations, presented in parallel columns. Written by Lutheran theologians for lay readers and busy church workers. Includes quotations from prominent Reformers and articles about Reformation views. Excellent for Bible classes.

Dunker, Gary. *1 and 2 Thessalonians: The Lord Is Faithful*. GWFT. St. Louis: Concordia, 2007. ✠ Lutheran author. Eleven-session Bible study, including leader's notes and discussion questions.

Kuske, David. *1 & 2 Thessalonians*. PBC. St. Louis: Concordia, 2005. ✠ Lutheran author. Excellent for Bible classes. Based on the NIV translation.

Life by His Word. St. Louis: Concordia, 2009. ✠ More than 1,500 reproducible one-page Bible studies covering each chapter of the canonical Scriptures. Page references to *The Lutheran Study Bible*. CD-Rom and downloadable.

Morris, Leon. *1 and 2 Thessalonians*. TNTC. 2nd ed. Grand Rapids: Eerdmans, 1984. ✠ A careful, popularly written exposition with attention to all the salient aspects of these two letters. His more detailed work is listed below under Academic Resources.

Nadasdy, Dean, and Roger Sonnenberg. *Ephesians, 1 & 2 Thessalonians*. Leaders Guide and Enrichment Magazine/Study Guide. LL. St. Louis: Concordia, 2011. ✠ An in-depth, nine-session Bible study with individual, small group, and lecture portions.

Church Worker Resources

Marshall, I. Howard. *1 and 2 Thessalonians*. NCBC. Grand Rapids: Eerdmans, 1983. ✠ A careful exposition, including introductory articles on the problems at Thessalonica, stressing the unity of 1 Thessalonians.

Academic Resources

Auberlen, Karl August, and J. Riggenbach. *1 and 2 Thessalonians*. LCHS. New York: Charles Scribner's Sons, 1868. ✠ A helpful older example of German biblical scholarship, based on the Greek text, which provides references to significant commentaries from the Reformation era forward.

Bruce, F. F. *1 & 2 Thessalonians*. WBC. Waco, TX: Word, 1982. ✠ Verse-by-verse commentary done in Bruce's usual thorough manner with careful attention to the meaning and implications of the Greek.

Donfried, Karl Paul. *Paul, Thessalonica, and Early Christianity*. Grand Rapids: Eerdmans, 2002. ✠ Provides an overview of perspectives in Pauline studies, including the "New Look at Paul." Based on scholarly essays.

Frame, James Everett. *A Critical and Exegetical Commentary on the Epistles of St. Paul to the Thessalonians*. ICC. Edinburgh: T&T Clark, 1912. ✠ An old standard, still a helpful resource.

Lenski, R. C. H. *The Interpretation of St. Paul's Epistles to the Colossians and Thessalonians*. Minneapolis: Augsburg, 1946, 2008. ✠ A standard resource by a noteworthy Lutheran interpreter, concerned with being faithful to the text and with its implications for today.

Malherbe, Abraham J. *The Letters to the Thessalonians*. AB. New York: Doubleday, 2000. ✠ Verse-by-verse commentary prepared by a critical scholar who argues that Paul wrote the Letters to the Thessalonians.

Milligan, George. *St. Paul's Epistles to the Thessalonians: The Greek Text, with Introduction and Notes*. London: Macmillan, 1908. ✠ Available in reprinted editions, this verse-by-verse commentary remains a valuable resource.

Morris, Leon. *The First and Second Epistles to the Thessalonians*. NICNT. Rev. ed. Grand Rapids: Eerdmans, 1991. ✠ A careful, detailed exposition with attention to all the salient aspects of these two letters.

2 THESSALONIANS

Faith growing, love increasing

The city of Thessalonica, named after a sister of Alexander the Great, was built within sight of one of the great religious landmarks of ancient Greece. Southward, across the Thermaikos Bay, the people could see the distant slopes of Mount Olympus, traditional home of the gods in their culture. (The city of Thessalonica is not to be confused with the region of Thessaly, which encompasses the fertile plains beyond Olympus.) From the founding of Thessalonica in 315 BC, its inhabitants stood within sight of what they regarded as divine. The community of Jews who settled at Thessalonica were likewise zealous, having persecuted Paul, Silas, and others for teaching that Jesus was the Christ (Ac 17:2–9, 13). Not surprisingly, the Christians at Thessalonica demonstrated an intense piety as well as deep curiosity about the return of Jesus.

Historical and Cultural Setting

According to reports that reached Paul at Corinth (we do not know how; perhaps the congregation wrote to him), the Christians of Thessalonica were still standing firm under persecution (2Th 1:4). But false notions "concerning the coming of our Lord Jesus Christ and our being gathered together to Him" (2:1) had gained currency in the Church. Those who advocated these notions apparently appealed to some alleged prophetic utterance ("spirit") or teaching or writing of Paul's to support them (2:2). The resultant excited, almost hysterical, expectation (2:2) had led some to abandon their regular occupation and to lead an idle and disorderly life in dependence upon the charity of the church (3:6–12). Others, it would seem, struck by the high demands of the first letter (the demand that they be found "blameless" at the coming of the Lord, 1Th 3:13; 5:23), had grown fearful and despondent concerning the coming of the Christ; for them, they felt, it would mean not deliverance, but judgment and destruction.

View from the top of Mount Olympus down toward the Aegean Sea, Gulf of Salonika.

Composition

Author

Some critical scholars have seriously questioned the authenticity of 2 Thessalonians, which unanimous tradition attributes to the apostle Paul. The chief arguments against Pauline authorship are listed below, followed by further considerations.

Argument: The second letter largely repeats the first, and this marks it as a forgery.

The statement is an exaggeration; about one third of the second letter is parallel to the first, and even this does not give the impression of mechanical copying, such as might be expected from a forger, for the material occurs in a different order from that in the first letter.

Argument: The second letter teaches differently about the end times from that of the first. The first letter stresses the fact that the coming of the Lord will be like that of a thief in the night, while the second points to certain events as signs that must precede and will therefore forewarn of the second coming.

It should be noted that this same double emphasis is found in Jesus' own teaching concerning His return (Mt 24:6–8, 36). Paul does not abandon the teaching of the first letter in the second; he simply defines it more sharply by the statement that certain events must precede the second coming of Jesus. Neither Jesus' nor Paul's words provide a means of forecasting the end.

The strongest arguments for authenticity (besides the unanimous testimony of the Early Church) are the lack of any motive for a forgery, and the genuinely Pauline tone and character of the second letter. Even some of the scholars who question the authenticity of the letter admit that there is nothing in it that could not have come from the pen of Paul.

Paul celebrated the growing faith and love among the Thessalonians (2Th 1:3).

Date of Composition

Paul evidently wrote the Second Letter to the Thessalonians not long after the First, perhaps a few months later, c AD 52, at Corinth.

Purpose/Recipients

Paul's second letter is his answer to the congregation's concerns about the return of Christ. It therefore sounds two notes. For those who indulge in overheated fantasies about the end times, there are sobering words that point to the events that must necessarily precede the coming of the Christ in glory (2Th 2:1–12). For the despondent and the fearful there is an eloquent and reassuring recognition of the new life that God has worked in them and a comforting emphasis on the certainty of their election by God (1:3–12; 2:13–15). Paul turns the church from both excitement and despondency to that sober and responsible activity which is the hallmark of the genuinely Christian hope. The hoping church turns from preoccupation with itself to God; the church must pray "that the word of the Lord may speed ahead and be honored" (3:1). The hoping church must work for its living in sober industriousness and work for its own health as the Church of God. It must discipline and correct all those whose lives are a departure from the apostolic word and example and are therefore denials of the real character of the Church (3:6–15).

Literary Features

Genre

Like Paul's first letter, 2 Thessalonians is an exhortation on how readers are to conduct themselves in view of Christ's second coming.

Characters

Paul makes special reference to apostasy and the exaltation of the **"lawless one"** (2:3–10), who must arise before Christ returns in judgment. Though Paul's descriptions of these future events are unique, the same themes are taught in other parts of Scripture. According to the Early Church Father Irenaeus (*ANF* 1:535–56), the lawless one corresponds to the "spirit

---

OVERVIEW

Author
Paul the apostle

Date
c AD 52

Place
Thessalonica

People
Paul; Silvanus; Timothy; Thessalonian Church; persecutors

Purpose
To correct misunderstandings about Christ's return that had arisen after Paul and his co-workers left Thessalonica

Law Themes
Steadfastness; affliction; eternal destruction; man of lawlessness; idleness

Gospel Themes
The Gospel message; God's righteousness; Jesus gathers us; the Spirit sanctifies us

Memory Verses
Grow in faith and increase in love (1:3); stand firm (2:15)

TIMELINE

AD 33	Resurrection of Jesus
AD 47–48	Paul's first missionary journey
AD 49–51	Paul's second missionary journey
c AD 52	Paul writes 2 Thessalonians
AD 52–55	Paul's third missionary journey

of the antichrist" (1Jn 4:3; cf 1Jn 2:18) and the beast (and/or the prostitute "Babylon"; Rv 13:1–10; chs 17–18).

Narrative Development or Plot

Since 2 Thessalonians is written as a letter, it does not have a storyline or plot. However, the book does describe the perils and some events leading up to Jesus' second coming (ch 2).

Resources

On the similarity between 1 and 2 Thessalonians, see "Author" above (p 580).

Text and Translations

The text of 2 Thessalonians is well established through a wealth of early manuscripts and from Early Church Fathers who cite the letter. As with Paul's other letters, scholars discuss the possible influence of the early heretic Marcion on causing some of the textual variants.

Doctrinal Content

Summary Commentary

1:1–2 Paul greets the Christians in Thessalonica as fellow members of the Body of Christ (the Church) and blesses them with God's grace and peace.

1:3–12 Paul gives thanks for God's grace at work among the Thessalonians, by which He has created faith and love in them. He points to the persecuted Thessalonians as examples for other Christians of their time and ours. God's judgment will be carried out by the Lord Jesus at His second coming on the Last Day.

Ch 2 Paul warns the Thessalonians not to be misled regarding the second coming of Christ, thinking that the day of the Lord has already come. He describes those apocalyptic events yet to take place before the return of Jesus, specifically the revelation of the man of lawlessness. He also calls on the Thessalonians to stand firm in the faith the Lord has given them. He reminds them that both their calling and comfort have God as the source.

Ch 3 Paul requests prayer for his missionary work and obedience to what he has commanded them. Those who are idle are to be avoided and even denied fellowship in order that this might cause them to repent, amend

OUTLINE

I. The Greeting (1:1–2)

II. The Thanksgiving (1:3–12)

- A. Thanks for Faith and Love (1:3–4)
- B. Encouragement of the Discouraged (1:5–10)
- C. Petition for Worthy Conduct (1:11–12)

III. Exhortation and Encouragement about the End Times (ch 2)

- A. Events Preceding the Coming of the Day of the Lord (2:1–12)
- B. Encouragement and Thanksgiving (2:13–17)

IV. Apostolic Commands (3:1–15)

- A. Request for Prayers (3:1–5)
- B. Discipline of the Disorderly (3:6–12)
- C. Admonition to Do Good (3:13–15)

V. Conclusion (3:16–18)

- A. Prayer for Peace (3:16)
- B. Greeting (3:17)
- C. Benediction (3:18)

their ways, and return to their fellow believers. Paul concludes his letter with a prayer for peace and, in his own hand, a blessing of grace.

Specific Law Themes

With greater sternness than Paul expressed in his first letter, he urges the Thessalonians to remain steadfast in the faith, despite the afflictions they may experience. He describes the righteous judgment of God when those who do not know God will face eternal punishment. Paul also describes the coming of a deceiver—the man of lawlessness—whom Satan will raise up. At the end of the letter he rebukes those who are idly waiting for Christ's return rather than supporting themselves.

Specific Gospel Themes

Paul celebrates the fruit of the Gospel message as the Thessalonians grow in faith and love. In righteousness, the Lord will eternally separate believers, who enjoy His presence, from unbelievers, who will not. In this way, the Lord gathers us up and sanctifies us with His Spirit, delivering us from evil. In concluding, Paul comforts the congregation and expresses his confidence in the Lord's work among them.

Specific Doctrines

Second Thessalonians is an outstanding example of the spiritual tact of the apostle, which enables him to quell the fevered excitement of a hope grown hysterical without quenching the fervor and the life-shaping force of that hope, and to instill sobriety without robbing the Christian hope of its intensity, leaving both fear and faith to do their salutary work. His emphasis on working industriously in this connection (an emphasis which he spelled out in his life, too, by supporting himself) is a part of the apostolic recognition of the order established by God the Creator. It remains one of the great safeguards of Christian sanity over against all false spiritual contempt for the gifts and claims of God's created world.

Grinning death boasts that he can snuff out the lives of even the most powerful "in the blink of an eye." Paul teaches believers to be ready for Judgment Day not through fear but through the hope in Christ Jesus, who rose from the dead.

Key Texts

In the opening of the letter, Paul gives thanks to God, who is causing the faith and the love of the Thessalonians to grow (1:3). He describes the benefits of Word and Sacrament ministry leading to ongoing sanctification.

At the heart of the letter is a prophetic warning about the corrupting influence of the "lawless one." The teaching about the end times is an amplification and an enrichment of what Paul has given the Church in the first letter, particularly in the second chapter.

This was for many medieval theologians, Lutherans, and other reformers the classic passage affirming that the papacy is the Antichrist (2:3–4). The passage renews and explicates the warning of Jesus, who taught His disciples that wheat and weeds must ripen together till the harvest; it reminds the Church that the satanic counterthrust is inevitable and constant wherever God's Word grows and God's reign is established. Any shallow ecclesiastical optimism that bows the knee to the idol of Progress, and any churchly piety that becomes comfortably at home in this world, is a denial of the revelation on which the life of the Church is built.

Application

1:1–2 Christian believers are called out of worldliness to lives of holiness. We are connected to the Holy One, to the Lord Himself.

1:3–12 We must set an example to others in what we believe and in what we say and do for them; i.e., by living in faith and in love. In this way, we will be, as Luther puts it, little Christs, "[helping] our neighbor through our body and its works" (AE 31:367). God's judgment will be carried out by the Lord Jesus at His second coming on the Last Day. This is bad news for those who do not believe, for those who reject God's grace in Christ (1:8), as "they will suffer . . . away from the presence of the Lord" (1:9). As believers, we live in a state of continual readiness for this day (cf Mt 24:36–51; 2Co 6:2). Jesus will be glorified in us, and we in Him (2Th 1:12); by His grace, God will judge believers worthy to inherit heaven; and by His power, He will bring our faith to its heavenly fulfillment (vv 11–12).

Ch 2 We must be on guard against deception. There is much false teaching, especially regarding the end times. Our only protection against falsehood is to cling to the Word of God: read the Bible, pray based on the Word, and continue to hear the Word in the communion of saints. The God who has elected us unto salvation keeps us steadfast in the faith (cf 1Th 5:23–24). The doctrine of election is a doctrine of the Gospel, by which we know that our salvation is guaranteed (Eph 1:14) because it depends on God alone as He has chosen us before the foundation of the world (Rm 8:28; 9:11).

Ch 3 We are called to listen to those whom God has given to teach and preach the pure Word (Heb 13:17; cf Ac 5:27–32). Laziness is a serious sin against the God who created us and gave us talents and abilities. It is a sin against the Body of Christ, against our brothers and sisters in the Lord, to whom we have been joined and with whom we are to be co-workers. Our prayer for God's peace and grace in our lives is no mere wish. We do have peace with God and with one another through the blood of Christ; by the grace of our Lord, this is a peace that passes all understanding and remains steadfast regardless of external assaults by the devil (cf Eph 2:11–21; Col 1:19–20; Jn 14:27).

Canonicity

Like Paul's other biblical letters, which were collected and copied as authoritative already in the middle of the first century AD (cf 2Pt 3:15–16), 2 Thessalonians quickly gained canonical status (*homologoumenon*).

Resurrection of Christ; part of the winged altar (1508–10) by Lucas Cranach the Elder.

Lutheran Theologians on 2 Thessalonians

Luther

"In the first epistle [5:2], Paul had resolved for the Thessalonians the question of the Last Day, telling them that it would come quickly, as a thief in the night. Now as is likely to happen—that one question always gives rise to another, because of misunderstanding—the Thessalonians understood that the Last Day was already at hand. Thereupon Paul writes this epistle and explains himself.

"In chapter 1 he comforts them with the eternal reward of their faith and of their patience amid sufferings of every kind and with the punishment of their persecutors in eternal pain.

"In chapter 2 he teaches that before the Last Day, the Roman Empire must first pass away, and Antichrist set himself up as God in Christendom and seduce the unbelieving world with false doctrines and signs—until Christ shall come and destroy him by his glorious coming, first slaying him with spiritual preaching.

"In chapter 3 he gives some admonitions, especially that they rebuke the idlers who are not supporting themselves by their own labor. If the idlers will not reform, then the faithful shall avoid them. And this is a stiff rebuke to the clergy of our day." (AE 35:387–88)

Gerhard

"The occasion for the writing of 2 Thessalonians was this: Some of the Thessalonians were understanding what the apostle had written in c. 3–4 of the first Epistle regarding the immediate coming of Christ as if the Day of the Lord were already upon them. In this Epistle, the apostle wanted to resist this false opinion.

"It consists of three chapters and the same number of parts. The first of these is of praising, in which the apostle commends the Thessalonians for their faith, love, constancy, and patience and offers them comfort for opposing persecutions. The second part is of correcting, in which he forewarns against the error that Christ's coming would happen soon and teaches that the Antichrist must be revealed first. The third is of disciplining, in which he urges them toward Christian virtues." (ThC E1 § 265)

Last judgment.

Questions People Ask about 2 Thessalonians

Providing for the Future

Matthew 6:31 says: "Therefore do not be anxious, saying, 'What shall we eat?' or 'What shall we drink?' or 'What shall we wear?' "

Second Thessalonians 3:12 advises: "Now such persons we command and encourage in the Lord Jesus Christ to do their work quietly and to earn their own living."

How can these words of Jesus and those of Paul be harmonized? Jesus apparently teaches improvidence, while Paul condemns it. Does our Lord in Mt 6:31, 34 urge us to be lazy, shiftless, or wasteful? Not at all. What He is saying is that we must not be overly concerned about the cares of this life. This is the attitude that the Bible teaches in a number of places. Psalm 127:2 says: "It is in vain that you rise up early and go late to rest, eating the bread of anxious toil; for He gives to His beloved sleep." Psalm 55:22 enjoins: "Cast your burden on the LORD, and He will sustain you; He will never permit the righteous to be moved." Philippians 4:6 warns: "Do not be anxious about anything, but in everything by prayer and supplication with thanksgiving let your requests be made known to God."

Does the text from 2 Thessalonians then advocate being a miser or being worried and anxious about earthly possessions? Hardly. It simply urges all Chris-

tians to work diligently in order that they and the members of their household may not suffer want or become burdens to other people or to the government. Thus while both texts given above speak of our attitude toward earthly possessions, each one treats a different aspect of the subject. Jesus forbids an anxious striving for this world's goods. Paul forbids indolence. The higher unity in which both these texts meet is proclaimed by Paul in 1Co 7:29–31:

> This is what I mean, brothers: the appointed time has grown very short. From now on, let those who have wives live as though they had none, and those who mourn as though they were not mourning, and those who rejoice as though they were not rejoicing, and those who buy as though they had no goods, and those who deal with the world as though they had no dealings with it. For the present form of this world is passing away.

In other words, we Christians are to work diligently, but we are not to become the slaves of our work; we are to do our full duty in our calling here on earth, but we must remember that our real home is above; we are to labor for our daily bread and still bear in mind that it is God who provides everything that we need. Although these passages seem at first to be inconsistent with each other, they form two sides of the Christian life for which we all should strive.

An Israeli man cooking flatbread.

Further Study

Lay/Bible Class Resources

Deterding, Paul E., and Edward A. Engelbrecht. *Colossians, Thessalonians.* RHBC. St. Louis: Concordia, 2012. ✠ Verse-by-verse commentary on the ESV and KJV translations, presented in parallel columns. Written by Lutheran theologians for lay readers and busy church workers. Includes quotations from prominent Reformers and articles about Reformation views. Excellent for Bible classes.

Dunker, Gary. *1 and 2 Thessalonians: The Lord Is Faithful.* GWFT. St. Louis: Concordia, 2007. ✠ Lutheran author. Eleven-session Bible study, including leader's notes and discussion questions.

Kuske, David. *1 & 2 Thessalonians.* PBC. St. Louis: Concordia, 2005. ✠ Lutheran author. Excellent for Bible classes. Based on the NIV translation.

Life by His Word. St. Louis: Concordia, 2009. ✠ More than 1,500 reproducible one-page Bible studies covering each chapter of the canonical Scriptures. Page references to *The Lutheran Study Bible.* CD-Rom and downloadable.

Morris, Leon. *1 and 2 Thessalonians.* TNTC. 2nd ed. Grand Rapids: Eerdmans, 1984. ✠ A careful, popularly written exposition with attention to all the salient aspects of these two letters. His more detailed work is listed below under Academic Resources.

Nadasdy, Dean, and Roger Sonnenberg. *Ephesians, 1 & 2 Thessalonians.* Leaders Guide and Enrichment Magazine/Study Guide. LL. St. Louis: Concordia, 2011. ✠ An in-depth, nine-session Bible study with individual, small group, and lecture portions.

Church Worker Resources

Marshall, I. Howard. *1 and 2 Thessalonians.* NCBC. Grand Rapids: Eerdmans, 1983. ✠ A careful exposition, including introductory articles on the problems at Thessalonica, stressing the unity of 1 Thessalonians.

Academic Resources

Auberlen, Karl August, and J. Riggenbach. *1 and 2 Thessalonians.* LCHS. New York: Charles Scribner's Sons, 1868. ✠ A helpful older example of German biblical scholarship, based on the Greek text, which provides references to significant commentaries from the Reformation era forward.

Bruce, F. F. *1 & 2 Thessalonians.* WBC. Waco, TX: Word, 1982. ✠ Verse-by-verse commentary done in Bruce's usual thorough manner with careful attention to the meaning and implications of the Greek.

Donfried, Karl Paul. *Paul, Thessalonica, and Early Christianity.* Grand Rapids: Eerdmans, 2002. ✠ Provides an overview of perspectives in Pauline studies, including the "New Look at Paul." Based on scholarly essays.

Frame, James Everett. *A Critical and Exegetical Commentary on the Epistles of St. Paul to the Thessalonians.* ICC. Edinburgh: T&T Clark, 1912. ✠ An old standard, still a helpful resource.

Lenski, R. C. H. *The Interpretation of St. Paul's Epistles to the Colossians and Thessalonians.* Minneapolis: Augsburg, 1946, 2008. ✠ A standard resource by a noteworthy Lutheran interpreter, concerned with being faithful to the text and with its implications for today.

Malherbe, Abraham J. *The Letters to the Thessalonians.* AB. New York: Doubleday, 2000. ✠ Verse-by-verse commentary prepared by a critical scholar who argues that Paul wrote the Letters to the Thessalonians.

Milligan, George. *St. Paul's Epistles to the Thessalonians: The Greek Text, with Introduction and Notes.* London: Macmillan, 1908. ✠ Available in reprinted editions, this verse-by-verse commentary remains a valuable resource.

Morris, Leon. *The First and Second Epistles to the Thessalonians.* NICNT. Rev. ed. Grand Rapids: Eerdmans, 1991. ✠ A careful, detailed exposition with attention to all the salient aspects of these two letters.

Three depictions from the life of Paul: preaching (top), surviving viper attack on Malta (middle; Ac 28:1–6), and healing people on Malta (bottom; Ac 28:7–9).

The Pastoral Letters

1 Timothy, 2 Timothy, and Titus

Among the letters of Paul, the Pastoral Letters connect Paul the writer closely with Paul the worker, who is portrayed in the Book of Acts. We see Paul consumed in the white heat of ministry—the missionary, the organizer, and the discipliner at work. Missionaries have always found these letters indispensable and have often understood them better than the armchair interpreters back home. Consecrated pastors and teachers have found in them their own New Testament within the New Testament and have lived by them soberly and successfully in the daily round of their duties. These letters hold before the Church and her teachers an ideal of a ministry and a teaching that have on them the imprint of godliness and sublimity just because they are down-to-earth; they walk on the ground, where people are, where the Son of God, the descendant of David, walked and worked for the salvation of all. Indeed, not the least of the services rendered to the Church by the Pastoral Letters is the instilling of a healthy contempt for all brilliant and speculative theologies that fail to edify.

The Pastoral Letters are Pauline barley bread, honest workman's food, rough and plain. They do not have the great sustained flights of letters like those to the Romans or Ephesians or Colossians; neither do they have the transfixing impact of letters like that to the Galatians. But if they usually walk, they never crawl; and the worker is bidden again and again to lift up his eyes and to walk by the light of the glory of God that shines from above. These letters abound in clear and keen formulations of the truth that we live and work by, the sort that deserve and demand to be gotten by heart. It is hard to imagine the Holy Christian Church living without these words: Paul's thanksgiving to Jesus Christ, who came into the world to save sinners and made Paul the example in which all sinners might see spelled out the grace of God (1Tm 1:12–17); the proclamation of the grace of God that has burst upon all men like a sunrise for their deliverance and remains their trainer in sobriety, righteousness, and godliness (Ti 2:11–14); the sure saying which comforts all who endure and die with Christ in the assurance that they shall live and reign with Him (2Tm 2:11–13); the great words on the inspired usefulness of Scripture (3:16–17).

Preaching, Teaching, and Scripture

Paul refers to himself in the Pastoral Letters as "preacher and apostle and teacher" (2Tm 1:11; cf 1Tm 2:7), and it is the teaching aspect of his apostolate that these letters show us most clearly and fully. There is in them a strong and persistent emphasis on teaching—formulated, defended, applied to life, teaching to be preserved and handed on to faithful men for the enduring health of the Church (cf 1Tm 1:11; 4:6; 6:3; 6:11–14; 2Tm 1:13; 3:10; 4:3; Ti 1:9; 2:10). But the teaching apostle is not essentially different from the herald (preaching) apostle; the trainer of the Church remains what the founder of the Church is, namely, "set apart for the Gospel of God" (Rm 1:1).

One should not drive too sharp a division between preaching and teaching. The content of the teaching that is to motivate and mold the conduct of those who have in repentance and faith obeyed the initial Gospel call is not essentially different from the content of the missionary Gospel that proclaimed Jesus as Christ and Lord. The apostles summoned people to repentance and faith and to the Baptism that incorporates them in the new people of God. Here as there, in the teaching as in the proclamation (*kerygma*), "the truth is in Jesus" (Eph 4:21). As examples in the Pastoral Epistles show, the worship life of the Church is controlled by the basic fact of the Gospel: the Church prays for all people because Christ Jesus died for all people (1Tm 2:1–6). Timothy's conduct in the Church of the living God has its norm and standard in the truth that the Church has, proclaims, and defends: the fact of the incarnation of the Son of God (3:15–16). The line between the true teacher and the heretic is determined by the fact that his words agree or do not agree "with the sound words of our Lord Jesus Christ" (6:3). The honesty and fidelity of the Christian slave has its source in the fact that the transforming and training grace of God has appeared to *all*, that our "great God and Savior Jesus Christ" has died in order "to purify for Himself a people . . . who are zealous for good works" (Ti 2:9–14). The act of teaching is anything but a merely intellectual one, and is far removed from the secular idea of developing a potential that is in mankind and needs only to be called into active play. Teaching in the New Testament sense is the shaping of the whole person, including especially one's will. This shaping is done not by human persuasion using the tools of human wisdom but by divine revelation. The content of the teaching is simply the Gospel revelation, with all that serves and supports that revelation (the Old Testament, both Law and Promise); it is the Gospel as a formative and disciplinary power, "the word of God . . . *at work in you believers*" (1Th 2:13; emphasis added).

Our written Gospels, too, belong under this heading of apostolic "teaching." They are the written result, the precipitate in writing, of the "apostles' teaching" that Luke speaks of (Ac 2:42) as the first and basic formative element in the life of the first church. The Gospels are not primarily the apostolic preaching (*kerygma*), as we see it reflected in the sermons of Peter in the Book of Acts or see it summarized in Pauline passages such as 1Co 15:1–8, proclamations of the basic facts that summon people to the obedience of faith; they are the expansions of that proclamation, the apostolic teaching that builds up the Church already called into being by the proclamation.

1 TIMOTHY

Godliness with contentment

The Book of Acts does not provide history for the period in which the writing of the Pastoral Letters falls; therefore, we must reconstruct the history of this period entirely from hints given in the letters themselves. The following order of events is drawn from all three letters to provide general historical background from the close of the Book of Acts to Paul's martyrdom.

1. That Paul was released at the end of the two years' imprisonment recorded in Ac 28:30 (AD 60) seems certain. There is really no evidence at all that his first Roman imprisonment ended in martyrdom. Paul apparently did not remain long in Rome after his release; the jealousies and frictions to which he alludes in his Letter to the Philippians (Php 1:15–17) would make it advisable for him to leave soon.
2. Whether Paul ever carried out his intention of going to Spain (Rm 15:28) must remain in doubt. The Captivity Letters (see pp 534–36) say nothing of an anticipated Spanish voyage, and the Pastoral Letters likewise say nothing. Neither did the Spanish church preserve any tradition that attributed its origin to the missionary work of Paul. On the other hand, Paul's journey to Spain is attested by early and reliable Roman sources like the Letter of Clement of Rome to the Corinthians, written within a generation after the events (AD 96), and the Muratorian Canon (about AD 200). The apoc-

The Good Shepherd (fresco); Roman (third century AD), from the Catacomb of Priscilla.

OVERVIEW

Author
Paul the apostle

Date
AD 65

Places
Ephesus; Macedonia

People
Paul; Timothy; Hymenaeus; Alexander

Purpose
To encourage and instruct Timothy as he called the Ephesians to be faithful to God's Word

Law Themes
Charged/appointed with service; threat of false teachers; management

Gospel Themes
The glorious Gospel; salvation through Christ, our Mediator; hallowed by God's Word/grace

Memory Verses
Chief of sinners (1:15–16); one Mediator (2:5–6); the mystery of godliness (3:16); contentment (6:6–8)

TIMELINE

AD 33	Resurrection of Jesus
AD 52–55	Paul's third missionary journey
AD 57–58	Paul journeys to Rome
AD 65	Paul writes 1 Timothy
AD 68	Martyrdom of Peter and Paul

ryphal Acts of Peter (written about AD 200) also refers to the Spanish voyage of Paul, and no one in antiquity seems to have questioned it. If Paul did make the voyage, it was probably soon after his release from imprisonment (AD 60).

3. Paul intended to revisit his former mission fields in Asia and Macedonia (Phm 22; Php 2:24), and the Pastoral Letters indicate that he carried out this intention. He returned to the East by way of Crete, where he remained for a time as missionary. He left Titus in charge of the task of consolidating the church there when he himself proceeded eastward (Ti 1:5).
4. Paul may have touched at Ephesus. If he did, he could not have remained there long. The instructions that he gave Timothy, whom he left in charge at Ephesus, indicate that much work still remained to be done there (1Tm 1:3).
5. Paul himself proceeded from Ephesus to Macedonia, and from there he wrote the First Letter to Timothy (1Tm 1:3).
6. Paul wrote the Letter to Titus either from Macedonia, just before his departure for Nicopolis, or during the journey to Nicopolis, where he planned to spend the winter. There were several prominent cities called Nicopolis; the one referred to in the Letter to Titus is probably Nicopolis in Epirus. Titus was to join Paul in Nicopolis when relieved in Crete by Artemas or Tychicus (Ti 3:12).
7. During the interval between the writing of the Letter to Titus and the Second Letter to Timothy, Paul visited Troas, Corinth, and Miletus (2Tm 4:13, 20).
8. Paul was again arrested (whether in the East or at Rome can hardly be made out) and imprisoned at Rome. This time his imprisonment was much more severe than AD 58–60, and he saw no hope of an acquittal. In his Second Letter to Timothy he summons his "beloved child" to him once more before the end.
9. This second imprisonment in Rome ended in the martyrdom of Paul. It took place under Nero, certainly, but hardly during the great Neronian persecution of AD 64. Paul would not have summoned Timothy, the man to whom he looked for the faithful continuation of his work, to a certain death in Rome; neither would it be like Paul to lament that none of the Roman Christians had stood by him at his first hearing if those Christians were at that time dying for their faith. The writing of the Second Letter to Timothy and Paul's death must be dated

after the great persecution under Nero, perhaps even so late as AD 68, the last year of Nero's reign.

Historical and Cultural Setting for 1 Timothy

Paul, on his way to Macedonia, has left Timothy at Ephesus with instructions to "charge certain persons not to teach any different doctrine" (1Tm 1:3). Paul does not describe this "different doctrine" systematically, but from his attacks upon it in 1:3–7; 4:1–3, 7; 6:3–5, 20–21 and from the tenor of his instructions for the regulation of the life of the Church, it is clear that Timothy must do battle with a deeply troubling heresy.

Church Fathers such as Irenaeus and Tertullian believed the heresy was an early stage of "Gnosticism" that was to become in its fully developed form the most serious threat to the Church in their generation. (Gnosticism is not so much a system as a trend or current of thought that produced a great variety of systems, often by combining with some already existing religion. It was emerging as a corrupting force before the great Christian-Gnostic systems of the second century appeared; we have already seen something like it in the heresy that threatened the church at Colossae.) However, since the 1945 discovery and subsequent study of actual Gnostic writings, the Nag Hammadi Codices, it seems better to characterize the heresy Paul combats as a mixture of Jewish beliefs with philosophical ideas that have some similarities with later Gnosticism.

Composition

Author

Critical scholars have called into question the authenticity of the Pastoral Letters on a number of counts, chief among them: (1) the historical setting of the letters; (2) the type of church organization presupposed by the letters; (3) the nature of the heresy combated in the letters; (4) the doctrinal substance of the letters; and (5) the style and language of the letters. The following paragraphs will describe each concern and provide broader consideration.

The historical setting. It is argued that the journeys and activities presupposed by the Pastoral Letters cannot be fitted into the life of Paul as known from his undoubted epistles and from the Book of Acts. It is usually assumed that the Roman imprisonment of AD 58–60 ended in Paul's death.

Over against this, one may urge that there is good reason to believe that Paul's imprisonment ended in his release; both Festus and Agrippa deemed him innocent, and no ancient source actually says that Paul was executed after his two years' imprisonment in Rome. Assuming, then, that Paul was released from prison in AD 60, the years between that date and the death of Paul (which may have occurred as late as AD 68) leave ample room for the activities presupposed by the Pastoral Letters, even if we cannot reconstruct the history of this period with absolute accuracy. (See pp 597–99.) It should be noted, on the positive side, that the personal notices in these letters are so true to the life and character of Paul that even many of the convinced opponents of the authenticity of the letters are inclined to believe that a later forger has made use of fragments of genuine Pauline correspondence.

Church organization. The church organization presupposed by the letters, it is urged, is too far advanced and too well established for the first century. It is assumed, therefore, that a writer of the late first or early second century wrote the letters in Paul's name in order to get apostolic sanction for contemporary arrangements in the church.

It may be said in reply that we hear of the appointment of elders in the churches as early as the first missionary journey (Ac 14:23). Paul speaks of "shepherds" and "teachers" in his Letter to the Ephesians (Eph 4:11) and addresses the overseers and deacons of Philippi in his Letter to the Philippians (1:1). Moreover, the organization presupposed in the letters is not elaborate and is not fixed with legal precision. The terms "elder" and "overseer" (which were later distinguished) are still used interchangeably (Ti 1:5, 7), and the concern of the letters is always for the *function* of the office as a power to edify the Church, not for an exact definition of its rights and powers.

The nature of the heresy combated in the letters. It is asserted that the false teaching attacked by the author can only be the great second-century Gnostic systems.

It is true that the false teachers and teachings attacked in the Pastoral Letters have some similarities with later Gnosticism. However, the heresy combated by the Pastoral Letters has a strongly Judaic coloring, something that is not broadly characteristic of second-century Gnosticism. There is no indication in the letters that the teachings under attack are the full-blown systems that divided the second-century Church. The teachings seem rather to be half-formed and ill-formed; and while some of the teachers have been excommunicated, many of them are still, apparently, working within the Church.

The doctrinal substance of the letters. Judgment in this area is bound to be somewhat subjective. For example, the fact that the work of the Holy Spirit receives relatively little emphasis has been used as an argument against the authenticity of the Pastoral Letters. These letters abound in teaching so completely Pauline in content and formulation that it has no real parallel except in the accepted letters of Paul. It should be remembered also that these letters were written to addressees and for purposes quite different from those of Paul's other letters. In general, a judgment like that of an able modern commentator would seem to be fair and reasonable: there is nothing in the Pastorals that Paul could not have written; there is much that only he could have written.

The style and language of the letters. The style resembles, as one would expect, the practical and hortatory portions of the other Pauline Letters rather than that of the doctrinal portions. Besides, Paul's style varies considerably from letter to letter and even within a single letter, so that arguments based on style must be used with considerable caution.

The vocabulary presents the greatest difficulty. Over 36 percent of the words that make up the vocabulary of the Pastoral Letters are not found in any of the other Pauline Letters. This large percentage of new words is in part explained by the newness of the subject matter of these letters, but only in part; for the little words (connectives, prepositions, etc.) that have no connection with the subject matter have changed too. How can one account for so radical a change?

First, Paul's vocabulary changes considerably within the range of his undoubtedly genuine letters, too, though not as radically as in the case of the Pastoral Letters. Second, part of the change may be accounted for by the fact that Paul quotes or paraphrases "sure sayings" of the Early Church more freely here than anywhere else in his writings. Third, it must be remembered that Paul probably spoke and wrote Greek as a second language, which he picked up largely by ear. His language would change more readily than that of a born Greek under changing conditions and surroundings. Thus his long stay in Rome would tend to make his Greek more like that spoken in Rome. And as a matter of fact the new words in the Pastoral Letters are found in much greater frequency in those Early Church Fathers who are connected with Rome than in non-Roman writings. All in all, there is no conclusive evidence to overthrow the early and practically unanimous testimony of the church that the Pastoral Letters are Paul's.

Date of Composition

Paul likely wrote 1 Timothy in AD 65 after leaving Timothy at Ephesus, where he received the letter (1:3). For more on Paul's travels during this period, see pp 597–99.

Purpose/Recipients

Paul wrote to Timothy in order to combat a heresy. The trend of thought in the heresy at Ephesus would lead inevitably to an utter distortion of all that "the Gospel of the glory of the blessed God" (1Tm 1:11) proclaimed. God the Creator disappears—all the good gifts of food and drink that He gives are suspected and feared; all the salutary orders that He has established in this world (marriage, family, government) are despised and ignored. The Old Testament, which rings with glad adoration of the God who made the heavens and the earth and blesses people within the orders of this world, must either be ignored or have its obvious sense interpreted away by allegorizing "myths and endless genealogies" (1:4). The Law becomes the arena of speculation and vain discussions, not the voice of God that calls the sinner to account and condemns him. In terms of this kind of thought, there can be no real incarnation of the Son of God; for how can the divine, which is spiritual, enter into union with matter, which is of itself evil? And when sin is not recognized as a person's guilt, there can be no real redemption either. Where knowledge is made central in a person's religious life, and self-redemption by way of ascetic exercise is made the way of salvation, there is no possibility of that pure Christian love that "issues from a pure heart and a good conscience and a sincere faith" (1:5). A narrow and sectarian pride takes its place (6:4, 20; cf 1:3–7). Where the teaching office becomes a wordy, speculative, disputatious purveying of "knowledge" to a select coterie of initiates, it is bound to become corrupted; it appeals to the pride, the selfishness, and the mercenary instincts of mankind, and the teacher becomes that ghastly, demon-ridden caricature of the true teacher that Paul has described in 4:1–2.

Timothy's task will be to let the fresh and wholesome winds of "sound doctrine" into the house of God, whose air has been infected by morbid and infectious mists. In opposition to the demonic denial of God the Creator and the rejection of His good gifts, he must present the glorious Gospel of the blessed God "who gives life to all things" (6:13). God still has upon His every creation the mark of His primeval "very good!" (Gn 1:31), and the creation is even in its fallen state "made holy by the word of God and prayer" (1Tm 4:5). In opposition to "irreverent, silly myths," Timothy must gratefully adore the Creator. In opposition to the misuse of the Law, he must present the right and lawful use and let the sinner hear the fearful verdict of God in order that he may give ear to God's acquittal in His Gospel (1:8–11).

In opposition to the rarefied and unreal Christ of speculation, Paul must present "the *man* Christ Jesus" (2:5), the Christ Jesus who really entered into history under Pontius Pilate (6:13) and died a real death upon the cross for the sins of all people (2:6). He must present this Christ as the whole content of the truth that the Church upholds and guards, the mystery of God "manifested *in the flesh*" (3:16). In opposition to self-redemption by means of knowledge and ascetic practices, he must present redemption as the sole act of the Christ who came into the world not to impart higher knowledge but "to save sinners" (1:15), the Christ "who gave Himself as a ransom for all" (2:6). In opposition to Gnostic exclusiveness, Paul must present the all-embracing grace of God. And in opposition to their narrow sectarian pride, he must present the Gospel of universal grace (2:4), and thus make of the Church a Church that can pray wholeheartedly "for *all* people" (2:1), a Church that lives in the "love that issues from a pure heart and a good conscience and a sincere faith" (1:5).

Jesus, our ransom, suffering on the cross; by Coppo di Marcovaldo (c thirteenth century).

To the imposing picture of these brilliant, speculative, disputatious, and mercenary men, Timothy must present the picture of the true teacher. He must, first of all, himself *be* that picture; he dare not let himself be drawn down to the level of his opponents and fight demonic fire with fire; he must do battle, "holding faith and a good conscience" (1:19); he must, as a good minister of Jesus Christ, not allow himself to be infected by what he opposes but must continue to be "trained in the words of the faith and of the good doctrine" that he has followed hitherto. He must train himself, athlete-like, in godliness (4:6–8). Thus he will be able to fight the good fight of faith as a "man of God," standing in the succession of Moses and the prophets, devoted to God's cause (6:11–12; cf 6:3–10), laying hold even now of that eternal life that shall be his in fullness at the appearing of the Lord Jesus Christ (6:11–15). He must himself be all that the Gnostic teachers are not; and he is to see to it that the men who oversee the church's life and administer the church's charity, the overseers and deacons, are men of like character. They need not be brilliant men; they must be good men. It is enough if an overseer be "able to teach" (3:2); he need not be a brilliant speaker or a captivating personality. The qualifications that Paul sets up for overseers and deacons are singularly sober and down to earth, but the moral standards that he sets up for them are awesomely high (3:1–13). Paul wants men whom the grace of God has "trained," as he puts it in his Letter to Titus (Ti 2:11–12), seasoned, selfless, wise, and gracious men whose faith has borne fruit in their homes, in their marital fidelity, and in the training of their children (1Tm 3:2, 4, 12).

Literary Features

Genre

Paul writes Timothy a letter that sums up once more the oral instructions already given him (1Tm 1:3). This letter will give his work the sanction and authority of Paul, "an apostle of Christ Jesus by command of God our Savior and of Christ Jesus our Hope" (1:1). Paul is in effect telling the Church of Ephesus what he had once told the Corinthians: "He is doing the work of the Lord, as I am. So let no one despise him" (1Co 16:10–11).

Characters

Timothy had a great piece of work assigned to him, and he was a good man for the task. He was both Jew and Greek (Ac 16:1). He had lived with the Old Testament from childhood (2Tm 3:15). Prophetic voices had assigned him to this "good warfare" (1Tm 1:18). God had given him the requisite gifts for it (4:14), and his whole history had been one that fostered those gifts. He had been Paul's almost constant companion for a dozen years (Ac 16:1). The apostolic "pattern of the sound words" (2Tm 1:13) had become a part of his makeup, and the apostolic example had been constantly before him (3:10–11, 14). Paul had employed Timothy as his emissary before this, though never for so extended and difficult a mission as this one. When Paul was prevented from returning to Thessalonica, he sent Timothy to the young and troubled church to establish the believers in their faith and to exhort them (1Th 3:1–2). He had sent Timothy to Corinth during that troubled period when the Corinthians were becoming drunk on the heady wine of the new teaching, to remind them of the apostle's "ways in Christ" (1Co 4:17; 16:10). He had sent him to Philippi from Rome during the time of his imprisonment and had commended him to the Philippians with the finest tribute that can be paid to a servant of God in the Gospel: "I have no one like him, who will be genuinely concerned for your welfare. For they all seek their own interests, not those of Jesus Christ. But you know Timothy's proven worth, how as a son with a father he has served with me in the Gospel" (Php 2:20–22).

If Paul was a fond father to Timothy, he was not a blind one. He knew his beloved child's weaknesses: Timothy was still young and apparently conscious of it as a handicap (1Tm 4:12). He was inclined to be timid (cf 1Co 16:10, 11; 2Tm 1:7). Besides, his health was not of the best; his stomach troubled him (1Tm 5:23).

Narrative Development or Plot

Since 1 Timothy is written as a letter, it does not have a storyline or plot.

Resources

See "Genre" above.

Text and Translations

The text of 1 Timothy is well established through a wealth of early manuscripts and from Early Church Fathers who cite the letter. As with Paul's other letters, scholars discuss the possible influence of the early heretic Marcion on causing some of the textual variants.

Different sizes and styles of Greek amphoras.

Outline

I. The Power of the Pure Gospel (ch 1)
- A. Greeting (1:1–2)
- B. The Task at Hand (1:3–11)
- C. The Power of the Gospel (1:12–17)
- D. Some Opponents of the Gospel (1:18–20)

II. The Church's Organization (chs 2–3)
- A. Good Order in the Church (ch 2)
  1. Good order in public worship (2:1–7)
  2. Good order in the Church's ministry (2:8–15)
- B. Qualifications for Offices (ch 3)
  1. The pastoral office (3:1–7)
  2. Deacons and deaconesses (3:8–13)
  3. The Church: the community of faith (3:14–16)

III. True versus False Teaching (ch 4)
- A. Doctrines of Demons (4:1–5)
- B. True Godliness (4:6–10)
- C. Paul's Charge to His Fellow Pastor Timothy (4:11–16)

IV. Exhortation to Christian Living (chs 5–6)
- A. Positions in the Church (5:1–6:2)
  1. The shepherd (pastor) and various classes of sheep (Christians) (5:1–2)
  2. The order of widows (5:3–16)
  3. Pastor Timothy and other pastors (5:17–25)
  4. Slaves and their masters (6:1–2)
- B. True Godliness (6:3–21)
  1. The importance of sound teaching (6:3–5)
  2. Contentment as a way of life (6:6–10)
  3. Personal note to Timothy (6:11–16)
  4. A word to the wealthy (6:17–19)
  5. A heartfelt farewell (6:20–21)

Doctrinal Content

Summary Commentary

Ch 1 The work of the Gospel ministry carried out by Paul and Timothy flows from God's command. The words they speak are His words, not their own. Their competence for ministry comes from God, who called them to His service. Paul writes this Epistle to stop the teaching of false doctrine among the Ephesian churches and to promote the teaching of sound doctrine. God's patience and mercy are at work to save all sinners, whether they are blinded by ignorance (like Paul was) or have actively rejected the faith (like Hymenaeus and Alexander).

Chs 2–3 The Gospel affirms the unique vocations God assigned to men and women at creation. Only qualified men may serve as pastors of God's flock. Deacons were faithful men, entrusted with special responsibilities for service to their fellow Christians. (The calling of deaconess is referred to in Rm 16:1 rather than here.) A confession of the mystery of godliness concludes the section dedicated to the Church's organization (chs 2–3).

The sarcophagus of Junius Bassus (d 359) includes this depiction of the fall into sin following Satan's temptation of Adam and Eve.

Ch 4 God daily and richly provides us with all that we need. To reject God's good gifts, or to receive them thanklessly, is a sin against His graciousness. Paul prepares Timothy to contend against the "teachings of demons" (v 1). Pastors are to command and teach true doctrine, while condemning doctrine that is false and deceitful.

Chs 5–6 Paul describes how to work respectfully with other members of the congregation. When Christians interact with one another in ways that are honorable and pure, they beautifully reflect God and the faith they confess. But the Church is burdened and liable to be reviled by unbelievers when honor and purity are lacking. Rather than being content with what we have, we by nature covet the things we do not have. Those who covet often see money as a solution to all of life's problems. But those who love money are in grave danger; they risk losing their faith in Christ. As a true man of God, Timothy is to flee every corrupting influence and keep God's command, faithfully guarding that which has been deposited with him.

Specific Law Themes

The Lord charges His servants with challenging duties, appointing them to withstand false teachers and to manage the work of the Church effectively.

Specific Gospel Themes

Through the glorious Gospel, the Lord saves both those who receive the Word and those who proclaim it. Christ is our Mediator with the heavenly Father, who hallows all things necessary to our life and salvation.

Specific Doctrines

The major emphasis in 1 Timothy is on sound doctrine in distinction from the false teaching that had afflicted the congregation at Ephesus. In keeping with the Old Testament doctrine of creation, Paul notes the goodness of God's created gifts and order, which the Lord blesses and sanctifies through prayer. To ensure sound doctrine and faithful practice, the Church requires qualified leaders: overseers and deacons who commend the truth of the Gospel through godly lives. Paul also includes much practical counsel on how to work with various persons in the church.

Key Passages

While combating the false teachers, Paul distinguishes the purposes of the Law from sound doctrine of the Gospel (1:8–11). This passage emerged in the early centuries of the Church as key for the doctrine of the Law and also for the Law and Gospel/promises distinction. False teachers will misuse the Law to introduce "teachings of demons" (4:1–3) that will afflict the Church in the last days. Yet the Church may live and pray confidently for all people and governments (2:1–2), for it is God's will to save all people through the one mediator, Jesus Christ (2:4–5).

Application

Ch 1 We should not judge the effectiveness of those called to serve as Gospel ministers only according to their personality traits or other outward characteristics. Ministers should first of all be regarded according to how faithfully they proclaim the Gospel message entrusted to them. Our sinful nature often leads us to be unconcerned about the doctrines God has given us in His Word. When this happens, we are guilty of being poor stewards of the Gospel. Yet, in the good news of Jesus Christ, we are given a pure heart, a good conscience, and a sincere faith—all of which enable us to receive God's gift of sound doctrine with thanksgiving and eagerness.

Chs 2–3 Our sinful nature may sometimes bristle at the roles and responsibilities God has given us, causing us to fail to see that God has given us His divine design for male and female because He loves us and always wants what is best for us. We must always be on guard against this kind of sin, especially as we are gathered for public worship. Jesus faithfully fulfilled the divine role assigned to Him as the one mediator between God and all people. He willingly submitted Himself to death as the sacred substitute for sinners. Through faith in Him, we receive forgiveness of sins, and we rejoice to serve Him in earthly vocations characterized by thanksgiving, modesty, and self-control.

We should honor and uphold the qualifications that God has set forth for those who would serve in the Office of the Public Ministry, always remembering that the pastoral office is a divine institution—a gift from God for His Church. The Lord Jesus has given this office and its qualifications because He loves us and always desires what is best for us. Christians today are also privileged to serve others through special congregational offices and service organizations. In truth, God calls every Christian to follow His example of self-giving service. Jesus came to serve sinners like us with His forgiveness and salvation (Mt 20:28). We are not free to amend or depart from God's revealed will concerning the outward organization of His Church, because it is the pillar and buttress of the truth—the Church of the living God that confesses the Gospel of Jesus Christ to a fallen world. By grace, the Savior's truth has been made manifest to us and, through faith, we will follow Him in glory.

Ch 4 Because of Jesus' sacrificial death for our sins, God does not reject us but receives us as His own children through faith. The doctrines of Scripture are God-given, because He loves us. Each individual doctrine testifies to and supports the most important doctrine of all—that we are saved by grace, for Christ's sake, through faith.

Chs 5–6 Our dear Lord Jesus has made every Christian worthy of eternal honor by His sacrificial death and resurrection. Through faith in Him, even dishonorable sinners are regarded as God's pure and beloved children. Nothing can separate us from His love. As He tenderly cares for us through His Word of promise, we are able to enjoy lives of godliness with contentment. All that we can take with us when we leave this world is the life and immortality that Jesus has given us through faith—and that is more than enough!

Canonicity

Like Paul's other biblical letters, which were collected and copied as authoritative already in the middle of the first century AD (cf 2Pt 3:15–16), 1 Timothy quickly gained canonical status (*homologoumenon*).

In 1Tm 5:1–16, the apostle Paul provides special instruction on the care of widows, one of common challenges facing congregations in the first century AD.

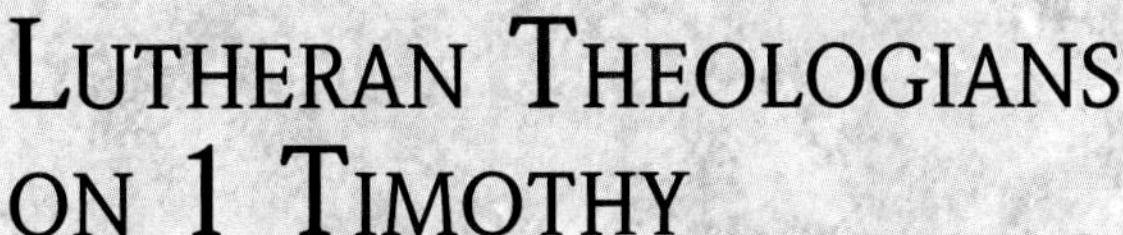

Lutheran Theologians on 1 Timothy

Luther

"This epistle St. Paul writes in order to provide a model to all bishops of what they are to teach and how they are to rule Christendom in the various stations of life, so that it may not be necessary for them to rule Christians according to their own human opinions.

"In chapter 1 he charges that a bishop keep true faith and love and resist the false preachers of the law who, beside Christ and the gospel, would also insist on the works of the law. In a brief summary, he comprehends the entire Christian doctrine concerning the purpose of the law and the nature of the gospel. He offers himself as an example to comfort all sinners and those with troubled conscience.

"In chapter 2 he charges that prayer be made for all stations of life. He also commands that women are not to preach or wear costly adornment, but are to be obedient to men. [For Luther's intent, see Eph 5:21–33.]

"In chapter 3 he describes the kind of persons that bishops, or priests, and their wives ought to be, and also the deacons and their wives. He praises those who desire to be bishops of this kind.

"In chapter 4 he prophesies of false bishops and the spiritual estate which is opposed to that spoken of above, who will not be persons of that kind, but instead will forbid marriage and foods, and with their doctrines of men inculcate the very opposite of the things Paul has described.

"In chapter 5 he gives orders as to how widows and young women should be looked after, and which widows are to be supported from the common funds; also how godly bishops or priests are to be held in honor, and blameworthy ones punished.

"In chapter 6 he exhorts the bishops to hold fast to the pure gospel and to promulgate it by their preaching and living. They are to avoid senseless and meddlesome controversies which are only raised for gaining worldly reputation and riches." (AE 35:388)

For more of Luther's insights on this book, see *Lectures on 1 Timothy* (AE 28:215–384).

Gerhard

"At one time the Donatist Petilianus considered Paul's disciple Timothy to be a layman, according to Augustine (*Contra liter. Petiliani*, bk. 3, c. 106). It is evident from the Epistles written to him, however, that he was a distinguished light of the Eastern Church, the bishop of Ephesus for forty years, as some think. The apostle had put this disciple of his in charge of the congregation at Ephesus that he [Paul] had planted. In this Epistle, then, [Paul] is instructing [Timothy] how he ought 'to conduct himself in God's house' and how he must perform his duty correctly.

"It consists of six chapters and is entirely of teaching, for he is instructing Timothy regarding ecclesiastical *duties, persons,* and *virtues.*" (ThC E1 § 266)

Further Study

Lay/Bible Class Resources

Guthrie, Donald. *The Pastoral Epistles.* TNTC. Grand Rapids: Eerdmans, 1957. § A helpful resource with emphasis on the exposition of the text. Surveys the various suggestions as to authorship. Holds to Pauline authorship.

Henricks, Michael, Erik Rottmann, and Robert Baker. *Timothy, Titus, Philemon.* Leaders Guide and Enrichment Magazine/Study Guide. LL. St. Louis: Concordia, 2005. § An in-depth, nine-session Bible study with individual, small group, and lecture portions.

Life by His Word. St. Louis: Concordia, 2009. § More than 1,500 reproducible one-page Bible studies covering each chapter of the canonical Scriptures. Page references to *The Lutheran Study Bible.* CD-Rom and downloadable.

Mueller, A. C. *1 and 2 Timothy, Titus: Keeping the Faith.* GWFT. St. Louis: Concordia, 2006. § Lutheran author. Thirteen-session Bible study, including leader's notes and discussion questions.

Schuetze, Armin. *1 & 2 Timothy, Titus.* PBC. St. Louis: Concordia, 2005. § Lutheran author. Excellent for Bible classes. Based on the NIV translation.

Church Worker Resources

Luther, Martin. *Lectures on 1 Timothy.* Vol. 28 of AE. St. Louis: Concordia, 1973. § The great reformer's comments and practical insights from 1527–28. Delivered while the plague threatened Wittenberg.

Academic Resources

Johnson, Luke Timothy. *The First and Second Letters to Timothy.* Vol. 35A of AB. New Haven, CN: Yale University Press, 2001. § Argues that each letter must be treated on its own terms and that they are based on existing Greco-Roman letter genres. Supports Pauline authorship, seeking to overturn the conventional wisdom of critical views. Thorough commentary.

Kelly, J. N. D. *The Pastoral Epistles.* Black's New Testament Commentary. Grand Rapids: Baker, 1981 reprint. § An excellent resource for the patristic background related to the letters, by the author of *Early Christian Creeds* and *Early Christian Doctrines.* Still good, though it is now more than 40 years old.

Knight, George W., III. *The Pastoral Epistles.* NIGTC. Grand Rapids: Eerdmans, 1992. § Commentary focused on the Greek text. Evangelical writer supporting Pauline authorship. He provides a very solid and competent treatment of basic exegetical issues.

Lenski, R. C. H. *The Interpretation of St. Paul's Epistles to the Colossians, to the Thessalonians, to Timothy, to Titus, and to Philemon.* Minneapolis: Augsburg, 1961. § A standard resource by a noteworthy Lutheran interpreter, concerned with being faithful to the text and with its implications for today.

Lock, Walter. *The Pastoral Epistles.* ICC. Edinburgh: T&T Clark, 1924. § A concise, helpful resource. However, Lock is uncertain about Pauline authorship.

Mounce, William D. *Pastoral Epistles.* WBC. Nashville: Thomas Nelson, 2000. § Thorough argument for Pauline authorship from a well-known evangelical interpreter. Extensive bibliographies.

van Oosterzee, Johannes Jacobus. *1 and 2 Timothy.* LCHS. New York: Charles Scribner's Sons, 1868. § A helpful older example of German biblical scholarship, based on the Greek text, which provides references to significant commentaries from the Reformation era forward.

Towner, Philip H. *The Letters to Timothy and Titus.* NICNT. Grand Rapids: Eerdmans, 2006. § Rejects the categorization of these letters as "pastoral epistles," emphasizing the need to treat each letter individually. Thorough commentary from an evangelical interpreter interacting with recent publications as well as the Greek text.

2 TIMOTHY

God's purpose and grace

While searching for Paul, Onesiphorus would tread the broad streets of Rome, passing beneath the archways of its aqueducts and walking beside its grand colonnaded porticos. But the prison where Paul was held would be out of the way, along an alley or even in a cave, requiring all of Onesiphorus's diligence to find his colleague.

The fact that Onesiphorus of Ephesus had to search earnestly to find Paul in prison at Rome (2Tm 1:16–17) tells us more about Paul's circumstances at the end of his life. The Romans did not typically hold prisoners for long periods of time. But Paul's case seems exceptional, since he received more than one hearing (4:16) and expected an extended stay in chains, requiring support from his fellow workers (4:9–13). With the Lord's help, Paul successfully defended himself so that he "was rescued from the lion's mouth" (4:17).

Historical and Cultural Setting

Paul could have little hope of ultimate acquittal from his detractors; he was at the end of his course. And he was virtually alone; only Luke was with him. He longed to see "his beloved child" Timothy once more and bade him come to Rome before the winter made travel by sea impossible (1:4; 4:9, 21). He had to reckon with the possibility that Timothy might not reach Rome in time; and so he put in writing all that he hoped to tell Timothy in person if and when he arrived.

OVERVIEW

Author
Paul the apostle

Date
AD 68

Places
Ephesus; Thessalonica; Galatia; Troas; Corinth; Miletus

People
Paul; Timothy; Lois, Eunice; Hymenaeus, Philetus; Paul's numerous co-workers

Purposes
To build up Timothy for service in the face of persecution and to appeal for him to visit Paul at Rome

Law Themes
Judgment Day; suffering for the Gospel; charges and commands

Gospel Themes
The appearing of our Savior; sound words of the Gospel; the gift of the Spirit; the good deposit; rescue

Memory Verses
God's purpose and grace (1:8–9); the value of Sacred Scripture (3:16–17)

TIMELINE

AD 33	Resurrection of Jesus
AD 52–55	Paul's third missionary journey
AD 57–58	Paul journeys to Rome
AD 68	Paul writes 2 Timothy
AD 68	Martyrdom of Peter and Paul

Ruins of the Roman forum.

Composition

Author

The apostle Paul, a Jew from Tarsus who studied under the Rabbi Gamaliel at Jerusalem, was regarded as the author of the letter by early Christians. On questions raised by modern critical scholars, see pp 599–602.

Date of Composition

Paul wrote this letter to Timothy in AD 68, not long before Paul was executed for ministering the Gospel.

Purpose/Recipients

The theme and mood of 2 Timothy are noticeably different from that of 1 Timothy. The letter is more concise and earnest. The writer has a single point to make, and he makes it simply and effectively. His advice is to beware of false teachers and to hold on to the simple Gospel. The second letter does not contain the many directions for congregational administration found in the first one. The writer limits this letter to the central thought almost exclusively.

Literary Features

Genre

The letter is, as Bengel has put it, Paul's "last will and testament," in which he bids Timothy preserve the apostolic Gospel pure and unchanged, guard it against the increasingly vicious attacks of false teachers, train men to transmit it faithfully, and be ready to take his own share of suffering in the propagation and defense of it. The most personal of the Pastoral Letters is therefore in a sense "official," too, for Paul cannot separate his person from his office. The man who has been "set apart for the Gospel of God" (Rm 1:1) remains one with that Gospel in life and in death.

Characters

Paul addresses the letter to **Timothy** (see pp 604–5) but also mentions **Onesiphorus** (see p 637), **Luke** (see pp 269–70), and others.

Narrative Development or Plot

Since 2 Timothy is written as a letter, it does not have a storyline or plot. However, Paul does relate some personal history regarding Timothy and himself, especially in chs 1 and 4.

Resources

Paul writes this letter from personal history, the "pattern of the sound words" (1:13), and references to the movements of his colleagues and opponents (4:9–21).

Text and Translations

The text of 2 Timothy is well established through a wealth of early manuscripts and from Early Church Fathers who cite the letter. As with Paul's other letters, scholars discuss the possible influence of the early heretic Marcion on causing some of the textual variants.

Laurel wreath, like those presented to victorious atheletes.

Doctrinal Content

Summary Commentary

Ch 1 Paul addresses Timothy tenderly, referring to him as his "beloved child" and speaking God's grace, mercy, and peace to him. Alone in prison and abandoned by many of his friends, Paul fondly remembers the encouragement he received from Timothy's sincere faith. Exhorting Timothy never to be ashamed of the faith he has been given, Paul exults in the promise of Christ, for whose sake he is imprisoned.

2:1–4:8 Using several comparisons (soldier, athlete, and farmer), Paul calls Timothy to find other faithful men who are able to share in the pastoral office. He reminds Timothy that he and his fellow pastors must remain focused on their task of proclaiming God's Word. They must not get bogged down in quarrels or give in to the temptations of the flesh (such as temper), but be generous and kind to all. Although Paul writes these words specifically about temptations that attack the pastoral office, they clearly apply to all Christians. Men such as Jannes and Jambres allowed themselves to be enticed, and in so doing they disqualified themselves regarding the faith. Paul points to himself as an example for Timothy. He speaks about the great work the Gospel has produced within him. Faced with the thought of his imminent death, Paul impresses upon Timothy the importance of carrying on where Paul will leave off, preaching the Word faithfully.

4:9–22 In closing, Paul requests that Timothy visit him at Rome, confident that his fellow Christian will prove faithful. Paul asks Timothy to greet the other Christians at Ephesus, whom Paul had earlier grown to love.

Specific Law Themes

As Paul faces the possibility of public execution, he warns about the approach of Judgment Day and how all will face God's justice. He reflects on what it is like to suffer for the Gospel, preparing Timothy for similar trials. He charges and commands Timothy regarding his duties before God and His people.

Specific Gospel Themes

Paul rejoices that Jesus is returning as the Savior, to rescue His people. The message of Christ is "sound," granting spiritual health and life. The Lord has prepared Timothy for the challenges ahead by giving him the Holy Spirit, who is a deposit or guarantee assuring the believer of God's mercy.

The Bible is the source and norm of doctrine and practice in the Church.

Specific Doctrines

Like 1 Timothy, this letter also serves as an effective antidote against false teachers and against those who argue that purity of doctrine is relatively unimportant to the Church. It also provides a powerful call to lives of selfless sacrifice and devotion by those who follow Timothy into the pastoral office.

Key Passages

Two passages in this letter emphasize the importance of Holy Scripture for the ministry and the life of the Church. One must handle the Scripture rightly (2:15) to be a faithful worker. In the

Outline

I. Not Ashamed of the Ministry of the Gospel (ch 1)
- A. Greeting (1:1–2)
- B. The Family of Faith (1:3–5)
- C. An Unashamed Ministry (1:6–14)
- D. Ashamed versus Unashamed (1:15–18)

II. Charge to Faithful Ministry in Hard Times (2:1–4:5)
- A. Laboring in the Truth (2:1–7)
- B. The Gospel of the Truth (2:8–13)
- C. Laboring for the Truth against Error (2:14–21)
- D. Laboring with the Truth for Those in Error (2:22–26)
- E. Opposition to the Truth (3:1–9)
- F. "Continue in What You Have Learned" (3:10–17)
- G. Final Charge to Timothy (4:1–5)

III. Paul's Farewell (4:6–22)
- A. Paul's Impending Martyrdom (4:6–8)
- B. Final Greetings and Requests (4:9–22)

Lutheran tradition, this is associated with distinguishing Law and Gospel. Paul also describes various uses of the Holy Scripture (3:16–17), a passage much discussed in view of modern criticism of the Bible and the doctrines of inspiration, biblical inerrancy, and authority.

Application

Ch 1 As you speak to others, especially your fellow Christians, season what you say with God's Word. Remind them of the grace that is theirs in Christ (e.g., "The Lord be with you"; "God's peace to you"). Instead of feeling self-conscious about being Christian, we must share in Paul's forthright confession: "I am not ashamed, for I know whom I have believed" (v 12). Our Lord Jesus Christ will never let us go.

2:1–4:8 Christians—including pastors—need one another, bearing one another's burdens. When God's Word is front and center in our minds and on our tongues, it acts powerfully to create ongoing repentance and faith. God's baptismal gift of the Holy Spirit creates within us an ongoing desire for repentance and forgiveness. Although we may regularly fall into sin (such falls are easy for all Christians), God calls us to faith again through His Word, reminding us of the forgiveness and cleansing that are ours in Christ Jesus. Our fellow Christians want to learn the faith from us, and they watch us in the same way that Timothy watched Paul. God's Word sometimes cuts like a knife when it exposes our sin. But after the Law comes the Gospel of peace, binding up the wounds inflicted by the Law with the sweet Gospel, which proclaims Christ's forgiveness for all our sins.

4:9–22 We should not hesitate to ask others for their help, particularly when our need is great. Probably they are more than ready to give us aid and require only to know our need. There is no Christian who lives to himself or herself alone. We are a family, joined together in Christ! God has given fellow Christians to us whom we will find gathered with us in worship. As we partake of the Word and the Sacraments in the communion of saints, our gracious heavenly Father will lighten our loads and lift our burdens.

Canonicity

Like Paul's other biblical letters, which were collected and copied as authoritative already in the middle of the first century AD (cf 2Pt 3:15–16), 2 Timothy quickly gained canonical status (*homologoumenon*).

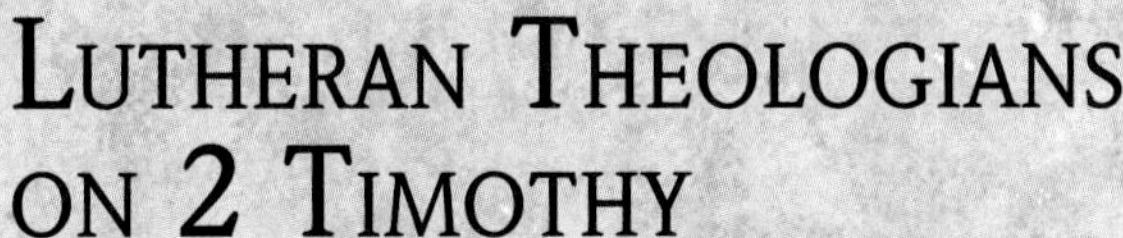

Lutheran Theologians on 2 Timothy

Luther

"This epistle is a farewell letter, in which St. Paul exhorts Timothy to go on propagating the gospel, even as he has begun. This is quite necessary, since there are many who fall away; and false spirits and teachers keep springing up all around. Therefore it is incumbent upon a bishop always to be alert and to work at the gospel.

"But he prophesies especially, in chapters 3 and 4, concerning the perilous time at the end of the world. It is then that a false spiritual life will lead all the world astray, with an outward show, under which every sort of wickedness and wrong will have its fling. Sad to say! we now see this prophecy of St. Paul all too amply fulfilled in our clergy." (AE 35:389)

Gerhard

"With regard to time, this is the last Epistle of St. Paul. He wrote it to Timothy a few days before his blessed departure [*analusis*] from his captivity at Rome.

"It consists of four chapters and falls into three parts. In the first, he encourages Timothy to guard the soundness of doctrine with great zeal and not to allow any perils to move him from his confession. In the second, he forewarns him of misleading spirits that already at that time were springing up in the Church. In the third, he explains his own situation to Timothy and asks Timothy to come to him, to bring Mark with him, and to bring some of his own things to him." (ThC E1 § 267)

Questions People Ask about 2 Timothy

Scripture, Inspired and Profitable

One of the chief passages to cite here is 2Tm 3:16: "All Scripture is breathed out by God and profitable for teaching, for reproof, for correction, and for training in righteousness." It is the text from which the term *inspiration* has been derived. According to the context, Paul has in mind particularly the Old Testament Scriptures, which Timothy had known from childhood (3:15). But the text could include also part of the New Testament which already had been written and circulated, for Paul in 1Tm 5:18 includes under Scripture a citation from Jesus found in Lk 10:7: "The laborer deserves his wages."

Some versions, as Luther does, render 2Tm 3:16 thus: "Every Scripture given by God is profitable for teaching, for reproof, for correction, for instruction in righteousness." The apostle here presents teaching on the origin of the Scriptures, which he has spoken of in the preceding verse. There he has given them the attribute "sacred." Here he calls them "inspired of God." Literally translated, this term means God-breathed. It is a beautiful figure that he uses, signifying that just as our breath proceeds from us, so the Scriptures have come from God.

If the objection is made that Paul, according to the latter translation, does not ascribe this quality to all the Scriptures, but that his meaning could be: If a Scripture is inspired of God, then it is likewise profitable, etc., and that hence we are not justified in basing on this passage our doctrine of the inspiration of the Bible or any part of it, we must reply that Paul certainly does not wish to make merely a hypothetical statement. On the contrary, when he follows up his remark on the power of the Holy Scriptures in v 15 with the declaration that every God-breathed Scripture is also profitable for doctrine, etc., the unbiased reader at once perceives that the apostle is alluding to the very writings which he has spoken of before in such high terms and that he merely varies the expression, using "God-breathed" instead of "sacred." Every such God-breathed Scripture as he has made mention of is also profitable for doctrine, etc. That is his meaning.

Further Study

Lay/Bible Class Resources

Guthrie, Donald. *The Pastoral Epistles*. TNTC. Grand Rapids: Eerdmans, 1957. ♦ A helpful resource with emphasis on the exposition of the text. Surveys the various suggestions as to authorship. Holds to Pauline authorship.

Henricks, Michael, Erik Rottmann, and Robert Baker. *Timothy, Titus, Philemon*. Leaders Guide and Enrichment Magazine/Study Guide. LL. St. Louis: Concordia, 2005. ♦ An in-depth, nine-session Bible study with individual, small group, and lecture portions.

Life by His Word. St. Louis: Concordia, 2009. ♦ More than 1,500 reproducible one-page Bible studies covering each chapter of the canonical Scriptures. Page references to *The Lutheran Study Bible*. CD-Rom and downloadable.

Mueller, A. C. *1 and 2 Timothy, Titus: Keeping the Faith*. GWFT. St. Louis: Concordia, 2006. ♦ Lutheran author. Thirteen-session Bible study, including leader's notes and discussion questions.

Schuetze, Armin. *1 & 2 Timothy, Titus*. PBC. St. Louis: Concordia, 2005. ♦ Lutheran author. Excellent for Bible classes. Based on the NIV translation.

Stott, John R. W. *The Message of 2 Timothy*. The Bible Speaks Today. Grand Rapids, MI: Zondervan, 1973. ♦ Commentary from a noted evangelical, originally published under the title "Guard the Gospel."

Church Worker Resources

Luther, Martin. *Lectures on 1 Timothy*. Vol. 28 of AE. St. Louis: Concordia, 1973. ♦ The great reformer's comments and practical insights from 1527–28. Delivered while the plague threatened Wittenberg.

Academic Resources

Johnson, Luke Timothy. *The First and Second Letters to Timothy*. Vol. 35A of AB. New Haven, CN: Yale University Press, 2001. ♦ Argues that each letter must be treated on its own terms and that they are based on existing Greco-Roman letter genres. Supports Pauline authorship, seeking to overturn the conventional wisdom of critical views. Thorough commentary.

Kelly, J. N. D. *The Pastoral Epistles*. Black's New Testament Commentary. Grand Rapids: Baker, 1981 reprint. ♦ An excellent resource for the patristic background related to the letters, by the author of *Early Christian Creeds* and *Early Christian* Doctrines. Still good, though it is now more than 40 years old.

Knight, George W., III. *The Pastoral Epistles*. NIGTC. Grand Rapids: Eerdmans, 1992. ♦ Commentary focused on the Greek text. Evangelical writer supporting Pauline authorship. He provides a very solid and competent treatment of basic exegetical issues.

Lenski, R. C. H. *The Interpretation of St. Paul's Epistles to the Colossians, to the Thessalonians, to Timothy, to Titus, and to Philemon*. Minneapolis: Augsburg, 1961. ♦ A standard resource by a noteworthy Lutheran interpreter, concerned with being faithful to the text and with its implications for today.

Lock, Walter. *The Pastoral Epistles*. ICC. Edinburgh: T&T Clark, 1924. ♦ A concise, helpful resource. However, Lock is uncertain about Pauline authorship.

Mounce, William D. *Pastoral Epistles*. WBC. Nashville: Thomas Nelson, 2000. ♦ Thorough argument for Pauline authorship from a well-known evangelical interpreter. Extensive bibliographies.

Towner, Philip H. *The Letters to Timothy and Titus*. NICNT. Grand Rapids: Eerdmans, 2006. ♦ Rejects the categorization of these letters as "pastoral epistles," emphasizing the need to treat each letter individually. Thorough commentary from an evangelical interpreter interacting with recent publications as well as the Greek text.

van Oosterzee, Johannes Jacobus. *1 and 2 Timothy*. LCHS. New York: Charles Scribner's Sons, 1868. ♦ A helpful older example of German biblical scholarship, based on the Greek text, which provides references to significant commentaries from the Reformation era forward.

TITUS

Saved according to His mercy

Nicopolis was a Roman colony on the west coast of Greece, on the isthmus separating the Ambracian Gulf from the Ionian Sea. The city would serve as winter quarters for Paul and his colleagues in AD 68 before his arrest and second imprisonment at Rome. Paul was on his way to Nicopolis, perhaps along the road from Macedonia, when he paused to write this letter to Titus, his representative serving congregations on the island of Crete. Paul urged Titus to sail to Nicopolis and join him for the winter (3:12).

Historical and Cultural Setting

The Letter to Titus is quite similar to 1 Timothy in its occasion, purpose, and content. Paul had worked for a while as a missionary on the island of Crete together with Titus, the prudent, able, and tactful Gentile companion who had rendered him such valuable services at the time when the relationship between the Corinthian Church and Paul had been strained to the breaking point (2Co 2:13; 7:6; 8:6; 12:18). At his departure from Crete, Paul left Titus in charge of consolidating and organizing the newly created Christian communities. His task resembled that of Timothy at Ephesus in that the faith and life of the Church were being endangered by the rise of false teachers, more pronouncedly Judaic in their teaching than those at Ephesus (Ti 1:14; 3:9). The situation was further complicated in Crete, however, by the fact that solid organization was lacking in these newly founded Christian communities, and the pagan envi-

OVERVIEW

Author
Paul the apostle

Date
AD 68

Places
Crete; Nicopolis

People
Paul; Titus; Artemas; Tychicus; Zenas; Apollos

Purpose
To guide Titus's teaching and administration for the Christians on Crete

Law Themes
Be above reproach; rebuke; the pure and the defiled; submissiveness; devotion to good works

Gospel Themes
Election; soundness; God's grace; redemption; washing and renewal; justification

Memory Verses
Redeemed and purified (2:14); renewal by the Holy Spirit (3:4–7)

TIMELINE

AD 33	Resurrection of Jesus
AD 57–58	Paul lands on Crete on way to Rome
c AD 64	Paul leaves Titus on Crete
AD 68	Titus written
AD 68	Martyrdom of Peter and Paul

Sailboats at Crete.

ronment was particularly vicious (1:5, 12–13). Whereas Timothy was to restore order in established churches, Titus had to *establish* order in young churches. It was a task that called for all his courage, wisdom, and tact.

Composition

Author

The apostle Paul, a Jew from Tarsus who studied under the Rabbi Gamaliel at Jerusalem, was regarded as the author of the letter by early Christians.

Date of Composition

Paul wrote this letter to Titus in AD 68, not long before Paul was executed for ministering the Gospel.

Purpose/Recipients

Paul wrote to Titus to encourage him in this difficult assignment, to aid him in combating the threatening heresy, to advise him in his task of organizing and edifying the churches, and, not least, to give Titus's presence and work in Crete the sanction and support of his own apostolic authority. This last intention of the letter is evident in the salutation, which dwells on Paul's apostolate (1:1–3), and in the closing greeting, "Grace be with you *all*" (3:15), which shows that the letter addressed to Titus is intended for the ear of the churches also.

Paul intercedes for a sinner. Sixth century; Lyon, France.

Literary Features

Genre

As noted above, this letter is similar to 1 Timothy in content. Luther described it as an exhortation.

Characters

Paul mentions **Titus** 15 times in his letters, most often when Titus was sent to Corinth to solve the problems there and then rejoined Paul in Macedonia (2Co 2:13; 7:6, 13–14; 8:6, 16; 12:18). Titus was a Gentile convert to Christianity who became Paul's friend and helper. According to the letter, Paul left his colleague behind in Crete to organize the churches there (Ti 1:4–5). The last mention of Titus indicates that he went to Dalmatia (2Tm 4:10). According to tradition, Titus was the bishop of Crete.

Narrative Development or Plot

Since Titus is written as a letter, it does not have a storyline or plot.

Resources

Because of similarities between the letter to Titus and 1 Timothy, it is possible that Paul drew on his earlier correspondence with fellow workers when writing to Titus.

Text and Translations

The text of Titus is well established through a wealth of early manuscripts and from Early Church Fathers who cite the letter. As with Paul's other letters, scholars discuss the possible influence of the early heretic Marcion on causing some of the textual variants.

Doctrinal Content

Summary Commentary

1:1–4 Paul opens his Letter to Titus and the churches on Crete with a greeting that asserts his authority, recaps God's plan for salvation, and notes his personal bond with Titus.

1:5–3:11 Step by step, Paul outlines the requirements for those who wish to lead as stewards of God's Church. Then he turns his focus to the false teachers, who do not measure up in understanding or teaching the truth, in their corrosive behavior, or in their motives. Self-controlled, godly living is beneficial regardless of our age or status in life, and it is important to our family relationships as well as to our witness as a Christian. God brings us out of sin and into new life in Christ, beginning with the cleansing and rebirth He provides in Baptism. This is all accomplished by the Father, Son, and Holy Spirit, not by anything we can do on our own. Those who stray away from God's truth and stir up division among God's people must be disciplined by the Church.

Titus 3:4–7 presents one of the most compelling statements about justification in the New Testament, describing God's benefits to us in Holy Baptism through His Holy Spirit.

3:12–15 Paul's closing remarks mention four co-workers who, with him, spread the Gospel and minister to churches in various locations. Paul and the others could not perform such ministries without the help of other Christians, so his closing includes instructions for their support.

Specific Law Themes

Paul charges Titus with being above reproach so that he may commend the pure and rebuke the defiled. He emphasizes the need for submissiveness among God's people in their various circumstances of life. Believers must devote themselves to good works.

Specific Gospel Themes

The doctrine of election was an important element of Paul's message to Titus, for his comfort. As with Timothy, Paul urged the soundness of God's Word and grace for granting spiritual health. Chapter 3 beautifully summarizes the redemption in Christ through the washing and renewal of Holy Baptism. Paul makes justification the basis of the Christian life.

Specific Doctrines

This letter has taken its place alongside 1 and 2 Timothy as a valuable, practical church manual. Its inspired combination of teaching about Jesus Christ with practical guidance serves as a model for Christian pastors.

Key Passages

Luther made frequent reference to Ti 1:2, emphasizing the reliability of God's Word, both the Law and the Gospel. Titus 3:4–7 presents one of the most compelling statements about justification in the New Testament, describing God's benefits to us in Holy Baptism through His Holy Spirit.

Outline

I. Opening Salutation (1:1–4)

II. Body (1:5–3:11)

- A. Appointment and Qualifications of Elders (1:5–9)
- B. Elders' Duty to Refute False Teaching in Crete (1:10–16)
- C. Instructions to Various Groups regarding Christian Living (2:1–10)
- D. Theological Basis for This Christian Living (2:11–15)
- E. General Instructions about Living as Christians in Society (3:1–2)
- F. Theological Basis for This Christian Living Grounded in Holy Baptism (3:3–8)
- G. Final Instructions about Dealing with False Teaching and Teachers (3:9–11)

III. Closing (3:12–15)

- A. Personal Instructions (3:12–14)
- B. Greeting (3:15)

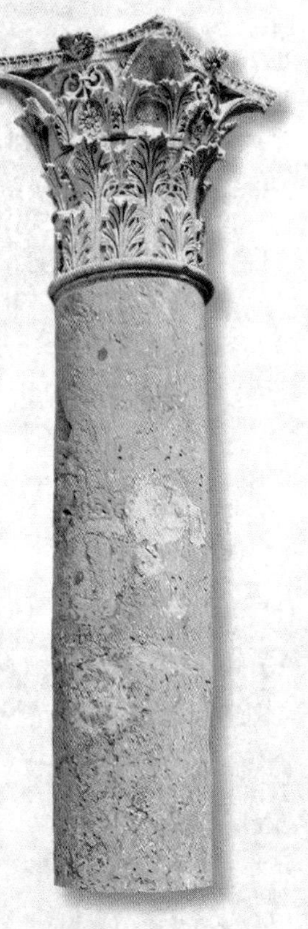

Application

1:1–4 God saves us from sin and condemnation and makes us fit for His kingdom. The only logical response to such love, grace, and generosity is, like Paul, to overflow with His praises and share this joyous news with others. Through Jesus Christ, the Father rescues us from our shortcomings yesterday, today, and tomorrow.

1:5–3:11 As living, active members of God's Church, potential leaders should aspire to know and understand His truth and to serve in the roles He provides. They and their families need to live a godly life that avoids empty talk, deceit, and any teaching that turns away from God's truth. Purity is a tall order, though, and we cannot make ourselves pure. Our lifestyle, relationships, and behavior must not discredit the Gospel. This sets a very high bar, indeed, and one that we cannot reach without a lot of help. However, God trains us for the present time and gives us hope for the future. He redeems and purifies us to make us His children. We are committed and fervent in our beliefs, but we also check ourselves, our words, and our behavior against God's trustworthy Scripture. We pay attention to the guidance, counsel, and teaching of our pastor and elders.

3:12–15 Whether or not we personally work in outreach ministry, we need to support others as they evangelize, teach, and minister in Christ's name. God, who redeemed us with the precious blood of Jesus and saw to it that we received His dear message, will give us opportunities to serve and support others. What a privilege to serve with our brothers and sisters in Christ in God's kingdom!

Canonicity

Like Paul's other biblical letters, which were collected and copied as authoritative already in the middle of the first century AD (cf 2Pt 3:15–16), Titus quickly gained canonical status (*homologoumenon*).

Titus was the apostles' representative to the Christian congregation on the island of Crete.

Lutheran Theologians on Titus

Luther

"This is a short epistle, but a model of Christian doctrine, in which is comprehended in a masterful way all that is necessary for a Christian to know and to live.

"In chapter 1 he teaches what kind of man a bishop, or pastor, ought to be, namely, one who is pious and learned in preaching the gospel and in refuting the false teachers of works and of man-made laws, those who are always warring against faith and leading consciences away from Christian liberty into the captivity of their own man-made works, [as if these works,] which are actually worthless, [should make them righteous before God.]

"In chapter 2 he teaches the various estates—the older, the younger, wives, husbands, masters, and slaves—how they are to act, as those whom Christ, by his death, has won for his own.

"In chapter 3 he teaches Christians to honor worldly rulers and to obey them. He cites again the grace that Christ has won for us, so that no one may think that obeying rulers is enough, since all our righteousness is nothing before God. And he forbids association with the obstinate and with heretics." (AE 35:389–90)

For more of Luther's insights on this book, see *Lectures on Titus* (AE 29:1–90).

Gerhard

"Titus, to whom this Epistle was written, was bishop of the church of Crete, a faithful minister and dear friend of the apostle (2 Cor. 2:13; 7:6). The apostle sent him this Epistle from Macedonia. It has nearly the same theme as 1 Timothy.

"It consists of three chapters and the same number of parts. The first teaches what sort of persons should be elected to the episcopate and diaconate. The second prescribes to individuals their duties. In the third he gives Titus advice about his office.

"But yet, at one time, Marcion rejected these entire Epistles to Timothy and Titus, according to Epiphanius (*Haeres.* 42) and Jerome (commentary on Titus); however, they have always been considered canonical by the common approval of the entire Church. Augustine, *De doctr. Christ.*, bk. 4, c. 16: 'Paul wanted him on whom the persona of a teacher has been imposed in the Church to have always before his eyes these three apostolic Epistles.' " (ThC E1 § 268)

Paul wrote that Titus should "hold firm to the trustworthy word as taught" (1:9).

Further Study

Lay/Bible Class Resources

Guthrie, Donald. *The Pastoral Epistles*. TNTC. Grand Rapids: Eerdmans, 1957. ❧ A helpful resource with emphasis on the exposition of the text. Surveys the various suggestions as to authorship. Holds to Pauline authorship.

Henricks, Michael, Erik Rottmann, and Robert Baker. *Timothy, Titus, Philemon*. Leaders Guide and Enrichment Magazine/Study Guide. LL. St. Louis: Concordia, 2005. ❧ An in-depth, nine-session Bible study with individual, small group, and lecture portions.

Mueller, A. C. *1 and 2 Timothy, Titus: Keeping the Faith*. GWFT. St. Louis: Concordia, 2006. ❧ Lutheran author. Thirteen-session Bible study, including leader's notes and discussion questions.

Schuetze, Armin. *1 & 2 Timothy, Titus*. PBC. St. Louis: Concordia, 2005. ❧ Lutheran author. Excellent for Bible classes. Based on the NIV translation.

Church Worker Resources

Luther, Martin. *Lectures on Titus*. Vol. 29 of AE. St. Louis: Concordia, 1968. ❧ The great reformer's lectures, first published in the twentieth century. Luther treats the Letter to Titus as an exhortation.

Academic Resources

Kelly, J. N. D. *The Pastoral Epistles*. Black's New Testament Commentary. Grand Rapids: Baker, 1981 reprint. ❧ An excellent, less technical resource for the patristic background related to the letters, by the author of Early Christian Creeds and Early Christian Doctrines. Kelly affirms Pauline authorship. He reads 3:5 as a reference to Holy Baptism.

Knight, George W., III. *The Pastoral Epistles*. NIGTC. Grand Rapids: Eerdmans, 1992. ❧ Commentary focused on the Greek text. Evangelical writer supporting Pauline authorship. He provides a very solid and competent treatment of basic exegetical issues. In particular, he does a very good job in arguing that the household code (Grm, *Haustafel*) of 2:1–10 is not simply a culturally contingent expression of first century AD Greco-Roman values. However, he does not read 3:5 as a reference to Holy Baptism.

Lenski, R. C. H. *The Interpretation of St. Paul's Epistles to the Colossians, to the Thessalonians, to Timothy, to Titus, and to Philemon*. Minneapolis: Augsburg, 1961. ❧ A standard resource by a noteworthy Lutheran interpreter, concerned with being faithful to the text and with its implications for today.

Lock, Walter. *The Pastoral Epistles*. ICC. Edinburgh: T&T Clark, 1924. ❧ A concise, helpful resource. However, Lock is uncertain about Pauline authorship.

Marshall, I. Howard. *The Pastoral Epistles*. ICC. Edinburgh: T&T Clark, 1999. ❧ Marshall denies that Paul wrote Titus, but seeks to affirm that Titus is based on authentic Pauline materials. He provides a very solid and competent treatment of basic exegetical issues. However, he does not read 3:5 as a reference to Holy Baptism.

Mounce, William D. *Pastoral Epistles*. WBC. Nashville: Thomas Nelson, 2000. ❧ Thorough argument for Pauline authorship from a well-known evangelical interpreter. Extensive bibliographies. He provides a very solid and competent treatment of basic exegetical issues, though he does not read 3:5 as a reference to Holy Baptism.

Quinn, Jerome D. *The Letter to Titus*. Vol. 35 of AB. New York: Doubleday, 1990. ❧ Quinn denies Pauline authorship. However, he is excellent on lexical issues, the Greco-Roman background, and epistolary features as he displays impressive and useful scholarship. He reads 3:5 as a reference to Holy Baptism, and his treatment of this verse is very helpful.

Towner, Philip H. *The Letters to Timothy and Titus*. NICNT. Grand Rapids: Eerdmans, 2006. ❧ Rejects the categorization of these letters as "pastoral epistles," emphasizing the need to treat each letter individually. Thorough commentary from an evangelical interpreter interacting with recent publications as well as the Greek text.

van Oosterzee, Johannes Jacobus. *Titus*. LCHS. New York: Charles Scribner's Sons, 1868. ❧ A helpful older example of German biblical scholarship, based on the Greek text, which provides references to significant commentaries from the Reformation era forward.

PHILEMON

Receive your brother

Paul's experience under house arrest at Rome is well described by his frequent companion, Luke, in the last chapter of Acts (cf Phm 24). Paul had to pay his own expenses for the house while being allowed to receive guests and to teach them about Jesus, the Messiah. He wrote this letter to Philemon, who lived in Colossae, Asia Minor. One of Paul's prison companions, Epaphras, was also from Colossae.

Historical and Cultural Setting

Epaphras was not Paul's only visitor from Colossae; there was another visitor of quite another kind, a slave named Onesimus (ironically misnamed, as it turned out; Onesimus means "useful"). Onesimus had run away from his master Philemon, lining his pockets for the journey with his master's goods, as was the usual practice of runaway slaves (Phm 18). Somehow he reached Rome, and somehow he came into contact with Paul. Paul converted him and grew very fond of the young slave who now earned the name "useful" in his ready service to Paul (v 11). He would gladly have kept Onesimus with him, and since the master, Philemon, was also a convert of his, he might have made bold to do so. But Paul honored all legitimate ties, including the tie which bound a slave to his master, as hallowed in Christ (Col 3:22; Eph 6:5). He therefore sent Onesimus back to Colossae with Tychicus, the bearer of his Letter to the Colossians (Col 4:7–9), and wrote a letter to Onesimus's master in which he anticipated for the runaway a kindly and forgiving reception. We can measure the strength of the bond between the apostle and his converts by the confidence with which Paul makes his request, a request all the more remarkable in the light of the fact that captured runaways were usually very harshly dealt with. Paul goes even further; he hints that he would like to have Onesimus back for his own service (Phm 13–14; 20–21).

Well-preserved ruins of Roman homes in the recovered city of Pompeii, Italy.

OVERVIEW

Author
Paul the apostle

Date
c AD 60

Places
Likely written at Rome

People
Paul; Timothy; Philemon; Apphia; Archippus; a house church; Onesimus; Epaphras; Mark; Aristarchus; Demas; Luke

Purpose
To reconcile Philemon to his runaway slave, Onesimus, who had become a Christian

Law Themes
Usefulness; imprisonment; service; debt; partnership

Gospel Themes
Comfort/refreshment; reconciliation; forgiveness

Memory Verses
Receive your brother (17–18)

TIMELINE

AD 33	Resurrection of Jesus
AD 57–58	Paul journeys to Rome
c AD 60	Paul writes Philemon
c AD 64	Paul assigns Titus to Crete
AD 68	Martyrdom of Peter and Paul

Composition

Author

The apostle Paul, a Jew from Tarsus who studied under the Rabbi Gamaliel at Jerusalem, was regarded as the author of the letter by early Christians.

Date of Composition

The letter was likely written during Paul's captivity at Rome, c AD 60 (cf Ac 28:30). On the flight of Onesimus and Paul's request for lodging in case he should be released from prison, see pp 534–36.

Purpose/Recipients

Philemon's slave, Onesimus, had run away with stolen money. Somehow he had made contact with Paul in prison and had been persuaded that his duty as a Christian was to return to his master. Paul tactfully urges Philemon, his dear friend, to receive the runaway back "no longer as a bondservant but more than a bondservant, as a beloved brother" (v 16).

A Roman slave necklace with an inscription denoting the owner.

Literary Features

Genre

The Letter to Philemon is, besides 2 Timothy, the only personal letter from Paul that we have—the First Letter to Timothy and the Letter to Titus are official letters. One of the valuable insights that the Letter to Philemon affords is that there is no separation between the official Paul and the person Paul; for both, life has one content and one meaning: "For to me to live is Christ" (Php 1:21).

Characters

Philemon's slave, **Onesimus**, apparently robbed his master and then ran away to Rome. In Rome he came in contact with Paul and became a Christian. Paul persuaded Onesimus to return to Philemon and wrote the Letter to Philemon on Onesimus's behalf (cf Col 4:9).

Narrative Development or Plot

Since Philemon is written as a letter, it does not have a storyline or plot, though it relates elements of Onesimus's story as a runaway slave.

Resources

The letter is evidently not drawn from other texts but from the apostle's heart and experience.

Text and Translations

The text of Philemon is well established through a wealth of early manuscripts and from Early Church Fathers who cite the letter.

Doctrinal Content

Summary Commentary

1–3 Paul begins with a short (compared to his other letters) and yet personal greeting. His greeting begins and ends with Jesus Christ, the focus of Paul's life.

4–22 Paul gives thanks for his friend Philemon's love and faith. Apparently, he has heard enough to know that this is real and not for show. He makes a plea for the freedom of Onesimus and bases his case on grace, love, and friendship.

23–25 Paul mentions five friends who serve with him or support him in the Gospel ministry. This is only part of the network of God's people, which includes Onesimus and Philemon.

Specific Law Themes

Paul describes his imprisonment and suffering for the Gospel as a basis for shaping Philemon's attitude toward his runaway slave. He calls believers to a life of service, to a sense of debt to one another, and he fosters a partnership among people in all estates of life.

Specific Gospel Themes

Philemon offers comfort and refreshment to Paul, as one believer to another. The letter provides for reconciliation and forgiveness between brothers, as the Church is a brotherhood in Christ.

Specific Doctrines

Luther portrays Paul in this letter as being a "Christ" for Onesimus, pleading his cause with his master as if he had no rights; "What Christ has done for us with God the Father, that St. Paul does also for Onesimus with Philemon. For Christ emptied himself of his rights [Phil. 2:7] and overcame the Father with love and humility, so that the Father had to put away his wrath and rights, and receive us into favor for the sake of Christ. . . . For we are all his Onesimus's, if we believe" (AE 35:390). All men are runaway slaves of God! Only such a man who has come back to God as God's runaway slave and has been welcomed like a son—only a man like Paul—can write a letter like the Letter to Philemon.

Roman key.

Personal letter though it is, the Letter to Philemon is an important document to illustrate the early Christian attitude toward social problems. It is noteworthy that Paul does not plead for Onesimus's liberation; whether he stays with Philemon or returns to Paul, Onesimus is to remain a slave. There is nothing like a movement to free slaves, even Christian slaves of Christian masters, either here or elsewhere in the New Testament. But a Gospel which can say to the master of a runaway slave that he is to receive him back "forever, no longer as a bondservant but more than a bondservant, as a beloved brother" (vv 15–16) has overcome slavery from within and has therefore already rung the knell of slavery.

Paul established the essential principle that Christians must regard other Christians as men and women "in Christ," and that this view must override every other question of social status or condition. But it is also true that Paul did not launch a frontal attack on the institution of slavery. Paul's confidence rested in the power of the Gospel, working as a leaven in society through the influence of committed and persistent Christians.

Outline

I. Opening Salutation (vv 1–3)

II. Thanksgiving for Philemon's Faith and Love (vv 4–7)

III. Appeal to Philemon on Behalf of Onesimus (vv 8–20)

IV. Concluding Remarks and Greetings (vv 21–25)

Application

1–3 Focus on Jesus should be present in our own friendships and greetings, both with other Christians and with those who do not yet know the Lord. We have opportunities to introduce people to our Lord and Savior. The Lord's grace and peace will strengthen our faith and equip us for all good service.

4–22 We should consider what people see in our lives, and how it might affect them. God can make our life of faith into an effective witness to Christ's glory. Through the Gospel, He already works effectively in us. Jesus has called us friend; to whom should we extend friendship in His name? As our friend, His grace and love give us salvation and the hope of eternal life.

23–25 Cherish the network of fellowship and support at your church and do not take it for granted. God has called us into His kingdom and made us part of His family, and He will help us and use us to help and encourage one another.

Canonicity

Like Paul's other biblical letters, which were collected and copied as authoritative already in the middle of the first century AD (cf 2Pt 3:15–16), Philemon quickly gained canonical status (*homologoumenon*).

The light of the Gospel was penetrating all levels of imperial Roman society, from the grandest centers of power to the lowly prison cell where Paul shared the Gospel with the runaway slave, Onesimus. Pictured here is the Pantheon in Rome.

Lutheran Theologians on Philemon

Luther

"This epistle gives us a masterful and tender illustration of Christian love. For here we see how St. Paul takes the part of poor Onesimus and, to the best of his ability, advocates his cause with his master. He acts exactly as if he were himself Onesimus, who had done wrong.

"Yet he does this not with force or compulsion, as lay within his rights; but he empties himself of his rights in order to compel Philemon also to waive his rights. What Christ has done for us with God the Father, that St. Paul does also for Onesimus with Philemon. For Christ emptied himself of his rights [Phil. 2:7] and overcame the Father with love and humility, so that the Father had to put away his wrath and rights, and receive us into favor for the sake of Christ, who so earnestly advocates our cause and so heartily takes our part. For we are all his Onesimus's if we believe." (AE 35:390)

For more of Luther's insights on this book, see *Lectures on Philemon* (AE 29:91–105).

Gerhard

"The apostle calls Philemon his 'fellow worker' (v. 1), namely, in preaching the Gospel. From this it appears that he was the minister of the church at Colosse (v. 17). Anselm calls him a bishop; Jerome, an evangelist. The occasion for the writing of this Epistle was this: Onesimus, Philemon's servant, had secretly escaped from his master and had stolen some things from him. He went to Rome, was there converted to the Christian faith, and became a faithful servant to Paul in his imprisonment (Col. 4:9). Wanting to repay this faithfulness, the apostle earnestly intercedes for him with Philemon.

"This treatise is divided into the proposition or explanation of his petition, the confirmation of his petition, and the confutation in which he removes the charge against Onesimus and promises that he himself will make satisfaction for him.

"The Anomoeans held this Epistle in contempt as 'written in human fashion,' as Epiphanius relates (*Haeres*. 76). The devout ancients, however, who list the canonical books of the New Testament, do not omit this Epistle." (ThC E1 § 269)

Roman fresco of a conversation between a family and their slave.

Further Study

Lay/Bible Class Resources

Doyle, Thomas. *Colossians, Philemon: Take a New Look at Christ*. GWFT. St. Louis: Concordia, 1994. ❧ Lutheran author. Thirteen-session Bible study, including leader's notes and discussion questions.

Henricks, Michael, Erik Rottmann, and Robert Baker. *Timothy, Titus, Philemon*. Leaders Guide and Enrichment Magazine/Study Guide. LL. St. Louis: Concordia, 2005. ❧ An in-depth, nine-session Bible study with individual, small group, and lecture portions.

Kuschel, Harlyn J. *Philippians, Colossians, Philemon*. PBC. St. Louis: Concordia, 2004. ❧ Lutheran author. Excellent for Bible classes. Based on the NIV translation.

Life by His Word. St. Louis: Concordia, 2009. ❧ More than 1,500 reproducible one-page Bible studies covering each chapter of the canonical Scriptures. Page references to *The Lutheran Study Bible*. CD-Rom and downloadable.

Wright, N. T. *Colossians and Philemon*. TNTC. Downers Grove, IL: InterVarsity Press, 1987. ❧ Compact commentary based on the NIV but interacting with other English translations. A popular but generally helpful evangelical treatment of the text.

Church Worker Resources

Luther, Martin. *Lectures on Philemon*. Vol. 29 of AE. St. Louis: Concordia, 1968. ❧ The great reformer's comments on Paul's personal letter.

Academic Resources

Bruce, F. F. *The Epistles to the Colossians, to Philemon, and to the Ephesians*. NICNT. Grand Rapids: Eerdmans, 1983. ❧ An up-to-date, invaluable resource.

Lenski, R. C. H. *The Interpretation of St. Paul's Epistles to the Colossians, to the Thessalonians, to Timothy, to Titus and to Philemon*. Minneapolis: Augsburg, 1961. ❧ A standard resource by a noteworthy Lutheran interpreter, concerned with being faithful to the text and with its implications for today.

Lightfoot, J. B. *St. Paul's Epistles to the Colossians and to Philemon*. Grand Rapids: Zondervan, 1957 reprint. ❧ Still a helpful resource; includes the views of some of the Early Church Fathers.

Martin, Ralph. *Colossians and Philemon*. NCBC. Rev. ed. Grand Rapids: Eerdmans, 1981. ❧ An important resource; includes an analysis of the nature of the Colossian heresy, and a careful study of the provenance of these two letters.

Moule, C. F. D., ed. *The Epistles of Paul the Apostle to the Colossians and to Philemon*. Cambridge Greek Testament Commentary. Cambridge: Cambridge University Press, 1957. ❧ Known for its careful study of the Greek text by a master exegete.

Nordling, John G. *Philemon*. CC. St. Louis: Concordia, 2004. ❧ Most thorough commentary on the Greek text from a Lutheran theologian and classicist. The best resource available.

O'Brien, Peter T. *Colossians, Philemon*. WBC. Waco, TX: Word, 1982. ❧ Includes a full discussion of the pros and cons of debated matters, such as that of authorship, the setting of the letter, and the like.

van Oosterzee, Johannes Jacobus. *Philemon*. LCHS. New York: Charles Scribner's Sons, 1868. ❧ A helpful older example of German biblical scholarship, based on the Greek text, which provides references to significant commentaries from the Reformation era forward.

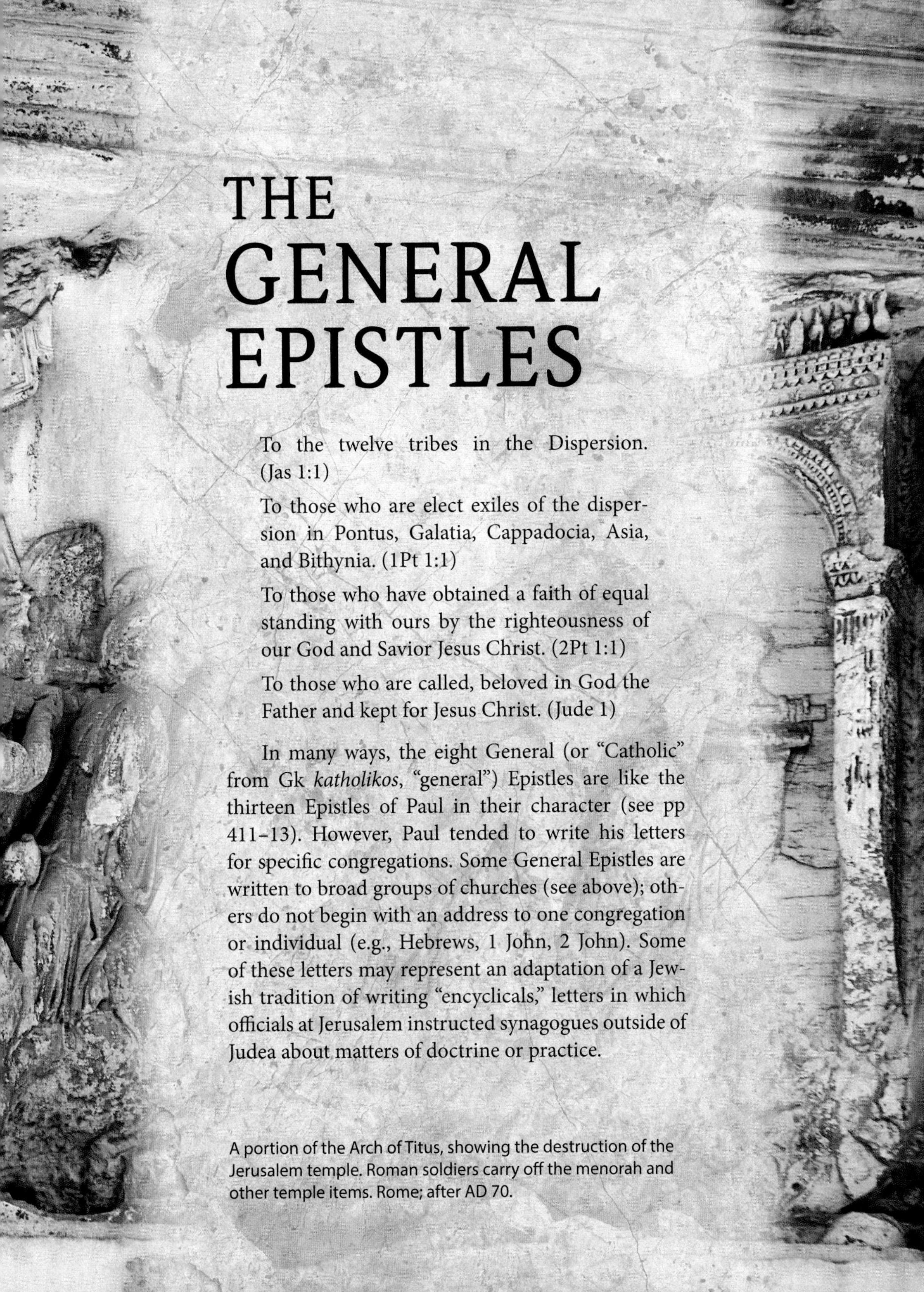

THE GENERAL EPISTLES

> To the twelve tribes in the Dispersion. (Jas 1:1)
>
> To those who are elect exiles of the dispersion in Pontus, Galatia, Cappadocia, Asia, and Bithynia. (1Pt 1:1)
>
> To those who have obtained a faith of equal standing with ours by the righteousness of our God and Savior Jesus Christ. (2Pt 1:1)
>
> To those who are called, beloved in God the Father and kept for Jesus Christ. (Jude 1)

In many ways, the eight General (or "Catholic" from Gk *katholikos*, "general") Epistles are like the thirteen Epistles of Paul in their character (see pp 411–13). However, Paul tended to write his letters for specific congregations. Some General Epistles are written to broad groups of churches (see above); others do not begin with an address to one congregation or individual (e.g., Hebrews, 1 John, 2 John). Some of these letters may represent an adaptation of a Jewish tradition of writing "encyclicals," letters in which officials at Jerusalem instructed synagogues outside of Judea about matters of doctrine or practice.

A portion of the Arch of Titus, showing the destruction of the Jerusalem temple. Roman soldiers carry off the menorah and other temple items. Rome; after AD 70.

The apostle John wrote letters of instruction and encouragement as well as the Gospel that bears his name. Sixth-century mosaic; Ravenna, Italy.

The Collection of the General Epistles

The General Epistles have a different history from other books of the New Testament. The Pauline Epistles were brought together as a unit very early in the history of the Church, as Papyrus manuscript 46 shows (c AD 200; the Book of Hebrews was often grouped with the Pauline Epistles, see pp 651–53). The Gospels, too, were brought together as a "Gospel Book," sometimes with Acts (e.g., Papyrus 45, third century AD). The General Epistles were also brought together—typically with Acts—but this collection formed much later (e.g., Gk ms E, sixth century AD; Papyrus 74, seventh century AD).

The collection of the General Epistles was probably a matter of convenience. Since the Gospels and the Pauline Epistles formed natural collections, the remaining books were also brought together over time. This collection of the General Epistles as a unit probably took longer because they came from a variety of authors. Also, in some regions, church leaders were not convinced about the authenticity of all the letters.

Disputes over the General Epistles

Before studying the General Epistles, readers should gain some understanding of their history in the life of the Church. In the fourth century AD, when Eusebius wrote his *Church History*, he distinguished between "agreed-upon" writings (Gk *homologoumena*) and "spoken-against" writings (Gk *antilegomena*) in the General Epistles. Eusebius made this distinction based on whether or not a letter was universally received and used in the churches. Never disputed in the Early Church, 1 Peter and 1 John were received in the same way as the Pauline Epistles (see above; see also pp 411–13).

> Among the disputed writings, which are nevertheless recognized by many, are extant the so-called epistle of James and that of Jude, also the second epistle of Peter, and those that are called the second and third of John, whether they belong to the evangelist or to another person of the same name. (*NPNF*2 1:156)

Elsewhere, Eusebius pointed out that Hebrews and Revelation were disputed (*NPNF*2 1:134, 156).

During the Reformation, Luther and others had the difficult task of reviewing all these matters and making decisions about what books would be published in new editions of the Bible. Regarding the General Epistles, Luther noted in his preface to Hebrews:

> Up to this point we have had [to do with] the true and certain chief books of the New Testament. The four which follow [Heb, Jas, Jude, Rv] have from ancient times had a different reputation. . . . We should not be deterred if wood, straw, or hay are perhaps mixed with [the works of the apostles; cf 1Co 3:12], but accept this fine teaching with all honor; though, to be sure, we cannot put [Hebrews] on the same level with the apostolic epistles. Who wrote [Hebrews] is not known, and will probably not be known for a while; it makes no difference. We should be satisfied with the doctrine that he bases so constantly on the Scriptures. For he discloses a firm grasp of the reading of the Scriptures and of the proper way of dealing with them. (AE 35:394–95)

Luther considered the books based on their history, their qualities as literature, and their use in the life of the Church. First, note that Luther accepted the Epistles of Peter and John without hesitation. Also note that Luther added some distinctions to those made by Eusebius. Luther distinguished between (1) writings that were clearly from apostles and represented apostolic doctrine (Grm *apostolisch*) and (2) writings that had disputed authorship and focused on the Law rather than on Christ (see pp 690–91). (3) Finally, Luther emphasized the importance of doctrine based "constantly on the Scriptures" over against issues of authorship or literary style.

Vulgate and English Bibles	Erasmus's New Testament and Luther Bibles
Hebrews	1 Peter
James	2 Peter
1 Peter	1 John
2 Peter	2 John
1 John	3 John
2 John	Hebrews
3 John	James
Jude	Jude
Revelation	Revelation

Based on his review of the General Epistles, Luther ordered the books differently than what we find in English Bibles. He placed the most disputable books last. Luther's order is still found in modern editions of the German Bible.

With characteristic vigor, Luther pointed out what he believed were weaknesses in Hebrews, James, Jude, and Revelation. But with characteristic conservatism, Luther also kept them in the New Testament, cited them as authoritative, and preached from them. He held within himself a freedom to critique books of Scripture as literature, yet to honor them as God's Word. The Epistle that caused Luther the most trouble was James. On that history, see pp 690–91. To learn more about how books were recognized as Holy Scripture, see pp 6–10.

Studying the General Epistles

The history of the General Epistles should not overwhelm or trouble students of Holy Scripture. Read, mark, learn, and inwardly digest these letters just as you would any other book of Scripture. The Lutheran Church has received them as books of the New Testament and as God's very Word.

However, learn also from the example of history—these books have confused some students of Scripture in the past. In Luther's day, James was the book that led to the most confusion. In our day, Revelation is hotly disputed and horribly misinterpreted. Disputed books should not be among the first books a Christian studies. Be certain that you have a clear understanding of the Gospels, Acts, the Pauline Epistles, 1 Peter, and 1 John before taking up any disputed books of the General Epistles. The great Lutheran theologian Johann Gerhard put it this way:

> For the sake of instruction, therefore, we can distinguish between canonical books of the New Testament of the first rank and of the second rank [*primi et secundi ordinis*]. Canonical books *of the first rank* are those about whose authors or authority there has never been any doubt in the Church but have always been considered canonical and divine by unanimous agreement. Such are the Gospels of Matthew, Mark, Luke, and John; the Acts of the Apostles; Paul's letter to the Romans, the two to the Corinthians, one to the Galatians, one to the Ephesians, one to the Philippians, one to the Colossians, two to the Thessalonians, two to Timothy, one to Titus, one to Philemon; 1 Peter; and 1 John. Canonical books *of the second rank* are those about whose authorship some in the Church had doubts at some time. Such are the Epistle to the Hebrews, the letters of James and Jude, 2 Peter, 2 and 3 John, and Revelation. . . . Augustine, *De doctr. Christ.*, bk. 2, c. 8: "The catechumen will maintain this method concerning the canonical writings: that he will prefer those that all the churches accept to those that some do not accept." (ThC E1 § 242)

IC

HEBREWS

Jesus, the founder and perfecter of our faith

The title "To the Hebrews" is not part of the original letter itself, but was probably added in the second century when the New Testament letters were gathered into a collection. Moreover, there is no salutation which identifies the readers. The destination of the letter must therefore be inferred from the letter itself.

Historical and Cultural Setting

Where these Jewish Christians lived cannot be definitely made out. Italy is the most likely place, and within Italy, Rome. The letter contains greetings to the church from "those who come from Italy" (Heb 13:24), evidently from members of the Jewish Christian Church who are now with the author and are sending greetings to their home church. This is confirmed by the fact the Letter to the Hebrews is first quoted and alluded to by Roman writers, namely Clement of Rome and Hermas. These readers have their own assembly (10:25) but are also connected with a larger group, as the words "greet *all* your leaders and *all* the saints" (13:24; emphasis added) indicate. It has therefore been very plausibly suggested that the recipients of the Letter to the Hebrews were one of the house churches to which Paul refers in his Letter to the Romans (Rm 16:5, 14–15).

Mosaic of Jesus Christ in Hagia Sofia, Istanbul, Turkey; sixth century AD.

OVERVIEW

Author
Unknown; see "Author" below

Date
Before AD 70

Places
The temple; Jerusalem (Salem); Italy

People
"Us" (writer and colleagues); brothers; leaders; martyrs; high priests; "those who serve the tent"; travelers from Italy; Timothy; numerous biblical figures

Purpose
To exhort the brothers, washed with pure water and partaking of the altar, that Christ is their High Priest and all-sufficient sacrifice for sin

Law Themes
Retribution for disobedience; slavery to death and the devil; an unbelieving heart; rebellion; obligation to sacrifice; repentance from dead works; crucifying Jesus again; the living God's vengeance; struggle against sin; discipline; obedience to leaders

Gospel Themes
God spoke through Jesus; purification for sins; inheriting salvation; our High Priest and Mediator; sanctification; God's promises; Melchizedek; sprinkled and washed; assurance of faith; the founder and perfecter of our faith; the great Shepherd

Memory Verses
God spoke through His Son (1:1–4); God's living Word (4:12–13); Christ's blood purifies us (9:13–14); faith defined (11:1–3); run with endurance (12:1–2)

TIMELINE

AD 33	Resurrection, Ascension, Pentecost
AD 49	Jerusalem Council
AD 68	Martyrdom of Peter and Paul
AD 70	Romans destroy Jerusalem
AD 96	Clement of Rome cites Hebrews

These Christians had in the past given evidence of their faith and love (Heb 6:10). They had stoutly endured persecution and had courageously aided others under persecution (10:32–34). Their believing courage had not failed them in times of crisis, but it was failing them in the long-drawn, unending struggle with sin (12:4). They were growing dispirited and slack (12:12); the continuous pressure of public contempt, particularly the contempt of their fellow Jews (13:13), had revived in them the old temptation to be offended at the weakness of the Christ they believed in, at His shameful death, and at the fact that the Christ did not fulfill their Judaic expectation and "remain forever" on earth (cf Jn 12:34) but was removed from sight in the heavens. They had ceased to progress in their faith (Heb 5:11–14) and were neglecting the public assembly of the church, which could strengthen them in their faith (10:25). Some had perhaps already apostatized (6:4–8); all were in danger of falling away (3:12) and reverting to the old faith (13:9–14). Judaism—with its fixed and venerable institutions, its visible and splendid center in the Jerusalem temple and its worship, its security and exemption from persecution as an approved religion under Roman law—must have had for them an almost overwhelming fascination.

Composition

Author

The letter does not name its author, and there is no consistent tradition in the Early Church concerning the authorship. In the East, the letter was regarded either as directly written by Paul or as in some sense owing its origin to Paul. Origen of Alexandria reflects this tradition; he says of the letter: "Its thoughts are the thoughts of the apostle, but the language and composition that of one who recalled from memory and, as it were, made notes of what was said by the master. . . . Men of old times handed it down as Paul's. But who wrote the epistle God only knows certainly." The Western Church did not attribute the letter to Paul; Tertullian of Carthage assigned it to Barnabas, while in Rome and elsewhere the letter was anonymous.

The fact that the author counts himself and his readers among those who received the word of salvation at second hand from those who had heard the Lord is conclusive evidence that the author is not Paul (Heb 2:3), for Paul appeals repeatedly to the fact that he has seen the Lord and has received the Gospel directly from Him (1Co 9:1; 1Co 15:8; Gal 1:11–12). The general character of the theology of the letter and the author's acquaintance with Paul's companion Timothy (Heb 13:23) point to someone who moved in the circle of Paul's friends and co-workers. The characteristics of the letter itself further limit the possibilities, indicating that the author was in all probability a Greek-speaking Jewish Christian, thoroughly at home in the Old Testament in its Greek translation, and intimately acquainted with the whole worship and cultus of the Jews, a man capable, moreover, of the most finished and literary Greek in the New Testament. Barnabas, the Levite from Cyprus (Ac 4:36) and companion of Paul, would be a likely candidate for authorship. Whether Tertullian attributed the letter to him on the basis of a genuine tradition or was making a plausible conjecture cannot be determined. Apollos, whom Luther suggested as the possible author, is even more likely. He was associated with Paul, though not in any sense a "disciple" of Paul, and Luke describes him as a Jew, a native of that great center of learning and rhetoric (Alexandria), an eloquent man, well versed in the Scriptures, and "fervent in spirit" (Ac 18:24–25), all characteristics that we find reflected in the Letter to the Hebrews.

Luther's conjecture remains the most reasonable of all the ancient and modern conjectures, which have attributed the letter to a great variety of authors—Luke, Clement of Rome, Silvanus, Aquila and Priscilla, Priscilla alone, etc. But Origen's word still holds: "Who wrote the epistle, God only knows certainly." More important than the man's name is the kind of man he was—an earnest teacher of the church, deeply conscious of his responsibility, whom the Holy Spirit moved to employ all his resources of language and learning in order to restore to health and strength the weak and faltering church.

Date of Composition

Since Clement of Rome quotes Hebrews in his Letter to the Corinthians of AD 96, the letter must be earlier than that date. There is no evidence that enables us to determine exactly how much earlier the letter was written. Timothy is still alive at the time of writing (Heb 13:23), but since he was a young man when Paul first took him as his companion in AD 49 (Ac 16:1–3), he may have lived to the end of the first century or beyond. The readers have been converted by personal disciples of the Lord (2:3), and a considerable time has elapsed since their conversion: they have had time for development and growth (5:12). Some of their first leaders are now dead (13:7). They have endured one persecution (probably the Neronian persecution; AD 54–68) and are apparently facing another (10:36). All this points to the latter half of the first century. Since the author dwells on the fact that the old system of priesthood and sacrifice was destined to be superseded by a greater and more perfect priesthood and sacrifice, it would seem strange that he does not mention the fall of Jerusalem (which put an end forever to the old cultus) if that event had taken place. The argument from silence is strong in this case, and a dating before AD 70, probably shortly before, seems very probable. But it should be said that many scholars today are not inclined to attach much weight to this argument; they argue that the author is thinking not of the Jerusalem temple and its worship, but of the worship practices as he knows them from the Old Testament, and date the letter somewhere in the 80s.

Purpose/Recipients

Many modern scholars are inclined to see in the readers not Jewish Christians in danger of relapsing into Judaism, but Gentile Christians (or Christians in general) in danger of lapsing into irreligion. And they have often argued their case with considerable ingenuity. But it is difficult to see why the letter should in that case be from beginning to end one great and emphatic exposition of the superiority of the New Testament revelation over that of the Old Testament. Why should an appeal to *Gentile* Christians in danger of apostasy take just this form? Jewish Christians seem more likely to be the recipients of the letter.

The purpose of Hebrews is practical, like that of every book of the New Testament. Its aim is to strengthen faith and hope, to inculcate stout patience and a joyous and resolute holding fast to the Christian confession. The message that provides the basis for the exhortation and the impetus and power for the fulfillment of the exhortation has three primary characteristics: (1) it is founded on the Old Testament; (2) it is centered in Christ; and (3) it is marked by an intense consciousness of the fact that all days since the coming of the Christ are last days.

Literary Features

Genre

The Letter to the Hebrews is not so personal as a letter of Paul's. It is more on the order of a sermon (cf 13:22, "my word of exhortation"), and it is more literary, with its high stylistic finish and its strictly unified theme. Still, it is not merely an essay in letter form, but a genuine letter. It grows out of a personal relationship between the author and his readers. The author has lived among the people whom he is now addressing, and though he is at the time of writing separated from them, he hopes to be restored to them soon (13:18–19, 23). The content of the letter indicates that these readers were

Outline

The pastoral intent of the writer dictates the structure of his letter; instruction alternates regularly with admonition, warning, and appeal. The indicatives that expound the surpassing significance of Christ as God's last word to mankind are always followed by the imperatives that summon people to heed that word.

I. Introduction/Theme: Christ Is the True and Final Revelation of God (1:1–3)

II. Jesus' Superiority (1:4–10:18)

- A. Over the Angels (1:4–2:18)
- B. Over Moses (3:1–4:13)
- C. Superiority of Jesus' Priesthood: Jesus, the New Melchizedek (4:14–7:28)
- D. Superiority of Jesus' Sacrifice (8:1–10:18)

III. Exhortation to Faithfulness (10:19–12:29)

- A. Invitation to Faithfulness (10:19–39)
- B. Old Testament Examples of Faith: Following in the Faith of Our Fathers (ch 11)
- C. Jesus as the Ultimate Example of Faithfulness (12:1–13)
- D. Warning against Disobedience, Using Old Testament Examples (12:14–29)

IV. Final Exhortations (13:1–19)

V. Blessings and Greetings (13:20–25)

Jewish Christians, so that the title given by the men of the second century is fitting.

The letter is therefore basically just what its author calls it, a "word of exhortation" (13:22), an appeal to "hold fast the confession . . . without wavering" (10:23; cf 10:38; 3:14). The author points his readers to Jesus and urges them to look to Jesus, "the founder and perfecter of our faith, who for the joy that was set before Him endured the cross, despising the shame, and is seated at the right hand of the throne of God" (12:2). They are to consider Him with the eyes of faith and find in Him the strength to overcome their weariness and faintheartedness (12:3). The whole long and detailed exposition of the high priesthood of Christ is anything but a merely informative theological treatise. It is wholly pastoral and practical in its aim and intent. The author is a leader like the leaders whom he describes in his letter (Heb 13:17); he is keeping watch not over the theology of his people, but over their souls, as one who will have to give an account of his leadership.

Place of the Old Testament

The message is, first, founded on the Old Testament. It is to a large extent an interpretation and exposition of Old Testament Scriptures. It has been likened to a Christian sermon or a series of sermons on selected Psalms (Pss 2, 8, 95, 110). The letter therefore contains high testimony to the inspiration and authority of the Old Testament. In the first verse, the whole Old Testament is designated as the very voice of God speaking to mankind, and throughout the letter, words that men of God spoke of old are presented as spoken by God Himself (e.g., Heb 1:5, 6, 13; 5:5) or by Christ (e.g., 2:11–13; 10:5–7) or by the Holy Spirit (3:7–11; 10:15–17).

Typology

The author's characteristic use of the Old Testament is that which has been termed the typological use; that is, he sees in the history and the institutions of the old covenant events, persons, and actions which are typical, foreshadowings and prefigurings of that which was to become full reality in the new covenant. In one sense the whole epistle is a set of variations on a theme from Paul: "These [the Old Testament sacral institutions] are a shadow of the things to come, but the substance belongs to Christ" (Col 2:17). Thus Melchizedek, both priest and king, is divinely designed to point beyond himself to the great High Priest Jesus Christ (Heb 7:1–10:18). The fate of God's people in the wilderness, their failure to attain to the promised Sabbath rest, points beyond itself to the eternal Sabbath rest that awaits the New Testament people of God (3:7–4:13). This view and use of the Old Testament

Sixth-century mosaic showing the sacrifices by the priest-king, Melchizedek of Salem. The center of the altar has bread and wine. On the left, Abel offers a lamb. On the right, Abraham offers Isaac.

never degenerates into mere allegory; that is, the Old Testament figures are never merely symbols of eternal truths, as in the allegorizing interpretation of the Jewish philosopher Philo. Rather, the Old Testament history is always taken seriously as history. As history, it points beyond itself to the last days. This use of Scripture is therefore an eloquent expression of the faith that God is Lord of all history, shaping all history for His purposes and leading all history toward His great redemptive goal. The Old Testament is therefore of abiding value and enduring significance for the people of God in the last days, for it enables them to see the whole sweep and direction of the mighty redeeming arm of God.

Christ, the Son of God

The message is, secondly, centered in Christ. Christ, the Son of God, dominates the whole, and Christ colors every part of the whole. He stands at the beginning of history as the Son through whom God created the world; He stands at the end of all history as the divinely appointed "heir of all things" (1:2). He dominates all history and rules the whole world, "uphold[ing] the universe by the word of His power" (1:3). He is God's ultimate and definitive word to mankind (1:2), and His high priestly ministry is God's ultimate deed for mankind—a whole, assured, eternal deliverance from sin. That high priestly, atoning ministry spans the whole of Jesus' existence: His entry into mankind, His sacrificial suffering and death, His entering into the heavenly Most Holy Place, His presentation of His sacrifice at the throne of God, and His return in glory to the waiting people of God are all high priestly acts (e.g., 2:17–18; 4:14; 9:11–14; 9:28).

His high priestly ministry marks Him as full partaker in the Godhead and as completely one with mankind. Indeed, no letter of the New Testament is so full of the humanity of Jesus as the Letter to the Hebrews. Since Jesus is both Son of God and a Priest fully one with mankind, His priesthood and His sacrifice have a real and eternal significance, and top and supersede every other priestly ministration. The impression of the incarnate Christ is upon His people; His history of suffering and triumph is their history; His obedience and fidelity to the Father make possible their faithful obedience to God. His entering into the Holy Place gives them access to the throne of God.

The Last Days

The message is, third, marked by the consciousness that the days since God spoke in His Son are "these last days" (Heb 1:2). Christ has appeared "at the end of the ages to put away sin by the sacrifice of Himself" (9:26). It is the beginning of the end; the new world of God has become a reality in the midst of the old, and people "have tasted . . . the powers of the age to come" (6:5) even now. What former ages had possessed in an imperfect form, a form that itself pointed to a fuller realization, is now a present blessing—a better covenant (7:22), better sacrifices (9:23), a better possession (10:34), and a better hope (7:19). People still hope, and the full realization of all that Christ has wrought is still to come. But the day is drawing near (10:25) when all that is now a sure hope shall be fully realized. This "last days" character of Jesus' work (its eschatological character) gives it a final, once-for-all character and makes the decision of faith one of terrible urgency; eternal issues are being decided now, in faith or unbelief. Seen in this light, the sternness of the warnings in 6:4–8 and 10:26–31, warnings that at first glance seem to preclude the possibility of a second repentance, is not strange. (These warnings seemed to Luther to be "hard knots" and made him dubious about the letter.) God has spoken His last word, and the time is short; people must not be left under the delusion that they can coolly and deliberately sin and then repent in order to sin again. Such sinning is the last step on the way toward apostasy; it is the expression of an "evil, unbelieving heart" (3:12) that cannot find the way to repentance because it has deliberately cut itself off from God, the Giver of repentance.

Characters

See "Christ, the Son of God," under Genre above.

Narrative Development or Plot

Since Hebrews is written as a letter, it does not have a storyline or plot. However, ch 11 does extensively recount the lives and faith of God's people as models of faith for the recipients of the letter.

Resources

As noted above, much of the letter's content may come from a sermon on various aspects of the Old Testament, with ch 13 added as the author's letter-conclusion.

Text and Translations

The text of Hebrews is well established through a wealth of early manuscripts dating as early as c AD 200 (Papyrus 46) and from Early Church Fathers who cite the letter. It was often included in the collection of Pauline Epistles.

Doctrinal Content

Summary Commentary

Ch 1 Jesus, through whom the Father created all things, and by whose Word all things are sustained, clearly reveals the gracious will of the Father to us. Although Jesus is heavenly like the angels, He is no mere creature.

Ch 2 Christians need God's Word, spoken by Jesus and attested by those who heard Him. The Father and the Holy Spirit also bear witness. Jesus, as true man, willingly humbled Himself to taste death. As resurrected Lord, and as our firstborn Brother (v 11), He serves as our High Priest to intercede for us before the Father.

3:1–4:13 Though Moses was a faithful servant in God's household, Jesus is the faithful Son. God's people missed rest in the Promised Land through their unbelief. This is a warning to us.

4:14–6:20 Jesus Christ, our true High Priest, shares our humanity and knows the weaknesses that we experience. Being one with the Father, He is the source of God's full forgiveness. Christians grow in maturity by building on the basic teachings of the faith and connecting God's promises with the new way of life that He gives. Those who reject God's promises should fear the just judgment of God. As heirs of Abraham, those who trust in Christ Jesus share in the blessing of life promised to Abraham. They experience unending stability and security through the Son's gracious access to the Father.

Ch 7 Melchizedek, both priest and king, showed the true nature of his authority by receiving tithes from the patriarch Abraham and blessing him. As both king of righteousness and king of peace, Melchizedek foreshadowed Christ's work of justification. Though the Levitical priesthood could not bring the fullness of God's salvation, Jesus, the sinless and perfect Priest, serves eternally as the One who brings our needs to the Father.

An ancient baptistry of an early church in the Negeb south of Israel.

8:1–10:18 The old covenant, because it could not permanently address the problem of sin, would "vanish away." As Priest, Christ came to establish an everlasting covenant and atonement for our sins. The Holy Place of the tabernacle was a picture of the old covenant and the old sacrificial system. But the Most Holy Place was a picture of heaven and of Christ's new covenant. Christ will come from His heavenly sanctuary and take us to Himself with joy. Christ offered up only one sacrifice for the sins of the world—Himself. He "perfects" or completes us by applying the benefits of His sacrifice to us in Holy Baptism and in His Holy Supper.

10:19–12:29 All Christians need patience through many sorrows. God calls us to do His will, bearing our crosses patiently, and He equips us with His Word and Spirit. Faith trusts even without sight what God has set forth in His Word. True faith is active in love and is steadfast under persecution. The Christian life is an endurance race, run with remembrance of the saints who have already finished. God sees you as holy through Christ's sacrifice and disciplines you to struggle against sin. The unpleasant discipline shows that the Lord loves you as a true child. The Son of God's speaking and presence are the center of worship.

Ch 13 To obtain pure hearts, Christ sacrificed Himself on the cross. By His blood, shed on the cross, Jesus our Shepherd redeemed us and made us well-pleasing to His Father. Hebrews sets forth God's grace in Christ, earned on the cross, ratified in the new covenant, and distributed in Word and Sacrament.

Specific Law Themes

Drawing heavily upon Old Testament teachings and examples, the writer to the Hebrews describes the thoroughness of the Law's retribution for disobedience. The fear of punishment and death results in a lifelong slavery. Unbelieving, rebellious hearts still feel the need to sacrifice and to appease God's wrath against them. In contrast, God calls all sinners to repent of their dead works and false worship. Believers, too, are called to continue in a life of daily repentance lest they fall from grace and crucify Jesus again in their rejection of Him as the only Savior. God's vengeance against sin is real; He calls us to struggle against sin, to live in discipline and obedience.

Specific Gospel Themes

The writer to the Hebrews opens with a distinctly Christ-centered message to his readers: God spoke through Jesus and sent Him to purify us from our sins. We inherit salvation through our great High Priest and Mediator, who sanctifies us with His blood. God is faithful to His Old Testament promises as the example of Melchizedek shows us, whose ministry foreshadowed the eternal priesthood of Jesus. We are sprinkled and washed in the blood of Jesus, who grants us assurance of faith. Indeed, He is the perfecter of our faith, the great Shepherd of our souls.

Specific Doctrines

The Letter to the Hebrews is surely a part of the story of how the Word of the Lord grew and prevailed. Here if anywhere in the New Testament we are made conscious of the fact that God's speaking is a mighty onward movement, an impetus of revelation which is designed to carry people with it from glory to glory. And here it is impressed upon us that if a person resists that impetus, he does so at his own deadly peril; we are warned that stagnation and retrogression invite the destroying judgment of God. But the letter is itself also the proof that God does not abandon the weak and sickly stragglers of His flock; He sends forth His Word and heals them.

The Holy Spirit descending on Mary and the apostles.

In Hebrews, several Old Testament passages are directly ascribed to the Holy Spirit as author. Thus when Psalm 95:7–11 is quoted, the passage is introduced by the words "As the Holy Spirit says" (cf Heb 3:7; cf 10:15). Many more passages of like tenor could be mentioned, but those that we have cited should suffice to show that, according to the New Testament, the Old Testament writings owe their origin to God, particularly to the Holy Spirit.

Also here one could add the great themes listed above under "Genre": typology, Christology, and the last days. These are all major themes of the book and of Christian doctrine.

Key Passages

The opening verses of Hebrews have contributed to our understanding of both Christ and the Holy Trinity (1:1–4), distinguishing Jesus from all other beings, including the most glorious angels. The letter is especially focused on Jesus' unique role as a sinless High Priest, sympathizing with our weaknesses while giving us confidence that we will receive mercy in the Father's presence (4:14–16). Such confidence is likewise fostered through the Sacrament that Christ instituted for cleansing our hearts and minds: Holy Baptism (10:22). This allows us to approach the Lord with our prayers, trusting by faith in Him. Faith is the topic of ch 11, a great catalog of the faithful. Interpreters have focused especially on the teachings of 11:4–6, which teaches that righteousness is received through faith, without which it is impossible to please God. Faith leads to the fulfilling of God's Law through acceptable worship and good works. In another popular passage, marriage is briefly commended through a firm teaching of the Sixth Commandment (13:4).

Application

Ch 1 Jesus is the firstborn Son of the Father, who shares with us all that the Father has. He frees us to receive God's ministry, including the ministry given through the angels.

Ch 2 Ignoring God's revelation of how to be saved is frightening. Jesus gives the Church pastors, teachers, and other leaders to spread the Word. He likewise gives us brothers and sisters to encourage us in our life of faith. He will always provide all that is needed to receive the gift of life. Without a Savior, we would live in slavery to the fear of death. But Jesus has taken the consequence of our sin and removes our fear. Knowing our weaknesses, He will always help us when we are tempted.

3:1–4:13 Since Jesus calls you to your heavenly home, you can be confident that you will share in God's glory. However, be careful not to boast of your own faithfulness. Only God is holy and righteous. In Christ, you freely share in God's holiness. He is calling you to glory. God calls us to trust Him and to enter into the rest that He has enjoyed since the completion of creation. In Christ Jesus, we have rest from the accusation of the Law. The Holy Spirit leads us to trust in Christ, granting us everlasting peace.

4:14–6:20 If we approach God confident in our own goodness, we will be condemned according to the strictness of the Law. But Christ Jesus is gentle and understanding. He forgives us, gives us confidence before the Father, and helps us in all our needs. If we fail to be fruitful in love, mercy, and generosity, we become like thorns and thistles, fit only for His fire. However, we can be confident that God, who has given us the gift of salvation, will grow the fruit of the Spirit in our lives. If we doubt God's Word, we act as if God were a liar and miss the blessings that flow from a trusting relationship with Him. As we trust God's promises, we see that God tells the truth, and we share in the blessings of eternal life.

Ch 7 As Abraham gave offerings and respect to Melchizedek, greater respect is due to our High Priest, Christ. He serves without end to lead us into His kingdom. In Him we have access to God's blessings. His perfect work reminds us that death will always cut short even the best effort that anyone makes to serve God. However, Jesus freely brings us God's eternal blessings through His sacrificial death.

8:1–10:18 Old Testament services pointed ahead to Christ, while New Testament services celebrate His work, distribute His benefits, and anticipate His return. Christ is the true Priest who sacrificed Himself to reconcile us to the Father. Our greatest joy should be Jesus and His priestly ministry, for

He delighted in us, making us the heirs of His last will and testament. Whenever you study the Word or hear it at church, expect the Lord to change your life and strengthen your faith, for He desires to change your heart and mind by grace.

10:19–12:29 God has promised eternal salvation to all who steadfastly confess Christ. By His resurrection, Christ conquered death and now provides His Holy Spirit to strengthen us. But most of all, we look to Jesus and His cross. In Him, our race is already won. Put your faith into practice by encouraging others and by doing works of service. The Lord is ever serving you, granting repentance, taking away your sins, and equipping you for a godly life. When God the Son spoke the Law, His people were terrified. But His sprinkled blood speaks better things to us: forgiveness, life, and salvation.

Ch 13 Instead of sacrificing bulls and goats, we should offer up true speech about God to praise Him and do good works to serve our neighbor. These sacrifices please God when they come from hearts trusting in Christ. We should pray for ourselves and others that God would equip us for all good works to do His will. By His blood, shed on the cross, Jesus our Shepherd redeemed us and made us well-pleasing to His Father. By holding

Marble statue depicting Jesus as the Good Shepherd; early Byzantine.

fast to the teaching of this sermon and by receiving God's grace through faith, we have fellowship with the writer of Hebrews and all the saints, and look forward to our inheritance with them in heaven.

Canonicity

Churches of the Eastern Roman Empire (Greek- and Syriac-speaking) have always welcomed Hebrews as part of the New Testament. However, the anonymity of the sermon and some challenging content limited its approval for public reading in churches of the Western Roman Empire. Yet, the book was highly regarded (e.g., cited by Clement, bishop of Rome, c AD 96), and by the fourth century, it became part of the Western canon of Scripture. Nevertheless, it is classified among the books spoken against (*antilegomenon*).

Stained glass window depicting the Ascension of Christ.

Lutheran Theologians on Hebrews

Luther

In Luther's preface to Hebrews, cited below, he reflects some of the historic concerns raised about the book, which was not at first universally received as an apostolic letter or as a book of Holy Scripture. Though Luther notes the book's "hard knots" and "straw" weaknesses, he elsewhere cites Hebrews as authoritative teaching (e.g., AE 2:393; 4:405–9; 35:247; 37:293). He sees the Holy Spirit bearing witness through the book (AE 2:387; 20:292) and refers to it as "Holy Scripture" (AE 41:19; cf 2:294). The Lutheran Confessions cite Hebrews as God's Word alongside other texts of Holy Scripture (e.g., FC Ep I 5). For more about the book's canonicity, see p 665.

"The author of the Epistle to the Hebrews—whoever he is, whether Paul or, as I think, Apollos—quotes [the Old Testament] most learnedly." (AE 8:178)

"If you would interpret [the Books of Moses] well and confidently, set Christ before you, for he is the man to whom it all applies, every bit of it. Make the high priest Aaron, then, to be nobody but Christ alone, as does the Epistle to the Hebrews [5:4–5], which is sufficient, all by itself, to interpret all the figures of Moses. Likewise, as the same epistle announces [Hebrews 9–10], it is certain that Christ himself is the sacrifice—indeed even the altar [Heb. 13:10]—who sacrificed himself with his own blood. Now whereas the sacrifice performed by the Levitical high priest took away only the artificial sins, which in their nature were not sins, so our high priest, Christ, by his own sacrifice and blood, has taken away the true sin, that which in its very nature is sin. He has gone in once for all through the curtain to God to make atonement for us [Heb. 9:12]. Thus you should apply to Christ personally, and to no one else, all that is written about the high priest." (AE 35:247–48)

"Up to this point we have had [to do with] the true and certain chief books of the New Testament. The four which follow have from ancient times had a different reputation. In the first place, the fact that Hebrews is not an epistle of St. Paul, or of any other apostle, is proved by what it says in chapter 2[:3], that through those who had themselves heard it from the Lord this doctrine has come to us and remained among us. It is thereby made clear that he is speaking about the apostles, as a disciple to whom this doctrine has come from the apostles, perhaps long after them. For St. Paul, in Galatians 1[:1], testifies powerfully that he has his gospel from no man, neither through men, but from God himself.

"Again, there is a hard knot in the fact that in chapters 6[:4–6] and 10[:26–27] it flatly denies and forbids to sinners any repentance after baptism; and in chapter 12[:17] it says that Esau sought repentance and did not find it. This [seems, as it stands, to be] contrary to all the gospels and to St. Paul's epistles; and although one might venture an interpretation of it, the words are so clear that I do not know whether that would be sufficient. My opinion is that this is an epistle put together of many pieces, which does not deal systematically with any one subject.

"However that may be, it is still a marvelously fine epistle. It discusses Christ's priesthood masterfully and profoundly on the basis of the Scriptures and extensively interprets the Old Testament in a fine way. Thus it is plain that this is the work of an able and learned man; as a disciple of the apostles he had learned much from them and was greatly experienced in faith and practiced in the Scriptures. And although, as he himself testifies in chapter 6[:1], he does not lay the foundation of faith—that is the work of the apostles—nevertheless he does build well on it with gold, silver, precious stones, as St. Paul says in I Corinthians 3[:12]. Therefore we should not be deterred if wood, straw, or hay are perhaps mixed with them, but accept this fine teaching with all honor; though, to be sure, we cannot put it on the same level with the apostolic epistles.

"Who wrote it is not known, and will probably not be known for a while; it makes no difference. We should be satisfied with the doctrine that he bases so constantly on the Scriptures. For he discloses a firm grasp of the reading of the Scriptures and of the proper way of dealing with them." (AE 35:394–95)

For more of Luther's insights on this book, see *Lectures on Hebrews* (AE 29:107–241).

Gerhard

In describing the Letter to the Hebrews, Gerhard occupies himself with two issues: (1) the canonical character of the book, and (2) whether the apostle Paul wrote the book. For both topics, Gerhard quotes extensively from ancient and Reformation era authorities, as well as his contemporaries. Rather than cite all this material, included below are Gerhard's conclusions on these two topics.

"We show our agreement with this latter position and claim that the Epistle to the Hebrews is (1) a letter of Paul himself; (2) canonical, but it is of the second rank because some people in the Church once had doubts about it; (3) written in Greek.

"Clement of Alexandria (*Stromat.*, bk. 4), Eusebius (*Hist. eccles.*, bk. 3, c. 32), Jerome (*Catal. script. illustr.*), and certain others of the ancients think that it was written in Hebrew and was translated into Greek by Luke or Barnabas. We think, however, that it is more likely that Paul himself wrote it in Greek: (1) Because the Greek language at that time was familiar to most Jews, especially to those who were living in Asia Minor. (2) Since Peter and James wrote their Epistles addressed to the scattered Jews in Greek, it is likely that Paul did the same thing. (3) Since Paul wrote all the rest of his Epistles in Greek, it is likely that in this Epistle, too, he used the same character of speech followed by the canonical books of the New Testament. (4) With this Epistle, the apostle wanted to advise not only the Hebrews but also other nations, among whom the Greek language was in use. (5) The style and diction of this Epistle have the flavor of Greek eloquence, not of Hebrew. (6) Had the Epistle been written in Hebrew, Hebraisms ought to appear here and there in the Greek translation. Hebraisms, however, are less frequent in this Epistle than in the rest. (7) There is no ancient writer who testifies that he saw a Hebrew copy of this Epistle. (8) The Old Testament Scriptures are quoted in it not according to the Hebrew sources but according to the Septuagint translation. (9) The Hebrew name Melchizedek is translated as 'king of righteousness' and Salem as 'peace.' This, however, in no wise fits, if he wrote in Hebrew. (Cf. Franciscus Junius, *Paral.*, bk. 3, on c. 9 of this Epistle, p. 479.)

"The subscript shows that it was sent from Italy through Timothy. Chrysostom adds that it was written from prison in Rome.

"Athanasius explains the theme of this Epistle in his *Synopsis* in this way: 'Because the Jews were devoting themselves to the Law and its shadows, for this reason the apostle Paul became the teacher of the Gentiles and was sent to the Gentiles to preach the Gospel to them. When he had written to all the Gentiles, now, finally, he writes also to all the Hebrews—those of the circumcision who had believed. He writes to them this Epistle that is filled with statements and proofs of the coming of Christ and the Law's shadow, which Christ's coming brought to an end.' Thomas notes: 'This Epistle was written against the errors of certain people who, after their conversion from Judaism to faith in Christ, wanted to observe the legal matters of the Old Testament along with the Gospel, as if the grace of Christ were not sufficient for salvation.' The aim and sum of the entire Epistle consists in this: that Jesus Christ, true God and true man, was promised in the Old Testament and revealed in the New as the Messiah, the only prophet, priest, and king of the Church; that He was foreshadowed by the Levitical ceremonies; that by Him the entire Church of God must be illumined and sanctified; that embracing His Gospel by faith, we should produce fruits worthy of the Gospel.

"It consists of thirteen chapters in which are discussed (1) Christ and His person and office; (2) the duties of Christians by which they must show their gratitude to their Redeemer, to which pertains also patience, which must be shown in persecutions suffered because of Christ." (ThC E1 § 278)

Questions People Ask about Hebrews

Impossible to Restore to Repentance

Hebrews 6:4, 6 says: "For it is impossible, in the case of those who have once been enlightened, . . . and then have fallen away, to restore them again to repentance."

Matthew 18:21–22 records Peter asking: " 'Lord, how often will my brother sin against me, and I forgive him? As many as seven times?' Jesus said to him, 'I do not say to you seven times, but seventy-seven times.' "

Jesus' answer to Matthew implies that there is every opportunity for repentance when someone falls away. However, Heb 6 seems to say that it is impossible to restore a brother who has fallen away.

How important it is that we understand the basis for this encouragement in Hebrews not to fall away from faith in Christ but to continue to grow in Him. There is a frightful end in store for those who hear the Good News again and again but do not believe in Jesus and follow Him. Those who believe in Jesus but then fall away and repudiate Him, the crucified Messiah, have no alternative means to repent and be saved. In rejecting Jesus, such people are "crucifying once again the Son of God" (Heb 6:6); they are repeating the same act of rejecting Jesus as those who actually nailed Him to the cross.

So long as they continue to crucify God's Son "once again" and subject Him to "contempt" by denying Him in whom they once believed, they cannot find a new way to repent and be saved. Of course, the moment they stop crucifying Jesus anew—as soon as they repent and put their trust in Him once again—they will be forgiven. The eagerness of God to receive back repentant sinners is illustrated in Jesus' memorable parable of the prodigal, or lost, son in Lk 15:11–32.

The point of Heb 6:4–6 is to warn wavering Christians not to persist in a refusal to acknowledge faith in Jesus, in a failure to draw near to God through Him. This would be absolutely the wrong response to the Word revealed from heaven. The short parable of verses 7–8 makes that clear.

Was Esau Not Permitted to Repent?

Hebrews 12:17 reads: "For you know that afterward, when he desired to inherit the blessing, he was rejected, for he found no chance to repent, though he sought it with tears."

Second Peter 3:9 affirms: "The Lord is . . . not wishing that any should perish, but that all should reach repentance."

It is the earnest will of God that all should repent, says the one text. The other seems to say that even though Esau wished to repent, he found no chance, that is, no opportunity, for repentance. A careful study of Heb 12:17 will show that we are not dealing with a real discrepancy here. The Greek word for repentance literally means a change of mind or heart. If we translate the passage from Hebrews literally, it reads: "For you know that afterwards also, when he wished to inherit the blessing, he was rejected; for he did not find room for a change of heart, although he sought it [namely, the change of heart] with tears." The mind that Esau wished to see changed was that of his father. The Genesis account indicates this very clearly (Gn 27:36–38). When Esau said to his father, "Have you not reserved a blessing for me?" the reply was, "Behold, I have made [your brother] lord over you. . . . What then can I do for you, my son?" Then Esau said to his father, "Have you but one blessing, my father? Bless me, even me also, O my father!" "And Esau," we read, "lifted up his voice and wept." The father had given the blessing to Jacob. To make the father change his mind and become willing to take away the blessing from Jacob or at least to give an equally glorious one to Esau, that was the object of the latter's entreaties and tears, and this change of mind he did not succeed in bringing about. If Esau longed for the change of his own heart, he certainly found it. We may agree with Luther in the opinion that Esau did repent and was saved. Hebrews 12:17, then, does not speak at all of repentance in the sense of seeing one's sinfulness and becoming a believer in Christ, and thus it does not contradict the great comforting Gospel truth that God's heart is yearning for the repentance of every sinner.

Further Study

Lay/Bible Class Resources

Grothe, Jonathan, Arnold Kuntz, Robert Smith, and Terry Small. *Hebrews*. Leaders Guide and Enrichment Magazine/Study Guide. LL. St. Louis: Concordia, 2005. ❧ An in-depth, nine-session Bible study with individual, small group, and lecture portions.

Guthrie, Donald. *The Epistle to the Hebrews: An Introduction and Commentary*. TNTC. Grand Rapids: Eerdmans, 2002. ❧ Comments on the Christological emphases of Hebrews.

Kramin, Howard. *Hebrews: The Fulfillment of Faith*. GWFT. St. Louis: Concordia, 1996. ❧ Lutheran author. Twelve-session Bible study, including leader's notes and discussion questions.

Lauersdorf, Richard E. *Hebrews*. PBC. St. Louis: Concordia, 2005. ❧ Lutheran author. Excellent for Bible classes. Based on the NIV translation.

Life by His Word. St. Louis: Concordia, 2009. ❧ More than 1,500 reproducible one-page Bible studies covering each chapter of the canonical Scriptures. Page references to *The Lutheran Study Bible*. CD-Rom and downloadable.

Church Worker Resources

Brown, Raymond. *Christ Above All: The Message of Hebrews*. Downers Grove, IL: InterVarsity Press, 1982. ❧ Brown was among the leading scholars of the day, but he writes as a man of the Church. He is very easy to understand, and a good conversation partner when you get stuck in your own thinking.

Luther, Martin. *Lectures on Hebrews*. Vol. 29 of AE. St. Louis: Concordia, 1968. ❧ The great reformer's lectures from 1517–18, early in his career, after posting the Ninety-five Theses. The lectures extend through Heb 11:26, omitting comment on the end of the book.

Academic Resources

Attridge, Harold. *Hebrews: A Commentary on the Epistle to the Hebrews*. Hermeneia. Philadelphia: Fortress, 1989. ❧ Of all the scholarly commentaries on Hebrews, this is probably the best. Attridge is particularly helpful in showing the literary and theological setting of the sermon, and in the exploration of the work's Christology.

Bruce, F. F. *The Epistle to the Hebrews*. NICNT. Grand Rapids: Eerdmans, 1990. ❧ A helpful resource, carefully expounding the many analogies drawing heavily on the Old Testament and their fulfillment in Christ (typology).

Buchanan, George Wesley. *To the Hebrews*. AB. 2nd ed. New York: Doubleday, 1972. ❧ Buchanan treats the epistle as a "homiletical midrash" and is adept at bringing out the many Old Testament allusions in Hebrews.

Ellingworth, Paul. *The Epistle to the Hebrews*. NIGTC. Grand Rapids: Eerdmans, 1993. ❧ Well worth consulting due to undeniable scholarship. Ellingworth seeks to make clearer the relationship between God and Christ.

Hagner, Donald A. *Hebrews*. New International Biblical Commentary on the New Testament. Peabody, MA: Hendrickson, 1990. ❧ Divided into thematic sections; brief and to the point. Keeps in mind the Christological emphasis of Hebrews. Used best as a supplemental resource.

Hughes, Philip Edgcumbe. *A Commentary on the Epistle to the Hebrews*. Grand Rapids: Eerdmans, 1987. ❧ Heavy in theological emphasis and the role of Hebrews in church history; language rather complex.

Koester, Craig R. *Hebrews*. Vol. 36 of AB. New York: Doubleday, 2001. ❧ This commentary is among the best of the most recent. Koester sees the sermon as forming a community of the faithful. Still, he does not see it as a Eucharistic community, and therefore misses the presence of Christ in the worship that is being described.

Lane, William L. *Hebrews*. 2 vols. WBC. Dallas: Word, 1991. ✠ This is a good example of solid, evangelical scholarship, though Lane is often overly technical and grammatical. His work is good for reference because of its thoroughness and serious attention to the text. As with much evangelical scholarship, it does not take seriously enough the churchly setting of the work.

Lenski, R. C. H. *The Interpretation of the Epistle to the Hebrews and the Epistle of James*. Minneapolis: Augsburg, 1966. ✠ A lucid exposition with emphasis on the Christological content of the writer of Hebrews. Careful attention to typology.

Moffatt, James. *A Critical and Exegetical Commentary on the Epistle to the Hebrews*. ICC. Edinburgh: T&T Clark, 1924. ✠ Helpful because of its philological emphasis. Use with discernment.

Moll, Carl Bernhard. *The Epistle to the Hebrews*. LCHS. New York: Charles Scribner's Sons, 1868. ✠ A helpful older example of German biblical scholarship, based on the Greek text, which provides references to significant commentaries from the Reformation era forward.

Montefiore, H. W. *The Epistle to the Hebrews*. Black's New Testament Commentaries. New York: Harper & Row, 1964. ✠ Holds that Hebrews was addressed to the Church at Corinth. Includes helpful introductory articles with stress on Apollos as the most probable author, with careful attention to typology. Use with discernment.

VanHoye, Albert. *Structure and Message of the Epistle to the Hebrews*. Rome: E. Pontificio Instituto Biblico, 1989. ✠ VanHoye's work shows the liturgical function of the sermon to the Hebrews.

Westcott, Brooke Foss. *The Epistle to the Hebrews: the Greek Texts with Notes and Essays*. 2nd ed. Grand Rapids: Eerdmans, 1973. ✠ Although somewhat dated, still a helpful resource with special reference to the Greek and the Early Church Fathers.

JAMES

Steadfast under trial

In the Letter of James, we see most clearly how constant and severe the struggle for renewal of strength and purpose must have been among the first Christians. The high qualities of this new life were not the once-for-all and static possession of the Church. They had to be constantly reclaimed and reasserted in repentance under the implanted Word of the Lord. The letter also shows how vigorously the leaders of the Judaic churches aided those churches in that struggle, with what agonized and conscientious consecration they strove to keep the Word once implanted in the Church implanted and active in the hearts of the members of the Church. We see what a concentrated energy of inspired pastoral wisdom, "wisdom from above," went into the human word that ensured the growth of the Word of the Lord and gave it firm and deep roots in the lives and words and deeds of people.

The Letter of James shows us more clearly than the Book of Acts another important feature in the life of the Early Church: how thoroughly apostolic the "apostles' teaching" (Ac 2:42) was—the mark of the apostle is that he is the voice and the representative of the Lord who sent him (Mt 10:40; Lk 10:16; Jn 13:20; 2Co 13:3), and we can see in the Letter of James how the very words of Christ were the basic substance of the apostolic teaching, the air that the Early Church breathed and lived by.

Fragment of plaster found in the destruction of a Herodian era house in Jerusalem, depicting the menorah that stood in the temple.

OVERVIEW

Author
James, brother of the Lord

Date
c AD 50

Places
The "Dispersion"

People
James; "the twelve tribes in the Dispersion"; rich and poor church visitors and believers; sick Christians; elders of the Church

Purpose
To impart the Lord's wisdom to the congregations dispersed among the Gentile nations

Law Themes
Must keep the whole Law; death; works required for salvation; sinners judged by Law as transgressors; faith apart from works is dead

Gospel Themes
Good and perfect gifts from the Father of lights; brought forth by the Word of truth; heirs of the Kingdom; counted righteous; the coming of the Lord, compassionate and merciful; forgiveness; because of Christ's death and resurrection, sinners are judged under the "law of liberty"

Memory Verses
The crown of life (1:12); the Father of lights (1:16–17); the tongue (3:1–12); fervent prayer (5:13–18)

TIMELINE

AD 33	Resurrection, Ascension, Pentecost
AD 41	Martyrdom of James, brother of John
AD 49	Jerusalem Council
AD 62	Martyrdom of James, brother of the Lord
AD 70	Romans destroy Jerusalem

Historical and Cultural Setting

All manner of theories have been advanced to account for the Judaic and Christian aspects of the letter. Some scholars, for instance, have suggested that the letter is really a Jewish writing lightly worked over to make it Christian, or that it incorporates an earlier Jewish work with Christian additions and modifications. Such theories are, of course, almost purely conjecture and do not carry us any further toward understanding the epistle in a really historical sense. One fruitful suggestion that has a solid basis in the facts of James's history is the following: James was a brother of Jesus and had witnessed Jesus' work, but had not come to faith in Him until he was confronted by Him as the risen Christ, the "Lord of glory" (Jas 2:1). After his conversion, James worked in Jerusalem and sought to win Israel for the Christ and therefore kept the Church of Jerusalem within the framework of Judaism; he stayed in Jerusalem and confronted Jerusalem with the Christ until his countrymen killed him.

This history turned James away from all speculative wisdom and from everything that smacked of generality and theory. He saw in Jesus' death and resurrection that he, James, with his ideas about God and Christ, had been in the wrong and that Jesus, who wholly loved God in word and deed, in life and in death, was in the right. He had seen how the "wise and understanding" (3:13) of his people had rejected Jesus because their theoretical knowledge about God had blinded them to God's presence and God's action in Jesus before their very eyes and in their very midst. And James saw that because Israel's teachers and leaders thought they knew what the Messiah should be, they persisted in rejecting the Messiah proclaimed by the apostles and so led their people to refuse Him. James had learned, both in his own life and in the life of his people, how thoroughly a presumptive knowledge of God can lead a person astray and turn someone from God as He actually reveals Himself.

What James held fast as the best and dearest possession that Jesus had left him was Jesus' call to repentance, that call which condemned Israel's pride and Israel's religious hypocrisy and proffered Israel God's grace. Only by repentance (which in Jesus' proclamation always includes faith) can someone come to God. The Church can remain the 12 tribes of God's people only by repentance; it can hope to win Israel only as a perpetually repentant Church, as the Church that itself heeds Jesus' call of "Repent, for the kingdom of heaven is at hand" (Mt 4:17). James taught his readers to heed and live it in the whole compass of the Church's life—for only so will Judaism be brought to see that God is in the midst of the Church.

Composition

Author

The only indications of authorship in the letter itself are (1) the name James in the salutation and (2) the general tone and character of its content. If we ask which of the various men named James in the New Testament could expect to be recognized and identified when he calls himself simply "James, a servant of God and of the Lord Jesus Christ" (1:1) and could speak with such massive authority to Judaic Christianity as he does in this writing, the most probable answer is James, the brother of the Lord. (The much debated question whether the brethren of the Lord were His cousins, half brothers, or full brothers need not detain us here. The last alternative, that they were the children of Joseph and Mary, would seem to be the most probable; that they were His half brothers is possible; the theory that makes them His cousins is beset by almost insuperable difficulties.)

Pomegranate coin used in Israel at the time of the Great Revolt (AD 68). The text is in ancient Hebrew script.

James had, like his brothers, refused to accept his brother as the Christ during His lifetime (Jn 7:5). It was apparently not until the risen Lord appeared to James that his doubts were overcome and he became the servant of Him whom he henceforth called "the Lord Jesus Christ" (cf 1Co 15:7; Ac 1:13–14). Active in the life of the Church from the beginning, he seems to have confined his work to Jerusalem. Possibly he undertook missionary journeys within Israel, like his brothers (1Co 9:5, which refers to the missionary travel of others). At any rate, it was in Jerusalem that he became and remained prominent. As early as AD 44, he was the acknowledged leader of the Jerusalem Church, as Peter's words in Ac 12:17 show: about to leave Jerusalem after his deliverance from jail, Peter bids the people assembled in Mary's house to tell of his release and departure "to James and to the brothers." At the Apostolic Council, the voice of James is the final and decisive voice in the discussion (Ac 15:13–29). When Paul at the end of his third missionary journey reports to the Jerusalem Church and brings the gifts of the Gentile Church to the saints at Jerusalem, he reports to James (Ac 21:18–19). The picture we have of James in Acts is confirmed by what we find in the letters of Paul, who can refer to him simply as "James" and reckon on being understood (1Co 15:7); he practically ranks him with the apostles in Gal 1:19, and even mentions him before Peter and John as one of the "pillars" of the Church (Gal 2:9). James is, for Paul, so integral a part of the life of the Jerusalem Church that he can describe Jerusalem Christians who came to Antioch by saying, "Certain men came *from James*" (Gal 2:12). Jude can in his letter identify himself to his readers by calling himself "brother of James" (Jude 1).

A later Jewish-Christian tradition preserved for us by Eusebius (*NPNF*2 1:125–26) pictures James as a paragon of Judaic piety in the sense that he was deeply interested in, and devoted to, the ritual side of that piety; but none of the New Testament notices of him confirms this. He is, according to the New Testament, a Christian Jew, devoted to his mission to Israel and therefore faithful to the temple and to the Law so long as the temple stands and there is an Israel that will hear him. Reliable tradition has it that he was faithful to his people to the end and died a martyr's death in c AD 62. So strongly had his piety and his love for his people impressed men that even pious Jews called him "the Just" and saw in the Jewish wars and the fall of Jerusalem God's righteous visitation upon Israel for putting this righteous man to death.

Theories and Arguments Denying Authorship by James

The theories can be roughly divided into two classes. According to one, James's letter is viewed as an earlier Jewish writing, worked over and Christianized by a later writer, not James the brother of the Lord. According to the other theory, the letter is considered to be a Christian work of the late first century or the first half of the second century, written either by an otherwise unknown James or by someone who wanted to have his work accepted as the work of James the brother of the Lord. These theories are highly conjectural and need not detain us long.

The specific arguments used to disprove the authorship of James the brother of the Lord are of greater concern. They are chiefly the following:

a. The absence of an early and definite tradition assigning the letter to James the brother of the Lord.
b. The absence of any emphasis on ritualism in the letter—the fact that there is no mention of circumcision, the Sabbath, clean and unclean food, etc.
c. The absence of concrete references to Jesus' history and Messiahship.
d. The high quality of the Greek employed in the letter.

As for (a): It may be admitted at once that the ancient tradition that assigns the letter to James is not very early (c AD 200) or very strong, whatever the reason may be. But if the evidence in tradition is relatively slight, it must also be noted that there is no evidence whatever for anyone else as author, so that the tradition must be allowed to stand until conclusive reasons for denying the letter to James can be advanced.

With regard to (b): The absence of any reference to ritualism is not by any means conclusive evidence against the authenticity of the letter. There is nothing in the New Testament evidence to indicate that James was a rabid ritualist who could not speak to the Church without touching on circumcision and the like. Indeed, the fact that he gave Paul "the right hand of fellowship" (Gal 2:9) and his words in Ac 15:13–21 would seem to indicate that James, while he earnestly sought to keep Judaic Christianity Judaic in order not to forfeit its missionary opportunity in Israel, had no particular interest in Judaic ritual as such. The picture of James as a passionate devotee of ritual stems from second-century heretical Jewish-Christian sources, which moreover tend to discredit themselves by their fanciful and legendary character.

Ruins of Sepphoris, a hellenized city near Nazareth where Jesus and James grew up.

With regard to (c): The absence of concrete and clear references to Jesus' history is more serious. James does, of course, state the Messiahship and Lordship of Jesus in emphatic and weighty terms (Jas 1:1; 2:1), and the fact that his work is permeated by the words of Jesus must be allowed due weight. But when we ask why James should have said this much and no more, we can only guess in answer. Theoretically, it is highly unlikely that the apostle Paul, who said, "for to me to live is Christ" (Php 1:21), should have written a whole chapter on love without once referring explicitly to Christ as the very embodiment and the sole source of that love. And yet Paul has done just that in 1Co 13.

With regard to the fourth argument, (d), the allegation that the Greek employed in the letter (correct, cultured, eloquent, and in some respects literary rather than popular) is impossible for a Galilean Jew, it must be remembered that such verdicts can never be certain. They might be more certain if we knew just what Greek James heard in Galilee and in Jerusalem, what Greek books he read or heard quoted, what kind of mind and memory James had—was it perhaps one like Shakespeare's, which sponged up and retained everything once heard, seen, or felt, and retained it with remarkable fullness and fidelity? We can point to the following facts: Greek was widely used in Galilee, with its many Hellenistic cities; Jesus no doubt knew Greek. According to Acts, Greek was so commonly known in Jerusalem that Paul might have addressed the mob at the temple court in that tongue; they were both surprised and pleased when Paul spoke Aramaic (Ac 22:2). The Jerusalem Church had a component of Greek-speaking Jews in it from the very beginning (6:1). If James wished to address Christian Jews outside Jerusalem and outside Israel, he could address them only in Greek if he wished to be understood by all. For James the brother of the Lord, leader of the Jerusalem Church and head of Judaic Christendom, Greek was a natural and necessary second language. It is precarious to make assertions as to how well or how ill he may have spoken it.

This winter storm is part of the "early . . . rains" James and other Israelite writers describe.

Arguments Supporting Authorship by James

On the other hand, the authenticity of the letter is strongly supported by (a) the simplicity of the self-designation, James (1:1); a later writer seeking to impersonate James would almost certainly have emphasized the fact that he was the brother of the Lord. (b) The free way in which the words of Jesus are used in the letter; a later writer would more probably have drawn upon the Gospels and have quoted more directly. (c) The points of agreement in language and thought between the letter and the speech of James (and the letter that he suggested) at the Apostolic Council (Ac 15:13–21, 23–29); this argument is not, of course, in itself conclusive, but it is remarkable that within the limited scope of the few sentences in Acts the points of contact with the letter of James should be so many (e.g., the use of "name," Jas 2:7; 5:10, 14 with Ac 15:14, 17, 26; the use of "brother," Jas 2:5 with Ac 15:13; the use of "keep," Jas 1:27 with Ac 15:29). (d) The peculiarly Israelite coloring of a number of expressions in the letter: "the early and the late rains," specific to Israel's agriculture (Jas 5:7) and "three years and six months" as the duration of the drought invoked by the prayer of

Elijah (5:17; the account in 1Ki 17:1 and 18:1 does not speak so precisely). Jesus, too, uses the same expression with reference to this drought in Lk 4:25. It seems to be not a popular exaggeration of the Old Testament narrative, but a popular Israelite expression for "a couple of" (as the half of seven, the number of completeness).

Date of Composition

The letter is apparently addressed to Judaic Christians of the early days, during the period covered by Ac 1–12. The Church is still firmly enmeshed in Judaism, a part of historic Israel, so much so that one modern scholar has argued that the letter is addressed to *all* Israel, stressing all that Christians and Jews have in common, and is intended to be a missionary appeal, by way of admonition and a call to repentance, to all Jews. Although this theory amounts to an overstatement of the case and can hardly be accepted in the form in which it is advanced, it does call attention to the essentially Judaic character of the persons addressed, and it recognizes the fact that there are portions in the letter that address the readers particularly as members of historic Israel. Judaism may not yet have definitively expelled the new community. Furthermore, there is no indication in the letter of the tensions and difficulties that arose when Gentiles came into the Church in large numbers, those tensions that eventually gave rise to the Apostolic Council (Ac 15) and occasioned Paul's Letter to the Galatians. A date prior to Paul's first missionary journey is therefore most probable, c AD 50; and the phrase "twelve tribes of the dispersion" is intended to designate the new people of God at a time when it consisted primarily and predominantly of converted Jews.

Purpose/Recipients

The Letter of James is addressed to Jewish Christians. The words of the salutation, "To the twelve tribes in the Dispersion" (Jas 1:1), in themselves do not necessarily mark the readers as Jewish, since the New Testament constantly appropriates the titles and attributes of Israel for the New Testament people of God (cf Gal 6:16; Php 3:3; 1Pt 1:1, 17; 2:9–10; Rv 7:4; 14:1); but these words are part of the generally Judaic coloring of the letter. The situation presupposed among the Christians addressed in the letter—that of a poor, tired, oppressed, and persecuted Church—corresponds to what we know of the Jerusalem Church of Ac 1–12; and what held for Jerusalem very probably held for other Jewish churches in Israel and in the Dispersion also. The sins that the letter particularly deals with are the sins of Judaism in their Christianized form; the problem of sexual license, for instance, that looms so large in Gentile Christianity and is constantly dealt with in letters addressed to Gentile churches, is not touched on here, while the prime sin of Israel under the leadership of scribe and Pharisee, that of cleavage between profession and practice (Mt 23:3), which evoked Jesus' most stringent polemics, is scored heavily by James. The place of worship is called by the same name as the Jewish synagogue (Jas 2:2; "assembly" translates Gk *synagoge*), a practice that was long observed in Judaic Christianity, but was never frequent elsewhere in Christendom. The author takes all his examples from the Old Testament (Abraham, Rahab, Job, the prophets, Elijah), and this tells us something about the readers as well as the author.

Byzantine era Jewish synagogue in Capernaum. Synagogues were naturally the first places where Christian teaching spread.

The Epistle of James shows that the author is acquainted with the situation of his readers, but no reference is so specific that it enables us to point to any particular event or set of circumstances as the immediate occasion for writing. Still, it is probably not accidental that the epistle opens with a summons to find cause for joy in "trials of various kinds" (1:2) and closes with an admonition to restore the brother who "wanders from the truth" (5:19). The "twelve tribes" are under the twin pressures of poverty and persecution; they are tempted to grow depressed, bitter, and impatient—depressed at the fate of the doomed people of which they remain a part, a fate that loomed ever more clearly and more terribly against the stormy skies of Israel; bitter at the fact that they are offering the grace of God in vain to this doomed people; and impatient for the "times of refreshing" and the restoring of all things (Ac 3:19–21), which the resurrection of Jesus Christ from the dead had promised and assured.

They were tempted, in this apathetic slackening of their energies, this decrease in their Christian stamina, to relapse and accommodate their life to the life of the world that pressed on them from every side and sought to put its mark and impress upon them. For them, accommodation to the "world" meant, of course, accommodation to the Judaism from which they had escaped, Judaism with its distorted piety, its encrusted and inactive faith, its superficial and fruitless hearing of the word, its arrogant and quarrelsome "wisdom," its ready response to the seduction of wealth, its mad thirst for liberty. The danger of apostasy was for members of this Church anything but remote and theoretical; it was immediate and real (Jas 5:19–20).

In such a situation, in a Church beset from without and within, faced with the necessity of constant correction and discipline, it is small wonder that the love of many grew cold, that the Church was troubled by inner dissensions, that men were ready to speak against and to judge one another, that the spontaneous mutual ministrations of the first glad days were in danger of lapsing and being forgotten.

Literary Features

Genre

To these Judaic churches in this characteristically Judaic situation, the leader of Judaic Christianity addressed a thoroughly Judaic letter, or rather, a homily in letter form. The letter is a letter chiefly in form—and even the letter form is not complete; the personal conclusion, characteristic of Paul's letters, is absent here. A phrase such as "Listen, my beloved brothers" (2:5) shows that we have to do with a writing that is simply the extension of the spoken "implanted word"; and the whole style of the letter bears this out. The leader and teacher whose word is the vehicle of the will of God to the Jerusalem church is speaking to the Judaic churches in Judea, Samaria, Galilee, Syria, Cilicia—perhaps the letter went even further afield than that.

The "miscellaneous" character of James's admonitions has often been exaggerated, sometimes in the interest of theories concerning the origin of the book. This miscellaneous character is more apparent than real, being due to the Semitic habit of thought that sets down related thoughts side by side without explicitly coordinating them or subordinating one to the other as we are accustomed to do. James's call to repentance breaks down, upon closer investigation, into six rather massive units, each of which again usually has two aspects.

Content and Form

Two things stand out at once as characteristic of this letter; it is practical in content and poetic in form. Both these qualities put the work of James into the literary classification of the Christian "psalm." Paul speaks briefly of this form of edifying speech in 1Co 14:26 and more fully in Eph 5:19 and Col 3:16. In the first passage, the psalm (or "hymn," as the ESV translators have rendered it) is coupled with "a lesson" over against three other forms of utterance that are clearly very closely related to one another: "a revelation, a tongue, or an interpretation." The purpose of all these is "building up," or edification (1Co 14:26). Since Paul goes on to regulate the utterance of revelation, tongue, and interpretation in the interest of an orderly and edifying worship by the congregation (1Co 14:27–31), we may assume that both the psalm and the lesson (to which he devotes no further attention) were less problematic. This is confirmed by the other two passages, in which the psalm appears as a form of inspired teaching and admonition "in all wisdom" (Col 3:16), in which Christians admonish one another. The psalm, it would seem, was a poetic form of the "word of Christ" (3:16) that addressed itself particularly to the practical problems of Christian living, as the immediate context of the passages in both Ephesians and Colossians shows (3:12; 3:18; Eph 5:15–18, 21). The Letter of James, with its 54 imperatives in 108 verses, is very decidedly "teaching and admonition" in poetic form. As such it naturally bears a strong resemblance to what is called the "Wisdom Literature" of the Jews, such works as the Book of Proverbs and Ecclesiastes in the Old Testament and apocryphal works such as the Wisdom of Solomon and Ecclesiasticus. Indeed, the letter is strongly Old Testamental in tone and content, much more so than the number of actual quotations from the Old Testament (only five) would seem to indicate. A glance at the margins of a cross-reference Bible will show how rich the letter is in allusive reminiscences of the Old Testament.

Harvesting olives.

Style

James's style has been well characterized as energetic, lively, and vivid. James dislikes the abstract and likes to make his meaning clear by images that he often expands into little narratives, such as that of

Outline

As noted above, the "miscellaneous" character of James's writing has challenged those who would present the letter in outline. The following is one example of how the content may be divided.

I. Greeting (1:1)

II. Perfection through the Implanted Word (1:2–21)
- A. Trials Result in Blessing (1:2–12)
  - 1. Trials and testing (1:2–4)
  - 2. Endurance comes only from God (1:5–8)
  - 3. The crown of life (1:9–12)
- B. Being Saved from Death (1:13–21)
  - 1. The source of temptation (1:13–16)
  - 2. Birth by the implanted Word (1:17–21)

III. Works Done by Those in Whom the Word Has Been Planted (1:22–2:26)
- A. Consistency of Word and Deed (1:22–2:13)
  - 1. The cause of inconsistency (1:22–25)
  - 2. Examples of inconsistency (1:26–2:7)
  - 3. Inconsistency results in condemnation (2:8–13)
- B. Living Faith (2:14–26)
  - 1. Faith leads to action (2:14–19)
  - 2. Examples of faith (2:20–26)

IV. Humbling Oneself in Light of the Coming Judgment (3:1–5:6)
- A. Call to Humility for the Sake of the Community (3:1–18)
  - 1. Proper and improper speaking (3:1–12)
  - 2. God's wisdom produces right speaking (3:13–18)

B. The Basis of God's Judgment (4:1–12)
  1. Selfish behavior destroys the individual and community (4:1–4)
  2. Prophetic call to repentance (4:5–10)
  3. God alone is the Judge (4:11–12)
C. Judgment on the Proud Person of Wealth (4:13–5:6)
  1. Becoming proud in self-sufficiency condemned (4:13–17)
  2. Becoming rich at the expense of others condemned (5:1–6)

V. Proper Speaking While Waiting for the Lord (5:7–20)
  A. Patience in View of the Lord's Return (5:7–12)
  B. Faithful Prayer in the Community (5:13–20)

the farmer waiting for the harvest (5:7). Or, he makes his point by means of crisp and telling dramatic sketches, such as the scene of fuss and flutter when the rich man makes his appearance in the Christian assembly (2:2–4). James buttonholes his reader by means of questions, direct address, and imperatives; no one daydreams while this prophetic preacher is speaking. None of these devices is a merely literary device, however; all are in the service of an inspired and passionate pastoral concern.

Characters

The contrasting estates of **the rich** and **the poor** show up constantly in the letter (1:9–11; 2:1–7, 15–16; 5:1–6), spanning many other themes. Persons of both estates are members of the churches to which James writes. He urges especially the rich to have compassion and due regard for their poorer brethren.

Narrative Development or Plot

Since James is written as a letter, it does not have a storyline or plot. However, as noted above, James tells stories about the rich and the poor (2:1–17), final judgment (5:1–6), and the patient farmer (5:7).

Resources

As noted above, the book may be based on a sermon. See p 684.

Text and Translations

The text of James is well established through a wealth of early manuscripts dating as early as the third century (Papyrus 20) and from Early Church Fathers who cite the letter.

Doctrinal Content

Summary Commentary

Ch 1 James writes to struggling Christians who are facing many trials and temptations. Those who face such challenges may be tossed about (vv 5–8) and eventually destroyed by sin (v 15). Those who seek God's wisdom endure trials (vv 2–4) and become stronger. James encourages Christians to return to the Word, take comfort in the Gospel, and live righteous lives focused on service toward others.

Ch 2 James rebukes an act that is inconsistent with the righteous life: judging others based on their appearance, wealth, or status. He also discusses a false understanding of faith: mere knowledge that has no application or effect on the one who has it. True faith and its response of true good works cannot be separated. Works naturally follow faith.

3:1–5:6 There are only two ways to live: by the "wisdom" of the world or by God's wisdom. James condemns the worldly pattern of selfishness, deception, hurtful words, and other evil behaviors. Using the language of the Prophets, he teaches that rejecting God's ways is spiritual adultery. Planning can be good stewardship, but not if our plans crowd out the things God would have us do. James reminds us to seek what "the Lord wills." He condemns the wealthy for living as if this life is all there is to live for and as if Christ will not return. God's Word repeatedly warns against this attitude.

5:7–20 The return of Jesus in glory shapes the Christian life. James calls sinners to repentance, and he exhorts the entire congregation to do the same.

Specific Law Themes

James teaches the unified character of the moral law of God. He calls us to keep the whole Law lest we break it and die in our sins. Sinners are judged by the Law, which reveals them to be transgressors. Faith apart from works is a dead faith. God expects us to be fair, care for the poor, tame our tongues, and to use them to pray diligently.

Specific Gospel Themes

Every good and perfect gift comes from the Father of lights who shines upon us graciously. He brought us forth through the word of truth. Because of Christ's death and resurrection, we are judged under the "law of liberty." We are heirs of His kingdom, counted righteous, awaiting the coming of our compassionate and merciful Lord who forgives us.

Specific Doctrines

The Letter of James proclaims Jesus as Lord and Christ, with divine authority; James's first word is a confession to God and to Jesus, and his relation is the same to both. He is "a servant of God and of the Lord Jesus Christ" (1:1). Jesus is "the Lord of glory" (2:1), just as God is "King of glory" and "God of glory" in the Old Testament (Ps 24:7; 29:3). Jesus is the object of faith (Jas 2:1); and He is Lord to the glory of God the Father, to the glory of the God whose nature is that He is the Giver of good gifts (1:5, 17), the God who has given to people the supreme gift of new life in the "word of truth," the Gospel (1:18). The presence and work of the Spirit is touched on too. God has made the Spirit to dwell in the men who constitute the new 12 tribes in the dispersion whom James is addressing (4:5). The wisdom that is God's gift to the believer (1:5–6) is in complete contrast to the "earthly, *unspiritual*, demonic" wisdom of natural man (3:15); it is wisdom that comes down "from above" (3:17)—we are reminded of the combination used by Luke in Acts: "Spirit and wisdom" (Ac 6:3, 10). The consciousness of living in the world's last days finds the most explicit and vigorous expression. Christ is the Author of life, of the new and eternal life, in James as in the first apostolic proclamation. The word of truth that proclaims Him and presents Him produces a new birth; and James views this new life as the "firstfruits," the beginning and the pledge of the renewal of all life (Jas 1:18). The new people of God await the "coming of the Lord" as the farmer waits for the harvest that will crown his year and his labors (5:7). The poor and oppressed people of God are "heirs of the kingdom" (2:5) and look forward to the crown of life that God will give to those who love Him (1:12).

Repentance

The characteristic thing about this letter is the fact that these great, fundamental statements are so rigorously and completely subordinated to the one imperative that is based upon them: to the command, "Repent!"

James's whole letter is one great call to repentance, repentance as the Old Testament prophets, John the Baptist, and Jesus Himself had proclaimed it:

the turning of the whole person wholly to his God, in a complete and radical break with his evil self and his evil past, a turning in submissive trust and obedience, a turning that is always ultimately God's own act (cf Ac 5:31; 11:18). James stands in the New Testament as a prophet, and his cry is the prophet's cry: "Turn!" (cf, e.g., Jer 25:5).

The Words of Jesus

The work is anything but a mere continuation of the Old Testament-Judaic Wisdom tradition. What gives the Letter of James its distinctive flavor and its distinctive content is not the influence of the Old Testament or anything in the tradition of Judaism. It is, rather, the all-pervasive influence of the words of Jesus, whom James calls Lord. Though James never quotes Jesus directly, he is constantly recalling and echoing words of Jesus in a way that shows they were for him and his hearers the basic and self-evident influence in their lives, the authority beyond which there is no appeal. Cross-references and statistics (a recent study lists 26 allusions to the words of Jesus in the letter) cannot really convey the true and full impression; the best way to measure the impact of Jesus upon James is to come fresh from a reading of the Gospel according to Matthew to the Letter of James. Then one can see how the Lord, who is so rarely mentioned by James, nevertheless casts His bright light across every page and can see that James's work is essentially the recalling of the words of the Lord Jesus Christ, with comment and explication that applies the Word to His Church here and now.

Fourth-century sarcophagus depicting Jesus Christ teaching the apostles.

Even in literary form, James bears a strong resemblance to Jesus. His imagery, like that of Jesus, is drawn largely from the outdoors—the stars of the heavens, the sea and the winds, the fields and the sun, fig tree and vine, the early and latter rain and the harvest, fountains, the morning mist, the horse, the birds and beasts and fish and creeping things, the forest and the forest fire. Some of James's images may be due to the direct influence of Jesus; other similarities are due, no doubt, to their common experience as men of Galilee. Furthermore, Jesus' words are poetic; the Beatitudes are direct descendants of the Psalter, and scholars have found that the Lord's Prayer, for instance, when translated back into Jesus' mother tongue, comes out as Semitic poetry. James's words, too, have a pronounced poetic rhythm throughout. Even a translation will give one the feel of it, especially if one reads aloud and notes the natural division suggested by the sense.

James, Peter, and the Reformation

At the time of the Reformation, the place of James in the Church's canon (that is, the collection of sacred books which are authoritative for the faith of the Church) was again questioned, not only by Luther, but also by Roman Catholic scholars such as Erasmus and Cajetan. Luther's objection to James is well-known; it is based chiefly on Jas 2:14–26, which to Luther seemed to be in irreconcilable conflict with Paul and the Gospel of salvation by grace through faith without the works of the Law. But James's words on faith and works are not aimed at Paul; neither do they really contradict Paul's teaching. The idea that faith is merely the certainty that God is one (2:19) has nothing to do with Paul; neither was Paul the first to see in Abraham the exemplar of saving faith—the rabbis had done that before him, as had Jesus Himself (Mt 8:11; Jn 8:56). The polemics of James *may* be directed at a watered-down and distorted version of Paul's Gospel, such as might have been reported in Jerusalem from Antioch when Paul was preaching there (Ac 11:25–26). But it is more likely that James is combating not a doctrine, but a practical threat to faith that came to his readers from their Judaic past and their Judaic surroundings. Jesus had said of the teachers of Judaism that they professed without practicing (Mt 23:3)—what would be more natural than a recurrence of this Judaic fault in a Christianized form in Judaic Christianity? It should be noted, moreover, that the bold but monumentally simple argument of James would be pitifully weak, if not malicious, as a refutation of Paul's teaching. And the James whom we know from his letter is neither weak intellectually nor malicious morally. James is not attacking Paul.

Neither does James, at bottom, contradict Paul. Both Paul and James are moved to speak by love. Paul emphasizes the fact that our salvation is wholly God's grace and entirely His doing, and that faith is therefore first and foremost pure receiving. Paul will leave no desperate sinner outside God's call of grace. James emphasizes the fact that faith is union and communion with

God and commits us wholly, with all our thoughts and all our doing, to God; James will allow no brother to destroy his faith and himself by making of faith an intellectual acceptance of doctrinal propositions and emptying it of love and works. Paul speaks to the sinner's desperation; James speaks to Christian complacency. When James is speaking to the repentant sinner, he makes no mention of works but bids such a one in his desperation draw near to God, in the assurance that God will draw near to him like the father of the returning prodigal son (Jas 4:8). James describes redemption as a new birth from God, solely by the will and word of God (1:18); and he describes God's love for mankind as God's sole and sovereign choice, as God's election (2:5). Paul, on the other hand, can combine his own characteristic emphasis with that of James in a single sentence: "By grace you have been saved through faith. And this is not your own doing; it is the gift of God, not a result of works, so that no one may boast. For we are His workmanship, *created in Christ Jesus for good works*, which God prepared beforehand, that we should walk in them" (Eph 2:8–10; emphasis added).

Luther, who objected so strenuously to James's conception of justification by faith, has given us a description of faith that would delight the heart of James:

> Faith, however, is a divine work in us which changes us and makes us to be borne anew of God, John 1[:12–13]. It kills the old Adam. . . . O it is a living, busy, active, mighty thing, this faith. It is impossible for it not to be doing good works incessantly. It does not ask whether good works are to be done, but before the question is asked, it has already done them, and is constantly doing them. Whoever does not do such works, however, is an unbeliever. He gropes and looks around for faith and good works, but knowd neither what faith is nor what good works are. (AE 35:370)

And the first of Luther's theses, which makes repentance the beating heart of the Christian existence, might serve as a title to the Letter of James. The presence of this letter in the canon is a perpetual reminder to the Church not to misconstrue Paul by making him the advocate of a lazy and workless faith, a reminder to hear and be guided by the real Paul, the Paul who entreats us "not to receive the grace of God in vain" (2Co 6:1).

Key Passages

The first two chapters of the book have been more important for the Lutheran tradition than the rest of the book. In 1:14–15 one finds a clear description of how desire progresses to become temptation, sin, and finally death. This devastating process occurs within the human heart, the result of original sin. The Law is so fragile in our sinful hands that just one sin shatters the entire Law (2:10). In contrast to the devastating effects of sin and death, God's goodness shines forth without shadow or change; He bestows on us every good and perfect gift (1:17). A controversial passage has been 2:17, which teaches that faith without works is dead, a matter much discussed during the Reformation, which requires careful discernment still today. Saving faith is never mere assent to God's existence—even demons so believe (2:19)! Faith is that trust which leads to good works.

Application

Ch 1 God gives His struggling children the crown of life not because of their strength but because of His grace. In that grace, we can follow Him and live confidently in this world of struggles and uncertainty. We also know the kind of lives God calls us to lead. Yet too easily we turn away from that calling. God, who implanted His Word in us and justified us in Christ, now calls us to bless others. He honors us by using us to bring His love to all people, especially those whom the world ignores.

Ch 2 The desire for wealth leads us to lift up the wealthy and look down on the poor. This is not God's way. He shows no partiality but calls all people to faith in Christ and grants the same gift of salvation to all. James calls us to look at one another as those for whom Christ died because the name of Christ has been given to us in Baptism (v 7). He gives all His people a new identity that the world cannot give. We live together in Him, serving and building up one another until His return. Faulty understanding of faith is just as wrong as the opposite error: focusing on actions alone apart from faith in Christ. God has given us a great gift—through Christ Jesus, He has forgiven us and declared us righteous and holy. He now blesses us by calling us to serve Him in the lives of those around us. A living faith leads us to gladly share with others what we have freely received in Christ.

3:1–5:6 Christians, too, struggle with sin and are even tempted to present themselves as holier than others. How different is the wisdom of God! He has purified us in Christ and freed us from the stain of the world. We now walk in the works He has prepared for us to do. James does not call us to turn to ourselves and do more works to be forgiven but instead calls us to return to the Lord in repentance. Even when we are unfaithful, God remains faithful. He has already purchased us by the blood of Christ. His love does not depend on our faithfulness or works but on His faithfulness and His work in Christ.

Like James's first readers, we strive to be self-sufficient and to develop detailed plans for our lives. It is easy to think that James's words do not apply to us because there is always someone wealthier, someone greedier. But Scripture teaches, "You know the grace of our Lord Jesus Christ, that though He was rich, yet for your sake He became poor, so that you by His poverty might become rich" (2Co 8:9). In Christ, we have the riches that come from God alone—above all, the gift of faith. He will give us the crown of life.

5:7–20 Confidence in His return (vv 7–8) gives us a perspective on how we relate to one another (v 9) and our sufferings (v 10). God promises to remain with us and restore us to Himself (v 11). In our shortsighted, self-focused lives, we dwell on our own problems and try to deal with them ourselves. The quicker we get out of a mess, the better. But this is not God's perspective. He looks at the true goal: eternal life with Him. Consequently, our sufferings can be borne with patience. He gives faith to sustain us through suffering and confidence to endure all things until He comes again. God continuously sends into our lives those who pray for us, sing praise with us, and speak God's words of forgiveness to us. As His people, healed in body and soul, we may approach His throne of grace with confidence.

Canonicity

James was classified among the books spoken against (*antilegomenon*) in the Early Church. However, it gradually gained broad acceptance. For Luther's changing opinion about the book, see below.

Lutheran Theologians on James

Luther

In 1522, Luther made harsh statements about the Epistle of James. These statements have become notorious among scholars who have sometimes taken them out of context. The statements derive from Luther's frustration with opponents who used Jas 2 to attack what Luther had learned about justification and sanctification while carefully studying the Epistles of Paul. The chief problem is raised by the way James and Paul use the same term (*faith*) and the same Old Testament history (examples from Abraham's life) to illustrate very different points about the Christian life.

Critics have been delighted that Luther described James as an "epistle of straw" and have used this statement as justification for launching attacks on other New Testament documents and doctrines. However, a patient consideration of Luther's statements yields the following important points:

1. Luther's description of the book changes. In some cases, Luther describes James as the work of an apostle (e.g., his postil of 1536; WA DB 41:578–90), but in other cases, he argues that it was not written by an apostle.
2. When Luther describes James as "straw," he is referring to its mundane, moral topics and not to its truthfulness. In medieval Wittenberg, straw was appreciated for its usefulness (e.g., Luther's mattress was stuffed with straw), but it was also characterized as having low

value (cf 1Co 3:12). So in his Preface to the New Testament, Luther is making a contrast between James and other New Testament epistles and is not dismissing James outright.

3. In Luther's Preface to James, he describes the epistle as "a good book, because it sets up no doctrines of men but vigorously promulgates the law of God" (AE 35:395). But Luther also notes that the book lacks teaching on Christ, whom the apostles were to preach.
4. Despite his strong opinion and suggestion that the Lord's brother James may not have written the book, Luther retains it as a New Testament Epistle. As the points above show, Luther was inconsistent in his opinions about James.

Luther wrote most harshly about James early in his career, while struggling against Rome and Andreas Carlstadt. Following the Antinomian Controversy, Luther showed new interest in the epistle. In 1533, he urged Christians in Leipzig to hold to the Apology of the Augsburg Confession, in which Philip Melanchthon provided a careful explanation of James's arguments about faith and works (Ap V 123–32), the issue in James that Luther found so troubling. During the 10 years after Luther wrote his prefaces to the New Testament, we have no sermons on James from him. But in 1536, Luther wrote a postil commentary on Jas 1:17–21. He preached on Jas 1 in 1535, 1536, 1537, and twice in 1539. Although Luther never fully reconciled himself to the challenges presented by Jas 2, it appears that he became more comfortable with the book in his mature years.

Below are quotes from Luther's prefaces of 1522 and 1546, which are presented for historical purposes only.

"In a word St. John's Gospel and his first epistle, St. Paul's epistles, especially Romans, Galatians, and Ephesians, and St. Peter's first epistle are the books that show you Christ and teach you all that is necessary and salvatory for you to know, even if you were never to see or hear any other book or doctrine. Therefore St. James' epistle is really an epistle of straw, compared to these others, for it has nothing of the nature of the gospel about it." (AE 35:362)

"Though this epistle of St. James was rejected by the ancients, I praise it and consider it a good book, because it sets up no doctrines of men but vigorously promulgates [*treibet*] the law of God.[1] However, to state my own opinion about it, though without prejudice to anyone, I do not regard it as the writing of an apostle; and my reasons follow.

"In the first place it is flatly against St. Paul and all the rest of Scripture in ascribing justification to works [2:24]. It says that Abraham was justified by his works when he offered his son Isaac [2:21]; though in Romans 4[:2–22] St. Paul teaches to the contrary that Abraham was justified apart from works, by his faith alone, before he had offered his son, and proves it by Moses in Genesis 15[:6]. Now although this epistle might be helped and an interpretation devised for this justification by works,[2] it cannot be defended in its application to works [Jas. 2:23] of Moses' statement in Genesis 15[:6]. For Moses is speaking here only of Abraham's faith, and not of his works, as St. Paul demonstrates in Romans 4. This fault,[3] therefore, proves that this epistle is not the work of any apostle.

"In the second place its purpose is to teach Christians, but in all this long teaching it does not once mention the Passion, the resurrection, or the Spirit of Christ. He names Christ several times; however he teaches nothing about him, but only speaks of general faith in God. Now it is the office of a true apostle to preach of the Passion and resurrection and office of Christ, and to lay the foundation for faith in him, as Christ himself says in John 15[:27], 'You shall bear witness to me.' All the genuine sacred books agree in this, that all of them preach and inculcate [*treiben*] Christ. And that is the true test by which to judge all books, when we see whether or not they inculcate [*treiben*] Christ. For all the Scriptures show us Christ, Romans 3[:21]; and St. Paul will know nothing but Christ, I Corinthians 2[:2]. Whatever does not teach Christ is not yet[4] apostolic, even though St. Peter or St. Paul does the teaching. Again, whatever preaches Christ would be apostolic, even if Judas, Annas, Pilate, and Herod were doing it.

---

1 The translator does not consistently handle Luther's use of Grm *treiben*, but renders it negatively when Luther uses the verb regarding teaching the Law. Readers should note that Luther did not oppose strongly teaching the Law (e.g., nearly half of Luther's Large Catechism expounds the Ten Commandments).

2 Melanchthon provided a very helpful explanation of the text in Ap V 123–32, which became standard among Lutherans.

3 Grm *Mangel* often describes a lack of something, a weakness.

4 Luther's earlier version of the preface (1522) lacks this qualification. He at first dismissed James as not apostolic. In 1546, he characterizes the book as not on equal standing with apostolic teaching.

"But this James does nothing more than drive [*treibet*] to the law and to its works. Besides, he throws things together so chaotically that it seems to me he must have been some good, pious man, who took a few sayings from the disciples of the apostles and thus tossed them off on paper. Or it may perhaps have been written by someone on the basis of his preaching. He calls the law a 'law of liberty' [1:25], though Paul calls it a law of slavery, of wrath, of death, and of sin.

"Moreover he cites the sayings of St. Peter [in 5:20]: 'Love covers a multitude of sins' [I Pet. 4:8], and again [in 4:10], 'Humble yourselves under the hand of God' [I Pet. 5:6]; also the saying of St. Paul in Galatians 5[:17], 'The Spirit lusteth against envy.' And yet, in point of time, St. James was put to death by Herod [Acts 12:2] in Jerusalem, before St. Peter. So it seems that [this author] came long after St. Peter and St. Paul.

"In a word, he wanted to guard against those who relied on faith without works, but was unequal to the task.[5] He tries to accomplish by harping [*treiben*] on the law what the apostles accomplish by stimulating people to love. Therefore I cannot include him among the chief books, though I would not thereby prevent anyone from including or extolling him as he pleases, for there are otherwise many good sayings in him."[6] (AE 35:395–97; see also AE 4:133–34; 54:424–25)

Despite Luther's early, harsh opinions and influence as an interpreter, the Lutheran Church has held that James is rightly part of the New Testament, citing its authority in the Book of Concord. See pp 647–48.

5 In 1522, Luther had continued, "in spirit, thought, and words. He mangles the Scriptures and thereby opposes Paul and all Scripture." These comments placed James outside of Scripture. Luther deleted these words for the 1530 edition.

6 In 1522, Luther had continued, "One man is no man in worldly things; how, then, should this single man alone avail against Paul and all the rest of Scripture?" Luther deleted these words for the 1530 edition.

Gerhard

Most of Gerhard's comments are devoted to the canonical character of the letter. He recites arguments for and against its apostolic authority, quoting numerous sources. He concludes:

> "We deem that this Epistle is both canonical and apostolic; that it was written at Jerusalem, inasmuch as it is likely that James was bishop of the church at Jerusalem; that he wrote it not long before his blessed death so that the faithful Jews might have the instruction of their apostle and bishop sealed in writing, with which they would be instructed even after his death.
>
> "It consists of five chapters in which the faithful who already for a long time have been established in the instruction of Christ (1) are dissuaded from various vices unbefitting their profession of faith and (2) are, on the other hand, exhorted to the virtues worthy of their profession. "(ThC E1 § 282)

Road to Jerusalem leads from the heights of the Mount of Olives down to the Kidron Valley and then rises up to the temple mount. The Golden Gate, east wall of the temple, is in the far background.

Further Study

Lay/Bible Class Resources

Eschelbach, Michael, and Milton Rudnick. *James and Jude*. Leaders Guide and Enrichment Magazine/Study Guide. LL. St. Louis: Concordia, 2003. ✎ An in-depth, nine-session Bible study with individual, small group, and lecture portions.

Groth, Lorraine. *James: How Faith Works*. GWFT. St. Louis: Concordia, 1994. ✎ Lutheran author. Thirteen-session Bible study, including leader's notes and discussion questions.

Jeske, Mark A. *General Epistles*. PBC. St. Louis: Concordia, 2005. ✎ Lutheran author. Excellent for Bible classes. Based on the NIV translation.

Life by His Word. St. Louis: Concordia, 2009. ✎ More than 1,500 reproducible one-page Bible studies covering each chapter of the canonical Scriptures. Page references to *The Lutheran Study Bible*. CD-Rom and downloadable.

Moo, Douglas J. *James*. TNTC. Downers Grove, IL: InterVarsity Press, 2009. ✎ Less helpful, but his discussion on 5:13–18 is especially good (and practical) and should be consulted on the problematic passage.

Church Worker Resources

Kistemaker, Simon J. *James, Epistles of John, Peter and Jude*. NTC. Grand Rapids: Baker, 1996. ✎ Treats James as New Testament proverbs or wisdom literature. Focused on providing application.

Academic Resources

Chilton, Bruce, and Craig A. Evans, eds. *James the Just and Christian Origins*. Vol. 98 of Supplements to Novum Testamentum. Leiden: Brill, 1999. ✎ A historical investigation of James and early Jewish Christianity.

Chilton, Bruce, and Jacob Neusner, eds. *The Brother of Jesus: James the Just and His Mission*. Louisville: Westminster, 2001. ✎ Eight essays by Jewish and Christian scholars of biblical history and literature.

Davids, Peter H. *The Epistle of James*. NIGTC. Grand Rapids: Eerdmans, 1982. ✎ Places the letter in the social setting of Jewish Christians in the middle of the first century. The commentary portion is less helpful.

Johnson, Luke Timothy. *The Letter of James*. Vol. 37A of AB. New York: Doubleday, 1995. ✎ What is especially helpful, in contrast to other commentaries, is that it has a good grasp of the original context for the letter and that it takes in the entire argument of the letter on its own terms. It does not read James as an anti-Pauline polemic.

———. *Brother of Jesus, Friend of God: Studies in the Letter of James*. Grand Rapids: Eerdmans, 2004. ✎ A collection of scholarly essays that challenge the assumptions of critical scholarship in James.

Lange, John Peter, and J. J. van Oosterzee. *The Epistle General of James*. LCHS. New York: Charles Scribner's Sons, 1867. ✎ A helpful older example of German biblical scholarship based on the Greek text, which provides references to significant commentaries from the Reformation era forward.

Laws, Sophie. *The Epistle of James*. Black's New Testament Commentary. San Francisco: Harper & Row, 1980. ✎ Favors a Roman origin for the letter, by an anonymous writer who assumes the well-known name of "James." Use with discernment.

Lenski, R. C. H. *The Interpretation of the Epistle to the Hebrews and the Epistle of James*. Minneapolis: Augsburg, 1966. ✎ A standard resource by a noteworthy Lutheran interpreter, concerned with being faithful to the text and with its implications for today. Concerned to bring out the message of James with stress on the faith lived in life.

Mayor, Joseph B. *The Epistle of St. James: The Greek Text with Introduction, Notes, Comments and Further Studies in the Epistle of St. James*. Rev. 3rd. ed. Grand Rapids: Zondervan, 1954. ✎ An old standard; very detailed and sometimes complex.

Wall, Robert W. *Community of the Wise: The Letter of James*. The New Testament in Context. Valley Forge, PA: Trinity Press International, 1997. ✎ A canonical reading of James, pursuing its meaning and application for today's readers. Sees James and Paul answering compatibly on issues of faith and works.

1 PETER

Called into His marvelous Light

On its way to the sea, the Tiber River bends westward toward Vatican Hill. Above the river once arose a circus arena, the site of chariot races for emperors Gaius and Nero. Today the site is dominated by the Basilica of St. Peter, which commemorates the site of Christian martyrs whom Nero condemned. Beneath the basilica's main altar one finds a humble mausoleum and chapel dedicated to Peter, where he was likely laid to rest.

In this letter, Peter sends greetings to his readers from her "who is at Babylon, who is likewise chosen" (1Pt 5:13). This no doubt refers to a church (the Greek word for church is feminine), and the church referred to is in all probability the church at Rome. Christianity seems to have taken over this name for Rome from late Judaism. Babylon had been branded by Old Testament prophecy as the embodiment of world power at enmity with God and His people. Peter is, in using this name for Rome, reminding his readers that the hostile world, which now has power to impose the fiery ordeal upon the scattered and homeless people of God, is doomed to destruction under the judgment of God. The letter was thus written at Rome.

Historical and Cultural Setting

As for the circumstances that prompted Peter to write to Gentile churches, some of which had their origin in Paul's missionary labors, one can only guess. Commentators on 1 Peter have wondered whether Peter may have written at Paul's suggestion. Paul, about to

Ancient bridge over the Tiber River by St. Peter's Basilica in the Vatican, Rome.

OVERVIEW

Author
Simon Peter the apostle

Date
Before AD 67

Places
Pontus; Galatia; Cappadocia; Asia; Bithynia

People
Peter; exiles of the Dispersion; unbelievers; Gentiles; governmental leaders; servants; wives and husbands; elders of the Church; younger believers; Silvanus; "she who is at Babylon"; Mark

Purpose
To instruct and encourage the Lord's people as they endure suffering for the sake of righteousness

Law Themes
Sin; ignorance of foolish people; perishable; disobeying God's Word; darkness; judgment; fiery trials

Gospel Themes
Christ bore our sins in His body; He suffered for us; He ransomed sinners; He is imperishable; Christ's death involved a righteous man dying for unrighteous people (the great exchange); marvelous light; stand firm in God's grace; God's Word is the living and abiding Word; good news; royal priesthood; holy nation; chosen race

Memory Verses
Ransomed by Christ's blood (1:17–19); the chosen people (2:9–10); healed by Christ (2:24–25); Baptism now saves you (3:18–22)

TIMELINE

AD 33	Resurrection, Ascension, Pentecost
AD 41	Peter imprisoned at Jerusalem
AD 49	Jerusalem Council
AD 68	Martyrdom of Peter and Paul
AD 70	Romans destroy Jerusalem

leave for Spain in AD 61 or 62, having heard of the situation of the churches of northern Asia Minor, may have laid it upon Peter's heart to write to them a circular letter, just as Paul himself had written somewhat earlier to a group of churches in Asia Minor (Letter to the Ephesians). This receives some confirmation from the fact that Silvanus, Paul's longtime companion, had a part in the writing of the letter. Peter's words, "By [or "through"] Silvanus, a faithful brother as I regard him, I have written briefly to you" (5:12), probably indicate that he was more than merely a secretary to Peter. Perhaps he acted as translator; Peter as a Galilean would know Greek but was doubtless more at home in Aramaic. Or perhaps Silvanus worked more freely, carrying out Peter's general instructions as to content and submitting his work to Peter's supervision, a practice common in ancient letter writing. Silas as the trusted companion of Paul and a man endowed with the gift of prophecy (Ac 15:32) may have been called into the consultation between Peter and Paul when the letter was planned and was thus acquainted with its purpose and content from the outset.

Sea of Galilee.

Composition

Author

The authenticity of 1 Peter is questioned by some scholars on the grounds that (a) the Greek of the letter is too delicately idiomatic and literary to be the work of a Galilean fisherman like Peter; (b) that the letter borrows from the Letter of James and from Paul to an extent that makes authorship by one of apostolic stature unlikely; (c) that the persecution the letter has in view is of a kind not possible within the lifetime of Peter, since persecution for the "name" itself (that is, for merely being a Christian) did not take place before the time of Emperor Domitian (AD 81–96) or even that of Trajan (AD 98–117).

a. We should remember that we really have no way of knowing how much Greek Peter could or did know. Peter's home country, Galilee, was more open to Greek influence than any other part of Israel. The part that Silvanus, the Roman citizen and the companion of Paul on his mission to the Gentiles, had in the composition of the letter must be reckoned with also.

b. The so-called dependence of Peter's first letter on other New Testament writings can easily be overstated. Not every similarity between New Testament writings is proof that one of the authors drew upon the work of the other. The apostles and other leaders of the Early Church did not merely read one another's letters in studious seclusion; these men heard and knew one another; they confessed together, worked together, and above all, they had one Lord and possessed one Spirit. Moreover, they lived for and with the Church, enriching the life of the Church and being enriched by it (cf Rm 1:11–12), so that whatever one apostle gave the Church became the property of all. The question of the interrelationship of the apostolic writings cannot be determined by the study of the coincidences of language in the writings alone; the whole historical picture must be considered. Thus considered, the coincidences between Peter and John (who is closely associated with Peter in the Book of Acts) is in many ways as striking as that between Peter and Paul or Peter and James: both Peter and John link Christ closely with the hope and the predictions of the Old Testament prophets (1Pt 1:10–12; Jn 12:41); both portray Jesus as Lamb and Shepherd (1Pt 1:19; 5:4; Jn 1:29; 10:11); both see the office and duty of apostles and elders as one of tending the sheep of Christ (1Pt 5:2; Jn 21:16); both see in the death of Christ the basic norm for Christian conduct (1Pt 2:21–25; 3:17, 18; 1Jn 3:16; 4:9–11); and both describe themselves as "witness" and "elder" (1Pt 5:1; 1Jn 1:1; Jn 1:14; 19:35; 2Jn 1; 3Jn 1). One can hardly, therefore, draw long conclusions from a limited number of literary coincidences between the Letter of Peter on the one hand and the Letter of James and the letters of Paul on the other, even if some of these coincidences are very close.

c. As was noted above, the kind of persecution indicated by the letter does not demand a dating later than the lifetime of Peter. Nothing in it points so definitely to a persecution of the type that occurred under Domitian and Trajan as to demand a dating under one of these Emperors. It should be remembered that from the point of view of the apostle and the Church, *every* persecution was a persecution for the sake of the "name" of Christ, whatever reason might be put forward by the persecuting power itself.

Positively, there are two features of the letter that speak strongly for authenticity. One is the claim of the writer to be an eyewitness of the sufferings of Christ (1Pt 5:1), a claim supported by many little touches throughout the letter. The other is the amount and kind of agreement between the letter of Peter and the sermons of Peter as recorded by Luke in the Book of Acts. Neither of these would, of course, *prove* that Peter wrote the letter; but they do indicate that there is no reason to doubt the early, widespread, and clean-cut tradition that Peter wrote the letter.

Date of Composition

The place of writing helps fix the time of writing. There is no reason to doubt that Peter reached Rome and died a martyr's death there. But Peter did not reach Rome until the latter years of his life, after Israel had been called to repentance and had been called in vain. Since the persecution to which the letter refers does not seem to be an official one like that under Nero, and since Peter can still call for absolute loyalty to the state (1Pt 2:13–17), a date before the Neronian persecution of AD 67 is probable.

Purpose/Recipients

The First Letter of Peter is addressed to the Christians of five provinces of Asia Minor. Peter calls them "exiles of the Dispersion" (1Pt 1:1), a term that suggests "the Dispersion of the Jews" and might naturally be thought to imply Jewish Christian readers, especially since Peter was primarily the apostle to the circumcised (Gal 2:7–9). But the letter itself shows that the readers have a Gentile background (e.g., 1Pt 1:14; 2:9–10; 4:3–4); they are therefore "exiles of the Dispersion" in a figurative sense, strangers and sojourners on this earth (1:17; 2:11), dispersed in an unbelieving world. There is nothing to indicate that Peter and his readers knew each other personally.

The Christians addressed are undergoing some form of persecution (3:16–17) and are perhaps being threatened by an even severer form of persecution (4:12–19). They are being slandered, ridiculed, and suspected of disloyalty to the state (4:14, 16; 4:4; cf 2:13–17); but there is nothing to indicate a full-scale official persecution. We hear nothing of a demand for emperor worship, for instance; nor is there any hint of confiscation of property, imprisonment, or martyrs' deaths. Yet it is a time of severe trial; they are going through a "fiery trial," perhaps the first great ordeal they have been called upon to endure, since they are finding it "strange" (4:12). And Peter

Regions and Cities of Asia Minor
Black Sea
THRACE
MYSIA
Troas
Assos
Adramyttium
Pergamum
Thyatira
Smyrna
Sardis
Ephesus
Magnesia
Miletus
Rhodes
Macestus River
Rhyndakos River
Hermus River
Cayster River
Maeander River
ASIA
Cotiaeum
Aezani
PHRYGIA
Hierapolis
Laodicea
Colossae
Lycus River
BITHYNIA
Sangarius River
Tembris River
Tolistobogii
Pessinus
Cilician Road
Antioch
Lake Limnae
PISIDIA
Lake Caralis
PAMPHYLIA
Perga
Side
LYCIA
Mediterranean Sea
CILICIA TRACHEIA
LYCAONIA
Iconium
Lystra
Derbe
Tectosages
GALATIA
Ancyra
PAPHLAGONIA
Halys River
Trocmi
Tavium
PONTUS
Lake Tatta
CAPPADOCIA
Cilician Gates
Tarsus
CILICIA PEDIAS
Amanus Gates

Outline

I. Apostolic Salutation (1:1–2)

II. Introductory Thanksgiving (1:3–12)

A. God to Be Praised for New Life in Christ (1:3–5)

B. Christians Are Strengthened and Sustained in Their Suffering by Joy and Hope (1:6–9)

C. Salvation Was Foretold by the Prophets (1:10–12)

III. Christians Are to Lead Holy Lives (1:13–2:10)

A. Newfound Status Demands That Christians Be Holy, as God Is (1:13–16)

B. Believers Are Mindful of the Price of Their Redemption (1:17–21)

C. Christians Turn Away from Malice as They Mature in Faith and Love (1:22–2:3)

D. As Living Stones in God's Temple, His Royal Priesthood and Chosen People, Christians Proclaim His Excellencies (2:4–10)

IV. Specific Instruction and Encouragement for Holy Living (2:11–4:11)

A. The Purpose of Holiness (2:11–12)

B. Christians Submit to Civil Authorities (2:13–17)

C. Household Slaves Submit to the Authority of Their Masters (2:18–25)

D. A Wife Yields to Her Husband's Authority as Head of the Household (3:1–6)

E. A Husband Demonstrates Godliness by Respecting His Wife (3:7)

F. Humility, Unity, a Tender Heart, and Brotherly Love Characterize Christian Brotherhood (3:8–12)

G. Christian Virtue Sends a Powerful Message to Outsiders and Gives Opportunity for Witnessing (3:13–17)

H. Jesus Was Treated Unjustly and Then Gloriously Vindicated (3:18–22)

I. Jesus' Example Inspires His People to Overcome Surrounding Evil (4:1–6)

J. Nearness of the End Stimulates Christians to Faithfulness (4:7–11)

V. Joy Amid Suffering and Further Clarifications about What Is Expected of the Community (4:12–5:11)

A. Suffering for the Sake of Christ Is a Sharing in Him (4:12–19)

B. Elders Have Special Responsibilities and Promises (5:1–4)

C. Younger Men Are to Submit Humbly to the Community's Elders (5:5)

D. Concluding Exhortation to Humility and Trust (5:6–11)

VI. Final Greetings (5:12–14)

A. Silvanus's Help (5:12)

B. Other Brothers from the Church in "Babylon" (Rome) Send Greetings (5:13)

C. The Holy Kiss and the Peace of Christ (5:14)

writes to them out of the riches of the grace that he has himself experienced, out of the fullness of the glorious hope which Christ has implanted in him, to encourage them in steadfast endurance in the strength of that grace and for the sake of that hope. He writes to admonish them to a life that befits the great salvation that is in store for them, a life whose moral beauty is to be in itself a proclamation of that salvation to the world about them. He writes in order to make these afflicted brothers see once more the full, eternal dimensions of the true grace of God, in order that they may stand firm in it (5:12).

Literary Features

Genre

The comprehensiveness of the letter is taken into account by those scholars who have suggested that 1:3–4:11 represents a baptismal homily, or address, which laid before the newly converted all that their new life in the

North African baptistry at the Church of Vitalis, Sbeitla, Tunisia.

Church conferred upon them as God's gift, and all that it asked of them as the response of faith and hope to that gift. Others have taken the whole letter as a record of an early Christian service of worship, beginning with an address to the newly baptized converts (1:3–4:11) and concluding with an address to the whole church (4:12–5:11). One may say that the compressed fullness of the letter marks it as the production of a worker who knows how to utilize his time; one sees in the "luminous" power of Peter's sentences the hallmark of that composed and settled intellectual strength that results from a life of constant prayer.

Characters

In view of eternity, Peter graciously describes the **believers** who receive his letter (2:9–10), while further describing their earthly sojourn as citizens, workers, and spouses (2:11–3:7).

Narrative Development or Plot

Since 1 Peter is written as a letter, it does not have a storyline or plot.

Resources

See reference to a baptismal address under "Genre" above.

Text and Translations

The text of 1 Peter is well established through a wealth of early manuscripts dating as early as the third or fourth century (Papyrus 72) and from Early Church Fathers who cite the letter.

Doctrinal Content

Summary Commentary

1:1–2 Peter writes to Christians who struggle because they live in this world but are really citizens of heaven. He reminds them of their election in Christ and of His gifts of forgiveness, life, and salvation.

1:3–12 Through Jesus Christ, we now have a living hope and know the promise of God that we will live in Him forever. We can face any trial or challenge, knowing that we are safe in His care.

1:13–25 In God's love, before the world was made, He determined to send His Son, the unblemished Lamb, to be our sacrifice. Now through His Word, He calls us to life and sets us apart to His glory and for the service of our neighbor.

2:1–12 Christ, the light of the world, has called us out of darkness into His light. He makes us His own, gives us a place as citizens of His kingdom, and empowers us to live as His royal priesthood. We are not alone but are part of His people, a holy nation.

2:13–25 Scripture never teaches that those who follow Jesus will be immune to suffering. Just as Jesus, our sinless Savior, faced unjust suffering and death, so we may be called to take up our own cross to follow Him.

3:1–7 God's divine order calls men to love their wives sacrificially and to care for them. Wives are called to love their husbands and be subject to them.

3:8–22 In the midst of trials, we may be tempted to feel self-pity and despair. But God calls us to something greater. Our powerful Lord forgives us in our Baptism and gives us His life.

4:1–11 Christ suffered in the flesh and became sin (2Co 5:21) in our stead. He now calls us to live the new life He has given us as stewards of His gifts.

4:12–19 God permits suffering in our lives for a variety of reasons. Sometimes it comes as a direct result of our own sin in order to discipline us. Other times it is an effect of being God's child in a world that wants to crush His Church. Although we do not know God's hidden will, we trust He has only the best in mind for us.

5:1–11 The chief Shepherd calls undershepherds to teach, preach, administer the Sacraments, and guard His sheep, always keeping in mind that sin and the devil seek to entrap them.

5:12–14 Peter encourages these persecuted Christians to stand firm in the one thing that is truly trustworthy: God's grace in Christ.

Specific Law Themes

Sin leads to our punishment and persistently troubles us. Our ignorance makes fools of us, so that we face perils and fiery trials. Disobeying God's Word leads us into darkness, for which we must finally face God's judgment.

Specific Gospel Themes

Thanks be to God, Christ bore our sins in His body. He suffered for us that He might ransom us—the righteous for the unrighteous, the imperishable Savior rescuing perishable sinners. Marveling in His light, we stand firm in God's grace. His living and abiding Word is our good news. We are a royal priesthood, a holy nation, a chosen race in Christ.

Specific Doctrines

The First Letter of Peter is often, and rightly, called the "Letter of Hope." Hope in the full Christian sense of a serene and confident dependence on God, hope based on the unshakable certainty of the resurrection of the dead which is begun and guaranteed in the resurrection of Jesus Christ, and hope as a mighty energizing power for the whole life of men in the Church is certainly a dominant note of the letter. But such convenient catchword summaries are necessarily oversimplifications and can serve to conceal from the student the variety and riches of the letter. These qualities of variety and richness have been noted by many students of the letter. Erasmus called it "an epistle sparse in words, crammed with content." Luther included 1 Peter in his list of the prime and capital books of the New Testament. Anyone looking for a key book that will unlock for him the meaning of the whole New Testament would do well to give his days and nights to this letter.

Key Passages

Peter credits the beginning, middle, and end of our salvation to faith alone, since God's power calls us to faith and guards us in the faith unto the salvation He will reveal in eternity (1:5). Even now God builds His Church into a spiritual house and priesthood through Jesus Christ, who is the chosen and precious cornerstone of Old Testament prophecy and the foundation of our faith (2:5–6). Although we are God's dear people, Peter also warns us that God's judgment will begin with the household of God (4:17) lest we despise the Gospel. Not only do we need to guard against our own weaknesses, but we must not overlook the fact that the devil is our vigilant adversary who stalks us like a lion (5:8).

Eighth-century fresco of the crucifixion.

Application

1:1–2 Apart from God's grace in Christ, this sinful world has no hope in the midst of trials, persecution, and eternal death. God, through His Son, brings reconciliation and forgiveness of sin for all who believe by grace through faith that Christ is Savior. In Him we have grace and peace.

1:3–12 We are born in sin and continue to commit sins in this fallen world. By ourselves, we have no hope of salvation or blessings. But God foretold His gracious plans through the prophets. In the fullness of time, He sent His Son to be our Redeemer. He has given us the gift of His Holy Spirit, that we might be brought to faith and persevere in the faith.

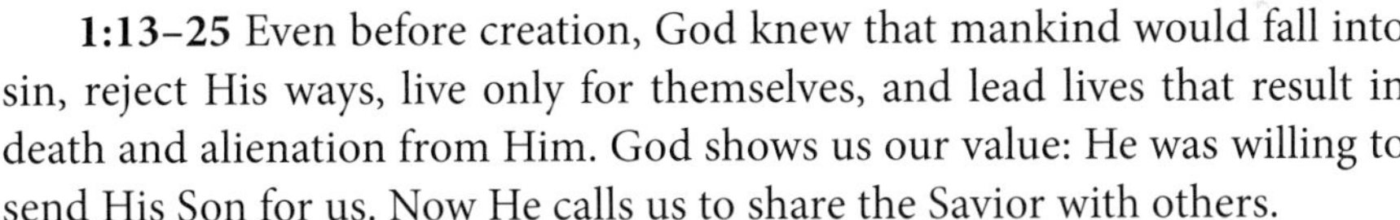

1:13–25 Even before creation, God knew that mankind would fall into sin, reject His ways, live only for themselves, and lead lives that result in death and alienation from Him. God shows us our value: He was willing to send His Son for us. Now He calls us to share the Savior with others.

2:1–12 Like all people, we were born in sin and lived in the darkness of the world. Now that same Savior calls us to tell others of His love. Through our words and actions, we proclaim the life and salvation that is ours in Jesus.

2:13–25 If God gives us a cross to carry, He also promises to give us the strength to bear it by faith. Christ our Shepherd calls us by name, brings us into His fold through the Gospel, and cares for us in the midst of suffering. We are honored to follow Him.

3:1–7 Sadly, sin affects marriage and families. We sometimes view God's gift as a burden or hardship. When a believing wife speaks the Gospel gently to her unbelieving husband and demonstrates her faith in action, the power of the Gospel may lead him to salvation. When a husband truly loves his wife and treats her with honor, the family is strengthened, and all are blessed. When our families fall short of this calling, our gentle heavenly Father calls us to follow Him and is ever prepared to forgive us.

3:8–22 Jesus Christ is our Savior. He suffered and died for us. He rose to give us life. His power and authority is above all others. He places us in the Church, where we may support and bless one another. And He blesses us by allowing us to tell others about the life we have in Him so that they, too, may share in His blessings.

4:1–11 Everything we have, even our lives, are used to benefit the Church and our neighbor. Through our words and actions, we bring Christ to a world that is dead in sin so that some may come alive in Christ, even as we have been made alive.

4:12–19 He will strengthen, uphold, and bless us in the midst of persecution. He will use any afflictions we face for our good or for blessing others. With our eyes on the cross, we can endure. Our God will preserve us, and He has prepared an eternal home for us in heaven for the sake of Christ.

5:1–11 The devil and false teachers, even though they are damned, would lead us astray through sin and temptation and take us to hell. By the Gospel, we have fervent love for one another because we share the same faith, Baptism, and Spirit. We will endure by God's power.

5:12–14 Jesus suffered for us at the hands of evil men. Yet He trusted in His Father with unswerving faith. Whatever trials or difficulties we may face, we can likewise rely on the true grace of God and on the bond of love in our Christian family. Through Jesus, we truly have peace.

Canonicity

The First Letter of Peter was regarded as authoritative at an early date and was never questioned (*homologoumenon*).

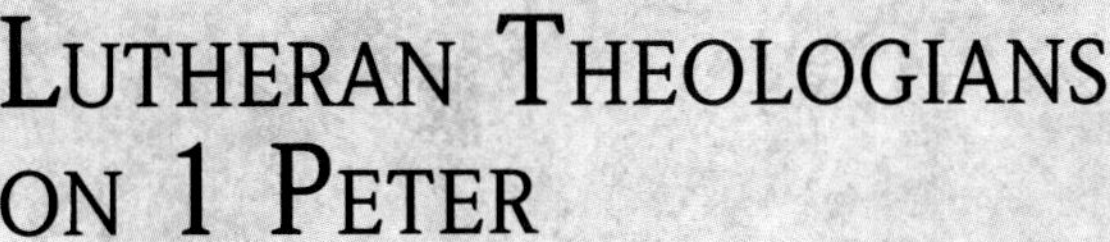

Lutheran Theologians on 1 Peter

Luther

"This epistle St. Peter wrote to the converted heathen; he exhorts them to be steadfast in faith and to increase through all kinds of suffering and good works.

"In chapter 1 he strengthens their faith through the divine promise and power of the salvation to come. He shows that this salvation has not been merited by us but was first proclaimed by the prophets. Therefore they ought now to live new and holy lives, and forget the old life, as those who have been born anew through the living and eternal Word of God.

"In chapter 2 he teaches them to know Christ as the Head and the Cornerstone, and like true priests to sacrifice themselves to God as Christ sacrificed himself. And he sets about giving instructions to the various estates. First he teaches in general subjection to temporal rulership; afterward he teaches in particular that servants are to be subordinate to their masters and [even] to suffer wrong from them, for the sake of Christ who also suffered wrong for us.

"In chapter 3 he teaches wives to be obedient, even to unbelieving husbands, and to adorn themselves with holiness. Likewise, husbands are to be patient with their wives and bear with them. And finally, all in general are to be humble and patient and kind to one another, as Christ was because of our sins.

"In chapter 4 he teaches us to subdue the flesh with sobriety, watchfulness, temperance, prayer, and to find comfort and strength through the sufferings of Christ. He instructs the spiritual rulers to inculcate the words and works of God alone, and each to serve the other with his gifts; and not to be surprised but to rejoice, if we have to suffer for the name of Christ.

"In chapter 5 he exhorts the bishops and priests as to how they are to live and to tend the people. He warns us against the devil, who without ceasing pursues us everywhere." (AE 35:390–91)

For more of Luther's insights on this book, see *Sermons on the First Epistle of St. Peter* (AE 30:1–145).

Gerhard

"In its inscription this Epistle is called 'catholic' because it was written not to some one person—like Paul's Epistles to Timothy, Titus, and Philemon—nor to some one particular church—as Paul's to the Romans, Corinthians, etc.—but to converts from the Jews who were scattered here and there, as the inscription reveals. Yet certain matters in this Epistle occur that pertain chiefly to Gentiles (c. 2:5, 10; c. 4:3), namely, because converted Jews, along with those of the Gentiles who had been converted, were making up one Church and were embracing one another as brothers (1:14, 18). The apostle himself explains the aim of his writing toward the end of the Epistle. He says, 'By Silvanus, a faithful brother as I regard him, I have written briefly to you, exhorting and declaring that this is the true grace of God in which you stand' (5:12). He had two purposes especially in this Epistle: (1) to bear witness to the converted Jews that the teaching regarding the grace of God through Christ, which they had embraced by faith and in the confession of which they were standing fast, is the one, indisputable way of salvation, heavenly truth, and immovable doctrine. (2) To exhort them both to persevere steadfastly in this faith and to live a life worthy of that confession and pleasing to God.

"In 5:13 he greets those to whom he has written in the name of 'the church that is gathered at Babylon,' from which one concludes that Peter wrote this Epistle in the city of Babylon. The question arises, however, whether we should take the name 'Babylon' properly for the city of Egypt or metaphorically for the city of Rome. Those who claim the former use the following arguments: (1) It fits with the apostleship of Peter, inasmuch as he was especially appointed for the Jews (Gal. 2:7), a great number of whom were living in those eastern regions and especially in Babylon. (2) We should not abandon the literal sense unless necessity itself compels us, none of which appears here. . . .

"Concerning this first Epistle of Peter, Eusebius witnesses (*Histor. eccles.*, bk. 3, c. 3): 'There never was in the Church any controversy about it as if it were not of Peter, who gives it his own name. For this reason it should be listed among the canonical books.' For this reason we also place it among the canonical books of the first rank. Among the ancients it is called the 'Epistle to the Pontians' [*Epistola ad Pontios*], as is evident from Tertullian (at the end of his *Scorpiac. adv. Gnosticos*) and Cyprian (*Testimonia*, bk. 3, c. 36), because Pontus is named in the first place among the regions to which it was sent: 'to the exiles of the dispersion in Pontus, Galatia,' etc. (1 Pet. 1:1).

"In the theme that he placed at the beginning of his paraphrase of this Epistle, Erasmus suspects that 'Peter had written to the same people still another letter before this first Epistle' because he says at the end of this Epistle: 'By Silvanus . . . I have written briefly to you' (1 Pet. 5:12). However, the words of his second Epistle clearly refute this opinion: 'This is now the second letter I have written to you, beloved' (2 Pet. 3:1). He ought not have said 'second' but 'third' had he already written them two. Therefore when he claims that he has written by Silvanus, he is speaking not about another but about this first Epistle. (Cf. Heb. 13:22; 2 John 12.) From the words of 1 Pet. 4:16—'But if as a Christian'—one gathers that this Epistle was written after the disciples already had begun to be called 'Christians.' Luke mentions when this happened (Acts 11:26).

"It consists of five chapters and contains, besides the preface and conclusion, (1) a remembrance of the spiritual benefits of God and (2) an exhortation to the true use of those benefits and to the pursuit of piety that is worthy of Christians." (ThC E1 §§ 270, 272)

Further Study

Lay/Bible Class Resources

Grudem, Wayne. *1 Peter*. TNTC. Downers Grove, IL: InterVarsity Press, 1988. ❧ Compact commentary interacting with key terms in the Greek text and a variety of English translations. Unlike other volumes in TNTC series, this book often references a broad variety of ancient texts in exploring context and meaning.

Jeske, Mark A. *General Epistles*. PBC. St. Louis: Concordia, 2005. ❧ Lutheran author. Excellent for Bible classes. Based on the NIV translation.

Life by His Word. St. Louis: Concordia, 2009. ❧ More than 1,500 reproducible one-page Bible studies covering each chapter of the canonical Scriptures. Page references to *The Lutheran Study Bible*. CD-Rom and downloadable.

Marth, David, Lenore Buth, Roland Ehlke, and Lane Burgland. *1 and 2 Peter*. Leaders Guide and Enrichment Magazine/Study Guide. LL. St. Louis: Concordia, 2001. ❧ An in-depth, nine-session Bible study with individual, small group, and lecture portions.

Mounce, Robert H. *A Living Hope: A Commentary on 1 and 2 Peter*. Eugene, OR: Wipf & Stock, 2004. ❧ Concise, evangelical commentary from New Testament scholar and translator.

Scharlemann, Martin. *1 Peter: God's Chosen People*. GWFT. St. Louis: Concordia, 1994. ❧ Lutheran author. Thirteen-session Bible study, including leader's notes and discussion questions.

Stibbs, Alan M. *The First Epistle General of Peter: An Introduction and Commentary*. TNTC. Grand Rapids: Eerdmans, 1988. ❧ Still a very helpful resource, though originally published in 1959. The introductory articles show an intimate knowledge of the variety of critical hypotheses. Holds to the Petrine authorship and the unity of 1 Peter.

Church Worker Resources

Luther, Martin. *Sermons on the First Epistle of St. Peter*. Vol. 30 of AE. St. Louis: Concordia, 1967. ❧ The great reformer's sermonic commentary from 1522–23. Luther described the letter as pure Gospel and one of the best writings of the New Testament.

Patterson, Paige. *A Pilgrim Priesthood: An Exposition of the Epistle of First Peter*. Eugene, OR: Wipf & Stock, 2004. ❧ Written from both a scholarly and practical perspective, including devotional content.

Academic Resources

Achtemeier, Paul J. *1 Peter: A Commentary on First Peter*. Hermeneia. Minneapolis: Fortress Press, 1996. ❧ Along with Elliott's volume in the Anchor series, this is probably the best and most up-to-date English language commentary on 1 Peter. The excurses alone (there are 14 in all) are worth reading.

Bigg, Charles. *A Critical and Exegetical Commentary on the Epistles of St. Peter and St. Jude*. ICC. 2nd ed. Edinburgh: T&T Clark, 1902. ❧ Extensive introductory articles on the witness of the Church Fathers, authorship, and parallels with other New Testament writings. Though now over a century old, this remains a classic. Especially useful are the lexicographical remarks and table of similarities between 1 Peter and the Pauline corpus. Bigg holds to the Petrine authorship of both letters, and stresses that Jude was written after 2 Peter.

Davids, Peter H. *The First Epistle of Peter*. NICNT. Grand Rapids: Eerdmans, 1990. ❧ An evangelical reading, and not sacramental in a Lutheran sense. This tendency is naturally evident in the remarks on 3:21. Very respectful of biblical authority, however, and worthwhile.

Elliott, John H. *I Peter: A New Translation with Introduction and Commentary*. Vol. 37B of AB. New York: Doubleday, 2000. ✠ Arguably the best and most thorough commentary available in English by perhaps the world's most respected authority on 1 Peter. Elliott's sociological insights break new ground in Petrine studies. His challenging position on the famous "royal priesthood" passage (2:9–10) also needs to be taken seriously.

———. *A Home for the Homeless: A Social-Scientific Criticism of 1 Peter, Its Situation and Strategy*. Eugene, OR: Wipf & Stock, 2005. ✠ Reads the epistle in light of Peter's address to "elect exiles" (1:1), examining the social context of the letter. First published in 1981.

Fronmüller, G. F. C. *The Epistles General of Peter*. LCHS. New York: Charles Scribner's Sons, 1867. ✠ A helpful older example of German biblical scholarship, based on the Greek text, which provides references to significant commentaries from the Reformation era forward.

Goppelt, Leonhard. *A Commentary on I Peter*. Edited by Ferdinand Hahn. Translated and augmented by John E. Alsup. Grand Rapids: Eerdmans, 1993. ✠ Goppelt's expertise in typology and valuable excurses make his volume useful reading.

Kelly, J. N. D. *The Epistles of Peter and of Jude*. Black's New Testament Commentary. Grand Rapids: Baker, 1969. ✠ Holds to the unity of 1 Peter and feels that the case for Petrine authorship is strong. In his view, Jude was written prior to 2 Peter, with the latter written by an unknown author.

Lenski, R. C. H. *The Interpretation of I and II Epistles of Peter, the Three Epistles of John, and the Epistle of Jude*. Minneapolis: Augsburg, 1966. ✠ A standard resource by a noteworthy Lutheran interpreter, concerned with being faithful to the text and with its implications for today.

Michaels, J. Ramsey. *1 Peter*. WBC. Waco: Word Books, 1988. ✠ A conservative, evangelical treatment. Michaels' comments on Christ's descent to hell are especially well considered and balanced.

Selwyn, Edward Gordon. *The First Epistle of St. Peter: The Greek Text with Introduction, Notes, and Essays*. Second Edition. New York: St. Martin's Press, 1947. ✠ Though older now, this work remains valuable.

SALVSMVNDI
+SANCTVS
APOLENARIS

2 PETER

A sure prophetic word

The historical contours of 1 Peter are tolerably distinct; we can answer with considerable assurance most of the questions that historical inquiry raises concerning it. The Second Letter of Peter, however, is wrapped in mystery, and the reconstruction of its historical background is beset at almost every point with perplexing uncertainties. While the place of the first letter in the canon has always been an assured one, the second letter has the weakest historical attestation of any book in the New Testament. There are indications that the letter was known and used in the second century, but there is no unmistakable evidence that it was known as a letter of Peter and used as such in the church before the time of Origen (AD 185 to 254), who referred to the letter and considered it apostolic, but was aware of the fact that its place in the canon was in dispute (see Origen's *Commentary on John*; *ANF* 9:346–47). (One may conjecture that the weakness of historical attestation is due to the fact that the second letter was designed for Jewish Christian readers; the gulf between Judaic Christianity and Gentile Christianity widened with the years, and books peculiar to Judaic Christianity might for that reason remain relatively unknown to the Gentile churches for a considerable period.)

Historical and Cultural Setting

The authenticity of 1 Peter, though questioned by modern critical scholarship, is actually quite solidly established by the external and internal evidence, whereas the authenticity of the second letter was questioned even in the Early Church and is denied by the great majority of scholars today. The circle of readers for whom the first letter was intended is clearly defined by the letter itself;

Dome of the aspe in the sixth-century Basilica of Saint Apollinare, in Classe near Ravenna, Italy.

OVERVIEW

Author
Simon [Simeon] Peter the apostle

Date
c AD 68

Places
Mount of Transfiguration; Sodom and Gomorrah

People
Simeon Peter; Jesus; false prophets/teachers; the unrighteous; the apostles; Paul

Purpose
To warn against false teachers who promoted sinful lifestyles and questioned whether Jesus would return in judgment

Law Themes
Exhortations to virtue; warnings against false prophets; ignorance; nearsightedness; forgetfulness; fiery judgment; destruction of the ungodly

Gospel Themes
God's sure Word; the Spirit's work; Christ cleansed us from our former sins; eternal kingdom; God promises new heavens and a new earth; God does not wish any to perish

Memory Verses
A sure prophetic word (1:19–21); new heavens and a new earth (3:13)

TIMELINE

AD 33	Resurrection, Ascension, Pentecost
AD 41	Peter imprisoned at Jerusalem
AD 49	Jerusalem Council
AD 68	Martyrdom of Peter and Paul
AD 70	Romans destroy Jerusalem

the address of the second letter is very general: "To those who have obtained a faith of equal standing with ours" (2Pt 1:1), and leaves the location of the readers uncertain. The words, "This is now the *second letter* that I am writing to you, beloved" (3:1) make it likely, but not certain, that its destination is the same as that of the first letter. Concerning the time and place of writing of the second letter, we can only say that it must be dated toward the close of Peter's life and that it was therefore probably written from Rome and addressed to the church in Asia Minor (cf 1Pt 1:1). We can see what sort of tendencies and difficulties occasioned the second letter, but we cannot fix them as to place and time with any precision.

Composition

Author

The majority of scholars today regard 2 Peter as a second-century work, written by one who wishes to invoke the authority of Peter to aid him in dealing with the dangers and difficulties confronting the Church in his day. The letter, they say, is not a malicious forgery; the use of Peter's name is not designed to deceive anyone. It is merely the author's way of saying, "This is what the apostle Peter would say to our situation if he were still with us today." It is commonly described as an example of the testamentary literature of this era (as in a "last will and testament" document; cf 2Pt 1:12–15 where Peter mentioned he was facing death).

This position is supported by a massive array of arguments, and the case is generally conceded to be proved beyond reasonable doubt. And yet there is room for reasonable doubt. The greatest difficulty about the theory that 2 Peter is a forgery is to discover a motive for the forgery. Men who write in the name of others, especially great authorities, have a reason for doing so. In the case of 2 Peter such a reason is hard to discover. The author is not using an apostle's authority to support a heresy, as is so often the case with early forgeries. He is not indulging in a romantic glorification of an apostle as the *Acts of Paul*, for instance, does. The allusions to Peter's life and experience remain within the limits of what we know of Peter from the Gospels. And the writer imports nothing from a later time and experience (anachronisms) into the picture of the apostle.

There have been similar cases in the history of New Testament scholarship where theories about a late date for a document were overturned; there was, for instance, a time when practically nobody who was anybody in the world of scholarship cared to defend the authenticity and first-century origin of the Gospel of John, while today further study and new discoveries have put the matter in a different light. This example shows that evidence needs to be sifted. The impressive list of arguments against authenticity for 2 Peter contains items of varying strength and validity. Some of the arguments are strong, and honest scholarship should not evade the fact that we are confronted by genuine reasons for uncertainty in this matter.

Strong Arguments

The argument based on differences between the first and the second letter in vocabulary and style is strong. The two letters are clearly quite different. One may conjecture that the differences in language and style are due not only to the different situation presupposed by the two letters, but also to the fact (as Jerome already suggested) that Peter employed a different helper for the second letter, that the associate "through" whom Peter wrote his second letter was a man different from Silvanus, the secretary "through" whom he wrote the first letter. But again this is conjecture; and we are left with unsolved problems.

For the argument based on the relationship between 2 Peter and Jude, see "Resources" below.

Epistles Likely Prepared through a Scribe (Amanuensis) or with Co-Authors

Although an apostle might handwrite his closing greeting (e.g., 1Co 16:21; Gal 6:11; Col 4:18; 2Th 3:17; Phm 19), much of the writing for New Testament letters was done through scribes. This may explain why some letters from an author may read quite differently from other letters he sent.

Epistle	Scribe	Co-senders	References
Romans	Tertius		Rm 16:22
1 Corinthians	Unnamed	Sosthenes	1Co 1:1; 16:21
2 Corinthians		Timothy	2Co 1:1
Galatians	Unnamed		Gal 6:11
Philippians		Timothy	Php 1:1
Colossians	Unnamed	Timothy	Col 1:1; 4:18
1 Thessalonians		Silvanus, Timothy	1Th 1:1
2 Thessalonians	Unnamed	Silvanus, Timothy	2Th 3:17
Philemon	Unnamed	Timothy	Phm 19
1 Peter	Silvanus		1Pt 5:12

Weaker Arguments

Other arguments used to support the thesis that 2 Peter must be a second-century non-Petrine work are less strong. Arguments on what the letter does not say are of dubious validity; it is argued that the second letter is less profoundly Christ-centered than the first letter, that the second letter is more somber about the approaching end of all things than the first letter.

The argument from silence is always dubious; Paul, for instance, is silent on the Lord's Supper in all his letters except 1 Corinthians, but this neither calls into question the authenticity of the other letters nor does it prove anything concerning the importance that Paul attaches to the Lord's Supper. Similarly, the fact that the second letter quotes and recalls the Old Testament less often than the first letter does not have much weight, especially when we consider that the second letter contains one of the most powerful statements in the whole New Testament on the authority and the inspiration of Old Testament prophecy (2Pt 1:19–21). Neither is the alleged fact that the author speaks of Paul's letters as a *collection* known to the Church (3:16) sufficient to prove a late date and exclude Peter as the author. The phrase "in all his letters" does not necessarily imply that everyone everywhere in the Church knew the collected letters of Paul. And to argue that Peter could not have ranked Paul's letters with "the other Scriptures" (that is, the Old Testament) involves the whole question of apostolic authority. If Paul himself considered the word that he spoke to be no less than the Word of God (1Th 2:13; 1Co 7:40; 14:37), there is no reason why Peter, who gave Paul the right hand of fellowship (Gal 2:9), should not have placed the same value on it.

Date of Composition

There is no denying the fact that the letter is very weakly attested by name in the Ancient Church; and it is difficult to see why it should have been less widely acknowledged than 1 Peter if it is a genuine work of the apostle. However, Curtis Giese points out:

> Second-century authors allude to portions of 2 Peter without stating 2 Peter as the source. These allusions appear in, for example, *Shepherd of Hermas*, *2 Clement*, the *Epistle of Barnabas*, Justin Martyr, Aristides, Theophilus, the *Letter of the Churches of Lyons and Vienne*, Irenaeus, Melito, and the *Apocalypse of Peter*. Even *1 Clement* from about AD 95 may allude to it. While this evidence does not guarantee Petrine authorship, it places the existence of 2 Peter in the first century AD, which enables one to rationally assert that the author is the apostle of Jesus. (CC 2Pt/Jude, pp 8–9)

Salt formations on the Dead Sea shore.

A difficulty that is usually overlooked by those who assign 2 Peter to the second century is the fact that it was just in this period that heretical sects were producing pseudoapostolic works in support of their heresies. The Early Church had every reason to be cautious and critical about works that claimed to be Peter's; and the Church was cautious, as the history of 2 Peter in the canon shows. The fact that this letter did nevertheless impose its authority upon the Church under just these circumstances must be given due weight.

Purpose/Recipients

As noted above, a primary reason for writing 2 Peter was to warn against false teachers. The letter clarifies specific teachings on morality and the promised return of Christ.

Literary Features

Genre

Some scholars classify 2 Peter as an example of testamentary literature, though the argument seems driven more by the opinion that the book was written in the second century than by the nature of the document itself. It is more reasonable to view the letter as exhortation and instruction, similar to other New Testament letters.

The parable of the Good Shepherd separating the sheep from the goats; sixth-century mosaic in the Saint Apollinare Basilica, Ravenna, Italy.

OUTLINE

I. The Apostolic Salutation (1:1–2)

II. Exhortation to Godliness (1:3–21)

- A. Content of This Exhortation (1:3–11)
- B. Necessity of This Reminder (1:12–15)
- C. Certain Basis of the Exhortation in the Revelation of Christ and Scripture (1:16–21)

III. Warning against False Teachers (ch 2)

- A. Anticipation of False Teachers (2:1–3)
- B. God Delivers the Righteous and Punishes the Ungodly (2:4–10a)
- C. Denunciation of the Motives, Character, and Message of the False Teachers (2:10b–22)

IV. Answers to Skepticism regarding the End of This World (3:1–10)

V. Final Exhortation on the Basis of Christian Expectation and Hope (3:11–18)

Characters

The letter devotes considerable space to describing **persons who have fallen away from the faith**. Giese summarizes the descriptions as follows:

> These apostates apparently originated from within the community (2 Pet 2:1) rather than from the outside, as did the heretics who had infiltrated the church of Jude's readers. Although once adherents of apostolic Christianity, they have now become heinous apostates (2 Pet 2:20–22). The major tenant of their aberrant teaching involves denial of Christ's second coming and the subsequent judgment (2 Pet 2:1–10; 3:3–7). . . . With greed and deception in their hearts, they intentionally wish to lead Christians astray (2 Pet 2:1–3). A great enticement offered by these teachers is unbridled immorality as an acceptable expression of Christianity (2 Pet 2:13–14). . . . However, 2 Peter lacks major tenets of Gnosticism. The errorists'

> teaching is not characterized by cosmic dualism, including a distinction between the OT God and the God of the NT. A disdain for the material and rejection of Christ's resurrection do not appear in the epistle. (CC 2Pt/Jude, pp 12–13)

Giese concludes that the apostates were not Gnostics but may have been influenced by Epicurean teachings, though one cannot definitely confirm the school of thought from which they came.

Narrative Development or Plot

Since 2 Peter is written as a letter, it does not have a storyline or plot. However, the book does include reference to the story of Jesus' transfiguration, which confirms the certainty of Jesus' words (1:16–21). The last chapter gives a prophetic account of how the Day of the Lord will come about and why it has not come yet (ch 3).

Resources

The relationship between 2 Peter and the Letter of Jude is usually considered one of the strong arguments against the authenticity of 2 Peter. The Letter of Jude and 2Pt 2 are so similar in language and thought that there is obviously a historical connection between the two; they can hardly have originated altogether independently of each other.

Most scholars today argue that 2 Peter is the later of the two documents and has incorporated the Letter of Jude. The arguments used to prove the dependence of Peter's second letter on Jude cannot be discussed in detail here. But it should be noted that this theory of borrowing on the part of a second-century writer leaves a good many unanswered questions. For example, if Jude is the earlier document and 2 Peter the later, why is it that Jude's account of the false teachers is the darker and more sinister of the two? In Jude, the false teachers are compared not only to Balaam, but also to Cain and Korah—why should a second-century writer, engaged in so desperate a struggle against such a dangerous heresy that he must invoke the name of Peter in order to combat it, tone down the indictment of Jude?

Note also that Jude twice (Jude 4 and 17) refers to an older apostolic writing that predicts the errorists who at Jude's time are present in the Church. The Second Letter of Peter answers to that document; it predicts future errorists (2:1, 3) whose coming and working Jude notes as present in his time. It would seem to follow that Jude knew and prized as apostolic a document that must have been very similar to 2Pt 2. If 2 Peter is not apostolic but later than Jude, the original apostolic document referred to by Jude (Jude 4 and 17) must have been lost early and without leaving a trace.

Text and Translations

As a shorter, later attested letter, 2 Peter includes some challenging readings. Nevertheless, the text of 2 Peter is well established from the fourth century onward through manuscripts such as Papyrus 72. Church Fathers as early as Origin (third century) cite the letter by name.

Doctrinal Content

Summary Commentary

1:1–2 Peter greets his readers with a salutation that affirms their standing in Christ. All who confess Christ possess "a faith of equal standing."

1:3–15 Peter affirms the greatness of the Christian hope, and he encourages his readers to make their calling and election sure by giving evidence of their faith with good works.

1:16–21 Peter had seen a glimpse of our Lord's glory on the holy Mount of Transfiguration.

Ch 2 Our Lord says, "In the world you will have tribulation. But take heart; I have overcome the world" (Jn 16:33; cf 2Pt 2:9).

Ch 3 Knowing that this world will not last, we are to live lives of holiness, hastening the coming of the Lord. Our Lord's patience is essential to our salvation in the sense that He is giving us time to repent.

Thirteenth-century icon showing the Transfiguration of Christ.

Specific Law Themes

In this letter, Peter exhorts his hearers to virtuous lives and warns them against false prophets. Christians struggle against their ignorance, nearsightedness, and forgetfulness of the Lord. The ungodly face destruction and fiery judgment.

Specific Gospel Themes

God's sure Word is the result of the Holy Spirit who carried along the prophets. Christ has cleansed us from our former sins, providing for us an eternal kingdom. Indeed, He promises us a new heavens and a new earth. He does not wish for anyone to perish.

Specific Doctrines

Peter makes a noteworthy statement about the holy penmen of God of the Old Testament when he says: "Men spoke from God as they were carried along by the Holy Spirit" (2Pt 1:21). The preceding verse shows that the apostle is discussing the Holy Scriptures ("knowing this first of all, that no prophecy of Scripture comes from someone's own interpretation," v 20). How did these Holy Scriptures originate? Holy men of God spoke, but they spoke as the Spirit of God moved them. What they said was in a sense their own product, and yet we have to say that it was not only their own product, but also the Word of the Holy Spirit.

Key Passages

Election is a dominating topic of ch 1; the Lord calls us to faith but also equips us to bear the fruit of faith, making our calling and election sure (1:8–10). With this teaching of God's election, the letter also teaches that God desires the repentance of all people (3:9), a paradoxical truth that should compel us to proclaim God's promised salvation to all.

Application

1:1–2 Our hold on faith in Christ can weaken as we are tempted into "false belief, despair, and other great shame and vice" (see SC, Sixth Petition). Thanks be to God that our Lord's grace and peace toward us is even greater than our sins, and that He is ever at work through His Word and Sacraments to strengthen our hold on faith.

1:3–15 We are saved by faith alone, but faith is never alone. In spite of our many failures to bear God-pleasing fruit, our Lord strengthens us daily through Holy Baptism.

1:16–21 We have the prophetic Word of God, on which the faith and hope of our Lord's triumphant return in glory depends. By God's grace in Christ, we are now "a holy nation, a people for His own possession" (1Pt 2:9).

Ch 2 The devil, the world, and our own sinful nature are ever seeking to overcome us through our tribulations (see SC, Sixth Petition). The way of escape is through His Holy Word and Sacraments, for this is how He strengthens and keeps us firm in His Word and faith (see SC, Third Petition).

Ch 3 We are often distracted by "the cares of the world" (Mt 13:22). Despite our many failures, the Lord graciously forgives our sins and renews us in the faith. He will preserve us unto the end.

Do we use the time allotted to us to take sin and salvation seriously, or do we neglect our worship and prayers and our Lord's gracious call to repent? Make daily repentance part of your life. The patient Lord is ever working to restore fallen sinners and to strengthen them in the stability of their salvation.

Canonicity

The Church cannot erase the line between *antilegomena* and *homologoumena*. The Church cannot rewrite or unwrite history. And the weakness of the historical witness to 2 Peter and the difficulties posed by its peculiar history and its peculiar character cannot and should not be simply ignored. But a coolly rational balancing of probabilities will never see the whole of the problem and will not find the whole answer.

The most important fact about 2 Peter is, in the last analysis, the fact that it has in generation after generation "strengthened the brothers" of Peter in a genuinely apostolic way. The Church has been strengthened for battle and heartened in its hope by the living words of this letter, words that are as clear and sure as the history of the letter is dark and uncertain. Whatever the historical difficulties attending it, 2 Peter has had, and has, an undeniable part in that peculiar history that gives meaning to all history, the history of the growing and victoriously prevailing Word of the Lord.

For more on the canonical issues, read Gerhard's comments below.

Lutheran Theologians on 2 Peter

Luther

"This epistle is written against those who think that Christian faith can be without works. Therefore he exhorts them to test themselves by good works and become sure of their faith, just as one knows trees by their fruits [Matt. 7:20].

"He begins accordingly by praising the gospel over against the doctrines of men. He says that people ought to hear the gospel alone and not the doctrines of men. For, as he says, 'No prophecy ever came by the impulse of men' [II Pet. 1:21].

"For this reason he warns in chapter 2 against the false teachers who are to come. They are preoccupied with works and thereby deny Christ. He threatens these men severely with three terrible illustrations and depicts them so clearly with their avarice, pride, wickedness, fornication, and hypocrisy that one must plainly see he means the clergy of today. For these have swallowed the whole world in their greed and are wickedly leading an irresponsible, fleshly, worldly life.

"In chapter 3 he shows that the Last Day will come soon; and though in the sight of [*fur*] men it may seem a thousand years, yet in the sight of [*fur*] God it is as one day. He describes what will happen at the Last Day, how everything shall be consumed by fire. However, he also prophesies that at that time people will be scornful and, like the Epicureans, will think nothing of faith.

"In summary, chapter 1 shows what Christendom was to be like at the time of the pure gospel. Chapter 2 shows how it was to be in the time of the pope and the doctrines of men. Chapter 3 shows how, after this, people will despise both the gospel and all doctrine, and will believe nothing—and this is now in full swing—until Christ comes." (AE 35:391–92)

For more of Luther's insights on this book, see *Sermons on the Second Epistle of St. Peter* (AE 30:147–99).

Gerhard

"In the early Church some people had doubts about the latter Epistle of Peter as well. Consequently, we place it also among the canonical books of the second rank. Eusebius, *Hist.*, bk. 3, c. 3: 'One Epistle of Peter, which is called "the Former," was accepted without controversy. The old presbyters used it in their writings without any hesitation. But we have accepted that the one which is called "the Latter" is not legitimate and canonical. Yet because it seems useful to many, it is used along with other Scriptures.' And later: 'Regarding those letters that are attributed to Peter, of which I realize that only one of them was held to be truly an epistle of that man in the estimation of the ancient presbyters, let this still be said.' In the same book, c. 22, after enumerating the canonical books of the first rank, he adds: 'Those that are spoken against, though they are well-known to many, are these: the Epistle attributed to James, the Epistle of Jude, 2 Peter, and 2 and 3 John.' Book 4, c. 24, from Origen in his explanation of Psalm 1: 'Peter left behind one Epistle about which there is definite agreement. But let it be that he also left a second one about which there is controversy.' Didymus, Jerome's teacher, concludes his brief commentary on this Epistle in this way: 'Therefore one must be aware that this Epistle has been falsified. Although it was published, that is, read in the churches publicly, nevertheless it is not in the canon.' Jerome, *Catal. viror. illustr.*, on Peter: 'Most deny that the second Epistle of Peter is his.' It is omitted in the Syriac paraphrase.

"Of the more recent writers, Cajetan reflects doubt about it in his commentary on this Epistle. Erasmus, on 2 Peter 3: 'There was controversy about this second Epistle of Peter as to whose it was. The difference of style both in the words and in their sense is too clear to ignore. Consequently, when he witnesses here that he was an eyewitness of the vision on the mountain, then mentions an earlier Epistle, and finally calls Paul a brother, what Jerome says about the interpreter does not displease me.' The words of Jerome, Epistle 150 *ad Hebidiam*, q. 11, read as follows: 'Blessed Paul had Titus as his interpreter, just as blessed Peter had Mark, whose Gospel was composed as Peter told it and Mark wrote it. Finally, the two Epistles that are called Peter's differ between themselves in style and character, as well as in the structure of the words. From this we understand that he used different interpreters in view of the necessity of his subject matter.' In *Contra D.*

Mentz., p. 161, Pistorius admits that 'for some time there was doubt about this Epistle.'

"There are ready arguments, however, to persuade that this is an apostolic Epistle and that Peter wrote it. (1) Its author in clear words calls himself 'Simon Peter, servant and apostle of Jesus Christ.' (2) It was entitled as written to the same people as was the first, namely, to the Jews scattered throughout the Roman Empire who had been converted to Christ and whose apostle Peter was. (3) The spirit in it is apostolic. (4) Its style and composition are in conformity with those of the first Epistle. The authors of the *Hist. Magdeb.*, cent. 1, bk. 2, c. 4, col. 54: 'Besides this one, which is said to lack the testimony of antiquity, the other seems to me to lack nothing to be considered a genuine Epistle of Peter, for its style and composition do not differ greatly from the first.' (5) The author of this letter says that 'the putting off of his tabernacle had been declared by Christ' (2 Pet. 1:14). With these words he is undoubtedly looking to Christ's prediction in John 21:18. (6) He says that he was an eyewitness of the transfiguration on the mountain (2 Pet. 1:16). But now, Peter was there along with James and John. (7) He mentions a prior Epistle (2 Pet. 3:1). (8) He calls Paul his 'beloved brother' (2 Pet. 3:15). (9) It is placed in the canon under Peter's name by the Council of Laodicea (canon 59), the third Council of Carthage, Athanasius (*Synopsis*), the Damascene (bk. 4, c. 18), Epiphanius (*Haeres.* 76), Jerome (*Ad Paulin.*), Augustine (*De doctr. Christ.*, bk. 2, c. 8), Gregory (*In Evangel.*, homily 18), etc. In his commentary, Bede wonders 'in what way there could be doubt regarding the author of this Epistle, since he expresses his name and testifies in clear words that he was on the mountain with the Lord.' Origen and Jerome in many places cite testimonies from this Epistle as from Holy Scripture. Luther (*Praefat. epist. ad Hebr.*) places it among the canonical books.

"To that which some argue to the contrary, that is, *the diversity in style from the first Epistle*, we respond with a denial. Even if there were a diversity of style here, the same things also occur in the Pauline Epistles. Jerome claims that this came from a difference of interpreter (*Ad Hebidiam*, q. 11). Because for some time there was doubt about it in the early Church, this argues that it should be referred to the canonical books of the second rank.

"It was written to the same people as was the first, namely, to the converted Jews (3:1), which is also concluded from 1:19. It consists of three chapters in which are added to the apostolic introduction (1) an exhortation to a zeal for continuing and persevering in the faith; and (2) a warning to watch out for both seducers as well as mockers and scorners who deny the final coming of Christ. The whole Epistle concludes with a doxology worthy of the apostle." (ThC E1 § § 283–84)

Mosaic portrait of Saint Peter in byzantine basilica of Saint Vitalis, Ravenna, Italy.

Further Study

Lay/Bible Class Resources

Dunker, Gary. *2 Peter and Jude: Contend for the Faith*. GWFT. St. Louis: Concordia, 2009. ❦ Lutheran author. Eleven-session Bible study, including leader's notes and discussion questions.

Green, Michael. *2 Peter and Jude*. TNTC. Grand Rapids: The Tyndale Press, 1968. [1987.] ❦ Concise, evangelical commentary. Green argues that 2 Peter is a first-century document, written by Peter, perhaps with a different secretary than he employed for 1 Peter. He favors the proposal that 2 Peter and Jude both depend on a third, underlying source. Green brings forth insights from classical, patristic, and, to a degree, rabbinic studies; he identifies the Asiatic Greek style of the epistle.

Jeske, Mark A. *General Epistles*. PBC. St. Louis: Concordia, 2005. ❦ Lutheran author. Excellent for Bible classes. Based on the NIV translation.

Life by His Word. St. Louis: Concordia, 2009. ❦ More than 1,500 reproducible one-page Bible studies covering each chapter of the canonical Scriptures. Page references to *The Lutheran Study Bible*. CD-Rom and downloadable.

Marth, David, Lenore Buth, Roland Ehlke, and Lane Burgland. *1 and 2 Peter*. Leaders Guide and Enrichment Magazine/Study Guide. LL. St. Louis: Concordia, 2001. ❦ An in-depth, nine-session Bible study with individual, small group, and lecture portions.

Mounce, Robert H. *A Living Hope: A Commentary on 1 and 2 Peter*. Eugene, OR: Wipf & Stock, 2004. ❦ Concise, evangelical commentary from New Testament scholar and translator.

Watson, Duane F. "2 Peter" in *The New Interpreter's Bible*. Vol. XII. Nashville: Abingdon Press, 1998. ❦ Based on the NIV and NRSV; provides an evangelical commentary.

Church Worker Resources

Luther, Martin. *Sermons on the Second Epistle of St. Peter*. Vol. 30 of AE. St. Louis: Concordia, 1967. ❦ The great reformer's sermonic commentary from 1523.

Academic Resources

Bauckham, Richard J. *Jude, 2 Peter*. WBC. Vol. 50. Waco: Word Books, 1983. ❦ Bauckham assigns 2 Peter to an anonymous Roman author, at the end of the first century, who borrows freely from Jude. He understands the letter to be an example of the sort of "testamentary literature" that even the first century reader would recognize to be a pseudepigraph. Bauckham views the author's opponents as libertine skeptics.

Bigg, Charles. *A Critical and Exegetical Commentary on the Epistles of St. Peter and St. Jude*. ICC. 2nd ed. Edinburgh: T&T Clark, 1902. ❦ Extensive introductory articles on the witness of the Church Fathers, authorship, and parallels with other New Testament writings. Though now over a century old, this remains a classic. Especially useful are the lexicographical remarks and table of similarities between 1 Peter and the Pauline corpus. Bigg holds to the Petrine authorship of both letters, and stresses that Jude was written after 2 Peter.

Davids, Peter H. *The Letters of 2 Peter and Jude*. Pillar New Testament Commentary. Grand Rapids: Eerdmans, 2007. ʂ Using rhetorical and narrative analysis, Davids argues that these letters are coherent documents addressed to the concerns of local churches.

Fronmüller, G. F. C. *The Epistles General of Peter*. LCHS. New York: Charles Scribner's Sons, 1867. ʂ A helpful older example of German biblical scholarship, based on the Greek text, which provides references to significant commentaries from the Reformation era forward.

Giese, Curtis P. *2 Peter and Jude*. CC. St. Louis: Concordia, 2012. ʂ Thorough historical and theological exposition of the Greek texts from a Lutheran theologian, describing the letters' mutual focus on the end times and warnings against false teachers. The best all-around volume.

Kelly, J. N. D. *The Epistles of Peter and of Jude*. Black's New Testament Commentary. Grand Rapids: Baker, 1969. ʂ Holds to the unity of 1 Peter and feels that the case for Petrine authorship is strong. In his view, Jude was written prior to 2 Peter, with the latter written by an unknown author.

Lenski, R. C. H. *The Interpretation of I and II Epistles of Peter, the Three Epistles of John, and the Epistle of Jude*. Minneapolis: Augsburg, 1966. ʂ A standard resource by a noteworthy Lutheran interpreter, concerned with being faithful to the text and with its implications for today.

Stoeckhardt, George. *Lectures on the Second Epistle of St. Peter*. Translated by H. W. Degner. Lake Mills, IA: Graphic Publishing Co., 1967. ʂ Sound theologically, from a learned and experienced Lutheran exegete at Concordia Seminary.

1, 2, AND 3 JOHN

God is love

From the heights of the great theater, one may look down the Arcadian Way to the harbor that made Roman Ephesus the first city of Asia. Its temple to Artemis, one of the Seven Wonders of the World, drew innumerable visitors and fostered trade. The Church, too, prospered here, where the apostle John preached and taught.

The Book of Revelation and other early Christian sources describe the woes John faced in the last years of his life when the emperor Domitian exiled him to the rocky island of Patmos. Tradition indicates that at the end of the first century John was the last of the apostles, all others having died as martyrs. After returning from exile, John completed his years in Ephesus, from which he most likely wrote these letters.

Historical and Cultural Setting

The Gospel of John was to some degree polemical. It was probably not directly occasioned by false teaching, but some characteristic accents and features of the Gospel are most readily understood as John's answer to a false teaching that perverted the true Gospel. The First Letter of John is wholly and vigorously polemical. It is aimed at false teachers, and although the letter never enters into a detailed refutation of their error, much less a full presentation of their teaching, the general character of the heresy can be ascertained with tolerable accuracy from hints given in the letter.

False teachers had arisen within the Church. "They went out from us," John writes, "but they were not of us; for if they had been of us, they would have continued with us. But they went out, that it might become plain that they all are not of us" (1Jn 2:19). At the time John wrote, they had separated themselves from the Church—or had been expelled. "You are from God and have overcome them," John tells the Church (4:4). These false teachers

The great theater of Ephesus, along the Arcadian Way.
John likely wrote his letters at Ephesus.

OVERVIEW

Author
John, apostle and evangelist, called "the elder"

Date
AD 85–95

Places
Various churches, perhaps in Asia Minor

People
John the elder; the brethren (children, fathers, and young men); antichrists; false teachers; various "spirits"; the elect lady, her children, and her elect sister; deceivers; Gaius; brothers who are strangers; Gentiles; Diotrephes; Demetrius; friends

Purpose
To establish and encourage the faith of John's contemporaries in the wake of rising controversy because some had left Christian congregations or had troubled them

Law Themes
Sin; walking in darkness or light; God's commands; hatred; death; deceit; antichrist(s); love one another; lawlessness; deceivers; wicked works; imitate God, not evil

Gospel Themes
Christ, the atoning sacrifice; our advocate; eternal life; God perfects His love in us (sanctification); light; born of God; children of God; truth; fellowship; abiding in Christ's teachings; Christ has come in the flesh

Memory Verses
Confession of sins (1Jn 1:7–9); Jesus, our advocate (2:1–2); the Son destroys the devil's work (3:8); God is love (4:7–12); true God and eternal life (5:20); beware of false teachers (2Jn 9–11)

TIMELINE

AD 33	Resurrection, Ascension, Pentecost
AD 49	Jerusalem Council
AD 70	Romans destroy Jerusalem
AD 95	Revelation written
AD 132	Bar Kokhba revolt begins

had apparently constituted themselves as a separate community; they continued to make vigorous propaganda for their cause (cf 2Jn 7 and 10) and still constituted a threat to the Church (1Jn 2:27; 3:7).

They were a real threat, for they were very "religious" men. They were "spiritual" men and claimed the prophetic authority of the Holy Spirit for their teaching (1Jn 4:1). They propagated a high and solemn sort of piety, a piety that claimed immediate communion with God and operated with slogans such as "I know Him," "I abide in Him," "I am in the Light" (2:4, 6, 9), and "I love God" (1Jn 4:20). They likely felt themselves and professed themselves to be a new elite in Christendom, the "advanced" type of Christian. John is probably referring to them in his second letter when he speaks of those who "[go] on ahead" and do not abide in the doctrine of Christ (2Jn 9). It was no wonder that they deceived many and that many who remained in the Church were perhaps not fully convinced that the Church had been in the right when it separated itself from them. Or there might well have been some who were still secretly attracted to this brilliant new theology.

Composition

Author

The First Letter

There can be little doubt that the first letter is by the same author as the Gospel of John. The first words of the letter (1Jn 1:1–4) seem expressly designed to recall the opening of the Gospel. First John and the Gospel of John have so many traits of language and style in common and have so large an agreement in substance that only common authorship serves to explain them, as most modern scholars also have recognized. One also answers the question of the authorship of the First Letter of John when one answers the question of the authorship of the Fourth Gospel. Those features that are peculiar to 1 John are readily explained by the particular purpose of the letter.

The Second and Third Letters

The second and third letters are not so well attested in the Early Church as the first letter. There was, in fact, some doubt as to their authorship. But the evidence of the letters themselves indicates that they are both by the same author. Compare, for example, 2Jn 1 and 3Jn 1; 2Jn 4 and 3Jn 3–4; the negative statement of 2Jn 10 and the positive statement of 3Jn 8; 2Jn 12 and 3Jn 13–14.

The evidence further indicates that the two shorter letters are by the same author as the First Letter of John. Compare 1Jn 2:7 with 2Jn 5; 1Jn 2:18 and 4:1–3 with 2Jn 7; 1Jn 2:23 with 2Jn 9; 1Jn 3:6–9 with 3Jn 11. In the light of such evidence one can understand why Eusebius, surveying the situation in the Church as it had developed by the beginning of the fourth century, included the smaller letters of John among those books of the New Testament "that are controverted by some, *yet recognized by most*."

Since the author of both these short letters designates himself simply as "the elder," some scholars are inclined to ascribe these letters to an "elder" or presbyter John, distinct from John the apostle. But there are two difficulties in the way of interpreting "elder" as a description of office, that is, as presbyter. For one thing, there were so many presbyters in the churches of Asia that the mere designation of "elder" could hardly serve by itself to identify a man. For another, the kind of authority exercised by the "elder" of the letters in congregations obviously not his own far exceeds that which any mere presbyter might exercise or aspire to. It is more natural to see in this word *elder* a self-designation of the apostle in the later days of the Church when the men of the older apostolic generation had become few and were distinguished from others by their age. According to tradition, John outlived his co-apostles and could therefore have been known as "*the* elder" (the outstanding man of the first generation) in the churches to which he ministered in his old age.

As the last of the apostles, John aptly described himself as "the elder," wisened by a lifetime of preaching the Gospel.

Date of Composition

Date of First John

What can be said certainly is that the letter dates from John's long ministry in Asia Minor, which presents a wide margin, from about AD 70 to about AD 100. The date of Cerinthus helps to narrow down the date of the letter somewhat more. Cerinthus was a contemporary of Polycarp, who died about AD 150. His activity as false teacher would thus probably fall into John's later years, somewhere between AD 90 and 100.

Date of Second John

The second letter is probably to be dated about the same time as the first. The designation of "elder" would seem to indicate that John had outlived his generation and had become the grand old man of the Church in Asia Minor.

Date of Third John

The third letter probably dates from the same period as the first and second letters. Some scholars think that the letter to the church referred to in 3Jn 9 may be our Second Letter of John. This cannot be either proved or disproved.

John described Jesus as a flesh-and-blood man who shared in our joys and woes.

Purpose/Recipients

The false teachers deceived many, but they could not deceive the heart of John, for that heart was in fellowship with the Father and with His Son, Jesus (1Jn 1:3). The eyes that had seen the Word of life in the flesh (1:1) saw these men for what they were. They are, in John's clear vision, not prophets of God, but false prophets (4:1); their words are inspired not by the Spirit of truth, but by the spirit of error (4:6); they are not the Christ's, but the very embodiment of the Antichrist of the last days (2:18), impelled and informed by the spirit of the Antichrist (2:22; 4:3), who inspires the lie.

What was this lie? They denied not the deity, but the full humanity of the Christ. They denied that Jesus, the man in history, was the Christ, the Son of God (1Jn 2:22; cf 4:3, 15; 5:5); they denied that Jesus was the Christ who had come "in the flesh" (1Jn 4:2; cf 2Jn 7). We get a hint of how far this denial went in the words of John that state positively the significance of the Christ who came in the flesh: "This is He who came by water and blood—Jesus Christ; not by the water only but by the water and the blood" (1Jn 5:6). These words are in themselves somewhat obscure, but they become clearer against the background of the heresy that they combat. That heresy was most probably the heresy of Cerinthus and his followers, of which Irenaeus has left us a description (*ANF* 1:352). Cerinthus, according to Irenaeus, taught that Jesus was a man among men, a superior man but still merely man, the son of Joseph and Mary; at His Baptism the "heavenly Christ" descended upon Him in the form of a dove and enabled Him to reveal the hitherto unknown God and to perform miracles; at His Passion, however, the "heavenly Christ" again left Jesus, and only Jesus the man suffered and died. In other words, the Christ came "by water" (the Baptism of Jesus), but did not come "by blood" (the Passion and death of Jesus). The cross of Jesus, the shed blood of the Son of God, which the apostolic witness celebrated as the crown and culmination of the ministry of Christ, was thus ignored or relegated to the background. The blood of Jesus, the Son of God, was no longer the blood that "cleanses us from all sin" (1Jn 1:7).

Where the cross is not taken seriously, sin is no longer taken seriously either. Men, whose proud piety centers in their assumed *knowledge* of God and ignores the cross in which God has revealed Himself as both the Judge of sinful man and the Forgiver of sinners, can think of sin as something that need not concern them; they can deceive themselves and say that they have no sin; they can say, "We have not sinned," and thus make a liar of God, who has in the cross declared that all people have sinned (1Jn 1:8, 10) and has in the cross given His Son as the "propitiation . . . for the sins of the whole

Outline

1 John

I. Prologue (1:1–4)

II. In the World, Not of It (1:5–3:12)

A. Because His Blood Cleanses Us from All Sin (1:5–2:2)

B. Because the True Light Is Already Shining (2:3–11)

C. Because the World Is Passing Away (2:12–17)

D. Because It Is the Last Hour (2:18–29)

E. Because Even Now We Are His Children (3:1–12)

III. In Him Who First Loved Us (3:13–5:21)

A. So We Love and Do Not Hate (3:13–24)

B. For Ours Is the Spirit of Truth (4:1–6)

C. Ours Is a God Who First Loved Us (4:7–10)

D. So Our Love Is His Love (4:11–21)

E. For His Is the Testimony of the Spirit, the Water, and the Blood (ch 5)

2 John

I. Greeting (1–3)

II. Walking in Truth and Love (4–11)

III. Final Greetings (12–13)

3 John

I. Greeting (1–4)

II. Support and Opposition (5–12)

III. Final Greetings (13–15)

world" (2:2). Such a piety can be comfortable in this world; the offense of the cross is gone, and the lives of Christians are no longer a walking indictment of the sins of the world. The world that does not recognize the children of God (3:1), but rather hates them (3:13), can come to terms with these men and with the Christ whom they proclaim: "They are from the world; therefore they speak from the world, and the world listens to them" (4:5).

Over against these men John asserts, with all the concentrated power that this inspired Son of Thunder can command, the full reality of the incarnation, the fact that life and communion with God are to be found in Jesus, the Christ who came and died for people's sin in the flesh, or they will not be found at all; that any claim to know and love God which does not produce a life of righteousness and love is a blank lie; that the child of God cannot ever, without denying himself and his God, be at home in the world which is in the power of the evil one. The letter is controversial and polemical, but it is not merely or one-sidedly polemical. John meets the danger that threatens the Church by a powerfully positive restatement of what the Christian life really is, a passionate appeal to recognize in action the full measure of the gift and the full extent of the claim of that grace of God which has given us fellowship with the Father and with the Son.

Occasion, Purpose, and Content of the Second Letter of John

The second letter was occasioned by the activity of false teachers, most probably the same group that John dealt with in his first letter. There is the same emphasis on the commandment of love (vv 5–6), the same emphasis on the reality of the incarnation of the Son of God (His "coming . . . in the flesh," v 7), the same designation of the false teaching as deceit and the work of the Antichrist (v 7), the same insistence on the fact that no one can know the Father except through the incarnate Son (v 9). The letter contains one of the sternest warnings in the New Testament against participating in, or furthering, the activities of those who pervert the Gospel (vv 10–11). It is this furthering of the work of the false teachers that is referred to, of course, in the words, "Do not receive him into your house or give him any greeting" (v 10); evangelists, who had no missionary fund to draw on, were dependent on the hospitality of Christians as they moved from place to place, as the Third Letter of John shows.

Recipients of the Second Letter

The Second Letter of John is addressed by one who calls himself simply "the elder" to "the elect lady and her children" (2Jn 1). This is probably a figurative way of addressing a church (the word for church is feminine in

John likely addressed the Church as the "elect lady," as Paul described the Church as the Bride of Christ. Praying woman on the fourth-century "Sarcophagus of the Trees."

Greek), rather than a literal address to some Christian woman and her children. The very broad statement of the salutation, "whom I love in truth, and not only I, but also all who know the truth" (2Jn 1) is more suitable to a church than to an individual. The expression in v 4, "I rejoiced greatly to find some of your children walking in the truth," is most naturally understood of a church, some of whose members had resisted the inroads of the heresy that was then ravaging the church of Asia Minor. The greeting of v 13, "The children of your elect sister greet you," also seems to be more naturally taken as a greeting from a sister church in whose midst the Elder is writing. And finally, the content of the letter (the renewal of the commandment of love and a stern warning against false teachers) seems eminently suitable as a message to a church. Besides, if the "elect lady" is an individual, why is she not named, as Gaius is named in the Third Letter of John?

Occasion and Purpose of the Third Letter

The Third Letter of John gives us another glimpse into the apostolic activity of John in his latter years. If the first and second letters dealt with heresy, the third letter deals with a missionary problem. The recipient of the letter, "the beloved Gaius" (v 1), had distinguished himself by his loyal support of some traveling evangelists (vv 5–8). These evangelists had meanwhile reported to their home church, probably at Ephesus, and had there testified to the love that Gaius had shown them (v 6). He had done so in the face of grave difficulties; a certain Diotrephes had sought, and was at the time of writing still seeking, to put himself in control of the church to which Gaius belonged and had refused to welcome the missionary brethren. He went even further than that and sought to stop those who wished to receive the missionaries and "put them out of the church" (vv 9–10). In so doing he was consciously opposing the Elder himself (v 9).

Literary Features

Genre

A challenge for any interpreter is determining the character of the First Letter of John. Although the early Christians referred to it as a letter, it does not include the typical greetings and conclusions found in most other New Testament letters. Like Hebrews, 1 John has the character of a sermon. This has led commentators to suggest that 2 John may have served as a cover letter for the sermon that is 1 John, with the third letter being an accompanying private letter. This well-crafted theory has much to commend it, though one must also agree that it remains a theory until some specific evidence for or against it comes to light.

The first two letters of John have a polemical quality, describing and warning against false teachers, though also admonishing the hearers to love God and one another. The third letter describes more practical matters, such as mission and church life.

Characters

On John, "the elder," and the false teachers, see "Historical and Cultural Setting" above. On "the elect lady," her sister, and children, see "Recipients of the Second Letter" above.

Narrative Development or Plot

Since 1 John is written primarily as a doctrinal letter, it does not have a storyline or plot. The second and third letters contain story elements, referring to actions of false teachers and hostile fellow workers. In each case, the story elements become occasions for teaching the readers about truth and faithfulness.

Resources

On the possibility that 1 John is a sermon, see "Genre" above. On the interrelationship between the Gospel of John and the letters, see "Author" above.

Text and Translations

The letters of John are largely well preserved, with a portion of 1 John appearing early in Papyrus 9 (third century) and the other letters appearing in the earliest uncial manuscripts (fourth century). However, 1 John includes two problematic readings. The first is 3:21, where scribes become confused about the meaning of "if our heart does not condemn us."

A notorious addition appears at 5:7, which is only found in four late Greek manuscripts that may have been translated from a Latin text. The reading does not appear in any Greek Church Fathers or early versions. It first appeared in a fourth century apologetic work attributed to the Spanish heretic Priscillian. It was likely a gloss or commentary on "the Spirit and the water and the blood" (5:8), interpreting them as symbolizing the Trinity "in heaven, the Father, the Word, and the Holy Ghost: and these three are one" (5:7 KJV).

Egyptian water clock.

Doctrinal Content

Summary Commentary

1 John 1:1–4 John begins this letter much like his Gospel account, with the Eternal Word, who was always with the Father and was working with the Father at creation. But here John's point is that this same Word who is "eternal life" is the crucified and risen Lord Jesus Christ, whom all the apostles had physically seen, heard, and touched.

1:5–3:10 John writes about faithfulness in our walk with God. God sees our true nature, and in Christ He reveals His nature, which is both just and gracious to us. Only true children who know Jesus as their Savior can truly walk as Jesus walked and love one another as Jesus has loved them. Jesus has shown us the love of God on the cross. This is the love the Law commanded but we could never fulfill. But more than that, it is the love that the Gospel imparts to those who love their brother and abide in the light so that there is in them nothing that would cause them to fall away from faith in Christ. True Christians abide in Christ through faith in Him and all His teachings. There are many antichrists, false teachers who infiltrate the Church and attempt to draw Christians away from the true Christ.

3:11–4:21 Our heart condemns us when we look at our brother, see his needs, and yet excuse ourselves from acting in love. However, in Christ we know that we have passed out of death into life; that is, we have true saving faith, because we love our fellow Christians. Whenever a teacher speaks of a "Christ" or a "Jesus" or a "God" who comes to us without human flesh, know this: it is a demon speaking through a man, a demon who is seeking to destroy faith everlastingly. "Whoever greets him takes part in his wicked works" (2Jn 11).

Ch 5 The children of God bear the family traits of their Brother, Jesus. He has faith, love, and victory over the world. The testimony of the apostles, the life of Jesus, and the work of the Spirit testify that God has given us life in His Son. Knowing that we have eternal life in Jesus gives us confidence to ask for anything, and we can be certain that we shall receive what we ask according to God's will, especially when we pray for our brother for Jesus' sake.

2 John The apostle John and all who truly know Christ as the Father's Son in human flesh love one another in truth. We walk in love and truth only by remaining faithful to Christ's teaching that He is God in human flesh who came to save us. Those who depart from Christ's teaching do not have God the Son or the Father or eternal life. Those who support them share in their wicked work and will share in their punishment as well. The apostle is planning to come and set straight all outstanding issues. Until then, the congregation has his warning and admonition to stand firm in the faith.

3 John The apostle prays that Gaius might be physically as healthy as he is spiritually healthy. Whatever flattery or intimidation people may use to get their way, there always comes a day when their works are brought into the open—when they will be shamed before God and His faithful. John gives Christ's blessing of peace and extends the greetings of all of Gaius's friends in Ephesus. John withholds all that he might say about Diotrephes until he meets with Gaius face-to-face.

Specific Law Themes

In the opening of the first letter, John quickly comes to the topic of sin and the fact that all people are sinners, persons who have walked in darkness. He confronts the reader with God's commands, including those against hatred, death, and deceit. John warns that many antichrists have come, spreading lawlessness, making people wicked and turning them into deceivers. In contrast, God commands that His people love one another and imitate God, who is love.

Specific Gospel Themes

Christ is our atoning sacrifice who takes away all our sins. He is likewise our advocate with the Father, who pleads for us. His gift is eternal life, love that He perfects in us, and the light of His truth. Since we are born of God, we are children of God, to whom He grants truth and fellowship. The Lord calls us to abide in the teachings of Christ, who has come in the flesh.

Specific Doctrines

The First Letter of John is written to Christians, to people whose faith is being endangered by heresy and is being tried by temptation. Although the usual letter forms (salutation, close, etc.) are missing, it is nevertheless a genuine letter, written for a specific situation by a father in Christ to his "children," and it is pervaded by an intense personal and pastoral concern for these "children."

In its white-hot passion for the truth, for a Christian Gospel and a Christian life that is genuine, whole, and uncompromised, it remains a tonic and bracing word for the Church always. It summons a congregation grown easy and comfortable to think penitently of the basic facts and the basic laws of its existence. Nowhere is black so black and white so white as in this letter; the antithesis of truth/lie, Christ/Antichrist, God/devil leaves the congregation no possibility of doubt as to where she must stand. And the letter likewise leaves no doubt that the Church *can* stand where she must stand; the greatness of God's enabling gift is lettered out in pithy statements that are as profound as they are brief and pointed. Perhaps no New Testament book of like compass has furnished so many brief sayings, sayings that Christians can lay up in their hearts, to live by and to die on, as this First Letter of John (e.g., 1:5, 8; 2:2, 9–11, 15–17, 23; 3:1, 2; 4:1–3, 7–12, 19; 5:3–5, 11–12).

Key Passages

Although only five chapters in length, 1 John has contributed significantly to theological reflection. In 1Jn 1:8 and 2:16, the doctrine of original sin and its effects upon all people is plainly taught. Also affirmed is that God created all things good. Just as sin affects all people, God intends that the Gospel belongs to all people (1Jn 2:2). The Father sent the Son to destroy the works of the devil (3:8), who would trap people in sin or bend them back to sin through lust (2:16). Believers must test the spirits to see whether they are from God (4:1). Christ gives fellowship with God (1:7) and provides new life, freeing the conscience from the burden of sin and fostering the confidence of forgiveness (3:21–22). The believer trusts in God through faith (5:10) and shows love for Him through keeping His commands (5:3).

The two shorter letters have some similar themes about the Church and its fellowship. John describes himself as elder (2Jn 1), which is associated with the office of pastor in other New Testament letters. Since the medieval era, the references to "antichrist" have garnered special attention (1Jn 2:18, 22; 4:3; 2Jn 7). Confrontations with false teachers and cults continue to make 2Jn 10 relevant.

Application

1:1–4 We owe the Eternal Word our perfect obedience. Despite our disobedience—our lack of recognition and faithfulness of our Creator—the Eternal Word came not to condemn us but to save us.

1:5–3:10 For those who confess their sins, God is always faithful to His promise to forgive. This is just and right because of His Son, who has paid the price for our sins. In Him, we love our fellow Christians. The new commandment, "love one another as I have loved you" (Jn 15:12), is rooted in Jesus' work, which frees us from guilt. His atonement for our sins empowers us to love as He loves. Our sinful flesh and the world entice and tempt us with their glittering promises. But none of it provides for forgiveness, peace, and contentment. No one born of God wants to give in to sinning. Those who give themselves over to sin will not be exonerated by the excuses they put forward. Through daily repentance and the practice of righteousness, we show ourselves to be true children of God and will not be ashamed when our Lord Jesus appears on the Last Day. Then we will be like Him and see Him as He is in all His glory.

3:11–4:21 Jesus laid down His life for us. His love for us has covered all our sins. God is greater than our heart, and His sure and certain promises of salvation give us confidence to come before Him. Faith in the heart cannot be seen; it can only be shown through acts of love. The greatest testimony is the true flesh-and-blood testimony of God's love manifest in Jesus. Whenever we do not treat our brother with love as Jesus has loved us, we fear God's punishment. Because He sent His Son to take away our sins, we gain confidence to stand before God without fear.

Ch 5 The world tempts us to think of our Lord's Commandments as a burden, too hard and too heavy for us to bear. The world seems too much for us to overcome. But our Lord Jesus has overcome the world for us. He has fulfilled all of God's commandments for us. He made Himself our human

Brother, that through Him we might become the children of His Father and share in His great family of love. This testimony is in stark contradiction to all who teach that God's Son did not suffer in the flesh or that He comes to us apart from the flesh of His humanity. All wrongdoing is sin, and any sin could lead to death if not for the Righteous One, Jesus Christ, who cleanses us from all sin by His blood. Not only can we be confident of our own forgiveness in Him who is the genuine Savior and the true God, but we can also pray even for our brother who sins and be certain that God desires his repentance and life because of Jesus.

2 John Those who know Jesus know the truth and, along with Jesus, they have grace, mercy, and peace. Cling to the truth that Jesus still comes to us in human flesh so that you may walk in love and in truth. The Father, Son, and Holy Spirit are ever with you to care for you. You, too, have the apostle's testimony and all of Holy Scripture. Abide in God's revelation and beware of strange teachings that diminish the person and work of Jesus, who is your salvation and joy.

3 John Our heavenly Father is on our side at all times, no matter what suffering we face. He sent Jesus as our great physician to heal us from sin and the afflictions we experience in a sin-broken world. We need not fear the threats and plots of power mongers who conspire against us and would try to harm our reputations and have us cast out because we show love and support for God's ambassadors. God will bring their threats and accusations into the light. Trust the Lord to protect you when you support the truth. He will deliver you by His Son, who is "the way, and the truth, and the life" (Jn 14:6).

CANONICITY

Like the Gospel of John, the First Letter of John was readily accepted by the Early Church (*homologoumenon*). However, the matter is somewhat different for the other two letters, since some doubted whether they were truly written by the apostle (*antilegomena*). For more on this issue, see "Author" above.

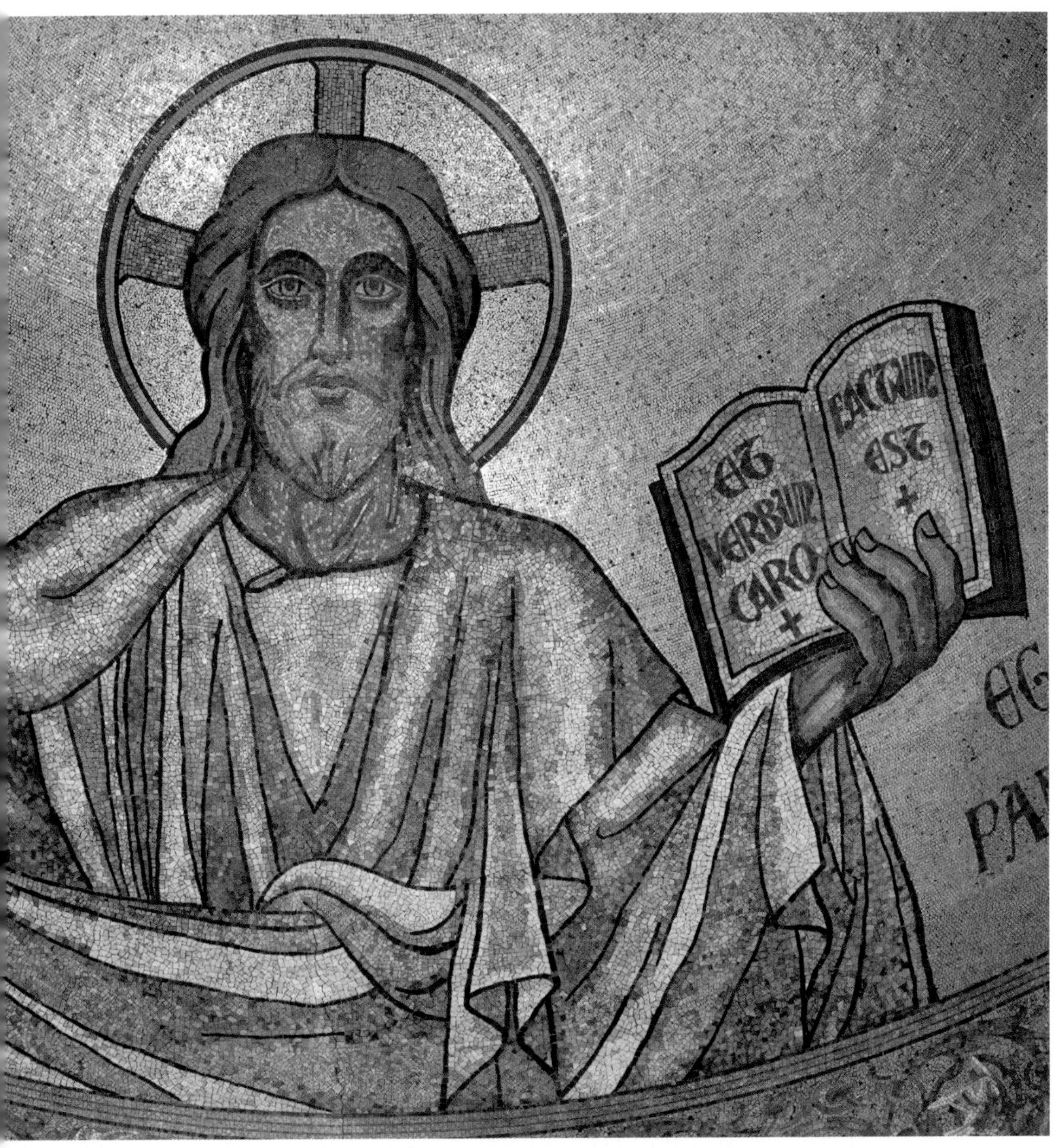

In the apostle John's Letters, he emphasized an opening point of His Gospel: Jesus the Word became flesh.

Lutheran Theologians on 1, 2, and 3 John

Luther

"The first epistle of John is a genuine apostolic epistle and ought to follow right after his gospel. For as in the gospel he promulgates faith, so here he opposes those who boast of faith without works. He teaches in many different ways that works are not absent where faith is; and if they are absent, then faith is not genuine but is lies and darkness. He does this, however, not by harping on the law, as the epistle of James does, but by stimulating us to love even as God has loved us.

"He also writes vigorously here against the Cerinthians, against the spirit of Antichrist, which was beginning even then to deny that Christ has come in the flesh, and which is today for the first time really in full sway. For although people do not now publicly deny with their lips that Christ has come in the flesh, they do deny it with their hearts, by their teaching and life. For he who would be righteous and saved by his own works and deeds is as much as denying Christ, since Christ has come in the flesh for the very purpose of making us righteous and saving us without our works, by his blood alone.

"Thus the epistle fights against both parties: against those who would live in faith without any works, and against those who would become righteous by their works. It keeps us in the true middle way, that we become righteous and free from sin through faith; and then, when we are righteous, that we practice good works and love for God's sake, freely and without seeking anything else.

"The other two epistles are not doctrinal epistles but examples of love and of faith. They too have a true apostolic spirit." (AE 35:393)

For more of Luther's insights on 1 John, see *Lectures on the First Epistle of St. John* (AE 30:217–327).

Gerhard

"At one time there was no less doubt about 2 and 3 John than there was concerning Hebrews, James, and 2 Peter. Eusebius, bk. 3, c. 21: 'The ancients, as well as the more recent, accept the first Epistle of John without any hesitation, but they speak against the other two.' In the same book, c. 22: 'Those that are spoken against, though they are well-known to many, are these: the Epistle attributed to James, etc., and 2 and 3 John, whether they are the work of that evangelist or of someone else with the same name as his.' Book 6, c. 24, from Origen: 'John left to us an Epistle with only a few verses. Let the second and third also be added (since they say those are not completely genuine), yet both do not have a hundred verses.' Jerome, *Catal. viror. illustr.*, on John: 'There are also two other Epistles of John that are claimed to belong to John the Elder, whose grave still today is at Ephesus. Some think that they are two memoirs of John the Evangelist.' (Eusebius, *Hist.*, bk. 3, c. 36, also decided, in accord with the opinion of Papias, that there are two Johns, namely, the apostle and the elder.) Erasmus, in his commentary: 'The authorities are agreed that 1 John is the work of that John whom Jesus loved most and that John the Elder wrote the latter two Epistles, not John the apostle.' In his commentary, Cajetan denies that they are canonical." (ThC E1 § 285)

Further Study

Lay/Bible Class Resources

Jeske, Mark A. *General Epistles*. PBC. St. Louis: Concordia, 2005. ❦ Lutheran author. Excellent for Bible classes. Based on the NIV translation.

Life by His Word. St. Louis: Concordia, 2009. ❦ More than 1,500 reproducible one-page Bible studies covering each chapter of the canonical Scriptures. Page references to *The Lutheran Study Bible*. CD-Rom and downloadable.

MacKenzie, Cameron, and David Loy. *1, 2, 3 John*. Leaders Guide and Enrichment Magazine/Study Guide. LL. St. Louis: Concordia, 2012. ❦ An in-depth, nine-session Bible study with individual, small group, and lecture portions.

Maxwell, David R. *1, 2, and 3 John: Love and Hate, Light and Darkness*. GWFT. St. Louis: Concordia, 2008. ❦ Lutheran author. Eleven-session Bible study, including leader's notes and discussion questions.

Stott, John. *The Letters of John*. TNTC. Downers Grove, IL: InterVarsity Press, 2009. ❦ A careful evangelical exposition written in simple style. Carefully surveys various views on authorship and accepts the apostle John as author.

Church Worker Resources

Marshall, I. Howard. *The Epistles of John*. NICNT. Grand Rapids: Eerdmans, 1978. ❦ Holds that the three letters were written by the same person but is uncertain whether he can be definitely identified as the apostle John. Otherwise a helpful resource.

Smith, D. Moody. *First, Second, and Third John*. Interpretation. Louisville: Westminster, 1991. ❦ Regards the letters and Gospel of John as the greatest theological and ethical developments in the New Testament. The series is designed for assisting those teaching and preaching.

Academic Resources

Braune, Karl. *The Epistles General of John*. LCHS. New York: Charles Scribner's Sons, 1867. ❦ A helpful older example of German biblical scholarship, based on the Greek text, which provides references to significant commentaries from the Reformation era forward.

Brooke, Alan England. *A Critical and Exegetical Commentary on the Johannine Epistles*. ICC. New York: Charles Scribner's Sons, 1912. ❦ A helpful resource. Holds that John's Gospel and the Johannine letters were written by the same author, who may not have been the apostle. Introductory articles include valuable parallels between the epistles and the Gospel.

Brown, Raymond E., trans. *The Epistles of John*. Vol. 30 of AB. Garden City, NY: Doubleday, 1982. ❦ Attempts to reconstruct the Johannine community responsible for the letters and the Gospel of John. An exhaustive, critical study that must be used with careful discernment.

Bultmann, Rudolf. *The Johannine Epistles: A Commentary on the Johannine Epistles*. Hermeneia. Philadelphia: Augsburg Fortress, 1973. ❦ A classic, critical work from a leading German figure of the twentieth century, with which other commentaries interact.

Culpepper, R. Alan. *The Gospel and Letters of John*. Interpreting Bible Texts. Nashville: Abingdon Press, 1998. ❦ A scholar of Johannine literature relates the Gospel and the letters, arguing for their common origin.

Kistemaker, Simon J. *James, Epistles of John, Peter and Jude*. New Testament Commentary. Grand Rapids: Baker, 1996. ❦ Introductory articles carefully analyze various theories on authorship, concluding that the apostle John is the author.

Kysar, Robert. *1, 2, 3 John*. Augsburg Commentary on the New Testament. Minneapolis: Augsburg Fortress, 1986. ❦ Lutheran author who has written extensively on Johannine studies, including numerous practical resources. Argues that one cannot be certain of the traditional view that the apostle John wrote the letters.

Lenski, R. C. H. *The Interpretation of I and II Epistles of Peter, the Three Epistles of John, and the Epistle of Jude*. Minneapolis: Augsburg Fortress, 1966. ❦ A standard resource by a noteworthy Lutheran interpreter, concerned with being faithful to the text and with its implications for today.

Lieu, Judith M. *The Second and Third Epistles of John: History and Background*. Edinburgh: T&T Clark, 1986. ❦ One of the most thorough commentaries on these two letters, including significant treatment of Church Fathers.

Painter, John. *1, 2, and 3 John*. Sacra Pagina. Collegeville, MN: Michael Glazier, 2002. ❦ Higher critical in orientation. Relates themes of the letters to the Gospel of John, uses a socio-rhetorical method.

Schnackenburg, Rudolf. *The Johannine Epistles: A Commentary*. New York: Crossroad, 1992. ❦ A critical treatment that does not hold that these letters were also written by the same author or community that developed the Gospel of John. Significant theological reflection from a critical viewpoint.

Schuchard, Bruce G. *1–3 John*. CC. St. Louis: Concordia, 2012. ❦ A thorough, conservative, and recent commentary on the Greek text from a Lutheran interpreter who supports apostolic authorship and accents the letters' opposition to false teaching. Draws together the best elements in other resources.

Westcott, Brooke Foss. *The Epistles of St. John: The Greek Text with Notes and Essays*. 2nd ed. Eugene, OR: Wipf & Stock, 2001. ❦ A classic resource from an influential nineteenth-century scholar.

JUDE

Built up in your most holy faith

Several passages in the New Testament refer to the narrow circle of relationships that made up the first followers of Jesus (Lk 1:39–45; Jn 1:29–51; 21:1–3). The small-town, largely Galilean roots of the movement stayed with the people even as they spread in all directions with the message that Jesus was the Christ. The Lord's immediate family was near the heart of that circle; Mary, His mother, believed the unique testimony about her firstborn Son, which she would have shared with other family members. The little book of Jude assumes that familiarity (v 1), presenting readers today with tantalizing questions.

Historical and Cultural Setting

We know so little of the life and activity of Jude that any attempt to fix the place of writing or to localize the church or churches addressed is bound to be guesswork. Nevertheless, some observations about the historical setting may be considered. For example, one may note that the letter lacks any overt influences from two major events of the era, which were for Judaism like World Wars I and II in our modern era: (1) the destruction of Jerusalem and the temple in AD 66–70, and (2) the Bar Kokhba or Second Jewish Revolt, which began in AD 132. Also, the letter has some relationship to 2 Peter (see "Resources" below) so that the date one assigns for 2 Peter can affect how one thinks about the historical situation for Jude. Further, as noted under "Author" below,

Arbel Cliff overlooking the Sea of Galilee, near where Jesus conducted His ministry.

OVERVIEW

Author
Jude

Date
c AD 68

Places
Egypt; Sodom and Gomorrah

People
Jude; James; false brothers and teachers; the apostles; doubters

Purpose
To warn fellow Christians about the dangers posed by the ungodly false teachers

Law Themes
The ungodly pervert God's grace; contend for the faith; God destroys unbelievers; blaspheming; eternal chains; gloomy darkness; stained by the flesh; judgment; eternal fire; way of Cain condemned

Gospel Themes
Called and beloved by God; peace; salvation; mercy of our Lord; present you blameless; God, our Savior

Memory Verse
Built up in the faith (vv 20–23)

TIMELINE

AD 33	Resurrection, Ascension, Pentecost
AD 49	Jerusalem Council
AD 68	Martyrdom of Peter and Paul
AD 70	Romans destroy Jerusalem
AD 132	Bar Kokhba revolt begins

the writer for Jude claimed to be a "brother of James," which if accepted as the half brother of Jesus, would also narrow down the date. Although these observations do not fix the date of the letter, one might argue that the letter was written before the fall of Jerusalem in AD 70, nearer the lifetimes of the apostles Peter and James.

Composition

Author

The author calls himself simply "Jude, a servant of Jesus Christ and brother of James" (Jude 1); he does not call himself an apostle, and the way in which he speaks of the apostles makes it clear that he is not one of them (v 17). He cannot therefore be identified with the apostle Judas, the son of James (Lk 6:16). "Brother of James" serves to identify him, and there is really only one James so generally known in early Christendom as to serve as identification, and that is James the brother of Jesus, the "pillar" and head of the Jerusalem Church (Gal 1:19; 2:9; cf 1Co 15:7; Jas 1:1). Jude is, then, one of the brothers of Jesus; we find his name listed in Mk 6:3 and Mt 13:55. Luke refers to these brothers as a group, and he associates them with the Twelve during the early days in Jerusalem (Ac 1:14). We learn from Paul (1Co 9:5) that these brothers of Jesus were active in missionary work. Jude, like the other brothers of Jesus, had not believed in Jesus during the time of His ministry on earth (Jn 7:5). Perhaps it was the example and the witness of his brother James after the resurrection (1Co 15:7) that won him for the faith. Nothing more is known of him.

Fourth-century mosaic in the Hagia Sophia of Mary, mother of Jesus, James, and Jude.

It is at first glance surprising that he does not call himself "brother of Jesus" in order to identify himself. But James, it should be noted, is similarly reticent; he, too, calls himself not brother but "servant" of Jesus (Jas 1:1). The men of the Early Church remembered the word that the Lord had spoken concerning His disciples: "Whoever does the will of My Father in heaven is My brother" (Mt 12:50); they knew that faith—and only faith—established the tie that bound a man to Jesus and made him an obedient son of God.

Date of Composition

Curtis Giese observes:

> If one accepts the authenticity of the epistle, . . . then the book must be dated to the historical lifetime of Jude, the half-brother of Jesus. Since the order in which the siblings are named likely indicates birth order, Jude may be the youngest (Mt 13:55) or perhaps the second youngest (Mk 6:3) sibling of Jesus. He might have been born as late as AD 10, and he could have died around AD 70. . . . Evidently 2 Peter was written in the early 60s AD (and no later than AD 65), and Jude probably wrote his epistle not long before the composition of 2 Peter (ca. AD 60–64). (CC 2Pt/Jude, pp 18–19)

Purpose/Recipients

Jude leaves us in no doubt as to what occasioned his writing. It was the appearance and the activity of men who answered Paul's question, "Are we to continue in sin that grace may abound?" (Rm 6:1) in a way that was the very opposite of Paul's answer, "No!" These were men who saw in the freedom that Christ had won for them not a freedom *from* sin, but the freedom *to* sin. Jude calls them "ungodly people, who pervert the grace of our God into sensuality and deny our only Master and Lord, Jesus Christ" (v 4). There was, moreover, nothing furtive or apologetic in their assertion and proclamation of this liberty; they did so quite openly and, indeed, arrogantly (vv 4, 8, 13, 16, 18–19). They had not broken with the Church, but carried on the propaganda for their views within it—they had "crept in unnoticed" (v 4), were present at the common meals of the Church (v 12), and created divisions within the Church (v 19). The images that Jude uses to describe them indicate that they set themselves up as teachers of the Church—they are clouds, from which people might expect water; trees, from which people might expect fruit; stars, from which the sailor expects guidance (vv 12–13).

Literary Features

Genre

Jude is a letter of admonition.

Characters

Jude centers his attack on the impiety of these **false teachers**; he does not honor whatever theological "system" they may have had by describing and refuting it—he is following the guidance of the word of his brother and Lord, Jesus ("You will recognize them by their fruits," Mt 7:16), in pointing to the evil fruits of this bad tree. But that they did have a system by which they defended and asserted their vicious liberty is evident not only from the fact that they appear as teachers, but also from other indications in Jude's letter. Jude speaks of their "dreams" (v 8); this would indicate a speculative kind of theology, perhaps akin to the emphasis on "knowledge" with which the brilliant and irresponsible misleaders of the Corinthian Church had justified their claim to liberty; their arrogance and their mercenary character (vv 11, 16) would also characterize them as men of similar bent. When Jude calls them "worldly people, devoid of the Spirit" (v 19), he is ironically using terms that Gnostics later used; they, of course, described the simple Christian who had only faith as "worldly" (unspiritual) and themselves, the men of knowledge, as "spiritual."

Ripe figs in a tree ready for harvest.

The very vehemence with which Jude exposes these teachers is indication enough that they were persuasive and impressive men, and therefore a fearful threat to the Church. They were all the more fearful a threat because they would not break with the Church; Jude therefore insists that the Church break with them. He rouses holy fear in his readers; they are called upon to do battle for that which the Lord and His apostles have given them (v 3) and to avoid all contact and compromise with the false teachers, lest they fall under the judgment of God that once struck a disobedient Israel, doomed the disobedient angels, destroyed Sodom and Gomorrah, and will surely destroy these destroyers of the Church of God (vv 5–7, cf vv 13–15). Even their attempts to save those believers who have not yet succumbed completely to the propaganda of the doomed teachers are to be marked by this holy fear: "Save others by snatching them out of the fire; to others show mercy with fear" (v 23).

But fear is not Jude's only weapon; he instills also the high confidence of faith. The arrogant, contentious, and mercenary blasphemers are surely doomed (v 4); judgment awaits them, and they will perish in their pride (vv 11, 14–15). His readers are forewarned by the apostolic word (vv 17–18); and, above all, they have their security in the love of God as people "beloved in God the Father and kept for Jesus Christ" (v 1). And so the letter closes with a doxology filled with the exuberant confidence of hope: "Now to Him who is able to keep you from stumbling and to present you blameless before the presence of His glory with great joy, to the only God, our Savior, through Jesus Christ our Lord, be glory, majesty, dominion, and authority, before all time and now and forever. Amen" (vv 24–25).

Narrative Development or Plot

Since Jude is written as a letter, it does not have a storyline or plot. However, the book does include the brief story of how false teachers have crept into the congregation receiving the letter (vv 3–4). Jude then uses numerous Old Testament stories to characterize the false teachers.

Resources

The Letter of Jude and 2Pt 2 are so similar in language and thought that there is obviously a historical connection between the two; they can hardly have originated altogether independently of each other. For more on this matter, see "Resources" on p 726.

Text and Translations

The text of Jude is well established from the fourth century onward through manuscripts such as Papyrus 72. Difficult readings occur in vv 5, 22–23.

Doctrinal Content

Summary Commentary

1–2 Despite the stumbling faith of Jude's readers, he begins with comfort and encouragement. He greets the whole congregation as God's chosen people, even though false teachers exist among them.

3–16 Jude flatly condemns the activities of the ungodly, while gently rebuking the godly for tolerating them. He candidly points out that the Gospel itself is at risk for corruption. He also refers the people back to their catechesis in the Old Testament history of God's wrath and grace. Jesus Himself condemned the Israelites for their sins and also acted as their Savior. Then Jude mercilessly describes the sins of the ungodly without explicitly nam-

Outline

I. Greeting (vv 1–2)

II. Judgment on False Teachers (vv 3–16)

III. A Call to Persevere (vv 17–23)

IV. Closing Doxology (vv 24–25)

ing them or their group. He knows that the congregation will read his letter publicly, in the hearing of these false brothers.

17–23 Christians, who have the full salvation already delivered to them in Scripture, need not fall into deceptions.

24–25 Jude emphasizes that salvation is not based on our own reason or strength but is wholly the Father's work in Christ.

Specific Law Themes

Jude describes how the ungodly pervert God's grace through blaspheming and wander in the way of Cain. He warns that God will destroy the unbelieving while pointing to the chains, darkness, and fire of eternal punishment. He admonishes the congregation to snatch people stained by the flesh away from the coming judgment.

Specific Gospel Themes

Jude refers to his readers as those called and beloved by God, bidding them God's mercy, peace, and salvation. Although much of the letter describes God's judgment, his closing doxology beautifully prays that the Lord would present them blameless in God's presence in eternity.

Specific Doctrines

When Jesus warned His disciples against false prophets, He gave them only one simple test by which they were to distinguish the false prophets from the true: "You will recognize them by their fruits" (Mt 7:16). The test seems almost absurdly simple when one considers the history of error in the

Tullian prison on the Forum in Rome, where Peter may have been imprisoned.

Church, error in its various, ever new, and plausible disguises. But the little powerful Letter of Jude is living proof that Jesus' confidence in His followers was not misplaced. Endowed with the Spirit of Jesus, Jude rightly saw and roundly declared that what these men produced was not a fruit of the Spirit; for the Spirit teaches men to call Jesus Lord and to live under His Lordship (1Co 12:3), and neither the brilliance nor the persuasiveness nor the arrogant boldness of these men could conceal from the keen eye of faith the fact that they did deny Him whom they professed as their only Master and Lord, Jesus Christ. Thus the Word of the Lord prevailed, and the presence of Jude in the canon is an assurance that it will continue to prevail.

Key Passages

Angels are an important element in this short letter (vv 6, 9), therefore, theologians have sought its insights for that portion of Christian doctrine. They have also used Jude's vigorous polemical language in disputes.

Application

1–2 View and address your congregation as godly and beloved, even if troubled by divisions or false teachers. For the Lord has called them by the Gospel.

3–16 The Lord certainly calls us to work patiently with those who err. But we can never compromise the Gospel, which is the basis of our salvation. You never outgrow the catechism basics of Bible stories and Law and

Gospel, by which the Lord grants constant blessings. Jude apparently trusts that the congregation will take all necessary action to correct the problems. By not naming names, he leaves the congregation to work with individuals at its discretion. This will grant opportunity for confession and absolution.

17–23 We have been warned about false teaching and the deception of sin that leads to death. Likewise, the Lord has taught us the path of righteousness by which His Spirit leads us in the Gospel of grace and peace.

24–25 As the Lord grants you opportunity, share the message of salvation with boldness, for it truly comes from the Lord and He truly works through that testimony, leading those who repent to great joy.

Canonicity

The genuineness of the Epistle of Jude was questioned in the Early Church (*antilegomenon*), but its attestation became quite strong. According to some ancient authorities, doubts concerning the epistle were occasioned by its use of noncanonical writings, such as the *Book of Enoch* (vv 14–15) and the *Assumption of Moses* (v 9). It may be that such apocalyptic writings were being used by the false teachers and that Jude in quoting these writings was meeting them on their own ground. It is noteworthy that he uses these writings only insofar as they serve to enforce the call to repentance, that is, as warnings against any proud self-assertion.

Lutheran Theologians on Jude

Luther

Reflecting on various statements from the Early Fathers, Luther concluded that St. Jude did not write this letter. Many modern scholars would agree. However, one should note that Luther assumed the writer of Jude had copied 2 Peter. This is not necessarily the case.

"Concerning the epistle of St. Jude, no one can deny that it is an extract or copy of St. Peter's second epistle, so very like it are all the words. He also speaks of the apostles like a disciple who comes long after them [Jude 17] and cites sayings and incidents that are found nowhere else in the Scriptures [Jude 9, 14]. This moved the ancient fathers to exclude this epistle from the main body of the Scriptures. Moreover the Apostle Jude did not go to Greek-speaking lands, but to Persia, as it is said, so that he did not write Greek. Therefore, although I value this book, it is an epistle that need not be counted among the chief books which are supposed to lay the foundations of faith." (AE 35:397–98)

There is good reason to suppose that St. Jude would have known Greek, which was commonly spoken in Judea and was also used in Persia.

For more of Luther's insights on this book, see *Sermons on the Epistle of St. Jude* (AE 30:201–15).

Gerhard

"The following . . . prove that this Epistle is apostolic: (1) The inscription. The author clearly calls himself 'Jude, a servant of Jesus Christ and brother of James.' (2) The subject matter. This Epistle agrees with both the thoughts and words of 2 Peter, of which it contains something like a brief summary and epitome. (3) The testimonies of the ancients. . . .

"The stronger arguments in support of the contrary are as follows: (1) 'In Holy Scripture there appear no traces of the accounts that this Epistle cites. Where is the account of the argument between the archangel Michael and the devil about the body of Moses?' We respond. Just as Paul cites the names of the mages Jannes and Jambres from tradition (2 Tim. 3:8), so also does Jude, regarding that argument of the archangel Michael and the devil. Furthermore, traces of that history are extant in a canonical book. Deuteronomy 34:6 mentions that the Lord buried the body of Moses in the valley of Mount Nebo and that the Israelites did not know the location of that tomb. The devil, therefore, seems to have wanted to reveal this to the Israelites so that they might establish an idolatrous worship of it, just as they later abused the golden serpent to the point of idolatry. The archangel Michael, however, prohibited the devil. At one time there was a writing called . . . 'The Departure of Moses from This Life.' . . . In it are contained the things cited in this passage about Moses' body. Some understand that argument as though the angel would have offered a service in burying Moses but that the devil was not willing to endure this; so the devil made the accusation that Moses belonged to him because of his murder of the Egyptian, and consequently the devil would not allow Moses to have an honorable burial. The earlier explanation, however, is the more simple.

"(2) 'The author of this Epistle takes testimony from the Book of Enoch, which is apocryphal.' We respond. Tertullian (*De habit. muliebr.*) and Bede (commentary on this Epistle) contend that the true Book of Enoch was still extant in the hands of men at Jude's time. Jerome (on Titus 1) and Augustine (*De civ. Dei*, bk. 15, c. 23; bk. 18, c. 38) respond: 'Even in the apocryphal books there is some truth, and Jude took this from an apocryphal book.' Nevertheless Jude did not consequently give his approval to the entire book, because the apostle proffers testimonies even from heathen poets yet did not intend to assign canonical authority to them. Some respond that Jude is not looking so much to a prophecy of words [*verbale*] as to a prophecy of things [*reale*], that is, to the order among the patriarchs. Just as bodily death, because of sin, held dominion over the first six fathers of the Church—namely, Adam, Seth, Enosh, Kenan, Mahalalel, and Jared—but could not exercise its power and dominion in the case of the seventh—Enoch—so also for the six thousand years during which this world will stand, it will hold sway over all men; but in the seventh millennium, which will be the beginning of eternal, heavenly life, it will lose its sting and be abolished completely. (Cf. Chunmannus Flinspachius, *De conject. extr. tempor.*) However, because Jude says explicitly: 'Enoch prophesied also of these, saying: "Behold, the Lord came," ' others make the more probable claim that Jude is speaking about a prophecy of words which, though not put into writing by Enoch, nevertheless could certainly have been known to Jude by the revelation of the Holy Spirit.

"(3) 'The author does not call himself an apostle.' We respond. Neither James nor John in their inscriptions call themselves 'apostle.' In the Epistle to the Philippians, Paul calls himself 'a servant of Christ,' which Jude also does here and adds 'the brother of James,' from which its apostolic authority is gathered clearly. In both letters to the Thessalonians, Paul omits the word 'apostle,' yet no one on this account doubts the authority of those Epistles.

"(4) 'The author signifies that he lived after the apostles: "Be mindful of the words foretold by the apostles of our Lord Jesus Christ" (v. 17).' We respond. This proves that this Epistle was written after the Petrine and Pauline letters in which those prophecies are extant (1 Tim. 4:1; 2 Tim. 3:1; 2 Pet. 2:1). By no means, however, does he exclude himself from the number of the apostles with these words. Jude came after some of the apostles—Peter, Paul, and James—but not after them all, because John still survived.

"(5) 'Jude taught in Persia; therefore he would have written in Persian, not in Greek, if he were the author of this Epistle.' We respond. The Epistle of Jude is a catholic one, that is, written not to a particular church but to all the faithful. Therefore the author wanted to use the most common language of that time (that is, Greek) in his writing. When Paul wrote to the Romans, he used the Greek language, not the Roman one. Clearly the Holy Spirit wanted Greek to be the authentic language in the New Testament, just as he wanted Hebrew to be the authentic language in the Old Testament.

"Therefore we accept the Epistle of Jude among the canonical books, but of the second rank. Its author Jude had three names, for he was also called Thaddaeus and Lebbaeus (Matt. 10:3; Mark 3:[18]). This Epistle seems to have been written to the same people as 2 Peter, namely, to those especially who from their circumcision had believed the things he signified in v. 17: 'Be mindful of the words foretold by the apostles of our Lord Jesus Christ. They told you that in the last days scoffers will come,' words that are in 2 Pet. 2:1. He indicates this in v. 5: 'I want to warn you, though at one time you knew all things.' You see, this fits the Jews aptly, who were imbued with a knowledge of sacred history from the beginning of time. It also has the same theme as has 2 Peter, along with which it uses the same ideas and words.

"Some people think that these Epistles of Peter and Jude were directed especially against the Gnostics. Their heresy, however, came after the times of the apostles, as is evident from Irenaeus and Epiphanius. Therefore it is more correct to claim that they were written against the followers of Simon Magus and the Nicolaitans, whose shameful heresy began to creep in far and wide after the deaths of the apostles. That is why Epiphanius (*Haeres.* on the Gnostics, who took their beginning from Simon Magus), after mentioning the wicked passions of that former sect, adds: 'Disturbed as He was about these people, the Holy Spirit said to the apostle Jude: "Whatever as mute spirits they knew naturally, such things are corrupted in them." ' In this Epistle, therefore, Jude exhorts those who were converted from Judaism to be steadfast in the faith, and he forewarns them of seducers who would corrupt the doctrine of the person of Christ, who would transfer the grace of God and spiritual freedom into license of the flesh, who would deny subjection to the magistracy, and who would stir up dissensions in the Church. Jude frightens them terribly and threatens God's judgment against them with the examples of the Israelites in the wilderness, of the wicked angels, and of the people of Sodom. Finally, he also teaches how they should be wary of deceits through their faith and prayers." (ThC E1 §§ 288–90)

Further Study

Lay/Bible Class Resources

Dunker, Gary. *2 Peter and Jude: Contend for the Faith.* GWFT. St. Louis: Concordia, 2009. ➳ Lutheran author. Eleven-session Bible study, including leader's notes and discussion questions.

Green, Michael. *2 Peter and Jude.* TNTC. Grand Rapids: The Tyndale Press, 1968. [1987.] ➳ Green's introduction includes a concise review of the arguments regarding the authorship and date of 2 Peter and its relation to Jude. He favors the proposal that 2 Peter and Jude both depend on a third, underlying source. Green has a good command of the patristic evidence.

Jeske, Mark A. *General Epistles.* PBC. St. Louis: Concordia, 2005. ➳ Lutheran author. Excellent for Bible classes. Based on the NIV translation.

Life by His Word. St. Louis: Concordia, 2009. ➳ More than 1,500 reproducible one-page Bible studies covering each chapter of the canonical Scriptures. Page references to *The Lutheran Study Bible.* CD-Rom and downloadable.

Rudnick, Milton, Earl Gaulke, Michael Eschelbach, and Edward Engelbrecht. *James and Jude.* Leaders Guide and Enrichment Magazine/Study Guide. LL. St. Louis: Concordia, 2003. ➳ An in-depth, nine-session Bible study with individual, small group, and lecture portions.

Academic Resources

Bauckham, Richard J. *Jude, 2 Peter.* WBC. Waco: Word Books, 1983. ➳ Bauckham assigns 2 Peter to an anonymous Roman author at the end of the first century, who borrows freely from Jude. He understands the letter to be an example of the sort of "testamentary literature" that even the first century reader would recognize to be pseudepigraphal. Bauckham views the author's opponents as libertine skeptics.

Bigg, Charles. *A Critical and Exegetical Commentary on the Epistles of St. Peter and St. Jude.* ICC. 2nd ed. Edinburgh: T&T Clark, 1902. ➳ Extensive introductory articles on the witness of the Church Fathers, authorship, and parallels with other New Testament writings. Though now over a century old, this remains a classic. Especially useful are the lexicographical remarks and table of similarities between 1 Peter and the Pauline corpus. Bigg holds to the Petrine authorship of both letters, and stresses that Jude was written after 2 Peter.

Davids, Peter H. *The Letters of 2 Peter and Jude.* Pillar New Testament Commentary. Grand Rapids: Eerdmans, 2007. ➳ Using rhetorical and narrative analysis, Davids argues that these letters are coherent documents addressed to the concerns of local churches.

Fronmüller, G. F. C. *The Epistle General of Jude.* LCHS. New York: Charles Scribner's Sons, 1870. ➳ A helpful older example of German biblical scholarship, based on the Greek text, which provides references to significant commentaries from the Reformation era forward.

Giese, Curtis P. *2 Peter and Jude.* CC. St. Louis: Concordia, 2012. ➳ Thorough historical and theological exposition of the Greek texts from a Lutheran theologian, describing the letters' mutual focus on the end times and warnings against false teachers. The best all-around volume.

Kelly, J. N. D. *The Epistles of Peter and of Jude.* Black's New Testament Commentary. Grand Rapids: Baker, 1969. ➳ Holds to the unity of 1 Peter and feels that the case for Petrine authorship is strong. In his view Jude was written prior to 2 Peter, with the latter written by an unknown author.

Lenski, R. C. H. *The Interpretation of I and II Epistles of Peter, the three Epistles of John, and the Epistle of Jude.* Minneapolis: Augsburg Fortress, 1966. ➳ A standard resource by a noteworthy Lutheran interpreter, concerned with being faithful to the text and with its implications for today.

REVELATION

Jesus is coming soon

Far from the shores of Galilee, the elderly apostle John trod the rugged hills of Asia Minor where he based his last years of ministry at the harbor city of Ephesus, according to early tradition. Disciples of John the Baptist, teachers such as Apollos and St. Paul, as well as others, had planted the congregation at Ephesus perhaps 40 years earlier (Ac 19–20). It prospered and became an important center for the faith. However, as the Church grew, so also grew formal opposition to its message and organization. Like the other apostles, John did not escape notice but participated in their suffering, though God preserved His life so that John might leave to the Church this capstone revelation.

Historical and Cultural Setting

Domitian was the first Roman emperor to make an issue of emperor worship; and since the emperor cult was propagated with great zeal in the province of Asia, the collision between the emperor, who laid claim to worship as "Lord and God," and those who would call no one Lord but Jesus and would worship Him alone, proved to be inevitable in Asia. That John should have been banished from Ephesus to Patmos, off the coast of Asia, "on account of the word of God and the testimony of Jesus" (Rv 1:9); that Antipas should have died a martyr's death at Pergamum in Asia (Rv 2:13); that the souls of those who had been slain for the witness they had borne should cry aloud for vindication (Rv 6:9–10)—all this fits in naturally with the historical situation in Asia in the latter years of Domitian's reign. The payment of divine honors to the emperor was made the test of loyalty; the Christian had to refuse, and that refusal made him liable to the penalty of death.

Coin featuring Roman emperor Domitian.

The visions given to John made it unmistakably plain to the churches why the Christian had to refuse and die. These visions wrote out in letters

Beaches of Patmos, Greece. Domitian exiled John to this island.

of gold and fire the promise that such dying was not defeat but triumph, a triumph which the Church shared with the Lamb that was slain, with Him who is King of kings and Lord of lords, whose people go His way through death to victory and royal reign.

Author

The Gospel and the three letters of John give a unified impression; in thought and language they are patently the creation of one man. The Revelation to John diverges strikingly in both thought and language. Many conceptions that are central for the Gospel and the letters are absent from Revelation (e.g., light, truth, grace, peace, the only Son, the Paraclete or Counselor as a title of the Holy Spirit; the antitheses light/darkness, above/below, lie/truth). Instead of the simple and correct Greek of the other works, Revelation has the strangest, harshest, and least "correct" Greek in the New Testament; it is Hebrew thinking transferred directly to Greek, and the most elementary laws of Greek grammar seem to be arbitrarily violated.

Common Themes with Johannine Works

But if the divergences in thought are striking, a closer examination reveals that the agreements between Revelation and the other Johannine works are no less so. The Gospel and Revelation agree in their view of the predicament of mankind. For the Gospel, man as man is in darkness and the world as world is under the judgment of God. This is what Revelation, too, declares with its visions of judgmental riders, trumpets of doom, and bowls of wrath. If in the Gospel Jesus calls those who oppose Him children of the devil and sees the world which hates Him under the dominion of the prince of this world, the devil, Revelation makes plain that the powers that persecute the Church get their will and impetus from Satan. In both the Gospel and Revela-

OVERVIEW

Author
John the apostle

Date
AD 95

Places
Patmos; Ephesus; Smyrna; Pergamum; Thyatira; Sardis; Philadelphia; Laodicea; the Euphrates; Jerusalem; Mount Zion; Armageddon

People
John; seven congregations in Asia; false teachers (Nicolaitans; the "synagogue of Satan"; Jezebel)

Purpose
To comfort suffering Christians and encourage their faithful witness with prophetic portraits of the victory that is already ours in the risen and living Lamb of God, Jesus Christ

Law Themes
Deception of false prophets; call to repentance; beasts; dragon (Satan); God's wrath; plagues; torment; woe; bottomless pit; tribulation; Babylon the great; second death; judgment; call to patient endurance

Gospel Themes
Word of God; made a kingdom, priests; Jesus' love; Lamb of God and numerous titles for the Savior; Spirit and authority of God; truth; Christ who conquers; Lord God Almighty; tree of life; Bride of the Lamb (Church); God is faithful and true; water of life

Memory Verses
Be faithful (2:10); Jesus at the door (3:19–20); the song and new song (4:11; 5:9–10); heaven's bliss (7:15–17); conquering Satan (12:10–11); marriage of the Lamb (19:6–9); Christ coming with recompense (22:12–15)

TIMELINE

AD 33	Resurrection, Ascension, Pentecost
AD 49	Jerusalem Council
AD 70	Romans destroy Jerusalem
AD 95	Revelation written
AD 132	Bar Kokhba revolt begins

tion, the line between the Church and the world, between those who are Christ's and those who are not, is most rigorously drawn, with no compromise or mediation. The Gospel speaks in terms of light, truth, life, and love as contrasted with darkness, lies, death, and hate; Revelation draws the same line between the white-robed, adoring saints of Christ united with God in the light, and the world bewitched by magic, worshiping the beast, subject to the dark dominion of the devil and under the wrath of God.

And even the language, for all its strangeness and harshness, does not exclude a common authorship of the Gospel and of Revelation. This Greek is not bungler's Greek; if it is strongly Semitic, the Greek of the Gospel and the letters is, despite its superior smoothness and correctness, strongly Semitic too. If it diverges from the normal laws of the Greek language, it does so intentionally and with powerful effect; it consciously recalls the language of the Greek Old Testament and has a marked poetic rhythm. Scholars are not so ready as they once were to say that the Greek of Revelation is impossible for the author of the Gospel. Given the difference in kind between the two works, the difference between the ecstasy of apocalyptic vision and the quieter, reverent eyewitness report, the difference is not so startling as it at first appears to be. And Revelation has in common with the Gospel a whole series of terms and conceptions that are found only in the Gospel of John: Jesus as the Word of God, Jesus as the Lamb of God, Jesus as the Shepherd, the Water of life, and the true worship of God independent of any temple (Jn 4:20–24; Rv 21:22). This does not exhaust the resemblances, but will suffice to indicate the state of the case.

There is one more link between Revelation and the Gospel of John—the link of personality. Some have found it impossible to think that the high serenity of the Gospel and the furious intensity of Revelation should be the product of one mind and heart. The two books are not, of course, merely the product of human personality; but the problem remains, for when God speaks through men, He does not blank out human personality, but uses it.

One should not forget what an amazing range of experiences the life of this passionate Son of Thunder comprehended. John had seen the Word made flesh and had beheld His glory. John had drawn on the fullness of the grace and truth incarnate in Jesus; he had seen the only Son of God go down before the hatred of those who resisted the light and loved darkness. John had seen Him who had proclaimed Himself to be the resurrection and the life risen from the dead, in the unbroken splendor of His eternal life. He had proclaimed this Prince of life to Jerusalem, and John had seen his own brother killed in the renewed collision between the truth and the lie. He had

Road through Galilee.

seen the fury of Nero break upon the Church of Rome, and he had seen the judgment of God visited upon Jerusalem and the temple. The high serenity of the Gospel is not the serenity of ignorance or illusion, but the serenity of knowledge, the knowledge of the man who knows Jesus both as the Life of the world and as the Judge of mankind. Only those who shut their eyes to half of John's Gospel, to the dark and fearful shadow of judgment cast by the true light of the world, can think it impossible that John the son of Zebedee, a Galilean, should have written both it and Revelation. In both works the judgment and the grace of God go hand in hand and move step for step toward God's wondrous goal. And in both there speaks a man whose vision of the Christ—whether that be the Christ thirsty and weary beside a well in Samaria or the Christ who breaks the seals of God's book and executes His sure and terrible decrees—has given him a unique and enduring authority, the authority of one who can step before the churches with the simple self-disclosure, "I, John."

Conclusion

The question of the authenticity of the works attributed to John, especially the Gospel, has been for more than a century one of the most warmly debated questions in the field of New Testament studies. Since the question is in the main the same for all the works (though the question concerning Revelation has its own difficulties too), and since the decision concerning the Gospel will largely determine the decision on the other works, it can be treated as

one question. The debate has been a long and involved one and has never been conducted along purely historical lines, but has been deeply influenced by theological considerations (that is, by the nature of the religious content of the books). Therefore, only the main lines of argument can be noted here. The validity and strength of the ancient tradition that assigns these works to John the son of Zebedee, the apostle and eyewitness of Jesus, is the first fact to be noted, and the arguments used to discredit that tradition must be the beginning student's first concern. He can judge the strength and weakness of the theologically colored arguments only after he has become thoroughly acquainted with the works themselves.

Date of Composition

The Church Father Irenaeus's statement (*ANF* 1:559) that Revelation was written toward the close of the reign of the emperor Domitian (AD 81–96) gives us the most probable date for the book, AD 95 or 96.

Purpose/Recipients

The situation that called forth the writing is made clear by the writing itself: the churches are being troubled by false teachers (Rv 2:6, 14–15), slandered and harassed by Jews, the "synagogue of Satan" (2:9; 3:9), and are undergoing a persecution (1:9) that has already cost the lives of some faithful witnesses (2:13; 6:9–10) but has not yet reached its height (6:11). To these

Continued on p 778.

Outline

Revelation is a series of visions. The first two visions describe Jesus appearing to John and messages that Jesus asks John to share with seven churches. Chs 4 and 5 are the heart of the book, revealing the worthiness of Jesus, who will save His people and judge the world.

Chs 6–21 are scenes of the end-times judgment. Three of Revelation's end-times scenes are clearly structured in seven parts (6:1–8:5; 8:6–11:19; 15:1–16:21). The other visions lack this sevenfold structure. The vision of 12:1–14:20 is clearly delimited by the sevenfold visions that come before and after it. Interpreters divide up 17:1–20:8 in different ways.

I. The Prologue: The Revelation of Jesus Christ (1:1–8)

II. The Visions Given to John (1:9–22:5)

- A. The Glorified Son of Man and the Seven Letters (1:9–3:22)
    1. The appearance of Christ to John on Patmos to commission John to record the vision (1:9–20)
    2. The letter to the Church in Ephesus (2:1–7)
    3. The letter to the Church in Smyrna (2:8–11)
    4. The letter to the Church in Pergamum (2:12–17)
    5. The letter to the Church in Thyatira (2:18–29)
    6. The letter to the Church in Sardis (3:1–6)
    7. The letter to the Church in Philadelphia (3:7–13)
    8. The letter to the Church in Laodicea (3:14–22)

B. The Heavenly Sanctuary and Divine Throne (chs 4–5)
   1. God (the Father) enthroned and worshiped as Creator (ch 4)
   2. The Lamb (the Son) enthroned and worshiped as the Passover/Atonement sacrifice (ch 5)

C. The First Scene of the End Times: Christ Opening the Seven Seals (6:1–8:5)
   1. The opening of the first four seals (6:1–8)
   2. The opening of the fifth and sixth seals (6:9–17)
   3. The sealing of the 144,000 faithful on earth (7:1–8)
   4. The myriads of the faithful in heavenly bliss (7:9–17)
   5. The opening of the seventh seal (8:1–5)

D. The Second Scene of the End Times: The Blowing of the Seven Trumpets (8:6–11:19)
   1. The blowing of the first four trumpets (8:6–13)
   2. The blowing of the fifth and sixth trumpets (ch 9)
   3. The recommissioning of John (ch 10)
   4. The measuring and witness of the Church (11:1–14)
   5. The blowing of the seventh trumpet (11:15–19)

E. The Third Scene of the End Times: The Battle between the Triune God and the Anti-Trinity (12:1–14:20)
   1. The woman in travail and the dragon (12:1–6)
   2. The war in heaven and defeat of Satan (12:7–17)
   3. The two beasts: a false christ and a false spirit (ch 13)
   4. The Lamb and true Church (14:1–5)
   5. The seven angels and the harvest of the earth (14:6–20)

F. The Fourth Scene of the End Times: The Pouring Out of the Seven Bowls of Wrath (chs 15–16)

G. The Fifth Scene of the End Times: Babylon the Prostitute Overthrown (chs 17–19)

H. The Sixth Scene of the End Times: The Final Judgment (20:1–21:8)

I. The Final Scene: The New Jerusalem as the Bride (21:9–22:5)

III. The Epilogue: Come, Lord Jesus! (22:6–21)

churches John, himself in banishment on the island of Patmos "on account of the word of God and the testimony of Jesus" (1:9), writes the account of the visions vouchsafed to him there, the record of "the revelation of Jesus Christ, which God gave Him to show to His servants" (1:1). He writes in order to strengthen them in their trials, both internal and external, to hold before them the greatness and the certitude of their hope in Christ, and to assure them of their victory, with Christ, over all the powers of evil now let loose upon the world and, to all appearances, destined to triumph on earth. The book is thoroughly practical, like all the books of the New Testament, designed to be read in the worship services of the churches, as the first of the seven beatitudes that the book pronounces shows: "Blessed is the one who reads aloud the words of this prophecy, and blessed are those who hear, and who keep what is written in it, for the time is near" (1:3).

Fifth-century bronze cross with the Greek letters for Christ, *alpha* and *omega*.

Composition

Literary Features

Genre

Revelation is, in form, a letter addressed to seven churches in the Roman province of Asia (Rv 1:4), complete with salutation and closing benediction (1:4; 22:21). With its visions of riders, trumpets, and bowls, of dragon and beasts, its use of number symbolism, and its mysterious and suggestive style generally, Revelation strikes the modern reader as strange and bizarre; even Luther at first wrote, "My spirit cannot accommodate itself to this book" (AE 35:399), though he later changed his mind (see pp 791–93). Much in the book that puzzles us today was familiar to John's first readers; much that we can gain access to only by laborious study and by a gradual process of sympathetic immersion into this alien world spoke directly to them. They had been familiarized with the imagery of John's vision by a form of Judaic religious literature known as "apocalyptic."

Apocalyptic literature elaborated certain elements or aspects of Old Testament prophecy, found in such passages and books as Isaiah 24–27, Zechariah 9–14, Ezekiel, Joel, and Daniel. It sought to interpret all history on the basis of purported visionary experiences of the author. It was especially interested in the end of history (eschatology) and the ushering in of the world to come. It utilized pictures, allegories, and symbols (which soon became traditional); numbers, colors, and stars were in these images endowed with a profound significance. Books of this type were the *Book of Enoch*, *Jubilees*, *4 Esdras*, and *The Assumption of Moses*.

Formally, Revelation belongs to this class; apocalyptic, as it were, furnished the familiar vocabulary of its speech. But Revelation is set apart from the general run of apocalyptic literature by profound differences. Apocalyptic literature itself drew heavily on the Old Testament; John draws even more heavily. No other New Testament book can compare with it in the number of allusions to the Old Testament. In fact, it is the Old Testament itself and not apocalyptic literature that constitutes the immediate background and the richest source for Revelation. Revelation is at bottom much more deeply akin to the Old Testament than it is to the apocalyptic literature that it resembles so strongly on the formal side. Other differences are equally striking. Apocalyptic works are generally pseudonymous; that is, they claim some great figure from Israel's past, such as Enoch, as author; and the past course of history as known to the actual author is made a prediction in the mouth of the purported author. John, however, writes in his own name. Apocalyptic literature has speculative interests and seeks to calculate the times and seasons of the world's last days and the world's end. John has no such speculative interest; he aims not to satisfy people's curiosity but to give them hope and courage, and he does not attempt to calculate the approach of the end. "I come quickly," is the burden of the revelation of Christ as given to John. The visions of apocalyptic literature betray their origin; they are fantasies. The visions of John have on them the stamp of genuine visionary experience; they are not products of the study. If apocalyptic may be termed literary meditation on prophetic themes, Revelation is genuine prophecy, a prophecy that uses apocalyptic motifs and forms insofar, and only insofar, as they are legitimate explications of Old Testament prophetic themes and are germane to its own thoroughly Christ-centered proclamation. The Lord, in speaking through John, speaks in human language, but He does not think merely human thoughts.

The peculiar advantage or virtue of utterance in this form lies not in the precision and clarity with which the utterance can be made, but in the power with which the thing said can be brought to bear on the whole person—on mind, imagination, feelings, will. His whole inner life is caught up in the moving terror and splendor of these visions, and the course and bent of his life are determined by them as they could hardly be determined by any other kind of communication. But just this characteristic of the book has given rise to widely divergent interpretations of the book; people have attempted, usually in a one-sided fashion, to be more precise in their interpretation of the book than the book itself by its very nature can be. One group of interpreters has fixed on the fact that the visions have their occasion and basis in real historical events and interprets the book wholly in terms of what had already happened at the time of writing; they see no real prediction anywhere in it, but merely an interpretation of past events in the guise of prediction. This, of course, ignores the prophetic claim of the book itself. Others refer everything but the content of the first three chapters to the very end of time, to the period immediately preceding the advent of Christ, and think of it as still awaiting fulfillment. This ignores the fact that for the author himself all time since the ascension of Christ is the time immediately preceding the advent of Christ and makes the book largely irrelevant for the very people for whom it was first written. Others again see in the visions a more or less detailed predictive portrayal of the successive events of universal history or of the history of the Church to the end of time; here again one must ask how such a series of predictions was to be of any aid and comfort to the troubled churches of Asia in AD 95. Still others renounce all attempts to relate the message of the book *directly* to history and see in the visions rather the enunciation of general principles that will hold good throughout history. But the book itself, with its life-and-death involvement in the crisis of AD 95, is anything but the enunciation of abstract principles.

Each of these attempts to interpret the book is, in its one-sidedness, a falsification. A true interpretation will, with the first group, look for the roots of the work in the history contemporary with it, for the book was obviously written for the Church's encouragement and strengthening at a certain time and place. It will, with the second group, recognize the fact that the prophecy embraces all time between the now of the Church and the return of the Lord of the Church. It will, with the third group, take seriously the relevance of the book to all history; but it will, with the last group, be inclined to see in it not a blueprint of history but a divine light that strikes history and illumines where it strikes, a pointing finger of God to guide people through history and judgment to the end. If the book is so viewed and so taken to heart, its value for the Church and the individual will not depend on the completeness of one's comprehension of every detail of its imagery.

Characters

Ninth-century ivory carving of the archangel Michael defeating the dragon, Satan.

In Rv 12:9 we read this remarkable statement: "And the great dragon was thrown down, that ancient serpent, who is called the devil and Satan, the deceiver of the whole world—he was thrown down to the earth, and his angels were thrown down with him" (cf also 20:2). The fact that **Satan**, or the devil, is here called "that ancient serpent" makes it certain that it was the devil who led our first parents into disobedience. And when Paul in Rm 16:20 says: "The God of peace will soon crush Satan under your feet," he is using figurative language, picturing the way in which serpents frequently are killed. Evidently Satan is thought of as a noxious reptile, the head of which is crushed by vigorous stamping of the feet. Although not mentioning the serpent, Jesus is clearly referring to the sad episode in Eden when He says to the unbelieving Jews: "You are of your father the devil, and your will is to do your father's desires. He was a murderer from the beginning, and does not stand in the truth, because there is no truth in him. When he lies, he speaks out of his own character, for he is a liar and the father of lies" (Jn 8:44). The devil, the father of lying—no one can fail to connect the expression with the story related in Gn 3. It is clear that our Lord ascribes the first lie of which the Bible makes mention to the devil. Hence divine revelation, while not entirely removing the veil that for us lies on the fall of humanity, has lifted it sufficiently to let us catch important glimpses of what occurred in the Garden of Eden.

If anyone should ask why the serpent, if it was the mere tool of Satan and therefore innocent, was cursed, the reply is that this was done to bring home to people the enormity of the wrong that had been committed, a wrong so great that the instrument of sin was branded as such for all time to come. Whenever we see a serpent, we are to be reminded of the woe that came upon the human race through the wiles of the tempter, whose design, let us remember, still is to work the ruin of human beings. The charge that God was unjust in thus inflicting a penalty on a dumb, innocent creature is easily met. The serpent by no means is conscious of its cursed state; the sentence that was spoken did not render it unhappy or miserable. To speak of injustice here is as much off the mark as would be the charge that a farmer is unjust toward his horse if he does not provide for it the glittering harness that can be seen on the horses of his neighbor.

On the question whether the serpent—cursed by God to go on its belly and to eat dust all the days of its life (Gn 3:14)—ever did have a different posture, the commentators are not agreed. Some think that originally it moved about in an erect position. It seems that such a view is not necessarily implied in Gn 3:14. The curse of God merely makes the serpent odious to us and leads us to regard its method of locomotion as a mark of degradation quite fitting for an animal that had been used by Satan for vile purposes. We may, as something analogous, point to eclipses, which are a natural phenomenon and have occurred since time immemorial. Who would assume that they did not happen before the prophets and Christ made mention of them as signs containing an important message for us? Thus the serpent may have moved on its belly from the beginning, but ever since the curse this mode of locomotion is a stigma, branding it as the instrument of Satan in the temptation.

Narrative Development or Plot

John narrates the visions he sees, which present different aspects of the world's rebellion, the Church's service, God's mercy, and His judgment. Each visionary scene presents a different view of the one judgment to come (see outline above). They drive toward the Last Day as the consummation of history and redemption, climaxing in chs 20–22, with consequences of eternal punishment for the wicked and eternal life for those righteous through faith in Jesus Christ. To explore further how the visions relate to one another and to broader history, see the Revelation study notes in *TLSB*.

Resources

On the significance of apocalyptic books and the Old Testament for Revelation, see p 779.

Text and Translations

One fragment of Revelation possibly dates from as early as the second century (Papyrus 98). The overall text is well established through a variety of witnesses. It includes no major variants.

Doctrinal Content

Summary Commentary

1:1–8 As John begins relaying the prophetic word that God gives through him, he pronounces a blessing upon all who will listen and take to heart this revelation. John praises the one true God—the Father, Son, and Holy Spirit—while simultaneously clarifying the identity of God's people: they are the "kingdom" and "priests" for whom He will soon come.

1:9–3:22 John describes his awesome vision of the risen and exalted Christ. Jesus is such an imposing figure that John instinctively falls down before Him, trembling with fear. Jesus encourages the Ephesian believers to avoid false teachers, return to their first love, and be zealous for good works. He promises the Church at Smyrna the crown of eternal life if it will faithfully endure the persecution it was suffering. Jesus urges the congregation in Pergamum to repent of the pagan practices into which they were slipping and to follow the example of one who stood fast, even to the point of death. Just as He warns the Ephesians, so He also admonishes the Thyatirans. They must avoid idolatrous worship and sexual immorality. Jesus exhorts the congregation at Sardis to wakefulness and renewed vigor. He assures the struggling Church in Philadelphia that their faithfulness to Him will be fully vindicated and rewarded. He rebukes the Laodicean Church for growing self-satisfied and indifferent to the faith.

Chs 4–5 John describes the heavenly worship he saw in the Lord's throne room, where all the saints and angels adore the Lord. The character of heavenly worship powerfully underscores the glory of Christ's redeeming work. The historical setting is the Ascension and enthronement of Christ.

6:1–8:5 John describes in symbolic language the calamities God will unleash upon the earth in the end times. The ferocity and totality of these predicted calamities move reflective people to shudder and repent. John's vision depicts God placing a protective seal on His people and thus marking them as those who will be delivered from the great final conflagration. John gives a glimpse of the glory that is Christ's. After finishing his vision of the seven seals being broken, John transitions to another vision, which depicts the end times with successive trumpet blasts.

8:6–11:19 In this vision, John describes catastrophes that will accompany the end times. John describes his prophetic commissioning. Using the figure of twin witnesses, John describes the response of a hostile world to the preaching of God's Word. John describes the transition from Satan's temporary rule of the world to the consummation of God's reign.

Chs 12–14 John portrays God's people as a struggling woman who is stalked by the devil and forced to flee into the desert. God's people have to contend with demonic onslaughts. John depicts the cosmic struggle between the forces of good and of evil and the damage it continually threatens to inflict upon the Church. In order to bolster his attacks against God and His people, the devil enlists the aid of a hideous beast, which represents worldly power and political authority run amok. In order to make his attacks against God's people even more devastating, Satan enlists the assistance of another beast, this one representing deceit and corruption from within the Church. John relates a vision in which those who have been delivered by the Lamb stand gathered around God's throne, singing a heavenly song of praise. John also relates a vision of three angels warning the world against the disaster that will come upon those worshiping the beast. He describes the final judgment in terms of a harvest and treading of a winepress.

Roman bowl.

Chs 15–16 This vision begins with a scene of joyous celebration but then continues with a description of the angels bearing the seven last plagues of God's wrath being sent out. As the bowls of God's wrath are poured out, all those worshiping false gods and refusing to repent of their sins are afflicted with terrible plagues. As the Lord pronounces the end of the outpouring of His judgment, the created order itself begins to come unhinged.

Chs 17–19 John describes the great end-times battle between the dominant world power and God. He describes the collapse and judgment of Babylon, the great oppressor of the innocent and exploiter of the weak. The heavenly chorus praises God for the collapse and destruction of the great prostitute Babylon. God follows up His victory over Babylon by solemnizing the marriage of His Son to His Bride, the Church. In the great final battle between good and evil, Christ returns and begins to destroy the remaining enemies of His rule once and for all.

20:1–21:8 Because Jesus has bound Satan and severely limited his power to harm the people of God, the faithful actually share in Jesus' rule throughout the entire New Testament age. However, in the last little bit before the end, all hell will break loose as Satan will be released and will thus wreak destruction. Happily, those remaining in the Lord will not be overcome.

Even as John affirms that there will be a "little while" of suffering before the end of all things and the judgment, he assures the faithful that this will result in the ultimate destruction and removal of Satan and his lies. Finally, John describes the judgment and overthrow of death. The climax of this book and indeed all of history at last comes clear: the restored heaven and earth is presented to God's resurrected people.

21:9–22:21 John continues his description of the glorified Church by focusing upon the splendor of the city in which God's people will dwell eternally. John describes our life in heaven as having no hunger, darkness, loneliness, or pain, but rather eternal joy in the presence of the one true God. By offering a vision of the new creation soon to be revealed, Revelation draws us on toward our blessed hope in Christ. To Him be power and glory throughout the ages!

Specific Law Themes

Through the letters to the seven churches, Revelation begins with a call to repentance. It then describes many hazards for believers, such as false prophets, beasts, and the dragon (Satan). The book also vividly describes God's wrath, plagues, and woes of His judgment against sin, including a bottomless pit, eternal torment, and the second death. The saints are urged to exercise patient endurance under the trials they face.

Specific Gospel Themes

As surely as Revelation is filled with fearful and threatening images, it is likewise filled with words of God's mercy and hope. He has made His people a kingdom and priests. They are surrounded with the love of the risen and ascended Savior, who receives titles extolling His grace through the prophecies. Christ is the conqueror of evil, who reigns with the Spirit and authority of God. The Lord God Almighty has prepared a tree of life and water of life for His Bride, the Church. He is faithful and true to His promises.

Specific Doctrines

On the significance of Revelation and its teaching, commentator Louis A. Brighton writes:

> The book of Revelation is the last book of the Bible. Whether it was written last or not, the church was led to place it at the end of the canon because she saw in it the completion of God's revelation. *Nothing further would be revealed* by God until the second coming of Jesus Christ. Revelation is thus the culmination of the entire story

> of salvation contained in the Bible. It is the end point of all that is written in both the OT and NT. For it draws all of revelation, both prophetic and apostolic, to its final goal: the exalted reign of Jesus Christ as King of kings and Lord of lords (19:11–16) and the fulfillment of the promise of the new heaven and earth (21:1).
>
> As the last book of the Bible and the completion of God's revelation to his church, it is the lens through which the entire Scripture is to be viewed. *Revelation reveals and confirms that Christ was prophetically promised and that his incarnation, death, and resurrection happened so that God's creation could be restored to its original glory and righteousness.* Revelation thus points to the *final meaning* and the *final answer* to all that is revealed in the Bible. In addition, as the last book, Revelation puts an imprimatur on all of God's revelation, a *final confirmation* of the divine truth and origin of God's spoken and written Word. This finality points to the *urgency* of the last times, in which all things will be brought to an end—an urgency which reminds the Christian to hold fast to the faith (2:10) and which encourages the church to complete her mission (10:11). (CC Rv, p 1)

Key Passages

The imagery of Revelation fills modern discussion with beasts, visions of doom and bliss, hell and heaven. Perhaps the most influential chapter historically is ch 12, which describes Satan as a red dragon and depicts the warfare between the evil angels and the holy angels. God's eternal essence is the subject of 1:8, and the chapter is often key theologically for describing the person and work of Jesus. The letters to the seven churches describe the need for ongoing repentance, especially 2:5 and 3:19. In chs 4–5, the image of the Lamb and adoration of Him illustrates how the New Testament doctrine of justification is rooted in the Old Testament doctrine, where the sacrifices anticipated the sacrifice of Jesus for our sins. Many modern liturgical passages, hymns, and songs are based on the songs in this portion of the book.

Application

1:1–8 Despite the promised opening blessing, people are resistant to hearing unsettling prophecies, let alone acting upon them by making changes in their lives. But take heart! Jesus Christ stands at the center of this and every other Scripture. His first coming resulted in forgiveness and life for you, and His second coming will perfect the new creation. Given our continual failure to live up to such a high calling, we need to hear again and again the truth of our identity in Christ. When the Gospel of God's grace is preached, the Church may speak a hearty "Amen" in its conviction that Jesus will return and then perfect our redemption.

1:9–3:22 Jesus is not merely about overwhelming power and glory. He was made like us in every way except without sin. Having overcome death and the grave, He now promises to share His eternal life and glory with us. In many parts of the world, the Church is still undergoing persecutions today. All Christians need to remain similarly watchful, for we, too, easily lapse into spiritual lethargy and even death—even while having the reputation of being strong. Sustained by the Word and Sacrament, however, we can remain healthy even unto life everlasting.

Chs 4–5 Regular worship is a serious matter, required by one of the Ten Commandments and described as the activity of heaven. Sadly, many people do not even feel a twinge of conscience while skipping divine services. Even while present, they may fail to focus on the promised blessing in such services. Yet, Jesus continues to call us back to His presence. In fact, His forgiveness and promise of eternal life is the first order of business in the Divine Service. Apart from Him, our fallen world has no hope. However, because Jesus was slain and then conquered death, His people are ransomed and have the hope of glory.

6:1–8:5 The Lamb who has taken away the sins of the world stands ready to forgive those who repent and restore them. His second coming is for the final deliverance of His people, not their destruction. Given the signs that daily surround us, God could release the devastating winds of His judgment at any moment. Yet God holds back now because He is "patient toward you, not wishing that any should perish, but that all should reach repentance" (2Pt 3:9). How incredible to be part of that blessedness! Drawn onward and upward by the magnificence of this hope in Christ, God's people join in the heavenly chorus even now. The visions are frightful, since we all know

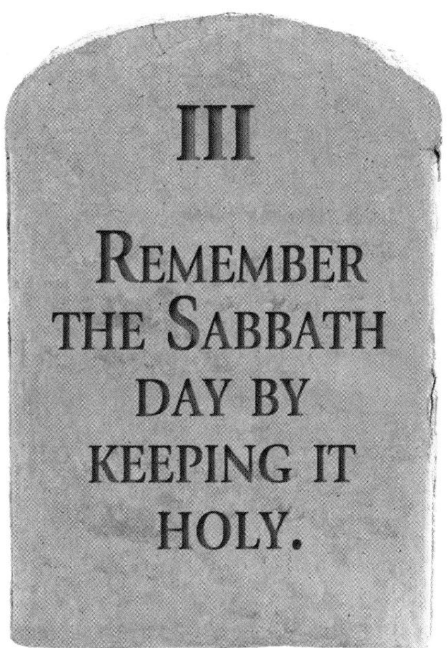

Christ depicted as the Lamb of God (Agnus Dei) surrounded by four archangels. San Vitale mosaic, sixth century; Ravenna, Italy.

in our hearts that we cannot stand before God in the judgment. Fortunately, we have one who stands beside us as our advocate—Jesus Christ—celebrated in chs 4–5. His blood cleanses us from all unrighteousness.

8:6–11:19 Precisely because our sworn enemy is so cunning and powerful, it is comforting to hear that Christ has already overcome him and will defeat him once and for all on the Last Day. On the one hand, the content of John's prophecy is bitter, for it reveals God's wrath against a hostile world. On the other hand, the Word he brings from God is the sweetest possible message, for it delivers Jesus' salvation to many peoples. Though ample opportunity is given for people to receive the blessings of repentance and the Gospel, most choose to reject the Church and persecute it. However, the apparent triumph of the Gospel's enemies is never the last word. Jesus' promise stands true: those remaining faithful unto death will be given the crown of life (2:10). For now, people can refuse to obey God. But such resistance will someday be met with an irresistible outpouring of wrath and judgment. Christ's people need not fear that day. Instead, they may long for the day when God will be all in all, and perfect harmony will again prevail.

Chs 12–14 At times we may struggle and despair, wondering whether God even remembers us. Yet He unfailingly preserves us in our wilderness sojourn, richly and daily providing everything we need through His Spirit, Word, and Sacraments. This depiction makes clear that although Satan cannot overcome the Church, he nonetheless tries his hardest to drag down with him as many as possible. It is most comforting to know, therefore, that Jesus has already defeated Satan and forgiven our sins, so that we can never be lost. In Christ, those who remain faithful to God and His Word will be blessed, entering into eternal rest when they pass out of this world. Those in

Christ need not worry over God's wrath, for instead of your blood flowing from God's winepress, Jesus' blood was poured out from the cross for you. His sacrifice for your sin removes the penalty of eternal death from you.

Chs 15–16 Unfortunately, the most sublime moments of rejoicing are followed by dreadful calamities, and hope is ever threatened by evil and judgment. Given this sad state of affairs, the Church needs to hear over and over again that there is "now no condemnation for those who are in Christ Jesus" (Rm 8:1). Tragically, there are even some within the Church who persist in this or that vice, stubbornly refusing to repent, and so put their very salvation in peril. Through Baptism, however, the Lord clothes His people with the perfect righteousness of His Son. The Holy Spirit leads God's children away from the plagues of judgment and keeps them on the winning side in the final battle.

Chs 17–19 This vision reminds us that earthly power structures, when built upon idolatrous worldviews and characterized by ungodly ambitions, are not morally neutral but rather stand in opposition to God and His Church. In the end, however, the King of kings and Lord of lords will get the victory and share it with the faithful, so that they reign with Him eternally. As modern, Western Christians hear the charges against Babylon, they note that some strike very close to home, especially greed and an addiction to luxury. The Church must remember where its true treasures are to be found. Whoever has Jesus can look forward to enjoying eternal splendor and joy in heaven. Some may be reluctant to join in this praise, still feeling sympathetic to Babylon and thus exhibiting a shameful self-centeredness. But Christ frees us from tyranny's grip and promises to share the spoils of His victory with us. Thus, we can heartily join in this praise now and forever. The faithful know that Jesus will come to right wrong and redress evil, and that He freely pardons all who embrace His mercy.

20:1–21:8 The second death has no power over those whom God's Spirit has regenerated and kept in the true faith. Consider how near we may be to the end of the age. Yet also consider what good news this is for believers! Christ comes to save and deliver us once and for all from every sin and evil. Since our first parents fled from the Lord in the garden (Gn 3:24), all their sinful descendants have been shutting their eyes and ears to the somber truth about the last judgment (cf Heb 10:31). However, Christ has covered us in the mantle of His righteousness. Consequently, our bodily resurrection will be unto glory and eternal bliss in God's presence. Such a magnificent future and hope call us to rise above the ugliness and sin of this fallen world, because impenitence and a lack of vigilance can still lead to the shipwreck of our souls. At the same time, God is faithful and so will unfailingly fulfill the purposes for which His Son became man; He will remove the curse that so sorely afflicts us.

21:9–22:21 On the one hand, the incredible beauty of the heavenly Jerusalem stretches our imaginations beyond what they can comprehend; on the other hand, the stern warnings about the impure, false, and detestable seem all too familiar. Yet God will overcome all evil, including that in our lives, for He who has written our names in the Book of Life will Himself see us home. How, then, can so many people fail to see the blessedness Jesus has laid out for us along the straight and narrow way that shortly leads to unceasing bliss? In many cases, the answer is simply that people do not appreciate the greatness of God's grace and the magnificence of the glory that awaits the faithful. Inspired by God's Word and preserved by His Spirit, however, we may already rejoice with those who have gone before us. Because John's message is about the ultimate triumph of good over evil, it is always relevant and all the more as the world slides further into chaos and corruption.

Canonicity

The Book of Revelation was welcomed by the western churches but questioned by some Christians in the east, who doubted that it was truly from the apostle John. For example, Revelation does not appear in the Syriac Peshitta translation.

Lutheran Theologians on Revelation

Luther

"There are many different kinds of prophecy in Christendom. One is prophecy which interprets the writings of the prophets. Paul speaks of this in I Corinthians 12 and 14, and in other places as well. This is the most necessary kind and we must have it every day, because it teaches the Word of God, lays the foundation of Christendom, and defends the faith. In a word, it rules, preserves, establishes, and performs the preaching ministry.

"Another kind foretells things to come which are not previously contained in Scripture, and this prophecy is of three types. The first expresses itself simply in words, without images and figures—as Moses, David, and others of the prophets prophesy about Christ, and as Christ and the apostles prophesy about Antichrist, false teachers, etc. The second type does this with images, but alongside them it supplies their interpretation in specific words—as Joseph interprets dreams, and Daniel both dreams and images. The third type does it without either words or interpretations, exclusively with images and figures, like this book of Revelation and like the dreams, visions, and images that many holy people have had from the Holy Spirit—as Peter in Acts 2[:17] preaches from Joel [2:28], 'Your sons and your daughters shall prophesy, and your young men shall see visions, and your old men shall dream dreams.' So long as this kind of prophecy remains without explanation and gets no sure interpretation, it is a concealed and mute prophecy and has not yet come to the profit and fruit which it is to give to Christendom.

"This is the way it has been with this book heretofore. Many have tried their hands at it, but until this very day they have attained no certainty. Some have even brewed it into many stupid things out of their own heads. Because its interpretation is uncertain and its meaning hidden, we have also let it alone until now, especially because some of the ancient fathers held that it was not the work of St. John, the Apostle—as is stated in *The Ecclesiastical History*, Book III, chapter 25. For our part, we still share this doubt. By that, however, no one should be prevented from regarding this as the work of St. John the Apostle, or of whomever else he chooses. . . .

"We can profit by this book and make good use of it. First, for our comfort! We can rest assured that neither force nor lies, neither wisdom nor holiness, neither tribulation nor suffering shall suppress Christendom, but it will gain the victory and conquer at last.

"Second, for our warning! [We can be on guard] against the great, perilous, and manifold offense that inflicts itself upon Christendom. Because these mighty and imposing powers are to fight against Christendom, and it is to be deprived of outward shape and concealed under so many tribulations and heresies and other faults, it is impossible for the natural reason to recognize Christendom. On the contrary, natural reason falls away and takes offense. It calls that 'the Christian Church' which is really the worst enemy of the Christian Church. Similarly, it calls those persons damned heretics who are really the true Christian Church. This has happened before, under the papacy, under Mohammed, indeed with all the heretics. Thus they lose this article [of the Creed], 'I believe in the holy Christian Church.' . . .

"This is why natural reason cannot recognize it, even if it puts on all its glasses. The devil can cover it over with offenses and divisions, so that you have to take offense at it. God too can conceal it behind faults and shortcomings of all kinds, so that you necessarily become a fool and pass false judgment on it. Christendom will not be known by sight, but by faith. And faith has to do with things not seen, Hebrews 11[:1]. Christendom joins with her Lord in the song, 'Blessed is he who takes no offense at me' [Matt. 11:6]. A Christian is even hidden from himself; he does not see his holiness and virtue, but sees in himself nothing but unholiness and vice. And you, stupid know-it-all, would behold Christendom with your blind reason and unclean eyes!

"In a word, our holiness is in heaven, where Christ is; and not in the world, before men's eyes, like goods in the market place. Therefore let there be offenses, divisions, heresies, and faults; let them do what they can! If only the word of the gospel remains pure among us, and we love and cherish it, we shall not doubt that Christ is with us, even when things are at their worst. As we see here in this book, that through and beyond all plagues, beasts, and evil angels Christ is nonetheless with his saints, and wins the final victory." (AE 35:399–411)

Gerhard

In the *Theological Commonplaces*, numerous pages are devoted to the question of whether Revelation is canonical, beginning with quotations from Eusebius who described the early reactions to the Book. Gerhard argued, "It can be demonstrated with substantial arguments that the Book of Revelation is canonical and was written by the apostle John" (ThC E1 § 293). He then listed the following reasons for accepting the book: (1) its inscription in John's name, (2) its style, (3) the circumstances of place and time, (4) comparison of its visions with Old Testament visions, (5) fulfillment of its prophecies, (6) its fulfillment of Daniel 12, (7) its quality, (8) usefulness, and (9) the testimony of the ancient fathers. Gerhard noted that the Latin fathers agreed on the canonicity of the book but that the Greeks did not. He finally cited and refuted writers of his era who rejected the book.

Fresco of Daniel, whose prophecies found fulfillment and affirmation in the Revelation of Jesus Christ.

Further Study

Lay/Bible Class Resources

Brighton, Mark. *Revelation*. RHBC. St. Louis: Concordia, 2012. § Verse-by-verse commentary on the ESV and KJV translations, presented in parallel columns. Written by a Lutheran theologian for lay readers and busy church workers. Includes quotations from prominent reformers and articles about Reformation views. Excellent for Bible classes.

Franzmann, Martin H. *The Revelation to John: A Commentary*. St. Louis: Concordia, 1976. § Simple notes and reading guides.

Griffin, Dale E., Julene Dumit, and Rodney L. Rathmann. *Revelation: Worthy Is the Lamb*. Updated edition. GWFT. St. Louis: Concordia, 2004. § Lutheran authors. Thirteen-session Bible study, including leader's notes and discussion questions.

Kettner, Edward G., Walter W. Stuenkel, and Edward Engelbrecht. *Revelation*. Leaders Guide and Enrichment Magazine/Study Guide. LL. St. Louis: Concordia, 2005. § An in-depth, nine-session Bible study with individual, small group, and lecture portions.

Life by His Word. St. Louis: Concordia, 2009. § More than 1,500 reproducible one-page Bible studies covering each chapter of the canonical Scriptures. Page references to *The Lutheran Study Bible*. CD-Rom and downloadable.

Morris, Leon. *The Revelation of St. John*. TNTC. Grand Rapids: Eerdmans, 1969. [1987.] § A helpful resource by a careful Johannine scholar.

Mueller, Steven P. *Revelation: An Introductory Course*. Leader Guide and Study Guide. Journeys through God's Word. St. Louis: Concordia, 2000. § Lutheran theologian writing for beginners in Bible study.

Mueller, Wayne. *Revelation*. PBC. St. Louis: Concordia, 2004. § Lutheran author. Excellent for Bible classes. Based on the NIV translation.

Strelan, John G. *Where Earth Meets Heaven: A Commentary on Revelation*. Eugene, OR: Wipf & Stock, 2007. § Originally published in 2007 by Open Book, a Lutheran publisher in Australia.

Church Worker Resources

Becker, Siegbert W. *Revelation: The Distant Triumph Song*. Milwaukee: Northwestern, 1985. § A careful exposition from a Lutheran theologian, who stresses that a millennial view is not in keeping with the text and message. The apostle John identified as author. Surveys and analyzes the validity of other suggestions as to authorship.

Boring, M. Eugene. *Revelation*. Interpretation. Louisville: Westminster, 1989. § Presents the book as a narrative or drama to be understood as a whole. Written from a critical perspective but intended for preachers and teachers.

Brighton, Louis A. *Revelation*. Concordia Popular Commentary. St. Louis: Concordia, 2010. § A distillation of Brighton's excellent academic commentary (see entry at right).

Hendriksen, William. *More Than Conquerors: An Interpretation of the Book of Revelation*. Grand Rapids: Baker, 1998 reprint. § A careful exposition of the text, keeping in mind the apocalyptic literary form and John's true message. Written from an amillenial perspective. A classic resource first published in 1940.

Academic Resources

Aune, David E. *Revelation*. 3 Vols. WBC. Dallas: Word Books, 1997–98. § A technical, critical commentary on the Greek text of Revelation by an expert in apocalyptic literature.

Bauckham, Richard. *The Climax of Prophecy: Studies on the Book of Revelation*. Edinburgh: T&T Clark, 1993. § Collection of essays exploring historical and literary features as they contribute to theology of the book. Note especially the first chapter on the structure of Revelation.

———. *The Theology of the Book of Revelation*. Cambridge: Cambridge University Press, 1993. § An extremely helpful volume that summarizes the numerous theological themes in their literary context and concludes that Revelation is a literary masterpiece.

Beale, G. K. *The Book of Revelation*. NIGTC. Grand Rapids: Eerdmans, 1999 § An analysis of the book based on the grammar and structure of the Greek text.

Beasley-Murray, George. *The Book of Revelation*. NCBC. Rev. ed. Grand Rapids: Eerdmans, 1981. § Opts not to identify author; needs to be clearer on his understanding of Revelation 20. Premillennial view. Otherwise helpful.

Brighton, Louis A. *Revelation*. CC. St. Louis: Concordia, 1999. § The best all-around commentary, prepared by a Lutheran theologian who has devoted his life to the study of Revelation. Describes the importance of Revelation's structure and symbolism; amillennial.

Harrington, Wilfrid J. *Revelation*. Sacra Pagina. Collegeville, MN: Liturgical Press, 1993. § Written from a critical perspective by a Dominican priest.

Hemer, Colin J. *The Letters to the Seven Churches of Asia in Their Local Setting*. Grand Rapids: Eerdmans, 2001. § Examines the locations and associated imagery for the cities mentioned in Rv 2–3.

Koester, Craig R. *Revelation and the End of All Things*. Grand Rapids: Eerdmans, 2001. § Helpful introduction on the history of interpretation from a critical, Lutheran theologian and Johannine scholar. The discussion of the millennium in Revelation 20 is not helpful.

Krodel, Gerhard A. *Revelation*. Augsburg Commentary on the New Testament. Minneapolis: Augsburg Fortress, 1989. § Liberal Lutheran scholar who provides a helpful critique of Bengel's millennial views, Luther, as well as many other interpreters.

Lange, John Peter. *The Revelation of John*. LCHS. New York: Charles Scribner's Sons, 1874. § A helpful older example of German biblical scholarship, based on the Greek text, which provides references to significant commentaries from the Reformation era forward.

Lenski, R. C. H. *The Interpretation of St. John's Revelation*. Minneapolis: Augsburg Fortress, 2008. § A standard resource by a noteworthy Lutheran interpreter, concerned with being faithful to the text and with its implications for today.

Mounce, Robert H. *The Book of Revelation*. NICNT. Rev. ed. Grand Rapids: Eerdmans, 1998. § Tentatively suggests John the apostle as author. Holds to an earthly millennium as proper interpretation for Revelation 20 (pre-millennial, post-tribulation view of rapture). Use with discernment.

Prigent, Pierre. *Commentary on the Apocalypse of St. John*. Tübingen: Mohr Siebeck, 2001. § Revised edition by a French scholar of Revelation, exploring the book in view of its Jewish and Greco-Roman historical and cultural environment.

Resseguie, James L. *The Revelation of John: A Narrative Commentary*. Grand Rapids: Baker, 2009. § Explores the canons of narrative criticism such as setting, rhetoric, point of view, character, and plot. Written by an evangelical scholar.

Sweet, J. P. M. *Revelation*. Westminster Pelican Commentaries. Philadelphia: Westminster, 1979. § Especially helpful for insight into Jewish apocalyptic thought as reflected in Revelation. Holds to an unknown author. More precise definitions of some terms would have been helpful. Use with discernment.

3

ARCHAEOLOGY AND THE BIBLE

Publications such as *Biblical Archaeology Review*, *Bible and Spade*, and various news outlets continuously release reports about developments and discoveries in the land of the Bible. It is important that we are clear about the relationship between the Bible and "biblical archaeology" (a term created by scholar William F. Albright). At least, that was the common label until recently. That label is still perfectly acceptable in church-related contexts. However, in academic circles the terms "Near Eastern archaeology," "Syro-Palestinian archaeology," or the like have come to be preferred.

The reasons for the change in terms are probably twofold. One is simply the increasing secularism that has no particular regard for Holy Scripture. The other is the frequent misuse of the assumption that archaeology proves the Bible true, an idea that we must examine further. For example, if we are speaking of the most important theological message of the Bible (the Gospel), no human study or research can prove (or disprove!) it. We confess that it can be learned and believed only by faith, by the gift of the Holy Spirit in Word and Sacrament. Similarly, if the subject is the external facts mentioned in the Bible (persons, events, places)—even if archaeology authenticated all of them—saving faith would not necessarily follow.

Since the Bible does speak of historical events, external confirmation can only be welcomed (objective knowledge). Biblical teaching is not mythology, or something that happens only in the hidden recesses of the human heart (subjective knowledge). Readers should come to this topic with realistic expectations. Since much of biblical history recounts private, individual actions or events that took place in small communities, we should not be surprised that much of what the Old Testament describes is not normally accessible to any human research.

Restorer working on artifact fragments from a burial chamber possibly belonging to King Herod (36–1 BC) or someone he honored. Biblical archaeology pieces together information from the material culture of the Near East, which scholars then seek to interpret.

Organizing Our Thoughts

For the Old Testament entries, we shall focus on major sites in the historical land of the Bible between the Jordan River and the Mediterranean Sea, moving from north to south. (Other information known from Israel's neighbors, as well as chance finds, often of unknown provenance, also remains relevant to biblical studies.) In many cases, simply having a positive identification for these most ancient sites is significant, all the more so if one likewise discovers important artifacts. For the intertestamental era and for the New Testament, the presentation will be chronological because the circumstances are different from the Old Testament era.

Major Old Testament Sites

Tel Dan. We begin near one of the major sources of the Jordan, which lends its name to the phrase, "from Dan to Beersheba." This phrase appears at Jgs 20:1 and eight other places in the Old Testament, encompassing all of Israel from north to south. The most significant find at Dan was an Aramaic text from about 830 BC, describing military operations of an Aramean king against various enemies, including the "house of David." Before that find, some skeptics had doubted that David even existed, or they thought that at best he was a very insignificant figure.

Podium of the ruler in Tel Dan.

One of the most prominent features on the surface of Dan is a huge, complex rectangular site usually considered a *high place*. The phrase represents the traditional translation of the Hebrew *bamah*. The "high" refers to ceremony, not elevation, though both connotations would apply at Dan. The excavated site uncovered an altar and shows other evidence of sacrificial activity; the Old Testament frequently refers to such activity at high places. According to Jgs 18, the migrating Danites brought worship equipment along with them, probably leading Jeroboam later to erect at Dan one of the golden calves for worship in the Northern Kingdom at the end of the tenth century BC (1Ki 12:25–33).

Hazor. Moving south along the west side of the Jordan, we meet another prominent site, described when Joshua conquered and burned it (11:11) as having formerly been "the head of all those kingdoms" of Upper Galilee (11:10). We are not given details of the subsequent history of the area, except that it became part of the inheritance of Naphtali. Later we meet it under the control of "Jabin king of Canaan" (Jgs 4:2) whose defeat is narrated in some detail in Jgs 4. The city was probably sacked again then.

Hazor's Solomonic city gates. Hazor is the largest archaeological site in Israel, first mentioned in Egyptian documents in nineteenth century BC. The location also contains fifteenth-century BC Cannanite ruins.

The site consists of the upper city, a mound of about 25 acres, and a lower city of about 170 acres enclosed by steep slopes and earthworks. The latter was destroyed about the time of the Israelite invasion and never rebuilt, but the upper city was rebuilt, and excavations expose structures from the time of Solomon (1Ki 9:15), though the city's later history plays no significant role in the biblical narrative.

Samaria. Crossing the Valley of Jezreel, we ascend to the Judean highlands, the country's central spine where Israelite life was centered for several centuries. Samaria is the first major site along this route. The hill on which it sits was not significantly occupied until Omri purchased it in the early ninth century (1Ki 16:23–24). He made it his capital, replacing Tirzah to the east. Extensive later ruins have prevented thorough excavation of the earliest city. On the acropolis, however, royal buildings and a casemate wall of the Israelite period were uncovered. Omri's initial constructions were continued under his successors, Ahab, Jehu, and Jeroboam II, though levels have often been unusually difficult to distinguish, until the Assyrians eventually destroyed the ancient city.

Special mention should be made of the Samaria ostraca, 66 pen and ink inscriptions on potsherds. Their content is not significant, because they are merely records of fine wine and oil sent to the capital during the reign of Jeroboam II (793–753 BC). But because they represent the earliest corpus of ancient Hebrew writing, they tell us much about the history of Hebrew writing, spelling, place and personal names, etc.

The origins of the "Samaritans" remain uncertain (mentioned in the Old Testament only in 2Ki 17:29), but are most likely to be found in a remnant left behind after Shalmaneser of Assyria conquered the area, probably augmented by people from eastern regions to replace those he had taken captive (17:3–41). In the face of steady persecution by later conquerors, the number of Samaritans has steadily dwindled; today the community numbers only a few hundred, with a synagogue atop Gerizim and some members in a suburb of Tel Aviv.

Shechem. A little further south we meet the most important ruins of ancient Shechem, at the eastern end of the strategic pass between Mount Ebal to the north and Mount Gerizim to the south. Although excavations show settlement already in Chalcolithic times (fourth millennium BC), it enters biblical history when Abraham stops there and God repeats His promise to Abraham (Gn 12:7). His grandson Jacob settles at Shechem more permanently on his return from Haran, even purchasing land (33:18–20). Shechem later became the place to bury the bones of Joseph, which Israel had brought along from Egypt (50:25; Jsh 24:32). The city of Shechem is at the center of the detailed narrative of Jgs 9 where Abimelech, a renegade son of Gideon, slaughtered all but one of his brothers and made himself ruler over the city, until a military campaign against a neighboring city eventually led to Abimelech's death.

The city gate of Shechem.

Historically noteworthy is the ceremony of antiphonal blessing and cursing, six tribes on Mount Gerizim for blessings and six on Mount Ebal for the curses. Moses had commanded the ceremony in his farewell address (Dt 27:11–26) and its fulfillment is recorded in Jsh 8:33–35. Before his death, Joshua gathered all the tribes together again at Shechem (24:1–28).

All of this may explain why archaeology shows little or no destruction at Shechem during the time of the Israelite invasion; the city is not included in the list of cities conquered by Joshua (Jsh 12:7–24). Apparently, the city passed into Israelite hands with minimal difficulty. Shechem played no major role thereafter, except at the division of Israel and Judah after the death of Solomon (1Ki 12:25).

Archaeologically of great interest is the huge cyclopean wall apparently built around the city, its height probably increased by courses of mudbricks on top of it. Two gates, each rebuilt a number of times, are prominent: the East Gate opening toward the plain, and the Northwest Gate, with a small temple found in one of its side chambers. In the acropolis area of the city stand some of the foundations of a massive temple, probably that of "El Berith" (i.e., "The god of the covenant"), where the Shechemites had taken refuge from Abimelech, but which Abimelech set on fire, killing about a thousand men and women (Jgs 9:49).

Shiloh.

Shiloh. As we move south, we come to the ruins of the city of Shiloh, where the ark, apparently after moving to various sites after the conquest, came to be housed more prominently, and where a permanent temple (Hbr *hekal*) was erected. Excavations there did not lead to the ark's discovery, but that proved nothing. Apparently after the Philistine victory and the capture of the ark, it was housed in various places until David brought it to Jerusalem (2Sm 6). The Philistine victory took place at the edge of the hill country, with the Israelites encamped at Ebenezer (1Sm 4:1) (possibly identified with a small village today called 'Izbet Sarta) and the Philistines below at the springs of Aphek (New Testament Antipatris).

Jericho. Settlement by a perennial spring is dated already in the eighth millennium BC, and Joshua confronted an ancient and formidable city, as recounted in Jsh 2–6. Many skeptics doubt the historicity of the biblical narrative, often even claiming that the city was uninhabited at the time. The best solution to the problem seems to be that the remains of the city Joshua conquered have simply eroded away. It is evident to the naked eye that much erosion of the mound has taken place.

Well at Gibeon, circling down to a spring pool.

Ai. The historical problems are even greater with Ai. The very word means *ruin* (always written with the definite article in Hebrew). Archaeological evidence indicates that it had long been in ruins at the time of Joshua. Current excavations are still going on, seeking for an alternative location, but a satisfactory site is yet to be found.

Gibeon. Two sites with similar names deserve mention as we approach Jerusalem. Gibeon, about 5 miles north, first appears when the people of the city tricked Joshua into making a treaty with them as vassals (Jsh 9). Additionally, when the neighboring kings, including Adoni-zedek of Jerusalem, attempted to punish them for allying themselves with the Israelites, God led to their defeat by means of a hailstorm and a miraculous extension of daylight (Jsh 10:11–14).

After Saul's death and David's accession, a contest of 12 representatives from Saul and David's men was held "at the pool of Gibeon" (2Sm 2:13). David's representatives won. The "pool" is also mentioned in Jer 41:12. It is probably the over 80-foot complex of the stepped pit and tunnel that leads to a spring-fed pool, which may still be visited today. A great "high place" also existed at Gibeon, the site of an inaugural dream and a divine promise to Solomon (1Ki 3:3–15).

Gibeah. Closer to Jerusalem and today virtually swallowed by its suburbs. Gibeah first figures in the atrocity of Jgs 19, resulting in the decimation of the tribe of Benjamin, and the aftermath recounted in Jgs 20–21. Later, in effect, it became Saul's capital during his reign.

Jerusalem. Easily the most important city on the Jordan's West Bank. Unfortunately, however, excavation is unusually difficult because of continuous occupation and/or debris from various sackings over the centuries. Until David's capture, the city was in the hands of native people called Jebusites, and the city itself was called Jebus. After reigning seven years at Hebron, David moved to Jerusalem, close to the Benjamin-Judah border, in order to unify the northern and the southern tribes. But first he had to capture the city. Second Samuel 5:8 indicates that the city was captured by climbing up the water shaft from the subterranean pool fed by the Gihon Spring at the foot of the hill. There is such a shaft, but it has never been demonstrated precisely how the feat of climbing up and surprising the Jebusites was accomplished.

One particularly large wall (often called "the Broad Wall" [cf Ne 3:8; 12:38]) is prominent among the many smaller ones on the eastern slope, but whether it was David's, Solomon's, or Hezekiah's construction is uncertain. It may have been part of the palace David built for himself. Mention must also be made of Hezekiah's Tunnel, built when Sennacherib's invasion was imminent. The Gihon Spring, Jerusalem's major source of water (except for collected rainwater) was in the Kidron Valley on the east side of the city of David. Apparently, a channel along the outside of the hill to the Pool of Siloam was built earlier. But all of this was accessible to any invader. Hence Hezekiah's men tunneled under the hill from the Gihon Spring to the Pool of Siloam on the west side of the city (2Ki 20:20). The "Siloam Inscription" was inscribed in the tunnel wall by the diggers or engineer directing it. Ottoman Turks later cut it out, and it can be seen in an Istanbul museum.

A portion of the Broad Wall in the middle of the Jewish Quarter.

Whenever possible, Israeli archaeologists have cleaned all the structures built up to the temple barrier (Gk *temenos*). The current walls of the "Old City" are the work of the Turkish sultan Suleiman the Magnificent (AD 1542). There never has been any doubt where the temple stood, but so many destructions and rebuildings have intervened that it is doubtful if any remains of the first (Solomon's) temple will ever be found. The Muslim "Dome of the Rock" (whence Muhammad is said to have ascended into heaven) occupies the site today. The exact location of the temple in relation to the protruding bedrock, which gives the site its popular name, cannot be ascertained.

The city of David stepped-stone retaining wall in the area of Jebus.

Zion. In 2Sm 5:7, we are told "David took the stronghold of Zion, that is, the city of David." This is the first time we meet the term "Zion," which would eventually be expanded to apply to the entire city of Jerusalem, including various theological implications. The "city of David" was only a southern spur of the mountain, south of the later location of the temple, with the Kidron Valley on the east and the Tyropean Valley (today nearly filled in) to the west. The label "Ophel" is also applied to this area (cf 2Ch 27:3; 33:14; Ne 3:26–27; 11:21). Perhaps the name was more prominent in postexilic times, or it may simply be an alternate term for the whole "city of David" or the northern portion where it widens to join the temple platform.

Millo. This is still a third term we have to puzzle over in connection with early Jerusalem, appearing in seven Old Testament passages. Etymologically, it would seem to mean "fill[ing]." It has been subject to various interpretations, none of them certain. Perhaps it was merely a predecessor term for "Ophel" (see "Zion," above). Most likely it seems to refer to the repair of the many terraces built along the steep eastern ridge of the city of David—where most excavation has taken place because of lack of current habitation. Building or repair of these terraces is apparently mentioned in 2Sm 5:9 and 1Ch 11:8 (David); 1Ki 9:15, 24; 11:27 (Solomon); 2Ch 32:5 (Hezekiah).

Bethlehem. Some 5 miles south of Jerusalem, just past Rachel's tomb (Gn 35:19–20). Mention of a cave or grotto as the location of Christ's birth is found already in Justin Martyr (Dialogue 78), however, there are skeptics who doubt the accuracy of the tradition. One may point out that the general description in tradition from Justin is the opposite extreme from the later Byzantine fashion, which would show us the exact spot where Jesus was born (in a grotto underneath the altar of the Church of the Holy Nativity). After the second Jewish revolt in AD 135, under Bar Kokhba, all Jews were banned from Bethlehem until Helena, mother of Constantine, built the Church of the Nativity. After the Samaritan revolt in AD 529, Bethlehem was rebuilt by Justinian and spared by Persian invaders because of paintings of Persians (the Wise Men) on its walls in 612 (otherwise the Persians savaged Christian monasteries, churches, etc.).

Hebron. Nearly 20 miles SSE of Jerusalem. It is reported to have been built seven years before Zoan (known in Gk as Tanis; cf Nu 13:22), the Hyksos capital in Egypt, a date that excavation supports. Otherwise archaeology has little to contribute. It is especially associated with Abraham, who purchased the burial cave of Machpelah (Gn 23:9). Herod built the great *haram* or enclosure over the site, and in Byzantine times the massive church was added. Tourists are shown the cenotaphs allegedly directly above the patriarchal graves below. It has been impossible to test the accuracy of such claims. As noted above, David originally reigned seven years in Hebron before moving his capital to Jerusalem. Under the name of el-Khalil ("the friend" of Abraham, after Is 41:8) it is one of the four sacred cities of Islam. It is also fanatically contested by some orthodox Jews today.

One of the remains of a well at Beersheba.

Beersheba. Having sampled major sites "from Dan to Beersheba" (Jgs 20:1; 1Sm 3:20, etc.) we finally arrive at the southern terminus of biblical Israel some 50 miles south of Jerusalem. There is a Tell es-Seba outside the modern city with some very unique artifacts and clear evidence for occupation, but otherwise evidence indicates that the biblical city is to be situated where the modern city is located and where earlier remains are found. "Beer" means *well* in Hebrew, and "sheba" means either *oath* or *seven.* The Bible puns on those meanings (cf Gn 21:25–31; 26:31–33), but it is uncertain that they really meant to explain the origin of the name. Nehemiah 11:7 describes resettlement after the exile. The site's importance lay in its location on a trade route to Egypt. It has many patriarchal associations, but none that archaeology elucidates.

The Intertestamental Era

As noted above, the Old Testament survey provided the reader with a listing of the chief cities of the Holy Land. In this section, we continue the presentation of sites but use a chronological method of organization. The intertestamental era may be divided into Persian, Hellenistic, Hasmonean, and Roman/Herodian periods. Below are some of the important sites of these periods.

Samaritan Temple. Excavations on Mount Gerizim have confirmed the existence of a fifth century BC temple that was built before the second temple in Jerusalem and rivaled it. Although the Hasmoneans later destroyed the Samaritan temple, a new temple was built late in the second century BC. Among the finds at Mount Gerizim were thousands of animal bones (indicating sacrifices) and hundreds of inscriptions.

Wadi ed-Daliyeh. Bedouins discovered a cave north of Jericho, which included the remains of c 300 people. Discovered among their possessions were the Samaritan Papyri, which includes documents of everyday life and refers to or portrays a variety of gods. Researchers conclude that the people in the cave were Samaritans who fled from Alexander the Great's troops (c 332 BC). Alexander's troops settled in Samaria and built large, round towers to refortify the city.

Hellenistic fresco in Mareshah.

Mareshah. Under the Hellenistic rulers, Mareshah became a major city in southern Israel, northeast of Lachish. Idumaeans and Sidonians settled there and created a Greek-style city centered on a marketplace (Gk *agora*). Below the city are numerous caves from which building stones were excavated. Inhabitants used the caves as work and storage spaces for raising doves, pressing olive oil, and creating other products. Some of the caves are burial tombs that include Hellenistic paintings.

Jerusalem Tombs. The continuation of Hellenistic influence can be seen in a number of Hasmonean period tombs found around Jerusalem. Among the earliest are the tomb of Benei Hezir (second century BC) and Jason's tomb (first century BC). They include Greek-style pillars; Jason's tomb is topped with a pyramid. These Hellenized features continued to be used for major monuments in the region during the Roman period.

Nabatean Petra. The origins of the Nabateans remain unresolved. However, by the late fourth century, these Semitic people established themselves at Petra in the red sandstone hills south of the Dead Sea. Like others in the region, they adopted the Hellenized style that adorns their finer tombs, such as the famous Khazneh (Arabic, "treasury") tomb, which was the burial place for one of their kings.

The Treasury, the most well-known building in the city Petra, Jordan.

Dead Sea Scrolls and Qumran. The most important find of the intertestamental era is the Dead Sea Scrolls. Since the scrolls are described in *ALEN*, pp 336–37, only the most basic facts are included here. The Qumran community was located near the northwest corner of the Dead Sea where c 800 scrolls or portions of scrolls were discovered in caves below the settlement. The scrolls date from c 250 BC to c AD 70. Most are in Hebrew and Aramaic, but a few are in Greek. Scribes hid or stored these scrolls in clay jars, which preserved them. Apart from one copper scroll and some papyri, the scrolls are made of sheep or goat leather. Their influence on our understanding of the text of the Old Testament, intertestamental history, and the emergence of Judaism and Christianity has been enormous. Ironically, the settlement at Qumran was rather small. It may have accommodated 100 to 150 people. Most scholars hold that the inhabitants were related to Zadokite priests who lost their status at the Jerusalem temple. Some Zadokites may have founded the Jewish sect of the Essenes, who are thought to have inhabited the Qumran community.

Herod's Building Projects. Archaeological sites for the Early Roman period are dominated by the building program of Herod the Great, whom the Romans crowned and supported as king of Judea. When Herod took Jerusalem in 37 BC, he soon began an aggressive building project that transformed the city. In honor of Mark Antony, Herod built the Antonia Fortress just north of the Temple Mount. He added defensive towers and walls around the city. On the west side he built a palace for himself. He enlarged the Temple Mount and its surrounding wall and redesigned the temple itself. Herod also built the city and harbor of Caesarea Maritima, the desert fortress of Masada, and the fortress/palace of Herodium, as well as other projects.

The New Testament Era

Excavations from the first century at various biblical sites have yielded a rich harvest of artifacts that support our understanding of the biblical record very directly. Here the spade has indeed proven to be "the Bible's best friend," as the hard evidence from 20 centuries ago has provided foundations, structures, inscriptions, coinage, material items, and even bones that correspond to those mentioned in New Testament texts. We list below only the most important correlations between archaeological finds and the New Testament record. The artifacts are arranged not in terms of importance or date of discovery, but as they relate chronologically to the life of Christ and the birth of the Church.

Capernaum Synagogue. A fourth-century Jewish synagogue dominates the excavations at Capernaum, the hub of Jesus' Galilean ministry. While He did not teach in this structure, it was constructed over the basalt rock foundations of the earlier synagogue in Jesus' day, which has been partially excavated.

The remains of St. Peter's house in Capernaum.

House of Peter. One block south of the synagogue are the ruins of a first-century two-room house. Scholars have identified it as Simon Peter's, where Jesus lived during His Galilean ministry, a claim that may seem too good to be true. But strong evidence supports the authenticity of this site, including (1) a hexagonal wall constructed around the site by Constantine (the first Christian emperor), (2) graffiti from Christian pilgrims on the plastered inside walls, and (3) the house's use as the earliest church in Galilee.

The Galilee Boat. In 1986, during a spring drought that lowered the water levels on the Sea of Galilee, a buried ship's hull was discovered and carefully excavated. Marine archaeologists dated the craft to a two-century period between 100 BC and AD 100. The hull is 27 feet long and 7.5 feet wide, and could have held 15 people. The boat's design shows that it was used for fishing and so helps explain many of the maritime scenes in Jesus' Galilean ministry, including the calming of the storm (Mk 4:35–41).

Pool of Siloam. The site of Jesus' miraculous cure of the man born blind in Jn 9, the Pool of Siloam is situated near the end of Hezekiah's Tunnel in Jerusalem, but it used to disappoint pilgrims because of its small size, more like a catch basin. However, the true pool in Jesus' day was discovered farther south in the Silwan (Siloam) Valley in Jerusalem, and it is six or seven times larger than the traditional small pool.

Tomb of Lazarus.

Burial Site of Lazarus. Certainly one of Jesus' most spectacular signs, the raising of Lazarus (Jn 11:1–44) is supported archaeologically by the excavation of a tomb site at Bethany from the first century, as indicated by its depth and the presence of an ante-chamber in addition to the burial chamber. For centuries it was also a magnet for Christian pilgrims, as the façade demonstrates, and the Arabic name for Bethany, el-'Azariyeh ("Place of Lazarus") is further support in view of the antiquity of the name change.

Pool of Bethesda. John reported that there is a pool named "Bethesda" near the Sheep Gate in Jerusalem. He proceeded with the story of Jesus healing the invalid who could not reach the water in time for a cure (Jn 5:1–17). Scholars sometimes use this as evidence for an early dating for the Fourth Gospel because this pool was filled with debris from the destruction of Jerusalem in AD 70. Deep excavations at Jerusalem uncovered the very pool at the location specified by John.

Bones of Joseph Caiaphas. For some reason, this spectacular discovery has gone largely unnoticed. In 1990, a burial site south of the temple area in the Old City of Jerusalem was accidentally discovered. This burial cave dates to the first century AD as indicated by the 12 limestone ossuaries inside, space-saving bone boxes that Jews used for the dead only in the first century. One of the ossuaries was magnificently carved with fluted borders and extraordinary circular designs, indicating that some VIP was inside. On the other side of the ossuary, inscribed twice in Aramaic, was the name of Joseph Caiaphas. Further testing of the bones confirmed that these were indeed the remains of the Sanhedral high priest who indicted Jesus before the tribunal of Pontius Pilate on Good Friday—the first authenticated remains of a biblical character ever discovered.

Inscription dedicated to honoring Emperor Tiberius, with the name Pontius Pilate, prefect of Judea (AD 26–36).

"Pontius Pilate" Stone. Critics of the Bible used to claim that Pontius Pilate, the Roman governor who sentenced Jesus to the cross, was not a historical figure. But in 1961, an Italian archaeological team was digging at the ruins of the very theater in Caesarea on the Sea where Herod Agrippa I was killed (Ac 12:20–23) when they uncovered a 2- by 3-foot stone inscribed with 2-inch Latin lettering, which translates: "To the People of Caesarea, Pontius Pilate, Prefect [Governor] of Judea, has presented the Tiberieum." This was a structure in honor of the Emperor Tiberius and is again a prime example of how archaeological finds strongly support the biblical record against its critics.

Bones of Crucifixion Victim. Some biblical critics have also denied that Jesus could ever have been nailed to a cross, as reported in John's Gospel. He must only have been tied, they argued, since fragile human flesh could not be supported by a nail or spike. Yet in 1968, a cave with 36 ossuaries was discovered in northeastern Jerusalem. One of these contained the bones of a man named Yehohanan ben Hagkol, whom pathologists later identified as a man in his late twenties who had been crucified by nailing, as evidenced by nail grooves in the wrists, both legs broken to induce death, and a large rusty spike still lodged in his heel bones. This, the first crucified victim ever discovered, again underscores the accuracy of the Gospel records, even the detail of how the malefactors crucified on either side of Jesus had their legs broken.

House of Judas. Strong evidence indicates that the very place where Saul spent three agonizing days after Jesus' appearance to him on the road to Damascus is authentic (Ac 9:8–19a). The "street called Straight" on which the house was located is unquestionably authentic. It was the main east-west thoroughfare in ancient Damascus, with a gate at its eastern end built by the Roman emperor Hadrian. The street is still there, and today the Arabs call it *Darb al-Mustaqim*, the "Straight Way," and parts of Hadrian's gate still stand at its eastern end. One block west of it, on the north side of the street, a stone Christian cross marks the entrance way to a subterranean chapel marking the house of Judas, with a mosaic of Ananias baptizing Saul of Tarsus.

Statue Base of Sergius Paulus. He was the Roman governor of Cyprus before whom Paul appeared early in his first missionary journey (Ac 13:4–12). Although the statue that it supported is now missing, the base of a statue of Lucius Sergius Paulus was discovered in the Roman Forum, indicating that he was also "Curator of the Beds and Banks of the Tiber"—a flood control commissioner—prior to his governorship of Cyprus.

Philippi Bema. The *bema*, or tribunal, where the city fathers sentenced Paul and Silas to be beaten and thrown into jail has been discovered in the marketplace (Gk *agora*) in the ruins of ancient Philippi (Ac 16:16–24). Even the prison itself has been identified, though this claim is questionable.

Athenian agora.

Athenian Agora. Easily the intellectual and cultural center of the ancient world in Paul's day, Athens was one of the centerpieces of the apostle's second missionary journey. Its great agora (marketplace, forum) continues to be excavated, and it was here that Paul was depressed by the rampant idolatry and shrines to the gods and goddesses of Greek mythology (Ac 17:16–34).

Areopagus at Athens. The culmination of Paul's visit to Athens was his famed address at the Areopagus—"Mars Hill" in Latin. This rocky protuberance from the Acropolis still stands northwest of the Parthenon. At its base, Paul's address, in the original Greek, is inscribed on a bronze plaque (Ac 17:22–31).

Corinth Bema. On the south side of the Corinthian agora, the very *bema* has been discovered where the Roman governor Gallio, in the first test case for Christianity, decided in Paul's favor (Ac 18:12–17). Gallio's name also shows up in four fragments of a letter written to him by the Roman emperor Claudius. When this was discovered at Delphi, across the Gulf of Corinth, it provided the great chronological fulcrum for dating the life of St. Paul. Gallo was governor only one year in Corinth during AD 51–52.

Erastus Inscription. At the end of his Letter to the Romans, Paul sends greetings to the Roman Christians from their fellow believers in Corinth. Among them was "Erastus, the city treasurer" (16:23). Critics used to howl at what they termed Paul's exaggerated claims of political connections—until Erastus's name showed up in stone at the ruins of a white marble plaza northwest of the agora. In 5-inch Claudian lettering, it translates to: "Erastus, the city manager of Corinth, paved this plaza at his own expense." Even a solitary name in the New Testament can be confirmed archaeologically.

Temple of Artemis. One of the traditional Seven Wonders of the World, the great Temple of Artemis was four times the size of the Parthenon at Athens. Only one column stands today in the sprawling ruins of Ephesus, but it was silver shrines or models of this temple that were hawked to pilgrims worshiping at the Artemis Temple (Ac 19:24–27).

Great Theater. When Paul's preaching curtailed the sales of these models, the noisy riot of the silversmiths took place when they all flocked to the great theater at Ephesus and chanted, "Great is Artemis of the Ephesians!" for some two hours (Ac 19:28). The great theater there has been excavated on the western side of a hill overlooking the city and remains the largest theater of antiquity. It is still in a state of remarkable preservation.

Temple warning.

Temple Warning for Gentiles. At the close of his third missionary journey, Paul brought the collection of Gentile Christians to the Jewish Christians in Jerusalem. Here he was arrested, Ac 21:27–36 tells us, because Ephesian Jews claimed Paul had taken a Gentile beyond the sacred limits into areas reserved only for Jews. Two signs, inscribed with warnings of death for such trespass, have been discovered—one with the inscription intact, the other partially so.

Caesarea Floor Mosaic. Luke reports Paul's two-year imprisonment at Caesarea after he refused to bribe the Roman governor Felix to secure his release (Ac 24). Felix is well-known in Roman history as brother of Pallas, the wealthiest man in Rome, and the imperial treasurer under Nero. At Caesarea has been discovered the mosaic floor in the central area of Paul's prison, at the base of Herod the Great's palace. The inscription reads: "Good luck to the captain of the guards."

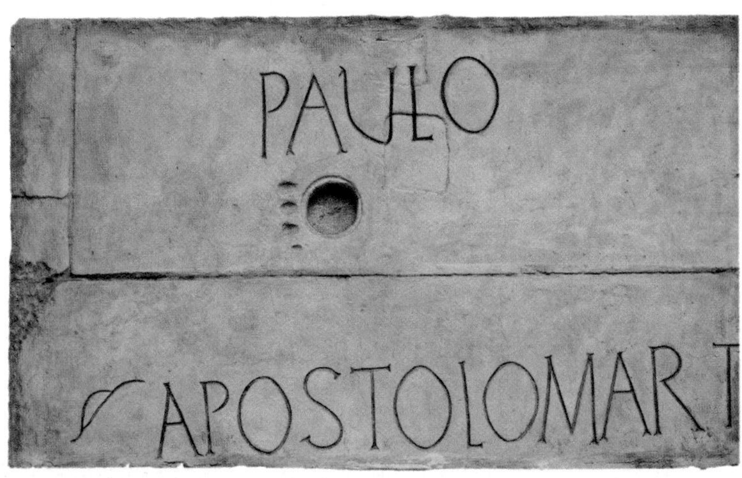

Inscribed stone probably made during the reign of Constantine (AD 280–334). The round opening is to touch the relic. Found at the Church San Paolo furio le Mura, Rome, Italy.

Probable Burial Site of Paul. According to earliest church tradition and supported by the testimony of Eusebius, Paul was beheaded on the Ostian Way several miles from the Ostian Gate at Rome. Constantine erected the Basilica of St. Paul (Outside the Walls) at his burial site nearby. Under the high altar (or the basilica) is a limestone sarcophagus inscribed with Latin datives: "To [or For] Paul, Apostle and Martyr." Because of the long tradition at this site and the fact that no other place has ever been claimed as Paul's burial site, many scholars deem it authentic.

In addition, extensive excavations have taken place at nearly all the sites and cities that Paul visited on his missionary journeys: Salamis, Paphos, Perga, Antioch in Pisidia, Tarsus, Troas, Philippi, Amphipolis, Apollonia, Thessalonica, Cenchreae, Miletus, Ptolemais, Caesarea, Malta, Syracuse, and Puteoli, in addition to the major cities cited earlier. Some absolutely authentic sites Paul visited that have not yet been excavated include Iconium, Lystra, Derbe, and Berea.

Cities of Revelation. As for the rest of the New Testament, most of the "Seven Cities of Asia Minor" mentioned in the Book of Revelation have also been excavated. All of these stand as mute witnesses to the geographical accuracy of the New Testament.

Common Archaeological Periods

In Ancient Near Eastern archaeology, the earlier periods are named for the material culture (Neolithic through Iron below) and then named for the dominant political culture (Assyrian through Roman, etc.). As a result, dates for the Iron Age and the Assyrian and Babylonian Periods overlap.

The dates given below reflect those used in scholarly publications. However, readers should be aware that not all scholars work with the same range of dates for the various periods.

Approximate Dates	Material-Based Periods	Politically-Based Periods	Approximate Dates
8500–4300 BC	Neolithic Period		
4300–3300 BC	Chalcolithic Period		
3300–2150 BC	Early Bronze Age		
2150–1550 BC	Middle Bronze Age		
1550–1200 BC	Late Bronze Age		
1200–586 BC	Iron Age	Assyrian Period	732–604 BC
		Babylonian Period	604–539 BC
		Persian Period	539–332 BC
		Early Hellenistic Period	332–167 BC
		Late Hellenistic (Hasmonean) Period	167–40 BC
		Early Roman (Herodian) Period	40 BC–AD 70
		Middle Roman Period	AD 70–180
		Late Roman Period	AD 180–330

Helpful Resources

The above listing of sites and artifacts is by no means exhaustive, and there are many other touch points between the sacred and the secular evidence, such as from numismatics (the study of coins), climatology, and related historical evidence. Excavation reports are usually quite technical—and useful only for specialists in the field. To the ordinary student, biblical dictionaries, encyclopedias, and periodicals (of which there are many) may be helpful. Here are some recommendations:

Biblical Archaeology Review. Washington DC: Biblical Archaeology Society, 1975–. ♘ Popular style; use with discretion. The general editor is Jewish.

Bible and Spade: A Quarterly Digest of Biblical Archaeology. Burnt Hills, NY: Word of Truth Productions, 1972–. ♘ Popular style; use with discretion. The general editor is a Christian.

Freedman, David Noel, ed. *Anchor Bible Dictionary*. 6 Vols. New York: Doubleday, 1992. ♘ Extensive entries, though many are vitiated by historical-critical speculations.

Maier, Paul L. *In the Fullness of Time: A Historian Looks at Christmas, Easter, and the Early Church*. Grand Rapids: Kregel, 1997. ♘ Well written history, which comments on archaeological artifacts and sites of the New Testament Era.

Marshall, I. Howard, A. R. Millard, J. I. Packer, and D. J. Wiseman, eds. *New Bible Dictionary*. 3rd ed. Downers Grove, IL: InterVarsity Press, 1996. ♘ Briefer than the *Anchor Bible Dictionary* but also more conservative in approach, and hence more helpful.

Master, Daniel M., ed. *The Oxford Encyclopedia of the Bible and Archaeology*. Oxford: Oxford University Press, 2013. ♘ Two volumes, including 130 essays researched, written, and reviewed by scholars. More focused in scope than *The Oxford Encyclopedia of Archaeology in the Near East*.

Mazar, Amihai. *Archaeology of the Land of the Bible, 10,000–586 B.C.E.* Vol. 1. New Haven: Yale University Press, 1992. ♘ Overview from the dawn of civilization in the region through the Babylonian conquest of Judah.

Meyers, Eric M., and Mark A. Chancey. *Archaeology of the Land of the Bible: Alexander to Constantine.* Vol. 3. New Haven: Yale University Press, 2012. ♘ Overview of intertestamental, New Testament, and early Jewish and Christian subjects.

Meyers, Eric M., ed. *The Oxford Encyclopedia of Archaeology in the Near East.* 5 Vols. Oxford: Oxford University Press, 1996. ♘ A thorough academic resource that encompasses biblical archaeology into the broader field of Near Eastern archaeology.

Stern, Ephraim. *Archaeology of the Land of the Bible: The Assyrian, Babylonian, and Persian Periods (732–332 B.C.E.).* Vol. 2. New Haven: Yale University Press, 2001. ♘ Overview of Assyrian, Babylonian, and Persian Periods, which bridges from the Mazar volume to the Meyers and Chancey volume.

———, ed. *The New Encyclopedia of Archaeological Excavations in the Holy Land.* 4 Vols. Jerusalem: Carta, 1993. ♘ A thorough academic resource treating c 420 sites.

Horace D. Hummel
Edward A. Engelbrecht
Paul L. Maier

ANCIENT LITERATURE AND THE HOLY SCRIPTURES

The following list briefly describes texts that biblical scholars and students commonly consult when seeking a broader understanding of the times in which the Scriptures were written. These are the writings of Israel's neighbors, who prospered and suffered alongside God's people, leaving behind their unique stories and religious views. Because scholars have titled these compositions and transliterated their proper nouns with different spellings, these appendices often include more than one title for a work. There is no standardization for titling to date. (See *SBL Handbook of Style*, 8.3.17.)

To read selections from these documents, learn more about them, or to explore other documents, the following resources are recommended and cited throughout the list:

ANEP Pritchard, James B., ed. *The Ancient Near East in Pictures, Relating to the Old Testament*. 2nd ed. With Supplement. Princeton: Princeton University Press, 1969.

ANET Pritchard, James B., ed. *Ancient Near Eastern Texts Relating to the Old Testament with Supplement*. 3rd ed. Princeton: Princeton University Press, 1969.

CS Hallo, William W., and K. Lawson Younger Jr., eds. *The Context of Scripture*. 3 Vols. Leiden: Brill, 2003.

OCD Simon Hornblower and Antony Spawforth, eds. *The Oxford Classical Dictionary*. 3rd rev. ed. Oxford: Oxford University Press, 2003.

Further resources on ancient literature and the Bible are found in *The Apocrypha: The Lutheran Edition with Notes* (abbreviated as *ALEN*). It includes entries especially for the intertestamental era, the New Testament, and early Christianity, such as the Elephantine Papyri, the Cairo Genizah Documents, the Dead Sea Scrolls, other early Jewish manuscript discoveries, Philo, Josephus, the Old Testament Pseudepigrapha, Rabbinic literature, New Testament Apocrypha or Pseudepigrapha, and the Nag Hammadi Codices.

Model of an Egyptian scribe (c 2494–2345) using his garment as a writing table.

Sumerian Literature

Ebla Tablets, *CS* 3:235 ❦ Mid third millennium BC. A vast collection of records and letters that characterize civilization in Mesopotamia before the appearance of Israel's patriarchs. Cf with Gn 1–11.

The Sumerian King List, *ANET* 265 ❦ Late third millennium BC. A list of the rulers of Ur, where Abram began his life.

Lamentation over the Destruction of Sumer and Ur, *CS* 1.166; *ANET* 611 ❦ Early second millennium BC. A poem describing how the Sumerian gods decree and carry out judgment against sin. Comparable with biblical laments.

The Laws of Lipit-Ishtar, *CS* 2.154 ❦ 1934–1924 BC. Legal code of the ruler of Isin. Comparable with stipulations in the Law of Moses.

Egyptian Literature

The Famine Stela, *CS* 1.53; **Seven Lean Years Tradition**, *ANET* 31 ❦ Set in twenty-eighth century BC. A description of seven years when the Nile was low, leading to famine, which has similarities to the setting for the story of Joseph in Gn 41.

The Protests of the Eloquent Peasant, *ANET* 407 ❦ Twenty-first century BC. The story of a peasant who went down to Egypt in search of food and faced ill treatment. Comparable with events from the story of Joseph.

A Dispute over Suicide, *ANET* 405 ❦ End of the third millennium BC. A man dialogues with his soul about weariness with life. Also known as "Dialogue of a Man with His Soul (Egyptian 'Ba')." Comparable with elements of the Book of Job.

Sinuhe, *CS* 1.38; **The Story of Si-nuhe**, *ANET* 18 ❦ Circa 1960 BC. The story of an Egyptian who volunteered to go into exile in Asia, which describes the region of Canaan and its inhabitants.

Harper's Songs, *CS* 1.30–31 ❦ Middle kingdom period. Songs from the tomb of King Intef and from Neferhotep. Comparable with elements of Ecclesiastes and Job.

Two Hymns to the Sun-god, *CS* 1.28; **The Hymn to the Aton**, *ANET* 369 ❦ Circa 1380–1362 BC. A hymn associated with the heretic king Amenhotep IV, who changed his name to Akhenaton and introduced worship of one god in Egypt. Comparable with elements of the Psalms.

The (Israel) Stele of Merneptah, *CS* 2.6; **Hymn of Victory of Mer-ne-Ptah**, *ANET* 376 ❦ Circa 1230 BC. This hymn includes the earliest discovered reference to Israel by name outside the Bible.

The Two Brothers, *CS* 1.40; **The Story of Two Brothers**, *ANET* 23 ❦ Manuscript dated c 1225 BC. A story of false accusation against a younger brother, whose experiences have parallels with the experiences of Joseph at Potiphar's house (Gn 39).

The Report of Wenamun, *CS* 1.41; **The Journey of Wen-amun to Phoenicia**, *ANET* 25 ❦ Circa 1100 BC. The travel account of an Egyptian official who was sent to Phoenicia to obtain lumber.

The Campaign of Sheshonk I, *ANET* 263 ❦ Late tenth century BC. A list of cities pharaoh subordinated in Asia, including locations in Israel. Cf 1Ki 14:25–28.

Instruction of Amenemope, *CS* 1.47; **Instruction of Amen-em-Opet**, *ANET* 421 ❦ Circa seventh or sixth centuries BC. This collection of wise sayings relates closely to Pr 22:17–24:22 in its content and style.

Akkadian Literature

Gilgamesh, *CS* 1.132; **The Epic of Gilgamesh**, *ANET* 72 ❦ Beginning of the second millennium BC, though the earliest tablets date from the middle of the second millennium. Describes the hero, Gilgamesh, who meets the survivor of a great flood, with elements comparable to the story of Noah.

Epic of Creation (Enuma Elish), *CS* 1.111; **The Creation Epic**, *ANET* 60 ❦ Early second millennium BC, though all texts were prepared much later. The account describes the Old Babylonian understanding of creation.

Laws of Eshnunna, *CS* 2.130 ❦ Eighteenth century BC legal code for an Amorite city. Stipulations comparable with the Law of Moses.

The Laws of Hammurabi, *CS* 2.131; **The Code of Hammurabi**, *ANET* 163 ❦ Circa 1700 BC. The legal code of the Old Babylonians, with parallels to the Law of Moses.

The Mari Letters, *ANET* 482 ❦ Circa 1700 BC. A vast collection of letters found at the palace of King Zimri Lim. Written by Amorites, they have cultural parallels with the biblical era of the patriarchs.

Atra-hasis, *CS* 1.130; **Atrahasis**, *ANET* 104 § Seventeenth century BC. A Mesopotamian account of mankind's sins and a great flood, with parallels to the account of Noah's flood in Gn 6–9. The story appears in Old Babylonian and later versions.

Nuzi [Tablets] Akkadian, *ANET* 219 § Mid second millennium BC. Legal documents with parallels to patriarchal and Israelite practices.

Tell El-Amarna Letters, *CS* 3.92; **The Amarna Letters**, *ANET* 483 § Circa 1350 BC. A collection of letters that belonged to the royal archives of Amenhotep III and his son Akhenaton. Written in Akkadian with Canaanite influences. Includes cultural elements like those in the Old Testament historical books.

Ludlul Bel Nemeqi, "I Will Praise the Lord of Wisdom," *ANET* 596 § Late second millennium BC. An Akkadian wisdom text that refers to Marduk and resembles biblical wisdom texts.

The Descent of Ishtar to the Underworld, *CS* 1.108; **Descent of Ishtar to the Netherworld**, *ANET* 106 § End of the second millennium BC. A myth in which the goddess of fertility enters the realm of the dead but returns to the land of the living. Elements describe Near Eastern fertility myths and rites.

Babylonian Theodicy, *CS* 1.154; *ANET* 601 § Early first millennium BC. A poetic dialogue between a sufferer and a friend, with themes comparable to the Book of Job.

The Dialogue of Pessimism, *ANET* 600 § Early first millennium BC. A conversation between a master and a servant in which the master proposes actions but then decides against carrying them out. Comparable with elements in the Book of Job.

Birth Legend of Sargon of Akkad, *CS* 1.133; **The Legend of Sargon**, *ANET* 119 § First millennium BC. The mother of the legendary figure sets him adrift on a river, similar to the story of Moses.

Shalmaneser III's Black Obelisk, *CS* 2.113F; **Shalmaneser III, Annalistic Reports**, *ANET* 278 § Circa 837 BC. Annals describing and depicting events of his reign, including the subordination of Jehu, king of Israel.

Sargon II: The Fall of Samaria, Annalistic Reports, *ANET* 284 § Circa 722 BC. An inscription from Cyprus, which describes his victory over Samaria.

Sennacherib, The Siege of Jerusalem, *ANET* 287 § 701 BC. A prism-shaped tablet including his annals of the siege.

Historical Documents of Nebuchadnezzar II, Varia, *ANET* 308 § After 587 BC. A description of the rations received by Jehoiachin, former king of Judah who was exiled to Babylon.

So-Called Nabonidus Chronicle, *ANET* 305 § Circa 540 BC. Also known as the "Verse Account." The chronicler criticizes the reign of Nabonidus, who lost Babylon to Cyrus the Great. Comparable with elements of the Book of Daniel.

Cyrus Cylinder, *CS* 2.124; **Cyrus**, *ANET* 315 § Circa 530 BC. Describes the accomplishments of Cyrus the Great. Comparable with events in Ezra.

Neo-Babylonian Tax Receipt (Murashu Tablets), *ANET* 221 § Circa 430 BC. A business document of the city of Nippur. Refers to Israelites settled in exile.

Hittite Literature

Many of the Hittite treaties were recorded in Akkadian as the language of international relations. See "Akkadian Literature" above.

Plague Prayers of Mursili, *CS* 1.60 § Circa 1300 BC. A ruler's requests for the gods to end an ongoing plague.

Treaty between Mursili and Duppi-Tesub, *CS* 2.17B; **Treaty between Mursili and Duppi-Tessub of Amurru**, *ANET* 203 § Circa 1300 BC. An example of a suzerain-vassal treaty, which bears similarities to the biblical covenants, includes history, legal clauses, invocations of the divine, and curses and blessings.

Treaty between the Hittites and Egypt; Treaty between Hattusilis and Ramses II, *ANET* 199 § Circa 1280 BC. An example of a parity treaty, which bears similarities to the biblical covenants. The text exists in Hittite and Egyptian versions.

Helpful Resources

Mendenhall, George E. "Covenant" in *Anchor Bible Dictionary*, ed. David Noel Freedman. New York: Doubleday, 1992. See 1:1179–1202.

Mendenhall, George E. *The Tenth Generation: The Origins of the Biblical Tradition*. Baltimore, MD: Johns Hopkins University Press, 1974.

West Semitic Literature

Ras Shamra Tablets (Ugaritic Letters), *CS* 3.45 § Second half of the second millennium BC. Royal and courtly correspondence, revealing the everyday life of rulers and officials. Comparable with the culture of ancient Israel.

Corpus Inscriptionum Semiticarum § Circa 2000 BC to AD 622. A modern publication of ancient inscriptions in various Semitic languages.

Khirbet Qeiyafa Ostracon (Hebrew) § Tenth century BC. Discovered in Elah Valley in 2010. Describes ethical leadership and mentions offices described in the Bible.

The Inscription of King Yehawmilk, *CS* 2.32; **Yehimilk of Byblos Inscription** (Canaanite), *ANET* 653 § Tenth century BC building dedication. Comparable with biblical dedication and prayer texts.

The Gezer Calendar (Hebrew), *CS* 2.85; *ANET* 320 § Circa 925 BC. A brief school exercise text including a poem about seasons for planting and harvesting in Israel.

The Inscription of King Mesha (Moabite), *CS* 2.23; **The Moabite Stone**, *ANET* 320 § Circa 830 BC. A stele describing the king's accomplishments against the people of Israel.

The Ostraca of Samaria (Hebrew), *ANET* 321 § Eighth century BC. A collection of potsherds used for record keeping at the royal archive of Israelite kings.

Kuntillet ʿAjrud Inscriptions (Hebrew), *CS* 2.47 § Circa 700 BC. Dedication texts to Yahweh, which refer to his Asherah consort, illustrating the mixing of biblical and Canaanite religions.

The Siloam Tunnel Inscription (Hebrew), *CS* 2.28; **The Siloam Inscription**, *ANET* 321 § Circa 700 BC. A description of how King Hezekiah's workmen hewed a water conduit that brought the flow of the Gihon Spring within the walls of Jerusalem.

The Words of Ahiqar (Aramaic), *ANET* 427 § Circa 700 BC. Wise sayings from the Assyrian court. Comparable with biblical wisdom texts.

Lachish Ostraca (Hebrew), *CS* 3.42; *ANET* 321 § Circa 589 BC. Administrative letters written on potsherds. Israelite correspondence.

Corpus Inscriptionum Iudaicarum § Third century BC to eighth century AD. A twentieth-century publication of ancient Jewish inscriptions in various languages, include Greek, Latin, Aramaic, and Hebrew.

Persian Literature

Behistun Inscription § Circa 521 BC. Darius I describes his rise to power. Because the inscription was written in Old Persian, Babylonian, and Elamite, scholars were able to decipher cuneiform for the first time.

Greek Literature

Corpus Inscriptionum Graecarum § From circa eighth century through the Roman era. Nineteenth-century publication that is now supplemented by *Inscriptiones Graecae*. Illustrates personal, local, regional, and imperial interests of Greek-speaking people.

Homer, *OCD* 718 § Second half of the eighth century BC. His epic poems, the *Iliad* and the *Odyssey*, were like Scripture to the ancient Greeks and treat events of the Trojan War and its aftermath.

Alcaeus, *OCD* 51 § Seventh century BC. Poet of Mytilene. Wrote hymns for the gods.

Theognis of Megara, *OCD* 1503 § Circa 550 BC. Elegiac poet and aristocrat whose sayings are similar to Solomonic wisdom.

Herodotus of Halicarnassus, *OCD* 696 § Circa 425 BC. Greek historian who described various cultures around the Mediterranean basin, including the Judeans.

Xenophon of Athens, *OCD* 1628 § Fourth century BC. Greek historian who served as a soldier in Asia and fought the Persians.

Manetho of Heliopolis, Egypt, *OCD* 917 § Early third century BC. Egyptian priest who wrote a history of Egypt beginning with their myths and traced rulers and events to c 342 BC. Invaluable for establishing historical events across nearly 3,000 years.

Berossos of Babylon, *OCD* 239 § Early third century BC. Wrote history of Babylon, preserved in fragments.

Septuagint translation, *OCD* 1391 § Second century BC. Greek translation of the Old Testament attributed to 72 scribes.

Polybius, *OCD* 1209 § Second century BC. Described the rise of Rome during the intertestamental era.

Diodorus of Agyrium, Sicily, *OCD* 472 ❧ First century BC. Wrote universal history, beginning with mythology and reaching 60 BC.

Oxyrhynchus Papyri ❧ From first century AD to sixth century AD. Nineteenth and twentieth century publications of ancient Greek and Latin documents found at an Egyptian dump. They illustrate everyday life in the Roman Empire.

Ptolemaeus of Mende, *OCD* 1271 ❧ First half of the first century AD. Attributed the exodus to the time of King Amosis (Ahmose I, sixteenth century BC).

Strabo of Amaseia, *OCD* 1447 ❧ First century AD. Geographer who described places around the Mediterranean.

Philo Judaeus of Alexandria, *OCD* 1167 ❧ First century AD. Commentator on books of Scripture. See *ALEN*, pp 340–45.

Josephus, Flavius, *OCD* 798 ❧ First century AD. Described Israelite history for Greek readers. See *ALEN*, pp 346–51.

Cassius Dio, *OCD* 299 ❧ Circa AD 164–post 229. Greek senator who wrote a Roman history, which corresponds with intertestamental and New Testament events.

Pliny the Younger, *OCD* 1198 ❧ Early second century AD. Lawyer, official, and correspondent who described conditions in the Roman Empire and mentioned interactions with Christians.

Plutarch of Chaeronea, *OCD* 1200 ❧ Early second century AD. Biographer and moralist, who described figures of the intertestamental era, such as Alexander the Great.

Hegesippus ❧ Second century AD. Jewish convert to Christianity who wrote memoirs about the Early Church. Eusebius of Caesarea preserved fragments of Hegesippus's work in his *Church History*.

Arrian of Nicomedia, *OCD* 175 ❧ Second century AD. Historian in the manner of Xenophon; he described the campaigns of Alexander the Great.

Helpful Resources

Loeb Classical Library. Cambridge: Harvard University Press.

Latin Literature

Tullius Cicero, Marcus, *OCD* 1558 ❧ 106–43 BC. Roman orator and politician, who served as consul and in a variety of other offices. His writings are a resource for historical information during the intertestamental era.

Livy, *OCD* 877 ❧ 59 BC–AD 17. Patriotic Roman historian who describes the state's development from its ancient mythology to the early empire, with the latter books corresponding to the intertestamental era.

Oxyrhynchus Papyri ❧ From first century AD to sixth century AD. Nineteenth- and twentieth-century publications of ancient Greek and Latin documents found at an Egyptian dump. They illustrate everyday life in the Roman Empire.

Corpus Inscriptionum Latinarum ❧ First century BC to medieval. Vast collection of Latin inscriptions illustrating personal, local, regional, and imperial interests of Roman citizens.

Tacitus, *OCD* 1469 ❧ Circa AD 56–post 118. Roman historian, whose writings correspond with the New Testament era.

Suetonius, *OCD* 1451 ❧ Circa AD 70–c AD 130. Roman biographer, who describes Roman leaders during the New Testament era.

Severus, Sulpicius, *OCD* 1398 ❧ Circa AD 360–c AD 420. Christian Roman historian and chronologist.

Helpful Resources

Loeb Classical Library. Cambridge: Harvard University Press.

THE CHURCH FROM AGE TO AGE

This brief article, encompassing more than 2,000 years of history, will help you appreciate the many challenges that students of God's Word have faced in sharing the Bible's message. It is drawn from *The Church from Age to Age: A History from Galilee to Global Christianity* (Concordia, 2011). Read it as a companion to the article on "How the Bible Came to Us" (p 827).

The Early Church (to AD 250)

In many ways, Jesus did not create something new when He created the Church. His first followers were part of God's Old Testament people, the Old Testament Church, if you like (e.g., Mt 4:18–25). But in other ways, Jesus introduced changes that distinguished His New Testament people and caused the Church to grow. During the Old Testament, only one nation followed the Lord: Israel (Dt 7). But Jesus extended the Church to all nations (Mt 28:19–20). During the Old Testament, only certain leaders were filled with God's Spirit. But through Jesus, the Holy Spirit came upon all flesh and dwells in believers (Jl 2:28–29; Jn 1:33; 7:39; 14:17; 20:22; Ac 2). He transformed old covenant rites (Ex 12; Jer 31:31–33; Ezk 36:25–27) into the cleansing of Baptism and the new covenant of His body and blood.

On mission journeys, the apostles Peter, Paul, and others administered these changes during the all-important beginnings of Christianity. In the second generation came the Church Fathers who continued to testify about Jesus. They defended the Church against those who would defame the faith. To that end, the Lord led them to collect the apostolic books of the New Testament canon, to prepare the Creed, and a church government that grew with the churches and guided them, despite the horror of persecutions.

The Church in a Changing World (250 to 600)

After the extraordinary conversion of Constantine (312), the first Roman emperor to convert to Christianity, the persecutions were finally halted. The faith went on to conquer Rome itself! Although the empire declined and fell to Germanic invaders (e.g., the sack of Rome in 410), the invaders were, in turn, conquered by Christ through Christian missionaries.

Christ calling His disciples. The pile of fish in the foreground illustrates the parable of the net (Mt 13:47–50).

As dark ages blanketed Europe, the Church and its priests and monks, as the only educated class, saved civilization in the West, while Christians of Asia and Africa continued to thrive. The Syrian, Egyptian (Coptic), and Ethiopian Christians translated the Bible into their languages and spread the Gospel ever further eastward and south until the suppressive *dhimma* status under Islam.

The Church of the Middle Ages (600 to 1400)

The Medieval Church and its papacy were challenged by their own successes as *the* dominant forces in Western civilization, much as the patriarch of Constantinople was in Eastern Orthodoxy. This was the era of powerful popes and soaring cathedrals, yet also a time when too close a link between church and state led to increasing doctrinal error and moral corruption.

In 632, with the death of the Muslim prophet Muhammad, Christianity had to face—and still faces—its greatest confrontation ever in Islam. Christendom was also weakened by the Great Schism—the huge split between the Eastern and Western Churches (1054), as well as the failure of the Crusades and the fall of Constantinople to the Muslim Turks in 1453. Although Syrian missionaries carried the Gospel as far east as China, vast cultural and political changes led to decline in eastern churches and to the isolation of African Christians from the Christians in Europe.

The Renaissance and Reformation (1300 to 1600)

The Renaissance ("rebirth") in Europe brought on a change in culture from a totally religious worldview to a secular alternative. A great constellation of scholars, artists, sculptors, and authors pioneered the new learning, and popes patronized them in hopes of saving the Renaissance for the Church. What happened instead was the secularization of the papacy, as well as moral and theological crises in the Western Church that demanded reform.

Peter Waldo in France, John Wycliffe in England, Jan Hus in Bohemia, and Savanarola in Italy attempted such reforms. All had failed, with the reformers themselves often burned at the stake. It was left to Martin Luther—the providential person at the perfect time—to inaugurate the Protestant Reformation, which transformed much of northern Europe and caused a revitalization of western Christianity that would propel it around the globe.

Orthodoxy and the Enlightenment (1600 to 1800)

Along with the Reformation in Europe, the emergence of Roman Catholicism at the Council of Trent (1545–63) and the Counter-Reformation caused the religious wars of the seventeenth century. These wars showed Christendom at its worst. Although the Thirty Years' War finally ended in 1648, religious hatred and persecution continued in Europe for many years. Fears of new conflicts encouraged a stolid form of orthodoxy. This faith of the head provoked a reaction emphasizing a faith of the heart called *Pietism* in Germany and *Methodism* in England. Meanwhile, the discovery of the Americas gave Roman Catholic missionaries the opportunity to spread the Christian message to other continents, though they often resorted to coercive methods like those used against Protestants in Europe—and sometimes worse.

The European Enlightenment of the eighteenth century became a powerful secularist challenge to all branches of Christianity. While some leaders of the Enlightenment, such as Isaac Newton, remained Christian, others, such as François Voltaire, ridiculed the faith and led others to do so as well.

Christian Churches in Modern Times (1800 to World War I)

The American, French, and Latin American revolutions rocked the world. Napoleon tried to redraw the map of Europe. All branches of Christendom were impacted by these events and also by the many political and social uprisings that punctuated the nineteenth century.

Even more so than previously, the Church now had to meet a fourfold ideological challenge from Rationalism, the theory of organic evolution, materialist philosophy, and biblical higher criticism. Christian reaction to these ideas ranged from militant denial to accommodation, and the debate continues to this day. But this was also the time of intense missionary activity across the world and a response to Matthew 28 not seen since the earliest missionaries from Rome and Constantinople. The Church used the newly invented forms of transportation and communication to spread the Gospel.

Global Christianity (The World Wars to the Present)

The global mission outreach of Christendom, restarted so strongly in the nineteenth century, has continued and even accelerated to the present day because the Church has capitalized on the communications revolution. Much as the printing press made the Reformation possible, so, too, radio, television, the Internet, and other technological gifts have transformed the way Christians spread the Gospel.

The worldwide response has been phenomenal, especially in Africa and the southern hemisphere. A strong ecumenical movement is also contributing toward at least a partial fulfillment of Jesus' prayer "that they might all be one." To that end, Christians cooperate on developing Bible translations and publications, which spread the teachings of Jesus to those who have not yet heard or believed.

HOW THE BIBLE CAME TO US

Today almost every person on earth can obtain a copy of the Bible and read it in his own language. It can be purchased for very little money, and thousands of copies are given away for free. However, the Bible was not always so easily obtained and read. There were times when only rich people could own a copy of the Scriptures; the common people knew the Bible from hearing it read during the church's liturgy. At times, most people could not understand the language in which the Bible was available. In some countries the people were not even permitted to read it.

How different it is today! Now we hear much about the "open Bible." Most everyone can read it. How was this great change brought about? How the Bible came down to us is indeed a most interesting story.

Ancient Manuscripts of the Bible

The oldest manuscripts of the Bible still in existence are among the Dead Sea Scrolls, penned between c 250 BC and c AD 70. The original copies of the biblical books—scrolls and letters written by men such as Moses, Isaiah, Matthew, and Paul—disappeared in ancient times. Some of them were likely worn out by persistent use, as happens with Bibles today. Those of the Old Testament may have been destroyed at Jerusalem in 587 BC when the temple treasury was burned; those of the New Testament may have been burned during the persecutions of the first three centuries AD.

After the Roman era of persecution, Constantine the Great (d AD 337) commissioned 50 complete copies of the Bible in Greek for use in the new churches he was constructing, many of which commemorated sites in the Holy Land. Eusebius of Caesarea (c 260–c 340) received Constantine's request and oversaw the completion of the volumes. These 50 Bibles are early examples of a *pandect*, a complete Bible in one volume, an important step toward creating the Bible as we know it today. However, for most of the ancient and medieval eras, such massive books were too expensive to purchase and too difficult to carry about. Individuals might have a copy of

A workman operates a replica of a Gutenberg press, which was used to print Bibles in the fifteenth century.

a biblical book or a collection of books, but only churches and monasteries had complete Bibles. One extreme example, the famous Old Latin Bible known as Codex Gigas, has pages 3 feet high and 20 inches wide; it is too large for one person to carry.

Medieval Manuscripts

Before the invention of printing (AD 1436) all books had to be copied by hand. From the sixth century to the tenth century AD, Jewish scribes known as the Masoretes used painstaking care in copying the Hebrew Old Testament. If the copyist made several mistakes, the whole page would be rejected, and he began all over again. An example of their careful work is seen in Codex Leningradensis (AD 1008), which has commonly served as the text for modern Hebrew Bibles. A comparison of the Dead Sea Scrolls with the work of the Masoretes demonstrates their remarkable care, which preserved the Hebrew Scriptures for thousands of years. Scribes spent their whole lives in copying the Bible by hand. That was slow and difficult work.

A breakthrough came in the thirteenth century when Christian scholars and scribes at the University of Paris developed what is called the Paris Bible. This was a one-volume Latin Bible written in tiny letters on thin parchment. The little Paris Bibles made it possible for many more people to have their own copy of the Bible, renewing and broadening study of the Bible that would become an important contribution to the Reformation. In fact, the 1287 constitution of the Augustinians included a stipulation that novices should diligently read the Bible, a rule Johann von Staupitz enforced in the case of Martin Luther, who received a little red-bound copy of the Bible upon entering the Erfurt monastery. A second technical breakthrough came with the invention of moveable type, resulting in Gutenberg's printing of the Latin Bible in c 1455.

Modern Bible Publication

The Renaissance search for better and earlier biblical manuscripts started just before the Reformation when European scholars rediscovered the study of Greek and Hebrew. For example, Desiderius Erasmus sought copies of Greek manuscripts to publish his Greek New Testament, which Luther used for his German translation of the Bible.

In the eighteenth century, Lutheran New Testament scholar Johannes Albrecht Bengel (1687–1752) introduced the first scientific study of the biblical text. His discoveries inspired others to search for earlier and better biblical manuscripts.

In the middle of the nineteenth century, German scholar Constantin Tischendorf (1815–74) discovered a very old copy of the Bible on Mount Sinai: Codex Sinaiticus. This pandect Bible is probably very similar to the ones made by Eusebius in the fourth century on behalf of the Roman Emperor Constantine. Codex Sinaiticus contains most of the Old Testament and the whole New Testament in Greek. Altogether, scholars today draw on thousands of Greek manuscripts of the Bible—most made between AD 500 and AD 1200—when preparing a new edition of the Bible.

Early Translations of the Bible

The Hebrew Old Testament was translated into Greek about 285 BC, as a tradition says, by 72 Jewish scholars in Egypt. This translation is known as the Septuagint (abbreviated LXX), that is, the work of the Seventy. Between AD 100 and AD 300, the whole Bible was translated into Syriac, Egyptian, Latin, and other languages. About AD 400 the Church Father Jerome made a new translation of the Bible into Latin, called the Vulgate, that is, the popular version. An edition of the Vulgate is still the authorized Bible of the Roman Catholic Church. The difficult work of translating the Bible into language after language continued down the centuries.

One of the best translations of the Bible into a modern language is that of Dr. Martin Luther, completed in 1534 with a team of scholars such as Philip Melanchthon. It became the popular German Bible, and it also had a great influence upon the translators of the English Bible.

The English Bible

The history of the English Bible is fascinating. Parts of the Bible were rendered into English before the Reformation. However, these versions were not accurate, and their English was difficult to understand. The man who gave his life in order to give the English people a good translation of the Holy Scriptures was William Tyndale, who greatly depended on Luther's German translation. Tyndale was persecuted in England by the supporters of the pope and had to flee to Germany, where he translated and published the New Testament. Copies were smuggled into England, but Tyndale was captured, strangled, and burned at the stake.

In 1611 appeared the King James or Authorized English Version, which was greatly influenced by Tyndale's work. This translation was made at the request of King James I. To this day it has remained the most popular English Bible. The work was done by some of the best scholars of England. A Revised Version was produced by a number of British and American scholars near the close of the nineteenth century. However, this revised version suffered from controversy due to the influence of liberal and critical scholars who contributed to it. As a result, English readers have seen a nearly constant number of new English translations ever since. The English Standard Version (ESV), used in this companion, is translated in the tradition of the King James Bible and presents the best balance between literal faithfulness to the Hebrew, Aramaic, and Greek texts of the Bible while presenting very readable, current English.

Lutheran Bible Translators, founded in 1964, is an example of an organization committed to making the Bible available to the millions of people around the world who may have access to the Bible through a foreign language they have studied but who would benefit from reading the Bible in their mother tongue.

Worldwide Distribution of the Bible

No book in the world has been copied with such painstaking care, none translated with such great labor, none printed and distributed with such holy zeal and amazing diligence as the Bible. Two events, the printing press and the Reformation, helped to spread the Bible over the world. Since Gutenberg's time, billions of copies of the Bible have been printed. The cost of Bibles has been greatly reduced.

The Bible societies, since 1804, have been active in having the Bible translated into all languages and in distributing it throughout the world. The worldwide distribution of the Bible is an important part of the missionary work of the Christian Church. We have the Bible by the grace and providence of God. We can show our gratitude to Him for this blessed gift by using it faithfully and by giving it to others. Our efforts to bring God's Word to others will never be in vain. (Cf Is 55:11; 1Co 15:58.)

Adapted and updated from J. M. Weidenschilling, *Our Bible: A Guide to the Study of the Holy Scriptures* (St. Louis: Concordia, 1945), 65–68.

A shepherd frees a sheep from tangling vines. Christ our Good Shepherd frees us from the ways of the world to practice and live in the teachings of His wholesome Word.

GREEK-ENGLISH
NEW TESTAMENT

HOLY
BIBLE

תורה
נביאים
וכתובים

BIBLIA
HEBRAICA

BIBLE DICTIONARY AND INDEX

This Bible dictionary is for use especially with the English Standard Version (ESV). It includes entries for the sixty-six canonical books of Scripture as well as the Apocrypha. The entries are focused on more common biblical content, themes, and the content of the Bible Companion rather than on rarely mentioned persons or places in the Bible.

Readers should note that biblical names come from Hebrew, Canaanite, Egyptian, Assyrian, Babylonian, Aramaic, Persian, Greek, Latin, and other languages. Spellings are often affected as names were picked up from one language and used in another. In many cases it is difficult to determine the meaning of ancient names due to spelling changes or to imprecise understanding of terms.

Erwin L. Lueker and colleagues originally wrote entries for the earliest version of this dictionary: *The Concordia Bible Dictionary*, a KJV/RSV edition released in 1963. That content was rereleased in the *Companion Dictionary of the Bible* in 1985. Rev. Roy Askins, Laura L. Lane, and I revised and updated the content yet again for publication in *Concordia's Complete Bible Handbook*, 2nd ed. For the present volumes, I have added entries from the vocabulary lists of *The Lutheran Study Bible*, *The Apocrypha: The Lutheran Edition with Notes*, as well as additional entries based on the text of the current volumes.

The General Editor

A

AARON (AIR-uhn; of uncertain meaning; if Egyptian, "the name is great"). Moses' assistant, the first high priest (Ex 4:14–17; 7). Aaron was born in Egypt. His family was from the tribe of Levi, the descendants of one of the twelve sons of Jacob (Ex 6:19–20). Miriam was his older sister, and Moses was his younger brother (Nu 26:59).

Aaron was praised because he spoke well in public (Ex 4:14). At God's command, Aaron spoke to the people for Moses because Moses did not believe himself to be a good public speaker.

During a battle in the wilderness between the children of Israel and the Amalekites, Aaron helped Hur hold up Moses' hands (Ex 17:12). While Moses was on Mount Sinai receiving the Ten Commandments, the people became impatient, so Aaron made a golden calf for an idol (Ex 32). Aaron and Miriam criticized Moses because of the foreign woman he had married (Nu 12:1).

Moses anointed Aaron and Aaron's sons to the priesthood (Nu 3:1–3). The Lord confirmed Aaron as His high priest when the staff with Aaron's name on it blossomed (Nu 17). Because Aaron and Moses doubted God at Meribah, they were not allowed to enter the Promised Land (Nu 20:12–13). Aaron's son Eleazar followed him as high priest. Aaron died at age 123 and was buried on Mount Hor (Nu 20:22–29). See 1:59, 64–65, 86–88, 99–102, 106–7, 113, 127, 129, 134–40, 368–69, 581, 703; 2:666.

AARONIC BENEDICTION. See 1:137.

AARON'S STAFF (OR ROD). When Aaron's staff swallowed the staffs of the magicians and sorcerers summoned by Pharaoh, God demonstrated His supremacy over the gods of Egypt (Ex 7:8–13). Later, by making the staff with Aaron's name on it blossom, God proved Aaron's authority. This staff was placed before the ark of the covenant (Nu 17; Heb 9:4). See 1:75, 88, 135, 138, 369.

ABASE. To humble or make low. The proud and wicked are to be abased (Jb 40:11). God abases the priests who fail to preach His Word (Mal 2:9).

ABBA (AB-ah; Aramaic "father," comparable with Eng "papa" or "dad"). Conveys childlike intimacy and confidence (Mk 14:36; Rm 8:15; Gal 4:6). Expresses the deep, loving relationship Jesus had with the Father and which believers now share. *Ab* or *abi* are also used to form proper names, e.g., Abraham.

ABEDNEGO (ah-BED-ne-go; "servant of Nego"). The Babylonian name given to Azariah, one of Daniel's friends (Dn 1:7). Abednego was thrown into the fiery furnace for not worshiping the golden idol set up by King Nebuchadnezzar (Dn 3). *See also* AZARIAH 5.

ABEL

1. (AY-buhl; perhaps meaning "son" or "vapor"). The second son of Adam and Eve. Abel was a keeper of sheep. When God was pleased with Abel's sacrifice, Abel's brother, Cain, became jealous and murdered him (Gn 4:1–8). In the NT, Abel is described as a righteous man because, by faith, he offered God "a more acceptable sacrifice than Cain" (Heb 11:4). See 1:13, 32, 417; 2:657.
2. (AY-buhl; meadow). A prefix for the names of towns and places (Gn 50:11; Jgs 7:22). See 1:199.

ABHORRENCE (ab-HAWR-uhns). Aversion or loathing; shrinking or withdrawing from someone or something that is disgusting. Believers abhor wicked, unholy things and sins (Dt 7:26; Ps 119:163). The wicked abhor both God's Law and the person who speaks God's truth (Lv 26:43; Am 5:10). God abhors those who worship false gods and break His Law (Lv 26:30).

ABIATHAR (ah-BIGH-ah-thahr; "father of abundance"). The son of the high priest Ahimelech. When Saul put Abiathar's father and 84 other priests to death, Abiathar escaped and fled to David's camp for protection (1Sm 22:20–23). He became David's counselor and with Zadok brought the ark of the covenant to Jerusalem (1Ch 15:11–14; 27:34). Toward the close of David's reign, Abiathar joined with Joab in supporting David's son Adonijah as the next king. Solomon became the new king, however, and expelled Abiathar from office (1Ki 1:7, 19, 25, 41–42; 2:26–27). See 1:310, 338, 751, 755, 797.

ABIJAH (ah-BIGH-jah; "the Lord is father").

1. A descendant of Aaron's son Eleazar. When David organized the priests into 24 divisions, the eighth division was named after Abijah (1Ch 24:10; Ne 12:17). Zechariah, the father of John the Baptist, belonged to this division (Lk 1:5).
2. The second son of Samuel. Because Abijah was a wicked judge, the elders asked for a king (1Sm 8:1–5). See 1:277.
3. The son of Jeroboam I (1Ki 14:1–18).
4. The son of Rehoboam and Maacah. Abijah was also known as Abijam. After his father died, Abijah became the next king of Judah. In an effort to

regain the ten northern tribes, he made war on Jeroboam I. Abijah reigned three years, following in the wicked ways of his father, and then he died (1Ki 15:1–8; 2Ch 12:16; 13). See 1:401.

5. The wife of Ahaz and mother of Hezekiah (2Ch 29:1).

ABIMELECH (ah-BIM-uh-lek; "my father is king").

1. The king of Gerar who made a covenant with Abraham (Gn 20; 21:22–34). See 1:703.
2. The king of Gerar who made a covenant with Isaac (Gn 26:1–33). He may have been the same person as the king who made the covenant with Abraham. See 1:28.
3. Gideon's son by his concubine (Jgs 8:31). See 1:233, 238; 2:800–1.
4. The son of Abiathar and grandson of Ahimelech the priest. Abimelech, who is sometimes referred to as Ahimelech, was a priest during David's reign (1Ch 18:16).
5. The name given to the Philistine king (probably King Achish, 1Sm 21:10) in the title of Psalm 34. It is thought that Abimelech was the throne name or title of Philistine kings.

ABNER (AB-nur; "father is light"). The son of Ner and commander of his cousin Saul's army (1Sm 14:50–51; 17:55; 26:5–14). When Saul died, Abner brought Ish-bosheth, Saul's son, to Mahanaim and made him king over Israel (2Sm 2:8–9). Then Abner and his men met David's army in combat at the pool of Gibeon and were defeated (2Sm 2:12–17). Later, Abner quarreled with Ish-bosheth and left his camp to join with David. Although David received him in peace, David's commander, Joab, and Joab's brother Abishai murdered Abner because he had killed their brother in the battle at Gibeon (2Sm 3:6–30). David mourned for Abner and described him as a prince and great man (2Sm 3:31–39). See 1:280, 294.

ABOMINATION (ah-bahm-i-NAY-shuhn). That which is disgusting, loathsome, detestable, particularly in a religious context. The term is applied to animals the Israelites were not allowed to eat, pagan practices, and idolatry (1Ki 11:5). Cf "tainted" and "detestable" in Lv 7:18, 21; Dt 29:17; Hos 9:10. See 1:117, 184, 240, 309, 603, 633, 742, 804, 810; 2:88.

ABOMINATION OF DESOLATION. This is mentioned in Dn 9:27; 11:31; 12:11, and may refer to the time when Antiochus IV Epiphanes desecrated the sanctuary by putting an idol to Zeus on the altar where sacrifices were offered. Ultimately, Daniel's prophecy concerning the abomination of desolation finds its fulfillment in messianic times. See 1:824, 835.

Christ also referred to the abomination of desolation (Mt 24:15–16; Mk 13:14). Here Jesus announced a new desolation and destruction of the Jerusalem temple, which would be carried out by the Romans in AD 70. This event would end all temple worship and sacrifice. However, these desolations are but a taste of what lies in the future (cf 2Th 2:3–4). In a figurative sense, this term is applied to the neglect of the Gospel in the Church. See 1:824.

ABRAHAM (AY-brah-ham; "father of multitudes"). The son of Terah and founder of the Hebrew nation. Abraham's name, before God changed it, was Abram. Abram and his family descended from Shem and lived in Ur of the Chaldeans. Abram had two brothers, Nahor and Haran. After Haran died, Terah, Abram, Abram's wife, Sarai, and Haran's son, Lot, left Ur for Canaan. But when they arrived in Haran, a city in Mesopotamia, they settled there instead. When Terah was 205 years old, he died in Haran (Gn 11:27–32).

After Terah's death, the Lord told Abram to leave his country, his family, and his father's house for a land the Lord would show him. He also promised to make of Abram a great nation and bless him and all the families of the earth in him. So Abram, now 75 years old, left Haran with Sarai, Lot, and all their possessions and began the journey to Canaan. In Canaan Abram pitched his tent by Shechem's holy place, the oak of Moreh. The Lord appeared to him there and promised to give the land to Abram's descendants. Then Abram built an altar to the Lord both there and, a little later, east of Bethel. When a famine came to the land, Abram went to Egypt. In order to be well received by Pharaoh, Abram told Sarai to say she was only his sister. Not realizing she was also Abram's wife, Pharaoh decided to marry Sarai because her beauty pleased him. When plagues fell on his household, however, Pharaoh found out that Abram had deceived him. He told Abram to take his family and many possessions and leave (Gn 12).

Abram and his family returned with Lot to the altar near Bethel. Because of bickering and fighting between their herdsmen, Abram and Lot decided to part ways. Lot, given his choice of the land, chose the Jordan Valley and pitched his tent as far as Sodom. The Lord repeated his promise to bless Abram, who moved to the oaks of Mamre at Hebron (Gn 13).

When four kings defeated five other kings in the territory where Lot lived and took Lot captive, Abram chased after the enemies, recovered the goods they had stolen, and rescued Lot. After this Abram received a blessing from Melchizedek, the priest and king of Salem (Gn 14).

Then God made a covenant with Abram, sealing His promise to make of Abram a great nation by giving him and his descendants the land of Canaan (Gn 15). But when Sarai did not become pregnant, she thought she could not have children of her own, so she gave her maid, Hagar, to Abram. He and Hagar had a son whom they named Ishmael (Gn 16). Then God changed Abram's name to Abraham and promised that His everlasting covenant would be fulfilled in Isaac, his son with Sarai. He made circumcision the sign of the covenant (Gn 17). God also changed Sarai's name to Sarah.

While Abraham was sitting at the door to his tent by the oaks of Mamre, the Lord appeared to him and told him that Sarah would bear him a son within the year. When Sarah heard this, she laughed because she thought she was too old to have a baby. The Lord rebuked her for laughing and told her nothing was too difficult for Him (Gn 18). When Abraham was 100 years old, Isaac was born. Soon after that Hagar and Ishmael were cast out (Gn 21).

Then the Lord tested Abraham's faith in His promise by commanding Abraham to sacrifice his son Isaac. At the last minute the angel of the Lord stopped Abraham from doing this. He told Abraham not to harm Isaac and provided a ram for sacrifice instead (Gn 22).

Because Abraham did not want Isaac to marry a Canaanite woman, he sent his servant back to his homeland to get a wife for Isaac. The servant returned with Rebekah, Abraham's great-niece. She became Isaac's wife (Gn 24). When Abraham was 175 years old, he died and was buried in the cave of Machpelah (Gn 25).

God called Abraham, who is later described as the friend of God, from a family that served idols (Jsh 24:2). God took the first step in making the covenant with Abraham, a covenant in which He bound Himself to give without receiving anything in return. Circumcision is a sign of His covenant (Rm 4:11).

By faith Abraham was just, as God wanted him to be, and thus became the father of all believers (Rm 4; Gal 3). This faith showed itself in works (Jas 2:21). In Christ, Abraham's offspring from all nations of the earth are blessed (Gal 3:16). Believers are the spiritual sons and heirs of Abraham (Rm 4:13–14; Gal 3:29). See 1:17, 21–28, 34–35, 49, 51, 53–55, 122, 399, 703; 2:146, 190, 219–20, 423, 506–7, 660, 696, 800, 805.

ABRAHAM'S SIDE. A term for everlasting life (Lk 16:22). Perhaps the place of honor at the heavenly banquet (cf Mt 8:11).

ABRAM (AY-bruhm; "exalted father"). *See* ABRAHAM.

ABSALOM (AB-sah-luhm; "father is peace"). The handsome son of David and Maacah (2Sm 3:3). When Amnon, his half-brother, raped Absalom's sister, Absalom killed him. Then Absalom fled to Geshur, where he stayed for three years (2Sm 13–14).

Four years after his return to Jerusalem, Absalom made plans to seize the throne from his father, David. To this end, he gathered people around him who were unhappy with David's rule. Ahithophel advised Absalom to attack David before the king had time to regroup his followers, but Hushai cautioned Absalom to wait. He told Absalom that he would need a big army to defeat David's able warriors (2Sm 17).

The two armies met in the forest of Ephraim, where Absalom's men were defeated by David's. When Absalom was fleeing, his hair became tangled in an oak branch. While he was hanging from the tree, Joab killed him with three spears. When David heard that Absalom died, he grieved for his son (2Sm 18). See 1:281, 287, 295, 301, 304, 315, 331.

ABSTINENCE (AB-stuh-nuhns). The act of abstaining from or not partaking of something. There are various examples of abstinence in the OT. The Israelites were to abstain from eating fat and blood, certain kinds of meats, parts of the offering sacred to the altar, and meats consecrated to idols (Ex 34:13–15; Lv 3:9–17; 11). Abstinence also was commanded under some special circumstances (Jgs 13:14; Nu 6:3; Jer 35:6; Lk 1:15).

In matters that are neither commanded nor forbidden, the NT does not command abstinence. It allows one freedom to decide for oneself as long as the decision is made in love and does not go against one's conscience (Ac 15; Rm 14:1–3; 1Co 8). The NT opposes sects that live by the Law (Col 2:16; 1Tm 4:1–4). See 2:552–53.

ABYSS (ah-BIS). When the NT speaks of "abyss," it refers to Satan's domain, hell (Lk 8:31; Rm 10:7). It is the source of all evil (cf "bottomless pit" in Rv 9:1–11; 11:7; 17:8; 20:1, 3). See 1:536, 575.

ACCURSED. Hbr *cherem*, one meaning of which is "something devoted to God for destruction" (Lv 27:28–29; Dt 7:26; Jsh 6:17) and thus "cursed" (cf Rm 9:3; 1Co 12:3; 16:22). Gk *anathema*; used in LXX. *See also* CURSE. See 1:120–21, 158, 214, 222–23; 2:296, 508.

ACHAN (AY-kan; "trouble"). A descendant of Judah who went against God's command and stole spoils of war at Jericho. For this sin Achan was stoned to death in the Valley of Achor (Jsh 7; 22:20). See 1:210, 218, 223–24.

ACHOR (AY-kawr; "trouble"). The valley south of Jericho where Achan was stoned to death (Jsh 7:24–26; 15:7; Is 65:10; Hos 2:15). Today this valley is identified with el-Buqeiʿa, which is about 10 miles south of Jericho. See 1:210.

ACTS, BOOK OF. See 2:359–409.

ADAM (AD-uhm; "human being," "man"; from the word for "ground"). The first human being. God created Adam in His own image. He placed him in the Garden of Eden and gave him dominion over animals and all other creatures. God made Eve from one of Adam's ribs so that Adam would have a helpmate. God told Adam and Eve to have children and rule over the earth. When Adam and Eve broke God's commandment by eating the fruit of the tree in the middle of the garden, God drove them out of Eden. Adam died when he was 930 years old (Gn 1–5). See 1:22, 32–35, 40–41, 44–46, 381, 411–12, 1002; 2:219.

Paul says that the first man, Adam, is the source of sin and death, and the second man, Christ, is the source of life and righteousness (Rm 5:12–21; 1Co 15:22, 45; cf Eph 4:22–24; Col 3:9–10). See 1:563, 836; 2:425, 429–30.

ADIAPHORA (ad-i-AF-o-rah). A term the church uses to refer to matters that are neither commanded nor forbidden by Scripture. In these matters individuals have freedom to make their own decisions or choices as long as they act in love and do not violate their consciences (Rm 14:3; 1Co 6:12; 8; 10:23; Col 2:16–17; cf AC XV and Ap XV). *See also* LIBERTY. See 2:470.

ADONAI (AD-o-nigh; "lord"). The Hebrews spoke this word whenever they saw the consonants YHWH, which spell Yahweh, the word for "Lord." When the vowels of the word *adonai* are placed with the consonants of YHWH, this results in the word *Jehovah*.

ADONIJAH (ad-o-NIGH-jah; "Yahweh is my lord"). The fourth son of David. Encouraged and supported by Joab and Abiathar, Adonijah proclaimed himself king. David, however, appointed Solomon as the new king (1Ch 23:1; 28:5). Solomon first pardoned Adonijah but later had him executed (1Ki 1–2). See 1:321, 338, 341.

ADOPTION. OT passages describing God's relation to Israel (Ex 4:22–23; Hos 11:1) certainly informed Paul's expression in the NT (Rm 8:15, 23; 9:4; Gal 4:5; Eph 1:5). Gk *huiothesia*, "placing as a son," a Greco-Roman legal term signifying the granting of the full rights and privileges of sonship in a family to which one does not belong by birth (Ex 2:10; Est 2:7; Acts 7:21). Paul says believers are adopted children of God. They have become members of God's family, the true Israel (the Church), by the work of the Holy Spirit, who brought them to faith in Christ (Rm 8:14–17; 9; Gal 3:26–28). That Christians have the Holy Spirit in their hearts witnesses to the fact that they are children and heirs of God (Gal 4:4–7). *See also* HEIR. See 2:499.

ADULTERY. In the OT, adultery refers to sexual intercourse between a man and another man's wife (Dt 22:22–24). Under the Law of Moses, the two people who had committed adultery were punished by death (Lv 20:10; Jn 8:3–5). Symbolically, adultery expressed the sins of God's people Israel when they worshiped idols (Jer 3:9; Ezk 23:36–49).

Jesus interprets the Sixth Commandment as forbidding all kinds of sexual indecency in both deed and thought (Ex 20:14; Mt 5:28). The NT lists adultery, or sexual immorality, among the sins of the flesh (Gal 5:19). See 1:92, 137, 294–97, 629, 634–35, 686, 805, 807, 861; 2:121, 335, 687.

ADVENT OF CHRIST. This term refers to Christ's coming in three ways: (1) The coming of Christ in the flesh—as the baby born in Bethlehem, the one who lived on earth, who died, and who rose again (Zec 9:9; Mt 21:1–5; Lk 2). (2) The spiritual coming of Christ in the hearts of people through faith and His presence in the Church (Jn 14:18, 23). (3) Christ's return for judgment at the end times (Mt 24:30). *See also* PAROUSIA. See 1:841–42; 2:277, 279, 780.

ADVERSARY (AD-vur-ser-ee).

1. A political or personal enemy (1Ki 11:9–43).
2. An enemy of God and His people. The devil especially is an adversary of God and His people (1Tm 5:14; 1Pt 5:8). See 1:46, 514; 2:189, 521, 711.

ADVOCATE (AD-vo-kayt). Someone who pleads the cause of another (1Jn 2:1). Often this word refers to the Holy Spirit and is translated as *comforter, counselor*, or *helper* (Jn 14:16). See 1:518; 2:641, 748, 788.

AENEAS (i-NEE-uhs; "praise"). A paralyzed man at Lydda who was healed by Peter (Ac 9:32–35). See 2:376, 385.

AGABUS (AG-ah-buhs; possibly "love" or "passion"). A prophet who came to the church at Antioch while Paul and Barnabas were there and prophesied worldwide famine. Later Agabus warned Paul that he would be arrested in Jerusalem (Ac 11:28; 21:10–11). See 2:372, 389–90.

AGAPE (Ah-GAH-pay). *See* LOVE; LOVE FEAST.

AGED. Old age was regarded as a token of God's favor, and the elderly were respected for their wisdom (Jb 5:26; 15:10; 32:4; Zec 8:4). Young people were commanded to honor them (Lv 19:32).

AGRAPHA (AG-rah-fah; "unwritten"). Sayings ascribed to Jesus that are not recorded in the Gospels (Jn 21:25; Ac 20:35).

AGRICULTURE. After the conquest of Canaan, Joshua allotted the conquered territory to nine and one-half tribes. The tribes of Reuben and Gad and the half-tribe of Manasseh had already received their allotment under Moses (Jsh 13–14; Nu 32). Joshua also gave each household a small section of land to be its inheritance forever. These family plots were improved over the years by the generations that followed. The people removed boulders, cultivated the ground carefully, and built terraces (Is 5:1–2).

After the first rainfall, the ground was cultivated. They cultivated either by hand with a shovel and mattock or else by a plow drawn by a donkey, cow, or ox. Sometimes a heavy, forked branch of a tree was used as a plow. At other times branches were bound and pegged together so that one long end became the tongue, a shorter end became the plowshare (which might be shod with stone or iron), and a third end became the handle to steer the plow.

After the plow had torn up the ground, large lumps were broken up with a mattock and then raked fine with a harrow, a bundle of brushwood, or a wooden platform shod with stones or iron spikes.

The farmer sowed the grain by hand, taking it from a basket or from folds in his garment. After sowing the ground, he harrowed it again or drove his animals back and forth over the ground to trample in the seed.

Ripe grain was cut with a sickle. Some early sickles were made from the lower jawbone of donkeys or cows. Other people at this time used more advanced sickles of bronze or iron set in wooden handles. These instruments eventually replaced the more primitive ones.

After the reaper cut the grain, he raked it up and tied it into bunches with its own straw. Fallen or missed grain was left for poor gleaners (Ru 2:2–3). The grain was transported from the field to the threshing floor on a rack fixed to a cart or bound to the back of a donkey. Sometimes this rack was carried on a litter-like frame by two women.

The threshing floor was a roughly circular plot of clay or a limestone rock carefully patched and leveled. Workers opened the bundles of grain and spread them about a foot deep over this area. Then unmuzzled cows, calves, sheep, and donkeys trampled the grain out of the straw (cf Dt 25:4). A primitive threshing sled or wooden flails were also used. Grain was winnowed by tossing the straw and grain into the air with a wooden shovel or fork. Then it was cleansed with a sieve. After this the grain was washed, dried, and stored in insect-proof jars.

In Scripture, the processes of agriculture are often applied to the spiritual realm (Mt 3:12; 9:37–38; 13:18, 39; Jn 4:35; Gal 6:7).

See 1:17, 96, 171, 240, 258, 317, 408; 2:200, 303, 585, 760.

AH. *See* WOE.

AHAB (AY-hab, "father's brother"; "uncle"). After his father, Omri, died, Ahab became the seventh king of Israel (1Ki 16:29). He ruled for 22 years and was more evil in God's eyes than all the kings who had gone before him. Ahab married Jezebel, a princess from Tyre who worshiped the pagan idols Baal and Astarte. Ahab began to worship these gods with his wife. He built an altar to Baal and killed the prophets of the Lord. On Mount Carmel, the prophet Elijah demonstrated to Ahab and all the people that Baal and his prophets were false.

Later Ahab had his eye on Naboth's vineyard and sulked when Naboth refused to sell it to him. So Jezebel arranged to have Naboth killed. Then Ahab claimed the vineyard as his own. Because of this wicked act, God sent Elijah to tell Ahab that dogs would lick Ahab's blood in the same place where Naboth had been killed (1Ki 21:1–19). This prophecy came true when Ahab died in battle from an arrow wound and his chariot was taken to the pool of Samaria, where dogs licked the blood off it (1Ki 22:33–38). See 1:309–10, 324–25, 332–34, 343–46, 366–67, 388–89, 402, 886, 923.

AHASUERUS (ah-haz-yoo-EE-ruhs; Persian for "mighty man").

1. The father of Darius the Mede (Dn 9:1). See 1:845–46.
2. The Persian king who married Esther (Est 1:2, 19; 2:16–17). The Hbr name in the Book of Esther corresponds to the Aram and Babylonian spelling of Xerxes, who reigned from 486 to 465 BC. For this reason it is believed that Ahasuerus and Xerxes were the same man. He is called Artaxerxes in Old Grk Est. See 1:426, 459–78; 2:105, 108–9. *See also* ARTAXERXES.

AHAZ (AY-haz; shortened form of "Ahaziah").

1. The idolatrous son of Jotham. When his father died, Ahaz became the twelfth king of Judah. During his reign, Judah became a vassal of Assyria. Ahaz turned his back on God and built altars to worship false gods. When he died, he was buried in Jerusalem (2Ch 28:22–27). Isaiah, Hosea, and Micah prophesied during the reign of Ahaz. See 1:347, 376–77, 402, 418, 715–16, 726–29, 853–54, 902, 922–23.
2. The son of Micah and great-great-grandson of King Saul (1Ch 8:35–36; 9:42).

AHAZIAH (ay-ha-ZIGH-ah; "Yahweh took [in protection]").

1. The son of Ahab and Jezebel. When his father died, Ahaziah became the eighth king of Israel. He was wicked and worshiped the idol Baal-zebub. When Ahaziah became sick, Elijah delivered a message to him from God: he was going to die since he did not worship the true God (1Ki 22; 2Ki 1; 2Ch 20). See 1:333–34, 344–46, 372.
2. The son of Jehoram and sixth king of Judah. He was also known as Jehoahaz and Azariah (2Ch 21:17; 25:23). His rule was wicked in the eyes of the Lord (2Ki 8:25–9:28; 2Ch 22). See 1:374, 402.

AHIJAH (a-HI-ja; "brother of Yahweh").

1. The son of Ahitub and great-grandson of Eli, the priest. Ahijah was the high priest at Gibeah (1Sm 14:3, 18).
2. A scribe or secretary of King Solomon (1Ki 4:3).
3. A prophet at Shiloh. He told Jeroboam that the kingdom of Israel was going to split at Solomon's death and that Jeroboam would rule over the ten northern tribes (1Ki 11:29–39). Later, when Jeroboam's son became sick, Jeroboam sent his wife to the prophet. Ahijah told her that the child would die because of Jeroboam's wickedness (1Ki 14:6–16). A record of events in the "prophecy of Ahijah the Shilonite" is referred to in 2Ch 9:29. See 1:323, 332, 396.

AHIMELECH (ah-HIM-uh-lek; "brother of the king").

1. A priest at Nob who helped David by giving him holy bread and a sword. When Saul heard this, he ordered his soldiers to kill Ahimelech and the priests with him (1Sm 21:1–9; 22:9–19). See 1:276.
2. *See* ABIMELECH 4.

AHITHOPHEL (ah-HITH-o-fel; "brother is folly"). One of David's counselors. Although Ahithophel's counsel was wise, he was untrustworthy. When Absalom decided to overthrow his father, Ahithophel joined forces with Absalom, advising him how to go about the task. However, when Absalom took Hushai's advice instead, Ahithophel went home and hanged himself (2Sm 15:12, 31; 16:23; 17:1–23; 1Ch 27:33). See 1:287.

AI (AY-igh; "ruin"). A city about 1½ miles from Bethel. In the conquest of Canaan, Joshua and the Israelites attacked Ai twice, the second time successfully. Ai is mentioned numerous times in Scripture (Gn 12:8; 13:3; Jsh 7; 8; 9:3; 10:1–2; 12:9; Ezr 2:28; Ne 7:32; Jer 49:3). See 1:199–201, 210–11, 218; 2:802.

AIJALON (AY-jah-lahn; "deer field"). A town in Dan (Jsh 19:42; 21:24; Jgs 1:35; 1Sm 14:31; 1Ch 6:69; 8:13; 2Ch 11:10; 28:18). During a battle, Joshua told the sun to stand still in Gibeon and the moon in the Valley of Aijalon (Jsh 10:12). See 1:211.

ALABASTER. Carbonate of lime, a white or cream-colored mineral that is easy to carve. It resembles marble and was popular for making perfume vases (Sg 5:15; Mt 26:7; Mk 14:3; Lk 7:37). See 2:57.

ALEXANDER (al-eg-ZAN-dur; "defender of men").

1. Alexander the Great, king of Macedonia. He was born in Macedonia (now Greece) in 356 BC and died in Babylon (now Iraq) in 323 BC. One of the greatest generals of all time, Alexander was responsible for the spread of Greek culture in Asia and Egypt. See 1:383, 425, 429, 461, 806, 824; 2:4, 12–13, 85.
2. The son of Simon of Cyrene (Mk 15:21).
3. A person who tried to quiet the riot of the silversmiths at Ephesus (Ac 19:33).
4. The coppersmith who did Paul "great harm" (2Tm 4:14). He may be the same Alexander whom Paul speaks against in 1Tm 1:20. See 2:597.

ALEXANDRIA (al-eg-ZAN-dri-ah). The Egyptian city founded by Alexander the Great in 332 BC. It was a center for Greek culture and was noted for its libraries, architecture, and commerce. Because many Greek-speaking Jews lived in Alexandria, a translation of the Hebrew text of the Bible into Greek was undertaken. This text, the Septuagint, was begun in the third century BC and completed before 132 BC. Later Alexandria became a Christian center noted for its scholarship and textual criticism (Ac 6:9; 27:6; 28:11). See 2:27–28, 72, 93–94, 127, 151, 234, 255, 374.

ALLEGIANCE (uh-LEE-juhns). The act of being loyal to kings and to God (1Ch 12:29; Is 19:18).

ALLEGORY. A figure of speech that represents a deeper spiritual reality. The word *allegorically* is used only once in the Bible (Gal 4:24), but as a figure of speech it is used frequently, for example, "vine" in Jn 15. See 1:45, 243, 686–91, 916–18; 2:119, 505, 657, 779.

ALMIGHTY. Hbr *shaddai*, which is not well understood. The tradition of translating it as "almighty" comes from the LXX, which has Gk *pantokrator*. In the OT, it often appears in passages about blessing and fruitfulness (e.g., Gn) as well as in passages about God's power to destroy or judge (e.g., Jb). God identified Himself to Abram by this name (Gn 17:1; cf Ex 6:3). Appears more often in 2Macc and Rv. See 1:96, 249–50, 496; 2:396, 785.

ALMS (AHLMZ). Gifts, freely given, to the needy. In the OT, almsgiving was a duty that God commanded His people to perform (Dt 15:11; Lv 19:9). Later it became an important religious duty (Ps 112:9). During the exile and its aftermath, Israelites suffered great poverty. As a result, they appreciated the value and kindness of charitable gifts in a new way. Almsgiving is an important theme in both Tobit and Ecclesiasticus. (On the theological issues raised with almsgiving, see Tob 12:9.) Christ and the apostles encouraged the giving of alms (Mt 25:35–36; Mk 9:41; Ac 24:17; Rm 15:25–27; 1Co 16:1–4; 2Co 9:7–9). Containers for receiving alms stood in the temple (Mk 12:41). See 2:46, 58, 375, 495.

ALPHA (AL-pha). The first letter of the Greek alphabet. When *alpha* is used with *omega* (the last letter of the alphabet), it means the beginning and the end (Rv 1:8; 21:6; 22:13; cf Is 41:4; 44:6). See 1:1004; 2:xix, 778.

ALPHABET. Letters used in writing and printing. Picture writing known as pictograms have been found in Israel from the fourth millennium BC, and hieroglyphics from the end of the third millennium. The Serabic alphabet, for example, which was found at Sarabit al-Khadim in the Sinai Peninsula, dates from between 1850 and 1500 BC. It is an early example of Semitic writing. The KJV records the letters of the Hebrew alphabet in Ps 119. The alphabet found on the Moabite stone closely resembles OT Hebrew. *See also* WRITING. See 1:150, 488, 601, 784–85, 792; 2:xix.

ALPHAEUS (al-FEE-uhs; "leader").

1. The father of James (the Less) and Joses (Mt 10:3; Mk 3:18).
2. The father of Matthew the tax collector (Mt 9:9; Mk 2:14). See 2:187.

ALTAR (high). An elevation made usually of earth or stone, though other materials were sometimes used (Ex 20:24–26). According to an ancient OT principle, an altar was erected wherever the Lord showed Himself (Gn 8:20; 12:7; 26:25; 35:1). The tabernacle had two altars. The first was the altar of burnt offering (Ex 27:1–2). All sacrifices were offered at this altar. These sacrifices were to remind Israel that it had access to God only through atonement. The second altar was the altar of incense (Ex 30:1–10). It symbolized adoration. See 1:28, 66, 72–73, 174–75, 199, 237, 241, 297–98, 305, 359, 439, 994; 2:4, 79, 460–61, 798.

AMALEKITES (AM-ah-lek-ights). An ancient group of nomads who descended from Esau (Gn 36:12). They were called first of the nations (Nu 24:20) and lived south of Canaan in the Sinai Peninsula, penetrating north into the Arabah. Traditionally they were enemies of Israel (Ps 83:7). The Amalekites were defeated by Gideon, Saul, and David (Jgs 7; 1Sm 15; 30:18). See 1:81, 127, 179, 279, 290–92, 307; 2:114, 224.

AMANUENSIS (ah-man-you-EN-sis). Latin, "by the hand" of another writer, a secretary or clerk. This technical term refers to the practice of ancient writers dictating their texts to scribes. See 1:433; 2:721.

AMASA (AM-ah-sah; "burden"). David's nephew and Joab's cousin (2Sm 17:25; 1Ch 2:17). Although Amasa was the captain of the rebel forces under Absalom, David forgave him and made him the commander-in-chief of his army in place of Joab (2Sm 19:13). Later, Joab, pretending to greet Amasa with a kiss, struck him with a sword and killed him (2Sm 20:4–13). See 1:281.

AMAZIAH (am-a-ZIGH-ah; "Yahweh has carried").

1. The son of Joash and ninth king of Judah. Amaziah became king after his father was murdered. Once he was firmly in power, Amaziah had his father's murderers put to death. He led an army against the Edomites, defeated them, and captured their capital. Later, he fought against Jehoash, king of Israel, but was defeated and taken prisoner. Some years later, Amaziah was murdered at Lachish (2Ki 12:21; 14–15; 2Ch 24:27; 25–26). See 1:346, 402; 2:220.
2. Priest of an idolatrous shrine of Bethel whom Amos confronted (Am 7:10–17). See 1:881, 883, 889–90.

AMBASSADOR. An envoy or messenger of great power (Is 18:2; Ezk 17:15). Paul called himself an ambassador of Christ (2Co 5:20; Eph 6:20). See 1:367, 449; 2:85, 491, 525, 530.

AMEN (AY-MEN; "true"). From Hbr *'aman*, "to be strong" or "trustworthy." Derives from synagogue services.

1. Amen is a name for Jesus. It emphasizes that He is the truth (Rv 3:14).
2. The word *Amen* is spoken when one wants to express "so be it." It indicates confirmation or agreement (Nu 5:22; Dt 27:15–26; Mt 6:13; 1Co 14:16). God's promises are described as "Yes" or "Amen" (2Co 1:20). *See also* FAITHFULNESS. See 1:695; 2:761.

AMMONITES (AM-un-ights). The people who lived east of the Dead Sea and the Jordan River. Their capital city was Rabbah (Dt 3:11), which is modern day 'Amman. Saul defeated the Ammonites in battle, and David took their capital (1Sm 11; 2Sm 12:26–31). The Ammonites worshiped idols and were fierce enemies of Israel (Dt 23:3–6; Jgs 3:13; 1Sm 11:1–11; Ne 4:3–9; Jer 49:1–6; Ezk 25:1–7; Am 1:13; 1Macc 5:6–7; cf Jth 7:17–18). The Moabites and Ammonites were descendants of Lot, Abraham's nephew (Gn 19:36–38). See 1:167, 231, 238, 240, 290, 293, 400, 768, 867; 2:17, 22.

AMON (A-mun; "skilled workman").

1. The fifteenth king of Judah. He was the son and successor of King Manasseh and the father of King Josiah. Amon worshiped idols. He was murdered by his servants (2Ki 21:19–26; 2Ch 33:21–25). See 1:348, 403.
2. The ancient Egyptian city of Thebes. It was a center for the worship of the sun-god Amon (Jer 46:25; cf Na 3:8).

AMORITES (AM-o-rights). A powerful nation in Canaan that occupied both sides of the Jordan River (Gn 10:16; 14:7; Nu 21:26–31; Jsh 5:1; 13:15–21). When Samuel judged Israel, Israel had peace with the Amorites (1Sm 7:14). Solomon made the Amorites his slaves (1Ki 9:20, 21). See 1:129–30, 139, 140, 225, 879.

AMOS (AY-mus; "burden-bearer"). A shepherd of Tekoa who became a prophet to Israel during the reigns of Uzziah and Jeroboam II. His prophecy is recorded in the Book of Amos. See 1:133, 351, 708–9, 880–81.

AMOS, BOOK OF. See 1:878–93.

AMOZ (AY-mahz; "strong"). Isaiah's father (Is 1:1). See 1:717.

AMPLIATUS (am-pli-AY-tuhs; "enlarger"). Paul's friend at Rome to whom he sent a greeting (Rm 16:8).

AMULETS (AM-yuh-lets). Charms people wore to protect themselves against sickness, accident, sorcery, and evil spirits (Is 3:20).

ANACHRONISM (ah-NAK-kro-ni-sim). Presention of historical information out of chronological sequence. See 2:405, 720.

ANALOGY OF FAITH. A term that means there is agreement or harmony among scriptural teachings. According to this rule, the interpretation of each Bible passage should harmonize, not conflict, with the totality of scriptural teachings (Rm 12:6). See 2:24, 47, 58, 147.

ANANIAS (an-ah-NIGH-uhs; "Yahweh is gracious").

1. A member of the Church in Jerusalem. Ananias died suddenly after he and his wife tried to deceive and cheat the church (Ac 5:1–6). See 2:375.
2. The disciple at Damascus who was sent to restore Paul's sight (Ac 9:10–20; 22:12). See 2:367, 811.
3. A high priest before whom Paul was tried (Ac 23:1–5; 24:1).

ANATHEMA (ah-NATH-i-mah). In the OT, anathema is a vow by which persons or things were devoted to God. Nonliving things devoted to God were given to the priests (Nu 18:12–14); living things were killed (Lv 27:28–29). Later, anathema removed a person from the community of faith (Ezr 10:8). In the NT, anathema is a solemn curse that implies separation (Rm 9:3; 1Co 12:3). See 2:508.

ANATHEMA MARANATHA (ah-NATH-i-mah mar-ah-NATH-ah). This is a term that means accursed person (1Co 16:22), lit, "the Lord comes to curse" that person. *See also* MARANATHA.

ANATHOTH (AN-ah-thahth; "answers" or "of [great goddess] Anat"). A Levitical city in Benjamin, noted as the birthplace of Jeremiah (Jsh 21:18; Jer 1:1; 11:21–23; 29:27). Today it is identified with 'Anata. See 1:338, 755, 766.

ANCESTOR. The far more common term is "fathers," based on the Hbr *aboth*. Often refers to wise, authoritative leaders of the past who had a special relationship with God. Gk *progonos* and *gonos*, "forebearer, parent," or forms of the word for "father" (*patros*). Cf Jsh 19:47; Jgs 18:29; Heb 7:10. *See also* FATHER 1. See 1:25, 167, 392; 2:194, 219–20.

ANCIENT OF DAYS. A name Daniel applies to the Lord to inspire awe and reverence for Him and to convey His majesty (Dn 7:9–22). See 1:834–35, 838.

ANDREW (AN-droo; "manly"). The brother of Simon Peter (Mt 4:18; Mk 1:16–18). Andrew came from Bethsaida and was a fisherman by trade (Jn 1:44). He was a disciple of John the Baptist but was directed by John to Jesus as the Lamb of God. Convinced that Jesus was the Messiah, Andrew brought his brother Peter to Jesus (Jn 1:35–42).

Later, Andrew became a permanent disciple of Jesus and was appointed an apostle (Mt 4:18–19; 10:2; Mk 1:16–17; 3:18; Lk 6:14; Ac 1:13). When Jesus asked how He could feed a great number of people, Andrew called Jesus' attention to a boy with five loaves and two fish (Jn 6:8–9). Andrew and Philip told Jesus about some Greek people who wished to see Him (Jn 12:20–22). Andrew was also one of the disciples who asked Jesus about the destruction of the temple (Mk 13:3–4). According to tradition, Andrew was crucified on November 30 in Achaia on a cross shaped like an X. See 2:319.

ANGEL (Hbr *mal'ak*; Gk *angelos*, "messenger").

1. Unseen, spiritual, holy, heavenly beings who continually do God's bidding (Ps 89:5, 7; 104:4; Mt 4:6; 22:30; Heb 1:14; 2:7) often as a messenger or warrior. Angels protect and serve those who fear God (Gn 48:16; Ps 34:7; Is 63:9). They differ in rank and dignity (cf "prince" in Dn 10:13, 21; see also Lk 1:19, 26; Rm 8:38; Eph 1:21). The OT speaks most often of good angels but does refer to evil angels or spirits (e.g., Lv 16:8; 17:7; Dt 32:17). Intertestamental books include frequent references to angels and demons (e.g., in Tobit, Raphael and Asmodeus are important characters); the writers emphasize the role of angels as mediators (2Macc 11:6). Angels are likewise mentioned some 50 times in the Dead Sea Scrolls. Alongside increasing interest in angels, some intertestamental writers downplay their role and importance, likely because of the influence of Greek rationalism/philosophy (e.g., Josephus changes OT accounts about angelic messages into visions; cf also Ac 23:8). See 1:46–47, 87–88, 333–34, 353, 359, 414, 503, 587, 800, 827, 834–38, 987–88, 998, 1007; 2:43–46, 169–73, 277, 493, 783–84.
2. An "angel of the LORD" may refer to an angel who carries out God's will (1Ki 19:5, 7). Frequently, however, when the angel of the LORD is mentioned in the Bible, it refers to a distinct person and yet a being who is of the essence of the Lord, who reveals God, and who has the Lord's name and presence (Gn 16:10, 13; 18:2–4, 13–14, 22:11; Ex 3:2; 23:20–21; 32:14). For these reasons the "angel of the LORD" is often identified with the Second Person of the Trinity, the preincarnate Son of God. See 1:243, 334, 389, 405, 988, 1007.
3. Evil angels are fallen spirits (2Pt 2:4). *See also* DEMONS; SATAN. See 1:46–47, 503, 507, 535–36; 2:781.
4. Human messengers who bring God's Word to the world. The "angels of the seven churches" are representatives of the churches mentioned in the Book of Revelation. John may be referring to the pastors of those churches (Rv 1:20; 2:1, 8, 12, 18; 3:1, 7, 14). See 1:1007.

5. John the Baptist is called a messenger (or angel) who was sent to prepare the way for Christ (Mt 11:10; Mk 1:2; Lk 7:27).

ANGER. Reaction of people against unfavorable situations (Gn 30:2; 1Sm 17:28). It may be evil or a reaction to evil (1Sm 20:34; Jn 2:15; 2Co 12:20). Human anger is described as a work of the flesh (Gal 5:20). *See also* WRATH. See 1:291, 446, 584; 2:207, 547.

ANKLET. An ornamental metallic or glass ring that was worn around the ankle (Is 3:18).

ANNA (AN-ah; "grace").

1. The wife of Tobit who must work to provide for the family when Tobit becomes blind. See 2:43.
2. The prophetess who thanked God when she saw the infant Jesus in the temple (Lk 2:36–38). See 2:277.

ANNAS (AN-uhs; "merciful"). The high priest at Jerusalem from AD 6–c 15 (Lk 3:2). He was appointed by Quirinius and deposed by Valerius Gratus. Annas was the father-in-law of Caiaphas, the high priest before whom Jesus was tried (Jn 18:13). Five of Annas's sons were also high priests. During the time when they and Caiaphas held office, Annas was also regarded practically as high priest, perhaps because he was the head of the family and therefore the most influential member (Ac 4:6). See 2:301–2, 337.

ANOINT. To apply oil to a person or thing. A common custom among Egyptians, Hebrews, Greeks, and Romans, anointing was done for several reasons.

1. Sometimes it was simply a part of grooming. After washing or bathing, people anointed themselves (Ru 3:3). Anointing was also an expression of joy (Ps 23:5; 45:7).
2. Hosts anointed their guests as an act of courtesy or respect (Lk 7:46).
3. Anointing was also done as an act of consecration and at a person's induction to the office of priest or king (Gn 28:18; Ex 30:23–26; 40:15; 1Sm 9:16). See 1:137, 273, 277–79, 283, 293, 299–300, 409, 584, 588; 2:190, 203, 237, 336.
4. The sick were anointed as an act of healing (Jas 5:14).
5. Christ was anointed with the Holy Spirit (Lk 4:18; Ac 4:27; 10:38; cf Ps 45:7; Is 61:1). *See also* ANOINTED ONE. See 2:381, 386, 389.
6. God anoints Christians with the Holy Spirit in Baptism. See 1:112.

ANOINTED ONE. Hbr *mashiach*, a chosen person, distinguished by anointing with oil (cf 1Sm 10:1). Prophets and even Cyrus, king of Persia, were titled this way (1Ch 16:22; Is 45:1). However, the title is most commonly used of kings Saul and David in 1 and 2 Samuel. Before Saul and David were chosen as kings, Hannah prayed that the Lord would rule the earth through "His anointed" (1Sm 2:10), a prophecy about the Savior from David's line (Ps 2:2; 45:7; Is 61:1; Dn 9:25–26). *See also* CHRIST; MESSIAH. See 1:301–2, 835, 837–38; 2:246.

ANT. The ant is held up as an example of diligence and wisdom (Pr 6:6–8; 30:24–25).

ANTELOPE. This is one of the animals God's people in the OT were allowed to eat because it was ceremonially fit for food (Dt 14:5; Is 51:20).

ANTICHRIST (AN-ti-krighst; "against Christ"). One who is both an enemy of Christ and a usurper of His rights and names. In the NT, John alone uses the word *antichrist* (1Jn 2:18, 22; 4:3; 2Jn 1:7). The other passages in Scriptures that speak about an antichrist were applied early in the history of the Church to the Antichrist (Dn 7–8; 2Th 2:3–12; Rv 13; 17–18). See 1:562; 2:581–82, 585, 741, 746–49.

ANTILEGOMENA (an-ti-lee-GAHM-i-nah; "spoken against," "questioned"). Those books of the NT that were not received as canonical by the Church everywhere until the latter part of the fourth century. They include James, Jude, 2 and 3 John, 2 Peter, Hebrews, and Revelation. See 2:157, 161–63, 647, 693, 729.

ANTIOCH (AN-ti-ahk; from "Antiochus," Syrian king).

1. A city in Syria on the south bank of the Orontes. It was founded around 300 BC by Seleucus Nicator. In 64 BC, Pompey made Antioch the seat of the legate of Syria and a free city. Both Barnabas and Paul worked in Antioch, and it was in Antioch that the followers of Jesus were first called Christians (Ac 11:19–26; 13:1–3; 14:26; 15; 18:22; Gal 2:11). Today Antioch is called Antakya and is located in Turkey. See 1:498; 2:367, 374, 377, 388, 423, 503.
2. A city in Pisidia, Asia Minor, which was also founded by Seleucus Nicator (Ac 13:14–52; 14:21).

ANTIOCHUS (an-TIGH-o-kus).

1. Antiochus III, called the Great, was the king of Syria from 223 to 187 BC. He was the sixth ruler

of the Seleucid dynasty ("king of the north," Dn 11:14–19). See 2:51, 79–80.

2. Antiochus IV, whose given name was Epiphanes, was the son of Antiochus III. He was the eighth ruler of the Seleucid dynasty, reigning from 175 to 164 BC. He was both an intolerant and energetic ruler. See 1:458, 835; 2:4, 13, 79–85, 93, 96–97, 103, 135–36.
3. Antiochus V, whose name was Eupator, was the son of Epiphanes. He ruled only two years, 164–163 BC, before he was slain. See 2:83, 96–97.

ANTIPAS (AN-ti-pas; "like father").

1. A Christian who suffered martyrdom at Pergamos (Rv 2:13). According to tradition, he was a bishop who was burned in a brazen bull under Domitian. See 2:771.
2. Herod Antipas, the son of Herod the Great. See 2:188, 195.

ANTIPATER (an-TIP-ah-tur; "like father"). The father of Herod the Great.

ANTIPATRIS (an-TIP-ah-tris). A city Herod the Great built between Caesarea and Jerusalem. Herod named the city after his father. Paul was a prisoner there (Ac 23:31). See 2:801.

ANTITYPE. A perfect thing that is represented or prefigured by a type (1Pt 3:21). For example, Christ is the antitype of the paschal lamb (type). See 2:272. *See also* TYPE.

ANTONIA (an-TO-ni-ah). A fortress on the northwest side of the temple. It was rebuilt by Herod the Great and named by him in honor of Mark Antony. Roman soldiers who watched over the temple area were housed there (cf "barracks" in Ac 21:31–40; 22–23). See 2:807.

APOCALYPSE (ah-PAHK-ah-lips; "uncover").

1. Another name for the Book of Revelation. See 2:771–95.
2. A general name for pseudepigraphal books dealing with the end times, such as *Ezra Apocalypse*. *See also* APOCALYPTIC LITERATURE. See 1:455; 2:722.

APOCALYPTIC LITERATURE. There are two types of apocalyptic literature: canonical and uncanonical. The first includes Daniel and Revelation. These books reveal events of the end times, judgment, and the hereafter.

The uncanonical apocalyptic literature appeared during the period of late Judaism and early Christianity. It includes works such as *1 and 2 Enoch*, the *Apocalypse of Peter*, the *Ascension of Isaiah*, the *Assumption of Moses*, the *Book of Jubilees*, and the *Shepherd of Hermas*. See 1:455, 809, 817–21, 823, 839, 843, 985; 2:779.

APOCRYPHA (ah-PAHK-ri-fah; "hidden"). A term the Church Fathers used for writings that were either difficult to understand or obscure, and for books whose authorship was unknown. Gradually the term came to be used for those books that were outside the canon. During the time of the Reformation, the uncanonical books that appeared in the Vulgate (the Latin translation of the Bible by Jerome), but did not appear in the Hebrew OT, were classed as apocryphal. They included Judith, the Wisdom of Solomon, Tobit, Ecclesiasticus, Baruch, the Letter of Jeremiah, 1 and 2 Maccabees, Old Greek Esther, Susanna, Bel and the Dragon, the Prayer of Azariah, the Song of the Three Holy Children, the Prayer of Manasseh, 1 and 2 Esdras, 3 and 4 Maccabees, and Psalm 151. See 1:xxviii, 454–56, 463, 831–33; 2:3–153.

APOLLOS (ah-PAHL-us; "belonging to Apollo"). A well-educated Jewish man from Alexandria. John baptized him, and Aquila and Priscilla instructed him more accurately in the Christian faith (Ac 18:24–28). Apollos then became an eloquent preacher and a friend of Paul (1Co 1:12; 3:4–22; 4:6; 16:12; Ti 3:13). See 2:28, 378, 447, 450–51, 455, 519, 653.

APOSTASY (ah-PAHS-tah-see). Forsaking the Lord or departing from the faith (Jer 2:19; 5:6; Heb 6:6). The Scriptures contain many warnings against apostasy (Heb 6:1–8; 10:26–29; 2Pt 2:15–21). An apostate, one who forsakes the Lord, should not be confused with an errorist or a heretic. The latter, unlike an apostate, still professes faith, even though he or she rejects a particular teaching or teachings of the Church. See 1:66, 231, 323, 687, 789, 860–61, 886; 2:98, 658, 683, 725–26.

APOSTLE (Hbr *shaliach;* Gk *apostolos,* "one sent forth").

1. In one sense the NT uses the word *apostle* as the official name for Jesus' twelve disciples: Simon Peter, Andrew, James, John, Philip, Bartholomew (perhaps another name for Nathanael), Thomas, Matthew (Levi), James the son of Alphaeus, Thaddeus,

Simon, and Judas Iscariot (Mt 10:1–4). Judas Iscariot's place was taken by Matthias (Ac 1:15–26). Later, on his way to Damascus, Paul also was called to be an apostle (Ac 9; 1Co 1:1; 2Co 10–12).

The apostles were eyewitnesses to Jesus' ministry and miracles (Ac 1:21–22). Through them, Christ established His Church (Mk 16:20; Acts), and through their written and spoken testimony, Christ laid the foundation of the Church (Eph 2:20). The apostles went with the full authority of Christ, their sender, to proclaim the Gospel. See 1:453, 889, 994; 2:157–58, 188–89, 302, 354, 367–68, 384–85, 411–12, 594–95.

2. In a general sense, the NT uses the word *apostle* to refer to anyone commissioned to preach the Gospel (cf Rm 10:13–15; "messenger" in 2Co 8:23; Php 2:25). See 1:747; 2:677.
3. Christ is referred to as an apostle (Heb 3:1).

APOSTOLIC MINISTRY. Gk *apostole*, a technical term for the office and work of an apostle of Christ (Ac 1:25; Rm 1:5; 1Co 9:2). *See* APOSTLE. See 2:321.

APPEAL.

1. In ancient Israel appeals were made to the head of the tribe. At Moses' time, Moses himself first handled all appeals. But when this became too burdensome for him, he appointed judges for this purpose (Ex 18:13, 26). Later, difficult decisions were made at the sanctuaries (Dt 17:8–11). Both judges and kings handled appeals (Jgs 4:5; 2Sm 15:3). Jehoshaphat established courts and delegated his authority of appeal to judges (2Ch 19:8). These courts were reestablished by Ezra (Ezr 7:25). After the Sanhedrin was instituted, it became the highest court of appeal for the Jews. Roman citizens could appeal to the emperor (Ac 25:11–12). See 1:297; 2:379.
2. A general appeal before God, usually for mercy or vindication. Moses made several such appeals to God on behalf of Israel (Nu 14:13–19), and frequently they occur in the Psalms (Ps 18:6). See 1:138–39, 575–76, 787; 2:507.

AQUILA (AK-wi-lah; "eagle"). A Jewish man who was born in Pontus. He was a tentmaker by trade (Ac 18:1–3). With his wife, Priscilla, Aquila was a prominent co-worker of Paul (Ac 18:18–19, 26; Rm 16:3; 1Co 16:19; 2Tm 4:19). See 2:418, 423, 435–36, 519, 522, 653.

ARABAH (AR-ah-bah; "desert"). The name of the valley between the Dead Sea and the Gulf of Aqaba (Dt 1:1, 7; 11:30; Jsh 3:16; 1Sm 23:24, 2Sm 2:29; 2Ki 14:25; Jer 39:4; Ezk 47:8). See 1:895, 905.

ARABIA (ah-RAY-bi-ah; "desert"). Originally, the northern part of the peninsula between the Red Sea and the Persian Gulf (Is 21:13; Jer 25:24) but later the entire peninsula (Ne 2:19; 6:1 Ac 2:11; Gal 1:17; 4:25). See 1:25, 413, 498, 844; 2:411.

ARABS. The tribal people to the east and south of Israel (Ne 4:7), which might include nomadic people (2Macc 12) or the settled Nabateans (1Macc 5). They had various political loyalties, siding with the kingdoms of the Ptolemies or Seleucids as it served their interests (cf 1Macc 12). See 1:262, 623, 896.

ARAM (AY-ram).

1. A son of Shem (Gn 10:22, 23; 1Ch 1:17). See 1:497.
2. The area where the Aramean people (Syrians) lived. It extended from the Lebanon Mountains to beyond the Euphrates River and from the Taurus Mountains to south of Damascus. Several divisions of the Aramean people are mentioned in the OT (Gn 31:20, 24; Dt 26:5; 1Ch 7:14). See 1:281, 768, 879, 905.

ARAMAIC (ar-ah-MAY-ik). A Semitic language in Aram that spread to all of southwest Asia. It was incorrectly called Chaldee on the basis of Dn 2:4–7:28. Aramaic inscriptions from as early as 850 BC still exist today. Parts of the OT are in Aramaic (Dn 2:4–7:28; Ezr 4:8–6:18; 7:12–26; Jer 10:11). Jesus also spoke Aramaic. See 1:215, 281, 428–29, 437–38, 830–32, 906, 972; 2:xviii, 8, 187–88, 351–53.

ARARAT (AR-ah-rat). A name for Armenia and its mountain range, especially its two peaks, which are 14,000 and 10,000 feet high (Gn 8:4; Jer 51:27). Armenia is a mountainous country north of Assyria, between the Black Sea and the Caspian Sea, and extends from the Caucasus Mountains to the Taurus Mountains. See 2:39.

ARCHAEOLOGY (ahr-kee-AHL-o-jee). A study of the material remains of the past. Biblical archaeology is concerned with Israel and the ancient countries with which the Hebrews and early Christians came into contact.

Modern archaeology is usually traced to Napoleon's 1798 expedition to Egypt. About 100 scholars went with him on this trip to study the Egyptian monuments. C. J. Rich, of the East India Company in Bagdad, made the first excavations in Mesopotamia, and in 1838 and 1852, Edward Robinson of

Union Theological Seminary made observations in Israel.

From these beginnings biblical archaeology developed. Although earlier excavations (1800–1890) were mainly concerned with finding objects of interest, the scientific aspects of archaeology soon developed (1890–1915). The results of biblical archaeology often are used in Bible dictionaries. See 1:7, 15, 199–200, 322–25, 384, 429, 553, 624, 869; 2:797–815.

ARCHANGEL (ARK-AYN-juhl). Chief angel (1Th 4:16; Jude 9). *See also* ANGELS 1. See 1:587; 2:765–66, 781.

ARCHELAUS (ARK-eh-LAY-us). *See also* HEROD 2. See 2:195, 298.

ARCHERY. The art or practice of shooting with a bow and arrow, the weapons used in ancient times. Some famous archers were the Philistines, the Benjaminites, the Medes, and the Elamites (1Sm 31:3; 1Ch 8:40, Is 13:18; Jer 49:35). The word *arrow* is used figuratively for deep trouble, danger, power, and a wicked tongue (Jb 6:4; Ps 91:5; 127:4; Jer 9:8). *Bow* is also used figuratively (Ps 78:56–57). A *quiver* is a case for carrying arrows (Gn 27:3). See 1:344.

ARCHITECTURE (AHR-kuh-tek-chur). The art or science of building. Hebrew architecture, in the proper sense of the word, came into being around the time of the kings. David built a house trimmed with cedar, and Solomon built palaces and a harem (2Sm 7:2; 1Ki 7). The palaces of later kings were showier, often decorated with ivory (cf Am 3:15). The temple, city gates, pillars, and the like offered further opportunity for architectural development and achievement. See 1:323, 360.

Jesus' disciples admired the splendor of Jerusalem under Herod (Mk 13:1). For examples of early architecture, *see also* HOMES. See 2:394.

ARCHIVES. A place for storing official papers (Ezr 5:17; 6:1). See 1:288, 339, 437; 2:8–9.

AREOPAGITE (ar-i-AHP-ah-jight). A member of the court that met at the Areopagus or Mars Hill in Athens (Ac 17:34).

AREOPAGUS (ar-i-AHP-ah-guhs). Hill of Ares or Mars, the Greek god of war. The Areopagus was also a council during Paul's day (Ac 17:19–34). Its chief concern was with education and religion. See 2:366, 379, 811.

ARIEL (AIR-i-el; "altar hearth of God").

1. A leader whom Ezra sent to obtain ministers for the house of God (Ezr 8:16).
2. A poetic name for Jerusalem (Is 29:1–10).

ARIELS. Although sometimes translated as "heroes" or "sons of Ariel," the meaning of this word is unknown (2Sm 23:20; cf 1Ch 11:22).

ARIMATHEA (ar-i-mah-THEE-ah; "height"). The home of Joseph, who buried Jesus in his own new tomb (Mt 27:57; Lk 23:50). See 2:337.

ARIOCH (AR-i-ahk). The captain of Nebuchadnezzar's guard (Dn 2:14).

ARISTOBULUS (ah-ris-to-BYOO-luhs; "best counselor"). A Christian at Rome. Paul sent greetings to his household (Rm 16:10). See 2:13, 96.

ARK ("chest"). The name given to three vessels in the Bible:

1. The floating home God commanded Noah to make in order to save himself, his family, and certain animals from the flood. The ark was made of gopher wood and was about 450 feet long, 75 feet wide, and 45 feet high (Gn 6–8). See 1:26, 47–49.
2. The basket into which baby Moses was placed (Ex 2:3–10 KJV).
3. The ark of the covenant, a chest about 3¾ feet long and 2¼ feet wide. It was made of acacia wood and lined and covered with gold. The solid gold lid of this chest was called the Mercy Seat. It had two cherubs on it, one on each end. Poles passed through two golden rings at the bottom of the ark so that the ark could be carried (Ex 25:10–22). The ark held manna, the stone tablets of the Law, Aaron's staff, and the Book of the Law (Ex 16:33; 25:21; 31:18; Nu 17:10; Dt 31:26; Heb 9:4).

   The ark went before Israel in its wilderness journeys "to seek out a resting place for them" (Nu 10:33). Priests carried it into the Jordan River, where it halted the waters so that the people could cross over on dry land into Canaan (Jsh 3:11–17). In the days of Eli and Samuel, the ark was kept in the temple at Shiloh (1Sm 3:3).

   Once the Israelites carried the ark into battle for good luck, but the Philistines defeated them and captured the ark (1Sm 4). Convinced by ill fortune, however, that the ark was too dangerous to keep, the Philistines soon returned the ark to the Israelites at Beth-shemesh (1Sm 6:12–20). When 70 of the men there died because they had looked into the ark, the people at Beth-shemesh asked the people of Kiriath-jearim to come and take it (1Sm 7:1–2).

David brought the ark to Jerusalem (2Sm 6:12–23). Later it was placed into the Most Holy Place in Solomon's temple (1Ki 8:1–9).

The ark is also called the "ark of testimony" and the "ark of God" (Ex 25:16, 22; 1Sm 3:3). See 1:73, 75–76, 137, 289, 294, 359–60, 368–69; 2:159, 801.

ARM. In Israelite thought, an image of strength. *See also* HAND; RIGHT HAND. See 1:49, 179, 261, 733, 957, 991; 2:210, 387, 396, 657.

ARMAGEDDON (ahr-mah-GED-on; "hill of Megiddo"). The name the NT gives to the final battlefield for the forces of good and evil (Rv 16:16).

Har-Magedon in Aramaic, the name may be derived from the hill on the southern rim of Esdraelon where many battles were fought. It was on this plain that Barak defeated the Canaanites and Gideon defeated the Midianites (Jgs 5:19; 7). Both Ahaziah and Josiah were killed there (2Ki 9:27; 23:29). See 2:772.

ARMENIA (ahr-MEE-ni-ah). *See* ARARAT.

ARMLET; BRACELET. A piece of jewelry usually worn on the upper arm (2Sm 1:10).

ARMOR; ARMS. Weapons used in battle. The offensive weapons, or arms, of the Hebrews included swords, javelins, spears, bows and arrows, slings, engines, darts, hammers, battle-axes, and battering rams (1Sm 13:19; 17:6; 2Sm 2:23; 2Ki 3:25; 2Ch 26:15; Jb 41:26; Jer 51:20; Ezk 4:2).

The defensive weapons, or armor, that the Hebrews used included coats of mail, greaves and war boots, helmets, bucklers, shields, girdles, and breastplates (1Sm 17:5–6, 38; 1Ch 5:18; 12:24; Is 9:5; 59:17). See 1:151, 283, 576; 2:167, 528–29.

ARMOR-BEARER. Someone who carried an officer's armor, guarded him, and helped him in whatever way he could. Abimelech, Jonathan, and Saul each had an armor-bearer (Jgs 9:54; 1Sm 14:7; 31:4)

ARMORY. A place where weapons were kept (Ne 3:19; Is 39:2; Jer 50:25; cf Sg 4:4).

ARMY. In order for the children of Israel to defend themselves against hostile attacks, they organized themselves into armies. In the wilderness they marched according to tribes. All males, except for the Levites, could be called into the army at age 20 (Nu 1–2). In time of war, the number of fighting men were gathered for war by inspectors (Dt 20:1–9; 2Ki 25:19). Army divisions were subdivided into companies of thousands and hundreds under their respective captains and still further into families (Nu 2:34; 31:14). The kings also had bodyguards (1Sm 13:2).

The first standing army in Israel was organized during the reign of Saul (1Sm 13:1–2). A captain of the host, or commander, was in charge of this army (1Sm 14:50). The army first consisted of infantry, or foot soldiers (1Sm 4:10), but in time horsemen and chariots were added (2Sm 8:4; 1Ki 10:26, 28–29).

The Roman army consisted of legions, which were divided into cohorts (Ac 10:1; 21:31). Cohorts were further divided into three maniples, and each maniple into two centuries (Mt 8:5; 27:54). See 1:69–70, 206, 209–10, 280–81, 311–17, 766–68, 871; 2:20, 114, 298–99.

ARNON (AHR-nahn). The river flowing east of the Jordan into the Dead Sea. The Arnon formed a natural boundary, first between the Amorites and Moabites (Nu 21:13; Jgs 11:18) and later between Israel and the Moabites (Dt 2:24; Jsh 12:1). See 1:140.

AROD (AY-rahd). A son of Gad and the forefather of the Arodites (Nu 26:17). He is referred to as Arodi in Gn 46:16.

AROER (ah-RO-ur; "juniper").

1. A Reubenite town on the Arnon (Dt 2:36). During Jehu's time, King Hazael of Syria took Aroer from Israel, but later it fell back to Moab (2Ki 10:33; Jer 48:19–20). Today it is called 'Ara'ir.
2. A town 12 miles southeast of Beersheba in the southern part of Judah (1Sm 30:26–28).

ARPACHSHAD (ahr-PAK-shad). The son of Shem and an ancestor of Abraham (Gn 11:10–13).

ARPAD (AHR-pad). A city in the northern part of Syria near Hamath (Jer 49:23).

ARROWS. *See* ARCHERY.

ARSENAL. *See* ARMORY.

ARTAXERXES (ahr-tugh-ZURK-seez; "Arta's kingdom").

1. The Persian king who stopped the rebuilding of the temple (Ezr 4:7, 23–24). His name was probably Smerdis.
2. Longimanus, the Persian king who reigned from 464 to 424 BC. He sent Ezra to Jerusalem and was also a friend to Nehemiah (Ezr 7; Ne 2:1–8). See 1:191, 423–51, 464–66, 997.
3. *See* AHASUERUS.

ARTEMIS (AHR-ti-mis). The Greek goddess of the moon, woods, and fields corresponding to the Roman Diana. She was a hunter and a symbol of chastity. The Artemis worshiped in Ephesus was a combination of Artemis and Ashtoreth (Ac 19:24–28). See 2:522, 737, 812.

ARUBBOTH (ah-RUB-uth). A district assigned to Ben-hesed to provide food for Solomon's court (1Ki 4:10).

ARUMAH (ah-ROO-mah). A place near Shechem where Abimelech lived (Jgs 9:41).

ASA (ay-SAH; physician). The son of Abijah and the third king of Judah. Asa was the first of the five kings of Judah who did "what was good and right in the eyes of the Lord" (2Ch 14:2). Asa began his reign with 10 years of peace, during which time he made many religious reforms (2Ch 14:1, 3–5; 15:1–17).

Then Zerah, the Ethiopian, waged war upon Judah, but with the Lord's help Asa and his armies defeated them (2Ch 14:9–15). Later in his reign Asa purchased the help of Ben-hadad of Damascus against Baasha of Israel (1Ki 15:16–22; 2Ch 16:1–10). In his later years, Asa was not as true to the Lord as he had once been. He died in the 41st year of his reign. See 1:343–44, 370–71, 390, 401–2.

ASAHEL (AS-ah-hel; "God has made").

1. The nephew of David and a brother of Joab. Asahel was killed by Abner (2Sm 2:18–23). See 1:294.
2. A Levite and teacher of the law under Jehoshaphat (2Ch 17:8).
3. An overseer of the temple in Hezekiah's reign (2Ch 31:13).

ASAIAH (ah-SAY-yah; "Yahweh has made"). An officer who was sent by Josiah to ask Huldah the prophetess about the Law (2Ki 22:12, 14; 2Ch 34:20).

ASAPH (AY-saf; "collector").

1. A Levite, the son of Berechiah. Asaph sounded the cymbals before the ark when it was brought to the city of David (1Ch 15:16–19). He was then given the permanent job of sounding the cymbals for religious functions (1Ch 16:4–5, 7).

   Asaph's family, with him as the head, was one of the families in charge of music and song (1Ch 25:1–9). Like the other chief singers, Asaph was called a seer (2Ch 29:30; Ne 12:46). Psalms 50 and 73–83 are called Psalms of Asaph. See 1:409, 542–41, 550, 552, 570.
2. The father of Joah, Hezekiah's recorder (2Ki 18:18; Is 36:3, 22).
3. A keeper of the royal forest in Israel under Artaxerxes Longimanus, king of Persia (Ne 2:8).

ASCENSION. Forty days after His resurrection Christ returned to His Father in heaven. The ascension marks the end of Christ's bodily ministry on earth (Mk 16:19; Ac 1:1–12; Eph 4:8–10; 1Pt 3:22). See 1:815; 2:277, 286, 314, 367, 783.

ASCENTS, SONG OF. The title given to Psalms 120–134. Some scholars think these psalms were named this because they may have been sung on the 15 steps that led from the court of women to the court of men. Others think that the word *degrees*, or *ascents*, refers to the way the poetic thought of the music advanced. See 1:543, 570, 583–84, 601–3.

ASENATH (AS-i-nath; "devotee of Neith, Egyptian goddess"). The daughter of Potiphera, priest of On. Pharaoh gave her to Joseph to be his wife (Gn 41:45, 50). They had two children, Manasseh and Ephraim (Gn 46:20). See 1:52.

ASHAN (AY-shuhn; "smoke"). A town assigned to the tribe of Judah that was later transferred to Simeon (Jsh 15:42; 19:7; 1Ch 4:32). It was made a city of refuge and given to the Levites (1Ch 6:59).

ASHARELAH (ash-ah-REE-lah). A son of Asaph. Asharelah was in charge of temple music (1Ch 25:2).

ASHBEL (ASH-bel; possibly "man of lord"). The second son of Benjamin (1Ch 8:1).

ASHDOD (ASH-dahd). One of the five chief cities of the Philistines. It was situated between Gaza and Joppa, and was the center of worship for the god Dagon (Jsh 13:3; 1Sm 5). Although assigned to Judah, it was never taken by that tribe (Jsh 15:46–47). When the Philistines captured the ark at Ebenezer, they carried it to Ashdod but soon returned it (1Sm 5–6). Uzziah, king of Judah, broke down the wall of Ashdod, and a number of years later it was captured by Sargon II of Assyria (2Ch 26:6; Is 20:1). In 630 BC, Ashdod was partially destroyed by Psammetichus of Egypt. In NT times it was called Azotus (Ac 8:40). See 1:211.

ASHDODITES (ASH-dahd-ights). The people who lived in Ashdod (Ne 4:7).

ASHER (ASH-ur; "happiness").

1. The eighth son of Jacob (Gn 30:12–13; 35:26). See 1:393, 399.

2. The territory along the seashore north of Carmel that was given to the tribe that descended from Asher (Jsh 19:24–31). See 1:213.

ASHERAH (ah-SHER-rah). A Canaanite goddess of sex and war. She was the wife or sister of El. *Asherah* means goddess or wooden image. Cf Dt 16:21; 1Ki 15:13; 16:33. See 1:230, 638.

ASHERIM (ah-SHER-rim). The plural form of Asherah. See 1:370.

ASHERITES (ASH-ur-ights). The people from the tribe of Asher (Jgs 1:32).

ASHEROTH (ah-SHER-rahth). The feminine plural form of Asherah.

ASHES. People in Bible times sat in or sprinkled themselves with ashes to show humiliation, grief, or penitence (2Sm 13:19; Est 4:3; Jb 2:8; Jer 6:26; Mt 11:21). When people felt depressed, they demonstrated this by eating ashes (Ps 102:9). Because of the ageless custom of burning captured cities, the expression "to reduce to ashes" implied complete destruction (Ezk 28:18; 2Pt 2:6). The ashes of a red heifer were used for cleansing the unclean (Nu 19:17–22). See 1:132, 510.

ASHKELON (ASH-kuh-lahn). One of the five chief cities of the Philistines. It was located about 12 miles north of Gaza. During the time of the judges, the tribe of Judah captured Ashkelon, but the Philistines soon got it back (Jgs 1:18; 14:19; 1Sm 6:17). Ashkelon's destruction is foretold in both Zep 2:4 and Zec 9:5. In AD 1270, the Bibars destroyed it. See 1:211; 2:196.

ASHKENAZ (ASH-kuh-naz). Noah's great-grandson (Gn 10:3). His descendants (Scythians) lived near Ararat.

ASHPENAZ (ASH-pi-naz; may mean "chief of the household"). The chief of the eunuchs in Babylon during Nebuchadnezzar's time. Ashpenaz gave Daniel and his friends their new names (Dn 1:3, 7).

ASHTORETH; ASHTAROTH (ASH-to-reth). A Canaanite goddess who was worshiped particularly at Sidon (1Ki 11:5, 33; 2Ki 23:13). During the time of the judges the people of Israel periodically stopped worshiping the Lord and served Ashtoreth instead (Jgs 2:13; 10:6). Toward the end of his reign Solomon built altars in Israel for the worship of Ashtoreth (1Ki 11:5; 2Ki 23:13).

Ashtoreth has been equated with Ishtar of the Babylonians, Astarte of the Greeks, and Venus of the Romans. The plural form of her name is Ashtaroth. Her male partner was Baal. *See also* ARTEMIS. See 1:240, 283.

ASIA (AY-zhah). When the NT speaks of Asia, it may be referring to either Asia Minor (Ac 19:26), Proconsular Asia (Ac 20:4; 1Co 16:19), or more restricted areas (Ac 2:9). See 1:17, 100, 425; 2:234, 499–500, 519–22, 704, 771–72, 813.

ASP. A poisonous snake (Dt 32:33; Rm 3:13; cf Is 11:8). *See also* SERPENT.

ASRIEL (AS-ri-el). A descendant of Manasseh and founder of a family (Nu 26:31).

ASSEMBLY. Hbr *qahal*. The term would not immediately have sacred association; it could simply mean "assembly." Gk *ekklesia*, "ones called out" for a public gathering. The author of 1Macc uses "great assembly," which could include priestly leadership and decision makers (4:59; 5:16; 14:19, 28, 44; cf Ecclus 6:34; 7:14). It became the common NT term for not only a local congregation but also for the universal Church (Eph 1:22). *See also* GREAT CONGREGATION. See 1:267, 289, 332, 400, 407, 547, 659; 2:651–52, 682, 686.

ASSHUR (AHS-shoor). The second-named son of Shem (Gn 10:22). The people who descended from Asshur settled in Assyria. *See also* ASSYRIA.

ASSHURIM (uh-SHOO-rim). An Arabic tribe that descended from Abraham (Gn 25:3).

ASSOS (AS-ahs). A seaport of Mysia in Asia Minor (Ac 20:13–14). See 2:388.

ASSYRIA (uh-SIR-i-ah). The country that dominated the biblical world from the ninth to the seventh century BC. At its height, Assyria encompassed the land between the Black Sea, the Caspian Sea, the Persian Gulf, and the Mediterranean Sea (including Egypt). Its capital city was Nineveh. Semitic in origin, it appears that the people of Assyria were originally colonists from Babylonia (Gn 10:11). They wrote with ideograms and syllabic signs. Chief among their gods were Asshur, Anu, Bel, and Ea.

The kings of Assyria often invaded Israel (2Ki 15:19, 29; 16:7–9; 2Ch 28:20). In 722 BC, the Assyrians finally carried the Israelites into captivity (2Ki 17:6; 18:11).

In 612 BC, Nineveh fell to the Medes, and after the battle of Carchemish in 605 BC, the Assyrians as a nation ceased to exist. See 1:25, 322–25, 345, 347–48, 352, 373, 727–31, 935–43; 2:17–21, 799–800, 814.

ASTROLOGERS (as-TRAHL-o-jurs). People who tried to predict the future by studying the stars (Dn 2:27; 4:7; 5:7, 11). See 1:847.

ATHALIAH (ath-ah-LIGH-ah; "Yahwah is great"). The wicked daughter of Ahab and Jezebel. Under Athaliah's influence, her husband, King Jehoram, introduced Baal worship to Judah. Later, when her son King Ahaziah was killed, Athaliah seized the throne and reigned for six years. While trying to stop a rebellion, she was killed by her guard (2Ki 11; 2Ch 22–24). See 1:346, 372–74, 402, 867.

ATHARIM (ATH-ah-rim). The route the Israelites followed when approaching Canaan (Nu 21:1).

ATHENS (ATH-enz; "city of Athena"). In ancient times Athens was the capital of Attica; today it is the capital of Greece. Located near the Gulf of Aegina, Athens grew up around the 512-foot-high rocky hill known as the Acropolis. It was connected to the harbor Piraeus by 5-mile-long walls. Athens was a center for both learning and civilization. During his second missionary journey, Paul visited the city and spoke to a group of people on the Areopagus (Ac 17:19–22). See 2:365–66, 379, 388, 454, 563–64, 811.

ATONEMENT (ah-TONE-muhnt; Hbr *kaphar*, "ransom, reconciliation." The word may be related to the idea of covering something, a sense that appears in other Semitic languages). Moses closely relates atonement to the idea of redemption, where an innocent life is offered as a substitute for a guilty life (e.g., the transfer of guilt to the sacrificial animal in Lv 1:4; 4:4; 16:21). Also, Jacob is described as reconciling with his brother, Esau, by offering him a gift as atonement (Gn 32:20). Atonement brought cleansing (Lv 16:30). It was the focus of a major annual ritual, the Day of Atonement, when the blood of a sacrifice was sprinkled on the "place of atonement," the cover of the ark of the covenant. Less common term in the Apocrypha.

Atonement is the removal of the separation that exists between God and people because of sin. It is accomplished by the life and death of Jesus in humanity's place. Cf "reconciliation" in Rm 5:11. *See also* DELIVER. See 1:73–75, 99, 102–16, 137, 142, 144, 178, 403, 439–41, 603, 808–9; 2:272–73, 553, 660, 749.

ATONEMENT, DAY OF. A Hebrew festival held on the tenth day of the seventh month. It was observed with fasting, humiliation, and sacrifice for sin (Ex 30:16; Lv 16; 23:27–32). See 1:75, 105–7, 110; 2:51.

ATTAI (AT-ay-igh; "timely"). A son of Rehoboam and Maacah (2Ch 11:20).

ATTALIA (At-ah-LIGH-ah). A seaport on the coast of Pamphylia (Ac 14:25). See 2:388.

AUGURY. Using signs or omens to predict the future. This practice was forbidden (2Ki 21:6; 2Ch 33:6). *See also* ENCHANTMENT; MAGIC.

AUGUSTUS (aw-GUS-tuhs; "venerable"). The title of Gaius Julius Caesar Octavianus, the first Roman Emperor, who reigned from 27 BC to AD 14. Christ was born during his rule (Lk 2:1). See 2:186, 297–99, 391.

AVENGER OF BLOOD. When a person was murdered, it was the duty of the person's nearest relative to pursue the murderer and obtain satisfaction for the relative's death, generally by killing the murderer (Dt 19:6). The person who made satisfaction for a relative's death in this way was known as the avenger of blood. See 1:142.

AVVA (Av-AH). A city of the Assyrian Empire. People from Avva helped colonize Samaria (2Ki 17:24).

AVVIM, AVVITES (AV-im, AV-vights).

1. Indigenous people who lived in Gaza before the time of Moses (Dt 2:23).
2. A town probably named after the Avvites (Jsh 18:23).

AZARIAH (az-ah-RIGH-ah; "Yahweh has helped").

1. The prophet who met King Asa on his return from victory over Zerah. Asa followed Azariah's advice by putting away idolatry and restoring the altar of God. A national reformation followed (2Ch 15:1–8). See 1:372, 401–2.
2. A son of Obed and another of Joash's captains. He also helped restore the throne to Joash (2Ch 23:1). See 1:396.
3. A son of Jeroham and one of Joash's captains. He helped place Joash on the throne (2Ch 23:1).
4. The son and successor of Amaziah. Azariah was the tenth king of Judah (2Ki 14:21; 15:1–7; 1Ch 3:12). He is also referred to as Uzziah. See 1:346, 373, 375, 715, 879, 890.
5. The Hbr name of Abednego, one of Daniel's friends (Dn 1:7; 2:17). Azariah was thrown into

the fiery furnace for not worshiping the golden idol set up by King Nebuchadnezzar (Dn 3). See 1:823, 833; 2:136.

6. The name taken by the angel Raphael in Tobit. See 2:45.

AZARIAH, PRAYER OF. See 2:135–41.

AZAZEL (ah-ZAH-zel). The word occurs only in Lv 16, where its meaning is unknown, though several have been suggested: (1) a solitary place; (2) a scapegoat, or goat that was allowed to run away; (3) a devil or demon of the wilderness; (4) dismissal or removal.

AZGAD (AZ-gad; "strong of fortune"). The head of a family of Israelites, a large number of whom returned from Babylon with Zerubbabel (Ezr 2:12; 8:12; Ne 7:17).

AZMAVETH (az-MAY-veth; "deathly strong").

1. One of David's warriors (2Sm 23:31). His sons joined David's army at Ziklag (1Ch 12:3).
2. David's treasurer (1Ch 27:25). Perhaps the same as 1.
3. A village of Judah or Benjamin situated between Geba and Anathoth (Ezr 2:24; Ne 12:29).

AZOTUS (ah-ZO-tuhs). *See* ASHDOD. See 1:915; 2:367.

AZUBAH (ah-ZYOO-bah; "forsaken"). King Jehoshaphat's mother (1Ki 22:42; 2Ch 20:31).

AZZUR (AZ-ur; "helper"). The father of the false prophet Hananiah (Jer 28:1).

B

BAAL (BAY-uhl; "lord," "possessor").

1. A common name for "god" among the Phoenicians. It was also a name used for the master of the house and a person who owned land or cattle (cf "owner"; Ex 21:28; Jb 31:39). See 1:16; 2:xviii.
2. The storm god of the Phoenicians and Canaanites. Baal was said to give increase to families, crops, fields, and flocks. He was worshiped on high places with self-torture and human sacrifices (Jer 19:5). Often he was associated with the goddess Ashtoreth (Jgs 2:13; 6:30; 1Ki 16:32–33).

   Early in their history, the Hebrews were attracted to Baal worship (cf Nu 22:41; Dt 4:16; Jgs 2:13; 6:28–32). Altars to Baal were built in Israel. Jezebel in Israel and Athaliah in Judah championed Baal worship (1Ki 16:31–32; 18:17–40; 2Ki 11:18; 2Ch 17:3; 21:6; 22:2). Numerous times the altars and images of Baal were torn down and destroyed, and the people of Israel returned to the Lord; yet Baal worship persisted in Judah and Israel (2Ki 21:3; 23:4–5; 2Ch 28:2; Jer 19:4–5; Hos 2:8). See 1:141, 146, 237, 240–41, 333, 343, 346, 351, 366–67, 860.
3. Often *Baal* is combined with other words or syllables in the names of people and places, e.g., Baal-hazor.

BAAL-BERITH (BAY-uhl-BEE-rith; "Baal of the enclosure"). The god worshiped at Shechem (Jgs 8:33; 9:4).

BAAL-HAZOR (BAY-uhl-HAY-zawr; "Baal of a village"). A place near Ephraim, where Absalom had a sheep farm. It is here that he had his half-brother Amnon murdered (2Sm 13:23).

BAALIS (BAY-ah-lis). A king of the Ammonites (Jer 40:14).

BAAL-PERAZIM (BAY-uhl-pi-RAY-zim; "Baal of openings"). A place where David defeated the Philistines (2Sm 5:20; 1Ch 14:11). See 1:293.

BAAL-ZEBUB (BAY-uhl-ZEE-bub; "Baal of flies"). The name by which Baal was worshiped in Ekron (2Ki 1:2–6). *See also* BEELZEBUL. See 1:333.

BAAL-ZEPHON (BAY-uhl-ZEE-fahn; "Baal of the north"). A place near which the Israelites camped before crossing the Red Sea (Ex 14:2, 9; Nu 33:7).

BAANAH (BAY-ah-nah; "son of affliction"). An officer in the army of Ish-bosheth, Saul's son. Baanah and his brother killed Ish-bosheth (2Sm 4:2–12).

BAASHA (BAY-ah-shah). The son of Ahijah of the tribe of Issachar. Baasha became the third king of Israel while Asa was king of Judah. Baasha began a long war with Asa. He built Ramah to block the flow of traffic in and out of Judah (1Ki 15:16–17). Baasha ruled Israel for 24 years (1Ki 15:27–34; 16:7). See 1:343, 345, 370–72.

BABEL (BAY-buhl; "gate of [god] Bel"; Hbr wordplay with "confusion").

1. A city in the Plain of Shinar (Gn 10:10).
2. The tower of Babel was a brick structure built on the Plain of Shinar. As a result of this building project, God confused people's language and scattered the people over the face of the earth (Gn 11:4–9). See 1:36.

BABYLON (BAB-i-lahn; Gk form of "Babel"). An ancient city-state on the Plain of Shinar; first mentioned as "Babel" in Gn 10:8–10.

Babylon began its rise to power in the nineteenth century BC. The great Hammurabi became its ruler in the eighteenth century BC, but it did not reach the height of its power until Nebuchadnezzar II, who reigned from 605 to 562 BC. Then in 538 BC, Babylon was conquered by Cyrus of Persia.

Babylon was noted for its temple of Bel (or Marduk) and the Ishtar Gate, as well as for its ziggurats, hanging gardens, bridges, palace, and overall strength and splendor. The prophets often spoke about it (Is 13–14; 21; 46–47; Jer 50–51). In the NT, Babylon is used figuratively for that which opposes God both within and without the Church (1Pt 5:13; Rv 14:8; 16:19; 17:5; 18:2, 10, 21). See 1:391, 413, 729–32, 734, 844–49, 908–9; 2:4, 12, 72–73, 117–19, 701, 784.

BABYLONIA (Bab-i-LO-ni-ah). A region of West Asia, the capital of which was Babylon. Babylonia was also called Shinar (Gn 10:10; 11:2; Is 11:11) and the land of the Chaldeans (Jer 24:5; Ezk 12:13). See 1:25, 322, 348–49, 373, 413, 753–55, 795–97, 844–49; 2:61–63, 71–72, 814.

BACA (BA-kah; "weeping" or "balsam tree"). An unidentified valley in Israel that was named for its balsam trees, which produced a tearlike gum. Some people identify Baca with Rephaim because of the balsam trees there (2Sm 5:22–24). It is usually interpreted figuratively, however, to describe any vale of tears (Ps 84:6).

BACKBITE. To speak evil of someone (Pr 25:23; cf "slander" in Ps 15:3).

BACKSLIDING. From Hbr *shub* (*see* TURN). Describes a person turning away from the Lord to follow his own way (Is 57:17; Ezk 37:23). *See also* APOSTASY. See 1:733.

BAG. Used for carrying weights, stones, and money (Dt 25:13; 1Sm 17:49; 2Ki 5:23). Judas's "moneybag" was probably a chest (Jn 12:6; 13:29). See 2:258, 312.

BAKER. Some people in Israel earned their living by baking (Jer 37:21). Often rulers had their own bakers (Gn 40; 1Sm 8:13). See 1:30.

BALAAM (BAY-lahm; possibly "Baal of the people"). The son of Beor, probably a Midianite (Nu 31:8; Dt 23:4). Balaam was the diviner hired by King Balak of Moab to curse Israel. God, however, used Balaam to bless Israel instead (Nu 22–24).

Before leaving the king of Moab, Balaam told him that the Lord would surely curse the Israelites if Balak could get them to worship false gods (Nu 31:15–16; Rv 2:14). Balak did this. To avenge themselves, the Israelites warred against the Midianites, killing their kings and Balaam (Nu 31:8). See 1:139–41, 146; 2:726.

BALAK (BAY-lak; "destroyer"). The king of Moab. He hired Balaam to curse Israel (Nu 22–24; Jsh 24:9; Jgs 11:25; Rv 2:14). See 1:139–41.

BALANCE. An instrument for weighing (Lv 19:36; Ezk 45:10; Am 8:5). In a figurative sense, the word *balance* is used for measuring the worth or trouble of people (Jb 6:2; Ps 62:9; Dn 5:27). It is also a symbol of fair dealing (Jb 31:6; Pr 11:1).

BALDNESS. Natural baldness is not mentioned often in the Bible. Sometimes it was connected with leprosy or misery (Lv 13:40–43; Is 3:24).

Shaving the head was a sign of mourning (Jer 16:6; Ezk 7:18). The Israelites were forbidden from doing this because they were a holy people (Dt 14:1–2). However, it was sometimes a punishment used for captives (Dt 21:12). When a Nazirite shaved his head, it marked the end of his vow (Nu 6:9, 18). See 2:488.

"Baldhead" was a term of ridicule (2Ki 2:23).

BALM. The resin or gum of trees that at one time grew in Gilead (Gn 37:25; Jer 8:22; 46:11). This balm or ointment was used to heal wounds (Jer 51:8). It made up part of the export trade of Canaan (Gn 37:25; Ezk 27:17). See 1:592.

BALSAM TREE. An unidentified plant in Israel (2Sm 5:22–24; 1Ch 14:14–15).

BAMAH (BAH-mah; "high place"). A place where idols were worshiped (Ezk 20:29). See 2:798.

BAMOTH (BAY-mahth; "heights"). A camp of the Israelites located in the land of the Moabites (Nu 21:19–20).

BAND. The tenth part of a Roman legion, a cohort or battalion (2Sm 23:13, 1Ch 12:21; Ezr 8:22). *See* ARMY; COHORT.

BAPTISM (bap-tiz'm). When the word *baptism* appears in Greek translations of the OT, it often means to dip, bathe, or wash (cf Ex 30:17–21; 2Ki 5:14).

Ezekiel prophesied the coming of Baptism to Israel (36:22–29). The Jews baptized proselytes; ceremonial washings were also common (cf Mk 7:3–4; Heb 9:10).

John's Baptism was connected with repentance so that those baptized might be spiritually prepared to recognize and receive the Messiah. It worked the forgiveness of sins (Mt 3; Mk 1:4–8; cf Ezk 36:25) but was distinguished from the Baptism Jesus instituted (Lk 3:16; Jn 1:26; Ac 1:5; 11:16; 19:4–6).

The Baptism Jesus received from John was unique because Jesus was without sin and therefore had no reason to repent. It signified His public entrance into His work of saving the world from sin (Mt 3:13–15; Mk 10:38; Lk 12:50).

In Christian Baptism an individual participates in the death and resurrection of Christ (Rm 6:3–11; Col 2:12) and is made a member of Christ (1Co 1:13; Gal 3:27; Eph 4:5). Baptism works the forgiveness of sins, delivers one from spiritual death and the devil, and gives eternal salvation to all who believe in Christ (Ac 2:38; 22:16; 1Pt 3:21). Baptism also makes an individual a member of the Body of Christ, the Church (1Co 12:13; Gal 3:27–28; Eph 5:26), and bestows the Holy Spirit (Ac 3:28; 1Co 12:13). The blessings of Baptism are received by faith (Rm 6:1–11).

Christian Baptism must include the application of water in the name of the triune God—the Father, Son, and Holy Spirit (Mt 28:19) as Jesus instituted it. The practice by which the water is applied to the individual, however, can vary (Jn 3:23; Ac 2:38; 8:12, 36; 10:47–48; 16:15, 33; cf Ezk 36:25; Heb 10:22). The NT does not restrict Baptism on the basis of age or mental ability but commands Baptism for all nations (Mt 28:19). *See* CLEAN. See 1:36, 111–12, 178, 215, 563, 591–92, 597, 740, 809, 811; 2:196, 204–5, 249–50, 333–34, 350, 384, 445, 464–66, 709, 728, 741.

BARABBAS (bah-RAB-bas; "son of Abba" [father]). The prisoner that the mob in Jerusalem asked Pilate to free instead of Jesus (Mt 27:16–26; Mk 15:7–15; Lk 23:18–25; Jn 18:40). See 2:204, 284, 337.

BARACHEL (BAR-ah-kel; "blessed of God"). The father of Job's friend Elihu (Jb 32:2, 6). See 1:504.

BARAK (BAIR-uhk; "lightning"). The Israelite whom Deborah, the prophetess and judge, summoned to lead an army against Sisera, commander-in-chief of the king of Canaan. Under Barak's leadership the Israelites defeated the Canaanites and killed Sisera (Jgs 4; 5:1, 12; Heb 11:32). See 1:217, 237, 243.

BARBARIAN ("rude"). At first, anyone who did not speak Greek was called a barbarian. The name was used to imply vulgarity and lack of culture. Later, barbarians were those people outside the Greco-Roman culture. When the NT talks about barbarians, no insult is intended (Rm 1:14; Col 3:11; cf Ac 28:4; 1Co 14:11). See 2:424, 429.

BAREFOOT. To go barefoot was a sign of either distress or of reverence for a holy place (Ex 3:5; 2Sm 15:30; Is 20:2–4). See 1:730.

BAR-JESUS ("son of Yeshua"). A Jewish magician and false prophet in the court of Sergius Paulus, also known as Elymas. When Bar-Jesus tried to hinder the conversion of Sergius Paulus by interfering with Paul's work, he was struck blind for a while (Ac 13:6–12).

BAR-JONAH (bahr-JO-nah; "son of Jonah" or "son of John"). The apostle Peter's last name (Mt 16:17).

BARLEY. A cereal grain grown in Israel and neighboring areas (Lv 27:16; Ru 1:22). The Hebrews called it the hairy, bristling thing. It was made into cakes or loaves and was often eaten by the poor (Jgs 7:13; 2Ki 4:42; Jn 6:9). See 1:263–64.

BARNABAS (BAHR-nah-buhs; "son of exhortation"). A Levite from Cyprus whose last name was Joses (Ac 4:36–37). Barnabas was Paul's friend and coworker (Ac 9:27). He helped Paul at Tarsus and went with him on his first missionary journey and to the council at Jerusalem (Ac 11–15). Because of a disagreement he had with Paul over John Mark, Barnabas separated from Paul before the second missionary journey (Ac 15:36–41). However, in his epistles Paul speaks highly of Barnabas (1Co 9:6; Gal 2:1, 9, 13; Col 4:10). See 2:234, 367–68, 388–89, 502–3, 652–53.

BARSABBAS (BAR-sab-uhss; "son of Sabas").

1. The last name of Joseph, one of the men nominated by the apostles to take the place of Judas Iscariot (Ac 1:23).
2. The last name of Judas, a member of the church at Jerusalem. He was sent on their behalf to Antioch with Silas, Paul, and Barnabas (Ac 15:22). Judas and Joseph Barsabbas may have been brothers.

BARTHOLOMEW (bahr-THAL-o-myoo; "son of Tolmai"). One of the 12 apostles (Mt 10:3; Mk 3:18; Lk 6:14; Ac 1:13). Bartholomew may have been the last name of Nathanael (Jn 1:45).

BARTIMAEUS (bahr-ti-MAY-uhs; "son of Timaeus"). A blind beggar at Jericho (Mk 10:46–52). See 2:247, 307–8.

BARUCH (BAIR-uhk; "blessed").

1. Jeremiah's friend, scribe, and fellow prisoner (Jer 32:12; 36:4–32; 43:3–6). Other apocryphal books are attributed to Baruch as well. *See also* BARUCH, BOOK OF. See 1:433, 647, 753–60, 768; 2:62.
2. One of Nehemiah's co-workers. He helped in rebuilding the wall of Jerusalem (Ne 3:20; 10:6).

BARUCH, BOOK OF. See 2:61–69.

BASEMATH (BAS-i-math; "fragrance," "balsam").

1. A Hittite wife of Esau (Gn 26:34). She is referred to as Adah in Gn 36:2.
2. Ishmael's daughter. She was Esau's last wife (Gn 36:3–4, 13, 17). She is also referred to as Mahalath (Gn 28:9).
3. One of Solomon's daughters (1Ki 4:15).

BASIN. A type of bowl used in the OT for various rituals in worship (Ex 30:17–21; 40:30). Some basins were very large (1Ki 7:38). See 1:72, 454.

BAT. This animal is classed among the fowls in the OT and is considered unclean (Lv 11:19; Dt 14:18).

BATH. *See* MEASURES 3c. See 1:398.

BATHE. Bathing and cleanliness were practiced by the Hebrew people from earliest times (Ex 2:5; Sg 5:3, 12; cf Ru 3:3; 2Sm 12:20). They associated bathing with cleanliness before God. It held a chief place in their rituals (Lv 13–16; 17:15–16). *See also* WASHING. See 2:21.

BATHSHEBA (bath-SHEE-bah; various etymologies: "daughter of oak," "of an oath," "of abundance," or "of the seventh day"). The wife of Uriah the Hittite, an officer in David's army (2Sm 11:3–4). As a consequence of David's adulterous relationship with Bathsheba, she conceived a child (2Sm 11:1–5). So David arranged Uriah's death on the battlefield in order that Bathsheba might become David's wife (2Sm 11:6–27). Four sons, including Solomon, were born to David and Bathsheba (2Sm 5:14; 1Ch 3:5). See 1:281, 294–96, 299, 338.

BDELLIUM (DEL-i-uhm). The name the Greeks gave to a fragrant gum resin. The OT lists it with precious stones (Gn 2:12; Nu 11:7).

BEARD. A badge of manly dignity. Tearing, cutting, or neglecting one's beard was a sign of mental abnormality, affliction, or mourning (1Sm 21:13; 2Sm 19:24; Jer 41:4–5). When greeting another person, it was customary to take hold of his beard (2Sm 20:9). Men also swore oaths by their beards (cf Mt 5:36). Lepers were not allowed to have beards (Lv 14:9). The Egyptians shaved their beards (Gn 41:14). Shaving the corners of the beard, a practice followed by some nationalities but forbidden to the Israelites, was probably part of a heathen religious act (Lv 19:27; Jer 9:26). See 1:15; 2:177.

BEAST.

1. A mammal, not man, distinguished from birds and other land animals (Gn 1:29–30). See 1:45–46, 48, 117, 669, 834.
2. Wild animals (cf Is 13:21; Mk 1:13). See 2:521.
3. Animals, including birds and reptiles (cf Ec 3:18; Ac 28:5).
4. A destructive power that is an enemy of God's kingdom and people (Dn 7; Rv 13:1–10; 17:3–18). *See also* LEVIATHAN. See 1:505–7.
5. In Rv 13:2–18, a beast identified with the Antichrist fights Christians and persuades people to worship the first beast. See 1:507, 836; 2:582, 784–85.

BEATITUDES (bee-AT-uh-toods). Declarations of blessedness (Mt 5:3–11; Lk 6:20–22). Isolated beatitudes appear throughout the NT (cf Mt 11:6; 13:16; Lk 7:23; Jn 20:29; Jas 1:12; 1Pt 3:14; Rv 1:3; 14:13). *See also* BLESSING. See 2:185, 190, 197, 690, 778.

BECHER (BEE-kur; "firstborn" or "young camel"). The second son of Benjamin (Gn 46:21).

BED. Poor people and travelers often slept on the ground or a mat (Gn 28:11; Mt 9:6). Early beds were made of wood, iron, and even ivory (Dt 3:11; 2Ki 1:4, 6; Am 6:4). They had a mattress, pillow, and covering (1Sm 19:13; Is 28:20). At times, beds had ornamental trimmings and canopies (Est 1:6; Am 6:4). *See also* HOMES; LITTER. See 1:334, 607, 690.

BEE. Many Bible passages speak of bees (Dt 1:44; cf Ex 3:8; 1Ki 14:3; Ezk 27:17). These insects are plentiful in Israel, where they nest in rocks, woods, and the remains of dead animals (Jgs 14:8; cf 1Sm 14:25; Ps 81:16).

BEELZEBUL (bee-EL-zee-bul; "lord of the fly"). The prince of the demons (Mt 10:25; 12:24; Mk 3:22; Lk 11:15, 18–19). Jesus identified him with Satan (Lk 11:18). *See also* BAAL-ZEBUB. See 2:200.

BEER (BEE-ur; well).

1. A place where Israel set up camp (Nu 21:16–18). See 2:805.
2. A place to which Jotham fled (Jgs 9:21).

BEER-LAHAI-ROI (BEE-uhr-lah-high-roy; "well of living one who sees me"). The well where the Lord appeared to Sarah's handmaid, Hagar, and where Isaac lived for awhile (Gn 16:6–14; 24:62; 25:11).

BEERSHEBA (BEE-uhr-SHEE-bah; "well of oath" or "of seven"). A town in southern Judah. The expression "from Dan to Beersheba" is used to designate the northern and southern extremities of Israel (2Sm 3:10). Abraham made a covenant with Abimelech there, and Isaac's servants dug a well there (Gn 21:31; 26:33). See 1:29, 333; 2:196, 798, 805.

BEHEMOTH (bi-HEE-mahth). From common plural Hbr word for "animal" or "beast." Scholars often suggest that the animal being described is a hippopotamus. Cf Jb 40:15–24. See 1:505–7, 513.

BEKA (BEE-kah). Half a shekel (Ex 38:26).

BEL (BEHL; "lord"). The patron god of Babylon (Is 46:1). The Hebrews called him Merodach (Jer 50:2). See 2:127–32.

BEL AND THE DRAGON, BOOK OF. See 2:127–33.

BELIAL (BEE-li-uhl; "useless"). In the OT, the word *Belial* is not a proper noun but one that means worthlessness, wickedness, or restlessness (cf Dt 13:13; Jgs 19:22; 1Sm 2:12). Belial is personified in 2Co 6:15.

BELL. Bells of gold were attached to the priests' robes (Ex 28:33–35; 39:25). People also wore bells on their ankles and put them on horses (Zec 14:20; cf Is 3:16–18).

BELLOWS. A device made of skins and used for blowing the fire of a furnace (Jer 6:29).

BELOVED. Hbr *dod,* which appears most often in Sg; Gk forms of *agape* or *prosphile*. The OT background conveys an exclusive love or jealous love, which distinguished it from Greek ideas of love. In the NT it describes fellow Christians. *See* LOVE. See 1:82, 264, 681–83, 689–90, 693; 2:257, 443, 605, 615, 761.

BELSHAZZAR (bel-SHAZ-ur; "may Bel protect the king"). The son of Nabonidus, the grandson of Nebuchadnezzar, and the last ruler of the Neo-Babylonian Empire (Dn 5). See 1:413, 829, 834, 844–45; 2:63.

BELTESHAZZAR (bel-ti-SHAZ-ur; "may Bel protect his life"). The name Nebuchadnezzar gave to Daniel (Dn 1:7).

BENAIAH (bi-NAY-yah; "Yahweh has built"). The son of Jehoiada, the priest (1Ch 27:5). Benaiah was known for his brave deeds (2Sm 23:20–21; 1Ch 11:22–23). He was captain of David's bodyguard and, later, commander-in-chief of Solomon's army (2Sm 8:18; 1Ki 2:34–46). See 1:338.

BEN-AMMI (ben-AM-ee; "son of my kindred"). Lot's son, the ancestor of the Ammonites (Gn 19:38).

BENE-JAAKAN (BEE-ni-JAY-ah-kuhn; "sons of Jaakan"). A place in the wilderness where the Israelites camped (Nu 33:31–32).

BEN-HADAD (ben-HAY-dad; "son of Hadad"). The name of two or three Syrian rulers.

1. Ben-hadad I was king of Damascus at the same time as Asa ruled Judah. Ben-hadad helped Asa oppose Baasha, king of Israel (1Ki 15:18–21; 2Ch 16:1–6).
2. Another king named Ben-hadad defeated King Ahab of Israel (1Ki 20:1–34). Then in the days of Jehoram he again attacked Israel (2Ki 6:24–7:20; 8:28). He was killed by Hazael, who took over his throne (2Ki 8:7–15). Some people identify him with Ben-hadad I. See 1:336, 343–44.
3. Ben-hadad II, son of Hazael. When Jehoahaz ruled Israel, first Hazael and then his son Ben-hadad II attacked the 10 tribes (2Ki 13:3–13). On three different occasions, however, Josiah was able to defeat Ben-hadad II and recover the cities of Israel (2Ki 13:22–25).

BENJAMIN (BEN-jah-muhn; "son of right hand").

1. The youngest son of Jacob and Rachel. Just before she died, Rachel named him Ben-oni (son of my sorrow), but Jacob renamed him Benjamin (Gn 35:16–20). Jacob loved Benjamin very much (Gn 42). See 1:31.
2. The tribe that descended from Benjamin (Gn 49:27). When Joshua divided the land among the 12 tribes, the tribe of Benjamin received territory between Judah and Ephraim (Jsh 18:11–28). Saul, the first king of Israel, and Paul, the apostle, were

Benjaminites (1Sm 9:1–2; Php 3:5). See 1:204, 239–40, 278, 399, 751; 2:802–3.

BENJAMIN, GATE OF. A gate in Jerusalem (Jer 20:2).

BEN-ONI (ben-O-nigh; "son of my sorrow"). *See* BENJAMIN 1.

BEOR (BEE-awr; possibly "torch"). Balaam's father (Nu 22:5; 2Pt 2:15).

BERA (BEE-rah). The king of Sodom in the days of Abraham (Gn 14:2).

BERACAH (BER-ah-kah; "blessing").
1. A Benjaminite who helped David at Ziklag when David was fleeing from Saul (1Ch 12:3).
2. A valley in Judah near Tekoa. Jehoshaphat celebrated his victory over the Ammonites and Moabites there (2Ch 20:26).

BEREA (bi-REE-ah). A city in Macedonia (Ac 17:10–14; 20:4). On his second missionary journey Paul started a church there. See 2:388, 563, 813.

BERNICE (BUR-NEE-si; "bringing victory"). The oldest daughter of Herod Agrippa. She and her brother Agrippa listened to Paul's defense at Caesarea (Ac 25:23; 26:30). See 2:380.

BERYL (BER-il). One of the precious stones in the high priest's breastpiece (Ex 28:20; 39:13).

BETHANY (BETH-ah-ni; probably "house of dates" or "of figs"). A village on the Mount of Olives about two miles from Jerusalem (Mt 21:17; Lk 19:29). Bethany was the home of Mary, Martha, and Lazarus (Jn 11:1). Today it is el-'Azariyeh. See 2:171, 286, 314, 809.

BETH-AVEN (beth-AY-ven; "house of wickedness").
1. A town east of Bethel, near Ai (Jsh 7:2).
2. Ironic pun on the name Bethel, "house of God" (Hos 4:15). See 1:853.

BETH-CAR (BETH-kahr; "house of the ram" or "of pasture"). A place to which the Israelites pursued the Philistines (1Sm 7:11).

BETHEL (BETH-uhl; "house of God"). A town about 10 miles north of Jerusalem (Gn 28:19). Abraham camped near it (Gn 12:8). Originally it was called Luz by the Canaanites, but after his vision Jacob renamed it Bethel and built an altar there (Gn 28:11–19).

In the division of territories Bethel was assigned to Benjamin (Jsh 18:13). Later the tribe of Ephraim captured it (Jgs 1:22–26). The ark was brought to Bethel from Shiloh (Jgs 20:26–27). When Jeroboam was king, he set up a golden calf in Bethel and made it a center of idolatry (1Ki 12:25–13:32). The children of Bethel mocked Elisha (2Ki 2:23–24). Its ruins are called Beitin. See 1:29–30, 880–81, 989.

BETHESDA (bi-THEZ-dah; probably "house of grace" or "of mercy"). A spring-fed pool at Jerusalem that had five porches (Jn 5:2). In 1888, such a pool, probably Bethesda, was found near St. Anne's Church in Jerusalem. See 2:323, 330, 809.

BETHLEHEM (BETH-li-hem; "house of bread").
1. A town 5 miles south of Jerusalem. Originally it was called Ephrath or Ephrathah, but after the conquest of Canaan, it was renamed Bethlehem in Judah to distinguish it from Bethlehem of Zebulun (Jgs 17:7). In Mi 5:2 it is referred to as Bethlehem Ephrathah. Bethlehem was the burial place of Rachel, the home of Ruth, and the birthplace of David and Jesus (Gn 35:19; Ru 1:19; 1Sm 17:12; Mt 2:1–2). See 1:257–58, 261, 923–24, 928–30; 2:196, 277, 300, 804–5.
2. A town in Zebulun (Jsh 19:15).

BETH-PEOR (beth-PEE-awr; "house of the opening"). A place in Moab where Israel camped while fighting Sihon and Og (Dt 3:29; 4:46; Jsh 13:20). Moses was buried in the valley opposite Beth-peor (Dt 34:6).

BETHPHAGE (BETH-fah-jee; "house of figs"). A village near Bethany not far from the descent of the Mount of Olives (Mt 21:1; Mk 11:1; Lk 19:29).

BETHSAIDA (beth-SAY-i-dah; "house of fishing").
1. A city on the Sea of Galilee, probably near Capernaum (Jn 1:44; 12:21). Bethsaida was the home of Peter, Andrew, and Philip. Along with Chorazin and Capernaum, Bethsaida was rebuked by Jesus for not receiving His teachings (Mt 11:21; Lk 10:13).
2. Another Bethsaida on the east side of the Sea of Galilee where Jesus fed 5,000 people (Lk 9:10–17). Also where He restored sight to a blind man (Mk 8:22–26). See 2:199, 240.

BETH-SHAN, BETH-SHEAN (beth-SHAN, beth-SHEE-uhn; "house of rest"). A fortress city strategically located at the junction of the Jezreel and Jordan valleys. Dating to the early part of the third millenium BC, Beth-shan was under Egyptian rule for three centuries. Under Joshua, Beth-shan was allotted to the tribe of Manasseh. The tribe found the city too formidable to conquer, however, because of the Philistines who held the city with their chariots of iron (Jsh 17:11–16). After Saul died on Mount Gilboa, the Philistines hung his body on the wall of Beth-shan, put his armor in the temple of Ashtoreth, and placed his head in the temple of Dagon (1Sm 31:10–13; 1Ch 10:10). See 1:37, 279.

BETH-SHEMESH (beth-SHEE-mesh; "house of sun"). A city in northern Judah set aside for priests (Jsh 15:10; 21:16). There Jehoash, king of Israel, defeated Amaziah of Judah and took him prisoner (2Ki 14:11, 13). While Ahaz was king, Beth-shemesh was occupied by the Philistines (2Ch 28:18). During one battle the Philistines captured the ark of the covenant, but a plague convinced them to return it. They put the ark on a cart pulled by cattle and headed it toward Beth-shemesh (1Sm 6:1–21).

BETHUEL (bi-THYOO-uhl; "house of God"). The nephew of Abraham and father of Laban and Rebecca (Gn 22:20–24; 28:5).

BETROTHAL (bi-TROTH-uhl). *See* MARRIAGE. See 1:858; 2:194, 472–73.

BE WITH. Found in numerous Hbr expressions of encouragement for God's people, which often also threaten defeat or punishment for enemies of God's people. In biblical theology, God fills the whole universe with His presence (Jer 23:23) and providential goodness (Mt 5:45; Ac 17:24–28; Rm 1:20). However, God is specially present with His saving power and grace where He promises to be present, in His Word (Ex 3:12; cf Jsh 1:5). These promises anticipate the greater day of Immanuel, which means "God with us" (Is 7:14; Mt 1:23; cf Mt 28:20). Jesus is present according to His grace wherever His Gospel and Sacraments are present. See 1:206, 403; 2:204, 229, 619.

BIBLE ("book"). The name given to the collection of 39 OT and 27 NT books. *See also* CANON. See 1:xxv–xxviii, xlvii–li, 5–11.

BIDKAR (BID-kahr). Jehu's aide (2Ki 9:25).

BIER (BEER). A stretcher used to carry the dead to their graves (2Sm 3:31; 2Ch 16:14; Lk 7:14).

BILDAD (BIL-dad). A Shuhite who was one of Job's three friends (Jb 2:11). Bildad made three speeches (Jb 8; 18; 25). See 1:504, 508–12.

BILGAH (BIL-gah; "gleam"). The head of the fifteenth division of priests during David's time (1Ch 24:14).

BILHAH (BIL-hah). Rachel's handmaid and Jacob's concubine. Bilhah was the mother of two of Jacob's sons, Dan and Naphtali (Gn 29:29).

BINDING AND LOOSING. *See* KEY. See 2:488.

BIRD. The Bible mentions a number of birds, classifying them as clean and unclean (Lv 11:13–19; Dt 14:11–19). It particularly describes the characteristics of the eagle, hawk, and ostrich (Jb 39:13–30). Cf Mt 6:26. People in Bible times ate bird eggs (Is 10:14; Lk 11:12). See 1:48, 106, 158.

BISHLAM (BISH-lam). A Persian officer who complained to Artaxerxes about the rebuilding of Jerusalem (Ezr 4:7).

BISHOP. From Gk *episkopos*; "overseer." *See* ELDER. See 1:369; 2:234, 611–12, 627, 698.

BITHYNIA (bi-THIN-i-ah). A country in northwest Asia Minor whose capital was Nicaea. Although Paul and his companions wanted to bring the Gospel to Bithynia, they did not, because the Holy Spirit was leading them to Europe instead (Ac 16:6–10). Nevertheless, there were Christians in Bithynia in the first century. Peter greets them in his letter (1Pt 1:1). See 2:564, 645, 701.

BITTER, BITTERNESS.

1. The opposite of sweet (Ex 15:23). See 2:261.
2. Sorrow, trouble (Ex 1:14; Jb 7:11). See 1:513, 517, 602; 2:260, 788.
3. Inner displeasure (Eph 4:31). See 1:257.
4. Evil (2Sm 2:26).
5. Hostile wickedness (Ac 8:23). See 1:895; 2:304, 488.
6. Wickedness that corrupts (Heb 12:15).

BITTER HERBS. Plants such as lettuce, endive, horseradish, and watercress. The Israelites ate bitter herbs in the Passover feast to remind themselves of their slavery in Egypt (Ex 12:8; Nu 9:11). See 1:71.

BITUMEN (bi-TYOO-muhn; "slime"). A mineral pitch or asphalt used for sealing together wood, bricks, and the like (Gn 11:3; 14:10; Ex 2:3). Bitumen pits were located along the Euphrates and Dead Sea.

BLASPHEMY (BLAS-fi-mee). Speaking evil of God (cf Ps 74:10; Rv 16:9). Blasphemy was punished by stoning (Lv 24:16). False charges of blasphemy were brought against Naboth, Stephen, and Jesus (1Ki 21:10–13; Mt 26:65–66; Ac 6:11). See 1:102–3, 107, 776; 2:191, 222–23, 248, 284, 313, 762.

BLASPHEMY AGAINST THE HOLY SPIRIT. *See* SIN, UNPARDONABLE.

BLEMISH. Any spot or deformity (Lv 21:18–20; 22:20–24). See 1:1006; 2:709.

BLESS. Eng term includes a variety of ideas. Hbr *barak*, "To bestow ability for success" (from the greater person to the lesser) or "to praise a person's ability for success" (from the lesser person to the greater). Gk *eulogeo*, "praise" or "speak well of." Hbr term refers to bending the knees, perhaps to kneel and receive a pronouncement of inheritance with all its wealth (cf Gn 27). At the time of death and on special occasions, parents bless their children (Tob 9:6; 10:11; 11:17; 1Macc 2:69). Hbr sense fills Gk term. The LXX translators usually viewed the term as a description of praise or congratulation for someone. Common in worship contexts, expressing thanks and praise (Ps 34:1; 145:1, 10; Tob 8, 13; Pr Az). The term is used most often in the Apocrypha in the expression, "Blessed is . . . " Israelites used prayers based on the *berakah* ("blessed") pattern (Dn 2:20–23; 2Co 1:3–4; 1Pt 1:3–5). "Bless the Lord" can also mean "greet." *See also* CURSE. See 1:490; 2:138.

1. God blesses (Gn 12:1–3; 2Sm 6:11). See 1:26, 34–36, 141–42, 342, 583–84; 2:383.
2. Godly people can give blessings by asking God to bestow His favor on an object or person (Gn 12:2; 27:28–29; Nu 23–24). See 1:558, 599–600; 2:345, 692.
3. God's blessing can also be a direct application of His grace through the Word (Gn 48:17–19; Nu 6:22–27; cf Mt 19:13). See 1:739, 976; 2:397.
4. Well-known blessings include the Mizpah, the Aaronic blessing, and the apostolic blessing (Gn 31:49; Nu 6:22–27; 2Co 13:14). See 1:142.

BLESSED. Hbr *'ashrey*; Gk *makarios*. Translates "happy, blissful," having God's gifts or escaping the disappointments of life (Ecclus 25:23; 45:7; Gk of 2Macc 7:24). In Ecclesiasticus, the term describes one who receives the benefits of wisdom. Tob 13:14 describes a person who is happy despite bad circumstances, similar to Jesus' beatitudes in Mt 5; Lk 6. Cf Wis 2:16. See 1:27–28, 143–47, 411–14, 615, 805; 2:197, 778.

BLINDNESS. Since blindness was common in Bible times, blind beggars are often mentioned in the Scriptures (Mt 9:27; 12:22). Some ancient tribes blinded the people they captured (Jgs 16:21; 1Sm 11:2). God told the Israelites to be kind to blind people (Lv 19:14; Dt 27:18). See 1:243–44, 604; 2:43, 198, 307–8.

BLOOD. Because blood contains the essence of human and animal life and is necessary for that life, the two were often thought of as the same thing (Gn 9:4; Lv 17:11, 14; Dt 12:23). The Israelites were forbidden to eat blood or the flesh of animals from which the blood had not been carefully removed (Gn 9:4; Ac 15:20, 29).

Under Mosaic Law the blood of animals was used in all offerings for sin, for "without the shedding of blood there is no forgiveness of sins" (Heb 9:22). These OT offerings pointed forward to Christ's supreme sacrifice on Calvary that took away the sins of the world. The expression "the blood of Christ" refers to His atoning death (1Co 10:16; Eph 2:13; 1Pt 1:2, 19). See 1:74–75, 115–18, 144, 594, 615–16; 2:210, 212, 248, 296, 461–62, 661, 741–42, 788–89.

BLOODGUILT. The guilt of murder (Ex 22:2–3; 1Sm 25:33; Hos 12:14). See 1:863.

BLOT. To destroy or abolish. To blot out sin is to fully remove it (Is 44:22). To blot people out of God's book is to cut them off from fellowship with God and His people and to give them over to eternal death (Ex 32:32; Ps 69:28). See 1:40, 593; 2:214.

BOANERGES (bo-ah-NUE-jeez; "sons of thunder"). A name Christ gave to James and John (Mk 3:17). See 2:187.

BOATS. Biblical references to boats within Israel are not numerous because the Hebrew people were mostly farmers, not seagoers. There were small fishing and passenger boats on the Sea of Galilee, however, and perhaps small boats or ferryboats on the Jordan River (2Sm 19:18; Mt 4:21; 9:1; Mk 1:19; Jn 6:17).

Solomon built a fleet of ships at Ezion-geber on the Red Sea (1Ki 9:26). His fleet sailed the Mediterranean with the Phoenician navy of King Hiram (1Ki 10:22; 2Ch 9:21). Later Jehoshaphat and Ahaziah also built ships at Ezion-geber (2Ch 20:35–37).

The Bible frequently refers to the ships of other nations (Pr 31:14; Ps 107:23). Luke's account of Paul's voyage to Rome is a good picture of the adventures at sea during NT times (Ac 27–28). See 1:500; 2:151.

BOAZ (BO-az; perhaps from Hbr term for "strength").

1. A wealthy Bethlehemite who was a relative of Elimelech, Ruth's father-in-law. Boaz married

Ruth. They had a son, Obed, who became David's grandfather. Obed was an ancestor of Jesus (Mt 1:5). See 1:253–67, 518.
2. The left pillar in the porch of Solomon's temple (1Ki 7:21; 2Ch 3:17). See 1:359.

BODY OF CHRIST. Gk *soma christou.* Paul repeatedly describes the Church as the Body of Jesus, believers united under one head. *See* MEMBER; CHURCH; and FELLOWSHIP. See 2:398, 460–61, 466, 525, 600.

BOIL. An inflamed, open sore (Ex 9:8–11). Boils were a common symptom of leprosy (Lv 13:18–20). Hezekiah and Job suffered from boils (2Ki 20:7; cf Jb 2:7). See 1:88.

BONE. Often used figuratively to show a close relationship (Gn 2:23; Jgs 9:2; 2Sm 19:12). See 2:249, 337, 508.

BOOK. *See* WRITING.

BOOK OF THE LAW. Used at the close of Deuteronomy, referring to all or part of that book (Dt 29:21). However, in later Scripture, it may refer to the five books written by Moses. See 1:189–90, 209, 389, 403, 753.

BOOTH. A temporary hut or shelter, usually made of tree branches (Gn 33:17; Lv 23:34, 42; Jb 27:18; Is 1:8). *See also* HOMES; BOOTHS, FEAST OF. See 1:253, 887.

BOOTHS, FEAST OF. The third yearly festival of the Jewish people, commemorating the tent life of Israel. The people celebrated this festival by building booths or huts from the branches of fruit and palm trees (Ex 23:16; Lv 23:34–43; Dt 16:13–15; 31:10–13; Ne 8). Other names for this festival are the Feast of Ingathering, the Feast of the Lord, and the Feast of Tabernacles (Ex 23:16; Lv 23:34, 39). See 1:107, 168, 434–35, 665; 2:334–35.

BOOTY. Spoils of war. It consisted of everything of value in a conquered town. At the conquest of Canaan the Israelites were told to kill all living things and destroy all idols and the places where idols were worshiped (Nu 33:52). Often the army took the spoils and divided them among themselves, the rest of the people, and the Levites (Nu 31:26–47). David made a law that the troops who guarded the baggage should share in the spoils of war equally with those who did the fighting (1Sm 30:21–25). See 1:222, 279; 2:789.

BOTTLE. *See* FLASK.

BOTTOMLESS PIT. *See* ABYSS. See 2:772, 785.

BOW.
1. *See* ARCHERY.
2. A bodily posture that demonstrates respect or obedience to God, an idol, an earthly ruler, or another person (Gn 43:28; Ex 18:7; 2Sm 1:2; 2Ki 5:18, Mi 6:6). See 1:80, 179, 559, 838.

BOWING. A combination of bending the knee and moving the head forward. Bowing was a respectful way to greet someone (Gn 23:7; Php 2:10). See 1:45, 559; 2:114, 382, 386, 585.

BOX.
1. A flask or jar for holding oil or perfume (Is 3:20). *See also* FLASK.
2. A container for giving offering (Mk 12:41, 43; Lk 21:1).
3. A container fastened to the cart on which the Philistines returned the ark (1Sm 6:8, 11, 15).
4. A container for holding bones. See 2:374, 809–10.

BOZRAH (BOZ-rah). A city in Edom (1Ch 1:43–44). Both Amos and Jeremiah predicted its destruction (Jer 49:13, 22; Am 1:12). Today it is called Buseirah.

BRAMBLE. *See* THORNS AND THISTLES.

BRANCH. A title applied to the Messiah as David's offspring (Jer 23:5; 33:15; Zec 3:8; 6:12). A branch is also a symbol of prosperity (Gn 49:22). See 1:753, 769, 987–91.

BREASTPIECE, BREASTPLATE.
1. A sacred article of dress worn by the high priest (Ex 28; 29:5).
2. Armor designed to protect the body in battle (1Ki 22:34; Is 59:17; Rv 9:9). See 1:310–11.

BRIMSTONE. *See* SULFUR.

BROOK. A small stream that usually flows only during the rainy season (Dt 2:13). The Kishon and Kidron were brooks (1Ki 18:40; 2Sm 15:23). See 1:295, 332, 366.

BROOM. A bush with many, almost leafless, branches and pinkish white flowers (1Ki 19:4–5; Jb 30:4; Ps 120:4).

BRONZE SERPENT. When the children of Israel complained in the wilderness against God and Moses, God sent fiery serpents against them. Many of the people died. Then God told Moses to make a serpent of bronze (or copper) and set it on a pole. Whenever a person who had been bitten by a snake looked at this bronze serpent, he or she lived (Nu 21:5–9). This bronze serpent was a type of Christ (Jn 3:14). See 1:139, 145–46.

BROTHER. Heb *'achim;* Gk *adelphoi.*

1. A male who shares the same parents or the same mother or father as his siblings (Gn 27:6; 38:1; Jgs 8:19). See 1:23, 28–32, 49–50, 119–20; 2:85–86, 758–59.
2. A male relative, such as a nephew or cousin (Mt 12:46).
3. Someone from the same tribe (Nu 8:26; Ne 3:1).
4. Someone from the same country (Mt 5:47). See 1:141.
5. A friend or companion (Jb 6:15; Ne 5:10). See 2:229.
6. Someone who is greatly loved (2Sm 1:26). See 1:682, 690.
7. A peer (Mt 23:8).
8. All men (Mt 5:22; 18:35). See 1:638.
9. A fellow Christian (Rm 8:29; Eph 6:23). By grace and in Baptism, the Father adopts Christians into the sonship that belongs to Jesus by nature (Gal 3:25–29). This makes people unrelated by blood true siblings to one another. See 1:412; 2:201, 205, 397, 564, 638.
10. A co-worker in Christ's mission (Php 4:21), whether male or female.
11. A man who led a congregation (1Co 12:1).

BROTHERS OF THE LORD. James, Joseph, Simon, and Judas are referred to as the Lord's brothers (Mt 13:55). Sisters of Jesus are also mentioned in Mt 13:56. There are differences of opinion as to whether these are full brothers and sisters, cousins, or children of Joseph by a former marriage. See 2:360, 676–80.

BUCKLER. *See* ARMOR; ARMS.

BULL. A male ox or cow (Ps 22:12; Ezk 43:19). Oxen were used for plowing, threshing, pulling wagons, and bearing burdens (Nu 7:3; Dt 22:10; 25:4; 1Ch 12:40). People also ate them and sacrificed them (Dt 14:4; 1Ki 1:9). See 1:78, 116–17, 848; 2:664.

BULRUSH. A marsh plant, such as the papyrus, or a swamp plant, such as the reed or rush (Ex 2:3; cf Is 18:2; 19:15).

BURDEN. Hbr *massa'* (cf Zec 9:1; 12:1). Also translated "oracle" (Is 13:1; Mal 1:1), emphasizing that what the prophets spoke were words of the Lord and not their own words. The translation "burden" emphasizes that the prophet must deliver a word of judgment on the Lord's enemies (Jer 23:33). See 1:444, 664, 890; 2:198, 290, 398, 507, 589–90, 748–49.

BURIAL. The people of Israel nearly always buried their dead, usually within 24 hours. When a person died, his or her body was washed, wrapped in a cloth or closely bound in bands, and, if the person had been wealthy, anointed with spices and perfumes (Jer 34:5; Mt 27:59; Jn 11:44; 12:7; Ac 9:37). The body was then carried on a bier to the grave (2Sm 3:31; Lk 7:14). Although holes in the ground were sometimes used as places of burial, often the grave was a cave or hole cut out of rock (Gn 25:9–10; Mt 27:60).

When a person died, friends expressed their grief by loudly weeping and wailing (Mk 5:38). Often professional mourners were hired (Jer 9:17). See 1:27, 32, 53; 2:248–49, 337, 406, 805–7, 809, 813.

BURNT OFFERING. *See* SACRIFICE. See 1:103, 117, 122–23, 762; 2:67–68.

BUSHEL. *See* MEASURES 2d.

BY FAITH. Gk *ek pisteos*. Paul's use of this expression is based on Hab 2:4; cf Rm 1:17; Gal 3:11; Heb 10:38. Faith serves as the instrument of key gifts in Paul's teaching: life, justification, righteousness, and blessing. See 1:216, 954–55; 2:437, 510, 662, 691.

BY NO MEANS. Gk *me genoito*, "may it not be." See 1:111.

BYWAY. Paths off the main roads. Byways were traveled to escape danger (Jgs 5:6). Figuratively, byways or side roads describe departure from the way of God (cf Jer 18:15).

C

CAESAR (SEE-zur). A title given to all the Roman emperors after Julius Caesar (Mt 22:17; Jn 19:15; Ac 17:7). The NT mentions by name Caesars Augustus, Tiberius, and Claudius (Lk 2:1; 3:1; Ac 11:28). Nero, the Caesar under whom Peter and Paul were martyred, is also referred to in Ac 25:8. See 1:328, 552; 2:186, 236, 391.

CAESAREA (Ses-ah-REE-ah; "for Caesar"). A city built between 25 to 13 BC by Herod the Great. Located about 23 miles south of Mount Carmel, Caesarea was the Roman capital of Israel. It was the home of Cornelius, in whose house Peter preached to the Gentiles (Ac 10:1, 24; 11:11). Philip also stopped in Caesarea at the end of his preaching tour (Ac 8:40).

Paul visited Caesarea a number of times (Ac 9:30; 18:22; 21:8, 16). The Roman commander at Jerusalem also sent Paul to Caesarea to be heard by Felix. From there Paul was sent to Rome (Ac 23:23, 33; 25). Today Caesarea is known as Kayseri. See 2:195, 274, 367, 388–89, 534, 813.

CAESAREA PHILIPPI (Ses-ah-REE-ah fi-LIP-igh). A city at the foot of Mount Hermon. Philip the Tetrarch, Herod's son, enlarged the city and called it Caesarea Philippi to distinguish it from the other Caesarea. Peter made his well-known confession, "You are the Christ, the Son of the living God," in Caesarea Philippi (Mt 16:13–20). See 2:240.

CAIAPHAS (KAY-yah-fahs). The son-in-law of Annas. Caiaphas was the high priest during Jesus' public ministry and crucifixion (Mt 26:3, 57; Lk 3:2). After Jesus raised Lazarus from the dead, Caiaphas advocated putting Jesus to death. Caiaphas was afraid that the people would believe in Jesus, which would lead to the destruction of their holy place and nation by the Romans (Jn 11:45–50). So he and the chief priest planned Jesus' death (Mt 26:3–5). After Jesus' arrest, He was brought before Caiaphas. Caiaphas declared Jesus guilty of blasphemy and sent Him to the Roman governor Pilate with the recommendation that Jesus be put to death (Mt 26:57; Jn 18:28).

Caiaphas also took part in the trial of Peter and John (Ac 4:6–22). See 2:301–2, 310, 809–10.

CAIN (KAYN; from term for "acquire"). The oldest son of Adam and Eve. He made his living by farming. Cain killed his brother Abel (Gn 4). *See also* ABEL 1. See 1:26, 32, 50; 2:762.

CALEB (KAY-luhb; "dog"). The son of Jephunneh and one of the twelve spies whom Moses sent into Canaan (Nu 32:12). When the spies returned, only Caleb and Joshua encouraged the people to take the land (Nu 13:6–14:9). Because of his faithfulness, Caleb was allowed to enter the Holy Land. When the land was distributed, Caleb received Hebron (Jsh 14). See 1:129, 138, 213, 219.

CALENDAR. *See* TIME. See 1:107, 473–74, 790; 2:224, 311.

CALF. A young bull or cow. The Hebrews considered a "fattened calf" to be the best possible food (Gn 18:7; 1Sm 28:24; Lk 15:23).

While Moses was receiving the tablets of the Law on Mount Sinai, Aaron made an image of a calf out of gold and set it up in the wilderness for the people to worship (Ex 32:4).

Jeroboam also set up two golden calves, one at Bethel and one at Dan (1Ki 12:28–29). At first these images were viewed as symbols of God, but soon they came to be worshiped as common idols. Calf worship was denounced (Hos 8; 10; 13). See 1:73, 78, 167–68; 2:423.

CALL (ON). Hbr *qara'*, "to call upon," "name," or "summon." "Call on God's name" describes speaking God's name in prayer, repentance, or consulting the Lord by Urim and Thummim, administered by the high priest. Gk *(epi)kaleo*, "to summon," and thereby "to choose." Common LXX rendering of a Hbr expression for prayer. See Jth 6:21; Wis 7:7; Ecclus 46:5, 16; Bar 3:7. See 1:576, 583, 769–70; 2:251, 253, 288, 397.

CALVARY (KAL-vah-ree). *See* GOLGOTHA. See 1:113, 144, 206.

CAMEL. In Bible times one-humped Arabian camels or dromedaries were valued animals. Some were used as pace animals and were frequently found in caravans, carrying heavy loads of goods across the hot, sandy land (2Ki 8:9). Others were bred for riding, often traveling 60 to 75 miles per day (Is 66:20).

Camels were considered a source of wealth (Jgs 7:12; 2Ch 14:15; Is 30:6). Abraham had camels among his livestock (Gn 12:16). Job had 3,000 camels before he lost everything and 6,000 after God restored his fortune (Jb 1:3; 42:12).

Because camels were unclean, the Israelites were not allowed to eat them (Lv 11:4). They did make clothing, however, from the camels' hair (2Ki 1:8; Zec 13:4; Mt 3:4).

CAMP, ENCAMPMENT. The place where an army or other body of transient people set up their tents (Ex 14:9; 1Sm 4:1, 5; 2Ki 7:7). Camps were erected both for short periods of time and as temporary dwellings.

When the Israelites were in the wilderness, they kept clean and orderly camps. They patterned their camps after a square, with the tabernacle and Levites in the center and an equal number of tribes on each side (Nu 1:47–2:34; 3:14–39). See 1:29, 127, 131–40, 155, 795; 2:801.

CANA (KAY-nah). A town in Galilee near Nazareth. Jesus performed two miracles here (Jn 2:1–11; 4:46). See 2:306, 327, 333.

CANAAN (KAY-nuhn; from term for "lowlands").

1. One of Ham's sons (Gn 10:6). His descendants occupied Canaan and took their name from that country (Gn 10:15–19).
2. Canaan, one of the old names for Israel, was the country between the Jordan and Mediterranean (Ex 6:4; Nu 34:3–12). After the people of Israel captured the land, it was referred to as the Holy Land (Zec 2:12). See 1:17, 25–32, 158–89, 199–242, 271–73; 2:799.

CANAANITE (KAY-nahn-ight). A person who lived in Canaan (Gn 10:18–20; Nu 13:29; Jsh 11:3). The Canaanites were talented people who early developed arts and sciences. Their languages included Phoenician and Ugaritic. Their religion, however, was immoral, centering around war gods and fertility goddesses. They worshiped such well-known deities as El, Baal, Astarte, and Asherah. See 1:166–242, 506, 647; 2:200.

CANDACE. Title of a queen of Ethiopia mentioned in Ac 8:27. See 2:41.

CANON. The collection of books of the Bible accepted by the Church as genuine and inspired. By NT times the 39 books of the OT were already recognized as canonical (cf Rm 3:2). Although a few of the 27 NT books were questioned for a while, they gradually found their way into the canon. See 1:xxvi–xxviii; 2:6–10, 156–64.

CAPERNAUM (kah-PUR-nay-uhm; "town of Nahum"). A city on the northwest coast of the Sea of Galilee (Mt 4:13; Jn 6:24). Capernaum had its own customs station and synagogue (Mt 9:9; Lk 7:5). It was the headquarters of Jesus and the apostles, and the scene of many miracles (Mt 9:1; Mk 2:1). See 1:935; 2:328, 244, 278, 319, 808.

CAPPADOCIA (Kap-ah-DO-shi-ah). A province in the eastern part of Asia Minor. People from Cappadocia were present when the Holy Spirit descended upon the disciples at the Feast of Pentecost (Ac 2:9). Later Peter wrote a letter to the exiles of the Dispersion that included those who lived in Cappadocia (1Pt 1:1). See 2:645, 701.

CAPTAIN. As a military title, *captain* was applied broadly to any officer who held a leadership position, from a commander-in-chief to a commander of the guard (Gn 37:36). The captain of the temple was not a military officer but a priest who was in charge of the temple guard (Ac 4:1). See 1:368, 758; 2:813.

CAPTIVITY. Hbr *galah*; Gk *aixmalosia*. Through Moses (Dt 28:41), the Lord warned that Israel would be taken from the Promised Land if they disobeyed the covenant (*see* PORTION). The prophets later announced the captivity, and Jeremiah gave it special emphasis. In the OT, Hbr *galuth* was used almost exclusively for the Judean exiles who suffered the Babylonian captivity. Tobit, however, describes the experience of the Northern Kingdom of Israel using the equivalent Gk term (3:4, 15; 13:6; 14:5). Over a period of years the 10 tribes of the Northern Kingdom (Israel) were taken prisoner by the Assyrian kings Tiglath-pileser, Shalmaneser, Sargon II, and Esarhaddon (2Ki 15:29; 17:3, 6; 19:37; Is 20:1). The Southern Kingdom (Judah) was taken captive in stages by King Nebuchadnezzar of Babylon (2Ki 24:10–17; 25:8–11; 2Ch 36:17–21). The prophets Ezra and Nehemiah describe the return of God's captive people to their homeland. See 1:lxxxiv–lxxxviii, 381, 402–3, 439, 745, 896; 2:62–63.

In the NT, unbelievers are described as captives of the devil and his kingdom (Gal 4:3, 8). But Jesus announced that He came to set people free from the devil and sin (Lk 4:18). By His death and resurrection Jesus captured sin, death, and the devil (Eph 4:8). See 2:214, 524, 534–36.

CARAVAN (KAR-ah-van). A group of traveling merchants, pilgrims, or others who joined together for a mutual purpose or for protection. These people often used camels, donkeys, and horses to carry their goods (Gn 37:25). They followed regular routes, such as the one leading from Damascus across the Jezreel Valley to the Mediterranean Sea (Jgs 8:11; Jb 6:18–19). See 1:621; 2:66, 196.

CARBUNCLE (KAHR-bung-k'l). A precious gem in the high priest's breastpiece (Ex 28:17; Ezk 28:13; Is 54:12).

CARCHEMISH (KAHR-kuh-mish). A Hittite city on the west bank of the Euphrates River (2Ch 35:20; Is 10:9). In 605 BC, Nebuchadnezzar of Babylon defeated Egypt in a battle at Carchemish (Jer 46:2). See 1:413, 751, 824, 844, 947.

CARMEL (KAHR-mel; "garden").

1. A mountainous range of hills in the territory of Asher in Israel. It averages 1,500 feet in height and runs 12 to 15 miles in length. This range forms the southwest boundary of the Jezreel Valley, and on its northwestern end, it juts into the Mediterranean Sea (Jsh 19:26; 2Ki 2:25; Jer 50:19). Elijah

defeated 850 heathen prophets on Mount Carmel (1Ki 18). See 1:213, 266.

2. A town in Judah about 7 miles southeast of Hebron (Jsh 15:55). It was the home of Nabal, the first husband of David's wife Abigail (1Sm 25:2–44). See 1:211, 276.

CARPENTER. A general term for a builder who worked in wood, stone, and metal (2Sm 5:11; 2Ch 24:12; Is 44:13). Joseph, Mary's husband, was a carpenter (Mt 13:55; Mk 6:3). *See also* TRADE.

CART. A two-wheeled vehicle for carrying people or freight. Carts were pulled usually by oxen (1Sm 6:7–16; Am 2:13).

CASSIA. (KASH-i-ah). An aromatic wood used in anointing oil. It probably tasted like cinnamon (Ex 30:24; Ps 45:8; Ezk 27:19).

CASTLE. A fortified building or stronghold (Ne 7:2; cf 1Sm 22:4–5). See 1:560.

CATTLE. A term broadly used in the OT to include large or small domestic animals, such as horned cattle, horses, donkeys, camels, sheep, and goats (Lv 19:19; Nu 32:26; Ps 50:10; Jb 1:3). Cf "livestock" in Gn 1:24–25; Ex 12:29; Nu 20:19. See 1:90–91, 307, 505, 664.

CAVE. A hollow place or cavern in the side of a hill or cliff. Caves are often found in areas of limestone, of which Israel has a great deal. The people in Bible times used caves as dwellings, as places of refuge, and for burials (Gn 19:30; 23:1–20; 49:29; Jgs 6:2; cf 1Sm 14:11; Mt 27:60). *See also* HOMES. See 1:53, 210–11, 276; 2:804–7, 809–10.

CEDAR. Most often the cedar referred to in Scriptures is the tall tree found in Lebanon. The wood of this tree was prized for its use in palaces, temples, idols, and ship masts (2Sm 5:11; 1Ki 5:5–6; Is 44:14–15; Ezk 27:5). See 1:132, 621, 691, 802.

CENCHREAE (SEN-kri-ee). A harbor of Corinth visited by Paul (Ac 18:18). Phoebe was a deaconess or servant of the Christian church there (Rm 16:1). See 2:388, 420, 441, 813.

CENSER. A container for burning incense. Censers for the tabernacle were made of copper; those for the temple were made of gold (Lv 16:12; Nu 16:39; Ezr 1:9).

CENSUS. A numbering and registration of people. The OT records several censuses (Ex 30:12–14; Nu 1:2–3; 26:51; 1Ki 5:15; 1Ch 21:1–6; 27:24; 2Ch 2:17–18). The NT mentions the Roman censuses in Lk 2:1 and Ac 5:37. See 1:129–36, 296, 316; 2:297–99, 405.

CENTURION (sen-TYOO-ri-ahn; "hundred"). A Roman officer in command of 100 soldiers (Mk 15:39; Lk 7:1–10; Ac 10:1). See 2:221–22, 279, 284.

CEPHAS (SEE-fuhs; "rock"). The Aramaic name Jesus gave to Peter (Jn 1:42; 1Co 1:12). See 2:302, 450–51, 503.

CHAFF (CHAF). The leftover part of winnowed grain (Jb 21:18; Ps 1:4; Zep 2:2); also straw or dry grass (cf Is 5:24; Jer 23:28). Figuratively, the word *chaff* often refers to something that has no value or is bad (Mt 3:12).

CHALDEA (kal-DEE-ah). Originally the southern part of Babylonia on the Persian Gulf; later, nearly all of Babylonia (Is 48:20; Jer 50:10; Ezk 11:24). See 1:815, 847, 953.

CHALDEANS (kal-DEE-ahnz). People who came from or lived in Chaldea. Their roots can be traced beyond 1000 BC. In the eighth century BC, Chaldean kings conquered and ruled Babylon and began to extend their rule over the then-known world (2Ki 24:2; 25; Is 13:19–22; Jer 21:4–14; Dn 1:4). Chaldeans were noted astronomers (Dn 2:2; 4:7). *See also* BABYLONIA. See 1:795, 804, 847, 947–54; 2:71.

CHALKSTONE. Limestone rock used to make mortar (Is 27:9). *See also* LIME.

CHAMBERLAIN (CHAYM-bur-lin). An important officer, good at keeping secrets, who served a ruler (2Ki 23:11; Ac 12:20). The chamberlain looked after the private chambers or rooms of the ruler's palace.

CHARIOT. A two-wheeled vehicle for travel and war (Gn 41:43; 46:29; 2Ki 5:9; Ac 8:28). Israel's enemies used chariots (Ex 14:7; Jsh 11:4; Jgs 4:3; 1Sm 13:5). Beginning with the time of David, Israel also used them (2Sm 8:4; 1Ki 9:19; Is 31:1). See 1:90, 217, 314–15, 804–5, 845; 2:701.

CHARMER. *See* MAGIC.

CHASTISEMENT (CHAS-tiz-muhnt). Refers to the punishment endured by Christ for sin (Is 53:5) as well as the suffering endured by Israel at God's hand (Lm 4:6). See 1:241, 989; 2:709.

CHEBAR (KEE-bahr). A river of Chaldea on whose banks Ezekiel had visions (Ezk 1:1, 3). See 1:795.

CHEDORLAOMER (ked-or-la-O-mer; possibly "servant of [god] Lagamar"). The king of Elam against whom Abraham fought (Gn 14). See 1:25.

CHEMOSH (KEE-mahsh; possibly means "subdue"). The god of Moab who was worshiped with child sacrifices (Nu 21:29; 2Ki 3:27). To please one of his foreign wives, Solomon built a place to worship Chemosh (1Ki 11:7). Later King Josiah destroyed this place of idol worship (2Ki 23:13). See 1:324.

CHERETHITES (KER-i-thights). A Philistine tribe that lived in southwest Canaan (1Sm 30:14; Ezk 25:16). Some were members of David's guard (2Sm 8:18; 15:18). See 1:281.

CHERITH (KEE-rith). A brook east of the Jordan where Elijah hid during the first part of the famine he had predicted (1Ki 17:3, 5). See 1:332, 343.

CHERUB (CHER-uhb). The plural form of this word is cherubim (CHER-ah-bim). The Bible pictures cherubim as winged, heavenly beings with the faces of men and the bodies of lions. Ezekiel describes them as four-winged and four-faced (Ezk 1:5–12; 10:1–22). See 1:800–801.

When God drove Adam and Eve out of the Garden of Eden, He put cherubim at the entrance of Eden to guard it (Gn 3:24). To adorn the ark of the covenant, craftsmen made two golden cherubim and placed them on top of it (Ex 25:18–22; 37:7–9; Heb 9:5). Cherubim were also embroidered on the curtain and veil of the tabernacle (Ex 26:1, 31). Solomon placed two cherubim in the Most Holy Place in the temple (1Ki 6:23–28; 8:7). See 1:75, 359–60.

The Bible pictures the Lord as living between cherubim and as riding on them (Nu 7:89; 2Sm 22:11; Ps 18:10; 80:1). See 2:492–93.

CHIASM. A literary device found in both Hebrew and Greek, in which words or content are first presented and then represented in reverse order. See for example the listing of "heart . . . ears . . . eyes" in Is 6:10a followed by the reverse order of "eyes . . . ears . . . hearts" in Is 6:10b. Such structure likely helped speakers remember points in the texts and recite them with rhetorical force. This structure may also appear across larger texts such as chapters and books.

CHIEF. Hbr *nasi'*; like "head," used variously with "father's house," "tribe," and with military units. See 1:71, 151, 281; 2:204, 336, 709.

CHIEF OFFICERS OF THE TEMPLE. The high priest and other temple officials. Sadducees seem to have dominated these positions during the first centuries BC and AD. *See* SADDUCEES and ZADOKITES.

CHIEF PRIEST. *See* PRIEST.

CHILEAB (KIL-i-ab). A son of King David and Abigail (2Sm 3:3).

CHILION (KIL-i-on; "pining," "frail"). A son of Elimelech and Naomi (Ru 1:2). See 1:257.

CHINNERETH, CHINNEROTH (KIN-i-reth, KIN-i-rahth; "harp").

1. A fortified city of Naphtali on the northwest shore of the Sea of Galilee (Jsh 19:35).
2. The region around the city of Chinnereth. It is often identified with the Plain of Gennesaret (1Ki 15:20; Mt 14:34).
3. An old name for the Sea of Galilee (Nu 34:11; Jsh 11:2). *See also* GALILEE, SEA OF. See 1:213, 854.

CHLOE (KLO-ee; "green grass"). A Christian woman well-known to the Christians at Corinth (1Co 1:11). See 2:452–53.

CHOOSE. Hbr *bachar*, "select." The Hbr root may mean "to look at carefully." The LXX translators use Gk *eklektos* freely for a wide variety of Hbr terms, esp in Ezekiel. Moses uses this term often in Deuteronomy, where the Lord explains that He chose Israel to be His holy people (Dt 14:2; Gn 12:1; cf Ecclus 47:22). His choice was based on His great love, not on Israel's merits (Dt 7:6–8). The idea is closely related to holiness (cf Ecclus 49:6). The Greek term in the Apocrypha also describes select troops (1Macc 9:5). Key NT term used of Christians (1Th 1:4; 2Th 2:13; 1Pt 1:1–2; Rv 17:14). *See also* CHOSEN. See 1:22, 158, 175–77, 804; 2:287, 384.

CHOSEN. Key NT description of Christians (1Th 1:4; 2Th 2:13; 1Pt 1:1–2; Rv 17:14). Although God chose us "before the foundation of the world" (Eph 1:4), His choice was not arbitrary. He chose us to be saved by Christ and in union with Christ, who Himself is God's "Chosen One" (Lk 9:35; 1Pt 2:4–6). God chose us in love, not anger or judgment; Paul speaks only of a choosing for redemption. Cf Rm 8:29–33; 11:5; Jn 15:16. See 1:15, 32, 183, 471; 2:377, 427, 527, 564, 573, 710.

CHRIST (KRIGHST). *See* JESUS CHRIST; MESSIAH.

CHRISTIAN (KRIS-chuhn; "belonging to Christ"). A follower of Christ. The disciples were first called Christians at Antioch, Syria (Ac 11:26; 26:28; 1Pt 4:16).

CHRIST JESUS. Used c 80 times in the NT, always by the apostle Paul. On its meaning, *see* JESUS CHRIST. See 2:603.

CHRONICLES, FIRST AND SECOND BOOK OF (KRAHN-i-k'lz). See 1:381–421.

CHRONOLOGY (kro-NAHL-o-jee). The science of dating biblical events. To arrive at these dates, scholars use statements in the Bible, for instance, Lk 3:1–2, as well as historical events and dates. The chronology of a man named Ussher is one well-known system of dating biblical events. However, many scholars do not agree with all of his dates.

Dates often given for key events are approximately 2100 to 1800 BC for the time of the Patriarchs, 1446 (or sometimes 1290) BC for the exodus, 1048 to 587 BC for the period of the kings, around 740 to 600 BC for the captivity of Israel, 587 to 538 BC for the captivity of Judah, and 2 BC for the birth of Christ. *See also* TIME. See 1:lxxiii–xcix.

CHURCH. Gk *ekklesia*, "ones called out" for a public gathering. The term would not immediately have sacred association in the minds of Gentile converts; it could simply mean "assembly." The Church is the collected gathering of God's people. In the OT, the word used for "church" means assembly or congregation (Dt 23:2; Ezr 10:8; Ps 149:1). The NT speaks of the Church both as the Christians gathered in a specific place and as all Christians everywhere of all time (Mt 16:18; Ac 5:11; 8:1; 1Co 10:32). It is most often used by Paul for a local congregation, but also for the universal Church (Eph 1:22).

The Church, the Body of Christ, draws its life and nourishment from the Gospel in the Word and Sacraments. It passes on its life by preaching and sharing the Sacraments (Mt 28:19, 20; Ac 20:28; 1Co 4:17; 2Co 8:18).

According to the NT, the Church belongs to God in Christ (Ac 20:28; 1Co 1:2; Gal 1:22; 1Th 2:14). It is described as the fellowship of God's people, the new Israel, the Bride of Christ, the Body of Christ, and a building of which Jesus Christ is the chief Cornerstone (Rm 12:5; Gal 6:16; Eph 2:20–22; 4:4; 5:25–33; 1Pt 2:9). *See also* FELLOWSHIP. See 1:xxxvii–xxxviii, 615–16, 692–93; 2:187, 201, 374–76, 383–87, 450–55, 489, 524–25, 530–31, 593–95, 600, 782–86, 823–25.

CIRCUMCISION (sur-kuhm-SIZH-uhn; "cutting around"). Removal of the foreskin of the penis. God instituted the rite of circumcision upon Abraham and his descendants (Gn 17:10). It showed that He would be their God and that they were to belong to Him, worshiping and obeying only Him. While in the wilderness, Moses made circumcision a legal institution (Lv 12:3; Jn 7:22–23). The Hebrew people looked down upon those who were not circumcised (Jgs 14:3; 15:18; 1Sm 14:6). Some other nations, such as the Egyptians, also practiced circumcision. See 1:30, 96.

Christians in the NT era refused to force Gentiles to submit to circumcision (Ac 15:1–5; Gal 5:2). See 2:296, 376, 425, 500–5.

God circumcises the heart by purifying it so that it will be able and willing to love God (Dt 10:16; 30:6). See 1:178.

CISTERN. A hole dug in the earth or rock to hold rainwater or water from a spring (Pr 5:15; Ec 12:6; Is 36:16; Jer 2:13). Empty cisterns were sometimes used as prisons (cf Gn 37:22–24). See 1:282, 767.

CITIZEN, CITIZENSHIP.

1. An inhabitant of a city or country (Lk 15:15). See 1:401; 2:708.
2. A Roman citizen had special rights, including the right to appeal to the emperor. The rights of Roman citizenship belonged to those who were born Roman citizens, who purchased citizenship, or who received citizenship through special service or favor (Ac 16:37–39; 22:25–29; 23:27). See 2:379, 417, 539.
3. Christians are citizens of heaven, together with the saints (Eph 2:19; Php 3:20). See 1:354; 2:208, 545, 709.

CITY OF GOD. *See* JERUSALEM; ZION.

CITY OF REFUGE. *See* REFUGE, CITIES OF.

CLAUDIUS (KLAW-di-uhs). The Roman emperor from AD 41 to 54. Claudius took over after Caligula. He banished all the Jews from Rome (Ac 18:2). See 2:195, 295, 418, 811–12.

CLAUDIUS LYSIAS (KLAW-di-uhs-LIS-i-uhs). *See* LYSIAS, CLAUDIUS.

CLEAN. Hbr *tahor*, "pure, genuine"; frequently translated by Gk *katharizo*. An essential concept governing the Israelites' relations with Gentiles, as occurs especially in 1Macc and 2Macc. The Lord gave Israel specific laws, customs, and rituals that distinguished it from other nations. These practices often involved washing or eating things that were regarded as clean and avoiding things that were regarded as unclean. However, the laws were not exclusively devoted to hygiene. These matters receive special attention in Lv 11–15. *See* HOLY. (Modern Hbr uses "kosher" ["legal, permitted"] to describe this idea.) "Clean" designates that which is acceptable to God; "unclean" refers to the opposite, that which cannot be presented to God or used by human beings. It has nothing to do with hygiene and everything to do with status before God. Unclean food (such as pork) must not be eaten; unclean people (due to disease or a variety of other conditions) cannot enter the temple or touch others; unclean animals will not be offered as sacrifices. Regarding NT use, *see* BAPTISM. See 1:102–12, 118–19, 137–44, 591, 810–11; 2:97–98, 207, 246, 426, 627, 662.

CLEOPAS (KLEE-o-pas; shortened form of "Cleopatras," which means "of renowned father"). One of the two disciples to whom Christ appeared on the way to Emmaus (Lk 24:18). See 2:286.

CLOPAS (KLO-pahs; possibly a Semitic name). Another name for Alphaeus. He was the husband of one of the Marys who stood beside the cross (Jn 19:25).

CLOUD. Most of the time when the Bible refers to clouds, it is speaking figuratively. Clouds show God's power and wisdom (Ps 135:7; Na 1:3). Sometimes they stand for a great number or for great trouble or danger (Is 44:22; 60:8; Ezk 30:3; Heb 12:1). Clouds are also a sign of God's presence (Is 19:1). See 1:137, 341–42, 834–35; 2:190, 202, 314.

COAT. *See* DRESS.

COCK. A male chicken. Cockcrowing is mentioned in Mt 26:34, Mk 13:35, and Lk 22:34. It refers to the time between midnight and 3 a.m. See 2:260–61.

COHORT. Roman military unit (Ac 10:1; 21:31; 27:1). *See also* ARMY; BAND.

COL-HOZEH (kahl-HO-ze; "all-seeing"). Baruch's father (Ne 11:5).

COLONY. A settlement of Roman citizens in a conquered territory (Ac 16:12). Often the colonists were retired Roman soldiers who settled in places where they could keep the enemies of the empire in check. See 2:442, 539, 625.

COLOSSAE (ko-LAHS-ee). An old city of Phrygia. Paul began a church at Colossae on his third missionary trip (Col 1:2). See 2:234, 522, 551–52, 635.

COLOSSIANS, LETTER OF PAUL TO THE (ko-LAHSH-ahnz). See 2:551–61.

COMFORT. Hbr *nacham*, "to be sorry," "to regret," or "to pity," and numerous other Hbr terms. Gk *parakaleo*, "encourage," "feel sorry." The stimulus described leads to acts of care for those who are hurt. Isaiah especially emphasizes that the Lord comforts His people (cf Is 40:1; 49:13; 51:3, 12, 19). Often means to encourage or exhort in the Maccabean books (*Theological Dictionary of the NT* 5:778; cf 1Macc 12:9). In Josephus the term can mean an encouraging summons and was used for calling on God in prayer. On Jesus' unique use for the Holy Spirit, see Jn 14:16, 26; 15:26; 16:7. *See also* REPENTANCE; RELENT. See 1:511, 521–22, 591–92, 609, 740–41, 936, 958; 2:330, 336, 489, 628.

COMING. Gk *parousia*; commonly described a royal visit. Used 18 times in the NT for Christ's reappearing in glory for the Last Day. See 2:580–82, 585, 786–87.

COMMANDMENTS. Hbr *mitswah*; *pequdim*. Gk *entole* in LXX. Philo and Josephus seldom use the term, preferring "law." Common in Ecclus (cf ch 29). The Ten Commandments served as major categories of the Law under which other commands could be arranged. Rabbis mention 613 commandments in the Law of Moses, which were subdivided as prescriptions and prohibitions. *See also* DECALOGUE. See 1:71–72, 167; 2:200, 202, 246, 300, 514–15.

COMMONWEALTH. *See* CITIZEN; CITIZENSHIP.

COMMUNION. *See* FELLOWSHIP; LORD'S SUPPER.

COMPASSION. *See* MERCY. See 1:729, 899–900; 2:189, 287, 461.

CONANIAH (kahn-ah-NIGH-ah; "Yahweh strengthens"). A Levite who was in charge of the offerings and tithes during King Hezekiah's reign (2Ch 31:12–13).

CONCUBINE (KAHNG-kyoo-bighn). A lesser wife who was often taken from among the purchased slaves or captives (Gn 16:1; Jgs 8:31). Although her status was lower, her rights were protected by the law (cf Ex 21:7–9; Dt 21:10–14). See 1:30, 239–40, 245, 342, 676.

CONDEMN. Gk *katakrino*, a legal term embracing both sentence and punishment (cf Rm 8:1). *See* JUDGE; WEIGH. See 1:37, 288, 357–58, 603, 764–65, 887–88; 2:203–4, 338–39, 430, 789.

CONDUIT. A channel cut in the rock or made underground for the purpose of moving water from one place to another (2Ki 18:17; 20:20; Is 7:3; 36:2).

CONFESS. Gk *homologeo*, lit, "to say the same thing."

1. To acknowledge publicly or make known as one's own. One confesses Christ by acknowledging one's faith in Him and His Gospel and by obeying Him (Mt 10:32; Lk 12:8; Rm 10:9). One confesses one's sins by admitting them, either publicly or privately, to God or another person (Ps 32:5; Jas 5:16; 1Jn 1:9). See 1:38, 591; 2:207, 209.
2. To acknowledge, praise, and thank God (Is 48:1; Dn 9:4). See 1:440, 732.
3. To declare openly one's faith (Heb 3:1; 4:14). See 1:219; 2:209–10, 338.

CONGREGATION. The Hebrew people viewed as one holy, religious group (Nu 16:3). Sometimes the word *congregation* refers to an assembly of all the people (Ex 12:6; 35:1); sometimes it refers to the people even when they are not assembled (Ex 12:3; Lv 4:13). The leader of the congregation often represented it (Jgs 21:10–20). It may also refer to a group of Christians gathered in a particular location. *See also* CHURCH; GREAT CONGREGATION. See 1:xxxvi–xxxvii, 101, 138, 659, 666; 2:7, 441–46, 783.

CONSCIENCE (KAHN-shuhns). A sense of right and wrong with an inner urge to do right and a guilty feeling if one goes against one's own standard of right and wrong (Ac 23:1; 1Tm 1:5; 1Pt 3:16). A "weak" conscience has a faulty norm (1Co 8:10–13). All people have a "conscience" (2Co 4:2), whether Christian (1Co 8:7) or non-Christian (Rm 2:14–16; 1Co 10:29). It is not separate from an individual but is shaped by a person's experience (2Co 5:11). See 1:93; 2:488, 494, 602–3, 748–49.

CONSECRATE (KAHN-si-krate). To set someone or something aside for God. The firstborn, whether man or beast, were set apart for the priesthood (Ex 13:2). Precious metals, persons, nations, fields, and cattle were consecrated to God (Nu 6:2–13; Jsh 6:19; 2Ch 29:33; cf "devoted" in Lv 27:28).

All Christians are consecrated or set aside for God (1Pt 2:9). There are also special consecrations. For example, Barnabas and Paul were set aside for the work of the ministry (Ac 13:2). *See also* HOLY; ORDINATION. See 1:73–74, 82, 101–2, 142–43; 2:447, 540, 593.

CONSERVATIVE. In biblical interpretation, describes those who hold to traditional interpretation and application of the Scriptures as God's very Word rather than merely as man's word. See 1:7–8.

CONTRITION (kun-TRISH-uhn). A sure knowledge of one's sin, grief because of it, and fear of God's punishment (Ps 51:17; Is 57:15; Lk 15:18; Ac 2:37). Contrition comes before forgiveness (Ps 34:18; Is 66:2). See 1:591, 733.

CONVERSION (kun-VUR-shuhn). An act of God's grace by which a sinful person is turned around and brought into Christ's kingdom (cf Col 1:13). Conversion is accomplished by the Holy Spirit, who brings the person to faith in Christ through the Word (Ps 51:13; Is 55; Jn 3:16; Ac 3:19; 11:21; 15:3; 26:18; Rm 1:16; 2Co 3:16; 1Pt 2:25). See 1:439, 520, 549, 741, 910; 2:340, 370, 823.

CONVOCATION. A meeting of the people that was called for the purpose of worshiping God (Lv 23:2–8; Nu 28:18–25). See 1:279, 659.

CORAL. The Hebrews highly valued coral, ranking it with precious stones (Jb 28:18; Lm 4:7).

CORBAN (KAWR-ban). An offering or sacrifice to God (cf Lv 1:2–3; 2:1; 3:1; Nu 7:12–17). In Mk 7:11, corban refers to money or service dedicated to God.

CORD. Cord was made of flax, animal hides, date tree fibers, or camel hair. It was used for holding together tents, binding prisoners, scourging, and making ship ropes (Ex 35:18; Jn 2:15; cf Jgs 15:13; Ac 27:32).

CORINTH (KAHR-inth). A wealthy, worldy Greek city on the isthmus connecting Peloponnesus and the mainland. Corinth was destroyed by the Romans in 146 BC and rebuilt by Caesar in 46 BC. Paul began a church there (Ac 18:1). See 2:442–44.

CORINTHIANS, FIRST LETTER OF PAUL TO THE (KO-RIN-thi-ahnz). See 2:441–77.

CORINTHIANS, SECOND LETTER OF PAUL TO THE (KO-RIN-thi-ahnz). See 2:479–97.

CORNELIUS (kawr-NEEL-yuhs; "of a horn"). A Roman centurion and the first Gentile convert (Ac 10). See 2:376, 385.

CORNERSTONE. The foundation stone laid at the corner of a building as its starting point (Jb 38:6; Is

28:16). Christ is the Cornerstone of the Church (Mt 21:42; Eph 2:20; 1Pt 2:5–7). See 1:735, 1004; 2:710.

COS (KAHS). An island in the Aegean Sea mentioned in connection with Paul's third missionary journey (Ac 21:1).

COUNCIL.

1. A group of people gathered for discussion and decision making (Gn 49:6; Ac 25:12). See 2:377.
2. The Sanhedrin and lesser courts (Mt 26:59; Mk 13:9; Ac 5:34). The Sanhedrin was the highest Jewish court during the Greek and Roman periods for enforcing Mosaic Law. It was made up of the high priest, elders, and scribes—the maximum number being 71. The high priest was in charge of this council. During Jesus' time, this council had jurisdiction over Israel (Mt 5:22; 26:59; Mk 14:55; 15:1; Lk 22:66; Jn 11:47; Ac 4:15; 6:12). *See also* APPEAL. See 2:15, 204, 248.
3. Ecumenical councils were gatherings of Early Church leaders to decide matters of doctrine and teaching. Scholars recognize seven ecumenical councils beginning with the Council of Nicaea (AD 325) and ending with the Second Council of Nicaea (AD 787). See 1:685.

COURIER. A messenger (Est 8:10, 14). See 1:754.

COURT, COURTYARD. The enclosed yard of a house, palace, or prison (2Sm 17:18; Jer 32:2), or the outer area of the tabernacle and temple (Ex 27:9; 1Ki 6:36). *See also* HOMES.

COURTS OF THE LORD. In the OT, the various courtyards that surrounded the tabernacle and temple were restricted by the various standards of holiness. To enter these holy places was to enter God's presence (2Ki 21:5; Ps 84:2). See 1:82, 639, 807, 812; 2:4, 159, 382, 401.

COVENANT (KUHV-i-nahnt). Hbr *berith;* Gk *diatheke,* "treaty," "covenant," or "disposition." Gains a nearly exclusive religious sense in Jewish writers. (E.g., Philo uses a different Gk term for non-religious agreements.) The Hbr root term never appears as a verb in the OT. The noun commonly appears with the verb "cut." In the Apocrypha, the covenant of the fathers is the basis of Israel's hope (Ecclus 44–50; 44:20; Wis 18:22). A mutual agreement between two or more tribes, nations, or individuals to do or refrain from doing something. People called upon God to witness the pacts they made with others (Gn 21:27; 31:50; Jsh 9:6; 1Sm 20:8).

The covenants God made with Noah and Abraham were pledges of His grace (Gn 9:9–16; 15:7–21). In the covenant God made with Israel, He promised to continue being their God and to care for them. They in turn promised to be His people and keep His commandments (Ex 24). The prophets spoke of a new covenant that would center in a person (Is 42:6; 49:8; Jer 31:31–34). The idea of covenant has been falsely associated with "dispensations," as though God worked differently with people at different times in history. Although the OT covenants with God have different stipulations, they are always based on God's two ways of working with mankind (cf *TLSB* note, Ex 34:6–7).

In the NT covenant, one is placed into a right relationship to God through the work of Christ (2Co 3:6–18; Heb 7:22; 8:6–13). The New Covenant stresses the forgiveness of sins accomplished through the shedding of Christ's blood (Mt 26:28; Rm 11:26–27). This leads to a new, holy life (Gal 5:22–26; Heb 8–10). *See also* BAPTISM; CIRCUMCISION; LORD'S SUPPER; PASSOVER. See 1:xliv–xlv, 23, 32–33, 71–74, 171–75, 547; 2:190, 381–82, 656, 660–61.

CREATION. An act of God by which He calls something into being (Gn 1–2). God is the one who does the creating (subject); the object of His creation is an entirely new thing. God creates by His Word (Jn 1:3; Eph 3:9; Heb 1:2). See 1:13–14, 24–26, 34–35, 43, 482, 581–85; 2:99, 387, 603, 785.

CREATOR. *See* MAKER.

CRETANS, CRETE (KREE-tahns). Crete is an island in the Mediterranean Sea about 165 miles long and 6 to 35 miles wide. Paul began a church there (Ac 27:7–13; Ti 1:5–14). It also is called Caphtor (Jer 47:4).

The people of Crete were referred to as Cretans. They were known for being good sailors and skillful archers. According to Paul they were also untruthful (Ti 1:12). Some Cretans were present in Jerusalem on the Day of Pentecost (Ac 2:11). See 1:281.

CRISPUS (KRIS-puhs; "curled"). A ruler of the synagogue at Corinth who was brought to the Christian faith by Paul (Ac 18:8; 1Co 1:14). See 2:442.

CROCUS. *See* ROSE.

CROSS. The cross commonly was found in four forms: (1) The simple upright beam; (2) St. Anthony's cross, which was in the form of the letter T; (3) St. Andrew's cross, which was in the shape of an X; and (4) the Latin cross, with the crossbeam near the upper part of the upright beam ✝. The Greek cross ✙ and the double and triple crosses were additional forms. The cross upon which Christ died may have been of the Latin type (Mt 27:32–35).

The word *cross* is often used figuratively for the Gospel, for Christ's sufferings, and for that which is suffered as, and as a result of being, a disciple (Mt 16:24; Gal 6:14; Eph 2:16). See 1:115–16, 536, 594–95; 2:204, 249, 252–54, 351–53, 462–64, 557–58, 660–61.

CRUCIFIXION (kroo-sah-FIK shuhn). A method of killing a person by hanging the person on a cross. Crucifixion was practiced by the Egyptians, the Persians, the Greeks, the Romans, and other old civilizations (Gn 40:19). Jesus was crucified by the Romans (Mt 27; Mk 15; Lk 23; Jn 19). See 2:248–49, 261–62, 284, 351–53, 464, 670.

CUBIT (KYOO-bit). *See* MEASURES 1d.

CUP. A small drinking vessel made from a horn or of clay or metal (Gn 44:2; 1Sm 16:13; Mt 26:27). Figuratively, the word *cup* is used to express one's lot in life (Ps 11:6; Mt 26:39; Mk 10:38). *See also* HOMES. See 1:191, 770; 2:314, 454, 488.

CUPBEARER. An officer who was in charge of wines and drinking vessels in a royal household (Gn 40; 41:9; 1Ki 10:5; 2Ch 9:4). Nehemiah was the cupbearer of King Artaxerxes (Ne 1:11). See 1:30, 449, 466.

CURDS. *See* FOOD.

CURSE. Translated from several Hbr terms, two in particular:

(1) Hbr *'arar*, "to bind" or "restrict," as with a law or spell. This term pronounces punishments, threats, and restrictions. (2) Hbr *qelalah*, from a word for "light" or "slight," which describes lowering of status from favored or blessed to cursed. Forms of Gk *kataraomai*. In the OT background, the Lord uses the curse terms especially to describe applications of His Law and its penalties. The opposite of bless. On the human level, to curse means to wish evil, harm, or suffering on someone (Gn 9:25; 49:7); on the divine level, it implies judgment.

All ancient people used curses (cf 1Sm 17:43) but typically regarded them as magic formulas that, if pronounced properly, would obligate the gods to harm someone.

God cursed the serpent and the earth after Adam and Eve's fall into sin (Gn 3:14, 17). God's curse was also spoken on various sins (Dt 27:15–26). Under the Mosaic Law, a person who cursed his or her parents was put to death (Lv 20:9). Christians are told to bless, not curse, those who curse them (Mt 5:11; Lk 6:28; Rm 12:14). See 1:32, 37, 139–42, 170–71, 220, 490, 511, 858; 2:247, 507–9, 512, 782.

CUSH (KUSH).

1. A son of Ham and grandson of Noah. Cush was the father of Nimrod (Gn 10:8; 1Ch 1:10).
2. The territory in the region of the Tigris and Euphrates Rivers (Gn 2:13). See 1:25.

CUSHITE (KUSH-ight). A person from Ethiopia (Nu 12:1). See 1:129, 295, 730.

CUTH, CUTHAH (KUTH, KYOO-thah). A city of Babylonia whose people worshiped Nergal. Sargon, king of Assyria, brought people from Cuth to colonize the area of Samaria that he had sacked in 722 BC (2Ki 17:24, 30).

CYPRESS. A tall fir tree (1Ki 5:8; Is 14:8).

CYPRUS (SIGH-pruhs). An island about 148 miles long and 50 miles wide in the Mediterranean Sea off the coast of Syria. It was famous for its copper.

Cyprus was the home of many Jewish people. Barnabas came from Cyprus, and Stephen preached there (Ac 4:36; 11:19–20). Paul, Barnabas, and Mark visited there on the first missionary journey (Ac 13:4; 15:39). See 1:25; 2:234, 653, 811.

CYRENE (sigh-REE-ni). The capital city of Cyrenaica (Tripoli) in northern Africa. It was colonized by Greeks (Mt 27:32; Mk 15:21; Ac 2:10). See 2:93–97.

CYRUS (SIGH-ruhs). Founder of the Persian Empire. Cyrus was a humane king. In 538 BC he catured Babylon and issued a decree allowing the captive Hebrews to go back to their native land and rebuild their temple (2Ch 36:22–23; Ezr 1:1–14; Is 44:28). Cyrus died in battle in 530 BC. *See also* DANIEL; EZRA. See 1:223, 381–83, 439, 845–46, 971–72; 2:4, 130.

D

DAGON (DA-gahn; may mean "grain" or "fish"). A pagan god with the body of a fish and the head and hands of a man. He was the god of natural powers, especially of grain. The Canaanites in Mesopotamia worshiped Dagon, and he was the national god of the Philistines. Temples were built to him at Ashdod and Gaza and in Israel (Jgs 16:21–30; 1Sm 5:1–7; 1Ch 10:10). Samson destroyed a temple to Dagon at Gaza (Jgs 16:30). See 1:239, 289.

DAMASCUS (Dah-MAS-kuhs). An old Syrian city situated on a plateau watered by the Abana and Pharpar Rivers (Gn 14:15; 2Ki 5:12). The plateau is about 2,300 feet above sea level and is at the eastern foot of the Anti-Lebanon Mountains. Damascus played an important part in biblical history. Both David and Jeroboam II captured it (2Sm 8:6; 2Ki 14:28). The rulers of Damascus who played a prominent role in the history of Israel and Judah were Rezon (1Ki 11:23–25), Ben-hadad (1Ki 15:19–20; 22:15–37; 2Ki 8:15; 2Ch 16:3), Hazael (2Ki 8:15; 13:22–25), and Rezin (2Ki 16:5, 7–8). Paul was converted to Christianity near Damascus (Ac 9:1–18). See 1:322–23, 730, 879; 2:20, 367, 375–76, 411, 810–11.

DAMNATION. Those who do not believe in Christ will be separated from God eternally and will receive awful punishment (Mt 23:33; Mk 16:16; 2Th 1:9). This punishment is described as imprisonment, outer darkness, and fire (Mt 5:25–26; 8:12; Mk 9:47–48). See 1:50, 224–25, 644; 2:214, 785.

DAN (DAN; "judge").

1. The fifth son of Jacob by Bilhah (Gn 30:5–6).
2. The tribe that descended from Dan and the territory allotted to it in Canaan (Nu 1:12, 38–39; Jgs 1:34–35). See 1:213, 342, 399; 2:798.
3. A city, formerly named Laish, which was in the extreme north of Israel. Members of the tribe of Dan captured and renamed it (Jsh 19:47; Jgs 18). See 1:6.

DAN TO BEERSHEBA. An expression used to refer to the length of Israel (Jgs 20:1; 1Ch 21:2). Dan was in the extreme north of Israel, and Beersheba was in the south. See 2:805.

DANCE. When people wanted to express joy or celebrate victory, they often danced (Jgs 11:34; Jb 21:11; Lk 15:25). Dancing as part of a religious ceremony or as an act of worship was common among the Hebrews (Ps 149:3). The women were usually the ones who danced, but occasionally men did as well (Ex 15:20; Jgs 21:21, 23). David, for instance, danced before the ark (2Sm 6:14–23). Dancing was also used for bad purposes (Ex 32:19; Mk 6:22). See 2:214.

DANIEL (DAN-yuhl; "God is judge"). A prophet who was born into a princely family of Judah around the time of Josiah's reformation. In 605 BC, when Daniel was just a young man, King Nebuchadnezzar's soldiers took him captive to Babylon (Dn 1:1, 3). Nebuchadnezzar's chief servant gave Daniel the Babylonian name Belteshazzar and trained him in the wisdom of the Chaldeans (Dn 1:4–5). Although he was in a foreign land, Daniel continued to have faith in the Lord.

God blessed Daniel with great learning and the ability to interpret dreams (Dn 1:17). Because of these abilities, Daniel held a high, powerful position in the Babylonian court under Kings Nebuchadnezzar, Belshazzar, Darius, and Cyrus. Throughout his life, Daniel showed concern for his people. See 1:373, 701–2, 823–25; 2:11, 117–18, 127–28, 135–36.

DANIEL, BOOK OF. See 1:823–49.

DARIC (DAR-ik). A Persian gold coin that had the picture of a king with a bow and javelin on one side and a square figure on the other side (1Ch 29:7; Ezr 2:69; 8:27; Ne 7:70–72). See 1:454, 977.

DARIUS (Dah-REE-uhs). A common name for the Medo-Persian rulers.

1. Darius the Mede. He was the son of Ahasuerus and the governor of Babylon under Cyrus (Dn 5:31; 9:1). He is mentioned often in the Book of Daniel (6:1, 6, 9, 25, 28; 11:1). Darius was tricked into writing a law that required everyone in the land to worship only him for 30 days. When Daniel broke this law by worshiping the Lord, he was thrown into a lions' den (Dn 6:4–24). See 1:826–27, 845–47.
2. Darius Hystaspes. He ruled from 522 to 486 BC and was the fourth and greatest king of the Persian Empire. He renewed the decree of Cyrus that allowed the Hebrews to return to their native land, and he helped them in rebuilding their temple (Ezr 4:5, 24; 5:5–7; Zec 1:1, 7; 7:1). See 1:426.
3. Darius the Persian. The last king of Persia, he reigned from 423 to 405 BC. He was defeated by Alexander the Great (Ne 12:22). See 1:429.

DAUGHTER(S) OF JERUSALEM/JUDAH/ZION. First appears chronologically in a psalm of David (Ps 9:14). Plural "daughters" occurs in Sg. Otherwise, these expressions are associated with the prophets and are very common in Lm. They may refer to the cities or towns surrounding Jerusalem (Ps 97:8) but often refer to the young women in and around Jerusalem who celebrated the victories of the city or mourned its siege and destruction. The important role of women as singers may stand behind these expressions (cf Ex 15:20–21; Jgs 11:34; 1Sm 18:6; Ps 68:25; Jer 31:4; Zep 3:14; Zec 2:10; 9:9). See 1:765, 679, 681, 786, 923.

DAVID (DAY-vid; "beloved"). The second king of Israel. He was from the tribe of Judah and was the youngest son of Jesse of Bethlehem (1Sm 16:1–13; 1Ch 2:13–15). After God rejected Saul as king, He sent the prophet Samuel to Bethlehem to anoint David as the next king (1Sm 16:13).

When Saul became troubled by evil spirits and bad moods, his servants told him to find a lyre player to soothe him. So Saul sent for David because he had heard that David had great musical gifts. David came and played the harp for Saul (1Sm 16:14–23). Later David killed Goliath, the Philistine warrior, when everyone else was afraid to fight him (1Sm 17).

David was loved by Jonathan, Saul's son, but feared and envied by Saul (1Sm 18). When Saul tried to take David's life, David fled to Gath, where he pretended to be mad (1Sm 18:1–3; 19–21; Ps 34 title). Living in a cave, David gathered 400 men around him who were unhappy with Saul's rule (1Sm 22). Among them was Abiathar the priest. With this group of men David protected the Israelites from the Philistines and bands of robbers. In return for this, the Israelites gave David and his men food (1Sm 23–25).

Informed of David's activities, Saul led his men in pursuit of David (1Sm 26). Eventually David left Judah and lived in Ziklag. Some time later the Philistines went to war with Saul. When David heard that Jonathan had been killed and that Saul had killed himself, he was sad (1Sm 27–30).

Then the tribe of Judah, to which David belonged, elected him king (2Sm 2–4). Ish-bosheth, Saul's son, was made king of the rest of the tribes. When Ish-bosheth was killed two years later, David was elected king over all of the tribes (2Sm 5). David set to work to unite the tribes into one kingdom. He took Jerusalem from the Jebusites and made it his capital. Then he defeated the Philistines (2Sm 5:17–25; 21:15–22; 1Ch 14:8–17). After this he brought the ark to Jerusalem, organized worship, and planned a beautiful temple (2Sm 6–7; 1Ch 13; 15–17; 22:7–10).

To ensure the safety of the nation of Israel and to keep it from being polluted by the idolatry of the surrounding countries, David waged war on and subdued the Moabites, Aramaens, Ammonites, Edomites, and Amalekites (2Sm 8; 10; 12:26–31).

David was a great king and a man of devout faith in God. Yet he was also a sinful human being. He committed a great sin when, after committing adultery with Bathsheba, he had her husband, Uriah, killed so that he could marry Bathsheba himself (2Sm 11:1; 12:23; 24; 1Ch 21; Ps 51). David also had many family problems (2Sm 12–19; 1Ki 1).

David reigned 40 years (2Sm 2:11; 5:4–5; 1Ch 29:27). Before he died, he said that Solomon should be the next king (1Ki 1–2).

David is referred to as the sweet psalmist of Israel (2Sm 23:1). Over 73 psalms are said to have been written by him. He was a man after God's own heart and an ancestor of Jesus (1Sm 13:14; Mt 22:41–45; Ac 13:36). See 1:280–82, 316, 399–400, 410–11, 551–53; 2:283–84, 798, 801–4.

DAVID, CITY OF.

1. A part of Jerusalem that David captured. He called it the city of David and made it his capital. It stood on the ridge south of the temple area (2Sm 5:6–9). See 1:330; 2:804.
2. Bethlehem, the birthplace or home of David (Lk 2:4). *See also* BETHLEHEM. See 1:260–61, 923–24; 2:196, 277, 804.

DAY. *See* TIME.

DAY OF ATONEMENT. *See* ATONEMENT, DAY OF.

DAY OF THE LORD.

1. In the OT, the day of the LORD refers to a day of victory for the kingdom of God, the day upon which evil is defeated. It is that day when God reveals Himself as the Lord, judges evil, and completes His work of redemption among people (Is 13:6, 9; Ezk 13:5; Zep 1:14). See 1:867–73, 895–97, 961–65.
2. In the NT, the day of the Lord refers to the day when Christ comes in the glory of the Father, the Day of Judgment. To those who do not trust in Christ, that day will be a day of terror (Mt 10:15; Rm 2:5–6; 2Pt 3:7, 12); to believers, it will be a day of great joy (Mt 16:27; 24:30; Jn 6:39; 2Co 1:14; Php 1:6, 10). *See also* PAROUSIA. See 2:362, 582–83, 726.

DAY'S JOURNEY. *See* MEASURES 1h.

DEACON (DEE-k'n; "minister" or "servant"). Gk *diakonos*, "servant" or "helper." Someone who serves (cf Lk 22:25–27; Mk 10:45). In the Early Church, deacons were chosen to relieve the apostles of caring for the physical needs of widows and other poor people

(Ac 6:1–6). Qualifications for the office of deacon are given in Php 1:1 and 1Tm 3:8–13. See 2:375, 604, 606–8.

DEACONESS (DEE-k'n-es). A female helper in the church (Rm 16:1). See 2:420, 423.

DEAD.
1. A lifeless body (Gn 23). *See also* BURIAL; DEATH.
2. People who do not have faith in Christ are spiritually dead (Eph 2:1). See 2:530.
3. Believers are dead to the Law (Col 2:20).
4. Faith that produces no works is dead (Jas 2:17). See 2:675.

DEAD SEA. *See* SALT SEA.

DEAD SEA SCROLLS. Scrolls that date from c 250 BC to c AD 70 and have greatly increased and influenced modern understanding of intertestamental history. Discovered in 1947 near Qumran, the find included about 800 scrolls or portions of scrolls. See 2:5, 807, 827.

DEATH. When life ceases. The Bible describes death as departure or separation from the body (Ec 12:7; 2Tm 4:6; cf 2Co 5:1–5). Death is a result of sin (Gn 2:17; Rm 5:12–14). Because all human beings are sinful, all will die (Heb 9:27). For those who believe in Christ, death is the beginning of eternal bliss (2Co 5:1; Php 1:23; 2Tm 4:6–8; Jas 1:12). See 1:32, 34–35, 44, 120–24, 311–14, 519, 661–62, 669; 2:203–4, 292, 310–11, 425–26, 785–89.

DEBORAH (DEB-o-rah; "bee" or "wasp").
1. Rebekah's nurse (Gn 24:59; 35:8).
2. A prophetess and judge of the Israelites who urged Barak to fight Sisera (Jgs 4:4–14). After the battle Deborah wrote a song of triumph for the victory (Jgs 5). See 1:229, 236–37, 487, 705; 2:17.

DEBT. That which is owed to another person. Within certain limits people who were unable to pay their debts could have their property, family, and even their own persons seized as payment (Lv 25:25–41; Dt 15:1–15; 24:6–13). See 1:107–8, 113, 163; 2:43, 637–38.

DECALOGUE (DEK-ah-log). The Ten Commandments, which God wrote on tables of stone and gave to Moses on Mount Sinai (Ex 20; 31:18; 32:15–19; Dt 10:1–5). The Ten Commandments form the basis of God's Law. In the OT they are also referred to as the "words" or "the covenant" (Ex 20:1; 34:28; Dt 4:13; 5:22). See 1:71–75, 102, 157.

In the NT they are called commandments (Mt 19:17; Eph 6:2). Jesus' interpretation of the commandments is found in Mt 5:17–48; 19:16–22; Mk 2:24–27; Lk 6:1–10; 13:10–16. Perfect love is the fulfillment of the commandments (Mt 22:35–40). See 2:197, 556, 747.

DECLARES THE LORD. The second most common indicator of a prophetic statement, occurring over 340 times in the OT. *See also* THUS SAYS THE LORD. See 1:670, 989.

DEDICATION. The act of devoting something to a holy use. For example, the people dedicated the tabernacle, the altar, and the temple, as well as other things, to God (Ex 40; Nu 7; Dt 20:5; 2Ch 24:7; Ezr 6:16–17). See 1:137, 341–42, 439, 614.

The Feast of Dedication, an annual festival of the Jewish people, was the occasion when they remembered the cleansing of the temple (Jn 10:22). See 2:97, 335.

DEEP.
1. The sea or its deepest part (Gn 7:11; Jb 38:30). See 1:49; 2:367.
2. *See* ABYSS.

DELILAH (De-LIGH-lah; possibly refers to dangling curls of hair). A Philistine woman from Sorek whom Samson loved. The Philistines bribed Delilah to discover the secret of Samson's strength (Jgs 16:4–20). See 1:239.

DELIVER. Hbr *padah*, *kaphar*, and *natsal*, "to rescue, save" as the Lord delivered Israel in the exodus from Egypt (cf NT use in Col 1:13). Forms of Gk *luō*, *hilaskomai*, and *hruomai* appears in the LXX to convey the wealth of OT imagery. In military contexts, the terms often describe the ransoming of prisoners. Moses closely related atonement to the idea of deliverance and redemption (where an innocent life is offered as a substitute for a guilty life; Lv 1:4; 4:4; 16:21). E.g., Jacob is described as reconciling with his brother, Esau, by offering him a gift as atonement (Gn 32:20). Such usage may stand behind the idea that alms atone for one's sins (Ecclus 3:30) or deliver one from death (Tob 4:10). Atonement brought cleansing (Lv 16:30; cf "clean" above). It was the focus of a major annual ritual, the Day of Atonement, when the blood of a sacrifice was sprinkled on the "place of atonement," the cover of the ark of the covenant. The Qumran community, removed from the temple, no longer had the usual sacrifices for atonement. They still believed they received God's atonement through his saving power, Spirit, or counsel. See Ecclus 51:2; 48:20; 49:10; 50:24; 51:2, 3. *See also* SAVE. See 1:63, 65, 574–75, 807, 871; 2:252–53, 430.

DELIVERED. Gk *paradidomi*, "to hand over" as one passes on a tradition. *See also* TRADITION; RECEIVED.

DEMAS (DEE-mas; possibly short for "Demetrius"). One of Paul's co-workers. Demas left Paul and went to Thessalonica (Col 4:14; 2Tm 4:10; Phm 24). See 2:551, 636.

DEMETRIUS (De-MEE-tri-uhs; "belonging to Demeter").

1. A silversmith at Ephesus (Ac 19:23–30). See 1:520–21.
2. Demetrius II Nicator was a Seleucid ruler during the intertestamental era. See 2:83–86.

DEMONS. Evil spirits who are against God and His work. Jesus called them unclean spirits (Mk 5:8). They form a hierarchy under Satan and take possession of persons in peculiar ways (Mt 8:16; Mk 1:32; Lk 8:36). See 1:565, 820; 2:44–45, 165–68, 200–201, 521, 607–8, 747.

DENARIUS (de-NAIR-i-uhs). A silver coin that looked like a dime. In NT times it was equal to a day's wage for people who worked on the land (Mt 20:2). The plural is *denarii* (Mt 18:28; Mk 6:37; Lk 7:41; Jn 6:7).

DESTRUCTION, SON OF. Found in the NT, this phrase refers to someone who spreads destruction and will ultimately be destroyed himself. Jesus calls Judas Iscariot by this title (Jn 17:12). Paul uses the same title to refer to the "man of lawlessness" (2Th 2:3). See 2:582–83.

DEUTERONOMY, BOOK OF (dyoo-tur-ON-o-mi). See 1:157–87.

DEVIL. *See* DEMONS; SATAN.

DEVOTE TO DESTRUCTION. Hbr *charam*, "to give over to the Lord by totally destroying" (Nu 21:2–3; Dt 7:2–6; 13:12–15). The related noun is *cherem*, "that which is to be given over to the Lord by destruction." The Lord declared the idolatrous Canaanites and some of their cities as *cherem*. The idea is related to but not the same as holiness (Lv 27:28–29), because both involve bans and restrictions. Things and persons associated with evil are forbidden to Israel and therefore destroyed; holy things may also be forbidden to Israel generally, yet are preserved for the priests and Levites. *See also* HOLY.

The command to devote the Canaanites to destruction has offended many modern interpreters who insist that a God of love would never give such a command. Such interpreters usually falsely conclude that the Bible does not describe real history at this point and must be interpreted allegorically, or the OT promotes bad ethics and should not be believed or followed. To be sure, war raises the greatest ethical issues, involving battle, refugees, prisoners, and occupation of conquered communities. See the issues raised by Midianite prisoners in Nu 31. Every modern military or police force wrestles with these issues. However, readers should also note that "pure" pacificism raises similar ethical issues, such as toleration for tyranny, murder, abuse, slavery, and moral compromise. Biblical history shows God advocating proactive resistance of evil, including the use of force at times. (Note that alongside the command to destroy the Canaanites, God also promises to drive out the Canaanites. So the command to destroy also services the purpose of driving the Canaanites away [cf Ex 23:27–31]). Interpreters who proudly dismiss the OT accounts fail to appreciate the depth of the issues and responsibilities for delivering people from evil. See 1:121, 213–16.

DEW. A heavy dew was considered a great blessing. It refreshed the earth and helped make it fertile (Gn 27:28; Jgs 6:37–40). The absence of dew was looked upon as evil (2Sm 1:21; 1Ki 17:1). Dew was considered a symbol of silent blessing (Dt 32:2; Ps 110:3). See 1:584.

DIADEM. A headdress worn by men, women, high priests, and kings (Is 28:5). The diadems of olden times were often made of silk and covered with gems. Cf "turban" in Jb 29:14; Is 3:23; Ezk 21:26. See 2:14–15.

DIAL. *See* TIME.

DIAMOND.

1. A precious stone (Ex 28:18; Ezk 28:13).
2. A symbol of hardness (Zec 7:12).

DIANA. *See* ARTEMIS.

DIDYMUS (DID-i-muhs; "twin"). The last name of the disciple Thomas (Jn 11:16; 20:24; 21:2).

DINAH (DIGH-nah; "judged").

1. Jacob and Leah's daughter. Shechem, a Canaanite prince, raped her (Gn 30:21; 34). See 1:30.
2. The name of Job's wife, according to Jewish tradition. See 1:504.

DIONYSIUS (digh-o-NISH-uhs; "devotee of Dionysus"). A member of the Areopagus, the supreme court at Athens. Dionysius was converted by Paul (Ac 17:34).

DISCIPLE ("learner"). A pupil. The prophets, Jesus, John the Baptist, and the Pharisees all had followers or disciples (Is 8:16; Mt 5:1; 9:14; 22:16). The word is used especially of Jesus' twelve disciples (Mt 10:1; 11:1; 20:17). *See also* APOSTLE. See 1:94–95, 344, 716; 2:188–91, 197–206, 229, 302, 380.

DISCIPLINE. Action taken for instruction and correction (Dt 8:5; Pr 13:24; 19:18; 1Co 11:32; Eph 6:4). Discipline is not merely punishment for sin, but for the purpose of building up and edification. *See also* EDUCATION. See 1:69, 303–4, 518, 637, 766, 861; 2:58, 453, 481, 660–61, 709.

DISEASE. The physical diseases and ailments mentioned in the Bible were generally the same as the ones existing today. They include fever (Mt 8:14), boils (Dt 28:27; Jb 2:7), gangrene (2Tm 2:17), dropsy (Lk 14:2), tumors (1Sm 5:6), dysentery (Ac 28:8), itch (Dt 28:27), scabs (Dt 28:27), leprosy (Ex 4:6), insanity (1Sm 21:15), plague (Ex 9:3), paralysis (Mt 9:2), worms (Ac 12:23), fractures (Lv 21:19), bruises (Is 1:6), lameness (Lk 14:21), illness (Jn 5:5), inflammation (Lv 13:28), discharge (Lv 15:2), sores (Is 1:6), and wounds (Lk 10:34). See 1:106–9; 2:208, 393.

Doctors are rarely mentioned in the OT (Gn 50:2; Jb 13:4). By NT times, however, medicine was a regular profession (Mt 9:12; Lk 4:23; Col 4:14). Figuratively, sin is described as a great disease (Is 1).

DISPERSION. The body of Israelites scattered about in lands other than their own. Through Moses, God warned the people that they would be scattered in other lands if they departed from the Mosaic Law (Dt 4:27; 28:64–68). These prophecies were largely fulfilled in the Assyrian and Babylonian captivities. Some scattering also took place due to smaller captivities or to migration and traveling. See 1:348–49.

In NT times groups of Jewish people could be found in nearly all parts of the civilized world (Jn 7:35; Jas 1:1; 1Pt 1:1). See 2:675, 681, 704.

DISTINGUISHING BETWEEN SPIRITS. The ability some Christians have that enables them to decide whether others speak by God's Spirit or by false spirits. This ability is given to them by the Holy Spirit (1Co 12:10).

DIVINATION (div-uh-NAY-shuhn). The practice of foretelling future events or discovering hidden knowledge (1Sm 6:2; Ezk 21:21; Dn 2:2). Divination was often practiced by heathen nations, but it was forbidden to Israel (Lv 19:26; Dt 18:10; Is 19:3; Ac 16:16). Rods, arrows, cups, a liver, dreams, and oracles were among the means used for divination (Gn 44:5; Dt 13:3; Is 41:21–24; Ezk 21:21; Hos 4:12). See 1:311–14, 706.

DOCTRINE. Something that is taught; instruction or teaching (Dt 32:2; Pr 4:2; Mt 15:9; 1Tm 1:3; 4:13; 2Tm 3:10; Ti 2:1). See 2:603–4, 608.

DOG. An unclean animal that ran wild in the streets and was generally despised (Ex 11:7; 22:31; 2Sm 3:8; Mt 7:6). Sometimes dogs were looked upon more favorably (Lk 16:21). To call someone a dog was an insult. Enemies, lustful people, those who did not appreciate holy things, teachers of false doctrine, Gentiles, and wicked people are referred to as dogs (Dt 23:18; Ps 22:16; Mt 7:6; 15:26; Php 3:2; Rv 22:15). See 1:333; 2:44, 46, 70–71.

DOOR. Biblical writers often use the word *door* figuratively. Christ says, "I am the door," that is, the way of salvation (Jn 10:9). The word *door* is also used to picture the entrance or way into a sinner's heart, the way to God's grace, and the entrance into heaven (Lk 13:25; Rv 3:20; 4:1). The picture of God opening a door is a way of saying that He provides the opportunity to preach the Gospel (Ac 14:27; Col 4:3). *See also* HOMES. See 1:178; 2:252, 398, 772.

DOORKEEPER. Someone who watches the gate of a city, temple, palace, house, or other private entrance to make sure that no unauthorized person goes through (Ps 84:10; Mk 13:34). Cf "gatekeeper" in 1Ch 9:21; Jn 10:3. See 1:394, 550.

DOORPOST. The framework around the doorway. Following an Egyptian custom, the Israelites often wrote important matters on their doorposts (Dt 6:9).

DORCAS (DOR-kuhs; "gazelle"). The Gk name for Tabitha, a Christian woman who lived at Joppa and was well-known for her deeds of love. Peter raised her from the dead (Ac 9:36–42). See 2:376, 386.

DOT. A small line or round mark used to tell one Hebrew letter from another (Mt 5:18; Lk 16:17). See 2:514.

DOTHAN (DO-thuhn; "two wells"). A place near Shechem and Samaria where Joseph was sold to the Ishmaelite traders and where Elisha had a vision (Gn 37:17–28; 2Ki 6:13–23). See 2:15.

DOVE. A gentle, timid bird that nests in holes in the sides of cliffs (Sg 2:14; Jer 48:28; Ezk 7:16; Hos 11:11).

Noah released a dove from the ark to see if the waters had subsided after the flood (Gn 8). At Jesus' Baptism the Holy Spirit appeared in the form of a dove (Mt 3:16). Poor people often sacrificed turtledoves (Lv 12:6–8; Lk 2:24). See 1:26, 612–13; 2:428, 741.

DOXOLOGY (doks-AHL-o-jee). Words or songs of praise to God (cf Ps 96:6; Lk 2:14; Rm 11:36; Eph 3:21; 1Tm 1:17).

DRAGON.

1. A sea monster (Is 27:1; cf Ps 74:13). *See also* LEVIATHAN.
2. A mythical monster used to picture Satan (Rv 12:3). See 1:507; 2:126–27, 781, 785–86.
3. Egypt (Ezk 32:2).

DRAM. *See* DARIC.

DREAM. Thoughts and ideas one has while sleeping. There are a number of times in the Bible when God revealed something to people, particularly His prophets, through a dream (Gn 20:3; 28:12; 37:5–11; 40:5; Dn 2; 4; Mt 1:20). The ability to interpret dreams was a special gift (Gn 40:5–23; Dn 4:19–27). See 1:30–31, 833–34; 2:106–11, 760, 791.

DREGS. The sediment or thick portion of wine that falls to the bottom (Ps 75:8; Is 51:17). "To settle on the dregs" is an expression for a lazy, luxurious, unhampered, stupid life (Jer 48:11).

DRESS. Adam and Eve made clothing out of leaves (Gn 3:7). Later, people made clothing out of animal skins, hair, wool, linen, and cotton (Gn 3:21; 38:12; Pr 31:13; Is 19:9; Mt 3:4; 7:15).

Men wore an inner tunic (Ex 28:4), an outer tunic (Lk 3:11), a mantle or cloak (Ex 12:34), breeches, a girdle or belt (cf 2Ki 4:29; Ac 12:8), a cap (Ex 28:40), and sandals (Mt 3:11). Women wore similar clothing. Theirs, however, was longer and made of finer material. Women also wore veils and ornaments (Gn 38:14; Is 3:18–23). See 1:477; 2:538–39.

DRINK. The Hebrew people drank water, milk, vinegar and oil, wine, and strong drink (Gn 14:18; 24:11–18; Lv 10:9; Jgs 4:19; Ru 2:14; Jn 2:3). Strong drink was anything of an alcoholic nature, such as barley beer, cider, honey wine, date wine, and raisin wine. See 1:191, 332, 627, 885; 2:261–62, 552.

Strong drink is frequently mentioned in the Bible, and abuse of it is warned against (Gn 9:21; Pr 20:1; Is 5:11; 24:20; Jn 2:1–11).

DRINK OFFERING. Pouring wine or some other liquid as an act of worship (Ex 29:40–41; Jer 44:17–25).

DROPSY. *See* DISEASE.

DROUGHT. A period of dryness due to lack of rain (Jb 24:19; Jer 51:43; cf Ps 32:4). Little rain falls in Israel from May to October. See 1:329, 340, 762; 2:680–81.

DRUSILLA (droo-SIL-ah). The daughter of Herod Agrippa I. She was first the wife of Azizus, king of Edessa, and later of Felix, the governor of Judea. Paul preached before Drusilla and Felix about judgment and righteousness (Ac 24:24–25).

DUMAH (DU-mah).

1. The son of Ishmael. The descendants of Dumah lived in the northwestern part of the Arabian peninsula (Gn 25:14; 1Ch 1:30; Is 21:11–12).
2. A town in Judah, 10 miles southwest of Hebron (Jsh 15:52).

DURA (DYOO-rah). A plain of Babylon. King Nebuchadnezzar set up an image made of gold on this plain (Dn 3:1). See 1:87, 593; 2:51, 105.

DYSENTERY. A disease caused by the inflammation and ulceration of the large intestine (Ac 28:8).

E

EAR. When priests were consecrated or lepers cleansed, blood was put on their ears (Ex 29:20; Lv 14:14). The Bible describes a disobedient person as having an uncircumcised or heavy ear; and an obedient person, an open ear (Is 50:5; Ac 7:51).

EARTH.

1. The world where we live (Gn 1:1). See 1:14, 271, 575–76; 2:474, 547.
2. Dry land (Gn 1:10).
3. The people who live in the world (Gn 6:11). See 1:22.

4. Soil (Ex 20:24).
5. Carnal or unspiritual things (Jn 3:31; Col 3:2). See 1:597; 2:198, 342, 688.

EAST. The direction toward the sunrise. The Hebrews faced toward the rising sun to determine direction (Gn 2:8; 3:24; Jsh 12:3). Traditionally, Christian churches (and graves) have been oriented toward the east because Christ, the sun of righteousness (Mal 4:2), rose at dawn in the east. Cf Ezk 8:16.

EAST COUNTRY. The region east of Israel, especially Syria and Arabia (Gn 25:6).

EAST WIND. A hot, dry wind from the east (Gn 41:23, 27; Ezk 17:7–10). See 1:89.

EASTER (possibly derived from "Eostre," Teutonic goddess of light and spring). The Christian celebration of Passover (Pascha), focused on the resurrection of Jesus. By the eighth century the name Easter was likely used in England because the celebration coincided with the spring Teutonic festival. See 1:74, 598–99, 693; 2:169–73, 320.

EASTERN SEA. *See* SALT SEA.

EBAL (EE-buhl). A mountain about 2,700 feet above the sea. It was separated from Mount Gerizim by the Valley of Shechem. Mount Ebal was the mount of cursing; Mount Gerizim was the mount of blessing (Dt 11:29; 27:12–26; 28; Jsh 8:30–35). See 1:170, 175; 2:800.

EBED-MELECH (EE-bed-MEE-lek; "king's servant"). An Ethiopian who heard that Jeremiah had been thrown into a dungeon. Ebed-melech obtained the king's permission to draw Jeremiah out (Jer 38:7–13; 39:15–18). See 1:767.

EBENEZER (eb-uhn-EE-zur; "stone of help"). A memorial stone that Samuel set up between Mizpah and Shen to show the place where the Israelites had defeated the Philistines (1Sm 7:12). See 2:801.

EBER (EE-bur; perhaps "one who crosses over"). A descendant of Shem. The Hebrews, the Joktanide Arabs, and the Arameans descended from Eber (Gn 10:21–30; 11:14–17; Lk 3:35). See 1:15.

EBIONITES. Hbr for "poor ones," a sect of Jewish Christians that flourished east of the Jordan River. They did not regard Jesus as the Son of God and of Mary but as a man God anointed as the Messiah (*NPNF*2 1:158–60). They rejected the Epistles of Paul and had their own version of a gospel (*ANF* 1:439–40). See 2:217.

EBONY. A heavy, hard, dark wood used for ornamental work (Ezk 27:15).

ECCLESIASTES, BOOK OF (e-klee-zi-AS-teez; "preacher"). See 1:653–73.

ECCLESIASTICUS, BOOK OF (e-klee-zi-AS-ti-cuss). See 2:51–59.

EDEN, GARDEN OF (EE-d'n; "delight"). The garden in which God put Adam and Eve was in the region of Eden (Gn 2:15). See 1:13, 22, 35, 46; 2:781.

EDOM (EE-duhm; "red").
1. The name given to Esau because he sold his birthright for a dish of red stew (Gn 25:30). 1:1000, 1002
2. The people who descended from Esau and their country, located in the southeastern part of Israel (Jgs 11:17; Nu 34:3; Ps 83:6). Later, the Greeks renamed this country Idumaea. See 1:895–902; 2:245.

EDOMITES (EE-duhm-ights). The descendants of Esau (Dt 23:7). They lived in the land of Edom, which they had taken from the Horites (Dt 2:12). When the Israelites were on their way to Canaan, they asked permission of the Edomites to pass through their country, but the Edomites said no (Nu 20:18–21). Saul fought against the Edomites, and David defeated them (1Ki 11:15–16; 1Sm 14:47; 2Sm 8:13–14). The Edomites were constant enemies of Israel (1Ki 11:14–22; 2Ch 21; 25; Is 34:5–8; 63:1–4; Jer 49:17). See 1:896–902; 2:83.

EDUCATION. In early times, Hebrew children were taught about God and their nation by their parents. Later, the Book of Deuteronomy was used as a textbook (Dt 4:9; 6:6–7). Moses and the prophets were also leaders in education. Before the exile, those who were considered wise became teachers. The Book of Proverbs contains ideas about the education of that period. See 1:631.

After the exile, Ezra added to the number of teachers (Ezr 8:16). He also encouraged people to read, something which only a few people had been able to do before (cf 2Ki 5:7; 22:8–10; 23:2). People who made their living at teaching taught in synagogue schools. See 2:52, 95.

Around 75 BC, compulsory education was begun. Students learned their work by memorizing what their teacher said.

EGLON (EG-lahn; "calflike").
1. A city in Canaan whose king, Debir, encamped against Gibeon. Joshua, through the Lord's help, routed the city's troops and executed the king (Jsh 10:1–28).
2. A king of Moab who captured Jericho and made Israel serve him for 18 years. Eglon was killed by Ehud, a judge of Israel (Jgs 3:12–30). See 1:237.

EGYPT (EE-jipt). A country largely in northeast Africa with a small part in the Sinai Peninsula. It is also called the country of Ham (Ps 105:23, 27; cf Gn 10:6). Egypt is watered by the Nile River, the longest river in the world. The river is divided into a narrow valley and delta, both of which are surrounded by desert. Egypt's rulers were called pharaohs. Its religion was polytheistic, that is, the people believed in many gods. Some of the well-known gods were Ptah, Ra, Thum, and Amon.

Egypt was a powerful kingdom during OT times. For many years the Hebrew people were slaves there until God sent Moses to free them (Ex 1–14). In NT times Egypt was a center of culture. See 1:16–32, 59–94, 321–23, 730–31, 806, 859–60; 2:93, 196, 300–1.

EKRON (EK-rahn). One of five chief Philistine cities. After the Philistines captured the ark of God, they brought it to Ekron (Jsh 13:3; 15:11, 45–46; Jgs 1:18; 1Sm 5:10; 2Ki 1:2–16; Jer 25:20; Am 1:8). Today this location is identified as Tel Miqne. It is located about 11 miles from Gath. See 1:211, 333.

EL (EL; "God," "divine being"). An ancient name for God that can be traced to the Canaanites. It is often used in forming other words, e.g., El-bethel (Gn 35:7). Elohim, the plural form of El, is the more common word for God in the OT. See 1:16, 496, 542.

ELAH (EE-lah; "oak," "terebinth").
1. The son of Baasha and fourth king of Israel. Elah was killed by Zimri (1Ki 16:8–10). See 1:343, 371–74.
2. The father of Hoshea, the last king of Israel (2Ki 15:30; 17:1; 18:1). See 1:375–76.
3. A valley southwest of Jerusalem where David killed Goliath (1Sm 17:2, 19; 21:9). See 2:153.

ELAM (EE-luhm; meaning uncertain). A son of Shem (Gn 10:22; 1Ch 1:17). Elam's descendants lived east of Babylonia and ruled it during Abraham's time. At that time the capital of Babylonia was Shushan (Ezr 4:9; Is 21:2; 22:6; Jer 49:34–39; Ezk 32:24; Ac 2:9).

EL-BETHEL (el-BETH-el; "God of Bethel"). The name Jacob gave to the altar he built at Bethel (Gn 35:7). See 1:30.

ELDAD (EL-dad; "God has loved"). One of 70 elders whom Moses appointed to help him (Nu 11:16, 26–29).

ELDER. Hbr *zaqen*; term related to "beard." Gk *presbyteros*. The term almost always occurs in the plural, describing leaders and representatives of the community. Used for various levels of tribal leadership. Elders were often associated with religious leadership and acted as counselors to rulers. In biblical times, the elderly were treated with great respect because of their wisdom and experience (Lv 19:32; Dt 32:7; Jb 32:6). An elder was one of the older men in his family or tribe who, by right of being firstborn, became its head (cf Ex 3:16; 19:7). The elder made all the major decisions for his family or tribe and was the leader in various activities (Gn 24:2; 2Sm 12:17; Ezk 27:9). Each city also had an elder who was called the elder of the city (Dt 21:3; 22:18). The elders became rulers of the synagogue. See 1:101, 129–30, 138, 796, 805.

In the NT, the terms *elder* and *overseer* are used to mean the same thing. The elder or presbyter was a man the apostles appointed in each Christian church to be its pastor (Ac 20:17, 28; 1Tm 5:17; Ti 1:5–9; 1Th 5:12; 1Pt 5:1–3). See 2:117–21, 222, 322, 600, 629–30, 738–40.

ELEAZAR (el-i-AY-zur; "God has helped"). The third son of Aaron. Because Aaron's two older sons had died, Eleazar took over the job of chief priest from Aaron (Ex 6:23; Nu 20:25–28). He helped Joshua divide the Promised Land among the tribes (Jsh 14:1). See 1:102, 129, 141–42.

ELECT, ELECTION. Election is the eternal act of God by which, out of His grace and for Christ's sake, He chooses from sinful people those whom He will save (the elect). God chose the people of Israel not because of the people's own goodness but because of His divine love (Dt 4:37; 7:7–8; 9:4–6; 10:15; 23:5). Although many of the people lost their faith and fell away from God, those who remained faithful to Him and trusted in Him received the blessings of election (Is 4:3; 37:31–32). The OT also talks about God choosing individuals (Ne 9:7; Ps 78:70; 105:26). See 1:77, 405, 471, 990.

The Gospels speak of Christ choosing disciples (Lk 6:13). They also note that the elect are the messianic community, those who have faith in Christ as the promised Messiah and Savior (Mt 24:22, 24; Mk 13:20–27).

The NT letters explain the doctrine of election. No one deserves to be saved. God, however, chooses from eternity those whom He will save. Those whom He will save are brought to faith in Christ Jesus by the Holy Spirit and are kept in faith by Him. They are placed in the company of other elect (Rm 9–11; 1Co 1:27–31; Eph 1:4–14; 1Pt 1:2). Election should not make the elect feel like they have "made it"; rather, their response will be thankfulness to God for His love and grace in choosing them (2Pt 1:10). Those who are of the elect are described as members of God's Church (Rm 8:33; 16:13; Col 3:12; Ti 1:1; 1Pt 1:1; 2Jn 13). See 2:425–26, 429, 530, 628, 691, 728.

EL-ELOHE-ISRAEL (el-e-LO-he-IZ-rah-el; "God, the God of Israel"). The name of Jacob's altar near Shechem (Gn 33:20).

ELEVEN, THE. After Judas betrayed Christ and then killed himself, the remaining disciples were called the Eleven (Mt 28:16; Mk 16:14; Lk 24:9, 33; Ac 1:26). See 2:194, 229.

ELI (EE-ligh; "elevated"). A descendant of Aaron (Lv 10:12). Eli lived at Shiloh and was both a devoted high priest and judge of Israel (1Sm 1:17; 2:20–30; 4:18). Eli's sons, who were also priests, acted shamefully; they had no regard for the Lord or His work. When Eli failed to discipline them, divine judgment was spoken against him and his household (1Sm 2:12–3:13).

In a battle between the Israelites and the Philistines, Eli's sons were killed, and the ark of the covenant was captured. When Eli heard the news, he fell backward, broke his neck, and died (1Sm 4). The priesthood passed from Eli's family to Zadok's (1Ki 2:27). See 1:253, 276, 288–89, 296, 299–301, 388.

ELI, ELI, LEMA SABACHTHANI (AY-lee, AY-lee, LEH-mah sah-bahk-TAH-nee). *See* ELOI, ELOI, LAMA SABACHTHANI.

ELIAB (i-LIGH-ab; "God is Father"). David's oldest brother (1Sm 17:13–14, 28; 2Ch 11:18).

ELIADA (i-LIGH-ah-dah; "God has realized"). One of David's sons (2Sm 5:16). He is referred to as Beeliada in 1Ch 14:7.

ELIAKIM (i-LIGH-ah-kim; "God raised").

1. The master of Hezekiah's household (2Ki 18:18, 19:2; Is 22:20). When Jerusalem closed its gates against the Assyrians, Eliakim was one of the men sent to receive a message from the leader of the invading army (2Ki 18:18, 26–27). After reporting to Hezekiah what the Assyrian leader had said, Eliakim was then sent to the prophet Isaiah for advice (2Ki 19:2; Is 37:1–7). Isaiah highly praised him (Is 22:20–25).
2. One of Josiah's sons. When he became king, he changed his name to Jehoiakim (2Ki 23:34; 2Ch 36:4).

ELIDAD (i-LIGH-dad; "God has loved"). A leader of the tribe of Benjamin who helped divide the land of Canaan among the tribes (Nu 34:21).

ELIEZER (el-i-EE-zur; "God is help").

1. Abraham's steward (Gn 15:2–3).
2. Moses' younger son (Ex 18:2–4; 1Ch 23:15–17; 26:25).
3. A chief whom Ezra sent to ask the Levites to return to Israel (Ezr 8:16).

ELIHU (i-LEE-hyoo; "He is my God"). One of Job's three friends (Jb 32–37). See 1:498–99, 512–13, 518.

ELIJAH (i-LIGH-jah; "my God is Yahweh"). A Tishbite and great prophet. When King Ahab, influenced by his wife Jezebel, made Baal worship the court religion, Elijah predicted a drought as punishment for forsaking the Lord. During the three years of dry weather, Elijah was fed by ravens at the brook Cherith. Later he lived in the house of the widow of Zarephath (1Ki 16:29–17:24). Then God told Elijah to go and show himself to Ahab.

Elijah proposed a test to Ahab to see whether Baal or the Lord was the true God (1Ki 18:1–19). On Mount Carmel two altars were prepared: one to Baal by his prophets, and the other to the Lord by Elijah. Only the altar of the Lord was consumed by fire. In this way God proved He was the only true God; Baal was a false one. Then Elijah put to death the 450 prophets of Baal (1Ki 18:20–40).

After this Jezebel plotted against Elijah's life. So Elijah fled to Horeb, where he heard the still, small voice of the Lord. Then Elijah was sent to anoint Hazael as king over Syria, Jehu as king over Israel, and Elisha as prophet in Elijah's place (1Ki 19). Elijah pronounced God's judgment on Ahab for the murder of Naboth (1Ki 21:17–29). At the end of his life, Elijah was taken to heaven in a whirlwind (2Ki

2:1–12). See 1:332–36, 343–44, 364–68, 1000.

In the NT, John the Baptist is referred to as Elijah (Mt 11:14; 17:10–13; Lk 1:17). See 2:175, 233, 277.

ELIM (EE-lim; "large trees"). An oasis in the desert where the Israelites camped during the exodus (Ex 15:27; 16:1; Nu 33:9). There were 12 wells and 70 palms there. Today it is the site of Wadi Gharandel. See 1:81.

ELIMELECH (i-LIM-uh-lek; "God is king"). Naomi's husband (Ru 1:1–3). See 1:257–61.

ELIPHAZ (EL-i-faz; "God is victorious").

1. The son of Esau and Adah (Gn 36:4; 1Ch 1:35–36).
2. The chief of Job's three friends. In his talks with Job, Eliphaz traced all suffering and distress to sin and told Job to make his peace with God (Jb 3–8; 15:22–24). God rebuked Eliphaz for saying this and told him to make a sacrifice (Jb 42:7–9). See 1:497–98, 508–12, 522.

ELISHA (i-LIGH-shah; "God is salvation"). The prophet who took Elijah's place as prophet to the Northern Kingdom. Elisha was the son of Shaphat and came from the tribe of Issachar. He prophesied during the reigns of Jehoram, Jehu, Jehoahaz, and Joash. During this time Elisha performed many miracles (2Ki 2–9; 13). See 1:334–37, 343–46; 2:175, 233.

ELISHAMA (i-LISH-ah-mah; "God has heard").

1. The captain of the tribe of Ephraim at the exodus and an ancestor of Joshua (Nu 1:10; 2:18; 7:48, 53; 1Ch 7:26).
2. Jehoiakim's scribe (Jer 36:12, 20–21).

ELISHEBA (i-LISH-i-bah; "God of oath"). Aaron's wife (Ex 6:23).

ELIZABETH (i-LIZ-ah-beth; "God is oath"). The wife of Zechariah and the mother of John the Baptist (Lk 1). See 2:277.

ELIZAPHAN (el-i-ZAY-fan; "God has protected"). The chief of the Kohathites when the Israelites were in the wilderness (Ex 6:22; Nu 3:30). He and his brother Mishael removed the bodies of Nadab and Abihu from the camp (Lv 10:4).

ELKANAH (el-KAY-nah; "God has acquired"). Samuel's father (1Sm 1:1–2:21). See 1:288.

ELKOSH (EL-kahsh). The place of Nahum's birth (Na 1:1). See 1:935, 943.

ELNATHAN (el-NAY-ahn; "gift of God").

1. The grandfather of Jehoiachin (2Ki 24:8; Jer 26:22).
2. One of the "men of insight" Ezra sent to Iddo to obtain priests for the house of God (Ezr 8:16).

ELOHIM (e-LO-heem). *See* EL. See 1:496, 531, 542–43, 570, 628.

ELOI, ELOI, LEMA SABACHTHANI (i-LO-igh, i-LO-igh, LEH-mah sah-bahk-TAH-nee; "My God, my God, why have You forsaken Me?"). Jesus' fourth cry from the cross (Ps 22:1; Mt 27:46; Mk 15:34). See 2:190.

ELYMAS (EL-i-mas; possibly Arabic for "wise"). *See* BAR-JESUS.

ELZAPHAN. *See* ELIZAPHAN.

EMBALM. To prepare a dead body with spices so that it will be preserved from decay. The Egyptians were noted for embalming. When Jacob died, Joseph had the Egyptians embalm Jacob. Joseph was also embalmed when he died (Gn 50:2, 26). See 1:21.

EMBROIDERY. The Hebrews and their neighbors did weaving, sewing, and artistic needlework (Ex 38:23; Jgs 5:30; Ps 45:13–14). They embroidered the hangings of the temple and the priests' clothing (Ex 26:36; 27:16; 28:33, 39; 39:29). See 1:72.

EMMAUS (e-MAY-uhs; "hot springs"). The village where two of Jesus' disciples were going on the day of Jesus' resurrection. It was near Jerusalem, though its exact location is unknown (Lk 24:13–33). See 2:286.

EMMER. An inferior type of wheat (Ex 9:32; Is 28:25; Ezk 4:9). *See also* FOOD 1.

ENCAMPMENT. *See* CAMP, ENCAMPMENT.

ENCHANTMENT. The use of magic arts, spells, or charms. Balaam's omens, sorcery, and serpent charming are some examples of enchantment (Nu 24:1; cf 2Ki 9:22; Ec 10:11; Is 47:9–12). The Egyptians practiced enchantment, but it was forbidden to God's people (Ex 7:11–22; 8:7; Dt 18:10–14). See 1:86–88, 175, 547–49, 645; 2:46, 389, 520.

END. Gk *telos*; in NT usage it can mean either "termination" (cessation) or "goal" (outcome). *See* PERFECT.

EN-DOR (EN-dawr; "fountain of Dor"). A village near Mount Tabor (Jsh 17:11; 1Sm 28:7; Ps 83:10). King Saul consulted with a medium from this village (1Sm 28). See 1:299, 311–14.

ENGEDI (en-GEE-digh; "fountain of a [goat] kid"). A town on an oasis on the western shore of the Dead Sea about 15 miles southeast of Hebron. It is fed by warm spring water (Jsh 15:62; 1Sm 24:1–7; Sg 1:14; Ezk 47:10). See 1:276, 292, 678.

ENGRAVING. To cut or etch letters or a design on a surface. This was a well-known practice in Israel and neighboring regions (2Ch 2:14). Examples of engraved articles include the Ten Commandments, stones and signets, and idols (Ex 20:4; 28:11, 36; 32:4, 16). See 1:62, 165–66, 173.

ENOCH (EE-nuhk; "dedicated").
1. The first son of Cain (Gn 4:17).
2. The father of Methuselah. After the birth of Methuselah, Enoch walked with God for 300 years, and then God took him to heaven (Gn 5:18–24; 1Ch 1:3; Heb 11:5; Jude 14).
3. A city built by Cain (Gn 4:17).

ENOS, ENOSH (EE-nahs, EE-nash). The son of Seth and grandson of Adam (Gn 4:26; 5:6–11; Lk 3:38).

EPAPHRAS (EP-ah-fras; shortened form of "Epaphroditus"). A Christian at Colossae who visited Paul when he was in prison (Col 1:7–8; 4:12; Phm 23). See 2:551–55, 635–36.

EPAPHRODITUS (I-paf-ro-DIGH-tuhs; "lovely"). A Christian who carried the gifts of the church at Philippi to Paul while Paul was in prison at Rome (Php 2:25–30; 4:18). See 1:539–44, 548.

EPHAH (EE-fah). *See* MEASURES 2d.

EPHES-DAMMIM (EE-fes-DAM-im; "boundary of blood"). A place in Judah between Socoh and Azekah. David fought Goliath there (1Sm 17:1). It is also referred to as Pas-dammim (1Ch 11:13).

EPHESIANS, LETTER OF PAUL TO THE (i-FEE-zhuhns). See 2:519–37.

EPHESUS (EF-uh-suhs). A city situated on the Cayster River about three miles from the Aegean Sea. Ephesus was the capital of the Roman province of Asia. It was a commercial city and melting pot of different people, languages, and backgrounds. The city was dedicated to the worship of the Phoenician goddess Astarte, associated with Artemis or Diana.

Many Jewish people who had Roman citizenship lived in Ephesus and had a synagogue there (Ac 18:19). On one of his missionary journeys Paul began a Christian church there (Ac 19:20; 1Co 16:8). See 2:322–25, 378, 435–36, 519–22, 736–37, 771–72.

EPHOD (EF-od; "garment"). An apronlike garment with shoulder straps and a belt. Made of gold, blue, scarlet, and fine-twined linen and beautifully adorned, it was one of the many garments worn by the high priests for worship (Ex 29). Later, others also wore ephods (1Sm 2:18; 2Sm 6:14; 1Ch 15:27). See 1:310.

EPHPHATHA (EF-ah-tha; "be opened"). Jesus spoke this when he healed a deaf man (Mk 7:34).

EPHRAIM (EE-fray-im; "doubly fruitful").
1. The second son of Joseph and Asenath (Gn 46:20). Jacob, Ephraim's grandfather, adopted both Ephraim and his brother Manasseh as his own sons. When the two sons were brought to Jacob on his sickbed, Jacob gave Ephraim the greater blessing, bestowing on him the birthright of the firstborn son (Gn 48:8–20). Ephraim's descendants were numerous (Nu 1:33; 26:37). See 1:21, 23, 52.
2. The tribe of Ephraim was given land west of the Jordan between Manasseh on the north and Dan and Benjamin on the south (Jsh 16). It became the dominant and centrally located northern tribe, the heart of the Northern Kingdom that was often called "Ephraim" (1Ki 12; Is 7:2; 11:13; Ezk 37:15–22). See 1:213, 219, 238–39, 271, 399, 730, 853–54.
3. A city near Absalom's sheep farm (2Sm 13:23).
4. A gate in Jerusalem (2Ki 14:13; 2Ch 25:23).

EPHRAIM, MOUNT. The central range of mountains in Samaria (Jer 4:15; cf Jsh 19:50; 1Sm 1:1).

EPHRATH (EF-rath; "fruitful"). An old name for Bethlehem (Gn 35:16, 19; 48:7). See 1:29.

EPHRATHAH (EF-rah-tha; "fruitful"). The wife of Caleb and mother of Hur (1Ch 2:24, 50; 4:4).

EPHRATHITE (EF-rah-thight). An inhabitant of Bethlehem (Ru 1:2).

EPICUREANS (ep-i-kyoo-REE-uhnz). The followers of Epicurus, a Greek philosopher who died in 270 BC. Epicurus taught that the chief purpose of human beings is to achieve happiness. He denied life after death (Ac 17:16–32). See 2:726, 730.

EPIPHANES (e-PIF-ah-neez). *See* ANTIOCHUS 2.

EPISTLE (i-PIS'l). A formal letter that contains Christian doctrine and instruction (Ac 15:30; Rm 16:22). The term refers particularly to the 21 NT books that are also called letters. These epistles are divided into Pauline and Catholic, or General, Epistles.

Paul refers to Christians as epistles written by the Holy Spirit (2Co 3:2–3). See 2:411–15, 645–49.

ERASTUS (i-RAS-tuhs; "beloved"). A convert of Paul. Erastus, who lived in Corinth, was with Paul at Ephesus (Ac 19:22; Rm 16:23; 2Tm 4:20). See 2:420, 812.

ESARHADDON (ez-ur-HAD'n; "Asshur has given a brother"). A son of Sennacherib and ruler of Assyria from 681 to 669 BC (2Ki 19:37; Is 37:38). Esarhaddon was one of Assyria's greatest conquerors. He rebuilt the city of Babylon, defeated Egypt and made it pay tribute, and took captive Manasseh, the fourteenth king of Judah (2Ch 33:11). See 2:15, 39.

ESAU (EE-saw; "hairy"). The firstborn of Isaac and Rebecca's twin sons (Gn 25:25). Esau sold his birthright to his brother, Jacob, for a bowl of lentil stew (Gn 25:29–34; 27:28–29, 36; Heb 12:16–17). Since lentil stew is red, Esau was referred to as Edom, which means red.

Esau married two Canaanite women and an Ishmaelite woman (Gn 26:34; 28:9; 36:2). He tried to kill Jacob for tricking him out of Isaac's blessing (Gn 27:41–45). Later he forgave his brother and warmly welcomed him back to Canaan (Gn 33). The country of Esau's descendants is called Edom (Gn 36). See 1:23, 27–30, 895–901, 1002; 2:667, 671.

ESCHATOLOGY (es-kah-TOL-o-ji; "doctrine of last things"). A study of the last things, such as death, resurrection, life after death, the second coming of Christ, Judgment Day, and heaven.

The OT emphasizes the destiny of God's chosen people and the Day of the Lord (Is 13:6, 9; Jl 3:14; Am 9:11–15; Zep 1:7). The resurrection of the body and life after death is talked about in Is 26:19–21 and Dn 12:2. See also Jb 19:25–26; Is 53:10.

The NT emphasizes Christ's return to judge the world (Mt 24:25–27; *see also* PAROUSIA). It also talks about the resurrection of the body and the end times, when the wicked shall be thrown into hell and those who believe in Christ shall enter the joy of the Father (Mt 5:29–30; 25:31–46; Rm 8:11; 1Co 15). See 1:721, 802; 2:194, 242, 362, 778–79.

ESHTAOL (ESH-tay-ol). A town 13 miles northwest of Jerusalem that was allotted to the tribe of Dan (Jsh 15:33; 19:41). Samson carried out his work in this area (Jgs 13:24–25; 16:31).

ESHTEMOA (esh-ti-MO-ah). A village 9 miles south of Hebron. It was given to the priests (Jsh 21:14; 1Ch 6:57).

ESSENE (e-SEEN). A Jewish sect in existence from the second century BC to the second century AD. They had settlements in Jerusalem, Judea, and around the Dead Sea.

Although the Bible does not speak of the Essenes by name, Josephus, Philo, and the Dead Sea Scrolls do talk about this group. The Essenes lived a simple life of sharing everything among one another. They believed that people should remain unmarried. While against slavery and animal sacrifice, they practiced cleanliness and tried to keep the Law. The Essenes also believed in life after death. Some scholars believe the Qumran community was an Essene settlement. See 1:311, 807.

ESTHER (ES-tur; "Ishtar," Babylonian goddess; "star"). A Jewish orphan maiden who was the cousin of Mordecai, a minor official of King Ahasuerus (Xerxes I). Ahasuerus ruled Persia from 486 to 465 BC. Esther became his wife, and when her people were going to be put to death, Esther saved them. Esther's Hbr name was Hadassah, which means "myrtle" (Est 2:7). See 1:192, 459–79.

ESTHER, BOOK OF. See 1:459–79.

ESTHER, OLD GREEK. See 2:104–15.

ETAM (EE-tam; "where birds of prey live"). Rock Etam was a place where Samson lived (Jgs 15:8, 11).

ETERNAL LIFE. Eternal life begins when the Holy Spirit by grace brings a person to faith in Jesus Christ, the Son of God and Savior of the world (Jn 1:4; 10:10; 17:3; Rm 6:23). Although the Christian already has eternal life, he or she will not experience it fully until the resurrection of the body and the life of the age to come (Mt 25:46; Jn 6:54; Rm 2:7; Ti 3:7). See 1:176–77, 596–97; 2:191, 201, 212, 252–54, 338–39, 510, 746–48, 782–83.

ETERNITY. Without beginning or end. Eternity is described as "forever" or "from everlasting to everlasting" (Ps 90:2). Only God is before and after all things (cf Jer 1:5; Ps 90; Rv 1:8; 21:6). His reign, power, and glory are eternal (Ps 29:10; Is 44:6; 57:15). See 1:13, 411, 636, 664–65; 2:429, 762.

ETHAM (EE-tham). The second place where Israel set up camp after leaving Egypt (Ex 13:20; Nu 33:6). See 1:81.

ETHBAAL (eth-BAY-uhl; "with Baal"). A king of Sidon who was the father of Jezebel (1Ki 16:31).

ETHICAL MONOTHEISM. Belief that there is one God to whom all human beings owe obedience, expressed especially through righteous acts rather than rituals. Biblical critics argued that later Israelite prophets invented this philosophical viewpoint. See 1:708–9.

ETHIOPIA (ee-thi-O-pi-ah; from Gk, possibly describing the dark complexions of the African people). A country in eastern Africa, south of Egypt. Both Cush, the Hbr name for this country, and Ethiopia refer to the same country (Gn 10:6–8; 1Ch 1:8; 2Ch 12:3; 14:9; Ezk 30:9; Ac 8:27). The people of Ethiopia were merchants (Is 45:14). They were also a strong military power (2Ch 14:9–12). *See also* CUSH. See 1:459, 734, 962; 2:41, 375, 824.

EUCHARIST. *See* LORD'S SUPPER.

EUNICE (YOO-nuhs; "victorious"). Timothy's mother (Ac 16:1; 2Tm 1:5). See 2:615.

EUNUCH (YOO-nuhk; literally "bedkeeper"). Hbr *saris*. A castrated man. Eunuchs were court officials and guardians of women and children (2Ki 20:18; Est 1:10–15; Dn 1:3; Ac 8:27). The Hebrews did not practice castration, nor did they permit eunuchs to enter the congregation (Dt 23:1). In the Israelite kingdom period, "eunuch" was the title of a minor official. In other nations, eunuchs served in more important administrative roles. (The term does not necessarily mean the official was castrated.) Philip baptized an Ethiopian eunuch after explaining what the eunuch was reading from Isaiah (Ac 8:26–40). See 1:823; 2:113, 225, 392.

EUPHRATES (yoo-FRAY-teez). A great river, 1,780 miles long, flowing from Armenia to the Persian Gulf. The Euphrates is one of the rivers that ran through Eden (Gn 2:14). In the OT it is frequently called the great river or the River (Gn 15:18; Dt 11:24). It was regarded as an ideal boundary of Canaan and of David's conquests (Dt 11:24; Jsh 1:4; 2Sm 8:3; 1Ch 18:3). See 1:17, 297, 331, 390, 795; 2:772.

EUTYCHUS (YOO-ti-kuhs; "fortunate"). A young man who went to sleep while Paul was preaching and fell from a third story window to his death. Paul brought him back to life (Ac 20:9–10). See 2:378.

EVANGELIST (i-VAN-juh-list; "publisher of good tidings"). Someone who preaches the Gospel (Ac 8:4–40; 21:8; 2Tm 4:5). The office of evangelist is mentioned in Eph 4:11. At a later date, the name evangelist was given to the writers of the four Gospels. See 1:453; 2:7, 176–77, 178–83, 234–38, 346–48, 389–90, 525, 743–44.

EVE (EEV; "life"). The first woman. God formed her out of Adam's side. She is the mother of all living beings (Gn 2:18–25; 3–4). See 1:22, 24, 35, 45–46; 2:288, 607.

EVERLASTING [ONE]. Gk *aionios*. A title for God favored by Baruch.

EVIL.

1. Anything not in harmony with the divine order; that which creates disorder in the universe (Gn 3; Jb 2:10; Ps 23:4; Pr 15:15; cf Lk 16:25). See 1:44–47, 223–34, 536, 891–92; 2:205–6, 311–12, 789.
2. *See* SIN, II.

EVIL-MERODACH (EE-vil-mi-RO-dak; "man of Marduk"). The king of Babylon from 562 to 560 BC. He reigned after Nebuchadnezzar (2Ki 25:27; Jer 52:31). See 1:353.

EXILE. *See* CAPTIVITY; DISPERSION.

EXODUS (EK-so-duhs; "a going out"). The departure of Israel from Egypt (Ex; Heb 11:22). See 1:39, 59–97, 171–72, 733; 2:27, 460.

EXODUS, BOOK OF. See 1:59–97.

EXORCISM (EK-sawr-siz'm). The driving out of demons and evil spirits by the use of God's Word, though some wrongly attempted it by magical spells and charms (cf Mt 12:27; Mk 9:38; Ac 19:13). See 2:165–68, 279–81, 395.

EXPANSE. The span of sky dividing the primeval waters so that part were above it and part were below it (Gn 1:6–7; Ps 19:1; Ezk 1:22–26).

EZEKIEL (i-ZEEK-yuhl; "God strengthens"). One of the OT prophets. He was a son of Buzi and from a priestly family (Ezk 1:3). Ezekiel was taken into captivity to Babylon in 597 BC with Jehoiachin (Ezk 33:21; 40:1; 2Ki 24:11–16). In Babylon, Ezekiel lived on the Chebar Canal, where he began his prophecies (Ezk 1:1, 3; 3:15). See 1:373, 701, 795–816; 2:779.

EZEKIEL, BOOK OF. See 1:795–816.

EZION-GEBER (EE-zi-on-GEE-bur). A place on the north end of the Gulf of Aqaba where the Israelites camped on their journey in the wilderness (Nu 33:35–36; Dt 2:8). Later, Ezion-geber was a naval port and copper refining center of King Solomon (1Ki 9:26; 22:48; 2Ch 8:17). Today it is identified with Tell el-Khel-eifeh. See 1:140, 331.

EZRA (EZ-rah; "help"). A Jewish priest, scribe, and prophet (Ezr 7:6–12). With the help of Artaxerxes, Ezra led a group of exiles back to Jerusalem c 458 BC. Ezra reformed Jewish life, worship, and government. He read the Law in public and rebuilt the temple (Ezr; Ne). See 1:382–83, 423–57, 777, 1006–8.

EZRA, BOOK OF. See 1:423–57.

F

FABLE.

1. A story in which animals and other objects in nature are made to act and speak as if they were human beings (Jgs 9:8–15; 2Ki 14:9).
2. A myth or fictitious story (1Tm 1:4; 4:7; 2Tm 4:4; Ti 1:14; 2Pt 1:16). See 1:485, 525–26; 2:255.

FACE.

1. Used both literally and figuratively. To fall on the face was an act of reverence, petition, or sorrow (Gn 17:3; Nu 14:5; Jsh 7:6). See 1:142; 2:455.
2. The face of God is God in His active presence (Nu 6:25–26). No one can see God's face and live (Ex 33:20). To seek God's face means to worship Him (Ps 27:8). See 1:51, 73, 523, 800, 815; 2:211, 385.

FAITH. Forms of Hbr *betach*; *'aman* and of Gk *pistis*, rendered often by English "trust." Hbr *'aman*, "to be steady, faithful, true," from which our term "Amen" comes. *Betach* is used negatively in the OT for false confidence. LXX tends to use "hope" (Gk *elpizo*) for sound confidence. OT term *'aman* becomes an important description of man's relationship to God (fear/trust is another). Man is to be faithful to God and His Law. The expression "keep faith" describes human relationships (Ecclus 27:17; 29:3; 1Macc 10:27). That belief and trust in the promise of God in Christ Jesus, worked by the Holy Spirit, through which a person is declared just, brought into a right relationship with God, saved (Rm 5:1; 1Co 2:10–13). A gift of God's grace (Eph 2:8–9), not a natural human power that we are to offer to God. Faith can be pictured as the hand that receives the blessings of salvation that God, out of grace, has provided in Christ Jesus.

In the OT, faith is described by the words *believe* (Ex 14:31), *trust in* (Ps 28:7), and *take refuge in* (2Sm 22:3). In the NT, the word *faith* occurs on nearly every page. It is described as belief and trust in Jesus Christ as the Lord, the one who paid for the sins of the world with His blood and His innocent suffering and death (Lk 24:46–48; Jn 3:16; 20:31; Ac 2:36; 16:31; Rm 10:6–15; Gal 2:20; 1Jn 1:7).

The Holy Spirit works faith in Christ in the individual through the Gospel and the Means of Grace, the Word and Sacraments (Rm 1:16; 10:17). Through faith in Christ, the individual dies, is buried, is raised, and lives with Christ (Rm 6:4, 8; Col 2:12; 3:3). See 1:xxxvi–xxxviii, 80, 178, 216–16, 358, 360, 403, 529–30, 735–36, 808; 2:280–83, 429, 437, 507–10, 660–62, 691.

FAITHFULNESS. From Hbr *'aman*, "to be steady, faithful, true," from which our term "Amen" comes.

FALL. The fall of humanity into sin is described in Gn 3. It was that act by which Adam and Eve turned away from God, yielded to temptation, and broke God's commandments. The fall involved not only Adam, but all of humanity, in sin, misery, and death (Rm 5:12–21).

As one man's fall affects all of humanity, so Christ's death and resurrection for the sins of the world brings God's grace to all (Rm 5:18). See 1:24–26, 35; 2:425, 430.

FALSE PROPHET. A person, not sent by or responsible to God, who performs signs and wonders to lead people astray (Jer 29:9; Ezk 13). *See also* PROPHET. See 1:169, 343–44, 366–67, 703–7, 762, 936; 2:727, 762–63, 785.

FAMINE.

1. A lack of food and drink caused by war or the absence of rain (Gn 12:10; 26:1; 1Ki 17:1–2; 2Ki 6:25). See 1:23, 25, 30–31, 253–62, 807; 2:390.
2. A lack of God's Word (Am 8:11–12).

FASTING. Partially or totally abstaining from food. Moses fasted on Sinai for 40 days and nights (Ex 34:28). In the OT, fasting was a sign of religious humiliation. At first, fasting was supposed to be done only on the Day of Atonement (cf "afflict yourselves" in Lv 16:29; 23:27–32). Later, days of national disaster and the like were added. See 1:471, 869, 871.

The disciples of John fasted, but not those of Jesus (Mt 9:14–15; Lk 5:33–35). Jesus fasted 40 days and nights in the desert (Mt 4:2). He approved of fasting, but not if it were done for show (Mt 6:16–18). See 2:197–98.

FATHER. This word has several meanings in the Bible.

1. It can mean one's own father (Gn 19:31), an ancestor (1Ki 5:1; Nu 18:2; Mt 3:9), or the founder of a community, tribe, or nation (Gn 10:21; 17:4–5; 1Ch 2:51; 4:14). See 1:53, 94–95, 223–24, 454; 2:45, 219–20, 304–6, 475–76.
2. God as Creator (Mal 2:10; Is 63:16) or Savior (Rm 8:15; Gal 4:6). God is the Father of Jesus (Mt 11:26; Mk 14:36). See 1:144–46, 591, 1002–3; 2:196–97, 257–58, 329, 350–51, 660–61.
3. A man who acts with fatherly kindness toward another person (Jb 29:16; Is 22:21); or a teacher (2Ki 2:12). See 2:605.
4. A father in the faith (1Co 4:15). See 1:334, 399, 432; 2:54, 447, 465.

FAVOR. Hbr *chen*, "approval" or "affection," related to the idea of grace. Often used in the Hbr expression "found favor in someone's eyes" (cf Gn 6:8; 39:21; Ex 3:21; 11:3; 12:36; 33:12). Common also in the writings of Solomon, especially Proverbs. Later Hbr uses the term in expressions of blessing and prayer. Qumran writings most often use Hbr *chesed* rather than *chanan*. Gk *charis* is common in Ecclus and 1Macc, though not a clearly theological term in the LXX as it would become in the NT, translated as "grace." *See* CHOOSE; GRACE. See 1:35, 512, 573–74, 661–62, 734–35, 879, 900; 2:210, 253, 437, 638.

FEAR. This word can mean reverence, terror, dread, trembling, or fright (Gn 9:2; Jb 41:33; Pr 29:25; Ac 10:2, 22). The "fear of the Lord," however, generally means to trust God, to show awe and respect for His holiness (Ps 34:11; Pr 1:7; Ec 12:13; cf Gn 20:11). Ecclus equates the fear of the Lord with wisdom (cf 1:11–21; 2:15–17). This wisdom aspect is not as prominent in the Dead Sea Scrolls. See 1:37–38, 76, 291, 481–83, 580–82, 627–28; 2:55–56, 252, 390–91, 760.

FEAST.

1. A lavish and costly meal that people attended with great joyfulness (Dn 5:1; Lk 5:29; Jn 2:1–8). See 1:26, 834; 2:45, 305.
2. A time when the Jewish people celebrate their religious festivals. Their major feasts included (a) the Passover, or Feast of Unleavened Bread (Lv 23:5–8; Nu 28:17–25); (b) the Feast of Weeks, Pentecost, Harvest, or Firstfruits (Ex 23:16; Nu 28:26–31); and (c) the Feast of Booths (Lv 23:34–36; Dt 16:13–17). See 1:74, 107, 980; 2:63, 94–98, 224, 334–35.

   Lesser festivals included (a) the Feast of Dedication, or Lights (Jn 10:22); (b) Purim (Est 9:21–28); (c) the Feast of Wood Offering (Ne 10:34); and (d) Sheep-Shearing (1Sm 25:4–11). See 1:467–69, 543–48.
3. The final end-time feast when all the hosts of heaven celebrate the complete victory of the Lamb of God. Prefigured in the Old Testament (Is 25:6–12), this feast for the faithful commences on Christ's second return (Rv 19:6–10). See 1:734; 2:202.

FELIX (FEE-liks; "happy"). A Roman procurator of Judea (Ac 23:26). See 2:272, 379, 813.

FELLOWSHIP. Gk *koinonia*, "sharing," "participation in a common thing." Christian fellowship shares the common bond of the Gospel, faith in Christ, and various spiritual gifts (1Co 12; Php 1:5–7; Phm). Fellowship is created by God, who calls Christians into participation in Christ so that they share in His work, blessing, and glory (Rm 6:3–8; 14:8; 1Co 1:9; 1Jn 1:3, 6–7). Through the work of the Holy Spirit believers have a oneness in Christ (Jn 17:11, 21–22; 2Co 13:14; Gal 3:28; 1Jn 1:7). The mark of fellowship is love (1Co 13:1–3; 1Pt 1:22). See 1:605; 2:205, 287, 386, 467, 748–49.

FESTIVAL. *See* FEAST.

FESTUS, PORCIUS (FES-tuhs, PAWR-shi-uhs). The Roman governor of Judea who came after Felix (Ac 24:27). See 2:379–80, 536, 600.

FETTERS. Chains for binding the feet of prisoners (Ps 105:18). Cf "shackles" in Jgs 16:21; 2Ch 33:11; Mk 5:4.

FIRE. A symbol of God's presence and a means of His judgment (Ex 3:2; 19:18; 2Pt 3:7). God's anger burns like fire (Ps 79:5). Christ will appear in fire (2Th 1:7–8).

Fire was used for cooking, for warmth, and to burn up sacrifices (Is 44:16; Jer 36:22). It was to burn continuously on the altar (Lv 6:9–13). See 1:70, 120–21, 137, 332–34, 366–68, 871–72; 2:663, 730, 762.

FIRSTBORN The first one born of a mother's offspring (Ex 12:12).

1. The firstborn son was privileged to receive a double portion of inheritance (Dt 21:17) and leadership over the family (Gn 35:23; 43:33; 2Ch 21:3). Sometimes the birthright was given to a younger son (Gn 25:23; 49:3–4). The term also signifies the preeminence of the exalted Lord Jesus and His relationship to the heavenly Father (Col 1:15, 18).
2. The firstborn of human beings and of animals belonged to God (Ex 13:2, 15). The firstborn of man was given to God as a priest. When the Aaronic priesthood was established, the Levites took the place of the Israelites' firstborn (Nu 3:12–13; 18:15–17).

   The firstborn of animals were given to the sanctuary. The clean were sacrificed; the unclean were either replaced by suitable sacrifices or killed (Ex 13:2, 13; 22:30; 34:19–20; Lv 27:26–29). See 1:69–70, 78, 119–20, 137, 169; 2:300, 663.

FIRSTFRUITS. The first ripe fruits, whether raw as in grain or fruit or prepared as in wine, oil, or flour. The first produce harvested each year was offered to the Lord with thanksgiving (Ex 23:19; 34:26; Lv 2:12; 23:10; Nu 18:12). The presentation of the firstfruits during the Feast of Weeks (Pentecost) included a liturgy (Dt 26:1–11). See 1:169, 1002; 2:688.

FISH.

1. The Sea of Galilee, filled with a great variety of fish, was the chief source of fishing for the people of Israel (Mt 4:18–22). Once the fish were caught, they were sold in Jerusalem (2Ch 33:14; Ne 13:16).

   The word *fish* is used figuratively for the Egyptians, the Church, and captives (Ezk 29:4–5; Hab 1:14; Mt 13:47–48). The letters of the Gk word for fish became a symbol for "Jesus Christ, God's Son, Savior." *See also* FOOD 3.

   The disciples were called "fishers of men" because they "caught" people with the Gospel (Mt 4:19; Mk 1:17). See 2:190, 244–45, 278, 319–20, 822–23.
2. The name of a number of larger sea creatures might also be translated as fish (cf Gn 1:21; Ezk 32:3). The Gk word used in Mt 12:40 means any large fish or sea creature. The word is also translated as great fish (Jnh 1:17). See 1:908–18.

FISH GATE. A gate of Jerusalem near the fish market (2Ch 33:14).

FLAGON ("skin"). A bottle or pitcher made of skin or earthenware (Is 22:24).

FLASK. An object or jar for holding oil or perfume (2Ki 9:1, 3; Mk 14:3). May also be a type of bottle (Jer 19:10–11).

FLESH.

1. The muscles or softer parts of any living thing (Jb 33:21; Lk 24:39).
2. All beings have flesh (Gn 6:13, 19; Ac 2:17; cf Rm 3:20). See 1:48; 2:376.
3. Meat (Ex 16:12; Lv 7:19). See 1:119.
4. Flesh as opposed to spirit (Jn 6:52; 1Co 5:5). See 2:251, 319, 333.
5. Our ordinary human physical condition (Gn 2:23; Mt 19:5–6; 1Co 6:16). See 1:243–44, 872; 2:212, 746–52.
6. Human nature deprived of the Spirit of God and corrupted by sin (Rm 7:5; 8:5–8; 2Co 7:1; Gal 5:16–20; 2Pt 2:9–10), which becomes the most important theological use of the term. See 1:304; 2:288, 423–24, 475, 508–11.

FLOCK.

1. Sheep (Lk 2:8). See 1:174, 990.
2. Israel as a covenant nation (Is 40:11). See 1:800, 989; 2:238.
3. The NT church (Mt 26:31; Ac 20:28–29; 1Pt 5:2–3). See 1:364; 2:212, 328–29, 661–62.

FLOOD.

1. Water, especially a river or the sea (Ex 15:8; Jsh 24:2; Ps 66:6). A flood is also anything overflowing, e.g., the overflowing of a body of water (Na 1:8; Lk 6:48). See 1:210.
2. The deluge in the time of Noah is referred to as "the flood." It is that event when God destroyed all living things on earth by water except the creatures in Noah's ark (Gn 6:9–9:17). See 1:26, 32, 47–49, 576.

FLOWING WITH MILK AND HONEY. Common OT expression encompassing both animal husbandry and agriculture. Describes the Promised Land as having every good quality in abundance. See 1:138–39.

FLUX. *See* DYSENTERY.

FOOD. The people in Bible times ate various kinds of food.

1. Bread and water were the "support and supply" of life (Is 3:1). Bread was made mainly from wheat. Sometimes barley, beans, lentils, millet, and emmer were also ground for bread or were eaten by the poor (Ezk 4:9).

Crushing the grain between two stones was one ancient method for grinding flour. The Canaanites used a rotary-type mill in which the cone of the upper millstone fit into a hollowed out spot in the lower millstone.

Once the grain was carefully sifted, it was ready to make into bread. Yeast, salt, olive oil, and water or milk were added to the flour to make the bread.

The people used different types of ovens to bake the bread. The simplest type was a slightly curved, circular sheet of iron that was heated over the fire. Then a thin layer of dough was placed on it to bake. Another type of oven was a dome of clay. The dough was placed under it, and then it was covered with fire. Community ovens were also used.

2. Wheat, barley, flour, parched grains, beans, and lentils were an important part of the Hebrew diet (Gn 25:34; 2Sm 17:28). The people also freely ate fish, melons, cucumbers, onions, garlic, and leeks (Nu 11:5; Is 1:8). Dill, mustard, and coriander seed provided strong flavoring for their foods (Ex 16:31; Is 28:25, 27; Mt 13:31). Cinnamon, mint, cumin, and saffron flavored both food and wine (Ex 30:23; Sg 4:14; Mt 23:23). In addition to these items, parsley, celery, lettuce, and cabbage were grown.

   One of the favorite dishes of the Israelites, which used many of the above items, was vegetable stew. Since good quality meat was scarce, the people ate it only on special occasions (Lk 15:23–24; Ex 12:3–10). At these times they might barbecue and serve whole animals (Gn 18:7; Lk 15:23). Poorer quality meats were stewed or used to flavor vegetable stew.
3. Fish were taken mainly from the Sea of Galilee (Mt 4:18), the Jordan River, and the Mediterranean Sea. They were roasted over charcoal (Jn 21:9) or salted and dried for later use (cf Mk 8:7–8). Wild or domestic birds and their eggs also provided a good source of protein (Ex 16:13).
4. Milk and milk products supplied the Israelites with protein, calcium, and fat. At mealtime the people, particularly the children, drank cow's, sheep's, or goat's milk (Gn 18:8; Dt 32:14; 1Sm 6:7; Heb 5:12–13). They ate curds of milk and cheese made from sour milk (Gn 18:8; 1Sm 17:17–18; Pr 30:33). Cream skimmed from the top of sour milk was churned inside a goatskin to make butter. See 1:103–5, 165, 847–48; 2:21, 130, 245–46, 426, 447, 460.

FOOL. A person who has no wisdom or understanding, or one who is lacking in morals or religion (Ps 14:1; 92:6; Pr 12:15; Jer 17:11; Lk 12:20). See 1:621–25, 633–43, 660–64; 2:31–33, 326, 461–63, 710.

FOOTMAN. A soldier who fights and marches on foot (2Ki 13:7). Cf "guard" in 1Sm 22:17.

FOREIGNER. Among the Israelites, anyone who was not part of their nation was a foreigner or stranger (Ex 12:45; Eph 2:12). The NT describes those who are not citizens of God's kingdom as foreigners or strangers (Eph 2:19; 1Pt 2:11). See 1:94, 168, 732, 927; 2:22, 71.

FOREKNOWLEDGE. God's eternal knowledge or foresight of all future events (Ac 2:23; 1Pt 1:2). *See also* ELECT, ELECTION. See 1:329; 2:386.

FORERUNNER. Someone who prepares the way (Heb 6:19–20). See 1:1000, 1004; 2:76, 296.

FORK. *See* WINNOWING FORK.

FORGIVENESS. Hbr *salach*, "to pardon"; *nasa'*, "to lift up, pardon"; Gk *aphiemi*, "to let go" or "dismiss" sin or debt. A consequence of justification. God's act whereby He ends the separation caused by people's sins and puts them back into a proper relationship with Himself. No one deserves to be forgiven, nor can anyone earn forgiveness (Mt 18:23–25; Eph 2:8). Rather, forgiveness is a gift of God, given out of grace for Christ's sake (Mk 2:5, 7, 10; Lk 24:47; Jn 20:23; Eph 1:7; 1Jn 2:12). As a result of Christ's forgiveness, we are to forgive our neighbor (Mt 6:12–14; Eph 4:32). Recognizing and being sorry for our sins precedes forgiveness (Ps 51; Is 57:15; Jer 14:20). *See also* REPENTANCE. See 1:116, 442, 599–600, 669–71; 2:196, 205, 222–23, 384, 466–67.

FORM CRITICISM. The interpretive practice of identifying and defining different types of stories in a text (e.g., legend, myth, saga, etc.), and determining how the community used them. Form critics usually assume the stories or accounts existed first in oral form before they were developed or edited as writing. See 1:204, 557, 710; 2:181–82.

FORTIFICATION, FORTRESS. Cities in ancient times were fortified with walls built of brick and stone. Jerusalem, Samaria, and Damascus were well-known fortified towns. God's protection is often pictured as a strong fortress (2Sm 22:2; Ps 31:3). See 1:217, 385, 559–60; 2:83, 195, 807–8.

FOR YOUR NAME'S SAKE. That is, "for the sake of the Lord's good reputation." The preciousness of God's name is illustrated by the way He guards it and by the delight He takes when people use His name well. Everything God does for His people reveals Himself and demonstrates His character. It brings glory to His name. *See also* NAME. See 1:170, 583, 800, 808.

FORTY. Often used with a length of time characterizing a critical period in redemptive history or a period of testing (Gn 7:12; Dt 9:11; Mt 4:2). See 1:92–93; 2:301, 350.

FOUNTAIN. Springs of water were of great importance in Canaan (Gn 16:7; Dt 8:7; 33:28; 1Sm 29:1). God, the source of grace, is described as having or being the fountain of life (Ps 36:9; Jer 17:13). Jesus told the woman at the well that the water He gives becomes a "spring of water welling up to eternal life" (Jn 4:14). See 1:48–49; 2:65, 689–90.

FOUR. Associated with the four corners of an object (Ex 27:2; Jb 1:19), directions of the compass (1Ch 9:24; Is 11:2; Zec 6:5), and the winds that blow from the four quarters of heaven (Jer 49:36). Four is therefore associated with the heavenly and earthly spheres of creation. See 1:813, 815.

FOWLER. A person who catches birds with a net or cords (Ps 91:3; 124:7).

FRANKINCENSE (FRANGK-in-sens). A fragrant gum resin from certain types of trees. It was an ingredient in meal offerings and in the oil used to anoint priests to their offices (Ex 30:34; Lv 2:1). Frankincense was also burned and poured on showbread (Lv 6:15; 24:7). *See also* SHOWBREAD. See 1:622.

FREEDOM. Gk *eleutheria*, "liberty," the opposite of slavery. A consequence of justification in the NT. *See also* FORGIVENESS. See 1:71, 360–61, 663; 2:425–26, 452–55, 637, 759.

FREE WILL. Verb and noun have the same Hbr root *nadab*, to "urge" or "volunteer." The expression "free will" can be confusing, as Scripture does not teach that the human will is free in spiritual matters but is bound due to the fall into sin. *See also* FREEDOM.

FRIEND(SHIP). Forms of Gk *philos*, which translates a variety of Hbr terms. Friends and friendship are major emphases in the Apocrypha, comparatively outnumbering the usages inthe OT. The prevelance of the terms are likely an example of Gk culture inserting its interests into intertestamental Judaism. In Ecclus the term is more typical for describing someone who should be a trusted companion, though the majority of sayings are warnings about untrustworthy friends (e.g., 6:5–17). In the Maccabean books, the sense is political since "friends of the king" is a title for the king's supporters. See 1:290–91, 302, 503–5; 2:79, 127, 336, 637–39.

FRIEND(S) OF THE KING. *See* FRIEND.

FRINGE. Tassels made of twisted blue thread that were fastened on to each corner of a garment. The Israelites wore these to remind themselves of the Law and their loyalty to the Lord (cf Nu 15:37–40; Dt 22:12). In the Gospels, the people seek to touch the fringe of Jesus' garments for healing (Mt 9:20; 14:36; Mk 6:56; Lk 8:44).

FRONTLET. Anything bound on the forehead. The Jewish people bound jewels or amulets between their eyes. Later they wore phylacteries (prayer bands) around their foreheads or on their left arms (Ex 13:9, 16; Dt 6:8; 11:18; Mt 23:5).

FRUIT. Gk *karpos* (singular). Spiritual fruit is the good works of a life produced and guided by God the Holy Spirit—in contrast to deeds (plural) of the self-indulgent life. See 1:40, 71, 356, 731; 2:202, 245, 321, 509, 728, 760.

FULLER. A person who bleaches, cleans, thickens, or dyes cloth (Mal 3:2; cf Mk 9:3). A fuller's field, the place where this work was done, lay outside the east wall of Jerusalem (cf "Washer's Field" in 2Ki 18:17; Is 7:3; 36:2).

FURNACE. People smelted iron, burned bricks, and melted silver and gold in furnaces or kilns (Dt 4:20; Pr 17:3; Ezk 22:20; cf "kiln" in Ex 9:8, 10; 19:18). The NT pictures everlasting punishment as a furnace of fire (Mt 13:42; cf Mt 25:41). See 1:826; 2:134, 138.

FUTURE LIFE. *See* ESCHATOLOGY; ETERNAL LIFE; ETERNITY.

G

GABBATHA (GAB-ah-thah). The place where Pilate held court and where Jesus was tried (Jn 19:13). See 2:262.

GABRIEL (GA-bri-uhl; "man of God"). The angel who interpreted visions to Daniel (Dn 8:16–27; 9:20–27) and announced the births of John the Baptist (Lk 1:11–22) and Jesus (Lk 1:26–38). See 1:820, 835–36; 2:277.

GAD (GAD; "good fortune").

1. Jacob's seventh son (Gn 30:9–11; 49:19).
2. The name of a tribe of Israel that descended from Jacob's seventh son (Nu 1:24–25; 26:15–18). This tribe settled east of the Jordan River (Nu 32). In 722 BC, Tiglath-pileser, king of Assyria, took this tribe into captivity along with the other nine northern tribes (1 Ch 5:26). See 1:31, 139, 164.
3. The name of a prophet who helped and wrote about David (1Sm 22:5; 2Sm 24:11–24; 1Ch 29:29). See 1:274, 298, 391, 396.

GADARENES (gad-ah-REENZ). The people who lived in the city of Gadara, about 6 miles southeast of the Sea of Galilee, or in the town of Gerasa on the east coast of the Sea of Galilee (Mt 8:28; cf Mk 5:1; Lk 8:26, 37). See 2:166.

GAIUS (GAY-yuhs).

1. A man of Macedonia who helped Paul at Ephesus (Ac 19:29).
2. A man from Derbe who helped Paul (Ac 20:4).
3. A Christian at Corinth who was baptized by Paul (1Co 1:14). See 2:420, 434.
4. The person to whom the Third Letter of John was sent (3Jn 1). Some scholars believe that some of these men may have been the same person. See 2:744, 747.

GALATIA (gah-LAY-shi-ah). A region of central Asia Minor (modern-day Turkey) named after the Gauls, who settled there about the third century BC. After the Romans captured the area in 64 BC, a Roman province called Galatia was formed. It included the region Paul visited on his first missionary journey (Ac 16:6; 18:23; Gal 1:2). See 2:388, 499–504.

GALATIANS, LETTER OF PAUL TO THE. See 2:499–517.

GALILEAN (GAL-uh-lee-uhn). A person from Galilee. *See also* GALILEE. See 2:196, 324, 503, 702.

GALILEE (GAL-uh-lee; "circuit," "district"). The name of the northernmost province of the three provinces of Israel. This name was already used in OT times (Jsh 20:7; 1Ki 9:11). Galilee was given to the tribes of Zebulun, Asher, and Naphtali (Jsh 19:10–16, 24–39). The land was fertile, and a number of important trade routes crossed the area (Is 9:1).

At the time of Christ, Galilee extended from Mount Hermon on the north to Mount Carmel on the south, and from the Jordan River on the east to the Mediterranean Sea on the west. Herod Antipas was its ruler. Jesus performed the major part of His ministry there. The twelve disciples, except Judas Iscariot, were all from Galilee (Mk 14:70). The leaders of Judea hated Galileans, who were known by the way they talked. See 1:352, 906; 2:195, 232–33, 238, 327, 679–80.

GALILEE, SEA OF. A freshwater lake fed by the Jordan River, which flows in at the north end and out at the south end. It is 13 miles long, 7 miles wide, and 160 feet deep at its deepest point. Its blue, fresh water is full of fish.

The Sea of Galilee is also referred to as the Sea of Chinnereth (Jsh 13:27) or Chinneroth (Jsh 12:3), the Lake of Gennesaret (Lk 5:1), and the Sea of Tiberias (Jn 6:1; 21:1). See 1:213; 2:232–33, 330, 809.

GALL.

1. A bitter material produced by the liver (Jb 16:13).
2. People thought that the poison of snakes was gall (cf Jb 20:14).
3. A poisonous, bitter-tasting plant (cf Hos 10:4).
4. Part of the drink the soldiers offered to Christ to lessen His suffering on the cross (Mt 27:34). See 2:261.
5. A symbol for a bitter, painful experience (Ac 8:23; cf "poisoned water" in Jer 8:14). See 1:789.

GALLEY. A low, flat-looking ship with a row of oars along each side. It was often rowed by slaves (Is 33:21).

GALLIO (GAL-i-o). The Roman proconsul (governor) of Achaia from AD 51 to 52. He was the brother of the philosopher Seneca. Gallio refused to hear the Jews' case against Paul in Corinth (Ac 18:12–17). See 2:441, 447, 811.

GALLOWS. An instrument used to hang people. Gallows (lit, "tree") are mentioned nine times in the Book of Esther as a means of execution. The word translated as gallows may refer to a pale or stake. See 1:649.

GAMALIEL (gah-MAY-li-uhl; "God has shown goodness"). The grandson of Hillel, the great Jewish teacher, and one of Paul's most influential teachers (Ac 22:3). Gamaliel was a Pharisee and a member of the Sanhedrin (Ac 5:34). He gave wise advice to the other leaders at the trial of Peter and the other apostles (Ac 5:38–40).

Gamaliel is considered one of the greatest Jewish rabbis. He is referred to as "rabban" (our teacher). See 2:405, 411, 419.

GAMES. Children often played in the streets (Zec 8:5). They played make-believe and kept birds (Jb 41:5; Mt 11:16–17).

Adult "games" included reveling (Jer 15:17), telling riddles (Jgs 14:12–19), playing music, dancing (Lk 15:25), racing (Ps 19:5), and using the bow and sling (1Sm 20:20; Jgs 20:16). Paul references Greek sports contests (1Co 9:24–27; 2Tm 2:5; 4:7–8). A board for an ancient game was found at Saul's castle in Gibeah. *See also* DANCE; MUSIC.

GATE. The door or entrance to the tabernacle, the camp of the Israelites, the temple, cities, houses, and prisons (Gn 19:1; Ex 27:16; 32:26; 2Ch 8:14; Ac 10:17; 12:10). Markets and courts, or places of judgment, were often near gates because many people walked past or met to talk or do business there (Dt 17:5; Ru 4:1–12; 2Sm 15:2; 2Ki 7:1).

A gate is a symbol of power (Gn 22:17; Mt 16:18). It also describes the beginning of something or the way to have access to something, for example, the gate of heaven (Gn 28:17), the gate of righteousness (Ps 118:19–20), the gates of the New Jerusalem (Rv 21:12, 21), the gates of death (Jb 38:17). See 1:356, 440, 620–21; 2:202–3, 226–27, 799–801.

GATH (GATH; "wine press"). One of the five great Philistine cities (Jsh 13:3), though its site is unknown. Gath was the home of Goliath (1Sm 17:4) and one of the places where David hid from Saul (1Sm 21:10). David later captured Gath (1Ch 18:1). See 1:276, 281, 290–92, 921.

GAZA (GAY-zah). The capital city of Philistia (Gn 10:19). It was given to Judah when Canaan was divided (Jgs 1:18). Gaza was the scene of Samson's death (Jgs 16) and the place near which Philip converted the treasurer of Ethiopia (Ac 8:26). See 1:211, 331; 2:196.

GAZELLE (gah-ZEL). The smallest of the Palestinian antelopes. This animal was considered ceremonially clean, i.e., one of the animals the Israelites were allowed to eat (Dt 12:15, 22). See 1:676.

GEHENNA. *See* HELL.

GENEALOGY (jen-ee-AL-o-jee; "birth record"). The tracing forward or backward of the ancestral relationships of tribes and families (Gn 35:22–26; Ne 7:5; Mt 1:1–16; Lk 3:23–38). Genealogies often contain gaps (cf Ex 6:16–24). See 1:35, 263, 386–89, 411; 2:219–20, 602.

GENERATION.

1. Creating or procreating (Gn 2:4). See 1:14–15.
2. Offspring or successions of offspring (Gn 5:1).
3. Age as a period of time (Gn 15:16; Dt 32:7; Ps 45:17).
4. People of a specific historical period (Lv 3:17; Mt 11:16; 17:17).

GENESIS, BOOK OF (JEN-i-sis; "beginning"). See 1:15–58.

GENNESARET (ge-NES-ah-ret).

1. The plain northwest of the Sea of Galilee (Mt 14:34; Mk 6:53).
2. *See* GALILEE, SEA OF.

GENTILES. Used primarily in the NT to refer to non-Jewish people (Mt 4:15; 10:5). It also may refer to non-Jewish people who worship false gods (Mt 6:7; 10:18). Now, in Christ, there is no distinction between Jew and Gentile (Ac 10:34–48; Rom 3:29; 9; 11). All are members of God's house through faith. *See also* NATIONS. See 1:441, 763, 912; 2:98, 222, 371, 398, 428, 525, 654.

GERASENES (GER-ah-seenz). *See* GADARENES. See 2:239, 280.

GERIZIM (GER-i-zim). A mountain about 2,850 feet high that stands opposite Mount Ebal. The blessings were read from Mount Gerizim; the curses, from Mount Ebal (Dt 11:29; 27:12). The Samaritans built a temple for themselves on Mount Gerizim (cf Jn 4:20). See 1:182; 2:800, 806.

GETHSEMANE (geth-SEM-ah-nee; "oil press"). An olive yard east of Jerusalem. It was the place of Jesus' agony and arrest (Mt 26:36–56; Mk 14:26–50; Lk 22:39–54; Jn 18:1–13). See 1:544; 2:190, 203.

GIANTS. People who are unusually tall and powerful. The Nephilim are the first giants mentioned in the Bible. They were on the earth in the days before the flood and in Canaan when the spies went through the land (Gn 6:4; Nu 13:33).

Giants known as the Rephaim (Gn 14:5; 15:20) lived in Canaan, Edom, Moab, and Ammon. At the time of the conquest, Og, king of Bashan, was the only one left of this race. His iron bedstead was about 13½ feet long (Dt 3:11; Jsh 12:4). The Anakim, another race of giants, were connected with the Rephaim because of their size (Nu 13:22; Dt 2:10–12). When the Hebrews captured Hebron, the Anakim who escaped destruction found refuge in Philistine cities. Goliath of Gath was probably one of these remaining Anakim (1Sm 17:4). See 1:296, 400; 2:153.

GIBEAH (GIB-i-ah; "hill").

1. A city of Benjamin a few miles north of Jerusalem (Jgs 19:13–14). It was the birthplace of Saul and the place where he lived after becoming king (1Sm 10:26; 15:34). Its modern-day site is Tell el-Ful. Excavation there has uncovered Saul's fortress-palace. See 1:285; 2:802.
2. Gibeah at Kiriath-jearim. It was the place where the ark was kept after the Philistines returned it (1Sm 6:21).

GIBEON (GIB-ee-uhn; "hill city"). A city in Benjamin that was given to the Levites (Jsh 18:20–28; 21:13–19). Originally it was a Hivite city. At the time of the conquest, the people of Gibeon made a treaty with Joshua under false pretenses. By doing this, they saved their city but brought slavery upon themselves (Jsh 9–10; 2Sm 21:1–9). See 1:210–11, 294, 401; 2:802.

GIBEONITES. Neither Israelites nor leaders, but Canaanites who became slaves. They cut wood and drew water for the Israelites (Jsh 9:21, 27). Other Canaanites who were spared during the conquest entered this type of service. *See also* GIBEON. See 1:210–11.

GIDEON (GID-ee-uhn; "cutting down"). The son of Joash of the tribe of Manasseh (Jgs 6:11). While threshing wheat, the angel of the Lord called Gideon to deliver his people. That night Gideon tore down his father's altar to Baal and built one to the Lord. The townspeople wanted to kill Gideon for doing this, but his father told them to let Baal defend himself if he were a god. Because of this incident Gideon was known as Jerubbaal, which means "let Baal contend against him" (Jgs 6:32).

Gideon defeated the Midianites and destroyed Succoth. When his people wanted to make him king, Gideon refused (Jgs 6–8; Heb 11:32–34). He was also called Jerubbesheth, meaning contender with shame (2Sm 11:21). Because of his work Gideon is regarded as one of the judges of Israel, even though he is not specifically called by that title. See 1:235–38, 241–44.

GIFTS. Gk *charismata*, gracious gifts or abilities from God, connected with an office of service in the congregation. *See also* GRACE. See 2:426, 461–62, 529.

GIHON (GIGH-hon; "gushing forth").

1. One of the four rivers of Eden (Gn 2:13).
2. A spring in the Kidron Valley near Jerusalem that supplied some of the water to that city. Hezekiah built the Siloam Tunnel to carry water from the Gihon to the pool of Siloam within the city walls of Jerusalem (2Ki 20:20; 2Ch 32:30). See 1:321, 338; 2:803.

GILBOA (gil-BO-ah). A mountain range overlooking the Valley of Jezreel. Saul and Jonathan died there while fighting the Philistines (1Sm 31). See 1:290, 480–81.

GILEAD (GIL-i-ad; "rough"). The name given to the land east of the Jordan River. It extended from the Sea of Galilee on the north to the Dead Sea on the south (Gn 31:21–25; Dt 3:12–17). See 1:136, 351, 853–54; 2:83.

GILGAL (GIL-gal; "circle," "wheel"). The place near Jericho that became Israel's base camp after the Israelites crossed the Jordan (Jsh 4:19–24; 9:6). Saul was crowned king of Israel at Gilgal (1Sm 11:15) and also had his kingship taken away there (13:4–15). See 1:210–11, 279.

GIVE THANKS. Gk *eulogeo*, "to praise," "bless" God in prayer (English "eulogy"). *See also* BLESS. See 2:139.

GLASS. By 1500 BC opaque glass was widely used by the Egyptians and Phoenicians (Jb 28:17). Clear glass was made in Roman times (Rv 21:18, 21). See 1:885.

GLEANING. The gathering of grain left in the fields or grapes left on the vines after harvest. According to OT law, owners of fields and vineyards were to leave leftover grain, grapes, and fallen fruit for the poor (Dt 24:19–21; Ru 2:2–3). See 1:258.

GLORY. The common Hbr term *kebod* refers to the "weight" or "weightiness" of something, and therefore its impressive appearance or "honor." Gk *doxa*, "reputation" or "reknown." The background for the Gk idea is significantly different from the Hbr.

The Gk stems from the verb *dokeo* ("to think") and means "opinion."

1. That which shows the greatness of someone or something. The glory of God is shown in and by His great miracles, His eternal perfection, His creation, and all His works (Ps 8; Mt 17:2; Jn 2:11). Moses introduces the expression during the exodus (Ex 16:7) to contrast the Lord's majesty with that of Pharaoh and Egypt. It comes to describe the visible manifestation of God's presence in the cloud and fire of the exodus. It is the splendor of God's presence that belongs *now* to believers in the promise, and that by His advanced preparation *will be* revealed to them and in them. The "glory" is a common topic in the hymns of Qumran. The Hbr sense dominates the use of the term in the Apocrypha. Most important, it is shown by His Son, our Lord Jesus Christ (Jn 1:14; 2Co 4:6). The glory of people is truly shown only by their relationship to God (2Co 3:18). See 1:386–87, 575; 2:196, 201–2, 333, 336, 688, 783.
2. That which is itself the greatness of someone or something. Here glory is spoken of as a possession of, or even part of, someone or something. Scripture speaks of God's glory and of the glory awaiting believers in the life to come (Is 42:8; Lk 2:9; Rm 8:18; Php 3:20–21). *See also* GLORY OF THE LORD.

GLORY OF THE LORD. Hbr *kebod yahweh*. The term *kebod* refers to the "weight" or "weightiness" of something, and thereby its impressive appearance or "honor." Moses introduces the expression during the exodus (Ex 16:7) to contrast the Lord's majesty with that of Pharaoh and Egypt. It comes to describe the visible manifestation of God's presence in the cloud and fire of the exodus (Ex 13:21). A human appearance in Ezekiel's visions (Ezk 1:28). Also, "glory of the God of Israel" (Ezk) and "Glory of Israel" (1Sm 15:29). It is the splendor of God's presence that belongs *now* to believers in the promise, and that by His advanced preparation *will be* revealed to them and in them. See 1:61, 73, 76, 408, 804–7; 2:387, 688.

GNOSTICISM (NOS-tuh-siz'm). A system of belief that reached its peak in the second to third century AD. According to Gnostics, salvation came by hating the world and everything physical and by escaping to the spirit world. Gnostics said Jesus came not to save people from sin but to show them how to escape to a spiritual world.

Gnosticism was a problem for Christians during the first few centuries after Christ. Some of the books of the NT seem to have been written in part to fight against it (Jn; Col; Ti; 2Pt; 1, 2, 3Jn; Jude; Rv). See 1:485; 2:9–10, 599, 601, 725–26.

GOAT. A valued animal that is mentioned many times in the Bible. Its hair was woven into cloth (Ex 35:26); its flesh and milk provided food (Dt 14:4); and the whole animal was used for sacrifice (Lv 3:12; 4:24; 9:15). *See also* AZAZEL.

Jesus used the goat as a symbol for those going to hell (Mt 25:32–33). See 1:71–72, 115–17, 835; 2:664, 724.

GOD. Gk *theos* translates three Hbr terms. (1) *'elohim* appears c 2,550 times in the OT. It is the first and most commonly used word for God in the OT (cf Gn 1:1). References to the true God always take singular verbs, even though *'elohim* is a plural noun. This grammar may signal God's unique majesty and trinitarian character. The Hbr term is occasionally used of men, such as judges (Ex 4:16; Ps 82:6). This may signal that Israelites understood *'elohim* to describe God's authority. (2) *'el* appears c 400 times, an ancient word for God appearing in every Semitic language except Ethiopic. It is especially common in Jb, appearing there more often than the other terms for God. (3) *'eloah* appears c 400 times. It is similar in spelling to the common Aram word for God. (Some have regarded *'eloah* as a singular form of Hbr *'elohim*, but this is not proven.) The term appears frequently in older poetry (cf Dt 32:15, 17; Jb uses it 41 times). Uses of *'eloah* outside of Jb associate the name with God's ability to defend His people. In the Apocrypha, the general name "God" is the second most common one, appearing about half as often as "Lord." The Being who is not limited in any way or by anything, who is not held by time or space, who possesses all power, knowledge, and wisdom, and who created the world and all people. God shows Himself through His creation, but because all people have fallen into sin, they exchange their knowledge of the true God for a lie and worship false gods (Rm 1:18–32; Ac 14:15–17; 17:22–31). Because of this, God chose to show Himself and His will to people through Jesus Christ so that they might know and believe in Him and be saved (Jn 1:14, 18; 2Co 4:6; 5:18–20).

The chief names for God in the OT are Elohim and Yahweh (*see* JEHOVAH). God is all-powerful; He is a spiritual being. Yet, the Bible describes Him as though He were a human person so that people can somewhat understand Him and talk about Him. For instance, Ps 145:16 speaks of God's "hand," even though God does not have hands as people do. Although Scripture often describes God as though He has a human body and human feelings or as acting in a human way (Gn 3:8; Ps 2:4; Zep 3:17), the only way He is truly like people is in Jesus Christ (Is 55:8–9; Jn 1:14).

The name God can rightly be used to refer to the entire Trinity or to any one of the three persons of the Trinity (Eph 1:3; Jn 1:1; Ac 5:3–4). *See also* GODS, FALSE; HOLY SPIRIT; JESUS CHRIST; TRINITY. See 1:24–26, 51, 70, 170, 496, 528; 2:74, 168, 338–39, 424–25.

GOD-FEARERS. NT term. Gentiles who believed that the God of Israel was the true God, but who had not received circumcision. *See also* PROSELYTE.

GOD MOST HIGH. *See* HIGH, MOST.

GOD OF HEAVEN. A later biblical term, appearing mostly at the time of exile and in the Apocrypha.

GOD OF HOSTS. The common OT name "Lord" or "God of hosts" (Hbr *yahweh tseba'oth*) is virtually absent from the Apocrypha, appearing in only one passage (1Esd 9:46). LXX translators preferred to substitute "almighty" for the Hbr term for "hosts," which was apparently too awkward for readers of Greek. See 1:276.

GOD OF ISRAEL. Common OT title that continued to be used in the intertestamental period. It emphasizes God's covenant bond with Abraham's descendants through the chosen seed, Jacob (Gn 32:28; 35:10). "Israel" remained the more common term for God's people even when Judeans or "Jews" were being described. *See also* HOLY ONE. See 1:51, 167, 757; 2:66, 132.

GODS, FALSE. Plural of Gk *theos*. Translates Hbr *elohim*. As in the OT, "gods" is the most common term for idols in the Apocrypa, due to its repeated use in Lt Jer. *See also* ARTEMIS; ASHERAH; ASHTORETH; BAAL; BAAL-ZEBUB; CHEMOSH; HADAD 1; IDOL; MERODACH; MILCOM; MOLECH; NEHUSHTAN; RIMMON; SAKKUTH; ZEUS. See 1:30, 365–66, 584; 2:21, 447, 465–66, 784.

GOG. The prince of Rosh, Meshech, and Tubal. The prophet Ezekiel described him as invading Israel in the last days (Ezk 38–39; cf Rv 20:7–10). See 1:811–12.

GOLD. A precious metal Israel obtained from foreign lands (1Ki 10:2; 22:48). The Israelites made ornaments, money, and temple furnishings out of gold (Gn 24:22; Ex 36:34–38; 1Ki 10:2; 22:48). Gold was a symbol of purity and perfection (Jb 23:10; Rv 21:15, 21). See 1:72, 359–60, 368; 2:258, 771–72.

GOLGOTHA (GOL-go-thah). A place outside the city gate of Jerusalem where Christ was crucified and near where He was buried (cf Mt 28:11; Jn 19:17–18, 41; Heb 13:11–13).

Another common word, *Calvary*, is the Latin rendering of the Gk word for skull. The Hbr word for skull, *Golgotha*, also refers to this place (Mt 27:33; Mk 15:22; Jn 19:17). Its name may be due to the shape of the hill or to the number of executions carried out there. *See also* CALVARY.

GOLIATH (go-LIGH-uth). The Philistine giant whom David killed (1Sm 17). See 1:290–91, 573; 2:153.

GOMER (GO-mur). The unfaithful wife of the prophet Hosea (Hos 1:3). See 1:855–60.

GOMORRAH (go-MAHR-ah). A city that was destroyed by fire (Gn 19:24, 28). It was on a plain that is now under the Dead Sea. *See also* SODOM. See 1:27; 2:760.

GOOD. That which is right, helpful, or better than others of its kind. The only true good is from God; in fact, God is good, and everything He does is good (Gn 1:31; Ex 18:9; Ps 118:1; Jer 32:40; Mk 10:18; Rm 7:12). Especially His plan of salvation is good. If a person wants to "do good," then he or she must have faith in and live for Jesus Christ (Rm 6; Gal 5:24–26). See 1:35, 584, 600, 614, 891–92; 2:197, 206, 252, 386, 483, 608.

GOPHER WOOD. The type of wood Noah used to build the ark. Bible scholars are not certain what kind of wood this was, but some think it may have been something like cypress (Gn 6:14).

GOSHEN (GO-shuhn).

1. The area in northeastern Egypt assigned to the Israelites (Gn 46:28). See 1:21, 29, 70.
2. An area in southern Israel, possibly named after the town of Goshen in the hills of Judah (Jsh 10:41; 15:51).

GOSPEL. Gk *euangelion*, "good news" or "message." Based on *aggelo*, "to bear a message." The Good News that God has forgiven all people because Jesus Christ has fulfilled the Law in their place and paid the penalty for their sin (Jn 3:16; Rm 1:16–17; 1Co 15:1–15; 2Co 5:18–20; Eph 2:8–9). Summarized by

Paul in 1Co 15:1–4; implications described in Rm 1:16. See 1:xxxii–xxxiii, 15, 34, 60, 294–95, 789; 2:204–5, 249, 287, 338.

GOSPELS. The first four books of the NT. Matthew, Mark, Luke, and John each wrote one of the books. They are called Gospels because they tell the Good News of how salvation was won for all people by Jesus Christ. The first three Gospels are referred to as the Synoptic Gospels because they can be placed side by side for comparison. The writers of all four of the Gospels are often referred to as evangelists. See 2:175–357.

GOVERNOR. Although this title is used for many officials in the Bible, it usually refers to someone who ruled a city or province and reported to the ruler above him (Gn 42:6; Ezr 5:14; Lk 3:1). See 1:424–25, 434, 976–77; 2:297, 379, 811–13.

GRACE. Gk *charis*. God's generous mercy toward undeserving people (Rm 5:12–21; Jn 3:16; Ti 3:3–7). God's free and undeserved favor toward sinful humanity is demonstrated in Christ's work of redemption. It is an unearned and undeserved gift. The word *grace* is sometimes used of a gift, quality, or virtue; saving grace, however, is none of these things. It is a quality within God. It is also referred to as God's steadfast love or faithfulness (2Sm 7:15; Ne 9:17; Ps 31:21; 42:8). *See also* FAVOR; MERCY. See 1:24, 109–11, 173, 614, 990; 2:205–6, 321, 428–29, 437, 443, 690–91.

GRACIOUS. From Hbr *chanan*, "to be gracious, generous, compassionate." An attribute of God celebrated in the Psalms. *See also* FAVOR. See 1:563, 582, 589–90.

GRAPE. *See* VINEYARD.

GRASS. Used in the Bible as the general name for all small green plants (Mt 6:30). Grass is also a symbol for the shortness of life (Ps 90:5–6; Jas 1:10–11). See 1:598.

GREAT CONGREGATION. From Hbr *qahal*, "assembly." The gathering of God's people at the tabernacle or temple. See 1:289, 400, 407.

GREECE (GREES). The name for the area in Bible times that included Macedonia, Achaia, and the islands of the Aegean Sea (Acts 20:2). Today Greece is the name of a modern country in southeastern Europe that is almost identical in location to the Greece of Bible times. See 1:464, 835; 2:481, 519, 562–63.

GREEK.

1. The language of Greece, from which the original language of the written NT came. See 1:52; 2:3–5, 185.
2. A person who was born in or lived in Greece (Acts 17:12). When Jews and Greeks are contrasted in the NT, the term *Greek* is used for a foreigner in general (Rm 1:16). Greek-speaking Jews were referred to as Hellenists. See 1:997; 2:3–5, 185.

GUILT. *See* CONSCIENCE; SIN, II. See 1:223–25, 577; 2:344, 428–29.

H

HABAKKUK (hah-BAK-uhk; "basil"). A prophet of Judah whose message of hope in God's grace is recorded in the Book of Habakkuk. Habakkuk prophesied about 605 BC while the temple was still standing (cf 2:20). See 1:947–59; 2:129–30.

HABAKKUK, BOOK OF. See 1:947–59.

HADAD (HAY-dad; "thunderer").

1. The name of the Aramean god of storm and thunder (like the Canaanite god Baal).
2. Possibly also a title, since several kings and princes of Edom had this name (1Ki 11:14–25; 1Ch 1:46, 50). See 1:323, 653.

HADES (HAY-deez). In classical Greek this word refers first to a person and then to the place in the depths of the earth where the spirits of the dead go. The Hbr word *Sheol* has a similar meaning. In the NT, Hades refers to the place of the dead (Lk 10:15; Ac 2:27; Rv 6:8). *See also* HELL; SHEOL.

HAGAR (HAY-gahr; "flight"). Sarah's Egyptian servant. Hagar took Sarah's place and had a son, Ishmael, for Abraham (Gn 16; 21:1–21). Hagar represents slavery under the Law (Gal 4:24–25). See 1:27; 2:507.

HAGGAI (HAG-ay-igh; "festive"). A prophet c 520 BC during the days of Darius (Hg 1:1). Haggai was a leader in rebuilding the temple (Ezr 5:1). His prophecy is recorded in the Book of Haggai. See 1: 445, 971–80, 983–85.

HAGGAI, BOOK OF. See 1:971–81.

HAGIOGRAPHA (hag-i-OG-rah-fah; "sacred writings"). The third main division of the Jewish OT. Its Hbr name is *Kethubim*, which means "writings." The

Hagiographa include Ruth, Chronicles, Ezra, Nehemiah, Esther, Job, Psalms, Proverbs, Ecclesiastes, Song of Solomon, Lamentations, and Daniel. See 1:491–92; 2:47, 57.

HAIL.

1. A word of greeting or respect for a superior. The soldiers who mocked Jesus addressed Him with this word (Mt 27:29). See 2:166.
2. Pellets of ice that fall from clouds like rain. God sent a plague of hail on Egypt (Ex 9:18–29). People feared hail because it destroyed their crops and hurt or damaged other things (Ps 78:47–48). See 1:90–91.
3. A symbol of God's judgment (Is 28:2).

HAIR. In OT times both men and women had long hair (2Sm 14:26). Nazirites, people who had made a special promise to God, were not supposed to cut their hair (Nu 6:1–5). *See also* NAZIRITE. Baldness was disliked and was used as a symbol for God's anger or judgment (Is 3:24; Jer 47:5). In NT times long hair was for women only (1Co 11:14–15).

Scripture forbids or warns against certain ways of wearing one's hair (Lv 19:27; 1Pt 3:3). It also mentions barbers and describes how hair was trimmed (Ezk 5:1; 44:20). See 1:238–39, 680, 853; 2:460, 468.

HALLEL (ha-LAYL; "praise"). The name given to certain psalms that played a special part in Israel's worship, e.g., Psalms 113–118. Jesus and His disciples probably sang the Hallel at the Last Supper. See 1:544, 582–83; 600–601.

HALLELUJAH (HAL-i-LOO-yah; "praise the Lord"). A call or command to praise God and His name. This word became an important part of the language of Israel's worship. It is found in the Book of Revelation (Rv 19:1, 3, 4, 6). See 1:558, 585–86.

HALLOW. To set apart as holy, for special use for or by God (Lk 11:2; cf Ex 20:11). See 1:108, 110, 803; 2:397–98, 608.

HAM (HAM; "black" or "hot"; also the Egyptian name for Egypt).

1. The third son of Noah (Gn 5:32). When Ham uncovered his father's nakedness, Noah spoke a curse on Canaan (Gn 9:21–27). Ham's sons were Cush, Egypt, Put, and Canaan (1Ch 1:8). Their descendants lived in South Arabia, Egypt, Ethiopia, and Canaan. See 1:26.
2. The poetic name for Egypt (Ps 105:23, 27).

HAMAN (HAY-muhn). The wicked prime minister under Ahasuerus. Haman tried to have all the Jews in Persia killed (Est 3:1). See 1:461–74; 2:104–9, 113–14.

HAMMER.

1. A tool used, much like today, for many tasks that required forceful blows, e.g., driving tent pins, tearing down buildings, shaping gold or other metals, and breaking rock (Jgs 4:21; 1Ki 6:7; Ps 74:6; Is 41:7).
2. A symbol of power or strength (Jer 50:23).

HAMMURABI (ham-uh-RAH-bi). A king of Babylon who ruled during the eighteenth century BC. He is known for the battles he fought, the cities he built, and the Code of Hammurabi, which was a set of laws he put together. See 1:16, 273; 2:818.

HANAMEL (HAN-ah-mel; "God has pitied"). The prophet Jeremiah's cousin. Before the siege of Jerusalem Jeremiah bought a field from him (Jer 32:6–12).

HANANIAH (han-ah-NIGH-ah; "Yahweh is gracious").

1. The false prophet who opposed Jeremiah (Jer 28:1–17). See 1:751, 765.
2. The Hebrew name of Shadrach, one of the three men thrown into the fiery furnace because he would not worship the golden image King Nebuchadnezzar set up (Dn 1:3–19; 3). See 1:823; 2:134.

HAND. Hbr *yad*, "hand," including the forearm.

1. Figurative for power, strength, or control (Ex 13:3, 14, 16; 1Sm 23:20; Ps 76:5). The phrase "hand of God" refers to God's actions or presence (1Sm 5:11; Ezr 8:22; 1Pt 5:6). The open hand stands for generous giving (Dt 15:8; Ps 145:16). See 1:167, 213, 218–19, 304, 448, 511, 521, 732, 805; 2:284, 386–87.
2. People gave directions by using their right hand for the south and their left hand for the north (Jb 23:9).
3. The Bible speaks of the right hand as the place of honor and authority (1Ki 2:19; Mt 25:33; Ac 2:33). See 1:521, 838; 2:292–93, 381, 389, 395–96, 656.
4. Hands were used to give a blessing (Mk 10:16; 2Tm 1:6). See 2:314.

HANNAH (HAN-ah; "grace"). Samuel's mother (1Sm 1–2). See 1:288, 296, 556.

HARAN (HAY-rahn; "road").
1. Abraham's brother (Gn 11:26–31). See 1:49.
2. A city in upper Mesopotamia where Abraham went after leaving Ur (Gn 11:31–32). See 1:17, 25, 29, 49; 2:800.

HARDNESS OF HEART. A condition of stubbornness and disobedience in which a person refuses to listen or change his or her mind (cf Pharaoh in Ex 7–10). Hardness of heart can prevent understanding and belief (cf Ac 19:9). People may harden their hearts against God or other people (Ex 8:32; Dt 15:7). God sometimes confirms their hardness of heart as punishment (Ex 10:1; Rm 9:18). See 1:67, 70.

HARLOT. *See* PROSTITUTE. See 1:863–64; 2:446–47.

HAROD (HAY-rod; "fear"). The spring or well where Gideon camped with his men (Jgs 7:1). See 1:244.

HARP. *See* MUSIC.

HARROW. A farming tool. The harrow was a toothed instrument that animals dragged along the ground to break up clods of earth after plowing (Is 28:24–25). *See also* AGRICULTURE.

HARVEST.
1. Refers to the physical gathering of goods (Ru 2). *See also* AGRICULTURE; ORCHARD; VINEYARD. See 1:258; 2:684.
2. Jesus describes the final judgment as a harvest (Mt 13:24–30). *See also* ESCHATOLOGY; JUDGMENT. See 2:585, 688–89, 784.

HARVEST, FEAST OF. *See* PENTECOST 1.

HASIDEANS. Or, Chasidim. Hbr "pious ones," mentioned in 1Macc 2:42 as a broad group of Jews who supported Judas Maccabeus in revolt against Antiochus IV Epiphanes. However, once the Hasideans gained their religious rights, they lost interest in advancing the Hasmonean dynasty. See 2:79.

HASMONEANS (haz-mo-NEE-ahnz). From Gk *Hasmonaios*, which likely refers to a place-name associated with the priest Mattathias, who led his family in revolt (AD 167) against Antiochus IV Epiphanes. Mattathias's son, Judas Maccabeus ("the hammer"), became the leader of the movement and established the Hasmonean dynasty (167 BC–AD 63) over Judea. *See also* MACCABEES. See 2:4, 13, 81, 806.

HATE.
1. To dislike or regard as ugly or wrong; to have feelings toward someone or something that are the opposite of love (Ps 45:7; Mt 24:10). See 1:30, 94–95, 470, 641; 2:201, 743.
2. To withdraw from or avoid someone or something so that a proper relationship with God can be kept (Am 5:15; Lk 14:26; cf Mt 10:37–39). See 1:576; 2:304–6.

HAZAEL (HAZ-ay-el; "God sees"). A great king of Syria whom God used to bring judgment upon Israel (1Ki 19:15–18). Hazael followed Ben-Hadad II, ruling Damascus from about 840 to 800 BC. Hazael captured Israel's land east of the Jordan, continually troubled Jehoahaz, and once even planned to attack Jerusalem (2Ki 10:32–33; 12:17–18; 13:3–7, 22–25). See 1:325, 334, 344.

HAZOR (HAY-zawr; "enclosure"). A city of northern Galilee near the headwaters of the Jordan River. Jabin was the ruler of Hazor when Joshua captured it (Jsh 11:1–14). Later it was given to the tribe of Naphtali (Jsh 19:36, 39). Another King Jabin of Hazor was defeated by Deborah and Barak (Jgs 4). See 1:28, 211, 881; 2:799.

HEAD. Hbr *ro'sh*.
1. A part of the body. See 1:179; 2:460.
2. A whole person (Pr 10:6).
3. The capital of a country or region (Is 7:8–9). See 2:799.
4. A leader in society (Is 9:14–15). Like "chief," general term used with "tribe," "clan," and "father's house." Indicates different leadership strata within a tribe. See 1:53, 152; 2:680, 758.
5. The name for one who has authority over others (Eph 5:23). See 1:496, 535, 631; 2:413, 527.
6. The expression "upon the head" refers to guilt, responsibility, or duty (Jsh 2:19; Ezk 9:10).
7. The expression "lift up the head" or the action of lifting up the head means to restore or renew favor, life, strength. (Gn 40:20–21; Ps 83:2). See 1:600.

HEAD OF THE CHURCH. Christ, who gives life, strength, and direction to every believer and who rules as the Head of the Body, the Church (Eph 1:20–23; 4:15–16). See 2:413, 525–27, 533, 713.

HEADBAND. Probably a sash or other piece of cloth worn around the head (Is 3:18).

HEAL. *See* DISEASE. See 1:108, 733; 2:244–50.

HEAR.
1. To receive sound by means of the ear (2Sm 15:10). See 1:403; 2:249.

2. To listen to God's Word and will (Mt 13:18). See 1:585; 2:209.
3. To understand and follow God's Word and will (Jn 8:47; 10:27). See 1:740; 2:291.
4. To listen to and approve as right (cf 1Jn 4:5). See 1:752; 2:336.
5. God's "hearing" describes His action of answering prayer (Ps 116:1). See 1:580; 2:291.

HEART.
1. A symbol for the life of the whole body (Jgs 19:5).
2. A word for describing the center of thought, understanding, decision making, emotion, will, and conscience (Dt 29:4; Ne 7:5; Is 44:18; 65:14; 1Co 7:37). Some Bible translations use the word *mind* instead of *heart* to describe these things. See 1:31–32, 160–61, 178, 180, 283, 607–8, 807, 869; 2:200, 292, 306–7, 671.
3. The place within us where Christ and the Spirit live (Eph 3:17; 2Co 1:22). See 1:219, 549; 2:572–73.

HEARTH (HAHRTH).
1. A portable fireplace (cf "fire pot" in Jer 36:22–23).
2. A fireplace on an altar (Ezk 43:15–16).

HEATHEN. *See* BARBARIAN; GENTILES. See 1:265; 2:127, 469.

HEAVEN (HEV-uhn).
1. The layer of air surrounding the earth and everything in it (Dn 7:13; Mk 14:62). See 1:226, 332–33; 2:386, 689, 785–86.
2. The upper or outer part of the universe and all that is in it; the firmament, especially the "waters above" (Ps 148:4; Is 40:22). See 1:48–49, 420.
3. The invisible world or universe from which God rules (Ezr 1:2; Ps 115:3); the home of angels (1Ki 22:19; Mk 12:25). Christ rules from heaven and receives believers there (Heb 8:1; cf Jn 14:1–3; Ac 7:55). *See also* PARADISE. See 1:37, 178, 344; 2:190, 203, 257–58, 314, 547, 785–87.

HEBREW (HEE-broo). The language in which most of the OT was written. Scripture refers to it both as the language of Canaan (Is 19:18) and as the language of Judah (2Ki 18:26, 28). The language is closely related to ancient languages from the region of Israel and is probably based on a Canaanite dialect adopted by the patriarchs.

The Hebrew alphabet, consisting only of consonants, came from the writing of the Phoenicians and was in existence by the fifteenth century BC. About AD 600 to 800, scribes known as the Masoretes added vowel sounds to the Hebrew text of the OT. See 1:cxii.

HEBREWS (HEE-broos). Abram is the first person in the OT to be referred to as a Hebrew (Gn 14:13). From that point on the name is given to his descendants in both the OT and the NT. Hebrew is another name for a person of the nation of Israel (e.g., a person who lives in the United States is referred to as an American).

The word *Hebrew* may come from a word that means to pass over, referring back to Abram's crossing of the Euphrates River after he had left home, or it may come from the name Eber, an ancestor of the Israelites (Gn 10:21). In ancient writings from Bible times the Hebrew people are sometimes linked with people known as the Habiru. See 2:451.

HEBREWS, LETTER TO THE. See 2:651–73.

HEBRON (HEE-brun; "place of alliance"). A city about 20 miles southwest of Jerusalem. It was originally called Kiriath-arba (Gn 23:2). Hebron played a large part in Abraham's life (Gn 13:18). The spies visited this place (Nu 13:21–22), Joshua conquered it (Jsh 10:36–37), and David was anointed as king and ruled Judah from Hebron for more than seven years (2Sm 2:1–4, 11). See 1:293; 2:802–3, 805.

HEDGE. A kind of fence or enclosure made of plants, often thorns (Is 5:5; Hos 2:6).

HEIFER. A young cow that has not produced a calf (Dt 21:3). A heifer is often used in metaphors (Jgs 14:18; Jer 46:20; 50:11). The Israelites used a red heifer for purification ceremonies and as a sin offering (Nu 19:1–10). See 1:131–32, 243.

HEIR. The individual to whom another person's wealth or possessions, the person's inheritance, is given after the person dies. When a man died, his inheritance was first divided among the sons of his legal wives (Gn 21:10; 24:36; 25:5). The oldest son usually received a double share and became the head of the family (Dt 21:15–17). *See also* FIRSTBORN. If the man had no sons, the inheritance was divided, in order, among his daughters, brothers, paternal uncles, or other relatives (Nu 27:8–11). See 1:27, 258.

In the NT, it describes the relationship of believers to the heavenly Father, based on grace (Rm 8:16–17). *See* PORTION for OT background. See 2:425, 507, 688.

HELL. Either the place of eternal punishment or the punishment itself. It is called Sheol in the OT, and it is the translation of the Gk word *Gehenna* in the NT. Hell is described as eternal punishment (Mt 25:46), a fire that cannot be put out (Mk 9:48), a place where worms continually eat and fires continually burn the damned (Is 66:24), a lake of fire (Rv 20:14), the outer darkness (Mt 25:30), and the furnace of fire where people cry out and grind their teeth (Mt 13:42, 50). Unbelievers are put in hell because they are under the wrath of God (Jn 3:36). *See also* HADES. See 1:184, 535; 2:215, 712, 784–85.**HELLENIST** (HEL-en-ist). Jews who accepted the Greek language and culture following the rule of Alexander the Great (356–323 BC). When the Ptolemies ruled Judea (323–198 BC), they encouraged Greek ways but did not force their religion on the people. After the Seleucids took over Judea (198 BC), they forced Greek ways on the people under threat of torture and death. This sharply divided the Jewish community. Acts reports that Hellenists readily converted to Christianity (Ac 6:1; 9:29), though the cultural conflict that divided Judaism likewise affected the Early Church. The Hellenist Christians actively spread the Gospel to Gentiles (cf Ac 11:19–20). See 1:656, 949; 2:3–5, 27–29, 80, 85–86, 95–97, 806–7.

HELMET. *See* ARMOR, ARMS.

HELPER. Sometimes Paraclete. One who is called to one's side or pleads one's cause before a judge. In 1Jn 2:1, the term is used of Christ. He is the believer's advocate with the Father; He pleads for the Christian before God. Elsewhere the word often refers to the Holy Spirit, who is the believer's Helper on earth (Jn 14:16, 26; 15:26; 16:7). It is He who indwells the Christian, bringing Christ and His work of salvation to remembrance; it is He who guides the believer into all truth. See 1:263, 583; 2:336.

HEM. The edge, fringe, or border of a piece of clothing (Ex 28:33–34; Mt 9:20). The Pharisees wore especially long fringes because they wanted to show off their obedience to the command in Nu 15:38–39 (cf Mt 23:5).

HEMLOCK. *See* GALL 3; WORMWOOD.

HEPHZIBAH (HEF-zi-bah; "my delight is in her").

1. The wife of Hezekiah (2Ki 21:1).
2. The symbolic name God gave to Israel to show His love and mercy for the covenant people (Is 62:4).

HERALD.

1. A messenger or someone who publicly announces decrees of the government or other news (Is 41:27; Dn 3:4). See 1:437.
2. Someone who spreads God's Word, especially someone who preaches it (2Pt 2:5). See 1:972, 1000; 2:279, 594.

HERD. *See* CATTLE.

HERDSMAN. A person in charge of cattle or pigs (Gn 13:7; Mt 8:30–33). The Israelites viewed this job favorably, but the Egyptians looked down on it (cf "shepherd" in Gn 46:34; 47:6). See 1:26, 880.

HERESY (HAIR-uh-see; "choice").

1. In the NT world, various schools of thought or belief were called heresies, that is, sects or parties within a larger system of belief. For instance, Sadducees, Pharisees, and Christians were all regarded as heresies, that is, sects or parties within Judaism (cf Ac 5:17; 15:5; 24:5, 14).
2. The word can describe differences of opinion, goals, or belief that cause divisions within the Church (cf 1Co 1:10; 11:18–19).
3. The word is used as a name for false, harmful teachings (2Pt 2:1). See 1:879–80; 2:160–61, 326, 599–602, 741.

HERITAGE. *See* PORTION. See 1:361–62.

HERMON (HUR-mun; "holy mountain"). A mountain about 9,100 feet high that stands approximately 30 miles southwest of Damascus and about the same distance northeast of the Sea of Galilee. Water runoff from the rain and snow on its slopes feeds the Jordan River.

Mount Hermon marked the northern extent of Israel's conquests east of the Jordan River (Dt 3:8). Some think it may be the mountain where the transfiguration of Christ took place (Mk 9:2). It is called Baal-hermon in Jgs 3:3 because it was a major center of worship of the false god Baal. See 1:140, 492–93; 2:150.

HEROD (HAIR-uhd; "heroic"). The family name of a line of rulers from Idumea (southeast of Israel) who ruled in Israel during NT times (55 BC–AD 93).

1. Although the line was begun by Herod Antipater, it was his son who was known as Herod the Great. Herod the Great was the Roman procurator of Judea in 47 BC and was king of the Jews for more than 30 years, from 36 to 1 BC (or 37–4 BC; there are different conclusions about the dating). To

stay on the good side of Rome and of the people in Israel, Herod rebuilt cities and temples, most important the temple at Jerusalem (Jn 2:20). To maintain his power he did many wicked things, often deceiving or killing people. He was the king who spoke to the Wise Men and had all the baby boys in Bethlehem killed (Mt 2:1–18). See 1:328; 2:159, 186, 195–96, 266–67, 806–8.

2. Herod Archelaus, the son of Herod the Great, was the ruler of Judea, Idumea, and Samaria from 1 BC to AD 6 (Mt 2:22; or 4 BC—AD 1). See 2:298–300.
3. Herod Antipas, another son of Herod the Great, ruled Galilee and Perea from 1 BC to AD 39 (Lk 3:1, 19; or 4 BC to AD 39). He was the ruler during Jesus' lifetime. Herod was rich and sly. Jesus referred to him as "that fox" (Lk 13:31–32). See 2:188, 195.
4. Herod Philip, yet another son of Herod the Great, is known only as the husband of Herodias. His brother Herod Antipas took Herodias from Herod Philip and married her himself (Mt 14:3–4). See 2:195.
5. Herod Philip II was not the son of Herod Philip but of Herod the Great. Herod Philip was his half-brother. Herod Philip II ruled Ituraea and other regions (Lk 3:1).
6. Herod Agrippa I, a grandson of Herod the Great, ruled different areas of the region of Israel from AD 41 to 44. He persecuted Christians. An angel of the Lord killed him because of his pride and wickedness (Ac 12:1–23). See 2:195, 376, 810.
7. Herod Agrippa II was a son of Agrippa I and a great-grandson of Herod the Great. He was king of the territory east of Galilee from about AD 50 to 70. Paul was brought before him (Ac 25:13–26:32). See 2:379–80.

HERODIANS (hi-RO-di-ahnz). The dynasty of Herod the Great and its political supporters. Descendants of Herod rule the region of Israel on behalf of the Romans (63 BC–AD 100). Cf Mk 3:6. See 1:896; 2:244, 806.

HERODIAS (hi-RO-di-as). Herod the Great's granddaughter. She left her first husband, Herod Philip, to marry her brother-in-law Herod Antipas (Mt 14:3–4). Herodias caused the death of John the Baptist (Mt 14:6–12).

HEZEKIAH (hez-i-KIGH-ah; "Yahweh is strength"). The thirteenth king of Judah. Hezekiah was the son of Ahaz and the father of Manasseh. He returned Judah to the worship of the true God after a long period of idolatry (2Ch 29–31). Under his direction many of the godly teachings of Solomon were written down (Pr 25:1). Judah prospered during his rule. Then Hezekiah became mixed up in a power struggle among Egypt, Assyria, and other nations.

Hezekiah strengthened the defenses of Jerusalem (2Ch 32:5–8). He also supervised the building of the Siloam Tunnel to bring water into the city (2Ki 20:20). When Sennacherib attacked, Hezekiah and the prophet Isaiah prayed to God for help, and God destroyed the attacking army (Is 36–39). See 1:347–48, 376–77, 402–4, 556, 625–26, 716–17, 726–27, 731; 2:803–4.

HIEROGLYPHIC (high-ur-o-GLIF-ik; "sacred carving"). A system of picture writing used in Egypt and other ancient nations. It is one of the earliest forms of writing. See 1:63.

HIGH, MOST. A name for God (Ps 9:2; 21:7; Lk 8:28). Melchizedek served God Most High (Gn 14:18–20). See 1:16, 577, 835–38.

HIGH PLACES.

1. Places of worship located on high ground. They usually had some type of altar and often one or more buildings (1Ki 12:31–32). Because the Canaanite high places brought the threat of idolatry and immorality, God commanded the Israelites to destroy them (Nu 33:52). But the kings of Israel, beginning already with Solomon, rebuilt the high places, sometimes to worship the true God but more often to worship false gods (1Ki 3:2, 4; 11:7; 2Ki 17:7–20). See 1:330, 370, 401; 2:798, 802.
2. The term *high place* eventually became a general name for any place of worship, even one in a valley (Jer 7:31). The place was considered high because of the lordship of the deity.

HIGH PRIEST. High priests were chosen from the line of Eleazar (Nu 20:25–28) and his son Phinehas. In later times, there appears to be more than one high priest (cf 1Ki 2:27, 35). One of Eleazar's descendants, Zadok (1Ch 6:1–15), headed the later succession of high priests. *See also* PRIEST; ZADOKITES. See 1:75, 78, 101, 299, 310, 402, 987; 2:301–2, 330, 656–63, 666.

HIGHER CRITICISM. Methods of studying a text that go beyond the basic ("lower") considerations of philology and textual criticism, by which manuscript copies are compared or studied to establish what the text is. Higher critical methods are hypothetical, seeking to discern the historical development of a text. They have included source criticism, redaction criticsm, form criticism, tradition criticism, and other methods based on assumptions about the evolution of texts and the communities that create them. Higher critical methods have led to numerous doctrinal issues and errors. See 1:5–11, 384–85, 708–13; 2:178–83.

HILKIAH (hil-KIGH-ah; "Yahweh is my portion"). One of Ezra's ancestors who was the high priest in the days of King Josiah (Ezr 7:1). Hilkiah found the Book of the Law in the temple (2Ki 22:4–14). See 1:348, 754–55; 2:117.

HILLEL, HOUSE OF. Disciples of Rabbi Hillel the Elder (active c 30 BC–AD 10). More tolerant toward Gentiles than the House of Shammai. Rabbi Gamaliel, with whom the apostle Paul studied (Ac 5:34; 22:3), may have been Hillel's grandson. See 2:411.

HINNOM (HIN-um). A valley south of Jerusalem where the Hebrews offered their children to the false god Moloch (Jsh 15:8; 2Ki 23:10; Jer 7:31; 19:2–6). It was also called Gehenna. Later this place became a dump for unclean matter; fires burned in it continually. For this reason the NT writers used the word *Gehenna* to name the place of the eternal destiny of unbelievers (cf "hell" in Mt 5:22, 29–30; 10:28; 18:9; 23:15, 33; Mk 9:43, 45, 47; Lk 12:5). *See also* HELL. See 1:753.

HIRAM (HIGH-ram; "my brother is exalted").

1. The king of Tyre who sent cedar and workmen to David for his house, and lumber and gold to Solomon for use in building the temple (2Sm 5:11; 1Ki 9:11–14). See 1:323, 341–42, 401.
2. The workman who made all the bronze items in or around the temple (1Ki 7:13–46). Both of these men were sometimes referred to as Huram.

HISS. A way of showing surprise or contempt (1Ki 9:8; Jb 27:23; Jer 19:8). It is sometimes translated as "scoff." See 1:789.

HISTORICAL CRITICISM. *See* HIGHER CRITICISM.

HITTITES (HIT-ights). The descendants of Heth (Gn 10:15). The Hittites were a great nation that at one time ruled a large portion of the ancient Near East. They are frequently mentioned in the OT (Gn 26:34). Archaeologists have discovered remains of the Hittite civilization and have learned their language. See 1:53–55, 63, 162, 322; 2:819.

HOLY. Hbr *qodesh*, "set apart." Gk *hagios*, "sacred" or "dedicated to God." God, uncreated and unique, is the only source of holiness. He hallows time (feasts), place (tabernacle/temple, called "the sanctuary"), people (priests/Levites/Israel), and the things and rituals that belong to them. That which is set apart to be used for or by God, or that which is recognized as partaking in God's holiness. God's very name is "holy" because He is perfect in every way and is "high above," or set apart from, all things (Is 57:15). God demands that His people be holy or set apart for Him (Lv 19:2; Nu 15:40). The holiness of God is imparted to people through His act of choosing them in grace and through His other mighty acts (Dt 26:18–19). It culminates in the saving work of Jesus Christ (Jn 17:19; 1Pt 2:1–10). Jesus is called the Holy One of God (Mk 1:24). The Apocrypha and LXX continue OT themes, choosing the rarer Gk term *hagios* over the common Gk term *hieros*, which might have introduced Gk religious ideals (Ezk LXX uses *hieros* for pagan sites, Ezk 27:6; 28:18; and 2Macc uses *hieros* for the temple). The OT and Apocrypha themes also stand behind NT teaching about salvation as (1) purification from sin and (2) election by grace. *See also* CHOOSE; CLEAN. See 1:99–107, 111–16, 599, 636, 742, 807, 988; 2:159, 200–1, 376, 475–76, 663, 709.

HOLY LAND. *See* CANAAN 2.

HOLY ONE. In the OT, this title is used 26 times in Is and only a few times elsewhere. Holiness includes all attributes of perfection that distinguish God from His creatures (*see* HOLY). Yet He condescended to enter a covenant relationship with Israel, His chosen servant for salvation. When Israel fell into sin, they had to fear God's holy wrath. In the Apocrypha, this title was favored by the author of Ecclus, Jesus son of Sirach. See 1:82, 644, 726, 733; 2:65, 166, 585.

HOLY ONES. *See* SAINT.

HOLY SPIRIT. The Third Person of the Trinity (Mt 28:19; 2Co 13:14). The Holy Spirit works through and is sent by God the Father and God the Son (Jn 15:26; Ac 1:8). The Holy Spirit is God and performs the works of God (Gn 1:2; Rm 8:9). He creates and sustains the universe and the Church (Gn 1:2; Jb 33:4; Ac 2). Moreover, each individual believer is created, or born again, through the Spirit, who works through water and the Word (Jn 3:3–8; 6:63; 1Co 12:13).

The Holy Spirit lives in the hearts of believers, strengthening and encouraging them in the faith and building them up in the unity of the Spirit and in the unity of the body of believers, the Church (Eph 4:1–6; 1Co 12; 2Co 1:22). The Holy Spirit also unites believers to God the Father and to Jesus Christ (Rm 8:14–17).

The Holy Spirit gave a special measure of understanding to the prophets, worked in a special way in certain leaders of God's people, and was given without measure to Jesus Christ (Jgs 3:10; Is 61:1; Lk 4:1; Col 1:19; 1Pt 1:10–12; 2Pt 1:21). The Holy Spirit dwells in believers (2Tm 1:14). He continues to give understanding of God and His will to believers and gives them all spiritual blessings (Jn 14:26; 16:13–15). See 1:112, 244–45, 302, 521–22, 606, 872, 874; 2:155, 222–23, 286–87, 333–40, 354, 374–76, 386–90, 473–75, 627–28, 728.

HOLY SPIRIT, SIN AGAINST. *See* SIN, UNPARDONABLE.

HOMES. Shepherds, exiles, outcasts, and lepers often lived in caves found throughout the limestone ridges of Canaan (1Ki 18:4; 19:9). People built temporary shelters, or booths (Is 1:8), by covering four upright poles with a network of sticks and leaves. Sometimes they made these shelters out of woven river reeds that they plastered with mud.

Nomadic people lived in tents (Gn 4:20), which were often woven from dark-colored goat or camel hair. These tents were usually very large. They had several supporting poles, sloping sides that were held in place by cords anchored in the ground with stakes, and curtains to divide up the living space inside (Is 54:2; Jer 10:20).

In sections of Canaan where building stone was readily available, people built homes out of blocks of limestone. Mortar made from lime and sand held these blocks together. In some areas of the ancient world people built homes made from clay bricks (Gn 11:3). They constructed doors from planks of wood or slabs of stone. The windows of their homes were usually very narrow; they were placed high up in the wall and fitted with wooden latticework (Pr 7:6). To make roofs for their homes, people laid beams across the tops of the walls. Then they covered these beams with a layer of branches laid crosswise, a layer of rushes and straw, and a layer of clay. More alternating layers of rushes and straw were added, and the roof was finished with a solid layer of clay. The walls extended about three feet above the roofline (Dt 22:8). The people often worked or stored things on their rooftops or went there to be alone or to enjoy cool breezes (Jsh 2:6; Ac 10:9). A stairway on the outside of the house led from street level up to the roof. Sometimes people built an upstairs room, or upper room, on one side of the building (2Ki 4:10; Mk 14:15; Ac 1:13). They also might make the one main room into two levels, the upper level for living quarters and the lower one for sheep and goats.

The furnishings of a typical house included mats or rugs woven from wool, grass, or straw. These were used for mattresses at night and in place of chairs during the day. A stove or fireplace for heating and cooking was located in the middle of the house. Sometimes it was only a hole in the earthen floor. Spoons, forks, and other utensils and pots and pans were made of copper. Knives were made of bronze or iron and had wooden handles. Plates, cups, bowls, jugs, and other containers were made of clay. People stored wheat in large pottery jars. Other things were stored by hanging them from the roof beams.

Wealthier homes had furniture—couches, beds, chairs—more like today's furniture. Often these homes had walled courtyards or consisted of a series of rooms built around an open court. As the nation of Israel grew richer, the wealthy and powerful people built big, beautiful mansions and palaces (1Ki 7:1–8; Am 6:4–8). See 1:341; 2:222, 238, 808.

HOMOLOGOUMENOM. A word that occurs only once, such as a term in Job and Song of Solomon that is found no where else in Hebrew literature. Such a word is often difficult to translate. See 2:156–64, 647, 729, 750.

HOMOSEXUALITY (HO-mo-SEK-shoo-AL-i-tee). The Bible never provides a detailed psychological answer for homosexuality but clearly condemns it as a corruption of God's created order (Rm 1:26–28; see also Gn 18–19; Lv 18:22; Jgs 19:22–23; 1Co 6:9–10; 1Tm 1:9–10).

HONEY. Wild honey, which was plentiful in Israel, was eaten in various ways (Ex 16:31; 1Sm 14:25). It was often a symbol of wealth and plenty (Nu 14:8). See 1:lxi, 138–39, 809; 2:161.

HOOKS. Hooks were used for fishing (Jb 41:1), hanging curtains (Ex 26:37), leading animals or prisoners (2Ch 33:11; Ezk 19:4), pruning and trimming (Jl 3:10), and hanging meat (Ezk 40:43).

HOPE. Hbr *batach*, the common OT term for "trust." Forms of Gk *elpis*, "confident trust" rather than wishfulness. A feeling of peace and joy; confident trust in what is not seen. The Christian's hope is centered in Jesus Christ (1Tm 1:1). It flows from the new, loving relationship a Christian has with God through faith in Jesus Christ (Rm 5:1–11). Faith, hope, and love are often linked in Scripture (1Co 13:7, 13; Heb 11:1; 1Th 1:3; 5:8). Christian hope looks beyond this life to the glory of heaven (cf 2Co 4:16–18). It takes Christ's resurrection as the promise of God that the Christian will also be raised to life eternal (cf 1Co 6:14). Christians who live in such hope are comforted in times of trouble and are motivated to live lives pleasing to God (Ps 43:5; 1Jn 3:1–3). See 1:253–54, 261, 511–12, 516–18, 786–89; 2:366, 393–95, 400, 568, 572–74, 658, 710–11.

HOR (HAWR; "mountain").
1. A mountain on the edge of Edom where Aaron died (Nu 20:22–29). See 1:140.
2. A mountain in northern Israel, probably in Lebanon, that was used to mark the northern boundary of Canaan (Nu 34:7–8).

HOREB (HO-reb; "dryness"). The mountain where the Law was given to Israel (1Ki 8:9). Also called Mount Sinai. See 1:172, 333, 343, 368; 2:150.

HORN. At first people blew on animal horns to give signals. They also made containers out of animal horns (Jsh 6:5; 1Sm 16:1). Later they made horns out of metal (cf Nu 10:2). The projecting corners of the altar in the tabernacle and the temple were called horns (1Ki 1:50). The horn was a symbol of honor and strength (Dn 7:7; Lk 1:69). Animals with horns are bold; in Israelite thought, a horned animal with its head held high symbolized strength and triumph. See 1:270–71, 329, 876–77.

HORSE. The Hebrew people during Jacob's time were familiar with horses (Gn 49:17). The Egyptians used horses mainly for war (Ex 14:9). The Israelites were ordered not to keep any horses captured in battle, and the rulers of Israel were directed not to keep large numbers of horses (Dt 17:16; Jsh 11:6). Later kings, however, did keep horses (1Ki 1:5; 4:26). See 1:90–91, 314–15, 334, 989.

HOSANNA (ho-ZAN-ah; "save now"). At Jesus' triumphant entry into Jerusalem the crowds chanted this as they waved palm branches (Mt 21:9–15). Usage of the word may have originated with Ps 118:25–26. See 1:583; 2:202.

HOSEA (ho-ZAY-ah; "salvation"). A prophet at the time of Kings Uzziah, Jotham, Ahaz, Hezekiah of Judah, and Jeroboam II of Israel (Hos 1:1). Isaiah, Amos, and Micah were other prophets at the same time as Hosea. Hosea's prophecy is recorded in the Book of Hosea. See 1:855.

HOSEA, BOOK OF. See 1:853–65.

HOSHEA (HO-SHEE-ah; "salvation"). The last king of Israel. Hoshea gained the throne by joining with a foreign king to assassinate Pekah, who was then king of Israel (2Ki 15:30). Hoshea placed himself under the control of Assyria by paying tribute to the king of Assyria, Shalmaneser V (2Ki 17:3). When Hoshea stopped paying tribute, the Assyrians conquered Israel and took the people captive. Apparently Hoshea was not as wicked as other kings of Israel (2Ki 17:2). See 1:347, 373–76, 854, 864.

HOSPITALITY (hos-puh-TAL-uh-tee). The readiness to help strangers by giving them food, clothing, shelter, or whatever else they might need. Hospitality is commanded in the Levitical law and is encouraged elsewhere in the OT and NT (Heb 13:2; cf Gn 18:1–8; Lv 19:34; Jb 31:32). See 2:305–6, 515.

HOST.
1. A great number. The host of heaven refers either to the numerous stars and other heavenly bodies that people often wrongfully worshiped or to the angels and the company of saints in heaven (Dt 4:19; 1Ki 22:19; Lk 2:13). See 1:186, 368.
2. One of God's names is Sabaoth, or Lord of hosts. He is named this because He rules over the angels, the stars, and all things (Is 40:26; cf Gn 28:12; Jb 37–39). *See* GOD OF HOSTS. See 1:272, 729–31.
3. Someone who shows hospitality. See 1:834; 2:338.

HOUSE.
1. The name for a family line (Ex 2:1; Lk 2:4). See 1:349; 2:396.
2. The name for the place where God makes His presence known, for instance, at Bethel, which means house of God, in the tabernacle, and in the temple (Gn 28:17; Ex 34:26; 1Ki 6:1). See 1:30, 113, 420, 976; 2:710–11.
3. *See* HOMES.

HOUSEHOLD. Hbr *beth*; Gk *oikos* or *oikonomia*, a core family group, including the slaves and children, sharing a home. Paul described a congregation as a household (Gal 6:10). *See also* CHURCH. See 1:27, 349, 631; 2:289–90, 413, 515.

HULDAH (HUL-dah; possibly Semitic for "mole," or a similar animal). A prophetess in the OT. She was the wife of Shallum (2Ki 22:14–20; 2Ch 34:22–28). See 1:348, 753.

HUMILITY. The opposite of pride; not thinking more of oneself than one should. Someone who is humble puts God and others ahead of self (Pr 15:33; Rm 12:3; cf Lk 18:9–14). See 1:244, 598, 732; 2:253, 330, 545–46.

HUNDRED. Used in round figures (cf Gn 15:13; Lv 26:8; Mt 18:12) and in expressions of uncertain amounts (Is 65:20), as also happens in other languages (e.g., the Eng expression "I've told you a hundred times" means "constantly"). See 1:150.

HUNTING. The Israelites hunted many types of wild deer, sheep, and birds (Dt 14:5; 1Sm 26:20). They used bows and arrows, slingstones, spears, nets, pits, and traps (Gn 27:3; Jb 41:28–29; Ps 9:15).

HUR.

1. The man who helped Aaron hold up Moses' hands at Rephidim so that Joshua was able to defeat the Amalekites (Ex 17:8–16). See 1:65.
2. A king of Midian (Nu 31:8).

HYMN. A song telling about God and praising Him (Ex 15:1–18; Dt 32:1–43; Jgs 5; 1Sm 2:1–10; Lk 1:46–55, 68–79). Christians are encouraged to worship God by using psalms, hymns, and spiritual songs (Col 3:16). See 1:404, 488, 553–62; 2:137–40, 530, 546.

HYPOCRISY (hi-PAHK-ru-see). To play a part; to pretend to be what one is not. In the Bible, hypocrisy usually describes a condition of pretending to have faith when no faith is present in the heart at all (Mt 23:28). It also refers to any type of trickery, lying, or falsehood (Mk 12:15). See 1:577; 2:188–89, 202–3, 375, 676.

HYSSOP (HIS-uhp). Although the Bible mentions this plant numerous times, it apparently is not always referring to the same type of plant. Ex 12:22 seems to speak of a bushy plant that the Israelites used to sprinkle blood on the doorposts at the first Passover. Jn 19:29 mentions a long stalk or stem as part of the hyssop plant that was used to put the bitter drink to Jesus' lips while He hung on the cross. The plant was used in certain religious ceremonies and also as a symbol of purification, correction, and forgiveness (Lv 14:4, 6, 49; Nu 19:6; Ps 51:7). See 1:132.

I

IBEX (IGH-beks). Probably a large, light-colored antelope. Since the ibex was classed among the clean animals, the Israelites were allowed to eat it (Dt 14:5). See 1:250, 956.

ICE. Snow and ice can be found on the higher mountains of Israel (Jer 18:14). Otherwise, snow and ice are rare except in the extreme north of the country (Jb 6:16; 37:6, 10).

ICHABOD (IK-ah-bod; "where is the glory?"). The son of Phineas and grandson of Eli. Ichabod was born after his father was killed in a battle with the Philistines, a battle in which the Philistines captured the ark of the covenant. Ichabod's mother named him as she did because she felt the glory had departed from Israel (1Sm 4:19–22). See 1:276.

ICONIUM (igh-KO-ni-uhm). A city on the southwestern edge of the central plain of Asia Minor (modern-day Turkey). Paul visited this city on his missionary journeys (Ac 13:51; 14:1–22; 16:2). See 2:377, 388, 499–500, 813.

IDDO (ID-o).

1. The name of a wise man who wrote down the events of the reigns of Solomon, Rehoboam, Jeroboam, and Abijah (2Ch 9:29; 12:15). See 1:190, 396.
2. The grandfather of the prophet Zechariah (Zec 1:1, 7). See 1:983.

IDOL, IDOLATRY (IGH-dol, igh-DOL-ah-tree). A false god or anything that is placed ahead of the true God is an idol. Worshiping a false God or placing a thing or person ahead of God is called idolatry. Often idols had names and were represented by pictures or some type of statue or figurine made of various materials and in varying sizes (Gn 31:34; Is 40:19–20; Dn 3:1). Idols and idolatry are forbidden and are spoken of as foolish, hateful, and horrible in Scripture (Ex 20:4–5, 23; Is 44:9–20; Ezk 37:23). For example, Hbr *gilulim*, "dung pellets" (always plural; related terms used in Jb 20:7; 1Ki 14:10; Ezk 4:12, 15; Zep 1:17). Expresses the utter derision the prophets felt toward pagan idols. One of 10 OT terms for idols; Ezk uses it repeatedly (38 of 47 appearances in the OT). Paul describes idols and idolatry as exchanging the truth about God for a lie (Rm 1:21–23, 25). See 1:73, 91–93, 174–75, 238–42, 805, 860–64, 992; 2:71–75, 127–31, 447, 464, 783.

IDUMEA (id-yoo-MEE-ah). The Greek name for Edom, the area south of Judah (Mk 3:8). See 1:498, 896; 2:186, 195.

IGNORANCE. A lack of knowledge. In the Bible ignorance is especially a lack of knowledge concerning the true God and His will. It is sometimes described as excusable and at other times as inexcusable (Ezk 45:20; Eph 4:18). See 1:728; 2:607, 727.

ILLYRICUM (i-LIR-i-kuhm). The name of a Roman province on the east coast of the Adriatic Sea, northwest of Greece. It was later called Dalmatia (2Tm 4:10). As far as we know, it is the northernmost part of Europe into which Paul traveled on his missionary journeys (Rm 15:19). See 2:419.

IMAGE. *See* IDOL, IDOLATRY. See 1:91–92.

IMAGE OF GOD. God created people in His image (Gn 1:26–27). Because God is a spiritual being and no person or thing can equal Him in any way, the likeness of people to God is spiritual, not physical, and is always "less than," not "equal to."

In the most proper sense, being created in the image of God means that people were created without sin. But this image was lost in the fall into sin. In the broader sense, the image of God refers to humanity's rationality and will, and still remains in people, though the presence of original sin has also corrupted that likeness (Gn 9:6; Jas 3:9). Christ is the image of God, and in Him we can see God (Jn 1:1, 14, 18; Col 1:15). Through Christ people regain the likeness to God (Rm 8:29). See 1:34–35, 529–30, 837; 2:191, 253, 547, 555–56.

IMMANUEL (i-MAN-yoo-uhl; "God is with us"). The name of the child whom the prophet Isaiah predicted would be born of a virgin (Is 7:14; Mt 1:22–23). This is an important prophecy predicting the birth of the Savior, Jesus Christ, the Promised One spoken of in many OT prophecies (Gn 3:15; Is 9:6–7; 11:1; Mi 5:2–3). See 1:715, 724, 727, 734, 738; 2:218.

IMMORTALITY (im-awr-TAL-uh-tee). *See* ESCHATOLOGY; ETERNAL LIFE. See 1:501, 669; 2:32–33, 99.

IMPERIAL GUARD. The bodyguard and household of the emperor in Rome (Php 1:13). See 2:540.

IMPUTATION (im-pyoo-TAY-shuhn). Placing the blame for something bad or the credit for something good on someone else. When Adam and Eve fell into sin, that sin was imputed to all, that is, the blame for it was placed upon all people. In the same way, when Christ paid the price for sin by His death and resurrection, that payment was imputed or credited to all who believe in Christ (Rm 5:12–21; 2Co 5:19–21). See 1:224, 564, 571.

INCARNATION (in-kahr-NA-shuhn). The term for what took place when the Son of God took on a human body and soul. The word itself does not occur in the Bible, but it is used properly in the Nicene Creed to describe Jesus' birth. *See also* JESUS CHRIST. See 1:76, 243, 532–34; 2:252, 284, 743.

INCENSE. Any substance that gives off a sweet smell when burned. Incense played an important part in Israel's worship. It was burned on the altar of incense morning and evening, carried into the Most Holy Place on the Day of Atonement, and used at other times as well. The incense the Israelites used is described in Ex 30:34–35. People also burned incense to worship false gods (Lv 26:30).

Incense is a symbol for prayer or worship (Ps 141:2; Rv 5:8). See 1:72, 407–8, 622; 2:45.

INCEST. Having sexual relations with members of one's own family. Incest is forbidden in Scripture (Lv 20:11–17, 19–21; 1Co 5:1). See 1:30, 49–50, 281; 2:456.

IN CHRIST. Can mean "by or through Christ," as the agent of our salvation. Christ is also the one in whom we find God's gifts. We are baptized "into Christ" (Gal 3:26–27) and experience what He has (Eph 2:4–6). *See* FELLOWSHIP. See 2:507, 527–29.

INDIA (IN-di-ah). The country on the east of the Persian Empire (Est 1:1). See 1:459.

INHERITANCE. *See* HEIR; PORTION. See 1:119–20, 168–69, 213; 2:292, 665.

INIQUITY (i-NIK-wi-tee). *See* SIN, II. See 1:222–23, 594, 739; 2:211, 406.

INK. A substance used for writing. Ink was made by mixing charcoal or lampblack (a fine black powder) with water and plant gum (Jer 36:18; 2Jn 12). See 2:799.

INN. Places where travelers can sleep at night. Hebrew hospitality made inns and hotels in our sense practically unnecessary. The inns in Lk 2:7 and 10:34 were probably more like private homes than places of business.

INSPIRATION (in-spuh-RAY-shuhn). The special way the Holy Spirit worked in certain people that caused them to act out, speak, or write God's Word (Mi 3:8; 1Co 2:13; 1Pt 1:10–11). When the Holy Spirit did this, the person who was inspired or motivated to act, speak, or write was certainly under the direction of God's power, but he or she was not a robot (Lk 1:1–4). See 1:8–9, 703–4, 817–19; 2:6–10, 351, 473–75, 622.

INTERCESSION. *See* PRAYER. See 1:36, 168, 703; 2:284, 659.

IN THAT DAY. *See* ON THAT DAY.

IOTA (igh-O-tah). The smallest letter of the Greek alphabet, particularly as a subscript (Mt 5:18; Lk 16:17). See 2:xix, 514.

IRON. Iron is mentioned already in Gn 4:22. The Hittite people passed the knowledge of ironworking to the Philistines. When David conquered the Philistines, the Israelites learned about ironworking as well. Tools, weapons, chariots, chains and shackles, and writing tools were all made from iron (Nu 35:16; Jsh 6:19, 24; 17:16; 1Sm 17:7; Jb 19:24; Ps 105:18). Iron is also a symbol of strength. See 1:217, 770; 2:312, 814.

ISAAC (IGH-sahk; "laughter"). Abraham's only son by Sarah (Gn 17:19). Isaac was the son of the promise, the one through whom God continued to work out His plan of salvation (Gn 21:12). Isaac showed himself to be a faithful, obedient son when God ordered Abraham to sacrifice him (Gn 22:1–18). Isaac married Rebekah and had two sons: Jacob and Esau. Rebekah and Jacob plotted together to trick Isaac into giving Jacob the blessing of the firstborn son (Gn 24–27). Isaac died at Mamre (Gn 35:27–29). See 1:27–30, 51, 122; 2:44, 423, 506, 657.

ISAIAH (igh-ZAY-yah; "Yahweh is salvation"). A prophet of Judah during the reigns of Uzziah, Jotham, Ahaz, and Hezekiah (Is 1:1). The year that Uzziah died, Isaiah saw a vision in the temple (Is 6). This is sometimes referred to as Isaiah's call to be God's prophet. Isaiah, who lived in Jerusalem, married and had two sons (Is 7:3; 8:3). Hezekiah sought the help of Isaiah when the Assyrians were about to attack Jerusalem (2Ki 19:1–7). See 1:347, 373, 716–17, 724; 2:381–82.

ISAIAH, BOOK OF. See 1:715–49.

ISCARIOT (is-KAR-i-ut). *See* JUDAS 2.

ISH-BOSHETH (ish-BO-sheth; "man of shame"). One of Saul's sons, originally called Eshbaal (1Ch 8:33). Ish-bosheth ruled two years at Mahanaim but was defeated by David's men. Later he was assassinated (2Sm 2:8–16; 3:6–15; 4:5–12). See 1:293–94, 372.

ISHMAEL (ISH-may-uhl; "God hears").

1. The son of Abraham and Sarah's maidservant, Hagar (Gn 16:3, 15; 17:25). Sarah became jealous of her stepson and demanded that Abraham send him and his mother away. Abraham was disturbed by this, but trusting God's word to him, he sent them away (Gn 21:8–20; cf Gal 4:21–31). Ishmael's descendants became a great nation (Gn 17:20; 25:12–16). See 1:27–28, 51.
2. The man who assassinated Gedaliah and caused Jeremiah to flee to Egypt (Jer 40:7–41:18). See 1:755, 758, 768.

ISHMAELITES (ISH-may-ul-ights). Descendants of Ishmael. The Ishmaelites were mostly traveling desert merchants and traders (Gn 37:25–28).

ISLAND.

1. Dry land surrounded by water (Ac 13:6). See 1:273; 2:41, 380, 625, 770–71.
2. Habitable land that once was water (Is 42:15).
3. Symbolic for faraway lands, whether islands or not. It often describes the majesty of God and the broad scope of messianic prophecy (cf "coastland" in Ps 97:1; Is 49:1).

ISRAEL (IZ-ray-el; "God strives"; "he strives with God").

1. The name given to Jacob at Penuel after he wrestled with a stranger (Gn 32:28). See 1:30–31.
2. The name of the nation composed of the descendants of Jacob and his 12 sons. Jacob and his sons founded the 12 tribes of Israel (Ex 3:16). The name Israel is used more than 2,000 times in Scripture to refer to the children, or nation, of Israel. See 1:32–33, 70–71.
3. The name given to the 10 northern tribes of Israel after Solomon's death when they revolted under Rehoboam and the kingdom split into two. The Northern Kingdom was called Israel to distinguish it from the Southern Kingdom, which was called Judah (1Sm 11:8). The capital of Israel was first Shechem (1Ki 12:25) and later Samaria (1Ki 16:24). When a remnant of the people returned to Canaan after the Babylonian exile, the name Israel was used again of all the descendants of Jacob and his sons (Ezr 10:10). See 1:294–96.

4. In the NT, Israel became a name for the Church, which constitutes believers from all nations (Ps 73:1; Rm 9:6–8; 11:25–36; Gal 3:26–29; 6:16). See 2:300, 328, 374, 396.

ISRAELITES (IZ-ray-uhl-ights). *See* ISRAEL.

ISSACHAR (IS-a-kahr; "hired laborer").

1. The ninth son of Jacob, the fifth by his wife Leah (Gn 30:14–18). A tribe of Israel was made up of Issachar's descendants. Jacob prophesied that Issachar's descendants would become slaves (Gn 49:14–15). See 1:31, 213.
2. The area southwest of the Sea of Galilee that was assigned to the tribe of Issachar (Jsh 19:17–23). It included the Plain of Esdraelon, also called the Valley of Jezreel (Jgs 6:33).

ITALY (IT-ahl-ee). The name of the whole peninsula of land that begins with the Alps on the north and juts southeastward into the Mediterranean Sea. The city of Rome is on the western shore of this peninsula (Ac 18:2). See 2:235, 651.

ITHAMAR (ITH-ah-mahr). The youngest son of Aaron (Ex 6:23). Ithamar was consecrated as a priest and directed the construction of the tabernacle (Ex 28:1; 28:40–29:9; 38:21). See 1:102.

ITTAI (IT-ay-igh). A powerful man from Gath who was loyal to David and led 600 of his men against Absalom (2Sm 15:18–22). See 1:281.

ITUREA (i-tyoo-REE-ah). A hilly area in the mountains of Lebanon, north of Israel. At one time warlike descendants of Ishmael lived there. Iturea was later also the name of a small Roman province (Lk 3:1).

IVORY. Both a symbol and a source of wealth, ivory was imported into Israel and used to decorate houses and furniture (1Ki 10:18, 22; Am 3:15). People also made many objects and implements out of ivory and decorated with it. See 1:360, 852–53; 2:351.

J

JABBOK (JAB-uk; "effusion"). An eastern tributary of the Jordan River that runs through Gilead. Cf Gn 32:22. It rises near Amman and flows through a deep canyon to join the Jordan about 23 miles north of the Dead Sea (cf Jgs 11:13). See 1:16.

JABESH-GILEAD (JAY-besh-GIL-i-uhd). A city east of the Jordan River and about 10 miles southeast of Beth-shan in the territory given to the tribe of Manasseh. All the men of this city were destroyed because they did not obey the command of God to assemble at Mizpah (Jgs 21:8–14). Later Saul freed the city from the Ammonites (1Sm 11:1–11). The people of this city remembered Saul and gave him a decent burial (1Sm 31:11–13). See 1:290, 293.

JABIN (JAY-bin; "he discerns").

1. A king of Hazor whom Joshua defeated (Jsh 11:1–14). See 1:208.
2. Another king of Hazor whose general, Sisera, was defeated by Deborah and Barak (Jgs 4). See 1:237.

JACHIN (JAY-kin).

1. The name of several minor OT characters, including a son of Simeon (Gn 46:10).
2. Jachin and Boaz were the names of the two large pillars that stood in front of Solomon's temple (1Ki 7:15–22). See 1:359.

JACOB (JAY-kuhb; "supplanter").

1. The son of Isaac and Rebekah and the younger twin of Esau (Gn 25:21–26). Jacob bought the birthright from Esau for a pot of lentil stew and, with his mother's help, tricked Isaac into giving him the blessing of the firstborn son (Gn 25:29–34; 27:1–41). Then Jacob fled to Haran. On the way he had a vision of a ladder reaching to heaven (Gn 27:42–28:22). At Haran Jacob worked for his Uncle Laban at least 20 years—14 years to earn the right to marry Laban's daughters, Rachel and Leah, and six more to acquire flocks of his own (Gn 29:1–30). Jacob had at least 12 sons and one daughter by his wives and his wives' maids. Leah was the mother of Reuben, Simeon, Levi, Judah, Issachar, Zebulun, and Dinah. Rachel was the mother of Joseph and Benjamin. Leah's maid, Zilpah, was the mother of Gad and Asher, and Rachel's maid, Bilhah, was the mother of Dan and Naphtali (Gn 29:31–30:24; 35:16–26).

   Jacob fled from Laban back to Canaan, wrestling with God one night on the way (Gn 30:25–32:32). Jacob reconciled with his brother, Esau, and settled in Canaan (Gn 33). Jacob worshiped the true God and was blessed by Him (Gn 35:9). God changed Jacob's name to Israel (Gn 35:10). See 1:16.

The story of Jacob's life overlaps in Genesis with the story of his son Joseph's life in Egypt (Gn 42–46). Before he died, Jacob gave a prophetic blessing to each of his sons (Gn 49). See 1:16–24, 27–32, 52–53, 897–99; 2:671, 800.

2. The name Jacob is also used as a symbol for the Israelites (Nu 23:10; Ps 59:13). See 1:806.
3. The father of Joseph of Nazareth and the paternal, earthly grandfather of Jesus (Mt 1:15–16). See 2:219.

JADDUA (ja-DYOO-ah; "well-known"). The name of the last high priest mentioned in the OT (Ne 12:11, 22). See 1:383, 429.

JAEL (JAY-uhl; "wild goat"). The wife of Heber. Jael killed Sisera, the general of Jabin's troops, with a tent peg (Jgs 4:17–27). See 1:237; 2:17.

JAIR (JAY-ur; "may Yahweh shine"). One of the judges of Israel (Jgs 10:3–5). See 1:238, 244.

JAIRUS (JIE-ruhs; the NT form of the name "Jair"). The ruler of the synagogue, probably at Capernaum, whose daughter was raised by Jesus (Mk 5:22; Lk 8:41). See 2:245, 320.

JAMBRES (JAM-breez). The name of one of the Egyptian magicians who opposed Moses (2Tm 3:8–9; cf Ex 7:9–13). See 1:153; 2:618, 766.

JAMES (JAMZ; the Hbr form of this name is Jacob).

1. The son of Zebedee who was called away from the family fishing business along with his brother to be a disciple (Mt 4:21). James, his brother John, and Peter formed the inner circle of disciples who were closest to Jesus. James witnessed the transfiguration of Jesus (Mk 9:2–9), the raising of Jairus's daughter (Mk 5:37–39), and Jesus' agony in Gethsemane (Mt 26:37). He was killed by Herod Agrippa I about AD 43. Jesus nicknamed James and his brother the "Sons of Thunder" (Mk 3:17). See 1:368; 2:320, 324–25.
2. The son of Alphaeus and Mary, another of the 12 disciples of Jesus (Mk 3:18; Ac 1:13). Often referred to as James the Less, he is distinguished from the other disciple named James as being either younger or smaller or both (Mk 15:40). See 2:169.
3. One of the brothers of the Lord (Mt 13:55). He apparently did not believe in Jesus as the Son of God until after His resurrection, possibly being converted by one of Jesus' postresurrection appearances (Jn 7:5; Ac 1:13–14; 1Co 15:5, 7). James became a leader of the Early Church, especially the church at Jerusalem (Gal 1:18–19; 2:12). He served as chairman of the Jerusalem council (Ac 15:13, 19–23). It is generally thought that James wrote the Letter of James (Jas 1:1). See 1:50; 2:252, 437, 503, 677–78, 758.

JAMES, LETTER OF. See 2:675.

JANNES (JAN-eez). The name of an Egyptian magician who opposed Moses (2Tm 3:8–9; cf Ex 7:9–13). See 1:153; 2:618.

JAPHETH (JAY-feth; "enlarged"). One of Noah's three sons and the father of Gomer, Magog, Madai, Javan, Tubal, Meshech, and Tiras (Gn 6:10; 10:2). His descendants occupied the islands and coastlands of the Gentiles; they were the Indo-European peoples (Gn 10:5). Japheth's obedient behavior brought him the blessing of his father (Gn 9:20–27).

JAPHIA (jah-FIGH-ah; "high place").

1. A king of Lachish whom Joshua put to death (Jsh 10:3–26).
2. A son of King David (2Sm 5:15).
3. An ancient town located near Nazareth (Jsh 19:12).

JASHAR (JAY-shur; "upright"). The author of a lost poetical book that was used in writing the historical books of the OT (Jsh 10:13; 2Sm 1:18). See 1:190, 205, 209, 339.

JASON (JAY-suhn; "healing").

1. Of Cyrene. A historian who wrote about the rise of the Maccabees. Second Maccabees is a summary and simplification of Jason of Cyrene's volumes. See 2:93–97.
2. A Christian who showed Paul hospitality at Thessalonica and received harsh treatment from the Jews (Ac 17:5–9). He is probably the same Jason mentioned in Rm 16:21.

JASPER. A type of quartz usually stained deep shades of red, brown, green, and yellow. In ancient times jasper included other types of rock as well. Jasper was used for decorative purposes (Ex 28:20; Ezk 28:13; Rv 4:3).

JAVELIN (JAV-lin). A short, light spear (Jb 41:26). *See also* ARMOR, ARMS.

JEBUS (JEE-buhs). The name of Jerusalem when occupied by the Jebusites (Jsh 15:63; 18:28; Jgs 19:10).

The city was small in comparison to the size of Jerusalem at Solomon's time. *See also* ZION 1. See 1:305, 657; 2:802–4.

JEBUSITES (JEB-yoo-zights). A mountain tribe of Canaan that lived at Jebus (Gn 10:16; 15:21; Nu 13:29; Jsh 11:3). Joshua killed their king and assigned their territory to Benjamin (Jsh 10:23–27; 18:16, 28). See 1:151, 294, 305, 621, 657; 2:802–4.

JECONIAH (jek-o-NIGH-ah; "Lord establishes"). A variant spelling of the name Jehoiachin. Jeconiah, or Jehoiachin, was a king of Judah (1Ch 3:16–17; Jer 24:1; 27:20; 28:4; 29:2). *See also* JEHOIACHIN. See 1:753; 2:61.

JEDIDAH (ji-DIGH-dah; "beloved"). The mother of Josiah (2Ki 22:1).

JEDIDIAH (jed-i-DIGH-ah; "beloved by Yahweh"). The name Nathan gave to Solomon (2Sm 12:25).

JEDP. A higher critical theory that claims multiple authors were responsible for compiling the Books of Moses. "J" refers to the Yahwist, "E" for the Elohist, "D" for the Deuteronomist, and "P" for the Priestly author. See 1:6–11, 196.

JEGAR-SAHADUTHA (JEE-gahr-say-hah-DYOO-thah; "heap of witness"). The Aramaic name Laban gave to the heap of stones he piled up as a memorial covenant between him and Jacob. Jacob called it Galeed (Gn 31:47–48).

JEHEZKEL (ji-HEZ-kel; "may God strengthen"). The head of the twentieth division of priests (1Ch 24:16).

JEHOAHAZ (ji-HO-ah-haz; "Yahweh has laid hold of").

1. The son and successor of Jehu and the eleventh king of Israel (2Ki 10:35; 13:1). Jehoahaz did what was evil in the sight of the Lord and continued the idolatry of Jeroboam. Because of this, God became angry with Israel and allowed Hazael, king of Syria, and Ben-hadad, his son, to campaign successfully against them (2Ki 13:1–9). See 1:346, 372.
2. The son and successor of Josiah and the seventeenth king of Judah. His reign of three months was evil. After this time he was deposed by Pharaoh Neco and taken captive to Egypt (2Ki 23:30–34; 2Ch 36:1–4). In 1Ch 3:15 and Jer 22:10–12 he is referred to as Shallum. He is also called a young lion (Ezk 19:1–4). See 1:348, 373.

JEHOIACHIN (ji-HOI-ah-kin; "Yahweh has established"). The son and successor of Jehoiakim and the nineteenth king of Judah. During his short reign of three months and a few days, he did that which was evil in the sight of the Lord. Then Nebuchadnezzar carried him away into captivity and put him into prison. When Evil-merodach ascended the throne of Babylon a number of years later, he released Jehoiachin (2Ki 24:8–16; 25:27–30; 2Ch 36:9–10; Jer 39:2; 52:28–34; Ezk 17:12). *See also* JECONIAH. See 1:348–49, 758–59, 798; 2:61.

JEHOIADA (ji-HOI-ah-dah; "Yahweh has known"). The high priest at the time Athaliah usurped the throne. Jehoiada's wife hid the young prince Joash while Jehoiada planned and carried out the revolt that led to Athaliah's overthrow. Then Joash became the rightful king. Jehoiada was Joash's uncle, and while Jehoiada lived, Joash was faithful to the Lord (2Ki 11:1–12:16; 2Ch 22:10–24:22). See 1:346, 402.

JEHOIAKIM (ji-HOI-ah-kim; "Yahweh has established"). The son of Josiah and the eighteenth king of Judah. His name was originally Eliakim. When his father died, the people put Jehoahaz, Jehoiakim's younger brother, on the throne. But when Pharaoh Neco took Jehoahaz captive to Egypt after three months, he made Eliakim, whose name he changed to Jehoiakim, the new king. Jehoiakim did what was evil in the eyes of the Lord and went back to idol worship. He also heavily taxed his people so that he could pay tribute to Pharaoh Neco.

In 605 BC, Nebuchadnezzar defeated Neco in battle at Carchemish and advanced on Jerusalem. Jehoiakim then became Nebuchadnezzar's servant and paid tribute to him. Three years later Jehoiakim rebelled against Babylonian rule. When he died, his body received the burial of a donkey (2Ki 23:34–37; 24:1–6; 2Ch 36:4–8; Jer 1:3; 22; 24–28; 35–37; 45–46; 52; Dn 1:1–2). See 1:348, 403, 754, 756, 758, 844, 951; 2:61, 220.

JEHOIARIB (ji-HOI-ah-rib; "Yahweh pleads"). The head of the first division of temple priests (1Ch 9:10; 24:7).

JEHORAM (ji-HO-ram). *See* JORAM. See 1:327, 344, 402.

JEHOSHAPHAT (ji-HAHSH-ah-fat; "Yahweh has judged"). The son of Asa and fourth king of Judah. Jehoshaphat reigned 25 years and is described as a good king. In the third year of his reign, he sent princes and Levites to teach the people the Law. He made peace with Israel and removed the high places and idols out of Judah. After visiting Ahab, king of Israel, Jehoshaphat was persuaded to join armies with Ahab against the Syrians. On Jehoshaphat's return home the prophet Jehu rebuked him for joining forces with Ahab and Ahaziah. Jehoshaphat died around 848 BC and was succeeded by his son Jehoram (1Ki 15:24; 2Ki 8:16, 26; 2Ch 17–21:1; Mt 1:8). See 1:344, 372, 388–90, 402.

JEHOSHAPHAT, VALLEY OF. A symbolic name for a valley where the Lord will gather all nations for judgment (Jl 3:2, 12). See 1:874–75.

JEHOSHEBA (ji-HAHSH-i-bah; "Yahweh is an oath," or "an abundance"). The wife of the high priest Jehoida and the daughter of Jehoram and sister of Ahaziah, both kings of Judah. When Jehoram was murdered, Jehosheba hid Joash, Jehoram's son, from Athaliah until Joash could safely be proclaimed king (2Ki 11:2). See 1:346.

JEHOVAH (ji-HO-vah). A common English word for one of God's names. It is a combination of the Hbr consonants YHWH (which were probably pronounced YAH-weh and mean "Lord") and the vowel points of *Adonai*, the word the Hebrew people said whenever they saw YHWH in the text. The Hebrews took seriously the commandment to keep God's name holy. That is why they spoke the word *Adonai* whenever they encountered God's name *YHWH* in their writings.

YHWH is derived from the verb *to be* and indicates God is eternal (Ex 3:13–15). It is God's personal name for Himself, the one He uses when dealing with His people. To know the name *YHWH* is to know God manifesting Himself to His people in grace and love (Ps 9:10; Jer 16:21). See 1:902.

JEHOVAH-JIREH (ji-HO-vah-JIGH-re; "Yahweh will provide"). The name Abraham gave to the place where he put Isaac on the altar (Gn 22:14).

JEHU (JE-hu; "Yahweh is He").

1. A prophet who rebuked Baasha and Jehoshaphat (1Ki 16:1, 7, 12; 2 Ch 19:1–3). See 1:190, 332, 365, 372.
2. The tenth king of Israel. He was a son of Jehoshaphat, a grandson of Nimshi, and a commander in Ahab's army. Because of Ahab's wickedness, God told Elijah to anoint Jehu king over Israel and commission him to destroy the house of Ahab (1Ki 19:16–17).

   After being anointed king, Jehu killed Jehoram of Israel (Ahab's son), Ahaziah of Judah, Jezebel (Ahab's wife), Ahab's heirs, and the prophets of Baal. Jehu, however, made no attempt to walk in the Lord's ways. He assembled all the people and said to them: "Ahab served Baal a little, but Jehu will serve him much" (2Ki 10:18). Jehu also paid tribute to Shalmaneser III, king of Assyria (2Ki 9–10; 2Ch 22:7–9). See 1:325, 345–46, 372; 2:799.

JEHUDI (ji-HYOO-digh; "Jew"). A messenger sent by the court of King Jehoiakim to ask Baruch for the scroll Jeremiah had written (Jer 36:14–23).

JEPHTHAH (JEF-thah; "he opens"). One of the judges of Israel. Jephthah was an illegitimate son who was driven from home by his brothers, the legitimate heirs. Jephthah went to the land of Tob, where he lived until the elders of the tribes of Israel called him back to fight the Amorites. Jephthah rashly promised God that, if he were permitted to win the war with the Amorites, he would offer as a burnt offering whatever first came to him from out of his house when he returned home. Jephthah did defeat the Amorites, and upon his return home was first greeted by his daughter, his only child. Because of his promise, Jephthah sacrificed her to the Lord. Jephthah judged Israel six years. Then he died and was buried in Gilead (Jgs 11:1; 12:7; Heb 11:32). See 1:122–24, 238, 271.

JERAHMEEL (ji-RAH-mi-el; "God has mercy"). One of the officers Jehoiakim sent to arrest Jeremiah and Baruch (Jer 36:26).

JEREMIAH (jer-i-MIGH-ah; "Yahweh founded"). One of the major Hebrew prophets. Jeremiah lived from about 640 to 580 BC. He was the son of Hilkiah, a priest of Anathoth in the territory of Benjamin (Jer 1:1). In the thirteenth year of King Josiah's reign, Jeremiah was called to prophesy by a vision in which God told him he was "to destroy and to overthrow, to build and to plant" (Jer 1:4–10).

Jeremiah continued in his prophetic office during the days of the last kings of Judah (Josiah, Jehoahaz II, Jehoiakim, Jehoiachin, and Zedekiah), approximately 50 years. He supported and probably assisted in Josiah's reforms (2Ki 23). He warned Jehoiakim not to be friends with Egypt and depend on it because the Chaldeans would be successful in their attack against Jerusalem. Jeremiah dictated a scroll of his prophecies to Baruch. When the scroll was eventually read to the king, he cut off a section at a time and threw it into the fire until the entire scroll was destroyed (Jer 36).

In the days of Zedekiah, the princes persecuted Jeremiah (Jer 37–38). After Jerusalem was captured in 605 BC by the Chaldeans, Nebuchadnezzar showed Jeremiah great kindness (39:11–12). Jeremiah finally moved to Egypt, where he probably died (43:6–7). See 1:325, 373, 755–56, 782.

JEREMIAH, BOOK OF. See 1:751–79.

JEREMIAH, LETTER OF. See 2:71–77.

JERICHO (JER-uh-ko; "moon-city"). A city near the Dead Sea about 825 feet below sea level and 6 miles west of the Jordan River. Jericho has been examined by archaeologists and is regarded as the oldest known city in the world.

Joshua conquered Jericho and later gave it to the tribe of Benjamin (Jsh 2–6; 18:21). Later, during Ahab's reign, Hiel rebuilt the city (1Ki 16:34). Jericho is frequently mentioned in the Scriptures (2Ki 2:1–22; 25:5; Ezk 2:34; Mt 20:29; Mk 10:46; Lk 10:30). See 1:121, 140–41, 207, 209–11, 255, 334; 2:246, 307–8, 801.

JEROBOAM (jer-o-BO-ahm; "he pleads people's cause" or "he enlarges").

1. Jeroboam I, the first king of Israel after the division of the kingdom. As a young man, Jeroboam was industrious and able. Solomon, who was busy in building operations in Jerusalem, made Jeroboam superintendent over all the forced labor assigned to the house of Joseph (1Ki 11:27–28). One day on the road outside Jerusalem, Jeroboam met the prophet Ahijah, who told him the kingdom would be divided, and Jeroboam would become king of 10 of the tribes (1Ki 11:29–40).

   When Solomon heard this news, he wanted to kill Jeroboam, and so Jeroboam fled to Egypt (1Ki 11:40). After Solomon's death, Jeroboam did become king of the 10 northern tribes. He made Shechem his capital and Tirzah the place where he lived. Jeroboam was afraid the people would be won back to the house of David and kill him if they went to Jerusalem to worship, so he built worship centers containing golden calves in Bethel and Dan (1Ki 12:25–33). The prophet Ahijah foretold Jeroboam's downfall (1Ki 13). See 1:323–24, 342–43, 345, 372, 653; 2:798.
2. Jeroboam II, the son and successor of Jehoash and the thirteenth king of Israel. Jeroboam was successful in war with Syria and other nations and extended Israel's territory. Amos prophesied during Jeroboam's reign against the moral corruption and idolatry that continued under Jeroboam. Hosea also began his prophetic work during Jeroboam's lifetime. Excavations at Samaria show the splendor of that time (2Ki 14:23–29). See 1:853–54, 878–79, 883, 905; 2:799.

JERUSALEM (ji-ROO-sah-lem). The capital of the united kingdom of Israel and Judah and of Judea. According to the Tel el Amarna letters it was originally called U-ru-sa-lim, which means "city of peace." It sits on a 2,550-foot-high rocky plateau 33 miles east of the Mediterranean Sea and 14 miles west of the Dead Sea.

Jerusalem's water is supplied by the Gihon Spring in the Kidron Valley and by En-rogel, a spring near the joining of the Kidron and Hinnom Valleys. There are reservoirs within the city. During Hezekiah's reign a tunnel was cut in the rock to conduct water from the Gihon to the upper pool of Siloam (2Ch 32:30).

The Jerusalem David took from the Jebusites consisted of only the southeast corner of present-day Jerusalem. Located on a hill south of Ophel, it was 1,250 feet long and 400 feet wide (1Ch 11:4–8). Solomon extended its walls to protect his palaces and temple (1Ki 3:1; 9:15). Manasseh also extended the wall of Jerusalem (2Ch 33:14). After it had been broken down by Nebuchadnezzar, Nehemiah rebuilt the wall out of old material, extending it on the north. Herod built or extended the walls as they were in the time of Christ. The modern walls of the city were built by Suleiman the Magnificent in AD 1542. The temple stood on Mount Zion.

In its history Jerusalem has been known by many different names. It is considered the Salem of Melchizedek (Gn 14:18). It is also called Salem (Ps 76:2), Jebus (Jgs 19:10–11), the city of David (1Ki 8:1; 2Ki 14:20; 2Ch 25:28), Zion (Ps 48:2), the city of God (Ps 46:4), the city of the great King (Mt 5:35), and the holy city (Ne 11:1). See 1:25, 294–96, 305, 320–22, 399–403, 432–37, 763–68, 803–6, 987–89; 2:195, 226–27, 247–48, 334–35, 377, 675–81, 802–4.

JERUSALEM, THE NEW. The city of God. It is described as coming down from heaven and as the mother of believers (Gal 4:26; Rv 21:2, 10). Cf Heb 11:8–10; 12:22–24. See 1:350, 795, 992; 2:777, 785.

JESHUA (JESH-yoo-ah; "Yahweh is salvation").

1. *See* JOSHUA.
2. The head of the ninth division of priests (1Ch 24:11; Ezr 2:36; Ne 7:39). See 1:424.

JESHURUN (JESH-yoo-run; "upright"). A poetical name for Israel that represents Israel as a righteous people (Dt 32:15; 33:5, 26; Is 44:2).

JESSE (JES-ee). The son of Obed and grandson of Ruth (Ru 4:17, 22; Mt 1:5). David was the youngest of eight sons (1Sm 16:11–13; 17:12). See 1:255, 290, 309, 729; 2:184–85.

JESUS CHRIST (JEE-zuhs KRIGHST). Used c 140 times in the NT, this name/title functions as a confession: "Jesus is the Christ." For the significance of this confession, *see* CHRIST. The biblical names and titles for Jesus tell us who He is and what He does for humanity. Some of the most important of His names and titles:

1. *Jesus.* The word *Jesus* is Gk for the Hbr name Joshua (*yehoshu'ah*), which means "Yahweh is salvation." An angel gave the name to Joseph to use with Mary's firstborn Son (Mt 1:21, 25; Lk 1:31), called "Jesus of Nazareth" because Jesus was a common name at the time (e.g., Ac 13:6). See 2:194, 277.
2. *Christ.* Christ is Gk for the Hbr name *Mashiah*, which means "Anointed One." Jesus is fully anointed with the Spirit of God (Jn 3:34). Thus, He is the promised Mashiah or Messiah (Mt 16:13–23; Lk 2:25–26; Jn 1:35–41). This name/title functions as a confession. *See also* MESSIAH. See 1:299, 301; 2:246.
3. *Logos.* Jesus is referred to as Logos, which in Gk means "word" (Jn 1:1–14; 1Jn 1:1; Rv 19:13). This name is used in the NT to identify Jesus as the eternal Second Person of the Trinity. As the Logos, Jesus is the living Word of God who creates and preserves life (Ps 147:15–18; Mt 8:24–27; 9:1–8; Jn 1:3; Col 1:15–20). The Spirit of the eternal Word also inspired the prophets of old (1Pt 1:10–11). See 1:xxxi, 533–34; 2:329–30.
4. *Son of God.* This title is applied to Jesus in a unique sense (Mt 11:27; 16:16; 21:33–41; Jn 1:14, 18; 3:16–18). It says that Jesus as the Son is equal to God the Father (Jn 10:30; 12:45; 14:8–11; 17). He is the Second Person of the Trinity, eternally born of God the Father (Jn 1:18; Rm 8:3). He has the same characteristics, works, and honor as God the Father (Mt 9:18; Jn 5:17, 21, 23, 25; 21:17; Col 1:15–20). See 1:298–99; 2:191, 200, 277, 284, 333–35, 657–58.
5. *Son of Man.* Jesus used this title to emphasize His humanity, especially in connection with His ministry (Lk 9:58; 19:10), power (Mt 9:6; 12:8), death (Mk 14:21; Lk 22:48; Jn 3:14), resurrection (Mt 17:9; Mk 9:9), ascension (Jn 6:62), and second coming and judgment (Mt 25:31). As the new Adam, Jesus brought into existence the new humanity (Rm 5:12–21; 1Co 15:22; Php 2:5–11). As man, He shared in the flesh and blood of man (Heb 2:14). Jesus is God and man in one person (Jn 1:14; Col 2:9; 1Tm 2:5). See 1:800, 834, 836, 838; 2:237, 333, 385, 393–94, 776.
6. *Servant of God.* Jesus is the Servant of God because He did what God willed, especially saving humanity (Mt 12:18; Mk 14:32–42; Jn 1:29; 4:34; 5:30). For this reason He is the ultimate fulfillment of Is 53 (Mk 8:31; 10:33; Rm 4:25). See 2:381.
7. *Savior.* Jesus is the promised Savior (Lk 2:11). Through His life, death, resurrection, and preaching He saves those who believe in Him from sin, wrath, and death (Mt 1:21; Lk 19:10; Jn 4:42; Ac 4:12; 11:14; 16:31; Rm 5:9–10; 10:9–10; 2Tm 1:10). See 1:223, 592; 2:277, 292, 374–75, 618, 785.
8. *Mediator.* Jesus is the Mediator between God and people (Gal 3:19; 1Tm 2:5; Heb 8:6; 9:15; 12:24). As Prophet, Priest, and King, Jesus brings people to God. (*See also* offices of Prophet, Priest, and King below.) See 1:38–39, 223, 521; 2:254, 280, 608–9, 661.
9. *Lamb of God.* Jesus is the Lamb of God sacrificed for the sins of the world (Jn 1:29, 36; Ac 8:32; 1Co 5:7; 1Pt 1:19; Heb 7:27). Cf Ex 12; Is 53:7. See 1:74, 109, 115–16, 742; 2:213, 329, 333, 773.

The work of Jesus Christ may be described in terms of the three offices He fills. As *Prophet*, Jesus announces the kingdom of God through His words and actions. He reveals to people God's anger over sin and God's love in Him. Christ carries on His prophetic work today through the preachers of the Church. As *Priest*, Christ fulfilled all righteousness and paid for the sins of all people by offering up to God the sacrifice of His own life, death, and resurrection in their place (Rm 4:25; 2Co 5:19; Heb 7). Now He continues to intercede for humanity before God the Father (Rm 8:34; 1Jn 2:1). As *King*, Christ rules the whole world through His power (Mt 28:18; Eph 1:22; Heb 1:3), the Church on earth through His grace (Mt 16:18–19; 28:19–20; Mk 16:15; Rm 1:16–17; 14:17–18), and the Church in heaven through His glory (Mt 25:34; Jn 17:24; 2Tm 4:18; Rv 5:12–13; 21:4). See 1:836, 977; 2:256, 669.

Further, the work of Jesus Christ may be described in terms of two states of being. During His state of *humiliation*, which began at the moment of the incarnation and continued through His death, Jesus in His human nature did not fully and always use all of the divine characteristics given to Him through His divine nature (Php 2:6–8). Beginning with His being made alive in the tomb and His descent into hell, Jesus in His human nature began to fully and constantly use all His divine characteristics (Php 2:9–11; Eph 4:8). This is called Christ's state of *exaltation*. See 2:254, 259, 296, 382, 545.

JESUS IS LORD. An early Christian confession (1Co 12:3; Php 2:9); a clear testimony to Jesus' divine nature (*see also* LORD). See 2:395, 520.

JETHRO (JETH-ro; "excellence"). A priest and prince of Midian and the father-in-law of Moses. After Moses fled from Egypt, he came to Midian, where he met Jethro. Jethro gave Moses his daughter Zipporah in marriage. Later, after Moses had led the Israelites out of Egypt and they were camping in the wilderness, Jethro came to Moses and gave him advice on how to govern the people (Ex 18).

Jethro was probably a surname or title; Reuel or Raguel was his personal name (Ex 2:18; Nu 10:29). See 1:65.

JEW (JYOO). Originally someone who belonged to the tribe or kingdom of Judah as opposed to those of the Northern Kingdom (2Ki 15:36; 16:6). After the Babylonian captivity, since the majority of the Israelites returning were from Judah, the meaning of the name Jew was extended. It was applied to any one of the Hebrew race who returned from captivity.

1. *Hebrew* denotes those who descended from Abraham; *Israel* denotes those who descended from Jacob; and *Jew* denotes those who descended from the tribe or kingdom of Judah. The word *Jew* is not applied to Gentile converts as *Israel* is. *See also* HEBREWS; ISRAEL.
2. Adherents of Judaism, a religion based on the beliefs of the Judeans and Israelites who maintained religious affiliation with the Jerusalem temple after the time of the OT.

JEZEBEL (JEZ-uh-buhl; uncertain meaning: "chaste" or "where is the prince?"). Ahab's wicked wife (1Ki 16:31). Jezebel's father was Ethbaal, the king of Tyre and Sidon and a priest of Astarte.

Jezebel worshiped the gods of her father. Ahab built altars to Baal in Samaria to please Jezebel, and 450 prophets of Baal and Astarte were invited to eat at her table (1Ki 16:31–32; 18:19). Jezebel killed the prophets of the Lord and opposed Elijah (1Ki 18:13; 19:1–2). When Ahab coveted Naboth's vineyard, Jezebel planned and carried out a way to have Naboth put to death so that Ahab could take over (1Ki 21).

Because of these murders and other wicked acts, Elijah prophesied that Jezebel would die and the dogs would eat her by the wall of Jezreel (1Ki 21:23). Eleven years after Ahab's death, Jehu killed Jezebel, and Elijah's prophecy was fulfilled (2Ki 9:7, 30–37). See 1:333, 343–44, 346, 351; 2:772.

JEZREEL (JEZ-ri-el; "God sows").

1. A city of Issachar about five miles north of Jerusalem (Jsh 19:18; 1Sm 29:1). The kings of Israel had a palace there (2Sm 2:9; 1Ki 18:45–46; 21:1). Naboth's vineyard was nearby. See 1:333, 345.
2. One of the two sons born to Hosea by Gomer (Hos 1:4). See 1:855–56.

JEZREEL, VALLEY OF. A plain 20 miles long and 14 miles wide between the ridges of Gilboa and Moreh (Jsh 17:16; Jgs 6:33; Hos 1:5). See 1:480–81, 621; 2:799.

JOAB (JO-ab; "Yahweh is father"). The son of David's half-sister Zeruiah and the brother of Asahel and Abishai (2Sm 2:18). Joab killed Abner out of vengeance for the death of his brother Asahel, whom Abner had killed at the battle of Gibeon (2Sm 3:22–39). David made Joab commander-in-chief of the armies of all Israel as a reward for his part in the attack on Jebus (1Ch 11:4–9). Under Joab's leadership, Israel defeated Syria, Edom, and Ammon (2Sm 10; 12:26–31).

Joab arranged Uriah the Hittite's death according to David's orders (2Sm 11). He killed Absalom and Amasa (2Sm 18:9–15; 20:4–13). When Adonijah tried to take the throne, Joab sided with him against David (1Ki 1). On his deathbed, David said he wanted Joab brought to justice for the unjust murders of Abner and Amasa. Solomon, carrying out this wish, had Joab put to death (1Ki 2:28–34). See 1:281, 294–96, 338.

JOASH (JO-ash; "Yahweh has given").

1. The son of Ahaziah and the eighth king of Judah (2Ki 11:2). When Joash was a baby, his father was murdered. Joash was saved from the same fate by his Aunt Jehosheba, the wife of the high priest Jehoiada: Jehosheba hid Joash in the temple for six years. Then through Jehoiada's efforts, Athaliah was put to death, and Joash was rightfully crowned king.

   Under the guidance of Jehoiada, Joash restored worship of the Lord. After Jehoiada's death, however, Joash turned his back on the Lord and led his people into idolatry. When Zechariah, Jehoiada's son, denounced Joash for his idolatry, Joash had him put to death. Joash reigned about 37 years. He was killed by his servants (2Ki 11–12; 2Ch 24). See 1:346, 372, 402.

2. The son of Jehoahaz and the thirteenth king of Israel. Joash followed in the sins of Jeroboam by continuing the worship of the calves at Bethel and Dan. He respected Elisha, however, and went to see him when the prophet was dying. Elisha told Joash to strike the ground with some arrows. The number of times Joash struck the ground symbolized the victories he would win over the Syrians, the Moabites, and Amaziah of Judah.

   Joash reigned about 16 years. He died in peace, and his son Jeroboam II took the throne (2Ki 13–14; 2Ch 25:17–28). See 1:867, 890.

JOB, BOOK OF. See 1:495–539.

JOBAB (JO-bab).

1. An Edomite king (Gn 36:33–34) associated with Job in Jewish tradition. See 1:498.
2. A king who joined with Jabin and Hazor to fight Joshua (Jsh 11:1).

JOCHEBED (JOK-i-bed; "Yahweh is glory"). The mother of Moses and Aaron (Ex 6:20; Nu 26:59). See 1:59.

JOEL (JO-el; "Yahweh is God"). The son of Pethuel and author of the second book of the Minor Prophets (Jl 1:1). Little is known about Joel outside of his prophecy. See 1:867.

JOEL, BOOK OF. See 1:866–77.

JOHANAN (jo-HAY-nuhn; "Yahweh is merciful"). A Jewish chief who warned Gedaliah, the governor of Judah, of a plot to murder him (2Ki 25:23; Jer 40:8–41:16). Later Johanan led Jeremiah and some other countrymen to Egypt (Jer 40–43). See 1:429, 768, 773, 782.

JOHN (JON; "Yahweh has been gracious").

1. The father of the apostle Peter (Jn 1:42; 21:15–17).
2. John the Baptist, the forerunner of Jesus. John was the son of Elizabeth and Zechariah, the priest, both of whom were descendants of Aaron (Lk 1:5–25, 56–80). Following the pattern of Elijah, John lived as a Nazirite in the desert (Mt 11:12–14; 17:11–12; Lk 1:17). He began his ministry in the fifteenth year of Tiberius Caesar in the region around the Jordan (Lk 3:1–3). John preached the Baptism of repentance and the coming of the kingdom of heaven (Mt 3:1–12; Lk 3:4–14). He baptized Jesus in the Jordan River and witnessed to Him as the promised Messiah (Mt 3:13–17; Mk 1:9–10; Lk 3:21; Jn 1:24–42).

   John rebuked Herod for living in sin with Herodias, Herod's sister-in-law. This made Herod angry, so he put John in jail (Mk 6:17–20). Because of what John had said to Herod, Herodias also had a grudge against John and wanted to kill him. She told her daughter, who had pleased Herod with her dancing, to ask for the head of John the Baptist on a platter. Her daughter did this, and Herod gave the order to behead John (Mt 14:6–12; Mk 6:21–28).

   Jesus highly praised John (Mt 11:7–14; Lk 7:24–28). See 2:196, 198, 245, 333.
3. John the apostle, a son of Zebedee and Salome and the brother of James (Mt 4:21; 27:56; Mk 15:40; Ac 12:1–2). John was from Galilee, probably Bethsaida, and was a fisherman by trade (Mk 1:19–20; Lk 5:10; Jn 1:44). John the Baptist introduced John the apostle to Jesus with these words: "Behold, the Lamb of God!" (Jn 1:35–36). John followed Jesus and was called by Him to be an apostle (Jn 1:43; 2:2, 12, 23; 4:5). Jesus named John and his brother James Boanerges, which means "Sons of Thunder" (Mk 3:17).

   John was among the three whom Jesus chose to be with Him at the raising of Jairus's daughter, at His transfiguration, and at Gethsemane (Mt 17:1; 26:37; Mk 5:37; 9:2; Lk 8:51; 9:28).

   One time when Jesus was rejected in a Samaritan village, John and James asked if Jesus wanted them to call down fire from heaven to burn the village. Jesus rebuked them (Lk 9:54). Another time John, James, and their mother asked Jesus for places of honor in His future kingdom (Mt 20:20–21; Mk 10:35–45). John helped prepare the Passover for Jesus and His disciples on the night before Jesus' crucifixion (Lk 22:8).

   John has been identified as the beloved disciple. At the Last Supper he sat next to Jesus (Jn 13:23). Later, when Jesus was taken prisoner, John followed the soldiers and was able to go along with Jesus into the court of the high priest (Jn 18:15–16). At the cross John stood near Mary, Jesus' mother. When Jesus asked John to look after Mary, John accepted the trust (Jn 19:26–27).

   John was the first disciple to believe that Jesus had risen from the dead (Jn 20:1–10). With the other disciples, he saw the risen Christ on the night of His resurrection and again a week later (Lk 24:33–43; Jn 20:19–30). After a night of fishing with the disciples on the Sea of Galilee, John was the first to recognize Jesus as He stood on the beach (Jn 21:1–7). After Jesus' ascension John waited for some time in the Upper Room in Jerusalem with the other apostles, and after Pentecost he became a missionary with Peter (Ac 1:13; 3:1–4:22; 8:14–17; Gal 2:9).

John lived to an old age. He wrote the fourth Gospel, the three letters bearing his name, and the Book of Revelation. See 2:280, 321–24, 338–39, 772.

JOHN, GOSPEL OF. See 2:319–57.

JOHN, FIRST, SECOND, AND THIRD LETTERS OF. According to the Early Church Fathers, the apostle John wrote these letters near the end of the first century. He wrote them to warn against false teachers (Gnostics) and to strengthen his readers in their Christian loyalty. The keynote of the letters is faith and love. See 2:737–55.

JOKTAN (JOK-tuhn). A person who descended from Shem through Eber (Gn 10:25–30). He is the ancestor of 13 Arabian tribes.

JONAH (JO-nah; "dove"). A son of Amittai of Gath-hepher and a prophet of Israel. Jonah predicted the recovery of the land of Israel to its ancient borders through the efforts of Jeroboam II. He also preached to Nineveh (2Ki 14:23–25; Jnh 1:1). His prophecy is recorded in the Book of Jonah. See 1:906–9; 2:201.

JONAH, BOOK OF. See 1:905–19.

JONATHAN (JON-ah-thuhn; "Yahweh has given").

1. The oldest son of King Saul (1Sm 13:16; 14:49; 1Ch 8:33). Jonathan was a great military commander. He successfully fought the Philistines (1Sm 13–14).

   Jonathan is best known for his devotion to David. Although Jonathan was the rightful heir to the throne, he stripped himself of his royal robe, girdle, and sword and pledged his loyalty to David (1Sm 18:4; 20:42). Later, when Saul wished to kill David, Jonathan defended him from Saul's anger (1Sm 19:1–7; 20). Jonathan was killed with Saul in a battle with the Philistines at Mount Gilboa (1Sm 31:2–10; 2Sm 1:17–27). See 1:289–91, 293–94, 301.
2. One of Mattathias's sons whose life and struggles are recorded in the Book of 1 Maccabees. He succeeded his brother Judas as leader of the Jews from 160 to 142 BC. He showed himself an astute leader. See 2:81, 85.

JOPPA (JOP-ah; "beauty"). An ancient walled seaport about 34 miles northwest of Jerusalem. It was assigned to the tribe of Dan. Simon Peter did missionary work there (Ac 9:36–11:18). Joppa, which is mentioned in both the lists of Thutmose III and the Amarna Letters, is modern-day Joffa (Jsh 19:46; 2Ch 2:16; Ezr 3:7; Jnh 1:3). See 1:905; 2:367.

JORAM (JO-ruhm; "Yahweh is exalted").

1. The son of Ahab and the ninth king of Israel. With the help of the kings of Judah and Edom, Joram defeated the Moabites (cf "Jehoram" in 2Ki 3:1–27). He was also undoubtedly the king to whom Naaman came to be cured of his leprosy and who sent the Syrians home unharmed (2Ki 5; 6:8–23). Jehu killed Joram and threw his body into Naboth's vineyard (2Ki 9:14–26). See 1:344–46.
2. The son of Jehoshaphat and fifth king of Judah. Shortly after Joram became king, he killed all his brothers and some other princes of Israel. Joram married a daughter of Ahab who led him into idolatry. During his reign, Joram was harassed by the Edomites, the Philistines, and the Arabs (cf "Jehoram" in 2Ki 8:16–24; 2Ch 21).

JORDAN (JAWR-d'n; "downrusher"). The most important river in Israel (Gn 13:10; Jsh 2:7; Jgs 3:28; Mt 3:13). It flows in a fissure extending from between the Lebanon and Anti-Lebanon Mountains through the Sea of Galilee to the Dead Sea and beyond. The Jordan Valley is 160 miles long, 2 to 5 miles wide, and as much as 1,292 feet below sea level. The river is 3 to 10 feet deep and about 100 feet wide. See 1:210–12, 334; 2:233.

JOSEPH (JO-zuhf; "he adds").

1. The son of Jacob and Rachel (Gn 30:22–24). Joseph was Jacob's favorite child (Gn 37:3–4). When Joseph was 17, his father sent him to the place where his brothers were looking after their flocks. Because his brothers were jealous of Joseph, they sold him into slavery to a caravan of merchants going to Egypt (Gn 37).

   In Egypt, Joseph became the slave of Potiphar, the captain of Pharaoh's guard. Falsely accused by Potiphar's wife, Joseph was put into prison for years. In prison Joseph became friends with the jailer. God gave Joseph the ability to interpret the dreams of the chief baker and chief butler who were in prison with Joseph. Two years later, when Pharaoh had two prophetic dreams, the jailer remembered Joseph and told Pharaoh about him. After Joseph correctly interpreted the dream,

Pharaoh made him a high officer in the kingdom (Gn 39–41).

When famine struck the land and Joseph's brothers came to Egypt for food, Joseph saved them from starving (Gn 42–45). Joseph arranged for his family to come to Egypt and settled them in Goshen (Gn 47). Joseph died at age 110. When the people of Israel left Egypt, they took Joseph's bones with them and buried them at Shechem (Jsh 24:32). See 1:16, 23, 30–32, 67–68.

2. The husband of Mary, Jesus' mother (Mt 1:16; Lk 3:23). Joseph was a carpenter who lived in Nazareth (Mt 13:55). When he found out that Mary was expecting a child, Joseph was going to put her away without public exposure. But when an angel assured Joseph that the child Mary was carrying was of the Holy Spirit, Joseph took her for his wife (Mt 1:18–25). Joseph took Mary with him when he went to Bethlehem to be taxed. There Jesus was born (Lk 2:4–6).

   Forty days after Jesus' birth, Joseph and Mary presented Jesus in the temple (Lk 2:22–40). When an angel warned Joseph in a dream that Herod was going to kill baby Jesus, Joseph fled with Mary and Jesus to Egypt (Mt 2:13–18). After Herod had died and the danger was past, they returned to Nazareth (Mt 2:19–23). When Jesus was 12 years old, Joseph and Mary took Him to Jerusalem (Lk 2:41–52). See 2:194, 196, 219–20, 277, 300.
3. Joseph of Arimathea, a member of the Sanhedrin and a secret disciple of Jesus. Jesus was buried in Joseph's new tomb (Mt 27:57–60; Mk 15:42–46; Lk 23:50–53). See 2:284–85.
4. A "brother of the Lord" (Mt 13:55; 27:56). He is also called Joses (Mk 6:3; 15:40, 47).
5. The personal name of Barnabas (Ac 4:36).
6. Joseph Caiaphas, the Sanhedral high priest who indicted Jesus (Mt 26:57). See 2:809–10.

JOSES (JO-seez; Gk for Joseph).
1. *See* JOSEPH 4.
2. *See* JOSEPH 5. See 2:233.

JOSHAPHAT (JOSH-ah-fat; "Yahweh has judged"). A priest who blew the trumpet before the ark when it was brought to Jerusalem (1Ch 15:24).

JOSHUA (JOSH-yoo-ah; "Yahweh is salvation." Later "Jeshua," "Jesus").
1. The helper and successor of Moses. Joshua, an Ephraimite, was the son of Nun (Ex 33:11; Nu 13:8, 16; 1Ch 7:27). Joshua commanded the Israelites in their attack against the Amalekites (Ex 17:8–16). As Moses' attendant, he went part of the way up Mount Sinai with Moses (Ex 24:13; 32:17). Joshua was also in charge of the tabernacle (Ex 33:7–11).

   As a leader of Ephraim, Joshua was among the spies sent to report on the land of Canaan. Of the 12 spies sent, only he and Caleb urged the people to go and take the land (Nu 13; 14:7–10). Moses appointed Joshua as his successor (Dt 31; Jsh 1). On the death of Moses, Joshua made plans for crossing the Jordan.

   After entering Canaan, Joshua conquered the land by leading the Israelites into a number of battles. Then he supervised the allotment of the conquered territory as it was divided among the tribes. Joshua asked for and obtained for himself the town of Timnath-serah (Jsh 19:50). He died at 110 years of age and was buried in Timnath-serah (Jsh 24:29). See 1:138, 141–43, 170, 206–7.
2. A high priest who, along with Zerubabbel, aroused the people to finish rebuilding the temple in 516 BC (Hg 1:1–15). Zechariah sees a visit of Joshua being judged in the place of Israel (Zec 3:1–10). See 1:974, 987–88, 990–91.

JOSHUA, BOOK OF. See 1:199–227.

JOSIAH (jo-SIGH-ah; "Yahweh supports"). The son of Amon and Jedidah and the sixteenth king of Judah. Josiah came to the throne of Judah when he was eight years old and reigned for 31 years (2Ki 22:1). In the eighth year of his reign he began to seek the God of David, and four years later he set about to suppress idolatry in Judah and Israel (2Ch 34:3).

In his eighteenth year of reign he decided to repair the temple. While engaged in this activity, workmen found the Book of the Law and handed it over to Shaphan, the scribe, who read it to the king. Josiah gathered together "all the elders of Judah and Jerusalem . . . the inhabitants of Jerusalem and the priests and the Levites, all the people both great and small. And he read in their hearing all the words of the Book of the Covenant that had been found in the house of the LORD" (2Ch 34:29–30). This reading of the Law stimulated worship reforms anew.

In 609 BC, Josiah's leadership was ended when Pharaoh Neco defeated and killed him in battle at Megiddo (2Ki 22–23; 2Ch 34–35). See 1:326, 348, 373, 389–90, 402–3, 752–56, 960–61; 2:149.

JOTBATHAH (JOT-bah-thah). One of the places Israel set up camp. It may have been near Ezion-geber (Nu 33:33–34; Dt 10:7).

JOTHAM (JO-thuhm; "Yahweh is perfect").

1. The son of Gideon. When Shechem made Abimelech king, Jotham told the parable of the trees and bramble (Jgs 9).
2. The eleventh king of Judah. He began reigning as a regent of his father, King Uzziah, while Uzziah was a leper. Later he was the sole king. Jotham is described as good because he followed the Lord. He fortified Jerusalem, built fortresses in Judah, and fought successfully against the Ammonites (2Ki 15:32–38; 2Ch 27).

   Jotham lived during the time of Isaiah, Hosea, and Micah (Is 1:1; Hos 1:1; Mi 1:1). He was an ancestor of Jesus (Mt 1:9). See 1:373, 375–76, 922–23.

JOURNEY. *See* MEASURE 1h.

JOY. Hbr *simchah*; Gk *euphosune, chara*; a mental and emotional appreciation for good things received. A result of God's grace toward believers mentioned especially in later OT historical books, wisdom literature, the prophets, and the NT book of Php. See 1:581, 679; 2:539, 545, 785.

JUBAL (JYOO-buhl). A son of Lamech and perhaps the inventor of musical instruments (Gn 4:19–21).

JUBILEE (JYOO-buh-lee; refers to ram's horn "trumpets"). Every fiftieth year in Israel was to be celebrated as a year of jubilee. This year was announced by a blast on the trumpet. Three things characterized this year: (1) The land rested for the year. (2) Property that people had to sell because of poverty was to be returned to them. (3) All Israelite slaves were to be set free (Lv 25:8–55; 27:16–25; cf Ezk 46:17). See 1:96, 107.

JUDAH (JYOO-dah; "praise").

1. The fourth son of Jacob and Leah (Gn 29:35). When Joseph's brothers were planning to kill Joseph, Judah suggested they sell him to the Ishmaelites instead (Gn 37:26–27). Judah married a Canaanite woman and had three sons with her. After his two older sons and his wife had died, he had twin sons by his daughter-in-law Tamar (Gn 38).

   Judah became a leader of his family (Gn 43:3–10; 44:16–34). Jacob bestowed the blessing of the birthright on Judah. This blessing is usually understood as a messianic prophecy (Gn 49:9–10). See 1:16, 24, 30–31.
2. The tribe that descended from Judah. It occupied the greater part of southern Israel (Jsh 15:20–63). David and Solomon were two kings of Israel who came from the tribe of Judah. Jesus also came from the tribe of Judah through Boaz, Jesse, and David (Lk 3:23–32). See 1:213, 219–20.
3. The kingdom of Judah, which began when the 10 northern tribes withdrew from Rehoboam around 912 BC and lasted until 587 BC when Jerusalem fell. In 538 BC, Cyrus permitted the Jews to return to their homeland (1Ki 12–22; 2Ki; 2Ch 11–36; Ezr; Ne). See 1:338–39, 345, 372–73, 401–3, 988–91; 2:61–62, 143–44, 800–801.

JUDAS (JYOO-dahs).

1. *See* JUDAH 1.
2. Judas Maccabeus, a son of Mattathias who, along with his brothers, helped organize a revolt and reclaimed Jerusalem in 164 BC (1Macc 3–4). In 160, he died in battle and was succeeded by his brother Jonathan. See 1:823–24; 2:80–85, 95–99.
3. Judas Iscariot, the disciple who betrayed Jesus (Mt 10:4; Lk 6:16). *Iscariot* is thought to mean "man of Kerioth." Judas was the treasurer for Jesus and the apostles (Jn 12:4–6; 13:29). He became greedy, however, and took money from the group moneybag for himself (Jn 12:3–8). Judas betrayed Jesus for 30 pieces of silver but then regretted his deed and hanged himself (Mt 26:47–49; 27:3–5; Ac 1:17–18). See 2:565, 203–4, 248, 284, 309, 336, 372, 406–7.
4. The brother of Jesus (Mt 13:55; Mk 6:3). *See also* JUDE, LETTER OF. See 2:758.
5. One of the 12 apostles. He was also apparently referred to as Thaddaeus since this name appears in lists in the place that corresponds to Judas (Mt 10:3; Mk 3:18). Judas was the son or perhaps brother of James (Lk 6:16).
6. A man in Damascus to whom Paul went after his conversion (Ac 9:11). See 2:810–11.

JUDE (JYOOD). *See* JUDAS 3; 4.

JUDE, LETTER OF. See 2:757–69.

JUDEA (jyoo-DEE-ah). The term used in Ezr 9:9 for the province to which the tribes of Judah and Benjamin returned. It is usually called Judah (Ezr 5:8; Ne 2:7).

At the time of Christ, Judea was the southern division of the three regions into which the Roman province of Israel was divided, the other two being Galilee and Samaria. Judea was about 55 miles long and wide. It was located east of the Jordan River and

Dead Sea, from Beersheba in the south to 10 miles north of the Dead Sea in the north. *See* JEW; JUDAH. See 1:439–40; 2:12–13, 195.

JUDGE. Hbr *shophet*. Elders served as officers of law courts in their communities (*see* ELDER). The judges (Jgs–1Sm 9) who led Israel during the tribal period were not officers of such courts, but temporary military saviors. The governors, leaders, and deliverers of the Israelites between the time of Joshua and Saul. They included Othniel, Ehud, Shamgar, Deborah, Barak, Gideon, Abimelech, Tola, Jair, Jephthah, Ibzan, Elon, Abdon, and Samson. The high priest Eli and the prophet Samuel also functioned as judges. The activity of the judges is described in the Book of Judges. Unlike local judges, priests, and kings, these tribal judges did not always come to their office because of tribal or family background; the Lord raised them up, or they were appointed by another Israelite leader (1Sm 8:1). See 1:234, 237–40, 277.

JUDGES, BOOK OF. See 1:229–51.

JUDGMENT. In the OT, the word *judgment* occasionally refers to the administration of justice (2Sm 15:4; 1Ki 3). It usually refers, however, to keeping people in a right relation to the covenant (Is 41:1; 58:2). The prophets describe God as bringing judgment upon a disobedient people. The purpose of God's judgment is to purify, not destroy, His people. God's judgment preserves a faithful remnant (cf Is 6:13). See 1:27, 234, 304, 513, 580, 662, 712–13, 725–31.

God's judgments point to the final judgment, the Day of the Lord, the day when His judgment will come upon all who are unjust and disobedient. On that day God will vindicate His divine rule (Is 25; Zec 14).

In the NT, the word *judgment* sometimes refers to the administration of law (Jn 18:31; Ac 23:3). Usually it refers to the judgment of God and includes the salvation of believers (Lk 18:1–8; Rm 1:18–32; 1Co 11:29–32; 2Th 1:5–10). God's judgment culminates in the final judgment (Mt 11:20–24; 25:31–46; Jn 16:11; 1Th 4:13–18). It belongs to God and is administered by Christ (Mt 18:35; Rm 14:10). God's judgment is salvation to believers, condemnation to unbelievers (Mt 25:31–46). God's judgment is based on whether an individual keeps the Law perfectly (Mt 25). But since the Law has been fulfilled only by Christ, a person's relationship to Him is the decisive factor (Mt 10:32–33; Rm 8:1–17; Gal 5:13–25). Gk *krino* and related forms that often connect with Paul's teaching about justification. Christians are to consider things in view of God's Word. *See also* CONDEMN; JUSTIFICATION; WEIGH. See 2:204, 247, 293, 394, 582–85, 772, 784–89.

JUDGMENT HALL. *See* PRAETORIUM.

JUDITH (JYOO-dith; "Jewess").

1. Esau's wife (Gn 26:34).
2. Judith is the main character in the apocryphal Book of Judith. She was a beautiful widow who delivered Israel from the Assyrian general Holofernes. *See also* JUDITH, BOOK OF. See 2:17.

JUDITH, BOOK OF. See 2:15–25.

JULIUS (JYOOL-yuhs; if Lat, "July"; if Gk, "soft-haired"). A Roman centurion of the Augustan band who conducted Paul and other prisoners to Rome (Ac 27).

JUSTIFICATION. Gk *dikaioo*, "to declare righteous or free." The basis for the dominant theological truth in Paul's Letters and the Scriptures. The gracious act of God by which He pronounces all people to be not guilty of their sin (2Co 5:19). The basis for His acquittal is that Jesus Christ fulfilled the Law in humanity's place and paid the penalty for all people's sin (Rm 5:12–20). An individual gains the benefits of Christ's substitutionary life and death through the instrument of faith, which God gives him or her by the Holy Spirit working through the Gospel (Rm 1:16; 3:21–25; 5:1; Eph 2:8–9). *See also* RECONCILIATION; RIGHTEOUSNESS. See 1:563, 665, 808–9, 955; 2:287, 425, 437, 504–7, 786.

JUTTAH (JUT-ah). A town in Judah about 5½ miles southwest of Hebron. It was assigned to the priests (Jsh 15:55; 21:16). It may be the same as the "town in Judah," where John the Baptist was born (Lk 1:39). Today it is known as Yuttah.

K

KAB. *See* MEASURES 2b.

KADESH (kay-DESH; "consecrated"). Known as En-mishpat in early times, Kadesh was in the desert about 70 miles south of Hebron (Gn 14:7). Hagar fled to the region around Kadesh (Gn 16:7, 14). Israel wandered in this area for 37 years, twice stopping to set up camp at Kadesh (Nu 13:25–26; Dt 1:46).

Miriam died at Kadesh (Nu 20:1). There, rather than speaking to the rock as the Lord had told him to do, Moses struck it to bring forth water (Nu 20:2–13). This displeased the Lord, and so the waters were called Meribah, which means strife. Kadesh is often called Kadesh-barnea (Nu 32:8; Dt 2:14). See 1:130, 134–35, 140, 157, 714–15.

KADESH-BARNEA (Kay-DESH-BAHR-ni-ah). *See* KADESH.

KARKOR (KAHR-kawr; perhaps "wells"). The place east of the Jordan River where Gideon attacked Zebah and Zalmunna (Jgs 8:10).

KEDAR (KEE-dur; "dark").

1. One of Ishmael's sons (Gn 25:13; 1Ch 1:29).
2. An Arabian tribe that descended from Kedar. The people of this tribe lived in black tents and had flocks and camels (Sg 1:5; Is 21:13–17; 42:11; 60:7; Jer 49:28–29). See 1:768.

KEDEMAH (KED-i-maa; "eastward"). Ishmael's son and the tribe that descended from him (Gn 25:15; 1Ch 1:31).

KEDESH (KEE-desh; "sacred place").

1. A Canaanite city northwest of Lake Huleh that Joshua conquered during his northern campaign. Having captured the city, Joshua put its king to death (Jsh 12:22). Kedesh was given to the tribe of Naphtali and made a city of refuge (Jsh 19:37). Years later Tiglath-pileser captured it (2Ki 15:29). Also called Kedesh-naphtali, it was the home of Barak (Jgs 4:6). See 1:211.
2. A town in southern Judah, probably the same as Kadesh.

KEILAH (ki-IGH-lah). A city in the lowlands of Judah (Jsh 15:44). David delivered it from the Philistines (1Sm 23:7–13). See 1:276, 285.

KENAZ (KEE-naz). A descendant of Esau and an ancestor of the Kenizzites (Gn 15:19; 36:15).

KENITES. A tribe of Midianites related to the Kenizzites (Gn 15:19). The Kenites had extraordinary skill in metal work. Moses' father-in-law was a Kenite (Jgs 1:16). Hobab the Kenite guided the Israelites on their march through the desert (Nu 10:29–32; Jgs 1:16; 4:11). The Kenites were on friendly terms with the Israelites. They settled in Wadi Arabah, near Hebron, in Naphtali, and in southern Judah (Nu 24:20–22; Jgs 1:16; 4:11; 1Sm 15:6; 27:10; 30:29).

KENIZZITES (KEE-niz-ights). Descendants of Kenaz (Gn 36:11). The Kenizzites were a tribe that lived in southern Canaan before Israel. It seems that they were conquered by and merged with the Edomites (Gn 15:19; Dt 2:12). Part of the tribe, however, may have merged with Judah. Caleb and Othniel were Kenizzites (Nu 32:12; Jsh 14:6; 15:17).

KERIOTH-HEZRON (KEE-ri-oth-HEZ-ron). A city in southern Judah (Jsh 15:25). Most likely Judas Iscariot came from there.

KETURAH (kuh-TYOO-rah; "incense"). Abraham's second wife. She was the mother of six sons, the ancestors of the eastern nations (Gn 25:1–6; 1Ch 1:32–33). See 1:51.

KEY. An Oriental key was made of a piece of wood. It had pegs to fit the corresponding holes in a wooden bolt (Jgs 3:25; Is 22:22). The key is a symbol of power and authority (Is 22:22; Lk 11:52; Rv 3:7).

The Keys of the Kingdom are power Christ gives to the Church through the apostles to open heaven by forgiving the sins of penitent Christians or to close heaven by retaining the sins of the impenitent (Mt 16:19; 18:18). See 1:811; 2:398, 638.

KID. A young goat used for sacrifice (Jgs 13:15–19). It was also a favorite food item (Gn 38:17; Lk 15:29).

KIDNEY. An internal organ that, along with the fat around it, was used for a burnt offering (Ex 29:13, 22; Lv 3:4–15). People regarded the kidney as the seat of emotion and desire (Jb 16:13). See 1:519.

KIDRON, BROOK. A valley and winter brook that begins northwest of Jerusalem. It then joins with the Valley of Hinnom and runs 20 miles to the Dead Sea. The Kidron was a burial ground and dumping place for destroyed idols and their altars (1Ki 15:13; 2Ki 23:6; 2Ch 29:16; 30:14). When David was being chased by Absalom, he fled across the Kidron (2Sm 15:23). Jesus crossed over it on His way to Gethsemane (Jn 18:1). See 1:295, 321, 338; 2:698, 803–4.

KING. Hbr *melek*; Gk *basileus*. The basis of one of the dominant historical and theological themes of Scripture. The Lord was the King of Israel (Dt 33:1–5; 1Sm 8:7; 10:19; 12:12). Later, the Israelites wanted to be like other nations and have a human king. So God allowed them to have kings to rule over them; nevertheless, these kings were accountable to the Lord. They were subject to democratic processes, the moral law, and prophetic warnings (2Sm 12; 1Ki 12:16; 21:20–24).

Israel had kings to rule them from about 1020 to 587 BC, beginning with Saul and ending with Zedekiah. Their kings had scepters, crowns, thrones, and palaces (1Ki 2:19; 7:1–12; 2Ki 11:12; Ps 45:6). The kings' officers included such people as army officers, a captain of the bodyguard, a secretary, overseers, and counselors (1Sm 14:50; 2Sm 8:17; 15:12; 20:23–24; 1Ki 4:6). See 1:277–82, 289, 330–34, 372–73.

KINGDOM OF GOD. This theological term refers to the fact that God is the Creator of the world and everything in it and rules over all things with unlimited power. He especially rules over His people as their Creator, Redeemer, and Sanctifier.

The development of this concept can be traced through the OT. God is described as King over the whole earth (Nu 23:21; Dt 33:5; Ps 47:7). Specifically, His Lordship over Israel, His chosen nation, is seen (1Sm 12:12; Is 44:6). In turn, the Israelites hoped for the coming of the kingdom of God—they looked for a redeemer or Messiah who would establish the kingdom of God.

During the time of the kings, these rulers were God's representatives, responsible to Him and ruling in His stead. David, for instance, was a type of ideal king or Messiah, ruling the kingdom subject to God's will and law. None of the kings, however, not even David, were perfect representatives of God. Nor were the people of Israel perfect. Thus it became clear that the kingdom of Israel did not equal the kingdom of God.

The prophets pointed out that God's kingdom is really a spiritual kingdom that includes all nations (Is 2:4; 9; 11; 61; Jer 23:5–6; Zec 9:10). The NT pictures God's kingdom as the Holy Spirit in the hearts of His people. Numerous Bible passages speak of the rule of God (Mt 12:28; Mk 4:11; Lk 9:27, 11:20). See 1:604, 828, 900, 928, 983.

When John the Baptist said the kingdom of God was near, he was telling people that God was laying the foundation for His rule in human hearts through the Messiah. Jesus is that Messiah. He is the fulfiller of the Kingdom and the one who brings God's kingdom to people (Mt 12:28; Lk 9:27; 17:20–21). Jesus said, "The time is fulfilled, and the kingdom of God is at hand; repent and believe in the Gospel" (Mk 1:15). People enter the kingdom of God by repenting of their sins and believing in Jesus as their Savior (Jn 3:3–5; cf "kingdom of heaven" in Mt 18:3–4). As members of the kingdom of God, the Holy Spirit works in them, and they become more and more Christlike (Mt 5–7; Lk 9:60–62).

The kingdom of God is, at times, spoken of as a future blessing and, at times, as a present reality (Mt 7:21; 8:11; Lk 16:16; 17:20). The Church proclaims the kingdom of God by witnessing to Christ. See 2:273, 279, 302–4, 362, 384–85, 395.

KINGS, FIRST AND SECOND BOOK OF. See 1:321–79.

KINGS OF JUDAH AND ISRAEL. These kings can be divided into three groups: the kings of the united kingdom of Israel; the kings of Judah, the Southern Kingdom; and the kings of Israel, the Northern Kingdom. See 1:372–73.

1. The kings of the united kingdom and the approximate dates they ruled were:

Saul	1048–1009 BC
David	1009–970
Solomon	970–931

2. The kings of Judah and the approximate dates they ruled:

Rehoboam	931–914 BC
Abijam	914–911
Asa	911–870
Jehoshaphat	873–848
Jehoram	853–841
Ahaziah	841
Athaliah	841–835
Joash	835–796
Amaziah	796–767
Azariah (Uzziah)	792–740
Jotham	750–735
Ahaz	735–715
Hezekiah	715–686
Manasseh	696–642
Amon	642–640
Josiah	640–609
Jehoahaz	609
Jehoiakim	609–598
Jehoiachin	598–597
Zedekiah	597–587

3. The kings of Israel and the approximate dates they ruled:

Jeroboam I	931–910 BC
Nadab	910–909
Baasha	909–887
Elah	886–885
Zimri	885
Tibni	885–880
Omri	885–874

Ahab	874–853
Ahaziah	853–852
J(eh)oram	852–841
Jehu	841–814
Jehoahaz	814–796
Joash	798–782
Jeroboam II	793–753
Zechariah	753
Shallum	752
Menahem	752–742
Pekah	742–732
Pekahiah	742–740
Hoshea	732–722

KIRIATH-ARBA (KIR-i-ath-AHR-bah; "city of Arba"). An ancient name for Hebron (Gn 23:2; Jsh 14:15; Jgs 1:10; Ne 11:25). See 1:25.

KIRIATH-JEARIM (KIR-i-ath-JEE-ah-rim; "city of thickets"). A Gibeonite town near Mount Jearim (Jsh 9:17). It was known by different names, e.g., Baalah (Jsh 15:9), Kiriath-baal (Jsh 18:14), and Baale-judah (2Sm 6:2). Kiriath-jearim was assigned to Judah first and then later to Benjamin (Jsh 15:60; 18:20). The ark of the covenant remained there for 20 years (1Sm 6:19–7:2). See 1:393.

KISH (KISH). A Benjaminite; the father of Saul (1Sm 9:3; 10:11; Ac 13:21). Kish was the son of Abiel; however, the Bible sometimes refers to him as the son of Ner (1Sm 9:1; 1Ch 8:33; 9:39). See 1:279, 653.

KITTIM (KIGHT-tim).

1. The descendants of Javan. These people lived on Cyprus and other islands and on the coasts along the eastern part of the Mediterranean Sea (Gn 10:4; Nu 24:24; 1Ch 1:7; Dn 11:30). The name Kittim was applied to these places too (cf Is 23:12; Jer 2:10). See 1:25.
2. Macedonia or the Macedonian people. *See also* MACEDONIA. See 1:949.

KNEADING BOWL. A shallow dish made of clay or wood that was used to knead dough (Ex 8:3).

KNEE, KNEEL. "To bend the knee" or kneel indicated an attitude of worship, prayer, awe, or subjection (Gn 41:43; 2Ch 6:13; Ps 95:6; Is 45:23; Mt 17:14; Php 2:10). See 1:600, 838; 2:143.

KNIFE. In ancient times knives were made of flint (Jsh 5:2–3). The Philistines used metal knives. These did not become common in Israel until the time of the later kings. Knives were used for killing, cutting, pruning, and shaving (1Ki 18:28; Is 18:5; Ezk 5:1). See 1:30; 2:620.

KNOW.

1. To trust in the word and works of Jesus Christ for the forgiveness of sin. See 2:215–16.
2. Verb used in a polite Hbr expression for sexual intercourse (e.g., Gn 4:1).

KNOW THAT I AM THE LORD. Phrase first spoken to Moses to describe a result of the exodus (Ex 6:7). However, over 80 percent of its OT uses are as a "recognition formula" in Ezk. When used in pronouncing judgment, it describes how the people must learn the truth through punishment (e.g., Eng expression "learn the hard way"). However, this phrase often follows announcements of God's mercy, affirming the sincerity of believers' repentance and faith. See 1:109, 142, 808.

KOHATH (KO-hath). One of Levi's sons (Gn 46:11; Ex 6:16–18; Nu 3:17). His descendants, the Kohathites, were one of the three divisions of Levites. Moses and Aaron were Kohathites (Ex 6:18–20). See 1:134, 550.

KORAH (KO-rah; "baldness"). A Levite who secretly plotted with Dathan and Abiram against Moses. As punishment for this, as well as to show that Moses was His appointed leader, God allowed the earth to open up and swallow Abiram and Dathan and their households and Korah and his servants. Korah's sons, however, were not destroyed (Nu 16). See 1:129, 132, 138–39, 570; 2:726.

KORAHITE (KO-ra-ight). Someone who descended from the Levite Korah. Heman and Samuel were both Korahites (1Ch 6:33–38). The Korahites became famous temple singers (1Ch 15:17; 16:41–42; titles of Ps 42; 44–49; 84–85; 87–88).

L

LABAN (LAY-buhn; "white"). Abraham's great-nephew and Rebekah's brother (Gn 24:29; 25:20). Laban lived at Haran (11:31–32; 24:4, 10). He allowed Rebekah to go with Abraham's servant to Canaan to become Isaac's wife (ch 24). Later, Jacob and Rebekah's son Isaac worked for Laban for 20 years. As payment for this service, Isaac received cattle and also his wives, Leah and Rachel (chs 29–31). See 1:28–29.

LABOR. The Bible describes labor as honorable (Ps 128:2; Pr 21:25; cf 1Th 4:11). God's work of creation is called work (Gn 2:2). Jesus points to God's continued work in the world, that is, His providential care, to defend working on the Sabbath (Jn 5:17). Workers were protected by laws (Dt 24:14) and were the subject of Jesus' parables (Mt 20:1). See 1:635, 661; 2:432, 572–73, 589–90.

LACHISH (LAY-kish). A royal city of the Canaanites located at Tell ed-Duweir, 30 miles southwest of Jerusalem and 15 miles west of Hebron. It was one of the largest cities of ancient Judah. Under Joshua, the Israelites captured Lachish and killed its king (Jsh 10:3–35). Years later, shortly after the division of the kingdom, Rehoboam strengthened the defenses of Lachish (2Ch 11:9). Amaziah, king of Judah, fled there and was slain (2Ki 14:19). Around 701 BC, Sennacherib, the king of Assyria, captured Lachish (2Ki 18:14, 17). Nebuchadnezzar destroyed Lachish along with Jerusalem two times: once in 597 BC and then again in 587 BC (2Ki 24–25; Jer 34:7). When the exiles returned from captivity, they once again lived in Lachish (Ne 11:30). The city, however, never regained its former importance.

Archaeologists have found many important items at Lachish. One find, the Lachish Letters, are written in Hbr and belong to Jeremiah's time. See 1:385, 445, 767; 2:806.

LAISH (LAY-ish; "lion"). A city in the extreme north of Israel. The people of the tribe of Dan captured it and renamed it Dan (Jgs 18:7–29). See 1:6.

LAMB. A young sheep. Lamb's meat was used for food and sacrifices, particularly at Passover (Gn 22:7; Ex 12:3–5; 29:38–41; Lv 3:7; 2Sm 12:4). Lambs used for sacrifices had to be perfect, without blemish. They pointed to Christ, the Lamb of God, who takes away the sin of the world (Jn 1:29; Rv 5:6, 8). Christians, particularly children, are compared to lambs (Jn 21:15). See 1:71, 74, 80, 115–17; 2:310–11, 333, 337–38, 772–73, 784.

LAMENTATIONS, BOOK OF. See 1:781–93.

LAMP. A container holding liquid and a wick. Lamps were burned to give light (Ex 27:20; 2Ki 4:10). Lamps in the tabernacle and temple were made of gold (Ex 25:31–40; 37:17–24). They burned olive oil (Ex 27:20). In the Bible a lamp is also a symbol for God's Word (Ps 119:105), His guidance (Ps 18:28), and wise leaders (Jn 5:33–35). See 1:72, 107, 819; 2:245, 329.

LANCE. A javelin or light spear (1Ki 18:28).

LANDMARK. An object, such as a stone or stake, that marked the boundary of an area of land. Landmarks were not to be removed (Dt 19:14; 27:17; Hos 5:10).

LANGUAGE. Words spoken or written to convey ideas. Language is a gift of God, but the differences among languages are a result of sin (Gn 11:1–9). Many languages were spoken during OT times. Sumerian, Akkadian, Egyptian, Phrygian, Phoenician, Canaanite, and Hittite are only a few. The chief languages spoken in Israel during NT times were Aram, Hbr, Gk, and Latin (Jn 19:20). See 1:829–33; 2:4–5, 351–53, 448–49, 829–30.

LAODICEA (lay-ahd-i-SEE-ah). A wealthy city located in the Lycus Valley of Asia Minor. It was probably founded by Antiochus II and named by him for his wife (Col 2:1; 4:15; Rv 1:11; 3:14–22). See 2:522, 551–53, 783.

LAPPIDOTH (LAP-i-doth; "torches"). Deborah's husband (Jgs 4:4). See 2:522, 551–53, 783.

LAST DAY. *See* JUDGMENT; ESCHATOLOGY. See 1:742; 2:587, 658, 788.

LAST TIMES. *See* ESCHATOLOGY.

LATIN (LAT-in). The language spoken by the Romans (Jn 19:20). See 1:572; 2:9, 351–53, 829.

LATTER DAYS. *See* ON THAT DAY.

LAW. Hbr *torah*, translated by Gk *nomos*. But in many passages that translation is inadequate, and "instruction" is preferable.

1. God's will for His creation, revealed to people in His judgments, words, rules, and acts (Ex 20:1–17; 21:1; Dt 7:6–16; Ps 19; 119; Is 1:10). See 1:71–73, 167–68, 583; 2:121, 197.
2. The Torah, the first five books of the OT (Mt 5:17; Lk 16:16). See 1:5–9.
3. The OT (Jn 10:34; 12:34).
4. The Ten Commandments given to Moses (Ex 20:2–17; Dt 5:6–21; Jn 7:19). The commandments summarize God's requirements of people—what their relationship to God, to one another, and to the rest of creation should be (Lv; Dt). See 1:xxxii–xxxiii, 71–72, 167.

Jesus showed respect and love for the Law. He pointed out its deeper meaning for people (Mt 5:17–48). Paul emphasized that the Law shows the sinfulness of people because they can never keep it perfectly. Moreover, the Law is unable to provide victory over sin (Rm 3–7; Gal). It does prepare one for the Gospel (Gal 3:24). *See also* APPEAL; JUDGMENT; RIGHTEOUSNESS. *See* 2:121, 197, 425.

The Law has three purposes or uses. It curbs sinful human behavior and preserves civil society (Gn 9:6; Rm 2:14–15; 1Tm 1:9). The Law also shows us our sin or acts as a mirror (Rm 3:20; 7:7). Finally, the Law guides and directs Christian behavior according to God's will (Ps 119:9, 105).

LAWLESS. Translates a variety of Hbr terms as well as Gk *anomos* and *anomia*. The common sense describes the breaking of God's Law or simple wickedness. It can also be used to describe the Gentiles, who did not have *torah* and thus violated it. See 1:87; 2:86, 581–84.

LAWYER. A professional interpreter of the OT, often a scribe (Mt 22:35; Lk 10:25). See 1:419.

LAYING ON OF HANDS. An act symbolizing dedication or blessing. It was used to dedicate priests to their office and animals to the Lord (Lv 1:4; Nu 8:5–20). Through the laying on of hands, blessings of various kinds were given and people were set apart for special service (Gn 48:5–20; Mk 10:16; Lk 4:40; Ac 6:6; 13:3; 1Tm 4:14; 2Tm 1:6; Heb 6:2). See 1:143, 375; 2:519.

LAZARUS (LAZ-ah-ruhs; form of "Eleazer").

1. The brother of Mary and Martha. After Lazarus died, Jesus came to his town and brought him back to life (Jn 11–12:11). See 2:330, 335–36, 809.
2. The name of the beggar in the parable Jesus told about a rich man and a beggar (Lk 16:19–31). See 1:312; 2:285.

LEAH (LEE-ah; "weak"). Laban's older daughter. Through a trick of her father, Leah was passed off on Jacob as his bride (Gn 29–30; 49:31). See 1:28–29, 95; 2:305.

LEADERS. Terms for Israelite leadership are often used interchangeably; offices are not easily ranked. However, during the tribal period (Ex 1 through 1Sm 8), the general order seems to be (1) elder of Israel, (2) tribal leader, (3) clan leader, (4) household leader, (5) household member, and (6) sojourner (cf Dt 29:10–11). On the organization of the people in the wilderness, cf Nu 1:2–18. 1Ki 8:1 gives an illustration of civil leadership in the kingdom period (1Sm 9 through 2Ch 36), stating, "Solomon assembled the elders of Israel and all the heads of the tribes, the leaders of the fathers' houses of the people of Israel." Most Israelite leaders could also act as military commanders. During the kingdom period, other administrative offices were added to supplement the traditional tribal administration. Regarding religious leaders, *see* LEVITES; PRIEST; PROPHET. See 1:137, 234, 296, 807, 988–90; 2:333–37, 572–73, 656.

LEAVEN (LEV-uhn). A substance used to make dough rise (Ex 12:15, 20; Mt 13:33). The Israelites removed leaven from their houses during Passover and did not use it in meal offerings (Lv 2:11). It was a symbol of corruption and moral influence, whether good or bad (Mt 13:33; 16:6, 12; 1Co 5:6–8). See 1:74; 2:306.

LEBANON (LEB-ah-nuhn; "white"). The snow-clad mountain ranges of Lebanon and Anti-Lebanon run 110 miles along the coast of Syria between the Taurus Mountains and the lower mountain ranges of Israel. Some peaks reach 10,000 feet. Mount Hermon is the southern spur of the Anti-Lebanon range. The Lebanons formed the northern boundary of Israel (Dt 1:7). They are known especially for their cedars (Jgs 9:15; 1Ki 5). See 1:100, 691; 2:150.

LEGION.

1. The largest single unit in the Roman army (about 6,000 men). See 2:221.
2. A great number (Mt 26:53; Mk 5:9). See 2:166.

LEHI (LEE-high; "jawbone"). The place where Samson killed the Philistines with a donkey's jawbone (Jgs 15:9–19). See 1:331.

LEMUEL (LEM-yoo-uhl; "belonging to God"). The unidentified king who wrote Proverbs (Pr 31:1–9). He may have been Solomon. See 1:623, 637, 644.

LEPROSY (LEP-ro-see). A dreadful skin disease. Leprosy usually began with scabs that scarred the skin and made the hair around the affected area turn white. Often raw flesh appeared (Ex 4:6; Lv 13:10, 14–16, 24).

The leprosy referred to in the Bible probably included skin diseases other than what is commonly known as leprosy today (Lv 13:14). The leprosy of garments may have been mold or mildew (Lv 13:47–59; 14:33–37). Jesus healed lepers (Mt 8:2–4; Lk 17:11–19). See 1:334, 344; 2:189, 198, 278, 282–83.

LETTER. *See* EPISTLE.

LEVI (LEE-vigh; "joined").

1. Jacob's third son by Leah (Gn 29:34). Born in Haran, Levi went with his family on the return to

Canaan. He joined his brothers in the plot against Joseph (Gn 37). Levi had three sons: Gershon, Kohath, and Merari (Gn 46:11; 1Ch 6:16–48). He died in Egypt (Ex 6:16). See 1:31.

2. Matthew, the Gospel writer, also went by Levi (Mk 2:14; Lk 5:27). See 2:187, 244, 302.

LEVIATHAN (li-VIGH-ah-thuhn). A sea monster (Ps 104:26). Poetical passages in the Bible describe it as somewhat similar to a crocodile or serpent (Jb 41; Is 27:1). Symbolically, Leviathan represents unrestrained power or evil (Jb 3:8; Ps 74:14; 104:26; Is 27:1). *See also* BEAST 4. See 1:505–7, 513.

LEVIRATE MARRIAGE (LEV-uh-rayt MARE-ij). When an Israelite man died without any male children, the nearest male relative was supposed to marry the deceased's wife. The first son born of this union was then the heir of the woman's first husband (Dt 25:5–10). See 1:119–20, 262–63.

LEVITES (LEE-vights). The descendants of Jacob's son Levi. Levi's three sons, Gershon, Kohath, and Merari, each became heads of a tribal family (Ex 6:16–25; Lv 25:32; Nu 35:2–8; Jsh 21:3). They became substitutes for the firstborn of their fellow Israelites in all duties pertaining to God (Nu 3:11–13; 8:16). Their duty was to preserve the law of the Lord and His worship (Lv 10:11; Dt 17:18; 31:9–13). Each family descending from the three sons had different duties assigned to them (Nu 3:5–39).

Aaron and Moses were Levites of the family of Kohath. The priests descended from this family through Aaron and his sons (Ex 28:1; Nu 18:7). They received no tribal territory but were assigned 48 cities and tithes (Lv 27:30–33; Nu 18:20–24; 35; Dt 10:9). See 1:67, 131–32, 136–38, 384, 405–10; 2:653, 660.

LEVITICUS, BOOK OF (li-VIT-i-kuhs). See 1:99–125.

LEVY. A contribution to the Lord taken from the spoils of war on at least one particular occasion (Nu 31:25–31).

LIBERALISM. In biblical studies, describes those who adopted the higher critical methods used to study the Holy Scriptures as though they were merely human texts. Common liberal views are that Israelite religion was originally more creative and flexible until the influences of priests and rituals taught rigid and dogmatic views and practices. See 1:6–11, 708–9; 2:829–30.

LIBERTY. Freedom, the opposite of slavery or bondage. Although the Israelites often were in bondage, they prized liberty. Those who had become slaves were to be freed in the year of jubilee (Lv 25:8–17).

OT prophecies about liberty have a spiritual meaning, which is fulfilled in Christ (Is 61:1, Lk 4:18; Jn 8:31–36). Jesus frees people from Satan, sin, death, judgment, fear, and the Law (Jn 1:29; Ac 26:18; Rm 6–8; Gal 3). In matters that are neither commanded nor forbidden in God's Word, a Christian has freedom (Rm 14; 1Co 8). *See also* ADIAPHORA. See 1:80, 889–90; 2:452–55, 683, 697, 760.

LIBYA (LIB-ee-ah). A country in North Africa west of Egypt (Ezk 30:5; Ac 2:10). See 2:94.

LIBYANS (LIB-i-uhns). People who live in Libya (Na 3:9). See 1:653.

LIEUTENANT (lu-TEN-uhnt). *See* SATRAP. See 1:845.

LIFE.

1. The Bible refers to the physical life of plants, animals, and humans as that quality which makes it possible for them to breathe, eat, grow, and reproduce (Gn 6:17; Ex 1:14; Jb 3:20–21; Ec 2:17). See 1:32, 35, 303.
2. The Bible also talks about the spiritual or eternal life of man. It is the gift of God that one has by grace through faith in Jesus Christ (Eph 2:8–10; Jn 17:3; 1Jn 5:12). The person who believes in Jesus as Savior never dies (Jn 11:25–26). See 1:32, 596–97; 2:191, 627.
3. Christ is the source of all life (Jn 1:4; 11:25; Col 3:4). See 2:291, 395–96, 774.

LIGHT, DARKNESS. God made natural light. It is a blessing that makes life as we know it possible. Light is often used to describe God, the highest good, from whom every good gift comes (Jas 1:17). Jesus is the light of the world (Jn 1:4–9). God's Word and believers are spoken of as lights (Ps 119:105; Mt 5:14–16). Living a godly life is described in terms of putting on the armor of light or walking in the light (Rm 13:11–14; 1Jn 1:7). See 1:144, 577, 591, 733, 819–20, 955; 2:207–8, 329, 338–39, 709–10.

Darkness, on the other hand, is symbolic of evil and all the results of the power of evil: spiritual blindness, evil deeds, death, hell, and suffering (Jb 10:21–22; Jl 2:2; Mt 22:13; Lk 22:53; Jn 3:19–20; 1Jn 1:6). See 1:46–47, 356, 733, 819–20, 871; 2:291, 327, 338, 341–42, 762, 772–73.

LIME. The mountains of Israel contain a large amount of limestone. The Israelites burned this limestone to make lime plaster and the like (Is 33:12; Am 2:1). See 2:809, 813.

LINEAGE. *See* GENEALOGY. See 1:235.

LINEN. A thread or cloth made from flax. Linen was used to make clothing, priestly garments, the temple veil, choir robes, and burial cloths (Gn 41:42; Ex 28:5–42; 2Ch 3:14; 5:12; Mk 15:46). It was a symbol of wealth and purity (Lk 16:19; Rv 19:8, 14). See 1:72.

LITTER. A couch or chair used to carry people (Sg 3:7; Is 66:20).

LIVER. An internal organ of the body. The liver was used in sacrifice and for divination (Lv 3:4–15; Ezk 21:21). It was thought to be the center of life and feeling (Pr 7:23). See 1:706; 2:45.

LIVING GOD. In contrast to dead idols, God is active on behalf of His people (Jsh 3:10; Mt 16:16). A special concern in the Apocrypha stories of Bel and the Dragon. See 2:130–31, 201, 488.

LO-AMMI (lo-AM-ee; "not my people"). The symbolic name of Hosea's third son (Hos 1:9). See 1:855–56.

LOANS. Something, especially money, that is lent. During OT times the Hebrews were encouraged to make loans to their needy neighbors. If the Israelites became poverty-stricken, they could sell themselves as servants. After seven years, however, Israelite servants were to be released, and in the year of jubilee their debts were to be canceled (Lv 25:39–41; Dt 15:1–11; 23:19). See 1:260.

The Israelites were not allowed to charge interest to other Israelites but could charge it to strangers. Charging interest on a loan was looked down upon (Ne 5:7; 10; Ps 15:5; Ezk 22:12).

LOGOS (LAHG-ahs). *See* JESUS CHRIST 3. See 1:533–34; 2:329.

LOIN. Part of the back of the body between the hips and false ribs. Before walking or working, a man usually tied loose clothing at his loins. See 1:762.

LOIS (LO-is; "pleasing"). Timothy's grandmother (2Tm 1:5). See 2:615.

LORD. Various Hbr and Gk names in the Bible are expressed by the English word *Lord*.

1. LORD (printed often in capital letters in the Bible) is God's personal name. It comes from the Hbr word *Yahweh*. Some Bible versions use *Yahweh* instead of LORD. See 1:6, 77, 272, 803.
2. Lord translates the Hbr word *ʾadon*. It means master or my master, my Lord, and denotes ownership by human beings or God (Ps 110:1; 114:7). See 1:582.
3. *Adonai* is the word the Israelites said whenever they saw the consonants of *Yahweh* (YHWH).
4. The Gk word *Kurios* is also translated as Lord. It is the word used for a human master or for God as the ruler (Mt 8:25; 21:9). It is also the word used for Christ, who by His death and resurrection is the Lord (Rm 14:9). *See also* JEHOVAH; JESUS CHRIST. See 1:902; 2:202.

LORD GOD.

1. Hbr *yahweh ʾelohim* (*see* LORD; GOD). Generally, OT authors use one or the other term, but 385 times they are used in combination ("Yahweh God," or perhaps "the God Yahweh"). Ezk uses this combination the most (217 times). In Gn 2–3, this combination is used 20 times and a few times thereafter (cf Gn 15:2).
2. The Gk expression *kyrios ho theos*. In the Apocrypha, the expression is commonly used in the context of prayer. See 1:46; 2:394, 785.

LORD OF HOSTS. *See* HOST 2.

LORD'S DAY. That day associated with the resurrection of Jesus and the outpouring of the Holy Spirit on the disciples (Ac 2:1–41). The Lord's day is the first day of the week. It was set aside for worship, though some people still observed the Sabbath (Ac 20:7; Rv 1:10; cf Rm 14:5; 1Co 16:2; Gal 4:10). *See also* SUNDAY.

LORD'S PRAYER. The prayer Jesus taught His disciples as a pattern for their prayers (Mt 6:9–13; Lk 11:2–4). See 1:50; 2:197, 208, 690.

LORD'S SUPPER. Christ instituted this supper on the night of His betrayal as a fulfillment of the Paschal Feast. It is a proclamation of His death for the sins of the world (1Co 11:26). In this meal Christ gives His body and blood together with the bread and wine (Lk 22:19–20; 1Co 10:16–17; 11:20–26). Before going to the Lord's Supper, believers in Christ are to examine themselves to see whether they are truly sorry for their sins, truly believe in Jesus Christ as Savior, and share the same confession of those at the altar (1Co 11:27–32). Christians who trust in the blessings Christ promises to give in this meal and partake of it in faith receive the forgiveness of sins, life, and salvation, and a strengthening of their faith.

The Lord's Supper is also called the breaking of bread (Ac 2:42; 20:7; 1Co 10:16), Communion (cf "participation" in 1Co 10:16), Eucharist (cf "blessing" in 1Co 10:16), and the table of the Lord (1Co 10:21). See 1:177, 412, 582, 639–40; 2:203, 248, 293, 454, 462, 722.

LO-RUHAMAH (lo-ryoo-HAY-mah; "no mercy"). The symbolic name given to Hosea's daughter (Hos 1:6, 8). See 1:855–56.

LOT (LOT; may mean "covering").

1. Haran's son; Abraham's nephew (Gn 11:27–31). Lot went with Abraham to Egypt and Canaan (Gn 13:1–7). In Canaan, Lot and his family settled in the Jordan Valley (Gn 13:8–13). Before the Lord destroyed Sodom and Gomorrah, He sent two angels to help Lot and his family escape. Only Lot and his two daughters made it to safety (Gn 19). Lot was an ancestor of Moab and Ammon (Gn 19:36–38). See 1:25–27.
2. A way people in Bible times decided an issue or figured out the divine will in a matter (Jsh 18:6–28; Jnh 1:7; Mt 27:35; Ac 1:26). *See also* PORTION. See 1:142, 279, 434; 2:106.

LOVE. Various types of love are referred to in the Bible. The OT talks about God's steadfast love for His covenant people (Hbr *'aheb*; Dt 7:7–9, 12). The Gk word *agape* represents God's undeserved love for sinful people (Jn 3:16; 1Jn 4:8). This is the kind of love Christians are to have—a self-giving, sacrificial concern for another person (Mt 5:44–45; 1Co 13; 1Jn 4). One may also have a noble, unselfish love or brotherly love (Jn 5:20; Ti 3:15). Those loved by God show love toward others. See 1:144, 580–85, 787; 2:343, 709, 737, 747–48.

LOVE FEAST. A common meal early Christians shared with one another that was connected with the Lord's Supper (Jude 12; cf 2Pt 2:13). These meals were held to express and deepen their brotherly love for one another.

LUKE. A doctor who was Paul's companion. Luke wrote the Gospel according to Luke and the Acts of the Apostles. From his writings it seems that he was a well-educated man. He was a Gentile Christian, probably a Greek, whom the NT mentions three times by name (Col 4:14; Phm 24; 2Tm 4:11). It seems Luke accompanied Paul on his missionary journeys at times. In Ac 16:6–10 we learn that he joined Paul at Troas. Later, when Paul was on his third missionary trip, Luke joined him again at Philippi (Ac 20:5–6). See 1:269–70.

LUKE, GOSPEL ACCORDING TO. See 2:267–317.

LYCAONIA (lik-ay-O-ni-ah; "wolf land"). A high, rugged tableland of Asia Minor that was annexed to Galatia in 35 BC. Paul visited this district and preached in three of its cities: Iconium, Derbe, and Lystra (Ac 13:51–14:23). See 2:502.

LYCIA (LISH-i-ah). A province of southwest Asia Minor (Ac 27:5).

LYDIA (LID-i-ah). A woman in Philippi who made her living by selling purple dyes. She was Paul's first convert in Europe to Christianity. Paul stayed in her house when he was in Philippi (Ac 16:14–15, 40). See 2:538–40.

LYRE (LI-er). A stringed musical instrument (1Sm 10:5; Ps 57:8; 71:22; Dn 3:5). *See also* MUSIC. See 1:540–41, 550, 556.

LYSIAS, CLAUDIUS (LIS-i-as KLAW-di-uhs).

1. A Syrian general defeated by Judas Maccabeus as recorded in 1Macc. See 2:85, 96.
2. The chief captain of the Roman soldiers in Jerusalem. He rescued Paul from a mob and sent him to Caesarea (Ac 21–24). See 2:379.

LYSTRA (LIS-trah). A Roman colony in Lycaonia (Ac 14:6–21; 16:1–2; 2Tm 3:11). See 2:377, 388, 499–500, 813.

M

MAACAH (MAY-ah-kah; perhaps "oppression").

1. David's wife and Absalom's mother (2Sm 3:3; 1Ch 3:2).
2. Rehoboam's wife, Abijah's mother, and Absalom's granddaughter (1Ki 15:2, 10, 13; 2Ch 11:20–22). She is also referred to as Micaiah (2Ch 13:2).

MAASEIAH (MAY-ah-SEE-yah; "work of Yahweh").

1. A captain who helped Jehoiada overthrow Athaliah (2Ch 23:1).
2. The governor of Jerusalem during Josiah's reign (2Ch 34:8).
3. A priest who was a co-worker of Ezra (Ne 8:4; 12:41).

4. The father of the false prophet Zedekiah (Jer 29:21).

MAAZIAH (may-ah-ZIGH-ah; "Yahweh is my refuge"). The head of the twenty-fourth division of priests (1Ch 24:18).

MACCABEES (MAK-ah-beez; may mean "hammer"). A Hasmonean Jewish family descended from the priest Mattathias (1Macc 2, esp v 4) that led a revolt against Antiochus IV, king of Syria. They won freedom for the Jews and ruled Judea from 164 to 134 BC.

The term *Maccabeus* was first given to Judas, the third son of the family who was a very effective military leader. Later it was used of his entire family, as well as others who had a part in the rebellion. The history of the Maccabees is found in the Books of the Maccabees in the Apocrypha. *See also* HASMONEANS. See 1:475; 2:81, 85–86, 95.

MACCABEES, FIRST BOOK OF. See 2:79–90.

MACCABEES, SECOND BOOK OF. See 2:93–103.

MACEDONIA (mas-i-DO-ni-ah). A country in the Balkan Peninsula north of Greece. Philip ruled Macedonia from 359 to 336 BC, and his son Alexander the Great ruled it from 336 to 323 BC. In 168 BC, Macedonia became a Roman province. Paul often visited there (Ac 16:9–12; 20:1–6; Rm 15:26; 1Co 16:5; 2Co 1:16; Php 4:15; 1Tm 1:3). See 2:4, 105, 388, 480–81, 539–40, 597–99.

MACHIR (MAY-kir; "sold"). The son of Manasseh (Gn 50:23). The Machirites descended from him (Nu 26:29). See 1:53.

MACHPELAH (mak-PEE-lah; "double"). A cave Abraham bought that was located in the western part of Hebron. Abraham, Sarah, Isaac, Rebekah, Jacob, and Leah were buried in this cave (Gn 23; 25:9–10; 49:30–31; 50:13). An Islamic mosque now stands over the site. See 1:27, 32; 2:805.

MAGDALENE. *See* MARY 3.

MAGIC. The use of spells, charms, and the like that supposedly gives one powers to make things happen in an unusual way (cf "magicians" in Gn 41:8; Ex 7:11, 22; 8:7, 18; Ac 13:6–12). Magic includes necromancy (trying to tell the future by getting messages from the dead; 1Sm 28:8), exorcism (driving out evil spirits; Ac 19:13), dreams (Dt 13:1–4), shaking arrows (Ezk 21:21), divination (trying to tell the future; Dt 18:10, 14), witchcraft (Lv 19:26; Is 47:9), astrology (believing that the sun, moon, and stars affect peoples' lives; Dn 2:27; 4:7), and divining by rods (Hos 4:12). See 1:547–48, 645–47, 711; 2:43, 46, 389, 520, 773.

MAGICIAN. A title the Babylonians, Medes, and Persians gave to their priests and learned men (Dn 2:2, 10; 5:11). The magicians studied astrology and astronomy and interpreted dreams and omens. They were important men who advised rulers.

When Jesus was born, the Wise Men, sometimes called Magi, came from the East to worship Him (Mt 2:1–11). In NT times the words *magi* or *magos* were also applied broadly to anyone who used the methods of these priests and learned men from the East (Ac 8:9; 13:8). *See also* WISE MEN. See 1:59, 70, 86–88; 2:196, 300.

MAGISTRATE. The chief official in a Roman colony (Ac 16:25–40). See 2:564.

MAGOG (MAY-gog; "Gog's land").
1. People who descended from Japheth (Gn 10:2; 1Ch 1:5).
2. Gog's land is often identified with Scythia, the place where the Magog lived, or with Lydia (Ezk 38; 39:1, 11). The word *Magog* is also used symbolically for the final struggle of the forces of evil against the people of God (Rv 20:7–9).

MAHALATH (MAY-hah-lath).
1. The daughter of Ishmael and wife of Esau (Gn 28:9). She is also referred to as Basemath (Gn 36:3).
2. The wife of Rehoboam (2Ch 11:18).
3. The title of Pss 53 and 88. The term probably refers to a familiar melody.

MAHANAIM (may-hah-NAY-im; "two camps"). A place east of the Jordan River on the boundary between Gad and Manasseh (Jsh 13:26, 30). After Jacob left Laban, the angels of God met him at Mahanaim (Gn 32:2). Later Mahanaim was assigned to the priests as a Levitical city (Jsh 21:38). Ish-bosheth ruled there, and when David was fleeing from Absalom, he went to Mahanaim (2Sm 2:8; 17:24; 1Ki 2:8). See 1:29, 293, 331.

MAHER-SHALAL-HASH-BAZ (MAY-hur-SHAL-al-hash-baz; "the spoil speeds, the prey hastens"). The symbolic name Isaiah gave to his second son (Is 8:1–4). See 1:724.

MAHLON (MAH-lon; "sickly"). The son of Elimelech and Naomi and the first husband of Ruth (Ru 1:2; 4:10). See 1:257.

MAID, MAIDEN.

1. A female servant or slave (Jb 19:15; Is 24:2). See 2:20–21.
2. A virgin (Gn 24:16) or young woman (cf 2Ch 36:17; Jer 2:32). See 1:680.
3. A prostitute (cf Am 2:7).

MAKER. Gk *poieon* and *ktistes*. Translates a variety of titles found throughout the OT, a consistent theme that did not gain a widely used Hbr expression. In the Apocrypha, the title is important to Ecclus and 2Macc and associated with God's authority. See 1:113, 482, 582, 739; 2:139, 253, 386–87.

MALACHI (MAL-ah-kigh; "my messenger"). A prophet who wrote the last book in the OT. Nothing is known about Malachi except what is written in his book. He is thought to have lived around the time of Nehemiah. See 1:998.

MALACHI, BOOK OF. See 1:997–1010.

MALCHIJAH (mal-KIGH-jah; "Yahweh is king").

1. The head of the fifth division of priests (1Ch 24:1, 9).
2. A prince into whose dungeon Jeremiah was thrown (Jer 21:1; 38:1, 6).

MALCHUS (MAL-kuhs; "king" or "counselor"). A servant of the high priest. On the night Jesus was betrayed, Peter cut off Malchus's ear in the Garden of Gethsemane (Jn 18:10).

MALTA (MAL-tah). The island where Paul was shipwrecked (Ac 28:1). See 2:380, 592, 813.

MAMMON (MAM-uhn; "wealth"). Riches, particularly those that make people greedy and selfish (cf Mt 6:24; Lk 16:9, 11, 13).

MAMRE (MAM-ri).

1. An Amorite living at Mamre. He helped Abraham (Gn 14:13, 24).
2. A place where Abraham lived that was near or in Hebron (Gn 13:18; 14:13; 18:1; 35:27; 50:13). See 1:25, 29.

MAN. A being that God created in His own image and likeness (Gn 1:26–27; 9:6; 1Co 11:7; Col 3:10). Man is dependent upon God (Mt 6:26–30; Ac 17:24–28). Man has a body (Mt 6:25), flesh (Rm 1:3), soul, spirit (Gn 2:7; Mt 10:28), and intelligence (Jn 12:40; Rm 2:15).

Man fell into sin and lost the image of God (Gn 3; Rm 5:15–21). As a result, man refuses to honor and thank God but worships created things instead (Rm 1:19–25). Because of sin man also dies (Rm 5:17). In His Law God shows man that he is a sinner, cut off and turned in the opposite direction from his Creator (Rm 7:14–24). But out of grace, God saves those who have faith in Jesus as their Savior and conforms them to His Son's image (Rm 5:15–21; 8:29; 1Co 15:48–49; Col 1:15; 3:10). See 1:24–26, 820, 836; 2:425, 547, 741.

MAN OF LAWLESSNESS. An enemy of Christ who makes himself out to be greater than God. He is found within God's temple and shows himself as God. He works with power and signs, bringing rebellion against God, deception, and delusion. The man of lawlessness will be uncovered at the end of time when Christ comes in glory (2Th 2:3–12; cf Dn 7; 1Jn 2:18). *See also* ANTICHRIST. See 1:581–83.

MAN, SON OF. *See* JESUS CHRIST. See 1:795, 836, 838; 2:237, 393–94.

MANASSEH (mah-NAS-eh; "cause to forget").

1. The first son of Joseph and Asenath (Gn 41:50–51). Manasseh and his brother, Ephraim, were blessed by Jacob (Gn 48:8–22). See 1:23, 52–53.
2. The tribe that descended from Manasseh (Gn 50:23; Nu 26:28–34; Jsh 17:1). See 1:139.
3. The son of Hezekiah and fourteenth king of Judah. Manasseh was a wicked ruler. He brought back many forms of heathen worship. As punishment for his evil ways and idol worship, God let Manasseh's enemies, the Assyrians, carry him into captivity (2Ki 21; 2Ch 33; Mt 1:10). See 1:348, 373, 403, 961.

MANASSEH, THE PRAYER OF. See 2:143–48.

MANASSITES (mah-NAS-ights). Descendants of Manasseh (Dt 4:43; 2Ki 10:33).

MANGER (MAYN-jur). A feeding place for cattle (Lk 2:7–16; 13:15). See 2:7, 296.

MANNA (MAN-ah;). A special food God miraculously provided for the Israelites while they were in the wilderness. It was white and finely flaked, like frost (Ex 16:14–36; Nu 11:7–9; Dt 8:3; Jsh 5:12). Jesus is described as the true manna from heaven (Jn 6:31–40). See 1:65, 75, 127, 368; 2:200–1, 280.

MANOAH (mah-NO-ah; "rest"). Samson's father (Jgs 13).

MARA (MAY-rah; "bitter"). The name Naomi gave to herself (Ru 1:20). See 1:257.

MARAH (MA-rah; "bitter"). A spring in the wilderness of Shur where the Hebrews found water (Ex 15:22–25; Nu 33:8–9). See 1:81.

MARANATHA (mar-ah-NATH-ah). An expression meaning "Our Lord come!" *See also* ANATHEMA MARANATHA. See 2:451.

MARK. The writer of the second Gospel. John was his Jewish name; Mark was his Roman name. Sometimes he is referred to by both names: John Mark (Ac 12:12, 25; 13:5; 1Pt 5:13). The young man mentioned in Mk 14:51–52 may be Mark.

John Mark's mother, Mary, had a home in Jerusalem (Ac 12:12–17). John Mark went with Barnabas, his cousin, and Paul, his spiritual father, on part of the first missionary journey (Ac 12:25; 13:1; Col 4:10; 1Pt 5:13). He left them, however, before the trip was over and returned to Jerusalem (Ac 13:13). This resulted in an argument between Barnabas and Paul (Ac 15:36–41). As a result, Barnabas let Paul go on the second missionary journey without him, and Barnabas took John Mark and went to Cyprus (Ac 15:39). Later Mark became Paul's helper (2Tm 4:11; Col 4:10; Phm 24).

According to tradition, Mark presented Peter's story of Christ in his Gospel (cf 1Pt 5:13). Mark is also said to have been the founder of the Church of Alexandria. See 2:234–35.

MARK, GOSPEL ACCORDING TO. See 2:233–65.

MARKET, MARKETPLACE. A place in cities where goods were traded or sold and where people came together to visit (Ps 55:11; Mt 11:16; Lk 11:43; Ac 16:19). Paul also reasoned and debated with those in the marketplace (Gk *agora*; AC 17:17). Archaeologists have excavated numerous sites that were marketplaces since every city or town had one. See 1:628, 630; 2:33–34, 379, 441, 806, 811.

MARRIAGE. A lifelong union between a man and a woman, instituted by God (Gn 1:26–31; 2:18–25; Mt 19:5). God provides blessings through marriage: children, help, and companionship (Gn 1:28; 2:18–24; 29:32; 30:1). Sexual relations between a husband and his wife are God pleasing (Pr 5:15–19; 1Th 4:1–5; Heb 13:4).

The union of one man and one woman until one of them dies is God's ideal intention for marriage (Gn 2:24; Pr 31:10–31; Mt 19:5–6; 1Tm 3:2). Nevertheless, men in Bible times sometimes had more than one wife (Gn 4:19; 30; 1Ki 11:3).

The Israelites were not allowed to marry Canaanites or close relatives (Lv 18; 20; Dt 7:3–4). There were also certain legal restrictions on marrying people of other nations (Dt 23:3–8). After the exile, Israelite men were told to divorce their foreign wives (Ezr 9–10).

Although divorce is not part of God's plan, it is allowed for certain reasons (Dt 24:1–4; Ezr 10:11–44; Mt 19:3–9). Unless one's husband or wife has been sexually unfaithful, to divorce him or her is adultery (Mt 5:31–32; 19:3–10; Mk 10:2–12; Lk 16:18).

In Bible times marriage customs differed from today. Fathers often picked wives for their sons. An engagement between a man and woman involved a legal agreement that was confirmed by an oath and dowry. After this the two were considered man and wife. They did not live together as man and wife, however, until they were actually married. When the bridegroom took his bride from her father's house to his own, the people joined in a marriage celebration (Is 61:10; Sg 3:11; Mt 25:1–13).

The Scriptures picture the covenant union between God and Israel as a marriage (Is 62:1–5; Jer 2:2). In the NT the Church is called the Bride of Christ (Lk 5:34; 2Co 11:2; Rv 21:2). See 1:24–26, 34, 49–50, 119–20, 240–41, 369–70, 679–80, 692, 1003; 2:224–25, 460, 472–73, 529–31, 784.

MARRIAGE, LEVIRATE. *See* LEVIRATE MARRIAGE.

MARTHA (MAHR-thah; "lady"). The sister of Mary and Lazarus (Lk 10:38–41; Jn 11; 12:2). See 2:330, 336.

MARTYR (MAHR-tur; "witness"). A person who witnesses to his or her faith in Christ by dying for it (Rv 17:6). Cf Ac 22:20. See 1:616; 2:371, 375, 399, 597–98, 737.

MARY (MAIR-ee; "rebellion"). Miriam in the OT. In the NT a number of women are named Mary.

1. Mary, mother of Jesus. She was the wife of Joseph, a descendant of King David (Mt 1:18–25; Rm 1:3) and a relative of Elizabeth, John the Baptist's mother (Lk 1:27, 36).

   Mary gave birth to Jesus in Bethlehem (Mt 1:18, 20; Lk 2:1–20). At the proper time Mary and Joseph brought Jesus to the temple in Jerusalem for His presentation to the Lord (Lk 2:22–38). Shortly after the visit of the Wise Men, an angel warned Joseph in a dream to flee to Egypt because Herod was going to kill Jesus. So Mary and Joseph took Jesus and went to Egypt (Mt 2:13–15). After Herod died, they returned to the land of Israel and lived in Nazareth (Mt 2:19–23; Lk 2:39–40). When Jesus was 12 years old, Mary and Joseph took Him to Jerusalem for the Feast of the Passover (Lk 2:41–50).

Mary was at the wedding in Cana where Jesus performed His first miracle (Jn 2:1–12). When Jesus was dying on the cross, He asked John to look after Mary (Jn 19:25–27). After Jesus' ascension Mary met with other believers in the Upper Room for prayer (Ac 1:14).

Mary is called blessed among women (Lk 1:28, 42, 48). She carefully considered and thought about Jesus' mission and work and believed in His powers (Lk 2:51; Jn 2:3–5). Jesus stressed His spiritual relationship to Mary rather than His earthly one (Mt 12:46–50; Lk 8:20–21; 11:27–28). See 1: 278; 2:169, 194, 196, 219–20, 277, 320, 677.

2. Mary, the wife of Clopas and mother of James and Joses (Mt 27:56; Mk 15:40). She was one of the women at Jesus' crucifixion and burial (Mt 27:61; Mk 15:47). Early on the morning of Jesus' resurrection she went to His grave only to discover that He was not there; He had risen (Mt 28:1; Mk 16:1; Lk 24:1). See 2:169.
3. Mary Magdalene, a woman who came from Magdala on the southwest coast of the Sea of Galilee. Mary became a devoted follower of Jesus after He cast seven demons out of her (Mk 16:9; Lk 8:1–2). She is often regarded as the sinful woman who anointed Jesus' feet and wiped them with her hair (Lk 7:37–50). No one knows this for sure, however, since the biblical account does not name this woman. Mary was among the women who witnessed the crucifixion and burial of Jesus (Mt 27:56, 61; Mk 15:40, 47; Jn 19:25). On the morning of His resurrection she went to His tomb (Mt 28:1; Mk 16:1; Lk 24:1; Jn 20:1). She was the first person to whom the risen Lord appeared (Mk 16:9; Jn 20:11–29). See 2:169, 243, 249, 337, 353.
4. Mary of Bethany, the sister of Lazarus and Martha (Jn 11:1). While Martha prepared the dinner, Mary sat at Jesus' feet and listened to His teaching (Lk 10:38–41). On another occasion Mary anointed Jesus' feet with oil (Jn 12:1–8). See 2:169, 280, 306, 335–36.
5. Mary, mother of John Mark and sister of Barnabas (cf Col 4:10). Mary lived in Jerusalem. When Peter was in prison, Christians met in her home to pray for his release. While they were gathered there, Peter surprised them by knocking at the door. After they had gotten over their amazement, they let Peter in and listened to him describe how the Lord had brought him out of prison (Ac 12:12–17). See 2:169, 234–35.

MASTER. Various words in the Bible are translated as master. Consequently, when the word *master* is used in English Bibles it may mean any of the following: master of a house or husband (Jgs 19:22; Mt 13:27); ruler, owner, or lord (Gn 24:14, 27; 39:20; 2Ki 19:4; Mt 24:45); superior or supervisor (Lk 5:5; 8:24). See 1:295, 488; 2:63, 208, 491, 525, 557, 635–38.

MATTANIAH (mat-ah-NIGH-ah; "gift of Yahweh"). The original name of King Zedekiah (2Ki 24:17). See 1:338.

MATTHEW (MATH-yoo; "gift of Yahweh"). The son of Alpheus. Matthew, who was also referred to as Levi, was a tax collector at Capernaum. One day Jesus called him to be His disciple (Mt 9:9–13; Mk 2:14–17; Lk 5:27–32). Along with the other 12 disciples, Jesus made Matthew an apostle (Mt 10:3; Lk 6:15; Ac 1:13). See 2:187–88.

MATTHEW, GOSPEL ACCORDING TO. See 2:185–231.

MATTHIAS (ma-THIGH-uhs; "gift of Yahweh"). The apostle whom the disciples chose to fill the place of Judas Iscariot after Judas killed himself (Ac 1:15–26). See 2:369.

MEASURES. Biblical measurements can be divided into three categories: length, dry ingredients, and liquids.

1. LENGTH
   a. A fingerbreadth equaled about three-fourths of an inch.
   b. A handbreadth equaled four fingerbreadths (about three inches).
   c. A span was the distance from the tip of the thumb to the tip of the little finger when the fingers were stretched apart (about 9 inches).
   d. A cubit equaled 6 handbreadths (about 18 inches).
   e. A reed equaled 6 cubits (about 9 feet).
   f. A pace was the distance of 1 step (about 30 inches).
   g. A little way (cf Gn 48:7) was the distance one could walk in 2 hours.
   h. A day's journey was the distance traveled in one day (about 20 miles).
   i. A furlong or stadion was about 600 feet.

j. A fathom was the distance between two hands when held wide apart (about 5 to 6 feet).
k. A mile was 1,000 paces (about 4,854 feet).
l. A Sabbath day's journey was 3,000 feet (Jsh 3:4).

2. DRY MEASURES
a. A handful was the amount that could be held in one hand.
b. A kab was equal to about 1 quart.
c. A seah was equal to 7 kabs (about 7 quarts).
d. An ephah was equal to about three-fifths of a bushel.
e. An omer was one-tenth of an ephah (about 2 quarts).
f. A homer was 10 ephahs, or the load of a donkey (about 6 bushels).
g. A choenix equaled about 1 quart.
h. A modius probably equaled about 1 peck.
i. A saton or measure equaled about a peck.
j. A cor equaled a homer (about 6 bushels).

3. LIQUID MEASURES
a. A log was the amount displaced by 6 hen's eggs (about one-third of a quart).
b. A hin equaled one-sixth of a bath (about 4 quarts).
c. A bath equaled 1 ephah (about 6 gallons).
d. A firkin was about 9 or 10 gallons.
e. A sextarius was about 1 pint.

MEDAD (MEE-dad). One of the elders Moses chose to help him govern the people. Medad was a prophet (Nu 11:26–27).

MEDAN (MEE-dan). The son of Abraham and Keturah (Gn 25:2; 1Ch 1:32).

MEDE (MEED). A person who came from Media (2Ki 17:6; Est 1:19; Is 13:17; Dn 5:31). See 1:826, 845–47; 2:18.

MEDIA (MEE-di-ah). A country in Asia northwest of Persia and south of the Caspian Sea. The people who lived there were famous for the horses they bred. In 612 BC, the Medes captured Nineveh. Under Nebuchadnezzar's rule, the Median Kingdom stretched from the Persian Gulf to the Caspian Sea (Est 1:3, 14, 18; 10:2; Is 21:2; Dn 8:20). See 1:461, 845–46; 2:39, 45.

MEDIATOR (MEE-di-ay-tur). A person who acts as a go-between (1Sm 2:25; Jb 33:23; Is 43:27). Christ is the mediator of the new covenant. Through Him God and people are brought back into a right relationship with each other (1Tm 2:5; Heb 8:6; 9:15; 12:24). *See also* JESUS CHRIST. See 1:38–39, 161, 298, 518; 2:280, 608–9, 661.

MEDICINE. In the Scriptures, the word *medicine* is used primarily in a figurative sense (Pr 17:22; 30:13; Jer 46:11). *See also* DISEASE; PERFUMER.

MEDITATE. Translates Hbr *hagah* and *siach*, terms about speaking. A person holds his attention by uttering words of Scripture or prayers to focus his thoughts. The Israelites meditated on God's Word by reciting it. The believer explores God's Word, since "there is always something left over to understand and to do. Therefore you must never be proud, as if you were already full" (AE 11:434). Luther suggests that this verb recalls the singing of the birds, "so the church continuously fills its mouth with preaching in joy and gladness like that of the little birds" (AE 11:437, n 23). See 1:217, 595.

MEDITERRANEAN SEA (med-uh-tuh-RAY-ni-uhn SEE). The sea that lies between Europe and Africa. It is also referred to as the sea, the Great Sea, the western sea, and the Sea of Philistines (Ex 23:31; Nu 34:6; Dt 11:24; Ac 10:6). See 1:17, 811; 2:5, 116–17, 798.

MEDIUM. A person who claims to be able to call forth the spirits of the dead for consultation (Lv 19:31; 20:6, 27; Dt 18:11; 1Sm 28:3; 2Ki 21:6). *See also* NECROMANCY. See 1:311–14.

MEGIDDO (mi-GID-o; "place of pleasant fruits"). A city that overlooked the Plain of Esdraelon. It was situated on two important trade routes (Jsh 12:21; 17:11; Jgs 1:27). Solomon strengthened its fortifications (1Ki 9:15). When Ahaziah, king of Judah, was wounded by Jehu's men, he fled to Megiddo, where he died (2Ki 9:27).

Megiddo was also the scene of a battle between Pharaoh Neco and King Josiah (2Ki 23:29; 2Ch 35:22). *See also* ARMAGEDDON. See 1:60, 211, 403–4, 754; 2:320.

MEGILLOTH. The five scrolls of biblical books read at the major Jewish festivals: Song of Solomon (Passover), Ruth (Weeks/Pentecost), Lamentations (Fall of Jerusalem), Ecclesiastes (Tabernacles), and Esther (Purim). See 1:255, 473, 491–92, 694.

MEHUJAEL (mi-HYOO-yay-el). Cain's grandson (Gn 4:18).

MELCHIZEDEK (mel-KIZ-uh-dek; "king of righteousness"). The king of Salem (Jerusalem) and priest of God. Melchizedek blessed Abram and received tithes from him (Gn 14:17–20). He is a type of Christ, the priest-king (Ps 110:4; Heb 5:6–10; 6:20; 7). See 1:25–26, 412; 2:657, 660–61, 668.

MEMBER. Gk *melos*, "limb or part of the body." *See* BODY OF CHRIST; CHURCH. See 2:501, 582.

MEMPHIS (MEM-fis; "place of good"). An ancient city of Egypt located on the Nile River about 10 miles north of Cairo. The prophets spoke of it negatively (Is 19:13; Jer 2:16; 44:1; 46:14; 19; Ezk 30:13, 16).

MENAHEM (MEN-ah-hem; "comforter"). The sixteenth king of Israel, who gained the throne by killing King Shallum. Menahem paid tribute to Pul (Tiglath-pileser) to keep him from invading the land. He also practiced calf worship. The Scriptures evaluate Menahem's reign by saying that "he did what was evil in the sight of the LORD" (2Ki 15:14–22). See 1:337, 373.

MENE, MENE, TEKEL, AND PARSIN (MEE-ni, MEE-ni, TEK-il, and PAHR-sin). Four Aramaic words that suddenly appeared on a wall at Belshazzar's feast (Dn 5:25–28). They probably mean "numbered, numbered, weighed, and divisions." See 1:834.

MEPHIBOSHETH (mi-FIB-o-sheth; "he scatters shame").

1. The son of Saul and Rizpah (2Sm 21:8). See 1:281.
2. Jonathan's son. He was accidentally crippled after Saul's death. David honored Mephibosheth and provided for him by giving him Saul's estates (2Sm 4:4; 9:6–13; 16:1–4; 19:24–30; 21:7). He is also referred to as Merib-baal (1Ch 8:34; 9:40). See 1:303.

MERAB (MEE-rab; possibly "increase"). Saul's daughter (1Sm 14:49). *See also* MICHAL. See 1:314.

MERATHAIM (mer-ah-THAY-im; "doubly stubborn"). A name for Babylon (Jer 50:21).

MERCY.

1. The Hbr word *hesed* means God's undeserved favor and love within the covenant relationship. *See also* STEADFAST LOVE. See 1:262, 711–12.
2. Various other Hbr and Gk words are translated into English as "mercy." Hbr *rachamim*, "tender mercy," "compassion" from the term for "womb"; it pictures the tender love a mother has for her children. Gk *eleos*, "pity," "compassion," moved by the troubles of others. They convey the idea of compassion or sympathy, pity, pardon or forgiveness, and showing favor (Gn 19:16; Dt 13:17; Jb 8:5; Ps 23:6; Mt 5:7; Col 3:12). See 1:35–36, 142, 907–11; 2:198, 204–5, 247, 489, 662.

MERCY SEAT. The covering of the ark (Ex 25:17–22; 26:34; 37:6–9). It reminded the people of God's gracious act of "covering" sin. On the Day of Atonement, the high priest burned incense before the Mercy Seat and sprinkled blood on it. By doing this, he made atonement for his sins and the sins of the nation in the presence of the Lord, who appeared in a cloud upon the Mercy Seat (Lv 16). The blood of Christ, shed for the sins of the world, is the real atonement (Heb 9). See 1:61, 73, 75–76, 589.

MERIBAH (MER-i-bah; "strife").

1. A place where God gave Israel water from a rock. It was near Rephidim (Ex 17:1–7). See 1:135, 139.
2. Meribah of Kadesh. *See* MERIBATH-KADESH.

MERIBATH-KADESH (MER-i-bath-kay-DESH; "strife of Kadesh"). A place near Kadesh-barnea in the Desert of Zin. The people of Israel were thirsty there, so God told Moses to speak to the rock. But Moses struck the rock instead. Water flowed from it for the people to drink. Because of his disobedience, however, Moses was forbidden to enter the Promised Land (Nu 20:1–13; Dt 32:51).

MERODACH (mi-RO-dak). Marduk, the chief god of the Babylonians (Jer 50:2).

MEROM (MEE-rom; height). A place north of the Sea of Galilee where Joshua defeated the kings of northern Canaan (Jsh 11:5–7). See 1:211.

MESHACH (MEE-shak). The Babylonian name given to Mishael, one of Daniel's friends (Dn 1:7). Because Meshach refused to worship the golden image King Nebuchadnezzar set up on the plain of Dura, he was thrown into a fiery furnace (Dn 3). See 1:823; 2:134, 136.

MESHULLAM (mi-SHUL-am; possibly "friend"). A common name in the OT. A number of men with this name lived during Ezra's time. Ezra sent one of them to get Levites for the temple in Jerusalem (Ezr 8:16).

MESHULLEMETH (mi-SHUL-i-meth; possibly "friend"). The wife of King Manasseh of Judah and mother of Amon (2Ki 21:19).

MESOPOTAMIA (mes-o-po-TAY-mi-ah; "between rivers"). The name applied to the upper part of the land between the Tigris and Euphrates Rivers (Gn 24:10; Dt 23:4; Jgs 3:8–11; Ac 2:9; 7:2). The Hebrews called it Aram-naharaim. Today it is Iraq. See 1:17, 25, 352; 2:20.

MESSIAH (muh-SIGH-ah; "anointed one"). In the OT this term describes any high official, such as a prophet, priest, or king, who was consecrated to his office by being anointed with oil. The term came to be used in a special sense, however, of a great prophet from David's family, anointed by God, and filled with His Spirit (Dt 18:15–18; 2Sm 7:12–14; Is 11:2). This Messiah would deliver God's judgment on the wicked, restore God's kingdom to the people of Israel, and enable them to live perfectly as God's chosen people. Moreover, He would usher in a time of universal peace, goodwill, and well-being (Is 11). Many nations would come to Him (Is 11:10; 60:1).

The OT also pictures the Messiah as the Savior and Suffering Servant, the one who would suffer and die for the sins of the people (Is 25:9; 53; 63:1–5). He would be the Creator of a spiritual kingdom for all people (Is 60; Jer 33:15–26).

Jesus fulfills the biblical prophecies concerning the Messiah. He is the Promised One of God (Lk 4:18; Ac 4:27). Through His threefold office of Prophet, Priest, and King, He ushers in God's spiritual kingdom. Through His suffering and death, He redeems people from their sins and brings peace and well-being between God and humanity (Lk 1:53; 7:18–25; Jn 3:16–21). *See also* ANOINT 5; JESUS CHRIST. See 1:22, 298–99, 410–11, 588, 733–34, 737, 807, 924, 991–92; 2:176, 190–91, 200–202, 249, 333, 383, 599.

METHEG-AMMAH (MEE-theg-AM-ah). A town that David took from the Philistines (2Sm 8:1). It was probably Gath (1Ch 18:1). See 1:293.

METHUSELAH (mi-THYOO-zuh-lah; possibly "man of the javelin"). The son of Enoch, father of Lamech, and grandfather of Noah. He lived 969 years, which is the longest recorded age of any person (Gn 5:21–27; 1Ch 1:3; Lk 3:37).

MIBSAM (MIB-sam; possibly "fragrant"). The fourth son of Ishmael and grandson of Abraham (Gn 25:13; 1Ch 1:29).

MICAH (MIGH-kah; "who is like Yahweh?").

1. A dishonest Ephraimite who worshiped idols and hired a wandering Levite as his priest (Jgs 17). See 1:239.
2. A prophet from Moresheth who wrote one of the shorter prophetic books in the OT (Mi 1:1; Jer 26:18). Micah began his work a little later than Hosea and Isaiah, prophesying during the reigns of Jotham, Ahaz, and Hezekiah. See 1:373, 922.

MICAH, BOOK OF. See 1:921–33.

MICAIAH (MIGH-KAY-yah; "who is like Yahweh?").

1. A prophet who predicted the death of King Ahab (1Ki 22:7–28; 2Ch 18:6–27). See 1:344, 367, 372, 402.
2. The man who reported Jeremiah's prophecies to the Jewish princes (Jer 36:11–13). See 1:706.

MICHAEL (MIGH-kuhl; "who is like God?"). An archangel who fought for Israel (Dn 10:13, 21; 12:1). Michael also disputed with the devil for Moses' body and defeated him, and successfully fought the dragon and the enemies of God's people (Jude 9; Rv 12:7). See 1:820, 827, 836; 2:765–66, 781.

MICHAL (MIGH-kuhl; "who is like God?"). The daughter of Saul and wife of David (1Sm 14:49; 18:20–27). *See also* MERAB. See 1:294, 314.

MICHMAS, MICHMASH (MIK-mas, MIK-mash; possibly "treasury" or "hidden place"). A town near the Mount of Bethel, about 7 miles north of Jerusalem. A notable battle between the Philistines and the Israelites occurred there. Through Jonathan's strategy the Philistines were defeated (1Sm 13–14). After the captivity Jewish exiles returned to Michmas and lived there (Ne 11:31). See 1:290.

MIDIAN (MID-i-uhn; "quarrels"). One of the sons of Abraham and Keturah (Gn 25:2).

MIDIANITES (MID-i-uhn-ights). A race of people that descended from Midian (Ex 3:1; Nu 22:4; Jgs 7:13). They were merchants who lived south of Moab and east of the Gulf of Aqabah, though the boundary of their land did shift (Gn 37:25–36). Moses fled from Egypt to Midian, where he married Zipporah (Ex 2–4). The Midianites were defeated first by the Israelites and then by Gideon (Nu 22–25; 31; Jgs 6–8). See 1:100, 127–28, 238, 895.

MIGHTY ONE. Hbr *'abbir*; Gk *dunastes*. Hbr term from Semitic root meaning "be strong." In the OT it appears only in poetic passages (cf Gn 49:24). Appears in Jesus son of Sirach's closing hymn about the fathers of Israel (Ecclus 46:5).

MIKLOTH (MIK-loth). David's chief officer (1Ch 27:4).

MILCAH (MIL-kah; "princess" or "queen"). A daughter of Haran, Abraham's brother, and the sister of Lot. Milcah married her uncle Nahor, and together they had eight children. Rebekah and Laban were her grandchildren (Gn 11:29; 22:20–23; 24:15, 24, 47).

MILCOM (MIL-kom; "king of the people"). A heathen god who was worshiped by the Ammonites (1Ki 11:5, 33; 2Ki 23:13; Jer 49:1, 3). Solomon introduced his worship into Israel. Milcom is sometimes identified with Molech. *See also* MOLECH.

MILE. *See* MEASURES 1k.

MILETUM, MILETUS (migh-LEE-tuhm, migh-LEE-tuhs). A city on the seacoast of Ionia about 36 miles south of Ephesus. Paul stopped there (Ac 20:15, 17; 2Tm 4:20). See 2:388, 598, 813.

MILLENNIUM (1,000 years). The term applied to that period, before or after the final resurrection and judgment, when Christ will supposedly appear on earth with the saints and rule for 1,000 years. It is based on a misinterpretation of Rv 20:1–7. See 1:823; 2:794, 795.

MINA (MIGH-nah). A Babylonian weight used in Israel that was equal to about 60 shekels (1Ki 10:17; Ezr 2:69; Ne 7:71). A light mina was about 500 grams, and a heavy mina was about 1,000 grams (Ezk 45:12). In the NT, it equaled about 100 drachmas (Lk 19:13–15). See 1:454.

MINISTER.

1. A person who serves or waits on another. Joshua was Moses' minister (Ex 24:13; Jsh 1:1). See 1:294, 726; 2:542.
2. A person who is active in service to God or the state. Priests performed a ministry (Ex 28:43; Dt 10:8). Prophets and kings were also consecrated for sacred service. *See also* KING; PRIEST; PROPHET. See 1:143, 807; 2:488, 603–4.
3. In the NT the usual word for ministry is *diakonia* or service. The NT distinguishes between the ministry or service rendered in the public sphere for the good of all, such as the government might perform (Rm 13:6), and the service or ministry rendered by God's special ministries in Word and Sacrament: apostles, evangelists, pastors, teachers, elders, bishops, and deacons (Lk 6:13; Ac 14:23; 21:8; Rm 12:7; 1Co 12:28–31; 2Co 6:13–10; Php 1:1; 1Tm 3:1–8; 5:17; 2Tm 4:5; Jas 3:1). While all Christians are called to speak the glory of Him who called them out of darkness, God especially calls the apostles and pastors to preach publicly (cf 1Co 1:17; 9:16; 1Tm 2:7; 2Tm 1:11; 4:2). See 2:312, 375.

MIRACLE. An event that causes wonder; something that takes place outside of the laws of nature (cf "sign" in Jn 4:48; Ac 2:19; 2Co 12:12).

The OT describes a miracle as an extraordinary manifestation of God's presence (Ex 4:21; 7:9; Ps 105:27; cf Nu 16:30; Jsh 10:10–14; 2Ki 20:8–11). God's people recognized miracles as God's work because of their faith in Him (cf Ex 7–12; Jgs 6:17–21, 36–40; 1Ki 18:38–39).

The NT depicts miracles as acts of power, signs, and wonders (Act 19:11; cf "signs" in Lk 21:25; Jn 2:11). Their significance could be understood only by those who had faith in Jesus Christ (Jn 6:26; 11:25–27, 38–40; 20:30–31). See 1:liii–lix, 86–89, 376–77, 911–12; 2:198, 227–28, 258, 272–73, 330, 333, 471–72.

MIRIAM (MIR-i-uhm; "rebellion"). The sister of Moses and Aaron. After the Israelites had passed unharmed through the Red Sea, Miriam led the women, with tambourines and dancing, in a song of victory (Ex 15:20–21). Miriam was a prophetess. When she criticized Moses for marrying a Cushite woman, she was punished with leprosy. But Moses asked God to make her better, and Miriam was healed after seven days (Nu 12:1–15). When Miriam died, she was buried at Kadesh (Nu 20:1). See 1:69, 129, 138, 705.

MISHAEL (MISH-ay-el; "who is like God?").

1. Moses' uncle (Ex 6:22; Lv 10:4–5).
2. The Hbr name of Meshach, one of the three men thrown into the fiery furnace for refusing to worship the golden idol King Nebuchadnezzar set up on the Plain of Dura (Dn 1:7; 3). See 1:823; 2:134, 136.

MISHMA (MISH-mah; "hearing" or "rumor"). A son of Ishmael and the founder of an Arabian tribe (Gn 25:14; 1Ch 1:30).

MITRE. *See* TURBAN.

MIZPAH, MIZPEH (MIZ-pah, MIZ-pe; "watch tower"). The heap of stones Jacob piled together in Gilead as a witness of the covenant between him and Laban. Laban called it Jegar-sahadutha; Jacob called it Galeed, which means "cairn of testimony."

The Mizpah blessing, "The Lord watch between

you and me, when we are out of one another's sight," was spoken there (Gn 31:44–49). The location may be that of Ramoth-gilead. See 1:279.

MOAB (MO-ab; according to LXX, "from father"). Lot's son by his daughter (Gn 19:30–38). Moab was the ancestor of the Moabites, people who lived on a well-watered tableland east of the Jordan (Nu 21:13–15). The Moabites were the ones who refused the Israelites passage through their land when the Israelites were on their way to Canaan (Jgs 11:17–18). Later they sent Balaam to curse Israel (Nu 22–24). During the period of the judges Moab controlled Israel for 18 years (Jgs 3:12–14).

David defeated the Moabites and made them pay tribute (2Sm 8:2, 12; 1Ch 18:2, 11). The Moabites were enemies of Israel (2Ki 1:1; 24:2; 2Ch 20:1–30). The prophets spoke against them in a strong way (Is 15–16; Jer 9:26; 48; Ezk 25:8–11; Am 2:1; Zep 2:8–11). Ruth, the mother of Obed and an ancestress of Jesus, was from Moab (Ru 1:4). See 1:140, 157–61, 254–61, 267, 293, 730, 805, 963.

MOABITE STONE (MO-ub-ight). A two-by-four foot black asphalt slab erected around 850 BC by Mesha, king of Moab. The stone, which is inscribed with the Moabite language (a language that is almost the same as Hbr), describes the events of 2Ki 3:4–27. See 2:820.

MOLECH (MO-lek; possibly "king"). A heathen god worshiped especially by the Ammonites. Sacrificing children to this god was a common worship practice. This practice was forbidden by Hebrew law (Lv 18:21; 20:1–5). Nevertheless, an altar was built to Molech in the Valley of Hinnom, and Manasseh worshiped him there, burning his sons as an offering to the god (2Ch 33:6).

When Josiah was king, he stamped out idol worship and tore down the altar built to Molech (2Ki 23:10). The prophets spoke strongly against the worship of Molech (Jer 7:29–34; 19:1–13; Ezk 20:26–39). This god is also referred to as Moloch (Ac 7:43).

MONEY. In early times bartering, or trading one thing for another, was the system of exchange. Cattle, produce, and weighed metal were used for this (Gn 13:2; 26:16; 1Ki 5:11; 1Ch 21:25). Coined money came into use after the exile (Ezr 1:4). To begin with, the Israelites used the coins of the country that had conquered them. During NT times coins from various countries were in use. *See also* MONEY-CHANGER. See 1:38, 110; 2:45, 190, 202, 292, 406, 482, 608.

MONEY-CHANGER. A person who for a fee changed foreign money into coins that could be used in the temple (Mt 21:12; Mk 11:15; cf Ex 30:13–15). See 2:202, 267.

MONOTHEISM (MON-o-thee-iz'm; "one God"). The belief that there is only one God. *See also* GOD; GODS, FALSE. See 1:500, 708–9, 718–19.

MONTH. *See* TIME.

MOON. The principal light of the night, given to mark seasons, days, months, years, and signs (Gn 1:14; Ps 104:19; Jl 2:10; Mt 24:29; Lk 21:25).

Many heathen nations worshiped the moon, but this practice was forbidden to the Israelites (Dt 4:19; 17:3). Nevertheless, during the period of the kings, moon worship was also practiced by some of the Israelites (2Ki 23:5; Jer 8:2). See 1:225–26, 837.

MORASHTITE (mo-RASH-tight). *See* MICAH.

MORDECAI (MAWR-di-kigh). A Benjaminite who was the uncle and foster father of Esther (Est 2:5–7). Mordecai saved King Ahasuerus's life by letting him know through Esther about two men who were plotting to kill him (Est 2:21–23). Mordecai also helped save the Jews from Haman's plot to destroy them (Est 3–10). The Feast of Purim reminds the Jewish people of this deliverance. See 1:459–72; 2:104–14.

MOREH (MO-re). An oak tree or plain near Shechem (Dt 11:30). Abraham camped there when he arrived in Canaan (Gn 12:6).

MORESHATH, MORESHETH (MO-resh-eth; "property"). *See* MICAH. See 1:921–23.

MORIAH (mo-RIGH-ah). The place where Abraham went to offer Isaac as a sacrifice to the Lord (Gn 22:2). It probably is the hill in Jerusalem on which Solomon built the temple (2Ch 3:1). See 1:25, 122, 305, 401.

MORNING. *See* TIME.

MOSES (MO-ziz; "drown out" or possibly "child" in Egyptian). The great Israelite leader, Lawgiver, and prophet through whom God delivered the Israelites from Egyptian slavery and prepared them for entrance into the Promised Land. Moses was born in Egypt to Israelite parents of the tribe of Levi. Since Pharaoh had ordered the death of all Hebrew baby boys, Moses' mother put him afloat in a basket on the Nile River. Pharaoh's daughter discovered baby Moses and adopted him as her own (Ex 2:1–10).

Moses received a fine education in the Egyptian court (Ac 7:22). This helped to prepare him for his later leadership of the Israelites.

When Moses was older, he killed an Egyptian who had struck one of Moses' Hebrew countrymen. The next day, fearing for his life, Moses fled to Midian.

Moses spent the next 40 years of his life in Midian. There he married Zipporah, the priest Jethro's daughter. Moses and Zipporah had two sons (Ex 2:11–25). The time spent in Midian was a period of preparation for Moses. He grew familiar with wilderness life, its climate, and resources. At the end of this period God spoke to Moses from a burning bush and called him as leader of Israel (Ex 3–4).

In a series of 10 plagues Moses countered Pharaoh's attempt to keep the Hebrew people as slaves in Egypt. Finally, when the Lord passed over the Israelites but put to death all the firstborn of the Egyptians, Pharaoh said the Hebrew people could go. The Passover was instituted to remind the Israelites of this event (Ex 5–15).

Moses led the Israelites through the Wilderness of Shur (Ex 15:22–26). At Sin, God provided manna for the people to eat (Ex 16). Next the Israelites traveled to Rephidim and from there to the wilderness at Sinai, where they set up camp (Ex 17–19:2).

At Sinai, Moses received God's Law for the people. It spelled out how they were to live in a covenant relationship with God (Ex 20–25). There Moses also received instructions for building the tabernacle and regulations for the priesthood and the altar (Ex 26–30). When Moses left the mountain and went back to the people, he found them worshiping a golden calf (Ex 32).

God renewed the covenant with His people (Ex 34). Then they began to build the tabernacle and make holy clothing for the priests (Ex 35–38:40; 39).

Moses took a census of the people (Nu 1–2). Later, at God's command, they left the wilderness at Sinai (Nu 10). At various times Moses' actions or leadership were opposed. Miriam and Aaron spoke against him for marrying a Cushite woman. God punished Miriam with leprosy for this act. But when Moses asked God to heal her, God did so after seven days (Nu 12). Later, Koran, Dathan, and Abiram also spoke out against Moses. Because of this, the Lord opened the earth and swallowed them up. In this way God showed the Israelites that Moses was indeed His chosen servant (Nu 16–17).

When they left Mount Hor to go around the land of Edom, the people once again spoke against God and Moses, saying, "Why have you brought us up out of Egypt to die in the wilderness?" (Nu 21:4–5). God punished them for their complaints and lack of trust by sending fiery serpents to bite them. Many of the people died. Moses prayed for the people and was told to set up a bronze serpent on a pole. Those bitten by real snakes would live if they looked at this bronze serpent (Nu 21:6–9).

Because Moses sinned at Meribah, he was not allowed to enter the Promised Land. Joshua, the man Moses named as the new leader of the Israelites, would be the one to lead the people into Canaan. God did allow Moses to see the Promised Land, however, before his death (Nu 20:27). Moses died on Mount Nebo (Dt 34).

Both the OT and NT indicate that Moses wrote the first five books of the OT called the Pentateuch (Gn–Dt; Lk 24:27, 44; Jn 5:45–47). After his death, Moses' greatness was recognized by all (Jer 15:1; Heb 3:2). Along with Elijah, Moses appeared on the Mount of Transfiguration with Jesus (Mt 17:3–4). Moses is the great Lawgiver with whom Christ is compared and contrasted (Ac 3:22; 2Co 3:12–18; Gal 3–4; Heb 3). See 1:5–7, 63, 67, 69–73, 159–60; 2:43, 300–301, 666, 764, 766.

MOST HIGH. Hbr *ʿelyon*; Gk *hupsistos* in LXX. Used four times in Gn 14:17–22 and c 40 times elsewhere in the OT (often in Ps and Dn), preferred in Lk/Ac. God is so far above us we cannot begin to comprehend Him. This title is especially common in Ecclus. See 1:16, 577, 835–38.

MOTHER. The Israelites, unlike many other nations, held mothers in respect (Ex 20:12). The word *mother* is sometimes used in a wider sense to mean grandmother or some other female ancestor (Gn 3:20; 1Ki 15:10) or a woman who acted kindly toward a person in need (Jgs 5:7).

It is also used figuratively for nation, city, and the new Jerusalem (Is 50:1; Gal 4:26–31; Rv 17:5). See 1:94–95, 169, 627, 644; 2:95, 219–20, 288, 304–5.

MOTHER-OF-PEARL. *See* ALABASTER.

MOUNTAIN. Much of Israel is hilly or mountainous. The best-known mountain range of Syria, the Lebanon range, formed the northwest boundary of the Promised Land (Dt 1:7; Jsh 1:4). The mountains consist of two ranges that begin at the northeast corner of the Mediterranean and extend northeast to southwest through Israel. During the Greek period the name Lebanon was restricted to the western range while the eastern range was called Anti-Lebanon. Often the peaks of mountains had names, for example, Mount Zion, Mount of Olives, Mount Hermon, Mount Tabor, and Mount Sinai. Many of these are no more than hills.

Mountains were places of refuge (Gn 14:10). They were used as lookouts and as sites for assemblies, camps, and cemeteries (Jgs 9:7; 1Sm 17:3; 2Ki 23:16; Is 18:3). Mount Ebal was the mountain from which the people recited the curses of the Law; Mount Gerizim, the blessings (Dt 27:4–26). Sinai and Zion were God's mountains (Ex 24:13; Ps 68:16; Is 27:13).

Mountains symbolize strength, persons in authority, proud persons, the righteousness of God, and the messianic reign (Ps 36:6; 72:3; Is 2:2, 14; Jer 3:23). See 1:73, 576, 583, 603, 962; 2:199, 201, 732.

MOURNING. During Bible times people showed grief for a dead person in the following ways: tearing their own clothing, putting on sackcloth and ashes, cutting their bodies, shaving their heads, crying loudly, and building fires (Gn 37:34; Ex 12:30; Dt 14:1; 2Ch 16:14; Mi 1:10). Often professional mourners were hired (2Ch 35:25; Mt 9:23). Mourning lasted 7, 30, or 70 days (Gn 50:3; Dt 34:8; 1Sm 31:13). See 1:294–95, 513, 786–87, 803, 809; 2:335–36, 590.

MULE. A cross between a horse and a donkey. It is not mentioned in the Bible before the time of David but was in common use then (2Sm 13:29; 18:9; 1Ki 1:33, 38, 44; Ezr 2:66).

MURDER. The act of killing another person. Murder is forbidden (Ex 20:13; Dt 5:17). During OT times those who did take another person's life received the death penalty (Gn 9:6; Ex 21:14). A person who killed someone else without meaning to do so could find freedom from the death penalty in cities of refuge (Nu 35:9–34; Dt 19:1–10). See 1:26, 222–23, 281; 2:211, 225, 781.

MUSIC. Music has existed from earliest times (Gn 4:21). Folk music celebrated victories (Jgs 5; 1Sm 18:6–7). Music was used at special occasions, such as feasts, weddings, and funerals (Gn 31:27; 2Sm 19:35; Jer 7:34; Mt 9:23).

David organized a sacred choir and appointed instrumental musicians (1Ch 6:31–48; 16). The use of these was continued by Solomon, Jehoshaphat, Hezekiah, Josiah, Ezra, and Nehemiah.

Various instruments were used in biblical times, for example, lyres, harps, trumpets, pipes, flutes, oboes, tambourines, and cymbals. During the NT period people played flutes at funerals and to accompany dancing (Mt 9:23; Lk 7:32). Harps were symbols of praise (Rv 5:8; 14:2). Music and hymns played an important role in the worship life of Israel (Mt 26:30; Eph 5:19). See 1:290, 386–87, 407–9, 612–13.

MYRA (MIGH-rah). A seaport of Lycia where Paul changed ships when he was being taken prisoner to Rome (Ac 27:5).

MYRRH (MUR). A yellow-brown resin used for perfume, embalming, and anointing (Ex 30:23; Sg 3:6; Mt 2:11; Jn 19:39; Rv 18:13). See 1:622; 2:261.

MYSTERY. In the NT, Gk *mysterion* is a "secret" previously kept hidden, but now openly revealed to all (1Co 4:1). God's plan of salvation was hidden in OT times in shadows and types. The mystery is revealed in the Word of God—in Christ (1Co 14:2). Pagan religions also used "mystery" for secret knowledge that was tightly controlled and limited to a few. Paul stresses that the revelation of Christ is for all people (Eph 3:9). See 1:87, 663, 838; 2:383, 429, 603.

N

NAAMAH (NAY-ah-mah; "pleasantness"). The wife of Solomon and mother of Rehoboam (1Ki 14:21, 31; 2Ch 12:13).

NAAMAN (NAY-ah-muhn; "pleasantness"). One of the commanders of Ben-hadad II. He was cured of leprosy by Elisha (2Ki 5:1–19; Lk 4:27). See 1:334, 344.

NABOTH (NAY-both). A man living in Jezreel who owned a vineyard near King Ahab's palace. When Naboth refused to sell Ahab his vineyard or exchange it for other land, Queen Jezebel plotted a way to get the land. She had Naboth stoned for blasphemy so that Ahab could take over the vineyard (1Ki 21:1–24; 2Ki 9:21–26). See 1:333, 344, 346, 351.

NADAB (NAY-dab; "generous").

1. A son of Aaron. He was a priest who went up Mount Sinai with Moses. When Nadab and his brother offered unauthorized fire on the altar, they were killed (Ex 6:23; 24:1, 9–11; 28:1; Lv 10:1–7; Nu 26:60–61). See 1:51, 102, 106–7.
2. The second king of Israel. He was the son of Jeroboam and the one who succeeded him to the throne. Nadab "did what was evil in the sight of the Lord." He reigned over Israel two years. Then

Baasha killed him and took over his throne (1Ki 14:20; 15:25–31). See 1:343, 372.

NAHOR (NAY-hawr; "snoring" or "snorting").
1. Abraham's grandfather (Gn 11:22–25; Lk 3:34).
2. Abraham's brother (Gn 11:26–29; 22:20; Jsh 24:2). See 1:49.

NAHSHON (NAH-shon). A leader of the tribe of Judah in the wilderness (Nu 1:7; 2:3; 7:12; 10:14). His sister married Aaron (Ex 6:23).

NAHUM (NAY-hum; "full of consolation"). A prophet from Elkosh who prophesied to Judah between 663 and 612 BC (Na 1:1; 3:8–11). He wrote the Book of Nahum. See 1:751, 936.

NAHUM, BOOK OF. See 1:935–45.

NAIN (NAY-in; "beauty"). A city in Galilee. Jesus raised a widow's son from death near Nain (Lk 7:11–17).

NAIOTH (NAY-oth; possibly "grazing places"). A place in Ramah where Samuel and his prophets lived (1Sm 19:18–20:1). See 1:276.

NAKED, NAKEDNESS. Without any clothing, without an outer garment, or poorly clothed (Gn 2:25; Mt 25:36; Jn 21:7).

Figuratively the word *naked* depicts a lack of power or spiritual poverty (Gn 42:9; Rv 3:17). See 1:24–25, 730, 927.

NAME. Two Hbr words are typically translated as "name": (1) *shem*, which may come from a root meaning "mark" or "brand," and (2) *zeker*, "remembrance," "memorial" (Ex 3:15). In biblical times a name often expressed something about the person named (Gn 2:20; Is 40:26). When an individual's name was changed, it reflected a change in the person's being. For instance, God gave Abram (exalted father) the name Abraham (father of a multitude) to show that He had established His covenant of grace with Abraham (Gn 17:5; 35:10). Naming someone expressed ownership or relationship. A name equaled one's reputation.

God's names reveal His nature (Ex 3:13–15), will (Ps 22:22; Jn 17:6, 26), and attributes (Ex 33:19; Ps 8:1, 9; 1Tm 6:1). God is present where His name is present (Is 18:7; 30:27). See 1:27, 30, 80, 143, 299, 582–83; 2:191, 288, 384.

NAOMI (nay-O-mi; "pleasantness"). Ruth's mother-in-law (Ru 1–2; 3:1; 4:3–17). See 1:257–65.

NAPHTALI (NAF-tah-ligh; "wrestling").
1. A son of Jacob and Bilhah (Gn 30:8; 46:24).
2. The tribe of Naphtali was given land in northern Canaan. Zebulun and Asher were to its west; the upper Jordan and Sea of Galilee to its east (Jsh 19:32–39). Barak came from this tribe (Jgs 4:6). Naphtali was the first tribe captured by the Assyrians under Tiglath-pileser (2Ki 15:29). See 1:213, 399; 2:39.

NATHAN (NAY-thuhn; "he gave").
1. A prophet during the reigns of David and Solomon. When David consulted him about building the temple, Nathan told David to leave this job for his son (2Sm 7:1–7). Nathan also rebuked David for his adultery with Bathsheba (2Sm 12:1–14). When David grew old and Adonijah tried to get his throne, Nathan stepped in and through Bathsheba secured the succession for Solomon (1Ki 1:8–45). Nathan also recorded the life of David and the history of the reign of Solomon (1Ch 29:29; 2Ch 9:29). See 1:281, 294, 300, 338, 589.
2. One of David's sons (1Ch 3:5; Lk 3:31).

NATHANAEL (nah-THAN-ay-el; "gift of God"). One of Jesus' 12 disciples (Jn 1:45–51; 21:2). It is thought that Nathanael and Bartholomew were the same person. See 2:329.

NATIONS. In the OT this word is often used for Gentiles, people who are not of the Jewish race (Ex 34:24; Is 43:9; Jer 10:1–25). See 1:76–77, 222–23, 441; 2:204, 287, 363.

NAVE (NAYV). The Holy Place of the temple (1Ki 6:3, 5, 17, 33; 2Ch 3:4–5, 13).

NAZARENE (naz-ah-REEN). Someone who came from Nazareth. Jesus was a Nazarene (Mt 2:23; Mk 14:67). See 1:131.

NAZARETH (NAZ-ah-reth). The town in Galilee where Mary and Joseph lived and where Jesus grew up (Mk 1:9; Mt 4:13; Lk 1:26; 2:4, 51). Jesus is often referred to as Jesus of Nazareth (Lk 18:37; Jn 1:45–46; Ac 2:22). See 1:911; 2:196, 258, 263, 300–301, 351–53, 679.

NAZIRITE (NAZ-i-right; "consecrated"). An Israelite who bound himself or herself by a vow to be set apart from others for the service of God, either for life or for a set amount of time. Nazirites could not drink alcoholic beverages or cut their hair. They also had to avoid contact with the dead and abstain from eating unclean food (Nu 6:1–21; Am 2:11–12). Samson and John the Baptist were both Nazirites from birth (Jgs 13; Lk 1:15). See 1:131, 133, 137, 238–39.

NEAPOLIS (ni-ap-O-lis; "new city"). The seaport of Philippi to which Paul sailed after being given a vision to preach the Gospel in Macedonia (Ac 16:11).

NEBAT (NEE-bat; "watched over"). The father of Jeroboam I (1Ki 11:26). See 1:330.

NEBO (KNEE-bo).
1. The Babylonian god of learning (Is 46:1).
2. The name of the mountain located in Moab that Moses climbed to view the Promised Land before he died (Dt 32:49–50; 34:1–5). *See also* PISGAH, MOUNT. See 1:63, 140, 199; 2:766.

NEBUCHADNEZZAR (neb-yoo-kuhd-NEZ-ur; "defend the boundary"). Nabopolasser's son and the ruler of the Neo-Babylonian Empire from 604 to 562 BC. In 605 BC, Nebuchadnezzar defeated Pharaoh Neco at Carchemish. Then in 603 BC, he made Jehoiakim his servant (Dn 1:1; 2Ki 24). After a few years of paying taxes to Nebuchadnezzar, Jehoiakim revolted. Nebuchadnezzar returned to Judah and in 587 BC destroyed Jerusalem and carried the people into captivity (2Ki 24:11–16; 25:1–21). Nebuchadnezzar is frequently mentioned in the OT (1Ch 6:15; 2Ch 36; Ezr 1:7; Ne 7:6; Est 2:6; Jer 21–52; Dn 1–5). See 1:373, 413, 767, 825–29, 833–34, 848–49; 2:20, 63.

NEBUSHAZBAN (neb-yoo-SHAZ-ban; "Nebo saves"). A rabsaris, an important officer in Nebuchadnezzar's court (Jer 39:13).

NECO (NEE-ko). *See* PHARAOH 8. See 1:403–6, 963.

NECROMANCY (NEK-ro-man-see). A form of witchcraft. A necromancer was a person who consulted the dead for information (Dt 18:11; 1Sm 28:1–25). *See also* MEDIUM.

NEGEB (NEG-eb; "dry"). A grazing region lying south of Hebron (Gn 12:9; 13:1; 20:1). See 1:25, 72; 2:660.

NEHEMIAH (nee-hi-MIGH-ah; "Yahweh comforts"). The son of Hachaliah and the cupbearer of Artaxerxes Longimanus (Ne 1:1; 2:1). When Artaxerxes found out that Nehemiah was distressed at Jerusalem's state of ruin, he allowed Nehemiah to return there. Nehemiah arrived in Jerusalem in the twentieth year of Artaxerxes' reign; in 445 BC, Nehemiah became the governor of Judah (Ne 2:1–10). He organized the Jewish community to carry out the task of rebuilding Jerusalem's walls (Ne 1–4; 6). He also instituted reforms and restored worship and the Law (Ne 5; 8–13). See 1:430–33.

NEHEMIAH, BOOK OF. See 1:423–57.

NEHUSHTAN (ni-HUSH-tuhn; "piece of bronze"). This was the name Hezekiah gave to the brass serpent made in Moses' time. Hezekiah destroyed it because the people were worshiping it rather than the Lord (2Ki 18:4).

NEIGHBOR. The OT describes one's neighbor as someone who lives nearby or as a fellow Israelite (Ex 11:2; Dt 15:1–11). The duty to love one's neighbor as oneself included both Israelites and foreigners (Lv 19:18–34). See 1:109, 636, 642, 733.

The NT describes one's neighbor as every person for whom Christ died, that is, everyone (Lk 10:25–37). Because Christ died for all, love is to be extended to everyone (Mt 5:43–48). Anything done for the neighbor is done for Christ (Mt 25:31–46). See 2:202, 221, 488, 664.

NEPHILIM (NEF-uh-lim). *See* GIANTS.

NER (NUR; "lamp").
1. The son of Abiel, father of Abner, and uncle of Saul (1Sm 14:50–51; 26:5, 14; 2Sm 2:8, 12).
2. Saul's grandfather (1Ch 8:33; 9:35–36, 39).

NERO (NEE-ro). The Roman emperor from AD 54 to 68. His full name was Nero Claudius Caesar Augustus Germanicus, but he was usually referred to as Caesar (Ac 25:11; Php 4:22). See 2:236, 391, 417, 598–99, 704, 774.

NEW BIRTH. *See* CONVERSION. See 2:321, 334, 688.

NEW MAN. This term refers to the Christian believer who is created anew by God's grace. Christ's death and resurrection makes the existence of this new man possible (Rm 5:10; 8:34–39). By faith in Christ, the believer dies to the old life and rises to the new life, becoming a new creature (2Co 5:17; Gal 6:15). Baptism works this conversion (Rm 6:1–4). The new man is a member of the Church, Christ's Body (Eph 2:15). His new life in Christ is shown in how he lives. It is constantly renewed in Christ (Rm 6:5–11; Col 3:10–11). See 2:425, 530.

NEW SONG. Hbr *shir chadash*, a song written to celebrate God's new work of salvation. The "old song" was the Song of Moses, which celebrated the redemption from Egypt (Ex 15:1–18). The "new song" in the Psalms often celebrated redemption from exile (cf Ne 12:27). Rv 5:8–9 says the "new song" is about the final redemption through Jesus. See 1:722; 2:772.

NEW TESTAMENT.

1. The books of the Bible from Matthew to Revelation. See 2:155–64.
2. The New Testament, or new covenant, is a term describing the work of Christ, by whose life, death, and resurrection God's grace is brought to all people (Jer 31:31–34; 2Co 3; Gal 4; Heb 7:20–22). The Holy Spirit brings people into this covenant by creating faith in their hearts by means of the Word (Jn 3:5; Rm 1:16–17; 15:16; 1Co 2:10; 2Th 2:13). The Lord's Supper is the NT made visible (Mt 26:26–28; 1Co 11:25). *See also* COVENANT. See 1:xxv–xxviii, 79, 115, 753, 769, 1004; 2:190, 485–86, 660–61.

NEW YEAR. *See* TIME.

NICANOR (ni-KAY-nawr; "conqueror").

1. A Syrian general defeated by Judas Maccabeus. See 2:85, 94–97.
2. One of the seven men chosen by the Church in Jerusalem to look after the widows and the poor (Ac 6:5).

NICODEMUS (nik-o-DEE-muhs; "victor over people"). A leading Pharisee and member of the Sanhedrin. He visited Jesus one evening and talked with Him. Jesus told Nicodemus about the new birth necessary to enter the kingdom of God (Jn 3:1–21). When Jesus was on trial before the Sanhedrin, Nicodemus spoke up for Him, though in a roundabout way (Jn 7:50–52). After Jesus' death, however, Nicodemus helped Joseph of Arimathea with the burial (Jn 19:39–42). See 2:330, 334, 337.

NICOLAITANS (nik-o-LAY-uh-tuhns). A Gnostic sect in the churches at Ephesus and Pergamum. Their teachings were harshly spoken against by John (Rv 2:6, 14–15). See 2:347, 772.

NICOLAUS (NIK-o-luhs, nik-o-LAY-uhs; "victor over people"). A proselyte at Antioch. He was one of the seven men chosen by the church at Jerusalem to take care of the widows and the poor (Ac 6:5).

NICOPOLIS (ni-KOP-o-lis; "city of victory"). A Roman town in Epirus that was founded by Caesar Augustus in 31 BC (Ti 3:12). See 2:598, 625.

NILE (NIGHL). The main river of Egypt and Africa. It is 4,050 miles long. The Nile's yearly overflow leaves deposits of rich soil that make the land of northern Egypt fertile.

The people in ancient times worshiped the Nile as a god. Moses was placed on the Nile in a basket made of papyrus (Ex 2:3). During one of the plagues the waters of the Nile were turned to blood (Ex 7:20–21). The Nile was also famous for the papyrus that grew along its banks. From it, the people made papyrus writing material (Is 19:7). See 1:17, 52, 70; 2:41, 196.

NIMROD (NIM-rod). A son of Cush. Nimrod was a hunter, builder, and founder of the kingdoms in Shinar (Gn 10:8–12; 1Ch 1:10; Mi 5:6). Many places in Mesopotamia were named Nimrod. See 1:7.

NINEVEH (NIN-uh-vuh). The capital of Assyria. It was located on the Tigris River and was founded by Nimrod (Gn 10:9–11). Sargon II, the ruler of Assyria from 721 to 705 BC, made Nineveh the capital of Assyria. From 705 to 626 BC, Nineveh was strengthened and made beautiful by Sennacherib, Esarhaddon, and Ashurbanipal. In 612 BC, the city was destroyed by the Babylonians, Scythians, and Medes. Nineveh is mentioned numerous times in the Bible (2Ki 19:36; Is 37:37; Jnh; Na; Zep 2:13; Mt 12:41; Lk 11:30, 32). See 1:905–12, 935–43; 2:15, 39, 45.

NOAH (NO-ah; "rest"). The son of Lamech (Gn 5:28–32). When Noah was 480 years old, God warned him that the world was going to be destroyed by water. Then He gave Noah instructions on how to build the ark. While building the ark, Noah warned people to repent of their wickedness (Gn 6:1–9, 12–22; 1Pt 3:20; 2Pt 2:5). After 120 years God led Noah, Noah's wife, their sons, and their sons' wives into the ark. Then God directed the animals into the ark. When all were safely aboard, God shut the door. In this way He saved Noah and his family from the flood, which destroyed everything outside the ark (Gn 7–8).

After the rain stopped and the waters went down, Noah, his family, and the animals were allowed to leave the ark. Noah and his family repopulated the earth (Gn 9:10). Noah lived to be 950 years old. See 1:23, 26, 32, 35–36, 47–48.

NO-AMON (no-AY-mon). *See* THEBES.

NOBLE. Translated from various Hbr terms, occurring mostly in later OT books. Indicates a free man, or a leader in fame or ability. See 1:434, 465, 677, 747.

NOD (NOD; "homeless"). The region east of Eden where Cain went to live after he had killed Abel (Gn 4:16).

NORTHEASTER. A tempestuous wind that eventually caused St. Paul to be shipwrecked on his journey to Rome (Ac 27).

NUMBERING. *See* CENSUS. See 1:316, 573.

NUMBER SYMBOLISM. The Israelites used number symbolism, as did many other ancient cultures. Ancient systems for counting probably developed from the 10 digits of human hands. As written language developed, ancient people commonly used the letters of their alphabets to represent numbers (this was true for the Hbr, Aram, and Gk languages). The use of letters as numbers caused numbers to become invested with greater symbolic meaning. The numbers presented in historical accounts of the Bible should usually be read as ordinary numbers; apocalyptic books such as Dn, Ezk, and Rv tend to use more number symbolism. The numbering of the days of creation may have provided symbolic meaning to some numbers, though Scripture does not emphasize this for each number. Sometimes, multiples of a number carry deeper meaning (Dn 9:24; Mt 18:22; Rv 13:18). However, biblical writers more often associated ideas with certain numbers in only a general way. Students of the Bible should beware of searching the Scriptures for hidden number symbolism because such speculating has led to false interpretations and false teachings in the past. Especially dangerous is the mixing of nonbiblical systems of number symbolism with interpretations of the Bible, as happened with the Jewish interpreter Philo of Alexandria, the Jewish Cabbala, and Christian allegorists. The Early Church Father Irenaeus strongly warned against the heretical Gnostic abuse of number symbolism, and his words provide appropriate caution today (*ANF* 1:393–96).

NUMBERS, BOOK OF. See 1:127–55.

NUN (NUN; "fish"). Joshua's father (Ex 33:11; 1Ch 7:27). See 1:223.

O

OATH. A solemn appeal to God, a person, or an object to witness the truth of a statement or the binding character of a promise (Gn 21:23; Ex 22:11; 2Sm 11:11; Mt 5:34). Oaths of the covenant were worked out in a careful and detailed way (Gn 21:28–31). Swearing by God's name showed loyalty to Him (Dt 6:13; 29:12, 14–21). Breaking an oath was regarded as sinful (Ecclus 23:9–11). See 1:77, 299, 602; 2:207, 805.

OBADIAH (o-bah-DIGH-ah; "servant of Yahweh").
1. One of Ahab's officers who was a friend to Elijah and the prophets of the Lord (1Ki 18:3–16). See 1:356.
2. A prophet of Judah who wrote the Book of Obadiah (Ob 1:1). See 1:372, 896.

OBADIAH, BOOK OF. See 1:895–903.

OBED (O-bed; "worshiper," "servant"). The son of Boaz and Ruth and the grandfather of King David (Ru 4:17, 21–22; 1Ch 2:12; Mt 1:5). See 1:255, 258.

OBED-EDOM (O-bed-EE-dum). A man from Gath into whose home David had the ark of the covenant carried after Uzzah had been struck dead for touching it. The ark remained in Obed-edom's house for three months, and God greatly blessed Obed-edom and all his household (2Sm 6:10–12).

OBEDIENCE. The act of obeying. The complete, willing response to God is the duty of all people (Dt 4:30; Jer 7:23; 1Jn 5:2). Man disobeyed God, however, and fell into sin (Gn 3). From that point forward the natural state of humanity has been disobedience toward God (Rm 1:24; 5:19). Christ obeyed the Father and obtained the forgiveness of sins for all people (Rm 5:19; Php 2:8; Heb 5:8). Throughout the Bible obedience is linked to faith (Rm 1:5; 1Pt 1:14). Christians show obedience in the home, to the state, in the church, and to others (Rm 13:1–7; Eph 5:21; 6:1; Heb 13:17; 1Pt 3:6). See 1:35, 174, 216–17, 307, 507; 2:220, 426, 613, 661.

OBEISANCE (o-BEE-suhns). *See* BOW 2.

OBEY. Gk *hypakouo*, based on the root word for "listening" (Rm 1:5). See 1:26, 37, 298, 834; 2:35, 251, 431, 788.

ODOR. Any smell, either pleasant or unpleasant (Jn 11:39; cf "aroma" in Gn 8:21; Nu 15:3–24).

OFFERING. *See* SACRIFICE.

OFFICES OF CHRIST. *See* JESUS CHRIST. See 2:256.

OFFSPRING. God made promises to Abraham (Gn 12:1–3, 7; 13:14–17; 17:8; 22:16–18; 24:7) about his "offspring" (singular "seed"; Hbr *zera'*), meaning either a single descendant or many descendants (collective sense; Gal 3:29). Gk *sperma*, "seed," denoting physical descent or ethnicity. In rabbinic fashion, Paul uses this grammatical point to prove a pivotal theological point. Through the one Seed (Christ), believers become the seed of Abraham. *See also* HEIR. See 1:22, 27–28, 32–34, 588.

OINTMENT. Usually perfumed olive oil was used to dress the hair and make the skin smell sweet, to prepare bodies for burial, and to anoint people (Est 2:3–12; Mt 26:6–13; Lk 23:56). The balm of Gilead and eye salve were two medicines (Jer 8:22; cf "salve" in Rv 3:18). *See also* MEDICINE; PERFUMER. See 2:248.

OLD TESTAMENT.

1. The 39 books from Genesis to Malachi that make up the first part of the Bible. Most of the OT was written in Hbr except for a few sections in Ezra and Daniel, which were written in Aramaic. See 1:xxv–xxviii, 1–3.
2. The covenant of Moses. *See also* COVENANT. See 1:69–74.

OLIVE. *See* ORCHARD.

OLIVES, MOUNT OF; OLIVET (AHL-i-vet). A ridge about one mile long on the eastern side of Jerusalem, separated from it by the Valley of Kidron. Gethsemane, Bethphage, and Bethany are on its slopes (2Sm 15:30; Zec 14:4; Mt 21:1; 24:3; Mk 11:1; Lk 22:39; Jn 8:1; Ac 1:12). See 2:274, 314, 698.

OMEGA (o-MEG-uh). *See* ALPHA. See 1:1004; 2:778.

OMER (O-mur). *See* MEASURES 2e.

OMNIPOTENCE (ahm-NIP-o-tuhns). All-powerful. Only God has limitless power and authority (cf Gn 17:1; Mt 19:26; Eph 1:21–22). See 1:249, 584; 2:228, 258.

OMNIPRESENCE (ahm-ni-PREZ-uhns). The attribute of being in all places at once. God is omnipresent; that is, He is everywhere (cf Ps 139:7–10; Pr 15:3; Ac 17:27–28). See 1:343, 420.

OMNISCIENCE (ahm-NISH-uhns). The term used to describe God's complete knowledge of all things (cf 1Sm 2:3; Mt 10:30; Ac 15:18; Eph 1:4). See 1:183, 584, 662–63; 2:259.

OMRI (OM-righ). The sixth king of Israel, who reigned from about 885 to 874 BC. Before gaining the throne, Omri was a general in the Israelite army of King Elah. During one battle news arrived that Zimri had killed Elah. At once the prophets and army proclaimed Omri the new king of Israel.

During his reign Omri moved the capital from Tirzah to Samaria. He is described as doing "evil in the sight of the LORD, . . . more evil than all who were before him" (1Ki 16:16–28). See 1:324, 343, 345, 372, 923; 2:799.

ON (ON). A city in the Delta of Egypt about 19 miles north of Memphis. It was also called Heliopolis (Jer 43:13). On was the main religious center for sun worship. Joseph's wife, Asenath, was the daughter of a priest of On (Gn 41:45, 50). See 1:29.

ONE. Typically represents uniqueness (2Sm 7:23) or unity (Gn 2:24; Ex 26:6). In the OT, related to Hbr *ro'sh*, "first in order; head, or chief."

ONESIMUS (o-NES-i-muhs; "useful"). Philemon's slave. It seems that Onesimus robbed his master and then ran away to Rome. In Rome he came in contact with Paul and became a Christian. Paul persuaded Onesimus to return to Philemon and wrote the Letter to Philemon on Onesimus's behalf (Col 4:9; Phm). See 2:535, 635–42.

ONESIPHORUS (on-i-SIF-o-rus; "profit bringing"). A Christian from Ephesus who ministered to Paul when Paul was in prison in Rome (2Tm 1:16–18; 4:19). See 2:615.

ON THAT DAY. Can simply mean "then," but appears often in the Prophets with reference to the "day of the LORD." Cf Is 24:18–20; 29:5–8; 66:15; Hos 3:5; Jl 2:30–3:16; Am 5:18–20; Zep 1:14–18; Zec 14:1–5.

ONYX (ON-iks). A precious stone, perhaps some type of quartz, which was put on the high priest's shoulder pieces and breastpiece (Gn 2:12; Ex 28:9; 35:9; 1Ch 29:2).

OPHRAH (AHF-rah). Gideon's hometown. It was located in Manasseh (Jgs 6:11, 24; 8:27, 32). See 1:241.

ORACLE (AHR-ah-k'l). A place, such as the Most Holy Place, a message or word of God, a prophecy or some other way in which God communicated His will to His people (2Sm 16:23; 1Ki 6; Is 14:28; 15:1; Ezk 12:10; Ac 7:38; Rm 3:2; 1Pt 4:11). *See also* BURDEN.

Heathen oracles are also mentioned in the Bible (cf Jgs 17:1, 5; 8:27; 2Ki 1:2). Israel is rebuked for consulting these false oracles (cf Hos 4:12; Hab 2:19). See 1:9, 139–41, 623, 703–7, 756–57, 763; 2:178–79, 448.

ORCHARD. The place where fruit- or nut-bearing trees are grown. Olives, figs, dates, pomegranates, citrus fruit, almonds, and walnuts were among the fruits and nuts grown in Israel.

The olive harvest began in August when the whitish fruit was knocked from the trees. The oil was taken out of the olives by placing the fruit in a stone basin or on a concave stone and then crushing it with another stone. Olive oil was used in ceremonial anointings, as fuel for lamps and torches, for anointing the body and head, and in salves for wounds (Ex 27:20; 29:7; 1Sm 16:13; Lk 7:46; 10:34). The olive was a symbol for peace, wealth, and success (Gn 8:11; Ps 52:8). See 1:677.

Various types of figs were grown in Israel (1Ki 4:25; Ps 105:33). The first crop was ready to harvest in May (Is 28:4; Na 3:12). The regular crop was ready in late July or mid-August, and sometimes a third crop was ready in late fall. The sycamore fig had smaller fruit (Am 7:14). Figs were dried for year-round use.

Date palms grew wild along the Mediterranean Sea, the Jordan Valley, and in desert oases. Dates were dried and caked for use in the winter. Palm tree branches were brought to Passover celebrations (Mt 21:8; Mk 11:8; Jn 12:13).

Pomegranates are often mentioned in the OT (Hg 2:19). The people made wine from the juice of this fruit (Sg 8:2). In a number of passages the pomegranate is referred to as an apple (Pr 25:11; Sg 2:3, 5; Jl 1:12).

Almonds and walnuts were both common in Israel. Almonds were particularly plentiful (Gn 43:11; Ex 25:33; Jer 1:11).

ORDINATION (awr-duh-NAY-shuhn). The act of conferring a sacred office upon a person. OT priests were ordained to office (Ex 28:41; Nu 3:3). Rams were sacrificed at these ordinations (Ex 29:22–34; Lv 8:22–33).

In the NT, deacons, missionaries, and elders were ordained to office, referred to as "laying on hands" (cf Ac 6:6; 13:3; 14:23). See 1:78, 143; 2:423.

ORPHA (AWR-pah). The daughter-in-law of Naomi and sister-in-law of Ruth (Ru 1:4–14).

OSNAPPAR (os-NAP-ur). The king of Assyria mentioned in Ezr 4:10. Osnappar is usually identified with Ashurbanipal, Sennacherib's grandson. Ashurbanipal ruled Assyria from 668 to 627 BC.

OTHNIEL (OTH-ni-el; "God is strength"). The son of Kenaz and first judge of Israel (Jsh 15:17; 1Ch 4:13). Othniel captured the town of Kiriath-sepher (Jsh 15:15–17; Jgs 1:11–13). Later he delivered Israel from the Mesopotamians (Jgs 3:8–11). See 1:235–37, 242.

OVERSEER. Gk *episkopos*, which is also translated as "bishop." This Early Church pastoral office was made up of Christian men responsible for the well-being of a group or groups in a congregation (Ti 1:5). See 2:542, 600, 604, 608.

P

PACE. *See* MEASURES 1f.

PADDAN-ARAM (PAD-uhn-AY-RAM; "plain of Aram"). The plain surrounding Haran in Mesopotamia. It was the home of Rebekah and Laban (Gn 25:20; 28:2–7; 31:18; 33:18; 35:9; 46:15). See 1:25, 29.

PAGAN. *See* GENTILES. See 1:547–48.

PAGIEL (PAY-gi-el). The chief of the tribe of Asher when it was in the wilderness (Nu 1:13; 2:27; 7:72, 77).

PALACE. *See* ARCHITECTURE; HOMES. See 1:359; 2:803, 807–8.

PALESTINE (PAL-uhs-tighn). The name comes from Philistia, the area along the coast where the Philistines lived (Ps 60:8). The older name for this region was Canaan (Gn 12:5). After the conquest it became known as the land of Israel (1Sm 13:19). The Book of Zechariah refers to it as the holy land (Zec 2:12), and during the Greco-Roman times it was called Judea.

Biblical Palestine was about 70 miles wide and 150 miles long. It lay south of the Lebanon Mountains, northeast of Egypt, north of the Sinai Peninsula, and east of the Arabian Desert. It was divided into five regions: the coastal plain on the west, the Shephelah, the central range, the Jordan Valley, and the eastern plateau.

Because of the variation in elevation from Mount Hermon's 9,101 feet above sea level to the Dead Sea's 1,290 feet below sea level, the climate of Palestine varies greatly. The mean temperature of Jerusalem is 65 degrees F, whereas the Jordan Valley is tropical in climate. There are two seasons: winter (November–April) and summer (May–October). Winter is mild and rainy; summer is hot and dry.

In the days of Abraham, Palestine was inhabited by the Canaanites, Amorites, Hittites, Horites, and Amalekites. The Israelites conquered Palestine under Joshua and under the judges and kings. From 587 to 166 BC, Palestine fell under foreign rule. Then the Maccabees reigned from 166 to 63 BC, at which time the Romans took over until AD 325. During NT times Palestine was divided into three parts: Judea, Samaria, and Galilee. See 1:848; 2:297.

PALSY. *See* DISEASE.

PALTI (PAL-tigh; "my deliverance"). The man to whom Saul gave David's wife Michal (1Sm 25:44).

PAMPHYLIA (pam-FIL-i-ah; "mingled races"). A coastal plain along the Mediterranean in southern Asia Minor. Some of the people at Pentecost were from Pamphylia (Ac 2:10). On his first missionary trip Paul preached at Perga, the chief city of Pamphylia (Ac 13:13; 14:24; 15:38). See 2:234.

PAPER. *See* PAPYRUS. See 1:489.

PAPHOS (PAY-foss). The capital city of Cyprus (Ac 13:6, 13). See 2:388, 813.

PAPYRUS (pah-PIGH-ruhs). An 8- to 10-foot-high sedge or reedlike plant that grew along the Nile River in ancient times. The people of that time made paper from this plant (Jb 8:11; Is 18:2). Moses' basket was probably made of papyrus (Ex 2:3). See 1:86, 489, 498; 2:345, 410–11.

PARABLE. A method of speech that compares two objects for the purpose of teaching a moral or religious truth (Mt 15:14–15; Mk 13:28). It is an earthly story with a heavenly or spiritual meaning. Although the events and characters in a parable are true to nature, not every detail of the story has a spiritual meaning. Rather there is only one main point of comparison (Mt 13; Lk 15). Jesus often spoke in parables to teach the people about Himself and the kingdom of heaven. Parables were also used in the OT (Ezk 17).

A parable differs from a fable, myth, allegory, and proverb. *See also* ALLEGORY; FABLE; PROVERB. See 1:238, 343, 650, 916–17; 2:200, 245, 280, 285.

PARACLETE (PAR-ah-kleet; "comforter"). *See* HELPER.

PARADISE (PAR-ah-dighs; "park"). A park, orchard, or pleasure ground. The Garden of Eden was a paradise (Gn 2:8–17; Rv 2:7). In the NT the word *paradise* is used to describe heaven, the home of those who die in Christ (Lk 23:43; 2Co 12:3–4; Rv 2:7). See 1:44, 677, 734; 2:284, 389.

PARBAR (PAHR-bahr; "open placed," "forecourt"). Some building or place on the west side of the outer court of the temple (cf "colonnade" in 1Ch 26:18).

PARDON. *See* FORGIVENESS; JUSTIFICATION. See 1:281–81, 929.

PARMENAS (PAHR-mi-nas; shortened form of "Parmenides," "steadfast"). One of the seven men chosen by the Early Church to look after widows and poor people (Ac 6:5).

PAROUSIA (pah-ROO-zhi-ah; "presence" or "coming"). A Gk word used in the NT to describe the second coming of Christ in glory and power to judge the world at the end of time (cf "coming" in Mt 24:27–39; 1Co 15:23; 1Th 4:15–17; Jas 5:8; 2Pt 3:4; 1Jn 2:28). *See also* ADVENT OF CHRIST 3; DAY OF THE LORD 2; JESUS CHRIST; JUDGMENT.

PARTICIPATION. *See* FELLOWSHIP. See 1:92, 848; 2:311.

PARTHIANS (PAHR-thi-uhns). People who lived in southwest Asia, southeast of the Caspian Sea. Today that country is Iran. Parthians were present on the Day of Pentecost (Ac 2:9).

PARTNERSHIP. *See* FELLOWSHIP. See 2:540, 637–38.

PASHHUR (PASH-ur).

1. A son of Immer. Pashhur was a priest. Because Jeremiah's prophecies angered Pashhur, he had the prophet beat and put in stocks (Jer 20:1–6).
2. The son of Malchiah. He was among the court princes in Zedekiah's reign who sought to put Jeremiah to death (Jer 21:1; 38:1, 4).

PASSION ("suffering"). The sufferings of Christ, beginning with His agony in the Garden of Gethsemane and ending with His death on the cross (Ac 1:3). *See also* JESUS CHRIST. See 1:744; 2:202, 213, 248–49, 284–86, 335–38.

PASSOVER. The first of three yearly festivals at which all the Jewish men were to come to the sanctuary

(Ex 23:14–17; Dt 16:16). It was instituted to keep alive the memory of the "passing over" of Israel when all the firstborn of Egypt were put to death (Ex 12; 13:3–9). The ritual involved with this feast is described in Ex 12:3–20. Passover began at sunset on the 14th day of Nisan (Lv 23:5). Passover is also called the Feast of Unleavened Bread (Ex 23:15; Dt 16:16). See 1:70–71, 74, 113, 206–7, 544.

Christ and the Lord's Supper are the Christian's Passover (Lk 22:1–20; 1Co 5:7). See 2:203, 248, 254, 284, 310–11, 459.

PASTORAL EPISTLES. The name given to three of Paul's letters: 1 Timothy, 2 Timothy, and Titus. These letters show Paul's concern for the pastoral work of the Church. See 2:593–95.

PATARA (PAT-ah-rah). A seaport on the southwest coast of Lycia (Ac 21:1). See 2:388.

PATH(S). *See* WAY(S). See 1:482; 2:6, 764.

PATMOS (PAT-mahs). A small island in the Aegean Sea off the southwest coast of Asia Minor. According to tradition the Emperor Domitian banished John there in AD 95 (Rv 1:9). See 2:737, 771, 778.

PATRIARCH (PAY-tri-ahrk; "father-ruler"). The father or chief of a race. The name is given to the fathers of the human race both before and after the flood (Gn 4–5; 11). Scripture also gives this name to the founders of the Hebrew race and nation: Abraham, Isaac, Jacob, the 12 sons of Jacob, and King David (1Ch 1:28, 34; Ac 2:29; 7:8–9; Heb 7:4). See 1:lxxvi–lxxviii, 15–17, 485, 495; 2:284, 660.

PAUL (PAWL; "little"). The apostle to the Gentiles (Rm 11:13; Gal 1:16; 2:2, 8–9).

Paul's given name was Saul. He was born in Tarsus to Jewish parents (Ac 21:39; 22:3). Paul's father was a Pharisee from the tribe of Benjamin (Php 3:5). He also held Roman citizenship, a privilege that he passed on to Paul (Ac 22:28; 23:6). Not too much is mentioned about Paul's relatives. From Ac 23:16, we learn that he had a sister and a nephew. Paul also mentions three relatives, two of which were Christians before Paul and well-known among the apostles (Rm 16:7, 11).

As a child, Paul was schooled in reading, writing, arithmetic, and particularly in religion. Later he went to Jerusalem and became a student of Gamaliel, a famous teacher known for his tolerant ways (Ac 5:34–40; 22:3). As a student of Gamaliel, Paul studied the Holy Scripture and its various interpretations by famous rabbis. After this Paul likely returned to Tarsus, where he learned the trade of tentmaking (Ac 18:3).

Paul was present at the stoning of Stephen, the first Christian martyr (Ac 7:58; 9:13; 26:10–11; Gal 1:13). Owing to his intense hatred of the Christians, a sect whom he thought to be a serious threat to the Jewish religion, Paul began to treat Christians in a cruel and harsh way. He sought them out in Jerusalem and other cities and then had them put in prison or even put to death (Ac 8:1–3; 9:1–2, 13–14; 22:1–5; 26:9–12).

One day while Paul was on his way to Damascus to arrest the Christians there, the glorified Jesus appeared to him and asked Paul why he was persecuting Him. Paul became a Christian and, a few days later, was baptized by Ananias (Ac 9; 22:1–16; 26:1–20; 1Co 15:8–10; Gal 1:12–16; Eph 3:1–8).

Then Paul went to Damascus, where he met with the Christian disciples and preached in the synagogues about Jesus, the Son of God (Ac 9:15; 26:16–20). After this Paul went to Arabia (Gal 1:17). Upon his return to Damascus, Paul continued to preach the Gospel but was forced to flee because of angry enemies who were trying to kill him (Ac 9:23–25). Paul then went to Jerusalem, and from there he set sail for Tarsus (Ac 9:26–30. Cf Ac 15:41). It seems that Paul spent a number of years there.

Barnabas brought Paul to Antioch to help him in serving the Christian Church there (Ac 11:25). When the church at Antioch heard that the believers in the church at Jerusalem were suffering from a famine, they took up a collection for them and appointed Paul and Barnabas to take it to them (Ac 11:29–30). Soon after their return from Jerusalem, Paul and Barnabas were sent on the first missionary trip to Asia Minor. John Mark went along with them on part of this journey (Ac 13:13–14). When they returned to the church at Antioch, they reported to it how God "had opened a door of faith to the Gentiles" (Ac 14:27).

Not long after this, Jewish Christians from the Church in Jerusalem came to Antioch. They said that Gentile converts must keep the Law. Paul went up to Jerusalem and attended the council, which reached a decision regarding Jewish laws for Gentile Christians (Ac 15).

Paul made two other missionary journeys, traveling to Asia Minor, Macedonia, and Greece (Ac 16–20). After his last trip, he went to Jerusalem for a visit. There he was almost killed by a mob. Roman soldiers came to break up the crowd, and they arrested Paul. Before taking him away, however, they allowed Paul to speak to his angry countrymen. Paul recounted to them his family background and how God had chosen him to tell others about Christ, the promised Messiah (Ac 21:37–22:21).

Paul was then sent before the Sanhedrin (Ac 22:30–23:10). Upon learning of a plot to kill Paul, the Roman officer in charge sent Paul to Caesarea. There Paul was brought before Felix, the Roman governor of Judea. Paul was kept under house arrest for a few years. When the new governor of Judea arrived to replace Felix, Paul was brought before him. His name was Festus. Paul appealed to his Roman citizenship and asked to be sent to Rome to be heard by the emperor (Ac 25:6–12). Before he was sent to Rome, however, Agrippa and his sister, who were visiting Festus, asked to hear Paul speak. After listening to Paul, Agrippa declared that he thought Paul was innocent. But since the appeal to Rome had already been made, Paul had to be sent there (Ac 26).

And so Paul was sent to Rome (Ac 27–28). It seems likely that Paul was set free after his first trial and made additional missionary journeys (Php 2:24; 1Tm 1:3; 3:14; 2Tm 4:20; Ti 3:12; Phm 22).

According to tradition Paul died in Rome around AD 68 (2Tm 1:8, 15; 4). He is the author of most of the letters in the NT. See 2:371, 375–80, 388, 391, 411–15, 419, 437, 442–44, 482, 592, 597–99.

PAULUS (PAWL-uhs). *See* SERGIUS PAULUS.

PEACE. Hbr *shalom*; Gk *eirene.* A word often used in the Bible in a variety of ways. It can mean a period of calm and quiet as opposed to war (Mt 5:9; 2Co 13:11; 1Tm 2:2). It is also used to describe that state of spiritual tranquility and harmony that God gives when He brings one into a right relationship with Himself (Nu 6:26). Christ is the Christian's peace with God (Eph 2:14–17). Through His death on the cross He has earned the forgiveness of sins for all people, making peace between God and people (Col 1:20). This peace is worked in believers by the Holy Spirit through faith and shows itself in their lives (Jn 20:19, 22; Rm 12:18; 14:19; 1Co 7:15; Gal 5:22; Eph 4:3; 1Th 5:13). See 1:26, 93, 110, 401, 578, 615–16, 736, 941; 2:209, 281, 429–30, 585–86.

PEACE OFFERING. An animal that was sacrificed to God as a thank offering for some blessing, as a result of some promise or vow made to God, or as an expression of love for God (Lv 3; Jgs 20:26; 2Sm 24:25). *See also* SACRIFICE. See 1:103–4, 110, 119.

PEDAIAH (pi-DAY-yah; "the Lord saved").
1. The grandfather of King Jehoiakim (2Ki 23:36).
2. Zerubbabel's father (1Ch 3:19).

PEKAH (PEE-kah; "opening"). The 18th king of Israel. Pekah gained the throne by murdering Pekahiah. He aligned himself with the king of Damascus against the king of Judah. Pekah reigned about 20 years and then was killed by Hoshea, who became the next king (2Ki 15:25–31; 16; 2Ch 28:5–15). See 1:347, 373, 375–76.

PEKAHIAH (pek-ah-HIGH-ah; "Yahweh has opened"). The 17th king of Israel. He took over the throne from his father, Menahem. He ruled about two years and then was murdered by Pekah, who wanted his throne (2Ki 15:22–26). See 1:347, 373.

PELEG (PEE-leg; "division," "channel"). A son of Eber (Gn 11:16–19; 1Ch 1:19, 25). "In his days the earth was divided" (Gn 10:25). This statement may refer to the time God confused the language and scattered the descendants of Noah. See 1:15.

PEN. Either a stylus or graving tool used for cutting letters on stone or a reed pen used for writing on papyrus (Jb 19:24; Ps 45:1; Jer 8:8; 3Jn 13). See 1:752; 2:799.

PENCIL. A tool that a carpenter used for marking lines (Is 44:13).

PENNINAH (pi-NIN-ah; "coral"). One of Elkanah's two wives (1Sm 1:2–6). His other wife was Hannah.

PENNY. Bronze or copper Roman coin worth a penny or less (Mt 5:26; 10:29; Lk 12:6; cf "copper coin" in Lk 21:1–4). *See* DENARIUS.

PENTATEUCH (PEN-tah-tyuk). The first five books of the OT: Gn, Ex, Lv, Nu, and Dt. The Hebrew people called this collection of books the Torah, or the Law. Both the OT and the NT speak of these books as being written primarily by Moses (Jsh 8:31; Ezr 6:18; Lk 24:27; Jn 5:45–47). See 1:5–9, 181–82, 196.

PENTECOST (PEN-ti-kawst; "50th day").
1. The Jewish Feast of Weeks, which was celebrated 50 days after the Feast of Passover (Ex 34:18–26; Dt 16:10). It is also known as the Feast of Harvest and the Day of Firstfruits (Ex 23:16; Nu 28:26). See 1:263–64, 491; 2:224.

2. The 50th day after Easter Sunday. On this day the Holy Spirit was outpoured on the disciples, and many people came to faith in Christ (Ac 2; 1Co 16:8). This first Pentecost fell on the same day as the Feast of Harvest. See 1:113, 872; 2:335, 354, 374–75, 389–90.

PENUEL (pi-NYOO-uhl; "face of God"). The place, east of the Jordan, where Jacob wrestled with God (Gn 32:31; Jgs 8:17; 1Ki 12:25). See 1:324.

PEOPLE OF THE LAND. General citizenry. However, in Jeremiah and Ezekiel, the expression may describe landowners who had political and cultural influence. See 1:267, 439, 869.

PERDITION (pur-DISH-uhn). *See* HELL; JUDGMENT. See 1:810.

PERDITION, SON OF. *See* DESTRUCTION, SON OF.

PEREZ-UZZA (PEE-rez-UZ-ah; "breach of Uzzah"). The name David gave to the place where Uzzah was struck dead for touching the ark of the covenant (2Sm 6:8; 1Ch 13:11). See 1:294.

PERFECT. Gk *teleios*, "something or someone complete." *See* END. See 1:670; 2:200, 443, 660.

PERFUMER. A person who mixed ointments and oils for the holy place (Ex 30:25, 35; 31:11; 37:29; Ne 3:8). They also made perfumes for burial spices and, according to excavation finds, medicinal herbs (2Ch 16:14).

PERGA (PUR-gah). A city of Pamphylia. Paul and Barnabas passed through Perga on their first missionary journey. This is also the place where John Mark left them to return home (Ac 13:13; 14:25). See 2:234, 388, 813.

PERGAMUM (PUR-gah-muhm). A city in Mysia in Asia Minor. It is the third of the seven churches of Asia mentioned in Rv 1:11; 2:12–17. Today it is called Bergama. See 2:771–72, 783.

PERSIA (PUR-zhah). To begin with, Persia was only the land around the Persian Gulf. Cyrus II, also known as Cyrus the Great, built the Persian Empire by conquering Media and Babylonia. This empire dominated Asia from 538 to 331 BC.

Cyrus allowed the Hebrew exiles in Babylonia to return to their land (2Ch 36:22–23; Ezr 1; Is 41:2; 44:28; 45). Darius I gave them permission to rebuild the temple at Jerusalem (Ezr 6). Darius's son, Xerxes I, was the next Persian ruler. He was probably the same person as the Ahasuerus mentioned in Est 1:1. Under Artaxerxes I, Ezra was allowed to lead more exiles back to Jerusalem. Nehemiah was also permitted to return to Jerusalem, where he organized the rebuilding of the city walls (Ezr 7–8; Ne 2:1–8). See 1:373, 381–82, 424–30, 463–66, 824, 845–47, 997; 2:104–6, 814.

PETER (PEE-tur; "rock"). One of the 12 disciples and a leader in the Early Church. He received the name Peter from Jesus at their first meeting. Peter's given name, however, was Simon or Simeon (Mt 4:18; Mk 1:16; Jn 1:41). He was also referred to as Cephas, which means "rock" (Jn 1:42; 1Co 1:12). Peter was the son of Jonas or John (Mt 16:17; Jn 1:42; 21:15–17). He lived in Bethsaida, where, together with his brother Andrew, he made his living as a fisherman on the Sea of Galilee (Mt 4:18; Mk 1:16; Lk 5:1–11; Jn 1:44).

Peter was first introduced to Jesus by Andrew and called to discipleship by Jesus at the Sea of Galilee (Mt 4:18–22; Mk 1:16–20; Jn 1:40–42). Later, along with the other 11 disciples, Jesus called him to be an apostle (Mt 10:2–4; Mk 3:13–19; Lk 6:13).

Because of Peter's personality, he seemed to be a natural leader among the disciples. On one occasion he walked on the sea toward Jesus. As his doubts began to grow, however, he began to sink, and Jesus had to put out His hand to save Peter (Mt 14:25–33). At Caesarea Philippi, when Jesus asked the 12 disciples what they thought of Him, Peter answered, saying, "You are the Christ, the Son of the living God" (Mt 16:16). Jesus praised Peter for his God-given confession of faith and said that He would build His Church on it (Mt 16:13–19; Mk 8:27–29; Lk 9:18–20). When Jesus began to tell the disciples about how He must suffer and die, Peter rebuked Him and said, "Far be it from You, Lord! This shall never happen to You." Jesus sharply scolded Peter for this (Mt 16:21–23).

Along with James and John, Peter was a member of the inner circle of disciples (Mt 16:15–16; 17:1). He was present at Jesus' transfiguration, in the Garden of Gethsemane, and at the high priest's palace, where Jesus was taken after His arrest (Mt 17:1; 26:37, 69; Mk 9:2; 14:33, 66; Lk 9:28; 22:54; Jn 18:16). While in the courtyard of the high priest's palace, Peter denied Jesus three times (Mt 26:69–75; Mk 14:70–72; Lk 22:59–62; Jn 18:26–27).

Peter was the first of the 12 disciples to whom Jesus appeared after His resurrection (Lk 24:34; 1Co 15:5). On Pentecost, Peter preached the Spirit-inspired message to the crowds of listening people (Ac 2). He was also one of the chief leaders in the Early Church (Ac 1–12; 15). According to tradition Nero had Peter put to death in Rome around AD 65. See 2:187, 201–4, 233–35, 238, 248, 260–61, 284, 336–38, 368–71, 375–76.

PETER, FIRST LETTER OF. See 2:701–17.

PETER, SECOND LETTER OF. See 2:719–35.

PHALANX. A Greek tactical battle line that came to use in Asia through the conquests of Alexander the Great.

PHANUEL (fah-NYOO-el; "face of God"). The father of the prophetess Anna (Lk 2:36).

PHARAOH (FAIR-o; "great house"). The title of Egyptian rulers (Gn 12:15; 41:39, 42; Ac 7:10). At birth individual names were given to the pharaohs, for instance, Pharaoh Neco and Pharaoh Hophra. A number of these Egyptian rulers are referred to in the Bible.

1. Pharaohs are mentioned in connection with Abraham and Joseph (Gn 12:14–20; 40–41). The names of these pharaohs are unknown. See 1:17, 30–31.
2. Also unknown is the name of the pharaoh of the oppression. He may have been Seti I or Thutmose III. See 1:60–61, 69–70.
3. Another pharaoh is mentioned when the children of Israel left Egypt under Moses. This ruler may have been Rameses II, Amenhotep II, Ahmose I, and Thutmose III. See 1:67–68, 70–71, 316.
4. Another pharaoh defeated the Canaanites of Gezer and gave the city as a dowry to his daughter, Solomon's wife (1Ki 3:1; 7:8; 9:16). See 1:323, 331.
5. Pharaoh Shishak, who began ruling Egypt during the latter part of Solomon's reign, used the division of the kingdom after Solomon's death for his own benefit. While the country was politically weakened, he invaded Jerusalem (1Ki 14:25–26; 2Ch 12:2–9).
6. Zerah invaded Judah in the days of King Asa but was defeated by him (2Ch 14:9–15; 16:8).
7. Before Tirhakah became pharaoh, he did battle with Sennacherib, king of Assyria (2Ki 19:9).
8. Pharaoh Neco killed King Josiah and, when Josiah's son, Jehoahaz, became king, Neco dethroned him and carried him off to Egypt. Next Jehoiakim was made king. In 605 BC Nebuchadnezzar, king of Babylonia, defeated Neco at Carchemish (2Ki 23:29–35; 24:7; 2Ch 35:20–36:4; Jer 46:2). See 1:403, 773, 963.
9. Pharaoh Hophra was the ruler of Egypt while Jeremiah was a prophet in Judah. Jeremiah spoke against him (Jer 44:30).

PHARAOH'S DAUGHTER.

1. The woman who found baby Moses on the Nile River and raised him as her own child (Ex 2:5–10). See 1:68, 85.
2. One of Solomon's wives (1Ki 3:1). See 1:621, 685.

PHARISEES (FAR-uh-seez; "separated"). One of the three leading Jewish parties during Jesus' time. It is believed that this strict and influential sect had its beginning during the time of the Maccabees.

The Pharisees believed that people had the ability to do good or evil, and that, by keeping the Law in an outward manner, they could of themselves earn God's favor. For this reason they stressed keeping God's Law and the oral law and put great emphasis on observing such rituals as washing, tithing, and fasting. They also avoided contact with non-Pharisees. They believed in the existence of angels and taught the immortality of the soul, two doctrines disputed by their rival party, the Sadducees (Mt 9:11–14; 12:1–8; 16:1–12; 23; Lk 11:37–54; Ac 15:5; 23:6–8). See *Ant*, 13:172, 288–98, 372–76; 18:12–15. See 2:85, 198–202, 206, 246–47, 328, 335.

PHILADELPHIA (fil-ah-DEL-fee-ah; "brotherly love"). A city of Lydia in Asia Minor. It was the location of one of the seven churches addressed in Rv 1:11; 3:7–13. See 2:326, 783.

PHILEMON (fi-LEE-mun; "friendship"). One of Paul's converts who lived in Colossae and had a church in his house. Paul addressed a letter to Philemon when he sent Philemon's runaway slave, Onesimus, back to him (Phm). See 2:535, 635–37.

PHILEMON, LETTER OF PAUL TO. See 2:635–43.

PHILIP (FIL-uhp; "lover of horses").

1. One of the 12 apostles. He came from Bethsaida on the Sea of Galilee and was likely a close friend of Andrew and Peter (Jn 1:44; 12:21). Philip was called to be a disciple near Bethany beyond the Jordan (Jn 1:41–43). Some time later Jesus called him to be an apostle (Mt 10:3; Mk 3:18; Lk 6:14).

   When Jesus was about to perform the miracle of feeding the 5,000, He tested Philip's faith by asking, "Where are we to buy bread, so that these people may eat?" (Jn 6:5–7). On the day of Jesus' triumphal entry into Jerusalem, Philip brought some Greeks who wished to meet Jesus to Him (Jn 12:20–23). While Jesus was talking to His disciples on the night before He was crucified, He told them that by knowing Him they knew the Father. Philip, however, did not understand this and asked Jesus to show them the Father (Jn 14:8–12). The last information the NT gives about Philip is that he was among the apostles in the upper room after Jesus' ascension (Ac 1:13).

2. The evangelist who came from Caesarea. Philip was one of the seven men chosen to look after the needs of widows and the poor in the Early Church.

   Philip preached the Gospel in Samaria. He cast out demons and healed sick people just as the apostles did. God used him to bring the Ethiopian eunuch to faith in Christ (Ac 6:5; 8:4–40; 21:8–9). See 2:367–68, 375.

PHILIPPI (fuh-LIP-igh). A Macedonian city that was made a Roman colony by Octavius and granted citizenship privileges. Paul visited this city and made various converts there, among whom were Lydia and the Philippian jailer (Ac 16:12, 20:6; Php 1:1; 1Th 2:2). See 2:269, 378, 388, 536, 539–42, 811, 813.

PHILIPPIANS, LETTER OF PAUL TO THE. See 2:539–49.

PHILISTIA (fuh-LIS-ti-ah). The land of the Philistines, an area along the coast of Canaan about 50 miles long and 15 miles wide. It extended from Joppa to south of Gaza and had five great cities: Gaza, Ekron, Ashdod, Ashkelon, and Gath (Jsh 13:2–3; 1Sm 6:17).

The Philistines were a non-Semitic people who came from Caphtor (or Crete) around 1175 BC. They were a warlike people, knowledgeable in making iron tools and weapons. Since Israel did not have these types of weapons until the time of David, the Philistines dominated them during the period of the judges (Jgs 13:1). Israel was set free from Philistine control by various deliverers, such as Shamgar, Samson, and Samuel (Jgs 3:31; 13–16; 1Sm 7:1–14). Later, the Philistines were defeated by Jonathan and conquered by David, who made them pay tribute (1Sm 13–14; 17–18). The Philistines regained their power during the period of the divided monarchy (1Ki 15:27; 2Ch 21:16; 28:18). See 1:276, 290, 352, 963; 2:153.

PHILISTINES (fuh-LIS-tinz). The people of Philistia. *See also* PHILISTIA. See 1:203, 239, 280–96; 2:801.

PHILOSOPHY (fuh-LOS-o-fee). The study of humanity's thinking about the meaning of life. In the Bible the word *philosophy* is used only in Col 2:8. Other passages in the NT, however, refer to various philosophical movements. The Epicureans and Stoics are mentioned in Ac 17:18. A chief threat to Christianity came from Gnostic (Col 2:8) and syncretistic thought (1Co 1:18–25; 1Tm 6:20). See 1:696–97; 2:378, 825.

PHINEAS (FIN-i-uhs).

1. The son of Eleazar and grandson of Aaron. Phineas ran a spear through an Israelite man and the Midianite woman he had brought into the camp. This ended a plague that had been sent as a judgment against the idolatry into which the Midianite women were leading the Israelites. For this reason God promised Phineas and his descendants an everlasting priesthood (Nu 25:1–8; 31:6; Jsh 22:13; Jgs 20:28). Except during the time of Eli, the descendants of Phineas held the high priesthood until AD 70.
2. A wicked son of Eli. Both he and his brother were unfaithful priests who were killed by the Philistines (1Sm 1:3; 2:34; 4:11–22).

PHOEBE (FEE-bi; "pure," "radiant"). A deaconess at Cenchrea. She was perhaps the first deaconess of the Christian Church and was highly spoken of by Paul (cf "servant" in Rm 16:1–2). See 2:420, 423, 436.

PHOENICIA (fi-NISH-i-ah; "bloodred" or "purple"). A country along the Mediterranean coast, about 120 miles long, that went from Arvad to the Ladder of Tyre. In the NT it extended to Dor.

The people who lived in Phoenicia were Semitic in background. They were well-known seagoers who founded Carthage and places in Spain and may even have reached England. Sidon was a city of Phoenicia. The Phoenicians were also famous shipbuilders and carpenters (1Ki 5:6; Ezk 27:9). Phoenicia was a trading center of the nations (Is 23:3; Ezk 27:25). Because the Phoenicians went to other lands and people from other lands came to Phoenicia, the Phoenician culture, its alphabet, dyes, numbers, weights, measures, and architecture spread.

The Phoenicians worshiped the idols El, Baal, Anath, Astarte, and Ashera. Jezebel, Ahab's wife, brought this worship to Israel (1Ki 16:31; 18:19). Hiram, one of the Phoenician kings, was friendly with

David and Solomon (2Sm 5:11; 1Ki 5:1–12; 2Ch 2:3–16). Another Hiram, a craftsman and architect, helped Solomon build the temple (1Ki 7:13–47; cf "Huram-abi" in 2Ch 2:13–14). After Elijah had told King Ahab about a coming drought, Elijah fled to Phoenicia, where a widow looked after him (1Ki 17:9).

Jesus visited the regions of Phoenicia and healed a Syrophoenician woman there (Mk 7:24–30). Paul visited the Christians in Phoenicia (Ac 15:3; 21:2–7). See 1:205, 352, 806, 811, 867; 2:240.

PHRYGIA (FRIJ-i-ah). A province in Asia Minor that once included the greater part of Asia Minor. It was obtained by Rome in 133 BC. Paul visited Phrygia on several of his missionary journeys (Ac 2:10; 16:6; 18:23). See 2:388, 551, 559.

PHYLACTERY (fi-LAK-tur-ee). *See* FRONTLET.

PIECE OF GOLD OR SILVER. A certain amount of precious metal, either in coin or uncoined form. The phrases "a piece of gold" or "a piece of silver" are used in the Bible because the exact amount of money is unknown. In the OT the original text often said "1,000 of silver," or "1,000 of gold" (Gn 20:16). In the NT a piece of silver commonly meant a drachma (Lk 15:8–9), shekel, or denarius (Mt 26:15; 27:3–9). See 1:150, 977; 2:40, 203, 228.

PILATE (PIGH-laht; "armed with javelin"). Pontius Pilate, the fifth procurator or representative of the Roman government in Judea (AD 26–36). Although Pilate found Jesus innocent of the accusations brought against Him, he nevertheless gave in to the people's wishes and condemned Jesus to death on the cross (Mt 27; Mk 15; Lk 3:1; 13:1; 23; Jn 18–19; Ac 3:13; 4:27; 13:28; 1Tm 6:13). See 2:204, 248, 284, 337, 352, 810.

PILGRIMAGE.

1. The Jewish people were expected to make the pilgrimage or trip to the temple in Jerusalem for the great feasts (Dt 16:16; Ps 120–134; Ac 2:5–11). See 1:99, 543, 566.
2. In the NT Christians are referred to as pilgrims or sojourners on the road to heaven (Heb 11:13; 1Pt 2:11). See 2:413.

PILLAR.

1. A monument that marked a sacred spot or a grave or was put up as a memorial (Gn 28:18; 31:45; 35:20; 2Sm 18:18). See 1:28, 370.
2. Pillars or columns that supported buildings (Jgs 16:25–30; 1Ki 7; 2Ki 11:14). See 1:341, 359; 2:806.
3. A pillar of cloud by day or fire by night that guided the Israelites during the exodus and showed God's presence (Ex 13:21; 14:19–24). See 1:137.
4. Leading apostles and teachers of the early Christian community in Jerusalem (Gal 2:9). See 2:321, 503, 758.

PINNACLE. Something shaped like a wing on a building, roof, battlement, or temple. The devil took Jesus to the pinnacle of the temple and said to Him, "If You are the Son of God, throw Yourself down" (Mt 4:5; Lk 4:9). See 2:196–97.

PIPE. A musical instrument of the woodwind category (Gn 4:21; Jb 21:12; 30:31). *See also* MUSIC.

PISGAH, MOUNT (PIZ-gah). Part of the Abarim mountain range that looks out over Jericho (Nu 21:20; 23:14; Dt 3:17; 4:49; 34:1; Jsh 12:3; 13:20). It is near Mount Nebo, the mountain from which Moses viewed the Promised Land (Dt 3:27). See 1:139–40.

PISHON (PIGH-shon). One of the four rivers of Eden (Gn 2:11).

PISIDIA (puh-SID-i-ah). An area in southern Asia Minor north of Pamphylia. Paul visited there on his first two missionary journeys (Ac 13:14; 14:24). See 2:377, 388, 489–500, 813.

PIT.

1. A hole that was dug for a well or cistern. Often these holes were used for prisons, burials, or traps (Gn 37:24; 2Sm 23:20; Ps 28:1; Is 24:22; Ezk 19:8). See 1:470; 2:802.
2. The word *pit* is also used in the OT to mean death, grave, or existence beyond death (Jb 33:18–30; Ps 28:1; 30:3; Is 14:15, 19). *See also* ABYSS; SHEOL. See 2:785.

PITCH. Asphalt or bitumen (Is 34:9). Pitch was used to make vessels watertight (Gn 6:14; Ex 2:3; Is 34:9). See 2:130.

PITHOM (PIGH-thom; "dwelling of Atum, sun-god"). An Egyptian store-city in Goshen. It held supplies of grain for armies and perhaps for caravans (Ex 1:11). See 1:62, 81.

PLAGUE. Something that causes trouble or suffering (Ex 11:1). Often a plague was a quickly spreading disease that made many people severely ill or caused them to die (1Sm 5; 2Sm 24:13–25). The ten plagues on Egypt were the means God used to convince the pharaoh to let the Israelites go (Ex 7–12). See 1:68–70, 86–89, 138, 866–71; 2:784–85, 792–93.

PLANE. A tree that grows along the water in Syria and Mesopotamia. The word *plane* is sometimes translated as chestnut or pine (Gn 30:37; Is 41:19; 60:13; Ezk 31:8).

PLEDGE.

1. Something given to be held as security for a loan (Dt 24:10–13, 17). *See also* LOANS. See 1:517, 581; 2:397.
2. A wager (2Ki 18:23; Is 36:8).

PLEIADES (PLEE-yah-deez; "cluster"). The stars in the constellation Taurus (Jb 9:9; 38:31; Am 5:8).

PLOW. *See* AGRICULTURE. See 1:243; 2:303.

PLOWSHARE. A stone or the point of a plow (1Sm 13:20; Is 2:4; Mi 4:3). *See also* AGRICULTURE.

POETRY. Features of Hebrew poetry include its rhythm, parallelism, alliteration, and rhyme or other wordplays. Jb, Ps, Pr, Ec, Sg, and sections in the prophets are examples of Hebrew poetry. See 1:487–90, 554–56, 783; 2:63.

POMEGRANATE (POM-eh-gran-it). *See* ORCHARD. See 1:408; 2:677.

PONTIUS (PON-shuhs). *See* PILATE.

PONTUS (PON-tuhs; "sea"). A region of northeast Asia Minor. During NT times it was a Roman province (Ac 2:9; 1Pt 1:1). Aquila, one of Paul's helpers, came from Pontus (Ac 18:2). See 2:645, 701, 715.

POOR. The OT speaks negatively about those who beg (Ps 37:25; Pr 20:4). Laziness, some great trouble or disaster, and cruel or unjust treatment are cited as causes of being poor (Jgs 10:6–17; Pr 10:4; 14:23; Is 5:8; Mt 23:14).

Although it is true that God promises to bless His people (Dt 28:1–14) and that hard work and wisely managing one's resources often benefit the person who does so, poor people were still present in Israel throughout its history. Laws protected the poor. For instance, when crops were harvested, some of the yield was to be left for the fatherless and widows (Lv 19:9–10; Dt 24:19–22). Every seventh year fields and orchards were to lie fallow so the poor could eat (Ex 23:11; Lv 25:6). During the Year of Jubilee, land that people sold because they needed the money was to be returned to them (Lv 25:8–30). The poor were to receive their wages on time, and they were not to be charged interest (Ex 22:25–27; Dt 24:14–15).

Scripture praises the person who has mercy on the poor (Ps 41:1; Pr 14:21; 29:7). See 1:82, 258, 574, 886; 2:46, 189, 305, 454, 686–88.

PORCH. A passageway from a street to the inner hall or an area protected by a roof, such as a veranda, a colonnade or portico, or a vestibule or hall (Jgs 3:23; 1Ki 7:6; 1Ch 28:11; Jn 5:2). See 2:382.

PORTION. Hbr *nachal*; *yarash*; *goral*, "lot." Gk *kleronomia*. By casting lots, the tribes of Israel were each given a portion of the Promised Land, though the priestly clan of the Levites was given God Himself, not land, as their inheritance (Dt 10:9; Ps 119:57). Inheritance is an important expression of God's graciousness in the OT. He gives lovingly and freely to His people as a father lovingly provides for his children. God's chosen people are His portion and treasured possession (Dt 32:9). Inheritance is an important theme in the accounts and references to the patriarchs. In later usage, "lot" took on a figurative meaning for an allotted punishment or reward (cf Wis 5:5; Ecclus 11:22; Qumran literature). In Qumran theology, inheritance is based on predestination. Cf Tob 3:15; 14:13; Ecclus 10:11. See 1:103–4, 213, 334, 410, 1004.

POST. A position from which soldiers would keep watch to protect the town or city (2Ch 23:18; Ne 7:3). Also figurative (Ezk 46:2). See 1:224.

POT. A clay or metal vessel used for holding liquid or dry ingredients (Jgs 6:19; 2Ki 4:38; Jb 41:20, 31; Lm 4:2). See 1:368–69, 805.

POTIPHAR (POT-uh-fur; "whom the sun god has given"). The captain of the pharaoh's guard during Joseph's time (Gn 37:36; 39:1). See 1:30, 38.

POTIPHERA (po-TIF-ur-ah; "whom the sun god has given"). The Egyptian priest of On, whose daughter, Asenath became Joseph's wife (Gn 41:45, 50; 46:20).

POTTER, POTTER'S FIELD, POTTER'S WHEEL, POTTERY. *See* TRADE. See 1:764, 771; 2:406.

POVERTY. *See* POOR.

PRAETORIAN GUARD (pri-TO-ri-uhn). *See* IMPERIAL GUARD.

PRAETORIUM (pri-TO-ri-uhm). The headquarters of a general.

1. The palace in Jerusalem occupied by Pontius Pilate (cf "headquarters" in Mt 27:27; Mk 15:16; Jn 18:28). See 2:235.
2. Herod's palace at Caesarea (Ac 23:35).

PRAISE THE LORD. Hbr *hallelu yah*, "praise Yah[weh]." An exclamation of thankful praise to the one true God. See 1:544, 581, 586.

PRAYER (PRAIR). Speaking with God. Moses' prayers were largely intercessory, that is, speaking to God on behalf of the people (Ex 32:11–13, 31–32; Nu 11:11–15; Dt 9:18–21). The Psalms are examples of the covenant people's prayers to their covenant God. These prayers are usually a result of some experience seen in its spiritual depth and are often closely related to sacrifice (Gn 12:8; 26:25) and the temple (1Ki 8:30, 33; Ps 5:7).

The NT teaches that prayer is to be spoken in the name of Jesus since sinful people cannot approach God on their own merits (Jn 14:13; 15:16). They approach only through Christ, who has bought humankind back from their sins and put them in a right relationship with God (Gal 4:1–7). Christ taught the disciples the Lord's Prayer (Mt 6:9–13; Lk 11:1–4). It is an example of proper approach and manner for speaking to God. Christ intercedes for believers before the Father (Rm 8:34; Heb 4:14–16; 7:25). The Holy Spirit, who dwells within all Christians, also intercedes for them according to the will of God (Rm 8:15–16, 26–27).

Prayers can be formal (Ps; Mt 6:9–13; 26:30) or spoken freely from one's own thoughts and concerns (Jn 17; Lk 18:13; 1Th 5:17). They can be said together by a large group of believers or alone by an individual (Mt 6:6; 14:23; Ac 1:14; Phm 4); they can be said at set times and places (Ac 2:42; 6:4; 16:13) or at all times and places (Eph 6:18; 1Th 5:17; 1Tm 2:8).

The Bible mentions various ways in which prayers can be said: with uplifted hands, while kneeling, while lying flat on the ground, or while standing (1Ki 8:54; Ps 28:2; Mt 6:5; 26:39; Ac 9:40; 1Tm 2:8). See 1:299–300, 609, 615; 2:64–65, 111, 135–36, 143–44, 197, 284, 306–7, 341, 690.

PREACHER, PREACHING. One who speaks God's message or the act of speaking for God.

In the OT, prophets proclaimed God's message—the Law and the Gospel. They spoke about God's will for people, proclaimed His judgment on those who had sinned, and spoke His promises (Ezk 20:46; Jer 11:6).

In the NT, preaching centered in the person and work of Jesus Christ (Ac 2:14–40; 3:11–26). Again, the message included both the Law and the Gospel (Mt 4:17; Lk 3:3–14; 4:18; Ac 2:14–40; 17:22–31). See 1:195, 406–7, 667, 706–9, 922–23; 2:176–77, 235, 257, 450–55, 594–95.

PREDESTINATION (pri-des-tuh-NAY-shuhn). God's act before the beginning of the world in choosing from sinners those whom He would save (Eph 1:4–5). God does this by (1) providing for the salvation of the world through Christ, (2) offering the merits and benefits of Christ's work to individuals through the Word and Sacraments, (3) working faith in the hearts of individuals through the Holy Spirit, (4) graciously receiving those who are sorry for their sins and who trust and believe in Christ as their Savior, (5) making individuals more and more holy by the Holy Spirit's work in them, (6) protecting them from the work of the devil and the sinful world, (7) keeping them in the faith until the end through the work of the Holy Spirit in Word and Sacrament, and (8) saving these individuals eternally (Mt 20:16; 22:14; Mk 13:20–22; Ac 13:48; Rm 8:28–30; 9:11; 11:15; Eph 1:4–5, 11; 2Th 2:13; 2Tm 1:9; 2:10, 19; 1Pt 1:2). *See also* ELECT, ELECTION. See 1:77, 404; 2:386, 533.

PRESBYTER (PREZ-buh-tur). *See* ELDER. See 2:322, 739.

PRESENCE. Hbr *panim*, "face," so "to be in front of someone/something." Gk *prosopon*. To "enter God's presence" typically refers to visiting the temple or tabernacle for worship. An advancing warrior naturally "faced" his enemies, so the Lord's "presence" or "face" is fearsome to His enemies. Forms of the Gk term are especially common in Jth, where the Gentile army covers the face of the earth, Judith enters the presence of their general, Holofernes (Jth 10:13–15), and Judith's face is the beautiful instrument by which Holofernes is deceived and defeated (Jth 13:16). *See also* BE WITH. See 1:61, 73, 143–44, 408, 420, 584, 807–8; 2:268, 343, 390, 762, 789.

PRIEST. One who represents the people before God. Originally individuals or heads of families carried out the work of a priest (Gn 4:3–4; 12:7; 13:18; 26:25; 33:20). Then through Moses God appointed Aaron and his sons and their descendants as priests (Ex 28:1). Aaronic priests had to meet high standards (Lv 21:16–24). Consecrated for this task, they wore special clothing in the sanctuary, taught the people, and inquired of God's will (Ex 28–29).

The priesthood was grouped into 24 divisions, each serving a week at a time (1Ch 24:1–19). Kings, judges, and prophets also made sacrifices to God (Jgs 6:17–21; 13:15–20; 2Sm 6:17; 1Ki 18:30–38).

The chief priest, or high priest, was in charge of all the other priests. He offered the sin offering, made sacrifice on the Day of Atonement, and discovered the will of God through Urim and Thummin (Lv 4; 16; Nu 27:21; Ne 7:65). The high priest wore the regular priestly clothing plus breastplate, ephod, sash, and turban (Ex 28). *See also* AARON. See 1:67, 73, 75, 106, 400, 751, 987.

In the NT, Jesus Christ is the only High Priest. Since He sacrificed Himself for the sins of the people and this sacrifice need never be repeated, there is no longer a need for the Levitical priesthood; it has been done away with in Christ (Jn 14:6; 1Tm 2:5–6; Heb 5:7–10). *See also* JESUS CHRIST (office of priest).

The NT also teaches the priesthood of all believers. Christians share in Christ's priestly activity by bringing the Gospel to people (Eph 2:18; Heb 10:19–25; 13:15; 1Pt 2:5, 9; Rv 1:5–6). See 2:97, 150–52, 204, 256, 301–2, 330, 336, 406, 656–63, 710, 783.

PRIEST, HIGH. *See* PRIEST.

PRINCE. A ruler or chief person, such as the head of a family or tribe, a king, a ruler, a governor, a magistrate, a satrap, or a royal descendant (Gn 25:16; Nu 22:8; 1Sm 9:16; 2Ki 10:13; 2Ch 12:5–6; Est 1). The Messiah is called the Prince of Peace (Is 9:6). The devil is called the prince or ruler of demons (Mt 9:34). See 1:234, 277, 552, 736, 807; 2:166–67, 200, 389, 773.

PRISCA, PRISCILLA (PRIS-kah, pri-SIL-ah; "ancient"). Wife of Aquila. Priscilla and her husband were tentmakers and Christian friends of Paul, whom they helped on a number of occasions (Ac 18:2, 18; Rm 16:3; 2Tm 4:19). They had a church in their house and together taught Apollos more about the Christian faith (Ac 18:26; 1Co 16:19). See 2:418, 435–36, 522, 653.

PRISON. A place where persons who are suspected of committing a crime or who have been accused of one are kept.

1. The oldest prisons mentioned in the Bible were wells or dungeons (Gn 37:24; Jer 38:6–13). During the period of the kings, prisons were located in the palace or in private houses (1Ki 22:27; Jer 32:2; 37:15). The Herods and Romans had royal prisons (Lk 3:20; Ac 12:4; cf "praetorium" in Ac 23:35). See 1:30, 758–59; 2:378, 530, 534–35, 541, 763.
2. Another word for "abyss," the place where Satan lives (1Pt 3:19; Rv 20:7). See 1:535.

PROCHORUS (PROK-o-ruhs; "leader of a chorus"). One of the seven men chosen by the Early Church to look after widows and probably the poor in general (Ac 6:5).

PROCONSUL (pro-KAHN-suhl). The governor of a Roman province administered by the Senate (Ac 13:7–8, 12). See 2:441, 565.

PROMISE. The most important promise in the Bible is God's assurance that He would send a deliverer, or Messiah, to save His people (Gn 3:15; 12:3; Rm 4:13; 9:8; Gal 3:14–19). The promises in the OT concerning the Messiah are fulfilled in Christ Jesus (Ac 13:23, 32–33; Rm 1:2–3; 15:8; Gal 3:14; 2Co 1:20). Those who believe in Jesus as their Savior are called heirs, or children, of the promise (Rm 4:16; Gal 3:16, 26–29; 4:28). By God's grace, through faith, they receive many blessings, including the forgiveness of sins, the indwelling of the Holy Spirit, and life everlasting (1Co 3:16; Gal 3:1–14; 1Jn 1:7). See 1:26–27, 104, 171–72, 731; 2:204, 336–37, 361, 389, 749, 786.

PROPHET (PRAHF-it; "seer," "announcer," "spokesman"). A person called by God to speak for Him to the people. Prophets spoke God's Word of judgment, calling people to account for their sins (2Sm 12; Is 58:1; Ezk 3:17), and His Word of mercy (Is 40; 53). Their work involved forth-telling and, to a lesser degree, foretelling. They constantly emphasized God's work in the course of history, particularly His plan of salvation through the Messiah, Jesus Christ.

The OT prophets came from all walks of life (Am 1:1). Many of them wrote books of the Bible that have been named for them. The OT also mentions schools of prophets (1Sm 19:19–20; 2Ki 2:3–5; 4:38; 6:1). See 1:xxvi, 372–73, 701–7; 2:3–5, 161, 256, 272–73, 728, 779–80.

PROPITIATION (pro-pish-i-AY-shuhn; "atonement"). The act of keeping God from being angry by satisfying His justice and holiness so that He can forgive sins. Sin causes a separation between God and people; it is necessary that human guilt be removed in order to restore a right relationship between them. In the OT, the sacrificial system served this function, though God also forgave people without sacrifices being offered (cf "atonement" in Lv 14:18; 17:11; 19:22; Is 6:7; 27:9; Ezk 16:63). These sacrifices pointed forward to the supreme sacrifice of God's Son, Jesus Christ, who died for the sins of the world. Christ's death and resurrection once and for all removed the barrier between God and all people (Rm 3:25; 1Jn 2:2; 4:10). See 2:741–42.

PROSELYTE (PRAHS-uh-light). In the OT, referred to as sojourners. *See also* SOJOURNER.

In the NT, proselytes included people who observed some or all features of the Jewish religion (Mt 23:15; Ac 2:11) and those who simply feared God (cf Ac 10:2). Some proselytes believed that the God of Israel was the true God, but they had not received circumcision. See 1:902; 2:538–39.

PROSTITUTE (PRAHS-tuh-tyoot). A person who offers sexual favors for money, especially a woman who offers herself to a man for money. There were both common and religious prostitutes in the ancient world (Dt 23:17–18; Hos 4:14). Scripture often speaks of prostitutes and prostitution as a symbol for disobedience and unfaithfulness (Ex 34:15; Ezk 16; 23; Hos 4:15). The sin of prostitution is forbidden in Scripture many times (Lv 21:7, 9, 14; 1Co 6:18–20). See 1:218, 805, 855; 2:194, 211, 453, 581–82, 784.

PROVERB (PRAHV-urb). Generally a short saying expressing a familiar or useful truth (Gn 10:9; 1Sm 10:12; Dt 28:37; Pr). See 1:485; 2:55, 328.

PROVERBS, BOOK OF. See 1:621–51.

PROVIDENCE (PRAHV-uh-duhns). The activity of God whereby He preserves, governs, and directs His entire creation (Jb 9:5; Ps 104:10–25; 145:15; Mt 4:4; 6:26–28; Lk 12:6–7; Ac 17:25–28; Heb 1:3). See 1:257, 441, 470–72, 911–12; 2:21, 400.

PROVINCE. A unit of a country, for instance, the provinces of the Roman Empire. Persian provinces were also called satrapies (Ezr 2:1; 5:8; Ac 23:34; 25:1). See 1:452, 465; 2:298, 704.

PSALMS, BOOK OF. See 1:541–619.

PTOLEMY (TAWL-i-mee). The common name of the Macedonian kings, descended from Ptolemy I son of Lagos. He ruled Egypt—after the death of Alexander the Great in 323 BC—until 30 BC, the year of Cleopatra's death. See 2:4, 28, 79, 86, 105–6, 150–52.

PUBLICAN (PUHB-li-kuhn). *See* TAX COLLECTOR.

PURE. Hbr *thahor*; Gk *katharizo*. Used in Moses and historical books to qualify the purity of gold. In wisdom and prophecy it describes God's Word and the ways of His people. Hbr used at Qumran to describe the special status of their community over against those who had a more common form of purity. Purity is a significant theme in 2Macc due to the purification of the temple (2:16–19; 10:1–9). *See also* CLEAN; HOLY. See 1:404, 439, 694, 860; 2:207, 465, 602–3.

PURIFIED. *See* PURE.

PURIM (PYOO-rim). A Jewish festival commemorating the deliverance of the Jews by Esther (Est 3:7; 9:24–32). The name comes from Pur, meaning "lot" (Est 9:24–26). See 1:461–67, 470–74; 2:106, 111.

Q

QUART. *See* MEASURES 2; 3.

QUEEN OF HEAVEN. A Semitic goddess of fertility. She was likely Astarte of Canaan or Ishtar of Babylonia (Jer 7:18; 44:17–25).

QUEEN OF THE SOUTH. The queen of Sheba (Mt 12:42; Lk 11:31. See also 1Ki 10:1–13; 2Ch 9:1–12). See 1:342, 390, 401.

QUIRINIUS, PUBLIUS SULPICIUS (kwigh-RIN-i-uhs PUB-li-uhs sul-PISH-UHS). The governor of Syria at the time Caesar Augustus issued the decree for the census in which Joseph enrolled (Lk 2:2). See 2:297–98.

QUIVER (KWIV-ur). *See* ARCHERY.

QUMRAN COMMUNITY. Jewish sect responsible for copying the Dead Sea Scrolls, led by "the Teacher of Righteousness." Flourished near the Dead Sea from the second century BC to c AD 70. The scrolls describe a people alienated from those who ran the Jerusalem temple (*see* ZADOKITES). They lived by a different calendar and by different laws. They awaited a Messiah. Some scholars believe they were Essenes, but others believe they were a distinct group. See 2:5, 311, 807.

R

RAAMSES (ray-AM-seez). A store-city the Hebrews built in northeast Egypt while they were slaves there (Ex 1:11). It was the capital of the Nineteenth Dynasty. It is also referred to as Rameses (Gn 47:11; Ex 12:37; Nu 33:3, 5). See 1:62.

RABBI (RAB-igh). Hbr *rab*, "great one"; means "my great one" and thus "my master/teacher." A title of respect the Jewish people gave to their spiritual leaders and instructors (Mt 23:7–8; Mk 10:51; Jn 1:38, 49; 3:2, 26; 6:25). The expression developed into a title describing teachers of the Law of Moses, Jewish traditions, and religious practices. Regarding an example of such teaching, see Luther's "Preface to the Book of Ecclesiasticus" (2:58). *See also* HILLEL, HOUSE OF; and SHAMMAI, HOUSE OF.

People addressed Jesus as "Rabbi" (e.g., Mt 26:25, 49; Mk 9:5; 11:21; 14:45), but He warned His disciples about accepting such a title (Mt 23:8). John explains *rabbi* and *rabboni* as meaning "master" (Jn 4:31; 9:2; 11:8; 20:16). See 1:433, 485; 2:411.

RABBONI (ra-BO-nee). *See* RABBI.

RAB-SARIS (RAB-sah-ris; "chief eunuch"). The title of Assyrian officials who held high positions in the court (2Ki 18:17; Jer 39:3, 13).

RABSHAKEH (RAB-shah-ke; "chief cup bearer"). The title of Assyrian military officials who held high positions (2Ki 18:17–37; 19:4–8; Is 36; 37:4, 8). See 1:731.

RACHEL (RAY-chuhl; "ewe"). The favorite wife of Jacob; mother of Joseph and Benjamin. Rachel was the younger daughter of Laban, Jacob's uncle. This made her Jacob's cousin (Gn 29–35; Jer 31:15). See 1:28–29, 37; 2:305, 804.

RADDAI (RAD-ay-igh; "Yahweh rules"). One of David's brothers (1Ch 2:14).

RAHAB (RAY-hab).

1. A woman who had a house on the wall of Jericho during the time of the conquest. For her help in hiding Israelite spies in her home, Rahab's life and the lives of her family were spared (Jsh 2:1–21; 6:17–25). She is likely the Rahab who married Salmon and became the mother of Boaz, an ancestor of Jesus (Ru 4:21; Mt 1:5). See 1:210, 217–18, 255.
2. Meaning "violent one." A mythical monster representing sea power and violence (Jb 26:12; Ps 89:10). The name is also applied to Egypt (Ps 87:4; Is 30:7). See 1:506, 516, 548.

RAIN. The rainy season in Israel extends from October through April. The early rain occurs in October and November (Ps 84:6; Is 30:23; Jer 5:24); the spring rain comes in March and April (Jb 29:23; Pr 16:15; Jer 3:3; Zec 10:1).

In the Bible *rain* is often a picture word for teaching and counsel, for the Word, for righteousness and peace, for blessings on believers, for judgments that destroy, and for nagging (Dt 32:2; Jb 20:23; 29:21–25; Ps 72:6; 84:5–6; Pr 19:13; Is 55:10; Ezk 38:22). See 1:48–49, 343, 514, 548; 2:680.

RAINBOW. The sign of God's covenant with Noah. The rainbow is a reminder that God will never again flood the whole earth (see "bow" in Gn 9:12–17). See 1:36, 145.

RAM. A male sheep. The ram was a source of food and sacrifice (Gn 15:9; 22:13; 31:38). The skins of rams were used as coverings for the tabernacle; their horns, for trumpets (Ex 26:14; Jsh 6:4–20). See 1:25, 27, 72, 298, 835, 876–77.

RAMAH (RAY-mah; "height").

1. A town of Benjamin 5 miles north of Jerusalem. It was near Deborah's palm tree and Rachel's tomb (Jsh 18:25; Jgs 4:5; 19:10–15; 1Ki 15:17–22; Jer 31:15; 40:1; Mt 2:18). Benjaminites lived in Ramah after the captivity (Ezr 2:26; Ne 7:30). Today it is called el-Ram. See 1:276, 371.
2. A town in the mountains of Ephraim. It was where Samuel was born, lived, and buried. In 1Sm 1:1 it is called Ramathaim-zophim to distinguish it from other towns of similar name. It may be the same as Arimathea, a place mentioned in the NT.

RAMESES (RAM-i-seez). *See* PHARAOH 3. See 1:321, 339, 653.

RAMOTH-GILEAD, RAMOTH IN GILEAD (RAY-moth-GIL-i-uhd; "heights of Gilead"). An Amorite city east of the Jordan and a Levitical city of refuge in Gad (Dt 4:43; Jsh 20:8; 21:38). It was the home of Jephthah and the place where Solomon's tax gatherer lived (Jgs 11:34; 1Ki 4:13). King Ahab was killed there (1Ki 22:1–38). It was also known as Ramah, Ramath-mizpeh, and Mizpah or Mizpeh (Jsh 13:26; Jgs 10:17; 2Ki 8:29). See 1:344.

RANSOM. The price paid for getting someone or something back (Ex 21:30. Cf 1Co 6:19–20). *See also* REDEMPTION. See 1:39, 263, 594; 2:191, 603, 710.

RAPHAEL (RAF-ay-el). An archangel who appears in the apocryphal Book of Tobit. See 2:43–46.

REAP. *See* AGRICULTURE. See 1:253, 471; 2:209.

REBA (REE-bah; possibly "fourth"). A Midianite king who, at Moses' command, was killed by Israel in Moab (Nu 31:8; Jsh 13:21).

REBEKAH (ri-BEK-ah; possibly refers to a "yoke" or the "ox" that bears it). The daughter of Bethuel, wife of Isaac, and mother of Esau and Jacob (Gn 22:23; 24; 25:21–26). See 1:27–30; 2:44.

RECEIVED. Gk *paradidomi*, a technical term for the handing on and receiving of a divinely given tradition (cf 1Co 15:1–3). *See also* TRADITION. See 2:411, 552–53.

RECONCILIATION (rek-UN-sil-i-AY-shuhn). The removal of the barrier, caused by sin, between God and humanity. Christ's death on the cross for the sin of the world is the way this barrier was removed. An individual appropriates the forgiveness earned by Christ for himself or herself by grace through faith (Rm 5:11; 2Co 5:18–19; Eph 2:16). See 1:39, 85, 112, 403; 2:176, 425, 488–90, 663.

RECORDER. An official of high rank who wrote down important events and kept the public documents (2Sm 8:16; 20:24; 1Ki 4:3; 2Ki 18:18, 37; 1Ch 18:15; Is 36:3, 22).

REDEEM, REDEMPTION (ri-DEEM, ri-DEMP-shuhn). Translates two terms. Hbr *ga'al*, "to ransom, deliver, buy back" (cf Ru 2:20). Hbr *padah*, "to ransom," used esp by Moses for the ransoming of the firstborn from sacrifice (cf Ex 13:13). The Lord redeemed Israel by rescuing them from slavery. Gk *apolytrosis* and related terms, "to buy back" a slave or captive, to set someone free. In the NT, "redeem" and "ransom" describe Jesus' work (Eph 1:7; 1Pt 1:18–19). The buying back of humanity from sin and death by Christ, who paid the price with His perfect obedience and His sacrificial death on the cross (Rm 3:24; Gal 3:13; cf "ransom" in Eph 1:7; 1Pt 1:18–19). *See also* ATONEMENT; DELIVER. See 1:60, 107, 258, 261–64, 515–18, 733; 2:293, 343, 429, 507, 711.

RED SEA. Body of water, 1,350 miles long, extending from the Gulf of Suez to the Indian Ocean. It has two arms: the Gulf of Suez and the Gulf of Aqabah. The name *Red Sea* may refer to either the Gulf of Suez (Nu 33:10–11), the Gulf of Aqabah (1Ki 9:26), the entire Red Sea (Ex 23:31), or nearby lakes. See 1:67–69, 71, 81, 88–89, 139.

REED. Tall grasses, flags, or rushes. *Reed* is used as a picture word for uncertain support, fickleness, and weakness or helplessness (2Ki 18:21; Is 36:6; 42:3; Mt 11:7; 12:20; Lk 7:24). See 1:489, 498.

REFINER. Someone who worked with precious metals (Mal 3:2–3). *See also* TRADE.

REFUGE, CITIES OF. Six Levitical cities designed to provide temporary shelter for those who had accidentally killed someone (Nu 35:6, 11–32; Dt 4:43; 19:1–13; Jsh 20). They were Kadesh (Naphtali), Shechem (Ephraim), Hebron (Judah), Golan (Manasseh), Ramoth-gilead (Gad), and Bezer (Reuben). *See also* MURDER. See 1:131–32, 142, 211–14.

REGENERATION (ri-jen-ur-AY-shuhn). To be born again, restored, renewed, completely made over. Regeneration is an act of God the Holy Spirit, who works through Word and Sacraments to bring a sinful, self-centered person into union with Christ Jesus through faith (Jn 1:13; 3:1–12; 1Pt 1:23). See 1:752; 2:223, 789.

REHOBOAM (ree-ho-BO-am; "enlarger of people"). Son of Solomon and Naamah (1Ki 14:21, 31; Mt 1:7). Rehoboam was the last king of the united kingdom of Israel. When he took over after his father's death, Rehoboam refused to listen to the people and lower their taxes. So the 10 northern tribes rebelled and made Jeroboam their king. Rehoboam became the first king of the Southern Kingdom of Judah, the two remaining tribes (1Ki 12; 14; 2Ch 10–12). Rehoboam made his kingdom and cities stronger. In the fifth year of Rehoboam's reign, however, King Shishak of Egypt captured the fortified cities of Judah and Jerusalem (1Ki 14:25–27). See 1:324, 342–43, 372, 390, 401.

RELENT. Hbr *nacham*. *See* COMFORT, which translates the same term. "The Lord relented/repented" is a metaphor of the Lord changing a previous pronouncement of judgment. The metaphor appears at some key junctures in Scripture: the flood (Gn 6:6), the Sinai revelation (Ex 32:12–14), and the institution of the monarchy (1Sm 15:11, 35). It also appears in psalmody and creedal statements (cf Ps 106:45; Jer 18:7–10; Jl 2:13; Jnh 4:2). In 35 examples, the

Lord is the subject of this verb. At first, these passages may appear to contradict other statements that He does not change previous decisions (Nu 23:19; 1Sm 15:29; Ps 110:4; Jer 4:28; 20:16; Ezk 24:14; Hos 13:14; Zec 8:14). However, the passages listed here divide into two types: (1) There are certain promises the Lord has made that He will never change. Five describe the Lord's refusal to change His decision concerning the judgment of 587 BC, and one (Ps 110:4) speaks of His unwillingness to change the eternal priesthood and order of Melchizedek. (2) Two passages speak of His refusal to change His will (Nu 23:19; 1Sm 15:29). These are statements of principle (i.e., God is not a man that He should go against a prior decision). He is constant with respect to His Gospel promises made to Abraham and David (cf Ezk 18:23, 32). He is unchangeable in His nature (Ps 102:27; Mal 3:6; Jas 1:17). See 1:517, 769, 887, 911; 2:692.

RELIGION. Humanity's recognition of its relationship to a supreme being and the expression of that relationship in faith, worship, and life. Religion may be true or false (Ac 17:22; 26:5; Rm 1:18–25; Jas 1:26–27). See 1:146–47, 547; 2:28–29, 157, 553, 599.

REMEMBER. Hbr *zakar*, "to recall" or "keep in mind." Gk *mimneskomai* in LXX. God could not forget His covenant with His people. When He "remembers" them, He actively works to keep His promise to protect and save them (1Macc 4:10; 2Macc 1:2). However, in the Apocrypha, the term most often introduces admonitions (e.g., Tob 4:4–5; Ecclus 28:6–7). See 1:36, 59, 219, 442, 436, 579–80, 861, 983; 2:65, 788.

REMNANT (REM-nuhnt). Hbr *she'ar*, "rest, remainder." Gk *kataleimma* in LXX. A common OT term that gained special use in the Prophetic Books. The term expressed God's condemnation (Is 10:22) or His mercy (Is 37:31). Though destruction would come upon God's chosen people, He would not annihilate them. God would keep His promises and preserve a remnant of those who would reconstitute the holy people. The Qumran community described themselves as a remnant. The term is not common in the Apocrypha, yet see the related idea in CAPTIVITY. In the NT the Church becomes the holy remnant. Something left over.

1. People who survived a period of deep trouble (Jsh 12:4; 13:12).
2. The small number of people who survive God's judgment and remain faithful to Him. Because of God's love for His people, believers will be added from all peoples to form the Church (Is 10:20–23; 11:11–12; Zec 8:12; Rm 9:27; cf Jer 32:38–39; Zep 3:13). See 1:246, 439, 724, 736, 769, 804–5, 887, 923–28, 965; 2:426.

REPENTANCE (ri-PEN-tuhns). Translates forms of Gk *strepho*; *metanoeo*. Related to Hbr *nacham* and *shub*. (*See* COMFORT, which translates the same Hbr term.) A total change of heart and life that God works in an individual who does not believe or trust in Him by turning him or her around to believe and trust in Him. Repentance includes both sorrow for one's sins and faith in Christ through whom forgiveness is granted (Mk 1:4; Lk 3:3, 8; Ac 5:31).

"The Lord relented/repented" is a metaphor of the Lord changing a previous pronouncement of judgment. The metaphor appears at some key junctures in Scripture: the flood (Gn 6:6), the Sinai revelation (Ex 32:12–14), and the institution of the monarchy (1Sm 15:11, 35). LXX uses *metanoeo* sparingly, though consistently for cases when God turns away from His wrath (e.g., Jer 4:28). Cf Jer 8:6; 18:8 in LXX (*Theological Dictionary of the NT* 4:989). In the Apocrypha, Gk *metanoeo* has fully come to mean "to convert" (Wis 12:10; Ecclus 44:16; 48:15). Philo and Josephus use the terms consistently with Gk tradition for change of mind and penitence. See 1:xl, 174, 299–300, 809, 943; 2:189, 278, 396, 414, 670–71, 688–89.

REPHIDIM (REF-i-dim). A place between Sin and Sinai where Israel camped (Ex 17:1; 19:2; Nu 33:14–15). See 1:81.

RESIN (REE-sen). An Assyrian city built by Nimrod. It was probably a suburb of Nineveh (Gn 10:11–12).

RESTORE THE FORTUNES. Yet another use of Hbr *shub*. Lit, "return the things turned over [to someone]." So, this is not a request for mere luck. The idea is closely related to the blessings of the new creation depicted as the new land of Israel (Ezk 47:3–12). In the NT, restoration describes what God effects through the coming of the messianic kingdom (cf Mt 17:11; Ac 1:6; 15:16; 1Pt 5:10). See 1:766, 795; 2:382, 393, 490.

RESURRECTION (rez-uh-REK-shuhn). A return to life after one has died. Because Christ rose from the dead, believers can be sure they, too, will rise from the dead and enjoy eternal life with Christ. The Bible describes the resurrected body as a spiritual body

(Rm 6:3–11; 1Co 15). All people, both believers and nonbelievers, will rise from the dead and be judged (2Co 5:10). See 1:519–20, 821; 2:169–73.

REUBEN (ROO-ben; "see a son"). Jacob's firstborn son by his wife Leah (Gn 29:32). Reuben brought mandrakes to his mother, which she used to get Jacob to make her pregnant so she could have another child (Gn 30:14–16). Reuben sinned by having sexual relations with his father's concubine (Gn 35:22; 49:3–4). When his brothers wanted to kill Joseph, Reuben spoke up and suggested that they throw him into a pit instead. Reuben's intention was to release Joseph and let him return home (Gn 37:22, 29–30).

Many years later when Joseph, whom they did not recognize, asked his brothers to bring Benjamin to Egypt, Reuben assured his father of Benjamin's safety (Gn 42:36–38).

The tribe of Reuben settled east of the Jordan River, an area suited for raising flocks and herds (Nu 1:20–21; Jsh 13:15–23). In her song Deborah refers to the Reubenites' lack of help in the battle with Sisera (Jgs 5:15–16). A number of years later the Assyrians took the Reubenites away into captivity (1Ch 5:26). See 1:31, 129, 139, 399.

REUBENITES (ROO-ben-ights). Descendants of Reuben (Nu 26:7; Jsh 1:12).

REUEL (ROO-el; "God's friend").

1. One of Esau's sons and the ancestor of the Edomite clan (Gn 36:4, 10, 13, 17).
2. The father-in-law of Moses (Ex 2:18). *See also* JETHRO. See 1:59.

REVELATION (rev-uh-LAY-shuhn). Gk *apokalypsis*, a disclosure of something previously hidden. The way in which God makes Himself and His ways known to people. God reveals something of Himself to all people through nature, their consciences, and history. God reveals Himself and His will in a special way to particular people at particular times through visions, phenomena, dreams, angels, words, prophecies, and by appearing in human form (Gn 16:9; 18:9; 28:12–16; Ex 3:4; 19:18; Is 6). In particular, God reveals Himself through the Bible and Jesus Christ, the Word made flesh. See 1:xxxi–xxxii, 8–9; 2:156–64, 595.

REVELATION, BOOK OF. See 2:771–95.

REWARD. Something given in return for something done. Being paid is a reward for work (Lk 10:7; 1Tm 5:18). God's punishment is the reward for people's sinfulness (Lk 23:41; cf "recompense" in Rv 22:12). The Bible also speaks about the reward of grace. Although people do not deserve it, God graciously provides for their salvation through Christ Jesus. Those who believe in Jesus receive life and salvation (1Co 9:18; Col 3:24). This new life shows itself in fruits of faith, the way in which God crowns His work in the believer (Mt 6:4; Mk 9:41; Lk 6:23; 1Co 3:14). See 1:76, 507, 520; 2:43, 198, 287, 293.

REZIN (REE-zin). Last king of Damascus. Rezin ruled Syria from 735 to 732 BC. He aligned his country with Israel against Judah. Tiglath-Pileser, king of Assyria, besieged Damascus and when he finally captured it, killed Rezin and took his people into captivity (2Ki 15:37; 16:5, 9; Is 7:1–9; 8:6–8). See 1:715.

RHODA (RO-dah; "rose"). A young woman who worked in the home of Mary, John Mark's mother. When Peter was miraculously released from prison and went to Mary's home, Rhoda opened the door when he knocked on it (Ac 12:12–15).

RHODES (RODZ; "roses"). An island at the southwestern tip of Asia Minor that is famous for its huge statue of Helios (Ezk 27:15). Rhodes was a center for commerce, literature, and art. Paul stopped there once (Ac 21:1). See 2:388.

RIDDLE ("dark or hidden saying"). In the Bible a riddle is any saying in which the meaning is not at first clear (Jgs 14:12–19; Dn 8:23). Proverbs, musical meditations, oracles, parables, and hard questions are all riddles (Nu 12:8; 1Ki 10:1; 2Ch 9:1; Ps 49:4; Pr 1:6). See 1:485, 630; 2:328.

RIGHT HAND. A phrase for describing God's activity in carrying out His purposes (Ex 15:6; Ps 98:1). Jesus' place at the right hand of God shows Jesus' power (Ac 2:25; 7:55–56; Heb 1:3). See 1:521; 2:292–93, 381, 425.

RIGHTEOUS. That which is right (Mt 27:19; Php 1:7) or in accordance with the Law and ceremonies (Mk 2:17; Lk 5:32; Rm 5:7). The term is particularly used to describe people who are in a right relationship with God through faith (Gn 15:6; Rm 1:17). *See also* RIGHTEOUSNESS.

RIGHTEOUSNESS (RIGH-chuhs-ness; "the quality of rightness"). Hbr *tsadik*; *rib*; *tsedaqah*, "blamelessness, honesty, justice." Gk *dikaios*/*dikaiosune* in LXX. An attribute of God praised especially in the Psalms. The expression "in Your righteousness deliver me" (71:2; cf 5:8; 31:1; 89:16; 119:40; 143:11) describes the psalmist asking God to keep His promise of salvation (see "righteous acts" and "deeds of salvation" in 71:15). He is the source of righteousness (4:1). The background for the Gk root term has to do with law, punishment for violating the law, and the virtue of keeping the law or custom. The Gk verb often means negatively "to condemn." Use of the term is significantly different in the LXX, influenced by the OT. In the LXX it is used for religious right standing before God. In fact, the term becomes more positive; it even describes God's work of salvation and can translate Hbr *chesed*, "steadfast love" (e.g., Gn 19:19). Cf 2Macc 1:25; Ecclus 18:2; Wis 1:8; 12:13. There is a theme of righteous suffering in Wis. The legal aspect persists in Tob. See 1:574, 584–88, 669–71, 711–12; 2:32–33, 423–25, 428–29, 548.

Jesus is our righteousness, the One who puts us in a right relationship with God (Rm 1:16–17; 3:21–26; 1Co 1:30; 1Pt 2:24).

RIMMON (RIM-un; "thunderer"). An Assyrian storm god (2Ki 5:18). See 1:992.

RING. A piece of jewelry (Jas 2:2; Lk 15:22). When rings were engraved with the symbol of the owner, they became symbols of power and authority. They were used as seals and signets (Gn 41:42; Est 3:10, 12; 8:2, 8, 10; cf "signet" in Dn 6:17). See 1:974; 2:46.

RIVER. A flowing body of water, such as a stream, a channel, or a brook (Gn 2:10–14; Ps 119:136; Ezk 47:1–12; Am 6:14). The word *river* is also a picture word for a great deal of good or evil (Jb 20:17; Ps 36:8; 69:2; Is 43:2). *See also* EUPHRATES; NILE. See 1:127–28, 140, 210; 2:12, 233.

ROAD. A path, a well-traveled road, or a highway made by a ruler or by people (Nu 20:17; 21:22; Dt 19:3).

The Romans built an elaborate network of roads across their empire. The ones in Israel were used by traders, armies, and travelers. Some well-known roads were those extending from Jerusalem to Jericho and beyond, from Jerusalem to Joppa, from Damascus to Ptolemais, from Ptolemais to Egypt, and from Galilee to Judea. See 1:631; 2:376, 539.

ROCK. Translates two terms: Hbr *sela'*, "rock" or "cliff face"; Hbr *tsur*, "massive rock" or "boulder." As a name for God, appears five times in the Song of Moses (Dt 32:4, 15, 18, 30, 31). Psalms use the terms interchangeably for a place of refuge or hiding. The Lord is "the Rock of my salvation" (89:26). *See also* ZION. See 1:71, 218, 583.

ROD. A branch, stick, staff, or shoot. A shepherd's rod was a sturdy club that he used for guiding, defending, and counting his flock (Ps 23:4; Ezk 20:37; cf Lv 27:32).

A *rod* or *shoot* is a picture word for the messianic ruler (Is 11:1). *Rod* is also a picture word for power and great trouble (Jb 9:34; Ps 2:9). See 1:86–88, 368–69, 967; 2:8, 156.

ROE. *See* GAZELLE; ROEBUCK.

ROEBUCK. A small deer (Dt 14:5; 1Ki 4:23). *See also* GAZELLE.

ROMAN (RO-mahn).

1. A person who was born in Rome or had Roman citizenship. *See* CITIZEN 2. See 2:235, 379.
2. A Roman official (Jn 11:48; Ac 28:17).

ROMAN EMPIRE. *See* ROME.

ROMANS, LETTER OF PAUL TO THE. See 2:417–39.

ROME (ROM). The capital of the Roman Empire, situated on the Tiber River in Italy about 17 miles from the Mediterranean Sea. Rome was founded in 753 BC. From 753 to 509 BC, it was a monarchy; from 509 to 31 BC, a republic; and from 31 BC until its fall, an empire.

The Roman Empire extended over the whole Mediterranean world, providing a large network of roads, peace, trade, and a common government. This aided in the spread of the Gospel.

Under Augustus, the provinces of the empire were divided into senatorial provinces ruled by a proconsul (Ac 13:7; 18:12; 19:38) and imperial provinces ruled by a governor (Mt 27:2; Lk 2:2; Ac 23:24).

Under Roman rule, cities, reservoirs, aqueducts, roads, and public buildings were constructed in Israel. The Bible refers to four emperors: Augustus (Lk 2:1), Tiberius (Lk 3:1), Claudius (Ac 11:28), and Nero (Ac 25:11–12). See 1:777; 2:297–99, 378–79, 391, 499, 806–7, 810–14.

ROSE. Many authorities believe roses grew in Israel during Bible times. The identity of the flower mentioned in Sg 2:1 and Is 35:1, however, is unknown. See 1:254, 611; 2:123.

RUE (RU). A plant grown for its use in medicine and seasonings (Lk 11:42).

RUFUS (RU-fuhs; "red"). Son of Simon of Cyrene (Mk 15:21). The Rufus mentioned in Rm 16:13 may be the same person.

RUHAMAH (roo-HAH-mah). Hosea's daughter. Her name means "she has received mercy" (Hos 2:1; cf Rm 9:25; 1Pt 2:10). *See also* LO-RUHAMAH. See 1:855–56.

RUSH. *See* PAPYRUS; REED.

RUTH (ROOTH; may mean "friendship" or "refreshment"). A woman from Moab who married Mahlon, a son of Elimelech and Naomi. When both Ruth and Naomi's husbands died, Ruth decided to return to Judah with Naomi. She told Naomi: "Where you go I will go, and where you lodge I will lodge. Your people shall be my people, and your God my God" (Ru 1:16). Ruth married Boaz and became the mother of Obed, an ancestor of both David and Jesus (Ru; Mt 1:5). See 1:257–58.

RUTH, BOOK OF. See 1:253–69.

S

SABAOTH (SAB-ay-ahth; "hosts"). A Hebrew name for God that means Lord of hosts. *See* HOST 2.

SABBATH (SAB-ahth; "rest," "cessation"). The weekly day of rest corresponding to the seventh day upon which God rested after creation (Gn 2:3; Ex 20:11; 31:17). The first time the Sabbath is mentioned by name occurs at the time when a double amount of manna was given on the sixth day to the people of Israel in the Wilderness of Sin. When they told Moses what had happened, he said: "This is what the Lord has commanded: 'Tomorrow is a day of solemn rest, a holy Sabbath to the Lord'" (Ex 16:23). The command to keep the Sabbath holy was repeated on a number of occasions (Ex 20:8–11; Lv 19:3, 30; 23:3; Dt 5:12–15).

The people observed the Sabbath by stopping their work, by gathering together for worship, and by increasing their offerings (Ex 16:29; 20:10; 35:3; Nu 15:32–36; 28:9–10; Am 8:5). The penalty for not observing the Sabbath was death (Ex 31:15).

The Day of Atonement on the tenth day of the seventh month was also a Sabbath (Lv 23:32).

The Sabbath Day is a picture for the believer's entrance into God's rest fulfilled in Christ (Col 2:16; Heb 4). See 1:34, 71, 94–96, 581; 2:198–99, 281, 334–35.

SABBATH DAY'S JOURNEY. *See* MEASURES 1l.

SABBATICAL YEAR (sa-BAT-i-kuhl yeer). Every seven years the Jewish people observed the Sabbatical year. During this year the land rested, the poor received what grew, and people in debt were released from what they owed (Ex 23:10–11; Lv 25:2–7; Dt 15:1–18). *See also* JUBILEE.

SABEANS (sah-BEE-uhnz). Semitic people who lived in southwest Arabia. The Sabeans or people of Sheba ran caravans in the Middle East. The Bible describes them as murderous bandits and slave dealers (Jb 1:15; Jl 3:8). The queen of Sheba who visited Solomon was queen of the Sabeans (1Ki 10; 2Ch 9; Mt 12:42; Lk 11:31). See 1:497.

SACKCLOTH. Coarse cloth made out of goat's hair and woven into sacks (Gn 42:25). People wore sackcloth to mourn a death (Gn 37:34; 2Sm 3:31; 2Ki 6:30; Ne 9:1; Jb 16:15; Mt 11:21; Rv 11:3). See 1:905, 911.

SACRAMENT (SAK-rah-ment). A word the Church uses to describe a sacred act instituted by God where visible means are connected to His Word. In a sacrament, God offers, gives, and seals to the individual the forgiveness of sins earned by Christ. *See also* BAPTISM; LORD'S SUPPER. See 1:110, 548–49, 808–9; 2:207, 284, 460, 728–29.

SACRIFICE (SAK-ruh-fighs). An act of worship where a person presents an offering to God. Sacrifices were practiced from ancient times and expressed thankfulness to God (cf "offering" in Gn 4:3–4; 8:20–22). They were offered on many occasions, for example, on a pilgrimage, at a time of rejoicing, when making a treaty, before battle, and after God had appeared to an individual (Gn 31:54; 1Sm 1:3; 20:6; cf Gn 12:7; 1Sm 7:9).

Sacrifices were offered for various purposes. Among the main ones mentioned in the OT are the sin offering (Lv 4), the guilt offering (Lv 5:15–6:7; 14:12; Nu 6:12), the burnt offering (Lv 1; 6:8–13), the peace offering (Lv 7:11–34), the meal and drink offerings (Lv 6), and the red heifer offering (Nu 19). Offerings were sacrificed upon the altar morning and evening, at each Sabbath and new moon, and at the three leading festivals (Ex 29:38–42; Nu 28–29).

All sacrifices point to and are fulfilled in Christ, the Lamb of God sacrificed for the sins of the world (Heb 9:10–28). See 1:104, 109–11, 115–24, 960; 2:207, 253–54, 426, 660–61, 786.

SADDUCEES (SAD-yoo-seez). Name thought to derive from Hbr "righteous" or from the Zadokite family. One of the three leading Jewish religious parties at the time of Christ. Although a small group, they were influential. Unlike the Pharisees, the Sadducees believed only what was in the written law; they held to the Law of Moses and the Oral Law. They were opposed to the traditions of the scribes and Pharisees. They denied belief in the resurrection, angels, and spirits (Mk 12:18; Lk 20:27; Ac 23:8). They stressed moral freedom. They also did not long for a Messiah the way other Jewish groups did. They were the second largest religious group in Judea. Both John the Baptist and Jesus spoke against them (Mt 3:7–8; 16:6, 11–12). See 1:182, 812; 2:52, 99, 201, 247, 379.

SAINT. In the OT, translates two terms: Hbr *qedoshim*, those "set apart, holy," God's chosen people who serve Him; Hbr *chasidim*, those "loyal, devout, faithful."

1. Those faithful to God in the OT are called saints (2Ch 6:41). See 1:522, 606–9, 836.
2. People, such as priests, who were set apart for God's service (cf "holy" in Ps 106:16; 1Pt 2:5).
3. Members of the Jerusalem congregation (Ac 9:13; 1Co 16:1). See 2:481–82.
4. Those who believe in Christ (Gk *hagioi*; Rm 1:7; 1Co 1:2; 2Co 1:1). See 2:424, 485, 783.

SAKKUTH (SAK-uth). A false god worshiped by Israel (Am 5:26).

SALAMIS (SAL-ah-mis). A city on Cyprus that Paul visited on his first missionary journey (Ac 13:5). See 1:464; 2:388, 813.

SALEM (SAY-lem; "peace"). The city of which Melchizedek was king. It was probably Jerusalem (Gn 14:18; Ps 76:2; Heb 7:1–2). See 2:657, 668.

SALMON (SAL-muhn). A genealogical father of Boaz (Ru 4:21; Mt 1:4; Lk 3:32). See 1:255.

SALOME (sah-LO-mi; "peaceful").

1. The wife of Zebedee and mother of James and John (Mk 15:40). Salome was among the women who witnessed the crucifixion of Jesus (Mt 27:56). Later she purchased spices to anoint His body (Mk 16:1). See 2:169, 320.
2. The daughter of Herodias. Salome's dancing pleased Herod so much that he granted her request for the head of John the Baptist (Mt 14:6; Mk 6:22).

SALT. Salt was used as a seasoning and preservative and for sacrifices (Lv 2:13; Nu 18:19; Jb 6:6; Mt 5:13).

Lot's wife was turned to salt (Gn 19:26). The site of Shechem was sown with salt to keep it from producing vegetation (Jgs 9:45; Ezk 47:11). The disciples of Christ are called the salt of the earth (Mt 5:13; Mk 9:50; Lk 14:34). See 2:74, 221, 282.

SALT SEA. The name given to the Dead Sea because of its high salt content. Fed by the Jordan River, the Salt Sea is 46 by 9½ miles long, 1,292 feet below sea level, and 1,300 feet deep. Since there is no outlet, the water is bitter and buoyant (Gn 14:3; Nu 34:3; Jsh 15:2). It is called by various names: Sea of Arabah (Jsh 3:16; 12:3), Sea (Ezk 47:8), and eastern sea (Ezk 47:18; Jl 2:20; Zec 14:8). See 1:27, 128, 807, 814; 2:263, 723.

SALVATION (sal-VAY-shuhn). Hbr *yeshu'ah*, "deliverance." Deliverance from any type of evil, both physical and spiritual (Ex 14:13, 30; Jb 22:29; cf Is 49:25). Sometimes translated as "victory" because of military imagery. Spiritual deliverance or salvation includes rescue from sin (Mt 1:21; Ac 4:12; Heb 2:10), death (Rm 6:9; 8:2; 1Co 15:54–57), evil (Gal 1:4; 2Tm 4:18), and the power of darkness (Col 1:13). It is a gift of God's grace through faith in Christ (Ac 16:31; Rm 5:1) and marks the entrance into spiritual, eternal life (cf Jn 5:24; Col 3:9–10). See 1:15, 32–33, 70–71, 563, 717, 732–34; 2:167, 253–54, 788–89.

SALVE. *See* OINTMENT.

SAMARIA (sah-MAIR-i-ah; "watch-mountain").

1. The capital city of Israel's Northern Kingdom. It was built by Omri on a tableland five and a half miles northwest of Shechem. Samaria is repeatedly rebuked for its luxury and evil ways (1Ki 17–19; 21; 2Ki 3:3–9; Is 7:9; Jer 31:5; Ezk 23:33; Hos 8:5–6; Am 3:1–12). Today it is called Sebastia. See 1:324, 344–45.
2. The entire area occupied by the Northern Kingdom of Israel, or the 10 tribes (1Ki 13:32). See 1:373, 755, 923–24.
3. The region where the Samaritans lived after they returned from captivity. *See also* SAMARITANS. See 2:195, 330, 389, 799–800.

SAMARIA, MOUNTAINS OF. *See* EPHRAIM, MOUNT.

SAMARITANS (sah-MAIR-uh-tuhns). In 2Ki 17:29 a Samaritan refers to a person belonging to the 10 tribes, or the old Northern Kingdom of Israel. Later

Samaritans descended from Israelites left behind after Samaria's destruction (722 BC) and included foreigners imported by Assyrian kings. They inhabited the area between Judea and Galilee (2Ki 17:24–34). Since all these people intermingled, they were despised by their Jewish neighbors to the south (Ne 4:1–3; Mt 10:5; Jn 4:9–26; 8:48).

Their observance of Judaism was regarded as corrupted. They accepted only the Five Books of Moses as authoritative, worshiped on Mount Gerizim, and rejected Jerusalem as the proper place of worship. See 1:353, 386, 971; 2:280, 290, 334, 375, 800, 806.

SAMOS (SAY-mahs; "height"). A mountainous island off the coast of Lydia. Paul stopped at Samos on his third missionary journey (Ac 20:15). See 1:519.

SAMOTHRACE (SAM-o-thrays). An island between Troas and Neapolis where Paul and his party spent the night on their voyage to Macedonia (Ac 16:11).

SAMSON (SAM-s'n; "sunlike"). A judge of Israel for 20 years. He was the son of Minoah from the tribe of Dan and a Nazirite from birth. Samson married a Philistine woman named Timnath. But later, when Timnath's father gave her to another, Samson burned the Philistine fields in revenge. Then the Philistines tried to capture him, but Samson broke the ropes binding him and, taking a donkey's jawbone, killed 1,000 Philistine men. Samson also performed great feats of strength. On one occasion he carried the heavy gates and two posts of the city of Gaza to the top of the hill that is before Hebron.

Samson fell in love with a Philistine woman named Delilah. She tricked him into telling her the source of his strength and then betrayed him into the hands of her countrymen. They cut off Samson's hair, blinded him, and put him to work grinding in the mill at the prison of Gaza.

On one occasion when the Philistines were making public sacrifice to their god Dagon, they called for Samson to make sport of him. Since his hair was beginning to grow, Samson was again fulfilling his Nazirite vow. He prayed to God, asking Him for strength one more time. Then Samson pushed against the pillars that supported the roof and brought the whole temple to Dagon down, killing himself and about 3,000 Philistines who were present (Jgs 13–16; Heb 11:32). See 1:239, 243, 245–46, 250.

SAMUEL (SAM-yoo-uhl; "God has heard"). Samuel is often referred to as the last of the judges and the first of the prophets after Moses (1Sm 3:20; 7:6; Ac 3:24). He was a Levite, the son of Elkanah and Hannah (1Sm 1:19–20). When he was still young, Samuel's mother brought him to Eli the priest, who educated Samuel and took care of him (1Sm 3).

Samuel anointed both Saul and David as kings of Israel (1Sm 10; 16:13). When Samuel died, all Israel mourned for him; the people buried him in Ramah, his home city (1Sm 25:1). See 1:277–78.

SAMUEL, FIRST AND SECOND BOOK OF. See 1:271–319.

SANBALLAT (san-BAL-uht; "Sin [the moon god] has given life"). A Persian officer who tried to defeat Nehemiah's plans for rebuilding the walls of Jerusalem (Ne 2:10; 4:1–9; 6:1–14; 13:28). See 1:435.

SANCTIFICATION (sangk-tuh-fi-KAY-shuhn). The Hbr word for sanctification means "separation from the world and that which is sinful" and "consecration to a sacred purpose by the Lord" (Ex 31:13; cf "consecrate" in 1Ch 15:14; 2Ch 5:11; 29:15).

In the wide sense the Gk word for sanctification includes the entire process of God's grace whereby spiritually dead people, through the work of the Holy Spirit in the Word and Sacrament, are reborn to spiritual life and made perfect in life eternal (Ac 26:18; Eph 5:26; 2Th 2:13; Heb 10:14).

In the narrower sense, sanctification is the spiritual growth, worked by God the Holy Spirit, that follows after a person has come to faith in Christ; it does not include justification itself (Rm 6:15–23; Gal 5:22–23; Php 2:13; 2Pt 3:18). See 1:78, 279, 414, 809; 2:204–5, 429, 570–71, 661.

SANCTUARY (SANGK-tyoo-air-ee). A holy place set aside for the worship of God. The sanctuary was the earthly place where God chose to dwell among His people. The Promised Land, the tabernacle, the whole temple, and particularly the Most Holy Place in the tabernacle and temple are called sanctuaries (Ex 15:17; Lv 4:6; 1Ki 6:16; 2Ch 20:8). Judah is also God's sanctuary (Ps 114:2).

The author of Heb explains that the earthly sanctuary was only a type of the true sanctuary—access to God through Christ, the believer's High Priest (Heb 8:1–5; 9:1–8). See 1:73, 112–13, 359, 579–80; 2:159.

SANDAL. Leather sandals usually fastened to the foot with straps known as thongs (Ex 3:5; Jsh 5:15; Is 20:2). Occasionally the Bible uses the word *shoe* rather than sandal (Ps 60:8; 108:9; Ezk 24:17, 23; Lk 15:22; Eph 6:15). See 1:206; 2:238, 258–59, 341.

SANHEDRIN (SAN-hi-drin; "sitting in council"). *See* COUNCIL 2. See 2:321, 390.

SAPPHIRA (sa-FIGH-rah; "lapis lazuli" gemstone). The wife of Ananias. Within a period of a few hours, both she and her husband fell dead at Peter's feet because they had lied (Ac 5:7–10). See 2:375.

SARAH (SAIR-ah; "princess").

1. The wife of Abraham and mother of Isaac (Gn 11:29; 21:2–3). Her given name was Sarai, but God changed it to Sarah (Gn 17:15–16). When Sarah's maid, Hagar, became pregnant with Abraham's child, she began to think she was better than Sarah. Sarah, in turn, treated Hagar cruelly and sent her away (Gn 16:5–16; 21:9–21).
   When Sarah was 90, God kept His promise to her and Abraham and blessed them with a son, Isaac. Sarah lived 127 years. After she died, Abraham buried her at Machpelah (Gn 23). The writer of Heb praises Sarah for her great faith (Heb 11:11). *See also* ABRAHAM. See 1:23, 25, 27; 2:503, 507.
2. A young woman who, after losing several husbands, married Tobias. See 2:42–45.

SARAI. *See* SARAH.

SARDIS (SAHR-dis). One of the seven churches to which Rv is addressed (Rv 1:11; 3:1–6). Sardis was a city of western Asia Minor located about 50 miles east of Smyrna. It was known for its manufacture of textiles, gold jewelry, and minted coins. Sardis was also a patron of the mystery cults. See 2:783.

SARGON II (SAHR-gahn). One of the kings of Assyria. He was born in 771 BC and died in 705 BC. In 721 BC, he took over the throne from his brother Shalmaneser V and completed the conquest of Samaria begun by Shalmaneser (2Ki 17:5; Is 20:1).
Sennacherib, Sargon's son, succeeded Sargon to the throne. See 1:921.

SATAN (SAY-tahn; "adversary"). The chief of the fallen angels, beings of great power (Lk 11:18; cf Mt 8:28–29; 9:34). Satan is the enemy of God, humanity, and all that is good (Jb 1:6, 12; 2:1; Zec 3:1).
Satan is named and described in other ways. He is called the devil (Mt 13:39; 25:41; 1Pt 5:8), a murderer and liar (Jn 8:44), Abaddon, or Apollyon, the angel of the bottomless pit (Rv 9:11), Beelzebul (Mt 12:27), Belial (2Co 6:15), the dragon (Rv 12), the evil, or wicked, one (Eph 6:16; 1Jn 2:13), the ruler of this world (Jn 12:31), the prince of power of the air (Eph 2:2), and a serpent (Rv 12:9). See 1:22–23, 367; 2:165–68, 196–97, 709–10, 766, 772–73, 781.

SATRAP (SAY-trap). An official person in the Persian Empire who was sent by the Persian king to rule several small provinces that had a combined government. These provinces were called satrapies, and the satrap had complete civil and military control over them (Ezr 8:36; Est 3:12; 8:9; Dn 3:3). See 1:465, 999.

SAVE. Hbr *palath* has sense of "escape." Hbr *yasha'*; *yeshu'ah*, "deliverance." Sometimes translated as "victory" because of military imagery. LXX uses forms of Gk *sozo*/*soteria*. God defeated Pharaoh and his army during the exodus, and subsequently conquered all enemies that would separate His people from Him. God's righteousness is victorious over wickedness, and thus salvation comes to His people solely because of Him. Most references describe the righteous being delivered from injustice or suffering. Salvation comes also through God's wisdom (Wis 9:18; 10:4). *See also* DELIVER.

SAVIOR. Hbr *moshia'*; Gk *soter*. In the OT, limited in use but preferred by Isaiah. In the Apocrypha, most common in 3Macc. The title becomes common for Jesus in the NT Epistles.

SAUL (SAWL; "asked").

1. The first king of Israel. Saul was the son of Kish and came from the tribe of Benjamin (1Sm 8–9). Samuel anointed him to be king of Israel, and then later, after Samuel had brought all the tribes of Israel together, the people chose Saul by lot to be their king (1Sm 9:27; 10:1–13, 17–27). Under Saul's leadership, the Israelites defeated the Ammonites, Philistines, Moabites, Zobah, and Amalekites (1Sm 11–14).
   When Saul disobeyed by offering the burnt offering himself rather than waiting for Samuel to do it, Samuel rejected him as the one from whom the kingdom of Israel would be established (1Sm 13:1–14). As Saul's power declined and David's popularity grew, Saul became jealous of David (1Sm 16–31). In a battle between the Israelites and Philistines, Saul was seriously wounded and killed himself by falling on his own sword (1Sm 31). See 1:278–80, 289–94, 311–14, 372; 2:802.

2. Paul's name was changed from Saul after the Lord called him to preach to the Gentiles. See 2:367, 375–77, 810–11.

SAVIOR (SAYV-yur).
1. One who saves from danger or evil (2Ki 13:5).
2. In Ps 106:21, God is referred to as Israel's Savior. Jesus is called our Savior (Lk 2:11; Jn 4:42; 1Tm 1:1; 2Pt 1:1). *See also* JESUS CHRIST; SALVATION. See 1:23, 473, 509; 2:209–10, 342, 711.

SAW. *See* TRADE.

SCAB. *See* DISEASE.

SCALES. *See* DISEASE; WEIGHT.

SCAPEGOAT. *See* AZAZEL.

SCHISM (SIZ'm). *See* HERESY. See 1:988; 2:824.

SCOURGING (SKURJ-ing). Severe punishment with a whip of cords or thongs (Mt 27:26; Mk 15:15; cf Mt 23:34; Jn 19:1; Heb 11:36). A person could be whipped no more than 40 times (2Co 11:24). It was unlawful to scourge a Roman citizen (Ac 22:24–25). See 1:941; 2:191, 222.

SCRIBE. A person who copied records, books, and the like before printing presses were invented. In Jewish times scribes served as recorders, secretaries, and clerks (1Ch 24:6; 27:32).

After the exile, scribes faithfully copied the Scriptures to preserve them for future generations. They became interpreters of the Law and powerful leaders in Israel (Ezr 7:6, 11; Ne 8:1–13; 13:13; Mt 16:21; 26:3; Ac 4:5). The title was associated with the priest Ezra in the fifth century (Ezr 7:11–12), describing him as a scholar of the Law of Moses. The rise of the scribes corresponded with increased interest in the Law, its interpretation, and application to Israelite life after the exile. See 1:191, 382, 433, 712; 2:189, 206, 412, 415, 557, 807.

SCRIPTURE. Something that is written down. The OT and NT of the Bible are called Scripture. See 1:xxv–xxviii, xliii–xliv; 2:6–10, 817.

SCROLL. A book made of sheets of skins, papyrus, or parchment sewn together to make a strip about 11 inches wide and several feet long. These sheets were rolled on sticks to make a book, a roll, or a scroll (Is 34:4; Jer 36; Ezk 3:1–3; Rv 5; 10:1–10). See 1:100, 463, 473, 701–2, 724, 993; 2:9, 501.

SCROLLS, DEAD SEA. Very old manuscripts first found in AD 1947 in caves around the Dead Sea. These manuscripts contained parts of the OT, commentaries, and other writings. See 2:5, 807, 827–28.

SCURVY. *See* DISEASE.

SEA. A large, deep body of water (Gn 1:26; Ex 10:19; Dt 30:13; Jb 12:8). *See also* GALILEE, SEA OF; MEDITERRANEAN SEA; MEROM; RED SEA; SALT SEA. See 1:27, 81, 88–89, 807; 2:42, 232–33, 809.

SEAL. A stamp or a ring with a raised design on it that was used to make an impression on something. People in authority used seals to secure or authenticate various items (Jb 38:14). At the request of some Pharisees, Pilate sealed Jesus' tomb so that His disciples could not break into it and take His body without someone knowing about it (Mt 27:66). See 1:210, 505, 754, 878; 2:254, 783.

SECOND COMING OF CHRIST. *See* ADVENT OF CHRIST 3; ESCHATOLOGY; PAROUSIA.

SECOND QUARTER. A suburb of Jerusalem (2Ki 22:14; 2Ch 34:22).

SECT (SEKT). A religious party that has its own set of beliefs. The Pharisees (cf Ac 15:5) and the Sadducees (cf Ac 5:17) were two sects of Judaism in Jesus' day. Some of the people in early NT times referred to Christians as a sect of the Nazarenes (Ac 24:5, 14). See 2:9, 322, 724, 807.

SEEK. Translates two OT terms: Hbr *baqash*, "look for"; *darash*, "care about, examine, inquire." Gk *zeteo*. The Lord is sought in three ways: (1) through calling on His name in prayer, (2) by consulting Him through Urim and Thummim administered by the high priest, and (3) through the study of His Word. A visit to the tabernacle or temple is frequently implied. Ecclus encourages seeking after wisdom. Unbelievers do not seek God. Believers seek Him in an attitude of repentance, not selfishness. *See also* CALL. See 1:175, 210, 357, 581, 965; 2:251, 287, 291.

SEER (SEE-ur). *See* PROPHET. See 1:190–99, 274, 703–5.

SELAH (SEE-lah; "may mean lift up"). This word is often found in the Psalms (Ps 9:16) as well as in Hab 3:3, 9, 13. The meaning of the word is uncertain, though it may be an instruction for singers or musicians. See 1:613, 951.

SELEUCIDS. Descendants and successive rulers from Seleucus I Nicator, who ruled Syria and Mesopotamia. See 1:832–25; 2:4, 13, 51, 79–80, 233.

SELEUCIA (si-LYOO-shi-ah). A seaport of Syrian Antioch about 16 miles west of Antioch. It was founded by Seleucus Nicator. Paul and Barnabas sailed from Seleucia on their first missionary journey (Ac 13:4). See 2:388.

SENATE. *See* COUNCIL 2. See 2:222.

SENNACHERIB (suh-NAK-ur-ib; "Sin, the moon god, has increased brothers"). The son of Sargon II and the king who ruled Assyria from 704 to 681 BC. After taking over the throne, Sennacherib dealt with revolts throughout his empire and extended the conquered territories of Assyria as far as the Mediterranean. During Hezekiah's reign, he invaded Judah. The Lord, however, saved Jerusalem by sending His angel to strike down the Assyrian army, forcing Sennacherib to return home (2Ki 18–19; Is 36–37). In his annals Sennacherib describes his victories in Judah. See 1:347, 389, 727, 935; 2:803.

SEORIM (si-O-rim). The head of the fourth division of priests (1Ch 24:8).

SEPHARVAIM (sef-ahr-VAY-im). A place near Riblah. The Assyrians brought people from Sepharvaim to colonize Samaria (2Ki 17:24–34; 18:34; 19:13; Is 37:13).

SEPTUAGINT (SEP-tyoo-ah-jint). The Gk translation of the OT, prepared at Alexandria, Egypt, in the third century BC. The abbreviation for this translation is LXX, which means 70. See 1:623, 763, 831–32; 2:829.

SERAIAH (si-RAY-yah; "Yahweh is ruler").
1. One of the men sent to arrest Jeremiah and Baruch (Jer 36:26).
2. A prince who was taken captive to Babylon when Jerusalem fell (Jer 51:59–64).

SERAPHIM (SER-ah-fim). An order of angels. Isaiah saw seraphim standing around God's throne (Is 6:2–7). See 2:492–93.

SERGIUS PAULUS (SUR-ji-uhs PAWL-uhls). The Roman proconsul of Cyprus, a senatorial province in Paul's time (Ac 13:7–12). See 2:811.

SERPENT. A snake, a creature that creeps on its belly (Gn 3:14). A number of serpents are mentioned in the Bible, for instance, the asp or perhaps cobra (Dt 32:33), the adder (Ps 58:4; 91:13), and the viper (Gn 49:17; Jb 20:16).

Serpents are a symbol of evil, great harmfulness, and poison (Gn 49:17; Ps 58:4; Pr 23:32; Mt 23:33). They are described as subtle and wise (Gn 3:1; Mt 10:16). A serpent deceived Eve (Gn 3). The bronze serpent Moses attached to the top of a pole when the children of Israel were in the wilderness was a type of Christ (Nu 21:4–9; Jn 3:14). When an Israelite who had been bitten by a real snake looked at the bronze serpent, he or she was healed. See 1:22, 24, 44–47, 86, 139, 514; 2:130, 781–82.

SERUG (SEE-rug). Father of Nahor and ancestor of Abraham (Gn 11:20, 23; 1Ch 1:26; Lk 3:35).

SERVANT. A general term used of both slaves and persons who worked for wages. The Israelites acquired slaves through purchase and war (Lv 25:44–45; Nu 31:25–47). When slaves had children, their children also were slaves (Gn 14:14; Ec 2:7). Israelites became slaves through poverty, theft, and birth (Ex 21:1–11; 22:3; Lv 25:39, 47; 2Ki 4:1). Laws in the OT protected servants (Ex 20:10; Lv 25:55). Often they were treated as members of the household (Gn 24; 30; 32:16; 1Sm 9:5, 8). See 1:22–23, 27, 220–21.

In NT times it was common practice for people to have slaves and servants (Mk 1:20; 14:66; Jn 18:10–18; Ac 12:13–15). Jesus was kind to servants (Mt 8:5–13), often referring to them in His parables (Mt 18:23–35; 24:45–51; Mk 13:34–37; Lk 20:9–16).

The NT stresses that faith in Christ removes the barrier between master and servant (Gal 3:28; Phm). See 2:221–22, 284, 376, 636–38.

SERVANT OF THE LORD, OF CHRIST, OF THE CHURCH. A title, more than a description of someone's function. Based on Nu 12:7–8, where God speaks of Moses' office.
1. Any agent of the Lord, such as Abraham, Moses, and the prophets (Ex 4:10; Ps 105:42; Zec 1:6). Chiefly, however, the term is used as a title for those who serve Christ (Rm 1:1; 2Co 11:23; Col 4:12; Ti 1:1; 2Pt 1:1; Rv 1:1). Most significantly, the title belongs to the Messiah in the Servant Songs in Is (Is 42:1–9; 49:1–13; 50:4–11; 52:13–53:12), and Jesus fulfilled this role through His suffering and death (Mt 12:18; cf Lk 22:37). See 1:189, 213, 299, 358, 732–33, 902; 2:200, 381–83, 677.
2. Ministers in the Church (Col 4:7; cf 1Th 3:2). See 2:303, 432, 491.

SERVANT, SUFFERING. *See* SERVANT OF THE LORD.

SERVICE. Gk *diakonia*; could refer to specific ministry in the Church or to Christian service in general. *See also* SERVANT. See 1:144, 443; 2:287, 436, 607, 687.

SET APART. *See* HOLY. See 1:95, 136, 636; 2:616.

SETH (SETH). The third son of Adam and Eve (Gn 4:25–26; 5:3–8; 1Ch 1:1; Lk 3:38). See 1:24, 26, 32.

SEVEN. Prominent in biblical order and design (such as the sevenfold lampstand). The most obvious association between the number seven and God's design is with the heavenly lights in the seven sunrises of the week (Gn 2:2–3; Ex 20:8–11), the moon's progress around the earth in c 28 days (7 × 4; Israel had a lunar calendar, Ex 12:2), and the seven visible "lights" in the sky (sun, moon, Mercury, Venus, Mars, Jupiter, and Saturn; cf Rv 1:20). In this way, seven has strong association with heaven, divine illumination, and the things of God. *See also* JUBILEE; NUMBERS; SABBATH. See 1:94, 107, 889, 989; 2:389–90, 670, 776, 783.

SEVENTY. *See* SEVEN.

SEVENTY-TWO, THE. Disciples sent on a special mission by Jesus (Lk 10). See 2:280, 296.

SHABBETHAI (SHAB-i-thigh; "of the Sabbath"). A Levite during Ezra's time who favored the position that the Israelites should divorce their foreign wives. Shabbethai also played a chief role in rebuilding the temple and reading the law (Ne 8:7).

SHADRACH (SHAY-drak). The Babylonian name given to Hananiah, one of Daniel's three friends (Dn 1:7). Shadrach was thrown into the fiery furnace for refusing to worship the statue that King Nebuchadnezzar had set up (Dn 3). See 1:823.

SHADES ("silent ones"). The dead in Sheol (Is 14:9; 26:14).

SHALLECHETH (SHAL-i-keth). The west gate of the temple (1Ch 26:16).

SHALLUM (SHAL-uhm; "recompense").

1. The 15th king of Israel. After killing Zechariah, Shallum ruled for one month and then was killed by Menahem (2Ki 15:10–15). See 1:330, 346, 373.
2. The son of Zadok, a high priest, and an ancestor of Ezra (1Ch 6:12–13; Ezr 7:2). In 1Ch 9:11 and Ne 11:11 he is referred to as Meshullam.
3. Husband of the prophetess Hulda (2Ki 22:14; 2Ch 34:22). He was probably Jeremiah's uncle (Jer 32:7).
4. Another name for Jehoahaz II, the son of Josiah. He was king of Judah (1Ch 3:15; Jer 22:11).
5. A ruler of half of Jerusalem who, with his daughters, helped repair the walls of Jerusalem (Ne 3:12).

SHALMAN (SHAL-muhn). *See* SHALMANESER 2.

SHALMANESER (shal-muhn-EE-zur). The title of a number of Assyrian kings.

1. Shalmaneser III, the first Assyrian king to come into conflict with the Israelites, ruled Assyria from 858 to 824 BC. He conquered the Hittites as far as the Mediterranean. The Syrian league was formed to stop him in the west. Among others, Ben-hadad of Damascus and Ahab of Israel opposed him. Nevertheless, Shalmaneser defeated Hazael, Ben-hadad's successor, and made Israel pay tribute. See 1:325.
2. Shalmaneser V was the king of Assyria from 726 to 722 BC. He besieged Samaria. The city likely fell to him shortly before his death, or it may have fallen to his successor, Sargon. After the fall of Samaria, the 10 northern tribes were carried into captivity (2Ki 17:3; 18:9). In Hos 10:14, Shalmaneser is referred to as Shalman. See 2:15, 39.

SHAMGAR (SHAM-gahr). The son of Anath. Over a period of time he killed 600 Philistines with an oxgoad, preparing the way for the deliverance of Israel by Deborah and Barak (Jgs 3:31). See 1:230, 234, 237.

SHAMMAI, SCHOOL OF. Disciples of Rabbi Shammai (c 50 BC–AD 30), founder of a school of Jewish thought. Strongly nationalistic and opposed to Gentile rule. See 1:665, 812.

SHAMMUA (sha-MYOO-ah; "one heard").

1. A Reubenite spy (Nu 13:4).
2. A son of David and Bathsheba (2Sm 5:14; 1Ch 14:4). In 1Ch 3:5 he is referred to as Shimea.

SHAPHAN (SHAY-fan; "rock badger"). A scribe and secretary during Josiah's reign. When the book of the Law was found, Shaphan first read it privately and then took it to King Josiah (2Ki 22:8–10). After hearing its contents, Josiah sent Shaphan, along with some others, to ask Huldah the prophetess what it meant (2Ki 22:14–20). See 1:753–54.

SHAPHAT (SHAY-fat; "he has judged"). The father of the prophet Elisha (1Ki 19:16; 2Ki 3:11).

SHARE. *See* FELLOWSHIP; TAKING PART.

SHAREZER (shah-REE-zur; "protect king"). The son and murderer of Sennacherib, the Assyrian king (2Ki 19:37; Is 37:38). See 1:983.

SHARON (SHAIR-uhn; "plain"). A coastal plain between Joppa and Carmel. It was about 50 miles long and 6–12 miles wide (1Ch 27:29; Is 33:9; 35:2; Ac 9:35). See 2:376.

SHAVEH, VALLEY OF (SHAY-ve). A place, probably near Jerusalem, where Melchizedek met Abraham (Gn 14:17).

SHAVSHA (SHAV-shah). One of David and Solomon's scribes (1Ch 18:16). He is probably the same person as the secretary Seraiah, the secretary Sheva, and the secretary Shisha (2Sm 8:17; 20:25; 1Ki 4:3).

SHEALTIEL (shi-AL-ti-el; "I have asked God"). A son of Jeconiah, or Jehoiachin, or possibly of Neri (1Ch 3:17; Mt 1:12; Lk 3:27). Shealtiel was probably the legitimate successor of Jehoiachin, and when Shealtiel died, the right to the throne passed to Zerubbabel (Ezr 3:2; 1Ch 3:17–19).

SHEAR-JASHUB (SHEE-ahr-JAH-shub; "remnant shall return"). A symbolical name Isaiah gave to his son (Is 7:3). See 1:715, 724, 736.

SHEBNA, SHEBNAH (SHEB-nah). King Hezekiah's secretary and the steward of his house. Isaiah rebuked him (2Ki 18:18–26, 37; 19:2; Is 22:15–25; 36:3, 11, 22; 37:2). See 1:726.

SHECHEM (SHEH-chem; "shoulder").

1. A town in the hill country of Ephraim in the pass between Mount Ebal and Mount Gerizim. Shechem was a Levitical city of refuge (Gn 12:6; 35:4; Jsh 20:7; Jgs 9:7; Ac 7:16).

   Shechem was the first place Abraham camped after leaving Haran. Although the Canaanites were in the land at that time, the Lord appeared to Abraham and told him He would give the land to Abraham's descendants (Gn 12:6–7). Later, Jacob bought ground at Shechem, and Joseph was eventually buried there (Gn 33:18–20; Jsh 24:32).
2. Today it is the site of Tell Balatah, located near Neapolis and Nablus. See 1:29–30, 53–55, 199–200, 216, 324, 345; 2:800–801.

SHEEP. Sheep were domesticated early (Gn 4:2). The patriarchs and their descendants herded flocks of these animals (Gn 12:16; Ex 10:9; 1Ch 27:30–31). Sheep were valuable property, since they were a source of food, clothing, and tribute (Lv 13:47; 1Sm 14:32; 2Ki 3:4). They were also used as sacrifices in worship (Ex 20:24; Lv 9:3). The sheep's horns were used for trumpets and as containers for liquids (Jsh 6:4; 1Sm 16:1). Sheepshearing time was an occasion for great festivity (1Sm 25:4, 11, 36).

Sheep and shepherds are often used in a figurative way in the Bible (2Ch 18:16; Ps 23; 119:176; Mt 9:36; Jn 10). See 1:141, 150, 766, 882; 2:201, 248, 259, 709.

SHEEPFOLD. An enclosure where sheep were kept, especially at night, for protection and when they were to be sheared (Nu 32:16; Jgs 5:16; 1Sm 24:3; Ps 78:70; Jn 10:1). See 1:744.

SHEEP GATE. One of the gates of Jerusalem (Ne 3:1, 32; 12:39). See 2:809.

SHEKEL (SHEK-uhl; "weight").

1. A weight used for metals. It weighed about half an ounce (Ex 30:13; 2Sm 14:26).
2. A coin (Mt 17:27). See 1:38, 317.

SHEM (SHEM). One of Noah's sons (Gn 5:32; 10:1; Lk 3:36). Shem received a blessing from God: from his line of descent would come the chosen people (Gn 9:21–27). Shem is the ancestor of the Hebrews, the Aramaeans, and the Arabs. See 1:26, 36, 301.

SHEMA (shi-MAH). A summary of the Ten Commandments, so named for the opening Hbr word, "Hear" (Dt 6:4). See 1:175.

SHEMAIAH (shi-MAY-yah; "Yahweh has heard").

1. One of God's prophets. Shemaiah told Rehoboam, king of Judah, not to attempt regaining control of the 10 northern tribes of Israel, which had revolted (1Ki 12:22; 2Ch 11:2; 12:5, 7, 15). See 1:324, 372.
2. The father of the prophet Uriah (Jer 26:20).
3. A false prophet among the exiles in Babylon who opposed Jeremiah (Jer 29:24–32).
4. One of the men Ezra sent to Iddo to ask for Levites and temple ministers (Ezr 8:16).

SHEMER (SHEE-mur; "guardian"). A person who owned a hill in Samaria that Omri, king of Israel, bought (1Ki 16:24).

SHEMINITH (SHEM-i-nith; "eighth"). A musical term. It may refer to an octave, a scale, or the strings of an instrument (1Ch 15:21; titles of Ps 6; 12). See 1:612.

SHEMUEL (shi-MYOO-uhl; "heard of God"). The Hbr version of the name Samuel. Various people in the OT are named Shemuel, among them, the prophet Samuel (1Ch 6:33; 7:2). *See also* SAMUEL.

SHENAZZAR (shi-NAZ-ur; "Sin [the moon god] protect"). A son of Jehoiachin (Jeconiah), who was likely born in captivity (1Ch 3:18). See 1:452.

SHEOL (SHEE-ol).

1. The OT name for the place where people go when they have died. It is translated in a number of ways, for instance, as grave and as the realm of the dead, a place full of darkness where the dead are (Dt 32:22; Jb 7:9; 17:16; 11:8; Ps 89:48; Is 38:10). See 1:821, 911; 2:32.
2. The people who are in Sheol (Is 14:9). *See also* ESCHATOLOGY; ETERNAL LIFE; HADES; HELL.

SHEPHATIAH (shef-ah-TIGH-ah; "Yahweh has judged").

1. One of David's sons (2Sm 3:4; 1Ch 3:3).
2. A prince who was among those who advised Zedekiah to put the prophet Jeremiah to death (Jer 38).

SHEPHELAH, THE (shi-FEE-lah; "low"). The land between the central highlands of Israel and the Mediterranean plain (1Ki 10:27; 1Ch 27:28; 2Ch 1:15; 9:27; 26:10; Jer 17:26; 32:44; Ob 19). See 1:921; 2:79.

SHEPHERD. A person who makes his living by looking after sheep. The shepherd was an important person in Bible times (Gn 29:6–7; 30:29–30; Ex 2:16–22). He led his sheep to pasture and water; he looked after them and protected them from danger (Gn 29:7; Ex 2:16; 1Sm 17:34; Ps 23; Jn 10:1–15). When a sheep was lost, the shepherd went out to search for it (Ps 119:176; Lk 15:1–7). At night, he brought the sheep home, checking to see they were all there by counting them as they passed under his shepherd's rod or staff (Lv 27:32; Ezk 20:37).

Shepherding was often dangerous work (Gn 31:40; 1Sm 17:34; Jn 10:11–13). For this reason a shepherd equipped himself with a sheepskin mantle, a crook, and a pouch in which he carried his slingshot, his food, and the oil for medicating scratches, cuts, and bruises on his sheep. Frequently, he was assisted in his work by a dog (Jb 30:1). The chief shepherd, overshepherd, or overseer was the person in charge of a number of shepherds and the flocks for which they cared (1Ch 27:30–31).

The word *shepherd* is also used figuratively in the Bible. God, a king, ministers, and Christ are all referred to as shepherds (Is 44:28; 56:11; Jer 23:4; 31:10; Jn 10:14; Heb 13:20; cf Ac 20:28–30). See 1:39, 146, 411, 575, 590, 687–88, 806–7, 880, 923–25; 2:201, 248, 277, 328–30, 335, 661, 709, 724.

SHEREBIAH (sher-i-BIGH-ah). A Levite who joined Ezra at Ahava on his return to Jerusalem. Ezra entrusted him with the gifts for the temple (Ezr 8:18, 24). Later, Sherebiah sealed the covenant with Nehemiah (Ne 8:7; 9:4–5; 10:12; 12:8, 24).

SHESHBAZZAR (shesh-BAZ-ur). A prince of Judah at the time Cyrus made the decree allowing the Jews to return to Jerusalem. Cyrus made Sheshbazzar a governor and gave him the sacred vessels for the temple. Sheshbazzar also helped lay the foundation of the temple in Jerusalem. He is often identified with Zerubbabel (Ezr 1:8; 5:14, 16). See 1:424, 437, 452.

SHIBAH (SHIGH-bah; "seven," "oath"). A well that Isaac's servants dug at Beersheba (Gn 26:31–33).

SHIELD. *See* ARMOR, ARMS. See 1:229, 575, 965.

SHIGGAION, SHIGIONOTH (shi-GAY-yahn, shig-i-O-nahth). A musical term perhaps referring to the music or meter of a piece (title of Ps 7; Hab 3:1). See 1:612.

SHIHOR (SHIGH-hawr; "pond of Horus"). *See* NILE.

SHILOH (SHIGH-lo; "peace").

1. A place about nine miles north of Bethel. It was the site of Israel's early sanctuary and the place where the ark of the covenant was kept for about 300 years (Jsh 18:1, 8–10; Jgs 21:19–23). Eli and Samuel lived at Shiloh and ministered in the temple there (1Sm 3). Shiloh was also the home of the prophet Ahijah. He was the one who told Jeroboam that God was going to make him king over the 10 northern tribes (1Ki 11:29–34; 14:1–18). By Jeremiah's time it seems that Shiloh lay in ruins (Jer 7:12–14; 26:6–9). See 1:245, 276, 282, 288–89, 553; 2:801.
2. A word of uncertain meaning. Many people think it refers to the Messiah (cf Gn 49:10). See 1:39.

SHIMSHAI (SHIM-shigh). A scribe and leader in Samaria who wrote a letter to Artaxerxes complaining about the rebuilding of the temple (Ezr 4:8–9, 17, 23).

SHINAR (SHIGH-nur). An alluvial plain of southern Babylonia where the cities Babel, Erech, Accad, and Calneh were located (Gn 10:10; Dn 1:2). The tower of Babel was built on this plain. During Abraham's time, Amraphel was king of Shinar (Gn 14:1, 9). Many years later, some of the Jews were taken captive to Shinar (Zec 5:11). See 1:823, 983.

SHIP. *See* BOATS.

SHITTAH, SHITTIM (SHIT-ah, SHIT-im; "acacia"). A tree that grew in the Jordan Valley, in the wilderness of Sinai, and in the area around the Dead Sea. The acacia was one species of shittah tree. Its wood was hard, fine grained, and insect repelling. The Hebrews used acacia wood to build the tabernacle, the ark, the altars, the tables, and the bars and pillars (Ex 25:5–28; 26:15–37; Is 41:19).

SHITTIM (SHIT-im; "acacias). The last place Israel camped before entering Canaan. From Shittim, Joshua sent spies to look over the defenses of Jericho, and then Israel broke camp to cross over the Jordan (Nu 25:1; Jsh 2:1; Mi 6:5). In Nu 33:49, it is referred to as Abel-shittim. See 1:140, 153.

SHOBAL (SHO-bal). The son of Hur and founder of Kiriath-jearim (1Ch 2:50; 4:1–2).

SHOBI (SHO-bigh; "one who leads captive"). An Ammonite who brought food and other provisions to David and the people with him when they stopped at Mahanaim (2Sm 17:27).

SHOE. *See* SANDAL. See 1:260; 2:258.

SHOWBREAD. A translation for the Hbr words that literally mean "bread of the presence" (Nu 4:7; 1Ch 9:32; 23:29; cf Ex 25:30; 35:13; 39:36). The showbread consisted of 12 loaves of fresh, unleavened bread that were placed in two stacks on the table of acacia wood in the Holy Place every Sabbath. The old loaves were eaten by the priests (Ex 25:30; 1Sm 21:1–6; Mt 12:3–4). See 1:72, 107, 291.

SHUA (SHU-ah). A Canaanite who was Judah's father-in-law (Gn 38:2).

SHUAH (SHU-ah; "sink down"). A son of Abraham and Keturah (Gn 25:2). An Arab tribe, probably the Shuhites, descended from him.

SHUR (SHOOR; "wall"). A region in the wilderness south of Israel and east of Egypt. The Israelites marched through this area for three days after crossing the Red Sea (Gn 16:7; 25:18; Ex 15:22).

SHUSHAN (SHU-shan; "lily"). *See* SUSA.

SHUSHAN EDUTH (SHU-shan-EE-duth; "lilies of the Testimony"). The title of Ps 60. Although its meaning is uncertain, it may be a musical term, perhaps referring to the melody.

SICARII (SICK-ar-ee). Jewish revolutionaries who expected a messianic king and supported their leader, Menahem, during the revolt against the Romans in AD 66. *See also* ZEALOTS.

SIDON (SIGH-d'n; "fishery"). An ancient Canaanite city situated on the Mediterranean coast about 22 miles north of Tyre. It was assigned to the tribe of Asher, but they never succeeded in conquering the Canaanite people living there (Jgs 1:31; 10:12; 18:7, 28). When Solomon was building the temple, he hired people from Sidon to cut timber for it (1Ki 5:6; 1Ch 22:4).

The Sidonians worshiped the false goddess Ashtoreth. Their religion corrupted the Israelites, who began to worship Ashtoreth also (1Ki 11:5). Jezebel, Ahab's wife, came from Sidon. Under her influence, Ahab built an altar to Baal in Samaria and worshiped him (1Ki 16:31). Sidon was spoken against by the prophets (Jer 27:3; Jl 3:4–6).

Sidon is also mentioned in the NT. Christ visited there, and Paul stopped at the port at Sidon (Mt 15:21; Ac 27:3). Today it is called Saida. See 1:213, 343, 730, 806; 2:246, 806.

SIEGE. Surrounding a city with an army in order to capture it. In Israel's early days, sieges lasted only a short time (2Ki 6:24; 2Sm 20:15). Later, siege engines, protected ladders, and battering rams were built to help the army take over the city (2Ch 26:14). *See also* ARMOR, ARMS; ARMY; WAR. SEE 1:402, 767, 798, 947; 2:20–21.

SIEVE. A utensil made of rushes, horsehair, or string that was used for sifting materials, such as grain (Is 30:28; Am 9:9).

SIGNET. *See* RING. See 1:974.

SILAS (SIGH-lahs; form of the name "Saul"). An important member of the Christian Church in Jerusalem. Silas went with Paul to Antioch to tell the Christians there the decision of the Jerusalem council (Ac 15:22, 27, 32). He also accompanied Paul on the second missionary journey (Ac 16–18). Silas is also referred to as Silvanus (2Co 1:19; 1Th 1:1; 2Th 1:1; 1Pt 5:12). See 2:368, 377–78, 388, 563, 570, 811.

SILOAM (si-LO-am; "shooting forth," "sent"). A pool at Jerusalem on the southern side of the temple. It received its water from En-rogel through a 1,780-foot tunnel built during Hezekiah's reign (Jn 9:7). In Is 8:6 it is referred to as Shiloah and in Ne 3:15 as Shelah. Today it is called Birket Silwan. See 1:384; 2:803, 809.

SILVANUS (sil-VAY-nuhs). *See* SILAS.

SILVER. A precious metal used from early times for money, ornaments, crowns, trumpets, vessels, and items in the tabernacle (Gn 23:16; 24:53; 44:2; Ex

26:19; 27:10; 38:19; Nu 10:2; Jb 28:15; Zec 6:11). Some idols were also made of silver (Ps 115:4). See 1:38, 72, 191, 454; 2:203, 228, 406, 520–21.

SIMEON (SIM-ee-uhn; "hearing").

1. One of Jacob and Leah's sons (Gn 29:33). Simeon and his brother Levi killed the people of Shechem because of what one of them had done to Dinah, their sister (Gn 34:24–31). During Israel's famine Joseph kept Simeon hostage in Egypt in order to make sure the rest of his brothers would return (Gn 42:24). When Jacob was dying, he foretold that the tribe of Simeon would be scattered in Israel (Gn 49:5–7). See 1:31; 2:22.
2. The tribe of Simeon. Members of this tribe descended from Simeon (Nu 1:22–23). The tribe of Simeon received cities and villages in Judah and in the neighborhood of Beersheba (Jsh 19:1–9; 1Ch 4:28–33). See 1:151, 213, 399.
3. A righteous and devout man to whom God revealed that he would not die until he had seen the Christ Child. When Mary and Joseph brought the baby Jesus to the temple, Simeon came in and recognized Him as the promised Messiah. He uttered the blessing known as the Nunc Dimittis (Lk 2:25–35). See 2:268, 277.
4. Simeon Niger, a Christian at Antioch (Ac 13:1).
5. *See* PETER.

SIMON (SIGH-muhn; "hearing").

1. *See* PETER.
2. The youngest son of Mattathias whose struggles with the Seleucids and Ptolemies are recorded in 1Macc (13–16). See 2:81, 86.
3. Simon the Canaanite, or Simon the Zealot, one of the apostles (Mt 10:4).
4. A brother of Jesus (Mt 13:55; Mk 6:3).
5. A Pharisee who invited Jesus to his home for a meal. While Jesus was there, a woman came in and anointed His feet (Lk 7:36–50).
6. The father of Judas Iscariot (Jn 13:2). See 2:165, 309.
7. Simon of Cyrene, the man who carried Jesus' cross for Him (Mt 27:32; Mk 15:21; Lk 23:26).
8. Simon Magus, a sorcerer of Samaria. When Simon saw that the Holy Spirit was given through the laying on of hands, he tried to buy the power from the apostles. Peter sharply rebuked him for this and told him to repent (Ac 8:9–24). See 2:389, 768.
9. A tanner at Joppa. Peter stayed at his house for many days (Ac 9:43).

SIN, I. A desert plain lying inland from the Red Sea. The Israelites passed through the Wilderness of Sin on their way from the Red Sea to Mount Sinai (Ex 16:1; 17:1; Nu 33:11–12). See 1:59, 81.

SIN, II. Sin is both doing what God forbids and failing to do what He commands (Rm 1:18–32; 1Jn 3:4). Since God's Law tells us what He wants us to do and not to do, sin is breaking God's Law. It is a condition as well as an act.

When Adam and Eve yielded to the devil's temptation and fell into sin, they lost the image of God; they were no longer holy and innocent. Because of their sin, they came under God's just anger and curse. Also by their act of disobedience, sin entered the world, and through it, misery, suffering, and death came upon the entire human race (Gn 3; Ps 51:5; Rm 3:9–23; 5:21; 6:6–17; 7:21–23).

From Adam all people receive both hereditary guilt (Rm 5:12) and a total corruption of the human nature, called original sin. Original sin is the evil condition of our nature that we have by being born of human parents also corrupted by sin. It consists of an alienation from God (Rm 1:18–24; 8:7) as well as a natural liking for doing evil (Rm 1; 7:14). It expresses itself in actual sinful deeds contrary to God's will as found in His law (Rm 3:20; 4:15; 7:7; 1Jn 3:4).

Sin is against God (Gn 39:9; 2Sm 12:13; Ps 51:4). Because of original sin, people by nature cannot fear, love, or trust in God or love their neighbor (1Jn). Because of sin everyone deserves temporal and eternal death. "The wages of sin is death" (Rm 6:23). Only through faith in Christ, who both kept God's Law perfectly and suffered the punishment for the sins of the world, does one escape the results of sin. "But the free gift of God is eternal life in Christ Jesus our Lord" (Rm 6:23). See 1:44–45, 299–300, 669–70, 2:222–23, 337, 424, 670.

SIN OFFERING. *See* ATONEMENT, DAY OF; SACRIFICE. See 1:103, 112.

SIN, UNPARDONABLE. A sin that excludes the possibility of repentance. The Bible often refers to this sin as the sin against the Holy Spirit. This sin is committed when the Holy Spirit has clearly revealed the divine truth to the sinner, and yet the sinner still consciously persists in his or her evil ways, opposing God and His will. It is the rejection of the Gospel by a hardened sinner who has been convinced of its truth (Mt 12:31; Mk 3:29; Lk 12:10; 1Jn 5:16). See 2:222–23.

SINAI (SIGH-nigh; possibly "Sin," a moon god). The mountain on which the Law was given. Mount Sinai was probably a peak in the mountain range Horeb (Ex 3:1; 17:6; Dt 1:6; 4:10). The Ten Commandments were given from its peak, and the covenant between the Lord and Israel was ratified at its base (Ex 20:1–24:8). The location of Mount Sinai is uncertain. The Sinai Peninsula lies between the Red Sea, the Gulf of Aqaba, and the Gulf of Suez. See 1:25, 33, 71–73, 79–81, 99–101; 2:829.

SIRAH (SIGH-rah). A well about one mile north of Hebron. Here, Joab killed Abner (2Sm 3:26).

SISERA (SIS-u-rah). A Canaanite who was the captain of the army of King Jabin of Hazor. Under Deborah's direction Barak united his forces and met with Sisera in battle. When Sisera's forces were killed or scattered, he ran away on foot. Jael, the wife of Heber, killed Sisera while he slept (Jgs 4–5; 1Sm 12:9; Ps 83:9). See 1:217, 226, 237.

SISTER.
1. Full sister or half sister (Gn 20:12; Dt 27:22). See 1:49–50, 126; 2:304–6.
2. Wife (Sg 4:9). See 1:675, 682.
3. A woman of the same tribe (Nu 25:18).
4. A female fellow Christian (Rm 16:1). See 1:412; 2:201, 397, 744.

SIX. The number of mankind, since God created Adam and Eve on the sixth day (Gn 1:24–27; Rv 13:18).

SLAVE. *See* MINISTER.

SLAVES. Israelites could be slaves for a time but were to be freed. Captives, such as Canaanites, might be enslaved permanently. *See also* GIBEONITES. See 1:94, 387, 882; 2:425, 507, 635–38.

SLEEP.
1. Physical rest (Ps 4:8; Pr 24:33; Jn 11:13). See 1:70, 476; 2:203, 248.
2. Death (1Ki 1:21; Ps 13:3; Jer 51:39; Jn 11:11). See 1:313; 2:576.
3. Spiritual laziness or stupidity (Rm 13:11; 1Th 5:6).

SMYRNA (SMUR-nah; "myrrh"). An ancient Ionian city about 40 miles north of Ephesus. After lying in ruins for a number of years, it was rebuilt by Alexander the Great in 320 BC. John addresses the church at Smyrna in Rv 1:11; 2:8–11. See 2:326, 783.

SNOW. Snow is common in the hilly country of Israel (2Sm 23:20; Is 55:10). It is often mentioned in poetical sections of Scripture and in metaphors (Jb 37:6; 38:22; Ps 51:7; 147:16; Is 1:18; Mt 28:3).

SOCIAL GOSPEL. Describing biblical faith and activies according to their social value rather than their theological truth, with the goal of achieving the rebirth of society. The Social Gospel Movement called for community involvement, response, and protest to address the excesses of industrialism during the nineteenth and twentieth centuries. See 1:709.

SODOM (SAHD-uhm). A city, along with Gomorrah, Admah, Zeboiim, and Zoar, that was located in the plain of Siddim (Gn 13:12). Although the exact site of Sodom is unknown, many think it was located on the southeast end of the Dead Sea. In Gn 14:2, it is described as a royal city. Abraham's nephew Lot lived there (Gn 13:11–13). When God destroyed Sodom because of its wickedness, only Lot and his two daughters escaped (Gn 19). The Bible repeatedly uses Sodom as an example of wickedness (Dt 29:23; Is 1:9; 3:9; Jer 50:40; Ezk 16:46; Mt 10:15; Rm 9:29; 2Pt 2:6). See 1:25, 27, 185, 768; 2:760.

SOJOURNER (so-JYOOR-nur). A stranger or foreigner in the land of Israel who obeyed certain rules (Ex 20:10; Lv 17:10, 15; 18:26; 20:2; 22:18; 24:16). Although there were exceptions (Dt 23:3, 8), they could become part of Israel if they underwent the rite of circumcision (Ex 12:48–49). *See also* FOREIGNER; PROSELYTE. See 1:257, 347, 361; 2:704, 708.

SOLDIER (SOL-jur). *See* ARMY.

SOLOMON (SAHL-o-muhn; "peaceable"). Third and last king of the united kingdom of Israel. Solomon was the son of David and Bathsheba. When Solomon was born, Nathan named him Jedidiah, which means "beloved of the Lord" (2Sm 12:24–25; 1Ki 4:1; 1Ch 3:5). After Solomon was made king, he put to death those who had plotted to take the throne from him: his brother Adonijah and Adonijah's followers Joab and Shimei. He also removed Abiathar, the priest, from office (1Ki 1:5–40; 2).

Solomon married numerous women, one of whom was the daughter of the Egyptian pharaoh (1Ki 3:1). Early in his reign Solomon was faithful to the Lord. He worshiped the Lord, offering up burnt offerings and praying to Him. When God told Solomon in a dream to ask whatever he wished of Him, Solomon chose wisdom so that he could rule his kingdom better (1Ki 3:3–12). God answered his request, blessing Solomon with "wisdom and understanding beyond measure. . . . He was wiser than all other men" (1Ki 4:29–31).

With the help of King Hiram of Tyre, Solomon built the temple in seven years. He also built a palace for himself (1Ki 5–8; 2Ch 2–7). Solomon showed wisdom in government and commerce (1Ki 4:2–19; 10:11–29; 2Ch 9:10–22). He also had interests and abilities in botany and zoology (1Ki 4:33). In addition to this, Solomon was a great writer. Among other writings, the Book of Proverbs and Psalms 27 and 127 were likely written by him.

In his old age, however, Solomon began to fall away from the Lord. Under the influence of his foreign wives, he was tempted to worship others gods; he built altars to Chemosh and Molech and worshiped Ashtoreth. The Lord grew angry with Solomon. As judgment on Solomon's idolatry, God said He would take the kingdom of Israel from Solomon's descendants. Only one tribe would remain for them to rule (1Ki 11:1–13). See 1:331–32, 338–39, 341–42.

SOLOMON, SONG OF. See 1:675–99.

SOLOMON, WISDOM OF. See 2:27–37.

SOLOMON'S PORTICO. A colonnade on the east side of Herod's temple (Ac 3:11; 5:12; cf Jn 10:23). See 2:385.

SON.
1. A male child; one's immediate descendant (Gn 27:1). See 1:23, 27, 70, 295; 2:51–53.
2. A descendant further removed than one's own child (2Ki 9:20; cf Mal 3:6). See 1:14; 2:190.
3. A spiritual son (2Ki 2:3; 1Tm 1:18; 2Tm 2:1). See 2:501, 605.
4. An address to a younger person (1Sm 3:6).
5. A member of a profession (Ne 12:28).
6. A follower (Nu 21:29).
7. An adopted son (Ex 2:10).
8. A native (Lm 4:2).
9. *See* JESUS CHRIST.

SON OF DAVID.
1. Messianic title, drawn from 2Sm 7:13–14. See 1:193, 349, 400, 771, 809, 812; 2:190, 220.
2. Solomon. *See also* SOLOMON. See 1:681.

SON OF GOD.
1. Adam (Lk 3:38). See 1:35; 2:219.
2. Angels (Jb 38:7).
3. Believers (Rm 8:14; 2Co 6:18; Gal 4:1–7). *See also* ADOPTION.
4. Used c 40 times in the NT. Emphasizes the fact that Jesus, a true man, is also eternally the true Son of God. *See also* JESUS CHRIST. See 1:301–2; 2:200–1, 236, 284, 657–58.

SON OF MAN.
1. A human being (Nu 23:19; Jb 25:6; Ps 8:4; Dn 8:17). Appears early in statements of non-Israelites (cf Nu 23:19; Jb 16:21; 25:6; 35:8), which may characterize their non-Hebrew language(s). However, c 85 percent of OT examples appear later in Ezk, who was exiled among Aram speakers in Babylon (cf Dn 7:13; 8:17). The expression is likely borrowed from Aram, where it simply means a human being, a person. See 1:517, 800, 836.
2. Used in a messianic sense in Dn 7:13–14. Jesus applies the term to Himself numerous times. Favorite self-designation of Jesus, used c 80 times in the Gospels but almost never in the rest of the NT. Its meaning varies somewhat depending on the context. Indicates that though Jesus is fully man, He is much more. As a messianic title, it combines the ideas of a servant who will suffer and die for all people (Is 53; Mt 20:28) and the exalted Son of Man, whose reign is everlasting (Dn 7:13–14; Mt 24:30). *See also* JESUS CHRIST. See 1:836; 2:237, 333, 393–94.

SONG. *See* MUSIC; PSALMS, BOOK OF.

SONG OF ASCENTS (DEGREES). *See* ASCENTS, SONG OF.

SONG OF SONGS. *See* SOLOMON, SONG OF.

SONSHIP. *See* ADOPTION; SON OF GOD.

SOOTHSAYER (SOOTH-say-ur). *See* DIVINATION. See 1:139.

SOPHERETH (so-FEE-reth; "office of scribe"). A name or title given to some of Solomon's servants (Ne 7:57).

SORCERER (SAWR-sur-ur). *See* DIVINATION; MAGIC. See 1:30, 86–88; 2:371.

SOSTHENES (SOS-thi-neez; "savior"). A ruler of the synagogue at Corinth (Ac 18:17). He may have been the man mentioned in 1Co 1:1, who was Paul's coworker. See 2:447, 721.

SOUL, SPIRIT (sometimes translated "life" or "ghost"). The word *soul* comes from the Hbr word *nephesh* and the Gk word *psuche*. The soul is not separate from the body; rather it is that which gives it life: it animates the flesh. It is the inner person as distinguished from the flesh (Jb 14:22). Through the breath of God, people and animals become living beings or souls (Gn 2:7). The soul is described as living and dying and as life itself (Gn 12:13; 44:30; Is 53:12; Ezk 18:4; Ac 20:10). The soul departs at death (Gn 35:18; Lk 12:20). The soul is the seat of the appetites, emotions, and passions (Ps 107:9; Mt 22:37; Lk 12:19; Jn 12:27). It can be lost and saved (Mk 8:35–36). See 1:160–61, 443, 520, 669; 2:99, 281, 771.

Spirit is a translation of the Hbr word *ruah* and the Gk word *pneuma*. It is often translated as breath or wind (Jb 15:30; 2Th 2:8). The spirit of life is created and preserved by God (Jb 10:12; 27:3; Zec 12:1). It is those inner aspects of one's personality and the seat of one's moral character (Ezk 11:19; 18:31; Mk 2:8; 1Co 5:3–5). The spirit returns to God at death (Ec 12:7; Mt 27:50; Jn 19:30). The Spirit of God gives special gifts to people (Ex 31:3; Jb 32:8). See 1:51, 512, 669; 2:328, 354, 485.

Some spirits are also wicked and evil. God sent a spirit to torture Saul (1Sm 16:14), Tobit contended with an evil spirit, and Jesus regularly cast out such evil spirits. *See also* DEMON; SATAN. See 1:290–91, 309; 2:244, 277.

At times soul and spirit are used as synonyms (Lk 1:46–47); at other times they are contrasted (1Co 15:44–45). Both demonstrate one life principle from two points of view. *See also* DEATH; ESCHATOLOGY; ETERNAL LIFE; HOLY SPIRIT.

SOVEREIGN. Gk *dunastes*. *See* MIGHTY ONE. See 1:504; 2:385–86.

SPAN. *See* MEASURES 1c.

SPICES. Pleasant-smelling gums, barks, and the like that were used during biblical times in ceremonies, in medicines, for embalming, for anointing, and for grooming oneself (Gn 37:25; 43:11; Sg 4:14; Mk 16:1; Jn 19:39–40). See 1:621; 2:320.

SPIDER. A spider's web is a picture word for the foolishness of wickedness (Jb 8:14; Is 59:5).

SPINNING. *See* TRADE.

SPIRIT. *See* HOLY SPIRIT; SOUL, SPIRIT.

SPIRIT, HOLY. *See* HOLY SPIRIT.

SPIRITUAL GIFTS. Gk *pneumatikon*, which can describe spiritual gifts, offices, works, or people, as in Gal 6:1. Gifts and abilities that the Holy Spirit gives to Christians to equip them for service in the Church (1Co 12). See 2:448–49, 471.

SPOIL. *See* BOOTY. See 1:294; 2:789.

SPOT.
1. A mark or blot that spoils an animal or person (Gn 30:32–39; Lv 13:2–39).
2. A physical or moral flaw (Lv 13). *See also* BLEMISH. See 1:762; 2:459.

STADIUM (STAY-di-uhm). *See* MEASURE 1i.

STAFF. *See* ROD. See 1:86, 138; 2:258–59.

STAIRS, STAIRWAY. *See* HOMES.

STANDARD. Banners that marked to which tribe each camp belonged (Nu 1:52; 2). See 1:552.

STAR. The Bible speaks of a star as any heavenly body except the sun and the moon. The Israelites recognized stars as the work of God and observed them from patriarchal times (Gn 1:16). For instance, God told Abraham his descendants would be as numerous as the stars, and Joseph dreamed the sun, the moon, and 11 stars had bowed down to him (Gn 15:5; 37:9).

Stars are also used as picture words for brightness, multitudes, and important persons (Gn 22:17; 37:9; Nu 24:17; Ps 147:4; 148:3; Dn 8:10; 12:3; Rv 6:13). The star of the east led the Wise Men to Bethlehem after Jesus was born (Mt 2:2–10). *See also* ASTROLOGERS; MAGICIAN. See 1:141, 467; 2:196, 779.

STEADFAST LOVE. The Hbr word for this is *hesed*. Although difficult to translate into English, *hesed* has the basic sense of that loving kindness, mercy, and faithfulness of God expressed in the act by which He chose Israel, established a covenant relationship with the people of Israel, promised them salvation, and bound Himself to loving them and showing them mercy. Those who have been called by grace into this covenant relationship with God respond in love to God and their fellow human beings (Gn 24:12–27; Ex 20:6; Ps 5:7; 26:3; Jer 16:5). Often this word is translated "loving kindness" or "mercy" as well as "steadfast love." *See also* GRACE; LOVE; MERCY. See 1:262, 299, 580–85, 712, 861; 2:430.

STEADFAST LOVE AND FAITHFULNESS. A common word pair in the Psalms, epitomizing the Lord's care for His people. *See also* STEADFAST LOVE; FAITHFULNESS. See 1:223.

STELE (STEEL). A monument erected for commemorative reasons, usually made of stone or wood. See 1:28, 31, 62, 323–24, 553.

STEPHEN (STEE-vuhn; "crown"). One of the seven deacons chosen by the Early Church to minister to the needs of the Greek-speaking widows and probably the poor in general. Stephen himself was likely a Greek-speaking Christian. The NT describes him as a man of great faith, wisdom, and power (Ac 6:3–8). Some people who belonged to the synagogue of the Freedmen, as well as Jews from Cyrene, Alexandria, Cilicia, and Asia, debated with Stephen. Accusing him of blasphemy against Moses and God, they stirred up the people to bring Stephen before the council (Ac 6:9–15).

Stephen gave a remarkable defense, explaining that Christianity was the fulfillment of Jewish history. His words angered his accusers, who took him outside the city and stoned him to death. The young man Saul (Paul) watched the proceedings and approved of Stephen's death (Ac 7–8:1). See 1:52–55; 2:368–69, 375, 389–90, 393–95.

STEW. A meal made of fruit and vegetables (Gn 25:29–30, 34; 1Ki 4:38–40; Hg 2:12). See 1:899.

STOICS (STO-iks; "porch [scholars]"). A school of Greek philosophy founded by Zeno. Stoics taught that virtue was the highest good. Through it they believed that one's actions were brought into harmony with nature and universal reason. Their religion was pantheistic, that is, they believed God is in everything.

Stoics were known for their austere ethics, for their rigid control of feelings, and for hiding their emotions. They were unmoved by pleasure or pain. When Paul was in Athens, he talked with some Stoics (Ac 17:18–32). See 1:696; 2:28, 32, 454.

STRAIGHT STREET. A street of Damascus (Ac 9:11). See 2:810–11.

STRONG DRINK. Any alcoholic beverage (Nu 28:7). It was usually made from grapes, barley, honey, or dates. Strong drink was forbidden to priests before they entered the sanctuary and to Nazirites (Lv 10:9; Nu 6:3; Jgs 13:4, 7; Lk 1:15).

STUMBLING BLOCK.

1. In OT usage, a stumbling block is any object that causes a person to fall (Lv 19:14).
2. In the NT, Jesus and the cross are described as stumbling blocks (1Co 1:23). God's way of salvation through Jesus and the cross does not meet people's expectations or wishes. Individuals cannot be saved through their own reason or works, only by grace through faith in Christ's redeeming work for them. This is a "stumbling block" for them. See 1:50; 2:191, 326, 429.
3. An occasion for inner conflict or sin (Rm 14:13; 1Co 8:9). See 2:761.

SUBMIT. Gk *hypotasso* and other forms of *tasso*, describes orderly relationships, not simply judgments of worth or importance. Cf Lk 2:51. See 1:131, 298, 513; 2:284, 386, 529–30, 609.

SUCCOTH (SUK-ahth; "booths").

1. The place east of the Jordan near Damiyeh where Jacob built a house for himself and booths for his cattle on his return from Mesopotamia to Canaan (Gn 33:17). Later, it was assigned to the Gadites (Jsh 13:27). During the time of Gideon, Succoth was an important town. When the people of Succoth refused to help Gideon, he punished the town severely (Jgs 8:5–16). See 1:29.
2. The first place Israel camped after leaving Rameses (Ex 12:37; 13:20; Nu 33:5–6). See 1:81.

SUFFERING. Gk *pascho* originally meant "experience" or anything "moving" (as in Eng "passion"). A result of the alienation between God and people caused by sin (Jb 10:2; Ps 51:4). Although the root cause for suffering is spiritual, people suffer both physically and morally (Gn 3:1–6; Jb; Mt 27:27–30, 39–44). Christ paid the penalty for the sins of the world by suffering and dying on the cross (Ps 22; Mt 27:45–46). Since it will not be until the next life that the effects of sin are totally removed, Christians still suffer in this world. Christian suffering, however, is understood by faith (Rm 8:24; 2Co 1:5–14). Suffering teaches Christians to rely on and trust in God. Paul writes: "We felt that we had received the sentence of death. But that was to make us rely not on ourselves but on God who raises the dead. He delivered us from so deadly a peril . . . [that] on Him we have set our hope that He will deliver us again" (2Co 1:9–10). People who do not believe in Christ will suffer eternally. See 1:303–4, 511–15, 536–37, 741, 787–89; 2:201, 204, 254, 337, 430–31, 657–58, 709, 783.

SULFUR. A chemical element commonly used figuratively for destruction and punishment (Jb 18:15; Ps 11:6; Is 34:9; Rv 21:8).

SUN. The greater light of the day created and preserved by God (Gn 1:16; Ps 74:16; 104:19; Jer 31:35; Mt 5:45). The sun helps crops and vegetation to grow but also burns them (Dt 33:14; Jnh 4:8). In OT days both the Hebrews and other nations worshiped the sun (2Ki 21:3, 5; 23:5; Jb 31:26–27).

The sun is also a picture word for the glory of Christ, heavenly beings, and the saints (Mt 13:43; 17:2; Rv 1:16; 10:1; 12:1).

When a person died before he or she reached old age, it was compared to the setting of the sun during daytime (Jer 15:9; Am 8:9; Mi 3:6). A darkened sun was symbolic of some great disaster or trouble (Ezk 32:7; Jl 2:10, 31). See 1:225–26, 376–77, 645–46.

SUNDAY. The first day of the week. At first, the early Christians worshiped on both the seventh day of the week, the Sabbath, and the first day of the week, the day upon which Christ rose from the dead. Eventually they stopped meeting on the seventh day. The word *Sunday* is of pagan origin. *See also* LORD'S DAY. See 2:223, 320.

SUPPLICATION (SUP-li-KAY-shuhn). A prayer for mercy or favor in some special need (Eph 6:18; 1Tm 2:1; 5:5; cf 1Ki 8:28–54; Jb 8:5; Ps 6:9). *See also* PRAYER. See 1:562; 2:589.

SUSA (SYOO-sah). The capital of Elam and later, under Cyrus, one of the capitals of the Persian Empire (Ne 1:1; Est 1:2; Dn 8:2). Today it is called Shush. See 1:459–62, 465.

SUSANNA, BOOK OF. See 2:117–25.

SUZERAIN-VASSEL. The title of a covenant or treaty between a greater authority (suzerain) and a lesser authority (vassel). The covenant describes the imbalance of power between the two authorities as well as the commitments of each to one another. The Sinai covenant may be described as such a covenant, with the Lord as the suzerain and Israel as the vassel. *See also* COVENANT. See 1:63, 162.

SWEARING. *See* OATH.

SWORD. *See* ARMOR, ARMS. See 1:166; 2:312.

SYCAMORE (SIK-ah-mor). A fig tree. It was valued for its small, edible fruit and light, durable wood (1Ki 10:27; 1Ch 27:28; Ps 78:47; Lk 19:4). *See also* ORCHARD. See 1:880.

SYNAGOGUE (SIN-ah-gog; "led together"). A Jewish place for worship and for social gathering. The synagogue served as the place for worship and instruction in both God's Law and the civil and moral law. The synagogue as a meeting place and building likely began during the captivity when people could not get to the temple in Jerusalem for worship (cf Ezr 8:15; Ne 8:2; 9:1). Such gathering places were found throughout the Mediterranean world, since they were typically established wherever 10 Jewish heads of household were present. The NT is one of the most important early witnesses to synagogue activity. The earliest Christian congregations were synagogues of Jews who believed Jesus was the promised Messiah.

The furnishings of the synagogue included a chest for the sacred books, a reading platform with a lectern, seats for the congregation, and lamps and trumpets. The ruler of the synagogue, the attendant, and the almoner were the officers in charge of the synagogue. When the people came for worship, they observed the following order of service: a reading from the Shema, prayer, a reading from the Law, a reading from the Prophets, and the benediction. *See also* EDUCATION. See 1:534, 573; 2:187, 278, 378, 519–20, 682, 775, 808.

SYRACUSE (SIR-ah-kyoos). A leading city on the east coast of Sicily where Paul stayed for three days on his voyage to Rome (Ac 28:12). See 2:813.

SYRIA (SIR-i-ah). In the OT Syria was called Aram. It was that territory bounded by the Taurus Mountains, the Euphrates River, the Arabian Desert, and the Mediterranean Sea. David conquered it, but under Solomon it became independent (2Sm 8; 10; 1Ki 11:23–25). Syria was a continual enemy of the Israelites (1Ki 15:18–20; 20; 22; 2Ki 6:8–33; 7; 9:14-15; 10:32-33; 13). See 1:314–15, 343–47, 373–74, 882; 2:43–44, 84–86, 297–98, 388, 824.

SYRIAC (SIR-i-ak). The language spoken in Syria; Aramaic (Dn 2:4). See 1:398, 499, 832; 2:139.

SYROPHOENICIAN (sigh-ro-fi-NISH-uhn). A person who lived in northern Phoenicia. The Syrophoenicians were absorbed into the Syrian kingdom (Mk 7:26). See 2:240.

T

TAANACH (TAY-ah-nak). A Canaanite city about 5 miles southeast of Megiddo. Joshua conquered Taanach and gave it to Manasseh and the Kohathite Levites (Jsh 12:21; 17:11; 21:25). The battle between Barak and Sisera was fought near Taanach (Jgs 5:19). See 1:211.

TABEEL (TAY-bi-el; "God is good"). The father of the one whom Rezin of Syria and Pekah of Israel proposed to put on the throne of Judah as their puppet king (Is 7:6).

TABERAH (TAB-i-rah; "burning"). A place in the wilderness where Israel camped. Here the fire of the Lord burned some people who complained. Taberah is also called Kibroth-hattaavah (Nu 11:3, 34; Dt 9:22).

TABERNACLE (TAB-ur-nak'l).

1. *See* TENT OF MEETING.
2. The movable sanctuary in the form of a tent. God directed Moses to make the tabernacle so that He would have a place to live as King among His people (Ex 25:8–9). Because it contained the ark and two tables, the tabernacle was sometimes referred to as the tent, or tabernacle, of testimony (Ex 38:21; Nu 9:15; 17:7; 18:2). Other names for it include the tent of meeting or the tabernacle of congregation, the house of the Lord, the sanctuary, and the temple (Ex 23:19; 25:8; 29:42, 44; 1Sm 1:9; 3:3).

   A description of the tabernacle is found in Ex 26:1–27:19. The tabernacle stood in a court that was 100 cubits long by 50 cubits wide. The court was enclosed by acacia pillars 5 cubits high that had silver bands and hooks connected at the top by silver-covered rods. From these rods hung sheets of fine linen, embroidered on the east entrance. The frame of the tabernacle was 30 cubits long by 10 cubits wide by 10 cubits high. It was made of gold-covered acacia wood, covered on the outside with double blankets of skin and on the inside with embroidered linen tapestry. The tabernacle was divided into the Holy and Most Holy Places by a linen veil embroidered with cherubim.

   The altar of burnt offering stood in the court between the court entrance and the tabernacle. A basin (the place where priests washed) stood halfway between the altar and the tabernacle. The table of showbread, the golden candlestick, and the altar of incense were kept in the Holy Place, while the ark of the covenant was kept in the Most Holy Place.

   The tabernacle was set up at Sinai the second year after the Israelites left Egypt (Ex 40:2, 17). During the time of the conquest the tabernacle was stationed at Gilgal and Ebal (Jsh 4:9; 8:30–35). Later, it was stationed at Shiloh, Nob, and Gibeon (Jsh 18:1; 1Sm 4:17, 22; 21:1; 1Ch 16:39; 21:29). Under David the ark of the covenant was moved to the new tabernacle in Jerusalem. When the temple was built, the ark was placed in it (2Sm 6:17; 1Ch 15:1). See 1:72–76, 136–37, 271, 390, 578–79; 2:660, 732.

TABERNACLES, FEAST OF. *See* BOOTHS, FEAST OF. See 1:491, 665.

TABITHA (TAB-i-thah; "gazelle"). *See* DORCAS. See 2:376, 386.

TABLE.

1. *See* SHOWBREAD; TABERNACLE.
2. A table spread with food (Jgs 1:7; 1Ki 2:7; Mt 15:27; Mk 7:28; Lk 16:21). See 1:303; 2:21, 189–90, 390.
3. *See* LORD'S SUPPER. See 1:112; 2:466.
4. A table the money-changers used for their business (Mt 21:12).
5. The two stone tablets of the Law are sometimes called the "tables of the law." See 1:84, 173.

TABOR (TAY-bur). A limestone mountain in Galilee about 6 miles east of Nazareth (Jsh 19:22). It is 1,843 feet above sea level. Barak gathered 10,000 men together on Mount Tabor (Jgs 4:6–14). Gideon's brothers were murdered there (Jgs 8:21). See 1:228–29.

TAHATH (TAY-hath). One of the places in the wilderness where Israel camped (Nu 33:26–27).

TAKING PART. Gk *koinonia*, "fellowship," "sharing." Christians share in (1) apostolic doctrine, (2) the Lord's body and blood in Holy Communion, and (3) specific acts of mutual love. *See also* FELLOWSHIP. See 1:605; 2:287, 386, 582–83.

TALENT. The largest metal weight in Bible times (Mt 25:14–30). A talent of gold was worth about 15 times as much as a talent of silver. A talent of silver represented wealth; a talent of gold meant fabulous riches. See 1:150, 398.

TALITHA CUMI (tah-LIGH-thah KOO-mi). An Aramaic expression that means "Little girl . . . arise" (Mk 5:41).

TAMAR (TAY-mur; "palm tree").

1. The wife of Er, son of Judah. When she was left a widow, Tamar tricked her father-in-law, Judah, into making her pregnant. She became the mother of Perez and Zerah (Gn 38:6–26; Nu 26:20–21; Mt 1:3). See 1:16, 30.
2. Absalom's sister (2Sm 13; 1Ch 3:9). See 1:295, 299.
3. The daughter of Absalom and mother of Maacah (2Sm 14:27; 2Ch 13:2).

TAMBOURINE (tam-boo-REEN). A percussion instrument used to mark time (Gn 31:27; Ps 81:2). See 1:541.

TANNER. *See* TRADE.

TAPHATH (TAY-fath; "drop"). Solomon's daughter (1Ki 4:11).

TARES. *See* WEEDS.

TARSHISH (TAHR-shish).

1. A place on the Mediterranean, perhaps in Spain or Tunisia (2Ch 9:21; 20:36–37; Ps 72:10). Jonah fled to Tarshish (Jnh 1:3). See 1:905, 907.
2. The "ships of Tarshish" were large, seagoing ships that carried refined ore or other cargo (1Ki 9:26; 10:22; 22:48; 2Ch 9:21).

TARSUS (TAHR-suhs). The chief city of Cilicia, located on the Cydnus River. It was a free city and a great commercial center. Known for its educational system, its schools were almost as good as those of Athens and Alexandria. Tarsus was the home of Paul, who no doubt benefited from all his city had to offer (Ac 9:11, 30; 11:25; 21:39; 22:3). See 2:367, 411.

TAX COLLECTOR. A person who collected taxes for the Roman government. The Romans used a tax-farming system, employing the natives of a particular country or area to collect taxes for them. For instance, in Israel the tax collectors were usually Jews. Tax collectors had two marks against them: not only were they collecting taxes, but they were doing this for Rome, a government hated by their fellow countrymen because of its control over their land. As a result they were also looked down upon, even hated, by their own countrymen (Mt 9:10; 18:17; Lk 3:12–13; 19:2). See 2:180, 186–89, 244, 282–83, 287.

TAXES. Under the judges, the Israelites paid taxes to support the priests and tabernacle.

Under the kings, taxes were collected from various sources to support the kingdom. These included the following:

1. Taxes in kind levied on the produce of fields and flocks (1Ki 4:7–28)
2. Military service (1Sm 8:12; 1Ch 27:1)
3. Special gifts (1Sm 10:27; 16:20)
4. Duties paid by merchants (1Ki 10:15)
5. Tribute and services exacted by subject people (2Sm 8:6, 14)
6. Monopoly of certain trade (1Ki 9:28; 22:48)

Under the Persian Empire, the satraps paid a fixed sum into the royal treasury. This sum was collected from the people by tribute, customs, and toll (Ezr 4:13, 20). The priests, Levites, and Nethinim, however, were exempt (Ezr 7:24).

The Egyptians and Syrians sold the right to tax to the highest bidder at auction. That person who promised to collect the most revenue from a province was authorized to do so and given military power to enforce his demands.

The Romans practiced tax farming (Mt 17:24; 22:17). *See also* CENSUS; TAX COLLECTOR. See 1:273, 280, 389–90, 440; 2:201–2, 297, 431.

TEACH. Gk *didasko*, commonly used by Paul to describe teaching and preaching. Also Gk *katecheo*, "to instruct" (Rm 2:18; 1Co 14:19; Gal 6:6), as in Eng "catechism" and "catechesis." Such instruction was not yet a highly structured ministry of the Word in the NT. *See also* PREACHER, PREACHING. See 1:298; 2:176–77, 191, 271–72, 500, 594–95, 607–8.

TEKOA, TEKOAH (ti-KO-ah). A town in Judah about 6 miles south of Bethlehem (2Sm 14:2, 4, 9). It was fortified by King Rehoboam and was the home of the prophet Amos (2Ch 11:6; Am 1:1). Today it is Tekia. See 1:878, 889–90.

TEL (tel). A mound covering an ancient city (Arabic spelling, "tell").

TEL-ABIB (tel-AY-bib; "grain heap"). A place on the Chebar Canal where Ezekiel lived (Ezk 3:15). See 1:795.

TEMAN (TEE-muhn; "south").

1. Esau's grandson and a prince of Edom (Gn 36:11, 15, 42; 1Ch 1:36).
2. A district in northern Edom where Teman's descendants lived (Ezk 25:13; Am 1:12). The people

of Teman were noted for their wisdom (Jb 2:11; Jer 49:7). See 1:497, 844; 2:61.

TEMPLE. Hbr *hekal*, "palace" or "temple," used for the holy place. Gk *hieros* and *naos*. In the Apocrypha, the former term is more common whereas the latter term is more common in the LXX for OT books. David wanted to build the temple so the Lord would have a permanent house instead of a tent. With this in mind, he gathered together the materials for it (2Sm 7; 1Ch 17; 22; 28:12–19; 29:1–9). But it was Solomon, his son, who actually built the temple on Mount Moriah with the help of Hiram of Tyre. The temple proper was 60 cubits long, 20 cubits broad, and 30 cubits high. It was built of stone from a quarry. The roof was made of cedar; the floor was carved with cypress overlaid with gold; and the inside walls were lined with carved cedar overlaid with gold.

The Most Holy Place, or inner sanctuary, was a cube, each side measuring 20 cubits. It contained two cherubim made of olive wood and overlaid with gold and the ark with the Mercy Seat.

The Holy Place, separated from the Most Holy Place by a cedar door and a veil, was 40 cubits long, 20 cubits wide, and 30 cubits high. It contained an altar of incense made of cedar and overlaid with gold, 10 golden seven-lamp candlesticks, and 10 tables for showbread.

On the east, west, and south sides of the temple was a three-story building containing rooms for officials and storage. On the north side before the front entrance was a portico with two pillars, Jachin and Boaz.

The temple had two courts: the inner, or upper, court for the priests, containing the altar of burnt offering and a molten sea, and around this inner court was the outer court for Israel (1Ki 6–8; 2Ch 3–7).

This temple, known as Solomon's temple, was burned by the Babylonians. Zerubbabel's temple was larger than Solomon's but less magnificent (Ezr 3–6).

Herod rebuilt, enlarged, and made Zerubbabel's temple more beautiful. Herod's temple had an outer court where Gentiles often gathered, a court of women, and an inner court. The gate called Beautiful was on the east side of this temple (Ac 3:2). *See also* NAVE. See 1:341–42, 350–51, 359–60, 400–401, 408, 439–41, 445, 807–8; 2:159, 247–48, 267–69, 382–83, 401, 803–8.

TEMPLE SERVANTS. A group of servants or slaves who performed menial tasks in the temple (1Ch 9:2; Ezr 2:43–58; 8:17–20; Ne 7:46–56). See 1:439.

TEN. Often associated with a group of persons in Semitic languages, though this association is not strong in the OT. Ten commonly represents completeness or constancy (Gn 31:7; *see also* multiples of ten—HUNDRED and THOUSAND). Tithing, based on giving the tenth part of a whole thing, is an important biblical practice in which offering the tenth represents thanks for the whole (Gn 14:20; 28:22; Lv 27:30–34; Nu 18:21–32; Dt 12:1–14; 14:22–29). The Ten Commandments (lit, "10 words") can stand for the whole of God's covenant (Ex 34:28; Dt 4:13).

TEN COMMANDMENTS. The Ten Commandments were given by God to Moses on Mount Sinai and written on tablets of stone (Ex 20; 31:18; 32:15–19; Dt 10:1–5). The Ten Commandments form the basis of God's Law. In the OT they are also referred to as "the words of the covenant" (Ex 20:1; 34:28). In the NT, they are called commandments (Mt 19:17; Eph 6:2). Jesus' interpretation of the commandments is found in Mt 5:17–48; 19:16–22; Mk 2:24–27; Lk 6:1–10; 13:10–16. Perfect love is the fulfillment of the commandments (Mt 22:35–40). See 1:71, 74–75, 77, 172–73, 637; 2:8, 531, 787.

TENT OF MEETING. A provisional tent where the Lord met with His people (Ex 33:7–11; 34:34–35). See 1:136–37, 139, 152, 401.

TERAH (TEE-rah; possibly "ibex").

1. The father of Abraham, Nahor, and Haran (Gn 11:26; 1Ch 1:26; Lk 3:34). Terah, who lived in Ur of the Chaldees, served idols (Jsh 24:2). He moved with Abraham and Lot from Ur to Haran, where he died at the age of 205. See 1:25–26, 49.
2. A place in the wilderness where Israel camped (Nu 33:27–28).

TERAPHIM (TER-ah-fim). Household idols. They were figurines in human form which varied in size (Ezk 21:21; cf Gn 31:19, 32–35; 1Sm 19:13).

TERTIUS (TUR-shi-uhs; "third"). Paul's scribe. At Paul's dictation Tertius wrote down Paul's Letter to the Romans (16:22). See 2:419, 721.

TERTULLUS (TUR-TUL-uhs; "little third"). The Roman lawyer hired by Jewish authorities to prosecute Paul before Felix (Ac 24:1–8). See 2:272.

TESTAMENT.

1. Will (Heb 9:16–17). See 2:214, 660.
2. Covenant (Heb 8:6–10). See 2:660.
3. The books of the Bible pertaining to the Old

Covenant (Genesis through Malachi) and the New Covenant (Matthew through Revelation). The Old and New Covenants are more accurate descriptions for the OT and NT. *See also* COVENANT.

TESTIMONY.
1. Divine commands (Dt 4:45; 6:17).
2. The Decalogue or divine law as found in the ark. The two tables of the law are called the testimony (Ex 25:16). See 1:7.
3. Legal evidence; witness (Mt 26:59). See 1:465, 636; 2:118–19, 204, 274, 771.

TETRARCH (TET-rahrk; "ruler of one quarter"). One who ruled over a small territory (Mt 14:1; Lk 3:1; Ac 13:1). See 2:195.

THADDAEUS (tha-DEE-uhs; "breast"). *See* JUDAS 4. See 2:302, 767.

THANKSGIVING. Gk *eucharistia*, "gratitude," "a prayer of thanksgiving." Eng "Eucharist." *See* BLESS. See 1:110, 409, 560–62, 739; 2:475–76, 568–69.

THEBES (THEEBZ). An ancient city of Upper Egypt referred to as No in the Bible. Thebes was built on both sides of the Nile and is well known for its temples and other ruins (Jer 46:25; Ezk 30:14–16; Na 3:8). See 1:731, 935–36.

THEOCRACY (thee-OK-rah-si; "ruled by God"). The form of government in the OT where God Himself ruled His people and where all power and authority rested in Him (1Sm 8:4–9; 12). See 1:272–73, 277, 453, 887.

THEOPHILUS (thee-OF-uh-luhs; "friend of God"). An unknown person, perhaps an official, to whom Lk and Ac are addressed (Lk 1:3; Ac 1:1). See 2:236, 270–73.

THERAPEUTAE. Jewish sect in Egypt known for its interest in healing. Praised by Philo of Alexandria in *On the Contemplative Life*.

THESSALONIANS, FIRST LETTER OF PAUL TO THE. See 2:563–77.

THESSALONIANS, SECOND LETTER OF PAUL TO THE. See 2:579–92.

THESSALONICA (thes-ah-lo-NIGH-kah; "victory of Thessaly"). A city on the Thermaic Gulf in Macedonia. Thessalonica was a commercial city, a chief port of Macedonia, and a free city in the Roman Empire. It was ruled by politarchs (Ac 17:1–8). Today it is known as Salonika. See 2:378, 388, 563–68, 574–75, 579.

THOMAS (TOM-ahs; "twin"). One of the twelve disciples. He was also known as Didymus, the Greek name for twin. Thomas showed great love for Jesus. When the other apostles were unable to talk Jesus out of going to Bethany to heal Lazarus because of the danger, Thomas said, "Let us also go, that we may die with Him" (Jn 11:16). Thomas doubted Jesus' resurrection since he was not present with the other apostles when Jesus showed Himself to them (Jn 20:24–25). Later, Thomas was with the apostles when Jesus appeared again; Thomas exclaimed, "My Lord and my God" (Jn 20:28). Thomas was with the apostles after the ascension (Ac 1:13). According to tradition Thomas preached in Parthia. See 2:326, 330, 338, 353.

THORNS AND THISTLES. There are 22 Hebrew words for thorns, thistles, briers, and so on that grow in great quantities in Israel (Gn 3:17–18). Figuratively, thorns and thistles are descriptive of a waste place, wickedness, divine visitation, a messenger of Satan, and troubles (Nu 33:55; 2Sm 23:6; Pr 22:5; 24:31; 2Co 12:7). See 1:306; 2:123, 663.

THOUSAND. Hbr *'eleph*; occurs most often in censuses and accounts of troop musters in Nu and other Historical Books. It is a technical military term similar to modern military terms such as division, brigade, and regimen (cf Nu 31, where 12,000 troops were mustered, a unit from each tribe). It described an Israelite tactical unit, which may not have included a literal 1,000 men. When Israelites heard or read the word *'eleph*, they did not necessarily think of the number 1,000. Like "ten" and "hundred," "thousand" can simply mean a large quantity, all of something, or constantly (Jb 9:3; Ps 50:10; 84:10; 90:4). This background is especially helpful for understanding the symbolism in Rv 7:4–8; 14:1–3; 20:2. See 1:150–53.

THREE. The first plural number in Hbr, since "two" in Hbr is dual. Three appears with examples of counsel (Gn 18:2; Dt 19:15; Jb 2:11; Ezk 14:14) and also represents a short, complete cycle of action (Nu 22:28; Est 4:16). The threefold repetition of God's name and His attributes also associates the number with God (Nu 6:23–26; Is 6:3) and points to Jesus' teaching about the Trinity (Mt 28:19). See 2:223–24, 244, 256.

THREE HOLY CHILDREN, SONG OF. See 2:135–41.

THRESHING, THRESHING FLOOR. *See* AGRICULTURE. See 1:262, 317.

THUNDER. In Israel thunder is rare in the summer. In Bible times, when thunder did occur, it served as a sign from God (1Sm 12:17–18). Thunder accompanied the giving of the Law (Ex 19:16; 20:18). Thunder is described poetically as the voice of God and is a picture word for glory and power (Ex 19:16; Jb 37:2; Ps 18:13; Rv 8:5).

THUS SAYS THE LORD. The most common indicator of a prophetic statement, used over 400 times in the OT, mostly in the Books of the Prophets. Indicates a personal, supernatural communication from God to the prophet (cf Zec 4:9). The prophets typically do not identify their statements as their own messages, nor as something resulting from a collaborative effort with the Lord. Such expressions affirm that the prophets truly spoke the Word of God, which must be fulfilled (cf Dt 18:15–22). *See also* DECLARES THE LORD; WORD OF THE LORD (THAT) CAME. See 1:704, 757, 973; 2:387.

THYATIRA (thigh-ah-TIGH-rah). A city of Asia Minor on the Lycus River in northern Lydia. It was known for its purple dyeing and weaving. Lydia, a seller of purple dye at Philippi, was from Thyatira (Ac 16:14). One of the seven churches mentioned in Rv was in Thyatira (Rv 2:18–29). See 2:783.

TIBERIAS (tigh-BEER-i-uhs). A city built by Herod Antipas on the western shore of the Sea of Galilee. Herod named the city after the ruling emperor at that time: Tiberius Caesar. After AD 70, Tiberias became a center for Jewish learning, and later the Sanhedrin was transferred there (Jn 6:1, 23; 21:1). Today it is called Tabariyeh. See 2:319, 404.

TIBERIUS (tigh-BEER-i-uhs). Tiberius Caesar was the second emperor of the Roman Empire. He was born in 42 BC and was the reigning emperor at the time of Christ's death (Lk 3:1; Jn 19:12, 15). See 2:391, 810.

TIBERIUS, SEA OF. *See* GALILEE, SEA OF.

TIBNI (TIB-nigh). Omri's unsuccessful competitor for the throne of Israel (1Ki 16:21–22). See 1:343, 372.

TIGLATH-PILESER III (TIG-lath-pigh-LEE-zur; "trust is [Ninip] the son of E-Sarra"). The Assyrian king who ruled Assyria from 744 to 727 BC. He extended the Assyrian Empire and was recognized as king even in Babylon, where he was referred to as Pul (2Ki 15:19; 1Ch 5:26). Tiglath-pileser broke the coalition of Uzziah, king of Judah, and made him pay tribute. Later, when Ahaz was king of Judah, Pekah of Israel and Rezin of Syria joined forces to conquer Judah. Ahaz paid Tiglath-pileser a large sum of money to defend him and his country from the armies of Pekah and Rezin (2Ki 16:7–10). See 1:322, 853.

TIGRIS (TIGH-gris). One of two rivers of Babylonia, the other one being the Euphrates. See 1:17, 853; 2:39, 45.

TIME. Time and seasons are mentioned early in the Bible (Gn 1:5, 14–16; 8:22; Ex 34:21; Ps 74:17). Ancient people calculated time by dating such things as important events, the reign of kings and rulers, and natural phenomena like earthquakes (Ex 12:40; 1Ki 6:1; 2Ki 3:1–2; Am 1:1; Lk 3:1–2). They followed a lunar year, consisting of 354 days, 8 hours, and 38 seconds. The lunar year was divided into 12 lunar months with seven intercalary months added over 19 years.

The Hebrew month began with the new moon. Before the exile the Hebrews used numbers to name the months; after the exile, they used names. The sacred year began with Nisan (March–April); the secular year, with Tishri (September–October). Months were divided into weeks of seven days. The week ended with the Sabbath (Ex 20:11; Dt 5:14–15).

The day was reckoned from either sunrise to sunset or dawn to darkness (Gn 1:5; 8:22; Ex 12:18; Jn 11:9). It was divided into morning, noon, and evening (Ps 55:17). Night was the time of darkness. It was divided into periods called watches (Ex 14:24; Jgs 7:19; Mk 13:35; Lk 12:38).

Sundials were used to divide the day (2Ki 20:11; Is 38:8). See 1:lxxiii–xcix, 376–77.

TIMNATH-SERAH (TIM-nath-SEE-rah). A city in Ephraim given to Joshua as his inheritance. It was his home and burial place (Jsh 19:50; 24:30). In Jgs 2:9, it is called Timnath-heres.

TIMOTHY (TIM-o-thee; "venerating God"). Paul's companion, assistant, and friend whom he affectionately spoke of as his "beloved and faithful child in the Lord" (1Co 4:17). Timothy's mother was a devout Jewish woman; his father was a Greek (Ac 16:1–3). When he was a child, his mother, Eunice, and grandmother Lois instructed Timothy in the

Jewish religion (2Tm 1:5; 3:15). Through Paul's witness to the Gospel, Timothy became a Christian (1Co 4:17; 1Tm 1:2). After his conversion, Timothy became active in Christian work at Lystra and Iconium. When Paul visited Lystra on his second missionary trip, he found Timothy well spoken of by the Christians in these places (Ac 16:1–2). Paul decided to take the young man with him, and Timothy was set apart for church work by the laying on of hands (1Tm 4:14; 2Tm 1:6). Paul also circumcised Timothy in order not to offend the Jews (Ac 16:3).

Paul frequently mentions Timothy in his writings (Php 1:1; Col 1:1; 1Th 3:2; 2Th 1:1; Phm 1). He also addresses two letters, 1Tm and 2Tm, to his friend. According to tradition, Timothy was a bishop at Ephesus. See 2:604–5.

TIMOTHY, FIRST LETTER OF PAUL TO. See 2:597–613.

TIMOTHY, SECOND LETTER OF PAUL TO. See 2:615–23.

TIRZAH (TUR-zah; "delightfulness"). A city that originally belonged to the Canaanites. Joshua captured Tirzah and killed its king (Jsh 12:24). Jeroboam I made Tirzah his capital, and it remained the capital of the kings of Israel until Omri built Samaria. Tirzah was located five miles east of Samaria and is probably modern-day Tell el-Far'ah. See 1:211, 324, 345, 371, 678; 2:799.

TISHBITE (TISH-bight). Elijah is referred to as a Tishbite, someone from the town of Tishbe or a town similar to that name (1Ki 17:1; 21:17; 28). See 1:351.

TITHE (TIGHTH). A tenth part of one's income. Abram gave tithes to Melchizedek; Jacob promised tithes to God (Gn 14:20; 28:22; Heb 7:2, 6).

According to Mosaic Law, a tenth of all produce of the land and herds was sacred to the Lord (Lv 27:30–33). This tithe was used to support the Levites (Nu 18:21–24). A tenth of it went for the priests (Nu 18:25–32). Additional tithes were used for festivals and for the poor (Dt 12:5–18; 14:22–29). The Pharisees also tithed mint, anise, cumin, and rue (Mt 23:23). See 1:28, 169, 998–99, 1002–3; 2:660.

TITTLE. *See* DOT.

TITUS (TIGH-tuhs). A Gentile convert to Christianity who became Paul's friend and helper. Titus went with Paul and Barnabas to Jerusalem at the time of the council. Since Titus was born of Greek parents, he was uncircumcised (Gal 2:3–5). This offended the Judaizers at the council; however, the Church refused to make Titus submit to circumcision, siding with Paul, who maintained the freedom of Gentiles from the Mosaic Law (Gal 2:1, 3–5). Titus was sent to Corinth to solve the problems there and then rejoined Paul in Macedonia (2Co 2:13; 7:6, 13–14; 8:6, 16; 12:18). Later Titus was left behind in Crete to organize the churches there. Paul wrote his letter to Titus while Titus was in Crete (Ti 1:4–5). The last mention of Titus indicates that he went to Dalmatia (2Tm 4:10). According to tradition Titus was the bishop of Crete. See 2:481–82, 626–27.

TITUS, LETTER OF PAUL TO. See 2:625–33.

TOBIT, THE BOOK OF. See 2:39–49.

TOMB. *See* BURIAL.

TOOTH. In the Bible a tooth illustrates the law of retaliation (Ex 21:24; Mt 5:38). When referred to in a figurative way, teeth also means "plenty" or "oppression" (Gn 49:12; Pr 30:14). The teeth of beasts are figurative for cruelty (Dt 32:24; Jb 4:10). Cleanness of teeth is a picture of famine; gnashing of teeth, a picture of rage or despair (Jb 16:9; Am 4:6; Mt 8:12).

TORCH. A light that could be carried from place to place (Jgs 7:16; Ezk 1:13; Dn 10:6; Jn 18:3). See 1:245.

TOWER OF BABEL. *See* BABEL 2.

TOWN CLERK. An official in Ephesus who was second in rank to the president of the council (Ac 19:35–41). See 2:521.

TRADE. In Israel trades were often carried out in the home. Mats and baskets were handwoven from straw or rushes. Wool, flax, and cotton were washed, combed, and spun into yarn. Then the yarn was woven on a loom into material.

Carpentry was also carried out in the home. The carpenter made agricultural machinery, woodwork for the house, furniture, and wooden utensils. Because of the lack of good timber in Israel, its carpenters could not produce as fine a product as carpenters from countries where good wood was plentiful. When David built his palace and when Solomon built the temple, they hired carpenters from heavily wooded Phoenicia, where the carpenter's trade had reached its height (2Sm 5:11; 1Ki 5:2–8).

Other trades in Bible times were those of the potter and brickmaker. Since Israel has a good supply of clay, many items were made from it (Gn 24:14–20;

Lv 6:28; 1Ki 17:12). Clay was dug from a field that became known as a potter's field because of it. Pottery was roughly shaped by hand or worked on a potter's wheel, then dried and baked in a kiln (Jer 18:3–6). Brick was molded in wooden molds and then baked in loosely built stacks or in kilns (Ex 9:8–10).

Metal casting and forging, tanning, stonecutting, gem cutting, leather working, and tent making were other common trades in Bible times. The leather worker made sandals, parts of armor, aprons, belts, shoes, and purses (Gn 3:21; 2Ki 1:8, Mt 3:4). Tentmakers used such items as knives, shears, and needles and thread to make their tents. The best tents were woven of goats' hair and were usually dark in color (Ex 25:4; Ac 18:3). See 1:61, 401, 622, 764, 868, 935; 2:40–41, 151, 441–42, 805.

TRADITION (trah-DISH-uhn).

1. Interpretations of the OT law (Mt 15:1–9; Gal 1:14). See 1:194, 433, 499; 2:200, 210.
2. Apostolic teaching or truths handed down in the Church by those who were witnesses to Christ (1Co 11:2; cf Lk 1:2; Rm 6:17; 1Co 15:3–9; 2Pt 2:21). See 2:291, 321–23, 813.

TRADITION CRITICISM. The attempt to discover the growth, combination, and reinterpretation of texts and motifs over time while considering the communities that created them. The method assumes that a text evolves over time as a community changes. See 1:710.

TRANSFIGURATION (trans-fig-yoo-RAY-shuhn). The name given to the time when Jesus was visibly glorified in the presence of His three disciples. Jesus' transfiguration likely occurred on Mount Hermon (Mt 17:1–13; Mk 9:2–13; Lk 9:28–36). See 1:313–14, 351; 2:201, 246, 280, 727.

TREASURE. Anything that is collected in storehouses, for instance, grain, wine, gold, or silver (1Ki 14:26; 15:18; Mt 2:11; 6:19).

Figuratively, treasure depicts God's resources in nature, God's peculiar people, piety, the Gospel, and Christ-centered wisdom and knowledge (Ex 19:5; Dt 28:12; Is 33:6; 2Co 4:7; Col 2:3). See 1:169, 239, 361, 962; 2:65, 126–27, 288, 485, 557–58.

TREASURY. The place in the temple where gifts were received (Mk 12:41; Jn 8:20; cf 1Ch 9:26; Lk 21:1). See 1:389, 454; 2:158–59, 807.

TRESPASS. *See* SIN, II.

TRIAL.

1. A testing, usually accomplished by a painful process, for the purpose of purifying or achieving good (1Pt 1:6–7; cf Ps 7:9; Zec 13:9). See 1:50, 166, 183, 521–22; 2:430, 521, 682, 709–10, 785.
2. An examination before a court to decide the guilt or innocence of the defendant (Mt 26:36–27:36). See 1:987; 2:203–4, 248–49, 379.

TRIBE. The 12 tribes of Israel (Jacob's name in Gn 32:28) came from Jacob's 12 sons, with Joseph's sons, Ephraim and Manasseh, forming two tribes (Gn 48:5; Nu 26:5–51; Jsh 13:7–33; 15–19). No tribal territory was given to Levi. The heads or elders of each tribe had great influence (1Sm 8; 2Sm 3:17; 2Ki 23:1). See 1:23, 212–13, 399–400; 2:676, 682, 688.

TRIBULATION (trib-yoo-LAY-shuhn). *See* SUFFERING. See 1:615–16; 2:727.

TRIBUTE. *See* TAXES.

TRINITY (TRIN-uh-tee). The Church's term for the coexistence of the Father, Son, and Holy Spirit in the unity of the Godhead: three distinct persons in one Divine Being, or Essence. The term *Trinity* does not occur in the Bible, but many passages support the doctrine of the Trinity (Dt 6:4; Is 48:16; Mt 3:13–17; 28:19; Jn 10:30; 2Co 13:14; 1Tm 2:5). See 2:196, 244, 340–41, 493, 746.

TROAS (TRO-as). A city of Asia Minor in the district of Mysia about six miles south of ancient Troy. It was founded by Alexander the Great (Ac 16:8–11; 20:5–10; 2Tm 4:13). See 2:388, 481, 813.

TRUMPET. A wind instrument made of metal or from the horn of a ram or goat (Nu 10:2). Trumpets were played to provide music; they were also sounded in battle and for other signals, such as an alarm or when a new king took the throne (Jgs 3:27; 1Ki 1:39; Is 18: 3; Hos 8:1; Am 3:6; 1Th 4:16). See 1:144, 217, 596; 2:576, 777–78, 783.

TRUST. *See* FAITH.

TRUTH. That which is eternal, ultimate, secure, steadfast, reliable. God is truth; He cannot lie (Ps 31:5; Is 65:16; Jn 17:3; 2Tm 2:13; Heb 6:18). Everything that comes from God is true (Ps 33:4). God has made known all that humanity needs to know for life and salvation. Truth is manifested supremely in Christ (Jn 1:14, 17; 14:6). The Holy Spirit imparts the truth of Christ (1Jn 2:20–22). God's Word is truth (Jn 17:17–19; 2Co 4:2; Gal 5:7; Eph 1:13; Jas 1:18). See 1:309–10, 367, 705–6; 2:6–7, 344, 424, 627, 682, 750.

TUBAL-CAIN (TYOO-buhl-kayn; possibly "territory of the smith"). A son of Lamech who worked in brass and iron (Gn 4:22). Tubal-cain represents the ancestor of all metalworkers.

TURBAN. A head covering worn by the priests as part of their official vestments. The words "Holy to the Lord" were written on it (Ex 28:4, 36–39; 29:6; 39:28–31; Lv 8:9).

TURN. Hbr *haphak* used of God punishing someone or something by overthrowing it (e.g., Sodom and Gomorrah). Also Hbr *shub*, "to turn, turn around." A very common OT verb, used over 1,000 times. Appropriately translated "repent" in more than 100 cases, most often in Jer (Is rarely uses the term this way). Repentance is God's work (Jer 31:18) that leads a person to renounce sin—requesting God's mercy and returning to His way (*see also* WAY). For a classic OT example, see David's confession and prayer in Ps 51; cf Ecclus 17:25–29. Forms of Gk *strepho* translate the Hbr term. However, Gk *metanoio* is not used for *shub* in LXX. Qumran follows OT usages. *See also* REPENTANCE. See 1:179, 332, 768–69; 2:205, 281.

TURTLEDOVE. A common type of pigeon in Israel that poor people used for sacrifices (Gn 15:9; Lk 2:24). See 1:613.

TWELVE. Associated with the sons of Jacob (Gn 35:22b–26), from whom descended the tribes of Israel (Ex 28:21; Nu 1:1–16). Twelve thus represents the people of God. This later applied to the NT people of God, the Church, led by the 12 apostles (Mt 19:28). See 1:212; 2:245, 280, 682.

TWENTY-FOUR. Twelve repeated (Rv 4:4, 10). *See also* TWELVE.

TWO. Hbr root term means "to repeat." The number's form is not plural but dual, a word form in Semitic languages used for pairs on the human body (arms, legs, etc.). However, the term also describes division, contrast, and distinction (1Ki 18:21; Jb 9:33). There may be an association with Day 2 of the creation, which describes separations (Gn 1:6–8).

TYCHICUS (TIK-i-kuhs; "fortune"). A disciple, messenger, and spokesman of Paul (Ac 20:4; Eph 6:21–22; Col 4:7–8). See 2:522, 524, 598, 635.

TYPE. Gk *typos*; of objects, a "shape" or "model"; of ideas, a "pattern," as in Eng "prototype." Paul saw in OT persons and events examples for teaching Christians (1Co 10:6, 11) and also prophetic prototypes of NT persons and events (Rm 5:14). *See also* ANTITYPE. See 1:122, 215, 299, 571, 717, 724, 800, 864; 2:119, 272.

TYRE (TIGHR; "rock"). An important Phoenician city on the Mediterranean Coast. It was built partly on the rocky mainland and partly on an island. Alexander the Great constructed a causeway to connect the two parts.

Tyre was a powerful merchant city (Is 23:8). David formed an alliance with Tyre (2Sm 5:11; 1Ki 5:1; 2Ch 2:3). A number of the prophets spoke against Tyre and its inhabitants (Is 23:1–17; Jer 27:3; Ezk 26–28). Jesus visited its region and was well received (Mt 15:21; Mk 7:24). Paul once stayed in Tyre for seven days (Ac 21:3–4). See 1:331, 401, 806, 912; 2:41, 246, 388.

U

UNBELIEF. A lack of faith; the rejection of God's promises and threats as found in His Word, and especially the refusal to believe and trust in Christ (Rm 11:20; Heb 3:19; cf Jn 3:36). See 1:240, 766–67, 789; 2:249, 258, 425–26, 659.

UNCIRCUMCISED.

1. Those who have not submitted to the Jewish rite of circumcision; Gentiles (Gn 34:14; Jgs 14:3; 1Sm 14:6; Rm 4:9). See 1:465; 2:507.
2. Ears that do not hear the truth (Jer 6:10; Ac 7:51).
3. Hearts that are not open to God (Lv 26:41; Jer 4:4; Ac 7:51). *See also* CIRCUMCISION.

UNCLEAN.

1. A number of food items were considered unclean in Bible times: animals that did not part the hoof and chew the cud; animals and birds that ate blood or the flesh of dead bodies; insects that did not have hind legs for jumping; and water creatures without scales or fins (Lv 11; Nu 19; Dt 14:1–21). See 1:112, 118–19; 2:21, 453.
2. Other forms of ceremonial uncleanness included leprosy, sexual discharge, and contact with the dead (Lv 11:24–15:33; 17:15; Nu 19:16–22). *See also* CLEAN. See 1:106, 137, 733; 2:200, 246, 475–76.

UNICORN (YOO-nuh-kawrn). *See* WILD OX.

UNKNOWN GOD. While Paul was in Athens, he

found an altar with the inscription "To the unknown god" (Ac 17:23). This was an altar built to appease any god that may have been overlooked. See 2:378.

UNLEAVENED. Bread without yeast. The Israelites ate unleavened bread at Passover as a reminder of the exodus (Ex 12:8; 13:3–10). See 1:74, 132, 207; 2:309–10.

UNRIGHTEOUS. *See* RIGHTEOUS; UNBELIEF. See 1:93; 2:425, 710.

UPHOLDS. Hbr *samak*, "sustain, support." The arms of the wicked will not support them before God on the Last Day, while the Lord's arms are under the righteous to hold them up. *See also* ARM; HAND; RIGHT HAND. See 1:193; 2:603, 657, 712.

UPPER CHAMBER, ROOM. *See* HOMES.

UR (UR). Abraham's native city. It was located in southern Babylonia near Uruk and was called Ur of Chaldeans (Gn 11:28, 31; 15:7; Ne 9:7). Today it is Tell Muggayyar. See 1:17, 25, 784.

URIAH (yoo-RIGH-ah; "Yahweh is light").

1. A Hittite, the husband of Bathsheba. After David committed adultery with Bathsheba, he arranged to have Uriah placed on the front line of battle so that Uriah would be killed (2Sm 11; Mt 1:6). See 1:281.
2. A prophet who was put to death by Jehoiakin after he predicted the destruction of Judah (Jer 26:20–23). See 1:751, 767.

URIM AND THUMMIM (YOO-rim and THUM-im; "lights" and "perfections"). Objects placed in the breastpiece of the high priest. Their exact nature is unknown. They were used, however, to determine the will of the Lord (Ex 28:30; Lv 8:8; Nu 27:21). See 1:310–11, 615.

UZ (UZ). The land of Job. Although its site is uncertain, Bible scholars usually locate it in the Arabian Desert next to Edom (Jb 1:1; Jer 25:20; Lm 4:21). See 1:496–99.

UZZAH (UZ-ah; "strength"). Son of Abinadab. When the oxen of the cart bearing the ark stumbled, Uzzah was struck dead for putting out his hand and touching the ark of God (2Sm 6:3–11; 1Ch 13:7–11). See 1:294, 393.

UZZIAH (u-ZIGH-ah; "Yahweh is strength"). Also known as Azariah, he was the son of Amaziah and the tenth king of Judah. Uzziah became king at the age of 16 and ruled Judah for 52 years (2Ki 14:21–22). He fought successfully against the Mehunim, the Arabs, and the Philistines. He strengthened his kingdom by developing agriculture, fortifying Jerusalem, and organizing the army (2Ch 26:1–15). "And his fame spread far. . . . But when he was strong, he grew proud, to his destruction" (2Ch 26:15–16).

Uzziah decided to burn incense to the Lord and went into the temple with that in mind. The priests told him to leave, for only they were set apart to burn incense. When Uzziah became angry with them, God struck him with leprosy. Uzziah remained a leper until the day he died (2Ch 26: 16–22). See 1:373, 375–76, 402, 715–17, 879.

V

VANITY

1. Something that is not profitable (Ec 1:2). See 1:658–60, 666–67.
2. That which is empty, nothing, worthless, futile, such as idols and lies (Ps 4:2; Jer 46:10–12; cf 2Ki 17:15; Is 41:29).
3. Human help is vain (Ps 60:11).
4. Sin (cf Ps 119:37; Rm 8:20).

VASHTI (VASH-tigh). The wife of Ahasuerus. She was the queen of Persia (Est 1:9–22). See 1:464, 469.

VEIL.

1. *See* DRESS. See 1:696–97; 2:454.
2. The curtain that separated the Holy Place from the Most Holy Place in the tabernacle and temple (Ex 26:31–35; 2Ch 3:14; Mt 27:51). See 1:72, 359, 445.

VICARIOUS SATISFACTION. The sacrifice of one life for another to atone for the sins of the one making the sacrifice or for someone on whose behalf the sacrifice is offered. The sacrifice bears the sin and guilt, acting as a substitute. This describes the sacrifice of Christ on behalf of mankind; He gave His life for the sake of all people and satisfied the justice of God. See 1:109–10, 563; 2:383.

VINE.

1. *See* VINEYARD.
2. Figuratively, a vine often depicts both Israel and happiness and contentment (1Ki 4:25; Ps 80:8; 128:3; Mi 4:4). Apostate Israel is pictured as wild grapes or a strange vine (Is 5:2; Jer 2:21). An emp-

ty vine is a picture of spiritual unfruitfulness (Hos 10:1). The vine of Sodom refers to godless people (Dt 32:28–33). The vine and branches are a picture of Christ and believers (Jn 15:1–6). See 1:805, 810; 2:336.

VINEYARD. The soil of Israel has always been good for cultivating grapes. When the Israelites arrived in Canaan, they expanded the grape industry already there (Nu 13:23–27). They cleared the land of stones, terraced it, planted choice shoots, and carefully cultivated and trained them (1Ki 4:25; Is 5:1–2; Hos 2:12; Mi 1:6). Often they built a wall around the vineyard and erected a tower (Is 5:1–7; Sg 2:15).

When harvesting began in June, bunches of grapes were gathered in baskets and taken to the winepress (Jer 6:9; Rv 14:14–20). The winepress was usually cut from solid rock, 6–12 feet in diameter and 1–2 feet deep, with a trench leading to a smaller container. Grapes were put in the winepress and trampled by men until the juice flowed into the lower container. This was one method of pressing grapes.

The grape juice was taken to the people's homes and allowed to ferment. The dregs were poured off, and then the wine was stored in large jars of stone or bottles of goatskins (Mt 9:17).

Fresh grape juice was also boiled down to make grape honey. Grapes were eaten raw in season or dried in the sun to make raisins (1Sm 25:18). See 1:171, 333, 344, 663, 730.

VIPER. *See* SERPENT. See 2:592.

VIRGIN MARY (VUR-jin MAIR-ee). *See* MARY 1.

VISION. An inspired dream or apparition (Nu 24:4; Is 6; Ezk 1; 8–10; Dn 7–8; Ac 10:9–16; 26:13–19; 2Co 12:1–4). See 1:28, 723–24, 800–805, 824–26; 2:778–80, 783–85.

VOW. Hbr *neder*. Gk *euche*, a vow or prayer. In OT, a peace offering (Lv 7:16; Nu 30:3–4) by which a worshiper is bound to God with a promise; a thank offering (Nu 21:1–3; cf Na 1:15) requesting God's favor and praising Him for success in fulfilling a promise (Ps 22:25; 50:14; 116:17–18). A vow and its offering are not distinguished. Clean animals or even service was offered with a vow. Both men and women made such vows (Nu 30). Related vows include the Nazirite vow (Nu 6) and "devotion to destruction" (cf Ecclus 16:9). In the Apocrypha, vows are often mentioned without the context of sacrifices. *See also* OATH. See 1:120–23, 131, 137, 141, 661; 2:207–8, 224, 491.

W

WAGES. In early times wages were often paid in trade (Gn 29:15, 20; 30:28–34). According to Mosaic Law a hired person was to receive his wages at the end of the day (Lv 19:13; Dt 24:14–15; Mt 20:8). Withholding wages was condemned (Jer 22:13; Mal 3:5). *See also* LABOR; SERVANT. See 2:622.

WALK. Hbr *halak*, can describe one's life or way of life (Gn 17:1), especially before God. Gk *poreuomai* often translates it in LXX. Gk *stoicheo*, "be in line with" or "keep in step with," is common in ethical sections of Paul's Letters (Eph 4:1, 17; 5:2; 1Th 4:1). *See also* WAY. See 1:81, 108, 283, 483, 535; 2:196–97, 334, 437, 692, 746–47.

WALL.

1. *See* HOMES.
2. In Bible times city walls were often made of clay (cf Ps 62:3; Is 30:13). Fortified cities, however, were surrounded by enormous stone walls (Ne 4:3; Is 2:15; Zep 1:16). See 1:216, 440, 516; 2:803–5, 808.
3. In the Bible walls are a symbol of strength, protection, and salvation (Is 26:1; Jer 15:20; Zec 2:5). *See also* FORTIFICATION, FORTRESS. See 1:602.

WAR. Before going to war, the Israelites consulted God's will and sought His help through prayer and sacrifice (Jgs 1:1; 20:2; 1Sm 7:9; 14:37; 1Ki 22:6).

As they were about to enter into battle, the Israelites, their commander, or a priest gave a shout or battle cry (1Sm 17:52; Is 42:13). Fighting was carried on by hand-to-hand combat (2Sm 1:23; 2:18). Strategies employed included double attacks, ambushes, surprise attacks, false retreats, and night attacks (Gn 14:15; Jsh 8:12; Jgs 7; 20:36; 2Ki 7:12). Some wars were decided by a single combat (1Sm 17).

After a battle, countrymen and enemies (if they were on their own soil) were buried and mourned (2Sm 3:31–39; 1Ki 11:15). Triumph was expressed, captives were killed or sold into slavery, and the booty was equally divided (Dt 20:16–18; Jsh 10:24; 1Sm 30:24–25; 31:9; Am 1:6, 9). *See also* ARMOR, ARMS; ARMY. See 1:215–16, 294–96, 577, 891, 978; 2:97, 86, 777.

WASHING. Cleanliness is stressed in the Bible. Frequent bathing or washing was necessary because of the warm climate. After a journey the people washed the dust from their feet, and before meals they washed their hands (Gn 18:4; Ex 30:19, 21; Jgs

19:21; Mt 15:2; Mk 7:3; Lk 7:37–44; 11:38; Jn 13:5–14). *See also* BATHE. See 1:112, 334; 2:246, 330, 573, 628.

WATCH.

1. A guard (Jgs 7:19; cf 2Ki 11:5; Ne 4:9; Mt 27:62–66). See 1:424, 690.
2. A lookout (1Sm 14:16; 2Sm 13:34; 2Ki 9:17; Is 21:8). See 1:730–31, 739, 800, 803; 2:203, 656.
3. The Hebrews divided the 12 hours of night into three watches (Ex 14:24; Jgs 7:19; Lam 2:19); the Romans, into four (Mt 14:25; Mk 13:35; Lk 12:38).

WATER. Because of the scarcity of water in Israel, it was greatly valued (Is 3:1; 33:16). Finding water was an important event; scarcity of water, a serious problem (Gn 6:7; Dt 28:12; 1Ki 17:1).

Water is also a picture for the messianic age, good news, life, and grace (Ps 23:2; Pr 25:25; Sg 4:15; Is 30:25; 32:2; 35:6–7; Jn 4:7–15). Negatively, it is a picture of trouble or misfortune (Ps 66:12; 69:1; Is 8:7). See 1:48–49, 88–89, 562–63, 602, 807; 2:207, 333–34, 741–42, 803.

WATER FOR IMPURITY. Water that was mixed with the ashes of a red heifer to remove impurity or sin (Nu 19). See 1:132.

WAVE OFFERING. The rite of waving the sacrificial portion before the Lord was regularly performed in the peace offering, the guilt offering of lepers, and the meal offering of jealousy (Lv 7:30, 34; 9:21; 14:12; 21; Nu 5:25). The sheaf of the first ripe grain as well as two loaves and two lambs at Pentecost were also waved before the Lord (Lv 23:10–11, 15, 20).

WAY(S). Hbr *Derek;* Gk *hodos,* "trodden path," used for a "pattern of behavior or custom." "The way of the Lord" is twofold: He punishes sinfulness, but He also shows mercy to the repentant (Ex 33:13). Very common term in LXX, especially in wisdom books and prophets; also occurs in the Apocrypha wisdom books. Often describes a way of life or contrasting ways of life between which people must choose (e.g., way of life and way of death). Qumran literature likewise includes these expressions and ideas. *See also* WALK. See 1:xl, 78, 82, 207, 483, 530–31; 2:176, 197, 380, 520, 687.

WEAVING. *See* TRADE.

WEDDING. *See* MARRIAGE. See 1:683–84; 2:333.

WEEDS. *Tares* in some translations. Probably a poisonous plant known as the bearded darnel. It is a grass that cannot be distinguished from wheat until the two are full grown (Mt 13:25–30). See 2:585.

WEEKS, FEAST OF. *See* PENTECOST 1. See 1:264; 2:224.

WEIGH. Gk *diakrino,* "to distinguish, to judge." *See* CONDEMN; JUDGE. See 1:580, 635.

WEIGHT. The Hebrews used stones for weights and balances for scales (Lv 19:36; Dt. 25:15; Pr 16:11). For the most part they followed the Babylonian system of weights where 60 shekels (.36 ounce) equaled 1 mina (about 1 1/12 pounds) and 60 minas equaled 1 talent (about 65 pounds). These were the regular weights and were called light shekels, minas, and standards.

There were also heavy shekels, minas, and talents, which were exactly double the weight of the regular standards above. See 1:317, 496.

WHALE. *See* FISH 2. See 1:916–18.

WHEAT. *See* AGRICULTURE; FOOD.

WIDOW. Widows were protected under Mosaic Law. They were to be treated with justice and special consideration (Ex 22:22; Dt 14:29; 24:19–21; 27:19; Ps 94:6; Ezk 22:7; Mal 3:5). If a married man died without a son, his brother was obligated to marry the man's widow (Dt 25:5–6; Mt 22:23–30). *See also* LEVIRATE MARRIAGE.

The NT Church also cared for its widows (Ac 6:1–6; 1Tm 5:3–16). Older, pious widows who had neither children nor grandchildren to care for them were enrolled, probably for special service (1Tm 5:9–10). See 1:119, 257–60, 343–44, 914–15; 2:35, 247, 306, 390, 611.

WIFE. *See* MARRIAGE.

WILDERNESS. Either a desert or a wild, thinly populated, uncultivated region used for pasturage. One of the chief wildernesses the Bible refers to is the place where the children of Israel wandered in the Sinai Peninsula (Nu 14:33; Dt 1:1; Jsh 5:6; Ne 9:19; 21; Ps 78:40, 52). See 1:81, 92–93, 126–28, 139–42, 292, 595; 2:244, 280, 350, 656, 788.

WILD OX. An animal, now extinct, that was known for its ferocity, strength, and speed (Nu 23:22; 24:8; Dt 33:17; Jb 39:9–10).

WILL.

1. Inclination or choice. God's will is that which He determines (Eph 1:11). It is revealed in His acts, His Law, and especially in Christ (Mt 6:10; Ac 22:14; Rm 2:18; 12:2; Col 1:9). See 1:173, 311, 512, 640, 775, 941; 2:248, 465, 608.

   Humanity's fallen or natural will cannot be good (Rm 8:7). God's grace alone is able to incline a person's will to good (Php 2:13). *See also* ELECT, ELECTION; PREDESTINATION; SIN, II. See 1:1004; 2:345, 425.
2. *See* TESTAMENT 1.

WIND. The Hebrews recognized four winds (Ezk 37:9; Mt 24:31). The wind that blew from the south was hot and dry; the wind from the north, cold (Sg 4:16; Lk 12:55; cf Jb 37:22). The west wind brought rain (1Ki 18:43–45; Ps 148:8). The east wind was hot and dry (Gn 41:6, 23, 27; Ezk 19:12; Hos 13:15; Jnh 4:8); it also had violent force (Jb 27:21; Ps 48:7; Is 27:8; Jer 18:17). See 1:89, 608, 761; 2:245, 787.

WINE, WINEPRESS, WINESKIN. *See* VINEYARD. See 1:39, 762, 954; 2:17, 248, 261, 333.

WINNOW, WINNOWING FORK (WIN-o, WIN-o-ing). A fork to throw threshed grain into the air to clean it of chaff (Is 30:24; Mt 3:12). *See also* AGRICULTURE.

WINTER. In Israel the winter season proper (December–February) is short. Scriptural references to the winter season, however, often include fall and seasons of seedtime (Gn 8:22; Ps 74:17; Zec 14:8; Mt 24:20). Although winters are usually mild, snow and hail occur in the higher regions. See 1:96; 2:445, 480–82, 625.

WISDOM. Hbr *chokmah;* Gk *sophia*. Skill, intelligence, judgment, understanding (Pr 10:1; 1Ki 3:28; 5:12; Dn 5:11; cf Ex 31:6). Wisdom is an attribute of God (Pr 3:19). It is the completeness and perfection of His knowledge (cf Jb 10:4; 26:6; Pr 5:21; Is 31:2). God's wisdom is seen in creation, especially His creation of man (Jb 12; 38–39; Ps 139:14). God's wisdom is far above that of people (cf Jb 11:6–9; Is 40:14, 28).

God gives wisdom to people (Pr 2:6). The fear of God is the beginning of wisdom (Pr 9:10). Since God's ultimate purposes in history are revealed in Christ, Jesus is wisdom (1Co 1:30; Col 2:2–3).

By faith in Christ, this wisdom becomes one's own and is expressed in one's life (1Co 1:19–24, Eph 5:15). The Bible contrasts this wisdom to a worldly understanding (1Co 1:19–26; Mt 11:25). See 1:481–86, 491–92, 528–34, 624–29, 645–47; 2:211, 332, 461–63, 530, 687–89.

WISE MEN. Those who served in the ruler's court to provide him with knowledge and insight (Jer 50:35; Dn 2:18). They were categorized together with sorcerers and magicians (Dn 2:27). It was these Wise Men who came from the east to see the infant Christ (Mt 2). *See also* MAGICIAN. See 1:86, 483–84, 833; 2:53, 196, 805.

WITCH, WITCHCRAFT. *See* DIVINATION; MAGIC.

WITNESS. Hbr *'ud*, "to repeat, retell, bear witness." In LXX, forms of Gk *martyreo*, "to testify," "bear witness." Used in legal contexts. Rooted in OT experience of the prophets, who were persecuted for testifying against Israel and calling the people to repentance. This experience of suffering for righteous testimony finds new emphasis in 1Macc 1–2 and 2Macc 6–7. These experiences laid the foundation for the Christian understanding of martyrdom. In fact, Heb 11:35 likely refers to the sufferings of the Maccabees. (Eng "martyr" is one who dies for his or her testimony.) See 1:142, 169, 517–18, 732, 809, 837; 2:157–58, 204, 323–25, 375.

WOE. Hbr *'oy* and *hoy*, also translated "oh!" or "alas." Interjection expressing sadness or warning. The prophets frequently begin pronouncements of judgment with this term, which may introduce a series of condemnations. See 1:706, 809, 859, 951–53; 2:189, 397, 785.

WOMAN. The helpmate of man. Together with man she forms a unity, created in the image of God, to rule over creation (Gn 1:26–28; 2:18–23). *See also* MARRIAGE. See 1:24, 34, 635; 2:201, 454, 460.

WOMAN IN LABOR. Common metaphor in the Prophetic Books; describes the greatest distress a person can experience.

WOMEN OF THE TABERNACLE. Mentioned only in Ex 38:8 and 1Sm 2:22, they apparently assisted the priests and Levites. However, their work is not described. Women could not serve as priests or Levites.

WORD. Hbr *deber*; noun from *'amar*. Important usage in OT wisdom literature. Gk *hrema*; *logos*. The Gk terms are used as synonyms in the LXX. God created the heavens and the earth by His Word (Gn 1). God's Word is His revelation to people (1Ki 6:11; 13:20; Jer 1:4, 11). By the Word, faith is created and the Church is built (Jn 14:26; Ac 4:29, 31).

God's Word came to people in various forms, for example, through speaking, writing, visions, and symbols (Jer 1:11; Jn 3:14–15; 20:31; 2Tm 4:2). His Word now comes to us through its written form in Scripture (2Tm 3:16) as proclaimed by His people. God's Word is dynamic, creative, and functional (Ps 147:15–18; Is 55:10–11; Mt 8:24–27; Rm 1:16).

Jesus Christ is the supreme revelation of God. He is the living Word (Jn 1:1–5; Rv 19:13). Wis 18:14–16, 22 anticipates the points in Jn 1. See 1:xvi, xxxi–xxxii, 9, 447–48, 533–34, 728–29, 769; 2:33, 209, 329–30, 359–60, 429, 585, 728, 773.

WORD OF THE LORD (THAT) CAME. Used over 100 times in the OT, mostly in the Books of the Prophets. Prophetic revelations are described as a "word" that God delivered to the prophets and through them. (Cf Jer 1:1–2; Ezk 1:3; Jl 1:1; Jnh 1:1; Mi 1:1; Zep 1:1; Hg 1:1; Zec 1:1; Mal 1:1). Sometimes the "word" is accompanied by a vision (Is 1:1; Ezk 1:1) or is somehow "seen" (Am 1:1; Mi 1:1; Hab 1:1). *See also* DECLARES THE LORD; THUS SAYS THE LORD. See 1:973.

WORD THAT CAME . . . FROM THE LORD. Introductory statement used by Jeremiah. *See* WORD OF THE LORD (THAT) CAME.

WORKS.

1. The works of God include creation, preservation, and redemption (Gn 1; Jb 37:14–16; Ps 104:24; 107; Jn 5:20–36; 14:10–12).
2. Whether a person's works are good or bad depends on that person's relationship to God. Only a person who believes in Jesus Christ as Savior can do good works in God's eyes, since good works are a fruit of faith (Jn 6:28–29; Rm 6; 14:23; Gal 2:20–21; Col 1:21–23). *See also* FAITH; FRUIT; JUSTIFICATION; SANCTIFICATION. See 1:22, 82, 178, 512, 559, 614, 809; 2:220–21, 437, 506–9, 687, 690–91, 694–97, 752.

WORLD.

1. The universe (Jn 1:10). See 1:22, 24, 43; 2:333.
2. The human race (Jn 3:16; 2Co 5:19). See 1:34; 2:254, 333–34.
3. The wicked; unregenerated; those who are opposed to God (Jn 15:18; 1Jn 2:15). The devil is the prince of this world (Jn 12:31). See 1:169; 2:254, 772, 784.
4. The earth (1Sm 2:8; Jb 37:12; Is 18:3). See 1:48; 2:339, 363.
5. The Roman Empire (Lk 2:1). See 2:267, 272.

WORMWOOD. A bitter plant that grows in desert places (Pr 5:4; Am 5:7; 6:12; Rv 8:11). See 1:789.

WORSHIP (WUR-ship; "to bow down," "kiss the hand," "to revere, work, serve"). The respect and reverence given to God or a god. The patriarchs worshiped God by building altars and sacrificing to Him (Gn 12:7–8; 13:4). Mosaic Law established the place for worship and set the times and forms for it. The prophets condemn empty ceremonies and people who try to cover an ungodly life (Is 1:11–17).

Worship in the NT is centered in and around the Word of God. It involved reading the OT and psalms, singing hymns and spiritual songs, teaching, praying, and celebrating the Lord's Supper (Lk 4:16–22; Ac 2:42; Rm 12:7–8; 1Co 11:23–24; 14:26; Eph 5:19). See 1:92–93, 107, 112, 386–87, 545–49; 2:10, 454, 464, 773, 783–84.

WRATH. Translates a variety of Hbr terms. Gk *orge*, used with *thumos*. The "anger" of God incited by sin, which offends God's righteousness and holiness. As a result, God judges or condemns sinners.

1. Anger of people. *See also* ANGER.
2. The reaction of a righteous God to evil (Dt 9:7, 22; Is 13:9; Rm 1:18; Eph 5:6; Rv 14:10, 19). See 1:70, 110–11, 222, 670, 732, 805–7, 911, 962–66; 2:189, 196, 475, 530, 661, 772–73, 784–85, 788–89.

WRITING. Probably invented by the Sumerians, who wrote in pictograms around 3000 BC. Their writing led to cuneiform, wedge-shaped letters written on clay. The Hebrews obtained their alphabet from the Phoenicians. Writing among the Hebrews was attributed to men of learning (Dt 17:18; 24:1, 3; Is 29:11–12). Writing materials included clay, wax, wood, metal, and plaster (Dt 27:2–3; Jsh 8:32; Lk 1:63). Later vellum, parchment, and papyrus were used (2Tm 4:13; 2Jn 12). A stylus was used to write on hard material; a reed pen, on parchment and papyrus (2Co 3:3; 2Jn 12). Ink was made of lampblack or soot. *See also* ALPHABET. See 1:lxxiii–lxxv.

WRITINGS, THE. *See* MEGILLOTH. See 1:491–92.

X

XERXES (ZURK-seez). *See* AHASUERUS. See 1:460–65; 2:105.

Y

YAHWEH. *See* LORD.

YEAR. *See* TIME.

YEAST. *See* LEAVEN.

YOKE. A wooden bar or frame with thongs that went around the necks of two draft animals and another thong that fastened to a wagon or plow. The yoke was used to join the animals together so they could draw the wagon or plow (Nu 19:2; Dt 21:3).

Figuratively, a yoke depicts subjection; the removal of a yoke, deliverance (Gn 27:40; 1Ki 12:4, 9–11; Is 9:4; Jer 2:20; Mt 11:29–30). A yokefellow is one's co-worker at a difficult task (Php 4:3). See 1:664, 864; 2:209, 398.

Z

ZACCHAEUS (za-KEE-uhs; "pure"). The chief tax collector of Jericho who climbed a sycamore tree to see Christ. Jesus told Zacchaeus to come down because He was going to his house that day. With joy, Zacchaeus came down. He became a follower of Christ (Lk 19:1–10). See 2:283.

ZACHARIAH (zak-ah-RIGH-ah). *See* ZECHARIAH 5.

ZADOK (ZAY-dok; "righteous"). A descendant of Aaron's son Eleazar (1Ch 24:3). Zadok was the son of Ahitub (2Sm 8:17). He was one of the young men, mighty in valor, who came to David at Hebron with the intention of making David king over Israel (1Ch 12:28). Later, after David had become king, Zadok was high priest with Abiathar (2Sm 8:17). He supported David during Absalom's rebellion and remained faithful to David in his old age when Adonijah tried to take over the throne (2Sm 15: 24–29; 19:11; 1Ki 1:7–8, 32, 45). See 1:182, 338, 755, 797.

ZADOKITES. Descendants of the high priest Zadok. In King David's time, there was more than one high priest. Zadok supported Solomon's succession as king and was made sole high priest (1Ki 1; 2:35). All high priests were Zadokites from c 970 BC until between 152 and 140 BC, when the Hasmoneans expelled the Zadokites from the temple and made themselves priests. The priests described in the Dead Sea Scrolls are called "sons of Zadok," since some Zadokites apparently retreated to Qumran after they were expelled. See 1:797, 807; 2:807.

ZALMONAH (zal-MUN-AH; "shady"). A place southeast of Edom where Israel camped (Nu 33:41–42).

ZALMUNNA (ZAL-mun-ah; possibly "shade denied"). One of the two kings of Midian whom Gideon put to death (Jgs 8:5–21; Ps 83:11).**ZAPHENATH-PANEAH** (ZAF-i-nath-pah-NEE-ah; possibly "the god speaks and he lives"). The name Pharaoh gave to Joseph (Gn 41:45).

ZAREPHATH (ZAR-i-fath). A Phoenician town 8 miles south of Sidon (1Ki 17:9–10; Ob 20; Lk 4:26). When the brook Chereth dried up, Elijah went to Zarephath. There a widow gave him a home until the famine was over (1Ki 17:8–24). See 1:332, 343, 914–15.

ZEALOTS (ZEL-uhtz). A Jewish party organized by Judas of Gamala in the time of Quirinius (AD 6) to resist Roman oppression. The apostle Simon, a member of this party, was referred to as the Zealot to distinguish him from Simon Peter (Mt 10:4; Mk 3:18; Lk 6:15; Ac 1:13).

ZEBEDEE (ZEB-i-dee; "Yahweh has endowed"). A fisherman, the husband of Salome and the father of James and John (Mt 4:21–22; 27:56; Mk 1:19–20; Lk 5:10; Jn 21:2). See 2:187, 319–21.

ZEBIDAH (zi-BIGH-dah). Jehoiakim's mother (2Ki 23:36).

ZEBOIIM (zi-BOI-im; "place of hyenas"). One of the five cities in the plain whose king was defeated by Chedorlaomer. God destroyed Zeboiim with Sodom and Gomorrah (Gn 10:19; 14:2, 8; Dt 29:23; Hos 11:8).

ZEBULUN (ZEB-yoo-luhn).

1. The tenth son of Jacob and sixth son of Leah (Gn 30:20; 35:23; Gn 46:14). In his blessing Jacob describes Zebulun as dwelling by the sea (Gn 49:13).
2. One of the 12 tribes of Israel that descended from Zebulun. After crossing over the Jordan into Canaan, Moses divided the tribes into two groups, one group to pronounce blessings, and the other

curses. Zebulun was one of the six tribes that stood on Mount Ebal to pronounce the curses (Dt 27:13). The territory allotted to Zebulun was between the Sea of Galilee and the Mediterranean Sea. It included Nazareth (Jsh 19:10–16; Is 9:1; Mt 4:12–16). See 1:213, 914–15.

ZECHARIAH (zek-ah-RIGH-ah; "Yahweh has remembered"). The name of numerous men in the Bible, including the following:

1. The 14th king of Israel. He came to the throne in the 38th year of Uzziah, king of Judah, and reigned six months. He was the son of Jeroboam II. Shallum murdered Zechariah in order to become the king himself (2Ki 14:29; 15:8, 11). See 1:346, 373.
2. A son of Jehoida, the high priest, and a priest like his father. He lived during the reign of King Joash of Judah. Zechariah was a reformer. On Joash's order Zechariah was killed in the court of the temple (2Ch 24:20–22). He is probably the Zechariah referred to in Mt 23:35 and Lk 11:51. See 1:402.
3. A prophet who advised King Uzziah (2Ch 26:5).
4. A minor prophet; the son of Berechiah and grandson of Iddo (Zec 1:1). He was a contemporary of Zerubbabel the governor and returned from the Babylonian captivity under his leadership. Zechariah also lived during the time of Jeshua the priest and Haggai the prophet. Along with Haggai, he exhorted the leaders of the Jewish colony to resume work on the temple. It is likely that Zechariah was a priest as well as a prophet (Ne 12:16). See 1:983–84.
5. The father of John the Baptist. Zechariah was a priest of the division of Abijah (Lk 1:5). He and his wife, Elizabeth, who was related to Mary of Nazareth, were godly people who lived in the hill country of Judea. One day while Zechariah was serving in the temple, an angel appeared to him and told him God had heard his prayer; he would have a son. And so, in their old age, Zechariah and Elizabeth became the parents of John the Baptist, the forerunner of Christ (Lk 1:5–25, 39–80). See 2:277.

ZECHARIAH, BOOK OF. See 1:983–95.

ZEDEKIAH (zed-i-KIGH-AH; "righteousness of Yahweh"). The son of Josiah and the last king of Judah. Because of Judah's wickedness, God allowed Nebuchadnezzar to come to Jerusalem and take Jehoiachin, Judah's king, to Babylon. Then Nebuchadnezzar placed Mattaniah, whom he renamed Zedekiah, on the throne as king. When Zedekiah rebelled a number of years later, Nebuchadnezzar seized him, put out his eyes, and took him to Babylon where he died (2Ki 24:17–20; 25:1–21; 2Ch 36:10–21; Jer 21–39; Ezk 17:15–21). See 1:348–49, 373, 758, 766–67.

ZEPHANIAH (zef-ah-NIGH-ah; "Yahweh hides").

1. The ninth minor prophet. Zephaniah was the son of Cushi and a descendant of Hezekiah. He prophesied during the time of Josiah, king of Judah (Zep 1:1). See 1:373, 961–62.
2. A priest, the son of Maaseiah. Zephaniah was one of those who carried messages between Zedekiah and Jeremiah (Jer 21:1; 37:3). After Jerusalem was captured by the Babylonians, Zephaniah was taken captive to Riblah, where he was put to death (Jer 52:24–25). See 1:751.

ZEPHANIAH, BOOK OF. See 1:960–69.

ZERUBBABEL (zuh-RUB-ah-buhl; "born in Babylon"). The son of Shealtiel and the grandson of King Jehoiachin (Ezr 3:2, 8; 5:2; Ne 12:1; Hg 1:1, 12, 14).

When Cyrus allowed the Jewish people to return to their homeland, he made Zerubbabel the governor of the colony. Zerubbabel led the first colony of captives back to Jerusalem (Ezr 2; Ne 7:7). With the support of Haggai and Zechariah, he supervised the rebuilding of the temple despite Samaritan opposition (Ezr 3–6; Hg 1:12, 15; 2:2–4; Zec 4:6–10). See 1:424, 437, 445, 452, 974.

ZEUS (ZYOOS). The chief god of the Greeks corresponding to the Roman god Jupiter (Ac 14:12–13). See 2:4.

ZIKLAG (ZIK-lag). A city in southern Judah located between Beersheba and Gath (Jsh 15:31; 19:5). Achish, king of Gath, gave it to David and his men when they were fleeing from Saul (1Sm 27:6; 30:1–2; 2Sm 1:1; 4:10). Today it is probably Tell el-Khuweiefeh. See 1:276, 292.

ZIMRI (ZIM-righ; "my help"). The fifth king of Israel. Zimri was a general under Elah, king of Israel. After murdering Elah, he set himself up as king in Terzah. Israel, however, proclaimed Omri the new king. When Omri marched against Zimri and captured his capital, Zimri set fire to the palace and died in its blaze. Zimri's reign lasted only a week (1Ki 16:9–20; 2Ki 9:31). See 1:141, 343, 345, 372.

ZIN (ZIN). A wilderness the Israelites crossed on their way to Canaan (Nu 34:3; Jsh 15:1). Kadesh was on the boundary of Zin (Nu 20:1). The Wilderness of Paran bordered it on the south (Nu 13:26). See 1:127.

ZION (ZIGH-uhn). A Hbr name that could be derived from a Semitic term for "defend" (as in a fortress) or "to be bald" (as in a defendable rocky space; *see* ROCK).

1. One of the hills on which Jerusalem stood. It is first mentioned in the OT as a Jebusite city. It was located on the southern spur of the eastern ridge of Jerusalem and received its water from Gihon Spring (Virgin Fountain) through an aqueduct. David captured the city, renamed it city of David, and made it his capital (2Sm 5:6–9; 1Ch 11:5–8). See 1:61.
2. After the temple was built on Mount Moriah and the ark brought to it, the name Zion was extended to include Moriah (Is 8:18; 18:7; 24:23; Jl 3:17; Mi 4:7).
3. David began an extension of the city, and the name *Zion* came to be used for the whole of Jerusalem (2Sm 5:9; 2Ki 19:21; Ps 48; 69:35; Is 1:8). See 1:350, 568, 737; 2:804.
4. Zion is a symbol of God's kingdom (Ps 76:2; Is 1:27; 2:3; 4:1–6; Jl 3:16; Zec 1:16–17; Rm 11:26). See 1:580, 717, 991.
5. Zion is the new heavenly Jerusalem (Heb 12:22–24; Rv 14:1; 21–22). See 1:728, 737; 2:65.

ZIPPORAH (zi-PO-rah; "sparrow"). The daughter of Jethro, the priest of Midian. She became Moses' wife (Ex 2:16–22; 4:25; 18:2–4). See 1:64.

ZOAR (zo-ur; "little"). One of the five cities of the plain on which Sodom and Gomorrah were located. When God's judgment was about to descend on the cities, Lot prayed for Zoar's safety, and it was spared destruction. Then Lot and his two daughters fled there, finding refuge in a cave where they stayed awhile (Gn 19:20–30). Zoar was originally called Bela (Gn 14:2, 8).

ZOPHAR (ZO-fur). One of Job's three friends who came to counsel him in his affliction (Jb 2:11; 11:1; 20:1; 42:9). See 1:504, 508, 511–12, 527.

ZORAH (ZO-rah; possibly "hornet" or "scourge"). A Canaanite city located at the highest point of the Shephelah about five miles northwest of Beth-shemesh. Manoah, Samson's father, came from Zorah, and Samson was buried near there (Jsh 15:33; 19:41; Jgs 13:2; 16:31; 18:2, 8, 11; 2Ch 11:10; Ne 11:29).

144,000. Multiple of *twelve* and a *thousand*, symbolizing all of God's people; Rv 7:4; 14:1–3. *See also* THOUSAND; TWELVE. See 2:777.

Art Credits

Editor's Preface
Olive tree © Shutterstock, Inc.

The Apocrypha and the Time Between the Testaments
P. 2. Greek amphora © Evangelos Kanaridis/iStockphoto.com.

Judith
P. 14 ivory Jewess © Erich Lessing/Erich Lessing Culture and Fine Arts Archive; p. 16 Judith with head of Holofernes © Erich Lessing/Erich Lessing Culture and Fine Arts Archive; p. 17 wine vessel © Zev Radovan/Bible Land Pictures; p. 22 bust of Ammonite king © Erich Lessing/Erich Lessing Culture and Fine Arts Archive.

The Wisdom of Solomon
P. 26 Rosetta Stone © Erich Lessing/Erich Lessing Culture and Fine Arts Archive; p. 29 Cleopatra VII, Bridgeman Art Library; p. 33 Anubis © Shutterstock, Inc.; p. 34 Plato © Shutterstock, Inc.

Tobit
P. 39 Seleucus I, Bridgeman Art Library; p. 40 silver tetradrachm © The Trustees of the British Museum. All rights reserved; p. 43 wall painting of Moses, Bridgeman Art Library; p. 46 ring, Clara Amit, Meidad Suchowolski, Miki Koren, Courtesy Israel Antiquities Authority; p. 48 Apamea © Shutterstock, Inc.

Ecclesiasticus
P. 50 Dura Europos wall, bpk, Berlin/Vorderasiatisches Museum, Staatliche Museum/Gudrun Stenzel/Art Resource, NY; p. 52 ossuary © Erich Lessing/Erich Lessing Culture and Fine Arts Archive; p. 57 alabaster figure © Erich Lessing/Erich Lessing Culture and Fine Arts Archive.

Baruch
P. 60 Persepolis gates © Shutterstock, Inc.; p. 65 golden deity head © Erich Lessing/Erich Lessing Culture and Fine Arts Archive; p. 66 Palmyra © Shutterstock, Inc.

The Letter of Jeremiah
P. 71 dog © Erich Lessing/Erich Lessing Culture and Fine Arts Archive; p. 72 cylinder seal, Art Resource, NY.

1 and 2 Maccabees
P. 78 tombs in Modi'im © Erich Lessing/Erich Lessing Culture and Fine Arts Archive; p. 81 Antiochus coin © Erich Lessing/Erich Lessing Culture and Fine Arts Archive; p. 86 terra-cotta elephant © Erich Lessing/Erich Lessing Culture and Fine Arts Archive; p. 91 Colombarium © Zev Radovan/Bible Land Pictures; p. 92 stone structure © Erich Lessing/Erich Lessing Culture and Fine Arts Archive; p. 95 menorah © Shutterstock, Inc.; p. 98 angel trampling Heliodorus © De Agostini Editore S.p.A.; p. 102 medieval manuscript © Erich Lessing/Erich Lessing Culture and Fine Arts Archive.

Old Greek Esther
P. 104 fresco of Mordecai and Esther © Zev Radovan/Bible Land Pictures; p. 106 myrtle wreath, Museum of Fine Arts, Houston, TX/Bridgeman Art Library; p. 114 Apadana columns © Ko Yo/Shutterstock, Inc.

Susanna
P. 116 wild lilies © Vadim Petrakov/Shutterstock, Inc.; p. 119 judgment of Daniel, Bridgeman Art Library; p. 122 fresco of Susanna, Alfredo Dagli Orti/ The Art Archive at Art Resource, NY; p. 124 mastic trees © Pali Michalis/Shutterstock, Inc.

Bel and the Dragon
P. 126 Achaemenid dragon © Erich Lessing/Erich Lessing Culture and Fine Arts Archive; p. 131 walking dragon, Bridgeman Art Library.

The Prayer and Azariah and the Song of the Three Holy Children
P. 134 fiery furnace, Gianni Dagli Orti/ The Art Archive at Art Resource, NY; p. 138 altar fragments, Clara Amit, Meidad Suchowolski, Miki Koren, Courtesy Israel Antiquities Authority.

The Prayer of Manasseh
P. 142 Mediterranean Sea © Shutterstock, Inc.; p. 145 woodcut from *D. Martin Luthers Werke: Kritische Gesamtausgabe: Die Deutsche Bibel* [Luther's Works, Weimar Edition: German Bible]. Weimar: Hermann Böhlaus Nachfolger, 1906–.

The Apocrypha in Other Christian Traditions
P. 151 fishing boats © iStockphoto LP; p. 153 Valley of Elah © Zev Radovan/Bible Land Pictures.

The New Testament Introductory Articles
P. 154 altar triptych © Erich Lessing/Erich Lessing Culture and Fine Arts Archive; p. 163 St. Athanasius, Bridgeman Art Library; p. 165 Jesus driving out unclean spirit, Bridgeman Art Library; p. 168 Christ driving out evil spirit, Bridgeman Art Library; p. 170 stone tomb © Mordechai Meiri/Shutterstock Inc.; p. 172 ivory carving © The Trustees of the British Museum.

The Gospels
P. 174 boat on Sea of Galilee © Asaf Eliason/Shutterstock Inc.; p. 177 portrait of Jesus, public domain; p. 180 mosaic © Doin Oakenheim/Shutterstock Inc.

Matthew
P. 184 Tree of Jesse, The Peirpont Morgan Library/Art Resource, NY; p. 186 Caesar Augustus © iStockphoto.com; p. 187 Theodotus inscription, courtesy Israel Antiquities Authority; p. 188 Matthew © ASP Religion/Alamy; p. 191 painting of Jesus, Bridgeman Art Library; p. 194 Adoration of the Magi, Bridgeman Art Library; p. 201 ostracon letter, Meidad Suchowolski, courtesy Israel Antiquities Authority; p. 203 Last Supper mosaic, Bridgeman Art Library; p. 204 fresco of Baptism, Bridgeman Art Library; p. 208 Christ healing the paralytic, Bridgeman Art Library; p. 213 sarcophagus, Bridgeman Art Library; p. 221 soldiers © Shutterstock.com; p. 226 Jesus enters Jerusalem, Bridgeman Art Library; p. 227 fig © Shutterstock Inc.

Mark
P. 232 Jordan River © Zev Radovan/Bible Land Pictures; p. 234 Mark © ASP Religion/Alamy; p. 235 Nero Caesar Augustus coin © Zev Radovan/Bible Land Pictures; p. 238 sandals © Zev Radovan/Bible Land Pictures; p. 244 fishing boat © Zev Radovan/Bible Land Pictures; p. 245 clay brick © Zev Radovan/Bible Land Pictures; p. 246 mikveh © Zev Radovan/Bible Land Pictures; p. 249 heelbone © Zev Radovan/Bible Land Pictures; p. 252 ossuary © Zev Radovan/Bible Land Pictures; p. 256 Christ victorious © De Agostini Picture Library/The Bridgeman Art Library; p. 260 pull toy, Cara Amit, courtesy Israel Antiquities Authority; p. 263 Dead Sea © Eldad Carin/Shutterstock Inc.

Luke
P. 267 Herodium © Yoel Harel/Alamy; p. 270 Luke © ASP Religion/Alamy; p. 273 road © Zev Radovan/Bible Land Pictures; p. 278 Capernaum synagogue © Hanan Isachar/Alamy; p. 279 Sepphoris mosaic © Zev Radovan/Bible Land Pictures; pp. 282–83 mosaic © Erich Lessing/Erich Lessing Culture and Fine Arts Archive; p. 290 catacomb portrait, Bridgeman Art Library; p. 293 temple stone, Courtesy Israel

Antiquities Authority; p. 297 gemstone, Yael Yolovitch, courtesy Israel Antiquities Authority; p. 301 Caiaphas ossuary © Zev Radovan/Bible Land Pictures; p. 304 sarcophagus © Erich Lessing/Erich Lessing Culture and Fine Arts Archive; p. 307 Jesus healing blind men, Album/Art Resource, NY; p. 309 death of Judas, Bridgeman Art Library; p. 313 crucifixion carving, Scala/Art Resource, NY; p. 314 Mount of Olives © Eldad Carin/Shutterstock Inc.

John

P. 318 Sea of Galilee © Sarah Coghill/Alamy; p. 320 fish mosaic © Zev Radovan/Bible Land Pictures; p. 321 John © ASP Religion/Alamy; p. 323 Last Supper © Zev Radovan/Bible Land Pictures; p. 327 ivory carving © Interfoto/Alamy; p. 330 sarcophagus © Erich Lessing/Erich Lessing Culture and Fine Arts Archive; p. 334 carrying cushion, Clara Amit, courtesy Israel Antiquities Authority; p. 335 fresco © Erich Lessing/Erich Lessing Culture and Fine Arts Archive; p. 337 dice © Zev Radovan/Bible Land Pictures; p. 340 water vessel © Zev Radovan/Bible Land Pictures; p. 345 Madaba mosaic © Kumar Sriskandan/Alamy; p. 351 ivory casket, Bridgeman Art Library; p. 355 Christ with disciples, Bridgeman Art Library.

The Acts of the Apostles

P. 358 Madaba Map © Zev Radovan/Bible Land Pictures; p. 361 "Sarcophagus of the Handing of the Keys" © Erich Lessing Culture and Fine Arts Archive; p. 365 Roman trireme © Erich Lessing Culture and Fine Arts Archive; p. 368 Peter and Paul © Erich Lessing Culture and Fine Arts Archive; p. 373 Sea of Galilee © Shutterstock, Inc.; p. 374 ossuary, Clara Amit, Miki Koren, Yael Yolovitch, courtesy Israel Antiquities Authority; p. 376 road to Damascus © Erich Lessing Culture and Fine Arts Archive; p. 377 map of ancient Antioch, from *Manual of Biblical Geography*; p. 378 Taurus Pass © Erich Lessing Culture and Fine Arts Archive; p. 379 map of Athens, from *Manual of Biblical Geography*; pp 382–83 the temple of Herod, from *Sacred Sites of the Gospels*; p. 387 Roman jug, Clara Amit, Miki Koren, Yael Yolovitch, courtesy Israel Antiquities Authority; p. 394 mosaic of basilica © Erich Lessing Culture and Fine Arts Archive; p. 399 St. Lawrence © Shutterstock, Inc.; p. 400 stone inscription Clara Amit, courtesy Israel Antiquities Authority; p. 407 Judas © Shutterstock, Inc.

The Epistles of Paul

P. 410 young Roman, Bridgeman Art Library; p. 412 coin © Zev Radovan/Bible Land Pictures; p. 413 Greek prayer © Erich Lessing/Erich Lessing Culture and Fine Arts Archive; p. 415 writing tools, Bridgeman Art Library.

Romans

P. 416 Appian Way © Rupert Hansen/Alamy; p. 418 plan of Ancient Rome, from *Manual of Biblical Geography*; p. 419 sword, Bridgeman Art Library; p. 423 mosaic of Abraham © Shutterstock, Inc.; p. 424 Roman mosaic © Alfio Ferlito/Shutterstock, Inc.; p. 428 mosaic of dove © Shutterstock, Inc.; p. 431 Paul's tomb © Erich Lessing/Erich Lessing Culture and Fine Arts Archive.

1 and 2 Corinthians

P. 440 Temple of Apollo © Jon Arnold Images Ltd/Alamy; p. 443 map of Corinth, from *Manual of Biblical Geography*; p. 446 plate © Erich Lessing/Erich Lessing Culture and Fine Arts Archive; p. 450 crucifixion © Vibrant Image Studio/Shutterstock, Inc.; p. 451 Rabbula Gospels, public domain; p. 453 sarcophagus © Erich Lessing/Erich Lessing Culture and Fine Arts Archive; p. 459 lamb © iStockphoto.com; p. 460 mosaic of Roman woman Photo credit: Bridgeman Art Library; p. 463 resurrection © Shutterstock, Inc.; p. 478 the Bema at Corinth © Zev Radovan/Bible Land Pictures; p. 481 leather pouch, Clara Amit, Miki Koren, Yael Yolovitch, courtesy Israel Antiquities Authority; p. 482 coin © Shutterstock, Inc.; p. 488 mosaic of Paul, Scala/Art Resource, NY; p. 492 Christ enthroned © Michal Durinik/Shutterstock, Inc.; p. 496 Greek coast © Shutterstock, Inc.

Galatians

P. 498 Lake Egridir © Erich Lessing/Erich Lessing Culture and Fine Arts Archive; p. 501 Torah scroll © Polyanska Lyubov/Shutterstock, Inc.; p. 506 floor mosaic © Zev Radovan/Bible Land Pictures; p. 507 Paul and Peter © Erich Lessing/Erich Lessing Culture and Fine Arts Archive; p. 509 Martin and Katharine Luther, Bridgeman Art Library; p. 511 fresco of Abraham © Renata Sedmakove/Shutterstock.com; p. 513 Paul © Zvonimir Atletic/Shutterstock, Inc.

Ephesians

P. 518 Ephesus, Turkey © Prisma Archivo/Alamy; p. 521 Ephesus theater © Shutterstock, Inc.; p. 522 Artemis statue © Valery Shanin/Shutterstcok, Inc.; p. 529 devil and sinner © Shutterstock, Inc.; p. 530 child being baptized © Erich Lessing/Erich Lessing Culture and Fine Arts Archive; p. 532 Paul © Shutterstock, Inc.; p. 534 men in chains, Bridgeman Art Library.

Philippians

P. 538 woman in purple © The Trustees of British Museum; p. 541 Paul's prison © Imagestate Media Partners Limited - Impact Photos/Alamy; p. 544 golden cross Photo credit: Bridgeman Art Library.

Colossians

P. 550 Trajan's Column © Shutterstock, Inc.; p. 553 Hierapolis © Bariş Muratoğlu/iStock.com; p. 556 mosaic cross © iStock.com; p. 560 the Resurrection © Lucinda Lambton/The Bridgeman Art Library.

1 and 2 Thessalonians

P. 562 Thessalonica, Greece © iStock.com; p. 567 Paul © Renata Sedmakova/Shutterstock, Inc.; p. 571 empty tomb © iStock.com; p. 575 Macedonian Bay © Panos Karas/Shutterstock, Inc.; p. 576 final judgment Photo credit: Bridgeman Art Library; p. 578 view from Mount Olympus © Miroslav Trifonov/Shutterstock, Inc.; p. 580 growing tree © Sunny studio - Igor Yaruta/Shutterstock, Inc.; p. 584 grinning death © Erich Lessing/Erich Lessing Culture and Fine Arts Archive; p. 586 resurrection of Christ, Bridgeman Art Library; p. 588 last judgment © Renata Sedmakova/Shutterstock, Inc.; p. 589 grapes © Shutterstock, Inc.; p. 590 cooking flatbread © Shutterstock, Inc.; p. 592 life of Paul, Bridgeman Art Library.

1 and 2 Timothy

P. 596 Good Shepherd fresco, Bridgeman Art Library; p. 600 feast of Corpus Christi © iStock.com; p. 603 Suffering Servant, Bridgeman Art Library; p. 605 Greek amphoras © Tansel Atasagun/Shutterstock, Inc.; p. 607 Adam and Eve © Erich Lessing/Erich Lessing Culture and Fine Arts Archive; p. 610 widow © Jose AS Reyes/Shutterstock Inc.; p. 614 Roman forum ruins © Shutterstock, Inc.; p. 617 laurel wreath © Miguel Garcia Saavedra/Shutterstock, Inc.; p. 618 Bible © Shutterstock, Inc.

Titus

P. 624 sailboats © JMWScout/iStock.com; p. 626 Paul © Erich Lessing/Erich Lessing Culture and Fine Arts Archive; p. 628 mosaic of dove © Shutterstock, Inc.; p. 630 island of Crete © Anilah/Shutterstock, Inc.; p. 632 man and Bible © Blend Images/Shutterstock, Inc.

Philemon

P. 634 ruins in Pompeii © Igor Stepovik/Shutterstock, Inc.; p. 636 Roman slave necklace, Scala/Ministero per I Beni e le Attivitá cultural/Art Resource, NY; p. 638 Roman key Photo credit: Clara Amit, Meidad Suchowolski, Miki Koren, courtesy Israel Antiquities Authority; p. 640 Pantheon © Martin Smeets/Shutterstock, Inc.; p. 642 Roman fresco © Shutterstock.com.

The General Epistles

Pp 644–45 Arch of Titus © Matt Ragen/Shutterstock, Inc.; p. 646 mosaic of John, Bridgeman Art Library.

Hebrews

P. 650 mosaic of Jesus ©Pavle Marjanovic/Shutterstock, Inc.; p. 657 sacrifices by Melchizedek, Alfred Dagli Orti/Art Resource, NY; p. 660 ancient baptistery © Novarc Images/Alamy; p. 662 Holy Spirit carving © INTERFOTO/Alamy; p. 664 marble statue, courtesy Israel Antiquities Authority; p. 665 stained glass window © Shutterstock, Inc.

James

P. 674 menorah carving © Zev Radovan/Bible Land Pictures; p. 677 pomegranate coin, Clara Amit, courtesy Israel Antiquities Authority; p. 679 ruins of Sepphoris © PhotoStock-Israel/Alamy; p. 680 winter storm © Shutterstock, Inc.; p. 682 Capernaum synagogue © Francesco Dazzi/Shutterstock, Inc.; p. 684 harvesting olives © Amit Erez/iStock.com; p. 689 Jesus teaching the apostles, Bridgeman Art Library; p. 694 hay bales © iStock.com; p. 698 road to Jerusalem © Erich Lessing/Erich Lessing Culture and Fine Arts Archive.

1 and 2 Peter

P. 700 Tiber River © Iakov Kalinin/Shutterstock, Inc.; p. 702 Sea of Galilee © Shutterstock, Inc.; p. 708 North African baptistry © Marcin Sylwia Ciesieslki/Shutterstock, Inc.; p. 711 fresco of crucifixion, Bridgeman Art Library; p. 718 Basilica of Saint Apollinare © Prisma Bildagentur AG/Alamy; p. 723 Dead Sea © Nickolay Vinokurov/Shutterstock, Inc.; p. 724 Good Shepherd Photo credit: Bridgeman Art Library; p. 727 Transfiguration of Christ © Erich Lessing/Erich Lessing Culture and Fine Arts Archive; p. 733 St. Peter © Shutterstock, Inc.

1, 2, and 3 John

P. 736 great theater of Ephesus © David Ball/Alamy; p. 739 man © Laurin Rinder/Shutterstock, Inc.; p. 740 Jesus' Baptism and crucifixion © Keith McIntyre/Shutterstock, Inc.; p. 744 "Sarcophagus of the Trees" © Erich Lessing/Erich Lessing Culture and Fine Arts Archive; p. 746 Egyptian water clock, Bridgeman Art Library; p. 751 mosaic of Jesus © Renata Sedmakova/Shutterstock, Inc.

Jude

P. 756 Arbel Cliff © Shutterstock, Inc.; p. 758 mosaic of Mary © Vladimir Wrangel/Shutterstock, Inc.; p. 760 ripe figs © iStock.com; p. 763 Tullian prison © Erich Lessing/Erich Lessing Culture and Fine Arts Archive.

Revelation

P. 770 beaches of Patmos, Greece © Shutterstock, Inc.; p. 771 Domitian coin © Paul Picone/Shuttersock, Inc.; pp. 774–75 road through Galilee © Shutterstock, Inc.; p. 778 bronze cross © Erich Lessing/Erich Lessing Culture and Fine Arts Archive; p. 781 carving of Michael © Erich Lessing/Erich Lessing Culture and Fine Arts Archive; p. 784 Roman bowl, Kren Miki, courtesy Israel Antiquities Authority; p. 787 stone tablet © iStock.com; p. 788 San Vitale mosaic photo credit: Alfredo Dagli orti/Art Resource, NY; p. 793 fresco of Daniel © Ivonne Wierink/Shutterstock, Inc.

Archaeology and the Bible

P. 796 burial chamber fragments © Eddia Gerald/Alamy; p. 798 podium © Hanan Isachar/Alamy; p. 799 Hazor's city gates © Zev Radovan/Bible Land Pictures; p. 800 Schechem's city gate © Erich Lessing/Erich Lessing Culture and Fine Arts Archive; p. 801 Shiloh © Hanan Isachar/Alamy; p. 802 well at Gibeon © Zev Radovan/Bible Land Pictures; p. 803 Broad Wall © Hanan Isachar/Alamy; p. 804 retaining wall © Hanan Isachar/Alamy; p. 805 Beersheba well © Hanan Isachar/Alamy; p. 806 fresco © Zev Radovan/Bible Land Pictures; p. 807 the Treasury © Shutterstock, Inc.; p. 808 St. Peter's house © Zev Radovan/Bible Land Pictures; p. 809 tomb of Lazarus © Erich Lessing/Erich Lessing Culture and Fine Arts Archive; p. 810 stone inscription © Erich Lessing/Erich Lessing Culture and Fine Arts Archive; p. 811 Athenian agora © Zev Radovan/Bible Land Pictures; p. 812 temple warning © Erich Lessing/Erich Lessing Culture and Fine Arts Archive; p. 813 stone inscription © Erich Lessing/Erich Lessing Culture and Fine Arts Archive; p. 814 glass bottle Photo: Mariana Salzberger, courtesy Israel Antiquities Authority; p. 814 bowl Photo: Mariana Salzberger, courtesy Israel Antiquities Authority.

End Matter Articles

P. 816 Egyptian scribe © Jose Ignacio Soto/Shutterstock Inc.; p. 822 Christ calling His disciples, Brenner, Adam (1800-91)/New Walk Museum & Art Gallery, Leicester, UK/photo © Leicester Arts & Museums/The Bridgeman Art Library; p. 826 Gutenberg press © Shutterstock, Inc.; p. 831 Stain Glass Window © Hemera Technologies/AbeStock.com/Thinkstock; p. 832 Bible © Magdalena Kucova/Shutterstock, Inc.